STARTING WITH
INGREDIENTS

STARTING WITH INGREDIENTS

QUINTESSENTIAL RECIPES
FOR THE WAY WE **REALLY** COOK

ALIZA GREEN

RUNNING PRESS

PHILADELPHIA · LONDON

© 2006 by Aliza Green
Cover and interior photographs © 2006 by Steve Legato,
except photo of quince © Image Source/Jupiter Images

Printed in the United States

9 8 7 6 5 4 3 2 1
Digit on the right indicates the number of this printing

Library of Congress Control Number: 2006921032

ISBN-13: 978-0-7624-2747-5
ISBN-10: 0-7624-2747-7

Cover and interior design by Amanda Richmond
Edited by Diana C. von Glahn
Typography: Nofret, Agenda, and Trajan

This book may be ordered by mail from the publisher.
Please include $2.50 for postage and handling.
But try your bookstore first!

Running Press Book Publishers
125 South Twenty-Second Street
Philadelphia, Pennsylvania 19103-4399

Visit us on the web!
www.runningpresscooks.com
www.runningpress.com

＊

To my children, Zachary and Ginevra Reiff, for being loving and understanding through all

the years of irregular meals, weird combinations of foods ("Mom, can't you make anything normal?"),

and the difficult hours of a chef. Zach, your sardonic sense of humor, clear intelligence, and insightful comments

keep me on my toes at all times. I wouldn't have it any other way. Ginevra, your caring, creativity, and willingness

to help me mean the world to me, and your exquisitely nuanced palate helps keep my cooking up to your high standard.

I know you both have a bright future ahead. I promise not to serve you "eggplant and kidney beans" anymore.

Acknowledgments

I could never have written this ambitious book without the help of many people. My husband, Donald Reiff, encouraged me every step of the way to follow my dreams. Although many people think he's lucky to be married to a chef, the truth is that it's often difficult, with scattered meals and odd combinations the norm. My heartfelt thanks go to my mom, Vivian Green, the other writer in the family, who gave me critiques (of my writing and my cooking) when I needed them and pats on the back when I needed those, too.

Clare Pelino and her highly competent staff at Profile Public Relations and Pro Literary Agency, including Jennie Hatton and others, worked with me to make this book the big success I know it's going to be. Clare's persistence and her confidence in my abilities helped me reach my lofty goals. Clare, I couldn't have done it without you.

Diana von Glahn, my feisty, energetic editor at Running Press, did a fantastic job in editing this 1,000 page plus manuscript without ever losing her cool or her wry sense of humor. She is an absolute dynamo, who has put together a fantastic cookbook list for Running Press this year. Go, Diana! Amanda Richmond took on the Herculean task of not only making sense of this giant book, but also making it readable and attractive. I'm thrilled with what she has done. Food photographer extraordinaire, Steve Legato, with whom I've enjoyed working on six books, did a superb job for this book.

Jon Anderson, Publisher at Running Press, had the vision to see this as a "big book" and worked to give it the attention it deserves. As a food lover and respected publisher, he made us all believe in the book and in Running Press. Craig Herman, Marketing and Publicity Director at Running Press, shared his great skill and experience, love of food, and caring personality to put together the fabulous marketing program for this book.

Sammy d'Angelo of Samuels & Son Seafood brought me the most beautiful fish and seafood imaginable. He and Joe Lasporgata, buyer at Samuels, have ruined me for anything but the best. Jim Conboy, owner, and Shawn Padgett, Director of Sales of the George Wells Company, provided much of the meats, poultry, and game for this book. In more than twenty-five years as a customer, I have continued to be impressed by their top quality products and their incredible service.

Ann Wilder of Vann's Spices provided me with the spices I use with abandon in my recipes. Ann is so knowledgeable and generous enough to share with others. Her spices just taste better. When I first started buying from Joel Assouline of CaviarAssouline, he delivered his specialty foods from the back of a Volkswagen bug. He's come a long way baby, with locations in Philadelphia and soon New York. I've always been able to call him for quick and accurate answers to my many questions.

In 1979, as Executive Chef of Ristorante DiLullo in Fox Chase, Philadelphia, I heard about Mark and Judy Dornstreich of Branch Creek Farm, who had started an organic farm. I quick called them and got my first delivery, eight bushels of sprightly spinach. Working with their produce made me understand just how good vegetables, herbs, greens, and edible flowers could be.

I met Glenn and Karen Brendle of Green Meadow Farm, Gap, Pennsylvania, during my tenure as chef of the White

Dog Café. Glenn brought me everything from double-fat yogurt, apple cider, and fresh sumac to wineberries, sweet corn, and brown eggs. It's people like this couple who enable chefs like me to show off. Paul Tsakos, of Overbrook Herb Farm, was the very first farmer I bought from, starting in the late 1970s. His baby white eggplants, ripe figs (in Philadelphia!), lush rosemary, and *fraises de bois* convinced me that local, fresh ingredients are essential to good cooking.

I was thrilled when I heard there was a farmers' market opening near my home that to hard-working founder Jim Kenney. I want to thank him and the farmers of the Glenside Farmers' Market, Glenside, Pennsylvania, for bringing the best in seasonal produce to market every week.

As one of the first customers of Albert Buehrer's former wholesale produce business, Indian Rock Produce, I was on the phone with him every day for many years. He taught me much of what I now know about produce, especially on the wholesale level. I wish him only good fortune in new endeavors.

Maria Teresa Berdondini, of Tuscany, by Tuscans brought me to visit artisanal Italian food producers and shared her superb Emilia-Romagna-style home cooking with me in Montecatini Terme, Italy. Maria Teresa knows everyone in Italy and is incredibly knowledgeable about my beloved Italian cuisine and wine.

Toto Schiavone and Claire DiLullo of Moonstruck Restaurant are proprietors of what started out as Ristorante DiLullo, where I became chef in 1979 and learned all about *la cucina Italiana*. I spent many years studying Italian and traveling to Italy and still love Italian food best of all. The two of them, and the late founder, Joe DiLullo, for giving me, as Joe once told me, " a chance to blossom."

Dr. Hansjakob Werlen of Slow Food Philadelphia put together a wonderful group trip to Campania, Italy, this past fall, which I joined. Having the chance to visit places like the Solagri lemon co-op and Vannulo, producers of superb *mozzarella di bufala* helped me with great stories and even better recipes.

Franz Sydow, with whom I've been working in Aruba on several projects, has shared his knowledge of island and Latin American food and wines. German and Luis Dao of Standard Seafood, Venezuela and Miami, arranged for me to visit Venezuela to learn about their farm-raised shrimp and Lake Maracaibo blue crabs.

Rodger Helwig, Marketing Director of Oso Sweet Onions, has given me the opportunity to represent outstandingly juicy, crunchy Oso Sweet Onions from Chile. Rodger has been a pleasure to work. I've learned so much from him, not just about onions, but also about the world of food, food marketing, and great wines.

My neighbors and friends have all been willing tasters through the years: Bill Brennan and Sherry Clearwater shared the Hungarian Mushroom Soup and tales of Middle European cooking; Al and Lynn Wagman brought me fresh-caught Jersey fish, garden tomatoes, and exquisite roses. Beth Saren and Windell Murphy and Joy and Barry Brommer have been eager tasters of whatever I've concocted.

For many years, Rima Synnestvedt has helped me deal with life's challenges while enjoying many meals and good bottles of wine together. I've prepared countless joint-venture meals with the highly creative Joy and Michael Irving including many of the recipes found in this book. Lester Kelner helped me to "find my bliss" in food writing, using my years of hard-won culinary experience. Martin Cherkes shared great jokes, good advice and annual seders. So many people have helped me on my way, please accept my apologies if I've neglected anyone.

7

Introduction

Starting with Ingredients is an ambitious book that brings together my love and in-depth, hands-on knowledge of ingredients with the clear, imaginative yet well-rooted and workable recipes I've developed through my wide-ranging culinary experiences. The best ingredients, treated with the respect they deserve and prepared with care and understanding, are the foundation of great food. Each of the one hundred chapters in this book focuses on a single ingredient, exploring its history and culture, freely garnished with abundant background information, variety descriptions, techniques, and more.

I've gathered a diverse collection of more than five hundred fifty recipes for dishes from appetizers to desserts and including drinks, breads, and preserved foods. The flavors and techniques are inspired by a world of ethnic traditions—Sicilian, Mexican, Spanish, Greek, Thai, Alsatian, Rumanian, Tunisian, Tuscan, Colombian, Jewish, and Vietnamese for starters. Dotted throughout are chef tips and trucs (tricks), stories, and suggestions to make it all work in the real world, where nothing is perfect and adaptability is key. In the recipes, foods are cured, pan-seared, baked, grilled, steamed, roasted, sautéed, hot-smoked, stir-fried, broiled, slow-cooked, and braised; some are never cooked at all.

Sidebars, recipes, and headnotes explain when, where and how to buy each ingredient, how to store and ripen it (if applicable), and best of all: how to cook fabulous, full-flavored dishes that will result in satisfying meals (and good leftovers). In my more than thirty years of professional cooking in every kind of kitchen from a dungeon to a palace, through a lifetime of intrepid travel,

voracious reading, language study, and culinary experimentation, my culinary drive has always been focused on knowing my ingredients: how and where they're grown or produced, who uses them and how, their roots in culture and history, and their individual character.

You could say (and you'd be right) that I'm a fanatic about ingredients. As a chef, I would do almost anything to get the best available and cook it fresh. I served hundreds of cases of fresh artichokes, each one prepped by hand, so many that our hands turned black. I would insist on personally cleaning fifty pound boxes of squid just to extract their ink sacs and use their contents to produce home-made squid ink pasta–nowadays, you just buy the ink. It's even shelf-stable. To make my lobster dishes, I dispatched and then cleaned dozens and dozens of lobsters, often getting pricked in the process by sharp lobster shells.

As a chef, when I wanted to serve zucchini blossoms, I found a local grower to pick only the plump, succulent female blossoms, not the more plentiful but hairier and less desirable males, in the early hours of the morning and deliver them the same day. I'd receive these delicate, short-lived beauties fully-opened and ready to stuff and serve that same night. When I wanted to make pomegranate sorbetto (one of the best flavors ever), I bought a case of "Wonderful" pomegranates, cut them open, picked out the seeds, crushed them, and finally sweetened the juice and made an exquisite ruby-red sorbetto.

I came up with my Trio Fries while working as a food consultant to the Dock Street Brewpub and Restaurant. This crispy fried combo of Idaho potato and boniato (Caribbean sweet potato) shoestrings mixed with thin

8

strips of leek won "Best of Philly" Awards three years in a row and consistently sold more than 2,500 orders a week. When a new chef attempted to remove them from the menu, customer outcry was so fierce that they were quickly reinstated. The Tunisian owners of A'propos Bistro taught me how to make preserved lemons, which I used to devise the Cinnamon and Preserved Lemon Grilled Chicken that became a big seller. To come up with the recipe for my incredibly moist (if I do say so myself) Jewish Honey Cake, fragrant with the perfectly balanced scents of coffee, clove, honey and orange zest, I baked cake after cake till I honed in on the intensity of flavor and lightness of texture I had enjoyed at Jewish holidays throughout my childhood. All of these recipes can be found within these pages.

Starting with Ingredients is the product of my endless culinary curiosity and long years of working to perfect my recipes. The headnotes are full of stories reflecting my years as a pioneering female chef in Philadelphia, a childhood spent living and traveling from Mexico to Brazil and Ireland to Israel, and working stints in kitchens from Bologna, Italy to San Juan, Puerto Rico. Many of these dishes were served to loyal restaurant customers, others are taken from newspaper columns, innumerable cooking classes, and from recipes that were shared with me by generous chefs, producers, and gifted home cooks.

My goal in this book is to draw readers of every experience level into the kitchen to explore familiar ingredients as well as new ones and learn about them on every level from visceral to cerebral. Cooking can be as therapeutic as massage or meditation and stimulating to all five senses. Actions like paring apples, pulling off the small hard bit of muscle called the "sweet meat" from the side of scallops, shredding ginger on a ceramic grater, dicing onions with a well-balanced sharp knife, and zesting the skin of lemons and oranges to release fragrant oil pockets all create their own rhythm. The satisfaction that follows from hands-on preparation of ingredients provides joy, and that pleasure is imbued in the dish.

There is nothing like preparing food from scratch to understand and appreciate the essence of the ingredient and its full potential. The broad range of recipes are sure to appeal to almost every palate and can be successfully prepared by real-life home cooks working in a non-dream kitchen. *Starting with Ingredients* is a book for food lovers; those who can't wait to get into the kitchen, not those who can't wait to get out. In fact, the hardest thing may be to choose which dish to make.

The imaginative but accessible recipes have clear, detailed, and easy-to-follow directions have been honed by my experience as a teacher, working hands-on with beginners, apprentices, experienced chefs both here and abroad and home cooks. All the recipes have been tested, not just in my own kitchen, but in restaurant kitchens, at innumerable cooking classes, in formal tastings, and in tasting dinners for friends and colleagues. First person anecdotes drawn from my years of food-obsessed travel, restaurant "cheffing" from the lowliest prep position to executive chef of several of Philadelphia's most prestigious restaurants, and my work doing television food styling for many of today's culinary stars add spice to the mix and bring the dishes to life.

Starting with Ingredients offers a new way to approach the kitchen with anticipation, confidence and joy for anyone who loves to cook. I hope that you, the reader, enjoy cooking and learning from this book as much as I did coming up with cooking and testing the recipes and sharing my hard-won knowledge. I love to hear from readers. Please write to me at www.alizagreen.com with comments, questions, and even criticism, and I'll be sure to answer you.

Contents

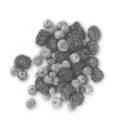

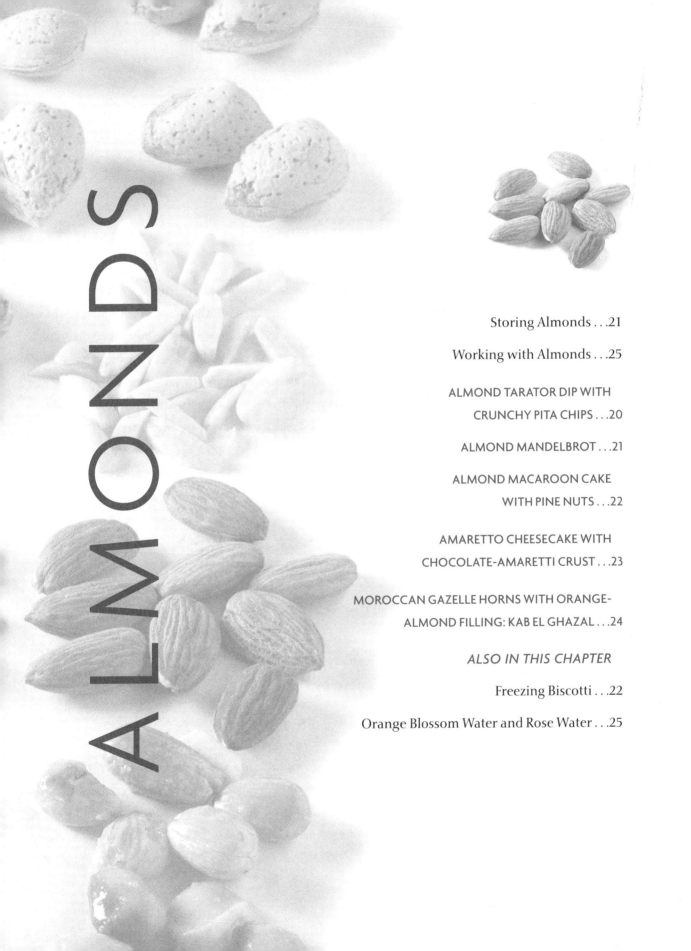

ALMONDS

ALMONDS

Almond joy—while I do love that combination of almonds, chocolate, and coconut, almonds give me much joy in the kitchen. These delicately flavored and highly versatile kernels of the pale green fruits of the beautiful almond tree have been cultivated since prehistoric times. As a young girl, I lived in Holland for a year where I fell in love with Van Gogh's paintings of almond trees in Provence enveloped in early spring with lovely soft pink blossoms. I get a nostalgic pang any time I see even a reproduction of one of the fourteen paintings he did on this subject.

The sweet almond, *Amgydalus communus*, belongs to the same family as the apricot, cherry, peach, and nectarine, but its pale green apricot-shaped fruit is leathery and can only be eaten when very young. The almond is essentially a fruit tree that puts all its energy into its kernel, rather than its flesh. The ancestors of the cultivated almond came from Western and Central Asia, where trees with small, dry fruits that produce bitter kernels are found. It is thought that millions of years ago, when the land rose up to form the mountains that separate Central Asia from China and Mongolia, the trees on the eastern side of the mountains evolved into the peach, which thrives at lower elevations in regions of higher humidity, while the almond developed along the fringes of the deserts and lower mountain slopes to the west.

Because almond trees need a temperate climate, they have long been cultivated in the Mediterranean; further north, the trees do not thrive. Today, almonds grow as far east as Afghanistan and Kashmir and as far west as California, where over half of the world's crop of this commercially most important nut is grown. Spain and Italy are the most important producers after the U.S.

In the Old Testament, Aaron's rod, which miraculously bore flowers and fruit, was made of almond wood. Phoenician traders introduced the almond tree into cultivation in Spain, and it was being grown in Provence as early as the eighth century BCE. The Greeks cultivated almonds, which they called *amygdalon*, the source of its name in modern European languages from *mandel* in German, to *mandorle* in Italian and *amande* in French. Italian musicians adopted the pleasing oval of the almond in designing the musical instrument that evolved in the eighteenth century into the *mandolino* or mandolin.

Almonds were of great importance in early Arabic and medieval European cookery in dishes such as blancmange, an almond milk pudding, common as recently as Victorian times. In Spain, days of fast meant not only abstaining from meat but also from the milk of animals, so that almond milk, made by grinding almonds and steeping them in water, was substituted. Almond milk is used today to make orgeat syrup used for milky white cooling drinks.

Sweet almonds, which come from the common almond tree, were developed by centuries of cultivation and breeding. Bitter almonds, their older ancestor, come from the bitter almond tree, *Amgydalus communus Amara*, and are used in small quantities for flavoring. However, even sweet almond trees sometimes yield bitter almonds, and some sweet almond cultivars smell faintly of bitter almond. Because they contain poisonous cyanide, it is illegal to sell bitter almonds in the United States. In Europe, they are sold at pharmacies and are added in small quantities to marzipan, amaretti biscuits, and amaretto liqueur for that edge of bitterness. In the United States, almond extract, also made from bitter almonds, is substituted for whole bitter almonds.

Almonds are sold in many forms. Young green almonds are the newest (and oldest) form of almonds found in season in early spring across the Mediterranean, and now starting to be available in the U.S. from specialty growers, especially in California. The inner green almond nuts are at their best when the seed case has just begun to plump, the interior is liquid, and there is no hint of a shell. The just-developed, soft, creamy "green" almonds (unripe, not green in color) are shelled and can be added to salads and other dishes, either raw or gently fried. They are a true seasonal delicacy that will hopefully become more common in the next few years.

Almonds may be found whole, either skin-on or blanched; slivered (in little sticks); sliced, either blanched or skin-on (my preference for their stronger flavor and more distinctive look); ground; or in almond flavoring. Blanched almonds, or almonds with their skins removed, are valued in baking for their light color, but as with all nuts, toasting enhances their flavor. Almonds are further prepared and sold as marzipan, almond paste, almond

extract, liqueurs, and almond milk. Store almonds in an airtight container in the freezer.

In California, nonpareil almonds are most common, because of their thin shells and smooth kernels. Mission almonds have a thick shell and dark brownish-red skin with a wrinkled kernel that is wider than that of the nonpareil. Because of their stronger flavor, they are used in snacks and ice creams, often toasted. In Spain, rounded, almost coin shaped Marcona almonds are grown only along its Mediterranean coast from Tarragona south to Málaga. Smooth and juicy with rich, sweet flavor, marconas are deep-fried in olive oil, sometimes with rosemary, until brown and crunchy, then sprinkled with sea salt. They are a perfect accompaniment to an aperitif or a glass of Spanish cava sparkling wine. Marcona almond trees bloom early, making them vulnerable to late spring frosts, so they are challenging to grow. But, because they grow inside a hard shell that resists insects, they can be grown without the use of pesticides.

Marzipan, a smooth, kneaded, stiff paste made of ground almonds and sugar, gets its characteristic flavor from bitter almonds and is often flavored with rosewater. Believed to have originated in Persia (today Iran), it was probably brought to Europe in the Middle Ages by Arab traders, where it became a specialty of the Baltic region of Germany, particularly in the town of Lübeck. The art of working with marzipan reached a high level in the convents of Sicily, where the sisters made small cakes of *marzapane*. Marzipan, rolled into thin sheets and glazed, is traditionally used to cover and decorate wedding cakes and to mold figures, such as tiny, lifelike fruits. In some places, marzipan is shaped into small figures of animals, such as pigs, to mark the New Year; in Italy, small marzipan fruits are eaten at Christmas. Almond paste is similar

19

to marzipan but less sweet and coarser in texture and mostly used for baking. Delicate and expensive, almond oil is extracted from bitter almonds and used in baking; the residue is steeped in water and distilled to make almond extract.

Ground almonds help give structure to cakes, used as an alternative to flour in Austro-Hungarian tortes and French flourless chocolate cake. Mixed with meringue, almonds add flavor and texture to light, crunchy *dacquoise* cakes (*see* Mocha Date Dacquoise, page 333). These same cake layers are also known as *Japonais* in French patisserie. A layer of absorbent frangipane, a mixture of almond paste and pastry cream, spread on the bottom of a fruit tart, prevents the fruit juices from making the pastry soggy. Macaroons, Chinese almond cookies, and financiers are just a few of the many kinds of cookies based on almonds.

Almonds were, and are, prized for their long-keeping qualities and concentrated food energy. In ancient times, nomads mixed ground almonds, chopped dates, bits of pistachios, sesame, and breadcrumbs and rolled the mixture into small balls to sustain them on long desert journeys. Today, we do the same thing with trail mix and granola (*see* Toasted Grain, Fruit, and Nut Granola, page 631).

Almonds, toasted or plain, add crunch to foods both savory and sweet, while ground almonds thicken creamy, rich Mediterranean sauces like Greek *skordalia*, Turkish *tarator*, Catalonian *romesco*, and Indian *korma*. These sauces probably originated in Persia, where almond trees have been cultivated for thousands of years

Almonds are just as versatile in sweets, especially those of Mediterranean, Middle Eastern, and North African origin. Almond milk, known in Arabic as *laban al loz*, is a popular cooling drink; in Sicily, almond milk is frozen into *granita*. French nougatine and praline marry the crunch of the nut with caramelized sugar, while honey and egg-white meringue mixed with whole toasted almonds are used to make Spanish *turrón* and Italian *torroni* that ranges from soft and fluffy to hard and crackling in texture.

Almond Tarator Dip with Crunchy Pita Chips

This Lebanese and Turkish dip or sauce, made with toasted and then ground almonds and livened up with lemon and garlic, is delicious with grilled or pan-fried fish, or steamed asparagus, green beans, fennel, or beets. Serve with Yogurt and Garlic Marinated Chicken Wings (see page 1016). The tarator also makes a great-tasting, if nontraditional, sandwich spread. Serve as a mezze (the Levantine equivalent to Spanish tapas) with Crunchy Pita Chips, vegetable crudités, and a bowl of mixed cured olives.

MAKES 3 CUPS

$1/2$ pound (2 cups) blanched almonds

3 to 4 slices country-style white bread, soaked in water and squeezed dry (about $1/2$ cup)

1 tablespoon crushed garlic

1 cup cold water

$1/4$ cup cider vinegar

$1/2$ cup extra-virgin olive oil

1 tablespoon kosher salt

Preheat the oven to 300°F. Toast the almonds lightly, about 20 minutes, or until lightly and evenly browned.

Place the toasted almonds, the bread, garlic, and half of the water in the bowl of a food processor and process until smooth and creamy. With the motor running, add the vinegar, olive oil, salt, and remaining water. Process again until well blended. Chill for 2 hours.

Crunchy Pita Chips

¼ cup extra-virgin olive oil

1 tablespoon chopped garlic

1 tablespoon ground cumin

½ teaspoon hot red pepper flakes

1 package pita breads, cut into 6 wedges each

Preheat the oven to 350°F. In a small bowl, combine the olive oil, garlic, cumin, and pepper flakes. Brush each pita wedge with the oil mix. Arrange in a single layer on a baking tray. Bake 6 to 8 minutes, then turn over and bake 2 to 4 minutes longer, or until lightly and evenly toasted.

STORING ALMONDS

It's best to store almonds and other nuts in a double zip-top freezer bag in the freezer, with all the air squeezed out, marked with the date. Ground almonds will tend to pick up freezer odors, so they are best kept frozen for several weeks at most.

Almond Mandelbrot

Anyone from an Eastern European Jewish background is probably quite familiar with biscotti, though by another name: mandelbrot or kamishbrot. Biscotti, mandelbrot, and kamishbrot are all twice-baked cookies; the first from Italy, the latter two from Eastern Europe. In German-speaking parts of Eastern Europe, they are called mandelbrot (almond bread), while in the Ukraine, a similar cookie called kamishbrot (or thuskamish) was served. In Eastern Europe, Jews dipped their mandelbrot into a glass of sweet tea, similar to the way Italians dip biscotti into espresso or sweet wine. There must be a connection. One theory is that Jews in Piedmont first tasted biscotti and brought them along when they migrated to Eastern Europe. Substitute whole hazelnuts for an equally delicious cookie.

21

MAKES 6 DOZEN

1½ pounds (6 cups) all-purpose flour, unbleached preferred

3 tablespoons baking powder

2 teaspoons ground cinnamon

1 teaspoon kosher salt

4 eggs + 1 egg, lightly beaten for glaze

2 cups granulated sugar

Grated zest of 1 lemon

1 tablespoon vanilla extract

½ pound (2 sticks) unsalted butter, melted and cooled

1 pound (4 cups) whole almonds with skin on, coarsely chopped

½ cup crystallized or raw sugar, for sprinkling

Whisk together the dry ingredients: flour, baking powder, cinnamon, and salt, and reserve.

Lightly beat the 4 eggs, sugar, lemon zest, and vanilla together, then stir in butter.

Stir in the dry ingredients, then stir in the almonds. Note: the dough will be stiff.

Preheat the oven to 325°F. Shape the dough into 4 to 6 evenly-shaped flat logs, about 2 inches wide and about 1 inch high. Place on Silpat or parchment paper-lined baking pans. (Flour your hands or rub lightly with oil to keep the dough from sticking.) Brush the logs with the beaten egg and sprinkle all over with the sugar.

Bake 25 minutes, until the outside of the logs are lightly browned. Remove from the oven and cool completely, overnight if desired. With a sharp knife, slice the mandelbrot on the diagonal, about between $1/4$ and $1/2$ inch thick.

Preheat the oven to 350°F., place the cookie slices back onto the baking pans, flat side down, and bake for 10 minutes. Turn the cookies and continue baking 5 to 10 more minutes, or until they are lightly browned all over. Remove and cool completely before storing in a tightly sealed container for up to 1 week.

FREEZING BISCOTTI

Like all biscotti, these mandelbrots freeze perfectly. Freeze the logs after they've been baked the first time, defrost and bake the second time for fresh-tasting, crunchy biscotti. Alternatively, freeze the dough or the shaped logs before baking, defrost, and then bake twice as directed in the recipe.

Almond Macaroon Cake with Pine Nuts

This buttery, rich cake has been a favorite of my son's since he was about fourteen. Serve it sliced and toasted with a scoop of butter almond ice cream for an indulgent treat or with strawberry, raspberry, or red currant fruit sauce for a lighter dessert. This cake also freezes very well, as long as it is tightly wrapped.

MAKES TWO 9–INCH DIAMETER CAKES

$1/4$ pound (1 cup) sifted cake flour

$1/4$ pound (1 cup) ground almonds or almond flour

$1 1/2$ teaspoons baking powder

1 teaspoon kosher salt

12 tablespoons ($1 1/2$ sticks) unsalted butter

1 pound almond paste

Grated zest of 1 orange and 1 lemon

$3/4$ cup (6 ounces) dark rum

8 eggs, separated

$1/2$ cup granulated sugar

1 cup pine nuts

Confectioners' sugar (for dusting)

Preheat the oven to 350°F. Prepare cake pans by spraying with nonstick spray. Sift together the dry ingredients: cake flour, almond flour, baking powder, and salt.

Using the paddle beater to a mixer, cream the butter, almond paste, orange and lemon zests until light and fluffy. Beat in the rum and then beat in the egg yolks, one at a time. Scrape out of the bowl and reserve. Clean the bowl very well (any oil will keep the meringue from achieving full expansion).

In a separate, clean bowl and using the whisk to a mixer, beat the egg whites until fluffy and then gradually beat in the sugar. Continue beating until the egg whites are firm and glossy and stick to the sides of the bowl.

Fold the dry ingredients into the creamed butter mixture, then fold in the meringue one-third at a time, so the batter doesn't deflate. Pour into the prepared pans. Sprinkle with pine nuts and bake 30 to 40 minutes or until set in the middle. When cool, remove from the pans and dust with confectioners' sugar.

Amaretto Cheesecake with Chocolate–Amaretti Crust

This is an old favorite from my days in the early 1980s as chef of Ristorante DiLullo. I wanted to combine the flavors of Italy (Amaretti biscuits are actually made from apricot pits and not almonds), amaretto liqueur, and bittersweet chocolate with the Jewish- or Italian-style cheesecake that many of my customers grew up eating. I've recently started to add crushed cocoa nibs to this cake for its crunchy texture and rich chocolate-cocoa fat flavor. The nibs are simply roasted and crushed cocoa beans. They can be purchased from specialty stores and chocolate and baking supply companies, many of them on the Internet.

MAKES ONE 9–INCH CHEESECAKE

Chocolate–Amaretti Crust

1 (7-ounce) package Amaretti biscuits (or almond biscotti)
$1/2$ pound semisweet chocolate, in bits or finely chopped
4 tablespoons unsalted butter

Grind the Amaretti (or biscotti) in food processor to crumbs. Melt the chocolate and butter together and then cool slightly. Combine the crushed Amaretti (or biscotti) and cooled chocolate. Press thecrust into the bottom of a 9-inch springform pan. Chill for at least 1 hour.

Amaretto Filling

1 pound cream cheese (at room temperature)
$1/4$ cup Amaretto liqueur
1 cup sour cream
$1/2$ cup heavy cream
$1/2$ cup granulated sugar
4 eggs
1 (3-ounce) package Amaretti biscuits, coarsely crushed
$1/4$ pound cocoa nibs, optional
1 teaspoon almond extract

Preheat the oven to 350°F. Using the paddle, beat the cream cheese and Amaretto liqueur until smooth and soft, scraping down the sides of the bowl once or twice. Add the sour cream, heavy cream, and sugar, and beat again until smooth. Beat in the eggs, one at a time. Lastly, fold in the crushed Amaretti, cocoa nibs, and the almond extract.

Pour into the chilled crust and bake at 350°F. for 30 minutes; reduce heat to 300°F. and bake 30 minutes longer, or until barely set in the middle. Cool completely before removing from the pan.

Chill in the refrigerator before slicing into 12 portions, using a hot, wet knife and rinsing the knife off under hot water in between each slice.

23

Moroccan Gazelle Horns with Orange–Almond Filling: Kab el Ghazal

These delicious pastries are thought to resemble the elegantly curved horns of gazelles found in Morocco. The pastries are served for special occasions such as weddings because they are admittedly time-consuming to make. The good thing is that the pastry and filling both freeze beautifully on their own and the baked Gazelle Horns can also be frozen.

MAKES 2 DOZEN

Pastry Dough

1 pound (4 sticks) unsalted butter, cut into bits

$3/4$ pound (3 cups) unbleached all-purpose flour

$1/2$ teaspoon kosher salt

2 eggs + $1/2$ cup ice water, lightly beaten together

Place the butter, flour, and salt in the bowl of a mixer and freeze for 30 minutes, or until the butter is firm and very cold. Using the paddle, beat until the bits are the size of oatmeal flakes. (Keep everything cold. Do not let the mixture get oily.)

Pour in the egg-water mix and beat only long enough for the dough to come together. Shape into a flattened block, transfer to a plastic freezer bag or wrap well in plastic and refrigerate until firm (at least 1 hour) before rolling out.

Orange–Almond Filling

$1/2$ pound (about 2 cups) blanched almonds

$1/2$ pound almond paste

$1/4$ cup chopped candied orange rind

4 tablespoons softened unsalted butter

1 egg

1 tablespoon orange blossom water

Lightly toast the almonds in a 325°F. oven for about 15 minutes, stirring once or twice. Remove from the oven and cool. Place the cooled almonds in the bowl of a food processor and grind to fine crumbs. Add the almond paste, candied orange rind, butter, egg, and orange blossom water and process until the mixture forms a smooth paste. Remove the mixture from the bowl and roll into a cylinder about $3/4$ inch in diameter. Cut the cylinder into 2-inch lengths and reserve.

Assembly

Pastry Dough

Orange-Almond Filling

2 tablespoons orange blossom water

1 cup confectioners' sugar

Roll out the dough on parchment or wax paper sheets to between $1/4$ and $1/8$ inch thick. Chill, then cut into 4-inch squares. Chill again.

Preheat the oven to 400°F. Arrange the dough squares on the diagonal on a board. Place one 2-inch-long cylinder of almond filling about halfway between the center line and the top point of each square. Fold over the point to cover the filling, then roll once. Lightly pinch together the edges, enclosing the filling completely, then continue folding. With the point-side down, gently form the cookies into crescent shapes.

Arrange the filled crescents on a buttered and floured or parchment paper (or Silpat)-lined baking sheet. (They won't expand much.) Bake 20 to 30 minutes, or until lightly but evenly browned.

Remove from the oven and, while hot, brush each horn with orange blossom water. Place the confectioners' sugar in a bowl and dip each brushed horn into the sugar to coat generously. Cool and serve at room temperature. The gazelle horns keep well for up to one week in a covered container.

WORKING WITH ALMONDS

To grind almonds without ending up with an oily mess, grind while frozen in the bowl of a food processor or in a meat grinder. Add the flour and/or sugar to the bowl while processing to get a finer grind without oiliness.

ORANGE BLOSSOM WATER AND ROSE WATER

In North Africa and the Middle East, pastries are traditionally scented with orange blossom or rose water, rather than vanilla, because these flavorings were local and inexpensive, whereas vanilla was (and is) quite expensive. Used in small amounts, flower waters add an exotic and haunting aroma to desserts. The best orange blossom and rose waters I have found are made by Cortas in Lebanon. Store in the pantry for up to one year.

25

APPLES

APPLES

Nothing says "home" better than the smell of baked apples with their brown sugar and butter stuffing bubbling up—in fact, home sellers may make a sale more quickly if the irresistible aroma of a baking apple pie wafts through the house as potential home buyers make their walk through. Unassuming but almost universally appealing apple desserts in this section include two "oldies but goodies": Apple Rum-Raisin Bread Pudding and Apple Caramel Bundt Cake.

Apples make a natural marriage with sugar, caramel, and honey. In Great Britain, apples are coated in toffee candy; in America, they are dipped in caramel and rolled in salted peanuts, or covered with a crackling red "apple-colored" sugar candy shell. Apple wedges dipped in honey are eaten during the Jewish New Year of Rosh Hashanah that falls in autumn to symbolize the hope of a sweet new year. Whether crunchy and raw as in the Autumn Apple Hazelnut Salad and Apple-Celery-Walnut Relish, or lusciously stuffed and baked as in the Lebanese Stuffed Baked Apples with Chicken, Golden Raisins, and Almonds, apples perform equally well in savory and sweet dishes

Though we think of apples as "all-American," they are just as common in the French kitchen, especially in the Atlantic region of Normandy, where apple orchards are abundant and apples go into chicken dishes, tarts, fresh and sparkling hard cider, and Calvados, a brandy distilled entirely from apples. In French cuisine, a dish with the word "Normand" in its name will include apples.

The small rounded apple, *Malus pumilla*, a fruit of ancient and mythical origins, has sweet, tart, and crunchy flesh dressed in blushing hues of ivory, pink, crimson, scarlet, gold, and green that may be solid-colored, streaked, speckled, or russeted or bi-colored. The smallest are squat, shiny Lady Apples, creamy yellow on the shaded side and deep glossy crimson on the sunny side, in season just in time for winter holiday fruit baskets; the largest are expensive, perfectly formed light red, golden-accented grapefruit-sized Fujis, prized for gift giving in the Asian community.

Apples originated in Kazakhstan as tiny sour fruits similar to crabapples that were carried east by traders on the Silk Road. As early as the second century BCE, people learned how to take cuttings of one tree and graft it onto suitable root stock, because the exact same type of apple won't grow from a planted seed. Emigrants to America brought along apple pips (or seeds) instead of cuttings, which could not have survived the long voyage. These seeds gave rise to entirely new varieties that were diversified by interbreeding with native American crabapples. As a result, American apples became a distinct group. These apples spread with the help of Johnny Appleseed, born John Chapman in Massachusetts in 1775, who collected apple seeds from local cider mills and planted

28

them on his travels through the East Coast region.

By the early 1800s, American nurseries offered about 100 apple varieties; by 1850, more than 500 varieties were being widely cultivated; and by 1872, Charles Downing described close to 1,100 apples in his book, *The Fruits and Fruit Trees of America*. Unfortunately, by the late nineteenth and early twentieth centuries, our incredibly rich and diverse apple culture began to decline. Our market system shifted overwhelmingly toward apples that could be grown in large-scale orchards, then packed and shipped across long distances or across the ocean. Flavor and texture inevitably lost out to appearance and durability.

Today, about 2,500 named varieties of apples are grown in the United States and more than 7,500 worldwide, but only 15 varieties account for more than 90 percent of our crop. In the past decade, the glossy but mealy and tasteless apples that once dominated the produce aisles of supermarkets are being joined by up-and-coming varieties like Braeburn, Cameo, Fuji, Gala, Ginger Gold, Honeycrisp, and Pink Lady.

Many old varieties have been preserved in home orchards by small-scale farmers, and in traditional communities such as those of the Amish and Mennonites, and there is a growing movement to bring back heirloom apples through organizations like Slow Food. Search out heirloom apples at local farmers' markets and older orchards to get the unique flavor and complexity of locally grown apples, which have adapted to a specific growing region, or even to the *terroir* (or special quality of the earth and environment) of an individual orchard.

All apples must be picked by hand because they are easily bruised. Apples should be fully ripe for best flavor; if overripe, they will be mealy and soft. There are crabap-

ples (small sour apples), eating (or dessert) apples, cooking (or baking) apples, and cider apples, though most apples in the U.S. are used for both eating and cooking.

According to the U.S. Apple Association, in 2002, Americans ate almost 16 pounds each of fresh apples and more then 26 pounds each of processed apples (juice, pies, dried, frozen, apple butter, apple jelly, cider, and more.) The most important apple-growing states are Washington, Michigan, and New York. Americans prefer red apples, and the Red Delicious is the most popular, though green Granny Smiths are gaining. Note that apple seeds contain cyanide, so avoid eating them.

HOW TO STORE APPLES

Apples may be left out for up to two days, but will tend to turn mealy. Store apples in the refrigerator for up to two weeks. For long-term storage, the apples must be absolutely sound with no blemishes or bruises, and must be kept in a dry and cool place without touching each other. Remove any spoiled apples because "one rotten apple spoils the whole barrel." Peeled, cooked apple wedges may be frozen and stored in an air-tight container or double plastic zip-top freezer bag.

How to Choose Apples

Choose apples with smooth, clean, shiny skin and bright, clear color, avoiding dull-looking, bruised apples or those with punctures, which result in decay spots. However, older heirloom varieties found at farmers' markets will often have odd shapes, small holes, or other blemishes; though less than perfect, they are well worth the effort of trimming because of their outstanding character.

Any brown soft spots can be easily cut away, especially if the apples are going to be baked or cut up, rather than eaten whole. If we buy only perfect shiny, red "teacher's pet" apples, we may end up with nothing but Red Delicious and possibly Golden Delicious and Granny Smiths. If the apple skin is slack rather than taut and wrinkles when you rub your thumb across it, it has probably been in cold storage too long or has not been kept cool.

Making Applesauce

Simmer cored and peeled (or not) apples into a thick chunky sauce with sugar, a bit of lemon and cinnamon stick or a couple of cloves, stirring often. To make the best-tasting applesauce (or apple pie), use as many different varieties of apples as you can find. Some will be sweet and soft; others crisp and tart; together they'll result in a complex, multidimensional flavor with some smoothness and some chunkiness to the texture. Crabapples, though small and tedious to trim, make outstanding applesauce; they require much more sugar than other types to cut their acidity. Though the sauce won't freeze completely hard, it will keep quite well in the freezer for up to three months.

THE MOST POPULAR AMERICAN APPLES IN ORDER FROM MOST TO LEAST

Red Delicious

Golden Delicious

Gala

Fuji

Granny Smith

McIntosh

Rome

Ida Red

Jonathan

Empire

York

Cortland

Northern Spy

Rhode Island Greening

Stayman Winesap

30

Common American Apple Varieties

Braeburn: This apple has a high-impact, rich, sweet-tart, spicy flavor that is aromatic, juicy, and crisp with a firm texture that makes it excellent for snacking and baking. Its color varies from orange to red over a yellow background. The Braeburn was introduced to the market in 1952 from New Zealand. It was discovered as a chance seedling, probably a cross of the Lady Hamilton and the Granny Smith. It is available year-round in supermarkets.

Cameo®: The Cameo®, formerly known as Carousel, is a relatively new apple variety that showed up in a Red and Golden Delicious orchard in 1987 in Washington state. Its attractive red has characteristic white spots on the skin and crunchy sweet-tart flesh. Shaped like a Red Delicious without the "sheep's nose" bumps on the bottom, Cameo® is an excellent all-purpose eating and cooking apple that keeps very well in storage, holds its texture for long periods and is sweet with a zingy crunch. It is available year-round in supermarkets.

Cortland: Cortland has very white flesh and is an excellent dessert apple. It was one of the earliest crosses made with the McIntosh early in the twentieth century. Its flavor is sweet compared to McIntosh, and it has a blush of crimson against a pale yellow background sprinkled with short, dark red stripes and gray-green dots. It is in season September through April.

Crabapples: Crabapples are the only apple native to North America. In order to qualify as a crabapple, the fruit must be two inches or less in diameter. Native American crabapples remain green even when ripe, but there are some hybrids and Asian varieties that turn red, yellow, and even purple when ripe. Crabapples are tasty, though quite tart, but they are excellent for making jellies and applesauce because of their high pectin content. Crabapples are generally found in fall and winter.

Crispin: Crispin is a 1930 cross of Golden Delicious and the Japanese variety Indo, originally named Mutsu and renamed Crispin in 1968. In Michigan, it is still widely known as Mutsu. The Crispin is one of the later varieties and works both as a fresh apple and a processing apple. It is typically greenish on the outside and creamy white on the inside with firm-textured, juicy flesh and moderately sweet flavor. It is in season from September through June.

Empire: Empire is a cross developed in New York in 1966 that combines the mild tartness of McIntosh with Red Delicious' sweetness. It is redder and firmer than McIntosh, and because it stores well, it provides the marketplace with a McIntosh-type apple well into the spring. Some claim that Empire's flavor, like fine wine, improves during storage. It is excellent for eating out of hand and in salads and for use in baking and cooking. Empire is a favorite in the United Kingdom, which imports much of its supply from Michigan. Empires are in season from October through July.

Fuji: This immensely flavorful variety was introduced to the U.S. from Japan in the 1980s, where it was developed in the 1930s as a cross of Red Delicious and Ralls Janet bred at a Japanese research station. Now the U.S. produces more Fujis than Japan, and the variety's popularity is growing every year. The Fuji is known for its firm, crispy texture and syrupy sweetness balanced by a tart edge. It holds its texture well when baked and works well in salads. Cool weather in the late fall helps develop its reddish-pink color and outstanding flavor. Fujis are available year-round though the huge, perfect specimens prized in the Asian community are to be found mostly in the fall. If I had to choose only one apple, it would be a Fuji.

Gala: The Gala is a cross of the superb Cox's Orange Pippin and Golden Delicious developed by New Zealand plant breeders in the 1970s. It has pinkish-orange stripes over a yellow background and crisp, sweet, aromatic flesh. It is best for snacking and salads and is found year-round in supermarkets.

Ginger Gold Apples: These apples were discovered in a Virginia orchard in the foothills of the Blue Ridge Mountains in the 1960s and may be a cross between a Golden Delicious and a Pippin. Sweet, tangy, and juicy, Ginger Golds are crisp and juicy with excellent flavor, round in shape with smooth, green-yellow skin tipped with a slight red blush. They are harvested in August and are in season until September.

Golden Delicious: The Golden Delicious originated in Clay County, West Virginia, from unknown parent-age, though some suspect the chance seedling can be traced to the French Golden Reinette and the Grimes Golden. Originally called Mullin's Yellow, it can be found year-round. The "Golden" is a good all-purpose apple with mellow, sweet flavor, used for baking and salads, although it can be somewhat dry in the mouth when eaten out of hand. Goldens hold their shape well when baked, and their flesh stays white longer than other apples when cut, two characteristics that make them desirable to chefs.

Granny Smith: The Granny Smith originated in Australia and is believed to be descended from French crabapples cultivated by Australian grandmother Maria Ann Smith in about 1868. Green, extremely tart, crisp, juicy, and versatile, Granny Smiths are a favorite for pies. They're also excellent for snacking and salads, for those who appreciate a firm, tart fruit. The deeper the green, the tarter and firmer the apple. Very green Grannys may be dry in texture. Granny Smiths are ubiquitous and may be found year-round.

Gravenstein: This outstanding summer apple has a long heritage in many countries, with names for it appearing in Russian, Italian, German, Danish, and English. Established in the 1600s, the Gravenstein came to America in the 1700s, where it is grown commercially mostly in California. It is a roundish, irregularly shaped apple with a very short stem; its color varies, but is usually a greenish yellow covered with broad red stripes. Gravensteins are excellent for sauce and pies and have crisp, juicy, aromatic flesh,

32

full of old-fashioned tart-sweet flavor. They may be found July through November, more commonly on the West Coast.

Honeycrisp Apple: The Honeycrisp was produced from a 1960 cross of Macoun and Honeygold as part of the University of Minnesota apple-breeding program. The skin of a Honeycrisp is mottled red over a yellow background. The fruit has an exceptionally crisp, sweet, and juicy texture and is in season July through November.

Ida Red: Ida Red is a cross of Jonathan with Wagener made at the Idaho Agricultural Experiment Station in 1942. It's a bright red apple that is firm and keeps well with tangy-tart flavor. Besides its excellence as a fresh apple, it is widely used in sauces and pies and for baking, because it holds its shape. It is in season October through June.

Jonagold: Jonagolds are a cross of Golden Delicious and Jonathan developed in a New York apple breeding program and introduced to market in 1968. This juicy, orange-tinted apple has a tangy-sweet flavor and is excellent for fresh eating, cooking, and pies. It is in season from mid-September through May.

Jonathan: The Jonathan was a chance seedling discovered in the 1820s in Woodstock, New York. It got its name from the man who first promoted it. This crimson apple with touches of green has a spicy tang that blends well with other varieties in sauces and cider. The Jonathan is suitable both for fresh eating

and for processing and is in season from November through January.

Lady Apple: Some people trace the origins of the Lady Apple back as far as Roman times to Appius Claudius, the Roman censor who constructed the Appian Way. A favorite French dessert apple, it was already grown in the gardens of Louis XIII at Orléans in the early 1600s. This tiny, flattish apple has shiny skin ranging in color from brilliant red to yellow with generous red blushing, usually creamy yellow on the shaded side and deep glossy crimson on the sunny side. Lady Apples have a sweet-tart flavor, perfect to pop right in the mouth, and tender, white, crisp, juicy, and faintly perfumed flesh. The best flavor is its skin, which should always be eaten. The petite size and exquisite coloring of this dessert apple make the Lady Apple as delightful to the eye as it is delicious to eat, and it is widely used for garnishing and decorating. A good keeper, it is in season in time for the winter holidays.

Macoun: The Macoun was developed at the New York State Agricultural Experiment Station in Geneva in 1932 and is named for a famous Canadian fruit breeder. This favorite East Coast apple is small to medium in size, with pale yellow skin almost completely blushed wine red, and tender, snow-white flesh. It's crisp, very juicy, sweetly tart, and aromatic. While it is considered an all-purpose apple, it is especially good for eating out of hand. Macoun apples are in season in October and November, mostly to be found on the East Coast.

McIntosh: In 1796, John McIntosh, who came from the Mohawk Valley in New York, homesteaded in Dundela, Ontario, not far from the St. Lawrence River. He transplanted wild apple saplings, one of which survived and produced fruit of such tangy flavor and fragrance that they became well-known in the region. Years later, his son propagated this apple, which became known as McIntosh Red. The variety is thought to be related to the Fameuse apple of the region. McIntosh has juicy white flesh and a rather tough skin that has mixed red and green coloring. It's a favorite apple for eating out of hand, but also is widely used in salads, sauces, and pies and is a mainstay in fresh cider. The McIntosh, immortalized though misspelled in the name of the Macintosh computer, is in season September through June.

Northern Spy: The Northern Spy is a venerable apple, discovered south of Rochester, New York, around the beginning of the nineteenth century as surviving sprouts of a seedling that had died. The Wagener is believed to be one of its forebears. Northern Spy is a late-season apple with a red blush over a yellow-green skin and yellowish flesh, used mainly for processing, because it holds its shape and flavor in cooking, although it has many fans for fresh eating. It is in season November through March.

Pink Lady®: The Pink Lady® is a cross of Golden Delicious and Lady Williams developed in a Western Australia breeding program and introduced to market in 1985. Firm, crisp flesh and a unique, tangy-tart, sweet flavor are characteristic of this apple, which can be enjoyed as a snack or used for baking. Pink Lady® is harvested in late October when crisp fall nights bring on the bright pink color that gives the apple its name. It is in season from the fall through the spring.

Red Delicious: Red Delicious was discovered as a chance seedling on the farm of Jesse Hiatt and was originally known as Hawkeye. Washington apple growers have been producing Red Delicious apples since the 1920s. America's classic snacking apple, the Red Delicious is heart-shaped with a characteristic four-bumped "sheep's nose" bottom, bright red, shiny, and sometimes striped. Crunchy with a mildly sweet, rather innocuous flavor, the Red Delicious is the most common apple by far in America, often reviled as an example of growing for perfect shape and deep red color, rather than complexity of flavor. It is, of course, available all year round.

Rome: The Rome apple is named not for the eponymous European city, but rather for its discovery in Rome Township, Ohio, in 1816. It is a round colorful apple, nearly solid red dotted with white "lenticels," the tiny dots that allow the apple to "breathe." With its firm flesh and tough, smooth skin, it is known as the "baker's buddy," because baking enhances its sweet flavor and it keeps its shape. Romes are rather bland to eat out of hand and may be mealy. Choose Romes that are firm with smooth skin and feel solid and heavy, not soft and light in the hand. Romes are in season from mid-October through June and are often quite large.

Stayman Winesap: The Stayman Winesap was developed from the Winesap to obtain larger size, better flavor, and better keeping qualities in 1866 by Dr. J. Stayman of Leavenworth, Kansas, and introduced to market in 1895 by Stark Brothers Nurseries. Medium to large in size, the Stayman's greenish-yellow skin is blushed with dull-red and darker red stripes. It surface is lightly russeted with heavy gusseting around the stem and is prone to cracking, which has discouraged commercial production. The white flesh is tinged a greenish-yellow and is firm, tender, and fine in texture with distinctive tart, wine-like flavor. It is excellent for fresh eating and also good for cooking. The Stayman Winesap ripens in late October and may be found through June.

Winesap: The Winesap is an eastern apple that is believed to be a native of New Jersey, where it was described in 1817 as "the favorite cider fruit" in the region. It is still commonly used to make cider. Winesap is good for eating fresh and for cooking because it has firm, crisp flesh and sweet, aromatic flavor. Its skin is deep red against a bit of yellow background, and is somewhat oblong in shape. It is in season from September through July.

York (or York Imperial): This apple originated in York, Pennsylvania, early in the nineteenth century. A medium-sized apple, it has yellow skin blushed with pinkish-red, faintly striped with bright red. Its flesh is yellowish in color, crisp, and moderately juicy and has a mildly acidic and sweet taste. It is in season from October through June.

Heirloom Apple Varieties

Ashmeads Kernels: This winter russeted variety from England that dates back to about 1700 has golden-brown skin. Its crisp, dense, yellowish flesh is characteristic of russet apples and is sugary and aromatic with concentrated flavor.

Caville Blanc d'Hiver: For French connoisseurs, the Caville Blanc d'Hiver, which was developed in France or Germany around 1598 is the finest apple for eating. It is best for tarts because its fine and tender flesh is sweet, lightly tart, and aromatic.

Chenango Strawberry: The Chenango Strawberry came from New York or Connecticut about 1850. It is medium to large in size and conical in shape with smooth, yellow- or green-tinted white skin striped with crimson. Its firm, tender, juicy flesh has a hint of the strawberries referred to in its name.

Cox's Orange Pippin: The fine Cox's Orange Pippin has been found in England since about 1830. Scarlet and yellow in color, and often striped with yellow, its flesh is firm, crisp, very juicy, and highly aromatic. This variety is prized in England as a dessert apple and is a personal favorite of mine.

Kandil Sinap: The creamy yellow Kandil Sinap came from Turkey or Russia, probably in the area of the Crimea on the Black Sea, in the early 1800s. It is tall, narrow, and cylindrical with a flattened bottom. Its creamy yellow, porcelain-like skin is blushed with brilliant red; its crisp, juicy, fine-grained flesh has good flavor.

Spitzenberg: The Spitzenberg, found in New York before 1800, is medium to large with a tough skin and russeted dots; its yellow-tinged flesh is firm, aromatic and lightly acidic. Many people believe that this variety is unexcelled in flavor or quality. It was Thomas Jefferson's favorite apple, and he really knew his fruits.

Autumn Apple–Hazelnut Salad

Apples and hazelnuts really complement each other in this crispy, refreshing, and colorful salad. In my days as chef of A'propos, with its New American/California-style cuisine, I developed this salad for my fall menu; simple as it is, it really took off. I love the idea of using apple cider cooked down to a thick syrup for the dressing; it adds an intense, concentrated apple flavor along with a welcome acidic edge. If you make the apple cider syrup in larger quantity, it will keep very well for up to one month, refrigerated. Use it to glaze ham, pork chops, roast chicken, or duck.

SERVES 6

Apple–Cider Dressing

2 cups apple cider

¼ cup cider vinegar

1 tablespoon coarse-grain mustard

¼ cup hazelnut oil (substitute canola oil or grapeseed oil)

½ cup canola oil

Kosher salt and fresh ground black pepper to taste

In a medium-size heavy pot, cook the cider until it's thick and syrupy, about ¼ cup in volume, paying close attention as it nears readiness so the syrup doesn't burn. Remove from heat, pour into a blender or food processor and add the remaining dressing ingredients, blending until smooth.

Salad

About 1 pound mixed salad greens (watercress, Boston lettuce, Belgian endive, red leaf, and radicchio)

3 assorted apples, preferably both red and green

Squeeze of fresh lemon juice

1 small red onion, peeled and thinly sliced and soaked in ice water 10 minutes

¼ pound (about 1 cup) hazelnuts, lightly toasted, skins rubbed off and roughly chopped

Wash and dry greens. Cut into bite-sized pieces. Cut down apples on all four sides, leaving a square core to be discarded. Dice the apples and toss with lemon juice.

Using just enough to coat lightly, toss the Apple-Cider Dressing with the greens and apples. Drain and rinse the onion, then sprinkle onto the salad along with the hazelnuts. Serve immediately.

Apple–Celery–Walnut Relish

This crunchy relish goes well with anything made from sharp cheese, such as the Farmhouse Cheddar Welsh Rabbit (see page 231) or grilled cheese sandwiches, or with turkey or chicken salad deli-style sandwiches (see Maple-Apple Smoked Turkey Breast, page 916). This dish was quite popular at the Dock Street Brewing Company and Restaurant where I developed an international brewpub menu and made my sandwiches on homemade bread. After all, beer is just liquid bread. The walnut oil isn't essential—while it enhances the flavor, vegetable oil can be substituted.

SERVES 6 TO 8

2 apples, preferably one red and one green, diced

3 ribs celery, diced

$1/4$ cup walnut oil

$1/4$ cup lemon juice

Kosher salt and black pepper to taste

$1/4$ pound (about 1 cup) toasted walnuts,
   coarsely chopped

$1/2$ bunch fresh chives, sliced

Combine the diced apples and celery in a bowl. Whisk together the walnut oil, lemon juice, salt and pepper and toss with the apple mix. Add the walnuts and chives and toss again.

Lebanese Apples Stuffed with Chicken, Golden Raisins, and Almonds

This is a Lebanese dish that follows the Middle Eastern and Levantine custom of stuffing vegetables or fruits and is often made with quince rather than apples. Large cooked apples are scooped out and filled with succulent chicken thigh meat, almonds, raisins, and rice, and then braised in a sweet-and-sour honey and cider vinegar syrup. It is a good dish to make for a crowd, or perhaps to bring to a potluck dinner, because it can be made ahead and takes well to reheating.

SERVES 8

Stuffed Apples

1 cup long-grain white rice

1 teaspoon kosher salt + salt to taste

2 tablespoon olive oil

1 onion, chopped

$1/2$ cup toasted almonds, chopped

$1/2$ cup golden raisins

$1/4$ cup cider vinegar

1 teaspoon ground cinnamon

$1/4$ teaspoon each hot pepper flakes, ground cloves,
   and ground black pepper

2 pounds chicken thigh meat, cooked and diced

8 large apples (12 ounces each), Fuji preferred

Syrup and Garnish

4 tablespoons unsalted butter

$1/4$ cup honey

$1/4$ cup cider vinegar

$1/2$ cup almonds, toasted and chopped + extra for garnish

$1/2$ cup golden raisins + extra for garnish

Butter a large baking dish, just big enough to hold the 8 apples, and set aside.

Preheat the oven to 350°F. In a medium pot, boil the rice with $1^{1}/_{2}$ cups water and salt for 6 minutes, or until half-cooked. Drain any liquid, rinse the rice under cold water, drain again and reserve.

Heat the olive oil, add the onion and cook five minutes, or until translucent. Stir in rice, almonds, raisins, cider vinegar, and seasonings: cinnamon, hot pepper flakes, ground cloves, salt, and black pepper to taste. Cook over high heat until most of the moisture has evaporated. Remove from heat, stir in chicken (and any cooking juices) and set aside.

Cut a 1-inch slice from the tops of the apples and reserve. Place the apples in a microwaveable dish with $1/2$ inch water on the bottom. Lightly prick the skin at 1-inch intervals.

Microwave the apples 8 minutes, or until somewhat softened. Cut out and discard the cores. Scrape out enough of the apple flesh to leave a $1/2$-inch thick wall.

Arrange the apples in the reserved baking dish and fill each apple with the reserved mixture. Set the reserved tops on top of the stuffed apples.

Melt the butter, honey, and cider vinegar together. Drizzle each apple with the mixture and bake uncovered 45 minutes, or until the apples are tender and glazed.

Transfer the stuffed apples to a serving dish. Strain any juices from the baking dish into a small pot, pressing down to extract the liquid and discarding the solids. Boil the liquid until thick and syrupy, about 5 minutes. Spoon the sauce over the apples. Garnish with toasted chopped almonds and golden raisins and serve.

USING LEFTOVER RICE

For many dishes that include rice, leftover rice that has been carefully refrigerated (because warm rice makes an especially good growing environment for bacteria) works best. Chinese fried rice should be made from day-old rice, and it is suitable to use for stuffing the apples above and for the fillings in the two stuffed cabbage recipes in the Cabbage chapter (*see* Sweet and Sour Stuffed Cabbage with Sauerkraut, page 194; and Stuffed Savoy Cabbage with Spicy Sausage and Pistachios, page 195). Or, add the rice to a soup pot. It will add body to a chunky soup. If you're making a puréed soup, it will thicken it and impart a velvety-smooth consistency.

Apple Rum–Raisin Bread Pudding with Butterscotch Sauce

Is there anything better than apples, butter, and caramel? This luscious rum-spiked bread pudding gets a topping of silky butterscotch sauce made from a layered mélange of honey, molasses, and caramel. Note that you will have extra Butterscotch Sauce. It keeps perfectly well for up to two months, refrigerated. Bring to the boil, whisking to recombine, before serving. Like all bread puddings, this one reheats beautifully in the microwave. I choose Fuji apples for most of my cooking and baking because they have the ideal combination of sweetness and tartness with a texture that holds up when cooked. Be sure to use bread with some body, not commercial white bread, which will turn to mush. I like to make a bigger batch of the rum-soaked raisins, to have some on hand to serve with a little of their syrup on vanilla gelato. (Requires make-ahead preparation).

SERVES 12

$^3/_4$ cup (about $^1/_4$ pound) golden raisins

$^1/_4$ cup light or gold rum

8 eggs

1 cup granulated sugar

1 teaspoon cinnamon

$^1/_2$ teaspoon allspice

1 quart half-and-half (or 3 cups milk and 1 cup heavy cream)

2 loaves (about 2$^1/_2$ pounds) stale country white bread, crusts removed and cut into 1-inch cubes

4 tablespoons unsalted butter, cut into bits + 2 tablespoons unsalted butter

6 large Fuji apples, peeled, cored, and diced

3 tablespoons dark brown sugar, packed

In a small bowl, soak the raisins overnight in the rum.

Lightly beat together the eggs, sugar, cinnamon, allspice, and half-and-half. Pour the egg mixture over the bread, lightly tossing to coat, and let soak in the refrigerator for 2 hours. Add the butter bits to the bread mix.

Preheat the oven to 350°F. Meanwhile, in a large sauté pan, cook the apples in the remaining 2 tablespoons butter and brown sugar until soft. Combine the bread mixture, raisins, and apples and spoon into a large baking dish.

Cover the dish with lightly oiled foil and bake for 45 minutes. Remove the foil and bake for 15 minutes longer, or until browned on top. Remove from oven, cool slightly, and then cut into 12 portions. Serve warm, topped with the Butterscotch Sauce.

Butterscotch Sauce

MAKES ABOUT 3 CUPS

1 cup granulated sugar

$^1/_2$ cup water

$^1/_2$ cup dark corn syrup

$^1/_4$ cup molasses (not blackstrap)

$^1/_4$ cup honey

1 cup heavy cream

$^1/_4$ pound (1 stick) unsalted butter

1 tablespoon vanilla

Combine the sugar and water in medium heavy-bottomed saucepan. Cook over low heat until the sugar dissolves, then raise heat to medium and continue cooking until the sugar turns golden brown. Keep shaking the pan to brown and melt sugar evenly. Do this carefully, as caramelized sugar is over 350°F.!

When the sugar is evenly browned to a rich color and just beginning to become red, carefully pour in the corn syrup, molasses, and honey (the sugar will bubble up and then subside). Then add the cream and butter and stir over heat, until combined and melted. Remove from heat and stir in the vanilla. Keep warm or reheat over low heat as needed.

Apple-Caramel Bundt Cake

One of my all-time favorite cakes, this recipe is adapted from one I cut out of the newspaper. Unlike most apple cakes, this one is made from grated apples, so the cake is moist as can be. Grating takes less time if you have a grater attachment for your food processor or mixer. I call for Fuji apples because I find that they have the perfect combination of crisp texture that holds it shape when cooked and well-balanced sweet-tart flavor. Double the recipe and make two cakes, if desired, because it freezes well.

MAKES ONE 10-INCH BUNDT CAKE, TO SERVE 12 TO 16

$^3/_4$ pound (3 cups) all-purpose flour

1 teaspoon baking soda

1 teaspoon kosher salt

1 teaspoon cinnamon

2 cups granulated sugar

3 eggs

2 teaspoons vanilla extract

$1^1/_2$ cups vegetable oil

4 large Fuji apples, peeled, cored, and grated

1 cup pecans, finely chopped

$^1/_4$ pound (1 stick) butter

$^1/_2$ cup dark brown sugar, firmly packed

1 tablespoon milk

Spread softened butter in Bundt pan. Dust with flour, shaking out the excess. Preheat the oven to 325°F.

Whisk together dry ingredients: flour, baking soda, salt, and cinnamon.

Beat sugar, eggs, and vanilla together until light and lemony colored. Slowly beat in the oil, allowing the oil to be absorbed before adding more (as if making a mayonnaise).

Gradually add the dry ingredients, then fold in the grated apples (with their juice) and the pecans.

Pour the batter into the prepared pan, banging down once or twice to remove air bubbles.

Bake 1 hour and 20 minutes, or until a toothpick stuck into the batter comes out clean and the cake has started to pull away from the sides of the pan.

Cool the cake somewhat and then turn it out upside down onto a cake rack placed over a baking pan. Cool until the cake is just warm, not hot.

Meanwhile, place the butter, brown sugar, and milk into a small pot and bring to a boil, whisking occasionally. Boil 2 minutes, or until the mixture is thickened and creamy looking. Cool the icing until it's firm enough to hold its shape and warm to the touch.

Spoon the icing over cake, allowing it to drip down the sides. If desired, scrape up the excess, using a rubber spatula, and spoon it over the cake again. Let cake cool completely before serving.

APRICOTS

APRICOTS

The delectable and exquisite apricot is as important in the kitchen dried as it is fresh and works equally well with sweet and savory dishes. A modern Jewish Carrot-Apricot Kugel (or pudding) is suitable for Passover but delicious any time of year, while chicken stuffed with apricots and spinach is a French-inspired dish adapted from the first cookbook I worked on with famed French chef, Georges Perrier.

On the sweet side, Apricot-Orange Hamentaschen Cookies, with a filling made from dried apricots, are a modern variation on the traditional tri-cornered cookies served for the Jewish holiday of Purim. Baked Apricots Stuffed with Almond Amaretto Cream are an Italian hot dessert made from fresh apricots.

The Romans named the fruit *Preacocium*, meaning "precocious," because it ripens earlier than other stone fruits. This richly sweet, aromatic fruit was first cultivated in China over 4,000 years ago. Cuttings of the golden fruit tree made their way across the Persian Empire to the Mediterranean, where they flourished. Apricots reached Italy as early as 100 BC and arrived in England in the thirteenth century. Spanish explorers introduced apricots to the New World, planting them in the gardens of Spanish missions in California, and by 1792, the first major planting of apricots was recorded south of San Francisco. Today, California produces more than ninety-five percent of the apricots in the United States.

Over four hundred growers produce apricots in orchards covering 21,000 acres in the San Joaquin Valley and northern California. Apricots are also a significant crop in British Columbia (Canada), Australia, Italy, the south of France, and Israel. Australian glazed apricots are highly sought after for their plump, satiny-glazed, soft texture, and rich color and flavor.

A cousin of the peach, the apricot, *Prunus armeniaca*, is smaller and has a smooth, oval pit that falls out easily when the fruit is halved. Like other stone fruits, apricots are sweetest—and most prone to bruising—when they're allowed to ripen on the tree. The small velvety-skinned fruit is smaller than a peach, orange-yellow when ripe, with flesh that tends to be dry, although some varieties are firmer, larger, and juicier.

The petite apricot is appreciated by fruit connoisseurs for delicate flavor, faintly fuzzed skin as smooth as a baby's cheek, and exquisite aroma. But, unless you can pick your own, you'll probably have to make do with the slightly underripe, more durable apricots sold in markets. Although apricots come to market fresh, large quantities are dried, canned, or used to make jams and jellies. Note that apricot jelly is rich in pectin and, when melted, makes a perfect glaze to brush over a fruit tart.

Choosing dried apricots

Whole dried, light-orange colored, wrinkle-skinned Turkish apricots are relatively inexpensive and easy to find, but I much prefer the deeply colored, melting California fruits dried in halves. I've found that the Trader Joe's stores have the best selection and quality (and the lowest prices) for California apricots. Try California slab apricots, which are made from very ripe fruit that have been dried, chopped, flattened, and cut into shape. Because they are processed from such ripe fruit, slab apricots are honey-sweet and soft and giving in texture, with intense apricot flavor. Their soft, luscious Blenheim come from that highly prized variety. Mariani is an excellent supermarket and warehouse-store brand.

MAKING CALIFORNIA DRIED APRICOTS

It takes about six pounds of fresh apricots to make one pound of dried apricots, which have more concentrated nutrients than any other dried fruit. Sweetly tart, dried apricots are superb in color, flavor, and texture and are extremely versatile in the kitchen. The fruits are picked at peak ripeness and halved, then arranged on trays, cut side up, and treated with sulphur dioxide (commonly used to keep yellow-colored dried fruits and white wine from darkening). The trays are rotated in the sun for about three days when the fruit is ready for washing and packing.

California Fresh Apricot Varieties

The most important apricot varieties in California are the Patterson, Blenheim, Tilton, and Castlebrite. The Patterson is a late-season, firm-medium apricot with good flavor, orange skin, delicate flavor, and possibly its most important quality for commercial success, excellent shelf life. The Blenheim, a medium apricot with intense flavor, is considered the king of apricots and is rarely to be found fresh outside of California. It also makes a superb dried apricot with soft, rich flesh, velvety skin, concentrated flavor, and pectin-rich body, making it well suited to purées, glazes, and tart fillings. Unfortunately, despite the Blenheims' superior flavor, it is rapidly disappearing from California orchards because of its fragility. The Tilton is a large, firm apricot with tart flavor. The Castlebrite is a medium-sized early apricot with bright orange skin with a red blush, firm flesh, and a tart flavor, unless it is very ripe.

Carrot–Apricot Kugel

This is a rather sophisticated version of the humble kugel, that hard-to-define Eastern European Jewish dish. A kugel, pronounced "koo-gel" or "ki-gel" and usually translated as "pudding," can be either a side dish or a dessert, always baked in a casserole dish. As a side dish, it may be made from potatoes, eggs, and onions; spinach and rice; noodles with cottage cheese and caraway; or, as here, carrots and apricots. As a dessert, it is usually made with noodles and various fruits and nuts in an egg-based pudding. Kugel made with noodles is called lokshen kugel (see Sweet Noodle and Cheese Kugel with Golden Raisins, page 780). For Passover, when observant Jews don't use corn products, potato flour may be substituted. Also, sweet Passover wine, a dessert wine or even brandy, may be substituted for the Madeira.

SERVES 8

¼ cup dried apricots (preferably California)

3 eggs, separated

¼ cup honey

Juice and grated zest of 1 lemon

Kosher salt and black pepper to taste

¼ teaspoon ground allspice

¼ cup Madeira

¼ cup cornstarch

1 pound shredded carrots

¼ cup granulated sugar

Soak the apricots in warm water to cover until soft, about 20 minutes. Preheat the oven to 350°F.

In a small heavy-bottomed nonreactive pot, simmer apricots in soaking liquid until quite soft, about 10 minutes.

Cool and chop. Combine the egg yolks, honey, lemon juice and zest, salt, pepper, allspice, apricots, and Madeira. Stir in the cornstarch and finally, fold in the carrots.

In a clean mixer bowl, beat the egg whites until soft and fluffy, gradually sprinkling in the sugar and continuing to beat until thick and glossy. Fold the egg whites into the carrot mixture in thirds. Spoon into a 2-quart nonstick sprayed casserole. Bake 45 minutes, or until golden brown, set in the middle and the mixture starts comes away from the sides of the pan.

GETTING HONEY OUT OF A JAR

To easily get to all the honey (or maple syrup, molasses, corn syrup, or other heavy syrup), heat the container briefly in the microwave, just long enough to liquefy the contents so that it pours out easily.

Fresh Apricot Season

In the United States, apricots from Chile are in season from mid-February through mid-March; California apricots are in season from mid-June through mid-July; and Washington apricots are in season from mid-July through mid-August. It's rare but rewarding to find a really wonderful fresh apricot on the East Coast because these fruits are too delicate to travel well cross-country. I have not yet had a Chilean apricot worth eating, so I generally avoid them.

Chicken Perrier

I call this dish "Chicken Perrier" because I adapted it from the first cookbook I ever worked on, Georges Perrier: Le Bec-Fin Recipes, *a book that I'm happy to say, continues to sell well. He calls it "Suprême de Poulet Farcie Parfumé au Vinaigre de Cidre." Chef Perrier uses an interesting technique here to obtain uniform, easily sliced portions (important for restaurant service, especially in one as high toned and elegant as his) of juicy chicken containing both white and dark meat surrounding the colorful stuffing. Because of the preparation work involved, I would serve this dish at a dinner party when you want an impressive, yet relatively inexpensive, make-ahead dish.*

Serves 6

Stuffing

$1/4$ cup dried apricots, diced, California preferred

$1/4$ cup golden raisins

1 pound fresh spinach (or Swiss chard, or frozen spinach leaves, rinsed and drained)

$1/4$ pound white mushrooms, trimmed and sliced

2 tablespoons unsalted butter

1 cup fresh tomatoes, diced

Kosher salt and ground black pepper to taste

Soak the apricots and raisins in warm water to cover until softened, about 20 minutes, and then drain. Remove stems and tough center ribs from the spinach (or chard). Wash in a large bowl of water. Scoop out spinach and cook in the water clinging to it until just wilted. Drain, rinse, and cool. Gently squeeze out some of the water and reserve. (If using frozen spinach, simply rinse under tepid water and squeeze out the excess liquid when the spinach comes to room temperature.)

In a medium skillet, sauté the mushrooms in butter until softened but not browned. Add the diced tomatoes and cook until the mixture is nearly dry. Add the apricots and raisins and cook 2 minutes longer. Season to taste with salt and pepper, then remove from heat to cool.

Chicken and Sauce

3 ($2^1/2$ to 3-pound) grain-fed chickens, cut in half and backbone removed (save for stock)

$1/2$ cup sliced shallots

4 tablespoons unsalted butter, divided

2 tablespoons granulated sugar

2 tablespoons cider vinegar

2 cups chicken stock

45

Cut each chicken half away from the rib cage. Remove the thigh and drumstick meat portion only from each half chicken, leaving the chicken breast and wing portion and the skin from the whole side of the chicken intact. Place the chicken breast skin side down on a cutting board. Using a thin, sharp knife, butterfly by slicing horizontally three-quarters of the way through the thickest portion of each chicken breast and spreading open to cover the extra skin. Remove the large bone from the thigh and place the meat on top of the breast.

Preheat the oven to 425°F. Season the chicken on both sides with salt and pepper. Divide the spinach into six portions and arrange each one directly over the thigh meat. Divide the apricot filling into six portions and spread out over the spinach. Roll up each breast towards the wing end and then tie with string as for a roast. Remove the large bone

from the thigh and place the meat on top of the breast.

In a large skillet, ideally cast-iron (for best browning), brown the chicken on all sides, placing the packets seam-side down to start. Transfer to a roasting pan just large enough to hold the chicken. Roast for 20 minutes, or until cooked through, indicating 165°F. on a meat thermometer. Remove the chicken from the oven, cool slightly, and remove the string or ties. Allow the chicken to rest 5 minutes longer and then cut each portion into 4 to 5 slices. The last slice will be connected to the first wing joint. Arrange on serving plates, preferably heated.

Meanwhile, in a medium sauce pot, sauté the shallots in 2 tablespoons of butter until well browned. Add the sugar and stir, cooking until the sugar caramelizes. Pour in the vinegar and chicken stock and boil until syrupy, about 10 minutes. Keep warm. Just before serving, beat in the remaining 2 tablespoons butter. Serve the sauce ladled over the sliced chicken.

46

VEGETABLE SCRAPS FOR STOCKS

In a good restaurant kitchen and a thoughtful home cook's kitchen, nothing that imparts good flavor is thrown away. Save all trimmings from aromatic vegetables including carrots tips and bottoms (not the rather bitter peelings), lighter-colored celery, celery root parings, the outer layers and stalks of fennel, pale green leek trimmings (dark green portions will be too strong), onion skins and roots, parsnip trimmings, mushroom stems; tomato cores, skins, and seeds; tender herb stems (such as basil, tarragon, dill, parsley, chives, cilantro, chervil, thyme), even corn cobs and potato or turnip trimmings.

Start one freezer bag with everything that will taste good in a basic chicken stock (carrots, celery, celery root parings, mushroom stems, and a smaller amount of herb trimmings from dill, parsley, thyme, and basil). When it gets full, start another, until you have two or three bags, to add to the pot along with chicken backs and necks for chicken stock.

Keep separate bags with tomato trimmings along with basil and tarragon sprigs, to simmer together, blend, and strain for homemade tomato puree. Save other vegetables for vegetable stock, just be sure not to use too many strong tasting Brassicas (cabbage family members); a good balance of sweet-and-savory tasting vegetables will work best.

Apricot–Orange Hamentaschen Cookies

Hamentaschen are special tri-cornered cookies baked to celebrate the joyous Jewish holiday of Purim, commemorating the saving of the Jews by the beloved and beautiful consort of the Persian King Ahasuerus, Esther, from the perfidious plot devised against them by Haman, the king's evil advisor. The Yiddish name of the cookies translates to "Haman's pockets." In Israel, they are known as osnei haman, *meaning "Haman's ears". Make these meltingly tender cookies with their brightly colored filling, and everyone will have a reason to celebrate. Here I use canned apricots to make the filling; dried apricots soaked in warm water to cover and simmered until soft can easily be substituted.*

MAKES ABOUT 4 DOZEN

Apricot–Orange Filling

2 (15-ounce) cans apricot halves, drained

1 (15-ounce) jar apricot preserves

1 small (6-ounce) can frozen orange concentrate
   (save 1 tablespoons for topping)

Grated zest of one orange

1 cup granulated sugar

Place all the filling ingredients in a heavy 2-quart saucepan. Stir to dissolve the sugar and bring to the boil. Simmer the filling 20 minutes, stirring occasionally, until mixture is thick. The filling is ready when you stir it with a wooden or plastic spoon and it leaves a line for a second or two that shows the bottom of the pot. Remove the filling from the heat, cool a little, then place it in a container and refrigerate until cold. (The filling keeps very well and can be made a week in advance.)

47

Dough

¹⁄₄ pound (1 stick) unsalted butter

1 cup granulated sugar

1 egg

¹⁄₂ pound (2 cups) all-purpose flour, preferably
  unbleached

2 teaspoons baking powder

¹⁄₂ teaspoon kosher salt

2 tablespoons orange juice

2 teaspoons orange zest

2 teaspoons vanilla extract

Using the paddle attachment to an electric mixer, cream
the butter and sugar until light and fluffy, then beat in the
egg. Whisk together the dry ingredients: flour, baking
powder, and salt. Stir half the flour mixture into the
creamed mixture. Beat in the orange juice, zest, and
vanilla, and then beat in the remaining flour mixture.

  To form hamentaschen, chill the dough until firm, and then
roll it out slightly more than ¹⁄₄-inch thick. Cut into 3-inch
rounds, dot each with a spoonful of apricot-orange filling,
and fold up the edges on three sides to form open triangles.
Bake at 375°F. for 20 to 25 minutes until delicately browned.
(Note: the unbaked cookies will freeze perfectly; bake from
frozen at 350°F., allowing 30 to 35 minutes for baking.)

Choosing Fresh Apricots

For fresh apricots, look for plump fruit with as much
golden orange color as possible. Blemishes, unless they
break the skin, will not affect flavor. Soft-ripe fruit has
the best flavor, but must be used immediately. Avoid
fruit that is pale yellow, greenish-yellow, overly firm
(unripened), shriveled, or bruised.

Baked Apricots Stuffed with Almond–Amaretto Cream

*When fresh apricots are in season, early in the summer, grab
those small, baby-skinned fruits, split them in half, pit, and
stuff them with this dreamy almond and amaretto filling.
Almonds and apricots marry very well; in fact, they are
closely related stone fruits. New-season almonds come into
season just before apricots. Cooking or baking really brings
out the flavor of fresh apricots; even a mediocre-tasting fresh
apricot will gain by cooking or baking as in this dish.*

SERVES 6

¹⁄₄ pound almond paste

4 tablespoons unsalted butter

¹⁄₄ cup granulated sugar

2 egg yolks

2 tablespoons all-purpose flour

1 cup skin-on whole almonds, toasted at 300°F.,
  cooled and then ground

¹⁄₄ cup Amaretto liqueur

4 egg whites

2 pounds fresh firm but ripe apricots, halved and pitted

¹⁄₂ cup confectioners' sugar, plus extra for sprinkling

Cream together the almond paste, butter, and granulated
sugar until light and fluffy. Beat in the egg yolks one at a
time. Stir together the flour and almonds and add to the
creamed mix. Stir in the Amaretto.

  In a separate clean bowl and using the whisk to a mixer,
beat the egg whites until fluffy and then gradually beat in
the confectioners' sugar. Continue beating until the
whites are firm and glossy and stick to the sides of the

bowl. Fold in the egg whites to the batter one-third at a time, so the batter doesn't deflate.

Preheat the oven to 375°F. Arrange the apricot halves cut side up on a buttered baking pan. Using a small ice cream scoop, fill each apricot with about 2 tablespoons of the filling. Sprinkle all with confectioners' sugar. Bake 20 minutes, or until the filling is puffed and browned and the apricots are soft. Serve immediately.

SCOOPS AND SIZES

Professional cooks and bakers know that round-bowl lever or squeeze-action scoops work well for many kitchen tasks besides scooping ice cream. Use them to quickly form equal portions of any medium-soft textured food mixture, from tuna salad to cookie dough. Portion cupcake and muffin batter evenly into baking tins with a scoop, or use it to form meatballs or dumplings. If you are left-handed like me, be sure to buy a universal-action scoop that you squeeze on the bottom rather than the kind with a side lever, which is suitable only for right-handers. Classic stainless steel scoops made for professional use will have a small number engraved into the inside of the rounded moveable strips, based on the number of portions per quart; thus a number 12 will make approximately 12 (2.7-ounce) scoops to the quart, while a number 24 will make 24 (1.4 ounce scoops). I use a number 40 scoop most commonly to make cookies. Oval and square-shaped scoops are also for sale; both work for fancy ice cream, whipped cream, and sorbet presentations.

Apricot–Black Walnut Crumb Bars

There is something about the combination of the tart, rich apricots and the sweet yet tannic native North American black walnuts that make these cookies really special. Bar cookies are a good choice when you want to make a lot of people happy with cookies, without a lot of work cutting and shaping. Although there is only a small amount of oatmeal called for here, it is essential to add body and crumbly, nutty texture to the shortbread and the crumb topping. These cookies will keep for about 1 week, refrigerated, and would be well appreciated at holiday time. Substitute well-drained canned apricots if you can't find dried California apricot halves; the light-yellow Turkish whole dried apricots will make disappointingly pale and not very tangy bars.

MAKES 1 HALF–SHEET PAN, OR 64 BARS

Apricot Filling

1 pound dried apricots, preferably California

1 cup orange juice + zest of 1 orange

1½ cups granulated sugar

1 tablespoon vanilla extract

Soak the apricots in warm water for 20 minutes to soften. Bring the apricots, their soaking liquid, orange juice and zest, and sugar to a boil. Reduce heat to a simmer and cook, stirring often, for 45 minutes, or until apricots have softened and started to disintegrate. Stir in vanilla, cool, and reserve.

49

Black Walnut Shortbread

1 pound (4 sticks) unsalted butter, softened

1 cup confectioners' sugar

1 pound (4 cups) all-purpose flour, preferably unbleached

1/4 cup heavy cream

1 cup oatmeal

1 cup chopped black walnuts

Beat together the butter and confectioners' sugar until creamy and light. Add the flour and cream and beat only long enough for the dough to form a ball. Remove from the mixer and divide into two portions: one-fourth and three-fourths.

Preheat the oven to 350°F. Line a half sheet pan or two 9 x 13-inch rectangular baking pans with parchment paper. Press the larger portion of dough onto the bottom(s) of the pan(s). Bake for 20 minutes or until the dough is lightly browned at the edges. Cool.

Combine the smaller portion of dough with the oatmeal and the black walnuts, mixing and crumbling together by hand for the crumb topping.

Arrange the reserved poached apricots along with their cooking syrup over the baked pastry layer and sprinkle the top with the black walnut crumb mixture. Place back in the oven and bake for 30 minutes, or until the crumbs are just starting to brown and the filling is bubbling. Remove from oven and cool to room temperature. Cut into 64 bars. Store in the refrigerator for up to 4 days.

BAKING APRICOTS IN THE OVEN

Like many delicate foods, apricots can be baked in an ovenproof casserole at low temperature (300°F.). They will hold their shape better because no stirring is necessary and will cook more evenly.

50

ARTICHOKES

ARTICHOKES

About 1635, the evocative artichoke was chosen by French artist Abraham Bossé to symbolize taste in a series of paintings depicting the five senses. The painting depicts a huge artichoke in a raised dish, while a regal lady stretches out her hand to pull out the first leaf. Appropriately, this queen of vegetables has a nutty, rich-tasting, and tender heart, surrounded by spiny armor.

The decorative artichoke, with its spiraled leaves, has a reputation as the sexiest of vegetables, thanks partly to Marilyn Monroe, who became California's first Artichoke Queen in February 1948. At the time, Monroe appeared in Salinas and Castroville, the center of America's artichoke industry, to promote diamond sales for a local jewelry store, where she attracted crowds so large that two policemen were assigned just to direct the crazed traffic in front of the store.

Miss Monroe seductively selected the lucky winner of a fabulous diamond ring in a drawing at the Vogue Theater (now the Globe—the most important artichoke variety). Witnesses vividly recall Miss Monroe's floor-length gown with its dramatically plunging neckline. The town was never again the same, and neither were artichokes. Before this history-making promotion, artichokes were often ignored in the grocers' shelf except in Italian neighborhoods. Suddenly artichokes were everywhere.

Artichoke's name in Latin, *Cynara scolymus*, derives from the mythological tale of the Greek god Zeus, who fell hopelessly in love with the beautiful young maiden Cynara. Unable to convince Cynara to leave her mother and her earthly home to become a goddess, Zeus became so enraged that he transformed her into an artichoke, forever holding captive her tender heart at the center of a protective crown of thorny leaves.

Caterina de Medici introduced the artichoke to France in the early sixteenth century, bringing it to court along with many other Italian gastronomic innovations including the fork and the sweet pea. She apparently couldn't get enough of them and ate so many that she *cuyda crever* ("could have burst" in medieval French). The artichoke was the passion of rulers: the Medici in Florence, Francois I and his court in Touraine, and Henry VIII in England. Francois' daughter-in-law, Henrietta Maria, queen of Charles I and daughter of Henri IV and Marie de Medici, kept a garden devoted to artichokes at her manor in Wimbledon.

Superb vegetable gardeners, Italians developed the fine varieties of artichoke that captured the fancy of Renaissance European courts. Even today, Italy has the largest repertoire of artichoke dishes. By 1629, the English herbalist John Parkinson asserted that even the youngest housewife knew how to cook artichokes and serve them with melted butter seasoned with vinegar and pepper.

52

The artichoke is a member of the very large *Compositae* (sunflower) family. It is the scaly-looking flower bud of a special thistle. If left on the branch, the bud will eventually open into huge beautiful violet-blue flower blossoms as large as seven-inches in diameter. The size of the bud depends upon where it is located on the plant. The largest artichokes are "terminal" buds, at the end of the long central stems. Lower down on the stem, the buds are smaller and are often sold as "baby artichokes."

A native of the Mediterranean, the Green Globe accounts for most of the artichokes grown in the Mediterranean and nearly all of those grown in California. The earliest cultivation of artichokes was by the Greeks , who improved the *kaktos*, the wild thistle of Sicily, known to the Romans as *caduus*. This thistle, also the ancestor of the cardoon popular in Provence, probably reached Sicily from North Africa, where it grows wild and is used to enrich the sauce for couscous.

Every artichoke grown commercially in the United States comes from California's Monterey County near the small town of Castroville, the self-proclaimed "Artichoke Capital of the World." At the annual Artichoke Festival in September, an Artichoke Queen is anointed.

Since the 1920s, Castroville has been known for producing artichokes in a crop now worth $50 million a year. Secrets of growing the Globe artichoke have been well kept by the Swiss-Italian families who planted artichokes along with the first vineyards in the Salinas Valley. The cool, misty sea air and alluvial soil filled with rich nutrients from two rivers (the Pajaro and Salinas) are one part of the secret; skilled, patient hand labor is another, because every artichoke is grown and harvested entirely by hand.

The Green Globe variety was first imported from Italy in the 1880s and Andrew Molera planted California's first artichokes in the 1920s. Today, more than three quarters of the world's crop is grown there. All artichokes, even on the same plant, grow to different sizes. The skilled pickers need to know when the 'choke is mature. The same field must be harvested every seven days during peak season, so labor represents about half the growing costs. Because artichokes are not grown from seed, after the harvest, the plant is trimmed to the nub so that it regenerates with a new crop.

The largest and most of the smallest artichokes are sold fresh, while about one-fourth of the crop is canned. Anyone who has been to an Italian produce market has probably been entranced by the classically beautiful long-stem artichokes. With about nine-inches of edible stem, tender as can be on the inside, they are now being marketed in the United States in specialty stores and are just as suited to a dinner table centerpiece as on the plate.

In Italy, land of artichoke lovers, the thistles are grown in the sunniest regions: Sicily, Sardinia, Lazio, and Liguria, where the season begins in December and January. One variety looks like a pinecone, purple in color and tender enough to be eaten raw. Another looks like a small chicken egg and is generally used to make artichoke hearts in oil. There are the large rounded Mamme; tender, tasty, and best boiled and others— pointed and with thorns, rounded and with smooth tips, thin or fat.

Italians attribute all sorts of magical and curative properties to artichokes. "They are good for your liver," and "they make other foods taste better." The phrase *la politica del carciofo* means a policy of dealing with opponents by picking them off at a time, as you would pick off each artichoke leaf. There is even an aperitivo called

53

"Cynar," made by infusing artichokes in alcohol, that is renowned for its beneficial medicinal properties. The manufacturer recommends Cynar as a calming influence effective against the stress of modern life.

British culinarian extraordinaire Jane Grigson paints a vivid word picture of artichokes in her classic *Jane Grigson's Vegetable Book*: "The artichoke above all is the vegetable expression of civilized living, of the long view, of increasing delight by anticipation and crescendo. No wonder it was once regarded as an aphrodisiac. . . . One cannot attack an artichoke with knife and fork and scoff it in three mouthfuls. It is first for admiration, then each leaf has to be pulled away for eating and dipped in sauce. When the leaves have gone, there is the fibrous and tickly choke to be removed before the gray-green disc—the *bonne bouche* (good mouthful)—can be enjoyed."

Perhaps danger is part of the irresistible appeal of the artichoke. The sharp thorns can prick the unwary, especially in large Green Globe artichokes. They are also the "enfant terrible" of food and wine pairing because they contain an acid called cynarin, which makes everything taste sweet after eating it.

Hidden deep within the leaves lies a trap: the hairy inedible choke lurking at the heart of the vegetable that camouflages the succulent base. The larger the artichoke, the more prominent the choke. Before cooking, remove the choke by scraping out with a stainless steel spoon (silver or aluminum will react and impart an unpleasant metallic taste) such as a serrated grapefruit spoon or a melon baller. Or, cook first and then scrape out the choke before serving.

When cutting an artichoke, be prepared with one or two cut lemons, taking precautions immediately to prevent them from blackening. Rub the cut edges with lemon and drop the cut artichoke into a bowl of water acidulated with lemon juice (or vinegar at a pinch) until you are ready to cook them. Don't cook artichokes in aluminum or they will react and turn black. Cut them with a stainless steel rather than carbon steel knife.

How the Artichoke Got its Name

The word artichoke came to us in the sixteenth century from the northern Italian *articiocco*. The earlier Italian word *arcicioffa* came from the Old Spanish *alcarchofa* through the Arabic *al-khashof*. The earliest English version was *artechock* but later changed to by association with choke, because of the inedible mass of immature florets inside the artichoke head.

EATING A WHOLE ARTICHOKE

To eat a whole steamed or boiled artichoke with a dipping sauce, pull away each leaf by the tip, dip the base in the sauce and draw the leaf through the teeth to scrape off the meaty flesh, piling used leaves on one side. If the choke is present, scrape out with the edge of a spoon and you're ready to enjoy the delectable artichoke heart (or bottom). My daughter especially enjoys eating whole artichokes, while disdaining pretrimmed artichokes because the fun is gone.

THORNS OR NO THORNS

You might see the rounded-end leafed variety of artichoke known as "thornless" artichokes in supermarkets with leaf ends that are split (like a cloven hoof). I find them inferior because their flesh tends to be mushy without the firm nuttiness of the true Green Globe artichoke. Identify the Globe artichoke by the pointed end, or thorn, on the tip of each leaf: if it sticks you, it's the real thing.

Choosing an Artichoke

Artichokes that are old will be tough, woody, and often have spread-apart leaves on tough stems. At their peak, they have tightly packed, crisp-textured leaves with bright coloring. Check the cut stem end for freshness. Avoid a blackened cut, which indicates an artichoke has been stored so long it will probably be bitter. Any brown, soft spots can be cut away, always using a stainless steel knife.

CARDOONS, ANOTHER MEMBER OF THE ARTICHOKE FAMILY

A relative of the artichoke, cardoon is similar to celery in appearance but with a nutty, somewhat bitter flavor. When planted, cardoons must be "blanched" or kept from the sunlight in order to cut down on their natural bitterness. Cardoons are quite popular in Northern Italy and are always included in *Bagna Cauda*, a hot anchovy, garlic, and butter mixture, sometimes flavored with rare white truffles used as a dip for vegetables in Piedmont. They are uncommon, though specialty stores are starting to carry them in season. You are most likely to find cardoons in December in areas with a large Italian population, because they are traditionally served for Christmas dinner.

To prepare cardoons, cut off the leaf stalk end and remove the remaining outer leaves and edges, including the inedible strings. Cut the inner stalks into pieces of desired length. Submerge the pieces immediately in vinegar and water before cooking in salted water with a touch of vinegar until soft and tender. Follow the recipe for Cauliflower au Gratin (*see* page 227), or the recipe for Swiss Chard Ribs au Gratin (*see* page 464), substituting cooked cardoons. Cardoons can be braised, or breaded and fried, or added to risotto.

55

Artichoke and Toasted Hazelnut Soup

About twenty years ago I traveled to San Francisco with the owners of the restaurant where I cheffed, along with the architect (whom I later married) to check out restaurants and equipment manufacturers. I was lucky enough to stay in the renowned Stanford Court Hotel, at that time owned by the influential hotelier, Jim Nassikas, who pioneered the idea that a hotel restaurant could be good enough on its own right to attract city residents. Here is my version of the silky, nutty-tasting soup that I enjoyed at the hotel's restaurant, Fournou's Ovens. I've used frozen artichoke wedges to make it easier and plenty of the hazelnuts, which I adore.

SERVES 6

2 large shallots, minced

2 tablespoons hazelnut oil

6 cups chicken stock

1 (12 ounce) bag frozen artichoke wedges

$1/2$ pound (about 1 cup) hazelnuts, lightly toasted, skins rubbed off, and ground

$1/4$ cup Wondra flour

$1/2$ cup heavy cream

$1/4$ cup dry sherry

Salt and black pepper to taste

1 bunch chives, thinly sliced

Sauté shallots in oil over medium-low heat until very soft. Stir in stock, artichoke hearts, and hazelnuts. Bring to a boil, reduce heat, and simmer 15 to 20 minutes, or until artichokes are tender.

Combine a little of the hot broth with the rice flour to dissolve. Stir into the soup, bring back to the boil, and then strain soup through a medium mesh strainer or food mill.

Return soup to pot. Stir in cream, sherry, and salt and pepper to taste. Simmer briefly to combine flavors. Sprinkle with sherry and chives and serve immediately.

Granulated Flour

Many chefs use granulated flour, sold under the brand name Wondra, because it is easily sprinkled into a soup or sauce for thickening. If you use ordinary flour, you will need to either mix it with butter (*beurre manié* in French) or cook it in butter (a French *roux*) to prevent lumps.

TOASTING NUTS

Toasting nuts really enhances their flavor and makes them extra crunchy. However, there is always a danger of burning them, because of their high oil content. I can't tell you how many trays of toasted nuts I had to discard during my chef days, because someone didn't use a timer.

To toast nuts, spread them out in a thin layer on a metal baking pan. Toast at 300°F. for 12 to 15 minutes, using a timer, and stirring once or twice so nuts brown evenly. The nuts should be noticeably browned and fragrant, but not at all dark brown or burnt. Cool to room temperature and then cover and store up to 1 week in the refrigerator. Soft, oily nuts like pine nuts, macadamia, and walnuts will toast quickest; harder nuts like hazelnuts and almonds will take a bit longer.

Italian-Style Marinated Artichoke Hearts

Many of us first got to know artichokes from the small jar of marinated artichokes in the "gourmet" section of the supermarket. Now that fresh artichokes are so common, it's worth making your own version, though admittedly it's a lot more work than opening a jar. I would also substitute frozen artichoke hearts for this dish. If you can find those sold by Green Giant or the Trader Joe's house brand, they are of superior quality.

Artichoke Cooking

1 (12 ounce) bag frozen artichoke wedges

Juice of 1 lemon

2 bay leaves

1 tablespoon each ground fennel seed and
   ground coriander seed

Kosher salt to taste

1 tablespoon each: chopped fresh thyme, oregano,
   and rosemary, or 1 teaspoon each dried thyme,
   oregano, and rosemary

Artichoke Marinade

1/4 cup red wine vinegar

1/2 cup extra-virgin olive oil

1 tablespoon chopped garlic

1 teaspoon celery seed

1/4 cup chopped Italian parsley

Kosher salt and freshly ground black pepper to taste

Combine Artichoke Cooking ingredients in a medium nonreactive pot and add enough cold water to cover. Bring to the boil, reduce heat, and simmer for about 10 minutes or until the artichokes are tender but not mushy. Drain the artichokes, discarding liquid.

Whisk together Artichoke Marinade ingredients and toss with artichokes. Marinate at least 1 hour before serving, or refrigerate for up to 1 week, allowing artichokes to come to room temperature before serving.

NONREACTIVE POTS

I avoid aluminum pots, because reactive foods (whether acidic like lemon, or basic like eggs) will discolor and pick up an unpleasant metallic taste. Many aluminum pans are coated, which helps protect from any reaction. However, these coatings eventually wear off or flake off in patches. It is particularly important to choose the right pot when making any cooked custard mixture, such as an ice cream base, pastry cream, crème brulée, and crème anglaise, or you could end up with a dingy gray liquid. While aluminum is inexpensive and lightweight, it also warps easily, so that in restaurant kitchens, the older aluminum pots will all be misshapen. Instead of aluminum, I go for steel-lined copper, old-fashioned cast-iron, French steel, or ceramic-lined steel or cast-iron pots. These last two, although not legal for use in commercial kitchens (because they can chip), are wonderful for the home.

Vinegar, which comes from the French: *vin aigre*, or sour wine, is nothing more than a further stage of alcohol. Alcohol is made by fermenting the sugars present in foods as varied as grapes, potatoes, persimmons, beer, and palm hearts by microscopic yeasts. While alcohol is resistant to most microbes, certain bacteria metabolize alcohol converting it to acetic acid. (Vinegar is diluted acetic acid, typically about 5 percent) There are different ways of producing vinegar.

The oldest method, dating back to the Middle Ages, is that used for the classic aged wine vinegars that originated in Orléans, France. There, vinegar is produced in wood barrels partially filled with wine to which is added a portion of the cloudy, stringy-looking "vinegar mother" (equivalent to a sourdough bread starter) that has been kept back from the previous batch. Other methods speed up the process, producing a more industrial and of course, less expensive, product. The better vinegars are aged longer, so their flavors are mellower and their acetic acid content lower.

Artichokes Roman Style

58

This typically Roman dish appears on the antipasti table of restaurants during artichoke season when the artichokes are young, tender, and plentiful. This is one of the first dishes I learned to make from Marcella Hazan, when she acted as consultant to Ristorante DiLullo, where I cheffed for six years. Come springtime in Rome, trattorias display a huge bowl of long-stem artichokes, braised as in this recipe, standing on their heads with their stems in the air. Look for the largest artichokes you can find or, if you find them, use the long-stemmed beauties now being marketed in specialty stores for this classic Roman dish.

SERVES 8

Juice of 2 lemons

8 large fresh artichokes

1/4 cup chopped Italian parsley

2 tablespoon chopped mentuccia
   (*see* Roman Mentuccia, page 59) or spearmint

2 tablespoons chopped garlic

Salt and black pepper to taste

1/4 cup extra-virgin olive oil

Have ready a bowl of cold water with half the lemon juice added. Using a stainless steel knife, slice off about 1/2 inch from the artichoke stems, so that no blackened ends remain. Pare the outer layer of dark green flesh away from the core of the stem, leaving only pale green to white core. Slice about 1-inch off the top of the artichoke. Turn the artichokes upside-down. Working in a spiral, pull one leaf at a time, breaking it back at the point where it meets the artichoke bottom. Keep breaking off leaves, going in order around the artichoke until all the leaves have been removed.

Now, using a sharp paring knife, pare away all the dark green outer skin from the artichoke bottom. You should have only light green flesh left. As you finish each artichoke, place in the lemon water. Using a melon baller, a grapefruit spoon, or a heavy stainless steel teaspoon, scrape out and discard the inner "choke." You will be removing the hairy portion in the center of each artichoke, which is inedible.

Preheat the oven to 400°F. Finely chop the parsley, mentuccia, and garlic, mix together and press the mixture into the bottom of each artichoke. Season with salt and pepper and place upside down in a deep oven-proof dish. Add olive oil and the remaining lemon juice to the pan and enough water to come halfway up the sides of the artichokes.

Cover the dish with foil and bake for an hour or until most of the liquid has evaporated and the artichokes are quite tender. Serve warm, drizzled with any pan juices, as an appetizer.

Roman Mentuccia

Italian *mentuccia* (English pennyroyal, *Mentha pugelium*) is essential to authentic Artichokes Roman Style (*carciofi alla Romana*). This highly potent herb, while in the mint family, more closely resembles savory and oregano in its strength. The smaller, slightly rounded leaves have a menthol-like fragrance. Unless you grow your own, substitute fresh spearmint.

Artichokes
Roman Jewish Style

Rome's ancient ghetto has been home to Jews for more than 2,000 years. In all that time, they have developed a typical cuisine, including this dish that I adore, called carciofi alla guidea *in Italian. The deep-rooted traditions of Roman Jewish food date back to the restrictions placed on them by the popes. Roman Jews became specialists at frying bits of fish and vegetables and were known as* friggitori, *or fry-cooks. They have perfected the art of frying, and it truly is an art, using good olive oil, so far from the awful-smelling recycled hydrogenated trans fats prevalent for deep-frying in America that it's hard to believe there is any relation between the two. You may have to go to Rome to taste the real thing: small golden, flower-like crispy baby artichokes fried in olive oil and sprinkled with salt.*

The petals are flattened out like a sunflower (in the same Compositae *family as the artichoke) and turn a deep golden brown from frying directly in the hot oil with no coating or batter. The artichoke's center will be moist; the outer leaves are paper-thin and crisp like the best potato chips. To recreate this marvelous dish as closely as possible to its original, I fry the artichokes twice, once to cook through and the second time to crisp them up, the same method used in Belgium for their wonderful "frites".*

SERVES 6

12 baby artichokes

Juice and zest of 2 lemons

1 tablespoon kosher salt

1 teaspoon freshly ground black pepper

3 cups olive oil (for frying)

59

Trim the artichokes with a small, sharp paring knife by pulling off a layer of the small tough outer leaves near the stem. Cut off and discard about $\frac{1}{2}$ an inch off the bottom of the stem. Pull off and discard the dark green tough outer leaves, then pare away the tough outer portion of the artichoke bottom. Using scissors, cut off and discard the tips of the inner leaves. Gently open up the leaves to expose the hairy choke inside. Using a small stainless steel spoon, scrape out and discard the choke. Place the artichokes in a bowl of lemon water until ready to cook.

Drain two artichokes and, holding one in each hand by the stem and bottom, gently knock the leaf parts against each other until the leaves open up a little. Repeat until all the artichokes are opened up (or tap lightly against a cutting board).

In a small bowl, combine the salt, pepper, and lemon zest. Sprinkle the mixture all over the artichokes.

Heat the oil in a heavy pan, large enough to cook the artichokes in a single layer (or do in 2 batches). Add the artichokes and cook over moderate heat for 20 minutes or until the bottoms and sides are well browned, turning so they brown evenly. During the cooking, sprinkle some cold water over the artichokes to produce steam so the insides will cook too. When the artichokes are cooked through and light brown in color, remove them from the pan. Reserve the pan with the oil until you're ready to serve.

When ready to serve, reheat the oil until shimmering hot and then pick up one artichoke at a time by sticking it with a fork. Placing the artichokes one by one into the hot oil, press the leaves down to the bottom of the pot using a spatula. The artichokes should look like flattened flowers. Allow them to cook until the leaves are golden brown and crispy. Drain on paper towels and serve immediately with wedges of lemon.

Stuffed Artichokes with Peppers, Pancetta, Pine Nuts, and Capers

While prepping a fresh artichoke is admittedly a time-consuming task, in this dish the reward is that the artichoke is stuffed to become a hearty main dish that can easily be made a day or two ahead of time and then baked before serving. Make this dish when large count artichokes (24 or 36 per case) are in the market. If the stuffed artichokes are cold from the refrigerator, allow about 1 hour for baking.

SERVES 8

Juice of 2 lemons
8 large fresh artichokes
$\frac{1}{4}$ pound pancetta, cut into small strips
2 tablespoons chopped garlic
2 tablespoons olive oil
2 roasted red peppers
$\frac{1}{2}$ cup small capers, drained
1 cup soft breadcrumbs
$\frac{1}{2}$ cup pine nuts, lightly toasted
$\frac{1}{2}$ cup chopped Italian parsley
Kosher salt and freshly ground black pepper to taste

Have ready a bowl of cold water with half the lemon juice added. Using a stainless steel knife, slice off the stems of the artichokes, so the artichokes lie flat. Slice off the tops of the artichokes leaving about $1\frac{1}{2}$-inches of leaves on the artichokes. Turn the artichokes upside-down. Working in a spiral, pull one leaf at a time, breaking it back at the point where it meets the artichoke bottom.

60

Keep breaking off leaves, going in order around the artichoke until all the tough dark green leaves have been removed and those that remain are light green and tender.

Now, using a sharp paring knife, pare away all the dark green outer skin from the artichoke bottom. You should have only light green flesh left. As you finish each artichoke, place it in the lemon water. Using a melon baller or a heavy stainless steel teaspoon, scrape out and discard the inner "choke." You will be removing the hairy portion in the center of each artichoke, which is inedible. Cook artichokes in a nonreactive pan with the remaining lemon juice and enough water to cover. When the liquid has evaporated, the artichokes should be just cooked through and tender. You may cook the artichokes up to 2 days ahead of time.

To prepare the filling, cook the pancetta in a small skillet over low heat until the bits are lightly browned and crispy. Add the garlic and cook 1 minute longer or until the garlic gives off its aroma. Remove from heat and stir in the remaining ingredients. Use this mixture to stuff the cooked artichoke bottoms.

When ready to serve, preheat the oven to 350°F. and arrange the artichokes in a single layer in a nonreactive baking dish just large enough to hold them. Bake 30 to 40 minutes or until browned and bubbling. Serve accompanied by a wedge of lemon.

Using artichoke stems

The stems of an artichoke contain a goodly portion of tender meat. To reach it, cut the stem so it has a flat end. Lay it upright on the cutting board and pare away the outer layer of tough dark green flesh. The pale green inner core will then be exposed. Either cook the trimmed stems in the pot when you're boiling artichokes or chop them up and add to the filling for the stuffed artichokes above.

Greek Artichoke Heart and Carrot Stew

During my trip to the Kalamata region of Greece, home of those delicious purple, pointy olives and superb olive oil, I enjoyed this dish at lunch at the airy and gracious Hotel Europa in Olympia, site of the ancient Greek games. It makes a lovely first course or a main dish for lunch, as it was served to us that day. The secret to this dish and much Mediterranean food, especially vegetable cookery, is serving food at room temperature—not icy cold or piping hot—so that the flavors are really brought out. This dish combines artichokes, young carrots, and garden peas, which come into season at the same time in spring.

SERVES 6

1/2 cup extra-virgin olive oil, preferably from Kalamata

4 carrots, peeled and sliced into rounds

2 pounds fresh peas, shelled (or 1/2 pound frozen baby peas)

1 (12 ounce) bag frozen artichoke wedges

Kosher salt and freshly ground black pepper to taste

1 bunch scallions, trimmed and sliced

2 tablespoons finely chopped dill

Juice of 1/2 lemon

In a heavy stewing pot, heat the olive oil and sauté the carrots until softened. Add the peas and artichokes and toss to coat with the oil. Pour in enough water to come about halfway up the vegetables. Season with salt and pepper. Cover and simmer over medium heat for about 15 minutes, or until the artichokes and peas are tender. (If using the frozen peas, add them to the pot after about 10 minutes of cooking the artichokes.)

Add the scallions, dill, and salt and pepper to taste. Just before serving, stir in the lemon juice. Remove and serve warm or at room temperature.

62

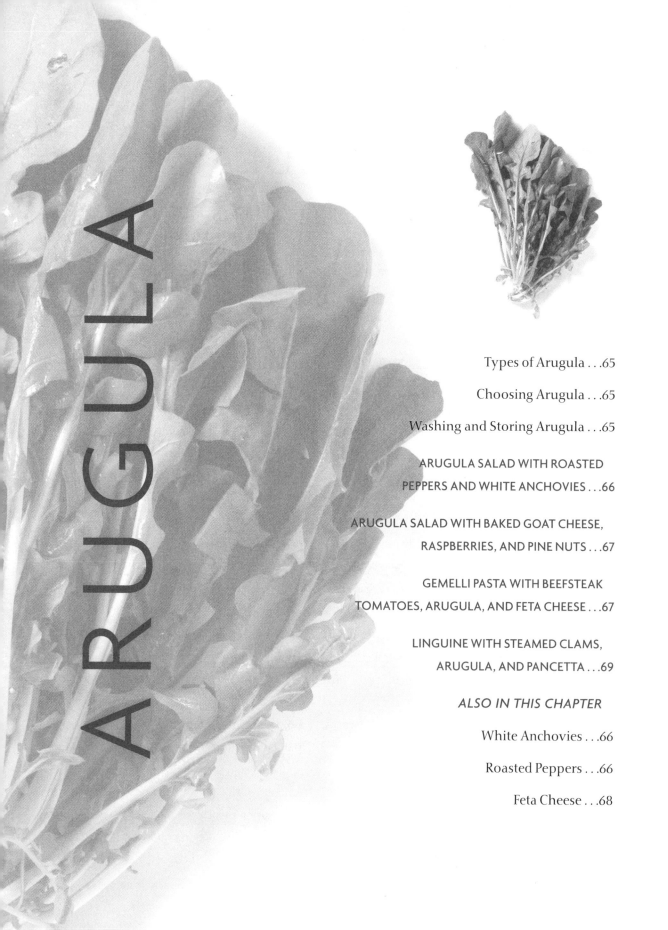

ARUGULA

ARUGULA

If I could have only one salad green, it would, without a doubt, be arugula. I crave arugula in salad and adore it cooked and added to pizza, in pasta, risotto, and frittatas. Uncooked, arugula marries especially well with slightly sweet and tangy foods as in my "California-Style" Arugula Salad with Baked Goat Cheese, Raspberries, and Pine Nuts, or with roasted peppers and anchovies as in the Arugula Salad with Roasted Peppers and White Anchovies.

Briefly cooked until it just wilts, arugula is potent enough to stand up to tangy, sharp feta cheese in my Gemelli Pasta with Beefsteak Tomatoes, Arugula, and Feta Cheese, and I find that it works especially well in my Linguine with Steamed Clams, Arugula, and Pancetta because it's potent enough to stand up to the salty clams and cured pancetta. If you're planning to cook it, allow at least one large bunch of arugula for only four people, as this strong yet fragile green collapses into practically nothing.

Both the ancient Egyptians and Romans considered arugula a potent aphrodisiac. It was consecrated to Priapus, the Roman fertility god and protector of gardens, who was unmistakable by virtue of his exaggerated phallus. Perhaps that association explains arugula's popularity today in Italy.

More properly known as *la rucola* in Italian, its name derives originally from the Latin *eruca*, meaning "caterpillar", which its rather hairy stems are thought to resemble.

Arugula is simply a Southern Italian dialect name that has become accepted in the United States. This quick-growing (and quick-spoiling) green has a mild to sharp bite with a mustardy tang. It will be milder and more tender early in the season, or if greenhouse grown, sharper if late in the season and field grown.

A member of the huge *Brassica* (mustard) family and a close cousin of the radish, arugula is a fresh, leafy green with slender, multiple-lobed leaves that resemble slender oak leaves. It is known in France as *roquette*, in Great Britain as salad rocket, and in the Middle East it is called *ghargir*. But it is in Italy that arugula really comes into its own as a salad and pasta green that shows up all over.

Native to the Mediterranean region, arugula grows wild throughout southern Europe. The young leaves are eaten raw in salad, while older leaves that have become too "hot" are delicious cooked and added to soups and sauces. The burning hot-mustard quality of late-season arugula may be the reason it is known as salad rocket in Britain.

Arugula was once found only in Italian markets, but now is sold at many supermarkets. It is a good bet for purchase at farmers' markets because it's so quick to spoil that supermarket offerings are too often less than stellar in quality. Later in the season, fieldgrown arugula may exhibit small insect holes. While perhaps unsuited to use in a salad, it works quite well as a cooked green.

64

TYPES OF ARUGULA

Arugula has many levels of intensity—from mild if it is greenhouse-grown or heavily irrigated, to extremely peppery if grown with a lot of sunlight. Baby arugula from California, sold cut and washed, is generally milder though it has a tendency to turn yellow in a few days. To prevent this, keep the arugula quite cold, even putting ice chips on top, as is done in wholesale markets with other perishable greens. Field-grown arugula will be stronger and may be extremely sandy. Some arugula, especially from local farms, is sold complete with roots. Hothouse arugula picked when very young is often added to mesclun or "spring mix" salad greens. Arugula is available year-round, but is more plentiful in late summer. When grown in very hot weather, arugula will have a strong biting taste and will be vulnerable to spoilage.

CHOOSING ARUGULA

Arugula is extremely perishable. Look for bright emerald-green leaves that are delicately crisp, avoiding arugula with yellowed, limp, or even slimy leaves. The younger (smaller) the leaves, the less likely they will have an excessively pungent flavor. Leaves that are 2- to 3-inches long will generally be young and tender. Older and larger leaves may be too pungent for salad and must be cooked. Arugula from local farms is often sold in bunches with the roots attached. This arugula has thin, easily bruised leaves and may develop rot where the bunches have been rubber-banded together. Pick up a bunch and sniff it before buying, avoiding any with a strong, unpleasant odor.

Washing and Storing Arugula

Because arugula is often grown in sandy soil, it is important to wash it well. Cut off and discard the stems and any broken, yellowed, or bruised leaves. Place the leaves in a large bowl of cold water and swish around vigorously to release sand. Gently lift leaves out of the water. Drain and spin in a salad dryer or spread out on paper or cloth towels to dry. To store, wrap washed and dried arugula in damp paper towels and place in a plastic bag. Refrigerate for up to three days. If the arugula has roots, wrap them first in paper towels. Put the wrapped arugula in a plastic bag and refrigerate up to two days.

65

Arugula Salad with Roasted Peppers and White Anchovies

This is a classic Italian salad that will never go out of fashion because of its perfect balance of flavor, texture, and color. The sweetness of the roasted peppers, which may be purchased if you're short on time, offsets the salty, inky-looking shiny black olives and pungent tiny green capers. Capers, which are the pickled or salted unopened bush of the Mediterranean caper bush, Capparis spinosa, *that grows wild all over the Mediterranean, are a typical flavor spiker, used where their intensity accents other more unobtrusive flavors.*

SERVES 4

$^1/_2$ pound baby arugula leaves, washed and dried

$^1/_2$ cup Red Wine Vinaigrette (recipe follows)

2 roasted peppers, red and/or yellow or orange,
   cut into thick strips (*see* Roasted Peppers, at right)

12 white anchovies (*see* White Anchovies, at right)

2 tablespoons oil-cured black olives, chopped and pitted

4 teaspoons capers, drained

Toss the arugula with most of the vinaigrette and arrange on salad plates. Alternate slices of roasted peppers on top of marinated arugula. Top each salad with 3 white anchovies, a portion of the black olives and the capers. Drizzle with a little of the remaining vinaigrette and serve.

Red Wine Vinaigrette

$^1/_2$ cup extra-virgin olive oil

$^1/_4$ cup red wine vinegar

1 tablespoon chopped marjoram or oregano, or
   1 teaspoon dried marjoram or oregano

1 teaspoon chopped garlic

Kosher salt and freshly ground black pepper to taste

Combine all the ingredients in a large bowl. Using a hand blender, blend to obtain a smooth, creamy dressing. The dressing will keep well for 2 weeks if tightly covered and refrigerated.

WHITE ANCHOVIES

One of the most delicious ways to eat anchovies is as "white anchovies", pickled in vinegar and oil (referred to as *boquerones* in Spain and *filetti di alici marinate* in Italy) instead of the more common dark salt-cured version. While these lightly cured small fish won't last as long as the darker version, they are quite delicate and mild enough to enjoy right out of the package. They will usually be found in clear plastic modified-atmosphere packaging in specialty markets. If you've never liked anchovies, give these a try, perhaps in your next Caesar salad or to top a pizza.

ROASTED PEPPERS

Preheat a grill, preferably charcoal, to white hot, or heat a broiler. Arrange 6 large, deep-red meaty peppers on a grill or under the broiler on high and cook until charred on all sides. Remove from grill, and cool until cool enough to handle. Rub off skin, rinsing hands occasionally in cold water to remove skin pieces. Remove and discard stem, seeds and white connective tissue. Avoid using water to rinse peppers as this washes off flavor. Slice peppers into strips and store for up to 1 week in refrigerator.

Arugula Salad with Baked Goat Cheese, Raspberries, and Pine Nuts

This salad goes back to my days as chef of A'propos Bistro on what is now Philadelphia's Avenue of the Arts. At that time, California cuisine was really making a splash, and after traveling out there a number of times, spending time in the kitchens of Campton Place and Chez Panisse, I was hooked on the fresh, colorful, simply presented seasonal style of cooking that fit in so well with my personal sensibility. Because I started working with local farmers in the Philadelphia area as far back as twenty-five years ago, I was primed for this type of food. Here soft, plump raspberries accent the mustardy greens, while tiny toasted pine nuts add a soft, almost buttery, crunch.

SERVES 4 TO 6

$^1/_2$ cup country or sourdough breadcrumbs

2 tablespoons chopped fresh strong herbs such as: marjoram, thyme, sage, rosemary, savory

2 tablespoons olive oil

4 to 6 ounces mild goat cheese, sliced into $^1/_2$-inch rounds using a hot, wet knife

2 bunches arugula leaves washed and dried

$^1/_2$ pint fresh raspberries

$^3/_4$ cup Raspberry Vinaigrette (*see* page 791)

$^1/_2$ cup pine nuts, toasted at 300°F. for 10 minutes or until lightly and evenly browned

Preheat the oven to 450°F. Mix together breadcrumbs, herbs, and olive oil and pat evenly to coat goat cheese rounds. Place goat cheese rounds on a piece of foil and bake until crumbs are browned and cheese is hot, about 5 minutes.

Meanwhile, arrange arugula on individual salad plates and scatter raspberries over top. Place a round of the baked goat cheese in the center of each salad, drizzle each salad with dressing, sprinkle with toasted pine nuts, and serve.

Gemelli Pasta with Beefsteak Tomatoes, Arugula, and Feta Cheese

Nothing beats a fresh tomato sauce made with summer's vine-ripened beefsteak tomatoes. Because they have such a thin skin, I don't bother peeling them, making it a lot easier to prepare this sauce. Also, because the tomatoes are only cooked briefly so their bright flavor shines, I use fresh tomatoes only for this dish. The twisted gemelli (or twins) soak up the sauce perfectly, but fusilli or rotini would also work well. The arugula and feta liven up the dish both in appearance and on the palate. Uncooked olive oil, with its full fruity and herbal character, enriches the sauce, but can be omitted for a lighter dish.

SERVES 4

Sauce

1 red onion, cut into strips

1 tablespoon chopped garlic

$^1/_4$ cup + 2 tablespoons extra-virgin olive oil

3 cups diced fresh tomatoes

Kosher salt and freshly ground black pepper to taste

1 pound gemelli pasta

1 bunch arugula, trimmed, washed and cut into wide strips

Scant $^1/_2$ cup oil-cured black olives, pitted and sliced

$^1/_2$ pound feta, rinsed and crumbled

Prepare the sauce by sautéing the onion and garlic in $^1/_4$ cup of the olive oil in a medium heavy-bottomed pot. Add the tomatoes, salt and pepper to taste and cook until thickened but the tomatoes haven't lost their shape, about 10 minutes. Reserve.

Bring a large pot of salted water to the boil. Add the gemelli and boil until *al dente,* firm and bouncy, and still yellow in color. Drain well. Toss the pasta with the remaining 2 tablespoons olive oil, arugula, olives, reserved sauce and the feta, and serve.

FETA CHEESE

This rich and tangy soft cheese is of humble origin—its name comes from the word "fetid" from the Latin *foetidus*, meaning to stink, or having a heavy offensive smell. (Some sources say its name comes from a Greek word meaning "to slice"; maybe both are true.) While some might call its characteristic aroma fetid and unpleasant, its international popularity belies this negative association. Feta cheese, which originated in Greece, is authentically made of sheep's milk, although much is now made with cow's milk or a mixture of the two, to cut down on cost.

Greek-made feta is so popular in its home country, where it's sold in special all-white dairy stores, that very little gets exported. Feta is aged (but not ripened) four to six weeks in a salty whey mixture. Actually a type of pickled cheese, feta's flavor becomes sharper and saltier with age. It is creamy white in color with small holes, a crumbly texture, and is normally found in square cakes that don't have any rind. It will be packed in the brine that helps preserve the cheese—because of the high percentage of salt—but also makes it taste stronger, the longer it stays in the brine.

In Greece, feta often goes into mezze—bar snacks like tapas—and elsewhere is used as a snackable cheese perfect to serve with drinks (bartenders love to serve salty foods like feta that get washed down by copious amounts of beverages like wine, beer, or ouzo). With its salty, uncompromising flavor, feta is used in a huge number of traditional Greek dishes, from Spanakopita (phyllo dough filled with spinach and feta) and Horiatiki (Greek salad) to Garides me Feta (shrimp with feta cheese and ouzo) and Beef Stifado (beef stew with whole small onions and tomato, mixed with feta just before serving).

Linguine with Steamed Clams, Arugula, and Pancetta

This was a perennially popular dish at my last restaurant, Stella Notte, a country Italian restaurant in Philadelphia's venerable Chestnut Hill section. Everything works together beautifully here to make a dish that is as eye-appealing as it is delicious. It's also one of those rare dishes that translates perfectly from the restaurant kitchen to the home kitchen. If you use red and yellow tomatoes, it will be even more striking. Note that if you don't have pancetta, bacon makes a good substitute.

SERVES 4

$^1/_2$ pound pancetta, frozen until firm and
   cut into very small dice
$^1/_2$ cup chopped shallots
4 dozen small clams, well scrubbed
1 tablespoon chopped garlic
2 tablespoons olive oil
1 cup dry white wine
1 cup bottled clam broth
1 pound linguine
2 bunches arugula, washed and trimmed of large ribs
Fresh ground black pepper, and hot red pepper flakes,
   to taste .
1 tablespoon vegetable oil
3 cups diced beefsteak tomatoes
4 tablespoons unsalted butter, for finishing

In a small pot, brown the pancetta bits in the oil, drain and reserve. Bring a large pot of salted water to the boil for the pasta.

In a large pot with a lid, such as a Dutch oven, sauté the shallots, garlic, and pancetta in the olive oil. Add the white wine, clam broth, and clams. Cover and bring to the boil, shaking occasionally until all the clams have opened.

Meanwhile, boil the linguine until *al dente*, firm and bouncy, and still yellow in color. Just before serving, add the arugula, pepper, and hot pepper flakes and swirl in the butter. Toss with linguine, surround with clams and serve immediately.

69

ASPARAGUS

ASPARAGUS

A plateful of asparagus makes any meal a special occasion. The tall, slender, regally crowned asparagus stalks are almost too decorative to eat. Asparagus, *Asparagus officinalis*, is a perennial plant in the lily family. An underground stem (or crown) produces edible shoots for about six weeks each spring. If left alone, the tips (actually branches-to-be) sprout into tall, feathery, dill-like fronds.

The ancient Egyptians and Greeks ate wild asparagus shoots as a rare spring delicacy and for nearly four hundred years, asparagus has been a cash crop in Venezia, the flatland surrounding Venice. Even back then, farmers knew they could get a high price for their asparagus if they brought it to Venice's main market at the Rialto Bridge. Louis XIV's royal gardeners cultivated great quantities of asparagus for the privileged few at the French Sun King's court. Because the shoots grow at different rates and must be harvested by hand, asparagus is a higher-priced vegetable. As a harbinger of spring, asparagus is a favorite at both Passover Seders and Easter Dinner, so prices may skyrocket at that time of year, especially if the two holidays coincide.

Lafcadio Hearn says in his 1885 cookbook, *La Cuisine Creole*, "the fresher this vegetable is the better . . . all stalks not crisp and tender should be thrown aside. Cut off nearly all the horny white parts and boil for twenty minutes or half an hour." By 1923, Fannie Farmer advises boiling asparagus for fifteen minutes or "until soft". She recommends Oyster Bay white asparagus, a vegetable that is being rediscovered today as American specialty growers are making it available. In contrast to today's lean leanings, both authors recommend serving asparagus in cream or butter or napped by Hollandaise sauce. Asparagus is rich in vitamins A and C and has long been famed as a diuretic—you've probably noticed the definite aroma that develops in your urine after eating asparagus. Note that it is perfectly appropriate to eat asparagus with the fingers and in my opinion, so many foods taste best eaten directly from the hand.

The word asparagus evolved from the old English "sparrowgrass." In England, "sprue" is the name for extra-thin spears, called "grass asparagus" or "spaghetti grass" here. Mild, creamy white asparagus is beloved in Alsace (France), Belgium, Germany, and Holland. Farmers bury white asparagus in earth to prevent it from developing green chlorophyll from the sunlight. Baby white asparagus is a pricy delicacy from Michigan hothouses. You might get to taste them at top restaurants, where shoots no thicker than spaghetti sometimes appear. Provençal and Italian cooks prize violet asparagus, now for sale here in specialty markets.

"Wild" asparagus is exactly the same species as the cultivated type. Birds scatter the seeds about the country.

My first taste of wild asparagus was in the back fields at Mark and Judy Dornstreich's Branch Creek Farm in Pennsylvania's Bucks County. The green tips poked through dirt and mulch. We cut them off and sampled them raw—crunchy, intensely green, with a sweet-bitter aftertaste, then feasted on a big plateful for dinner. Wild and cultivated may be the same variety but there's nothing like a vegetable straight from the ground for flavor.

Paul Tsakos is the quirky proprietor of tiny, jam-packed Overbrook Herb Farm in Montgomery County, near Philadelphia. He planted his asparagus bed about 20 years ago. In late April through May, Paul cuts about five pounds of shoots a week. As the plants get older and bigger, the shoots get fatter. He likes large asparagus because they're just as tender as skinny stalks and cuts them when they're about six-inches high. I don't spend much time thinking about the sex life of plants, but according to Paul, it's more important than I might realize. The new asparagus varieties are male only, so the plant uses its energy growing stalks with tight buds instead of making seeds. If you want to grow your own, be aware that you'll need patience. It takes four years to grow asparagus from seed and two to three years from crowns.

I have a well-worn copy of Euell Gibbons' 1962 classic *Stalking the Wild Asparagus*. In it, he describes how as a boy, he spied a clump of asparagus growing by the Rio Grande River. Noticing that old, dried stalks stood above every outcropping of new asparagus tips, he picked out dozens of old clumps. His pail was soon full, so off came his undershirt. Tied at the neck and sleeves, he filled up his makeshift sack.

For the next week his family ate fresh asparagus every day, "Boiled and buttered, creamed, on toast and in soup." Gibbons says, "I doubt that young people today can real-ize how good the first green vegetables of spring tasted in those days before quick freezing and fast transportation began furnishing us with fresh green vegetables all winter."

The next time he saw wild asparagus, Gibbons was a middle-aged man, driving along a country road in Pennsylvania. To be back in wild asparagus country again was like a welcome home. Gibbons' friends think it's so much simpler to buy your asparagus, but he "has a secret they don't know about. When I am out along the hedgerows and waysides gathering wild asparagus, I am twelve years old again and all the world is new and wonderful as the spring sun quickens the green things into life after a winter's dormancy. Now do you know why I like wild asparagus?"

In *Vegetables in the French Style*, Provençal master chef Roger Vergé declares: "I adore asparagus—white, green, violet, or wild. Nothing in the garden moves me more than seeing its pearly, delicate shoots rising from the ground." He skewers uncooked asparagus spears crosswise, using two to three thin bamboo skewers and then grills them. He first ate this dish on a trip to Japan. "They will grow nice and tender while remaining very slightly bitter." Rather than water-chilling cooked asparagus, Vergé spreads the stalks out to air-cool so as not to lose any of their mouth-cleansing slightly bitter flavor.

Vergé warns, "however you serve it, do not let your asparagus sit in water, this will damage both its texture and its flavor." Vergé describes the wild asparagus that grows in springtime in the Provençal scrubland, generally after regularly occurring fires. "It is dark green and very thin—no thicker than the tine of a fork. You eat only the tips." Serve wild asparagus with a sharp mustard vinaigrette. Try asparagus with a light, blushing Rosé wine from Provence.

73

Grilled Asparagus with Chunky Vinaigrette and Parmigiano Crisp

I adapted this from a recipe of San Francisco star chef, Bradley Ogden. He served a more elaborate version during the Book and the Cook Festival one year while I served as chef of A'propos Bistro in Philadelphia. I've added the Parmigiano Crisps, which are delicious and add welcome crunch to this dish. You could, of course, serve the salad without the crisps, or serve the crisps with cocktails or a glass of Prosecco. Note that it's difficult to make the crisps on a humid day.

SERVES 6 TO 8

Chunky Vinaigrette

1 cup brunoise (tiny diced) diced yellow, orange,
  and red pepper

$^1/_2$ cup drained capers

$^1/_4$ cup brunoise (tiny diced) preserved lemon
  (all white pith scraped off first)

$^1/_2$ small red onion, finely diced

$^1/_2$ cup finely diced celery and/or finely diced fennel

2 tablespoons red wine vinegar

$^1/_4$ cup extra-virgin olive oil

Freshly ground black pepper (salt is not needed)

Combine vinaigrette ingredients and reserve.

Parmigiano Crisps

$^1/_2$ pound Parmigiano-Reggiano (or Grana Padano), moist
  inner portion only, finely grated

Preheat the oven to 400°F. Set a 6-inch steel ring (substitute with a cleaned empty tuna can with both ends removed) on a Silpat sheet; sprinkle a thin layer of freshly grated Parmigiano cheese into the ring, making sure to cover evenly. Repeat, filling the tray. Remove the ring and bake until the cheese melts, bubbles, and begins to brown around the edges. Remove sheet tray from oven, cooling just long enough so the cheese is warm but pliable, and not floppy. Set cheese circles over a rolling pin to form curved shape, leaving until cool.

Store the Parmigiano Crisps in an airtight cookie tin for up to three days, separating with bubble wrap to keep them from shattering.

Assembly

$1^1/_2$ pounds asparagus spears, trimmed

2 tablespoons olive oil

$1^1/_2$ cup Chunky Vinaigrette

$^1/_4$ cup diced oil-cured black olives (for garnish)

6 Parmigiano Crisps

Preheat grill until white hot and no visible flames remain. Rub asparagus spears with oil to coat. Grill on all sides. Place grilled asparagus on plates with tips all facing the same way. Spoon $^1/_4$ cup Chunky Vinaigrette across the middle of each portion of asparagus and sprinkle with black olives. Cover the bottom end of asparagus with a Parmigiano Crisp and serve immediately.

PREPARING AND COOKING ASPARAGUS

Some people peel asparagus, but because I'm careful to buy young asparagus, I break off each stalk at its natural breaking point, where it toughens, and save the stalk ends for soup stock. Cooked whole, asparagus is elegant as can be. For quick cooking and best flavor, I slice them on the diagonal into 1-inch lengths, exposing the tender insides. Some asparagus, such as that grown in New Jersey, can be quite sandy. Be sure to wash the root ends well.

My English cookbooks recommend cooking asparagus by tying the bunches and standing them up in a tall pot with several-inches of boiling water on the bottom. Cover with a lid (or an upside-down pot or foil if the pot isn't tall enough). French and Chinese recipes call for cooking asparagus as quickly as possible to retain its fleeting flavor. The French cook asparagus in lots of boiling water, so that the water will return to the boil as quickly as possible. The Chinese stir-fry asparagus at high temperature in light soybean oil or steam cut asparagus in a vegetable basket steamer. My standard way is to bring about one-inch of (salted) water to the boil in a nonreactive skillet. I lay the trimmed asparagus spears down flat and quickly bring the water to the boil. Then I cook the asparagus spears 3 to 5 minutes, turning once or twice, or until bright green and crisp-tender. To microwave, cover whole or cut asparagus by about half an inch of salted water, then microwave on high 3 to 5 minutes.

CHOOSING ASPARAGUS

Buy firm and plump asparagus spears, avoiding any that are shriveled or stringy-looking. Check the tips since these deteriorate the fastest. If the tips are wet or at all slimy, don't buy the asparagus. Examine the cut bottoms; dried-out stalks mean old asparagus. Look for uniformly green stalks since the farther down the stalk the green goes, the more tender the asparagus will be. Young asparagus is long and green to the bottom. White feet on asparagus tell you it's overgrown. Because not enough tender green stalk appeared aboveground, its spear was cut below the ground. I prefer slender stalks because they're greener on the outside with less blander white inside.

French Vegetable Cutting Sizes

A *brunoise* is a $1/8$-inch cube; a *julienne* is a strip $1/8$-inch cubed on the end and 1 to 2-inches long; *small dice* is a $1/4$-inch cube; *medium dice* is a $1/3$-inch cube; *large dice* is a $3/4$-inch cube; a *tourné* vegetable has been trimmed to a seven-sided oval.

Parmigiano–Reggiano and Grana Padano cheeses

Parmigiano-Reggiano is a venerable cheese made from the milk of cows that eat only grass or hay and in its strictly delineated region—an area near Parma in the central Italian province of Emilia-Romagna. The long-aged cheese is made purely from milk and salt, and is in fact, entirely edible, rind and all. Genuine Parmigiano-Reggiano is stamped all over the rind with its name formed from dotted letters. Parmigiano is a grana cheese, meaning that it is finely grained. It is quite firm and craggy in texture with a tendency to break off in large shards, and has an intense and complex nutty flavor. Authentic Parmigiano can also be recognized by the tiny crunchy crystals of salt throughout. Aged about two years, this cheese is never inexpensive, but it is the standard by which all other grating cheeses are measured. Fresh cut in chunks, it also makes a superb table cheese, especially good with fruit or prosciutto. Grana Padano (meaning grainy cheese) from the Po Valley is a less expensive grana cheese made throughout the province of Emilia-Romagna. Aged for only about six months, simpler, and less concentrated in flavor, it makes a good alternative for use as a grating cheese.

Pizza Milanese with Asparagus, Prosciutto, Fontina, and Pine Nuts

This rich, high-style pizza befits the ultra-elegant city of Milano, Italy's fashion capital and home to some of its finest restaurants. This is a "white" pizza, in that it contains no tomatoes. Instead a layer of sweet caramelized onions is topped with salty prosciutto, fresh asparagus, richly melting Fontina cheese, and finally, a sprinkle of pine nuts for a bit of nutty crunch.

MAKES ONE 14–INCH PIZZA, TO SERVE 4

$1\frac{1}{2}$ cups asparagus cut on the bias into 1-inch sections

1 pizza round ($^3/_4$ pound, about half the recipe for Cornmeal Pizza Dough, *see* page 985; or $^3/_4$ pound purchased dough)

Cornmeal, for sprinkling

Olive oil, for brushing

3 ounces thinly sliced prosciutto, cut into thin strips

1 cup Caramelized Onions (*see* Alpine Mushroom Pizza, page 651)

1 cup shredded Fontina cheese

3 tablespoons pine nuts

Preheat the oven to 500°F., if possible with a pizza stone in the oven. Bring a medium pot of salted water to the boil. Add the asparagus and cook 2 to 3 minutes, or until brightly colored and crisp-tender. Drain and run under cold water to set color.

Stretch out pizza round to the size of wooden peel (*see* using a Wooden Peel, page 79) and sprinkle lightly with cornmeal. Alternatively, roll out the pizza and transfer it to a cornmeal dusted metal baking pan (a paella pan works well here). Brush lightly with olive oil, especially on edges.

Spread the dough with the caramelized onions, leaving a 1-inch border at the edges. Arrange the asparagus and prosciutto over top. Top with Fontina cheese and pine nuts.

If using the peel, transfer unbaked pizza to the pizza stone by placing the peel at a low angle to the stone and giving the peel a fast, vigorous thrust forward and then back, so that the pizza jumps onto the stone. Bake until bubbling and well browned, about 6 minutes. Cool slightly, then cut into 8 to 12 wedges.

SILPAT SHEETS

Silpat nonstick baking sheets are made of woven fiberglass coated with food-grade silicon. There is a whole branch of restaurant cuisine that has been enabled by these reusable sheets, allowing thin sheets of syrup-coated fruits and vegetables to be dried into crisps, Parmigiano cheese to be made into lacy crisps (*see* Grilled Asparagus with Chunky Vinaigrette, page 74), and fancifully-cut paper-thin wafer cookies to be made. Originally from France, these sheets are now available for the home in smaller sizes. They are wonderful for baking cookies, roasting meats, poultry, vegetables, and anything else that can be baked on a metal pan. They're easy to clean and can be reused two to three thousand times each. You'll never have to buy parchment paper and they eliminate the need for buttering and flouring. They are heat-resistant up to 480°F. There is one caveat: do not cut into the sheet. Remove the items from the sheets before cutting.

Asparagus Risotto

This springtime asparagus risotto combines two specialties of the Veneto (the region surrounding Venice): spring's fresh young asparagus and the rice that grows in the Po River Valley. I have made more than my share of risotti (plural of risotto) in my time. With six years as chef of a Northern Italian restaurant and two years as chef of a country-style Italian restaurant, not to mention all the years of travel to Italy, consulting, and teaching in between, I've really gotten a feel for this rather temperamental dish. A good risotto is firm but yielding (sounds like a good recipe for love-making), soft enough that it moves rather than being stiff and heavy. The rice itself should be barely cooked through with no pearly hard grain in the center, but neither should it be at all mushy.

SERVES 4

1/4 cup chopped shallots, green onion,
  or sweet white onion
2 tablespoons unsalted butter
1 cup risotto rice (Arborio, Carnaroli, or Vialone Nano)
1/4 cup dry white vermouth
3 to 4 cups simmering chicken stock seasoned with
  salt and pepper
1 pound asparagus, thinly sliced on the diagonal
2 to 3 ounces (1 cup) grated Parmigiano Reggiano
  (substitute Grana Padano or domestic Asiago)

In a 3- to 4-quart heavy-bottomed sauce pot, cook shallots in butter until transparent. Add rice and cook, stirring, until rice is transparent (about 3 minutes). Pour in vermouth and stir. Raise the heat, bring to the boil and cook

77

until liquid is absorbed, about 4 minutes. Reduce heat to a healthy simmer and, one ladle at a time, add simmering stock to rice. Stir after adding stock, and then allow stock to get fully absorbed before adding a second ladle.

After three ladlefuls have been absorbed, stir in the sliced asparagus and the final ladle of simmering stock. The rice should be firm, but not cooked through. At the last minute, stir in the grated cheese and taste for seasoning. Serve on hot plates since risotto tastes best piping hot.

ABOUT RISOTTO RICE VARIETIES

A true risotto must be made with special varieties of short to medium-grain rice raised specifically for this dish for hundreds of years in the wetlands of Italy's Po River Valley. Three varieties are best suited to making risotto: Arborio, Carnaroli, and Vialone Nano. Arborio is the most widely available outside of Italy, but Italian cooks tend to prefer Carnaroli and Vialone Nano for the firm yet creamy texture of the risotto they yield. Arborio has large rounded grains and good creamy texture, Carnaroli has a longer grain that tends to hold its shape well even when fully cooked, while Vialone Nano is said to have the creamiest, smoothest texture of all.

Joe's Asparagus with Brown Butter and Poppy Seeds

For years I had heard about the legendary restaurant, Joe's, in the unlikely location of industrial Reading, Pennsylvania. Joe's had one of the first fine American wine lists and specialized in wild mushroom dishes. On my first visit, a momentous occasion, I devoured three big fat asparagus spears anointed in brown butter and poppy seeds. This is my version of the dish, probably derived from owner Jack Czarnecki's Polish heritage. I remember it as a high point in asparagus cookery, though I ate it more than twenty years ago. The restaurant was opened originally as a working-man's saloon by Jack's great-grandfather and is now, sadly, closed. Mr. Czarnecki now runs the Joel Palmer House in Oregon's Willamette Valley with his wife, Heidi, in an area chosen for its outstanding wines and treasure-troves of his beloved wild mushrooms.

SERVES 4

2 tablespoons unsalted butter
1 tablespoon poppy seeds
Kosher salt and freshly ground black pepper to taste
Juice and grated zest of 1 lemon
1 bunch asparagus, trimmed

Place butter in a small heavy-bottomed pot, melt over moderate heat, then brown until nutty smelling and golden, not burnt. Add poppy seeds, season with salt and pepper and stir in lemon juice and zest. Meanwhile, steam or boil asparagus and drain well on paper towels. Toss well with the poppy seed butter and serve immediately.

78

Asparagus alla Parmigiana

My all-time favorite Italian cookbook is Le Ricette Regionale Italiane *(The Regional Recipes of Italy) by Anna Gosetti della Salda. Her treasure-trove of a tome, never translated, is my constant reference for authentic regional Italian dishes. I (loosely) translated her traditional recipe for asparagus that comes from the butter-and cheese-loving province of Emilia-Romagna, home of Bologna, Italian capital of gastronomy. Notice the large amount of asparagus called for, over half a pound per person. Italians do love their vegetables and eat them in quantity. Make a meal of this dish with a loaf of crusty bread and perhaps some sliced dry salami. For this dish, use genuine Parmigiano-Reggiano, or substitute Italian Fontina for a more melting version.*

SERVES 4

2 pounds (2 bunches) asparagus, trimmed so they're
  all the same length

4 tablespoons unsalted butter, softened

2 to 3 ounces (1 cup) finely grated Parmigiano Reggiano

Kosher salt, freshly ground black pepper, and grated
  nutmeg to taste

Preheat broiler. Steam or boil asparagus until firm but not fully cooked. Drain well and arrange the spears in layers in a shallow metal baking pan (such as a paella pan). Dot with butter bits, then sprinkle with grated Parmigiano Reggiano cheese. Broil on high for 5 to 10 minutes, or until browned and bubbling. Serve immediately in their dish.

USING PAELLA PANS FOR BROWNING AND GLAZING

When browning, broiling, or making a crusty gratin, I use my trusty steel paella pans. Inexpensive and widely available, these practically indestructible pans conduct heat beautifully, and with their wide surface area, there is lots of room for making those delicious browned crusts. Try making your next batch of nachos in a paella pan: roast small chickens or Cornish hens surrounded, if you like, with potatoes and other firm vegetables; or roast cut-up mixed vegetables (like eggplant, butternut, fennel, carrot, peppers, and onions) in one. Cut up yellow potatoes, mix with olive oil (or butter), garlic, and herbs like rosemary or thyme and roast until brown and crispy. Note that because these pans are made from steel, they can rust. To care for your pan, wipe dry immediately after washing and rub lightly with oil. If rust appears, wipe it off and rub the pan with oil. Eventually your pan will get a good seasoning that will prevent rust. A 15-inch diameter pan is most useful; small individual pans are good for things like roasting garlic cloves.

USING A WOODEN PEEL

A peel is a long-handled wooden board that is used to transfer pizza and bread dough to and from the oven.

79

AVOCADOS

AVOCADOS

The luscious avocado, *Persea americana*, is the most sensually pleasing fruit/vegetable around. It is technically a fruit and belongs to the *Lauraceae* family, along with bay laurel and allspice. Its Aztec name, *ahua-catl*, means testicle, referring to both the fruit's shape and the way it dangles from the tree in pairs. Along with its suggestive name, its plump, pear-like shape and creamy, spring-green flesh rich with natural oils naturally lead to its reputation as an aphrodisiac.

The overwhelming majority of avocados end up as guacamole, so be sure to try my Best Ever Guacamole with Lime. They lend their subtle, enticing flavor and unctuous texture to everything from soup like Chilled Avocado and Tomatillo Gazpacho to Avocado-Tequila Ice Cream. A fraternal rather than identical green pair appear in the Chayote and Avocado Salad with Salsa. Although avocados are most commonly eaten raw, they are also delicious heated. In the Yucatan Chicken Soup, the hot soup is poured over sliced avocado just to warm it through. Warmed avocado is combined with a light tomato cream sauce in Sautéed Striped Bass with Avocado in Rose Sauce.

The avocado was cultivated from the Rio Grande to central Peru long before the arrival of Europeans. Native to Central America, it migrated early to Mexico. Around Oaxaca, Mexico, avocado leaves are used in cooking for their licorice-like aroma. Chilean writer Isabel Allende, in her *Aphrodite: A Memoir of the Senses*, tells us that the avocado, "was taken to Europe by Spanish conquistadors, who were responsible for spreading its fame as a stimulant—so effectively that in the confessional, Catholic priests forbade it to their parishioners."

First known to English-speaking people by the evocative names "midshipmen's butter", "alligator pear", "vegetable butter", or "butter pear", the avocado was introduced into the United States in 1833 and crossed the border from Mexico into California about 1871. Today, California growers supply ninety-five percent of the nation's crop, with San Diego County, the avocado capital of the country, alone producing forty percent.

A single California avocado tree can produce up to 120 avocados every year. Avocados are available twelve months a year, thanks to the coastal California microclimate. They are grown commercially everywhere from North America to Israel, South Africa, New Zealand and Australia, though 90 percent of the world's crop comes from California.

Avocados have only been commercially available in Europe since the early 1900s. Because of their unfamiliar appearance and flavor, they were treated with suspicion at first. The Israelis started marketing them extensively to Europe in the 1960s. Avocados have since made a rapid advance into the cuisines of Western Europe and pyramids of avocados appear at fruit and vegetable stands across Europe.

Though rich in oils, avocados are nourishing and easy to digest. High in protein, they contain significant amounts of vitamins A, B, B2, C, and E, and minerals including potassium, phosphorus, magnesium, and iron. Avocados are good for both hair and skin, and their oil is used in many personal care products.

Avocado Varieties

Fuerte: Once the best-selling type, the Fuerte has thin green skin with a smooth surface and creamy, pale green flesh. Medium to large in size, it is pear-shaped with a medium-size seed, peels easily, and has excellent flavor. It is in season from late fall through spring.

Hass: The rich and buttery Hass now accounts for nearly 80 percent of California's total avocado crop. Its thick, pebbly skin turns from green and shiny to purplish-black and dull when ripe. Oval-shaped, with a small to medium-sized seed, the Hass peels easily because of its thick, pliable skin. In fact, a Hass is perfectly ripe when the peel and pit come away from the flesh easily and cleanly. A ripe Hass will also yield to gentle pressure when ripe, and the flesh will feel firm yet slightly giving. Avoid avocados with soft or mushy spots; these indicate the avocado is overripe. Hass are considered by many (including me) the avocado of choice, especially for Mexican dishes. It is now grown year-round in California.

Pinkerton: Pinkerton is the premium winter variety with medium-thick green skin, slight pebbling, and buttery-textured creamy, pale green flesh. It is in season in winter and spring.

Zutano: Zutano is one of the first varieties harvested when the season begins in September. Easily recognized by its shiny, yellow-green skin, it has pale green flesh with a light texture.

Florida and Caribbean Avocado: Florida and Caribbean avocados have deep green flesh covered with a smooth, shiny green skin with leathery, pliable skin, flesh that is low in oil, and non-aromatic leaves. The fruit is quite large with an equally large pit inside and a light taste and texture that is fruitlike rather than buttery. The majority of the avocados grown in the West Indies, Bahamas and Bermuda and the tropics of the Old World are of the Caribbean type.

Cocktail Avocado: The cocktail or "cuke" avocado is a seedless miniature Fuerte that resembles a small pickle. It has smooth green skin and pale green flesh with a creamy consistency. These cocktail avocados are actually freaks of nature that grow without a seed. Once thrown into the trash, these avocados are now occasionally harvested them and marketed, labeled as "Cocktail" or "Finger" avocados.

83

Yucatan Chicken Soup with Avocados and Lime

I served many bowls of this soup at West Philadelphia's now famed White Dog Café where it was always popular. It's always fun to eat soup with different textured garnishes. This soup has so much going on that it can easily be served as a meal in a bowl with a salad and maybe enough room for dessert. Though your own will have the best flavor and crunch, you may substitute purchased tortilla chips for speed.

SERVES 8

3 quarts chicken stock, preferably homemade
  (*see* page 991)
2 pounds boneless skinless chicken thighs
2 cups canola oil for frying
8 corn tortillas, sliced into strips
2 jalapeño peppers, seeded and minced
$\frac{1}{2}$ bunch cilantro, sprigs picked off
Juice of 4 key limes, or 2 limes
Kosher salt to taste
2 firm but ripe avocados, sliced

In a small pot, bring 2 cups of the chicken stock to the boil. Add the chicken and simmer 15 minutes, covered, or until thoroughly cooked. Cool in the liquid, then remove the thighs, trim, and cut into strips. Strain the cooking liquid through a dampened paper towel to remove any white coagulated bits, then add the chicken strips back into broth and reserve.

Meanwhile, heat the oil in a heavy pot or a wok until just beginning to smoke. Fry the tortilla strips until crispy and lightly colored. Keep stirring with tongs while frying to separate the strips. Scoop the tortilla strips out of the oil using a wire skimmer and then drain on paper towels.

Bring the remaining stock to the boil. Add the chicken strips and their liquid, the jalapeño, cilantro, lime juice, and salt. Simmer 5 minutes and taste for seasoning. Place a portion of avocado slices and tortillas crisps on the bottom of each of eight large soup bowls. Pour the soup over top and serve immediately.

CHINESE BRASS WIRE SKIMMER

An inexpensive Chinese brass wire and bamboo skimmer, also known as a spider, is best for scooping deep-fried foods from cooking oil. The brass wire repels oil so that the foods will be lighter. Almost any Asian market will sell them for about five dollars.

Chilled Avocado and Tomatillo Gazpacho

This smooth and velvety soup is a lovely cooling green color, perfect to serve on a summer evening. The pumpkin seeds add crunch along with their nutty flavor. You may also purchase toasted pumpkin seeds to use here. Increase the quantity of jalapeños if you like a hotter soup.

SERVES 6

2 large cucumbers, peeled and roughly chopped
3 firm but ripe avocadoes, 2 roughly chopped and 1 diced
Juice of 6 key limes, or 3 limes

3 cups cold chicken or vegetable stock

1 cup loosely packed cilantro leaves (about 1 bunch), washed and dried

1 green jalapeño or 2 serrano chiles, trimmed and seeded

1 bunch scallions, sliced, divided

6 medium to large tomatillos, 4 roughly chopped + 2 finely diced

Kosher salt to taste

2 tablespoons canola oil

$1/2$ cup raw pumpkin seeds (pepitas)

In a blender, puree the cucumbers, the roughly chopped avocadoes, lime juice, stock, cilantro, jalapeño, half the scallions, and the roughly chopped tomatillos. Season to taste with salt. Blend until smooth, straining if desired for smoother texture. Cover and then refrigerate until well chilled, about 2 hours.

In a small pan, fry pumpkin seeds in the oil until they pop and brown lightly. Drain and reserve.

Pour the chilled soups into serving bowls and garnish with remaining scallions, diced tomatillos, and pumpkin seeds.

Best Ever Guacamole with Lime

There are numberless guacamole recipes and I'm a big fan of almost any good homemade version. Years ago, TGIF had a reputation for having the best guacamole, made in-house. Now almost every chain restaurant that features guacamole serves it from the freezer. It's a far cry from the fresh version. In fact, the best Mexican restaurants prepare guacamole tableside. To keep the color, it's important to choose firm yet giving avocados and use plenty of fresh lime, as here. Adding the avocado pit to the bowl doesn't really help keep it green, but it doesn't hurt either. I generally buy underripe avocados several days before I'm going to need them and ripen them myself on the kitchen counter.

MAKES 1 $1/2$ CUPS, SERVES 6 TO 8

2 firm but ripe avocados, preferably Haas or Fuerte

2 tablespoons fresh-squeezed lime juice

1 teaspoon salt

$1/2$ cup finely diced white onion, red onion, or sweet onion

1 jalapeño pepper, seeded and finely diced (or 1 tablespoon drained pickled jalapeños, chopped)

$1/2$ cup seeded, diced, and drained ripe tomatoes

$1/4$ cup chopped cilantro

Peel the avocados and quarter them. Remove the pit and peel back the skin from each quarter. Using a heavy whisk, mash the avocado together with lime juice and salt, until you obtain small lumps and no large chunks remain. Stir in remaining ingredients. Cover tightly, pressing plastic wrap directly on the guacamole and reserve in refrigerator for up to two days.

Note: after a few hours, the Guacamole will discolor on top. Simply scrape off the darkened layer, which will have an off-taste, and use the remainder.

85

Sautéed Striped Bass with Avocado in Rose Sauce

This is a luxurious dish for a summer dinner when stripers are running. As far as I'm concerned, the magnificent striped bass is the king or queen of fish. It's not often available and quite pricey because of high demand. However, its cousin, the hybrid striped bass, is a good substitute. The licorice-flavored Pernod and tarragon underscore the faint anise note of the avocado.

SERVES 4

1½ pounds striped bass fillets (or farm-raised hybrid
    stripers, or black sea bass)
Kosher salt and fresh ground black pepper
2 tablespoons olive oil
2 tablespoons unsalted butter
¼ cup minced shallots
2 tablespoons Pernod
½ cup dry white vermouth
2 cups peeled and diced plum tomatoes
    (*see* Peeling fresh plum tomatoes, at right)
Juice of 1 lime
2 tablespoons chopped fresh tarragon
½ cup heavy cream
2 firm but ripe avocados, sliced

Season the fish with salt and pepper. Over high heat, heat the olive oil in a large skillet, preferably nonstick. Sauté the fish fillets about 3 minutes on each side, starting with the skin side down, until the flesh is white and opaque but moist. Using a slotted spatula, remove the fish from the pan, place on a platter, and keep warm.

Pour off and discard any fat in the pan.

In the same pan, heat the butter until foaming, then add the shallots and cook several minutes or until soft but not brown. Add the Pernod and vermouth, heat 1 minute, and then flame to cook off alcohol. Add the tomatoes to the pan and cook over high heat until the tomatoes soften. Stir in the lime juice, most of the tarragon and the cream and then bring to the boil. Season sauce to taste with salt and pepper.

Pour the sauce onto the bottom of four dinner plates, preferably heated and arrange the avocado slices around the plate. Top with the reserved fish fillets and garnish with the remaining tarragon.

PEELING FRESH PLUM TOMATOES

While I don't bother peeling thinner-skinned round tomatoes, plum tomatoes have thick, indigestible skin that should be removed. The skins will easily slip off of fully ripened tomatoes. To skin, bring a pot of water to the boil and have a bowl of ice mixed with water ready. Drop the tomatoes in the boiling water and allow them to cook only long enough for the skin to move easily against the flesh, about 1 minute. Immediately scoop the tomatoes from the pot (dumping them out will crush them) and drop into the ice water. When cool enough to handle, slip off the skins. Cut out the core, using a "tomato shark", small paring knife, or a small melon baller. If you care to remove the seeds, cut in half "through the equator" and lightly squeeze the seeds out of the exposed seed pockets. Strain the delicious liquid from the seeds if desired, then cut up the tomatoes and add back the strained juice.

86

Chayote and Avocado Salad with Salsa

The many aliases of the chameleon chayote include "vegetable pear", "mirliton" in Louisiana, "christophine" in France, and "custard marrow" in Britain, a name that surely doesn't do justice to this highly adaptable member of the gourd family. Similar to the avocado, with which it is paired here, the chayote's name is Aztec in origin and was eaten by both Mayas and Aztecs. Pale green to the avocado's deeper color, it is similar in size, and also has a large single central pit. Served cooked and stuffed, grilled, or steamed, chayote is also good raw and shredded as for coleslaw

SERVES 4

4 red, ripe tomatoes, seeded and diced

$1/2$ white onion, diced

2 jalapeño peppers, seeded and finely chopped

Juice of 2 limes

$1/4$ bunch cilantro, chopped

$1/4$ cup canola oil

Kosher salt to taste

2 chayote squash

2 firm but ripe Haas avocados

Prepare the salsa by combining tomato, onion, jalapeño, lime juice, cilantro, oil, and salt.

Bring a medium pot of salted water to the boil. Cook the whole chayote for 5 minutes, then cool and pare away tough outer skin. Remove seed pod and slice the flesh thinly.

Cut the avocados in half, remove the pit, and quarter. Peel back the skin from each quarter, then slice each quarter into 3 to 4 slices. Arrange alternating slices of chayote and avocado on individual salad plates. Spoon salsa over top and serve immediately.

Avocado–Tequila Ice Cream

The avocado is just as much a fruit as it is a vegetable. Here its incredibly rich, buttery flesh with its faint licorice flavor enhances an ice cream spiked with another Mexican specialty: tequila. Tequila is a native Mexican liquor distilled from the fermented juices extracted from the hearts of the blue agave, Agave azul tequilana weber. It got its name from the town of Tequila in the state of Jalisco, where production began more than 200 years ago. Tequila labeled añejo must be aged for a minimum of one year in white oak casks; silver tequila is aged in wax-lined vats. Use whichever tequila you have on hand here.

SERVES 8

2 large firm but ripe avocados, preferably Hass,
   peeled and quartered

1 cup + $1/2$ cup heavy cream

4 egg yolks

$1/2$ cup granulated sugar

$1^1/2$ cups milk

$1/4$ cup tequila

$1^1/2$ teaspoons vanilla extract

Combine avocados and 1 cup of the cream in a blender jar or food processor bowl. Blend or process until smooth. Remove and strain if desired for a smoother texture. Cover and reserve in the refrigerator.

Beat the egg yolks with the sugar. In a large Pyrex measure or bowl, scald the milk and remaining $1/2$ cup of cream in the microwave. Whisk a little of the hot cream mixture into the egg yolks to temper. Beat in the remaining hot cream and transfer egg mixture into a medium nonreactive pot. Cook, whisking, until the custard reaches 165°F., or until it thickens visibly.

Remove from the heat, stir in the tequila and the vanilla, cool over ice, and then chill in the refrigerator (*see* Cooling foods, page 238). Combine with the reserved avocado cream and freeze in an ice cream maker according to the manufacturer's instructions.

BANANAS & PLANTAINS

BANANAS & PLANTAINS

Bananas

Though I'm a fruit-loving fiend, as a child I always disliked bananas. Though bananas are by far America's favorite fruit, I was turned of by their penetrating, tropical aroma and would never eat them. Don't get me wrong, I enjoyed cooking with them and my feelings never extended to plantains, the starchy cousin of the banana with many disguises—ranging in color from green to gold to black—that is always cooked.

It took my stint at A'propos—at the time the "hottest" restaurant around—to realize what I was missing in the world of bananas. At the time, I served a wildly popular appetizer made from delectable deep-fried ninõs (small finger-size bananas) topped with sour cream and three kinds of caviar: sturgeon, salmon, and golden white fish—the recipe is included here. From ninõs, I progressed to firm, full-bodied red bananas. I tend to gravitate toward the more exotic bananas that are showing up more and more often in local supermarkets. Once in a while, I'll even enjoy a Yellow Cavendish, the American standard.

While it seems everyone has a recipe for banana bread because we need something to do with that readily over-ripening fruit, my Banana Oatmeal Quick Bread benefits nutritionally from the addition of oatmeal. Arañitas are crispy grated plantain fritters that fancifully resemble large spiders. Firm red bananas caramelize beautifully in the Red Bananas in Spiced Rum Syrup, a variation on the restaurant standard, Bananas Foster, a tableside specialty in old New Orleans.

The Latin name for the banana, *Musa sapientum*, recalls the legend that wise men would sit in the shade of the banana tree and eat its fruit. Bananas originated in Southeast Asia, where the wild fruits were known as monkey bananas. Alexander the Great's army encountered bananas in India where they had been known for several thousand years and brought tales of the new fruit back home to Greece in the fourth century BCE. The banana reached China about 200 CE. Because it had previously grown only in the south, it was long considered a rare, exotic fruit in northern China.

During the first millennium CE, the banana also arrived in Africa and traveled east through the Pacific islands. The Arabs spread banana cultivation throughout North Africa before 750 CE, but the fruit was unknown to Europeans until Portuguese sailors brought them to the Canary Islands around 1400. The Canaries have remained an important banana-growing area ever since. A Spanish missionary brought banana roots from the Canaries to America in 1516. The new plant spread so quickly through Latin America that early writers were convinced that it was known by the Incas.

During the nineteenth century, bananas began to be

shipped from the Canaries to Europe and from Cuba to the U.S., but high shipping costs made them an expensive luxury. In 1899 two American entrepreneurs formed the United Fruit Company which had and still has great influence in Central America and the Caribbean countries that became known as the "banana republics" (not a fashion store), because their entire economies revolved around bananas. The five biggest companies account for over eighty percent of the world banana trade: Chiquita (U.S.), Dole (U.S.), Fyffes (Ireland), Del Monte (Chile), and Noboa (Ecuador).

The banana plant is not a true tree, even though it may reach heights of 25 feet with leaves up to eight feet long and two feet wide. Bananas are thought to be one of the first species of plant domesticated by man and are a staple food to many peoples. They provide food, clothing, building materials, and cooking utensils to numerous cultures around the world. Bananas grow in large bunches or "hands," which are formed from the double rows of female flowers on each plant. Each flowering hand produces 200 to 300 individual fruits or "fingers." Under the immense weight of the fruit, the hands bend down towards the ground, making for easier picking.

Plantains

The Latin name for the banana's starchy cousin, the plantain, *Musa paradisiaca*, came about because of an Islamic myth, probably of Indian origin, that the banana (and not the apple) was the fruit of the tree of knowledge in the Garden of Eden (located in Sri Lanka according to the same legend). Furthermore, after the Fall, Adam and Eve covered their naked bodies with generously sized banana leaves, quite a bit more effective that the skimpier fig leaves of Western tradition.

Plantains start out starchy and hard like a vegetable and ripen to become soft and sweet like a fruit. In Spanish, green, or starchy, plantains are known as *platanos*; partially ripe plantains are known as *pintos* (painted), and fully ripened black-spotted yellow plantains are known as *maduros* (mature or ripe).

91

BANANA BLOSSOMS

Magnificent deep purplish-crimson banana flowers are used in many Asian cuisines as a vegetable. They are usually steamed or boiled first to get rid of their bitterness and then sliced and used in salads or cooked in curries or simmered in coconut milk. In Thailand, the blossoms go into fried noodle dishes and soup; in the Philippines, they go into kari-kari, a rich beef stew. Look for fresh and bright flowers in Asian markets. Wrap in plastic and store in the refrigerator for several days. To prepare the flower, remove and discard outer bracts until the inner, paler portion is revealed, like an artichoke. Steam for 20 minutes and cool before slicing.

Banana Varieties

Burro Banana: This short, stocky banana, also known as the Chunky, hails from Central America and Mexico and is three to five-inches long with squared sides. When ripened to a golden yellow with scattered black spots, it has a lively, lemony flavor and velvety flesh that is white to yellow in color, and soft in texture with some firmness toward the center. It may be eaten out of hand, baked, or added to fruit salads or desserts, and is in season year-round from Mexico.

Cavendish: By far the most common variety in the U.S., the Cavendish grows in large bunches of full-sized, sweet, smooth fruit with yellow skin that is slightly ridged on the edges. "Petites" are small versions of the Cavendish that are also known as "institutional" bananas because they are often included in school lunches. Gray-yellow or dull yellow bananas are an indicator of improper temperature handling and will probably not develop full flavor. Cavendishes are available year-round almost everywhere. The Guinea Verde is an unprocessed yellow Cavendish used as a starch, much like plantains.

Ice Cream Banana: This exotic banana has blue skin, a creamy texture, and a flavor that fancifully suggests smooth, luscious ice cream.

Macabu: These small, chunky bananas should be fully ripened until the yellow begins to turn black. The pulp will be firm, not mushy with a very sweet taste and creamy texture.

Manzano: This short, chubby banana is green when unripe, and black at its peak. Its flavor combines strawberries, apples, and bananas with flesh that is dryer than most bananas.

Niño: These mild, sweet, finger-sized baby bananas just over three-inches long originated in the jungles of Colombia where they are called *murapo*. Niños are also known as "lady bananas" in Spanish, no doubt in comparison to the unquestionably phallic "males".

Plantain: Large, firm, four-sided plantains start out starchy and hard like a vegetable and ripen to soft and sweet like a fruit. Starchy plantains can be thinly sliced, crosswise or lengthwise, and then fried in chips; they are also sold in bags like potato chips.

Firm-ripe plantains with mottled brown and yellow skins are the best for pan-frying. Sliced on the diagonal and fried until golden brown, they are delicious served with savory roasts. Fully ripe plantains that are nearly black are best broiled or pan-fried and are wonderful bathed in flaming rum sauce and served with ice cream or served as an ever-present Caribbean side dish. Plantains are available every day of the year at Latino markets.

Red Banana: Red bananas are four to six-inches long with maroon to dark purple skin with ripe and firm orange-tinted flesh that can be quite sweet and sticky They are well suited to caramelizing for desserts because they combine sweetness with firm texture.

Pan–Fried Baby Bananas with Crème Fraiche and Golden Caviar

Make this extraordinary restaurant-style dish when you want to impress your guests or serve it as an hors d'oeuvre at a party. It is actually easy to make and not expensive. The American golden caviar, also known as whitefish caviar, is the lightly salted, crunchy and colorful roe of the whitefish, a meaty freshwater fish found in all the Great Lakes. The tiny eggs are an almost iridescent, lovely pale orange to gold color, and they pop in your mouth with subtle flavor and fine crunch.

SERVES 6 AS AN APPETIZER

2 cups canola oil

1 bunch baby (niños) bananas, firm but ripe

Fleur de sel or kosher salt to taste

1 pint crème fraiche, or sour cream

2 to 3 ounces golden (whitefish) caviar

1 bunch chives, thinly sliced

In a large, heavy-bottomed pot or a wok, heat the oil until shimmering (365°F. on a frying thermometer). Meanwhile, peel the bananas. If they're small, leave them whole, otherwise, cut in half lengthwise.

Fry bananas until golden brown, scoop from oil using a wire skimmer, and drain on a wire rack.

Arrange bananas in an attractive pattern on individual serving plates. Sprinkle with salt, place a scoop of crème fraiche in the center of the bananas and top with several tablespoons of chilled golden caviar and sprinkle with chives. Serve immediately so that you eat hot bananas with chilled cream and caviar.

CHOOSING, RIPENING, AND STORING BANANAS

Choose plump, evenly colored yellow bananas flecked with tiny brown specks (a sign of ripeness). For plantains, buy them at any stage from green to black, but always choose plump, unshriveled bananas without mushy spots.

FLEUR DE SEL

Fleur de Sel (flower of salt in French) is a highly prized and highly priced artisanal sea salt that consists of "young" crystals that form naturally from the surface down of salt evaporation ponds in the Guérande region of France. High in mineral content and low in sodium, it is hand harvested under specific weather conditions by traditional *paludiers* (salt farmers). Chefs use it for sprinkling on foods just before serving so that it contributes crunchy texture and bold, explosive flavor as it melts on the tongue.

93

Banana Oatmeal Quick Bread

Banana bread is one of the easiest and tastiest of quick breads. Here I've added oatmeal for texture, buttermilk for flavor and lightness, and chopped pecans for richness. Be sure to spray your pans generously with nonstick spray, as the batter tends to be sticky, or if you prefer, smear the pans with softened butter and dust with flour. Quick breads like this one freeze very well.

Makes two 8–cup loaves

$3/4$ pound (3 cups) unbleached all-purpose flour

1 cup oatmeal, not instant

$1^1/2$ teaspoons baking soda

1 teaspoon kosher salt

$1/2$ pound (2 sticks) unsalted butter

2 cups granulated sugar

1 tablespoon vanilla extract

3 eggs

2 cups mashed very ripe bananas (ripe plantains
   or red bananas are also good)

2 cups buttermilk, preferably whole milk

1 cup chopped pecans

Preheat the oven to 325°F. Prepare loaf pans by spraying with nonstick spray. Whisk together dry ingredients: flour, oatmeal, baking soda, and salt, and reserve.

In a mixer bowl using the paddle attachment, cream butter, sugar, and vanilla until light and fluffy. Beat in eggs one at a time, then add bananas and beat again until creamy, about 1 minute.

Add dry ingredients mix to the creamed mix beginning and ending with the dry ingredients, and alternating with the buttermilk. Stir in pecans.

Transfer the batter to the pans and bake 45 minutes or until set in the middle and mixture has pulled away slightly from pan. Cool before removing from pans.

BUTTERMILK AND WHOLE BUTTERMILK

The cultured buttermilk commonly available in American supermarkets is not the same as "old fashioned buttermilk", which was actually the milky liquid left after churning butter. Farmers would let fresh milk sit for half a day to allow the cream to rise, which they would then skim off. Several days' worth of milking would be added until a goodly amount had accumulated, enough to churn a batch of butter. During this time, naturally occurring bacteria in the cream would cause it to sour slightly, also increasing the amount of butter that could be extracted from the cream. After the cream was churned and the butter "came", the remaining liquid was the buttermilk, which had the consistency of milk, though paler, with flakes of butter floating in it. Cultured buttermilk is not a byproduct of buttermaking, rather it is a special thick and tart milk product made by adding lactic acid to non-fat or low-fat milk. My preferred buttermilk is made by Sealtest and is made from whole milk, so that it is richer and creamier with the same tanginess as other types.

Crispy Fried Plantain "Spiders" (Arañitas)

Arañitas are spiders, a fanciful name given to this Caribbean dish of grated plantains formed into spider-shaped fritters. Because unripe plantains are so starchy, it's pretty easy to fry them crisp without sogginess. Serve Arañitas as an appetizer with your favorite salsa (see Pico De Gallo Salsa, page 120; Mango-Mint Chutney, page 575; Salsa Verde, page 586; Pineapple-Poblano Salsa, page 720; Spicy Grilled Vegetable Salsa, page 920), or as a side dish with Caribbean-style fish, seafood, or chicken. It can be a bit tedious to peel off the skin of an unripe plantain; follow the directions below to make it easier.

MAKES ABOUT 16, SERVES 8 AS AN APPETIZER

2 cloves garlic, mashed

2 teaspoons kosher salt

2 green plantains

3 cups canola oil for frying

Mash garlic with salt to a paste. Mix well with 2 cups water and set aside.

Cut off the tips off the plantains and slice down the side, being careful to cut only through the skin and not the flesh. Fill a bowl with hot water from the tap. Soak the plantains for 30 minutes to soften them slightly. Using a spoon, carefully separate the skin from the flesh. Discard the skin.

Using a mandoline or a box grater, shred plantain into long strips. Gently clump plantain strips together into patties, about 1½-inches around, leaving plantains strips sticking out on all sides of the patty.

In a large, heavy-bottomed pot, an electric deep-fryer, or a wok, heat the oil until shimmering (365°F. on a frying thermometer). Dip the Arañitas (patties) into reserved garlic water quickly and shake off excess liquid. Carefully, lay the Arañitas one at a time into hot oil (be careful not to throw them in, to prevent spattering). Fry until golden on both sides, about 4 minutes, remove, and place on paper towel or wire rack to drain excess oil. Keep warm in a 200°F. oven until all the Arañitas are cooked, and then serve immediately.

FRYING OILS

With all the furor about trans-fats and the health problems associated with them, I have never used any solid fat for deep-frying. My first choice is pure peanut oil, because of its high smoking point and good flavor. However, some people are allergic to peanut products. In that case, I would substitute canola oil (high in beneficial omega-3s), or the soybean oil (often labeled vegetable oil) commonly used in Chinese restaurants. Because canola and soybean are quite bland, I would flavor it with a small amount of extra-virgin olive oil if frying a Mediterranean style dish, or a little roasted sesame oil (as is done to make Japanese tempura) for an Asian style dish. Pure olive oil, which has been refined, not extra-virgin—which contains particles that burn easily—is also excellent for frying.

95

Red Bananas in Spiced Rum Syrup

Once, all sugar was sold in large, solid, tan-colored, cone-shaped "loaves", which had to be broken apart and crushed before use. In fact the famed Pão di Azucar in the harbor of Rio di Janeiro is a rock that gets its name from its resemblance to an old-time sugar loaf. Today, dark brown cakes of unrefined sugar known as piloncillo *are sold in Mexico; in Colombia, loaf sugar is called* panela. *Latin American markets often carry a wide selection of these unrefined dark sugars, each with its own characteristic flavor and color. Of course, you can easily substitute boxed dark brown sugar, actually white sugar coated in molasses.*

SERVES 6

1 1/2 cups panela, piloncillo, or dark brown sugar

2 whole cloves

1 stick cinnamon, preferably soft-stick or canela
   (*see* Cinnamon, canela, and cassia, page 297)

1 teaspoon whole allspice

Juice of one lemon

1/4 pound (1 stick) unsalted butter

1/4 cup dark rum

1/4 cup water

6 whole ripe red bananas, halved

Place the sugar, cloves, cinnamon stick, allspice, and lemon juice in a nonreactive skillet and heat until it turns into a thick syrupy brown caramel (about 5 minutes). Add the butter slowly and stir. Then add the rum and water. Whisk together and bring to a boil. When the mixture boils, add the banana halves. Reduce to medium heat and cook for one minute, shaking to coat the banana halves with the syrup. Immediately spoon onto the serving platter. (The spices are not mean to be eaten.) Serve hot with cinnamon, rum raisin, or vanilla ice cream.

DARK RUM

Rum is distilled from molasses and is made at proofs ranging from 80 to a "white-lighting" 151. White or silver rum is the lightest and best used for cocktails. Gold rums are multipurpose, while dark rums are excellent for cooking and baking. The most well-known dark rum, Myer's, is distilled in Jamaica.

BEANS

DRIED AND FRESH-SHELLED

BEANS
DRIED AND FRESH-SHELLED

Though coffee, vanilla, and chocolate are all known as beans, a bean is actually a double-seamed pod containing a single row of seeds (also called beans), which may be used for its edible pod, like green or wax beans; for shelling fresh, like the black-eyed peas and cranberry beans found in farmers' markets; and most commonly, to be cooked from their dried form. All common beans, *Phaseolus vulgaris*, originated in the New World in Central America, including kidney beans, black turtle beans, cranberry beans, and cannellini (or white kidney beans). Lima beans, *Phaseolus lunatus*, and the closely related larger, elongated runner beans popular in England and the famed French Tarbais were believed to have originated in Brazil, but new evidence points to Guatemala.

One of the world's most ancient foods, beans have been a staple of the diet for thousands of years because they are versatile, easy to grow, easy to store and carry for travel, inexpensive, and are packed with essential nutrients. No part of the bean is wasted, from its sprouts, tender young pods, and green seeds to its dry seeds to be stored for cold winter days.

Though we may think of beans as lowly, they have enjoyed high status and been credited with possessing great powers in other eras and cultures. Native Americans, such as the Algonquins, depended on corn and kidney beans for making their traditional succotash (cooked in bear fat)—a dish that's been adapted across America (minus the bear fat). Mexican cooks spoon a dollop of pinto or black bean "frijoles" onto every plate, or serve them refried the next day. In India, dark red kidney beans called *badi rajma* are a staple because of their heartiness. Perhaps it is their meaty look that makes them such a satisfying meat substitute.

Beans have been around so long that many techniques have evolved for improving their flavor and decreasing their notorious proclivity to induce intestinal gas. In Germany and Switzerland, sprigs of savory, known as *bohnenkraut* (bean herb), go into the pot when cooking beans. Mexicans invariably cook black beans with epazote, a resinous, almost turpentine-like herb that grows wild along roadsides, using the *olla* (earthenware pot) that is said to have its own gas-absorbing properties. Cooks in rural Italy faithfully cook their favored white cannellini and red-and-cream streaked borlotti and Romano beans with alkaline-rich greens like wild chicory, arugula, dandelion, or chard to neutralize the acidity of the beans.

What about using dried beans that have been canned, such as pinto, kidney, and black beans? By all means use them for their convenience, but be sure to try cooking your own and see if you don't prefer their texture and flavor. In a dish where beans are going to be cooked further, such as baked beans or beans and rice, canned will work fine. In soups it's hard to get a rich multileveled flavor of beans if they have not been cooked all the way from dried.

Today, America is by far the world leader in dry bean production, due largely to nearly perfect bean-growing conditions. The four corners area of Colorado is high in altitude and renowned for the high quality of its beans, especially pintos and the heirloom variety, Anasazi®.

Bean seeds are easy to save and can maintain their viability for years. Many heirloom varieties have striking markings or special characteristics that families and farmers wanted to save and share. Saving heirloom bean seeds promotes genetic diversity in our crops, thus helping our food supply stay healthy. Because beans are self-pollinating, insect cross-pollination is not common, so gardeners can save the seeds and expect them to remain true to type. The greater the diversity of seeds we have, the better the probability of overcoming the problems of any one plant. Generations of gardeners and small regional growers have saved seeds to preserve heirloom varieties that have performed best, developing resistances to local insect and disease problems, and becoming adapted to specific soils and climates.

Measuring Canned and Dried Beans

When soaked and cooked, most varieties of small dried legumes, such as navy beans, will at least double in size; medium- to large-size dried beans will triple in size. One pound of dried beans will yield about 6 cups of cooked. A 15-ounce can contains about $1^1/_2$ cups of drained beans; a 20-ounce glass jar of beans contains about 2 cups of drained beans.

CHOOSING DRIED BEANS

When shopping for dried beans, it pays to buy the best. Even a pound of "gourmet" beans works out to an inexpensive meal. Dried beans from the current year's crop take less time to cook, cook more evenly, and are easier to digest. If you buy dried beans from a place that doesn't turn over stock quickly, the beans may be up to ten years old! If you buy beans from an ethnic market, specialty market, or natural foods store that really moves its stock, you'll be more likely to get fresher beans. The older the bean, the more problems are likely to be experienced, both in cooking and in digesting. Many companies sell high-quality heirloom and specialty beans now through the Internet.

FROZEN BEANS

I often cook up a large batch of beans and freeze them in one-quart freezer bags. Opening a bag of these homemade precooked beans is as easy as opening, rinsing, and draining a can of beans. To freeze your own beans, cool them to room temperature and divide among labeled quart-size zip-top freezer bags. Squeeze out the excess air and seal well. I often double-bag my beans to give them extra protection from odors and freezer burn. Beans may be frozen for two to three months. Note: Label frozen legumes (and other foods) with the name and the date. Use an indelible marker that won't rub off. Believe me, you'll never remember what was in those bags a month later. Fresh-shelled beans can be frozen raw or cooked.

The next best thing to freezing your own beans is buying them already frozen. Most supermarkets carry baby Fordhook limas, while markets with a large southern or African-American clientele will often carry frozen black-eyed peas. I buy frozen pigeon peas (gandules) and favas from Latino and Mediterranean markets. Frozen green soy beans (edamame), which make a great addition to stir-fries, soup, and pasta, and frozen fava beans are sold at many Asian markets. Edamame are now available frozen in many supermarkets.

COOKING WITH CANNED BEANS

I highly recommend the excellent glass jars of cooked beans imported from Spain and sold at Whole Foods under their house brand, 365. They are firm, plump and whole, and taste so good you can eat them right out of the jar. I also recommend the large selection of canned and dried beans sold by the Puerto Rican company Goya. It's worth buying the best, especially since beans are a good value, no matter how you buy them. For more detailed information and lots of recipes, see my book, *Beans: More than 200 Wholesome, Delicious Recipes from Around the World*, also published by Running Press.

100

Bean Varieties

While there are thousands of varieties, here are descriptions of some of the most important beans along with a few heirlooms.

Black Turtle Bean: The black turtle bean is medium to small in size and turns a deep, dark purple color when cooked. Black beans are beloved in Cuba, Trinidad, Brazil, and Mexico, and have a meaty, mushroom-like flavor along with a fine-grained, velvety texture. Note that the black bean used in Chinese cooking (often fermented and salted) is actually a soybean, which may or may not be black to start. Dried black turtle beans are very likely to contain foreign matter, because dirt clumps or pebbles are easily disguised, so pick them over carefully.

Kidney Bean: I always seek out the large, almost purple-red dark red kidney beans called *badi rajma* in India for their robust, full-bodied flavor and soft texture that cooks up to a striking crimson color. The common lighter kidney beans share their robust, full-bodied flavor and soft, though meaty, texture but cook up to a more neutral light pinkish-red. Both types have thick skins so they require long cooking and they can be difficult to digest, but they hold their shape well in long-simmered dishes like chili con carne. As with all beans, fully cooking them until they are quite soft, but not mushy, will make them easier to digest.

Navy Bean: This small white bean was served so often to sailors that it became forever associated with the navy. Because of its small size, it took less time to cook on board ship than larger beans. For a similar reason, they are often used by commercial baked bean manufacturers. Navy beans have many names, including haricot, from the Aztec *ayacot*, Boston bean, white coco, pea bean, white pea beans, and *alubias chicas* (small whites) in Spanish. They work well for baked beans, salads, soups, stews, and purées.

Pinto Bean: This medium-sized, oval, mottled beige and brown bean common throughout the American Southwest has an earthy flavor and powdery texture and turns reddish brown when cooked. The best pintos are raised at high altitude; they are quicker cooking and easier to digest. Pinto means "painted" in Spanish; other colorful names include crabeye bean and gunga pea.

Appaloosa Bean: Though sometimes referred to as Anasazi® bean, growers insist the two beans are different. Also called red appaloosa, these beans have markings that are reminiscent of the appaloosa pony. Slender and oval with mottled burgundy to purple markings, this bean is recommended for slow-cooked casseroles because it holds its shape well and has a rich flavor. Appaloosas make a good substitute for black-eyed peas and may also be substituted for pintos, a close relation.

Black Calypso: This boutique bean, also known as Yin Yang, or Orca, with its dramatic black and white color patterns, was developed by growers in Europe where they are quite popular. They are smooth in texture with a mild, vegetable-like flavor. Cooking these beautiful beans in lots of water helps maintain their attractive markings.

Calypso Bean: This thin-skinned white bean with mustard colored splotches or "eyes" is a four-hundred-dred-year-old variety with many names, including Steuben yellow eye, molasses face, Maine yellow eye, and butterscotch calypso. It has a velvety texture, mellow flavor, and plumps up well and turns ivory to brown after cooking. It was supposedly the original bean used in colonial Boston for baked beans. In parts of the South, it is preferred for the Hoppin John, usually made with black-eyed peas.

European Soldier Bean: For perhaps obvious reasons, these oval, medium-size white beans with red markings in the "eye" reminiscent of a European toy soldier, were well known in early New England where British soldiers were known as "red coats". They are also said to resemble the uniform of soldiers in Napoleon's army. They have a slightly mealy texture and should be cooked whole in plenty of water to maintain their markings in slow-cooked dishes and soups.

Trout Bean: These white- and maroon-spotted heirloom beans are also known as Jacob's Cattle Bean, Coach Bean, and Dalmatian Bean. They do indeed resemble spotted Dalmatian dogs or cattle. Originally brought to the United States from Germany, where they are called *Forellen*, trout beans have been grown in New England since colonial times. Like other tepary beans, they are suitable for growing in desert climates and have a relatively short growing season. When cooked, they have a smooth texture and are good in salads, relishes, and soups.

White Runner Beans with Broccoli Rabe

Large, creamy white runner beans are shaped like an elongated oval and have a creamy texture and appealingly sweet flavor. They are quite popular in the Mediterranean: in Greece, they are known as gigandas, *in Spain similar varieties are called* judión *or* alubias. *In America, they're known as* emergos *while in Great Britain they are called "sweet white runners", because of their exquisite white flowers and seeds. Substitute white kidney beans, also known as cannellini beans. Substitute mustard greens, endive, arugula, spinach, or even dandelion greens for the broccoli rabe.*

Serves 8

1 pound dried white runner beans, soaked overnight in water to cover

1 whole peeled onion, stuck with 6 cloves

1 head garlic, top $1/2$ inch sliced off

3 bay leaves

Zest of 1 lemon, cut in strips using potato peeler

Several sprigs of thyme and/or marjoram tied with a string

1 small whole dried hot red pepper

$1/2$ cup extra-virgin olive oil, divided

Kosher salt and black pepper to taste

1 bunch broccoli rabe, bottom 1-inch cut off and discarded and sliced into 1-inch lengths

2 teaspoons chopped garlic

1 small red onion, diced

Preheat the oven to 300°F. Drain and rinse beans. Place the beans, onion, garlic, bay leaves, lemon zest, herb sprigs, hot red pepper, and $1/4$ cup of the olive oil in a large heavy ovenproof casserole with a lid. Cover with cold water and bring to the boil on top of the stove, skimming off any white foam.

Place covered casserole in the middle shelf of the oven and bake about 1 hour, add salt and pepper to taste, stir to combine, cover again and keep baking about 1 hour more, or until the beans are tender all the way through but still hold their shape. Remove from the oven, uncover and cool slightly. Remove and discard the onion, garlic, bay leaves, herb sprigs, lemon zest, and hot pepper. Avoid stirring, which will break up the beans.

Meanwhile, bring about 2-inches of salted water to the boil in a pot. Add the broccoli rabe and cook over high heat 2 to 3 minutes after the water comes back to the boil. Drain and rinse under cold running water to set the color.

In a large skillet or shallow pot, heat the remaining $1/4$ cup olive oil, add chopped garlic and cook until sizzling. Add the diced red onion and cook until the onions have slightly browned. Stir in the broccoli rabe and the cooked beans and continue cooking until thoroughly heated and then serve.

Diner–Style Black–Eyed Pea Soup

What good is a diner without a big bowl of hearty, rib-sticking bean soup? Here I use small black-eyed peas for their savory flavor and light, crunchy texture and because they hold up well to strong-tasting ingredients such as chiles, garlic, and smoked pork. These medium-sized, light cream-colored, nearly round beans have a small but prominent round black "eye" on the curved inner side. Black-eyed

peas were brought into this country by slaves from Africa and are still most popular in the South. Look for smoked pork bones at German and Amish butcher shops and markets catering to a southern and/or African-American clientele. For those who don't eat pork, smoked turkey drumsticks make a good substitute. It's important to remove all the thin, sharp bony tendons in the drumsticks from the soup; alternatively, tie the drumsticks to keep them whole.

SERVES 12

1 pound dried black-eyed peas

A small handful of thyme sprigs

2 bay leaves

2 smoked ham hocks

2 quarts Smoked Pork Stock (*see* page 995)

1 onion, diced

2 carrots, diced

4 celery ribs, diced

1 tablespoon canola oil

Kosher salt, freshly ground pepper,
    and hot red pepper flakes to taste

Pick through the peas, discarding any small stones or dirt. Cover the peas with cold water and soak overnight at room temperature. The next day, discard any floating peas, drain, and rinse.

Tie the thyme and bay leaves into a compact bundle with kitchen string. Place the herb bundle, ham hocks, and the stock into a large soup pot and bring to the boil. Reduce heat and simmer for $1^{1}/2$ hours, or until the hock meat starts to get tender. Add the peas along with enough cold water to cover and bring the liquid to the boil, skimming off any white foam. Reduce heat and simmer 1 hour longer, or until the beans are almost cooked through.

Meanwhile, in a skillet, cook the onions, carrots, and celery in the oil until soft, but not brown. Stir into the soup and simmer together 30 minutes longer, or until the beans are cooked through but still hold their shape. Remove and discard the herb bundle and season with salt, pepper, and hot pepper to taste before serving.

White Bean and Tomato Gratin

Here's a recipe where canned or jarred beans work well. This old-fashioned white bean gratin is the traditional accompaniment to roast leg of lamb in the south of France. It also goes well with roast pork, roast beef, or game birds.

SERVES 8

$1/4$ cup + 2 tablespoons extra-virgin olive oil

1 cup diced onion

2 tablespoons chopped garlic, divided

2 tablespoons chopped fresh thyme leaves
  (about $1/4$ bunch)

Grated zest of 1 lemon

2 bay leaves

2 cups chicken stock

6 cups cooked cannellini beans (four 15-ounce cans)

1 (15-ounce) can diced tomatoes

2 cups Japanese panko
  or homemade country style breadcrumbs

Heat $1/4$ cup of the olive oil in a sauté pan. Add the onion, 1 tablespoon of garlic, thyme, lemon zest, and bay leaves and cook for 2 to 3 minutes, stirring constantly, or until the aromas are released. Add the chicken stock and bring the mixture to a boil. Add the cannellini beans along with their cooking liquid and the tomatoes, and remove from the heat.

Preheat the oven to 375°F. Lightly rub the inside of a shallow 2-quart oval gratin dish or large shallow baking dish with a little oil. In a separate bowl, combine the remaining 2 tablespoons olive oil with the remaining 1 tablespoon of garlic, and the breadcrumbs. Spoon the bean mixture into the dish, spreading it out evenly with the back of the spoon. Sprinkle generously with the breadcrumbs. Bake the gratin for 1 hour, or until bubbling and browned on top.

CONTRONE BEANS FROM CAMPANIA, ITALY

Controne is a small town in the province of Salerno, famous for its white beans, called *fagioli di Controne*, which are much appreciated in the region. They are cultivated on the hilly area of Campania called the Alburni Mountains. An annual festival celebrating the beans is held every November in Controne. During those days, beans are the 'princes' of the menu and are served in traditional and newly creative recipes. Small, round, and very white, without spots or eyes, this bean has long been prized for its ease of digestion and for its thin, almost nonexistent, skin.

BEEF

BEEF

Beef, *Bos taurus*, is the meat of domestic cattle which are members of the larger *Bovidae* family along with goats and sheep. Our domestic beef cattle evolved about 8,500 years ago from the huge ancient aurochs, the last of which died out at the beginning of the seventeenth century in Poland. The English word "beef" comes from the French *boeuf*, first used for more expensive cuts while the older Saxon word, ox (plural oxen) was and is used for more plebian cuts like oxtail. Cattle is a broader term that includes beef cattle, humped cattle, water buffalo, bison, and yak—all so closely related they can usually interbreed. Tropical humped cattle, like Brahman and Africander, are in the closely related Bos *indicus* species.

Purebred cattle breeds have been selectively bred over a long period of time to possess distinctive traits and have the propensity to pass these traits to their offspring. The British Angus and Scottish Hereford breeds are both known for moderate size, easy fattening, and high marbling; American breeds (actually Indian in origin) such as Brahman and Africander, are raised in the South because they tolerate heat and humidity best. Continental breeds such as the French Charolais and Italian Chianina, known for their large size, lean meat, and low marbling, were originally draft animals. Texas longhorns, descendants of Spanish cattle brought over by the Conquistadores, are now seeing a revival. Beef cattle were first brought to the New World by European colonists, although the bison, often called buffalo, is native to North America.

Beef is eaten mainly in Northern Europe, North and South America, and Australia. Americans love beef: we eat about 60 pounds a year per person, but Argentineans beat us by far: they consume about 143 pounds a year per person in two or even three meals a day. Americans' appetite for beef grew with the enormous expansion of the Western cattle industry at the end of the nineteenth century, because of the introduction of railroad cattle cars and refrigerated cars that made it easier to ship the beef back east.

Beef usually comes from castrated males or steers (bullocks in Britain), slaughtered at 18 to 24 months of age when they weigh about 1,000 pounds. Each animal will yield about 450 pounds of meat. For commercial production, cattle are raised most of their life on grass and then "finished" (grown to maturity) by feeding on grain for about 100 days before slaughter in huge feedlots that house as many as 450,000 head of cattle.

All beef cattle start out eating grass; in the U.S., three-fourths of them are "finished" in huge feedlots where they are grain-fed mostly with corn; the remaining quarter are entirely grass-fed. Corn-fed beef is fattier and milder in flavor; grass-fed beef is leaner and more pronounced in flavor. In the U.S., antibiotics may be given to prevent or treat disease in cattle, although a "withdrawal" period is required before slaughter, and hormones may be used to promote growth.

The four largest packing houses alone account for more than 70 percent of the 35,000,000 cattle harvested annually in the United States, and much of the work that butchers used to do (breaking down quarter or half-carcasses) is now done at the packing house itself. This cuts costs because the least valuable parts—fat, bones, and trim—are trimmed before shipping. Ninety percent is sold as boxed beef rather than the old-fashioned beef hanging quarters or sides. After slaughter, the cattle are broken down into large primal cuts, vacuum-packed, and then boxed for shipping to wholesalers and supermarkets, where butchers cut them down into retail or food service cuts.

Only 10 to 12 percent of the animal represents the high-priced middle cuts from the rib and loin sections such as rib-eye, strip steak, and tenderloin. Fifty percent of all beef ends up as ground meat. The challenge today is to use more of the animal by cooking less-common cuts like tri-tip (from the sirloin), skirt and hanger steak (from the lower portion), and flat-iron, sometimes called French tip, and the shoulder tender, also called petite tender (from the shoulder).

GRADING BEEF

Grading is voluntary and is based primarily on the amount and distribution of marbling (the white flecks of fat) within the muscles. The greater the amount of marbling, the higher the grade, because marbling makes beef more tender, flavorful, and juicy. Much of today's supermarket meat is U.S.D.A. Choice; the most popular grade overall, and often bears a brand name such as Angus or Buckhead. Only about two percent of beef is graded U.S.D.A. Prime (so all those advertisements for "prime rib" are more than likely just plain beef rib). Prime beef is high priced and found in high-end butcher shops ("the carriage trade") and good steakhouses. Because of plentiful marbling, prime beef has outstanding flavor and texture (fat carries flavor). Wholesale cuts of prime beef will be marked with a purple shield. Because the entire animal receives the same grade, less expensive cuts of prime-graded steers may be worth seeking out.

Wet and Dry Aging of Beef

About ninety percent of American beef is shipped as boxed beef, wholesale cuts that are vacuum-packed and boxed for shipping. The retailer stores boxed beef under refrigeration until needed for sale, when the bag is opened and the meat cut. During the period meat is in the bag, averaging about seven days, it does age. This is referred to as "aging in the bag" or "wet-aging".

Dry-aging is an old-fashioned, expensive, and slow process done by top butcher shops and restaurant suppliers. Beef is dry-aged to develop additional tenderness and flavor in a special process using controlled temperatures and humidity, which can last anywhere from ten days to six weeks. The longer the aging, the more benefits in flavor and tenderness, but also the more shrinkage and trimming—as much as eighteen percent. The length of time and method of aging beef is strictly a personal preference.

Dry-aging results in a unique flavor that may be described as slightly "musty"; aficionados love this flavor, calling it "gamey" or intense. The tenderness effects of aging are more evident in older animals, though it also decreases the shelf life of products like ground beef. Beef that is not aged at all can be "metallic" tasting and lacking beefy flavor.

MAD COW DISEASE

Mad Cow Disease is the common name for Bovine Spongiform Encephalopathy (BSE), a progressive, degenerative, and fatal disease affecting the central nervous system of adult cattle. In December 2003, one U.S. cow was found to be affected with BSE, which has had a major impact on the beef industry and our large export market with Japan, which now bans all U.S. beef. In Japan, every single beef cow slaughtered is inspected for BSE; in the U.S., we test only about 20,000 animals a year, a small fraction of the beef harvested.

BSE is not destroyed by cooking, although research indicates that the organs and especially the brain and spinal cord are the main source of infectious prions (the diseased proteins). Limit risk by avoiding processed beef products that may contain nervous-system tissue, such as hot dogs, sausage, and hamburger (or buy hamburger ground to order). Both kosher and halal meat carry lower risk of Mad Cow, because it is forbidden to use animals that are ill or injured and the hand-slaughtering method ensures that brain matter does not contaminate the meat.

ORGANIC AND GRASS–FED BEEF

Organic and 100 percent grass-fed beef represent a small but growing category. Organic beef is grain-fed with organic grain and is mostly found in natural foods markets. Grass or pasture-fed cattle stay on their own farms their entire life, where they eat a variety of grasses. This type of beef is generally marketed directly to consumers through internet sales, farmers' markets, CSA's (community supported agriculture), and direct sales. Note that in beef-loving Latin America, all beef is grass-fed.

Farmers who raise pasture-fed beef believe that returning the land to a balanced state in terms of soil fertility with quality forages will lead to animal health, and the enhanced quality of our lives. Grass-fed beef is high in beneficial elements like vitamin E, beta-carotene, Omega-3 fatty acid, and CLA (conjugated linoleic aid), but is very different in consistency and marbling from the grain-fed beef most of us have grown up on. It must be cooked at lower heat and cooked until rare to medium-rare or it will be dry—having little natural fat for moisture.

KOSHER AND HALAL MEAT

Both Muslims and Jews have special religious laws for both the choice of animal and the slaughtering method. In both religions, it is forbidden to eat the meat of carnivores, or the meat from animals that have not been ritually slaughtered; blood is also forbidden. The words Kosher (for Jews) and Halal (for Muslims) both describe what is "fit and proper" to eat.

The term Kosher is used for food that Jews are permitted to eat under dietary laws derived from the Torah. Only mammals that chew their cud (ruminants) and have cloven hoofs are permitted (beef, veal, lamb, venison, goat, bison, and antelope) and only a trained kosher slaughterer (*shochet*) is permitted to kill the animal.

In kosher slaughter, the animal is killed by a quick, deep stroke across the throat with a razor-sharp, perfectly smooth blade, causing instantaneous death. Because the hind-quarters contain the forbidden sciatic nerve, which is time consuming to remove, the hind-quarters are usually sold to non-kosher butchers. (In Israel, where demand is high, this nerve is painstakingly removed so that both fore and hind-quarters cuts are available.)

The term Halal is used for food that is permitted to Muslims using laws derived from the Qur'an. The idea is to kill the animal as quickly and humanely as possible. The knife must be sharpened each time, but not in front of the animal, which must be fed and rested and must not be slaughtered in the presence of other animals. As in the laws of *Kashrut* (kosher-ness), the animal should be free from any apparent or hidden defects. Many, though not all, Muslims consider Kosher meat to be Halal; however, Halal meat is not considered Kosher.

ABOUT KOBE BEEF

Kobe beef comes from Wagyu cattle, a cross of native Asian, British, and European cattle first bred in the late 1800s in the Kobe Prefecture of Japan. Today's Wagyu (*Wa* means Japanese and *gyu* means cattle), is genetically predisposed to intense marbling. The animals are fed sake mash and beer and are sometimes massaged with sake, producing meat that is extraordinarily tender, finely marbled, and full-flavored, rivaling foie gras for richness and caloric content. Kobe beef graded A5 in Japan is twenty to twenty-five percent fat; in comparison, U.S. and Canadian Prime is only six to eight percent fat. However, the fat in Kobe beef is far less saturated so that it melts quickly on the palate, lending an intense beefy flavor. As you might expect, Kobe beef is also extremely expensive.

In 1976, four Wagyu bulls were imported into the U.S. Their progeny are sold as American Kobe. Wagyu cattle are now also born and raised in Canada and Australia. Land and grain are expensive in Japan, so many Japanese Kobe cattle, though born in Japan, were raised in California or Australia and then shipped back to Kobe, Japan, for finishing and slaughtering, allowing it to be called "Kobe Beef". Today, because of fears of Mad Cow disease, American-raised cattle are not allowed into Japan. This has led to a big increase in the marketing of American-raised Kobe to American consumers. That's why you'll see it more and more on restaurant menus.

Kobe beef should be seared quickly, like tuna or foie gras, so that it is blackened on the surface but extremely rare inside. It will be smooth, velvety, and incomparably sweet with a subtle tang that lingers on the palate. Kobe beef is usually sold frozen but does not suffer in texture or flavor because of its high percentage of marbled fat.

Carpaccio of Beef alla Veneziana

Carpaccio was created at the justly famed Harry's Bar, which overlooks the Venetian Grand Canal. The dish is named after Vittore Carpaccio, an Italian Renaissance painter known for his orangey reds. Here's a chance to make this world-famous restaurant dish in your home. Thinly sliced, very fresh, well-trimmed, and well-chilled lean beef from the sirloin top butt is pounded thin enough to be almost translucent. The beef is arranged on serving plates in a single layer, drizzled with a savory mustard sauce, and topped with Parmigiano cheese shavings.

SERVES 8

1 pound boneless sirloin top butt

1 tablespoon coarse mustard

2 egg yolks

2 tablespoons balsamic vinegar

$\frac{1}{2}$ cup extra-virgin olive oil

2 anchovies, chopped

2 shallots, chopped

Freshly ground black pepper (no salt)

Shaved Parmigiano-Reggiano cheese

Cornichon pickles, cut into fans

Trim the fat and any white connective tissue from the beef and freeze until firm yet pliable. Slice, using an electric slicer or electric knife, into paper-thin slices, arranging in a single layer on individual serving plates as you go. (If the slices are not thin enough, pound out between two sheets of wax paper.)

Make the dressing by placing mustard, egg yolks, and vinegar into the bowl of a food processor. Process briefly until sticky, then slowly start pouring in the olive oil. Continue until all the olive oil has been absorbed and the sauce has thickened. Stir in the anchovies, shallots, and black pepper. Drizzle in a decorative pattern over the beef. Garnish with Parmigiano shavings and cornichons.

PARMIGIANO SHAVINGS

Fresh-cut moist Parmigiano-Reggiano cheese can be made into decorative and delicious shavings using a potato peeler, cheese shaver, or if you have one, a deli-slicer set between zero and one on its dial.

CORNICHONS AND HOW TO CUT THEM

Cornichons are tiny French cucumber pickles flavored with tarragon and yellow mustard seeds with a sharp vinegary flavor. They are a traditional garnish for pâtés and terrines and are chopped up and added to French sauces like rémoulade. Slice into small fans by cutting four to six parallel slits three-quarters of the way from the bottom end towards the stem end. Spread out the slices to form a fan shape and arrange each cornichon on the serving plate.

Philadelphia Steak Sandwich with Provolone and Grilled Onions

The steak sandwich has become an icon of Philadelphia food and there are "Philly Steak Shops" across the country today. There, the sandwich is made on long, relatively soft Italian rolls. Mr. Pat Olivieri, the self-proclaimed "King of Steaks", claims to have invented the Philadelphia cheese steak sandwich during the Depression. According to the story, one day Olivieri threw a few thin slices of steak and some onions on the griddle and piled it all into a roll at his South Philly hot dog stand. A passing cabby offered to buy the sandwich and word began to spread. His stand later became Pat's King of Steaks, rival to Geno's right across the street. Today, Rick Olivieri, Pat's grandson, operates Rick's Steaks in Philadelphia's Reading Terminal Market, where there is always a line. Olivieri offers American cheese, provolone, mozzarella, Cheez-Whiz, known as the "reg", or pepper jack. I always go for the provolone.

SERVES 4

1½ pounds top round of beef, totally trimmed
  of fat and connective tissue

Kosher salt and freshly ground black pepper to taste

4 tablespoons canola oil

1 large Spanish onion, sliced

1 to 2 sweet green and red peppers and/or hot frying
  peppers (Cubanelle or Italian frying peppers), optional

1 cup sliced mushrooms, optional

4 crusty long Italian Rolls, split open

8 ounces sliced Provolone, or other preferred cheese

Wrap meat in plastic wrap or place in a freezer bag and freeze about 1 hour or until firm but not hard. Slice as thin as possible, preferably using an electric slicer or an electric knife. Alternatively buy thinly sliced "chip steak", usually sold frozen, and defrost in the refrigerator overnight until firm but pliable. Season with salt and pepper.

Preheat broiler. Heat an iron skillet or griddle over medium heat. Add 2 tablespoons of oil to the pan and brown the onions. Remove the onions and reserve. Brown the peppers and mushrooms and reserve.

Add the remaining oil and brown the slices of meat quickly on both sides. Sprinkle a little water on the meat to keep it from sticking to the griddle.

Meanwhile, open up the rolls, cover inside with cheese and broil briefly, just long enough to melt the cheese. Divide the meat among the four rolls. Top with onions, peppers, and mushrooms, close sandwich, press edges together and slice into two.

STEAK ROLLS IN PHILLY

A good steak sandwich roll is about nine-inches long, crusty on the outside and nicely chewy on the inside. Amoroso's Bakery is the best-known supplier of steak and hoagie rolls, but there are other bakeries in South Philly who make equally fine rolls such as Caccia's and Sarcone's. Many natives order their sandwiches "inside out" with the soft interior of the roll pulled out. Talk about fast food, a hot steak sandwich just off the grill will be rolled up tightly on the diagonal onto a square of foil-backed paper and then sliced in two, right through the foil. Eat it while it's hot.

Braciole of Beef Calabrese

The small stuffed beef rolls called "braciole" in Italy's southern province of Calabria have been transformed from tasty but tough bottom round or rump. By stuffing and braising this cut, the meat becomes juicy and tender nestled in a bubbling sauce infused with all the flavors of the braciole. Rump is an excellent cut to use here, because it consists of one larger muscle that can be easily sliced thinly. Braciole are an example of what happens in the search to make a smaller amount of meat go a long way. Braciole stuffed just like this are also made with pork, or with swordfish, in which case, they are cooked for far less time.

SERVES 6

2½ pounds beef bottom round

¼ cup olive oil, divided

Kosher salt and black pepper to taste

¾ cup Italian or country-style breadcrumbs

¾ cup grated Pecorino cheese

1 tablespoon chopped garlic

¼ cup chopped Italian parsley

4 each hard-cooked eggs, peeled and chopped

6 cups Marinara Sauce (*see* page 895)

1 pound spaghetti

Partially freeze the beef until firm but still pliable. Cut into 12 slices of about 3-ounces each, or have the butcher do this. Using the knobbed end of a meat pounder, pound the meat slices until thin and even. Rub with half the olive oil, and sprinkle lightly with salt and pepper (remember the cheese is salty).

Combine the breadcrumbs, cheese, garlic, parsley, and eggs. Place equal portions of this filling on each beef slice. Fold the edges under and then roll up each slice like an envelope, and tie with kitchen string.

Heat the remaining olive oil. Brown the braciole all over. Meanwhile, bring the Marinara Sauce to the boil and add to the pan. Simmer covered, or transfer to a 300°F. oven and bake covered, for 1 hour, or until the meat is tender when pierced.

Bring a large pot of salted water to the boil. Cook the spaghetti until *al dente*, firm and bouncy, and yellow in color. Drain and toss with some of the braciole sauce. Serve two bracioles per person accompanied by the pasta in sauce.

USING A MEAT POUNDER

A good, solid meat pounder is a kitchen essential. I use one made by Oxo that has a good heft and one smooth and one knobbed end. The smooth end is good for crushing small amounts of spices like peppercorns or allspice berries; the knobbed end is used to thin out and tenderize slices of meats like chicken, veal, turkey, and beef. Use a light even motion when pounding and keep moving the pounder in a circular pattern.

Braised Beef Cheeks with Juniper and Red Wine

The first time I prepared beef cheeks was during a special Book and the Cook Festival dinner when I was working with guest chef Jean-Georges Vongerichten. He had asked me to purchase one hundred pounds of beef cheeks. It took some doing, but I finally tracked down a huge box of frozen cheeks. I was doubtful, but with its bold, beefy flavor and rich, melt-in-the mouth, lip-smacking texture, this lowly cut was a revelation to me. Accompany with Potato Dumplings (see page 750), Spaetzle with Brown Butter, Chives, and Toasted Breadcrumbs (see page 172), or Horseradish Mashed Potatoes (see page 762). Double or even triple the recipe; it freezes beautifully.

SERVES 4

8 large beef cheeks, defrosted overnight
  in the refrigerator, if frozen

2 cups dry red wine

$1/2$ cup diced carrot

$1/2$ cup diced onion

$1/2$ cup diced white leek

3 cloves garlic, smashed

2 sprigs thyme

2 bay leaf

1 tablespoons crushed juniper berries

Kosher salt and fresh ground black pepper to taste

Flour, for dusting

$1/2$ cup olive oil, divided

2 cup veal or chicken stock

$1/4$ pound thick sliced bacon, cut into thin strips

Preheat the oven to 350°F. Trim any exterior gristle and fat from the cheeks. Do not trim the silverskin, which runs through the middle. Tie each cheek with butcher's twine, so that it holds its shape. Or ask the butcher to do this part.

Place the trimmed cheeks in a nonreactive container and add the red wine, carrot, onion, leek, garlic, thyme, bay leaf, juniper, salt and pepper. Cover and refrigerate overnight or up to 2 days.

Remove the cheeks from the marinade and pat dry. Strain the marinade, separately reserving the vegetables and the wine.

Season the meat liberally with salt and pepper, and dust with flour, shaking off the excess.

In a large Dutch oven or chicken fryer with a lid, preferably cast-iron, heat $1/4$ cup of the oil until shimmering. Place the meat in the pan without crowding and brown well on all sides. Work in batches if necessary. Remove the meat from the pan, reduce the heat to medium, then add the reserved vegetables and brown lightly.

Deglaze by adding the reserved marinade liquid, bringing it to the boil, and using a wooden spoon or rubber spatula, scrape off all browned bits from the bottom of the pot. Add the meat back into the pan and add the stock and bacon strips. Bring to the boil, skimming off any foam from the top and cover.

Meanwhile, preheat the oven to 300°F. Transfer the pot to the oven and bake 3 hours, or until the cheeks are soft when pierced. Remove the pot from the oven and allow the meat to cool in the liquid. When cool, refrigerate overnight.

The next day, pull off and discard any solidified fat from the top. When ready to serve, place the pot over low heat on top of the stove and warm just until the liquid melts. Remove the cheeks from the pot and then cut off the string. Put back in the pot and continue to heat until thoroughly hot. Serve with potato dumplings, spaetzle, or horseradish mashed potatoes.

Pan–Seared Fillet of Beef Forestiera

At the late country Italian restaurant Stella Notte where I cheffed in the early part of the naughts, this was one of those "can't take it off the menu" dishes. I also made it for the series of cooking classes I held in the restaurant and people flipped. It's no wonder—the combination of buttery beef tenderloin, earthy mushrooms, the salty-cured taste imparted by the pancetta, and the many-layered sauce all work together to make a truly wonderful dish, suited for a special occasion dinner, perhaps a Valentine's Dinner for two or a New Year's celebration. Accompany with Golden Potato Mash with Garlic and Green Olive Oil (see page 761).

SERVES 4

4 (6- to 8-ounce) fillets of beef
Kosher salt and freshly ground black pepper
3 tablespoons canola oil
$1/4$ pound pancetta, frozen until firm
    and cut into very small dice
$1/2$ cup sliced shallots
1 tablespoon chopped garlic
3 cups sliced mixed mushrooms
$3/4$ cup brandy
$3/4$ cup heavy cream
$1/2$ cup Demi-Glace (for richness, substitute beef stock,
    or porcini mushroom liquor)
Thinly sliced chives (for garnish)

Season beef on all sides with salt and pepper. Allow beef to rest at room temperature for about 20 minutes.

Heat oil in a large heavy-bottomed skillet, add beef and brown well on both sides. To the same pan, add pancetta and brown. Add shallots and garlic and cook together until the shallots are translucent but not browned. Add mushrooms, and sauté all together over high heat until well browned.

Averting your eyes, pour in the brandy and flame. When flames die down, add heavy cream and demi-glace and cook until liquid thickens. The beef should be medium-rare at this point. Serve immediately, sprinkled with chives.

114

Beef tenderloin and trimming

The baseball bat-shaped tenderloin is a little-used inner muscle that lies underneath the ribs alongside the backbone, beginning just past the ribs and running toward the rear, so that it is extremely tender. When cut through the back bone, its somewhat stringy pointed, smaller end becomes part of the T-bone steak, its larger, more rounded and tenderest middle section becomes part of the porterhouse. The largest portion at the butt end is part of the sirloin and is a bit chewier. Tenderloin is incredibly versatile and takes equally well to roasting, sautéing, and grilling and is prized for its mellow flavor, yielding texture, and ultra-fine grain. Though expensive, there's little waste, it's easy to prepare, cooks quickly, and is always a crowd pleaser. A well-marbled tenderloin will be succulent; if less-marbled, it can be dry and flavorless, especially if cooked beyond medium-rare. To trim, pull off all the outside fat, removing the chain (the long, thin muscle attached to the main portion of the fillet) and saving for another use. Using a sharp boning knife, cut away the thin, lengthwise ribbons of the "silverskin," the silvery white connective tissue encasing the larger end. Cut into individual steaks of anywhere from 4 to 12 ounces.

Homemade Demi-Glace

This basic "mother" sauce in French cuisine forms the backbone of many a sauce, particularly those meant for meat. There are a number of good commercial versions for sale. I recommend More than Gourmet or D'Artagnan. Here's a good recipe to make your own.

Makes about 1 quart

10 pounds veal marrow bones and, if possible,
  knuckle bones, cut into 2-inch lengths by the butcher
1 large yellow onion, unpeeled
2 carrots
2 ribs celery
2 tomatoes
2 tablespoons tomato paste
1 teaspoon black peppercorns
2 sprigs fresh thyme
1 bay leaf

Preheat the oven to 425°F. Place the bones in a large roasting pan. Roast until deep brown in color, taking care not to burn, which will cause bitterness, about 45 minutes, turning once or twice so the bones brown evenly.

Remove the pan from the oven. Transfer the bones to a large stock pot. Pour off any excess fat from the pan. Add the remaining ingredients to the roasting pan, stir to mix well and place back in the oven to roast for 15 to 20 minutes, or until medium-brown. Remove from the oven, and scrape the contents of the pan into the pot. Add a little water to the roasting pan and heat either in the oven or directly on the stove to melt any brown bits clinging to the pan.

115

Pour in enough cold water to cover the contents of the pot by about 4-inches and bring to the boil. Skim off any foam that comes to the top and reduce the heat to a bare simmer. Cover partially and simmer slowly overnight, or 12 hours. The next day, strain the liquid into another metal pot or stainless steel bowl and cool to room temperature, preferably by setting the container into a sinkful of ice mixed with water. Refrigerate overnight. The next day, remove and discard the solidified fat. The liquid should be jellied; if not, bring back to the boil and cook down until syrupy before using. Store in the freezer for up to 2 months or refrigerate for up to 2 weeks.

HANGER STEAK AND TRIMMING

The hanging tender, hanger steak, or *onglet* (in French) is a small, odd-shaped muscle that "hangs" from the diaphragm (or skirt steak). This popular bistro steak is best known in France though in recent years, it has been showing up on menus in the United States. Very dark in color and with a tendency to give off its juices, it has a pronounced grainy though quite tender texture and an outstanding full, beefy flavor. Hanger steak is best cooked rare to medium-rare and sliced thinly against the grain. There is only one hanger steak per animal; it weighs about one pound and consists of two small muscles with grain that runs in a V-shape joined by a tough elastic membrane that must be removed. Ask for hanger steak at your market. Trim the long, tough membrane from the center or ask the butcher to do this.

Seared Hanger Steaks with Shallots

Hanger steak is the newest fashion-steak seen on trendy menus in New York, Chicago, and San Francisco. What is it exactly? Actually a continuation of the very delicious skirt steak, which is the diaphragm, the hanger steak is also called the hanging tender. Here it is prepared in classic French bistro style. You may have to ask your butcher to order it in, because hanger steaks are in big demand for restaurants and there is only one of these smallish steaks per animal. Depending on the size, you may want to serve one or both sides of the two lengthwise sections formed once the hanging tender has been trimmed.

SERVES 6

6 (7-ounce) hanger steaks
Kosher salt and freshly ground black pepper
1 tablespoon canola oil
3 tablespoons unsalted butter, divided
3 shallots, thinly sliced, rinsed, and dried
2 tablespoons red wine vinegar
$1/2$ cup dry red wine
2 tablespoons chopped Italian parsley

Season beef on all sides with salt and pepper. Allow beef to rest at room temperature for about 20 minutes.

Heat a large, heavy-bottomed skillet over high heat, then add the oil. Add the steaks to the pan and brown evenly, turning as needed, until done, about 6 minutes for medium-rare. Remove the steaks from the pan and keep warm.

Add 1 tablespoon butter and the shallots to the same pan and cook, stirring, for 3 to 5 minutes, until the shallots

116

are softened but not browned. Add the vinegar and cook until it evaporates, then pour in the wine. Bring the wine to the boil and cook until syrupy. Off the heat, swirl in the remaining 2 tablespoons butter, then stir in the chopped parsley and season with salt and pepper.

Cut each steak on the bias into thin slices and fan the slices out on warm dinner plates. Ladle the sauce over the meat and serve immediately.

Grilled Skirt Steak with Argentinean Chimichurri Sauce

Skirt steak, the original "fajita", is one of the quickest and tastiest steaks to cook. My meat-loving daughter, Ginevra—a Leo—adores this cut. Not only does it have wonderful flavor, it is tender, juicy, and quite reasonable in price. Here I accompany it with the Argentinean version of Italian salsa verde (or green sauce), no doubt brought to Latin America by the many Italian immigrants to Argentina and adapted there to local tastes. The sauce is easy to make and its name is so much fun to say.

SERVES 4 TO 6

2 skirt steaks, trimmed

Kosher salt and freshly ground black pepper, to taste

2 tablespoons red wine vinegar

Juice of 1 lemon

$1/2$ cup + 2 tablespoons olive oil

$1/2$ cup minced red onion

2 teaspoons hot paprika

1 tablespoon crushed garlic

Leaves from 1 large bunch flat leaf parsley,

1 teaspoon ground black pepper

$1/4$ cup fresh oregano leaves

(or 1 tablespoon dried oregano)

Preheat a charcoal or gas grill until white hot and no visible flames remain. Season beef on all sides with salt and pepper. Allow beef to rest at room temperature for about 20 minutes.

Meanwhile, in a blender, combine vinegar, lemon juice, $1/2$ cup of olive oil, onion, paprika, and garlic. Blend to a thick puree. Add the parsley, pepper, oregano, and salt to taste. Blend again to a green puree. Store sauce refrigerated up to 2 days.

Rub steaks with 2 tablespoons olive oil and then grill to medium-rare only, about 6 minutes on each side. Remove from grill, drape with foil and allow steaks to rest about 10 minutes. Cut crosswise into three sections and then slice thinly across the grain.

Spoon the sauce over meat and serve extra on the side.

117

SKIRT STEAK AND TRIMMING

Skirt steak is a thin, long, fan-shaped muscle from the belly (or plate) of the beef cow. Moderately priced, it is one of the most flavorful of all steaks with a pronounced coarse, loose grain that takes well to marinating. Belt- or skirt-shaped and most popular in the Southwest and West, it the source of fajitas (belts in Spanish) and is the authentic meat for this dish. Cook quickly over high heat, preferably using natural charcoal or wood, to no more than medium-rare. A whole skirt steak will weigh about one pound and should require little in the way of trimming. Simply cut or pull off any larger strips of white fat and marinate or dry-rub with spices before grilling, broiling, or pan-searing (preferably in a cast-iron skillet for best browning). Allow the meat to rest for 10 minutes, cut crosswise into 2 to 3 sections and then slice each section thinly against the grain.

BEEF RIB–EYE AND "RIB LIFTER MEAT"

The naturally tender, luxurious beef rib is used to make the king of roasts: the standing beef rib on its long curved bones. At top butcher shops, whole prime ribs are used for dry aging and their price can be shockingly high. Surrounding the main muscle or "eye" is the fatty but very tasty meat called rib lifter, rib-eye lip, or deckle, excellent for stir-fries, chili, and stews.

A full 7-bone rib roast can weigh more than 15 pounds and can feed up to 20 happy people; a smaller roast should include at least three ribs. (Leftovers make out-of-this-world sandwiches.) Look for a bone-in rib-eye roast, which has been trimmed so that it is smaller, more compact, and easier to carve. The front section closer to the shoulder (or chuck) will be larger all around but with a smaller "eye" and more fat; the back section, though smaller all around, contains the largest portion of the largest "eye". Ask the butcher to remove the chine bones from the spine to make carving easier.

Roast Rib–Eye with Baharat

Baharat *simply means "spices" in Arabic and comes from the Arabic word for black pepper, which it always includes. Depending on what part of the world it comes from, baharat may also include everything from dried rose petals, chiles, cardamom, coriander, and cumin, to savory, mint, cinnamon, nutmeg, and allspice. Used especially to season meats, baharat is equivalent to the French* quatres épices *(four-spice) and Indian garam masala, both of which are also based on black pepper. Here baharat adds a wonderful fragrance and warm, rounded flavor to a simple but scrumptious rib-eye roast. Below is a recipe to make your own Turkish-style Baharat, but it can also be purchased from Middle Eastern markets like Kalustyans in Manhattan and Bitars in Philadelphia.*

SERVES 12 TO 16

$^1/_2$ cup olive oil
$^1/_4$ cup finely chopped garlic
Baharat seasoning
Kosher salt and freshly ground black pepper to taste
1 whole beef rib-eye, trimmed to main eye, outer
  "rib lifter meat" removed

Combine olive oil, Baharat, garlic, salt and pepper. Rub all over beef. Wrap in plastic wrap and marinate 24 hours, refrigerated. Remove the beef from the refrigerator about 1 hour before roasting.

Preheat the oven to 375°F. In a large, heavy-bottomed skillet, brown the beef on all sides. Transfer to a roasting pan just large enough to hold the beef. Roast fat-side up to medium-rare (the meat will be red with a warm, firmer

118

center and 135°F. to 140°F. on a meat thermometer) for 1 hour to 1 hour and 20 minutes, depending on the size of the roast. Remove roast from oven, drape with foil, and allow it to rest 15 to 20 minutes before slicing into individual portions. Serve with any pan juices.

Baharat Turkish Spice Mixture

1 tablespoon pickling spice

2 teaspoons dried savory

1 teaspoon each: dry mint, ground cumin, and ground black pepper

$1/2$ teaspoon each: ground cinnamon and ground nutmeg

Grind all together in a spice (or clean coffee) grinder until a fine powder. Store away from the light in an air-tight container.

USING A MEAT THERMOMETER

A reliable meat thermometer is an indispensable tool. Calibrate by plunging into boiling water; it should read 212°F.; adjust it by moving the small hexagonal wheel just under the dial. Stick the thermometer into the center of the thickest section of meat and wait until the dial comes to a stop. For a medium-rare beef roast, cook to between 130°F. and 140°F. Be sure to allow for carry-over heat—the heat that continues to cook meat even after it's removed from the heat. The larger the cut, the more carry-over heat. Remove a big roast from the oven when it is about 10 degrees under your ultimate goal. Always allow the meat to rest, draped with foil, for 10 to 25 minutes, before slicing. This allows the meat to come to a more even temperature throughout and the juices to get reabsorbed, so it will be juicier.

Grilled Tri–Tip Steak with Chili Rub

While I was working on my Field Guide to Meat, *my family ate meat almost every night. Tri-tip was a revelation to all of us. This neglected cut from the sirloin has been popular in California since the late 1950s when an enterprising butcher in Santa Maria decided to rotisserie-roast it. Tri-tip's popularity quickly spread throughout the central coast of California as a delicious and low-cost cut ideal for outdoor barbecues. Here I serve it Santa Maria-style with Pico di Gallo salsa. Accompany with cooked pinto beans, (traditionally pinquitos are used), and toasted, buttered sourdough bread to make a real Santa Maria barbecue.*

SERVES 6

2 tablespoons chili powder

Kosher salt and freshly ground black pepper to taste

2 tablespoons canola oil

1 whole tri-tip roast of beef

Preheat a charcoal or gas grill. In a small bowl, mix together the chili powder, salt, pepper, and oil. Rub this seasoned oil all over a whole tri-tip and leave to season and come to room temperature, about 30 minutes before cooking. Grill to medium-rare over indirect heat—with the lid on.

Alternatively, preheat the oven to 400°F. Preheat a large, heavy skillet, preferably cast-iron, until it begins to smoke. Brown the tri-tip on all sides, finishing in the oven for about 10 minutes to desired temperature. Allow the meat to rest 10 to 15 minutes, draped with aluminum foil. Slice thinly, against the grain, and accompany with the salsa.

Pico De Gallo Salsa

The name of this well-known colorful, chunky, uncooked sauce translates to "rooster's beak." It is known by this name in Texas; in Mexico, similar sauces are called simply "salsa" or "salsa Mexicana."

MAKES ABOUT 2 CUPS

2 to 3 large ripe beefsteak tomatoes,
   seeded and cut into small dice
1 tablespoon kosher salt
1 small sweet white onion, diced
2 fresh jalapeño or serrano chiles, seeded and finely chopped
$^1/_4$ cup fresh lime juice (about 2 limes)
$^1/_2$ cup chopped fresh cilantro leaves (about $^1/_2$ bunch)

Mix the tomatoes with the salt and allow them to drain in a colander to remove excess liquid for about 15 minutes. (Freeze the liquid to add to soup, stock, or tomato sauce.) Drain the tomatoes and mix with the remaining ingredients. Cover tightly, pressing plastic wrap directly on the surface of the salsa and refrigerate until ready to serve. The salsa will keep for 2 to 3 days, but will become more watery each day. If necessary, drain off this excess liquid before serving and taste. Because cold deadens flavor, it might need extra seasoning.

BEEF TRI-TIP AND TRIMMING

This well-flavored, easy-to-cook cut comes from the bottom of the sirloin (equivalent to the hip section) and is shaped like a large isosceles triangle. One tri-tip will feed four to six people and works well as a grilled, sliced steak or it can be pan-seared and then finished in a hot oven. It is only recently that I have started to see this cut on the East Coast, mainly at the Trader Joe's stores, where it is sold in convenient cryovac packaging. Great flavor, tender juiciness, and moderate price make this cut a winner. Ask your butcher to order it in. The only trimming this cut will usually need is removing a layer of excess fat from the outside.

Chinese Braised Short Ribs of Beef with Star Anise

Star anise has a particular affinity for beef and here, chunky, meaty short ribs are braised (which simply means cooking slowly in a small amount of rich liquid) with star anise, soy sauce, and Chinese black vinegar. Any special ingredients called for here are easily found in Chinese markets and nowadays, in many supermarkets. For several years, biting and slightly numbing Szechuan peppercorns were illegal to import into the United States. Now, because of better ways of processing the spice, they are once again coming into the country. French Pernod accentuates the licorice flavor here, but it can be omitted.

SERVES ABOUT 6

120

1/4 cup soy sauce

1/4 cup Chinese rice wine

2 tablespoons Chinese black vinegar (or balsamic vinegar)

2 tablespoons Pernod liqueur

2 cups chopped plum tomatoes

2 teaspoons ground cinnamon

Zest of 1 orange

1 tablespoon ground Szechuan peppercorns

2 tablespoons canola oil

6 short ribs of beef (about 5 pounds)

1 tablespoon chopped garlic

1 bunch scallions, thinly sliced

6 whole star anise pods for garnish

In a medium bowl, combine the soy sauce, rice wine, vinegar, Pernod, tomatoes, cinnamon, orange zest, and Szechuan pepper and reserve.

Heat the oil in a large Dutch oven or other heavy-bottomed pot with a lid. Add the ribs and brown well on all sides. Discard most of the fat, then add the garlic and cook for 1 minute while stirring until fragrant. Pour in the reserved sauce mixture, cover the pot, bring to a boil, then reduce heat and simmer at lowest heat 2 hours, or until the beef is tender and the liquid has thickened. Alternatively, preheat the oven to 300°F. and bake, covered, in the oven after bringing to the boil on top of the stove.

Remove the pot from the oven and allow the short ribs to cool to room temperature in their cooking liquid. Refrigerate overnight and the next day, remove and discard any solidified fat. Reheat thoroughly over low to moderate heat and serve garnished with scallions and one whole star anise pod, just for looks. Accompany with steamed rice.

Korean Braised Short Ribs

In recent years, short ribs have become the newest darling on menus. It used to be that such a homey cut would never be served in a restaurant with any sort of pretensions. That has changed totally. Now the emphasis is on using good technique to produce a well-flavored dish from the lowliest cuts. The best thing about this dish is that the short ribs don't even have to be browned. You just throw everything into a large heavy pot with a lid, bring to the boil on top of the stove, and then bake slowly.

SERVES 8

1/2 cup soy sauce, preferably dark soy

1/4 cup molasses, not blackstrap

4 tablespoons Japanese roasted sesame oil, divided

1 tablespoon chopped garlic

2 teaspoons dry mustard

1 teaspoon Korean red pepper flakes
  (substitute Italian hot red pepper flakes)

4 pounds cross-cut short ribs of beef

2 tablespoons sesame seeds, preferably Korean roasted
  sesame seeds

1 bunch scallions, thinly sliced

In a blender jar or food processor, combine the soy sauce, molasses, 2 tablespoons of the sesame oil, garlic, mustard, and red pepper. Blend all together to a paste, then transfer to a large bowl and stir in 2 cups of water. Combine the meat with the sauce mixture and place in a Dutch oven. The ribs should be just covered with liquid, otherwise add a little more water. Bring to a boil on top of the stove, uncovered.

121

BEEF

Transfer to a preheated 300°F. oven, cover, and continue to cook about 2 hours, or until the ribs are quite tender when pierced with a fork. Remove the pot from the oven, cool, and then refrigerate the contents of the pot up to 2 days.

Preheat the oven to 425°F. Remove and discard the layer of solid fat on top. Drain the liquid and place in a small pot and boil until somewhat thickened and well flavored. Keep the sauce warm. Place the short ribs bone-side down on a roasting pan, brush with the remaining 2 tablespoons of sesame oil and roast until the ribs are slightly crisped on the outside and hot on the inside, about 25 to 30 minutes.

Stir the sesame seeds and scallions into the sauce and pour over the beef. Serve immediately. The short ribs will keep up to one week if refrigerated and will freeze quite well.

122

KOREAN RED PEPPER FLAKES

One of the secrets of my kitchen is that I use brick-red flakes of Korean pepper for heat. Unlike most other dried chile flakes, only the flesh is used to make this potent seasoning used in huge quantities in Korean cooking. At my local Korean market, there is an entire aisle devoted only to red pepper.

BEETS

BEETS

Beets have undergone a total transformation from the pickled ones used as a cheap addition to salad bars and the mushy canned ones that no one looked forward to eating to today when they have become the fashionable chef's newest darling. Beets, *Beta vulgaris*, and their close cousins, Swiss chard and spinach, all descended from the sea beet, a wild seashore plant growing throughout Southern Europe that has been eaten since prehistoric times.

Not surprisingly, beets are most popular in northern and eastern Europe, where historically the selection of vegetables was limited. Three of the many versions of the hearty beet-based soup, borscht, are included in this section: a cold summertime version from the Catskill Mountains, a vegetable-laden version from Romania, and a rib-sticking version suitable for the bitterest cold day from the Ukraine.

In Italy, where they are passionate vegetable lovers, whole roasted beets are sold at the greengrocers. In this chapter, I combine roasted beets with licorice-scented tarragon. In Lebanon, lightly cooked beets are mixed with yogurt and mint, not very different from the Russian habit of mixing sour cream and beets.

Beets have the highest sugar content of any vegetable, although they are low in calories. The sugar that you buy at the grocery store may be actually beet sugar, extracted from the huge sugar beets grown in colder climates rather than cane sugar. (Beet sugar will be somewhat moister than cane sugar with the damp, sandy consistency of natural sea salt.)

The brilliant magenta color of beets comes from betacyanin, a water-soluble pigment. Because the natural acid in beets evaporates in heat, after long cooking, the beets eventually turn from magenta to orange. Beets have such concentrated color that they stay red when cooked even though a lot of color may leach out. Just look at your hands and the cutting board! (Fancy gold beets contain a different color compound, which is much more stable.)

Many colorful varieties of beets are to be found in supermarkets and especially at farmers' markets, including Chioggia beets from the Adriatic town just south of Venice that is also home to round Chioggia radicchio (*see* page 492). Also called Candy Cane beets, they are striped in concentric circles of red and white. A newer variety, the gold beet, has the advantage of not staining. There are even white beets, though I tend to go for the colorful ones. (Magenta was always my favorite color in the Crayola 64-color box; I still tend to dress in bold colors and to cook with bold flavors.) The availability of these tender baby and adolescent beets have inspired chefs to use them in all sorts of creative ways. They work especially well with walnuts and goat cheese. Beets are available all year long, but their peak season, particularly for local and specialty varieties, is June through October.

124

Choosing Beets

Medium-sized beets are fine for most cooking purposes but small, young beets (about $1^1/_2$-inches in diameter), usually sold with their tops, are tenderest and quickest to cook. Look for fresh-pulled beets with bright, dark green tops, called "bunch beets". However, those with wilted or deteriorated greens can be trimmed and used for their roots. Choose relatively smooth, hard, round beets with perky-looking rather than limp tap roots and deep red (or gold) color. The surface should be unbruised and free of cuts. Beets with no tops have been stored for weeks or even months; they are called "loose beets". Avoid overly large beets, because they are likely to be extremely dense with unpleasantly woody cores and may take hours to cook. However, larger beets will have the most intense color. It's best to choose beets that are similar in size so they will cook evenly.

Preparing and Cooking Beets

Scrub the beets gently without breaking the thin skin, again to keep the beets from bleeding. To keep their bright color (and to heighten flavor), beets are usually cooked with lemon juice, vinegar, or the old-fashioned "sour salt" (citric acid) used in Poland and Russia where fresh lemons were not available. Betacyanin, the coloring matter in beets, is quite sensitive to the relative Ph of the cooking liquid. Cooking beets in alkaline water will result in an off color, so always add a small amount of acid to the cooking liquid.

Roasting locks in nutrients and intensifies the natural sweetness of beets, but it's best to roast medium to medium-large beets, because all beets will shrivel up when roasted. Very large beets won't have enough natural moisture to roast; they should be boiled. To roast, wrap in foil, place in a baking dish and bake at 400°F. until tender when pierced, 1 to 2 hours, according to size.

To boil beets, prepare a large pot of salted water with a splash of vinegar or lemon juice. Add the beets, cover, and bring to the boil. Reduce heat to a medium boil and cook until the beets are tender when pierced, from 30 minutes to $1^1/_2$ hours.

To steam beets, bring 1-inch of water to the boil in a pot with a tight-fitting cover, and a vegetable steamer inserted. Add the beets, cover, and steam over moderate heat until tender when pierced, about 30 minutes. Steaming is best suited for smaller beets.

Peel beets while still warm, rubbing off the skin, which should slip away easily if the beets are thoroughly cooked. Wear gloves so your hands don't get stained. If the skin won't slip off, use a small paring knife or a vegetable peeler to remove the skin. Cut the beet in halves, quarters, wedges, slices, cubes, or julienne. If they're small enough, serve whole.

Roasted Beets in Honey–Tarragon Dressing

This is a good dish to make when you have larger beets that won't shrivel up into nothing when roasted. Because roasting concentrates their sweetness, the dressing contrasts this with sharp mustard, savory shallots, and a goodly amount of licorice-tinged tarragon. Substitute dill if fresh tarragon is not available. Grapeseed oil has a mild, faintly nutty flavor that makes it a good base for dressings. Substitute vegetable oil.

SERVES 6

2 pounds whole beets, greens cut off
   and reserved for another use
$1/2$ cup grapeseed oil
2 tablespoons coarse-grain mustard
1 tablespoon Dijon mustard
2 tablespoons finely chopped shallots
1 tablespoon chopped fresh tarragon,
   or 1 teaspoon dried tarragon
$1/4$ cup cider vinegar
2 tablespoons honey
Kosher salt and freshly ground black pepper
Sprigs of fresh tarragon (for garnish)

Preheat the oven to 400°F. Wrap the beets in aluminum foil. Roast for 45 minutes to one hour, or until they are tender when pierced. Cool enough to handle then peel by rubbing off their skins. (If your beets are different sizes, remove the smaller ones as they are done and continue cooking the larger ones. Do not cut the beets before cooking or the color will bleed out.)

Cut beets in half, through the root end, then cut into wedges like an apple. Whisk together remaining ingredients to make the dressing and toss with the beets. Garnish with tarragon sprigs.

Lebanese Shredded Beet Salad with Yogurt and Mint

This Schiaparelli-esque shocking pink salad is refreshing because of the cleansing mint and tang from the yogurt. It would make a good addition to a meal of mezze, the small dishes of salads and dips served in the Levant as a relaxing way to eat a meal with friends. Serve with Almond Tarator Dip with Crunchy Pita Chips (see page 20), Turkish Red Tabbouli Salad (see page 967), Tunisian Carrot Salad (see page 212), Grilled Octopus Salad with Kalamata Olives, Tomato and Cucumber (see page 204), and/or Crunchy Fried Cauliflower with Pomegranate Sauce (see page 164). If you don't grow fresh mint, look for high-quality whole leaf dried spearmint in Middle Eastern and North African groceries.

SERVES 6 TO 8

1 pound beets
2 teaspoons finely crushed garlic
2 tablespoons chopped fresh mint,
   or 2 teaspoons crumbled dried spearmint
Juice of 2 lemons (about $1/4$ cup)
Kosher salt and fresh ground black pepper
   to taste
1 cup plain yogurt, preferably whole milk
$1/4$ cup extra-virgin olive oil
Sprigs of fresh spearmint (for garnish)

Trim the beets and boil or steam until tender (about 25 minutes). Drain; skin while warm and trim off the ends. Coarsely grate the beets. In a medium bowl, combine the garlic, mint, lemon juice, salt and pepper. Add the beets, olive oil, and yogurt and blend well. Refrigerate about 1 hour until chilled. Serve garnished with fresh mint.

Cold Summertime Borscht

So that nobody should feel left out, along with the Farm Belt, the Corn Belt, the Bible belt, we Jews got the Borscht Belt, which got its name from the predominantly Jewish singers and stand-up comics who worked the cabarets of the summer resort hotels in New York's Catskill Mountains. According to one comedian of the time, the white line on Route 17, the direct route from Seventh Avenue to the Catskills, is made of pure sour cream. One of the typical dishes served in the family hotels and boarding houses filled with New Yorkers starved for fresh air was this unearthly magenta-colored, cold, clear borscht topped with a hot boiled potato and a dollop of rich sour cream. Part of the pleasure of the soup is to pull streaks of the white cream through the red soup and then astonish the palate by eating the chilled soup and hot potato together in one mouthful.

SERVES 8

1 pound medium beets

1 tablespoon cider vinegar

Kosher salt to taste

Juice of 1 lemon

8 small all-purpose potatoes, peeled and cut into half

2 cucumbers, peeled and diced,
  or 2 half-sour pickles, diced

½ bunch scallions, thinly sliced

2 tablespoons chopped dill

8 hard-cooked eggs, quartered
  (*see* Chopping Hard-Cooked Eggs, page 319)

1 cup sour cream

Place beets, vinegar, salt, and cold water to cover in a large soup pot and bring to the boil. Cook until the beets are tender when pierced, about 45 minutes.

Remove the beets from the pot, cool, peel, and coarsely grate. Return to the pot of water and add the lemon juice. Chill overnight in the refrigerator.

The next day, steam the potatoes until soft through. When ready to serve, pour the cold soup into individual bowls and top each portion with the cucumbers (or pickles), two hot steamed potato halves, a sprinkle of scallions and dill, 4 egg quarters, and a generous dollop of sour cream. Serve immediately.

127

STORING BEETS

Because the greens draw moisture from the root, cut off greens before storing, leaving at least an inch of the stem attached, to keep the beets from "bleeding" from the top. Cut away the greens and refrigerate the beet roots and greens separately. The leaves draw moisture from the roots; if left on, the roots will tend to soften and wither. Beets, especially those medium to large in size, may be stored inside a plastic bag in the refrigerator for up to three weeks.

Rumanian Beet Borscht
with Brisket and Sauerkraut

In typical Rumanian style, where vegetables grow profusely, this borscht contains a whole gardenful of vegetables— onion, carrots, parsnip, green cabbage, celery, green pepper, and tomato, flavored with plenty of chopped fresh dill. Serve this rosy-red soup with a dollop of brilliant white sour cream floating on top. It's a meal in a bowl that tastes as good as it looks. Some cooks add finely shredded raw beets to borscht just before serving to revive the color. This recipe does make a large batch, but this well-flavored soup freezes beautifully.

SERVES 8 TO 10

1 pound meaty beef bones (neck or shank)

Salt to taste

1 pound beef brisket (or other tough, flavorful cut used
  for pot roast, such as chuck or bottom round)

1 onion, sliced

3 carrots, peeled and grated

3 cups peeled and grated beets (about 1 pound beets)

1 cup peeled and grated parsnip

1 small green cabbage, shredded

3 ribs celery with leaves, chopped

1 green pepper, seeded and diced

1 (28-ounce) can tomato puree
  (or 1 box Pomi brand strained tomatoes)

Juice of 2 lemons (about $1/4$ cup)

$1/2$ cup chopped dill (about $1/2$ bunch)

2 tablespoons brown sugar

Fresh ground black pepper to taste

Place bones in a soup pot with water to cover by 2 inches. Add salt, bring to the boil and simmer 2 hours, skimming off any foam. Strain into a second pot. Add the brisket and 2 gallons water. Bring to the boil and skim. Add the onion and simmer 1 hour, uncovered.

Add remaining ingredients to the soup and simmer, with lid ajar for 1 hour longer. Remove the brisket, trim off fat, cut into small dice and return to soup. Season to taste with more salt and pepper.

AN OLD RECIPE FOR BORSCHT

While modern recipes for borscht (like mine) often include long lists of ingredients and specific instruction, old-fashioned cookbooks gave only minimal information. In my 1918 *Jewish CookBook*, the recipe for borscht in its entirety reads, "Cut one large beet and one-half pound of onions in thick pieces and put in kettle with one pound of fat brisket of beef. Cover with water and let cook slowly two hours, add three-fourths of a cup of sugar and a little citric acid to make it sweet and sour and let cook another hour."

Ukrainian Beet Borscht with Ham and Cabbage

It is the ruby-red beet root that is now the defining ingredient of borscht. This was not always so. The Russian name, borscht, means cow parsnip, *a root vegetable in the carrot family and presumably the soup's original base. Borscht is usually made with beef stock, though pork, ham, chicken, and goose are all used along with aromatics like dried mushrooms, dill, and caraway. Beet root, parsnips, carrots, turnips, Hamburg parsley root, and celery root all find their way into the pot of borscht. This hearty version from the Ukraine gets its deep flavor from beef stock and ham and includes those original parsnips.*

Serves 6 to 8

1 cup chopped onion

2 teaspoons chopped garlic

4 tablespoons unsalted butter

3 cups peeled and coarsely grated beets (about 1 pound)

2 cups peeled and grated parsnip

1 (15-ounce) can chopped plum tomatoes

1 tablespoon granulated sugar

$^1/_4$ cup red wine vinegar

1 tablespoon kosher salt

2 quarts beef stock

1 pound boiling potatoes, peeled and diced

1 pound white cabbage, cored and shredded

1 pound ham, diced

1 pint sour cream, for garnish

In a large soup pot, over moderate heat, cook the onions and garlic in the butter 6 to 8 minutes, or until softened but not browned. Add the beets, parsnip, tomatoes, sugar, vinegar, salt, and beef stock. Bring the mixture to the boil, then reduce heat and simmer, partially covered, for 45 minutes.

Meanwhile, bring a medium pot of salted water to the boil. Cook the potatoes until half-cooked, about 10 minutes, then stir in the cabbage. Cook together about 10 minutes, or until the potatoes and the cabbage are tender. Drain most of the water and add the potatoes, cabbage, and the ham to the soup pot. Cook together 10 minutes longer. Season and serve immediately, accompanied by a bowl of sour cream.

129

Beets and Greens

If you, like I do, enjoy visiting your local farmers market, you can buy beautiful young beets in season in the late summer with their sprightly tops. This dish is ideal because it uses both parts of the beets along with sharp-flavored turnip or mustard greens to lend a bit of bite to this dish. It's ideal for when the beets are quite small and the greens abundant and vigorous, usually in June.

SERVES 4 TO 6

2 bunches young beets with greens

1 bunch turnip greens, mustard greens, or kale

1 large white onion, chopped

2 tablespoons unsalted butter

2 tablespoons cider vinegar

Kosher salt and black pepper to taste

Trim the beets, leaving about 1 inch of tops. In a medium pot, boil the beets until just tender, about 20 minutes. Cool, peel, and cut into quarters.

Meanwhile, strip the greens from their stalks and wash in plenty of water. In a large skillet, cook onions until translucent in butter. Add the greens and simmer together about 10 minutes, or until tender. Add cooked beets and heat through. Sprinkle with vinegar and season to taste with salt and pepper.

130

BLUEBERRIES & BLACKBERRIES

BLUEBERRIES & BLACKBERRIES

Blueberries

Blueberries are America's best known native fruit—two others are cranberries and Concord grapes. These small, round, smooth-skinned berries are dusted, in most varieties, with a powdery whitish "bloom" on their deep-blue skins. Their sweet, appealing flavor is best when the berries are fully ripened. If overripe, their flavor will be overly sweet without the balancing edge of tartness. Both blueberries and their wild cousin, huckleberries, are native to North America and have been used extensively since Colonial times. Native Americans made pemmican by pounding dried buffalo meat, blue and other berries along with animal fat into a cake as their version of trail mix.

Low-bush blueberries, *Vaccinium angustifolium*, which grow only about one foot high, thrive in Eastern Canada and Maine. These small, intensely flavored blueberries are often marketed as wild blueberries or huckleberries. High-bush blueberries, *Vaccinium corymbosum*, grow as high as fifteen feet tall with berries that are larger and more innocuous in flavor. Blueberries have been commercially cultivated since the 1920s with Bluecrop the most important cultivated variety. New Jersey and Michigan are the country's leading producers.

Huckleberries, *Gaylussacia baccata*, the blueberry's wild and more intensely flavored counterpart, are used in similar ways. To add confusion, in some parts of the United States, blueberries and true huckleberries go by the same name. Blueberries are blue and have lots of tiny, soft seeds; huckleberries are purplish-black with fewer, harder seeds. The tiny dark bluish-purple whor-tleberry, *Vaccinium myrtilus*, resembles small blueberries and is known as the bilberry in Europe.

Blueberries may be found almost year-round because of imports, but home-grown American berries are in season from April to October with Canadian berries in season a bit later, from July to October.

132

Blackberries

Blackberries, *Rubus fruticosus*, members of the *Rosaceae* (or rose) family and the largest of the wild berries, can be up to one and a half-inches long and equally plump. Blue to purplish black in color with shiny skin and tart flavor, they grow on thorny bushes or brambles, which gives them their other name: brambleberry. Like raspberries and strawberries, each blackberry consists of clumps of fruits, each containing one prominent seed. They are delicious eaten out-of-hand, especially when fully ripe and tending toward red and purplish red, and excellent for cooking and baking, especially when slightly underripe.

The naturalized American blackberry, *Rubus laciniatus*, was gathered by Native Americans all over North America, and by the colonists as well. Blackberries are now widely cultivated in the United States, though Oregon and Washington are best known for the quality of their berries. Blackberries are in peak season from June through September, though because of imports from South America, Australia, and New Zealand, they are available occasionally throughout the year. Specialty berries are sporadically available in season on the East Coast but are more prevalent on the West Coast, especially in the Pacific Northwest where most types are grown. Loganberries are in season in June and July. Boysenberry and Marion-berry's short season lasts from mid-July to mid-August.

Choosing, Preparing, and Storing Blackberries

Look for berries that are plump with full, deep color and a bright, clean, fresh appearance and firm, though not hard, texture. Avoid overripe berries that are soft and may be moldy or leaky. If the hulls are attached, the berries are immature and were picked too early; their flavor will be tart. Refrigerate lightly covered and preferably in a single layer and use within a day or two. Do not wash until ready to use. Note that berries don't ripen after picking. Blackberries deteriorate quickly; plan to use them within a day or two after purchase. Just before using, place berries in a colander and rinse with a gentle stream of cool water and gently pat dry with paper towel.

My first baking project, which launched me on my lifelong career as a culinarian, was as an eleven-year old during a summer spent in Seattle the year of the World's Fair (1962). Blackberries grow abundantly there and in much of the Pacific Northwest, favoring its mild climate and notoriously common rain. With a friend, I picked buckets of blackberries from a huge and thorny backyard patch and proceeded to turn them into my very first pie. (What's a little pain in search of great ingredients?)

Blackberries and Related Varieties

Boysenberry: The Boysenberry is probably a blackberry crossed with a loganberry or red raspberry. It was found growing in the late 1920s on the abandoned farm of Mr. Boysen. This very large, reddish-purple berry is quite tart and has prominent seeds.

Evergreen Blackberry: The Evergreen blackberry, native to England and known there as cut-leaf or parsley-leafed blackberry, was brought to Oregon around 1850 by settlers from England. At the time, few growers were interested in blackberries because of their sharp thorns but after a Thornless Evergreen (also known as Black Diamond) was found in the 1920s and propagated, they became much more desirable.

Loganberry: Loganberries date from the 1880s when Judge Logan of California inadvertently crossed two varieties of blackberries with an old variety of red raspberries. His happy accident became the loganberry, now grown mainly for juice, pies, and wine. Loganberries make excellent jams and preserves. Juicy and sweetly tart, they turn purple-red when very ripe. Like others in this list, loganberries are rarely found outside of the West Coast.

Marionberry: This thorny native Oregonian is a cross between a Chehalem blackberry and an Olallieberry. The Marionberry is named after Marion County, Oregon, where it was first popularized. The fruit is dark red to black in color, medium to large, rounded, and somewhat longer than wide with medium seeds. Marionberries have excellent flavor with the taste of wild blackberries.

Olallieberry: The Olallieberry is grown mainly on the West Coast. This cross between a youngberry and a loganberry has a distinctive, sweet flavor and resembles a large, elongated blackberry. It's delicious both fresh and cooked and makes excellent jams and jellies.

Tayberry: This is a cross of a blackberry, raspberry, and loganberry. It has large, sweet red fruit and was first grown at Tayside, Scotland.

Youngberry: This is a hybrid blackberry with dark red color and sweet, juicy flesh.

Blackberry–Apricot Crisp

This home-style crisp is inspired by a dessert that I enjoyed at Chez Panisse in Berkeley, California more than twenty years ago. I'd have to call it perfect, but what made it so (and what makes the food there so very good), is that the fruits were at their peak of perfection. If apricots are out of season, substitute peaches. Serve with a small scoop of real vanilla ice cream that's almost melting.

SERVES 6

$1/2$ cup granulated sugar

$1/2$ cup sour cream

1 egg

$1/2$ teaspoon almond extract

1 teaspoon vanilla extract

2 tablespoons + $1/2$ cup all-purpose flour

8 to 10 firm, but ripe apricots, cut into wedges

1 ($1/2$ pint) container blackberries

4 tablespoons unsalted butter, cut into bits

$1/2$ cup oatmeal

$1/2$ cup roughly chopped almonds

$1/2$ cup light brown sugar, packed

Preheat the oven to 350°F. Whisk together sugar, sour cream, egg, almond extract, and vanilla. Stir in 2 tablespoons of flour. Combine with sliced apricots. Lightly fold in blackberries. Spoon mixture into the bottom of a shallow baking dish or into individual gratin dishes.

Using your fingertips, crumble together the $1/2$ cup flour with the butter, oatmeal, almonds, and brown sugar. Sprinkle over top of fruit. Bake for 30 minutes, or until bubbling. Serve while still hot.

134

Blackberry Panna Cotta

What is it about this simple dessert of flavored cream thickened with gelatin that has made it quite the rage? Twenty-five years ago when I cheffed at a wonderful Northern Italian restaurant, no one had ever heard of panna cotta ("cooked cream" in Italian) and it was a very hard sell. Years later when I went back into the kitchen, I couldn't keep enough panna cotta in the house and served it in different versions for every season. Like all gelatin desserts, this one tastes best if it is barely set and quite jiggly. Use sheet gelatin for best results (see Sheet Gelatin, below). Note that the key to the Italian flavor here is lemon zest, the best "free" seasoning in your kitchen.

SERVES 8 TO 10

3 cups heavy whipping cream

$3/4$ cup + $1/4$ cup granulated sugar

Pinch of salt

Grated zest of 1 lemon

Scrapings from 1 vanilla bean

3 sheets gelatin, soaked in cold water until softened
(or $1^1/2$ teaspoons powdered gelatin soaked in warm
water until softened and then heated until clear)

1 cup sour cream

2 cups blackberries

2 tablespoons kirsch (optional)

Have ready 8 to 10 (6- to 8-ounce) small metal timbale molds or use coffee cups. Spray molds lightly with nonstick spray and reserve.

In a nonreactive saucepan, warm the cream with the $3/4$ cup granulated sugar, salt, zest, and vanilla over medium-high heat. Do not let it boil. Take the cream off the heat, drain the gelatin sheets and then stir in until thoroughly dissolved (or stir in the melted powdered gelatin). Cool slightly, mix in the sour cream, and then pour into the prepared molds. Cool and then chill until fully set, at least 2 hours, and preferably overnight.

When ready to serve, mix the blackberries with $1/4$ cup granulated sugar and the kirsch. Unmold the molds by dipping very briefly in hot water or wrap in a hot towel just long enough for the panna cotta to start to come away from the sides of the mold. Turn upside-down and unmold directly onto individual serving plates. (Put the plates in the refrigerator to firm up if the panna cotta gets a little too warm.) Serve topped with the blackberries.

SHEET GELATIN

Gelatin is derived from collagen—present in skin, connective tissue, and bones, particularly from young calves or from gelatin-rich fish. Yes, it is the same collagen (or elasticity) that we lose as our skin ages. Transparent and almost colorless, unflavored gelatin in sold by Knox as a dehydrated powder in envelopes or in a bulk container. One envelope (about $2^1/2$ teaspoons) will gel 2 cups of liquid. European pastry chefs prefer using glassy-thin fragile sheets of gelatin, an extremely refined form of gelatin that results in a clearer, more delicately gelled product. Sheet gelatin is becoming more widely available in America and is sold by the Baker's Catalogue in packets of 20 sheets. It is, naturally, more expensive than powdered. Five sheets will gel 2 cups of liquid; each sheet is the equivalent of about $1/2$ teaspoon of powdered gelatin. To use the sheets, soak in cold water until they're soft and limp. Remove from water and drop sheets directly into hot liquid, stirring until they dissolve. For making panna cotta, where barely set, jiggly consistency is essential, sheet gelatin is ideal.

Blueberry Buckle

A buckle is one of those old-fashioned homey desserts with a humble name, like dowdy and slump, that originated in England and was brought over by the Colonists. Three hundred years later, it still tastes good and blueberry makes one of the best versions. When blueberries are in season and inexpensive, buy extra and freeze them in double plastic zip-top bags. Make this buckle with berries right out of the freezer; they'll start to bleed and turn the buckle an unpleasant gray color if allowed to defrost. Use white whole wheat flour here for lighter color (see Whole Wheat and White Whole Wheat Flour, page 228).

SERVES 8 TO 10

1 cup granulated sugar

$^1/_2$ pound (2 sticks) unsalted butter

2 eggs

6 ounces (1$^1/_2$ cups) all-purpose flour, preferably unbleached

2 ounces ($^1/_2$ cup) whole-wheat flour

$^1/_2$ teaspoon kosher salt

$^1/_2$ teaspoon baking soda

Few gratings fresh nutmeg

1 cup buttermilk

1 pint blueberries, picked over, washed and drained

Streusel Topping (recipe follows)

Preheat the oven to 375°F. Using the paddle attachment on a stand mixer, cream the sugar and the butter in a mixer until light and fluffy. Beat in the eggs, one at a time, continuing to beat until completely incorporated.

Whisk together the all-purpose flour, whole wheat flour, salt, baking soda, and nutmeg.

Beginning and ending with the buttermilk, alternate adding the buttermilk and the dry ingredients to the wet ingredients, beating only long enough to combine. Spoon half the batter into a nonstick sprayed 9 x 13-inch metal baking pan or a ceramic baking dish. Cover with half the blueberries. Repeat. Sprinkle streusel over top and bake for 35 to 45 minutes or until the blueberries bubble and the batter has set.

Streusel Topping

$^1/_2$ cup granulated sugar

2 ounces ($^1/_2$ cup) all-purpose flour, preferably unbleached

1 ounce ($^1/_4$ cup) whole wheat flour

4 tablespoons unsalted butter

2 teaspoons cinnamon

Combine the ingredients using a pastry blender or in an electric mixer with the paddle attachment until crumbly.

Blueberry Buttermilk Pancakes

Blueberry pancakes are classic breakfast food in America, to be found in diners across the country. The secret to good-looking pancakes is not to mix the blueberries with the batter, but rather to ladle in each pancake and then sprinkle with blueberries. That way you won't end up with grayish pancakes. Once you've made your own pancakes, you might as well go all the way and serve them topped with a pat of butter and pure maple syrup.

SERVES 6

¼ pound (1 cup) all-purpose flour, preferably unbleached

2 tablespoons cornmeal, preferably stone-ground

¼ cup brown sugar, packed

1 teaspoon baking powder

1 teaspoon baking soda

½ teaspoon kosher salt

2 cups buttermilk

1 large egg

2 tablespoons unsalted butter, melted

Unsalted butter, for frying, clarified if possible
  (*see* Making French-Style Clarified Butter, page 170)

1 pint blueberries, picked over, washed and drained

Whisk together flour, cornmeal, sugar, baking powder, baking soda, and salt in a large bowl.

Whisk together buttermilk and egg in medium bowl to blend; add to dry ingredients and stir until just blended but still lumpy. Gently mix in butter.

Heat a griddle or large nonstick skillet over medium heat. Brush a thin coating of butter onto the griddle and let melt. Working in batches, drop batter by small ladlefuls onto the griddle, evenly spaced. Sprinkle each pancake with 1 to 2 tablespoons of blueberries. Cook pancakes until light brown on bottom and bubbles form on top at the edges, about 3 minutes. Turn pancakes over and cook until they are just set in the middle, about 2 minutes. Transfer to plates, keeping warm in a 200°F. oven. Repeat with remaining batter, adding more butter to griddle as needed.

137

BLUE CHEESE

BLUE CHEESE

Blue cheese is something one either adores or despises. Because I go for intense flavors with a punch, I adore blue cheese in all its many forms, both for eating and for cooking. Cheese is the one indulgence I never want to give up. My introduction to the unique pleasure of eating moldy, stinky blue cheese occurred as a preteen when I was invited along with my parents to visit friends. In the middle of their coffee table was a top-hat-shaped wheel of Stilton cheese surrounded by British wholemeal biscuits—what we call crackers. All afternoon I sat close to that table and kept going back for more of this strange but fascinating cheese with its alluring nutty aftertaste. Ever since then, I've developed regular cravings for bold, even funky blue cheeses.

There is nothing wrong at all with limiting your enjoyment of these blue cheeses to eating them in their purest form, accompanied by their classic partners: Stilton with Port wine and walnuts in their shell, Gorgonzola with pears, Roquefort with Sauternes wine, and Cabrales with red grapes or figs. However, there is another whole world of pleasure for blue cheese lovers in cooking. Blue cheeses have a distinctive taste that doesn't get lost when used as an ingredient.

The assertive flavors and rich, creamy melting texture of classic blues like Gorgonzola, Roquefort, Stilton, and Cabrales pair well with a wide range of foods. Add them to starches like fresh and dried pasta, polenta, and gnoc-chi, use as a topping for pizza with fresh tomatoes or walnuts and caramelized onions, or serve with fruits like pears or figs. Add to all sorts of potato dishes and savory baked goods likes homemade crackers, flatbreads, and scones. All these starches provide the background to show off bold blues.

Many salads call for blue cheeses and in fact, you can top just about any green salad with small bits of your favorite blue cheese. California classic Cobb salad; a mixture of frisée and other bitter greens with pears and blue cheese; watercress with blue cheese and poached figs; or steakhouse-style salad of tomato wedges, red onions, and crumbled blue cheese all benefit by their addition of blue cheese. Although there are countless versions of the ubiquitous Buffalo-Style Chicken Wings, all of them must be accompanied by blue cheese dip and the celery sticks that are so well matched with the cheese.

My personal favorites for cooking and eating include the "three kings of blue cheese": Gorgonzola from Italy, Roquefort from France, and Stilton from England. Recently, I've become enamored of Spain's superb representative in this class of exalted blues, Cabrales, from the north Atlantic coast of Asturias. Each of the main cheese-making countries—from Great Britain to Denmark, France, Italy, Spain, and the United States—makes their own version. Some blues, like Gorgonzola, are made from cow's milk whether raw or pasteurized; Roquefort and other blues, especially in France, are made from sheep's milk. Cabrales and a few other blues are made from a blend of milks, mainly cow's milk but mixed with both sheep and goat's milk.

America's fast-growing artisanal food movement has brought us lots of new delicious choices. Maytag blue, produced in Maytag, Iowa (yes, it is the same town that Maytag appliances come from), with its sharp, biting flavor and crumbly texture, works well in blue cheese dips and sauces. Goat's milk blue cheese is a relative new-comer made by American artisanal cheesemakers like Rollingstone Chevre in Idaho and Westfield Farm in Hubbardston, Massachusetts.

Each blue cheese has a unique aroma, enticing when properly conditioned, though unpleasant if the cheese is overripe. Buy your cheese from someone who cares about quality because cooking will only accentuate any off flavors in your cheese. Next time you shop, pick up a half pound of so of your favorite blue cheese and try some of the many appetizing cooking and serving ideas here.

CHOOSING AND STORING ROQUEFORT

Good Roquefort should be crumbly but should hold together. The cheese should be ivory-colored without any yellow tint. The veins of greenish-blue mold (called the *persillade* or parsley in French) should be abundant and reach right to the edge of the cheese. Because Roquefort has no crust, you can use the entire piece that you buy; though it will be saltier near the edge. Rinse the cheese lightly under cold water to remove excess salt.

Avoid Roquefort with excess moisture leaking from it, which happens when the cheese is rewrapped in plastic over the foil. Because of its worldwide fame, good Roquefort is relatively easy to find. Just about any cheese store will carry the real thing. Though the price can be rather high, you don't need to use much to get the sharp, memorable flavor of genuine Roquefort.

Choosing and Storing Gorgonzola

This cow's-milk cheese is rich and creamy with a savory and pungent flavor. Because of its brine-washed rind, when Gorgonzola is aged over 6 months, its flavor and aroma can be quite strong, even down-right stinky. Because of this tendency, pay particular attention to the quality of any Gorgonzola you buy. Avoid Gorgonzola if the interior is turning gray or if it truly smells like dirty feet (actually the exact same bacteria produces the aroma).

There are two types of Gorgonzola: Dolce (sweet) and Mountain (aged). Gorgonzola Dolce is sweet with a creamy "paste" (interior) that makes this milder blue cheese an excellent choice for cooking. It is full-flavored with an ivory-colored interior that can be lightly or thickly streaked with bluish-green veins in layers. Mountain Gorgonzola has a crumbly, drier texture and potent blue flavor so that it is best served with fruits like pears and apples or with nuts and sweet wine. Both types work well in salads.

CHOOSING AND STORING STILTON

Stilton has characteristic radial veining that can look like shattered porcelain because of its extremely fine veins of mold. This gives Stilton its overall bluing—not just in pockets like other blue cheeses—and allows for even flavor. Good Stilton should have a dry, rough, brown rind and a creamy ivory interior that has plenty of bluing right to the edge. The cheese should be crumbly, but moist enough to hold its shape. Avoid Stilton that is darkened with a dry brownish crust. The best Stilton for cooking comes from the inner core of the cheese where it is creamiest.

Buy Stilton in larger pieces so that you will end up with a good-sized section of interior. Unfortunately the rind and hard portion near the rind isn't good for cooking, though some people enjoy eating it. To keep up with the strong demand for Stilton, some cheese that is of lesser quality can be found on the market. Poor-quality Stilton has insufficient blue veining because it hasn't been aged long enough, and a dry rather than creamy interior.

Choosing and Storing Cabrales

Cabrales, from Spain, is produced only in the village of the same name and three neighboring villages located on the northern spur of the Europa Peaks in eastern Asturias. A cylindrical wheel of Cabrales weighs about 4 to 8 pounds. Originally wrapped in maple leaves, today, like many other blues, most Cabrales is wrapped in foil, numbered, and stamped with the Cabrales *Denominación de Origen* logo.

Cabrales is piquant, acid, and creamy and is powerful enough to work well in cooking. A good Cabrales is completely grown with mold, with deep blue veining. The strong smelling rind is sticky and yellow; the interior is compact but very open, with lots of holes and blue veins. Cabrales is crumbly and fragile, drier than Roquefort and less salty. It is quite strong, with a higher proportion of blue type veining (actually closer to purple in color) than other blues. Avoid Cabrales if the interior is turning gray. The cheese should look fresh with intense, clear purple rather than murky or muddy-looking veins. Be on the lookout for artisanal Cabrales wrapped in natural maple leaves, rather than the more common foil wrapping.

142

Blue cheese tastes extra strong when heated, and can easily be overpowering, so it is best combined with starchy, bland foods like potatoes, fresh and dried pasta, polenta, or as a topping for pizza.

The exception to this rule is beef. Blue cheese and rare-cooked beef make a natural marriage that's seen over and over. A simple hamburger, sliced grilled flank steak, rib-steak, or tenderloin of beef topped with crumbles or thin slices of your favorite blue makes an earthy, satisfying dish with the rich heartiness of beef contrasted with the creamy piquancy of the blue cheese. My favorite hamburger is sprinkled with kosher salt and lots of freshly ground black pepper, pan-seared in a cast-iron skillet, then topped with Roquefort, broiled briefly to melt. I then put it into a heated, good-quality hamburger bun and top it with a slice of sweet onion and red ripe beefsteak tomato. Yum!

Almost all blue cheeses are quite high in fat, and act in cooking more like a ripened creamy butter than a cheese. For this reason, it's best not to cook blue cheese but rather gently melt it or bake it. If making a cream sauce, pull the sauce from the fire, then stir in bits of the cheese until melted. If necessary, place back on the fire just long enough for the cheese to melt.

When cooking with blue cheese, your dish will only be as good as the cheese. I do not recommend cooking with commercially produced, inexpensive blues, often sold crumbled. Any negative qualities to cheese (bitterness, overpowering moldiness, and sharpness) will be accentuated when the cheese is cooked.

I like to maintain the veined look of the blue cheese in my cooking. Even when I make a blue cheese dressing or dip, I puree only part of the cheese, folding in crumbled bits at the end. When making a sauce, I stir in the bits of cheese just before serving. I'd rather have attractive bits of blue showing than a uniformly grayish sauce.

Baby Spinach Salad with Crispy Prosciutto and Creamy Gorgonzola Dressing

Another winner of a salad from my chef days, here I combine crispy prosciutto and tender flat-leafed baby spinach leaves—which have the considerable advantage of being prewashed—with a creamy Gorgonzola dressing. Unfortunately, when Gorgonzola is good, it's very, very good, but when it's bad, it's horrible. Because Gorgonzola has never really caught on in the United States (and I mean the real thing; I haven't tasted much good domestic), the quality of this marvelous cheese can be poor. Substitute with Cabrales, if you need to. Serve any leftover Creamy Gorgonzola Dressing as a dip with Buffalo-Style Chicken Wings, or simply with carrot, celery, and cucumber sticks.

SERVES 4

1 large red onion, cut into rings and skewered (*see* Using skewers to keep onion slices together, page 144)

1/4 cup canola oil

Kosher salt and freshly ground black pepper, to taste

1/4 pound thinly sliced prosciutto, cut into strips

1 pound bag baby spinach leaves

1 cup Creamy Gorgonzola Dressing (recipe follows)

Preheat a grill or broiler. Brush red onion rings with a little oil and sprinkle on both sides with salt and pepper. Grill or broil on both sides and reserve.

In a medium skillet, gently fry prosciutto strips in a little oil (to supplement natural fat) until crispy, about 5 minutes. Drain and reserve.

Toss spinach with most of the dressing. Arrange in a soft mound. Arrange red onion rings over salad. Drizzle salad with remaining Creamy Gorgonzola Dressing. Sprinkle crunchy prosciutto over top and serve immediately.

Creamy Gorgonzola Dressing

$3/4$ cup buttermilk

$1/4$ cup red wine vinegar

2 tablespoons chopped shallots

2 tablespoons chopped dill

2 tablespoons Dijon mustard

Kosher salt and freshly ground pepper to taste

$1/4$ pound Gorgonzola cheese, in bits

Blend together the buttermilk, red wine vinegar, shallots, dill, mustard, and salt and pepper. At the last minute, add the cheese, blending briefly to combine, but still leaving bits of cheese.

144

USING PROSCIUTTO HOCK

If you live anywhere near a good Italian grocery, ask to buy their prosciutto hocks, left from slicing big legs of prosciutto. The inexpensive hocks contain plenty of meat, though in smaller pieces. It is perfect for this salad and other dishes that call for small pieces of prosciutto, like *paglia e fieno* (straw and hay), a dish of green and white pasta tossed with cream, bits of prosciutto, green peas, and cream. You'll need to cut away the rind (or skin), but don't throw it out. Italians call this *la cotenna* and add it to the pot when making *pasta e fagioli* (pasta and beans) for that inimitable lip-smacking quality.

Using Skewers to Keep Onion Slices Together

When grilled, onion slices pick up a delicious flavor. To keep the slices from falling apart, cut slices "through the equator" that are on the thick side (about $3/4$ of an inch thick). Run a water-soaked bamboo skewer horizontally through the slice, brush lightly with oil and grill on both sides.

Fettuccine with Gorgonzola and Red Onion Marmalade

This is one of those perfectly balanced dishes: the richness of the earthy, pungent Gorgonzola sauce is cut by the sweet-sour red onion marmalade, which also contrasts its deep burgundy color with the light cream-colored sauce. When I first started making this dish, I worked in a restaurant where we made all our pasta from scratch. While there is no doubt that homemade is better, there is good-quality packaged fettuccine available in many supermarket, both fresh (usually in modified atmosphere packaging) and frozen. Crème fraiche, a French-style tangy, ripened cream adds a little zip here; heavy cream is a perfectly good substitute. The Red Onion Marmalade keeps quite well and is delicious heated and served over a steak.

SERVES 4

1 cup crème fraiche (substitute heavy cream)

1/2 pound imported Gorgonzola Dolce, rind trimmed and cheese cut up

Freshly grated nutmeg, salt and black pepper, to taste

1 pound fresh fettuccine (spinach or egg)

1 cup Red Onion Marmalade (recipe follows)

Bring a large pot of salted water to the boil. Meanwhile, using a nonreactive sauté pan, gently heat the crème fraiche. Off heat, stir in the Gorgonzola cheese and let it melt. Swirl around and season with nutmeg, salt, and pepper.

Cook the fettuccine 1 to 2 minutes after the water comes back to the boil. Drain gently but thoroughly. Off heat, toss pasta together with sauce. Twirl pasta onto plates, preferably heated, forming a nest shape. Top with a generous spoonful of the Red Onion Marmalade in the center of the dish. Serve immediately.

Red Onion Marmalade

3 red onions, sliced

3 tablespoons unsalted butter

1/2 cup red wine

1 tablespoon balsamic vinegar

1 1/2 teaspoons chopped thyme (or 1/2 teaspoon dried thyme)

2 tablespoons honey

1/4 teaspoon ground allspice

Kosher salt and fresh ground black pepper to taste

In a large nonreactive skillet, sauté the onion in butter until softened but not browned. Add the red wine, balsamic vinegar, thyme, honey, allspice, and salt and black pepper to taste.

Bring to the boil, reduce heat and simmer about 30 minutes, or until the liquid is syrupy, stirring occasionally.

Potato Gnocchi with Gorgonzola, Leeks, and Spinach

Potato gnocchi are somewhat challenging to make if you didn't grow up with an Italian grandmother. I give a detailed recipe on page 824, but if you don't have the time or inclination to make it yourself, substitute one pound purchased potato gnocchi. In this dish, I combine potent Gorgonzola with Parmigiano-Reggiano or Grana Padano (see Parmigiano and Grana Padano cheeses, page 76); the Parmigiano provides the foundation flavor and mellows out the Gorgonzola.

SERVES 6 AS AN APPETIZER

$1/2$ cup heavy cream

Grated nutmeg and freshly ground black pepper to taste

6 ounces imported Italian Gorgonzola Dolce, trimmed of rind and cut up

2 ounces grated Parmigiano-Reggiano

1 pound potato gnocchi, purchased or homemade (*see* Potato Gnocchi, page 824)

2 leeks, sliced, washed, and drained

1 tablespoon unsalted butter

2 cups baby spinach leaves

In a large skillet, heat the cream, nutmeg and pepper. Simmer 5 minutes or until the cream has thickened slightly. Remove the pan from the heat and stir in both cheeses. Keep stirring until cheeses have just melted, placing pan back on the fire briefly if necessary. Reserve in the pan.

Meanwhile, bring a large pot with a wide surface full of salted water to the boil. Gently drop in the gnocchi and bring back to the boil. Cook over medium heat until the gnocchi float to the surface, and continue cooking 2 to 3 minutes, or until gnocchi are cooked through, with no raw, doughy inside when cut open. Drain the gnocchi using a perforated spoon, rather than dumping them into a colander, because they are quite delicate.

Meanwhile, in a small pan, cook the leeks in the butter until soft and translucent, about 5 minutes. Stir in the spinach leaves, turning them over until just wilted, and then reserve.

Gently spoon the gnocchi into the pan with the Gorgonzola Sauce, add the leeks and spinach and toss lightly to combine, using a wooden spoon or rubber spatula so as not to break up the gnocchi. Serve immediately, preferably in heated pasta bowls.

Iceberg Lettuce and Herb Salad with Stilton Cheese and Tomato

While iceberg lettuce doesn't have much to offer in the way of flavor, it sure is crisp. Here I combine crunchy, water-laden iceberg with tender, fresh herb leaves, nutty-tasting Stilton, and ripe beefsteak tomatoes for a lively salad. Inspired by the classic steakhouse salad of lettuce, blue cheese, tomato, and onion, this one gains another dimension by the addition of fragrant, palate-wakening herbs. Soaking the red onions in ice water makes them extra-crispy and mellows their bite. Tender herbs work best here; other possibilities include dill, chervil, young mint, and marjoram.

SERVES 4 TO 6

1/4 cup Sherry vinegar

1/2 cup extra-virgin olive oil

Kosher salt and freshly ground black pepper, to taste

1 head iceberg lettuce, cut into large squares

1 small red onion, thinly sliced and soaked in ice water
  to cover 15 minutes.

1/4 cup each: basil leaves, Italian parsley leaves,
  and cut chives

2 tablespoons each: tarragon and coriander leaves

1/4 pound Stilton cheese, cut into small cubes

2 large red-ripe beefsteak tomatoes, cored and
  cut into large chunks

Whisk together vinegar, olive oil, salt and pepper and
reserve. In a large mixing bowl, combine lettuce and herb
leaves. Toss lightly with the dressing and divide among 4
large plates. Top each portion with cheese and tomato.
Drain onions, pat dry and sprinkle onto salads.

BUYING AND TRIMMING
BEEF TOP SIRLOIN BUTT STEAKS

The top sirloin butt—yes, it is the butt—is a moderately priced, lean, beefy-tasting favorite among steak
lovers and may be found whole or cut into steaks. A
rather dense, boneless cut, it is well suited to marinades and spice rubs, needs little trimming, and is
suitable for steaks, kabobs, and fajita or saté strips.
Top sirloin steaks increase in size while decreasing in
tenderness as they get closer to the rump end. Steaks
off the front end can be juicy and flavorful; those
from the rump end tend to be chewier and drier.
Center-cut top sirloin butt steaks consist of a single
muscle; others are made up of several muscles.

Pan-Seared Sirloin Steaks with Herb Rub and Cabrales Cheese Topping

*Red meat is a surprising but recurring theme among blue
cheese recipes: grilled flank steak, rib steak, and filet all get
an extra kick from a topping of blue cheese. Here I combine
well-flavored, dense-fleshed sirloin with the wonderfully
nutty and firm blue cheese from Spain called Cabrales. It's
an excellent alternative to Roquefort, produced not that
far away. It's important not to overcook sirloin, because it
can get rather dry and mealy. When cooked to medium-rare
or less, it is a steak lover's dream.*

SERVES 4

2 tablespoon canola oil, divided

1 tablespoon chopped rosemary

2 teaspoons chopped thyme

Kosher salt and freshly ground black pepper to taste

4 (8-ounce) sirloin steaks

1/2 pound Cabrales cheese, trimmed and cut into bits

Combine 1 tablespoon oil, rosemary, thyme, salt and pepper. Rub all over steaks and allow them to rest at room
temperature for about 20 minutes.

Heat remaining 1 tablespoon oil in a large, heavy-bottomed skillet, add beef and brown well on both sides to
desired temperature (rare to medium-rare preferred).
Preheat broiler to high. Transfer steaks to a metal baking
pan and allow them to rest 5 minutes. Top with cheese
and broil for 2 to 3 minutes, or until cheese is bubbling.
Serve immediately.

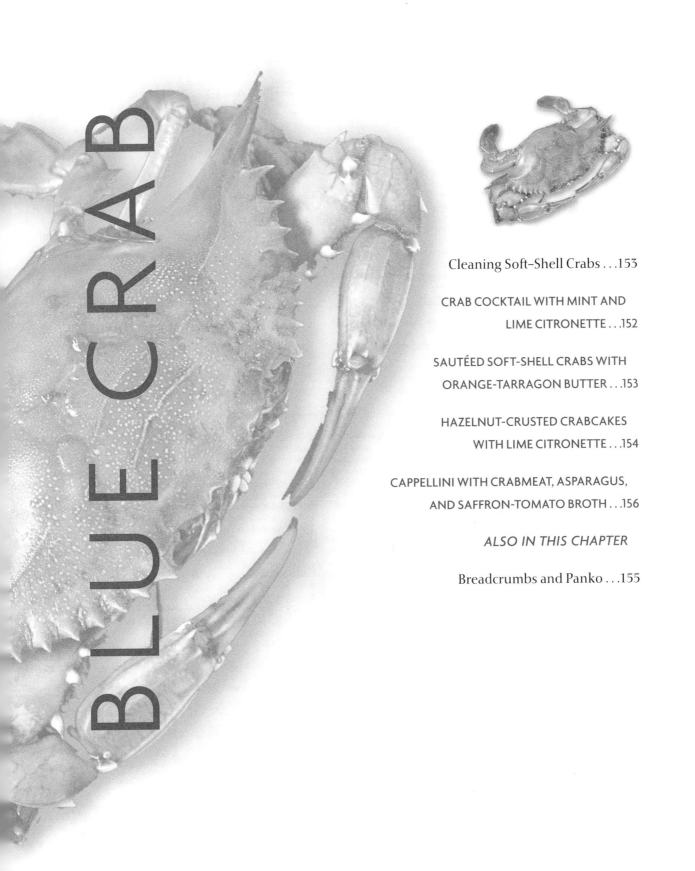

BLUE CRAB

BLUE CRAB

Brilliant white in color, mild and sweet in flavor, tender and succulent in texture, this can only be the East Coast's exquisite summertime delicacy, the blue crab. Its Latin name, *Callinectes sapidus*, tells us the essentials. *Callinectes* is Greek for beautiful swimmer; *sapidus* means tasty or savory in Latin. One of many species of edible crab worldwide, the blue crab can be found from Canada to South America and is harvested commercially from New Jersey to Texas.

As a crab lover, I am certainly not alone, because more than 60 million pounds of blue crabs were harvested from Chesapeake Bay in 2004. The "watermen" (the fishermen of the Chesapeake) harvest these wildly popular crustaceans at three stages in their lives: as adult hard shells, as peelers (just prior to molting, or shedding their shells), and then again just after they molt, as luscious soft-shell crabs. If you'd like to explore the fascinating life and lore of the blue crab and the Chesapeake watermen, pick up a copy of William Warner's classic Pulitzer Prize-winning book, *Beautiful Swimmers*.

Most of Chesapeake Bay's crabs are hard-shells sold by the bushel to restaurants or at streetside "crab shacks" for crab boil parties. Big, hard crabs sold by the bushel don't bring much money to the watermen, so another portion of the catch ends up steamed at picking houses where skilled hand-pickers, most of them women with their smaller hands, painstakingly remove the meat from frustratingly thin and brittle shells. Next it is packed into plastic containers for sale as fresh crabmeat (jumbo, lump, backfin, or claw) or pasteurized in cans. The most common type sold in retail markets, canned crab, is less desirable because the meat tends to get stringy after cooking in high-pressure retorts for canning, although the quality has improved.

Crab season, called "the run" or "the rush", usually starts in April in the shallow coastal bays and sounds of the Carolinas, moving up through the Chesapeake, cresting throughout its Tangier Sound by mid-May and reaching nearly to New England before it ends. Tinged with crimson and cerulean blue on their claws, blue crabs by the millions make their way up from their winter homes in the muddy bottom all the way up the coast.

The blue crab fishery has a venerable history in the Chesapeake Bay, with towns like St. Michael and Crisfield settled as far back as the early sixteenth century, but demand has grown dramatically in recent years. The market seems to have no limit. Crabs are getting harder to come by, not just because of a scarcity of crabs, but because more people want to eat them more often.

Fishermen on the Chesapeake pull drags along the shallow, muddy bottom of the bay's 9,000-mile in-and-out shoreline, popping crabs from their resting places. To catch crabs ready to molt (shed their outgrown shells), the watermen bait underwater traps with big male crabs.

Blue crabs mate from May through October when mature females are ready to mate after their winter spent in the mud. However, crabs can mate only when they are soft, so they must first shed their shells. Near to shedding time, the females swim upstream along the trail of pheromones released by the captured male, into the trap and are captured themselves.

Females swelled by eggs attached to the U-shaped aprons on their undersides are called "sponge crabs". The females release their eggs at the mouth of the Bay, where they float around until they are blown back into Chesapeake Bay. Then the eggs begin their movement back up the Chesapeake, subject to sea and tides. They may settle out in seagrass beds as they continue their evolution into adult blue crabs, a process that may take one year to eighteen months.

Over its two- to three-year life span, the blue crab (actually blue only on its claws with an olive-green top shell and a white underbelly) outgrows and sheds its shell about twenty times. Once the crab has molted, the new shell takes about four days to harden. Just after shedding, the blue crab's shell is soft enough to eat; that's when it's time for our annual rite: soft-shell season.

More than ninety percent of the nation's soft-shells comes from the 3,200 square miles of the Chesapeake Bay shared by Maryland and Virginia, where they fetch a much higher price than hard-shells. Watermen harvest the crabs as "peelers" (about to shed), "rank peelers" (within hours of shedding) and "busters" (in the process of shedding). Shedding crabs are stored until they're soft and then shipped to market on a bed of ice and cool sea grass. Because of the extreme perishability of the soft-shell, they must be alive until just before cooking.

Soft-shell crabs are almost entirely edible; their salty, sweet taste is redolent of the shallow marshes where they grow. Soft-shells can be rather intimidating to the uninitiated, but once you savor your first soft-shell, you'll be hooked (or netted). Soft-shell crabs are not separated by sex but by size. The largest soft-shells are called whales, next are jumbos, then primes, and the smaller hotels, usually the ones found for sale in retail markets.

To insure a healthy population of crabs, any crab, whether male or female, must measure at least five-inches across the top or it must be released. For hard-shell and picking crabs, the larger and therefore meatier and more desirable males are termed "jimmies". To tell female crabs from male crabs, turn them over so that you can see their "apron", the rounded section that ends with a prong or tab shape. The apron of the "jimmy" is T-shaped and is attached to the body and the prong shaped and narrow. On a young female or "she-crab", the apron is triangular in shape and is attached to the body. A mature female crab, or a "sook", has a semi-circular apron that is free of the bottom shell.

In the winter, the female crabs carry their roe—tiny orange eggs that account for the delicate color and flavor of classic Charleston She-Crab Soup. This soup recipe came about at a time when crabs were abundant. Today, to conserve the blue crab population and ensure their future, it is now illegal to harvest pregnant females with their eggs showing in a sponge-like protrusion on the underside of their bodies. The soup is now made with females whose roe are on the inside, not yet visible.

In the Chesapeake, blue crabs are a matter of pride; in Philadelphia, crabs are a matter of fiendish loyalty and fierce arguments. A good portion of the Chesapeake catch ends up on the plates of Philadelphia diners who seem insatiable in their appetite for blue crabs. In Italian

151

South Philly, hard-shell crabs simmered in spicy red sauce are served over spaghetti. In restaurants from Manayunk to Old City, soft-shell crabs are floured and pan-fried or battered and deep-fried for a scrumptious rich, melt-in-the-mouth tender indulgence.

Crab Cocktail with Mint and Lime Citronette

Buy the best-quality crab for this crab "cocktail". Pick it carefully by rolling each chunk of crabmeat lightly using your fingertips to locate any errant shell pieces. Break the crabmeat up as little as possible for best appearance. The chayote called for here is a type of squash, light green in color with a crispy, juicy texture when raw. Chayote is also called christophene (in the Caribbean) and mirliton (in Louisiana). Look for it in well-stocked supermarkets, and Asian and Latino markets (see Chayote and Avocado Salad with Salsa, page 87).

Serves 6

$1/4$ cup freshly squeezed lime juice

$1/4$ cup extra-virgin olive oil

Kosher salt and freshly ground black pepper to taste

1 pound jumbo-lump crabmeat, cleaned

1 chayote squash, peeled and cut into julienne strips

1 red pepper, cut into julienne strips

1 bunch chives, thinly sliced

2 tablespoons shredded mint

Mint sprigs for garnish

Whisk together lime juice, olive oil, salt and black pepper and reserve.

Combine crabmeat, chayote, red pepper, chives, and mint with dressing. Divide into six portions. Place in stem glasses such as wine goblets or martini glasses and serve chilled with a mint sprig for garnish.

Sautéed Soft-Shell Crabs with Orange-Tarragon Butter

Soft-shell crabs are wonderful to eat once you've gotten beyond the fear of biting into that whole animal. If you're like me, after bravely eating your first soft-shell crab, you'll be hooked. The tender and sweet meat bursts into your mouth with sweet, ocean-scented juice. The next scary thing is to learn how to clean soft-shells (or have your friendly fishmonger do it for you). Even pros can be intimidated by this procedure, though actually you can clean soft-shells in less time than it takes to explain the process (see Cleaning soft-shell crabs, at right).

SERVES 4

8 soft-shell crabs, cleaned

Kosher salt and freshly ground black pepper to taste

$1/2$ cup canola oil, divided

1 cup flour, for dusting

2 cups orange juice

$1/2$ cup Orange-Tarragon Butter

Sprinkle the soft-shells with salt and pepper. Heat half the oil in a large skillet, preferably nonstick. Dust each crab with flour and then sauté in hot oil starting with the upper-side down. (Stand clear because soft-shells tend to pop and splatter.) When the crabs are well browned, turn them over and cook on the second side. Remove from the pan, drain on paper towels, and keep in a warm place. Repeat with the second batch of crabs.

Pour off any excess oil from the pan. Add the orange juice and boil until syrupy. Add the crabs back into the pan along with the Orange-Tarragon Butter and swirl to combine.

Orange-Tarragon Butter

$1/2$ pound (2 sticks) unsalted butter, cut up and softened

Zest of 1 orange

1 bunch tarragon, leaves picked and roughly-chopped

Process butter with orange zest until smooth and creamy. Add tarragon and process until combined. Refrigerate or freeze, well-wrapped.

CLEANING SOFT-SHELL CRABS

Before anything, make sure the crabs are alive; they should wave their claws about. Note that if kept too cold, the crabs can die. The ideal temperature to store them is about 50°F. and they should be protected by layers of dampened newspaper.

Turn the crabs over so their undersides face you and their claws face away from you. Lift up the "tab" from the large, triangular apron shell and bend back. Twist and pull back to remove both the apron shell and the underlying intestinal vein at the same time.

Lift up the edges of the top shell. Scrape away and discard the inedible spongy "dead-man's fingers" (actually the gills) from both sides of the crab.

Lastly, slice off the front $1/4$- to $1/2$-inch strip at the front of the crab, including its eyes. Squeeze out the greenish bubble from behind the eyes and rinse the crabs in cold water.

Pat the crabs dry with a paper towel. Cover and refrigerate until you're ready to cook the crabs, which should be within 24 hours.

153

Hazelnut–Crusted Crabcakes with Lime Citronette

Crabcakes inspire endless arguments among opinionated aficionados but no matter what style you prefer, the best crabcakes start with the best crabmeat: jumbo lump, large meaty chunks of crab extracted from the body rather than the claws and packed fresh in one-pound plastic containers. Although all crabcakes must be made with some kind of binder to stick it all together, the less used, the better the cake. Baltimore-style crabcakes are bound with mayonnaise, breadcrumbs, or cracker crumbs, and Baltimore's classic Old Bay seasoning (a mixture of many spices, though celery salt dominates). Here I bind the crabcakes with a mixture of breadcrumbs, eggs, and sour cream and then roll them in breadcrumbs mixed with hazelnuts to make a crunchy crust and serve it with a lime and Dijon mustard dressing. The crabcakes can be formed a day ahead of time. Any extra dressing is delicious on grilled fish, steamed green beans, broccoli, or asparagus.

SERVES 6

Crust Mixture

2 cups hazelnuts
2 cups Japanese panko breadcrumbs

Process together hazelnuts and the panko and reserve.

Crabcakes

½ cup Japanese panko breadcrumbs
2 eggs
¼ cup sour cream
2 teaspoons kosher salt
¼ teaspoon freshly ground black pepper
2 teaspoons Spanish pimentón (or paprika)
Zest and juice of 1 lemon
1 small head fennel
1 tablespoon canola oil
1 bunch scallions, thinly sliced
2 pounds jumbo-lump crabmeat, picked over for shells

Whisk together breadcrumbs, eggs, sour cream, salt, pepper, pimentón, lemon zest, and lemon juice and reserve.

Cut up the fennel and then process it to a chunky paste or chop by hand. Sauté the fennel in the oil until transparent and slightly soft. Cool and then stir into breadcrumb mixture along with the scallions. Using a light hand, fold in the crabmeat.

Spread out about one-fourth of the crust mixture onto a baking pan. Scoop crabcake mixture into 4-ounce balls and lay into a separate pan filled with crumbs. Pat crumbs around outside of balls and form into hockey-puck-shaped disks. To make the cakes even and firm, use a 3-inch steel ring or a tuna can cut out at both ends to help shape the cakes and place them onto a wax-paper-covered pan. Cover and keep refrigerated until ready to cook, up to one day later.

Lime Citronette

¼ cup roughly chopped shallots
2 tablespoons chopped tarragon
¼ cup fresh lime juice
Finely grated zest of half a lime
2 tablespoons Dijon mustard
¾ cup extra-virgin olive oil
Kosher salt and freshly ground black pepper to taste

Blend shallots, tarragon, lime juice, zest, and mustard. Slowly pour in olive oil until thick and creamy. Season with salt and pepper.

Assembly

½ cup canola oil

12 crabcakes

Preheat the oven to 400°F. Heat oil until shimmering, preferably in a large nonstick skillet. Brown crabcakes well on bottom side before turning (using spatula). Brown again on second side, then transfer to a baking pan and finish cooking in the oven for about 10 minutes, or until firm but not at all dry.

Drizzle Lime Citronette over crabcakes just before serving.

BREADCRUMBS AND PANKO

There's a big difference in your results depending on what kind of breadcrumbs you choose. Homemade crumbs are always best and should be made from day-old bread with the crusts cut off. For the best crabcakes, process firm white sandwich bread (such as Pepperidge Farm's) and use for the binding; for crunchy texture, process stale baguettes, sourdough bread, or ciabatta bread. If you'd like, lightly brown the crumbs in olive oil with a little crushed garlic and use the crumbs Sicilian style instead of cheese when dressing pasta. For rich, soft texture, process brioche or challah bread. Commercial crumbs are generally quite fine in texture and include the crust of the bread so they turn dark easily if used for frying.

The best all-around type of breadcrumb to use is Japanese panko, made in a special process so that they are entirely white with a coarsely shredded flake-like consistency. Panko is used in Japan to give a specially crunchy coating that resists getting soggy. Because of its pure white color, foods breaded with panko can be fried longer without over-darkening. Panko is available in Asian markets and most supermarkets and is quite inexpensive.

155

Cappellini with Crabmeat, Asparagus, and Saffron–Tomato Broth

Crabmeat and asparagus go very well together. Here, they are mixed with a saffron-infused white wine and tomato sauce, with bottled clam broth added to accent the taste of the sea. Pernod, the Provençal licorice and anise-based drink, is wonderful with seafood, especially any dish with a Mediterranean character like this one. Cappellini (or angel hair) pasta works best with very liquid sauces, because it has a large surface area to absorb the sauce. The hair-like fine pasta would break up if mixed with a heavier sauce. One pound of crabmeat will suffice, but an extra half pound is even better.

SERVES 4

1 cup white wine

1 large pinch crushed saffron threads

2 tablespoons Pernod

2 cups bias-sliced asparagus

1 cup sliced scallions

$1/4$ cup extra-virgin olive oil

1 cup tomato sauce, purchased or homemade (*see* Marinara Sauce, page 895)

$1/2$ cup bottled clam broth

1 to $1^1/2$ pounds jumbo lump crabmeat

1 pound pasta cappellini

Combine the white wine, saffron, and Pernod and allow saffron to soak for about 15 minutes or until the liquid is golden in color.

Bring a pot of salted water to the boil.

Meanwhile, sauté the asparagus and scallions in olive oil. Add the saffron-wine mix, the tomato sauce, and clam broth to the pan and bring to the boil. Remove the pan from the stove, add crabmeat and reserve.

Meanwhile, cook the cappellini until *al dente*, firm and bouncy, and still yellow in color, about 2 to 3 minutes. Drain and toss with the sauce.

Serve in a large pasta bowl (preferably heated), making sure that crabmeat and asparagus shows on top of pasta.

BROCCOLI & CAULIFLOWER

BROCCOLI & CAULIFLOWER

Broccoli

Shortly after becoming president, George H. Bush declared, "No more broccoli on the White House menu," infuriating broccoli growers who sent tons of the vegetable to the White House in a humorous protest; broccoli was also forbidden on the Air Force One menu. I say, what's not to like? Broccoli is mild in flavor, appealingly firm without being fibrous, easy to prepare, versatile in the kitchen, not to mention reasonably priced and available year-round in every supermarket. Steamed and served with a Maltese Sauce, a blood orange-infused hollandaise, it is a classic. Served Italian style with an anchovy and lemon sauce, it plays with the palate. And my favorite member of this family, broccoli rabe, is a bold, pleasingly bitter vegetable that marries best with mild foods like pasta, or as in my recipe, with breaded fried chicken cutlets in a South Philadelphia-style sandwich.

Broccoli, *Brassica oleracea*, is a deep emerald-green vegetable that is part of the huge *Brassica* (or mustard) family and comes in tight clusters of tiny buds that sit on stout, edible stems. Broccoli's name comes from the Italian for "little arms of cabbage" and it is basically a cabbage in which flowers have begun to form but have stopped growing while still in bud. In spite of how immensely popular broccoli has become since it began to be commercially grown in California in the 1920s (where 90 percent of the crop is grown), America raises only green broccoli. Purple, green, or white flower heads may be found elsewhere. The main variety of broccoli grown in the U.S. is Calabrese—the name used for broccoli in Britain, deriving from the southern Italian province of Calabria.

CHOOSING BROCCOLI

Look for broccoli with tight, compact bud clusters with an even deep green color, or green tinged with purple. The buds should be tightly closed and the leaves crisp with stems that are a lighter green than the buds, relatively thin and easy to pierce with a fingernail. As broccoli grows, the stalks become larger and tougher. Avoid broccoli with large, thick, whitish rather than green stalks because they will be tough and woody with strong tasting florets. Stalks with yellowed or open bud clusters and stems will be hard and dry.

Broccoli and Friends

Broccoflower: Broccoflower is a hybrid mix of cauliflower and broccoli. The florets are bright green (lighter than broccoli) and packed into a round head like cauliflower. Its flavor and use are somewhere between broccoli and cauliflower.

Broccoli Romanesco: Broccoli Romanesco, common around Rome and just starting be found in the U.S., matures later in the year and displays distinctive yellow-green pointed spiral cones that are so other worldly looking, it's hard to believe it is simply a vegetable. Like broccoflower, its flavor and use are somewhere between broccoli and cauliflower.

Broccoli Rabe: Broccoli Rabe, meaning "turnip-broccoli" in Italian, is a nonheading variety of broccoli—also known as *broccoletti di rape*, *brocoletto*, *cima di rabe*, or *rapini*—that resembles broccoli florets on long, thin stems. Prized in Southern Italy and increasingly well-known in the U.S., where it was planted by immigrant Italian farmers, it has a bitter but zesty flavor and intense deep green color. Rapini is almost (or exactly) the same as broccoli rabe, depending on who you talk to. Small local farmers often sell what they call rapini, which consists mostly of leaves and with few of the florets that characterize broccoli rabe. It is closer in taste and use to mustard greens.

Chinese Broccoli: Chinese broccoli has broad, glossy, blue-green leaves with long, crisp, thick stems and a small head. Its flavor is similar to, though juicier and more tender than, broccoli.

Broccolini®: Broccolini is a trademarked name for Asparation or baby broccoli, a new hybrid that is a cross between broccoli and Chinese kale. Broccolini has a long, slender stem, reminiscent of asparagus, topped with small flowering buds that resemble a cross between broccoli florets and an asparagus tip. It is on the expensive side because of limited supply. Two California growers produce the vegetable, the Mann Packing Company which calls it "broccolini," and Sanbon Incorporated, which calls it "Asparation," the original name given to it by the plant's developer, the Sakata Seed company of Yokohama, Japan.

CHOOSING BROCCOLI RABE AND RAPINI

At the market, you'll usually find broccoli rabe sprinkled with ice because it yellows easily. Choose firm, green, small stems with compact heads and an abundance of florets with tightly closed dark green flower buds. "Andy Boy" is the brand of choice. Because it is quite perishable, sniff the stalks where they are tied together and avoid if it has an unpleasantly sharp, mustardy smell. Avoid rabe with yellowed flowers or stalks that are heavily split at the bottom, a sign of age. Choose firm rapini with relatively few buds and flowers. In hot summer weather, all members of the broccoli family tend to deteriorate.

Refrigerate all members of the broccoli family, unwashed, in a plastic bag in the refrigerator for up to 4 days. If the stalks are tough, peel before cooking. Broccoli rabe may be wrapped first in a wet paper towel to prevent wilting. It will keep up to two days refrigerated.

For Chinese broccoli, remove leaves and flower buds, and peel stems because the outer layer can be quite fibrous. Chop stems, leaves and buds before cooking.

For broccoli rabe, cut off the bottoms of the stalks (they're too tough to eat). Slice across into 1-to 2-inch lengths for ease of cooking. To cut down on bitterness, boil briefly in salted water for 2 to 3 minutes. Drain, rinse under cold running water to set the color and then drain and proceed with cooking.

For broccoli, boil stalks 3 to 4 minutes, florets for 1 to 1½ minutes; steam 5 to 6 minutes for stalks, 2 to 3 minutes for florets. Don't neglect the stalks; just peel and slice and add to the pot or use for stir-fries.

160

SEASON FOR BROCCOLI AND FRIENDS

Broccoli is available year-round, with peak season from October through April. Broccoli rabe is most plentiful between late fall and early spring, but is usually available year-round, except for the hottest summer months when you might find locally grown rabe in farmer's markets. Rapini is available from California August through March. Broccoli Romanesco may occasionally be found in American markets or at farmer's markets in early fall. Chinese broccoli is grown all year round in California. Broccolini and/or Asparation is occasionally available throughout the year.

Cauliflower

Cauliflower, *Brassica oleracea Botrytis group*, is basically white broccoli. Say cauliflower in French—*chou-fleur* (cabbage flower)—and it automatically becomes charming and attractive. So many food words sound so much better in French. Would you rather eat fat liver or *foie gras*? Call it a *ragout* and your plain old stew becomes something much more elegant and of course, anything sautéed is fancier than if it's merely pan-fried. *Mon petit chou*, a term of endearment in French, definitely loses its charm when translated to "my little cabbage".

In the sixteenth century, cauliflower (or cabbage flower) imported to Europe from the East, became the rage at the French court, served up in rich dishes with cream, sweetbreads, mushrooms, foie gras and truffles. In French cuisine, any dish described as "à la Du Barry"—named for the Comtesse du Barry, the favorite of King Louis the XV—invariably contains cauliflower.

Travel eastward to Egypt, Lebanon, and India, and

Choosing Cauliflower

Look for bright white, crispy heads with firm, green leaves surrounding the head. Old cauliflower will have tiny black mold spots on the white florets, with yellowed leaves.

bold flavors bring excitement to this mild, self-effacing vegetable. It's no wonder cauliflower is prepared in so many imaginative ways in the Eastern Mediterranean. This is the part of the world it was were first grown—perhaps in Cyprus—although no one is sure when. By the Middle Ages, Arab growers had highly developed cauliflower varieties. Even three hundred years ago, the best seeds for cauliflower came from the fabled Syrian culinary capital of Aleppo.

Growing cauliflower is demanding. Because of its delicate nature, much of the work of planting and harvesting must be done by hand. It must be protected from the sun to keep it creamy white by preventing the development of green chlorophyll. In older varieties, the farmer had to carefully tie the leaves over the cauliflower to keep the sun out. In modern cauliflower varieties, the leaves wrap over the flower portion on their own.

William Woys Weaver in his *Heirloom Vegetable Gardening* tells us, "In the nineteenth century, Suffolk County on Long Island was well known as the 'Cauliflower County' and from there the very best cauliflower grown in this country originated. . . . Cauliflower was a vegetable created by hands. It was a vegetable luxury, like a fine piece of furniture, or a hand-woven cloak." These days, most American cauliflower is grown in the coastal deserts of California. In the summer months, cauliflower still comes from Long Island, along with upper New York State and Michigan. Cauliflower grown in Ontario, Quebec, and the Maritime Provinces comes into the U.S. in season from Canada.

Cauliflower is a member of the *Brassica* family, along with its green cousin, broccoli. Like broccoli, cauliflower flowers have begun to form but have stopped growing at the bud stage. The thick stems under the buds store the nutrients, which would have gone into the flowers and eventually their fruits. Because of that, cauliflower is rich in vitamins and minerals. One serving of cauliflower can provide the entire daily requirement of Vitamin C and is also an excellent source of folic acid and dietary fiber.

According to British culinarian, Jane Grison, "A fresh cauliflower of quality looks and smells beautiful. The ones I like best are covered with a mass of creamy pointed whorls, gently studding the whole surface."

PREPARING CAULIFLOWER

Pull off and discard the green leaves, exposing the stem and core. Using a small, sharp paring knife, cut around the core in a cone shape, pull it out and discard. Separate the florets by cutting them apart. The outer florets will be larger and should be cut in halves or quarters; the inner florets will be grouped together on small stems and should be cut into matching sizes. While many recipes call for precooking the cauliflower, I prefer to cook it once only. The pleasing, slightly crunchy flavor is fresher tasting and less "cabbagy" when it is cooked briefly. To tone down the odor when cooking cauliflower, add celery seeds or leaves to the pot.

161

Broccoli Maltese

Maltese sauce is named for the small isolated island of Malta in the central Mediterranean, not too far from Sicily, where blood oranges grow abundantly. A hint of nutmeg enhances the aroma. Maltese sauce goes very well with fish and shell-fish and, although it is traditional for asparagus, it accents crisp-tender, bluish-green broccoli spears beautifully.

SERVES 4 TO 6

$^1/_2$ cup blood orange juice (freshly squeezed or
 purchased in bottles)
Grated zest of 1 blood orange (substitute zest of 1 orange)
2 tablespoons chopped shallots
1 teaspoon black peppercorns
2 egg yolks
$^1/_2$ pound (2 sticks) unsalted butter, melted and hot
Kosher salt, freshly ground black pepper, nutmeg,
 and cayenne pepper to taste
1 head broccoli, cut into small florets or spears
1 blood orange, cut into segments

In a small nonreactive saucepan, combine the blood orange juice and zest, shallots, and peppercorns and place over medium-high heat. Bring to a boil and cook down until syrupy, about 4 minutes. Remove from the heat and strain through a sieve into a medium Pyrex or metal bowl. Whisk in the egg yolks.

Set the bowl over a pan of simmering water (without the bowl touching the water) and whisk until the egg starts to thicken, about 2 to 3 minutes. Set the bowl to the side of the heat and slowly drizzle in about half the butter, whisking vigorously to incorporate. Return the bowl to the heat, whisk again, and when the egg starts to thicken again, whisk in the remaining butter, pulling the pan off the heat if the mixture starts getting too hot. Remove the sauce from the heat and season with salt, black pepper, nutmeg and cayenne to taste.

Meanwhile, steam the broccoli until brilliant green and crisp-tender, about 5 minutes. Drain well, patting dry with paper towels. Drizzle sauce over broccoli and garnish with blood orange segments.

Broccoli with Lemon–Anchovy Sauce

Broccoli is rather mild in flavor with a firm and pleasing tex-ture. It contrasts well with the bracing lemon and anchovy sauce here. Broccoli florets, the smaller side shoots that grow off the main stalk, are commonly found in supermar-kets at a lower price than the stalks. I always choose them, as long as their quality is good. Because they are more del-icate, the florets don't last quite as long as the stalks, but, for the same reason, they have excellent flavor and tender texture and don't need any peeling.

SERVES 4 TO 6

1 egg
4 anchovy fillets
Juice of 1 lemon
1 cup olive oil
$^1/_2$ cup oil-cured black olives, pitted and chopped
2 tablespoons capers, drained
1 head broccoli, cut into small florets or spears

162

Prepare the sauce as for a mayonnaise. Place the egg, anchovies, and lemon juice in the jar of a blender. Blend until smooth, then slowly pour in the olive oil until the sauce has thickened. Stir in the olives and capers and reserve.

Steam the broccoli until brilliant green and crisp-tender, about 5 minutes. Drain well, patting dry with paper towels. Drizzle sauce over broccoli.

Philadelphia Chicken Cutlet Sandwich with Broccoli Rabe

Go to sandwich shops like Tony Luke's in the Italian area of South Philadelphia or to Rocco's at Reading Terminal Market and you'll find great versions of this not-to-be-missed fried, breaded chicken cutlet, sharp provolone, and broccoli rabe sandwich. Although the steak sandwich (see Philadelphia Steak Sandwich, page 111) is more famous, I'd choose this Italian-style sandwich first any day. The fried long green Italian peppers are optional, but I always add them. They are normally not trimmed or seeded in Philadelphia, but you are welcome to do so.

SERVES 6

2 eggs, lightly beaten

$1/4$ cup milk

Kosher salt and freshly ground black pepper, to taste

$1/4$ teaspoon each: grated nutmeg and cayenne pepper

1 cup all-purpose flour

3 cups Japanese panko breadcrumbs

1 pound chicken cutlets

1 cup canola oil for frying

6 hot Italian frying peppers (optional)

1 bunch broccoli rabe, 1-inch cut off and discarded from the bottom, and sliced into $1/2$-inch lengths

6 long Italian rolls (hoagie rolls)

$1/2$ pound sharp provolone shredded

In a medium bowl, lightly beat together the eggs, milk, salt, pepper, nutmeg and cayenne. Place the flour in a second bowl and the breadcrumbs in a third bowl. Dip the cutlets, one at a time into the flour, shaking off the excess. Next, dip the cutlets into the egg, then coat with breadcrumbs. Arrange the cutlets on a wax paper-lined baking sheet in a single layer without touching each other and chill in the refrigerator to set coating about 30 minutes (or up to 1 day ahead).

When ready to cook, heat the oil in a heavy skillet or a wok until lively bubbles form when a cutlet is placed in the oil. Fry the chicken for about 5 minutes or until golden brown on all sides. Drain on a wire rack and reserve. Drain off most of the oil, then add the frying peppers and cook until peppers are tender and collapsed. Drain and reserve.

Meanwhile, bring a large pot of salted water to the boil. Add the broccoli rabe and cook 3 to 4 minutes or until crisp-tender. Drain and reserve, keeping warm.

Preheat the oven to 400°F. Open up the rolls. Lay 1 to 2 chicken cutlets in each roll, top with a frying pepper, spread with a layer of broccoli rabe, and top with shredded cheese. Arrange rolls on a baking sheet and bake about 5 minutes or until the cheese melts. Close rolls, pressing together to keep them closed and slice in half. Serve immediately.

163

Crunchy Fried Cauliflower with Pomegranate Sauce

The Indians and the Arabs know how to cook cauliflower properly without overcooking, taking best advantage of its mild, creamy, yet firm texture. My favorite way with cauliflower is to bread and pan-fry it, so that all its delicate flavor is retained on the inside with the crunchy outside providing that all-important contrast of texture. Here I serve the fried cauliflower with a simple, tartly delicious sauce made from pomegranate molasses. Although it is called molasses, this syrup is not at all sweet; it is made from the juice of special tart varieties of pomegranate cooked way down until the consistency is similar to that of molasses. Easily found in Middle Eastern groceries, it will keep indefinitely and is quite inexpensive. (Try using it instead of vinegar for your next vinaigrette dressing.)

Crunchy Fried Cauliflower

1 cup all-purpose flour
2 eggs, lightly beaten
1/4 cup milk
Kosher salt and freshly ground black pepper, to taste
1/4 teaspoon each: grated nutmeg and cayenne pepper
3 cups Japanese Panko breadcrumbs
1 head cauliflower, cut up into florets about 1 inch all around
2 cups canola oil for frying
Pomegranate Sauce (recipe follows)

Place the flour in a bowl. In a second bowl lightly beat together the eggs, milk, salt, pepper, nutmeg and cayenne, and place the breadcrumbs in a third bowl. Dip the florets, one at a time first into the flour, shaking off the excess. Next dip the florets into the egg mixture, letting the excess liquid drip off, and finally coat evenly with the breadcrumbs. Arrange the florets on a wax-paper-lined baking sheet in a single layer without touching each other and chill in the refrigerator to set coating about 30 minutes (or up to 2 days ahead).

When ready to cook, heat the oil in a heavy skillet or a wok until lively bubbles form when a piece of cauliflower is placed in the oil. Fry the florets in small batches, for about 5 minutes or until golden brown on all sides. Drain on a wire rack, keeping warm in a 200°F. oven until all the cauliflower is done. Sprinkle with salt and pepper before serving with Pomegranate Sauce.

Pomegranate Sauce

1 teaspoon finely chopped garlic
2 tablespoons pomegranate molasses
6 tablespoons extra-virgin olive oil

Whisk together (or blend) the garlic, pomegranate molasses, and olive oil until thick and creamy and reserve at room temperature.

Egyptian Cauliflower in Garlicky Tomato Sauce

Back in my early days as a budding cook, I had little funds for the cookbooks I loved (and still love) to read for inspiration, information, and recipes to try. One of the handful on my shelf in those years was Claudia Roden's wonderful A Book of Middle Eastern Food, with its charming drawings and outstanding recipes from the part of the world whose cuisine I still adore. This is my adaptation of her recipe that I still make and enjoy thirty years later. My dog-eared, stained copy of her book still has an honored place on my shelves.

SERVES 6

2 tablespoons extra-virgin olive oil
6 cloves garlic, cut into slivers
1 (28-ounce) can tomato puree
$1/4$ cup chopped Italian parsley
Kosher salt to taste
Crunchy Fried Cauliflower (*see* previous page)
Freshly ground black pepper

In a large skillet, heat the olive oil over moderate heat, then add the garlic. Fry until light golden brown, taking care not to allow the garlic to get overly dark (which will make it bitter). Add the tomato puree along with 1 cup of water, half the parsley and salt and bring the sauce to a boil.

Reduce the heat to a simmer and drop in the fried breaded florets. Simmer together for 20 minutes or until the sauce is thick enough to coat the cauliflower.

Transfer to a serving dish and sprinkle with the remaining chopped parsley and freshly ground black pepper and serve immediately.

Cauliflower Polonaise

Any dish that is called "á la Polonaise" in French cuisine has this garnish of butter-toasted breadcrumbs and chopped hard-cooked egg. Although other vegetables (like asparagus) are served in this style, somehow it just works perfectly with cauliflower. Here I toast homemade white breadcrumbs in butter for the extra-nutty, buttery-good flavor.

SERVES 4 TO 6

4 tablespoons unsalted butter
$1/2$ cup fresh white breadcrumbs, made from country-style bread or baguette
1 head cauliflower, broken into florets
2 hard-cooked eggs, shelled and chopped fine
$1/4$ cup finely chopped Italian parsley
$1/4$ teaspoon each: grated nutmeg and cayenne pepper
Kosher salt and freshly ground black pepper, to taste
6 lemon wedges

In a small pan, melt the butter and add the breadcrumbs. Cook over low heat, stirring constantly until golden brown.

Separately, steam the cauliflower over boiling water until crisp-tender, about 6 minutes. Drain well and add to the pan with the crumbs. Toss together to heat and lightly brown the cauliflower. Add the eggs, parsley, and seasonings and toss together again. Serve immediately with lemon wedges for garnish.

165

How to hard–cook, not boil, eggs

I never boil eggs, instead I hard-cook them in hot water resulting in creamy, not rubbery eggs. Place the eggs in a heavy saucepan, cover them with cold water, add salt (to help the shells separate from the egg), cover and bring to the boil. Boil for 1 minute, then turn off the heat. Let the eggs set in the covered pot of hot water for 8 to 10 minutes. Test by lightly cracking the shell all over. If the center feels liquidy, the yolk is not set. The yolks should feel soft but not mushy. Drain off the water and run the eggs under cold water to stop the cooking process. Store in the refrigerator up to 3 days.

166

BUTTER

BUTTER

One of the first things I learned as a chef was how dangerous my job could be to my waistline. After a few forays into a new size range for my wardrobe, I knew I had to get a handle (not a lovehandle; I already had those) on my eating habits. So, I learned the difference between tasting and eating: one is a bite, the other is a meal. I still indulged in rich foods, but I became very selective. I wouldn't waste calories on mediocrity. If I was going to eat it, it would have to be real, like butter.

I use pure butter for almost everything I bake, never shortening or margarine. Nothing else tastes like butter, performs like butter, or holds flavor better than butter. That's why it's so indispensable to chefs. Yes, it's high in calories, but I cook and bake with butter to get the most "bang for my buck".

The Normans first popularized buttermaking, from methods learned from the Danes, a people to whom dairying was long central to survival. By the middle ages, butter production had become common. Normandy is the center for the best butter in France, made from ripened cream, giving it a distinctive full flavor and ultra-smooth texture. This butter is also less watery than ours, making it preferable for pastry making. American butter is about 80 percent clear yellow butterfat, 18 percent water, and 2 percent milk solids; European butter and European-style butter (like Plugra) is higher in butterfat (and lower in moisture), making for lighter pastry and

cakes that rise higher. It also doesn't burn as easily, so you can cook at higher heat.

Shortening and margarine are just as calorific, but don't have the innate richly subtle, mouth-melting quality of butter. If I'm going to indulge in a buttercream-iced cake, I want to make sure it's made from real butter. I won't waste my calories on some fake "butter" sold to bakeries because it's cheap and never spoils. Butter is a very rich natural food with a high energy value. It has 750 calories per 100 grams, or about 100 calories per tablespoon, less than oil or lard, with Plugra at 130 grams per tablespoon. Like other animal fats, butter is saturated, meaning that it is solid at room temperature.

Table butter is emulsified (just like mayonnaise, hollandaise, peanut butter, and even soap). This sounds complicated, but it just means that the liquid portion is suspended in the fat, giving it a creamy, smooth consistency. You can make your own butter (on purpose or by accident) by beating heavy cream until the butterfat separates from the whey. If you beat ice-cold cream, you'll end up with a bowl of light, white clouds. If the cream is on the warm side, or the day is hot and humid, you might very well end up with a clump of yellow butter floating in milky liquid instead. Drain off the buttermilk, and voilà! You have just created butter. When the cream is cold, the globules of butterfat stay suspended in the milk. If it's warm, the fat molecules will start to clump

168

together, separating out of its suspension in the cream.

The color of butter ranges from creamy white to deeper golden yellow depending on the cow's diet. Nowadays, our butter is blended, so seasonal and regional changes are much less noticeable. Yellow butter comes from milk from a cow eating a diet rich in carotene. Note that butter absorbs unwanted flavors and odors easily, so keep it tightly covered and away from strong smells. It freezes especially well, but because it's so absorbent, the butter will taste unpleasantly "freezer-burned" if not protected from exposure to air while frozen.

I find the best nationally distributed butter to be Land O'Lakes from Minnesota. I've been spreading their sweet, unsalted butter on bread since I was a girl (I seem to remember a marble included in the package). I prefer unsalted butter, which is not, by the way, the same as sweet butter. In the past, butter was commonly made from soured milk, because a higher percentage of butter-fat could be extracted from it. Today, almost all of our butter now is made from sweet cream. However, the best butter will always be unsalted. With no salt to help pre-serve it and disguise any off flavors, the more perishable unsalted butter must be extremely fresh and of the high-est quality.

Although Americans are familiar with cow's milk but-ter, in Africa and Asia the milk of buffalo, camel, goat ewe, mare, and donkey is used to manufacture butters with distinct flavors. Rich-tasting sheep's milk butter is used in Greece and elsewhere in the Eastern Mediter-ranean to make pastries like baklava.

Butter browns foods best and its toasted nut flavor is especially important when cooking blander foods like eggs, pancakes, or French toast. As the butter heats, and the temperature reaches the boiling point of water, the liquid vaporizes, causing the butter to sizzle. As the tem-perature continues to go up, the small amount of white foam (milk solids) will turn brown and nutty flavored. This brown butter mixed with fresh sage leaves and Parmesan cheese makes a classic sauce for spinach or squash-filled ravioli, Parma style. Sizzled brown butter, called *beurre noisette* or hazelnut butter in French, accented with lemon and capers makes an unbeatable sauce for white-fleshed fish. Add toasted pine nuts and it becomes a Sauce Grenobloise, a fancy name for a simple sauce.

However, if the butter reaches too high a temperature, the brown bits will blacken and burn, making the whole dish taste bitter. In a recipe that dates back to the six-teenth century, the French sauce classically used for poached brains or skate fish, *beurre noir* (black butter), it isn't really burnt. The sizzled brown butter blackens when a few drops of vinegar are squeezed into the pan. This deglazes (or melts and liquefies) the solids or the browned bits, darkening them slightly while they mix with the butterfat to form a sauce.

Making pastry with butter is its own challenge. Because it's temperamental, costs more, and is vulnera-ble to spoilage, many commercial bakeries don't touch the stuff, relying on inert shortening with all that trans-fat we've been hearing about instead. No trouble, but no flavor. Since I've always been a purist, I've learned to work with butter. It didn't come easily.

When I first went to work at the old Garden Restau-rant, in 1977, I believed that I should be able to do every-thing or else I wouldn't be a "real chef". Hired in the height of summer, I proclaimed that I knew how to make puff pastry dough. Pastry chefs make this "laminated" dough by rolling out butter between layers of pastry dough, then turning, folding and rolling again. Each

169

folding and rolling out is called a "turn". Traditionally, the number of "turns" is six, so the dough will have about 700 layers.

The only problem is, you can't make puff pastry in a hot kitchen. I tried anyway. The butter kept breaking out of holes in the dough, getting greasier and slipperier by the minute as I struggled. Without refrigeration for the dough or air-conditioning for me, I was attempting an almost impossible task. I didn't know enough to know that my failure wasn't just due to my lack of experience.

Later I learned to make wonderful all-butter croissants by the five and six hundred while working at the Barclay Hotel. I would roll out the croissants, working all day in a forty-degree walk-in-refrigerator so everything would stay cold, including me. Such dedication! But the croissants were outstanding. Butter is incredibly versatile and can be a wonderful friend to the cook. Don't be afraid to live a little dangerously.

MAKING FRENCH–STYLE CLARIFIED BUTTER

To raise the low burning point of butter, I clarify it (or extract the pure butterfat). The easiest way to do this at home is to place one or two pounds of butter in a large Pyrex measuring cup. Melt it for about 2 minutes in your microwave, or until the layers separate. Note that if you heat the butter too much it will bubble up rather than separating, so be conservative with your microwave timing. Alternatively, place the butter in an ovenproof pot and bake in a slow (300°F. oven) to melt. After about 30 minutes, the butter will have separated into three distinct layers.

Carefully remove the pot from the oven so as not to disturb the layers. First skim off the flavorful foam, saving it to stir into mashed potatoes, to toss with noodles, or add to a creamy soup. Next, carefully ladle out most of the clear butterfat into a tall, narrow container. When you can't ladle off any more clear fat without stirring up the milky water underneath, slowly pour the remainder into a separate tall, narrow container. Cool both containers to room temperature and then refrigerate to solidify, several hours or overnight.

The first container, full of pure butterfat, will solidify into a grainy, yellow paste. In the second container, the liquid portion will remain on the bottom, while the remaining butterfat will solidify above. Remove this solid mass of butter, rinsing the bottom layer under cold water to wash off every last bit of milk. It's easier to clarify butter in a larger quantity, and because it keeps almost indefinitely, why not invest in a couple of pounds? Note that Plugra is now being sold in clarified form in glass jars at retail stores and is also available in 5-pound containers for food service.

Indian cooks use another method to make their cooking fat, called "ghee". Slowly melt the butter in a heavy-bottomed pot without heating it enough to make it sizzle. A layer of white foam will settle on the top. Remove this foam and save it to add to vegetables, noodles, or mashed potatoes. The butter will begin to crackle as the water cooks out. After the crackling stops (about 10 minutes), keep a careful watch on the butter as it keeps cooking.

You want to cook the remaining milk solids just until they brown to a deep golden color but never blacken. Turn off the heat, let the solids settle to the bottom and strain the "ghee" into a plastic container or a glass jar. This method gives "ghee" its nutty aroma. Sometimes aromatic coriander, curry leaves (which have a deep, earthy aroma like no other herbs I've ever come across), or basil leaves are added toward the end of buttermaking to make it aromatic.

Eggs "Benedito" with Sun-Dried Tomato Hollandaise

This was a very popular brunch dish at Stella Notte when I was chef there. It is, of course, a variation on the perennial favorite: Eggs Benedict. The sun-dried tomato hollandaise is just delicious and worth serving with other dishes, such as grilled beef or chicken or steamed vegetables. Thinly sliced pancetta works very well instead of the prosciutto, but if cut too thick, it will be tough and leathery.

SERVES 4

¼ pound prosciutto, thinly sliced

8 diagonal slices of Italian bread, toasted

2 tablespoons rice wine vinegar

½ teaspoon kosher salt

8 eggs

½ cup Sun-Dried Tomato Hollandaise

To crisp the prosciutto: Preheat the oven to 375°F. Arrange prosciutto slices in a single layer in a metal baking pan. Bake 10 minutes, or until crispy and brown. Drain off any excess fat and arrange on the toasts, keeping warm.

To poach the eggs: In a shallow, wide medium pan, bring to the simmer 2 to 3-inches of water along with the vinegar and salt. Swirl the water with a spoon to make a whirlpool and then drop one egg inside, repeating the swirling before adding each egg. Cook at a slow simmer for 2 to 3 minutes. The whites should be firm and set, the yolks liquidy in the middle.

Drain the eggs using a slotted spoon, patting dry with a paper towel and place one egg on each slice of toast with prosciutto. Top eggs with warm Sun-Dried Tomato Hollandaise and serve immediately.

Sun-Dried Tomato Hollandaise

2 egg yolks

½ cup Sun-Dried Tomato Pesto (*see* page 897)

½ pound (2 sticks) unsalted butter, melted

Kosher salt, freshly ground black pepper, and cayenne pepper, to taste

In a small nonreactive bowl, whisk together egg yolks, pesto, and 2 tablespoons warm water. Set the bowl over a pan of simmering water (without the bowl touching the water) and whisk until the egg starts to thicken, about 2 to 3 minutes.

Set the bowl to the side of the heat and slowly drizzle in about half the butter, whisking vigorously to incorporate. Return the bowl to the heat, whisk again, and when the egg starts to thicken again, whisk in the remaining butter, pulling the pan off the heat if the mixture starts getting too hot.

Remove the sauce from the heat and season with salt, black pepper and cayenne.

WORKING WITH HOLLANDAISE

If a hollandaise sauce breaks (or separates), most likely the moisture has evaporated. To bring it back, try adding a spoonful of hot water and then blending with an immersion blender. To keep this hollandaise and other delicate sauces such as the Maltese sauce (*see* page 162), store in a thermos or inside a bowl of hot but not boiling, water.

Spaetzle with Brown Butter, Chives, and Toasted Breadcrumbs

I've served these Spaetzle with Brown Butter in many a restaurant. Spaetzle are a popular German batter dumpling, an offshoot of the dish of ancient Italian origin: gnocchi. Spaetzle are delicious, easy to make, inexpensive, and reheat well. What more could a restaurant (or home) chef ask for? Try varying the recipe by substituting $1/4$ to $1/2$ cup of chestnut flour, buckwheat flour, or chickpea flour for the all-purpose flour. Serve the spaetzle with rich stews and goulash.

SERVES 6

$1/2$ pound (2 cups) all-purpose flour, preferably unbleached

2 teaspoons kosher salt

1 teaspoon grated nutmeg

2 eggs

$1/2$ cup milk

2 tablespoons unsalted butter

$1/2$ cup Japanese panko breadcrumbs

1 bunch chives, thinly sliced

Combine flour, salt, and nutmeg in a mixer bowl. In a separate bowl, whisk together eggs and milk. Using the paddle, beat in egg mix slowly until dough is smooth and halfway between a pancake batter and a dough in consistency.

Bring salted water to the boil in a large wide-mouthed pot. Press the spaetzle dough through the holes of a colander or through a spaetzle maker. Stir gently to prevent sticking. Spaetzle are ready when they float to the surface (about 5 minutes). Remove with a slotted spoon.

Meanwhile, melt butter and brown breadcrumbs in a skillet, stirring frequently until evenly toasted. Toss drained spaetzle with toasted crumbs and chives.

Rich Philadelphia Sticky Buns

The gooiest of sticky buns have been a Philadelphia specialty since the nineteenth century. Today, folks line up to snatch up warm sticky buns at the city's historic Reading Terminal Market. Unless you like to get up at the crack of dawn, you'll have to start these sticky buns the day before to have them ready first thing in the morning. To do so, prepare the buns all the way until they're cut and placed into the syrup-covered pan. Cover with plastic wrap and refrigerate overnight. The buns will continue to rise until they get cold enough for the butter to get firm. Remove from the refrigerator and allow them to rise further, if necessary, before baking. If you'd like, freeze half the rolled-out sticky buns. Defrost overnight in the refrigerator and allow buns to proof at room temperature for about 2 hours, or until puffy and light, before baking.

Makes 2 dozen

Sticky Bun Smear

3/4 cup dark brown sugar, packed

1/4 pound (1 stick) unsalted butter

3/4 cup light corn syrup

1 teaspoon cinnamon

Melt all ingredients together in a small pan. Spread a thin but even layer on bottom of two 9 x 13-inch baking pans, and reserve.

Sticky Bun Sprinkle

1 cup dark brown sugar, packed

1 cup golden raisins

2 cups chopped walnuts (or purchased walnut bits)

1 teaspoon cinnamon

Stir all together and reserve.

Assembly

2 pounds Brioche Dough (*see* page 987)

2 tablespoons unsalted butter, melted

Sticky Bun Sprinkle

Sticky Bun Smear

Divide the dough in half. Roll out each half into a rectangular shape to fit into 2 half-sheet pans or onto baking sheets.

Brush with melted butter and chill again until firm and cold but still malleable, about 15 minutes in the freezer, or 30 minutes in the refrigerator.

Working with one rectangle of dough at a time, sprinkle evenly with half of the sprinkle. Roll up like a rug and slice into 12 individual rings, each about 1 inch thick. Place in a baking pan covered with smear.

Allow buns to rise fully at room temperature for about 1 hour, until they are puffy and light and "kissing each other" (barely touching).

Preheat the oven to 350°F. Cover bun pans with foil and bake 30 minutes, remove foil and continue baking 10 minutes longer, or until lightly browned. Remove from oven, allow buns to cool slightly, then turn upside-down onto a serving platter. Serve while still warm.

173

Dutch Boeterkok with Almonds and Candied Ginger

Holland is rich in butter and this boeterkok (buttercake) is a prime example of the country's butter-rich baking tradition. Living in Holland as a young girl, I adored the Dutch butter cookies and ate so many that for years, I couldn't bring myself to eat another. This dense shortcake, reminiscent of the French Pithiviers (made with puff pastry instead of the rich cookie crust used here that is related to German muer-beteig pastry), has a wonderful almond filling. Candied ginger is quite popular in Holland, likely because of its history in Indonesia. My mother once won a dessert contest with a recipe for Dutch-style ice cream with a candied ginger topping, so this one's for her.

SERVES 12

Pastry

1/2 pound (2 sticks) unsalted butter, softened

1 cup granulated sugar

1/2 pound (2 cups) all-purpose flour, unbleached preferred

Pinch of salt

1 egg, lightly beaten

Almond Filling (recipe follows)

2 tablespoons chopped candied ginger

Using the paddle attachment to a mixer, cream butter and sugar until light and fluffy. Beat in flour along with the pinch of salt, beating only long enough to combine. Beat in egg, beating only long enough for the dough to come together.

Divide the dough in two, with one portion slightly larger than the other. Wrap each portion separately in plastic, pressing into a flat compact block, and chill until firm but malleable. Press the smaller portion into a 9-inch diameter French fluted tart part with a removable bottom (or a 9-inch removable-bottom cake pan). Roll the remaining portion of the dough between two sheets of wax paper into a 9-inch circle and reserve.

Preheat the oven to 350°F. Spoon the Almond Filling over the dough in the pan and spread it out in an even layer using the back of a spoon. Cover with the reserved dough circle and press so the filling is completely enclosed. Sprinkle with candied ginger and press lightly so the ginger stays on the top layer of pastry. Score lightly in a decorative pattern, if desired.

Bake 50 minutes or until golden brown. Remove from the oven and cool on a wire rack. Cut into thin wedges and serve.

Almond Filling

1 pound (2 cups) blanched almonds

1/4 cup granulated sugar

1 egg

Grated zest of 1/2 lemon

1 teaspoon almond extract

Place almonds and sugar in the bowl of a food processor. Process until almonds are in fine bits, add the egg, lemon zest, and almond extract and process again until well combined.

174

Candied or crystallized ginger is so good in desserts and can be chopped up and added to apple desserts, pound cakes, and shortbreads. Ginger, like bananas, is sold in "hands" and individual shoots are called "fingers." Look for pliable ginger that is thick but tender, without dried-out white areas. The ginger sold in gourmet shops is often overpriced. Asian markets are good places to find inexpensive candied ginger. Ginger preserved in sugar syrup is called young stem if made from the tips of the "fingers," called fingers if made from the mid portion of the "fingers," and cargo if it made from the main body. Trader Joe's sells excellent, soft, succulent ginger slices from Australia that are reasonably priced.

English Bread and Butter Pudding

In Great Britain, a pudding is any kind of dessert, a term that originated because of the long-time popularity there of all kinds of sweet puddings. The oldest puddings were made with meat, like French boudin blanc and German weisswurst. In Medieval times, puddings were boiled in a bag or casing, so that pease pudding, made from split peas, was called "dog's body" in the British navy. By the end of the nineteenth century traditional English puddings no longer included meat, though they were stilled boiled (like the plum pudding still served at Christmas time) and were dense and cake-like. In time, puddings evolved to sweet, soft, custard desserts like this one, which thriftily uses stale bread, though the Drambuie (a liqueur made from Scotch whiskey and heather honey) makes it luxurious.

SERVES 8

1 cup golden raisins

$^1/_4$ cup Drambuie

$^1/_4$ pound (1 stick) unsalted butter, soft and almost

melting, divided

1 loaf stale, firm white sandwich bread, crusts removed, sliced $^1/_2$ inch thick

$1^1/_4$ teaspoons ground cinnamon

8 egg yolks

$^3/_4$ cup granulated sugar

2 cups heavy cream

1 quart milk

$^1/_2$ teaspoon nutmeg

Drambuie Toffee Sauce (recipe follows)

Combine raisins and Drambuie in a small bowl and allow to soak about 30 minutes, or until plump.

Brush 2 tablespoons of softened butter over a 9 x 13-inch metal baking pan. Brush each slice of bread on both sides with butter. Layer buttered bread on the bottom of the baking pan, covering tightly. Sprinkle with raisins with their soaking liquid, and cinnamon, then repeat, finishing with buttered bread.

Beat egg yolks and sugar until the mixture forms a ribbon and the sugar is dissolved. Beat in cream, milk, and nutmeg and then pour mixture over the bread. Allow the pudding to rest at room temperature for 30 minutes or

175

until the bread has absorbed most of the liquid.

Preheat oven to 350°F. Bake covered with buttered foil, for 30 minutes. Remove foil and bake 30 minutes longer or until the top is golden and crisp. To serve, cut the pudding into squares and serve with hot toffee sauce poured over top.

Drambuie Toffee Sauce

Juice and grated zest of 1 lemon

1 1/2 cups granulated sugar

2 tablespoons Drambuie

1 cup heavy cream

Combine lemon juice and sugar in a medium-sized heavy saucepot. Cover and melt the sugar over low heat, shaking pot occasionally. Raise heat to moderate and continue cooking the sugar until it turns a deep, even, slightly reddish brown.

Averting your eyes, carefully pour in the Drambuie and light it with a match. When the flames die down, pour in the cream (it will boil up) and simmer together until the sauce is thick and bubbles appear all over the surface. Remove the sauce from the heat and stir in the lemon zest.

Galataboureko (Greek Semolina Custard–Filled Baklava)

In this delicious galataboureko, a creamy, sweetened semolina custard is baked between layers of phyllo and then soaked with cinnamon-scented sugar syrup. A borek is a pastry in which a filling—usually savory, but sometimes sweet, as here—is wrapped in thin sheets of phyllo dough, while galata *refers to the milk-based filling. In the Greek town of Ioannina, the capital of the Romaniot Jews, a community that traces its origins to Roman times, a slice of galataboureko was traditionally used to break the Yom Kippur fast, along with watered ouzo, the Greek anise-flavored liqueur. While no one knows exactly when the first Jews arrived in Greece, legend has it that they escaped from a slave ship traveling from Jerusalem to Rome.*

SERVES 10 TO 12

Filling

1 cup granulated sugar

1 cup fine semolina

5 cups milk

1 tablespoon brandy

4 large eggs, lightly beaten

Combine the sugar, semolina, and milk in a large saucepan and cook over medium heat, stirring, for about 15 minutes, until the mixture is thick and creamy. Stir in the brandy, remove from heat. Cool slightly and beat the eggs in vigorously so they are well combined. Place plastic wrap directly on the surface of the filling and cool to room temperature.

Syrup

2 cups granulated sugar

1 cinnamon stick

1 strip of orange zest

2 teaspoons lemon juice

Combine sugar and 1 cup water in a saucepan and cook over medium heat. As soon as the sugar dissolves and the liquid is clear, add the cinnamon, orange zest, and lemon juice. Raise heat, bring to a boil, lower heat and simmer for 10 minutes or until thick and clear. Remove and cool. Remove and discard the cinnamon and orange zest.

Assembly

1 pound phyllo dough (if frozen, defrosted overnight in the refrigerator), brought to room temperature

½ pound (2 sticks) unsalted butter, melted and clarified (*see* sidebar: Making French-style clarified butter, page 170)

2 teaspoons cinnamon

Preheat the oven to 350°F. Layer 8 to 10 sheets of phyllo, in pairs, on the bottom of 2 buttered 9 x 13-inch metal baking pans or one 12 x 18-inch half-sheet pan, brushing every other sheet lightly with clarified butter. Spread the filling evenly over the phyllo. Cover with 8 to 10 more layers of phyllo, brushing those pairs with butter, too. Gently score the galataboureko on the diagonal into diamond-shaped serving pieces.

Bake about 45 minutes, or until tops are lightly browned and the filling is bubbling. Remove from the oven and immediately pour the cooled syrup over the galataboureko, tilting the pan so that it seeps in all over. Cool and sprinkle with cinnamon.

SEMOLINA

Semolina is the heart of durum wheat that is more coarsely ground than normal wheat flour and often sifted to remove the floury bits, leaving only the grainier bits. It is very similar to and can be substituted by Cream of Wheat cereal. It is used in Middle Eastern pastry baking to thicken the filling for phyllo dough-based pastries such as galataboureko and pistachio baklava. In Rome, a similar mixture of semolina simmered in milk is mixed with eggs, poured out, chilled until firm, and then cut into rounds or lozenges. These gnocchi alla Romana are arranged in a baking dish, topped with butter and Parmigiano cheese, and baked.

177

BUTTERNUT
& OTHER WINTER SQUASH

BUTTERNUT
& OTHER WINTER SQUASH

Butternut squash, *Cucurbita moschata*, makes me think of a large animal's thigh bone because of its shape—a long, thin neck attached to a bulbous bottom—and its smooth fleshy-looking skin. A stalwart member of the huge squash family, the meat of the butternut is a deep, blazing orange with a dense, satisfying texture once cooked. Along with its other virtues—reasonable price, good availability, long-keeping quality, and versatility—butternut squash is an excellent source of beta- carotene and potassium and a good source of Vitamin C and folacin. Its main season runs from August through March, though these days, you will see them on sale just about all year around.

The word *squash* is derived from the Algonquin word *askutasquash*—something that is eaten green, or in an unripe state, like summer squash. The eastern woodland Indians seem to have enjoyed even field pumpkins when young and green. Today, when we say squash, we usually mean winter squash—like butternut, acorn, and spaghetti squash—which have a hard, inedible peel. Summer squashes—like zucchini and yellow crookneck—are entirely edible. The difference is also apparent in the seeds. Winter squashes have large, tough-skinned seeds that are edible only if roasted and shelled. Summer squashes have—ideally—smaller, tender-skinned seeds.

Roger Vergé, proprietor of the renowned Provençal restaurant, the Moulin de Mougins, waxes poetic about butternut squash in *Roger Vergé's Vegetables in the French Style*, where he captures the essence of this easy-to-love vegetable. "They have a gentle flavor, slightly sweet and deliciously soft—soft and warm, like my mother's hands, hands that transformed them into silken purées, luscious gratins, and sweet, creamy soups."

CHOOSING AND STORING BUTTERNUT SQUASH

Choose large butternuts with a relatively small bottom and a long "neck." This neck portion contains solid meat without any seeds, making it easy to cut up. The bottom end contains the seed cavity and is surrounded by flesh that is softer in texture with noticeable strings. The skin should be dry, uniformly hard, and free of soft spots and bruises. Despite the tough exterior (which preserves the squash during lengthy storage), butternuts need careful handling because they will bruise if roughly handled. To store for several weeks, keep in a cool, dry place with good air circulation. The soft, moist flesh surrounding the seedpod will deteriorate quickest. If that area is mushy, you've stored your squash too long. However, the "neck" area will probably be firm and quite usable.

PREPARING
BUTTERNUT SQUASH

One of the few disadvantages of this squash is that it can be difficult to peel. To eliminate this rather tedious step, some supermarkets now sell pre-peeled butternut squash chunks. If your butternut is whole, cut off a thin slice from the top and bottom end of the squash so it will stand upright. Cut in half at the point where the narrow neck meets the bulgy bottom, so you have one easy-to-peel cylindrical section and one more difficult-to-peel rounded section. Peel, using a standard swivel-bladed potato peeler, or use a paring knife. Or, avoid the question of peeling and roast the squash "in its coat." Once cooked, it's easy to pull the flesh away from the hard shell-like skin.

More Ways with Butternut

For a simple side dish, peel the squash, cut it into cubes and then steam until tender, but not mushy, when pricked with a fork. Roast butternut whole, after pricking in several places, at 375°F. for about 1 hour and 15 minutes. Or, cut butternut into halves, scrape out the seeds and connective tissue using a large spoon and bake at 375°F. for 45 minutes to 1 hour with brown sugar or maple syrup and a pat of butter in the cavity. Or, scoop out the flesh and mash, seasoning to taste with butter, salt, pepper, and a little nutmeg.

Shred raw, peeled butternut and mix with an equal amount of standard pancake batter, then cook these savory pancakes on a griddle and serve as a side dish. Cut peeled raw butternut crosswise into thin slices. Dip into chilled tempura batter and deep-fry for a delicious crispy fried vegetable. (Purchase tempura batter powder in Asian markets.) Or, dip the same slices first into flour, then beaten egg, and finally into breadcrumbs, and then chill to set the coating. Pan-fry in oil until crispy brown on both sides and serve as an appetizer with a spicy dip.

Add butternut squash along with cooked chickpeas (and five other vegetables such as zucchini, yellow squash, turnip, okra, and celery root) to make the traditional lucky-seven vegetables served with Moroccan- style couscous. Stir sticks or cubes of butternut into a sauce for braised lamb shanks or beef pot roast about 10 minutes before serving, adding texture, color, and sweetness.

Mix diced butternut with finely chopped garlic, chopped fresh rosemary, olive oil, salt and pepper. Spread in a single layer onto a baking pan and roast at 400°F. for about 45 minutes, shaking once or twice so the squash will brown evenly. Combine well-drained, cooked butternut purée with eggs and pumpkin pie spices (cinnamon, nutmeg, and cloves) to make squash pie.

COOKING BUTTERNUT IN THE MICROWAVE

To cook in the microwave, pierce a whole butternut squash in several places (to prevent the squash from exploding). Cook on high power for 8 to 12 minutes depending on size, or until tender when stuck with a fork through the thickest part of the neck. Turn over halfway through cooking. Let stand 5 to 10 minutes to cool. Cut in half, remove seeds, and serve, or scoop out flesh and mash.

Winter Squash Varieties

Some of the major winter squash species are: *Cucurbita maxima*, which includes varieties like Hubbard, Blue and Red Kuri, Rouge Vif d'Etampes, and Buttercup Squash; *Cucurbita moschata*, which includes varieties that grow only in warmer climates including Butternut, Winter Crookneck, some Pumpkins, and Calabaza; *Cucurbita pepo*, which includes Acorn Squash, Summer Squash, Carnival, Spaghetti, and Pumpkin; and *Cucurbita mixta*, which includes the Golden Striped and Green Striped Cushaw.

Acorn Squash: Acorn squash, which may be buff, orange, or dark green in color, is the most widely available small winter squash. It has smooth, sweetish flesh that is rather stringy; buff varieties have the most concentrated flavor. The skin is usually edible after baking, though it may have been waxed.

Buttercup Squash: Buttercup squash weigh two to four pounds, are stocky in shape with a beanie top like a turban. This top enlarges as the squash matures. Many people consider buttercup to be the best hard squash. When baked, the fine, dry flesh is smooth and tastes of roasted chestnuts and sweet potato.

Calabaza: Calabaza is a general name for warm-climate pumpkins. In the U.S., calabaza has become the name for a large round or pear-shaped squash with mottled skin that may be deep green-orange, amber, or buff and speckled or striated, but always relatively smooth and hard-shelled when mature. Calabaza is often sold in large wedges. Unlike other pumpkins, it is grown primarily in warmer climates and is thus available year-round, especially at Latino markets.

Carnival Squash: Carnival Squash is a trademarked name for a cross between an Acorn and a Sweet Dumpling squash and weighs two to four pounds. It is flattened in shape with ivy-green marbling mixed with orange. Its flesh is deep yellow and is sweeter and more concentrated in flavor than the Acorn, though a bit coarse in texture.

Delicata: Delicata is an old variety that has been revived. Petite to medium in size, this oblong squash has yellow skin with spruce-green stripes inside its prominent ridges. The abundant, light, sweet yellow flesh is fine and moist. It will not keep for long storage because of its relatively thin skin.

Green Striped Cushaw: Green Striped Cushaw is a longtime gardener's favorite and often shows up at farmers' markets. It has a bulbous bottom and thin neck with relatively thin skin and moist, rather coarse flesh.

Hubbard: Hubbard is a term for a group of large to huge squash that may be bluish, gray, orange, dark to light green in color and are mostly teardrop or top-shaped with dense flesh and may weigh up to 50 pounds! This squash was named after Mrs. Elizabeth Hubbard of Marblehead, Massachusetts, around 1850, who provided the seeds for this previously unnamed variety.

Italian Gourd Squash: The Italian gourd squash, *Lagenaria siceraria*, variously known as Italian Edible Gourd, Serpent of Sicily, or *Cucuzzi*, is in another botanical family entirely. This long, thin, serpent-like squash is used in the kitchen much like other winter squash. Its tender shoots, called *tennerumi,* are much appreciated in Sicily.

Jarrahdale Pumpkin: Jarrahdale Pumpkin is an Australian cultivar that looks like a smaller classic pumpkin with heavily lobed sides and a distinctive celadon-green, smooth, and relatively thin skin. Its deep orange flesh is extremely smooth and creamy.

Kabocha: Kabocha is a marketing name in the U.S. applied to many strains of Japanese pumpkin and winter squash with rough mottled skin, including Delica and green or orange Hokkaido. All have tough skin, deep flavor with honeyed sweetness, and fine grained, extremely dense sweet-potato-like flesh.

Kuri: Kuri, or Orange Hokkaido, is a teardrop-shaped Japanese squash with smooth, deep red skin and deep yellow flesh and is similar to the Golden Hubbard.

Pumpkin: A pumpkin is almost anything as long as it's a hard-skinned squash. What is considered "pumpkin" changes from country to country and region to region. In the U.S., the term generally means a large rounded orange squash of the type used for Jack O'Lanterns. Miniature pumpkins are cream or orange in color with sweet, firm, flavorful flesh. Some may have edible skin.

Rouge Vif d'Etampes: This striking persimmon-orange pumpkin has been cultivated in France since the mid 1800s and was later introduced to American gardeners. It weighs 15 to 20 pounds and has a dense, sweet flesh

and mild flavor. It's easy to see why it's also called *Cinderella pumpkin;* it would make a perfect coach.

Spaghetti Squash: Spaghetti Squash is grown specifically for its long, prominent, spaghetti-like fibers. It is usually golden yellow in color with lightly sweet, mild flavor and a thin, hard shell. The larger the squash, the thicker the strands, which may be steamed and dressed like pasta.

Sweet Dumpling Squash: Sweet Dumpling Squash is a Japanese variety that is solid and plump, warm cream in color with ivy-green stripes inside the ridges. Sweet Dumplings weigh about one pound each and ripen to butter and orange color. The pale yellow flesh is fine and dry textured like a potato with a fresh sweetness.

Turk's Head: Turk's Head is a medium-large old variety that is best known as a decorative squash, with its brilliant orange and dark green markings, that resembles a Turkish-style hat. Though edible, it has a hard, woody rind that is difficult to remove.

Zucca: Zucca (zucchini is a diminutive) is a hard Italian squash that may be squat or rounded, ridged and bumpy. Either orange or gray-blue with a green tinge, it is shaped like a giant zucchini with dense deep orange flesh. Available in late fall and winter, and like the Caribbean calabaza, it is often sold in sections. The delicious tender shoots, called *teneri di zucca,* may be found in local markets. In the central Italian region of Emilia-Romagna, the flesh of the dense sweet squash, called *zucca barucca,* fills delicious *tortelli di zucca* along with amaretti biscuits and Parmigiano cheese.

183

Curried Pumpkin and Apple Soup

Make this warm, bittersweet, orange-colored soup with a firm "sugar pumpkin"—a large pumpkin with a curved neck meant for cooking—rather than the common "jack-o-lantern" pumpkin, which tends to be stringy and not very meaty. Best of all is a French red pumpkin, Rouge Vif d'Etampes (see description on page 183). Serve with a dollop of unsweetened whipped cream swirled into the soup if you want to get fancy, and perhaps some diced apple for crunch. I have, on occasion, served this soup inside a baked red pumpkin as is done in the south of France, where the soup is actually cooked inside as the pumpkin bakes. This soup freezes beautifully; I always double this recipe to have a batch for the freezer. You can also garnish this soup with a dollop of yogurt or sour cream and a sprinkle of toasted chopped hazelnuts or walnuts.

SERVES 10

2 pounds sugar pumpkin, or substitute calabaza
   or butternut squash

1 large onion, peeled and quartered

2 apples, quartered and seeded

3 cups chicken stock

1 cup apple cider

$1/2$ cup heavy cream

2 teaspoons curry powder

1 teaspoon cinnamon

$1/2$ teaspoon allspice

Kosher salt and freshly ground black pepper to taste

Preheat the oven to 400°F. Prick the pumpkin all over and bake whole, in a metal pan, for 30 minutes. Add the onion and apples and bake together for 30 minutes longer or until the pumpkin is soft when stuck with a metal skewer. Remove from the oven. Split the pumpkin and remove and discard the shell and seeds.

In a large soup pot, bring the chicken stock and apple cider to the boil. Add the pumpkin, onion, and apples and bring back to the boil. Pour in the cream, curry powder, cinnamon, and allspice. Season to taste with salt and pepper. Blend until perfectly smooth or use a food processor and strain through a sieve to remove fibers. Serve immediately.

About S and B Curry Powder

In 1923, Minejiro Yamazaki established a spice business that evolved into today's S and B Foods. He made his success blending curry powder especially suitable for Japanese tastes. Available in Asian markets and sold in foil-sealed red and yellow tins, this is my all-time favorite curry powder, with a sweet-spicy, full-bodied, and perfectly balanced flavor. The care taken in the packaging reflects the high quality of its contents.

BLENDING AND PROCESSING SOUPS

When pureeing soups, either a food processor or a blender will work. For the processor, it's best to strain most of the liquid out, reserving it on the side to add back in later. If you want a really smooth soup, process and then strain through a food mill or a sieve. To puree in a blender, it is not necessary to strain out the liquid, simply blend all together. Blender-puréed soups will be smoother than processor-puréed soups and will usually not need to be strained.

Zucca Squash Risotto with Parmigiano and Sage

Zucca was the one of the few foods available during the period following Italy's surrender in 1943 and before its the liberation by the Allies. People subsisted for months on little else but boiled, unseasoned squash, a far cry from this delicate and richly flavored risotto. When finishing risotto, one of the goals is to "make the wave" (fare l'onda in Italian) by adding the cheese (and sometimes butter): the ideal risotto should be loose enough to move in wavelike fashion.

SERVES 4

4 tablespoons butter, divided

$1/2$ cup chopped shallots (about 3 shallots)

1 cup risotto rice

$1/2$ cup dry white vermouth

3 cups chicken stock (or vegetable stock) simmering

2 cups shredded butternut squash

Kosher salt, freshly ground black pepper, and freshly grated nutmeg to taste

$1/2$ cup freshly grated Parmigiano-Reggiano or Grana Padano cheese

1 tablespoon chopped sage leaves

2 tablespoons chopped Italian parsley

In a medium heavy-bottomed pot, melt 2 tablespoons of the butter and slowly cook the shallots over medium heat about 5 minutes, stirring frequently, until tender and transparent.

Stir in rice and cook 2 minutes, stirring constantly, until the rice is shiny but not browned. Add the vermouth and raise the heat to high. Cook until the vermouth has been absorbed and then reduce heat to medium. Stir in about 1 cup of the simmering broth and simmer uncovered, stirring occasionally, until most of the liquid is absorbed. Stir in 1 cup more of broth and simmer uncovered, stirring occasionally, until most of the liquid is absorbed.

Stir in remaining broth and butternut squash. Simmer uncovered about 10 minutes, stirring occasionally, until rice is tender but firm. Season to taste with salt, pepper, and nutmeg. Vigorously stir in the cheese and remaining 2 tablespoons butter (to form "the wave"), sage, and parsley. Serve immediately, preferably on heated plates.

USING DRY WHITE VERMOUTH

I use dry white vermouth in much of my cooking, because the herbs and spices used to make vermouth, which is simply white wine fortified with extra alcohol, add an extra layer of flavor. Also, vermouth is inexpensive and much more stable than wine because of its extra alcohol. It can be kept on the counter, ready to add to the pot, without refrigeration. Because it is stronger, use half as much vermouth as white wine, adding water to equal the same amount of liquid called for in the recipe. My preferred brand is Stock.

BUTTERNUT & other winter squash

Rosemary Roasted Butternut Squash

If you've never tasted roasted squash, you're in for a pleasing surprise. Roasting concentrates its flavor and because of its sweetness, the squash caramelizes along the edges. It's also easy to make and keeps well for two to three days for reheating. Try it on pizza along with other vegetables and ricotta cheese.

SERVES 6 TO 8

1/2 cup olive oil

1/2 cup chopped fresh robust herbs such as: thyme, marjoram, rosemary, and savory

2 tablespoons chopped garlic

Kosher salt and freshly ground black pepper

1 large butternut squash, pared and cubed
  (or 2-pounds bagged diced butternut)

Preheat the oven to 425°F. In a large bowl, combine the oil, herbs, garlic, salt and pepper. Toss with the squash until coated well.

Spread the squash out onto a shallow metal tray or pan (such as a jelly roll or lasagna pan), without crowding. (If the squash cubes are too close together they will steam in moist heat, rather than roasting in dry heat.) Roast for 20 minutes, then stir the squash so it will cook evenly. Place back in the oven and roast another 20 minutes or until the squash has shrunk and has well-browned edges. Remove from the oven and serve.

Sautéed Spaghetti Squash with Panch Phoran

Spaghetti squash has an interesting texture and mild flavor. Here it is seasoned with the aromatic five-seed mixture called panch phoran (panch means five) that comes from Bengal, a region in northern India famous for its distinct cuisine. Most commonly, it is usually a combination of equal parts hot black mustard seeds, pungent nigella seeds, warm-tasting cumin seeds, acrid fenugreek seeds, and licorice-like fennel. Panch phoran can be found in Indian groceries and is inexpensive. The seeds are left whole for their potent crunch and eye-catching look.

SERVES 6

1 spaghetti squash (about 2 pounds)

1 tablespoon chopped garlic

4 tablespoons unsalted butter, preferably clarified as ghee (*see* Making Indian-style Ghee, page 171)

2 tablespoons Panch Phoran (or 2 teaspoons each: celery, cumin, fennel, anise or caraway or other combination of seed spices)

1/2 cup chopped cilantro

Kosher salt and freshly ground black pepper to taste

Preheat the oven to 350°F. Prick the squash, then bake whole for 45 minutes or until soft when stuck with a fork. Cut in half and pull out the "spaghetti strands" using a fork. Be careful to avoid mashing up the strands.

Meanwhile, lightly brown the garlic in the butter and add the Panch Phoran. Heat briefly until the fragrance is released. Add the "spaghetti strands" and the cilantro. Season with salt and pepper, toss to combine and serve immediately.

Savory Calabaza Bread Pudding

Savory bread puddings have become quite fashionable in restaurants, partly because restaurants always have an all-too-ample supply of stale bread. Unlike many restaurant dishes, this one is easy to prepare at home. Bake it in an attractive oven-to-table ceramic dish and it will be fit for company. You can make the pudding up to two days ahead of time, baking it just before serving. Note that if the mixture is cold from the refrigerator, it will take about 1 hour and 15 minutes to cook through in the middle. Leftovers reheat beautifully in the microwave.

SERVES 8

2 tablespoons unsalted butter, divided

2 bunches scallions, thinly sliced

2 cups milk

1 cup heavy cream

6 eggs

Kosher salt, freshly ground black pepper,
  and grated nutmeg to taste

$3/4$ pound (about 12 slices) stale, firm white
  sandwich bread, cubed

2 pounds calabaza squash, peeled, seeded, and shredded

Preheat the oven to 325°F. Rub a 2-quart baking dish with 1 tablespoon of the butter. In a small pan, cook the scallions in the remaining butter until wilted and bright green, about 3 minutes, then reserve.

In a large bowl, whisk together the milk, cream, eggs, salt, pepper, and nutmeg and combine with the bread cubes. Allow the bread to soak up the liquid for about 15 minutes or until the bread is soft and the liquid is absorbed.

Stir in the shredded butternut and pour the mixture into the baking dish. Bake 45 minutes or until puffed in the center. Serve immediately.

Maple–Ginger Baked Acorn Squash

While visiting Quebec during the International Association of Culinary Professionals conference held in Montreal in 2003, I spent a lively and convivial evening at a Quebeçois maple syrup "sugar shack" where we warmed up with hot mugs of "caribou"—a highly potent mix of wine and alcohol named for the native caribou—and ate typical sugartime dishes like yellow pea soup, tourtiere (meat pie), and for dessert, pancakes with maple syrup. Here I use maple syrup to fill acorn squash halves. Though not traditional, maple and ginger go very well together.

SERVES 6

3 acorn squash, green or cream-colored

$1/2$ cup maple syrup

3 tablespoons unsalted butter

2-inch section of fresh ginger, peeled and grated

Kosher salt and freshly ground black pepper to taste

Prick the acorn squash 2 to 3 times (to prevent them from exploding), then microwave on high for 3 minutes. Split squash in half and, using a large metal spoon, scrape out and discard seeds.

Preheat the oven to 350°F. Meanwhile, in the bowl of a

food processor, combine maple syrup, butter, ginger, salt and pepper, and process until creamy. Divide maple-butter equally and spoon into the cavity of the acorn squash halves. Arrange the acorn squash in a tightly fitting baking dish and bake 45 minutes, or until lightly browned and soft when pierced with a skewer.

MAPLE SYRUP

Native American tribes taught the Colonists how to tap the abundant maple trees of the northern regions and boil their sap down to syrup. Using a tomahawk to split the bark and inserting a small piece of wood to direct the watery sap into a birch bark bucket, they then boiled the watery syrup down in an earthenware cauldron. Quebec, New York, Pennsylvania, and Vermont are known for their maple syrup and products like maple sugar and maple vinegar. It takes between twenty and fifty gallons of sap to produce one gallon of syrup, depending on the season. Maple syrup is graded from AA to A, B, and C according from the lightest and most delicate to the darkest and most robust. I prefer the B grade because it has strong flavor and deep color and also costs less than higher grades.

CABBAGE & BRUSSELS SPROUTS

CABBAGE
& BRUSSELS SPROUTS

Cabbage

Plentiful and cheap, cabbage has a negative reputation, especially among people old enough to recall the infamous smell of overcooked cabbage wafting through the hallways of boarding houses and tenement apartments. For centuries, cabbage was a staple that sustained European populations during great famines, so today we tend to stay away from it as a food of necessity, not choice. Though cabbage contains copious and pungent sulfur compounds that produce its unpleasant smell, if fresh, young, and cooked with imagination, cabbage is quite delicious, extremely versatile, and is rich in antioxidants.

Cabbage, *Brassica oleracea,* was highly valued by the ancient Egyptians and Greeks, and its cultivation goes back 4,000 years. It is thought that the Celts introduced cabbage to the British Isles as early as the fourth century BCE. The earliest headed cabbage, which gets its name from the French *caboche* or head, appeared in Northern Europe about 2,000 years ago.

Cabbage was the earliest cultivated vegetable in the huge *Brassica* family and is the ancestor of numerous relations such as cauliflower, broccoli, and Brussels sprouts. In the United States, the most common cabbages are compact heads of waxy, smooth, tightly wrapped leaves in colors ranging from almost white to green to red. It is most commonly used to make cole slaw, a dish brought to America by the early Dutch settlers. Its name derives from the Dutch koolsla, meaning "cool cabbage."

Chinese and Mongolian horsemen learned to preserve cabbage in brine, which sustained the builders of the Great Wall of China in the third century BC. This preserved cabbage was later brought to Europe by Hun and Mongol horsemen and evolved into sauerkraut. Today, in Germany and Alsace, sauerkraut ("sour cabbage" in German) is salted and naturally fermented cabbage prepared in big barrels as a wintertime vegetable and source of Vitamin C, served in huge platters as elaborate *choucroute garni,* or sauerkraut with garnishes that range from duck, goose, and sausage to fish and seafood.

> #### CHOOSING CABBAGE
>
> Choose cabbage that is heavy for its size, with fresh, crisp-looking leaves that are firmly packed. In green and Savoy cabbage, the darkest leaves are on the outside and will be pulled off at the market as the cabbage ages, so that light color indicates age. Avoid cabbage with yellowed leaves, a strong smell, or a woody, split core. Red, green, and white cabbage are available all year round.

Preparing Cabbage

For all cabbages, trim off and discard the stem end. Cut the core out in a cone shape and discard or grate for slaw. (It has a stronger taste). Slice or cut cabbage into thin wedges before washing. Discard any withered or stringy parts. For mildest flavor and tenderness, cut out and discard the fibrous thick ribs from the outer leaves. Store cabbage refrigerated and tightly wrapped for about a week.

Cabbage Varieties

Red Cabbage: Red cabbage, *Brassica oleracea Rubra*, dates back to the sixteenth century and is especially popular in Germany and Eastern Europe. Similar to red beets, its red coloring is highly sensitive to changes in Ph, and if cooked in even slightly alkaline conditions, it will turn an unappetizing blue-gray color. For this reason, all traditional recipes for red cabbage include acidic fruit, vinegar, lemon, or wine.

Savoy Cabbage: Savoy cabbage has a loose, full head of soft crinkled leaves varying from dark to pale green. It was first recorded in the sixteenth century as *chou d'Italie* or *chou de Savoy* and probably descended from the old Roman types. This epicurean cabbage is named for the region where it is thought to have originated, the Savoy, which straddles the Alpine regions of Italy and France. Mellow-flavored Savoy cabbage is considered superior by many (including me) but is less common. Savoy cabbage is intermittently available year-round with local Savoy sold in the fall. Look for small, deep-colored Savoy cabbage that is semi-solid, slightly cone-shaped, and fairly heavy in relation to size. Even green coloring means good flavor and vitamin content. The leaves should be fairly thick and pliable, crisp, not limp, and there should be no sign of browning.

Portugal Cabbage: Portugal Cabbage (also known as Braganza or Galician Cabbage, or Sea Kale)—*couve tronchuda* in Portuguese—has no head but large, wide, spreading leaves and thick, white fleshy ribs. It is essential to the Portuguese national soup Caldo Verde.

Brussels Sprouts

Brussels sprouts, *Brassica oleracea Gemmifera*, are miniature head buds of cabbage that grow in a spiral fashion up around a thick central stem. Brussels sprouts became known in Europe at the end of the eighteenth century and a little later in North America. Brussels sprouts originated in northern Europe and were a popular vegetable in Belgium by the sixteenth century. Thomas Jefferson introduced Brussels sprouts to North America in 1812. French settlers in Louisiana cultivated Brussels sprouts extensively so that they would have a continuous supply of miniature cabbages throughout the growing season. Commercial production began in the Louisiana delta in 1925. Today the sprouts are grown in California and New York, in Ontario, Canada, in Northern Europe, and Australia.

Choose Brussels sprouts with good green color that are firm in texture with compact leaves and clean butt ends. Avoid puffy, wilted, or yellowed Brussels sprouts or those that are overly large with woody, split stems. Peak season for Brussels sprouts is November and December when fresh Brussels sprouts on the stem may be found in farmers' markets. Many people believe that the sprouts are best after they have been exposed to frost.

CLEANING AND COOKING BRUSSELS SPROUTS

Pull off and discard any damaged or yellowed outer leaves and trim stem ends. Soak in cold water and drain. For larger sprouts, cut an X-shape into the trimmed stem so they will cook more evenly. Cook the sprouts only until crisp-tender, otherwise they will start to get an unpleasant sulfur smell.

Steam, boil, cook in the microwave, or pan-sear. Serve with toasted hazelnuts or almonds, with butter and lemon, with buttered toasted breadcrumbs, or in a cheese sauce. For lots more Brussels sprouts recipes, go to my favorite recipe Web site: www.fooddown under.com, where at last count, there were 179 Brussels sprouts recipes.

Braised Red Cabbage and Apples

This classic German-style side dish is easy to make and keeps and reheats well. It goes best with salty or smoky pork dishes, game birds, and rich, braised meats such as beef cheeks. Remember that red cabbage reacts readily so avoid cooking it in aluminum and always include an acid ingredient like the cider vinegar in this recipe. If you have any on hand, bacon fat gives it a wonderful smoky flavor.

SERVES 6

1 onion, diced

2 tablespoons bacon fat or canola oil

3 tart apples, peeled and diced

1 small head red cabbage, cored and shredded

$1/4$ cup cider vinegar

$1/2$ cup dark brown sugar, packed

Kosher salt and freshly ground black pepper to taste

Preheat the oven to 300°F. In a large Dutch oven, sauté onion in bacon fat or oil, caramelizing lightly. Add apples and sauté together several minutes, add shredded red cabbage and remaining ingredients and bring mixture to the boil. Cover and bake 45 minutes, or until cabbage is quite soft.

Cabbage and Caraway Strudel

I found a recipe for this cabbage strudel in a old Jewish cookbook when I was working on the menu for a large local diner. Like homemade fresh egg pasta in central Italy, strudel dough is traditionally hand-stretched (maintaining the texture of the gluten network that binds the dough) by skillful bakers over a large table covered with a tablecloth. Here I take the shortcut of using phyllo dough, a Greek version of the original paper-thin dough brought to Eastern Europe by the Turks.

SERVES 8 TO 12

1 head green cabbage, finely shredded

2 teaspoons kosher salt

1 large white onion, diced

4 tablespoons unsalted butter

1 1/2 teaspoons ground coriander, divided

1 1/2 teaspoons ground cumin, divided

1/2 pound (2 sticks) unsalted butter, melted and clarified (*see* Making French-style Clarified Butter, page 170)

1 pound phyllo dough, brought to room temperature (if frozen, defrost overnight in refrigerator)

1 cup homemade-style breadcrumbs, or Japanese panko

2 eggs whites, lightly beaten with 2 tablespoons water

Sprinkle cabbage with salt and let stand 15 minutes. Squeeze out excess liquid. Brown onion in butter, stirring until well caramelized. Remove onion from pan, and sauté cabbage until wilted, then combine with onion. Add half the coriander and cumin to the cabbage mixture and cool to room temperature.

Add the remaining coriander and cumin to the melted clarified butter. Overlap two phyllo leaves to make a long rectangle, then brush lightly with the seasoned butter and sprinkle with breadcrumbs. Repeat three times.

Preheat the oven to 350°F. Spread the cabbage mixture lengthwise down the center of the phyllo. Roll up, brush with more butter, then brush with egg white mixture. Cut bias slits 1-inch apart down each roll. Arrange on a lightly buttered metal baking sheet, curving into a long U-shape. Bake 45 minutes, or until well browned. Cool slightly and then cut apart into serving portions through the slits. Serve hot.

Sweet and Sour Stuffed Cabbage with Sauerkraut

Jewish style cabbage leaves stuffed with beef in a tomato-based sweet-and-sour sauce are known by many different names and are made in many versions depending on where your grandmother came from. In Poland and northern Russia, stuffed cabbage was known as holoptshes (the name used by my grandmother, who came from the Eastern Polish region of Galicia), holishkes and geluptze, all from the Russian goluptzi, *meaning "little pigeon." This fanciful name refers to the shape of the small bundles that are thought to resemble a small bird, the same way that Italians call small rolled-up and stuffed veal or beef cutlets* uccelletti scappati *(escaped birds). In the Ukraine the dish was called* prakkes, *a name derived from the Turkish* yaprak *(leaf).*

SERVES 8

2 pounds ground beef

1 cup diced onion

1 tablespoon chopped garlic

2 cups cooked rice (1 cup raw, simmered in $1^3/_4$ cups
   salted water until barely tender)

1 cup golden raisins

2 teaspoons kosher salt

2 eggs

$^1/_2$ teaspoon freshly ground black pepper

1 medium head green cabbage (about $2^1/_2$ pounds) prepared
   as in sidebar, Preparing Cabbage for Stuffing, at right

2 cups tomato sauce (purchased or homemade)

2 cups chicken stock

$^1/_2$ cup freshly squeezed lemon juice

$^1/_2$ cup dark brown sugar, packed

1 pound sauerkraut, rinsed and drained
  (fresh sauerkraut in plastic bag preferred)

Preheat the oven to 300°F. In a large sauté pan, brown the ground beef. Remove from the pan and reserve. In the fat remaining in the pan, cook together the onion and garlic until the onion is lightly browned. In a large bowl, combine the beef, onion and garlic, rice, raisins, salt, eggs, pepper, and cabbage heart. Place about $^1/_4$ cup of filling in the center of each cabbage leaf and fold up like an envelope.

In a medium pot, combine tomato sauce, chicken stock, lemon juice, brown sugar, and sauerkraut and bring to the boil. Spoon half of the sauce on the bottom of a large baking pan and arrange the stuffed cabbage rolls over top, seam-side down. Spoon remaining half of sauce over top. Cover with foil and bake for $1^1/_2$ hours, or until the cabbage rolls are quite tender and the liquid has mostly been absorbed.

PREPARING CABBAGE FOR STUFFING

Fill a large pot with water and bring to a boil. Cut out the core of the cabbage. Gently separate the leaves and pull them off, one at a time until the heart of the cabbage is left. Place the cabbage leaves in the water, then bring the water back to the boil. Cook 2 to 3 minutes or until wilted, stirring once so they will cook evenly. Skim the leaves from the water and rinse under cold water. Add the cabbage heart to the pot, bring back to the boil and cook 5 minutes. Remove from the water and rinse to cool. Cut out and discard the large center ribs of the cabbage leaves. (If the leaves are large, cut them in half. You should have cabbage leaves about 6 inches by 5 inches.) Chop up the cabbage heart and reserve to add to the filling.

194

Stuffed Savoy Cabbage with Spicy Sausage and Pistachios

Savoy cabbage makes an elevated version of the rather plebian stuffed cabbage, this version stuffed with fennel seed-studded Italian hot sausage, soft-textured rich green pistachios, rice, golden raisins, and piney rosemary. All the flavors work beautifully in this recipe adapted from one of Rosalind Creasy's, author of the wonderful Edible Garden *series. Like all stuffed cabbage dishes, this one reheats (and freezes) beautifully. Just add a little water to the pan when reheating for more moisture, or microwave. Shelled pistachios used to be hard to find outside of restaurant and bakery suppliers, but are now sold at warehouse clubs and at the Trader Joe's stores at reasonable prices.*

SERVES 8

1 pound hot Italian sausage, casing removed

1 cup diced red onion

1 cup diced roasted red pepper
   (purchased or homemade)

1 tablespoon chopped garlic

2 cups cooked rice (1 cup raw, simmered in $1^3/_4$ cups
   salted water until barely tender)

1 teaspoon cinnamon

2 tablespoons chopped fresh rosemary
   (or 2 teaspoons crumbed dried rosemary)

$^3/_4$ cup golden raisins

$^3/_4$ cup coarsely chopped shelled pistachios

2 tablespoons paprika

$^1/_2$ teaspoon hot red pepper flakes

2 eggs

2 teaspoons kosher salt

1 large green Savoy cabbage (about 2 pounds) prepared as
   in sidebar, Preparing Cabbage for Stuffing, at left

2 cups tomato sauce (purchased or homemade)

2 cups chicken stock

1 cup dry white vermouth

Preheat the oven to 300°F. In a large sauté pan, brown the sausage over medium heat, breaking up with a spoon as the sausage cooks. Remove the sausage from the pan. In the fat remaining in the pan, cook together the onions, roasted red pepper, and garlic until the onion is softened but not brown. In a large bowl, combine the sausage, onion mixture, cooked rice, cinnamon, rosemary, raisins, pistachios, paprika, hot pepper, eggs, salt, and chopped cabbage heart.

In a medium pot, combine tomato sauce, chicken stock, and vermouth. Spread about half the sauce mixture into the bottom of a large baking dish (such as a lasagna pan). Spoon about $^1/_4$ cup of filling in the center of each cabbage leaf. Fold the sides over and then roll up tightly like an envelope. Arrange the cabbage rolls seam-side down in the baking dish. Spread the remaining sauce over top and cover the pan with foil. Bake for 1 hour, uncover, raise the heat to 375°F. and bake 15 minutes more, or until the cabbage is soft and lightly browned.

195

Native to the Middle East, pistachios have been discovered by archaeologists in the ruins of villages dating back 9,000 years! Commercial plantings began in the 1800s in Iran, today the world's largest producer of pistachios. Pistachio trees, which may be as much as 30 feet high, take 10 to 15 years to begin producing significant quantities of nuts, often bearing a large crop one year and a small crop the next. Pistachio trees grow in Turkey, Syria, Afghanistan, Greece, Italy, and in California in areas with long, hot summers and cool winters.

Turkish and California pistachios are generally the only varieties available in the U.S.; those from Iran have been unavailable since the mid-1980s. The foremost pistachio supplier in the U.S. is the Zenobia Company of the Bronx, New York, which has been importing Turkish pistachios for over 60 years. Smaller and less open than California-grown pistachios and with darker shells, they have a richer, more distinctive taste. Turkish pistachios are left to dry with their outer husks on so that the shells darken but the flavor is protected. The best pistachios in Turkey come from the area around the city of Gaziantep, close to the Syrian border. Although pistachios in the shell, whether from Turkey or California, will have best flavor, the shelled pistachios found in many warehouse markets and specialty stores are much easier to use in the kitchen. The old practice of dying pistachio shells red has pretty much died out, so that the shells are now left their natural tan color.

Sautéed Savoy Cabbage, Leeks, and Carrots

Savoy cabbage, called la verza *in Italian, makes a delicious and unexpected side dish combined with nutty-tasting browned butter, mild onion-like leeks, and crunchy, sweet carrots. This sautéed cabbage is a good choice when you have a big crowd to feed or to serve for a buffet, because it's easy to make in a larger batch and holds up well if kept warm. Try it as a side dish for Thanksgiving.*

SERVES 4 TO 6

1 small head Savoy cabbage

4 carrots

2 leeks

4 tablespoons unsalted butter

Kosher salt and fresh ground black pepper to taste

Cut the cabbage into quarters and then cut out and discard the triangular core section from each quarter. Slice each quarter into thin strips and reserve. Peel and trim the carrots and shred on a box grater or cut by hand into matchstick strips.

Cut the leeks into 2 to 3 sections, pulling off and discarding the dark green outer leaves and cutting off a 1-inch portion from the bottom that includes the roots. (Save this in the refrigerator or freezer for soup stock, if desired.) Slice each section in half lengthwise and then cut into thin, matchstick strips. Fill a large bowl with cold water, add the leek strips and swish around vigorously to dislodge any dirt, which will fall to the bottom. Using a wire skimmer or perforated spoon, skim off the leeks and drain. Discard the water.

Melt the butter in a large, heavy-bottomed skillet over moderate heat. Continue to cook the butter until it browns and gives off a definite nutty aroma. Immediately add the cabbage, carrots, and leeks and sauté all together about 5 minutes, or until crisp-tender. Season to taste with salt and pepper, tossing with the vegetables to combine well. Serve immediately.

Farfalle with Brussels Sprouts and Hot Sausage

One of my problems is being ahead of the curve in my culinary tastes. Witness my first book, The Bean Bible, *published about five years ahead of the new interest in and stylishness of beans. The book I co-authored with Guillermo Pernot,* Ceviche, *won the prestigious James Beard award in 2002, but ceviche is only now becoming more mainstream. This dish of Brussels sprouts leaves mixed with Italian hot sausage and lusciously melting Italian Fontina cheese is another example. I started serving this dish twenty years ago. It's only now that Brussels sprouts have been popping up on trend-setting menus. It's still a wonderful dish, easy to make, colorful, and full of flavor. If you don't have the patience to pull off the whole leaves from the Brussels sprouts, simply trim and quarter. This is one of those wonderful dishes where you make the sauce while the pasta cooks.*

SERVES 4

1 pint Brussels sprouts, trimmed

1 pound hot Italian sausage, casing removed

2 tablespoons olive oil

1 small red onion, cut into strips

1 cup chicken stock

2 roasted red peppers, cut into strips (*see* page 66)

1 pound farfalle pasta

Kosher salt and freshly ground black pepper to taste

6 ounces Fontina cheese, frozen until firm and then shredded

2 ounces grated Parmigiano-Reggiano or Grana Padano

Bring a large pot of salted water to the boil.

Cut out the core of each Brussels sprout, releasing the leaves. Pull away the whole outer leaves of each sprout, cutting away more of the core to release more of the leaves as you work toward the center. Discard the pale green innermost portions of the sprout, or chop up finely to add to the sauce. You should have a nice pile of tiny, whole Brussels sprouts leaves.

In a large sauté pan, brown the sausage over medium heat, breaking up with a spoon as it cooks. Brown well, drain off excess fat and reserve.

Add the olive oil to the same pan, and sauté the red onion until lightly browned. Stir in the Brussels sprouts leaves and chicken stock and cook together about 5 minutes, or until the leaves are crisp-tender. Add the sausage bits and red pepper strips and bring back to the boil.

Meanwhile, cook the farfalle pasta until *al dente*—firm and bouncy, and still yellow in color—and drain well. Toss with the sauce mixture, season to taste with salt and pepper and toss with both cheeses. Serve immediately, preferably on heated plates.

Farfalle, Butterflies, and Bowties Pasta

The fancifully named *farfalle* translates to *butterflies* in Italian. The similarly shaped pasta, though with rounded rather than squared edges, is called bowties in Jewish cooking, as in Kasha and Bowties (*see* Kasha Varnishkes, page 509).

FONTINA CHEESE

One of the richest, most supple, and creamiest melting cheeses made is authentic Fontina d'Aosta, made in the Alpine valleys of Piedmont. This semi-firm cow's milk cheese is produced in large wheels of about twenty pounds and has a full-bodied flavor with hints of herbs, nuts, and fruit from the milk of cows that graze high in the mountains. It will naturally be more expensive than its imitators from Scandinavia sold in a red wax rind rather than the natural rind of the original. Fontina is a wonderful table cheese, always served at room temperature, and is outstanding as a cooking cheese. In Piedmont, it is melted in *fonduta,* the equivalent of Swiss fondue served with potatoes, polenta, and cardoon—the stalky, white, and bitter cousin of the artichoke. If you're lucky and happen to be in Italy in their winter season, the *fonduta* will be redolent of rare white truffle. Try it on pizza, or make it into smoked ham and Fontina panini sandwiches pressed on a grill.

Caramelized Brussels Sprouts with Balsamic Syrup

Caramelizing Brussels sprouts is the newest way to serve these suddenly stylish miniature cabbages. Who knows why the once maligned, indeed loathed, Brussels sprout went from reviled to revered in recent years. Here, balsamic vinegar is simmered with brown sugar and a little honey until it is dark and syrupy, reminiscent of the expensive, long-aged artisanal balsamic vinegars that can cost one hundred dollars a bottle. The crunchy, earthy-tasting sprouts are accented by a drizzle of this syrup. Extra syrup would also go well with other earthy roasted or pan-seared vegetables such as rutabagas, fennel, parsnips, or celery root, or with exotic cultivated or true wild mushrooms.

SERVES 4 TO 6

1 pint Brussels sprouts
2 tablespoons olive oil
Kosher salt and freshly ground black pepper to taste
1/4 cup Balsamic Syrup (*see* page 596)

Trim off the bottoms of the Brussels sprouts and slice in half "through the poles." Preheat a heavy skillet, preferably cast-iron, and then add the olive oil. Place the Brussels sprout halves cut-side down in the skillet and brown for 3 to 4 minutes. Turn sprouts over individually and continue cooking for about 2 minutes, or until crisp tender. Sprinkle with salt and pepper, arrange on serving plates and drizzle 1 to 2 tablespoons of the Balsamic Syrup over each plate. Serve immediately.

CALAMARI & OCTOPUS

CALAMARI
& OCTOPUS

As freedom loving and adventurous as we Americans are, we are quite squeamish when it comes to eating uncommon foods. In fact, we will eagerly order and eat "calamari" but will avoid "squid", though they are the exact same thing. I have to say I'm surprised at how popular octopus has become, especially in the new crop of Spanish tapas bars and modern Greek seafood restaurants like Molyvos in New York, Kokkari Estiatorio in San Francisco, and Estia in Philadelphia.

Squid are long, thin, ten-armed members of the *Cephalopod* class, closely related to octopus and cuttlefish, and a branch of the mollusks, which also includes snails, oysters, mussels, and clams. Instead of an outer shell, the squid has a thin, transparent, flat, pen-shaped "bone" inside. Young squid as little as one inch long are sought after for their tender texture and mild, delicate flavor. Larger squid are often tough and suitable for stuffing and braising and will have a more pronounced flavor.

Once cleaned, the bright white squid meat consists almost entirely of pure albumin protein (like that of egg whites). The squid may or may not have its thin outer layer of purplish skin. Both the "tubes," the cleaned tube-shaped bodies, and the tentacles are edible, though some restaurants serve only the bodies. Chewy whole dried squid are popular in Asian markets.

Calamares en su tinta (squid cooked in their own ink) is a popular Spanish dish, while in Venice I've had the pleasure of tasting the typical dish *risotto di seppioline*, baby cuttlefish cooked with their ink to make a delicately flavored, deep gray risotto. Cuttlefish, *sepia* in Italian, resemble squid but are shorter and broader, prized for their large dark ink-filled sacs. I must admit that although I have eaten and enjoyed fresh cuttlefish, when I ordered in a fresh case imported from Italy, I had a hard time getting past the scary look of their prominent teeth. Still, I adore sepia-tint photographs, made from cuttlefish ink sacs. The warm color is so appealing and its organic character is well suited to portraits.

In my earlier chef days, we had to clean all our squid by hand, so I am one fast squid cleaner. I would order in fifty-pound cases of fresh squid and clean them in order to extract each individual ink sac to make my squid ink pasta and risotto. Today, many restaurant seafood suppliers will clean them for you and you can buy small containers of squid ink. On the other hand, there is something really satisfying about taking that rather scary-looking sea creature and reducing it to its clean, white edible parts.

Octopus, like squid, are cephalopods, but the octopus has eight tentacles to the squid's ten. The most commonly found octopus size in the market weighs about three pounds before cleaning. It's best to purchase already-cleaned octopus. Fresh or frozen raw octopus is purplish or brownish-gray in color, but otherwise resembles the octopus as it is found alive in water. Like squid, all parts of the octopus can be eaten except for the eyes, mouth area, and inner organs, although the tentacles are the most tender portion.

Choosing Squid

Choose fresh squid with little to no smell and bright eyes. Because squid are quite perishable and also a bit tedious to clean, they are often sold already cleaned and frozen (often sold defrosted at fish counters). Store in the refrigerator in a bowl for up to 1 day and keep extra-cold by covering with a freezer gel-pack enclosed in a plastic zip-top bag to prevent leaking. All parts of the squid can be eaten except for the eyes, mouth area, inner organs, and the clear hard "bone" that stiffens the inside of the squid.

Cooking Squid

Squid can be cooked very briefly at high heat, in a skillet, on the grill, under the broiler, or in a hot oven, and they take well to marinating. Larger squid are often stuffed and braised slowly until tender. The countries of the Mediterranean (especially Spain, Italy, and Greece) have excellent recipes for squid. In Japan, squid is eaten raw in sushi; in China and Korea, it is often dried and eaten as a snack. My local Korean market sells dried squid cut to order into short slits in a special machine so that they can be pulled apart in a "jalousie" shape, with alteranating rows of small slits.

Cooking Octopus

Octopus are delicious when simmered at length at low heat in a flavored broth and then grilled. The Greeks famously beat fresh octopus on beachside rocks to tenderize them before cooking. Properly cooked octopus meat is firm, slightly chewy, and yet tender with a mild flavor that easily picks up smokiness from a charcoal grill.

Grilled Calamari and Corn Salad

Here I marinate tender young calamari and roast them together with sweet corn kernels. I then mix up the warm roasted mixture with crunchy licorice-like raw shaved fennel and strips of sweet bell pepper for a warm seafood salad that combines lively textures and colors. While I no longer have access to one, I originally served this dish roasted in a wood oven. The closest equivalent is to roast the calamari and corn on a perforated metal pan inside a covered grill, so that it will pick up the smoky charcoal notes that seem to go so well with calamari and octopus.

SERVES 4 TO 6

Calamari

Juice and zest of 2 lemons

1/2 cup olive oil

3 tablespoons finely chopped fresh oregano, or 1 tablespoon dried oregano

1 tablespoon ground fennel seed

1 teaspoon hot red pepper flakes

Kosher salt and freshly ground black pepper to taste

2 pounds cleaned small calamari, cut into 1/2-inch slices

Kernels cut from 2 ears corn

In blender jar, combine the lemon juice and zest, olive oil, oregano, fennel seed, pepper flakes, salt and pepper, and blend until creamy looking.

Combine half the marinade with the calamari and marinate at least 2 hours and up to 24 hours, refrigerated and tightly covered.

Preheat the oven to 450°F. Combine calamari and corn in a metal baking pan, such as a paella pan. Raise heat to the broil setting and broil 5 minutes or until calamari turns opaque and begins to curl and the corn is slightly browned, watching carefully so it doesn't burn. Alternatively, place the calamari and corn on a perforated metal pan (or failing that, a doubled piece of aluminum foil with some slits cut into it) and cook in a preheated covered grill.

Salad

1 bulb fennel, finely shaved and soaked in a bowl of ice water

1/2 red onion, cut into thin strips and soaked in a bowl of ice water

2 colorful sweet bell peppers, cut into thin strips

2 tablespoons chopped Italian parsley

Assembly

Drain the fennel and onion. Combine fennel, peppers, and onion with remaining marinade. Top with roasted calamari and corn. Sprinkle with parsley and serve immediately.

Crunchy Spiced Calamari

Deep-fried calamari are almost as popular these days as French fries. Here I make crunchy "dipped and dusted" calamari marinated in buttermilk, garlic, and smoky chipotle chile powder, drained and then tossed with granulated Wondra flour, which resists turning pasty. The easiest way to get good frying results at home is by using a classic steel wok that conducts heat very well and is shaped so that a smaller amount of oil can be used. Of course, if you own an electric deep fryer, by all means, use that. Accompany if you like with Romesco (see page 468), harissa (see page 703), flavored mayonnaise or simply lemon and lime wedges.

SERVES 6 TO 8

2 pounds cleaned small calamari,
  sliced into rings + tentacles

1/2 cup full fat buttermilk

2 teaspoons chopped garlic

1 tablespoon chipotle chile powder

2 teaspoons ground cumin

2 tablespoons sweet paprika

1 tablespoon kosher salt

1/2 teaspoon freshly ground black pepper

3 cups Wondra flour

3 cups frying oil (canola, peanut, or soy)

1 lemon and 1 lime, cut into wedges

Fine sea salt for sprinkling

Marinate calamari in buttermilk mixed with garlic at least 2 hours and up to 24 hours, refrigerated and tightly covered.

Combine chili powder, cumin, paprika, salt, pepper, and flour and reserve. In a large, heavy-bottomed pot, a wok, or an electric fryer, preheat oil to 365°F. on a frying thermometer, or until oil is thin and almost watery looking and shimmering.

Drain calamari well in a colander. Toss half the calamari in a large bowl filled with the spiced flour. Shake through a wire skimmer, colander, or large-holed sieve into a second bowl, or scoop out with your hands, shaking well to remove excess flour

Fry, without crowding, until golden brown, about 4 minutes, keeping warm in a 200°F. oven. Drain on paper towels, toss lightly with fine sea salt and serve immediately with lemon and lime wedges.

203

Chipotle Chiles

Chipotles are one of the flavors sweeping the U.S. today. They've even given their name to a quickly expanding chain of fresh Mexican restaurants. These tobacco-colored, brittle, and wrinkled finger-sized chiles are simply smoke-dried red, ripe jalapeños. When purchased whole, they smell quite smoky, even through the package. Chipotles in adobo have been rehydrated in a spicy tomato-based sauce and packed in small cans. Both the chipotles (with or without their seeds) and the packing liquid is used. Many specialty and Hispanic groceries carry this product. La Preferida, Embasa, and San Marcos are among the many good brands available.

Grilled Octopus Salad with Kalamata Olives, Tomato, and Cucumber

Baby octopus are sold frozen and already cleaned so they are really easy to cook. Defrost overnight in the refrigerator, drain, and rinse before cooking. Here the octopus is first poached to tenderize it and give it extra flavor. Greek style, it is then grilled briefly and mixed with a Kalamata olive, tomato, and cucumber salad. Marinate the olives one day ahead of time for best flavor, and make extra while you're at it, because they keep well and are delicious added to all kinds of salads or even in sandwiches. If small tomatoes are in season at the farmers' market, combine all different colors and shapes including grape, currant, pear, and cherry-shaped varieties.

SERVES 4

2 quarts Seafood Poaching Stock (*see* page 994)

12 cleaned frozen baby octopus, defrosted if frozen

$1/4$ cup extra-virgin olive oil

Juice and grated zest of 1 lemon

2 tablespoons red wine vinegar

1 teaspoon crushed hot red pepper flakes

2 teaspoons chopped garlic

1 tablespoon chopped fresh oregano, or 1 teaspoon
 dried oregano

Kosher salt to taste

$1/2$ cup Kalamata olives, pitted and roughly chopped

1 English cucumber, lightly peeled and diced

1 pint cherry tomatoes, halved lengthwise

$1/2$ cup thinly sliced red onion

In a large pot, bring the Poaching Broth to a boil. Add the octopus, stirring so they cook evenly. Simmer 5 minutes or until the octopus is just firm to the touch. Drain and reserve.

Whisk together the olive oil, lemon juice and zest, vinegar, red pepper flakes, garlic, oregano, and salt, and reserve. Toss half of this marinade with the octopus about 1 hour before serving.

Preheat a grill until red hot. Drain the octopus and grill about 5 minutes, until the bodies are lightly charred and the tentacles curl. Toss the grilled octopus with the olives, cucumbers, tomatoes, red onion and the reserved marinade and serve immediately.

PITTING OLIVES

To pit whole olives, using your curled fist, or the flat side of a heavy knife, press down heavily on each olive to break it open. Remove pits. Note that ripe purple to black olives will be much easier to pit than unripe green olives.

204

Braised Octopus Terrine with Fennel and Pomegranate Molasses Vinaigrette

Octopus and fennel make a natural marriage, because the clean, licorice taste of the fennel accents and refreshes any seafood or fish. What's unexpected here is the pomegranate. Pomegranate molasses, a concentrated reduction of special extra-tart pomegranates is found in Middle Eastern markets. It makes a wonderfully tart, fruity dressing for the slow-braised octopus, here mixed with diced vegetables and chilled until firm. The octopus has enough of its own natural gelatin to set into a sliceable terrine, as long as the vegetables and octopus are mixed together while still warm and then formed into a compact shape. If fresh pomegranates are in season, by all means sprinkle the terrine with the ruby-like seeds.

SERVES 6 TO 8 AS AN APPETIZER

Braised Octopus

2 cups red wine

2 cups red wine vinegar

2 carrots, diced

4 to 5 sprigs fresh thyme

6 crushed bay leaves

2 teaspoons crushed black peppercorns

4 pounds fresh or defrosted frozen cleaned octopus

4 ribs celery, diced

1 red onion, diced

1 cup fennel trimmings, finely chopped (from the stalks)

Kosher salt and freshly ground black pepper to taste

In a large soup pot, bring the red wine, vinegar, carrots, thyme, bay leaves, and peppercorns to the boil. Add the octopus and enough cold water to barely cover. Bring the liquid back to the boil, skimming as necessary. Reduce to lowest heat and simmer 2 to 3 hours or until tender.

Remove octopus from the pot and as soon as it is cool enough to handle, trim as necessary and cut into large chunks. Discard the remainder of the contents of the pot. Mix the octopus with celery, onion, and fennel, season to taste with salt and pepper and wrap in cheesecloth or a double layer of plastic wrap, and place in a 6-cup loaf pan to set the shape. Chill overnight to allow the natural gelatin in the octopus to set.

Fennel Salad and Assembly

3 heads fennel

1/4 cup freshly squeezed lemon juice

1/2 cup extra-virgin olive oil

Kosher salt and freshly ground black pepper to taste

1/4 cup pomegranate molasses

1/4 cup chopped shallots

1/2 cup fresh pomegranate seeds, optional, for garnish

Trim the fennel, saving the innermost green fronds for garnish.Using a French mandoline, Japanese Benriner cutter, or a very sharp knife, shave the fennel as thinly as possible. Soak the fennel in a bowl of ice water to cover for 20 minutes. Drain well, and spin-dry in a salad spinner.

Whisk together the lemon juice and 1/4 cup of the olive oil. Season to taste with salt and pepper and toss with the fennel.

Whisk together the pomegranate molasses, shallots, the remaining 1/4 cup of olive oil, and salt and pepper.

Unwrap the octopus terrine and slice into $1/4$-inch thick rounds. Arrange the fennel on the bottom of the plate and lay a slice of terrine over top. Drizzle with the pomegranate vinaigrette. Chop the fennel fronds and sprinkle over top along with the pomegranate seeds. Serve immediately.

206

CARROTS & PARSNIPS

CARROTS & PARSNIPS

Carrots

It's easy to see why the early Celts referred to carrots as "the honey underground." Honey-sweet carrots are brightly colored and crunchy, not to mention loaded with Beta-Carotene, from which we get Vitamin A. Equally delicious raw and cooked, carrots are often taken for granted because they are ubiquitous. Carrots are just about the most versatile, adaptable, and forgiving vegetable around. They're generally quite inexpensive, even when organically grown, and available year-round.

Carrots can be as fancy as the fresh-dug miniature carrots complete with their tops served peeled and steamed beloved by caterers (because they look good on the plate and keep their color, unlike green vegetables that tend to discolor). As long as I can remember, I've loved carrots—maybe it's because I generally go for "rabbit food" like salad greens, cucumbers, and apples. My perennial late-night snack after chef work was freshly cut carrot sticks, hard pretzels, and sliced extra-sharp cheddar cheese (with maybe a sour pickle too).

When my cupboard is bare and I have no more fresh vegetables, there's almost always a bag of carrots with which to make Carrot Confit—slow-cooked carrots with orange juice, lemon, and garlic, or a Tunisian carrot salad with mashed cooked carrots and caraway. I could make several kinds of shredded raw carrot salad, includ-ing one with currants and rosemary, or a French-style salad with tarragon, lemon, and Champagne vinegar.

Lovely carrot soup is accented with flecks of dill, an herb from the same family as the carrot. Carrot Apricot Kugel—a kind of baked pudding (*see* page 44) and carrot *tzimmes* are venerable dishes from the Jewish repertoire. I add carrots to any beef stew (especially goulash), cook them in my tomato sauce to accent the sweetness of the tomatoes, add them to vegetable soups and stir-fries, or cut them on the diagonal and brush them with rosemary oil for grilling. Carrots à la Vichy is a classic French carrot dish made of carrots cooked in bottled water from the spring at Vichy, butter, and sugar until a sweet, shiny glaze is formed.

Because of the inherent sweetness of carrots, they have long been used for candies such as Middle Eastern carrot halvah and carrot cake with cream cheese icing (*see* a variety on this theme on page 215). The Irish and English make sweet carrot pudding while the French make a Bavarian cream studded with candied carrot slivers. Early New Englanders gave carrot cookies as Christmas gifts; today we make carrot quick breads for holiday gifts.

The carrot, *Daucus carota Sativus*, is a biennial plant in the *Apiacea* family which produces an edible root, closely related to the (inedible) wild carrot, *Daucus carota*, known as Queen Anne's lace. This European wildflower is now a common plant of meadows and fields in eastern North

America. I have a big patch growing along my front sidewalk. Other close cousins of the carrot are celery, parsnip, and herbs like dill, fennel, chervil, and parsley.

First cultivated in Afghanistan in the seventh century, carrots slowly spread into the Mediterranean area. These early carrots had purple exteriors and yellow flesh. In the 1600s, the Dutch developed the bright orange carrot we know today to honor their royal House of Orange. All modern-day orange-colored carrots are directly descended from these Dutch-bred carrots. Orange may be the familiar color of carrots today, but the exotic "new" varieties of red, yellow, white, crimson, and purple-rooted carrots fetching high prices today actually developed much earlier. Carrots were formerly every color *but* orange: red, black, yellow, white, and especially purple.

The early British garden writer, John Parkinson, describes red, yellow, and white carrots and reports that the small-rooted "deepe gold yellow" variety is the best of all. He says that the carrot's fine-textured leaves "in Autumne will turn to be of a fine red or purple, the beautie whereof allureth many Gentlewomen oftentimes to gather the leaves, and stick them in their hats . . . in stead of feathers."

Early European settlers brought carrots to North America by the 1600s—one report has them growing in Virginia as early as 1609. Thomas Jefferson raised several types of carrots in his Monticello vegetable garden. In the 1800s, carrots were more important in this country for feeding cattle and other livestock than they were for the table. When Irish immigrant and nurseryman Bernard McMahon published "The American Gardener's Calendar" in 1806, he listed only two carrots: 'Early Scarlet Horn' and 'Long Orange'. The French were especially fond of carrots and it was the famed French seed company, Vilmorin, that introduced many varieties in the late 1800s, many of which, including the 'Chantenay', are popular today. Two billion pounds of carrots are grown annually in the U.S. alone, with California leading all other states in production. The town of Holtville, California calls itself "The Carrot Capital of the World."

CHOOSING, STORING, AND PREPARING CARROTS

Carrots are sold fresh in bunches and bags as well as canned, frozen, and dehydrated. The "bunch" carrots sold with their tops on are by necessity picked within days of sale. Not only do the tops wilt and deteriorate easily if allowed to sit around, they also pull moisture out of carrot root, making for wilted carrots. For the tenderest, freshest carrots, buy them in "bunches" with leaves that are bright green and perky. Remove the green tops before storing as they will reduce the carrots' shelf life.

Choose carrots with bright orange-gold color and good shape, avoiding any with the heavy lengthwise splitting that sometimes occurs. Look for organic carrots for sale in many supermarkets. For the bagged types, look for evenly sized carrots without broken-off pieces. The tops with their cut-off leaf ends should not be at all dark or slimy. (The top end is the part that deteriorates first.) Carrots will keep in the refrigerator in a plastic bag up to 10 days. The cheapest type are called "horse carrots", both for their overlarge size and because they are often given as a treat to horses.

When buying carrots, note that 1 medium bunch equals a 1 pound bag. One large carrot equals about $1/4$ pound, and makes about 1 cup of shredded carrot.

If I have extra carrots that are either wilted or broken, I freeze them in plastic bags and add them to my next batch of chicken stock. Although much of the nutrient value of the carrot lies in the skin, I do recommend peeling carrots because the skin is also where much of the sharp bitterness lies. Cook carrots in boiling salted water approximately 5 minutes, steam for 7 minutes, or shred and serve raw.

Baby Carrots

A special variety of carrot, called "caropak" are grown for mini-peeled carrots that have taken over lunch boxes. Caropaks are grown close together, which results in a smaller, more tender carrot and they grow to maturity in only 120 days, instead of the 140 to 150 days needed to grow other varieties. Ninety percent of all mini-peeled carrots are grown in the Central Valley of California and more than 25 percent of total fresh carrot production in California will go into these mini-peeled carrots.

However, most "baby carrots", especially the inexpensive brands, are actually larger carrots that have been cut and peeled. The carrots are first cleaned and sorted, then they are cut into 2-inch lengths and peeled. A final polishing process rounds their corners and, voila!, you have a "mini carrot." These minis are shipped worldwide. If your mini-peeled carrots ever turn white on the outside from refrigerator dehydration, just put them in cold water for a few minutes and they will become vivid orange again.

CHOOSING, STORING, AND PREPARING PARSNIPS

To choose, look for small to medium, well-shaped parsnips without pitting. Because it is the age rather than the size of the parsnip that determines tenderness, choose large squat parsnips to make preparation and cooking easier. Parsnips that have been stored too long may be tough and even woody. Avoid limp, shriveled, or spotted parsnips. The tops should show no signs of sprouting. Thin, long parsnips are apt to be stringy.

To store, wrap parsnips in paper towels, place inside a plastic bag and refrigerate in the coldest, moistest part of the refrigerator for up to one month. To trim, cut off ends and knobs. Peel like carrots before cooking if cutting into chunks for stew or roasting. Peel after cooking if you're going to mash them, to help preserve their color and flavor and save nutrients. Parsnips are almost always cooked, as they tend to be fibrous, particularly their cores. If the cores seem overly tough or stringy, cut them out and save them for soup stock. Boil, steam, or roast parsnips. Don't overcook as their flavor will be sweeter when just tender. The outer layer of raw parsnip may be shredded and added to coleslaw.

Parsnips

Parsnips, *Pastinaca sativa*, are root vegetables that look like ivory-colored carrots with a sweet, nutty, though distinctly earthy flavor. Parsnips have been cultivated in Europe since ancient times but became less important over the centuries as other sources of once-rare sweetness became more easily available. Europeans brought the parsnip to the United States in the early 1600s, but the sometimes maligned creamy-white root has never become an American favorite. Parsnips are complex and intense in flavor, combining sweetness and an earthy herbal complexity. They are in season after the first frost of the year converts the parsnip's starch to sugar. Note that parsnips and Hamburg or root parsley are quite similar in appearance, though only the parsnip is sweet.

Creamy Carrot–Dill Soup

Carrot and dill make a particularly good-tasting soup with lots of eye appeal in its cheerful orange tint. Make this soup in early spring when the weather is still cold and often miserably wet and you're starting to crave the brightness that warmer weather brings. Garnish with a small handful of raw shredded carrot, if desired.

SERVES 8 TO 12

2 sweet onions, diced

2 tablespoons unsalted butter

1 pound bag carrots, peeled and roughly cut

1 pound Idaho potatoes (about 2), peeled and roughly cut

1 quart chicken stock

1 teaspoon paprika

Kosher salt and ground white pepper to taste

2 cups milk

1 cup heavy cream

$1/4$ cup chopped dill + sprigs of dill for garnish

Sauté the onions and butter in a heavy sauté pan until translucent. Add the carrots, potatoes, chicken stock,

paprika, and salt and pepper to taste. Bring to the boil, cover, and reduce to a simmer for 35 to 40 minutes or until the carrots and potatoes are soft when pierced. Stir in the milk and cream.

Transfer the mixture to a blender and puree until smooth, straining for an even smoother texture. Serve, garnishing each portion with a sprig of dill. To store, cool the soup to room temperature before refrigerating for up to 5 days.

Balsamic Marinated Carrots and Parsnips

Make these marinated carrots and parsnips 2 to 3 days before serving for best flavor. Serve as part of an antipasto tray with thinly sliced prosciutto and cured hard sausage such as Genoa salami, assorted cured olives, and chunks of hard cheese like Pecorino Romano. Or top slices of fresh mozzarella with the marinated vegetables and their marinade. Remember to bring them to room temperature before serving, for best flavor.

SERVES 8 TO 10 AS A SNACK

1 pound each carrots and parsnips, peeled and trimmed

6 tablespoons extra-virgin olive oil

3 tablespoons balsamic vinegar

Juice of 1 lemon

1 tablespoon chopped fresh oregano,
   or 1 teaspoon dried oregano

2 teaspoons crushed garlic

Kosher salt and freshly ground black pepper to taste

Bring a medium pot of water to the boil. If the parsnips are large, it's best to cut out the cores as follows: Cut the parsnips in two. Cut on four sides around the smaller top portion, leaving the tough, stringy core center inside. Repeat with the larger second section, which will have a much larger core. (Save the cores for soup stock.) Slice the parsnips and carrots into bite-size portions.

Add the carrots and parsnips to the pot, bring back to the boil and cook until crisp-tender, about 5 minutes. Drain and reserve.

Meanwhile, whisk together the olive oil, vinegar, lemon juice, oregano, garlic, salt, and pepper. Toss with the carrots and parsnips while still warm, and marinate, refrigerated for 2 to 3 days before serving.

PRESERVED LEMONS

North Africans cure and preserve lemons by soaking them in brine or salting them and layering in olive oil to cure. Look for brightly colored preserved lemons, well-covered in brine without any white mold. Preserved lemons are sold in specialty foods stores and Moroccan stores. To use, scrape out the pulp and the inner white part of the rind, and slice or dice the cured yellow rind. The edible part is the yellow zest, not the lemon pulp, which is too salty to eat and should be discarded.

Tunisian Carrot Salad

Like many Tunisian salads, this one is based on a cooked vegetable, here carrots, mixed with aromatic seasonings and the country's high-quality, fruity olive oil. In Tunisia, mashed carrot salad like this one (or a similar one made with zucchini) is also used as a spread for their casse-croute sandwiches, an excellent and tasty alternative to high-fat mayonnaise. A name adopted from the French, meaning break-the-crust, casse-croute describes a kind of hero sandwich with canned tuna, potatoes, and salad on a French baguette served with spicy Harissa sauce. Use either purchased or homemade preserved lemon for the garnish. Because it is made from cooked vegetables, this salad will keep quite well for 4 to 5 days in the refrigerator.

SERVES 6

1 pound carrots
1 teaspoon minced garlic
3 tablespoons red wine vinegar
1 teaspoon Harissa sauce (page 703)
1 teaspoon ground caraway
2 tablespoons chopped cilantro
6 tablespoons extra-virgin olive oil
Kosher salt to taste
2 tablespoons chopped preserved lemon peel,
    about $1/2$ a lemon (*see* Preserved Lemons, at left)
2 tablespoons chopped oil-cured black olives
Sprigs of cilantro, for garnish

Wash, peel, and dice the carrots. Boil in water until tender, about 20 minutes. Drain and mix with the garlic, vinegar, harissa, caraway, cilantro, oil and salt. Garnish by sprinkling with the preserved lemon peel and olives and a sprig of cilantro for each portion.

Carrot Tzimmes (Sweetened Braised Carrots)

Tzim is cinnamon in Yiddish and it is as beloved in Eastern European Jewish cookery as it is in so many other parts of the world. The appreciation of cinnamon goes way back and was even mentioned in the Old Testament as "kinamon", although it's not certain that this is the same spice. So it's appropriate that this is a celebration dish served on Jewish holidays like Rosh Hashana (New Year) and Passover. While you don't have to use the chicken fat called for here, it is the characteristic cooking fat of this cuisine and is full of flavor. Old-time recipes call for dried ginger, because that's the only kind that was found in Poland. Now that fresh ginger is so common, I've modernized the recipe to use fresh ginger with its fuller, sweeter, more aromatic flavor.

SERVES 6 TO 8

3 pounds carrots, peeled and sliced
$1/2$ cup chicken (or duck or goose) fat (or canola oil)
2 cups orange juice
2 tablespoons chopped fresh ginger
$1/4$ cup honey
Kosher salt and freshly ground black pepper to taste

In a large pan, sauté the carrots in the fat or oil until crisp-tender. Add the remaining ingredients and a splash of water to keep it moist. Simmer, covered, for 30 minutes, or until the carrots are tender and the liquid has reduced to a glaze.

Moroccan Carrot Confit

Here carrots are made into confit, or preserve, by slow-cooking in cumin-scented orange juice, concentrating their flavor and infusing it with the typical flavors of Moroccan cooking. The carrot confit may be kept refrigerated for at least 1 week and reheated gently. As in much of the Mediterranean, cooked vegetables are usually served at room temperature to take best advantage of delicate flavors that are lost when eaten very hot or very cold.

SERVES 6 TO 8

3 pounds carrots, peeled and cut into 3-inch lengths
  (split in half, if large)
$1/2$ cup extra-virgin olive oil
Juice of 3 oranges (about $1 1/2$ cups)
Zest of 1 orange
1 tablespoon chopped garlic
1 teaspoon Aleppo pepper (or hot red pepper flakes)
1 tablespoon ground cumin
1 tablespoon ground coriander seed
1 tablespoon kosher salt
$1/2$ cup chopped cilantro

Preheat the oven to 275°F. Combine carrots, olive oil, orange juice and zest, garlic, pepper, cumin, coriander and salt. Place in a large casserole and cover tightly. Bring to a boil, then place in the oven and bake $1 1/2$ hours.

Uncover and bake 30 minutes longer or until the liquid evaporates and the carrots are very soft. Shake occasionally but don't stir as this will break up the carrots. Cool to room temperature and stir in chopped cilantro just before serving.

213

Carrot-Honey Mousse

I adapted this recipe from a dish Chef Georges Perrier serves at Le Bec-Fin in Philadelphia. With its "secret ingredient"—honey—it is one of his most requested recipes. It is also easy to make at home. Of course, part of what makes it so good is the large amounts of butter and cream used. Once in a while, it's good to splurge. Drying vegetables out in the oven is one secret of French kitchens, so that they are better able to absorb butter and cream. The same technique is used to make heavenly mashed potatoes. Serve this dish for a celebration dinner, perhaps for Christmas or New Year's. It can be made ahead and gently reheated in a double-boiler (or in the microwave).

SERVES 6 TO 8

3 pounds large sweet carrots, peeled

2$\frac{1}{2}$ cups heavy cream

4 tablespoons sweet butter

$\frac{1}{4}$ cup honey

Kosher salt and freshly ground white pepper to taste

Preheat the oven to 200°F. Cut off the tips and bottoms of the carrots (saving for stock if desired) and cut into rough chunks. Bring a large pot of salted water to the boil. Cook the carrots for 5 minutes or until tender. Drain, then place carrots on a baking pan and dry out in the oven for 30 minutes.

Heat the heavy cream to scalding. Remove carrots from the oven, then purée in a food processor, gradually pouring in the hot heavy cream, butter, and honey while the machine is running. Season with salt and pepper.

214

Spiced Carrot–Coconut Squares with Pistachios

In a case of necessity being the mother of invention, last time I set out to make these cake squares, I had run out of the more standard walnuts. Looking through my stash of nuts, I realized that pistachios might work really well, because they have a similar soft texture as walnuts with the added bonus of their green color and faintly exotic flavor. The aromatic cinnamon, cardamom, and ginger give the cake an Indian character, which works especially well because pistachios are also quite popular in that part of the world. Because this carrot cake is so rich, I make it in smaller squares iced only on top, rather than as a big, heavy layer cake. (see Fresh Frozen Grated Coconut, page 311).

Makes 24 squares

Cake Batter

$3/4$ pound shredded carrots

$1/2$ cup shredded frozen coconut,
   or substitute natural shredded coconut

$1/2$ cup golden raisins

2 tablespoons grated fresh ginger

$3/4$ cup chopped pistachios

$3/4$ pound (3 cups) all-purpose flour,
   preferably unbleached

1 teaspoon ground cinnamon (preferably milder
   true cinnamon, not cassia)

$1/2$ teaspoon ground cardamom

1 teaspoon baking powder

1 teaspoon baking soda

$1/2$ teaspoon kosher salt

4 eggs

$1^1/2$ cups granulated sugar

$1^1/2$ cups canola or vegetable oil

Prepare a 12 x 18-inch half-sheet pan or 9 x 13-inch rectangular cake pan by spraying generously with nonstick spray. Preheat the oven to 350°F.

Combine carrots, coconut, raisins, ginger, and pistachios and reserve.

Whisk or sift together the dry ingredients: flour, cinnamon, cardamom, baking powder, baking soda, and salt and reserve.

Beat eggs and sugar together until light colored and the mixture forms a ribbon. Gradually beat in the oil until the batter is thick, like mayonnaise.

Fold in the dry ingredients. Fold in the carrot mixture. Scrape batter into prepared pan. Bake 30 minutes (if using a half-sheet pan), 45 minutes (if using a 9 x 13 pan) or until set in the middle. Remove cake from oven and cool to room temperature before icing the top.

Cream Cheese Icing

$1/2$ pound (2 sticks) unsalted butter, softened

$1/2$ pound cream cheese, softened

2 cups confectioners' sugar

1 tablespoon vanilla extract

2 tablespoons brandy (optional)

$1/2$ cup shredded frozen coconut

$1/2$ cup chopped pistachios

Beat butter until soft, then add cream cheese, confectioners' sugar, vanilla, and brandy. Beat again until light and creamy, scraping down the sides several times to beat out any of the lumps that tend to form.

Chill the icing in the refrigerator for 1 hour until firm but spreadable. Spread the icing over top the cake in an even layer, sprinkle with coconut and pistachios and chill before cutting into serving squares.

215

AN ALTERNATE CAKE WITH CRANBERRIES

To make a moist, tart, cranberry-apple cake, substitute the carrots, coconut, raisins, ginger, and pistachios with a 12-ounce bag of fresh cranberries, 2 cups finely chopped apples (3 to 4 medium apples), 1 cup (6 ounces) Zante currants, and 1 cup (4 ounces) chopped pecans. Ice with the Cream Cheese Icing above, cut into squares and decorate with 1 whole pecan half set in the center of each square.

216

CELERY
STALK, ROOT, SEEDS, LEAVES

CELERY:
STALK, ROOT, AND LEAVES

Like its friend the carrot, celery is so common that we tend to take it for granted in the kitchen. However, its cleansing, slightly bitter flavor forms the foundation of much of European, North American, and even Caribbean cooking. An Italian *battuto* or *soffrito*, a French *mirepoix*, and a Caribbean *sofrito* all depend on celery for their base flavor. Raw celery has a special affinity for blue cheese, thus the celery sticks served with Buffalo-Style Chicken Wings and the celery stalks stuffed with blue cheese that I enjoyed at an outdoor restaurant on Copacabana Beach in Rio di Janiero.

Wild celery is a common plant in Europe and Asia, especially near the sea, and has been used since ancient times. It is mentioned in Homer's *Odyssey* as *selinon*, from which we derive its modern names. Celery was used originally as a seasoning because it was quite bitter, similar to the way we use celery seeds gathered from the ancient, hardy marsh plant known as smallage, or wild celery. The practice of earthing up or blanching celery to keep it out of the sun so it is milder tasting and lighter colored started in the sixteenth century, probably in Italy, where so many vegetables were developed (asparagus, broccoli, and sweet peas, among others).

Braised celery, slowly cooked in chicken broth and white wine, turns into a meltingly delicious accompaniment to roasts of meat and poultry. Celery root, whether shredded and raw, roasted in wedges, cooked with potatoes to make intriguing celery-infused mashed potatoes, or fried in paper-thin slices to make celery root chips, is my favorite in this family.

218

Celery Varieties

Pascal Celery: Pascal Celery is the standard green celery variety grown for sale in the fall. The more expensive Celery Hearts are simply the inner, mild-flavored, tender and almost stringless hearts of standard celery. Blanched Celery is a regional specialty of the Pennsylvania Dutch and can be found in late fall in some areas. In Britain, special varieties of celery that have long white, pink, or red stems are grown in trenches out of sunlight.

Choose celery with straight stalks and rigid ribs that snap crisply when bent. Their inside surface should be clean and smooth. The leaves should be fresh, well-colored, with no sign of wilting. Avoid celery that is overly large with dark-green stalks which may be bitter and/or stringy. Store celery in its perforated bag and refrigerate for up to 1 week; note that it is apt to freeze in a colder section of the refrigerator. Pascal celery may be found year-round. Blanched celery, a specialty type, can be found in late fall.

To remove strings, which are found on large outer stalks, bend back and snap a rib of celery—without removing it—at the point where it changes color from white to green. The strings will be exposed and can be gently pulled off the stalk. Cut off the base of the celery head and discard or wash and save for soup stock. Separate the individual stalks and wash, being especially careful at the base, which collects dirt. Cut off the tops below the point that they form a joint (which will be tough). Discard darker green leaves. You may choose to use the inner yellowy green leaves, which are more tender and milder in flavor. Use the celery raw or cooked.

Celery Root: Celery Root, or Celeriac, has a long history and was already being used by Arabs as a delicacy in the sixteenth century. It is very popular in the cuisine of Germany and France but until recently was not well known in American markets. Look for large, relatively smooth and uniform celeriac knobs for less waste. The leaf tops should be lively and green, never slimy. Avoid celeriac that is too small, because with its thick peel, there won't be much left. Note that very large celery roots will tend to have spongy centers, fine for cooking but not as good for use raw.

Celery root is a cold-weather specialty in season from November through April. To prepare celery root, cut off the top and a thin slice off the base. Pare away tough outer skin with a sharp knife (saving the flavorful parings to add to soup stock). Drop the peeled celery root immediately into cold water so the bare root doesn't oxidize. Shred for use raw, as in Celery Root Rémoulade, or cut up and cook in acidulated water until tender to the core when pierced.

Chinese Celery: The Chinese, who have been using wild celery since as early as the fifth century CE, independently developed their own special varieties of celery. Chinese Celery grows in individual branches rather than by the bunch. The stalks are thin, hollow, and juicy, with a strong flavor. It should be picked young.

Leaf Celery: Leaf celery, or cutting celery, is dark green and close to wild strains of celery. It is used in France and Italy to flavor soups and stews, similar to the use of the closely related herb lovage.

Creamy Three Celery Soup

Celery, potatoes, and leeks are a trio of humble peasant's ingredients, but together they make a satisfying home-style soup that is very warming on a cold winter's day. I use celery root, celery ribs, and celery seed to enhance and round out the celery flavor here. With such a simple soup, a good homemade stock will make all the difference between good and great.

SERVES 8

2 tablespoons unsalted butter

1 onion, roughly chopped

2 leeks, white and light green portions only,
  diced and washed

1 large celery root, pared and cut up

3 large Idaho potatoes, peeled and diced

2 quarts chicken stock, simmering

1 cup heavy cream

Kosher salt, ground white pepper, a pinch of cayenne, and
  freshly grated nutmeg to taste

1 teaspoon celery seed

2 ribs celery, chopped

In a soup pot, melt butter and cook onion, leek, and celery root until softened but not browned. Add potato and cook until potato is soft. Add chicken stock and continue cooking for another 10 minutes or until flavors come together. Pour in heavy cream and stir to combine. Pour the soup in a blender, blend the soup and strain. Season to taste with salt, pepper, cayenne and nutmeg, and celery seed. Stir in the celery, transfer back to the pot, and cook for 2 to 3 minutes until crisp-tender.

WASHING LEEKS

Cut leeks into desired shape: rings, strips, squares, or wedges (including the root ends to keep them together). Fill a large bowl (or a sink) with cold water. Place cut leeks into the bowl and swish around vigorously to encourage the sand to wash away and drop to the bottom of the bowl. Using a skimmer or your hands, scoop out the leeks and transfer to a colander to drain. If the water has a lot of grit on the bottom, repeat the process. Leeks will be especially gritty if they have been harvested in wet weather. You can clean the leeks 2 to 3 days ahead, drain well or spin in a salad spinner, and roll in paper towels before storing in a plastic bag in the refrigerator.

220

Alpine Mushroom, Celery, and Gruyère Salad

I first tasted this salad in a restaurant in Bergamo, a town in Lombardy north of Milan, Italy, where my entire meal consisted of wild mushroom dishes. This simple salad combines dense, nutty-sweet mountain cheese strips like Gruyère (called Groviera in the Italian version) with thinly sliced mushrooms, here woodsy tasting, brown-skinned baby bellas, colorful, lightly bitter radicchio, and crunchy, cleansing celery in a simple olive oil, lemon, and mustard dressing. Easy to make, it's an ideal salad to make in wintertime and substantial enough for a first course or for lunch.

SERVES 4 TO 6

Dressing

1/2 cup extra-virgin olive oil

1/4 cup freshly squeezed lemon juice

2 tablespoons grainy mustard

Kosher salt and freshly ground black pepper to taste

Whisk together the dressing ingredients and reserve.

Salad

1 pound button mushrooms, trimmed and sliced

1/2 pound crimini mushrooms, trimmed and sliced

4 ribs celery, thinly sliced on the bias

1/2 small red onion, thinly sliced

1 head radicchio, shredded

1/2 pound Gruyère cheese, sliced and cut into strips

Combine mushrooms, celery, red onion, and radicchio. Toss with the dressing. Top with the cheese and serve.

Poppy Seed Veggie Slaw with Celery Root, Carrot, and Kohlrabi

If you own a vegetable shredder, this is the perfect time to use it. I'll admit my old pro model R2 Robot Coupe is more powerful than a home version, but yours will also make short work of the prep here. For a more elegant version, cut everything using the julienne blade of a mandoline or a Japanese Benriner cutter. This makes a rather large batch of slaw, but it keeps well for up to a week. Serve it with sandwiches like the Smoked Turkey Reuben (see page 917), the Philadelphia Steak Sandwich (see page 111), or under Hazelnut-Crusted Crab Cakes (see page 154).

SERVES 8

Poppy Seed Dressing

3/4 cup canola oil

6 tablespoons cider vinegar

2 tablespoons granulated sugar

2 tablespoons coarse mustard

2 tablespoons poppy seeds

2 teaspoons celery seeds

Kosher salt and freshly ground black pepper to taste

Vegetable Mix

1 celery root, peeled and shredded

1 pound carrots, peeled and shredded

1 each: red, yellow, and green pepper, cut into thin strips

1 kohlrabi root, peeled and shredded

Whisk together dressing ingredients. Toss dressing with vegetables, season to taste and marinate for at least 30 minutes before serving.

Roast Chicken with Celeriac, Rosemary, and Apples

A perfectly roasted chicken is a thing of beauty, and if you follow this recipe and use the best-quality grain-fed chicken, you'll have delicious results, perfect for a late fall or winter dinner. Serve the chicken with its accompaniments over soft Mascarpone Polenta (see page 345), but it would also go well with simple steamed rice or even kasha. I used to make this dish in the wonderful wood-burning oven I had at my last restaurant, Stella Notte. Of course, it was even better roasted in that 600° to 700° degree oven where it could pick up the flavor of the oak we used for fuel. At home, roast in a covered grill, or at high heat in a preheated oven for best browning and richest flavor. Make sure that your oven is pretty clean before roasting at high heat, or you may smoke up your whole house.

SERVES 6

Apple Cider Glaze

2 cups apple cider

2 cups chicken stock

2 to 3 sprigs thyme

$1/2$ cup chopped onion

2 bay leaves

1 teaspoon peppercorns

1 teaspoon coriander seed

1 teaspoon fennel seed

Bring all ingredients to a boil and reduce until the liquid is syrupy and equals about 2 cups. Strain and reserve, keeping warp.

Marinated Chicken

$1/2$ cup finely minced shallots

2 tablespoons finely chopped rosemary

1 tablespoon kosher salt

$1/2$ teaspoon freshly ground black pepper

$1/4$ cup canola oil

3 broiler-fryer chickens, split in half and backbone cut away (save backbone for stock if desired)

Combine marinade ingredients and rub all over chicken halves. Refrigerate at least 2 hours and up to 2 days, covered and refrigerated.

Apples, Celery Root, and Red Onion

1 large celery root, pared and cut into wedges

2 large Fuji apples (or other firm, red-skinned apples), cored and cut into thick wedges

Juice of 1 lemon

2 small red onions, cut into wedges

Cook celery root for 2 minutes in boiling salted water. Drain and reserve. Toss apple wedges with lemon juice. Combine apples with red onions and celery root and reserve.

Assembly

Preheat the oven to 450°F. Drain the chicken halves, and arrange skin-side down in a large baking pan. Scatter apple mixture over top. Roast until the chicken is three-quarters cooked, about 30 minutes. Turn chicken halves over and complete cooking until the chicken skin is browned, and the chicken has reached 165°F. on a meat thermometer when measured at the thickest portion of the thigh, about 25 minutes longer.

To serve, place Mascarpone Polenta (*see* page 345) into a pasta bowl. Arrange chicken and vegetables over top. Ladle Apple Cider Glaze over top.

CHEESE

CHEDDAR, SWISS & JACK

CHEESE:
CHEDDAR, SWISS & JACK

I, for one, am crazy about cheese—it's one of my favorite ingredients in the kitchen. One of the most useful cheeses in the kitchen is rich, tangy cheddar, especially if aged to sharp or extra-sharp. Americans eat more than nine pounds of cheddar per year, per person, so I'm obviously not alone in my love of this satisfying cheese. There is both factory-made and artisanal cheddar in America, almost always made from pasteurized milk.

In the kitchen, I often use Cabot's Private Stock, aged eighteen months; or Cabot's Vintage, aged two years; Vermont Hunter, which has a distinctive pungent flavor not to everyone's liking, or their extra-sharp cheddar, which is relatively easy to find in supermarkets and warehouse club stores. If you happen to find it, Cabot's also makes small quantities of a five-year aged cheddar that is unbelievably concentrated in flavor, called Old School. The best thing is to try different types and ages of cheddar to find the one you like best, but in general if you're using it in the kitchen, a well-aged cheese works best.

When adding cheese to dishes, keep in mind that your goal is to melt it, not cook it, so melt gently over heat, or pull the dish off the fire and use its carryover heat to melt the cheese. Cheese that is heated to too high a temperature will turn grainy and unappetizing. Allow two to four ounces of cheese per person when making a main dish.

Cheddar, Swiss, and Jack Varieties

Cheddar: Cheddar is a cow's milk cheese with a texture that gets more and more crumbly the longer it is aged, usually between nine months and two years. It gets its name from the process of "cheddaring," or cutting up the curd into small bits. Cheddar cheese originated in England, but today it is produced all over the world. Because its name is not protected (like Roquefort or Gruyère) anyone can call their cheese "cheddar." Cheddar is a hard cheese, about forty-eight percent fat, traditionally shaped like a large drum with a natural rind and covered in cheesecloth. Natural cheddar is creamy white to pale yellow, but some cheddars have annatto added to make them orange (*see* Annatto Coloring, page 226).

Gruyère: Gruyère is named after the Swiss Alpine village Gruyères in the canton of Fribourg. Long ago, the forests of the region were called gruyères. Local cheesemakers used the forest wood to heat their cheese-cooking kettles, and eventually the cheese of

---

the region became known by this name. It is a traditional unpasteurized, cooked curd, whole raw cow's milk cheese with a hard, rusty-brown rind. At one time, Gruyère had lots of pea-sized holes, but today's technology has eliminated gas and hole causing bacteria from production. It is made in large flattened wheels and is similar to, but darker than, Emmenthal, with a dense, shiny, slightly creamy consistency and rich, nutty flavor. It is aged for three to ten months; the longer the aging, the deeper the flavor and the denser the cheese. With its strong flavor, this is the cheese of choice, along with Emmenthal, for fondue and to top French onion soup.

Comte: Comte, similar to Gruyère, comes from the French Alps. It is aged at least six months and up to one year. Comte has a deeper color and richer, nuttier flavor and its occasional holes are smaller.

Emmenthal: Emmenthal, or Emmenthaler, is produced in the valley of the Emme river in the canton of Bern, Switzerland, and in neighboring France and is made in huge wheels that weigh about two hundred pounds. This traditional, unpasteurized, cooked-curd cheese is made from partially skimmed raw milk from cows that graze on flavorful wild plants and herbs in high Alpine pastures. It has a firm consistency and large holes that are called *noix* (walnut in French). Its hard, thin rind is covered by paper with the producer's name on it. It has a pleasing, sweet aroma with overtones of hay and a fruity, slightly acidic flavor. It is considered to be one of the most difficult cheeses to be produced because of its complicated fermentation process that results in its characteristic holes.

Jarslberg: Jarlsberg is a similar style of cooked-curd cow's milk cheese made in Norway (Jarlsberg), though with a much milder, sweetly nutty flavor. It is produced in much smaller wheels of about twenty pounds. It is exported in great quantities, especially to the U.S., where it can be found in most supermarkets. While it doesn't have the fully developed character of the Alpine mountain cheeses on which it is modeled, it works well in the kitchen. Domestic Swiss is a mass-produced shiny, pale yellow with large holes and a sweet, innocuous flavor, good for children's sandwiches. It is acceptable, though not wonderful, in the kitchen, and is not suited to serving on its own.

Monterey Jack: Monterey Jack originated in California (location of the town of Monterey) and was originally developed in 1882 by a man of Scots origin, David Jacks. It is generally a soft, mild, buttery-tasting and creamy-textured cheese, good for melting. Common supermarket jack cheese is aged about six months; older types are rubbed with oil and black pepper to keep the rind soft. Jack is about twenty-five percent fat. I often use Jack cheese as a substitute (though less complex in flavor) for the more expensive and harder-to-find Italian Fontina.

Dry Monterey Jack: Dry Monterey Jack, a prize-winning cheese first made in 1915, is today made exclusively by the Vela Company in California. It is long-aged, with a firm texture and concentrated sweet, nutty flavor. Its dark, natural rind is hand-rubbed with oil, cocoa, and pepper and can be rather difficult to remove. The deep yellow, craggy-textured cheese is excellent for grating, well-suited to

225

Mexican- and American-style dishes, though not commonly available, at least on the East Coast. To me, this is America's finest grating cheese.

Shaker Herb and Cheddar Cheese Soup

This delicious herb-accented soup was inspired by the cooking of America's Shakers, known for their abundant use of fresh herbs. It was on the opening menu for The Azalea Restaurant at the Omni Hotel at Independence Park, a small boutique hotel for which I developed an entire regional menu. Make it in the summer when fresh herbs are abundant; dried just won't do here. Use any combination of tarragon, chervil, sorrel, dill, and chives; the more the better for a fragrant, cheesy soup. Buttery-tasting Yukon gold potatoes give a lovely color to the soup, but any type of starchy potato will work.

SERVES 8 TO 12

1 onion, diced

2 leeks, sliced

2 tablespoons unsalted butter

1 pound Yukon gold potatoes (2 to 3 medium potatoes), peeled and roughly cut

1 quart chicken stock

Kosher salt, grated nutmeg, and ground white pepper to taste

3 cups milk

$1/2$ cup heavy cream

$1/2$ cup chopped tarragon, chervil, sorrel, dill, and chives

2 cups shredded extra-sharp cheddar cheese

Sauté the onion and leeks in the butter in a large, heavy casserole dish until translucent. Add the potatoes, chicken stock, salt, nutmeg, and pepper to taste. Bring to the boil, cover and reduce to a simmer for 35 to 40 minutes or until the potatoes are soft when pierced. Stir in the milk and cream.

Transfer the mixture to a blender and puree until smooth, straining for an even smoother texture. Transfer back into the soup pot, add the herbs and stir to combine. Serve each portion topped with a small handful of cheddar to stir into the soup.

To store, cool the soup to room temperature before refrigerating for up to 5 days.

226

Cauliflower au Gratin

I adapted this old-fashioned dish from a recipe given to me by the owners of a huge Philadelphia diner called The Dining Car. They've been making it for years and customers keep loving it. The present diner was the last one built by the famous Swingle Diner Company of New Jersey. It was trucked to the site in 1980 where it's been operating 24 hours a day, 7 days a week, serving 15,000 loyal guests every week. This rich, creamy dish is great to serve for a party (or to bring to a potluck) because you can prepare it the day before up to the point of baking. Though a diner specialty, it is made with a classic French béchamel sauce enriched with cheese, usually Gruyère, in which case it is called Mornay sauce. Also in the French tradition is the use of white pepper, preferred in French kitchens for light-colored dishes. White pepper is hotter than black, because it has had its aromatic outer layer removed. Although the diner original called for Swiss cheese, French Gruyère not only tastes better, it's more authentically French.

SERVES 6

1 large head cauliflower

2 cups milk

3 tablespoons salted butter

4 tablespoons all-purpose flour

$1/2$ teaspoon each: dry mustard and grated nutmeg

Kosher salt and ground white pepper to taste

2 cups grated Gruyère cheese

$1/4$ cup freshly grated Parmesan cheese

Paprika (for dusting)

Cut the cone-shaped core out of the bottom of the cauliflower, cutting around the stem. Separate the cauliflower into 1- to 2-inch florets. Steam the cauliflower (or boil) until almost cooked. Drain and arrange in an ovenproof baking dish with low sides (such as a gratin dish).

Make the cheese sauce by heating the milk to scalding in a pot (or pour into a glass measure and heat in the microwave). In a separate medium-sized saucepan, melt the butter, then stir in the flour. Cook 3 to 4 minutes on medium low heat while constantly stirring. Add the hot milk to the pan while stirring or whisking until well combined.

Preheat the oven to 400°F. Cook the sauce for 15 minutes over low heat, stirring occasionally, until thickened and smooth. Remove from the heat and stir in the seasonings and Gruyère. Pour the cheese sauce over the cauliflower and sprinkle with the Parmesan cheese and the paprika. Bake 20 minutes or until browned on top and bubbling. Remove from the oven and allow to cool slightly before serving.

227

Cheddar Cheese Biscuits

For a cheddar cheese lover like me, these biscuits really take the cake. I like to serve them with hearty soups like the Rumanian Borscht (see page 128) and the Diner-Style Black-Eyed Pea Soup (see page 103). For the cheesiest flavor, use extra-sharp cheddar. For light and tender biscuits, work the dough as little as possible so the toughening gluten in the flour doesn't get activated. If using the non-aluminum baking powder, roll out, cut, and bake as soon as the dough is mixed, or the leavening power will start to dissipate.

MAKES 18 TO 24

3/4 pound (3 cups) white whole wheat flour

1 tablespoon granulated sugar

1 tablespoon baking powder

1 tablespoon kosher salt

1/2 teaspoon baking soda

1/2 teaspoon cayenne pepper

1/2 pound (2 sticks) unsalted butter, cut into bits and
   chilled in the freezer until firm

1/2 pound extra-sharp cheddar, grated

1 cup buttermilk

Preheat the oven to 400°F. Combine dry ingredients in a mixer bowl: flour, sugar, baking powder, salt, soda, and cayenne. Using the paddle attachment, cut in butter until the mixture resembles oatmeal. Add the cheddar cheese and pour in the buttermilk. Mix only enough for the dough to form a ball.

Roll out lightly on a minimally floured surface, and cut into 3-inch diameter biscuits. Arrange on nonstick-sprayed baking sheets and bake 20 minutes or until lightly browned. Serve warm.

Whole Wheat and White Whole Wheat Flour

White whole wheat flour is milled from a special variety of white winter wheat, so that it has the same nutritional benefits of common red whole wheat flour, but with milder flavor and an attractive creamy light tan color. It is sold by the King Arthur company and by Bob's Red Mill in many natural foods markets, or is available from their catalogues.

RUMFORD AND ALUMINUM IN BAKING POWDER

Rumford's Baking Powder is made by Hulman and Company, a family-owned business founded in Indiana in 1848. It is made from only three ingredients: calcium acid phosphate, baking soda, and corn starch. Most baking powders include bitter-tasting sodium aluminum sulfate to delay the reaction between the liquid and the powder until the product goes into the oven. Because it doesn't contain aluminum, Rumford's is faster acting then common baking powder. Two-thirds of its reaction takes place in the mixing bowl; the remaining third takes place in the oven. When using Rumford's, combine dry ingredients, then add wet ingredients, mixing no more than necessary after adding the liquid. Bake immediately in a preheated oven.

228

Ripe Tomato, Jack Cheese, and Dijon Mustard Tart

I first learned to make this savory tart while working on a consulting project for a company called Northern Italian Foods. While the company didn't go far, the tart is worth making, perfect to serve for lunch or brunch. I'd make it on Mother's Day when I usually prepare a simple brunch so that I can enjoy it myself, or for a tea party. Just be sure your tomatoes are big and juicy and your basil is fragrant. The tender, slightly tangy buttermilk pastry used here contrasts perfectly with the flavors and textures of the filling.

MAKES ONE 11- TO 12-INCH TART

1 pound Buttermilk Pastry (*see* page 988)

2 pounds firm red-ripe beefsteak tomatoes

2 teaspoons kosher salt

$^1/_4$ cup extra-virgin olive oil

1 tablespoon chopped garlic

1 cup fresh basil leaves

$^1/_2$ teaspoon freshly ground black pepper

$^1/_4$ cup Dijon mustard

1 pound Monterey Jack cheese, shredded

Roll out the dough on a floured board to a thickness of $^1/_8$- to $^1/_4$-inch and 12 to 14 inches in diameter. Drape into an 11- to 12-inch fluted tart-shell pan with a removable bottom. Chill in the refrigerator about 30 minutes.

Preheat the oven to 375°F. Line tart shell with heavy-duty foil and fill with beans. (You will have extra dough; bag and freeze for another time. Defrost in the refrigerator when ready to use.) Bake the shell 25 minutes, or until pale brown and fully cooked. Cool and remove beans.

Meanwhile, slice the tomatoes, sprinkle with salt and let rest at room temperature for 30 minutes. Drain. Place the olive oil and garlic in the bowl of a food processor. Process to a paste, add the basil leaves and black pepper and process again briefly until the mixture forms a bright green paste. Mix gently with the tomato slices.

Brush the entire insides of the pastry shell with the mustard. Cover with shredded cheese. Arrange the slices of the marinated tomatoes over the cheese. Bake 30 minutes or until filling is bubbling. Cool and then cut into 8 or 12 slices.

STORING EXTRA EGG YOLKS

Leftover yolks are a bit more difficult to save than whites (which can simply be frozen). To store yolks for up to 2 days, slip them into a small container and cover with a layer of water to protect the yolks from drying out. Cover and refrigerate. To freeze, mix the yolks with an equal amount of sugar, transfer to a small container and freeze. Use for custard, pastry cream, ice cream, or any other sweet preparation that calls for yolks, cutting down slightly on the amount of sugar called for in the recipe.

229

Cornmeal, Scallion, and Cheddar Cheese Soufflé

Many cooks get scared when they hear the word "soufflé", although they are really easy to make and much more do-able at home than in a restaurant where it's so difficult to control the timing. Because the beaten egg whites are what make the soufflé rise, I use more whites than yolks for fluffy texture. Here's a perfect place to use a few of those frozen egg whites you've accumulated (see Freezing Egg Whites, page 289). For best rising, the whites should be at room temperature.

SERVES 4

1 tablespoon unsalted butter

$1/2$ cup cornmeal, preferably stone-ground

3 egg yolks + 6 egg whites

3 bunches scallions, trimmed, sliced

$1/2$ pound extra-sharp cheddar cheese, grated

1 teaspoon kosher salt

$1/2$ teaspoon freshly ground black pepper

$1/4$ teaspoon cayenne pepper

Butter a shallow 2-quart baking dish. Preheat the oven to 400°F. Bring 2 cups of water to the boil. Slowly pour in the cornmeal, stirring all the time. (It's easier to do this if you pour the cornmeal from a Pyrex measuring cup.) Bring back to the boil, then simmer 10 minutes or until thick, whisking often to break up any lumps.

Remove from heat, and then beat in the egg yolks, one at a time. Stir in the scallions, cheddar cheese, salt, pepper, and cayenne and reserve.

In a dry, clean bowl, beat the egg whites until they're white and fluffy and stick to the sides of the bowl. Fold one quarter of the whites into the corn-cheese mix, repeat, and then fold the remaining half into the mix. Spread the mixture into the baking dish. Bake for 25 to 30 minutes or until puffed and moist but not liquidy in the center. Serve immediately.

Farmhouse Cheddar Welsh Rabbit

In the early 1990s, I worked on a consulting project for the Dock Street Brewpub, the first brewpub in the state of Pennsylvania. In fact, the owner fought a case all the way to the Pennsylvania State Supreme Court to be allowed to produce and serve the beer on the same premises.

Although Dock Street is no more, its legacy is going strong in the area. The menu of international, beer-friendly food included this very popular rendition of Welsh Rabbit. Sometimes it's called "rarebit" to make it fancier, but in reality, Welsh rabbit is a tongue-in-cheek name for a poor man's dish that never actually includes rabbit.

SERVES 6

1¼ pounds extra-sharp cheddar cheese, grated

¼ cup cornstarch

6 ounces (½ bottle) dark beer

2 tablespoons Pickapeppa (or Worcestershire) sauce

2 teaspoons dry mustard

½ teaspoon cayenne pepper

3 egg yolks

12 slices multi-grain bread, toasted

12 slices bacon, cooked until crisp

12 slices ripe tomato

Combine cheddar, cornstarch, beer, Pickapeppa, mustard, cayenne, and yolks in a heavy pot. Cook over moderate heat, whisking, until mixture thickens. Do not allow mixture to boil. Remove from heat and keep warm.

Preheat broiler. Place bread slices in individual gratin dishes. Cover with sliced crisp bacon and tomato slices and top with cheese sauce. Broil until bubbling, 3 to 5 minutes, and serve piping hot.

231

Pickapeppa Sauce

With its colorful, parrot-festooned label, Pickapeppa Sauce was created in Shooter's Hill, Jamaica, in 1921 and is still made there today. Prepared with cane vinegar and tamarind and aged in oak barrels, it is similar to A-1 and Worcestershire sauce in color and consistency, but sweeter and mellower in flavor. Pickapeppa is versatile in the kitchen and can be mixed with cream cheese for a quick dip, or added to barbeque sauce, cooked plantains, or bloody Marys.

PRE-SHREDDED CHEESE AND CELLULOSE

While it's a bit more work to shred your own cheese, look at the ingredients of any bag of pre-shredded cheese and you'll see cellulose added. While this is an inert ingredient, added to keep the cheese from clumping back together, I'd much rather be eating pure cheese than any additives.

Crumb-Topped Macaroni and Cheese

I find that the more kinds of cheeses I use, the better this mac and cheese tastes. I wait until I have lots of bits and pieces of various cheeses, but not too much of any one kind and then make this dish, so loved by my kids. When they were young, I had to buy them packaged macaroni and cheese, which was an embarrassment to me; as they got a little older, they started to prefer my homemade version. Now, I'm happy to say, that's all they'll eat. Many recipes call for making a béchamel sauce (or cream sauce). Here I use milk and eggs, which together with the cheese forms a custard while baking. It's easy, cheesy, and luscious. The crumb topping adds that little bit of crunch.

SERVES 6

4 eggs

2 cups milk

Kosher salt, freshly ground black pepper, fresh grated
   nutmeg, and cayenne pepper to taste

6 ounces Monterey Jack, shredded

6 ounces Emmenthal or other Swiss cheese, shredded

6 ounces sharp cheddar cheese, shredded

$1/2$ cup grated Asiago, or other sharp,
   grating cheese

1 cup homemade or Japanese panko breadcrumbs

3 tablespoons unsalted butter, melted

1 pound ridged penne pasta

Preheat the oven to 375°F. Whisk together eggs, milk, salt, pepper, nutmeg, and cayenne. Mix in the Jack, Swiss, and Cheddar cheeses. In a small bowl, mix together the breadcrumbs, Asiago, and butter and reserve for topping.

Bring a large pot of salted water to the boil. Cook the pasta for about 6 minutes or until mostly cooked with a small, hard, pearly core. Drain but do not rinse.

Combine cooked pasta with egg-cheese mixture. Transfer to an 8-cup (2-inch deep) baking dish. Top with crumb mixture and then bake 30 minutes or until bubbling and browned on top.

232

CHERRIES

SWEET AND SOUR

CHERRIES
SWEET AND SOUR

Blush, rose, and cerise, cherries are totally alluring with a short, sweet season that makes them even more desirable. As beautiful to look at as they are delicious to eat, it's no wonder these petite beauties are favored fruits of painters. I've had a lifelong love for cherries, and eagerly anticipate cherry season every year. (Maybe it's partly because I grew up in Washington, D.C., where the blossoming—though not fruiting—Japanese cherry trees were an annual delight.)

Because they must be picked and sorted by hand and are vulnerable to both cold and bruising, fresh cherries are a luxury crop. For cherry aficionados, the season is never long enough. Luckily, the crop which starts in California in June, continues up into Washington State, moves cross-country to Michigan, and on to Ohio and Pennsylvania and further east later in the summer.

I snatch up superb gold-to-rose pink Rainier cherries from California during their fleeting season as long as they in good condition (no bruising or soft spots). The fanciest cherries I ever bought were an 18-pound wood crate of "double-face packed 10-row Bing cherries from the O.G. Packing Company of Stockton, California. Ten-row means that 10 extra-large cherries fill one row across a wooden crate. Double-faced means that each individual cherry is sorted for size, color and quality and then hand-packed in tight, even rows, all facing the same way like cherry sol-

diers. These primo cherries (or cherry fruit, as they're called in the wholesale produce business) fetch a price to match. Later in the season come the smaller, thin-skinned sour cherries, best suited to making pies and other desserts and for savory dishes like my Duck Breast with Sour Cherry Sauce and Austrian Chilled Cherry and Red Wine Soup.

All of the more than 1,000 varieties of cherries—sweet, sour, and in-between—belong to the *Prunus* (or stone fruit) family, a huge group including peaches, apricots, almonds, and plums. Some of our contemporary varieties are the same ones known to the Romans, but cherries hybridize like crazy. The native habitat of the cherry tree is probably somewhere between the Caspian Sea and the Balkans. Cherries had spread throughout Europe, however, before agricultural history was recorded.

By Roman times, cherries were already being cultivated in Britain. By the time colonists were taking the cherry to New England, they had the choice of two dozen or more varieties. The old Anglo-Saxon word, *ciris*, was replaced in the fourteenth century by *cherise* borrowed from the French. English speakers quickly misinterpreted *cherise* as a plural, and so the new singular name "cherry" was coined. We use the modern French term *cerise* for an adjective meaning bright red.

Cherry color ranges from deep dark red, like my husband's favorite Oxheart cherries that grew profusely in the small upstate Pennsylvania town where he grew up, to light red and creamy white with a blush of yellow. Sour cherries—morello, or pie cherries (*griottes* in French)—come from the *Prunus cerasus*, which grows as a shrub or small tree, sometimes called the *gean* or *mazzard*, which are very old English names for the wild cherry. Sweet cherries come from the *Prunus avium* tree. Dukes or royales, which are crosses of sweet and sour cherries, are much more rare.

Cherries grow wherever winter temperatures are not too severe and summer temperatures are moderate. They require winter cold in order to blossom in early spring. In Asia, particularly Japan, cherry varieties are selected for the beauty of their flowers; most of them do not set fruit. These beautiful ornamentals were widely disseminated throughout the moderate-temperature areas of North America and Europe after 1900. The mayor of Tokyo presented the Japanese flowering cherries around the Tidal Basin in Washington, D.C., in 1912.

Cherry growers have always been a brave lot. The trees themselves are vulnerable to disease, and are very choosy about soil and climate. Cherries also demand careful hand picking and packing. As you may well have noticed, when buying loose cherries from the supermarket, they are easily bruised. Skilled cherry pickers work with tin buckets contoured to fit snugly against their bodies. They scramble up and down tall, slender ladders, plucking cherries from limbs heavy with shiny, ruby-colored fruit.

Next, workers must carefully pack and refrigerate the cherries before shipping.

Cherries are a big business. California produces a little more than a fifth of the country's entire sweet-cherry crop, ranking second to Washington, which is famed for the high quality of its cherries and picks about 78,000 *tons* of cherries each season. The first variety to be picked is the Chelan, followed by the Bing, Ranier, and others, with the peak of the season in early July.

Michigan produces more red tart cherries than any other part of the world and holds an annual Cherry Festival in the beautiful Lake Michigan resort town of Traverse City, "the cherry capitol of the world." Though the variety is now rare in its native France, Michigan raises a huge quantity of French Montmorency cherries. Montmorency was a pre-revolutionary French dukedom in the southwest of France, famous for its cherries and, so legend has it, for a duke who insisted on having them with everything.

Montmorencys have been cultivated in Michigan for more than a century, where they are used for pies, preserves, jellies, juice, and wine. These same tart cherries are transformed by sweetening and drying to sell as a delectable (and rather pricey) alternative to raisins. During my first pregnancy, I craved those same Michigan Montmorency cherries so much, I would buy them in the 10-pound food-service bags straight from the Cherry Coop in Michigan just to keep up with my appetite.

CHERRY VARIETIES

The Bing is the leading sweet cherry in North America. Its fruit is firm, juicy, and a deep mahogany red when ripe. Bings are exceptionally large fruits with an intensely sweet, vibrant flavor. The fabulous, though rare, Rainier has golden skin with a pink-to-red blush, clear flesh, very sweet, delicate flavor and fine texture. Delicately flavored with extraordinary sugar levels, the Rainier has flesh that is very firm, and finely textured, though easily bruised if not handled gingerly. For this reason, many supermarkets are reluctant to carry them. Check out farmers' markets and roadside farm markets for hard-to-find fresh sour cherries, the cherries of choice for cherry pie.

To Pit or Not to Pit?

Must you pit them? This seems to be largely a personal choice, with many people saying that half the fun of eating a cherry pie is lining the pits up around the edge of each plate so you can count them at the end. If you do not pit the cherries, remember to warn your guests. When removing the pit, hold the fruit over a bowl so that the juices are caught. I use a sharp paring knife to cut a slit into the indentation along one side and then cut halfway around the cherry. I then twist off the two halves and pop out the pit. Note that a pound of fresh cherries will yield about 2 cups of pitted cherries.

CHERRIES IN DISGUISE

Cherries turn up in all sorts of guises. Maraschino cherries are pitted, colored, and packed in flavored sugar syrup. Once upon a time, marasca (or maraschino) cherries were preserved in the liqueur of the same name. They eventually evolved into the garish, artificially colored cherries that are American bar and ice cream sundae standards. Glacé or candied cherries are seen most often decorating cakes at holiday time. The pits of Mahlab or St. Lucy's cherry lend their flavor to Middle Eastern and North African sweet pastries.

Three well-known liqueurs start with cherries: kirsch, maraschino liqueur, and Cherry Heering. Kirsch or *Kirschwasser*, originally from Germany, is a clear, white fruit brandy distilled entirely from wild European cherries. Its popularity is one of the reasons that Germany is by far the largest producer worldwide of both sweet and sour cherries. Add kirsch to flavor fruit desserts such as Black Forest Cake and my Cherry-Vanilla Ice Cream (page 239).

Maraschino liqueur, originally from Dalmatia (now in Croatia) is a bittersweet cherry liqueur made from wild Marasca cherries and their crushed pits, which give it a subtle bitter-almond flavor. The cherries are processed and distilled much like brandy, and later combined with pure cane syrup before it is aged and filtered. Cherry Heering from Denmark is a dark red, cherry-flavored liqueur.

236

CHOOSING AND STORING CHERRIES

Fresh sweet cherries should be firm, plump, bright and glossy with full color, plump, crisp green stalks, and a sweet taste. Smaller sour cherries should be firm, bright, and uniformly red or dark red. Avoid purchasing overmature cherries that are soft, dull, seeping, shriveled, or have any soft brown spots.

Cherries should be refrigerated as soon as possible.

Sort them carefully and place loosely in a shallow container so that air can circulate. Don't allow the weight of the cherries on top to crush those on the bottom. Wash cherries just before using. One of the best ways to preserve cherries for future use is to freeze them. The easiest way is to line a tray with wax paper and place the fruit in a single layer. Freeze, then transfer the frozen fruit to freezer bags and freeze.

Sour Cherry and Red Wine Soup

I found pitted sour cherries in the freezer case at a local Russian supermarket and immediately set out to make this cold fruit soup, made in many versions in Germany, Austria, and Poland. Maybe you have to grow up with it, but to me, a chilled bowl of clear, crimson-red fruit soup makes for a most refreshing first course. Chefs are now serving all kinds of fruit soups for dessert, so that's another possibility. Serve it with a crisp cookie such as biscotti (see Fig and Walnut Biscotti, page 371) as a dessert.

SERVES 8

1 cup granulated sugar

1 stick cinnamon, crushed

$1/2$ teaspoon ground allspice

$1/2$ teaspoon ground black pepper

6 cups pitted sour cherries, about 2 pounds
  (frozen or fresh)

$1/4$ cup cornstarch

1 cup dry red wine, chilled

1 cup sour cream

In a large nonaluminum soup pot, combine 2 quarts of water, sugar, cinnamon, allspice, and black pepper. Bring to the boil and then add cherries. Simmer 30 minutes and then strain by letting the liquid drain through a fine sieve. Discard the solids.

Mix the cornstarch with $1/2$ cup cold water to make a slurry (thin paste). Beat slurry into the hot soup while stirring constantly. Continuing to stir, bring the soup back to the boil and then remove from heat. Cool and then chill in the refrigerator. Just before serving, stir in the red wine. Top each serving with a spoonful of sour cream.

Contrary to what may be your first instinct, it is not a good idea to put hot food in the refrigerator to cool it down. By doing so, the heat given off will raise the temperature of everything in the refrigerator, forcing the motor to work harder and cutting down on the shelf-life of everything inside. The same holds true of the freezer, where condensing steam will form unwanted frost. Instead, make sure that food is at no more than room temperature before refrigerating.

In warm or hot weather, transfer hot mixtures to smaller metal bowls or a metal pot, preferably stainless steel, because metal is such a good heat conductor. Food stored in plastic, ceramic, or glass won't cool as quickly, and quick cooling is one of the goals in food safety. Sink the bowls or pot into a larger container or a sink full of ice mixed with water, which will cool things much more quickly than plain ice (because of greater contact with the surface). When the ice melts, ladle out some of the water and then add more ice. Alternatively, surround the food with water and freezer gel-packs.

Seared Duck Breast with Sour Cherry Sauce

Fresh sour cherries are in season briefly in mid-summer. Snap them up if you find them at a farmers' market . Otherwise, look for frozen pitted sour cherries or substitute dried Montmorency cherries, from the sour cherry capital of America, Traverse City, Michigan. Soak the dried cherries in the red wine and vinegar for about 1 hour to plump them up before sautéing. If Moulard duck breast is not available, substitute the more familiar and smaller Pekin duck breast. Accompany this dish with Savory Wild Rice Pancakes (see page 979).

SERVES 4

2 boneless breasts of Moulard ducks

Kosher salt and freshly ground black pepper, to taste

2 tablespoons unsalted butter

1 pound sour cherries, pitted and halved

2 tablespoons granulated sugar

$1/2$ cup red wine

2 tablespoons red wine vinegar

1 tablespoon demi-glace concentrate (optional)

1 cup chicken stock, heated

2 tablespoons butter to finish sauce (optional)

Cut light scores into the skin side of the duck, cutting all the way through the fat layer but without piercing the flesh. Season the breasts on both sides with salt and pepper and leave the duck at room temperature for about 20 minutes.

In a heavy skillet large enough to hold the cherries in one layer, melt the butter until sizzling. Brown the cherries in the butter together with the sugar until the sugar melts and caramelizes lightly. Pour in the red wine and the vinegar and then cook several minutes until syrupy.

Separately dissolve the demi-glace concentrate in the hot chicken stock, stirring until completely liquefied. Add the sauce mixture to the cherries in the pan and cook together 5 minutes over high heat, or until the sauce has thickened slightly. Taste for seasoning, adding salt and pepper and optional butter and keep warm.

Meanwhile, place the duck breasts skin-side down in a cold cast-iron or nonstick skillet. Cook on low to medium heat until the skin is crisp, pouring off the excess fat every so often. (Save the delicious duck fat for sautéing, as long as it hasn't burned.) Pour off the fat from the pan and turn the breasts over. Cook about 5 minutes longer or until the breasts are medium rare (145°F. on a meat thermometer).

Remove the duck from the pan, drape with foil, and allow the meat to rest five minutes. Using a sharp carving knife (or preferably an electric carving knife), carve the duck breasts on the angle into thin, even slices, paralleling the length of the breasts. Arrange the duck slices on large, heated dinner plates and pour the sauce over top.

Cherry Vanilla Ice Cream

Kirschwasser, or "cherry water", is an eau de vie or "water of life" made by distilling cherries, not by flavoring pre-made spirits such as vodka or brandy with cherry flavor, as is done for less expensive cherry-flavored spirits such as Cherry Heering. It has a full-bodied cherry fragrance, is not sweet, and a little goes a long way. Try adding a little to chocolate desserts, because chocolate and cherries go so well together. Or serve this ice cream with chocolate cake or brownies. Start this ice cream a day ahead of time to give the cherry pits time to steep in the milk and lend their intriguing, slightly bitter flavor to the ice cream.

MAKES ABOUT 2 QUARTS

1 pound cherries (mixed varieties if possible), pitted and halved, with pits reserved

2 tablespoons kirsch mixed with 2 tablespoons granulated sugar

3 cups milk

8 egg yolks

1½ cups granulated sugar

1 cup heavy cream

¼ teaspoon salt

Starting the day before you wish to serve the ice cream, soak the cherries overnight in the kirsch mixed with the sugar. Scald the milk with the cherry pits and allow to steep overnight, refrigerating after the mixture cools. The next day, strain out and discard the pits. Add to the milk any liquid that has accumulated in the cherries.

In the bowl of a mixer, combine egg yolks with the sugar. Using the whisk attachment, beat on moderately high speed for one minute, until light colored and the mixture forms a ribbon. Meanwhile, scald the cream. Reduce the mixer speed to low and slowly pour in the cream to temper (or slowly heat) the custard. Stir in the cherry-flavored milk.

Transfer the custard to a medium nonreactive pot. Stir in the salt, then return pan to medium heat. Cook, whisking, until the custard reaches 165°F., or until it thickens visibly. Cool thoroughly over a bowl of ice water and then freeze in an ice cream maker. Just before removing from the ice cream maker, stir in the soaked fruits. Cover tightly and store in the freezer for up to 2 weeks.

239

Chocolate–Cherry Crunch Cookies

Here's the classic combination of chocolate and cherries in a chunky, dark, rich, chewy cookie. I first tasted these cookies more than 20 years ago when I stopped by the late SoHo Charcuterie on the way to the airport in NYC for a trip to Italy. Those cookies sustained me through the flight and gave me a treat in my hotel room for the next few days as I nursed a bad cold. If you don't have bittersweet chocolate, cut down the sugar to $^3/_4$ cup.

Makes 4 dozen

1 pound bittersweet chocolate

$^1/_4$ pound (1 stick) unsalted butter

8 eggs

1 cup granulated sugar

1 tablespoon vanilla extract

$^1/_4$ pound (1 cup) all-purpose flour, preferably unbleached

2 teaspoons baking powder

$^1/_2$ teaspoon kosher salt

$^1/_2$ pound semisweet chocolate chips

$^1/_2$ pound walnuts, roughly chopped

$^1/_2$ pound sun-dried cherries

Preheat the oven to 300°F. Place the chocolate and butter in a heatproof bowl and melt over steaming water, or using moderate power, heat in the microwave until barely melted. Cool to room temperature.

Beat together eggs, sugar, and vanilla until light. Stir in chocolate mixture. Transfer to a large mixing bowl. Whisk together dry ingredients: flour, baking powder, and salt. Spoon into the batter, beating only until mixed. Stir in chocolate chips, walnuts, and cherries.

Drop batter by tablespoonfuls onto baking sheets sprayed with nonstick coating, or covered with silpat sheets and bake 15 minutes. The cookies should come away from the pan without sticking in the middle, but should be soft inside. Store at room temperature.

Dutch Cherry Vlaai

A vlaai is a sweet bread dough covered with fruit and baked, almost like a fruit pizza, that is typical of the southern regions of the Netherlands (Limburg and Brabant). It is made in many variations including rice, apricot, white chocolate, apple and rum, crumb, goose-berry, and this cherry version. This recipe was generously given to me by an accomplished Dutch physicist, Anneke Sengers, who has been a long-time family friend.

Serves 6 to 8

Bread Dough Crust

$^1/_4$ cup milk, lukewarm

5 tablespoons + $^1/_4$ cup granulated sugar, divided

1 teaspoon kosher salt

$2^1/_4$ teaspoons dried yeast (1 packet)

1 egg, lightly beaten

4 tablespoons unsalted butter, melted

½ pound (2 cups) all-purpose flour,
 preferably unbleached

Cherry Filling (recipe follows)

Combine the milk, 1 tablespoon sugar, and the salt in a bowl and then sprinkle in the yeast. Allow the yeast to proof; when it bubbles up, it is ready (about 5 minutes). Transfer the yeast mixture to a mixer bowl and stir in the egg and butter. Beat in the flour and continue beating until the dough is smooth and elastic (though it will be sticky). Cover and let the dough rise at warm room temperature until doubled in bulk, about 1 hour.

Punch down and then roll out on a flour-dusted surface to a circle about 12 inches in diameter. Spray the bottom of a 10-inch fluted tart pan with nonstick spray. Cover the bottom of the pan with the dough, which should reach 1 inch up the sides. Prick the inside of the dough and allow it to rise for another 30 to 45 minutes.

Preheat the oven to 400°F. Cover the dough with the Cherry Filling, leaving a 1-inch border around the edges. Make sure the cherries are packed closely together with most of their cut sides facing up. Brush the edge of the dough with the beaten egg. Sprinkle the fruit and the edge of the dough with 2 tablespoons of sugar. Bake 20 minutes, and then remove from the oven and sprinkle with the remaining 2 tablespoons of sugar. Return to the oven and bake 10 minutes longer or until the dough is puffed and browned and the filling is bubbling.

Cherry Filling

2 pounds sour cherries, pitted and halved (substitute
 sweet cherries mixed with the juice of 1 lemon)

1 egg, lightly beaten

½ cup granulated sugar

In a bowl, combine the cherries, egg, and sugar, and reserve.

UNBLEACHED FLOUR, CERESOTA, AND KING ARTHUR

I always choose unbleached flour except for the rare light sponge cake that needs bleached flour for lightness. I prefer—and have tested these recipes using—a good unbleached all-purpose flour, such as Ceresota (known as Hecker's west of the Mississippi), or King Arthur's from Vermont.

241

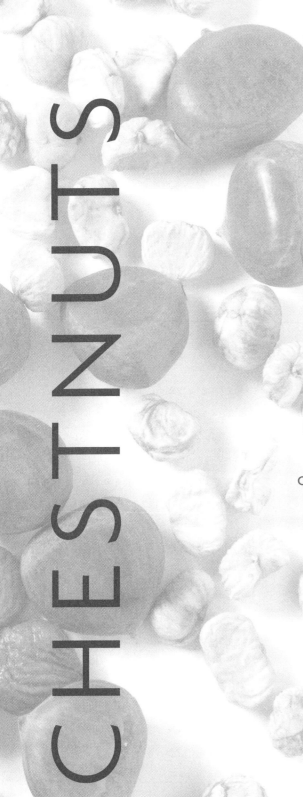

CHESTNUTS

CHESTNUTS

On the streets of Italy in November and December, while rain and cold wind may dampen the spirits, chestnut roasters on street corners ply their toasting, smoldering wares. Giant, soft, and creamy-sweet *marrone* (large chestnuts) are roasted over charcoal in huge tin pans, split open like a smiling mouth and arranged in orderly rows ready for the taking. Irresistible! Almost as irresistible are chestnut gelato, with pieces of candied *marrons* (commonly known as *marrons glacées*) folded in for texture, served with oven-roasted winter fruits; lentil soup with chestnuts; and baked apples filled with chestnut cream. In New York City, similar pans of fragrant roasting chestnuts help create that special holiday feeling. Chestnuts are abundant in the southern Italian region of Campania, which is where most of the world's chestnuts are grown today.

Chestnuts are a wonderful ingredient in the kitchen, whether for savory or sweet dishes, though less known in the U.S. than in Europe, probably because the magnificent groves of native American chestnuts died out early in the twentieth century. In Europe, chestnut season is a reason to celebrate, and greengrocers and restaurants make displays of the spiky split-open chestnut fruits, revealing the shiny, mahogany-skinned nuts inside. For both Native Americans and Europeans, chestnuts were an important food source. Chestnuts are starchier and contain less oil than other nuts, so chestnut flour is also made. Today, chestnuts go into soup, desserts, side dishes, stuffing, and dumplings.

The cultivated chestnut, *marrone* in Italian and *marron* in French, produces a single, large nut inside each case and is the type imported to the U.S. in season. The highest grade for chestnuts is AAA, which are largest and firmest but rarely found in the retail market. The wild chestnut, *castagna* in Italian and *châtaigne* in French, has several small nuts inside each case. Most fresh chestnuts in the U.S. are imported from Italy, but sweeter and less starchy Asian chestnuts with relatively thin skin come in from Asia and are also being grown in America. Dried chestnuts are commonly used in Asian and Italian cooking but only the Asian variety, *Castanea mollissima*, is commonly available in dried form.

While nothing beats the flavor of fresh-roasted chestnuts, even for a food fanatic like me, slitting, roasting, and then peeling the chestnuts while they're still hot enough to burn your fingers is a bit of a challenge. At home, I often use the vacuum-packed chestnuts from France and Italy that come in glass jars or vacuum-packed plastic packages.

PREPARING FRESH CHESTNUTS

Make a crisscross cut on the domed side of each chestnut with a small, sharp knife, taking care not to slip off the smooth, slippery shell. Roast at 425°F. for about 20 minutes, or until the chestnuts inside start to brown. Cool slightly and pull off the outer peels, taking care to also remove the brown inner skin as well. It's easiest to do when the chestnuts are quite warm, so work with only a few at a time, keeping the rest in the pot or oven, and work with heat resistant gloves to make peeling easier. Or, roast the cut chestnuts over the embers of a fireplace fire by placing them in a perforated steel chestnut roasting pan and shaking over the fire for about 15 minutes, or until all sides of the chestnut are darkened.

Buying Chestnuts

While there's no doubt that the best chestnuts are the ones you cook yourself, for most of us, the peeled, cooked chestnuts sold in glass jars at Trader Joe's and other places make a good substitute. They also sell Italian frozen roasted chestnuts still in their shells, but scored for relatively easy removal in the winter season. Chestnut purée, usually sweetened, is sold in cans from France, and expensive but exquisite *marrons glacés* (candied large chestnuts) and chestnut flour can be found in specialty stores, especially in winter.

Italian Chestnut Soup with Fennel

This fragrant, rich, and deep-flavored soup has a base of the salt-and-pepper cured pork belly called pancetta *in Italian. Bacon makes the best substitute, though if it is fatty, some of the fat should be discarded. Sweetly nutty Marsala wine (the dry type is best here) from the island of Sicily adds flavor and a slight kick; dry sherry, Madeira, or even Tuscan Vin Santo, a dessert wine made from raisin-grapes, will also work. Chestnuts and fennel are a natural pair; both are in season in autumn and in high demand in Italy, where most of the world's chestnuts are grown. The sweet, starchy-nutty chestnuts are lightened and accented by the fennel, both in its bulb form and its more intensely anise-flavored seeds.*

SERVES 6 TO 8

245

2 ounces ($1/2$ cup) diced pancetta (or bacon)
$1/2$ cup each: chopped celery, chopped onion, and
   chopped fennel (can be stalks)
2 whole cloves
2 bay leaves
1 tablespoon ground fennel seed
2 quarts chicken stock, preferably homemade
About 1 pound peeled cooked chestnuts
$1/2$ cup dry Marsala
$1/2$ cup heavy cream
Kosher salt and freshly ground black pepper to taste

In a large soup pot, heat the pancetta over moderate heat until the fat has rendered out. Add the celery, onion, fennel, cloves, bay leaves, and fennel seed, and cook, covered, for about 15 minutes, or until the vegetables have softened.

Add the chicken stock and chestnuts and bring back to the boil. Skim as necessary and simmer 45 minutes, or until the chestnuts are soft enough to break apart.

Pick out and discard the bay leaves and cloves. Blend the soup until smooth and velvety and then strain through a sieve or a food mill.

Transfer to a clean pot and add the Marsala and the cream. Bring back to the boil, season to taste with salt and pepper, and serve immediately.

MADEIRA WINE

Madeira wine is named after the Portuguese island that sits far out into the Atlantic off the coast of Morocco, where it is has been produced since about 1500. Madeira was a natural port of call for ships traveling to America or south around Africa to Asia, and ships invariably loaded up on the famed soft, fortified wine made there. By the eighteenth century, the British American and West Indian colonies drank Madeira as their only wine. It was used to toast the Declaration of Independence in 1776, and in 1789, the inauguration of George Washington. To make Madeira, wine is fortified with brandy, a practice that originally helped keep the wine from turning to vinegar on long sea voyages. It is then aged in wood by a complex method and heated either by the sun or by steam pipes, giving it its characteristic light, fruity, caramel flavor that makes it so good for cooking.

Madeira-Braised Chestnuts and Brussels Sprouts

In Great Britain, where Brussels sprouts have gone from the most hated vegetable to one of the most popular in just a few years, they are combined with chestnuts and served alongside a holiday roast turkey. Adding the Madeira (or dry sherry or dry Marsala) makes them just a bit sweeter and richer. If you buy cooked chestnuts, usually packed in glass jars, be sure they're unsweetened.

SERVES 4

1 pound Brussels sprouts, trimmed
2 cups cooked whole chestnuts (unsweetened)
3 tablespoons unsalted butter
2 tablespoons chopped shallots
$1/4$ cup Madeira
Kosher salt, grated nutmeg, and freshly ground black pepper to taste

Cut the Brussels sprouts in halves. Steam or boil in salted water for about 5 minutes, or until crisp-tender and bright green.

In a large skillet, melt the butter and keep cooking over low heat until the butter starts to brown and has a nutty aroma. Add the shallots and sauté briefly. Add the chestnuts, sprouts, Madeira, and seasonings and toss to combine.

Simmer together until the liquid in the pan is syrupy, about 10 minutes. Serve in a skillet.

Castagnaccio: Tuscan Chestnut Cake with Pine Nuts, Currants, and Rosemary

Castagnaccio, which lies somewhere between a sweet and a savory cake, is a popular afternoon snack for school children in the afternoon in Tuscany. It is dense and nutty and has a slight sweetness imparted by the chestnut flour, the currants, and the fennel seeds. Strutto (or melted lard) is the traditional fat used here, but olive oil makes a good substitute. For the best texture and browning, use a blue steel pan, such as those used for French fluted flan tarts. I also like to serve the Castagnaccio as a starchy accompaniment to hearty game dishes such as braised wild boar or venison in red wine sauce.

SERVES 6 TO 8

1 pound (4 cups) chestnut flour

$1/4$ pound (1 cup) pastry flour

2 teaspoons baking powder

Kosher salt to taste

$1/2$ pound currants, soaked in warm water to cover

$1/4$ pound pine nuts, lightly toasted

1 tablespoon finely chopped rosemary

2 tablespoons fennel seeds

$1/4$ cup melted lard or olive oil

Preheat the oven to 400°F. Whisk together the dry ingredients: chestnut flour, pastry flour, baking powder, and salt. Beat in enough cold water, about 2 quarts, to make a soupy mixture. Mix in half the currants, pine nuts, rosemary, and fennel seeds.

Brush a large shallow pan, such as a pizza pan, with melted lard or olive oil. Spread the batter into the pan, so that it is no more than one half inch-thick. Sprinkle remaining currants, pine nuts, and fennel over top and bake 20 minutes, or until set, and lightly browned on top. Remove from the oven, cut into thin wedges and serve while still warm.

Pumpkin Spice Roulade with Chestnut and Cranberry Fillings

This moist and fragrant cake was developed by the talented Robert Bennett, former pastry chef at the acclaimed Le Bec-Fin in Philadelphia and now judge for the International Pastry Cup. True to his American roots, Bennett came up with this roulade to serve at Thanksgiving. To me, it's a perfect combination of French techniques and American flavors. If you can't find sweetened chestnut puree, follow the recipe for Homemade Chestnut Cream (see page 279).

SERVES 10 TO 12

Cranberry Filling

1 cup orange juice

1 cup granulated sugar

1 (12-ounce) bag cranberries

In a medium heavy-bottomed nonreactive pot, bring the orange juice, sugar, and cranberries to the boil, stirring often and skimming as necessary. Simmer until the cranberries have burst and the sauce is thick, stirring occasionally, about 15 minutes. Cool to room temperature, and then refrigerate until chilled.

Chestnut Filling

1 cup sweetened chestnut puree

  (or Homemade Chesnut Cream, *see* page 249)

2 tablespoons gold rum

1 teaspoon vanilla extract

1 cup heavy cream

Beat together chestnut puree, rum, and vanilla and reserve. Separately beat the cream until light and firm. Fold the cream into the chestnut mixture, and refrigerate, tightly covered, until ready to use.

Pumpkin Spice Cake

$1/4$ pound (1 cup) cake flour, or 7 tablespoons

  all-purpose flour + 1 tablespoon cornstarch

1 teaspoon baking soda

1 teaspoon ground cinnamon

1 teaspoon ground ginger

$1/2$ teaspoon ground allspice

Pinch Kosher salt

3 eggs

1 cup + $1/2$ cup granulated sugar

$1/2$ cup canned pumpkin purée

$1/4$ cup golden rum

Preheat the oven to 400°F. Line a 12 x 18-inch half sheet pan or two 11 x 17-inch shallow jelly-roll pans with parchment paper or Silpat sheets.

Sift together the dry ingredients: cake flour, baking soda, cinnamon, ginger, allspice, and salt, and reserve.

Beat eggs and 1 cup sugar together until light colored and the mixture forms a ribbon. Reduce the mixer to low speed, then beat in the pumpkin. Fold in the dry ingredients.

Spread the batter out in the prepared pan(s) with a rubber spatula. Bake 8 to 10 minutes or until the center puffs up and the cake has started to come away from the sides of the pan. Remove cake from the oven and immediately turn out onto a wire cooking rack.

Meanwhile, in a small pot, bring the $1/2$ cup sugar and $1/2$ cup water to the boil. When the liquid is clear, remove it from the heat, stir in the rum, and set aside. When the cake has completely cooled, brush all over with the rum syrup.

Assembly

Pumpkin Spice Cake

Cranberry Filling

Chestnut Filling

Confectioners' sugar, for sprinkling

Spread one-half the Cranberry Filling evenly over the under side of the cake, making two smaller cakes if using the jelly-roll pans, and leaving a one-inch border on one long end of each cake layer. Spread the Chestnut Filling directly on top, again leaving a one-inch border on the same long end.

Starting on the filled end and rolling the long way, roll the cake(s) up tightly, ending with the plain border for the seam. Turn the cake(s) seam-side down and chill in the refrigerator for at least 2 hours, or up to overnight. Sprinkle with confectioners' sugar, slice on the diagonal using a serrated knife, and serve.

248

HOMEMADE CHESTNUT CREAM

3/4 pound shelled chestnuts, either
    vacuum-packed or roasted and shelled
1 cup granulated sugar
1 teaspoon vanilla extract

Combine the chestnuts and sugar along with 2 cups
of water in a medium heavy-bottomed nonreactive
saucepan. Bring to the boil and simmer over low
heat for 20 minutes, or until the chestnuts start to
break up into bits and the liquid has mostly evaporated. Remove from the heat and stir in the vanilla.
Transfer the mixture to the bowl of a food processor
and process till smooth. If there are any bits of skin
in the mixture, strain through a sieve or food mill.
Cool to room temperature and then refrigerate until
needed. The chestnut cream will keep in the refrigerator for up to two weeks and can also be frozen.

Chocolate–Chestnut Terrine

*This layered combination of chocolate and chestnut
accented by small bits of sun-dried fruits and pistachios is
a lighthearted variation on the classic terrine made from
ground, seasoned meat studded with bits of meats and
the same pistachios as here. This elegant terrine is a good
make-ahead dessert for wintertime holidays. It keeps
quite well for up to 1 week, refrigerated.*

MAKES ONE 8–CUP TERRINE, TO SERVE 12

1/2 pound dried California apricots, diced
1/4 cup brandy
2 pounds cooked chestnuts, divided (fresh or jarred)
1 cup + 3/4 cup + 3/4 cup granulated sugar
1 cup light cream
1 cup heavy cream
4 egg yolks
1/4 cup dark rum
1/2 pound semisweet chocolate, melted
1/4 pound (1 stick) unsalted butter
1/4 pound dried cranberries
1/4 cup peeled pistachios

Soak the apricots in brandy overnight. Simmer 1 pound of
the chestnuts in 1 cup of sugar and 1 cup water for 45 minutes, or until chestnuts are shiny but tender. Drain, and
break up any whole chestnuts into smaller bits.

In a non-reactive, heavy bottomed pot, scald the light
and heavy cream together, then whip the yolks with
3/4 cup sugar, and temper into the scalded cream. Heat
until the custard thickens perceptibly, and registers about
165°F. on a thermometer. Remove from heat and mix

249

custard with the remaining 1 pound of chestnuts and the rum. Process together until a smooth puree is obtained. Divide the mixture into two bowls, one with one-third and one with two-thirds of the mixture and reserve.

Combine the chocolate with the larger amount of chestnut cream.

In the bowl of a mixer, cream the butter and remaining $^3/_4$ cup sugar until light and fluffy. Add the smaller amount of chestnut cream and beat again to combine. Stir in the sweetened chestnut bits, drained diced apricots, cranberries, and pistachios.

Line an 8-cup loaf pan with wax or parchment paper. Spread half of the chocolate mixture on the bottom of the pan, tapping down to break up any bubbles. Cover with half of the chestnut-fruit layer; top with the remaining chocolate mixture, and then the remaining chestnut cream. Tap to remove any air pockets and refrigerate until firm, or overnight. Unmold and slice using a knife dipped in hot water.

CHICKEN

CHICKEN

According to Andre Simon's *Encyclopedia of Gastronomy*, written almost fifty years ago, "Everybody in America loves chicken, and more importantly, can afford it." Today, Americans consume more than 85 pounds of chicken per person, per year!

Chicken is perfect for easy home-style meals and because it is so versatile, your family won't get bored. It also has the highest percentage of protein (30) and the lowest percentage of fat (5) of any animal meat. Raising chickens is also an efficient use of our precious natural resources, because it takes only two pounds of grain to produce one pound of chicken meat as compared to four pounds for pork, and a full eight pounds for beef.

In the children's classic *Amelia Bedelia*, Amelia is directed by her new employers to "Dress the chicken!" Taking the instruction literally, Amelia dresses the chicken in a tiny polka-dot outfit. Instead, "dress" your chicken according to any of these international recipes that take advantage of the chicken's mild flavor and readiness to absorb flavors. You'll think plain chicken is for the birds.

The domestic chickens we know today are believed to have descended mainly from the Red Jungle Fowl, *Gallus bankiva*, of Southeast Asia where it exists in the wild. Domesticated chickens may have been kept in India as long ago as 3200 BCE, and in China and Egypt as early as 1400 BCE. The earliest domestication was for cockfight-ing rather than for food, which just shows that, to many, gambling is more important than eating! There are about 175 varieties of chickens, though the most common varieties in America are the Cornish (from Great Britain) and the White Rock (from New England). Specialty varieties include the Plymouth Rock, Rhode Island, the small but tasty Chinese Black Chicken with its black skin, and the South American Araucana, which lays the blue or green-ish eggs sometimes seen in farmers' markets.

Not all chickens are alike; in fact, chickens are raised and fed very differently. Some are free-range—not con-fined to a cage and able to roam around. Some are organic—every bit of their feed must be certified as organically grown. Grain-fed chickens have a diet of soy, barley, and corn. Free-range chickens are allowed access to the outdoors. They are generally tastier and more humanely raised, but not as tender and more expensive. Some "humanely raised" free-range chickens are given free access to clean ground, comfortable housing, and good feed and water.

Kosher chickens are presalted, fulfilling just one of the requirements to acquire this dietary designation. These birds must have no imperfections and are fed a vegetar-ian diet. Many people, Jewish or not, buy only kosher chickens because they are raised and processed with special care.

Commercial chickens are commonly fed a high-protein diet, often made from ground fish meal, to make them put on weight faster. (It takes longer to convert grain into flesh than to convert flesh into more flesh.) Because of consumer preference, in the Northeast, chickens are commonly fed marigold petals to make their skin yellow whereas in the South, white chickens are preferred.

A capon is a large chicken, actually a cockerel (young cock) that has been surgically castrated so it becomes larger and fatter than other fowl when fully developed. Although expensive, it has tender, succulent meat covered with soft, smooth-textured skin and has been specifically bred for well-flavored meat. A capon is under 8 months old and weighs 6 to 10 pounds. Its name comes from the Latin *capon, capo*, meaning to cut. Capons have been known since before the twelfth century. Roasting whole and stuffed is the method of choice for capons.

Cornish game hens look just like miniature chickens, which is just what they are. They were created in 1965 by chicken mogul Donald Tyson, who cross-bred White Rock and Cornish chickens with the goal of obtaining small, reasonably priced, individual chickens that would be especially well-suited to serve at large banquets. Two-thirds of Cornish game hens sold in the U.S. still come from Tyson Foods. For banquets and restaurant service, the birds are often partially boned (with only the rib cage removed) in a process called glove-boning (*see* page 269).

Cornish hens are quite meaty and relatively fatty, though tender and mild in flavor. They are easy to split in half and cut away the back bone before or after cooking, because their bones are relatively soft. The birds are sold whole, with or without a separate packet of giblets, and are available fresh or frozen. Frozen Cornish game hens, usually sold in pairs, are commonly found in supermarkets and warehouse club stores. I especially recommend the fresh Cornish hens sold by Bell and Evans, although they are higher in price, because they are incredibly tender, juicy, and the perfect size for one person.

The hens are five to six weeks old and weigh between one and two pounds, with the average size of one and a quarter pound a good size for one person. Larger hens can be served for two, allowing about one pound of hen per person. Because they are young and tender, fresh Cornish hens won't keep very well. Cook fresh hens within two days of purchase. To defrost hens, place them in a pan to catch any drips and refrigerate one to two days.

Poussin are very small, young chickens, which get their name from the French for unfledged—a bird that is too young to have developed feathers for flying. These individually portioned birds have very delicate, moist, subtly flavored lean meat and are most popular among French chefs. Poussin are very soft textured, with fragile flesh and bones; they are about 1 month old and weigh about one pound, perfect for a single portion.

Poussin are available in specialty markets and are most often roasted whole, often with a rich stuffing. They are rather high priced, but are still an accessible luxury food. Because they are so young, poussin are quite perishable. Store to 1 to 2 days refrigerated.

Freezing Chicken

Sometimes it makes the most sense to freeze chicken. For best results in freezing, it's important to lessen the "drip" (excess liquid) which affects the texture of the bird. Defrost as slowly as possible in a cold part of the refrigerator. Remember: the principle is "quick to freeze, slow to defrost." To prevent freezer burn, wrap tightly, freeze quickly, and maintain cold.

Names for Chicken

A cockerel is a male chicken under one year of age; a cock or rooster is a male more than one year old; a pullet is a female under one year, and a hen is a female over one year of age.

Dark and White Meat Chicken

Every cut of chicken has its own distinct flavor and texture. Because chickens do a lot of standing around and little flying, they have white, mild-flavored and tender breast meat. Their legs get much more exercise and because of this, need a larger oxygen supply. This capacity to store oxygen results in dark, firm leg meat with a stronger, gamier flavor. By using the right cooking method, the white meat will be flavorful and juicy and the dark meat will be tender enough to fall off the bone.

CHICKEN THIGHS

Darker meat chicken thighs may be less prized than the white breast meat, but for those of us who want both flavor and juiciness, chicken thighs are the only way to go. The rule is the more a muscle is used, the more flavor it gets. Chicken breasts are white and tender because the chickens don't fly anywhere. They do use their thighs, however, for walking around the chicken yard. As a result, their thighs have a more pronounced flavor. Because chicken thighs are a stronger-tasting meat to begin with and have more fat, which collects flavors, make a point of buying an all-natural chicken so the thighs will have a milder flavor than commercial chickens. I like the top-quality, creamy-skinned, grain-fed chicken from Bell and Evans, or another all-natural chicken, such as Bob Eberly's organic chickens.

Now that boneless, skinless chicken thighs are for sale in supermarkets, they're easier than ever to use. Trim off any visible fat, and marinate them in adobo, in vinaigrette dressing, or in buttermilk mixed with thyme and a little hot sauce and then grill them, spread out flat on the grill for faster cooking. Or steam the thighs; pick off the meat and discard any tougher connective tissue and you'll have the makings of the juiciest, best-tasting chicken salad ever. When you're making a slow-cooked braise, it's best to use chicken thighs on the bone (with or without their skin).

COOKING CHICKEN THIGHS

When roasting chicken, roast the thighs complete with skin and bones for the juiciest results. Spread the thighs out in a single layer into a shallow pan and roast in a pre-heated oven at 400°F. until the thighs are well browned, about 30 minutes. Remove the pan from the oven, pour off the fat that has accumulated, and then transfer the thighs to a plate to keep warm. Now, take a lesson from the pros and deglaze the pan. This just means melting off the browned solids that have stuck to the pan and boiling them with a liquid to form a natural pan sauce.

To deglaze the roasting pan, pour about 1 cup of water, stock, white wine, dry white vermouth, or even apple juice into the pan and place back in the oven for about 15 minutes. The liquid will soften the solids enough so that you can scrape them up with a wooden spoon or a rubber spatula. Pour the contents of the pan—including the browned bits—into a small pot and cook over high heat to evaporate some of the excess water and to thicken the sauce slightly. Serve the roast chicken thighs with some of the strained pan sauce poured over top. Add potatoes, polenta, or rice to absorb the delicious pan juices.

The only trick to cooking chicken thighs is how to tell when they're done. Because the meat is darker, it doesn't change much in color when it's fully cooked. If you're cooking the thighs on the bone, the meat should pull away easily from the bone when fully cooked. Otherwise, look for opaque meat, rather then translucent. As the proteins in the meat cook, they form a crisscross net. In raw meat, the proteins line up, so you can see through them. If you roast the thighs, the juices will run clear, rather than pink, when the chicken is cooked through. To be absolutely sure, a meat thermometer stuck into the thickest part of the thigh should read 170°F.

Chicken Types

Nowadays, there isn't a clear-cut difference between "fryers" and "roasters" since both are young enough to be tender. Most of the birds we eat are raised to be fully grown at 7 to 12 weeks. Large chickens, sometimes called "oven-roasters", are bred for an enlarged breast area. Older and tougher (but flavorful) stewing hens, available by special order, give great flavor to soup or sauce but their meat tends to be mealy.

For a special meal, try a capon (a neutered male bird) which can be quite large but still tender and quite succulent, though always high-priced, as befits this exotic creature. Unless you live in a rural community, it's rare to come across a cock, though this is actually the most flavorful bird of all, best for stews, like the French classic Coq au Vin (cock in wine sauce), or for the richest chicken soup you'll ever taste.

Broiler/Fryer: A young chicken about 13 weeks old with smooth-textured skin, relatively lean meat, and a flexible breastbone. It is quite versatile and can be cooked by almost any cooking method, especially by broiling or frying. It usually weighs between $2\frac{1}{2}$ and $3\frac{1}{2}$ pounds.

Roaster: A roaster is a young chicken, 3 to 5 months old, weighing $3\frac{1}{2}$ to 5 pounds. It has tender meat, smooth-textured skin, and a breastbone that is less flexible than broiler meat-type chicken. It is especially suited to roasting.

Stewing Chicken: A stewing chicken, hen, or fowl is a mature female chicken, often the by-product of egg production, that is over 10 months old and weighs up to

8 pounds. It has flavorful meat that is a bit chewier than that of a roaster and is best cooked by stewing or braising.

Common Cuts of Chicken:

- Half or split: broiler-fryers cut in half
- Breast half or breast split: broiler-fryer breasts on the bone
- Breast quarter: including breast, wing, and back
- Drumstick: the part of the leg below the "knee"
- Drummette: the meatiest top wing section adjoining the shoulder
- Leg quarter: the drumstick and thigh
- Cut-up chicken: broiler-fryers that are cut up and packaged with two breast halves, two thighs, two drumsticks, and two wings
- Chinese-cut chicken: hacked into bite-size pieces on the bone
- Chicken oyster: (*soy l'y laisse* in French: "the fool leaves it there") a choice morsel that is a muscle inside the hollow of the bones just above the tail at the point where the backbone and thigh meet. Each chicken contains two of these small walnut-shaped muscles on either side with rich flavor and smooth, dense flesh. The carver usually keeps it for him/herself or offers it to a special guest.

USING LEFTOVERS

In Medieval France, a large pot remained on the back of the range day and night, constantly replenished with scraps, recalling the story of Stone Soup, where a soup is made "out of nothing." This is truly elegant cooking with nothing wasted as each soup becomes the next. While cutting up the aromatic vegetables to finish one soup, I save the tasty trimmings in a well-sealed plastic bag for the next. Carrot, celery, onion, fennel ends, mushroom stems, turnip and celery root trimmings, parsnip tops, tender herb stems, tomato tops and seeds are all flavorful. Any chicken wings, backbones, and even roasted chicken carcasses are saved as well with a separate bag for trimmings and roast ends of beef. The next time I make chicken soup or beef stock, out comes my hoard to be put in a stockpot, covered with water, skimmed, and slowly simmered overnight on lowest heat with the lid slightly ajar.

Grandma's Jewish Chicken Soup with Matzo Balls

There's more than one way to make a good soup. Grandma would most likely use an entire stewing hen, and she'd leave the golden dots of fat in the bowl when serving for its extra richness. A Chinese cook would remove all the skin from a whole chicken, except for the skin covering the wings, so that there would be very little fat at the end. As for me, I make my broth restaurant style, using inexpensive and tasty but fattier backs and necks. I cool and then chill the soup overnight, spooning off and discarding the fat which rises to the top. (The fat may or may not solidify.)

Here I supplement the chicken with inexpensive turkey wings to impart full-bodied flavor and plenty of natural gelatin to the soup. A leftover roasted chicken carcass would make a wonderful addition to the pot. The matzo balls are simply dumplings made from ground-up matzo flatbreads. Some people like "sinkers;" some like "floaters," I go for "Mr. In-Between."

MAKES 3 QUARTS

5 pounds chicken backs and necks

2 pounds turkey wings

3 ribs celery, 1 whole and 2 finely diced

2 parsley roots, 1 whole and 1 peeled and thinly sliced

1 whole yellow onion

3 carrots, 1 whole and 2 peeled and thinly sliced

2 leeks, thinly sliced

2 to 3 sprigs dill +2 tablespoons chopped dill

1 cup mushroom stems (optional)

2 bay leaves

Kosher salt and freshly ground black pepper, to taste

Put the chicken parts and turkey wings into a large soup pot along with enough cold water to cover by 2 to 3 inches (about 1 gallon). Bring to the boil over moderate heat, skimming off any foam on top. When no more foam rises up, add 1 rib celery, 1 parsley root, the onion, 1 carrot, the dill sprigs, mushroom stems, and bay leaves. Bring back to the boil. Reduce heat to a bare simmer, cover with the lid slightly ajar and cook 4 to 6 hours, or up to overnight.

Cool, strain the solids and discard them. Chill overnight. Remove and discard the solid fat from the top. Bring the soup to the boil and add the diced celery, the sliced parsley root, the carrots, leeks, and the chopped dill. Bring to the boil, season to taste with salt and black pepper, add the poached matzo balls and simmer 10 minutes or until the vegetables are tender.

Matzo Balls

4 eggs, separated

3 tablespoons cold chicken stock

1/4 cup chicken fat or shortening, melted and cooled

1/2 cup finely diced onion

Generous amount of kosher salt and ground white pepper

1 1/4 cups matzo meal, enough to make a firm, yet slightly sticky dough

Whisk together the egg yolks, chicken stock, chicken fat, onion, and salt and pepper. Beat in the matzo meal and reserve.

Beat the egg whites until soft and fluffy but still glossy and firm enough to stick to the sides of the bowl. Fold the eggs into the yolk mix in thirds, so as not to deflate. Add a little water if the mixture is too stiff; add a little more matzo meal if it is too thin. Keep in mind that the mixture will stiffen as it sets and chills.

Chill mixture till firm, about 1 hour. Form into walnut-sized balls using an ice cream scoop to make it easier (size 40, meaning 40 portions to the quart, is perfect).

Bring a large, wide pot of salted water to the boil. Drop the matzo balls one by one into the water and boil until the matzo balls float to the top, 3 to 5 minutes. Scoop out with a perforated spoon or wire skimmer and drop directly into the pot of simmering chicken soup above, or rinse under cold water and reserve until you're ready to serve the soup.

257

Curried Chicken Salad with Apples

Here I use roasted chicken breast, cooked on the bone for moistness. Don't throw out the bones; save them in the freezer and add to your next pot of chicken broth. While the cilantro adds a haunting, pungent note to the salad, balancing the sweetness of the apples, it is always optional. No other herb creates as much controversy; people either absolutely love it or detest it. I, of course, crave cilantro and use it with abandon.

SERVES 8

4 pounds chicken breast on the bone

Kosher salt and freshly ground black pepper to taste

2 tablespoons curry powder

$1/2$ cup fresh lemon juice

1 cup mayonnaise (homemade or purchased)

$1/2$ head celery, thinly sliced

1 bunch scallions, thinly sliced

2 each: red and green apples, cut into $1/2$-inch dice

$1/4$ cup chopped cilantro (optional)

Preheat the oven to 400°F. Sprinkle the chicken breasts with salt and pepper and arrange in a single layer in a baking pan. Roast for 30 to 40 minutes, or until the chicken is completely opaque (165°F. on a meat thermometer). Cool and then, while slightly warm, pull the meat off the bones. Dice and reserve.

Whisk together the curry powder and lemon juice. Whisk together with the mayonnaise and salt and pepper to taste. Fold into the chicken and then add the celery, scallions, apples, and cilantro. Store in the refrigerator, tightly covered, for up to 4 days.

Chicken Salad with Grapes, Walnuts, and Horseradish–Mayonnaise

This café favorite gets its kick from horseradish-spiked mayonnaise. Use mixed green and red grapes for the most impact, pitting the grapes if necessary. Serve on a bed of radicchio if desired, and don't forget to reserve a few of the grapes and walnuts to sprinkle on top. Cooking chicken on the bone makes it much more moist and it won't shrink as much. It's just a bit more work to pull the meat off the bone, but then you get the bonus of the bones to be saved for stock.

SERVES 8

4 pounds chicken breast on the bone

1 cup mayonnaise (homemade or purchased)

$1/4$ cup prepared white horseradish

$1/4$ cup sour cream

Kosher salt and freshly ground black pepper, to taste

1 cup diced celery

$1/2$ pound each: red and green seedless grapes, halved lengthwise

$1/2$ pound walnuts, lightly toasted in a 300°F. oven

2 tablespoons thinly sliced chives

Preheat the oven to 400°F. Sprinkle the chicken breasts with salt and pepper and arrange in a single layer in a baking pan. Roast for 30 to 40 minutes, or until the chicken is completely opaque (165°F. on a meat thermometer). Cool and then, while slightly warm, pull the meat off the bones. Dice and reserve.

Whisk together mayonnaise, horseradish, sour cream, and salt and pepper. Fold into the chicken and then add the celery, grapes, walnuts, and chives, saving a bit of the grapes, walnuts and chives to sprinkle on top just before serving.

Chicharrónes de Pollo
with Ajili Mojili Sauce

Some years back, I acted as sous-chef to Chinese-Parisian chef Philippe Chin (now of Bambù in Augusta, Georgia) at the Vintage Wine and Food Festival in Puerto Rico. While there, I most enjoyed my meal at the restaurant called Ajili Mojili in San Juan, that serves made-from-scratch traditional island food in a wonderfully convivial atmosphere. This dish is inspired by one I ate there. Ajili-Mojili is an onomatopoetic word that seems to derive from the words for chili (aji) and mojo (salsa) that's as much fun to say as it is to eat. It is well-suited to party fare. Keep the chicken warm in a 200°F. oven until ready to serve. Substitute white meat chicken, if you'd like, which will take less time to cook.

SERVES 8

1/4 cup dark rum

1/4 cup soy sauce

1/4 cup lime juice

2 pounds boneless, skinless chicken thighs with
   visible fat snipped away with scissors

Kosher salt and freshly ground black pepper

1 cup all-purpose flour

1 quart frying oil (canola or peanut)

Ajili Mojili Sauce (recipe follows)

Combine the rum, soy sauce, and lime juice. Cut the chicken thighs into 3 to 4 lengthwise strips. Add the chicken strips to the rum mixture and marinate for 24 hours in the refrigerator. Drain well and pat dry with paper towels. Sprinkle the chicken strips lightly with salt and pepper and dust with flour.

In a large, heavy-bottomed pot, an electric deep-fryer, or a wok, heat the oil until shimmering (365°F. on a frying thermometer). Working in 3 to 4 batches, lay the chicken strips into the oil and turn with tongs as they brown. Fry until firm and well-browned, about 10 minutes. Using a wire skimmer, remove chicken from the oil and drain on a wire rack, keeping warm in a 200°F. oven. Serve with Ajili Mojili Sauce.

Ajili Mojili Sauce

3 large roasted red peppers (purchased or homemade)

1 chipotle in adobo, seeded if desired

1 tablespoon chopped garlic

1/4 cup rice vinegar

1 1/2 teaspoons crushed black peppercorns

1 1/2 teaspoons kosher salt

1/2 cup extra-virgin olive oil

Juice of 1 lime

1 cup diced red onion

Place the red peppers, chipotle, garlic, vinegar, crushed pepper and salt in the bowl of a food processor and process briefly until you have a chunky paste. Transfer the mixture to a bowl, whisk in the olive oil, and lime juice, stir in the red onion and refrigerate. Store refrigerated for up to 1 week.

259

260

Quesadillas Filled with Adobo Chicken

Quesadillas are such great party food, served in wedges, and everyone seems to love them. I like to use flavored tortillas, especially red or green chile, but plain flour tortillas will do just fine. The toasted pumpkin seeds (pepitas in Spanish) add nutty crunch and touches of deep, olive-green color. This recipe calls for Adobe Marinade from the Grilled Chicken Thighs Adobo on the next page. For the sauce, be sure to only use marinade that has not been mixed with raw chicken.

SERVES 6

1 package large flour tortillas

3 to 4 poblano peppers (1 pound), grilled, peeled, seeded, and cut into strips

1 large sweet onion, cut into wedges, grilled, then cut into strips

4 cups (1 pound) shredded cooked Chicken Thighs Adobo (*see* page 261)

6 ounces Monterey jack cheese, or sharp cheddar cheese, shredded

$1/2$ cup chopped cilantro

$1/2$ cup sour cream

$1/2$ cup reserved Adobo Marinade, from Grilled Chicken Thighs Adobo (next page)

2 teaspoons vegetable oil

3 tablespoons pumpkin seeds (lightly toasted in a 300°F. oven)

Arrange flour tortillas on the counter. Sprinkle one half of each tortilla with a portion of the poblano strips, onion strips, chicken, cheese, and most of the cilantro. Fold over the top half and press down to make large half-moons. Refrigerate at this point until ready to serve.

To serve, preheat a grill until evenly hot. Combine the sour cream and the reserved Adobo Marinade and set aside. Brush the tortilla half-moons with the oil and then grill on both sides. Alternatively, preheat a dry cast-iron skillet until smoking hot and lightly brown the filled tortillas on both sides. Remove from the stove, cut each tortilla into thirds and arrange on large plates. Drizzle with the sour cream sauce, and then sprinkle with the pumpkin seeds and the remaining cilantro.

PAN-SEARING IN A CAST-IRON SKILLET

So many dishes are best made in a old-fashioned cast-iron skillet, for best browning with little to no sticking and the added bonus for women especially, of getting just a little bit of necessary iron in your system from the pan. If you don't own one, a 9 to 10-inch or larger skillet can be purchased inexpensively in many hardware stores. Follow the directions for seasoning the pan and you'll have made a lifelong investment in kitchenware.

I bought my very best skillet about 20 years ago at a flea market. It must have been used for hundreds of meals before I rescued it from an ignominious end. Hardly a day goes by that I don't get out one of my trusty cast-iron skillets, ideal for pan-roasting and sautéing because they conduct heat so evenly and efficiently. After using the skillet, rinse briefly and then wipe out to dry and then rub with a lightly oiled paper towel. If any rust develops, rinse off the skillet, then wipe it with a lightly oiled paper towel until all the rust is removed. Rust is poisonous and should be removed before the pan is used.

Grilled Chicken Thighs Adobo

SERVES 8 TO 10

$1/2$ cup achiote paste (purchased at a Mexican grocery)

$1/4$ cup canola oil

$1/2$ cup cider vinegar

1 tablespoon ground toasted cumin

2 tablespoons finely chopped garlic

1 tablespoon dried oregano

1 teaspoon ground allspice

2 teaspoons kosher salt

2 pounds boneless, skinless chicken thighs (or 4 pounds bone-in chicken thighs, skin discarded)

Blend together the marinade ingredients: achiote, oil, vinegar, cumin, garlic, oregano, allspice, and salt. If you're making Quesadillas (*see* page 260), reserve $1/2$ cup of the marinade for the sauce. Combine the remaining marinade with the chicken and marinate, refrigerated, for 24 to 48 hours.

Preheat a grill and grill over indirect heat until thoroughly cooked. Alternatively, roast in a preheated 425°F. oven for about 35 minutes, or broil under high heat, turning once for about 20 minutes, or until the chicken is opaque. Serve with wedges of lime and rice for a simple meal or cool, then shred the chicken meat and use it to fill quesadillas.

261

High–Temperature Roast Chicken with Giblet Gravy and Two Variations

Although it may smoke up your house, especially if you haven't cleaned your oven recently, nothing beats the flavor of a high-temperature roasted chicken, all browned and juicy. This gravy was served at the late, lamented Quickie Chickie, a fast-food chicken project that I worked on. The concept and results were wonderful; the location not so good. You'll need a flat steel pan or a cast-iron skillet for best results.

SERVES 4

3- to 5-pound whole roaster chicken

Kosher salt and freshly ground black pepper to taste

Liquid to deglaze (chicken stock, water spiked with a
    little fruit vinegar, apple cider or other fruit juice,
    or vegetable juice)

Preheat the oven to 450°F. A high-temperature roast chicken will have a much deeper and richer flavor because of the caramelization of its juices, though it will tend to shrink more. Diffuse any smoke from the oven by turning on a fan and/or opening a window near the oven.

Season the chicken inside and out, using plenty of freshly ground black pepper and a sparing amount of kosher salt. Since kosher salt is formed into flaky crystals, it is less concentrated and is easier to sprinkle lightly.

Prep the chicken as follows: Fold the wings backwards and place underneath the chicken. Cut a slit in the skin just above the inner thigh. Criss-cross the legs, then push the opposite leg through the slit in the skin, securing the legs. Use a steel, cast-iron, or enameled steel pan just big enough to hold the bird to obtain the best color and flavor. A dark pan absorbs rather than reflects the heat, while metal conducts the heat much better than a glass or ceramic dish.

Place the chicken breast-side up and roast 1 hour to 1 hour and 15 minutes. Surprisingly, the difference in cooking time from a 3-pound to a 5-pound bird will only be about 15 minutes. After 30 minutes, carefully pour off and discard any excess fat. Place back in oven and continue to roast. Pour off the fat once more, during the last 15 minutes of cooking.

Test the readiness of the bird by piercing the inner thigh, since this part takes the longest to cook. Check the color of the juices that run out. If the juices are clear, rather than pink, this indicates that the flesh is cooked through. Remove the chicken from the roasting pan and place it on a heated serving dish.

Pour off any fat from the pan and add about 2 cups of deglazing liquid. Place the pan (metal only) directly on a stovetop burner and bring the liquid to the boil. Turn down the heat and simmer about 10 minutes, scraping up the browned bits by using a wooden spoon. Pour the liquid through a sieve, if desired, to remove any solid particles, and keep warm. Carve the chicken into serving portions and place back on heated platter, pouring deglazing liquid over top.

Giblet Gravy

½ pound chicken giblets

4 tablespoons chicken fat
   (substitute duck fat or butter), divided

1 cup diced onion

½ cup diced celery

1 ounce (¼ cup) all-purpose flour

1 quart rich chicken stock, simmering

Kosher salt and freshly ground black pepper

In a skillet, thoroughly brown giblets in 2 tablespoons of the chicken fat. Remove from pan, transfer to the bowl of a food processor and process briefly until chunky but not at all pasty or chop by hand.

Brown onions in remaining 2 tablespoons chicken fat, then add celery and cook until crisp-tender. Gradually stir in flour and cook together, stirring, for about 5 minutes to make a stiff paste that starts to come away from the bottom of the pan.

Slowly pour in chicken stock, whisking to combine. Bring to the boil, season with salt and pepper and add reserved giblets. Simmer 30 minutes, occasionally skimming off any scum or skin that forms. Season to taste with salt and pepper.

Variation 1: Roast Chicken with Forty Cloves of Garlic and Rosemary

SERVES 4

3- to 5-pound whole chicken

1 bunch fresh rosemary, leaves picked off of half the bunch

Kosher salt and freshly ground black pepper to taste

2 to 3 heads fresh garlic, peeled

Carefully separate, but don't remove, the skin from the flesh on the breast side of the chicken. Insert about half the rosemary leaves in the pocket between the skin and the flesh. Season the chicken with salt and pepper, then fill the cavity with the garlic before trussing.

Roast the chicken at 425°F. for about 45 minutes. Pour off any fat and then, using a wooden spoon, remove the garlic cloves from inside the chicken. Scatter the garlic around the chicken in the roasting pan and place it back in the oven for 30 minutes longer, browning the chicken and the garlic. If desired, deglaze the pan as in High-Temperature Roast Chicken recipe (*see* previous page).

Note: Look for firm heads of new crop garlic with no green sprouting. If you're using prepeeled garlic, make sure the cloves are plump and creamy-looking, and not at all shriveled or sprouted.

263

Variation 2: Roast Chicken with Lemon and Herbs

SERVES 4

3- to 5-pound whole chicken
Kosher salt and freshly ground black pepper to taste
2 whole lemons
$1/2$ cup roughly chopped fresh herb sprigs (sage, thyme, marjoram, tarragon, and lovage are all delicious)
Liquid to deglaze

Season the inside of the chicken with salt and pepper and place 1 whole lemon and about half the herb sprigs in the chicken cavity. Truss, then rub the chicken skin with the juice of the second lemon. Season with black pepper and a little salt and then place in roasting pan, scattering remaining herb sprigs around chicken.

Roast as in Basic recipe (*see* page 262) and remove from pan. Pour off any fat, deglaze with water or chicken stock and strain liquid before pouring over skinned and carved chicken.

COOLING SAUCES WITHOUT MAKING A SKIN

Sauces, especially those thickened with flour, will tend to form a skin as they cool. To prevent this, dot the surface of the sauce with small bits of butter, which will then melt and cover the surface. Alternatively, lay plastic wrap directly onto the surface of the sauce.

Tandoori Chicken with Red Onion Garnish

In tandoori cooking, marinated meats are lowered on long skewers into the intensely hot round tandoor oven. The meat picks up a wonderful flavor both from its marinade and from the super-hot smoky environment it's cooked in, not all that different from cooking in a wood-burning oven. Typically, a tandoor is dug into the ground or built into an enclosure, so that the heat can only escape through the open top. The direct heat of the fire is reflected by the sides, intensifying the heat further. Yogurt is the main ingredient in the marinade for just about any tandoori dish, because its natural acidity tenderizes the meat, while its thick consistency allows it to stick to the meat along with other spices. Tandoori dishes are commonly colored with red dye. I use inexpensive, natural ground annatto seed, sold in Latin American markets. Here, you'll want to use an outdoor grill fired with plenty of natural charcoal and allowed to burn until you start seeing white ash and little to no open flame. A gas grill will also work, though will produce a less smokey flavor.

SERVES 6 TO 8

12 skinless chicken thighs, on the bone
$1/4$ cup canola oil
1 onion, coarsely chopped
6 cloves garlic, peeled
2-inch piece of fresh ginger, peeled and sliced
Juice of 1 lemon
1 cup plain yogurt, whole milk preferred
1 tablespoon ground coriander

264

1 teaspoon each: ground cumin, turmeric,
 garam masala, mace, and nutmeg

1 teaspoon annatto powder (optional)

¼ teaspoon each: ground cloves, cinnamon,
 and cayenne pepper

1 tablespoon kosher salt

½ teaspoon freshly ground black pepper

Red Onion Garnish (recipe follows)

Make 2 diagonal slashes on each thigh, halfway to the bone. Make marinade by combining in a blender or food processor the oil, onion, garlic, ginger, lemon juice, yogurt, coriander, cumin, turmeric, garam masala, mace, nutmeg, annatto, cloves, cinnamon, cayenne, salt, and pepper. Purée until smooth.

Coat the chicken with the marinade, rubbing into the slashes. Cover tightly and marinate (refrigerated) for 24 to 48 hours. Turn several times to marinate evenly.

Prepare a hot charcoal fire and when coals have burned to embers, grill chicken over indirect heat (with the lid closed) for about 30 minutes, turning once or until thoroughly cooked. Alternatively, cook the chicken in a covered gas grill over high heat. Serve the chicken on a bed of Red Onion Garnish.

Red Onion Garnish

1 red onion (sliced paper thin)

1 teaspoon kosher salt

2 tablespoons sherry vinegar

Soak onion rings in ice water for 30 minutes. Dissolve salt in vinegar and place drained onion rings in vinegar. Marinate at least 30 minutes (at room temperature) and up to 4 hours (refrigerated).

Chicken alla Parmigiana

Chicken "Parm" is one of those dishes that has become so commercialized that it's difficult to remember just how good it can be. My version includes fresh slices of tomatoes and fresh mozzarella. Remember, the better the chicken you use, the better the results. If you make this dish in farmers' market season, combine red and yellow tomatoes for striking eye appeal. Don't be scared off by the long recipe; it's really not very difficult to make and everything can be made ahead of time.

SERVES 6 TO 8

Marinade for Tomatoes and Chicken

½ cup extra-virgin olive oil

2 tablespoons chopped garlic

Kosher salt and freshly ground black pepper to taste

½ cup basil leaves

4 beefsteak tomatoes, yellow and red if possible, sliced

Juice of 1 lemon

2 pounds boneless, skinless chicken cutlets

Place olive oil, garlic, salt and pepper in a blender and puree. Add basil leaves and blend long enough to make a green paste. Combine half the paste with the tomatoes and marinate at least 30 minutes and up to 1 hour at room temperature.

Add the lemon juice to the remaining paste and use to marinate the chicken cutlets about 15 minutes at room temperature.

265

Breaded Chicken

2 pounds Marinated Chicken Cutlets (*see* previous page)

1 cup all-purpose flour

3 eggs, lightly beaten

1/4 cup milk

Kosher salt and freshly ground black pepper to taste

1 teaspoon pimentón, substitute paprika

2 cups fresh Italian breadcrumbs or Japanese panko

1 cup grated mixed Romano and Parmigiano cheese

3 tablespoons chopped marjoram or oregano, or
   1 tablespoon dried oregano

Drain the chicken and pat dry. Place the flour in one bowl, in a second bowl lightly beat together the eggs, milk, salt, pepper, and pimentón. In a third bowl, mix the breadcrumbs, cheese, and oregano. Dip the chicken cutlets, one at a time, first into the flour, shaking off the excess, next into the egg mixture, letting the excess liquid drip off, and finally coat evenly with the breadcrumb mixture, patting lightly so it adheres.

Arrange the chicken on a wax-paper-lined baking sheet in a single layer without touching each other and chill in the refrigerator to set coating, about 30 minutes (or up to 2 days ahead).

Assembly

1 pound linguine

3 cups Marinara Sauce, simmering (*see* page 895)

1/2 cup olive or canola oil, divided

Breaded Chicken Cutlets

Marinated red and yellow tomato slices

1/2 pound sliced fresh mozzarella

3/4 cup grated Parmigiano Reggiano

Basil leaf, for garnish

Bring a large pot of salted water to the boil. Cook the linguine for about 8 minutes or until mostly cooked, but yellow in color and bouncy in texture. Drain and toss with the Marinara Sauce and keep warm. Preheat the broiler.

Meanwhile, in a large heavy-bottomed skillet, preferably cast-iron or nonstick, heat about half the oil until shimmering. Brown about half the chicken cutlets on both sides. Drain and transfer to a metal baking pan. Repeat with remaining oil and chicken. Top each chicken cutlet with 1 to 2 tomato slices, then 1 to 2 mozzarella slices, and finally, sprinkle with Parmigiano Reggiano cheese.

Brown chicken briefly under the broiler until the cheese melts and starts to brown. Arrange a portion of the sauced linguine in a nest-shape in the bottom of pasta bowls, preferably heated. Top each serving with 1 to 2 chicken cutlets. Garnish each portion with a basil leaf and serve immediately.

Southern-Style Skillet-Fried Cornish Hens

This idea came to me when I had to prepare a summer menu for one hundred guests to be served outside at a wonderful old home outside of Philadelphia. We set up a frying station outside with a heavy gas-powered burner and proceeded to fry up these delectable little chicken parts, a perfect size for party fare. Because Cornish hens are only sold whole, you'll have to cut them up yourself, unless you can talk the butcher into doing it for you. It's not at all hard, because the birds are so small and tender.

SERVES 8 TO 10

1 cup buttermilk

¹/₄ cup cayenne hot sauce (such as Crystal or Durkee's)

2 tablespoons chopped thyme (or 2 teaspoons dried)

2 tablespoons chopped marjoram (or 2 teaspoons dried)

1 tablespoon kosher salt

¹/₂ teaspoon freshly ground black pepper

5 pounds Cornish hens, cut into 8 pieces each, with backbone removed (*see* Cutting up a bird into eight pieces, at right)

4 cups Japanese panko breadcrumbs, divided

5 to 6 cups peanut oil for frying

In a large bowl, whisk together the buttermilk, hot sauce, thyme, marjoram, salt, and pepper and reserve. Marinate the chicken pieces in the buttermilk mixture for at least 1 hour at room temperature or up to overnight, refrigerated.

Drain the chicken, discarding the marinade. Place half the crumbs in a bowl. Heat the oil in a large (12-inch or more) cast-iron skillet or chicken fryer to 275°F. One by one, coat each piece of chicken thoroughly with the crumbs, patting crumbs onto chicken and shaking off the excess.

Place the chicken pieces in the oil, without crowding the pot, skin-side down, and fry until golden brown, then turn with tongs. Continue cooking until the internal temperature of the thigh meat reaches 175°F. and the chicken pieces are firm.

Using tongs or a wire skimmer, remove the chicken from the oil and drain on a wire rack, keeping warm in a 200°F. oven, if desired. Working in batches, continue with the remaining chicken, replacing the crumbs with the remaining 2 cups when they get wet. The chicken will take 20 to 25 minutes to cook through.

CUTTING UP A BIRD INTO EIGHT PIECES

Using a heavy chef's knife, poultry shears, or a cleaver, cut down along one side of the backbone all the way through until the bird splits in half. Open up the bird and, working from the inside, cut along the other side of the backbone all the way until the backbone is freed. (Save it to add to chicken stock.)

Jiggle the wings in their sockets at the neck end and cut between the wing and the neck to separate out the wings on both sides. Cut off the small third joint from the wing if desired.

Jiggle the thighs in their sockets and cut between the leg and the body on both sides. Jiggle the drumstick to find the place that it attaches to the thigh and cut to separate the thighs on both sides. Pull out and discard any fat pads from inside the thighs.

Turn the remaining breast portion over, skin-side down. Cut down the center of the keel (or breast bone) to divide into two individual pieces, for a total of 8 pieces of chicken: two wings, two drumsticks, two thighs, and two breasts.

267

Poussin with Cornbread Stuffing and Garlic Cream Sauce

This garlic-lover's dish can be made with either poussin or Cornish hens. The garlic is roasted and then simmered, taming any harshness and yielding gentle, rounded garlic flavor in the sauce. Because poussin are somewhat smaller than Cornish hens, the stuffing will be enough for eight birds, six if you're using Cornish hens. If desired, to make it easier for each guest to carve at the table, glove-bone the birds, removing the rib cage (see Glove-Boning a Bird, following page). Make this recipe when you have extra cornbread, fresh-made or in the freezer. It works perfectly using the Buttermilk Cornbread recipe (see page 341). You can also use purchased cornbread, just make sure it's not too sweet. Alternatively, roast the birds whole on the bone without stuffing and serve with the garlicky, creamy sauce.

SERVE 6 TO 8

Garlic Cream Sauce

2 tablespoons unsalted butter

$1/2$ cup peeled garlic cloves

1 tablespoon chopped thyme

1 cup chicken stock

$1/2$ cup heavy cream

Kosher salt, freshly ground black pepper
  and cayenne pepper, to taste

Preheat the oven to 375°F. Melt butter in a small skillet or pot and combine with the garlic cloves and the thyme. Spread out onto a small metal baking pan and roast for 30 minutes, stirring occasionally, or until the garlic is golden brown.

Remove the garlic from the oven and scrape the mixture into a medium pot. Add the chicken stock and bring to the boil. Cook until the liquid has been reduced by half. Add the heavy cream and reduce again by half.

Puree sauce until smooth in a blender. Season with salt, pepper, and cayenne and keep warm.

Poussin and Stuffing

4 tablespoons unsalted butter, softened, divided

$1/2$ cup chopped onions

$1/2$ cup sliced leek

$1/2$ cup chopped celery

1 tablespoon chopped garlic

2 tablespoons each: chopped sage and Italian parsley

6 cups crumbled Buttermilk Cornbread (see page 341)
  or purchased cornbread

Kosher salt, freshly ground black pepper
  and cayenne pepper, to taste

8 poussin, innards removed, and reserved for another use

Garlic Cream Sauce

In a skillet, melt 2 tablespoons of the butter and cook the onions, leek, celery, and garlic until softened but still brightly colored. Remove from heat and stir in sage and parsley. Combine with the cornbread and season with salt, pepper, and cayenne. Cool and reserve.

Rub poussin dry inside and out using paper towels. Season inside and out with salt, pepper, and cayenne. Stuff poussin with the cornbread mixture. Tie closed with butcher's string or FoodLoops (see Tying Birds for Roasting, following page). Rub birds with the remaining 2 tablespoons softened butter.

Raise oven temperature to 450°F. Arrange poussin in a metal roasting pan just large enough to hold them. Roast poussin about 40 minutes or until the thigh bones move easily in their joints.

Remove the pan from the oven and reserve the birds, keeping warm. Deglaze the brown bits from the bottom of the roasting pan with a little water and then strain and pour this liquid into the garlic cream sauce. Serve poussin accompanied by a sauceboat of the hot Garlic Cream Sauce.

TYING BIRDS FOR ROASTING

A quick way to close up the legs of birds is by cutting a slit into the skin alongside the thigh in the loose skin that lies between the thigh and the breast, about 1 inch from the edge. Pull one leg over the slit. Pull the other leg over the first leg and push the end into the slit, crossing over the other leg. (This is easier to do with bigger birds; smaller birds have more tender, easily broken skin.)

GLOVE–BONING A BIRD

Glove-boning is a way to remove the entire rib cage of any bird without cutting, basically by turning the bird inside out. It is used when you want to stuff the bird and makes it easy for the diner to cut up the bird.

First, find the place on either side of the neck where the collar (or wish-bone) attaches to the top wing joint. You can easily do this by jiggling the wing. Using a small, sharp knife cut between the wing joint and the collar bone to sever the tendons that connect them. You should be able to pull away the wings from the neck freely. Cut out and discard the collar bone.

Next, start to pull back the flesh and skin from the rib cage, using your hands to feel where the flesh attaches to the bones. Keep pulling away while turning inside out as you go. When the rib cage is completely exposed, cut away the tendons connecting it to the large thigh bone, freeing the rib cage from the legs.

Pull out the whole rib cage, twisting and working it gently until you can pull it free from the bird. You should have a whole bird without its rib cage, but with its legs and wings. Turn back right-side in and reserve. Season inside and out with salt, pepper, and a squeeze of lemon, if desired.

Just before roasting, stuff the bird without overfilling, because the stuffing will expand and the meat will shrink as it roasts. It's important that you stuff the bird right before you cook it, because of the dangers of bacteria growth once the stuffing has been placed inside the bird. Keep in mind that the smaller the bird, the more gently you have to work to keep from tearing the skin or flesh.

269

Roast Cornish Hen Stuffed with Spinach and Sausage

This is an oldie but-goodie dish that dates back to my days as a sous-chef at the Barclay Hotel on Philadelphia's Rittenhouse Square. The hotel kitchen was vast and stocked with a marvelous assortment of tri-ply copper and steel pots made by Legion Hotelware, dating back to the 1940s, when huge copper stockpots and copper fish poachers were still made. We would make huge batches of chicken stock in monster steam kettles, chicken á la king for seven hundred, and this chicken that was served in the hotel's dining room, which catered especially to the many hotel residents.

Suitably for a old-time dish, the sauce is basically a classic French velouté (velvety) sauce, thickened with a roux of flour cooked in butter. You'll have extra sauce. It will keep for about 1 week refrigerated. Use as a base for soup, add to a pasta dish, or serve over plain roast chicken.

SERVES 8

Sauce

1 quart rich chicken stock

1 pound mushrooms, caps and stems, divided

$1/2$ onion, peeled

3 to 4 sprigs each: fresh thyme, Italian parsley, and tarragon

$1/2$ cup dry white vermouth

$1/2$ cup chopped shallots

3 tablespoons unsalted butter

1 ounce ($1/4$ cup) flour

$1/4$ cup mixed chopped herbs: thyme, parsley, chives, and tarragon

Kosher salt and freshly ground black pepper to taste

Add the chicken stock, the mushroom stems, onion, herb sprigs, and vermouth to a large soup pot. Simmer together 2 hours, then strain, discarding solids.

Meanwhile, slice the mushroom caps and then sauté with the shallots in butter in a large skillet. Sprinkle in the flour, stir well to combine and cook together several minutes to eliminate the raw flour taste. Pour in the hot strained stock and simmer together 20 minutes, or until sauce is somewhat thickened and clear, skimming often to remove impurities and obtain a clear sauce.

Just before serving, stir in the chopped herbs and season with salt and pepper.

Hens and Stuffing

1 pound bag baby spinach

$1/2$ pound spicy Italian sausage

1 cup diced onion

$1/2$ pound mushrooms, trimmed and sliced

$1/2$ cup country-style breadcrumbs or Japanese panko

Kosher salt and freshly ground black pepper to taste

8 Cornish hens, glove-boned if desired (*see* Glove-Boning A Bird, page 269)

Wilt the spinach briefly, either by cooking in the microwave for 1 to 2 minutes or placing in a skillet with about half an inch of boiling water and stirring until evenly wilted. Drain, rinse under cold water to chill, squeeze out the excess water, and chop roughly.

Remove casings from sausage and sauté in a skillet, preferably cast-iron or nonstick, until well-browned and crumbled, breaking up with a wooden spoon as it cooks. Remove from pan and drain off most of the fat, reserving 2 tablespoons.

In the same pan, sauté the onion and mushrooms in the reserved fat. Combine the contents of the pan with the reserved spinach and the sausage. Stir in the breadcrumbs and season with salt and pepper. The stuffing should be softly bound, moist and juicy, not at all stiff. Cool the stuffing and then stuff the hens, just before roasting.

Preheat the oven to 425°F. Place the hens in a roasting pan just large enough to hold them. Roast for about 50 minutes, or until the juices from the thigh run clear when a thigh is pierced and a meat thermometer inserted into the thickest part of the thigh registers 175°F.

CHICKPEAS

CHICKPEAS

Chickpeas are about the best-tasting, most versatile legume in the kitchen, though dried chickpeas can be challenging to cook and canned chickpeas can be rather bland. One of civilization's oldest cultivated foods, the chickpea's unique curled-up shape has inspired its many fanciful names. Its Latin name, *Cicer arietum*, forever commemorates the large chickpea-shaped wart on the face of the famed Roman orator, Cicero, himself a chickpea lover. In Italy today, a *cicerone* (large chickpea) is a guide for sightseers, because these guides are typically glib and loquacious like Cicero. The word *arietum*, means ram-like (as in Aries, the zodiac sign of the ram) and refers to the chickpea's fanciful resemblance to a ram's head, complete with curling horns.

The Spanish word for chickpea, *garbanzo*, is said to derive from Greek and prehistoric German, which then evolved into the seventeenth-century English word *calavance*. Before that, the English name for chickpeas was *chichi*, derived from the Latin (and Italian) *ceci*. Their Portuguese name, *grao-di-bico*, means "grain in the beak". The Indian term, *gram*, refers to whole, rather than split, chickpeas, while *channa* (chickpea) *dal* is used for skinless, split chickpeas.

Not only are chickpeas tasty, versatile, and full of protein, they may even give a boost to your love life. There are many traditional beliefs that chickpeas increase energy and the sexual desires of both men and women. The sixteenth century North African Arab guide to lovemaking, *The Perfumed Garden*, claimed that eating chickpeas can cure impotence, and that they should be eaten as a sexual stimulant.

Chickpeas have a chewy, nutlike texture and a nutty, earthy flavor that makes them satisfying in hearty soups, one-pot-meals, stews, and pasta. They are basic to cuisines from India to the East and Portugal in the West, as well as throughout Latin America. In Israel, the small deep-fried spiced chickpea dumplings called falafel are the national dish while *hummus bi tahini*—a dip/spread of creamy mashed chickpeas, sesame paste, and lemon—is found on the table throughout the Levantine region from Lebanon to Israel, Jordan, and Palestine. In India, chickpeas have been part of the diet since the second millennium BCE, and because vegetarian cooking is so important there, chickpeas, with their high levels of vegetable protein, show up in all sorts of intriguingly spiced dishes. Because of Spain's long years of Arab influence, its cuisine is also full of chickpea dishes, including the Chickpea Soup found in this chapter.

In the Riviera regions of the south of France and the northern Mediterranean coast of Italy—particularly in the cities of Nice, France, and Genoa, Italy—the thin, wood-oven baked cake of chickpea flour brushed with olive oil called *farinata* in Genoa and *socca* in Nice are a not-to-be-

274

missed local specialty, best eaten hot out of the oven, where it is baked in huge metal pans. I've included a recipe on page 279. In India, chickpea flour becomes the batter for Indian-style tempura vegetables, while channa dal, split skinless chickpeas, are commonly used to make dal. In North Africa, chickpeas end up in many a couscous dish along with vegetables, lamb, chicken, and even fish. Roasted chickpea flour is even used to make crumbly cookies in Tunisia.

Chickpea Varieties

Black Chickpea: This small chickpea, also known as Black Garbanzo or Black Gram, is the size of a large pea and has black skin that bleeds slightly when cooked. It has an earthy, smoky flavor with a subtle sweet note and a firm texture. When split and skinned, they are known as *Channa Dal* or yellow split chickpeas and are the most popular legume in India.

Ceci Siciliani: Chickpeas were a staple food of the Roman Empire, especially in Sicily. There, a less than intense feeling of love is ironically referred to as *amuri e brodu di ciciri*—love and chickpea broth. This saying dates back to the thirteenth century, when rebellious Sicilians could easily identify hated French overlords by having them pronounce the word *ciciri* (chickpeas), whose sound they could never reproduce correctly.

Cicerchie: This heirloom chickpea dates back to ancient Roman times and is cultivated today primarily in Puglia and Umbria. Tiny, irregular, and somewhat flattened in shape, cicerchie range in color from cream to light gray to brown. They are high in iron, have a delicate flavor, and tender skin. They go well with game and are often pureed and served with bitter greens.

Desi Chickpea: These smaller, darker-skinned chickpeas are popular in India. Because they have a rather thick skin, they take a long time to cook.

Kabuli Chickpea (Garbanzo): This common variety, called *garbanzo* in Spanish-speaking countries, is tan to light brown when raw and golden brown, plump, and creamy when cooked. It has relatively thin skin.

275

Spanish Chickpea Soup with Garlic–Mint Pesto

This simple Spanish peasant soup shows how a few well-chosen ingredients can be transformed into a hearty and satisfying meal. The Spanish taste for chickpeas developed during the long years of Arab dominance in that country, where chickpeas were one of the many foods brought by the Arabs. The simple sauce made here is another variation on the theme of crushing fresh herbs with garlic and olive oil as in Pesto alla Genovese. Stir in the pesto at the last minute to release a heady aroma and infuse the soup with its bold, bright flavor. This is a very fast soup to make if you buy cooked chickpeas, either in glass jars or cans.

Serves 8

½ loaf stale Italian bread (about ½ pound), crust
   trimmed, cut into small cubes

¼ cup + ¼ cup extra-virgin olive oil

1 tablespoon + 1 tablespoon chopped garlic

¾ cup Italian parsley leaves

¾ cup fresh mint leaves, preferably spearmint

2 quarts chicken stock, preferably homemade

2 (19- or 20-ounce) jars (5 cups) cooked chickpeas
   with their cooking liquid

Kosher salt and freshly ground black pepper to taste

Preheat the oven to 350°F. Make the croutons by tossing the bread cubes with ¼ cup of the olive oil and 1 tablespoon of the garlic. Spread out in a single layer on a baking pan and toast in the oven for 15 minutes, stirring after about 10 minutes for even browning. Remove from the oven and reserve.

In a food processor or blender, blend the remaining ¼ cup olive oil with the remaining 1 tablespoon garlic, parsley, and mint to a thick green paste. Remove and reserve.

In a large soup pot, bring the stock to a boil and add the chickpeas. Reduce the heat and simmer for 15 minutes, then season with salt and pepper. To serve the soup, ladle the chickpeas and broth into bowls. Let each person add a spoonful of the mint pesto to their bowl, stirring to release the aroma. Then top with the croutons.

BUYING CANNED AND JARRED CHICKPEAS

I highly recommend the imported garbanzos in glass jars sold by The Spanish Table, www. spanishtable.com, or the jars of Spanish chickpeas sold at Whole Foods under the store's 365 Brand. Goya's canned chickpeas are a good choice that is less expensive and more easily found.

Chop–Chop Salad
with Chickpeas

As far as I can tell, chop-chop is a phrase that means quickly, deriving ultimately from Chinese. It has been adapted in California, where so many of classic American salads were developed (Crab Louis, Cobb Salad, Chop-Chop Salad, Caesar Salad from Tijuana just south of the border) to mean a salad cut into bite-sized bits. It is basically a salad made from leftovers and may include meats, cheeses, and eggs, so it really is a meal in a bowl. Though I can't verify this, my feeling is that Cobb Salad is a variation of Chop-Chop or the other way around. Cobb has specific ingredients, where the other is made with a whole slew of ingredients from what is on hand. Wherever it came from, this is one good salad and great for feeding a crowd. Feel free to improvise, always keeping in mind that you want contrasting flavors and textures. Serve with crusty semolina bread.

SERVES 8

Red Wine Vinaigrette

1 cup extra-virgin olive oil

6 tablespoons high-quality red wine vinegar

2 teaspoons chopped garlic

2 tablespoons chopped fresh marjoram or fresh oregano

1 tablespoon kosher salt

1 teaspoon freshly ground black pepper

Combine all the ingredients in a blender jar and blend until smooth. The dressing will keep well for 2 weeks if tightly covered and refrigerated.

Salad

1 head radicchio, shredded

1 head heart of romaine, cut into 1-inch-wide strips

1 head Belgian endive, cut into 1-inch-wide strips

1 head arugula, washed and dried

Red Wine Vinaigrette

1 1/2 cups (15-ounce can) cooked chickpeas,
   rinsed and drained

2 red beets, steamed or roasted
   and then peeled and diced

1/4 pound smoked turkey, diced

1/4 pound Genoa salami, diced

1/4 pound Stilton cheese, diced

1 pint grape tomatoes, sliced in half

4 hard-cooked eggs, quartered

Toss radicchio, romaine, endive and arugula with enough dressing to coat lightly. Arrange in a large salad bowl.

Separately toss the chickpeas and then the beets with a little more dressing. Arrange in a decorative pattern on top of greens.

Garnish with turkey, salami, Stilton, tomato, and egg quarters. Serve immediately.

USING AN IMMERSION BLENDER

A small, inexpensive immersion blender is perfect to make a creamy salad dressing that will emulsify (blend together) without having to add ingredients like egg yolk and mustard to help it along. Place all the ingredients into a Pyrex measure or other tall, rather narrow container and move the blender around until the dressing is creamy.

Arbes: Jewish Chickpea Snack

A small bowl of chickpeas was always on the table in Jewish restaurants so the hungry diner wouldn't have to wait to eat. After the circumcision ceremony (Bris milah), done when a baby boy is eight days old, boiled chickpeas are served, said to be a sign of mourning that the angel caused the baby to forget everything he learned in his mother's womb. At the other end of life, during the seven-day morning period called the Shiva (sheva is seven in Hebrew), round foods like hard-cooked eggs and boiled chickpeas called arbes in Yiddish and nahit in Hebrew are served, symbolizing the cycle of life and death. So chickpeas, one of our most ancient foods, carry all sorts of symbolic meaning, but they also make a great high-protein snack. Substitute drained and rinsed canned chickpeas if desired.

277

SERVES 8 TO 12

6 cups cooked chickpeas (four 15-ounce cans,
   three 20-ounce jars, or *see* recipe on page 278)

2 tablespoons sweet paprika

2 teaspoons onion powder

1 teaspoon garlic powder

Kosher salt and freshly ground black pepper to taste

Drain and rinse the chickpeas (saving any cooking juices for soup stock if desired). Toss the chickpeas well with paprika, onion, and garlic powder, and season to taste with salt and pepper. Serve at room temperature as a snack.

Tunisian Chickpea and Olive Salad

Tunisian cooking involves a heavy use of legumes, especially nutty, meaty chickpeas, which are quite high in protein. Here the chickpeas are flavored with warm cumin, sharp caraway, orange-scented coriander seed, lots of garlic, black bits of the oil-cured olives popular in North Africa and right across the water in Sicily, with chopped vegetables for color and texture.

SERVES 6 TO 8

$^1/_2$ cup lemon juice

$^1/_2$ cup extra-virgin olive oil

Kosher salt to taste

2 teaspoons ground cumin

2 teaspoons ground caraway

1 tablespoon ground coriander

2 tablespoons Harissa Sauce (purchased or homemade, *see* recipe on page 703)

1 tablespoon crushed garlic

6 cups cooked chickpeas (four 15-ounce cans, three 20-ounce jars, drained and rinsed, or *see* recipe at right)

1$^1/_2$ cups finely diced red onion, soaked in ice water 30 minutes and then drained

$^1/_2$ cup oil-cured black olives, halved

1 cup diced tomatoes

1 cup diced green pepper

$^1/_4$ cup each: chopped Italian parsley and cilantro

Whisk together the lemon juice, olive oil, salt, cumin, caraway, coriander, harissa, and garlic. Mix with chickpeas and most of the onion, olives, tomatoes, and peppers, reserving some to sprinkle on top. Serve immediately.

CHICKPEAS IN BROOKLYN

In his memoir of his childhood in Brooklyn, *A Walker in the City*, Alfred Kazin writes of "paper spills of hot yellow chickpeas. I still hear those peddlers crying up and down the street [in Yiddish], 'Arbes! Arbes! Hayse gute arbes! Kinder! Kinder! Hayse gute arbes!'" [Chickpeas, chickpeas, I've got good chickpeas! Children! Children! I've got good chickpeas.]

Cooked Chickpeas

Dry chickpeas are the most challenging of legumes to cook. Shriveled, dried-out chickpeas will never get soft, no matter how long you cook them. Check that your chickpeas come from a source that sells its stock quickly, such a Latin American, Indian, or Middle Eastern grocery, because all those cuisines have many dishes made from chickpeas. More than any other type of legume, chickpeas need to cook in softened water, without a lot of minerals. Most tap water is too hard—acidic and mineral laden—to cook them properly. To ensure that your cooking water is soft enough, add a pinch of baking soda. If the beans are still hard after cooking two hours, add a pinch more, but note that too much baking soda will make the beans mushy and their skins will slip off. Chickpeas produce a great deal of white foam when cooked; skim as needed.

SERVES 8 (MAKES 6 CUPS)

1 pound (2 cups) dried chickpeas, soaked overnight in cold water to cover

2 bay leaves

2 to 3 sprigs thyme

3 whole cloves garlic

2 whole cloves

1 small dried red chile pepper, or 1 fresh chile
   such as serrano or jalapeno, optional

1/4 to 1/2 teaspoon baking soda, depending
   on hardness of water

Kosher salt to taste

Drain and rinse the soaked chickpeas. Cover with cold water and bring to a boil. Boil for 3 to 5 minutes, skimming off and discarding the foam that rises to the top, then drain and rinse under cold water.

Make a spice sachet by combining the bay leaves, thyme, garlic, cloves, and chile pepper in a square of cheesecloth. Bring the corners together and tie with kitchen string. (Alternatively, add the seasonings to the pot and fish them out later by hand.)

In a large pot with a lid, cover the chickpeas with 2 quarts cold water. Bring to a boil, along with 1/4 teaspoon of baking soda. Skim off and discard the white foam that rises to the top. Cover, reduce the heat, and simmer for 1 hour, or until the chickpeas are starting to soften. (Alternatively, bake in a 300°F. oven.) Add salt to taste and continue to cook 1 1/2 to 2 hours, or until the chickpeas are tender to the core but not mushy. Cool slightly so the chickpeas firm up and then drain gently so as not to break them up, saving both the chickpeas and their cooking liquid. (The chickpea broth is excellent used as a vegetarian soup stock and has lots of natural soluble fiber; it will most likely gel in the refrigerator.) Remove and discard the spice sachet, or the loose spices, and cool.

Farinata:
Italian Chickpea Torte

This thin, flat, savory cake—made on both the French and Italian sides of the Riviera—is made with chickpea flour, which has a nutty flavor and dense texture. The French version, popular in Nice, is called socca. *According to the longtime editor of the magazine* La Cucina Italiana, *Anna Gosetti della Salda, the torte should ideally be baked in a wood-burning bread oven because of the smoky flavor it imparts and its high heat. It is generally not served at the table, but is tasted and savored throughout the day as a warm snack. Cut the torte into diamond shapes and accompany with an aperitif like Martini and Rossi, half sweet and half dry; Lillet with orange; Dubonnet; or a glass of Italian Prosecco (sparkling wine).*

SERVES 6

1 pound (2 cups) chickpea flour

2 teaspoons kosher salt

6 tablespoons extra-virgin olive oil, divided

1 large red onion, sliced paper thin

2 tablespoons finely chopped fresh rosemary
   (about 1/4 bunch)

Freshly ground black pepper to taste

Place the chickpea flour in a bowl. While whisking constantly, beat in 1 quart of cold water, enough to make a soupy consistency. Add the salt and let the batter rest in the refrigerator at least 1 hour or preferably overnight to allow it to thicken. Remove and discard any white scum that forms on the surface.

Preheat the oven to 450°F. Generously brush a 12-inch

round pizza pan with 1 tablespoon of the olive oil. Beat 4 tablespoons of the remaining oil into the chickpea batter. Pour the batter into the pan, cover with the onion slices and the rosemary, and place in the oven. Bake on the top rack for 10 to 15 minutes, or until the torte is golden and crispy. Drizzle the top with the remaining 1 tablespoon of oil, and sprinkle with black pepper. Cut immediately into circles or diamond shapes and serve warm.

CHICKPEA FLOUR

The lightest and most delicate-tasting chickpea flour that I've ever tasted comes from Europe, but the more common type available in Indian groceries, called Gram flour, will also work well. Bob's Red Mill (www .bobsredmill.com) sells good-quality garbanzo bean flour, available at natural foods markets; look at Indian groceries for "besan" flour. Store chickpea flour in the freezer, as it is prone to attract bugs.

BLANCHING CHICKPEAS

Chickpeas produce a great deal of white foam impurities when cooked, so it is best to blanch (pre-cook) them first. Soak them in cold water to cover overnight. Drain and rinse them, then transfer them to a pot, cover with cold water, and bring to the boil. Cook for 5 minutes, skimming off any white foam. Drain and rinse the chickpeas and then cook them a second time, either in more water with aromatics, or in broth.

FARINATA AT GENOA'S ANTICA SCHIAMADDA

While visiting the great seagoing port of Genoa, I made a pilgrimage to the famed, old Antica Sciamadda (Via San Giorgio, 14R), a small, unassuming shop that specializes in traditional farinata baked on huge steel pans in a wood-burning oven. The flat cake, with its lightly crunchy olive-oil-anointed crust, is made of specially milled chickpea flour, slowly cooked with water, spread out into a thin layer, brushed with local Ligurian extra-virgin olive oil, sprinkled with sea salt, and then baked fresh throughout the day. By order, it is cut out by hand in circular portions and eaten warm as is, or inside a round roll as a quick, tasty sandwich.

COOKING CHICKPEAS IN A PRESSURE COOKER

Because they give off so much foam, it's not a great idea to cook chickpeas in a pressure cooker. It's possible, though unlikely, that the valve could get clogged. If you're short on time, and wish to use your pressure cooker, make sure that you don't fill it more than half full, to give the beans plenty of room to expand, and press down on the valve occasionally to unclog it.

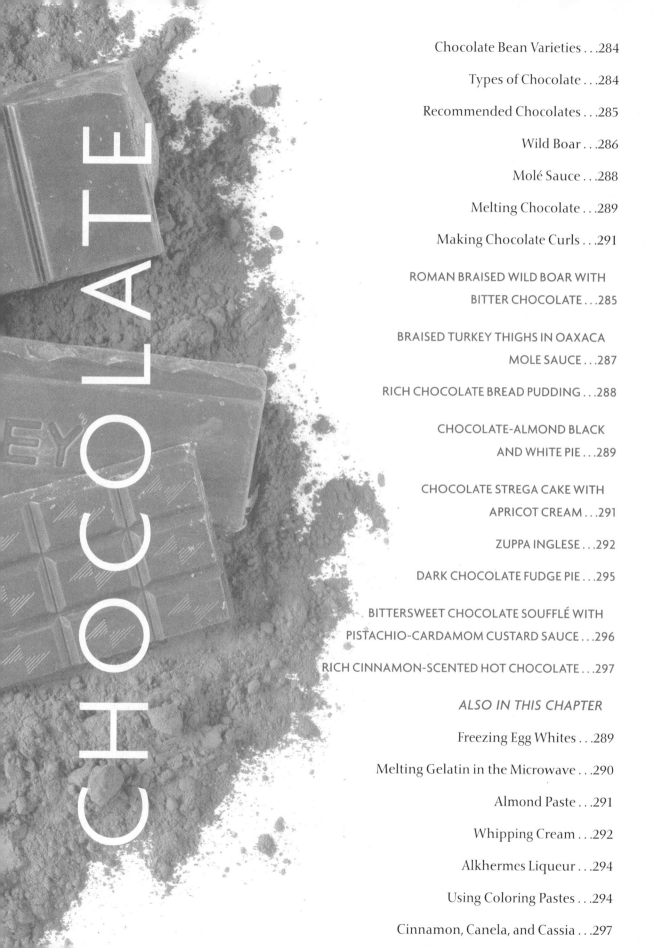

CHOCOLATE

CHOCOLATE

Imagine: Chocolate Passion, Chocolate Oblivion, Chocolate Sin, Chocolate Indulgence, Chocolate Torture, and finally, Death by Chocolate. There are no in-betweens here, chocolate's all about extremes. Chocolate lovers come in two flavors—milk and dark—which rarely intersect. We're talking fanatics here: chocolate weekends at hotels, chocolate cravings, chocolate binges. Several years ago when I consulted for Omni Hotels, I noticed that every menu listed Chocolate Ecstasy. When I asked why, I learned it was a must for single female travelers, perhaps as an out-of-town substitute for the real thing. Maybe we need a new twelve-step program, for those who can't control their desire for chocolate?

I got hooked on chocolate quite by accident, in the course of working on new products for a small Philadelphia company, Society Hill Snacks, started by Carmelita Thill, a leader of Philadelphia's Hispanic community. Thill brought the recipe for their toffee-roasted nuts from her native Venezuela forty years ago. While working with the company, I came up with two varieties of a chocolate bark that we called "Chocolate Mosaic", dark with sun-dried fruits and nuts, and milk with their toffee-roasted nuts.

As I learned the hard way, chocolate has its own secrets. I made tray after tray, and more trays than I want to remember became rejects (not that my husband and neighbors minded getting rid of the evidence). As Lindsey Shere says in her book, *Chez Panisse Desserts*, "Like iron pots and busy cooks, chocolate has temper." The chocolate reacted to everything: temperature, the humidity, the thickness, the cooling, the wrapping, the storing, and the packing. With advice from three experts, I learned to temper, or properly crystallize chocolate. Tempering makes the chocolate smooth and shiny, important for candy-making. Well-tempered chocolate breaks with a "good snap." Luckily, you won't need to temper the chocolate for any of these recipes.

Chocolate comes from the Aztec word, *xocalatl*; its scientific name, *Theobroma cacao*, means *food of the gods*. The Aztec king Montezuma believed chocolate to be a powerful aphrodisiac and is said to have drunk golden goblets of chocolate before visiting his wives. (It works as long as you believe it will.) The chocolate pod grows only in the tropics. Inside the pod is the chocolate bean, which has two main components: cocoa butter and chocolate liquor or solids. It's the combination of these two parts, with other ingredients, that determines the type of chocolate. In a method similar to roasting coffee, the cocoa beans are removed from their pods, fermented, dried and then roasted. The inner beans, or nibs, are ground to separate the cocoa butter and solids. The chocolate is then "conched" or finely ground in special machines, until the particles are micro-fine.

Chocolate is so voluptuous because it melts well below body temperature. Put a piece of chocolate on your tongue and it melts away quickly. The heat releases flavors and aromas. The chocolate then fills and coats your mouth with exquisitely smooth liquid cocoa butter that quickly disappears.

Europeans and Latinos think of chocolate as a restorative, concentrated, high-energy food that is often given to strengthen children. An Italian friend remembers eating chocolate, always dark with little sugar, for her health rather than as a treat. As a young child, I lived in Holland where I learned to cut neat squares of the Dutch favorite: white bread lathered with sweet butter and covered with chocolate sprinkles. Chocolate bars were standard issue in rations for American soldiers in World War II because they gave quick energy and didn't spoil in the heat.

Is it any wonder that the Italian *Bread and Chocolate* and the Mexican *Like Water for Chocolate* are two of my favorite movies? Sicily, Spain, and Mexico share a common heritage in their use of chocolate for cooking with strong-flavored meats like wild turkey and wild boar. Oaxaca, the center of Mexico's chocolate plantations, is also the originator of the sometimes chocolate-enriched molé sauces.

Chocolate companies endure: many of today's giants were founded in the early part of the nineteenth century. Coenraad Van Houten invented Dutch processing for cocoa in 1828. His method, called "Dutching", decreases acid and turns the cocoa a characteristic red-brown color. Milk chocolate was invented by a Swiss, Dr. Peter in 1818, which explains why milk chocolate is still most popular in Switzerland. Cadbury's, Nestlé's, and Lindt all date from the same time.

I often buy a large commercial block of chocolate, 5 kilos, or about 11 pounds. This kind of chocolate is easiest to break up using a fork-like ice chopper, an inexpensive and indispensable tool available at kitchen supply stores. Avoid chopping with a knife. I have a sizable scar that I got attempting to use a boning knife to break up my block of Peter's.

Wrap block chocolate back in its own paper or in heavy-duty foil. Keep it away from heat and light. Even better is to buy a 5 kilo box of small, easily-melted chocolate discs, now made by many fine chocolate companies and available at specialty stores. Because dark chocolate keeps for at least one year if covered and stored in a cool (not refrigerated) place, even 11 pounds is not too much to buy.

If you have a favorite chocolate cake recipe, try making it with great chocolate. All of a sudden, your cake will taste like your restaurant favorites. Low-grade chocolates just can't compare in flavor to specialty American brands and imports. Many of them depend on cheaper vegetable fats rather than on lusciously melting cocoa butter. It's like the difference between brand-name canned Robusta coffee and freshly ground Arabica beans. Once you've tasted the best, it's hard to go back to ordinary.

283

Chocolate Bean Varieties

The three major cacao varieties—Forastero, Criollo, and Trinitario—have been cross-bred and hybridized so that distinctions are not clear. The Criollo, know for its mild fruitiness, was the most important variety in Central and the northern portion of South America at the time of the Spanish explorers, but it now represents a tiny portion of the crop. The Forastero is by far the most common of the three varieties. It is believed to be indigenous to the northern Amazon River basin in what is now Brazil. Because of disease-resistance and high productivity, it represents close to ninety percent of the world crop. It tends to have earthy, relatively simple flavors with moderate acidity. The Trinitario is a spontaneous hybrid of Forastero and Criollo that appeared in Trinidad in the mid-1700s. It has flavor notes that range from spicy to earthy and fruity to acidic, because of its two forebears.

Types of Chocolate

Baking, bitter, or unsweetened chocolate (like Baker's chocolate squares) is unsweetened, made from cocoa and cocoa fat. Extra (expensive) cocoa butter is added to *couverture* or coating chocolate, used for fancy chocolate-dipped candies to insure shine and a clean break. Bittersweet, semisweet, and sweet chocolates each have different amounts of sugar added. Milk chocolate is enriched with milk solids and is generally quite sweet.

Not a true chocolate, white chocolate has had the chocolate liquor, or solid part removed. The remaining cocoa butter is mixed with milk solids and sugar. Because it has such a high fat content, white chocolate is notoriously temperamental. Lecithin, an emulsifier or stabilizer made from egg yolks, is added to keep chocolate smooth, along with real vanilla or artificial vanillin.

Much of the "chocolate" we eat really isn't. For "confectionery" or "summer coating", manufacturers replace expensive, finicky cocoa butter with easier-to-handle vegetable fats that melt at higher temperatures. While this enables a factory to run all year round, its waxy mouthfeel is a big disappointment for true chocolate aficionados. The chocolate morsels used for chocolate chip cookies are generally made from this type of "chocolate" for shelf stability.

284

285

Roman Braised Wild Boar with Bitter Chocolate

This is a traditional Roman dish that uses unsweetened chocolate to enrich and flavor the sauce along with candied fruits for bittersweet accent. It is said to date back to the Crusades, when knights returning home from the Holy Land brought back the taste for combining fruits with meat. Of course, the addition of chocolate dates the dish to sometime in the past five hundred years, when chocolate was brought back to Europe from the New World by Spanish explorers. I adapted this recipe from the wonderful book, Le Ricette Regionale Italiane (Italian Regional Recipes), written by Anna Gosetti della Salsa, first published in 1967 and still in print. This enormous and incredibly well-researched book has never been translated into English. In fact, at one time, my goal was to translate it myself—a formidable project, but one that still needs doing. Feel free to substitute pork shoulder for a milder-tasting but very tasty dish. The original recipe includes diced candied orange and citron; I've substituted grated orange zest and sun-dried cherries. Serve over soft polenta to soak up the rich juices.

SERVES 6

3 pounds wild boar shoulder (or substitute pork shoulder)

2 cups dry red wine

2 tablespoons red wine vinegar

1 onion, roughly chopped + 1 onion, diced

1 carrot, roughly chopped

2 ribs celery and/or fennel stalks, roughly chopped

2 bay leaves

Several sprigs thyme, or 1 teaspoon dried thyme

1 teaspoon crushed black peppercorns

5 whole cloves

2 tablespoons olive oil

2 tablespoons unsalted butter

2 tablespoons all-purpose flour, preferably unbleached

1 ounce unsweetened chocolate, grated

$1/4$ cup each: sun-dried cherries, cut up pitted prunes,
   Zante currants, and pine nuts

Grated zest of 1 orange

Kosher salt and freshly ground black pepper to taste

Trim off any excess fat from the meat and then cut into 1-inch cubes. Bring the wine, vinegar, the roughly chopped onion, carrot, celery (and/or fennel), bay leaves, thyme, peppercorns, and cloves to the boil in a nonreactive pot. Transfer to a large nonreactive bowl, cool completely and then add the boar. Weigh down with a plate to immerse completely, tightly cover and refrigerate overnight.

Pick the meat cubes out of the marinade, reserving both marinade and meat. Bring the reserved marinade to the boil, skimming off any foam and then simmer 30 minutes, or until the vegetables are soft.

Preheat the oven to 300°F. Pat the meat dry with paper towels. In a 3- to 4-quart Dutch oven (with a lid), heat the oil until shimmering and then brown the meat, working in batches so it doesn't steam. When all the meat is well-browned, drain off any excess oil from the pot.

Strain the simmered marinade into the pot and boil about 15 minutes, or until somewhat reduced. Add the browned meat, reduce heat, cover and bake 1½ hours, or until the meat is tender when pierced and the liquid is concentrated.

Meanwhile, in a large skillet, heat the butter and brown the diced onion. Stir in the flour and cook together 3 to 4 minutes to get rid of the raw flour taste. Stir in the chocolate, cherries, prunes, currants, and pine nuts. Add to the boar along with salt and pepper to taste. Bring the contents of the pot back to the boil, skimming if necessary. Reduce heat and simmer 10 minutes, or until the juices are syrupy. Serve over soft polenta.

Wild Boar

Wild Boar, *cinghiale* in Italian, is commonly sold in markets in Central Italy, in the provinces of Tuscany, Umbria, and Lazio (Rome). In Florence's wonderful San Lorenzo market, the first floor of the nineteenth century steel and glass building is filled with purveyors of game, many of them displaying terrifying-looking boar's heads to show that they carry the real thing. In America, "wild boar" is raised in Texas and is available from specialty purveyors like D'Artagnan (www.dartagnan.com).

Braised Turkey Thighs in Oaxaca Mole Sauce

There is a definite relationship between this dish and the Roman Braised Wild Boar with Bitter Chocolate above. Both show Spanish influences and through that, Arab flavors too. Moist, richly flavored meat from the thighs of the turkey, a bird native to Mexico, is put to excellent use here. Inexpensive and even better reheated, this is a dish not to be missed.

SERVES 8

2 quarts chicken stock

1 tablespoon kosher salt

2 bay leaves

8 turkey thighs

1 cup raw peanuts

1 cup blanched almonds

1/4 cup canola oil

1/4 cup sesame seeds (natural tan seeds with hull on preferred)

1 (2-inch) stick canela, also called soft-stick cinnamon

1 teaspoon anise seeds

1 teaspoon allspice berries

1 teaspoon black peppercorns

2 cups chopped plum tomatoes, fresh or canned

1/2 cup roughly cut onion

1/4 cup chopped garlic

3 dried chile mulatos or chile anchos, seeded and stemmed, then soaked in water to cover for 30 minutes, or until soft.

2 ounces unsweetened (baker's) chocolate

Bring the chicken stock, salt, and bay leaves to the boil in a large pot. Add the turkey thighs, bring back to the boil and then reduce the heat to a bare simmer. Cook 1 hour and then remove from the heat. Allow the thighs to cool about 30 minutes and then remove from the pot, reserving the liquid. Remove and discard the turkey skin. Place the skinned turkey thighs back into the liquid, cool and reserve.

Brown peanuts and almonds in 2 tablespoons of the oil. At the last minute stir in the sesame seeds and let them brown lightly. Remove from the heat and reserve.

Heat a small skillet (with no oil) and then add the canela, anise, allspice, and peppercorns, shaking the pan to toast the spices evenly. (The spices are ready when they start to give off a strong fragrance.) Remove from heat, cool to room temperature and then grind in a spice grinder (or crush using a mortar and pestle, a meat pounder, or a similar heavy object).

Scrape the reserved peanut mixture, tomatoes, onion, garlic, the drained chiles, and ground spices with about half the cooking liquid from the turkey into the bowl of a food processor. Blend until a smooth creamy paste is obtained.

Heat the remaining oil in a large skillet. Scrape the contents of the food processor into the pan and fry over medium heat, until fat rises to the surface, about 20 minutes. Stir in chocolate and remaining chicken stock and whisk together to make a smooth cream. Strain, if desired, through a sieve for a smoother sauce.

Preheat the oven to 325°F. Combine the sauce with the turkey thighs in an ovenproof casserole. Cover and bake for 1 1/2 hours or until the turkey is tender. Serve with steamed white rice or white hominy.

287

Rich Chocolate Bread Pudding

I adapted this recipe from one given to me by one of the most influential of woman chefs, Anne Rosenzweig, who worked with me on a special event during my stint as Chef/Partner at the White Dog Café in Philadelphia. Anne came down from New York, where she was then chef at the acclaimed Arcadia Restaurant, and brought along this recipe. The dinner turned out to be one of those nightmare-nights in the kitchen, with a special menu created for the evening that was brand-new to the not-yet-well-trained staff, but the recipes were wonderful and many of them I still use. I always regretted that Anne Rosenzweig's experience in my hometown was so unrewarding, because I so much admire her work. This bread pudding is rich as can be, so serve in small squares, always warm. If you want to really go all the way, make your own Brioche Dough (see page 987).

SERVES 12

2 pounds stale brioche or challah bread, crust removed, cut into cubes
2 cups + 1 cup heavy cream
1 pound semisweet chocolate, grated
½ pound bittersweet chocolate, grated
12 egg yolks (*see* Freezing Egg Whites, page 289)
1 cup granulated sugar
1 quart milk

Arrange brioche slices in a single layer in a baking pan. Bake at 350°F. for about 20 minutes, or until lightly toasted. Reserve.

In a large glass or ceramic bowl, scald 2 cups of cream in the microwave, or over a pot of scalding water. Add both chocolates and stir occasionally until the chocolate has melted completely.

In a mixing bowl, beat together the egg yolks and sugar until light. Meanwhile, scald the milk and the remaining 1 cup heavy cream in the microwave or in a small pot. Beat a small amount of the scalded cream mixture into the yolks to temper. Then beat in the remaining hot cream mix. Scrape the mixture into a nonreactive heavy-bottomed pot and heat until the sauce starts to thicken visibly and reaches 165°F. on a thermometer.

Remove the pot from the heat and whisk the melted chocolate into this custard. In a large baking pan, such as a lasagna pan, layer the warm chocolate custard with the brioche, beginning and ending with the custard. Pour plenty of custard over each layer so it will soak in. Allow the pudding to sit at room temperature for about 30 minutes, turning the bread chunks over so that they are completely saturated with the custard.

Preheat the oven to 325°F. Place the baking pan in another larger pan to make a water bath. In the larger pan, pour in enough hot water to come at least 1 inch up the sides of the smaller baking pan, cover the smaller pan with foil, and bake 1 hour or until the custard has completely set in the middle. Remove pudding from the oven and allow it to cool somewhat before cutting into serving pieces. Serve warm.

Chocolate–Almond Black and White Pie

In this updated version of a classic American pie, I use the same basic techniques for melting the chocolate and making the custard sauce base as for the Rich Chocolate Bread Pudding (see page 288). Once you know these basics, it's easy to make so many desserts. This one combines almonds and chocolate, a perfect flavor duo. You'll need to buy almond paste, available at many supermarkets or from baking supply companies such as The Baker's Catalog. Until I researched its name, I hadn't realized that Black-Bottom Pie, the original name for this pie, could be seen as derogatory. It seems its name, in use for about one hundred years, came from low-lying areas inhabited by black people. These areas were often called "black bottom." For an eye-catching presentation, decorate with chocolate curls.

Serves 12

Crumb Crust

2 cups chocolate cookie crumbs (made from a
   9-ounce package of chocolate wafer cookies)
1 cup finely ground almonds (about $1/2$ pound)
4 tablespoons melted unsalted butter

Preheat the oven to 350°F. Mix together crumbs, almonds, and butter and press firmly into a 9 x 2-inch deep fluted quiche pan with a removable bottom, or a 9 x 2-inch spring-form pan. Place in freezer to set for 30 minutes and then bake for 20 minutes or until set. Remove from oven and cool.

Chocolate and Almond Toppings

2 cups heavy cream, divided
$1/2$ pound bittersweet chocolate, grated
2 teaspoons unflavored gelatin powder
6 yolks + 4 whites
$3/4$ cup granulated sugar, divided
2 teaspoons vanilla extract
$1/4$ cup dark rum
7 ounces almond paste (one tube Odense almond paste)
1 cup heavy cream, whipped for topping
Chocolate curls (optional) for garnish

In a large glass or ceramic bowl, scald 1 cup of the heavy cream in the microwave or over a pot of steaming water. Add the chocolate and stir occasionally until the chocolate has melted completely. Reserve.

Soften the gelatin by sprinkling into $1/4$ cup cold water. Heat in the microwave on low power 1 to 2 minutes or until melted and clear. Reserve.

In a mixing bowl, lightly beat together the egg yolks and $1/2$ cup of the sugar. Scald the remaining 1 cup heavy cream. Beat a small amount of the scalded cream into the

yolk mixture to temper. Beat the remaining hot cream into the yolks. Scrape into a nonreactive heavy-bottomed pot and heat, while stirring often, until the sauce starts to thicken visibly and reaches 165°F. on a meat thermometer. Stir in the vanilla and rum.

Divide the custard into 2 bowls—one containing one-third and one containing two-thirds of the custard.

Make the black bottom: mix the larger part of the custard with the melted chocolate and cool until lukewarm. Pour into baked crust and refrigerate until partially set, about 1 hour.

Make the cream topping: Whisk the gelatin into the smaller part of the custard. Cream the almond paste in a food processor or mixer. When completely smooth, beat in a little custard making sure that the mixture is creamy and smooth, then continue to add the remaining custard to make a creamy, thick topping. Cool to room temperature.

In a clean mixer bowl, beat the egg whites with the remaining $1/4$ cup sugar until thick and glossy. Fold egg whites by thirds into the almond custard and spoon over the partially set black bottom. Chill the pie for several hours or overnight in the refrigerator.

Remove the pie from the pan and cut into 12 portions using a hot knife that has been rinsed and dried in between each cut. Garnish with whipped cream and chocolate curls.

MELTING GELATIN IN THE MICROWAVE

Gelatin melts perfectly in the microwave. Sprinkle the gelatin over water, whisking if necessary so that no lumps remain. When the water has completely absorbed the gelatin and no powder remains, heat in the microwave on low power 1 to 2 minutes or until the gelatin is melted and clear, but not bubbling hot.

Almond Paste

Almond paste is a smooth mixture of finely ground almonds, sugar, and almond flavoring. It is used in Scandinavia for cake fillings and for filling Danish pastry; in France, where it fills puff-pastry Pithiviers tarts; in England, where it is used to fill and ice wedding cakes; and in Italy, where it goes into many desserts, especially in Sicily. Its origin can be traced back to the Arabs.

Making Chocolate Curls

You'll need a thick block of chocolate (such as one broken from a 5-kilo block) at warm room temperature (75°F. to 80°F.). Using a potato peeler, peel long, narrow curls of chocolate from the block. Alternatively, use a sharp knife and scrape towards yourself with the knife, forming long, thin curls. If the chocolate is not warm enough, the chocolate will break up without forming curls. Warm in your hands to bring to temperature. Store the curls in a single layer in an airtight container at room temperature if the weather is cool, refrigerated if the weather is warm.

Chocolate Strega Cake with Apricot Cream

More of a fallen soufflé than a cake, this fragile, melting cake is redolent of dark chocolate and enriched by ground almonds. It is perfectly complemented by the sweet-tart apricot cream. But it's the haunting flavor of the Strega (witch in Italian) liqueur that makes this cake so bewitching.

Strega has been produced since 1860 in the town of Benevento, halfway between Rome and Naples. According to legend, it is the place where witches from all over the world gathered and prepared a love potion to unite forever those couples who drank it. Made from more than seventy herbs and spices, Strega gets its golden color from saffron, Note that the cake will fill a 9 x 2-inch cake pan and puff over the top. It can also be made in a 10-inch pan; just cut the baking time down to about 40 minutes. It would also work well as individual cakes, if you have small molds.

MAKES ONE 9–INCH CAKE, TO SERVE 12

Cake

$^1/_2$ pound (2 sticks) unsalted butter, softened

1 cup granulated sugar

6 eggs, separated

$^1/_2$ pound semisweet chocolate, melted and cooled
  (*see* Melting Chocolate, page 289)

Juice and grated zest of 1 orange

$^1/_4$ cup Strega liqueur

$^1/_2$ pound almond flour (or blanched almonds
  ground in a food processor)

2 tablespoons cornstarch

$^1/_4$ cup Dutch process cocoa

1 teaspoon baking powder

Pinch of Kosher salt

$^1/_4$ cup confectioners' sugar + extra for dusting

Apricot Cream (recipe follows)

Prepare a 9 x 2-inch cake pan by spraying with nonstick spray. Preheat the oven to 325°F.

Cream butter and sugar together until creamy and light. Beat in egg yolks, one at a time, until absorbed. Add

291

melted chocolate, orange juice and zest, and Strega, and beat just long enough to combine.

Whisk together the dry ingredients: almond flour, cornstarch, cocoa, baking powder, and salt and fold into the chocolate mix.

In another bowl, beat egg whites until they form soft peaks, then add confectioners' sugar and beat until firm and glossy. Fold into cake batter in thirds then spoon batter into the pan.

Bake for 50 minutes or until barely set in the middle. Remove from the oven and cool to room temperature before removing from the pan and turning upside-down. Note that the cake will fall as it cools.

To decorate the cake, lay a paper doily over top and dust with confectioners' sugar. Slice with a hot knife, rinsing under hot water and wiping dry in between each cut. Serve at room temperature with a dollop of the Apricot Cream.

Apricot Cream

$^1/_4$ cup dried apricots (preferably California), soaked in warm water to cover until soft

$^1/_4$ cup granulated sugar

1 cup heavy cream

2 tablespoons Strega liqueur

In a small heavy-bottomed nonreactive pot, simmer apricots in soaking liquid with the sugar until quite soft, about 10 minutes. In a blender, puree apricot mixture. Cool to room temperature.

In a chilled bowl, whip heavy cream until stiff but not at all yellow. Fold the cooled apricot puree and Strega liqueur into the cream; it puree should form streaks through cream. Serve on side of cake.

292

WHIPPING CREAM

To keep from making butter when you don't want to, chill both the cream and the mixer bowl in the freezer for about 30 minutes. The extra-cold cream will whip up stiff without breaking down. Also, beat the cream until soft peaks form before sprinkling in the sugar. Confectioners' sugar is best because its 3 percent cornstarch helps keep the fragile whipped cream from deflating. Always cover whipped cream tightly with plastic wrap, as the air bubbles it contains makes it very porous to extraneous odors.

Zuppa Inglese

Zuppa Inglese translates to English soup and is basically an English trifle consisting of layers of sponge cake soaked in a spiced liqueur syrup, interspersed with chocolate- and vanilla-flavored pastry cream, that have been lightened with whipped cream. This popular Italian dessert came about to please the many British people who would take their long summer "holidays" in Italy. Zuppa Inglese is one of those dishes that just doesn't work out in smaller quantities, but it makes an easy-to-serve dessert with a beautiful presentation for a large gathering. Assemble in a footed, straight-sided trifle dish so that the layers are clearly visible. Serve in scoops, using a large metal spoon. If you don't have cake flour, substitute three parts all-purpose flour mixed with one part cornstarch.

SERVES 15 TO 20

Vanilla Genoise

**MAKES ONE 12 x 18–INCH HALF SHEET PAN OR
TWO 11 x 17–INCH SHALLOW JELLY–ROLL PANS**

10 eggs

1 cup granulated sugar

1 cup cake flour

1 tablespoon vanilla extract

In a large stainless steel bowl, lightly beat together the eggs and sugar. Heat, while whisking often, in a double boiler until hot to the touch. Remove from heat and then beat, using the whisk attachment of an electric mixer until cool to the touch, light and thick. Sprinkle the flour over top and fold in along with the vanilla.

Spread the batter onto a parchment paper-lined half-sheet pan (or 2 jelly-roll pans). Bake at 350°F. or about 15 minutes or until lightly browned on top and slightly shrunken away from the sides. Cool before removing from pan. Split the cake in half horizontally to make 2 thin sheets of cake. (If using the jelly-roll pans, bake for about 12 minutes and don't split these shallower cakes.)

Pastry Cream

6 egg yolks

$^1/_2$ cup granulated sugar

$^1/_2$ cup pastry flour

2 cups milk, scalded

6 ounces semisweet chocolate, cut into bits and melted

2 cups heavy cream, whipped

Beat egg yolks and sugar together until light colored and the mixture forms a ribbon. Sprinkle in the flour and beat only long enough to combine well. Slowly beat in the milk to temper. Transfer the mixture to a nonreactive pot and cook over moderate heat, while constantly whisking, until the mixture thickens evenly and just comes to the boil.

Divide into 2 bowls, one third in one bowl and two-thirds in the second bowl. Stir melted chocolate into the bowl with the smaller amount. Cool both bowls over ice mixed with water, stirring occasionally to cool evenly and prevent a skin from forming. Fold half the whipped cream into each bowl and reserve.

Zuppa Syrup

I use whole spices here so that they don't darken the syrup. Substitute half the quantity of ground spices if desired.

$^1/_2$ cup granulated sugar

1 teaspoon ground cinnamon

1 teaspoon each: whole allspice, coriander, and anise

2 to 3 whole cloves

Zest of 1 orange in large strips (peel with a potato peeler)

$^1/_2$ cup dark rum

2 tablespoons rosewater

Small amount of rose coloring paste, enough to stick
  to the end of a wooden skewer

Bring the sugar, $1^1/_2$ cups water, cinnamon, allspice, coriander, anise, cloves, and orange zest to the boil, simmering until the syrup is completely clear, about 5 minutes. Remove from heat and then stir in rum, rosewater, and rose coloring paste. Cool, strain, and reserve.

Assembly

Large, straight-sided glass trifle bowl

Vanilla Genoise

Pastry Cream, vanilla and chocolate

Zuppa Syrup

Cut the cake to fit the bowl. Pieces are fine but reserve one whole circle of cake for the top. Spread half the vanilla cream into the bottom of the bowl. Cover with a layer of cake and moisten generously with syrup.

Cover with all of the chocolate pastry cream. Cover with a second layer of cake and moisten generously with syrup.

Cover with remaining vanilla pastry cream and a final layer of cake, preferably in one whole piece, and moisten generously with syrup. Wrap well with plastic wrap and refrigerate several hours to firm before serving. Use a large steel serving spoon to serve.

294

ALKHERMES LIQUEUR

In the classic recipe for Zuppa Inglese, a hard-to-find Italian liqueur called Alkhermes flavors the cake. It gets its bright red color from carmine, a natural dye extracted from the cochineal insect that lives in the prickly pear cactus. My version uses rose coloring paste and spices to approximate its color and flavor. Substitute a (very) few drops of red food coloring, or add a chunk of beet to the syrup.

USING COLORING PASTES

Professional cake decorators rely on coloring pastes with the thick consistency of oil paint, rather than water-based liquid food color. These small jars usually come in a set and are extremely concentrated. A small dip of a wooden skewer or toothpick (which can be thrown away after use) is usually enough. Buy a set of these pastes and they'll last for a very long time. Just be sure not to color anything inadvertently, because it will be very hard to get off.

Dark Chocolate Fudge Pie

This diner-style pie is a treat for the true chocolate fiend. A crumb crust made from stale brownies (or chocolate cookie crumbs) is filled with dark chocolate mousse, layered with chocolate fudge sauce, and to really put the icing on the cake, it is served with warm chocolate fudge sauce with whipped cream for lightness! This pie freezes very well; just defrost in the refrigerator. Cut the pie into serving portions while it is quite cold, using a knife dipped in hot water and wiped dry in between each slice.

MAKES A 9–INCH PIE TO SERVE 12

Brownie Crust

3 cups stale brownies or chocolate wafer cookies

1/4 cup dark brown sugar, packed

6 tablespoons unsalted butter, melted

Preheat the oven to 350°F. In the bowl of a food processor, process the brownies (or chocolate wafers) with brown sugar until finely crumbled. Add the melted butter and process briefly to combine.

Press firmly into a 9 x 2-inch fluted quiche pan with a removable bottom, or a 9 x 2-inch springform pan. Place in freezer to set for 30 minutes and then bake shell 20 minutes or until set. Remove from oven, cool, and reserve.

Hot Fudge Sauce

1/2 cup heavy cream

1/2 cup light corn syrup

2 tablespoons unsalted butter

1/2 cup Dutch process cocoa

2 teaspoons vanilla extract

1/2 pound semisweet chocolate

Combine cream, corn syrup, butter, in a medium heavy-bottomed pot and whisk together over medium heat until mixture comes to the boil. Remove from heat, whisk in cocoa, vanilla, and stir in chocolate until melted. Keep warm.

Mousse Filling

1/2 pound semi-sweet chocolate, chopped

12 tablespoons (1 1/2 sticks) unsalted butter

3/4 cup dark brown sugar, packed

3 egg yolks

1/4 cup hot, strong, brewed coffee

3/4 cup heavy cream, whipped

Melt chocolate and butter together in the microwave or in a bowl set over a pot of steaming water. Cool.

Meanwhile, whisk together the brown sugar, yolks, and coffee in a large bowl placed over a pot full of boiling water (as for making a hollandaise) and continue whisking until mixture is thickened and light. Remove from heat and fold cooled chocolate mix into the eggs, a little at a time, so the mixture doesn't deflate. Fold in the whipped cream.

Assembly

Mousse Filling

Brownie Crust

1/2 cup Hot Fudge Sauce

1 cup heavy cream, chilled

Spoon half of the Mousse Filling into the brownie crust, cover with Hot Fudge Sauce, and then spoon remaining mousse over top. Freeze until firm, about 2 hours.

Meanwhile, beat heavy cream until firm, but not stiff, and reserve. Using a hot knife, cut the pie into 12 portions. Serve a wedge of pie with a ladle of Hot Fudge Sauce over top and a spoonful of the whipped cream alongside.

Bittersweet Chocolate Soufflé with Pistachio–Cardamom Custard Sauce

SERVES 6 TO 10

10 ounces bittersweet (not unsweetened) chocolate, finely chopped or grated

$3/4$ cup heavy cream

$1/4$ cup + 2 tablespoons + 2 tablespoons granulated sugar

2 tablespoons unsalted butter, plus more as needed

2 tablespoons dark rum or brandy

1 tablespoon vanilla extract

6 eggs, separated

Pinch kosher salt

Pinch of cream of tartar

Confectioners' sugar

Pistachio-Cardamom Custard Sauce (recipe follows)

Combine chocolate, cream, $1/4$ cup sugar, butter, rum, and vanilla in a medium heavy-bottomed saucepan. Stir over low heat until chocolate melts and mixture is smooth. Remove from heat; cool to lukewarm. (Chocolate base can be made 1 day ahead. If so, warm over low heat just until lukewarm before continuing.)

Preheat the oven to 350°F. Butter eight 6- to 8-ounce ramekins or custard cups and sprinkle the insides with 2 tablespoons sugar. Whisk egg yolks into lukewarm chocolate base and reserve.

Beat the egg whites, salt, and cream of tartar in a large bowl until soft peaks form. Sprinkle in the remaining 2 table-spoons sugar and beat until firm and glossy.

Fold whites into chocolate base in thirds. Divide soufflé mixture among prepared ramekins; place on baking sheet. Bake soufflés until puffed but still moist in center, about 15 minutes. Sift powdered sugar over soufflés and serve immediately with Pistachio- Cardamom Custard Sauce.

Pistachio–Cardamom Custard Sauce

SERVES 8

2 cups milk

1 cup heavy cream

4 to 6 cardamom pods, crushed

6 egg yolks

$1/4$ cup honey

$1/4$ cup granulated sugar

$1/4$ cup shelled chopped pistachios (rinsed and dried if purchased salted)

Scald together the milk, cream, and cardamom and reserve.

Beat the egg yolks, honey, and sugar until light colored and the mixture forms a ribbon. Pour in about $1/2$ cup of the hot cream mixture while continuing to beat to warm the mixture. Pour in remaining milk-cream mixture and then transfer to a heavy-bottomed, nonreactive pot and heat until the custard visibly thickens and reads 165°F. on a thermometer. Immediately remove from heat. Strain mixture through a sieve and serve warm.

Rich Cinnamon–
Scented Hot Chocolate

The oldest way of using chocolate in Mayan and Aztec culture, where chocolate originated, was as a spiced drink. The solid form we crave came much later. In recent years, hot chocolate and its close cousin, hot cocoa, really got downgraded to where they were only made using of lesser quality packages. But, along with the explosion in espresso, cappuccino, and fine teas, inevitably there has been a resurgence in high-quality hot drinking chocolate, here scented with cinnamon and orange zest. Serve steaming mugs on their own on a cold winter's day or with a sugar cookie, perhaps as a personal reward after shoveling the walk. Just be careful not to burn your tongue—something I never manage not to do. If you substitute semisweet chocolate, cut the sugar by $1/4$ cup.

SERVES 8

1 quart milk

1 (3- to 4-inch) cinnamon stick, crushed

Grated zest of 1 orange

$3/4$ cup dark brown sugar, packed

2 cups heavy cream

$1/2$ pound bittersweet chocolate, grated or in bits
(about $1 1/2$ cups)

$1/2$ cup Dutch process cocoa

Combine milk, cinnamon, orange zest, and brown sugar in a medium heavy-bottomed nonreactive saucepan. Bring to a simmer over low heat, stirring often until bubbles form around edges of pan. Turn off heat, and steep for about 30 minutes, keeping in a warm place.

Place the cream in a Pyrex measuring cup (or other microwaveable container) and heat to scalding in the microwave (or place in another saucepan and heat on medium heat). Remove from microwave (or heat) and stir in the chocolate bits and cocoa. Allow the chocolate bits to melt for 2 minutes and then whisk together until you have a thick chocolate cream.

Strain the spiced milk through a sieve into the chocolate cream and then beat lightly together with the whisk. When ready to serve, reheat in the microwave (or a pot) for 2 minutes on medium power or until steaming hot.

CINNAMON, CANELA, AND CASSIA

Cinnamon, *Cinamomum zeylanicum*, is the soft, sweetly scented inner bark of the cinnamon tree and is related to the bay laurel, which originated in Sri Lanka (the former Ceylon). One of the world's oldest-known spices, cinnamon is beloved for its warm, sweet-spicy yet mild flavor. Vietnamese cinnamon, *Cinamomum loureirii*, is also highly regarded. In Latin America, true cinnamon is known as *canela* and may also be found under the name "soft-stick cinnamon." The rolls of bark, called quills, of true cinnamon are indeed soft enough to crush lightly by hand. Cassia or Chinese cinnamon, *Cinamomum aromaticum*, is similar to true cinnamon, with a bolder, harsher flavor. The bark is thicker and tougher with a dark brown, rough outer surface and the quills are thicker, hard and woody. Much of the "cinnamon" used in the United States is actually cassia. In Europe, it is illegal to sell cassia labeled as the more expensive cinnamon.

297

CLAMS

CLAMS

The sight of net bags full of silver-gray clams takes me immediately to summer days "down the shore" (as we say in Philly) in Jersey, Delaware, Nantucket, and Cape Cod, where hard-shell clams are sold in abundance. Nothing evokes the bracing, salty scent of the sea as much as steamed clams. The same clams, shucked and stuffed, Casino style, make a favorite appetizer, familiar from Italian-American restaurant menus. Clam chowders are a sure subject for controversy between those that favor tomato in a more Mediterranean-style chowder and those to whom tomato is anathema and only cream and salt pork are allowed. Clams on the half-shell are enjoyed by many, and are quite safe as long as they come from good, clean, water, preferably cold, and the clams themselves are tightly shut with a clean salt aroma.

Clams are bivalve mollusks of various species that live buried in mud or sand and have valves (the two halves of their shell) of equal size that are hinged together by a tough elastic ligament that acts like a rubber band. Clams propel themselves into the sand by using their muscular foot, which appears out their front end between the two shell halves. Clams can live up to one hundred fifty years or more (some larger quahogs found off the East Coast of the U.S. may be two hundred years old!) Clams are as highly valued today as they were when Native American tribes harvested them in abundance for food and trade.

They used the deep violet-colored inner portion of the large quahog (a Narragansett Indian name) shell as wampum, their form of money.

Native American tribes on Martha's Vineyard and in coastal regions of New England were baking clams on the beach long before the Pilgrims landed. They would dig a large pit in the sand and fill it with smoldering rocks. A section of rawhide would be boiled and then used as a cooking pot filled with clams, lobsters, mussels, fish, and seawater. The whole pit would then be covered with seaweed and allowed to steam. Modern-day clambakes are not that different, although corn on the cob, potatoes, and spicy Portuguese linguiça sausage are often added. The sausage pays homage to the history of the New England's fishing industry, where people of Portuguese descent sailed the majority of the fishing vessels off the coast of New England.

Most of the clams consumed in this country are surf clams or ocean quahogs, dredged in large quantities off the mid-Atlantic and New England coasts in annual harvests of about ninety million pounds of meat per year. The meat from these clams is cooked, sliced, diced, and used in processed products like breaded clam strips and canned chowders. The darker, stronger-smelling meat of ocean quahogs, usually labeled "ocean clam", is less expensive than that of surf clams, usually labeled "sea clam."

Clam Varieties

Cockle: The cockle is similar to the hard-shell clam, with two hinged, heart-shaped shells and prominent rib markings, which aid the animal in gripping the sand. Most of the cockles sold in the U.S. are flown in live from New Zealand. Those from the South Island are larger (15 per pound) than cockles from the North Island (20 to 25 per pound).

Geoduck Clam: Pronounced gooey-duck, this huge clam gets its name from a Nisqually Indian term meaning *dig deep*. Geoducks are found in Puget Sound in Washington State, and the inland waters of British Columbia and southern Alaska. The long, trunk-like siphon is covered by tough tan to brown skin; protruding from the shell is the edible portion. (In Chinese, its name means *elephant trunk clam*.) The edible meat below the skin is smooth and cream-colored.

Hard-Shell Clam: The hard-shell clam, *Mercenaria mercenaria*, is abundant from the Gulf of St. Lawrence as far south as Texas. Eastern hard-shells, especially smaller little necks, are the only clam commonly served raw on the half-shell. Also called the quahog, when larger, this clam has a thick shell that is grayish-white on the outside and white on the inside with a deep violet-colored patch near the rear. Hard-shell clams live in sandy-bottomed bays and coves and along beaches. Recreational fishermen gather the clams with rakes and hoes, or simply by probing the bottom with their feet. At low tide, gatherers can spot the siphon holes on the bottom that reveal their location.

The smaller the clam, the more expensive it will be with each size bearing a different name. Little Necks, named after Little Neck Bay on New York's Long Island, once a thriving center of the clam trade, are the smallest (and most expensive) hard clam, although some suppliers pick out an even smaller size called a "button neck." Little Necks average 10 to 12 per pound. The next size up, top necks, average 6 to 8 per pound. Cherrystones, named after Cherrystone Creek on Virginia's Eastern Shore, average 3 to 5 per pound. The largest size, called chowder or quahog, average only 1 to 2 clams per pound.

Mahogany Clams: With their attractive deep mahogany-brown shells, mahogany clam is a marketing name for small ocean quahogs, *Arctica islandica*, harvested off the New England coast. American Mussel Harvesters has trademarked the name "golden necks" for their mahogany clams. Mahoganies, which typically average about 25 per pound, are about the same size as Manilas, but cost less. Because they open up flat when steamed, instead of the familiar wedge-shaped opening of hard-shell clams, they are not as desirable in appearance.

Manila Clams: The Manila Clam, *Tapes japonica*, was accidentally introduced to the U.S. in the 1920s, when it traveled along with a shipment of seed oysters from Japan. These moderate-sized clams with streaked-brown, curved shells, are the most common clam on the West Coast. Harvested in both Washington and British Columbia, Manilas run about 20 clams per pound. Those harvested in Washington State come primarily from farmed beds, while those from British Columbia come primarily from natural beds.

Pacific Razor Clam: The Pacific razor clam, *Siliqua patula*, has a long, narrow, sharp-edged shell that suggests an old-fashioned straight razor. It is abundant on beaches from California to Alaska. The adult clams live right in the surf, and people dig for them at low tide when their holes are visible in the sand.

Soft-Shell Clam: Steamer clams, *Mya arenia*, also called Ipswich clams (for Ipswich, Massachusetts, which is famed for them), belly clams, longneck, manniñose, or steamer clams, are quite popular in New England. Although they are found from Newfoundland, Canada, to as far south as North Carolina, soft-shells are harvested commercially mostly in New Brunswick, Canada; Maine; and Massachusetts. These clams have long necks (or feet), large hanging bellies, and fragile shells that don't close completely. They average about 12 to 15 clams per pound.

Stimpson Surf Clam: The Stimpson surf clam, *Mactromeris polynyma,* from the Canadian Maritimes, is prized in Japan as a delicacy for the bright red to purplish black of the tips of its foot. In Japan, it is called *hokkigai* and is served as an expensive type of sushi. Look for frozen *hokkigai* in Asian markets.

Venus Clams: Venus clams, *Chione undatella*, are farmed in Mexico's Baja Peninsula and are new to the U.S. market.

West Coast Littlenecks: The West Coast littleneck, *Protothaca staminea*, (not to be confused with the East Coast two-word Little Neck), is harvested along with the Manila, but costs less because it takes longer to open when being steamed, and has a shorter shelf life.

STORING CLAMS

Cover clams with a clean wet towel to keep moist and store in a cool, dark area at 36°F. to 40°F. Don't use ice, as it will be too cold and the melting fresh water will shorten shelf life. Under ideal conditions, clams will stay alive for up to two weeks, although shelf life is shorter in summer after animals have spawned. Figure on three to four days shelf life in a home refrigerator.

EVALUATING CLAMS

A live clam will have a tightly closed shell, or will close readily if tapped. However, soft-shell clams do not close completely because the "siphon" or "neck" often protrudes from the shell. If the clam moves when touched, it is alive. Avoid eating clams with broken or damaged shells. Discard any clam if the meat is dry when the clam is opened, or the shell has dirt inside (called a "mudder"). The clam meat should be a creamy tan color with firm texture, its shell should be full of liquid, and it should smell fresh and briny.

CLAM YIELD

Although it will vary depending on the season (the yield and shelf life will be lower in the summer after clams spawn), one pound of hard-shell clams will yield about a quarter pound of meat, while a pound of soft shell-clams will yield 6 ounces to $\frac{1}{2}$ pound of meat.

CLAMS IN THE KITCHEN

Steamed until they pop completely open, little necks have a buttery-sweet, light flavor. Larger clams are stronger-tasting and chewier. Little necks are best for clams on the half-shell (raw) because they are the tenderest. But, they also may be steamed with garlic, olive oil, and a little white wine for a delicious dish. Try the Linguine with Steamed Clams, Arugula, and Pancetta (see page 69).

Cherrystones are typically stuffed and baked in their shells as for the Baked Clams wih Fennel, Roasted Peppers, and Lemon Zest (see page 306). Smaller chowder clams may be cut into strips and breaded for frying, dipped in batter (use the one in the Fish and Chips recipe, on page 319), chopped up and added to pasta, or used top a New Haven–style white clam pizza with plenty of garlic and parsley.

Steam clams in a small amount of liquid just until their shells fully open, removing each clam from the pot as its shell opens. Discard any clams that were not closed or which do not open after steaming for 5 to 10 minutes. When serving the clam broth, allow it to settle first, so that any sand can fall to the bottom, Strain the clam broth through a dampened paper towel laid into a sieve to remove any sand, or leave behind the last half cup of so of broth, which will contain most of any sand.

303

Clam and Mushroom Soup with Riesling

This soup is an unexpected, yet marvelous combination of fla vors. While you wouldn't necessarily think of combining clams and mushrooms, they work perfectly together. For restaurant service, I would steam open large, flavorful chowder clams, chop them up, mix with their liquor, and simmer together for about an hour, or until tender. Here, I've substituted the fresh chopped clams available in many markets. Canned clams make a merely acceptable substitute. The deep, earthy flavor of porcini mushroom "liquor," the liquid obtained by soaking them, imparts the mushroom flavor. The Riesling, a German grape varietal with fresh, herbal character, adds the coupe de resistance (the final fillip). Substitute dry white vermouth.

SERVES 8 TO 12

1 cup chopped shallots

1 cup diced onions

1 tablespoon chopped garlic

6 tablespoons unsalted butter

1 pound button mushrooms (white and completely
   closed), trimmed and quartered

$^1/_2$ pound shiitake mushrooms, stemmed and caps sliced

$^1/_2$ cup dried porcini mushrooms, soaked, cleaned, and
   chopped (*see* Reconstituting Dried Porcini, at right)

6 tablespoons flour

1 pint container chopped clams

1 quart chicken stock

2 cups clam broth, substitute more chicken stock

2 cups heavy cream, scalded

2 tablespoons each: chopped thyme and tarragon

Freshly ground black pepper to taste

1 cup Riesling wine

In a large soup pot, sauté the shallots, onions, and garlic in the butter until soft, but not browned. Add the button mushrooms, shiitakes, and the porcini, and sauté until the mushrooms give off their juices and the juices have evaporated, about 8 minutes.

Stir in the flour and continue to cook for 3 to 4 minutes while stirring to cook out the raw flour taste. Add the chopped clams with any liquid, the chicken stock, and the clam broth, and bring the soup to the boil. Pour in the cream, bring back to the boil and add the chopped herbs. Season to taste with black pepper and serve. (The clams are salty, so salt will probably not be needed.)

RECONSTITUTING DRIED PORCINI

Soak porcini in warm water to cover until soft, about 20 minutes. Scoop out the mushrooms, and reserve. Strain the mushroom "liquor" through a dampened paper towel laid into a sieve to remove any sand, and reserve.

CHOWDER IN *MOBY DICK*

In Herman Melville's 1851 sea-classic, *Moby Dick*, he writes of the Try Pots, a Nantucket chowder house. The inevitable menu was "chowder for breakfast, and chowder for dinner, and chowder for supper, until you began to look for fish-bones coming through your clothes." (Try pots were the large cauldrons used for melting and rendering whale fat for lamp oil.)

New England–Style Clam Chowder

Chowder in its numerable versions provokes both strong feelings and contradictory claims. Even the origins of the word chowder itself are disputed, although most believe the word comes from the French chaudière, *a large cauldron in which Breton sailors threw their catch to make a communal stew. Their custom was carried first to Newfoundland and Nova Scotia and then down into New England. In 1751, the* Boston Evening Post *published a recipe for chowder containing onions, salt pork, marjoram, savory, thyme, ship's biscuit, and fish, to which was added a bottle of red wine. Because of the crumbled common crackers, hardtack, or ship's biscuit they contained, early chowders were so thick that they were more like stew than soup, best for onboard consumption.*

SERVES 8

Milk Broth

1 quart milk

1 cup heavy cream

$1/2$ cup cut up onion or onion trimmings

Several sprigs thyme or marjoram

2 bay leaves

1 teaspoon ground allspice

In a heavy-bottomed pot, heat all the ingredients, stirring often, especially at the beginning, so the milk doesn't stick and burn. Simmer 15 minutes and strain through a sieve, discarding solids, then reserve.

Soup

$1/2$ pound bacon, cut into small strips

1 onion, peeled and diced

3 to 4 ribs celery, sliced

1 ounce ($1/4$ cup) flour

Milk Broth

1 pint bottled clam broth

2 large Idaho potatoes, peeled and diced

1 pint container chopped clams, scrubbed

2 tablespoons each: chopped Italian parsley and thyme or marjoram

Black pepper and cayenne pepper to taste

In a heavy skillet or in the microwave, cook the bacon until crispy and brown and the fat has been rendered (melted out). Strain and reserve the bacon bits. Separately reserve about 3 tablespoons of the fat, discarding the remainder or saving for another use.

Put the bacon fat in a large soup pot and cook the onion and celery until transparent. Add flour and stir to combine, cooking together 3 to 4 minutes to get rid of the raw flour taste.

Pour in the milk broth, the clam broth, and the potatoes, and bring to the boil. Simmer about 10 minutes or until the potatoes are tender. Add the clams, the reserved bacon bits and the chopped herbs. Bring back to the boil, season to taste with pepper and cayenne and then serve immediately. (The clams and broth are salty, so salt will probably not be needed.)

Portuguese Steamed Clams à La Cataplana

A cataplana is a round, domed set of two hammered copper bowls hinged together. It was introduced to southern Portugal by the Moors during their long reign, which started in the eighth century C E. Cataplana is most often used over an open fire or on the stovetop, and was originally filled only with clams and mussels because it was an ideal way to steam them open. Today, small bits of other quick-cooking foods are often added, such as the chouriço used here. While an authentic cataplana (sold by many cookware stores) makes a striking presentation, the dish can easily be prepared in a covered pot, preferably a heavy enameled cast-iron casserole, such as those made by Le Creuset. Substitute Spanish or Mexican fresh-type (rather than cured or smoked and dried) chorizo for the Portuguese chouriço. Serve with crusty bread to mop up the delicious juices.

SERVES 6

4 dozen little neck clams

3 tablespoons chopped garlic

$1/2$ pound Portuguese chouriço sausage, peeled and broken up, substitute Spanish or Mexican chorizo

$1/2$ pound smoked ham, diced

1 teaspoon hot red pepper flakes

$1/4$ cup olive oil

1 cup dry white vermouth

2 cups diced fresh tomatoes

$1/4$ cup chopped cilantro

Scrub the clams using an abrasive scouring pad, then soak for 30 minutes in cold salted water with a couple of tablespoons of cornmeal added. Remove clams from water, taking care to leave any sand undisturbed, and discard water.

In the bottom of a cataplana or a heavy casserole dish, sauté the garlic, chouriço, ham, and hot pepper flakes in olive oil. Pour in the dry white vermouth and quickly bring to the boil. Add the clams, diced tomato, and cilantro, cover and steam, shaking occasionally until the clams open. Serve in the cataplana or the casserole dish.

Baked Clams with Fennel, Roasted Peppers and Lemon Zest

This version of Clams Casino comes by way of two restaurants, each famed in its own time. The original was served at the Casino Restaurant in New York. As the story goes, in 1917, a society patron asked Julius Keller, the restaurant's maître d', to surprise her with a new dish. Keller presented her with clams baked on the half shell, topped with chopped bell peppers, herb butter, and bacon. By the twenties, Clams Casino was ubiquitous on restaurant menus. The second comes from the simply wonderful Italian restaurant, Al Forno (out of the oven) in Providence, Rhode Island, specializing in wood-oven cookery where they serve their own version called "Clams al Forno." Ask your fishmonger to "pop" the clams, cutting through the hard elastic muscle that joins the two sides of the clam shell to make it easier to open them at home.

SERVES 6

1 large roasted red pepper, diced

1 cup finely chopped fennel stalks

½ cup chopped Italian parsley

1 cup sourdough breadcrumbs

¼ cup extra-virgin olive oil

2 tablespoon chopped garlic

Grated zest of 1 lemon

2 teaspoons Korean red pepper flakes (*see* Korean Red
  Pepper Flakes, page 122) or hot red pepper flakes

½ teaspoon freshly ground black pepper

3 dozen cherrystone clams, well scrubbed and purged

¼ pound thick-sliced pancetta, cut into ½-inch squares

3 lemons, halved

Combine roasted pepper, fennel, most of the parsley, breadcrumbs, olive oil, garlic, lemon zest, red pepper, and black pepper.

Preheat the oven to 425°F. Open the clams, keeping all juices inside. Top each clam with a portion of the filling, mounding it up. Cover with several squares of pancetta. Arrange on a metal baking pan. Roast 15 minutes until crusty and bubbling. Sprinkle with remaining parsley and serve with lemon halves.

Broccoli Flan with Petite Clams in Lemon Butter Sauce

This is a lovely appetizer to serve to your most discerning friends. Broccoli and clams makes another unexpected yet felicitous combination of textures and flavors. I first tasted this dish in a restaurant in Italy and immediately set out to create my own version once I returned home. Here small broccoli custards, or savory flans, called sformati *in Italian, are steamed and then surrounded by rich, flavorful clams in the butter sauce called* beurre blanc *in French. The only hard part is finding the right little molds to make the flans. Pyrex custard cups, ceramic ramekins, foil custard cups, or even muffin tins will all work. Just be sure to coat them generously with nonstick spray first. Note that the flans may be made 1 to 2 days ahead and reheated at 50 percent power in the microwave for about 3 minutes or until steaming.*

307

SERVES 6

Broccoli Flan

2 cups broccoli florets and small, brightly colored stems

2 tablespoons chopped garlic

¼ cup extra-virgin olive oil

6 eggs, lightly beaten

1 cup heavy cream

1 cup milk

Kosher salt, freshly ground black pepper, freshly ground
  nutmeg, and cayenne pepper to taste

Preheat the oven to 325°F. Spray six 8-ounce glass custard cups, ceramic ramekins, or muffin tins thoroughly with nonstick spray and reserve.

Chop the broccoli florets in a food processor until very finely chopped. Measure out 4 cups broccoli and discard any excess. In a medium pot over low heat, cook the garlic in the olive oil until soft, but not brown, about 3 minutes. Add the chopped broccoli and cook together about 4 minutes, or until the broccoli is slightly softened, but still brightly colored.

Remove the broccoli from heat; stir in the eggs, cream, milk, and seasonings. Pour liquid into molds as full as possible. Place the molds into a baking pan large enough to hold them. Pour hot water halfway up the sides of the molds to make a water-bath. Cover the pan with foil that has been slashed in 2 or 3 places to allow excess steam to escape.

Bake 45 minutes or until the custards are just set in the middle. Remove the pan from the oven. Using tongs (or hot pads) remove the custard cups from the water bath and cool.

Cool slightly and then shake molds back and forth to loosen the contents. Remove flans from molds by turning upside-down and rapping sharply on the bottom.

Clams in Lemon Butter Sauce

2 dozen smallest clams, well-scrubbed
$1/4$ cup chopped shallots
Juice and grated zest of 1 lemon
$1/4$ pound (1 stick) unsalted butter, softened

Place the clams in a pot with a lid and about $1/2$ cup of water. Steam over high heat until the clams open, shaking occasionally so they steam evenly. Cool and then remove the clams from their shells. Strain the clam "liquor" through a dampened paper towel laid into a sieve and reserve.

Place clam liquor, shallots, lemon juice and zest in a saucepot and bring to the boil. Reduce until syrupy, or one quarter of its volume. Whip in the butter, arrange clams in their shells around the flans, serving an equal number for each guest, then ladle the sauce over the clams.

COCONUT

COCONUT

On a trip to Brazil, I sipped refreshing coconut juice right out of the green coconut hacked open in front of me by a man wielding a scary-looking, but no doubt effective, machete on Rio's magnificent Copacabana Beach. Tropical breezes, swinging hammocks, and coconuts all seem to belong together, and rightly so. Coconuts originated in Southern Asia but they floated easily to islands throughout the Indian Ocean, Africa, the islands of the Pacific islands, the coasts of the Americas, and the Caribbean. Intrepid Portuguese seamen began using the Spanish word coco, meaning *monkey's face*, for the coconut towards the end of the fifteenth century. In the sixteenth century, the Spanish introduced coconuts to Puerto Rico, and the Portuguese brought them to Brazil. Today, most American coconuts come from Honduras, the Dominican Republic, and Puerto Rico.

The fresh coconut, *Cocos nucifera*, in the market is the inner shell of a mature fruit; the large, fibrous husk is removed before shipping. The smooth, tough, green to reddish-brown husk turns gray as the coconut matures. Between the outer husk and the inner white coconut meat is a thick, loose layer of coarse brown fibers. Next comes the hard, woody shell that has three "eyes" at one end. Inside the hollow shell, a paper-thin brown coat adheres all-too-firmly to the solid and slightly fibrous white meat of the kernel. Inside there should be a small amount of liquid, which is generally discarded in a mature coconut because it no longer tastes good. (A coconut without any liquid is probably cracked and most likely spoiled.) Coconuts are high in saturated fats, so coconut fat, like butter, is solid at room temperature.

In a very young coconut, the inner kernel is soft and the liquid abundant, but unpalatable. As the fruit ripens to a "green coconut," the inner white kernel gradually hardens to a creamy, gelatinous texture and the liquid is transformed into the sweet, refreshing drink, called coconut juice or coconut water, that I enjoyed in Rio di Janeiro. Green coconuts are most commonly found in tropical coconut-growing countries. One kind of green coconut, called Sweet Young Coconut, is now imported into the U.S. from Thailand and is found in specialty and Asian markets. Coconut milk, or coconut cream, is extracted from the meat of the ripe coconut. It is sold in cans either plain (unsweetened) or sweetened, so check the can carefully. The unsweetened kind is what you want for cooking.

In the tropical regions where coconuts abound, unsweetened coconut cream is used much like heavy cream, to flavor, enrich, and thicken sauces. From Thailand and Sri Lanka to Bahia, Brazil, and Trinidad, coconut milk shows up in soups, sauces, drinks, and sweets. In many countries, including Mexico and Italy, a fresh coconut vendor on the street will sell juicy chunks of fresh mature coconut kept moist in ice water.

310

Coconut Season And Choosing A Coconut

Fresh mature and young, green coconuts are available year-round, with peak season September through April. Coconuts have a shelf life of about two months, but it can take more than that for them to reach the market because they are shipped by boat. It's likely that some of these coconuts will be moldy or dry inside, so it's important to check before buying. The coconut should feel heavy and you should be able to hear the juice sloshing inside when the fruit is shaken. Its three "eyes," or soft spots, should be dry. Avoid coconuts with moldy spots, any sour or alcoholic smell, or with "eyes" that are moldy and wet. Patches of staining are a sign that the liquid has escaped through a crack in the shell. Older coconuts will be grayish rather than rich brown in color. While newly matured coconuts will be light tan. Store a whole coconut up to 1 month in the refrigerator.

Frozen–Fresh Grated Coconut

While fresh-grated coconut is absolutely delicious, it is a real challenge to prepare. Instead I use frozen fresh-grated coconut sold in one-pound packages in the freezer case in Latin American and Asian groceries. It is inexpensive, easy to use, and far closer to the fresh in flavor and texture than either the fibrous desiccated coconut sold in natural foods stores or the preservative-laden, too-sweet sweetened shredded coconut sold in supermarkets. Look for the La Fe or Goya brand in Latin markets. Imported from Thailand, it is sold under various names in Asian markets.

OPENING A FRESH COCONUT

The coconut has three "eyes," one of which is soft. This is the one you want to poke open, using an awl or sharpening steel. Drain and discard the coconut liquid. Don't skip this step, because you will be baking the coconut next. If not opened and drained, the coconut could explode.

Preheat the oven to 350°F. Bake the coconut for 25 minutes, and then cool. The flesh will shrink away from the shell. Tap the shell with a hammer at the horizontal line that usually appears about one-third of the way down from the top until it cracks apart.

Insert a thin, flexible icing spatula between the shell and the meat to pop the meat away from the shell. Peel the dark skin on the coconut for snow-white coconut, or leave it on for a natural look. Note that peeling is easiest when the coconut is warm.

Cut shavings for garnish using a mandoline, Japanese Benriner cutter, or a meat slicer, or shred using a sharp box grater.

Caribbean Callalou Soup

Callalou is a delicious celebration soup made in different versions throughout the Caribbean islands. It gets its name from the special green leaves used in it, which may be taro, amaranth, or other island-specific greens. While the recipe uses okra, which is of African origin, it also uses coconut milk and crabmeat, which are native to the Caribbean. I served this soup at the Dock Street Brewing Company in Philadelphia in the early 1990s, where it was a big hit. While amaranth leaves are traditional, a mild tasting green like spinach, Swiss chard, Chinese spinach, or even beet greens will also work well. For those who don't want to eat pork, add diced smoked turkey leg or thigh. Fresh young okra is often found at farmers' markets and it is quite delicious. While a 12- to 16-ounce package of frozen sliced okra can be substituted, the frozen type tends to be slippery; fresh okra will be pleasantly chewy.

SERVES 8

½ pound bacon, cut into ½-inch strips

1 onion, diced

2 green bell peppers, diced

2 ribs celery, diced

2 tablespoons chopped garlic

2 tablespoons chopped fresh thyme,
   or 2 teaspoons dried thyme

1 pound okra, ends trimmed off, sliced ½ inch thick

6 cups chicken stock, purchased or homemade

1 tablespoon Jamaican Pickapeppa Sauce (*see* Pickapeppa Sauce, page 231), substitute Worcestershire Sauce

1 (14-ounce) can unsweetened coconut milk

2 bay leaves

1 pound bag fresh baby spinach leaves

1 pound best-quality crabmeat, picked over for shells

Kosher salt and freshly ground black pepper, to taste

In a heavy skillet or in the microwave, cook the bacon until crispy and brown and the fat has been rendered (melted out). Strain and reserve the bacon bits. Separately reserve the fat.

In a large soup pot, sauté the onion, peppers, celery, garlic, thyme, and okra together in most of the bacon fat until softened but not brown. Pour in the chicken stock,

Pickapeppa, coconut milk, and bay leaves and bring to the boil.

Just before serving add the spinach leaves, reserved bacon bits, and the crabmeat. Heat together until spinach is wilted, season with salt and pepper, and serve piping hot.

Crispy Coconut Shrimp with Marmalade– Mustard Dipping Sauce

A perennial bar menu favorite, these crunchy golden-brown shrimp with their easy sweet-sharp dipping sauce also work well as a lunchtime entree accompanied by steamed rice and cooked greens. Or, serve them as an hors d'oeuvre at a cocktail party, making sure that you have enough on hand, because they're liable to be snapped up almost instantly. Use the unsweetened desiccated coconut found in natural foods stores here. If you have a wok, you'll need less oil for frying, because of its rounded bottom.

SERVES 8

Beer Batter

3 eggs

4 cups beer

½ pound (2 cups) all-purpose flour, preferably unbleached

Lightly beat together the eggs and beer. Place the flour in a mixing bowl, making a well in the middle. Pour the egg-beer mix into the well, whisking to combine with the flour. Set batter aside to rest for 20 minutes in the refrigerator.

312

Shrimp

2 pounds shrimp (16 to 20 count per pound, extra-large)

¹/₂ pound (2 cups) all-purpose flour, preferably unbleached

Kosher salt, freshly ground black pepper, and
  cayenne pepper, to taste

2 pounds desiccated coconut

Peel and devein shrimp, leaving the last tail shell attached. Split the shrimp open down the middle, cutting as far as the tail shell, to butterfly. Press the shrimp lightly to flatten. Mix the flour with the salt, pepper, and cayenne.

Set up 3 bowls: one of flour, the second of batter, the third of coconut. Dip each butterflied shrimp first into flour, shaking off the excess. Then dip into the batter, allowing the excess to drip off. Then, place the shrimp into the bowl of coconut, patting all over so the coconut adheres well. Repeat until all the shrimp are coated. (You can refrigerate the shrimp at this point for cooking later the same day or the next day.)

Marmalade–Mustard Dipping Sauce

2 tablespoons grated ginger

2 tablespoons horseradish

1 cup orange marmalade

¹/₂ cup Dijon mustard

Whisk together all the dip ingredients and reserve.

Assembly

4 cups peanut oil, for frying

Coconut-breaded shrimp

Marmalade-Mustard Dipping Sauce

In a large, heavy-bottomed pot, an electric deep-fryer, or a wok, heat the oil until shimmering (365°F. on a frying thermometer). Working in 3 to 4 batches, lay the shrimp into the oil, turning with tongs as they brown. Fry until well-browned and crispy, about 5 minutes.

Using a wire skimmer, remove the shrimp from the oil and drain on a wire rack, keeping warm in a 200°F. oven. Fry in several batches, adding only enough shrimp at a time that won't crowd the pot, cooking until golden brown and crispy. This way your shrimp will be light without absorbing excess oil.

Serve Coconut Shrimp accompanied by a bowl of the Marmalade-Mustard Dipping Sauce

Dream Bars with Honey, Coconut, and Pecans

Dreamy these are, with their delectable combination of honey and coconut. And if that isn't enough, buttery pecans make it even better. Like all bar cookies, these are a great way to make a large quantity of cookies without a lot of work. The cookies will keep quite well for up to one week refrigerated and they freeze beautifully. Allow them to come to room temperature before serving. I like to use wildflower honey for its faint floral perfume, but any kind of light honey will work well. Use the unsweetened dessicated coconut sold in natural foods stores here rather than the preservative-laden sweetened coconut found in supermarkets.

MAKES 48 LARGER OR 72 SMALLER BARS

1½ pounds Sugar Pastry (*see* page 989)

6 eggs

1½ cups granulated sugar

1 cup honey

1 tablespoon vanilla extract

1 ounce (¼ cup) all-purpose flour,
  preferably unbleached

1½ teaspoons baking powder

1 teaspoon kosher salt

¾ pound (about 3 cups) shredded dried coconut

¾ pound (about 3 cups) chopped pecans

Preheat the oven to 350°F. Press the dough out into a parchment paper-lined 12 x 17-inch half-sheet pan or two 9 x 13-inch rectangular baking pans. Bake about 20 minutes, or until the dough is fully cooked and lightly browned. Remove from the oven and cool.

Meanwhile, prepare the filling: Whisk together by hand the eggs, sugar, honey, and vanilla extract just until well combined. Stir together the dry ingredients: the flour, baking powder, and salt.

Fold dry ingredients into egg mixture and then stir in the coconut and pecans. Spread mixture over top of the baked pastry in one or two pans. Bake 30 minutes, or until topping is lightly browned and thickened.

Cool to room temperature and then chill. Cut into 48 or 72 pieces, using a sharp wet knife. Bring to room temperature before serving.

HALF-SHEET PANS

Note: When baking bar cookies, I use commercial size half-sheet pans (12 x 18-inch). These heavy aluminum pans never warp, are inexpensive and available at restaurant supply houses. However, not every home oven is big enough, so alternatively use 2 shallower (9 x 13-inch) baking pans.

Creamy Coconut Tart

A mile-high coconut cream pie is a delight served in a good diner and delectable served at home. In this scrumptious almond-flavored version, I use unsweetened coconut milk to amplify the coconut flavor and rosewater for its heavenly perfume. Coconut and rosewater appear together in many Indian desserts for good reason. A bit of flour gives the filling body; cornstarch makes it light. The sugar crust is flavored with almond extract and vanilla; an idea that I got from a Chez Panisse recipe. There are three parts to this tart, although the pastry can easily be made ahead, but it's not a last-minute dessert.

MAKES ONE 9 x 2–INCH TART

1 pound Sugar Pastry (*see* page 989)

1 (13- to 15-ounce can) unsweetened coconut milk

1 cup heavy cream + extra (enough to make 3 cups
  liquid when combined with coconut milk)

2 eggs + 6 yolks

1 cup granulated sugar

2 tablespoons all-purpose flour

2 tablespoons cornstarch

2 teaspoons vanilla extract

1 tablespoon rosewater

Roll out the pastry dough and use to line a 9 x 2-inch deep fluted quiche pan with a removable bottom, or a 9 x 2-inch springform pan. Chill to allow the dough to relax, 30 minutes in the freezer or 1 hour in the refrigerator.

Preheat the oven to 375°F. Press heavy-duty foil into the shell and fill with beans. Bake 30 minutes or until pale brown and no longer raw and pasty. (For more information on blind-baking, *see* Blind-baking with beans, page 230.)

Remove to foil and beans and bake 5 to 10 minutes longer, or until the dough is light brown. Remove the shell from the oven. Cool the shell to room temperature and reserve.

Meanwhile, prepare the coconut filling: Scald the coconut milk and heavy cream. Beat together eggs, egg yolks, and sugar until light and fluffy and the mixture forms a ribbon. In a separate bowl, whisk together the flour and cornstarch and then add to the yolk-mixture, beating again until just combined. Slowly beat in the hot cream mixture and continue to beat until well combined.

Transfer the mixture to a large, heavy-bottomed non-reactive pot and bring just to the boil over moderate heat, whisking constantly until evenly thickened. Remove the pot from the heat and stir in the vanilla and rosewater.

Chill by transferring to a steel bowl placed inside a larger bowl filled with ice mixed with water, stirring the filling occasionally to cool evenly and prevent a skin from forming. Pour into the prebaked crust and reserve.

Coconut Topping

2 cups freshly grated coconut

1 cup heavy cream

$1/2$ cup granulated sugar

2 tablespoons dark rum

1 tablespoon vanilla extract

1 tablespoon rosewater

Preheat the oven to 375°F. In a medium nonreactive pot, simmer together the coconut, heavy cream, and sugar until thickened and the milk has almost completely evaporated. Remove from heat and stir in the vanilla, and rosewater. Cool and then spoon the topping over the coconut filling.

Place the tart on the top shelf in the oven and bake about 30 minutes, or until the topping is browned on top and set. Cool tart completely and then refrigerate until the filling is cold and set before cutting into (small) portions.

315

PARCHMENT PAPER

Lining baking pans with parchment paper (sold at cookware shops and well-stocked supermarkets) eliminates the need for buttering and flouring the pans. The dough never sticks and the paper is reusable.

COD, SCROD, & BACCALÀ

COD, SCROD & BACCALA

Three hundred years ago, the codfish was a hugely important, indeed essential, source of food. Historians theorize that the enormous stocks of cod on our side of the North Atlantic spurred the European colonization of America. Just think of "Cape Cod" in Massachusetts, where a model of a salted cod hangs in the State House in recognition of the wealth this cold-water fish brought to them. Early maps from the sixteenth century show a vaguely outlined North American continent labeled "Land of the Cod."

During the five recorded voyages by the Vikings to Greenland around the year 1000, they ate the air-dried cod (known as stockfish) already being produced in Iceland and Norway. In the same era, Basque fisherman were fishing for cod in a major way. They kept the location of their fishing grounds secret to insure their domination of the enormous market for cod salted for preservation with the salt the Basques had in abundance. Salt cod (the fish came from too great a distance to keep fresh) was essential because on the Catholic calendar of the time, almost half the days were meatless.

When in 1497 Giovanni Caboto (known as John Cabot), a Genovese who sailed across the Atlantic for King Henry VII of England, landed in what he called "New Found Land," which he promptly claimed for England, he noted that the seas were teeming with cod. And, not very many years later, when Jacques Cartier arrived at the mouth of the St. Lawrence and claimed it for the French, he noted 1,000 Basque fishing boats already there. So, the cod-rich area off the coast of Eastern Canada called the Grand Banks was apparently the secret location of the Basque wealth. By 1640, the inhabitants of the Massachusetts Bay Colony brought an incredible 300,000 cod to market annually.

Fresh cod became the fish of choice in New England, with salt cod being exported across the ocean. There are more than 200 species in 10 families of cod, nearly all living in the cold salt water of the Northern Hemisphere, including the Atlantic cod, the haddock, the pollock, the whiting, and the hake. Flaky white meat, high protein, and virtually no fat make cod very well appreciated. Scrod, which is simply young cod, or haddock, has a delectable succulence, and is highly prized in Boston. Cod on its own has a very mild flavor, so that it takes well to rich preparation and strong flavors. Cooked fresh, it tastes best if pan-seared, to make a tasty brown crust.

More About Cod, "The Fish That Changed The World"

To learn out more about the fascinating history of the cod, read *Cod: A Biography of the Fish that Changed the World* by Mark Kurlansky.

Broiled Boston Scrod with New England Egg Sauce

This dish dates back to my days consulting for Azalea Restaurant at the Omni Hotel at Independence Park. Egg sauces are quite old-fashioned and were brought over by the colonists from England. Here, I update this traditional sauce, adding lots of chopped fresh herbs to make a light, fresh, green sauce. Scrod is just young cod, or haddock, a close cousin, with a finer texture and milder flavor than full-grown fish. If you can't find scrod, any lean-white meat fish such as black sea bass or hybrid striped bass fillets would work well.

SERVES 4

2 pounds scrod fillet

Kosher salt and freshly ground black pepper to taste

4 tablespoons unsalted butter

Juice and grated zest of 1 lemon

1 tablespoon cornstarch

2 tablespoons chopped tender herbs, such as marjoram, Italian parsley, chervil, chives, and tarragon

3 hard-cooked eggs, chopped into small bits

Preheat the broiler to high. Sprinkle scrod with salt and pepper and dot with 1 tablespoon of the butter. Arrange scrod in a shallow metal pan. Broil 5 to 10 minutes, or until the fish flakes. Remove the fish from the oven and pour off any cooking juices a into small pot, keeping the fish warm. Bring the juices to the boil, adding the lemon juice, zest, and enough water to make $1/2$ cup of liquid. Mix the cornstarch with a little cold water to form a thin slurry. Pour the cornstarch mixture into the liquid while whisking and then continue to cook several minutes, whisking often, until the

liquid boils again and is thickened and shiny.

Remove the pot from the heat, whisk in the remaining 3 tablespoons butter and the herbs. Season to taste with salt and pepper and stir in the eggs. Pour the sauce over the fish and serve immediately.

CHOPPING HARD-COOKED EGGS

Use an egg slicer to cut up eggs into small bits. Put an egg through the wires going in one direction to make slices. Turn the egg around and put it through the wires crosswise to make small bits.

Fish and Chips with Homemade Tartar Sauce

This fish and chips was the number one dish at the Dock Street Brewing Company, where appropriately, we made the batter with beer lightened with beaten egg whites. In Great Britain, fish and chips is served with salt and malt vinegar, brewed from barley. The most common fish used for fish and chips in England is cod, but pollock, haddock, plaice, dogfish (shark), and skate are also common; beef tallow was long the frying fat of choice. In America, we have adopted the French tartar sauce for our fish and chips. Rather than serve more fried food, I like to roast golden potatoes in the oven as I'm preparing the fish. (see Rosemary and Garlic Roasted Gold Potatoes, page 758). Prepare the Tartar Sauce first, put the potatoes in the oven to roast, and then prepare the fish.

SERVES 6

Homemade Tartar Sauce

2 tablespoons chopped Italian parsley

2 tablespoons chopped green olives

2 tablespoons sweet pickle relish (purchased)

1 tablespoon drained capers

1/2 cup chopped pickles, either small kosher dills or
French cornichons

2 hard-cooked eggs, peeled and chopped

2 teaspoons dry mustard

2 teaspoons hot pepper sauce

1 cup mayonnaise, prepared or homemade

Kosher salt and freshly ground black pepper, to taste

Stir all ingredients together and reserve in the refrigerator.

Beer Batter and Frying

3 cups (2 bottles) dark beer

4 eggs, separated

1 teaspoon cayenne pepper

1/2 cup thinly sliced chives (optional)

1/4 pound (1 cup) all-purpose flour, preferably unbleached

2 teaspoons baking powder

2 pounds lean, firm white fish fillet, such as cod, halibut,
   scrod, haddock, or pollock cut into 12 pieces

Kosher salt and freshly ground black pepper, to taste

3 cups canola, peanut oil, or soy for deep-frying

Extra flour, for dusting

Beat together beer, egg yolks, cayenne, and chives. Stir
together flour and baking powder. Fold into the beer mix.
Just before using, beat egg whites until firm but not stiff
and fold into batter.

Cut the fish into evenly sized smaller portions of about
2 ounces each. Sprinkle with salt and pepper and keep cold.

In a large, heavy-bottomed pot, an electric deep-fryer,
or a wok, heat the oil until shimmering (365°F. on a frying
thermometer). Working in 3 to 4 batches, dust the fish
pieces with flour, shaking off the excess. One by one, dip
the fish into the batter, allowing the excess to drip off.

Lay the fish in the oil, turning with tongs as they brown.
Fry until firm and well-browned, about 6 minutes. Using a
wire skimmer, remove fish from the oil, drain on a wire
rack and sprinkle with salt, keeping warm in a 200°F. oven.
Serve with tartar sauce and Rosemary and Garlic Roasted
Golden Potatoes (*see* page 758).

FISH & CHIPS HISTORY

Fish and chips began with the originally Sephardic
Jewish dish, *pescado frito* (fried fish), that arrived in the
Netherlands and then England along with Spanish and
Portuguese Jews fleeing the Inquisition in the seventeenth and eighteenth centuries. By the middle of the
nineteenth century, deep-fried fish had become popular
in London and the surrounding region, while at the
same time fried "chipped" potatoes developed in the
north of England made with the potatoes that had been
introduced to England in the seventeenth century.
Deep-fried fish and chips had been eaten separately for
many years, but the first combined fish and chips shop
was probably the one opened in London in 1860 by
Joseph Malin.

Spanish Bacalao Stew

You'll have to start this rustic Spanish fish stew the day before by soaking the salt cod (or Bacalao) overnight in cold water to cover, (see Preparing Salt Cod on page 322). The oak-smoked Spanish paprika called pimentón *adds a deep, dark, smoky flavor. You could also make this stew with fresh cod, in which case, simmer the cod fillet in the sauce until it flakes, about 15 minutes, adding salt to the recipe, which it likely won't need if made with salt cod. Accompany the stew with steamed potatoes or rice to soak up the abundant delicious juices.*

SERVES 6

2 pounds salt cod fillet, soaked overnight
   in cold water to cover
¹/₄ cup extra-virgin olive oil
1 large Spanish onion, diced
2 large red bell peppers, diced
1 tablespoon chopped garlic
1 (28-ounce) can diced tomatoes (or 3 cups peeled
   and diced fresh plum tomatoes)
1 teaspoon crushed red pepper flakes
1 teaspoon pimentón
2 tablespoons chopped Italian parsley

Prepare the salt cod following the directions in Preparing Salt Cod on page 322.

Drain and rinse the salt cod and place in a large pot with cold water to cover. Bring to the boil, then reduce heat and simmer for 10 minutes, or until the fish flakes easily. Drain the fish, flake into large chunks, making sure to remove and discard bones (if any), and reserve.

Meanwhile, heat the olive oil in a large heavy-bottomed skillet. Add the onion and sauté until lightly browned, and then add the bell peppers, and the garlic. Cook together 2 to 3 minutes or until slightly softened, and then add the tomatoes, red pepper flakes, and pimentón. Simmer all together for 20 minutes, stirring occasionally, until the sauce has thickened.

Drain the salt cod, which should be just slightly salty to the taste, and add to sauce. Mix gently so as not to break up the fish. Cover and simmer for about 20 minutes, or until the fish flakes. Sprinkle with parsley and serve.

Finding and Choosing Salt Cod

Caribbean, Asian, Portuguese, and Italian markets are the place to find whole salt cod (Baccalà), but many supermarkets carry the filleted type, especially during the holiday season. Bone-in baccalà has more flavor and more natural gelatin to give extra body to the sauce. But, boneless, skinless fillets are easier to handle, especially for the Baccalà novice. The salt cod will keep perfectly for months if well wrapped and refrigerated. One pound of boneless fillet will yield 1¹/₂ pounds when reconstituted.

When purchasing Baccalà, look for ivory-colored flesh with a faint tint of green or yellow. Bright white color can mean that the fish has been artificially treated or is overly salty. Salt cod can be cooked directly in a sauce, as long as the liquid is kept to a bare simmer (boiling toughens salt cod and turns it stringy). Because of its strong flavor, a not-too-subtle red wine it the best choice for beverage.

The day before you cook with it, rinse the fish under cold running water until you no longer feel any hard crystals of salt on the surface. Place the fish in a large bowl and cover with cold water. Leave to soak overnight, refrigerated in hot weather, at room temperature in cold weather, changing the water once or twice during the soaking period. Drain the salt cod and place in a large pot with cold water to cover. Bring to the boil, then reduce heat and simmer for 10 minutes, or until the fish flakes easily. Drain the fish, flake into large chunks, making sure to remove and discard bones (if any), and reserve.

Note that boneless, skinless fillets shredded into flakes can be ready in 2 hours, while larger whole fish require up to 36 hours of soaking. Because there are so many methods of salt curing, there is no set rule for how long to soak the fish. Once the fish has soaked sufficiently, it will be plump and pliable and the soaking water will not taste unpleasantly salty.

Baccalà Cakes with Green Sauce

These simple salt cod (or Baccalà) cakes with potatoes and vegetables are served with a sharp green Italian-style herb and vinegar sauce. Make the cakes up to one day ahead. Just before you want to serve them, sauté the cakes until golden brown and crispy. If desired, keep the cakes warm in the oven for up to 20 minutes. Served with a tangy herbal green sauce, the cakes are also delicious served over your favorite tomato sauce.

SERVES 6

Green Sauce
MAKES 1 1/2 CUPS

1/2 cup extra-virgin olive oil

1 teaspoon chopped garlic

1 bunch Italian parsley

1/2 cup roughly chopped fennel stalks

1 bunch scallions, thinly sliced

3 tablespoons chopped fresh oregano,
  or 1 tablespoon dried oregano

1/2 cup roughly chopped cornichon pickles

Kosher salt and freshly ground black pepper to taste

Place olive oil and garlic in a food processor and process to a paste. Add parsley, fennel, scallions, and oregano and process again until smoother and bright green in color. Add cornichon pickles and salt and pepper and process again just long enough to chop up the pickles. Reserve.

Fish Cakes

1 pound golden potatoes, peeled

2 tablespoons unsalted butter, softened

1/2 medium onion, cut up

1/2 cup chopped celery

1/4 cup Italian parsley leaves

1 pound salt cod fillet, cooked and flaked
  (*see* Preparing Salt Cod, above)

Grated zest of 1 lemon

1/2 teaspoon freshly ground black pepper

2 eggs

1/2 cup fresh white breadcrumbs or Japanese panko

1/2 cup canola oil

322

Steam (or boil) the potatoes until quite soft, then drain. While still hot, mash the potatoes and butter together using a potato ricer or potato masher, and reserve.

Place the onion, celery, and parsley into the bowl of a food processor and process about 1 minute or until finely chopped, but not pasty. Combine the mashed potatoes, flaked salt cod, the onion mixture, lemon zest, black pepper, and the eggs. Form into cakes, using about 1/2 cup of the mixture for each cake, then place on a wax paper-lined pan and refrigerate until cold.

Dust the cakes evenly with the breadcrumbs, patting to set the crumbs, then shaking off the excess. Heat the oil, preferably in a cast-iron or nonstick skillet and add the cakes in a single layer. Cook over medium heat until browned on one side, then turn and cook on the second side. Drain on a wire rack (keeping the cakes warm in a 200°F. oven, if desired) and serve with the Green Sauce.

CHOOSING FRESH CRANBERRY BEANS AND THEIR SEASON

Cranberry beans come into season in October, but are sporadically available throughout the year, especially in Asian and Italian markets. When cooked, shelled cranberry beans lose their red color and turn a warm pink. When buying fresh cranberry beans, check inside if the pods are wilted and brown, because the beans inside may be perfectly sound; avoid buying if the beans have rusty brown spots. If you have extra, freeze either the shelled beans or the cooked beans in a double layer of plastic zip-top bags. Frozen edamame (green soybeans) make a good substitute.

Pan–Seared Cod with Fresh Cranberry Beans, Arugula, and Tomato

I served this rustic-yet-stylish dish at the sadly short-lived Avenue B restaurant on Philadelphia's Avenue of the Arts, made with the gorgeous, creamy-textured fresh cranberry beans I adore. An Italian favorite, these plump beans dappled with lovely pink and wine-colored splotches come inside of equally striking cranberry-streaked pods and taste something like creamy, smooth chestnuts.

SERVES 6

Cooked Fresh Cranberry Beans

2 pounds fresh cranberry beans, shelled
(2 to 3 cups shelled beans)
1/2 small onion, peeled but whole
1/2 head garlic, outer skin removed and 1 inch cut off
of the top end
2 bay leaves
4 sprigs thyme, tied with kitchen string
Kosher salt to taste

Combine the cranberry beans with 3 cups cold water, onion, garlic, bay leaves, thyme, and salt in a medium pot. Bring to a boil, skimming off any white foam. Reduce the heat, and simmer very slowly for 30 to 40 minutes or until the beans are quite tender but still whole. Leave beans in their cooking liquid to cool and reserve.

Cod and Assembly

6 portions (about 2 pounds) fresh cod fillet,
skin-on preferred

Kosher salt and freshly ground black pepper to taste

2 tablespoons olive oil

2 cups diced fresh tomatoes

2 cups Cooked Cranberry Beans

1 bunch arugula, trimmed, washed, and cut into 1-inch strips

Season the cod all over with salt and pepper and reserve.

In a heavy-bottomed skillet such as cast-iron or a non-stick skillet, heat the oil until shimmering. Place the fish skin-side down in the skillet. Cook over high heat 3 to 4 minutes until skin has a good brown crust, then carefully turn over and cook 3 to 4 minutes longer, or until the fish flakes. Remove the fish from the pan and keep warm.

Pour off the excess oil and add the tomatoes and cranberry beans along with about 1 cup of their cooking juice. Bring to the boil and cook together 5 minutes, or until thickened. Add the arugula, toss to wilt, and then spoon the mixture onto 6 serving plates. Top each portion with a piece of cod and serve immediately.

Salt Cod Bouillabaisse

Large boards of white salted fish—doesn't sound too appetizing, does it? Don't judge too quickly. Salt cod (or Baccalà) can be poached, fried, braised, roasted, grilled, baked, or mixed with other ingredients to make fritters, soups, and stews, like this variation on the classic Marseillaise fish stew that I adapted from The Wonderful Food of Provence. *This book, published in 1968, is a translation by Peta Fuller of Jean-Noël Escudier's original 1953 anthology of authentic Provençal recipes called* La Véritable Cuisine Provençale. *One of the many cookbook treasures I have picked up in my haunts of used book stores, this one is worth seeking out. A splash of Pernod, with its flavors of anise and star anise and so popular in the land of bouillabaisse, enhances the stew.*

SERVES 6

Toasts

1/4 cup olive oil

1 tablespoon finely minced garlic

1/2 loaf country-style bread, cut into 1/2-inch thick slices

Preheat the oven to 350°F. Combine the olive oil and minced garlic in a small bowl. Brush both sides of the bread slices with the oil-garlic mixture. Spread out onto a single layer on a baking sheet. Bake 10 minutes, or until lightly browned. Turn over and bake 5 minutes longer. Remove from oven and reserve.

324

Salt Cod Bouillabaisse

1 red onion, diced

1 fennel bulb, trimmed and diced

2 carrots, diced

1 tablespoon finely chopped garlic

$1/4$ cup extra-virgin olive oil

3 large gold potatoes (about $1/2$ pound) peeled
   and cut into thick slices

2 teaspoons chopped fresh, or $1/2$ teaspoon dried thyme

2 bay leaves

2 teaspoons grated orange zest

1 (28-ounce) can chopped plum tomatoes (or Pomi)

$1/2$ cup dry white vermouth

$1/4$ cup Pernod (optional)

4 cups water

$1^1/2$ pounds salt cod fillet, cooked and flaked
   (*see* Preparing Salt Cod, page 322)

Kosher salt, freshly ground black pepper, and hot red
   pepper flakes to taste

In a large soup pot, cook the onion, fennel, carrots, and
garlic in the oil until the onion is softened but not
browned. Add the potatoes, thyme, bay leaves, and
orange zest and toss. Add the tomatoes, vermouth,
Pernod, and water. Bring the mixture to the boil, then
reduce heat to medium and cook until the potatoes are
almost tender. Add the flaked fish and gently heat
together. Lay a slice of toasted bread in each of 4 large
soup plates, and ladle the bouillabaisse over top.

COFFEE

COFFEE

Coffee is both the fitting finale to a wonderful meal and a source of potent flavor for desserts and savory dishes. Think of coffee as a spice, rather than as a beverage, and it begins to make sense. Coffee often goes into barbecue sauce (along with just about everything else under the sun) and it is poured into the skillet with slices of salty country ham to make the red-eye gravy beloved in the South. In Sweden, another country that loves its coffee, leg of lamb is roasted with coffee to cut its fattiness. The lamb is first roasted on its own, then roasted further with sweetened creamy coffee. Finally, a bit of tart red currant jelly finishes the sauce.

The history of coffee is both fascinating and complex, and worthy of an entire book, so I've included only some highlights here. The coffee tree probably originated in the province of Kaffa in Ethiopia. The succulent outer flesh of the coffee bean was eaten by slaves taken from present day Sudan into Yemen and the Arab world, through the great port of the day, Mocha, a name that now refers to a coffee-chocolate mixture. Coffee was certainly being cultivated in Yemen by the fifteenth century and probably much earlier than that. Like that of rare spices from the East, the secret of coffee's origins was kept secret by the Arabs who traded in it. The beans themselves are sterile, but, although forbidden, eventually plants were smuggled out and were first planted in India.

The first coffeehouses were opened in the busy port city of Mecca on the Arabian Peninsula. These luxuriously decorated coffeehouses quickly spread throughout the Arab world as places for men to play chess, gossip, and listen to music, similar to the role they played later in Europe. Although banned at times because they became the center for political unrest, coffeehouses endured.

The Ottoman Turks introduced coffee to Constantinople where the world's first coffee shop, called Kiva Han, open in 1475. The Turks soon adopted coffee as a drink, adding spices such as clove, cinnamon, cardamom, and anise to the pot. According to Turkish law of the time, a woman was permitted to divorce her husband if he failed to provide her with her daily coffee. Coffee and spices still go together. After all, in a way, coffee is another spice brewed into a beverage. Bedouins have special coffee pots that hold a few whole cardamom pods in their spouts, flavoring the coffee as it trickles through them. In Ethiopia, coffee is toasted immediately before use, often along with spices such as cardamom.

Venetians trading with Arabs first brought coffee to Europe in 1615. The first coffeehouse opened in Venice in 1683, with the most famous, Caffè Florian in the Piazza San Marco, opening in 1720 and still open for business today. Don't miss visiting this window into the past if you get to Venice. The new drink was embraced wholeheartedly in the form of espresso, or pressure-brewed coffee.

In 1652, the first coffeehouse opened in England. Early coffeehouses became popular places for learning and discussion and were called "penny universities" (a cup of coffee cost one penny). A few years later, Lloyd's coffeehouse, which was frequented by merchants and maritime insurance agents, evolved into the famous insurance company, Lloyd's of London.

In 1690, the Dutch smuggled a coffee plant out of the Arab port of Mocha, and began cultivating it in their East Indian colony, Java, which became one nickname for coffee. In 1727, through another case of smuggling, this time from the French to the Brazilians, coffee began to be raised in Brazil. By 1907, Brazil accounted for ninety-seven percent of the world's harvest.

Coffee came to be cultivated in the Caribbean in the 1720s when a French naval officer serving in Martinique, Gabriel Mathieu de Clieu, acquired a coffee tree in Paris, which he took with him on the ship back. Although the ship was attacked by pirates, there was a terrible storm, and an enemy on board tried to kill the plant, the single plant survived and was planted in Martinique. By 1777, there were said to be eighteen to nineteen million coffee trees on Martinique.

In America, in 1886, a former wholesale grocer, Joel Cheek, named his popular coffee blend "Maxwell House," after the hotel in Nashville, Tennessee, where it was served. In 1900, Hills Brothers began packing roast coffee in vacuum tins and local coffee-roasting shops started to die out in America. Today, because fresh-roasted coffee is again in demand, small, artisanal coffee roasters can be found in many cities. Coffee sales boomed during Prohibition and during World War II, soldiers were issued instant Maxwell House coffee in their rations. By 1940, the U.S. was importing seventy percent of the world coffee crop.

Postwar, in Italy, Achilles Gaggia perfected an espresso machine for the coffee once made only on the stovetop in Southern Italy, opening the way to an entire industry. With the availability of steam in the machines, cappuccino, named for the robes of the Capuchin monks, developed. In 1971, Starbucks opened its first store in Seattle's Pike Place public market and started a nationwide craze for strong, fresh-roasted whole-bean coffee that seems to have no limit.

329

WHERE IS COFFEE GROWN?

Today, coffee is grown and enjoyed worldwide, and is one of the few crops that small farmers in third-world countries can profitably export. Coffee is the number one food product traded internationally. The top coffee-growing countries of the world today are Brazil, Costa Rica, Peru, Guatemala, Kenya, and Ethiopia, where the unique flavor profile of its wild coffee is highly prized. Some excellent coffee is raised in the central plateau of Mexico.

Arabica and Robusta Coffee Beans

The two most important species of coffee beans are *Coffea arabica*, and *Coffea robusta*. Arabica beans grow best at high altitudes and produce superior-quality coffees with mellow, rich flavor and complex aromas and about half the caffeine of robusta beans. Arabica production represents eighty percent of the world's coffee trade, however, only ten percent is suitable for specialty coffee companies. Robusta beans grow at lower elevations. The trees are easier to grow, with higher yields and better disease resistance than the Arabica. They have a woody, astringent flavor and are used for lower price and for higher caffeine. A small percentage is typically added to Italian espresso blends to increase the desirable *crema* or small bubbles produced when espresso is brewed properly.

ROASTING COFFEE

Coffee beans are quite fragile and easily broken, but the best-tasting coffees contain the maximum percentage of whole beans. Broken beans make for unevenly roasted coffee and therefore unevenly brewed coffee. As the beans age, they turn from green to yellow and at the same time lose their moisture. The skilled roaster must gauge the moisture content, ripeness, consistency, when it was picked, and where it was grown, to judge how best to roast the beans. Anywhere from three to six types of beans may be combined to make signature blends. According to some roasters, the best coffees are preblended and then roasted together so that the results are mellower, rounder, with more depth of flavor because of the exchange of flavorful volatile aromas during the roasting process. The best coffee is roasted in smaller batches at about 800°F., where all the various factors can be better controlled, using green (or unroasted) coffee beans that have been stored for less than one month before roasting.

330

Coffee and Spice–Rubbed Lamb Chops

In this Moroccan-style dish, coffee, cardamom, and ginger are mixed with a little honey and used to coat lamb leg chops. In Morocco, honey is a common seasoning for lamb and often combined with dates. Use either the small lamb T-bone chops from Australian or New Zealand lamb, often available at warehouse club stores, or lamb leg chops, a cut that is becoming more available at meat counters. Simply a slice cut through the leg including a round bone portion in the middle, it works well if marinated, because the leg is leaner than other parts of the lamb. Don't cook it more than medium-rare, or it will be dry. Other kinds of lamb chops would also work well here, but they will be fattier; or else ask for bone-in or boneless lamb sirloin chops, which will be similar to the leg chops.

SERVES 6

¼ cup finely ground coffee

Kosher salt and freshly ground black pepper to taste

2 tablespoons honey

1 teaspoon ground cinnamon

1 teaspoon ground cardamom

12 small lamb T-bone chops or 6 lamb leg chops, about ½ pound each

2 tablespoons canola oil

Combine the coffee, salt, pepper, honey, cinnamon, and cardamom. Rub chops all over with the mixture. Leave to marinate at room temperature for about 30 minutes, or cover and refrigerate up to overnight. If refrigerated, allow the chops to come up to room temperature, about 30 minutes, before cooking.

Preheat the oven to 400°F. Heat a large cast-iron or other heavy skillet. When it begins to smoke, add the oil, swirling to coat the bottom. Add the chops, browning well on all sides. If using leg chops, they will be thin enough to cook all the way in the pan; if using the T-bones, transfer the chops to a baking pan and roast 5 minutes, or until the chops are medium rare (135°F. on a meat thermometer).

Remove chops from the oven, drape with foil and allow them to rest for 5 minutes and then serve.

Tiramisu with Espresso Syrup

Tiramisu means—as many of us know by now—pick-me-up in Italian. Pick up a cookbook written in Italian and you won't be likely to find a recipe for this suddenly ubiquitous delectable dessert that is easy to make at home. Tiramisu was originally popularized by restaurants in the Veneto, the area surrounding Venice. It combines the love of layered desserts adopted from the British (think trifle) with typical Italian flavors of luscious mascarpone, sweetened espresso, and lemon zest. If you can get it, this is a good place to use fresh vanilla bean. The tiny black specks add visual interest, while the full, rounded fragrance and flavor of vanilla bean is highlighted in this simple dish. Because this dessert includes semi-cooked eggs, it is best avoided by anyone with a compromised immune system.

SERVES 8

¼ cup + 2 tablespoons + 2 tablespoons granulated sugar

¼ cup of water

1 cup strong brewed espresso

1 pound mascarpone

2 tablespoons light or gold rum

3 egg yolks

Grated zest of 1 lemon

Scrapings of 1 vanilla bean, or 1 tablespoon vanilla extract

2 egg whites

1 (12-ounce) package ladyfingers

Dutch-process cocoa, for sprinkling

Have ready a 2-quart serving bowl, preferably glass. In a small pot, bring ¼ cup of the sugar and ¼ cup of water to the boil and cook just until clear, 1 to 2 minutes. Remove from heat, mix with the espresso, and reserve.

Lightly beat together the mascarpone and rum and reserve.

Whisk together the egg yolks, lemon zest, vanilla bean scrapings, and 2 tablespoons sugar in a large steel bowl. Set the bowl over a pan of simmering water (without the bowl touching the water) and whisk until thick and light and firm enough to form definite streaks when stirred.

Cool mixture to room temperature, stirring occasionally. Fold into mascarpone in thirds.

In a clean bowl, whip the egg whites with the remaining 2 tablespoons sugar until firm and glossy. Fold into yolk and mascarpone mixture in thirds.

Brush the ladyfingers with the reserved espresso syrup. Spoon one-third of the mousse into the bottom of the serving dish, top with a layer of ladyfingers. Repeat layers, finishing with the mousse, then sprinkle with the cocoa. Cover tightly with plastic wrap and chill for at least 2 hours and up to overnight. Serve by spooning out of dish.

Coffee–Caramel Pots de Crème

Coffee and caramel have a natural affinity both in color and flavor. Here Kahlua, the Mexican coffee liqueur, flavors these rich and creamy little custards. In France, where pots de crème (pots of cream) originated, they are baked in individual cups that traditionally have lids. Because this is a rich dessert, a half-cup is a more than adequate portion. While sugar on its own has one single flavor component once cooked to caramel, it becomes a very complex ingredient, containing over 400 flavor components. Always pay special attention when working with caramel, it is over 365°F. You'll need six to eight 4- to 6-ounce individual custard cups. Demitasse cups would be perfect, with the custards mimicking a cup of coffee with cream.

SERVES 6 TO 8

2 cups heavy cream

1 cup granulated sugar

½ cup water

1 cup very strong brewed coffee

4 eggs + 4 egg yolks

¼ cup Kahlua liqueur

Preferably in a Pyrex measure, scald the cream in the microwave and reserve.

In a 3- to 4-quart heavy-bottomed, nonreactive pot with a lid, mix the sugar with the water. Bring to the boil, then cover and cook over moderate heat, shaking occasionally until the water cooks away and the sugar starts to turn brown. Continue cooking until the sugar browns and just begins to redden in color.

332

Immediately remove from the heat, pour in the coffee and then the cream, a little at a time. Note that it will bubble up vigorously and give off very hot steam. Stir until all the caramel has been dissolved, placing the pot back on the heat to melt if necessary.

Preheat the oven to 325°F. Lightly whisk the eggs and yolks in a large bowl. Slowly, while still whisking, pour in the hot caramel. Stir in the Kahlua, mixing well. Transfer the custard to a large Pyrex measuring cup or other container with a spout and pour into individual 4- to 6-ounce custard cups.

Place the custard cups into a baking pan, such as a lasagna pan. Pour hot water into the lasagna pan so that it comes about 2 inches up the sides of the custard cups. Cover with aluminum foil with several slashes cut into it to vent excess steam, and bake about 1 hour or until set in the middle. Remove the whole pan from the oven and then, using a heavy spatula, remove the custards from the bath. Cool and serve.

Espresso Granita

Once upon a time in Persia, sherbet (or sharbat) was an ice or snow-chilled sweetened fruit juice drink. The ice was brought down from the mountains and stored for the summer months using much the same method used by Alexander the Great, who is said to have dug out pits and covered them with oak branches so that he would always have cooling snow available. Ancient Greeks and Romans in Sicily adopted the custom of chilling their wine and mixing their fruit with snow they gathered from Mount Etna. In the two hundred years they ruled Sicily, the Arabs refreshed themselves in the torrid summers with sharbat, a preparation they brought with them from the east. Even

today, Sicily is famed for its granitas (grainys): frozen sweetened liquids broken up into glassy shards, especially one like this made from espresso.

SERVES 6

4 cups strong, hot, brewed espresso
1 cup granulated sugar
1 teaspoon grated lemon zest
1/8 teaspoon ground cinnamon
1 cup heavy cream, well-chilled
Strips of lemon zest, for garnish

Mix espresso, sugar, lemon zest, and cinnamon in a medium bowl until the sugar dissolves. Cool to room temperature. Transfer the mixture to a shallow metal baking dish and freeze until it has the consistency of shaved ice, stirring the mixture with a fork and breaking up frozen edge pieces every 30 minutes, for about 3 hours. (The granita can be made 6 hours ahead.). Before serving, stir again with a fork to break up the ice.

Beat the cream until it forms soft peaks form. Scoop the granita into bowls. Top each portion with a dollop of whipped cream. Garnish with strips of lemon zest and serve immediately.

Mocha–Date Dacquoise

I first tasted this crunchy, nutty confection (it's really too rich to call it a cake) filled with luscious Medjool dates at Joyce Goldstein's (now closed) wonderful restaurant, Square One, in San Francisco. I just had to try and recreate it for myself.

Coffee adds the bitter note that balances the honey-sweet dates, while the hazelnut dacquoise layers (nut-enriched meringues) bring the whole creation together into one delectable experience. Like any meringue-based dessert, it's best not to attempt this on a hot, humid day. It does keep well (and freezes well), so you can make it one to two days ahead of time. This is a good recipe to use any extra egg whites from the freezer. Defrost by placing them in a bowl of tap-hot water, swishing around occasionally so they melt evenly. You'll need several sheets of parchment paper, available at baking supply stores, to bake the meringue circles.

MAKES ONE 10-INCH CAKE, ENOUGH TO SERVE 12 TO 16

Dacquoise Cake Layers

1/2 pound (2 1/4 cups) confectioners' sugar

1/2 pound hazelnuts, preferably lightly toasted and skins rubbed off

1 cup egg whites (about 8), at room temperature

1/2 cup granulated sugar

Preheat the oven to 275°F. Line two 12 x 18-inch half sheet pans or two 11 x 17-inch shallow jelly-rolls pans with parchment paper. Using the bottom of a 10-inch cake pan for a guide, draw 3 circles onto the parchment paper with a pencil (cut smaller circles if using the smaller pans).

Grind together the confectioners' sugar and the hazelnuts in a food processor to a fine powder. Beat the egg whites until white and fluffy and then gradually sprinkle in the sugar. Continue beating until firm and glossy. Transfer to a large wide bowl. Fold the hazelnut mixture into the whites in thirds.

Divide the mixture into 3 portions. Spread one portion

onto each parchment paper circle, spreading out into an even circle with a rubber spatula. Bake 1 1/2 hours, rotating position halfway through. Cool and remove from the parchment paper. (Note: the meringues should be crunchy and pull away easily from the paper. If they are sticky, they need more time in the oven to dry.)

Mocha-Date Filling

3/4 pound Medjool dates

1 cup heavy cream

1/2 pound (2 sticks) unsalted butter

1 pound semisweet chocolate, in bits or grated

1/2 cup hot, strong coffee

1/4 cup coffee liqueur (or brandy)

Pit the dates by slicing lengthwise, opening up, and removing the long pit. Reserve 8 large dates in halves (a total of 16 halves) and cut the remaining dates into small pieces and reserve.

Heat the cream and butter together until the cream is steaming hot and the butter has melted. Remove from heat and immediately stir in the chocolate and the coffee. Stir occasionally until the chocolate has melted completely.

Whisk in the liqueur and allow the mixture to cool to room temperature, whisking occasionally so that it cools evenly. (Note, you may cool the mixture in the refrigerator, but be careful to whisk often and cool only until the mixture is firm enough to hold its shape and still maintain its shine.)

Assembly

Mocha-Date Filling

Dacquoise Cake Layers

Reserved chopped dates

Reserved date halves

Have ready a plastic gallon-size freezer bag with a pencil-sized hole cut out of one corner (or cut a larger hole and fill with a small pastry tip). Fill the bag with about three-quarters of the Mocha-Date filling and reserve. Fill a plastic quart-sized freezer bag with the remaining quarter of the filling and cut out a toothpick-sized hole out of one corner and reserve.

Pipe a small circle of Mocha-Date Filling onto a large flat cake plate to secure the cake. Press one Dacquoise Cake Layer, rough side up, onto the chocolate to secure. Pipe out half the filling from the bag, spreading all the way to the edge of the meringue circle using a rubber spatula to smooth it. Sprinkle the surface evenly with half the cut up dates.

Top with a second round of meringue, turning and gently pushing down so that it's well attached to the filling. Spread with the remaining filling and sprinkle with the remaining cut up dates.

Top with the third meringue circle, this time with the smooth side up, turning and gently pushing down to attach.

Using the smaller pastry bag (or equivalent) pipe lines of chocolate mixture across the top of the dacquoise. (If the chocolate is too hard, place the bag in the microwave for 1 to 2 minutes on low power to soften.) Turn the cake and pipe more lines at an angle to the first set.

While the chocolate lines are still soft, place the reserved date halves in an even circle around the outer edge of the dacquoise. Press down firmly to attach the dates. Refrigerate the dacquoise until ready to serve (up to 1 day ahead) or wrap well and freeze to serve at a later time. Use a serrated bread knife to cut the dacquoise into 12 to 16 wedges.

335

CORN & POLENTA

CORN & POLENTA

A creamy white-gold ear of freshly picked corn, shining with butter, defines summer for people in many regions of America. We tend to take the abundance of this all-American delicacy for granted since it's available all summer long. Sweet corn may be common in the U.S., but it's still exotic to most of the world. It's not too long ago that three-star French chefs discovered a "new" ingredient: sweet corn! Chinese restaurants add canned baby corn with abandon to stir-fries, and make soup with canned creamed corn. Around the world, people eat corn as a grain, not as a vegetable—in Italian polenta, Rumanian mamalinga, and Mexican tamales.

Corn is the New World's most important contribution to world diet. Originating in Central America, corn has been cultivated since at least 3500 BC. Very quickly, corn became the basic food plant of the Incas, Mayas, Aztecs, and North American native tribes. Because corn is relatively easy to grow, it allows the farmer the luxury of extra time. With the advent of corn, Native American civilizations began to flourish because people were able to think beyond mere survival. Columbus brought corn back with him to Europe and within one generation, farmers in Southern Europe were raising corn for grain, where it often was used to make polenta.

Polenta is both an ancient Old World dish and a modern New World dish. How is this possible? The early Romans ate a porridge they called *puls* or *pulmentum* made from grain—usually millet or spelt and sometimes chickpea flour. Gradually other grains came to be used; at first barley, then faro (another old type of wheat) and buckwheat (not wheat at all but the seeds of a plant related to rhubarb and sorrel). The Latin *pulmentum* evolved into *pollinta* and then into its modern form, *polenta*.

Pulmentum may not have been very inspiring, but it was nourishing fare for Roman soldiers on the road. Each soldier received about a kilo of grain every day, which he roasted on a hot stone, crushed and then stored. Whenever he camped for the night, he could boil the mixture, eat it hot as porridge, or eat it cooled and hardened into a heavy cake. To this day, we eat polenta in both versions, soft and creamy, or cold and firm enough to slice like a cake and then grill, fry, or bake.

Italians began eating cornmeal, *granoturco* (Turkish grain) in Italian, in about 1650, when cornmeal first reached Italy not from the west, but by way of the eastern Mediterranean, although it's not known just who brought it. Perhaps the Venetians exchanged Mexican maize for sugar cane. Because corn has a low vitamin content, anyone who eats little but corn is vulnerable to pellagra, a disease caused by vitamin deficiency. Native Americans knew they needed to complement corn with other vegetables and legumes, but as corn became a staple in certain parts of Europe, pellagra spread from Spain to the rest of Europe, particularly in northern Italy and Romania where polenta (or mamaliga) was a staple. Not something Americans need to worry about, with our typical high-protein diet.

ORIGIN OF THE WORD CORN

The English word corn originally meant any grain or grain-like object, like the corns of salt used to make corned beef. The more specific Aztec word *maize* is used in many languages for corn, including its scientific name: *Zea mays*.

Edna Lewis' Favorite Corn

Edna Lewis writes in her book, *In Pursuit of Flavor*, about her favorite varieties. She considers Country Gentleman and Silver Queen to be the best in white corn; Golden Bantam, Kandy Corn, and plain old Golden, to be the best yellow corn. She always serves corn as a separate course, "since you can't really eat anything else if you're concentrating on corn." These days, most farmers raise Silver King instead of the original Silver Queen, which loses its sugar very quickly.

VARIETIES OF SWEET CORN

Sweet corn is only one of five main types of corn: flint and dent corn (grown for animal feed), popcorn, flour corn, and sweet corn. Sweet corn, when picked young, acts as a vegetable rather than a grain because the translucent kernels of sweet corn store more sugar than starch.

People in the Mid-Atlantic states prefer white corn. Yellow corn is sought after in the Mid-West. Bi-colored corn is considered best in New England. Roadside stands in Massachusetts claim to have the sweetest "Butter and Egg" corn (bi-color). Modern corn varieties are hybrids, meaning they must be grown from special seed corn, a boon to seed companies. Miniature corn is just infant regular corn; the cobs are tender enough to eat.

Supersweet hybrids slow down the conversion of sugar to starch. Their golden-yellow kernels are twice as sweet as any other corn. The kernels actually get sweeter after harvest and stay sweet up to 14 days. This makes the supersweets ideal for freezing. However, to my taste, some of the special corn flavor is eclipsed by sugar in these varieties.

CHOOSING AND STORING FRESH CORN

To choose corn in the husk, pull back enough of the husk to expose the kernels. You should see full rows of pearly rounded teeth. If the kernels are flattened and tightly packed, the corn will be starchy because it's overgrown. Evenly spaced rows should be plump and milky all the way to the tip of the ear; the husk should be bright, green, and fit snugly against the kernels. The pale to deep gold silks should be dry, not soggy. Don't be scared off if you see a corn worm at the top of the ear. Just cut off the tip and enjoy. It has probably chosen the sweetest ear for you. Stay away from prehusked corn, since it's often old and deteriorates faster.

Because the sugars in older corn varieties convert so quickly to starch, buy corn as soon as possible after it's been picked, preferably from a market that buys locally grown corn in season, and with a high volume and quick turnover. Store the ears in plastic for one to two days in the refrigerator.

Preparing Fresh Corn

To prepare corn, pull back and tear off the husks. Rub off the pesky silks using a nylon scrubber, a soft toothbrush, or a vegetable brush. Remember, there is one thread for each kernel. To remove kernels from the cob, cut off the tip of the ear to make a flat end. Stand the cob upright, then use a small, firm-bladed knife to slice downward. Cut off 3 to 4 rows at a time. Don't cut too deeply into the cob, or the kernels will be woody. After cutting off the kernels, scrape the cobs downward to remove the corn "milk."

COOKING FRESH CORN-ON-THE-COB

I prefer to steam corn, for speedy and even cooking. Whether you boil or steam, don't salt the cooking water since this will toughen the skin. Cook corn until just tender, anywhere from 3 to 10 minutes. Don't overcook or the corn will be tough. The sweeter and younger it is, the faster the corn will cook. For extra corn flavor, remove the silks, replace the husks and then steam. Cover when steaming so the corn will cook evenly. If you have any leftover cooked corn, cut off the kernels and add them to salad, omelets, pasta, salsa, or soup.

340

Pennsylvania Dutch
Corn and Potato Chowder

This creamy meal in a bowl is packed full of chunks of potato, peppers, corn, and bacon, and is filling enough to serve at a Pennsylvania Dutch barn-raising. If you like, use double-smoked bacon for a more intensely smoky flavor. Double-smoked bacon is sold at the Pennsylvania Dutch or German butcher shops. (My favorite bacon is made by Nueske's in Wisconsin and is applewood smoked.) Either cooked or raw corn will work here, but the soup will taste best if made with fresh young corn cut from the cob. Because it contains both potatoes and cream, this soup does not freeze well. It will keep up to five days refrigerated.

SERVES 12

$^1/_2$ pound well-smoked country-style bacon strips, cut into $^1/_2$-inch slices

1 cup diced onion

$^1/_2$ cup diced celery

$^1/_2$ cup diced red pepper

$^1/_4$ cup diced green pepper

2 pounds gold or all-purpose potatoes, peeled and diced into $^1/_2$-inch cubes

3 cups (5 to 6 ears) whole kernel sweet corn (kernels cut off of leftover cooked sweet corn on the cob or raw corn cut from ears)

3 cups milk

1 cup heavy cream

Kosher salt and freshly ground black pepper to taste

Sauté bacon in a large soup pot until most of the fat is rendered. Add the onion, celery, red and green pepper and simmer until tender but not browned.

Add the potatoes and just enough water to cover. Bring to a boil, then simmer until the potatoes are soft.

If using raw corn kernels, add to the pot during the last five minutes of cooking the potatoes. If using cooked corn, add the corn kernels when the potatoes are soft.

Add the milk and cream. Heat slowly until the chowder is almost boiling. Season to taste with salt and pepper and serve.

Buttermilk Cornbread

This quick, basic but moist and delicious cornbread gets its tang from buttermilk and tastes best if made from stone-ground cornmeal. Old-fashioned stone-ground (also called water-ground) cornmeal retains some of the hull and germ of the corn so that it is more nutritious but also more perishable. It should be stored in the refrigerator or freezer. Industrial milling is done by huge steel rollers that remove almost all of the husk and germ. This type of cornmeal can be stored almost indefinitely in a cool, dry place. Cornmeal may be yellow, white, or blue, depending on the variety of corn. While any type may be used, I find the blue makes a very odd-colored cornbread. Use this recipe for cornbread used for stuffing either the Poussin with Cornbread Stuffing and Garlic Cream Sauce (see page 268) or the Stuffed Turkey with Achiote and Cornbread-Jicama Stuffing (see page 921). Note that stale cornbread works best for stuffings because it's easier to crumble and absorbs liquid readily.

MAKES ONE 9 x 13–INCH PAN CORNBREAD

10 ounces (2½ cups) all-purpose flour, preferably
  unbleached

6 ounces (1½ cups) cornmeal, preferably stone-ground

1 tablespoon baking powder

1 teaspoon baking soda

2 tablespoons granulated sugar

2 teaspoons kosher salt

2 cups buttermilk

¼ pound (1 stick) unsalted butter, melted

5 eggs

Preheat the oven to 350°F. Have ready a nonstick 9 x 13-inch baking pan, sprayed with nonstick baking spray.

Combine the dry ingredients in one large bowl: flour, cornmeal, baking powder, baking soda, sugar, and salt. Stir to mix and make a well in the center of the bowl.

In a separate bowl, lightly beat together the buttermilk, melted butter, and eggs. Pour the liquid mixture into the well in the dry mixture and whisk together until mostly combined. Using a rubber spatula, fold the batter together until no dry spots remain. Don't overbeat or you will toughen the cornbread.

Using the rubber spatula, spread the batter into the pan. Bake in the middle shelf of the oven for 40 minutes or until the center no longer jiggles and the cornbread comes away from the side of the pan. Cool before cutting into squares.

342

White Corn Cakes with Chives

These rich, buttery corn cakes include pureed corn to give them moistness and delicate, sweet "corny" flavor. Serve as a side dish or top with sour cream or crème fraiche and smoked salmon or smoked trout for a wonderful appetizer. Out of season, use frozen white corn, which is sweeter and more tender than yellow. A nonstick griddle is best for cooking the cakes, because it will give you plenty of flat surface. Next best is a nonstick skillet. I also like to serve these cakes with fresh tomato sauce.

MAKES 4 CUPS BATTER, ENOUGH FOR 16 LARGE OR 24 SMALL CAKES

2 ounces (½ cup) all-purpose flour

2 ounces (½ cup) cornmeal, stone-ground preferred

1 teaspoon baking powder

Kosher salt, freshly ground black pepper,
  and cayenne pepper to taste

3 cups young fresh corn kernels (5 to 6 ears of corn)

4 eggs, separated

¼ pound (1 stick) unsalted butter, melted and cooled

½ cup thinly sliced chives

Clarified butter, for brushing griddle
  (*see* Making French-style Clarified Butter, page 170)

Stir together dry ingredients: flour, cornmeal, baking powder, salt, pepper, and cayenne. Purée corn, egg yolks, and melted butter in the food processor. Pour into a mixing bowl and fold in dry ingredients. Stir in chives. Beat egg whites until light and fluffy, and then fold into the batter in thirds.

Heat a nonstick griddle or skillet over moderate heat. Brush lightly with clarified butter. Pour a scant (2-ounce) ladle of batter onto the griddle. Turn when the cake bubbles around the edges. Repeat until all the batter has been used. Keep the cakes warm in a 200°F. oven until ready to serve, up to one hour.

SERVING GRILLED CORN-ON-THE-COB

Serve with basil butter made by processing together softened butter, chopped garlic, and salt and pepper until very creamy, and then adding plenty of basil and processing until the butter is green.

In Mexico, grilled corn is served with mayonnaise to slather all over the ears. Next, ground chile ancho or a mixture of chile ancho and chile chipotle powders is sprinkled on top. Strong grating cheese such as Mexican queso añejo (aged cheese), Romano, or aged Gouda, goes over that and finally wedges of lime, which taste good on just about anything, are squeezed over the whole thing.

Smoky Grilled Corn-on-the-Cob

Because memory is reached directly through the infinitely variable sense of smell, the smoky aroma of grilled corn wafting by brings me back instantly to Mexico City, where I spent a summer living as a preteen. There, large metal drums would be transformed into charcoal braziers and ears of no-doubt starchy field corn would be grilled for a street snack that could be sold at a low price. Make grilled corn-on-the-cob when you have best-quality young, sweet ears of corn direct from the farmers' market. The hugely popular American summer treat, corn-on-the-cob, is prepared from the sweet corn that still only represents ten percent of America's corn crop.

SERVES 6

12 ears of sweet young corn
3 tablespoons unsalted butter or vegetable oil

To grill the corn, use either of the following methods:

For a moist, succulent ear, pull the green husks back to expose the silk. Do not remove the husks. Rub off the silk, using a damp paper towel, vegetable scrubbing brush, or clean plastic scouring pad. Spread the ear evenly with soft butter, then cover the ears again with the husks. Grill 20 to 30 minutes, or until steam escapes from husks.

For a smoky, slightly crunchy corn, remove husks and silk. Brush ears with oil and grill directly on grate. The longer this cooks over the fire, the smokier the taste. Turn frequently so the corn chars lightly, rather than burns. Cover the grill to intensify the smoky flavor. Cook for 10 to 15 minutes.

Confetti Cornbread

This colorful cornbread is extra moist because of the vegetables, which also add a nice crunch. If using frozen corn, rinse under warm water to remove the frost, which will also get rid of any freezer odors. Substitute diced sweet onion for the red onion, if desired. Like all corn-breads, this one tastes best served warm. It reheats well first in the microwave and then toasted briefly to crisp the top and can also be frozen successfully.

SERVES 12

1 small red onion, diced

2 colorful sweet bell peppers, diced

2 tablespoons unsalted butter + $1/4$ pound (1 stick) unsalted butter, melted and cooled

2 cups fresh or frozen corn kernels

$3/4$ pound (3 cups) all-purpose flour, preferably unbleached

6 ounces ($1^1/2$ cups) cornmeal, preferably stone-ground

2 teaspoons baking powder

1 teaspoon baking soda

$1/4$ cup granulated sugar

2 teaspoons kosher salt

2 cups buttermilk

6 eggs

Preheat the oven to 350°F. In a skillet, fry the red onion and peppers in 2 tablespoons butter until crisp-tender. Remove from heat, stir in the corn, and reserve.

Combine the dry ingredients: flour, cornmeal, baking powder, baking soda, sugar, and salt in a large bowl.

Lightly beat together the buttermilk, melted butter, and the eggs. Pour into the flour mixture and whisk together until just combined. Fold in the vegetables.

Coat a 9 x 13-inch baking pan with nonstick spray. Pour in the batter and bake 45 minutes or until the cornbread is set in the middle. Cool slightly before cutting into serving portions.

CUTTING THE KERNELS OFF THE COB

Cut off both ends of the cob, whether the corn is still wrapped in its husk or it has already been husked. If the husk is present, pull it off and then pull off the silks after slicing off the ends. Rub the ear vigorously with a brush or your hands to remove any remaining silk. (There is one silk for every kernel.)

Place the ear with its flat bottom end down on the cutting board. Holding the ear in one hand, and slice down using a sharp knife, cutting the kernels away from the cob, without going too close to the cob, which will result in woody kernels. Keep cutting away in strips around the ear of corn, five strips in all. Next, scrape up from the bottom of the cob toward the top to release any of the creamy corn "milk" still left on the ear. One ear of corn will yield about $1/2$ cup of kernels. Once cut, the kernels should be used within 2 days and should be stored in the refrigerator.

Mascarpone Polenta with Ground Fennel Seed

I flavor my polenta with licorice-like ground fennel seed. Although it's not traditional, the fennel flavor goes so well with the polenta, especially if it's to be served with a roast of meat or chicken. Lusciously rich mascarpone is stirred in to enrich the polenta, taking it a long way from la cucina povera, *the cooking of the poor, where it originated. If your polenta is fine-grained, it will take less time to cook and will probably need less water. I prefer to use just water, rather than stock, to make my polenta so the corn flavor is clear.*

SERVES 6

1 tablespoon extra-virgin olive oil

1 tablespoon ground fennel seed

Kosher salt to taste

1 cup medium coarse-grained imported Italian polenta

1/2 cup mascarpone

In a medium pot, bring 4 cups of water, olive oil, ground fennel, and salt to the boil over high heat. While constantly whisking, pour the cornmeal in a very fine stream into the water. Keep the water boiling as you add the cornmeal. Reduce the heat to low, hot enough to keep the polenta bubbling slowly and steadily and allow it to cook, whisking often (about every five minutes).

The polenta will thicken first on the bottom and outsides of the pan. Occasionally, using a rubber spatula, scrape the thickened polenta into the center of the pot and whisk to combine well. As the polenta thickens, you will most likely need to switch to a heavy wooden spoon or spatula to stir. Watch out though, because the thick polenta has a tendency to splatter.

The polenta is ready when it forms a mass that pulls away from the sides of the pan. Stir in mascarpone just before removing from heat, cover and allow the polenta to thicken slightly before serving in scoops.

TYPES OF POLENTA

While many chefs use ordinary cornmeal to prepare polenta, special varieties of hard corn are raised in Northern Italy and the surrounding region for polenta. This corn is milled in a particular way so that only the grainy bits are used, with the floury bits sifted out. This makes for lighter, never pasty, polenta. My preferred polenta is Polenta Tradition under the Croix de Savoie brand from the French Alps. Because the bits of grain are coarser, it takes longer to cook, but the flavor and texture are excellent. It is available from specialty stores and from Internet sites.

Leftover Polenta

Pour out any leftover polenta onto a nonstick-sprayed baking dish so that it is about 3/4-inch thick. Cover with plastic wrap and refrigerate. The next day or so, cut into squares and use for the Grilled Polenta with Mushrooms and Cherry Tomato Ragout below. Or, brush with olive oil or butter and sprinkle with grated Parmigiano-Reggiano. Arrange in a baking pan and bake at 400°F. for about 30 minutes, or until lightly browned on top and serve as a side dish.

345

Grilled Polenta with Mushroom and Cherry Tomato Ragút

Here, squares of cooked polenta are grilled and then topped with a sauté of woodland mushrooms. If you happen to be a mushroom hunter, or have access to true wild mushrooms, such as chanterelles, morels, or even porcini (boletes), this dish will be outstanding. Made with the more commonly available exotic mushrooms now widely cultivated, by all means substitute them with true foraged wild mushrooms. Serve as an appetizer or as a main dish for lunch.

SERVES 6

3 tablespoons extra-virgin olive oil, divided

1 tablespoon minced garlic

2 teaspoons chopped rosemary

1 pound mixed mushrooms (Portabella, crimini, and
   shiitake caps, trimmed and quartered)

$1/2$ cup dry red wine

1 pint red ripe cherry tomatoes, halved

Kosher salt and freshly ground black to taste

2 cups polenta cooked until firm, then poured into a pan
   to about $3/4$-inch thick, chilled and
   cut into 6 squares or rectangles

In a large sauté pan, heat 2 tablespoons of olive oil, the garlic and rosemary until the garlic sizzles. Add the mushrooms and cook over high heat, tossing vigorously, until the mushrooms brown. Add the red wine, cherry tomatoes, and salt and pepper. Cook all together over high heat, for 5 minutes, or until most of the liquid evaporates.

Season with salt and pepper and keep warm.

Wipe a grill or cast-iron grill pan with a paper towel dipped in cooking oil, then heat the grill until the oil begins to smoke. Brush the polenta pieces with the remaining olive oil and place on the grill at a 90-degree angle, then turn them a quarter turn (to make diamond shaped grill marks). Grill on both sides, and then place on individual serving plates (preferably heated). Cover with the mushroom ragout and serve immediately.

Serving Suggestions for Polenta

For soft polenta, serve with braised beef or beef stew with plenty of rich juices, or add butter and grated Parmigiano-Reggiano, Italian Fontina, or Gorgonzola (from Lombardy) for part of the Parmesan. Layer cold polenta with tomato or meat sauce, top with grated cheese, and bake like lasagna.

Polenta is not just for cold weather. Cooled and then grilled, baked or pan-fried, polenta takes on a different character, more suited to the outdoor cooking season. Fry small squares of cold polenta for salad croutons. Grill polenta for an appetizer topped with fresh chopped tomatoes, basil, and a little garlic next time you set up the barbeque.

346

Polenta Cake with Figs and Rosemary

Here, polenta makes a wonderful, slightly crunchy, dense but moist cake in the style of the Veneto, where crumbly cornmeal cakes and cookies abound. This is a cake for fig lovers, because diced dried figs are folded into the cake batter. If you don't care for figs, simply omit them from the cake and substitute an equal quantity of diced apples mixed with raisins or sun-dried cherries. This cake is also delicious toasted and served with warm fruit compote, such as pears poached in red wine syrup (see Red Wine and Cinnamon-Poached Pears, page 695). It freezes quite well if well wrapped.

MAKES ONE 9–INCH CAKE, SERVES 8

Polenta Cake with Figs

6 ounces (1$^{1}/_{2}$ cups) all-purpose flour

2 ounces ($^{1}/_{2}$ cup) polenta or cornmeal

1 teaspoon baking powder

Pinch kosher salt

3 eggs

1 cup granulated sugar

4 tablespoons unsalted butter, melted and cooled

$^{1}/_{4}$ cup extra-virgin olive oil

$^{1}/_{2}$ cup buttermilk

1 teaspoon vanilla extract

Grated zest of 1 lemon

1 teaspoon finely chopped fresh rosemary

$^{1}/_{2}$ pound dried figs, stems removed and chopped into small bits

Preheat the oven to 350°F. Spray a 9-inch springform pan generously with nonstick spray and reserve.

Whisk together the dry ingredients: flour, cornmeal, baking powder, and salt and reserve.

Beat eggs and sugar together until light colored and the mixture forms a ribbon. Gradually beat in the butter and oil until the batter is thick like mayonnaise. Add the buttermilk, vanilla, lemon zest, and rosemary, and beat until just combined. Allow the batter to rest at room temperature for 10 minutes to thicken. Gently fold in the diced figs.

Scrape the batter into the prepared pan and bake for 45 minutes or until light brown and firm. Remove from the oven and cool. Cut the cake into 8 slices and serve.

A COPPER POLENTA POT

Marcella Hazan vividly describes the ritual of making polenta in her *Essentials of Classic Italian Cooking*, paraphrased here: In northern Italy, only a few generations ago, in the Veneto and Friuli and much of Lombardy, polenta was the food that sustained life. Preparing polenta in the special tall, open-necked unlined copper pot called a *paiolo* (or cauldron) that hanged on a hook over an open wood fire was as holy as any religious rite. The polenta had to be stirred slowly and patiently with a heavy wooden spoon made of chestnut or acacia. The hearth was often large enough to include a bench on which the family could sit as they watched the golden polenta thicken to a quivering mass.

CRANBERRIES

CRANBERRIES

Remember when cranberries were a once-a-year treat reserved for Thanksgiving? Out of a can slipped a crimson, jellied cylinder ready for slicing in wobbly rings. Then, two things happened: Ocean Spray, the cranberry cooperative, came up with the brilliant idea of marketing cranberry-apple juice. At the same time, young American chefs discovered a new ingredient in their quest for inspiration: cranberries! They are a natural for chefs because their brilliant jeweled color brightens up any plate. Whether at home or in a restaurant, cranberries are versatile enough to fit into almost any part of the meal—and they freeze perfectly.

Cranberries, *Vaccinium macrocarpon*, belong to a family of low, scrubby, woody plants that thrive on moors and mountainsides, in bogs and other places with poor and acidic soil. Native to North America, they are closely related to the tiny, bright red lingonberries popular in Scandinavia and also to native American blueberries. People in the boggy lands of northern England and Scotland enjoyed smaller European cranberries sugared and baked into tarts. Here in America, the early settlers found big, plump cranberries, double the size of European varieties. Because their waxy skin contains a natural preservative, New Englanders valued them especially for long-keeping.

Cranberry farming is a whole way of life in Southern New Jersey, Massachusetts, and in Wisconsin between the Great Lakes. In South New Jersey, farmers cultivate cranberries by flooding the bogs with water to protect the perennial cranberry vines from freezing. In April, they drain the water, hoping that there will be no more frost. The cranberry plants bloom in late June and they're ripe by the end of September, when a year's worth of work is harvested in one three-week period.

In order to flood the land yearly, cranberry farmers have to maintain their own water supply. They use mechanical harvesters to detach the berries from their vines, then the reservoirs are opened, flooding the bogs. The cranberries float in acres of crimson which are rafted into collecting points on the water's edge. At the turn of the last century, there were about 10,000 acres of cranberry bogs in New Jersey. Real-estate developers transformed many of South Jersey's abandoned cranberry reservoirs into lakes, such as Medford Lakes, so now it's down to 3,000 acres.

Traditionally, cranberry season is between Labor Day and Halloween, but early-picked cranberries tend to be pale and super-sour. Later varieties are deeper in color and less acidic and bitter. Cranberries are at their peak in November, one reason they've come to be so closely associated with Thanksgiving. Cranberries from South Jersey bogs come to market "loose-packed" in heavy wooden crates. I always bought crate berries because they seemed to be plumper and riper. However, it's unusual for consumers to see wood-crate berries for sale since supermarkets sell almost all their cranberries packed in three-quarter-pound plastic bags.

CRANBERRY TIPS

- Look for brightly colored, brilliant red cranberries, not greenish or pale pink.

- Cranberries will keep in the refrigerator for at least 1 month.

- In season, buy extra bags of cranberries and freeze them for up to three months. Use them straight from the freezer but allow 10 to 15 minutes extra baking or cooking time.

- The more sugar you use in cooking cranberries, the tougher their skins will be.

- If you have a food processor, use it to chop cranberries quickly, pulsing them until chunky.

- Add a pinch of baking soda while cooking cranberries to neutralize some of their acid. You'll need less sugar to compensate.

- Only cook cranberries until they pop, otherwise they will get bitter.

Cranberry–Buttermilk Corn Muffins

Because muffins are usually quite sweet, tart cranberries provide a welcome contrast. If you make these muffins with stone-ground cornmeal, the full-bodied corn flavor perfectly balances the tart cranberry. Frozen cranberries will work perfectly here, just add them directly from the freezer, and inc-rease the baking time to about 35 minutes. These muffins will freeze quite well. To defrost, wrap them in foil and heat in a 350°F. oven for about 15 minutes, or until hot all the way through.

MAKES ABOUT 18

$1/4$ cup + $1/2$ cup granulated sugar

$1/2$ pound (2 cups) all-purpose flour, preferably unbleached

$1/4$ pound (1 cup) cornmeal, preferably stone-ground

2 tablespoons baking powder

1 teaspoon kosher salt

2 cups buttermilk

2 extra large eggs

1 ($3/4$ pound) bag cranberries

Crystallized or raw sugar, for sprinkling

Preheat the oven to 325°F. Prepare the muffin tins by spraying with nonstick spray and sprinkling with $1/4$ cup sugar.

Combine dry ingredients: flour, cornmeal, baking powder and salt and reserve.

Beat together the remaining $1/2$ cup sugar, buttermilk, and the eggs. Lightly beat in the dry ingredients, mixing only long enough to combine.

Stir in most of the cranberries, leaving aside a few handfuls to sprinkle on top of muffins.

Spoon the batter into the prepared tins and sprinkle with the crystallized or raw sugar. Bake 20 minutes or until the muffins are set in the middle and are starting to come away from the sides of the tin. Bake 35 minutes if the cranberries are frozen. Remove from the oven and cool before serving.

Cranberry–Tangerine Sauce with Cointreau

This simple, uncooked cranberry sauce is inspired by a recipe from Philadelphia master chef, Georges Perrier. He takes advantage of the high pectin content of cranberries that will naturally gel even without cooking. I've substituted tangerine juice and zest, because to me, that is the best-tasting juice with the most aromatic zest for orange. Tangerines are in season just at holiday time. If you see a good deal on cranberries, buy a couple of bags and freeze until needed. Mandarine Napoleon is a Belgian liqueur made from cognac flavored with essential oils of fragrant Sicilian tangerines. Here it makes quite a sophisticated cranberry sauce. Substitute Triple Sec, Cointreau, Grand Marnier, or even Cognac.

MAKES 2 CUPS

1 (12-ounce) bag cranberries
Juice and grated zest of 2 tangerines
1 cup granulated sugar
$^1/_4$ cup Mandarine Napoleon liqueur

The day before, process the cranberries until finely chunky, but not pasty. Mix well with the tangerine juice and zest, sugar, and liqueur. Chill overnight. The sauce will gel overnight. Serve cold.

Cranberry Ketchup

Indonesians first came up with the sauce called ke-tsiap, *which we call ketchup. British seamen brought* ke-tsiap *home with them where the name was changed to catchup and then finally ketchup. In Britain, the concentrated sauce was made in many versions using anchovies, walnuts, and mushrooms. It wasn't until the late 1700s that New Englanders added tomatoes to the blend, thereby making the sauce that conquered the world, wiping out all other versions. It's quite reasonable to make a cranberry ketchup, using many of the same spices as the more familiar tomato version. It's also a colorful accent to any grilled meat or poultry. Make a big batch and fill decorative bottles for holiday gifts. The ketchup will keep for at least 3 months in the refrigerator.*

MAKES ABOUT 1 QUART

3 (12-ounce) bags cranberries ($2^1/_4$ pounds)
1 large onion, cut up
2 cups dark brown sugar, packed
1 teaspoon allspice
1 teaspoon cinnamon
1 tablespoon kosher salt
$^1/_2$ teaspoon freshly ground black pepper
$^3/_4$ cup cider vinegar
1 teaspoon celery seeds
1 tablespoon whole yellow mustard seeds

In a large heavy-bottomed pot, combine the cranberries, onion, sugar, allspice, cinnamon, salt, pepper, and cider vinegar and bring to the boil. Reduce heat and simmer 1 hour, stirring often, or until thickened.

Transfer the sauce to the jar of a blender and blend until smooth. Strain to remove the skins. Wash out the pot and return the sauce to it. Stir in the celery and mustard seeds and simmer 1 hour longer, stirring often. Cool to room temperature before transferring to containers.

Chunky Cranberry–Fruit Chutney

This brightly colored sweet and spicy chutney is laden with dried and fresh fruit and gets its flavor from candied ginger bits, black mustard seed, cinnamon, cardamom, chipotle chile flakes, and exotic grains of paradise. While there is a long list of ingredients, once assembled, everything simply simmers together until thick and full-bodied (you could always leave out one or two ingredients, just not the cranberries or apples). Trader Joe's sells some of the highest-quality fruit, bright-colored and plump, at very reasonable prices, so stock up if there's a store in your area. Natural foods stores and Asian markets also carry a good selection of dried fruit. Look for candied ginger especially at Asian markets. I use orange marmalade here for its body and the slightly bitter taste of the peel; if you happen upon Korean citron marmalade meant to be mixed with hot water for tea, use that instead of the marmalade for a delicious twist. Serve with Galantine of Duck (see page 377) or Country Pate with Hazelnuts (see page 469). The chutney will keep well refrigerated for up to three months.

MAKES ABOUT 6 CUPS

1 cup cranberries

2 large apples, preferably Fuji or Granny Smith, peeled and cut into small dice

1/2 cup diced onions

1/2 cup golden raisins

1/2 cup dried cherries

1/4 cup dried blueberries or currants

1/4 cup orange marmalade

2 tablespoons chopped candied ginger

3/4 cup granulated sugar

3 tablespoons cider vinegar

2 tablespoons black mustard seeds

2 teaspoon chipotle chile flakes, or 1 chipotle in adobo, rinsed, seeded and chopped

1 1/2 teaspoons crushed grains of paradise

1 teaspoon cinnamon

1 teaspoon cardamom

1 teaspoon ground coriander

2 cups water

In a heavy-bottomed nonreactive pot, preferably enamel or stainless steel, combine all the ingredients. Bring to the boil, reduce heat and simmer, stirring often but gently, so as not to break up the fruits, for about 30 minutes, or until thickened. Remove from heat and cool to room temperature before storing in a covered container in the refrigerator.

353

HOW THE CRANBERRY GOT ITS NAME

Cranes and cranberries share large wetland bogs with other wildlife such as herons, egrets, frogs, muskrats, and waterfowl. People in New England believed that the cranberry blossom in silhouette looks just like the head of a crane, so a cranberry is really a "craneberry."

Belgian Endive Salad with Cranberry–Walnut Vinaigrette

Fruit vinaigrettes like this one use the natural thickening power of pectin (kind of like fruit gelatin) to make a smooth, creamy dressing without the usual egg. Because it is thick, this dressing is best drizzled over, rather than tossed with, the salad. I like to serve it with pale, creamy spears of Belgian endive. Even better would be the long, narrow radicchio called radicchio di Treviso *or the similar* American Endigia. *For more information, see* the Indivia and Radicchio chapter.

SERVES 6

$^1/_2$ cup cranberries, fresh or frozen

$^1/_4$ cup honey

$^1/_2$ cup cider vinegar

$^1/_2$ cup canola oil

$^1/_2$ cup walnut oil (substitute with $^1/_4$ cup walnuts plus $^1/_4$ cup canola oil)

Kosher salt and freshly ground black pepper

1 pound Belgian endive

$^1/_2$ cup chopped walnuts, lightly toasted

Combine the cranberries and honey in a small pot (with a small amount of water) or in a microwaveable container and heat just until the cranberries pop and turn bright red. Cool the mixture. Combine with the vinegar, canola and walnut oils, and salt and pepper to taste. Blend to a smooth purée, strain, and reserve.

Cut off about 1 inch from the bottom of the endive spears, and then pull off the whole leaves that come free. Again, cut off about 1 inch from the bottom of the spears and pull off the whole leaves. Continue until only the heart of the endive is left.

Arrange the endive leaves attractively on salad plates, drizzle the dressing over top, sprinkle with walnuts and serve.

GRAINS OF PARADISE

The small dark brown seeds called grains of paradise, *Aframomum melegueta*, resemble those of cardamom to which they are in fact related. They are also related, though less closely, to ginger. Their haunting flavor has a numbing quality like an aromatic black pepper with a gingery sharpness. This spice is mostly imported from Ghana where the seeds are chewed on cold days to warm the body, and it is most common in the cooking of North and West Africa. In fifteenth-century Europe, grains of paradise were an important spice, commonly flavoring beer. Today, it is the spice-of-the-moment and has seen renewed popularity.

CUCUMBERS

CUCUMBER

Cool as a cucumber indeed—because cucumbers are ninety percent water, they are indeed cooling to eat and they stay cool because of all the water they contain. This also makes them one of the more perishable vegetables around. Cucumbers are light and refreshing, most commonly used raw in cold soups and salads, but worth trying in a quick sauté with butter with a little tarragon or chervil, French style, to serve with fish.

The cucumber, *Cucumis sativus*, is an Old-World vegetable in the gourd family, that in America is most commonly oblong, dark green, full of seeds, with watery, mild flesh. The cucumber is one of the oldest cultivated vegetables and is believed to be native to India. It has been cultivated in western Asia for somewhere between three and four thousand years, so it's no wonder that there is so much diversity of varieties from Asian and Armenian to European and American. Columbus brought cucumbers to Haiti in 1494, and they quickly spread. When the first Europeans arrived, these Old-World cucumbers were already being raised by the Iroquois.

Although there are special kinds of cucumbers grown the world over, all of them have crisp texture, moist, cool flesh, and mild flavor. Note that when making a salad or relish with cucumbers, it's a good idea to lightly sprinkle the slices with kosher salt to draw out excess moisture to keep salad or relish from getting watery.

Cucumber Varieties

Armenian Cucumber: Armenian cucumbers, *Cucumis melo*, are actually in the melon family although they look and act like a cucumber. These long, thin, ribbed, chartreuse-colored coils have downy, almost nonexistent, skin and mild flavor with pale, crisp flesh.

Asian Cucumber: Asian cucumbers have concentrated crispness and deep flavor. They exist in a dramatic range of lengths, colors, and flavors, from mild to bitter and may have conspicuous dark or light spines, which are easily brushed off. Their flavor is rich, slightly earthy, and not sweet. Japanese cucumbers are a mild, narrow, thin-skinned variety with few seeds.

Common American Cucumber: American cucumbers are plump and rounded at the ends and grow up to about eight inches in length. They have a light, water-laden, refreshing flavor, and sweet, grassy aroma and are bred to have thick skin for better keeping and protection during shipping. Their smooth, dark green skin is often waxed to prolong shelf life, in which case, they should be peeled. Larger, local field-grown cucumbers can have a tendency toward bitterness, especially at their ends and they may also have tiny spines that should be rubbed off.

Greenhouse Cucumber: Because greenhouse-grown cucumbers originated in Holland, they're sometimes called Dutch cucumbers, but they're also known as English, European, seedless, or burpless cucumbers. They are smooth, lightly ridged, and dark green in color, and uniform in shape because they're grown in a totally controlled environment. Narrow and pointed at both ends, these cucumbers are usually one foot long, narrow, and ridged, and have small seeds, so they are more easily digestible. Because they have such thin, easily damaged skin, they are sold shrink-wrapped for better shelf-life. They have a pleasing, subtly sweet flavor, and firm, biting, juicy texture.

Lemon Cucumber: An heirloom variety sometimes found in farmers' markets, lemon cucumbers look more like a round lemon than a cucumber. This unusual cucumber has sweet flavor and an abundance of prominent seeds.

Middle Eastern Cucumber: Middle Eastern cucumbers, known as Persian cucumbers or Beit Alpha cucumbers in Israel, probably came from Israel in the early 1900s. Thin skinned and smooth, they are slightly ridged, slim, relatively small, and curved. Their sweet, pale green flesh is crunchy, juicy, and fine-textured, perfect for diced Middle Eastern or Israeli cucumber and tomato salad served with yogurt.

Pickling Cucumber: Pickling cucumbers—such as gherkins, American dills, and tiny French cornichons—are small and firm. Gherkins and cornichons are only one to two inches long; American dills are about twice that length. They have knobby warts or spines, pale stripes, and skin that ranges from cream to deep green with solid, biting, crisp texture and fresh, lightly sweet flavor. This type of cucumber is often called a Kirby, though this is a misnomer, because the original Kirby is no longer cultivated.

357

CHOOSING CUCUMBERS

Choose common cucumbers that are well-shaped, firm, and have deep green color. Choose hothouse cucumbers that are firm all the way to the tip, because this is the first place to spoil. Cucumbers are quite perishable because of their high water content. Exceptionally large cucumbers will spoil more quickly, have larger seeds, and tend to have spongy flesh. As the cucumber deteriorates, its flesh turns from the palest green towards yellow. With all varieties, the cucumber should be firm with no soft spoiled spots or any slipperiness to the skin. If there are only a few soft spots, you can cut them away.

Greek Cucumber–Yogurt Relish: Tzatziki

Tzatziki is so much fun to say, and just as pleasurable to eat, whether with warm pita bread or as an accompaniment to grilled lamb, for which it has a special affinity, served in kebobs or with Spicy Lamb Burgers (see page 518). Seedless cucumbers are preferred here because they won't make a watery relish. Kirbys will make a firmer relish, since their texture is closer to that of a zucchini, but they should be peeled. If you use garden cucumbers, it is best to remove the seeds. Try making the tzatziki with the wonderful, richly flavored Greek yogurt now available in some supermarkets, especially the one made with goat's and sheep's milk.

SERVES 8

2 seedless cucumbers, lightly peeled and grated

1 teaspoon kosher salt

1 cup plain whole-milk yogurt

Juice of 2 lemons

$^1/_2$ bunch scallions, thinly sliced

2 tablespoons each: chopped dill and parsley

Freshly ground black pepper to taste

Mix cucumbers with salt and marinate 15 minutes at room temperature, or until liquid comes out of cucumbers. Drain cucumbers, gently pressing out excess liquid. Combine with remaining ingredients and serve, or refrigerate up to 2 days.

Indian Cucumber–Yogurt Relish: Raita

In the same family of cooling salads as the Greek tzatziki above, raita is a fresh-made, rather than cooked, chutney that is served all over India. Here, instead of salting the cucumber to drain off the excess liquid, I drain the yogurt as is done in India and in the Middle East to make the labne, *sometimes called yogurt cheese. Indian yogurt is traditionally made from high-fat buffalo milk, the same milk that is transformed into the mozzarella di bufala of Campania, Italy (see the chapter on Mozzarella for more information). This raita is particularly refreshing because the cooling cucumbers and mint contrast with the warming cumin and hot green chiles. Use Indian cucumbers here if you happen to find them. If fresh mint is out of season, the best substitute is the dried whole-leaf spearmint sold in Middle Eastern markets for tea.*

1 cup plain whole-milk yogurt

2 large seedless English cucumbers, lightly peeled
   and grated

1 fresh green jalapeño or pasilla chile, seeded and minced

2 teaspoons ground cumin

2 tablespoons chopped mint leaves
   (or 2 teaspoons dried spearmint)

1 teaspoon kosher salt

Place a sieve lined with a clean and dampened cheese-cloth or cotton, linen, or muslin cloth over a large bowl. Place the yogurt into the lined sieve and allow it to drain for about 1 hour at room temperature, or up to overnight in the refrigerator. (This step is optional, but makes for a thicker raita with more body.)

Grate the cucumber, and add the chile pepper, drained yogurt, cumin, mint, and salt. Cover and refrigerate for at least 30 minutes before serving so the flavors combine. Store up to 2 days in the refrigerator. Serve cold with Indian curries and breads.

Chilled Cucumber–Buttermilk Soup with Toasted Walnuts

I've been making this tangy white soup every summer for years. It's easy to make and quite delicious. The toasted walnuts give it richness and a bit of crunch; the mint makes it even more refreshing. This is a good way to use the larger, seedy cucumbers you might have in the summer. Once the cucumbers are puréed, the seeds just add flavor, not toughness. I usually throw out the ends, because that's where cucumbers tend to be bitter. Try to get whole milk buttermilk for more body; I like the kind made by Sealtest sold at Whole Foods.

SERVES 8

359

3 cups buttermilk

1 cup sour cream

1 bunch scallions, trimmed, washed and thinly sliced

4 large cucumbers, lightly peeled, topped and tailed, cut
   into 1-inch chunks

$1^{1}/_{2}$ cups walnuts, lightly toasted in a 300°F. oven

$^{3}/_{4}$ cup lightly packed dill sprigs

Kosher salt and freshly ground black pepper to taste

Combine buttermilk, sour cream, scallions, and cucumbers in a blender jar and blend until smooth. Add walnuts and dill and blend again just until finely chopped, but still a bit chunky. Season to taste and serve chilled.

Sautéed Cucumbers with Fines Herbs

In this classic French dish, cucumbers are quickly sautéed and then mixed with the delicate tender herb combo called fines herbs. *Chopped dill, mint, and scallions would make a good substitute. Serve the cucumbers with fish and seafood dishes or with roast chicken. Add a touch of cream, if you like, in the French manner, to enrich the dish and bring all the flavors together. I've used the small Korean cucumbers that resemble baby seedless "Q's" with fine, thin skin and firm texture, with excellent results for this dish. They are small enough to simply slice whole before cooking.*

SERVES 4

3 tablespoons unsalted butter

2 seedless cucumbers, peeled and cut into
  half-moon slices

Kosher salt and freshly ground black pepper to taste

A pinch of mace

4 tablespoons chopped mixed fines herbs: tarragon,
  chives, chervil or thyme, and Italian parsley

Melt the butter in a large skillet. Add the cucumbers and cook until crisp-tender, about 5 minutes. Add the salt, pepper, mace, and finally the mixed herbs. Toss all together and serve immediately.

Thai Cucumber Salad

Cucumbers lend themselves so well to salads. Here is another version from Thailand with a sweet and sour dressing. Use firm seedless cucumbers or the small, thin-skinned Korean cucumbers, which don't need peeling. These can be found at Asian and Korean markets. This salad is an excellent accompaniment to Thai curries and grilled seafood, such as Thai Tamarind Grilled Shrimp (see page 868).

SERVES 6

$1/4$ cup rice vinegar

$1/4$ cup granulated sugar

$1/4$ cup soy or vegetable oil

2 tablespoons finely chopped or grated ginger

3 seedless cucumbers, peeled, and thinly sliced

Kosher salt and freshly ground black pepper to taste

$1/4$ cup chopped cilantro

Whisk together the vinegar, sugar, oil, and ginger. Toss with the cucumbers and season with salt and pepper. Just before serving, drain if necessary, and toss with the cilantro. Serve within one day, because the cucumbers will give off water and the salad will lose flavor.

360

Cucumber Dill Sauce

This is a chunky, cold sauce that is wonderful served with grilled rich-fleshed fish such as salmon, bluefish, or mackerel. If you like, substitute yogurt for all or part of the sour cream. Cucumbers naturally pair with dill, mint, chives, and tarragon. Any of them would work very well here.

SERVES 8

1 lightly peeled seedless cucumber

2 teaspoons kosher salt

2 cups sour cream

$^1/_4$ cup freshly squeezed lemon juice

2 shallots, finely minced

$^1/_4$ cup chopped dill

$^1/_2$ teaspoon freshly ground pepper

Grate cucumber and toss with salt. Allow cucumbers to soak 15 minutes at room temperature, or until water is released. Drain the cucumbers, gently squeezing out excess liquid.

Whisk together the sour cream, lemon juice, shallots, dill, and black pepper. Add the cucumbers. Serve cold or store in the refrigerator up to 2 days.

CUBAN CUCUMBER AND GARLIC SALAD

Make a quick Cuban-style cucumber salad by thinly slicing peeled and seeded cucumbers, and tossing them with lime juice, a little olive oil, fresh chopped garlic, salt, and hot red pepper flakes.

361

DATES & FIGS

DATES & FIGS

Dates

At age eighteen, I set off on a backpacking trip to the Canadian Rockies. How does this relate to dates? Like a nomad in times of antiquity, I found that dates were one of the best foods for a foot-traveller (like a backpacker or a desert nomad). Dates are compact, long-keeping, and highly nutritious. Best of all, they're sweet, rich, and delicious. These are not qualities normally found in freeze-dried or other camper-friendly food. I'll forever hold a place in my heart for the rectangular packages of gooey, sugary Iranian pressed dates (no longer available, as far as I know) that I carried with me across Canada.

The date palm was one of the fruits that grew in the Garden of Eden, located by legend near the junction of the Tigris and Euphrates rivers, in the heart of the Fertile Crescent. While the origin of the date palm is lost in antiquity, it is certain that it grew 4,000 to 5,000 years ago and that date gardens were well-established at that time throughout the region once known as Mesopotamia.

Dates, *Phoenix dactylifera*, were found buried with King Tutankhamen in Egypt. In Biblical times, Jewish girls were (and still are) named Tamara, from *tamar* or date in Hebrew, in a wish that they grow smart, tall, pretty, and fertile as the date palm. According to the Old Testament book of Samuel, "David [the king] blessed the people . . . . Then he gave a loaf of bread, a cake of dates, and a cake of raisins to each person in the whole crowd." Early Christians in Jerusalem carried fronds of date palm as they met Jesus upon his return to the city, and Christians still adorn their churches with palm leaves to celebrate the last Sunday before Easter, known as Palm Sunday. Mohammed said, "There is among trees one that is pre-eminently blessed, as is the Muslim among men; it is the date palm."

According to the Arabic proverb, the date palm grows best "with its head in fire and its feet in water." About 2,000 years ago, nomadic tribes slowly spread the date palm from the Middle East through the Sahara desert, planting the palms in oases. Moors from Arabia eventually brought date palms across North Africa to Spain. Spanish priests brought the palms with them to the New World. These trees are still found in the Caribbean, Brazil, and the Pacific Coast, although the trees don't bear fruit in these damp coastal climates. Early in the twentieth century, dates imported from the oases of North Africa were planted in California's southern desert, the Coachella Valley. These same date palms now produce about 35 millions pounds of dates annually.

All dates keep extremely well and do not need to be refrigerated. The sugar content of ripe dates is about eighty percent; the remainder consists of protein, fat, and minerals. Dates are high in fiber and an excellent source of potassium.

Figs

I couldn't possibly describe how to eat a fig better than the notoriously sexy British poet and writer, D.H. Lawrence. Here is part of a poem he wrote in 1921, while in Italy, a land of fig-lovers and lovers of figs in both its forms.

"The proper way to eat a fig, in society,
Is to split it in four, holding it by the stump,
And open it, so that it is a glittering, rosy, moist,
honied, heavy-petalled four-petalled flower.
Then you throw away the skin
Which is just like a four-sepalled calyx,
After you have taken off the blossom with your lips.
But the vulgar way
Is just to put your mouth to the crack, and take out
the flesh in one bite.
Every fruit has its secret.
The fig is a very secretive fruit.
As you see it standing growing, you feel at once it is symbolic:
And it seems male.
But when you come to know it better, you agree with the
Romans, it is female.
The Italians vulgarly say, it stands for the female part;
the fig-fruit. . . ."

Lawrence seems to have been pretty much obsessed with figs. Who can forget the scene in the 1969 movie based on Lawrence's book, *Women in Love*, in which a fig is eaten? It's pretty close to pornography with a fruit.

Today, the Italian word for fig still has two meanings, but it's important to use the proper gender: *il fico* (masculine) is the fruit; *la fica* (feminine) refers to a woman's genitals. When describing figs, it's almost impossible not to think in sensuous terms.

Figs, *Ficus carica*, are plump, soft, yielding fruits, oval to round with a protruding stem. When properly honey ripe, they are quite delicate in texture and flavor and filled with tiny, edible, crunchy seeds. Figs are native to Turkey and are one of the oldest fruits known. In the Old Testament, Adam and Eve covered their bodies with fig leaves. Later, Cleopatra hid the poisonous asp she used to end her life in a basket of fresh figs.

The dark-skinned Smyrna fig (from the area of Smyrna on the western coast of Turkey) was introduced to Mexico by the Spanish in the mid-sixteenth century. Franciscan monks brought them to their San Diego mission in the late eighteenth century. These dark-purple figs spread to missions along California's coast and became known as Mission figs. Almost all fresh figs consumed in the United States still come from California.

Figs don't ripen once picked, so they are harvested at their peak. The fruits are extremely fragile, and their skin bruises and tears easily. Cut open, fresh figs are alluring–juicy crimson or yellow flesh packed with minuscule edible seeds. A short season plus the difficulty in transporting figs make this highly perishable fruit a deservedly high-priced delicacy. But, luckily, figs are also delicious dried.

CHOOSING AND STORING FRESH FIGS

Fresh figs should be yielding, with a honey-sweet aroma. Always handle them carefully because their fragile skins bruise and tear easily. Because they are shipped ripe, it's common, and acceptable, for the base of the fig to tear slightly, or become sticky, and for the skin around the stem to be a bit shriveled. Ripe figs produce clear, sticky syrup from their bottom or blossom end. Store fully ripened figs in the refrigerator up to 2 days; bring to room temperature before serving.

CHOOSING AND STORING DRIED FIGS

The crown or string figs grown in the Kalamata region of Greece are imported from October through December and are honey-sweet. When buying packages of dried figs, the wrapping should be unbroken and the figs should be plump-looking and soft enough to give slightly when gently squeezed. Avoid moldy, hard, or sour-smelling dried figs. Dried figs are high in fiber and are excellent for snacks and for use in the kitchen.

Fig Varieties

Black Mission: Black Mission figs have dark purple skins with light strawberry colored flesh. They are in season from May through November and may be found in quart or pint-size baskets.

Brown Turkey: Brown Turkey figs are medium to large in size with copper-colored skin and whitish to pink pulp with few seeds. They are in season from May through December and are often found individually packed.

Calimyrna: Calimyrna figs get their name from a contraction of California and Smyrna. They are yellowish-green on the outside with pale pink flesh and are most often sold dried, in which case they will be light golden brown in color. Because they have thick skin, they are usually peeled when eaten fresh. They are in season in July and August.

Celeste: This small to medium-sized fig has purple-tinged skin and sweet, juicy, creamy white pulp. It is good fresh or dried. This type is often grown in backyard gardens.

Kadota: Kadota figs have green skins with amber-colored flesh and are slightly less sweet than the other two varieties and have few seeds. They are in season from May through October and are good both dried and fresh.

366

English Sticky Toffee Pudding

Date purée is a new product in the produce section that makes it easy to make this deliciously gooey English-style pudding that probably originated in Scotland. Toffee is what Americans would call butterscotch or caramel. Here, dates and the brown sugar combine to make the deep, dark toffee flavor with a dash of whisky to warm things up. This dessert is best served warm, but luckily it reheats beautifully in the microwave.

MAKES ONE 9-INCH PUDDING, TO SERVE 12

6 ounces pitted dates (or 6 ounces date purée)

10 ounces (2$\frac{1}{2}$ cups) all-purpose flour

1 tablespoon baking powder

2 teaspoons baking soda

Pinch of kosher salt

4 tablespoons + $\frac{1}{4}$ pound (1$\frac{1}{2}$ sticks) unsalted butter, divided

1$\frac{1}{2}$ cups well-packed dark brown sugar, divided

4 eggs

2 teaspoons vanilla extract

2 cups heavy cream, divided

2 tablespoons whisky (optional)

Prepare a 9 x 2-inch springform pan by spraying with non-stick coating. Cover the outside of the pan with aluminum foil. Preheat the oven to 350°F.

If you're using the whole dates, place them in a small pot and bring them and 1 cup water to the boil, then cook over moderate heat for about 10 minutes or until the dates are soft. Pour off any excess liquid. Cool and then puree in a food processor and reserve.

Whisk together the dry ingredients: flour, baking powder, baking soda , and salt, and reserve.

Cream 4 tablespoons of butter and $\frac{3}{4}$ cup of the brown sugar until soft and creamy. Beat in the eggs, one at a time, and then the vanilla. Mix in the date puree. Fold in the reserved flour mix. Scrape batter into prepared pan.

Place cake pan in a second, larger pan filled with hot water. Cover entire pan with foil and then steam-bake for 45 minutes or until the cake comes away from the sides of the pan and comes out dry in the middle when stuck with a skewer. Remove from the oven and cool to room temperature. When the cake is cool, remove from the pan (reserving the pan), and then slice horizontally into two layers.

In a small pot, bring the remaining $\frac{3}{4}$ cup dark brown sugar, remaining $\frac{1}{4}$ pound butter and 1 cup of heavy cream to a boil and cook together 5 minutes longer or until the mixture has thickened and thick bubbles cover the entire surface. Remove from the heat and stir in the whisky.

Place one layer of cake back into the cake pan. Drizzle half the sauce over the cake, cover with the second layer of cake and then drizzle the remaining sauce over top. Cover with foil and then place back into a 350°F. oven to bake for 30 minutes longer or until the sauce has been absorbed.

Using a whisk or an electric mixer, beat remaining 1 cup of cream until firm. Cut Sticky Toffee Pudding into wedges and serve warm with unsweetened whipped cream.

367

Date Varieties

Dates fall into three types: soft, semi-dry, and dry. Soft dates have soft flesh, high moisture content, and low sugar content. Semi-dry dates have firm flesh, fairly low moisture content, and high sugar content. Dry dates (also known as "bread dates") have a high sugar content, low moisture content, and dry, hard flesh.

Deglet Noor: The famed Deglet Noor, which make up 90 percent of California's crop, are a semi-dry date, originally imported from Algeria. They have a delicate flavor, firm texture, and are light red to amber in color.

Medjool dates: Large, candy-sweet Medjools originated in Morocco, where they were the ultimate delicacy for Moroccan royalty, who kept the fruit just for themselves. In the 1920s, disease threatened the Moroccan Medjool. In a radical move to save this precious fruit, the Chariff gave the United States eleven date palms from the Bou Denib oasis. They were successfully planted in the Coachella Valley.

Today, the Bard Valley Growers Cooperative produces most of the Medjools in the world today, which are sought after in America and the Middle East. Medjools ship well, which is why we see them in our supermarkets. In the midst of the darkest days of winter, it's a pleasure to see open red boxes of Medjools in the produce aisle at many of our local supermarkets. Medjools are not cheap and must be pitted for use in the kitchen, although it's easy: just cut a slit down the middle and pull out the large, hard pit.

Thoory: The Thoory is the staple date of the nomadic tribes of the desert countries and is often called "bread date" because it is so dry though also sweet and nutty.

Zahidi: The oldest-known cultivar, the semi-dry Zahidi, is consumed in great quantity in the Middle East. Introduced into California about 1900, it is sugary, medium-sized, cylindrical-shaped, and light golden-brown in color.

368

GROWING FIGS IN THE PHILADELPHIA AREA

I have a farmer friend of Greek and Italian background, Paul Tsakos of Overbrook Herb Farm, who grows figs of the smaller Celeste variety for sale to Philadelphia area restaurants. Like many Italians in the area, he protects his fig trees from the harsh winters by covering them in burlap and then bending them down and burying them. In Italian neighborhoods all over Philadelphia, it's not unusual to see one of the burlap-blanketed trees or else a long, mounded grave-like form where the tree has been buried.

Classic Date-Nut Bars

When, as a ten or eleven year old, I started doing the baking in my house, one of the first sweets I learned to make were these chewy, nutty bars. Like all bar cookies, they are easy to make in quantity and, because of the dates, they stay moist for days. These bars can be frozen (best to freeze before cutting) for up to two months before cutting and serving. It's a good thing I learned how to make them myself, because I used to sneak down into the basement where we kept a large chest freezer and steal the date-nut bars my mom had made ahead for the holidays. I prefer to chop up the dates myself, because I find the prechopped kind to be rather dry, and will always choose Medjools if I have the choice.

MAKES 24 BARS

$1/4$ pound (1 cup) all-purpose flour, preferably unbleached

1 teaspoon baking powder

$1/2$ teaspoon salt

2 eggs

1 cup granulated sugar

$1/2$ pound (2 sticks) unsalted butter, melted and cooled

2 cups chopped dates

$1 1/2$ cups chopped walnuts

Preheat the oven to 350°F. Sift together the dry ingredients: flour, baking powder and salt. Beat eggs and sugar together until light-colored and the mixture forms a ribbon. Add butter and beat again until well combined.

Stir in the dry ingredients and then stir in the dates and walnuts. Spread the mixture into a nonstick-sprayed 9 x 13-inch baking pan. Bake 30 minutes or until the mix-ture begins to pull away from the sides of the pan and the center is completely set. Cool and cut into 24 bars.

Walnut-Stuffed Baked Savory Figs

These luscious, sweet-savory baked figs complement game birds, especially duck, very well. Make them when fresh, ripe figs are in season, usually in the later summer and early fall. They're easy to make and quite wonderful. If you have black walnuts, combine them with the milder common English walnuts for extra flavor.

SERVES 8

8 large ripe figs

$1/2$ bunch scallions, thinly sliced

1 tablespoon chopped fresh thyme, or 1 teaspoon dried thyme

2 tablespoons unsalted butter

$1/2$ cup chopped English walnuts, lightly toasted (or use half black walnuts)

Kosher salt and freshly ground black pepper to taste

Split figs lengthwise and scoop out flesh, using a spoon, and reserve. Sauté scallions and thyme in butter until softened, then stir in fig flesh and cook together until liquid has evaporated. Remove from heat and stir in walnuts, salt, and pepper.

Preheat the broiler. Spoon the stuffing into the reserved fig shells. Broil until bubbling and browned and serve.

Fig and Prosciutto Pizza

I served this elegant Northern Italian-style pizza in the 1980s while chef of A'propos Bistro on what is now Philadelphia's Avenue of the Arts, where I baked it in a wood-burning oven. Figs and prosciutto are a classic combination of sweet and salty that has roots in ancient Roman cuisine. Serve this in small wedges as an appetizer with an Italian aperitivo such as Campari and soda or with a glass of sparkling Prosecco from the Veneto.

SERVES 2 TO 8

1 (12- to 14-inch) round of pizza dough or 2 (8-inch) rounds, (*see* Cornmeal Pizza Dough, page 985)

Extra-virgin olive oil

$1/4$ pound thinly sliced prosciutto

$1/2$ pound very ripe figs, use black Mission or yellow Kadota, or a combination

$1/2$ pound mascarpone, domestic or imported

$1/4$ pound walnuts, chopped

Fresh mint leaves for garnish

Preheat the oven to 500°F., heating pizza tile or ceramic bricks if available.

Brush the pizza round with the olive oil, leaving a 1-inch border without oil. Lay prosciutto slices all over pizza. Slice figs $1/4$ to $1/2$ inch thick. Arrange fig slices over prosciutto and brush with a little olive oil.

Spoon dollops of mascarpone in between fig slices and scatter walnuts over top.

Bake pizza 8 to 10 minutes until dough has bubbled and is brown and figs are caramelized along the edges. Cool slightly and then cut into serving portions. Garnish with mint leaves.

Fig and Walnut Biscotti

I have made these anise-scented biscotti over and over again, because they're just so good. Figs have a special affinity for anise, while the soft, rich walnuts balance their sticky-sweet chewiness. Use either anise seed ground in a spice mill, coffee grinder, or mortar and pestle, or anise extract. Because anise is such a favorite flavor in Italian baking, the extract can usually be found in Italian groceries. Note that the dough logs keep beautifully in the freezer if tightly wrapped. The baked logs can also be frozen, defrosting before slicing and rebaking.

MAKES 6 DOZEN

1 pound plump, moist dried figs

1½ pounds (6 cups) all-purpose flour, preferably
   unbleached

3 tablespoons baking powder

3 tablespoons ground anise seed (or add 2 teaspoons
   anise extract to the egg mixture)

½ teaspoon kosher salt

6 eggs + 1 egg lightly beaten, for glaze

2 cups granulated sugar

½ pound (2 sticks) unsalted butter, melted and cooled

1 pound walnut halves and pieces

½ cup crystallized or raw sugar

Stem the figs and then cut each fig into 6 to 8 small pieces.

Whisk together the dry ingredients: flour, baking powder, ground anise, and salt and reserve.

Preheat the oven to 350°F. Beat together the eggs and granulated sugar until light and fluffy, and then stir in melted butter. Stir in dry ingredients, then stir in figs and walnuts. (The dough will be medium stiff.)

Shape into 4 to 6 evenly shaped flat logs, about 2 inches wide and 1 inch high. Place on parchment paper-lined or Silpat-lined baking pans. (Flour your hands or rub them lightly with oil to keep the dough from sticking.) Brush the logs with the remaining egg and sprinkle all over with the crystallized sugar.

Bake 25 minutes, or until the outsides of the logs are lightly browned. Remove from oven and cool completely, overnight if desired. With a sharp knife, slice the biscotti on the diagonal, about between ¼ and ½ inch thick.

Place the cookie slices back on their flat sides onto baking pans and rebake in a 350°F. oven. Turn over after 10 minutes and continue baking 5 to 10 more minutes, or until lightly browned all over. Remove and cool completely before storing in a tightly sealed container for up to 1 week.

371

DUCK

DUCK

Duck lovers abound, myself among them, but even a dedicated food fiend like me doesn't often make a whole roasted duck because the process is rather messy. For this reason, duck is a popular restaurant dish, especially in Chinese restaurants. After all, the domesticated duck did originate in China. Although we often think of sweet glazes for duck, it also works well with savory garnishes as is more common in European cooking, like green peppercorns, juniper, or wild mushrooms. Recipes like those included in this chapter show the versatility of duck in its many guises.

Most birds sold now are actually ducklings, or young ducks. They have full-bodied flavor and tender, rosy-pink meat and are excellent for roasting. Unlike chickens and turkeys, ducks fly, so they develop breast meat that is as dark as their legs. More oxygen, delivered by the red blood cells, is needed by working muscles. Most breeds of duck develop a thick layer of fat beneath the skin to keep them warm in cold weather and buoyant while swimming, so they must be specially prepared and cooked to melt it away.

In any breed, the duck breast will be more finely textured and milder than the gamier and tougher leg meat. Duck breast may be steamed, pan-seared, broiled, or grilled to medium-rare, and then thinly sliced. Duck legs, cooked long and slow, will become tender and succulent without excess fat. (There is a very low incidence of salmonella in ducks, although to be certain of safety, the breast must be cooked to 165°F., the legs to 170°F.)

Fresh whole ducks may be available at holiday times, although they are commonly sold frozen. Look for good prices on frozen duck at Asian markets. To defrost, place the bird inside a pan to catch the drips, and defrost in the refrigerator for 48 hours.

Duck Breeds

Pekin duck: The most common duck in America is the white Pekin duck, first domesticated in China 2,000 years ago. The first domestic ducks were introduced to North America by Spanish explorers. In 1873, a Yankee clipper ship crossed the Pacific with about a dozen Pekin ducks on board, which became the start of America's duck industry. The term *Long Island duck* is reserved for Pekin ducks actually raised on Long Island, New York, the center for raising ducks in this country until the 1970s.

Moulard duck: The Moulard, not to be confused with the wild mallard duck, is a cross between a Muscovy male and a Pekin female artificially bred to produce an enlarged, fattened liver (foie gras). These ducks are essential to the Gascon cuisine of Southwest France. Their large breasts, when seared and served rare like a steak, are called *magret de canard*. The moulard is older and larger than other ducks, with strong-flavored meat with woodsy notes of berry and juniper. The drake (male) is about twice as large as the hen (female); a drake breast will weigh about 1 pound, the female breast will weigh half as much and will be much more tender. Those available in the market are generally from females.

Muscovy duck: The lean Muscovy duck, now Europe's and especially France's most popular breed, originated in Brazil. Its name comes from musk, because its meat, though excellent and pleasing most of the year, develops a pronounced musky flavor in the mating season. Muscovys were domesticated by South American Indians more than 2,000 years ago. Because they needed no protection against cold weather and didn't develop the thick protective layer of fat typical of other breeds, the Muscovy is by far the leanest domesticated duck. They have plump breasts and a rich, distinctive flavor. The smaller females are excellent for roasting; the drakes are larger and are often older so they are best-suited for braising.

Duck Legs Poached in Szechuan–Spiced Broth

Tougher duck legs are transformed here into tender, succulent meat with the deep, warm-spiced flavor of Szechuan cooking. The legs are slowly cooked in a potent simmering broth, called red cooking in Chinese cuisine. Once fully cooked, the meat is pulled off the bone and is ready to eat. It can be mixed with stir-fried Chinese vegetables, or heated with some of its own flavorful cooking liquid and served over steamed rice topped with sliced scallions. I also use the duck meat for the filling in the Szechuan Duck Spring Rolls (see page 376), a more elaborate recipe, but likely to be the best spring rolls you've every tasted. After use, the cooking broth can be boiled, strained, and refrigerated or frozen to use one to two more times. Moulard duck legs or even turkey legs would also work, though they would require a longer cooking time.

SERVES 6

2 cups soy sauce

1¹⁄₂ cups rice wine or saké

¹⁄₄ cup sherry

¹⁄₄ cup dark brown sugar, packed

3 cloves garlic

2 tablespoons unpeeled sliced ginger

1 tablespoon Szechuan peppercorns

1 tablespoon star anise

2 teaspoons dark sesame oil

6 duck legs

Combine everything but the duck legs in a medium pot and bring to the boil. Add the duck legs, bring back to the boil and simmer very slowly for 1¹/₂ hours skimming as necessary, or until the duck legs jiggle freely at the joint between the thigh and the drumstick.

Remove the duck legs from the stock. When cool enough to handle, discard the skin and then remove all the meat. Check over the meat, discarding any connective tissue. Pull the meat apart into bite-sized pieces and reserve for use in other recipes.

Szechuan Pepper

Essential to Szechuan cooking is the hot, tingly, and slightly numbing sensation called *ma* that is imparted by Szechuan pepper. These small, brownish, dried, red fruits have rough walls and split open to reveal tiny black seeds. After sorting to remove bits of thorn and the gritty-tasting seeds, they should be toasted in a dry skillet and crushed. Until recently, Szechuan pepper was banned in the U.S. because it carried a citrus tree disease. With new heat treatments, Szechuan pepper is once more being imported. Look for whole, deeply colored Szechuan pepper at Asian markets.

Browning Spring Rolls Evenly

To brown spring rolls evenly, weigh them down by pushing them under the surface of the oil with a Chinese brass wire skimmer. In a restaurant, chefs will place them in one wire fry-basket, fry lightly and then cover with a matching second fry-basket to keep them immersed in the oil so they brown on all sides.

Szechuan Duck Spring Rolls

I adapted this recipe from one given to me by Michael McNally, longtime chef and now owner of the London Grill, one of Philadelphia's most popular neighborhood restaurants. I used to hang out at the London in the early 1970s and listen to music. Today, people do the same thing, but the food is way better. You'll need to make the Duck Legs Poached in Spiced Broth (see page 375) to prepare these outstanding spring rolls. For the complete experience as served at the London, serve them atop the light and crispy Thai Peanut Slaw (see page 683).

MAKES 12

1 tablespoon dark sesame oil

2 cups shredded napa cabbage

2 cups shredded duck meat
 (*see* Duck Legs Poached in Spiced Broth, page 375)

1 package large (8-inch) spring roll skins,
 defrosted if frozen

1 egg lightly beaten with 2 tablespoons water (egg wash)

3 cups canola or vegetable oil

¹/₂ cup Hoisin Sauce

Thai Peanut slaw, optional (page 683)

Heat the sesame oil in a large skillet. Add the cabbage and stir-fry until lightly wilted but still crispy, about 2 minutes. Combine the cabbage with the duck and cool, reserving for the filling.

Place one spring roll skin on a board on the diagonal. Brush the underside of the top point with a little egg wash (for sealing). Spoon about ¹/₄ cup of the filling in an oblong shape in the center of the triangle formed by the bottom half of the spring roll skin, leaving at least 1 inch of

376

border around the edges. Pull the bottom point up over the filling and tuck under. Tuck the sides underneath the filling. Roll up the spring roll as tightly as possible from the bottom. Press the point down to seal with the egg wash and transfer (point side down) to a wax paper- or parchment paper-lined baking sheet.

Continue making spring rolls until all the filling has been used. (You can store the spring rolls in the refrigerator, on wax paper lightly covered with plastic wrap, for up to two hours at this point.)

When ready to serve, heat the oven to 200°F. Heat the oil in a wok until shimmering hot or 365°F. on a frying thermometer. (You can also fry in an electric deep fryer or a heavy deep pot, but you will need more oil.) Carefully lay one spring roll at a time into the wok, frying about four in each batch. Fry for about 4 minutes or until golden brown on all sides. Drain on a wire rack, transfer to a baking pan, and keep warm in the oven until all the spring rolls have been fried.

Using a serrated knife, slice the spring rolls in half on the diagonal. (If serving with Peanut Slaw, arrange a portion of slaw in a mound in the center of each plate. Place two or four spring roll halves with their slanted sides up around the slaw.) Drizzle the plates with a little Hoisin Sauce and serve immediately.

Galantine of Duck with Apples, Cherries, and Port Wine

For the thrifty yet discerning French, galantine is a wonderful way to make a duck and some ground pork into a marvelous dish. This classic French dish is made up of a boned bird (usually turkey or duck), a rabbit, or less often, a large fish, stuffed with a rich ground meat mixture studded with bits of pistachio, truffles, and the like. Here, I garnish the galantine with sweet-tart sun-dried cherries, bright green pistachio nuts, and chunks of apples for extra moistness. For the fanciest presentation, the galantine would be poached then glazed in aspic. Here I roast it, cool it to room temperature, and slice. With its beautiful presentation, it is ultimate party fare. It can be made several days ahead and serves a large group. Serve with Quince Mostarda (see page 770), Quince and Cherry Chutney (see page 772), or Chunky Cranberry-Fruit Chutney (see page 353). If you have a friendly butcher, ask him/her to glove-bone the duck, removing the rib cage, but leaving in the leg and thigh bones and the wing bones.

SERVES 12

$3/4$ cup sun-dried cherries

$3/4$ cup + $3/4$ cup port wine

2 tablespoons kosher salt

1 teaspoon freshly ground black pepper

1 teaspoon ground coriander

1 teaspoon ground cinnamon

$1/2$ teaspoon ground allspice

1 duck (about 5 pounds)

$1^1/2$ pounds ground pork, well-chilled

6 tablespoons chopped shallots

$^3/_4$ cup homemade-style breadcrumbs

3 eggs

$^3/_4$ cup heavy cream, chilled

Duck liver (if available), finely chopped

2 apples, peeled and diced, preferably Fuji
  or Granny Smith

$^3/_4$ cup pistachio nuts

Soak the cherries in $^3/_4$ cup of the port wine overnight or until plump and soft. Combine the salt, pepper, coriander, cinnamon, and allspice and reserve.

Pull out and discard the fat packets from inside the duck legs. Remove the ribcage of the duck, following the direction for glove-boning a bird (*see* Glove-Boning a Bird, page 269). Cut off the third joint of the wings (saving for stock if desired). Prick the breast all over to make it easier to melt out the fat. Sprinkle the duck inside and out with about one third of the spice mixture and reserve.

Prepare the stuffing (called the *forcemeat*): In a mixer, beat together the ground pork, shallots, breadcrumbs, and remaining spice mixture. Beat in the eggs, one at a time, beating at moderately high speed until the eggs have been completely absorbed. Beat in the remaining $^3/_4$ cup port wine and then beat in the cream, continuing to beat until the mixture is well combined.

Add the duck liver, apples, cherries with any soaking liquid, and the pistachios and beat briefly to combine. Sauté a little bit of the mix in a small pan and taste for seasoning (you don't want to sample raw pork.) Note that the galantine should be heavily seasoned, because chilling dulls flavors.

Preheat the oven to 400°F. Stuff the duck with the forcemeat and tie into a compact, even shape. Roast the duck, breast up for 45 minutes, pour off any fat from the

pan and return it to the oven. Reduce the heat to 350°F. and continue to roast for 30 to 45 minutes longer, or until the filling measures 145°F. on a meat thermometer inserted at the thickest point into the filling and the juices run clear when pricked the thickest part of the thigh, and the duck feels firm. Continue to pour off excess fat as it develops in the pan. (Save the drippings if desired and use to brown potatoes.)

Remove the duck from the oven, and cool to room temperature. Remove the twine from the duck and wipe off the skin to remove any fat. Serve in thin slices accompanied by chutney, if desired.

ANOTHER WAY TO PREPARE THE DUCK

Glove-boning a large bird such as a duck can be rather challenging because the duck has a lot of tendons connecting the meat to the bones that don't come away easily. Also, when turning the duck inside out, it is easy to tear the skin, especially along the backbone. An alternative method for preparing the duck is to cut the duck down the back, open it up flat and cut out and discard the backbone. Using a combination of a sharp boning knife and your fingers, remove the rib cage, cutting the tendons connecting it to the wing bones at the top end and to the leg bones at the bottom end. Flip the deboned bird over, sprinkle with the seasonings as above, and fill. Using a heavy needle and thread, sew the bird closed up the back and then roast. Just be sure to remove the thread before serving the duck.

Tea–Steamed Duck Breast with Spiced Fig Sauce

While duck is a delicious bird, it is a challenge to prepare in a home kitchen, because of all the fat it contains. Duck breast, on the other hand, is easy to make at home. Here I marinate the duck in an orange-soy mixture and then steam it over smoky Lapsang Souchong tea, which is my favorite drinking tea. The simple spiced fig sauce adds a perfect fruity note. If you're a fig lover like me, accompany the duck with scrumptious Walnut-Stuffed Baked Savory Figs (see page 369). Any kind of duck breast is suitable here, but you'll need to adjust the time accordingly.

SERVES 4

$1/4$ pound (1 cup) dried figs, stemmed

4 large Pekin duck breasts

Juice and grated zest of 1 orange

$1/2$ cup soy sauce

$1/4$ cup honey

2 tablespoons grated ginger

2 teaspoons chopped garlic

4 tablespoons Lapsang Souchong tea

Soak the figs in warm water to cover until plump, about 30 minutes.

Trim off any excess fat from the duck breasts. Score the skin lightly in a criss-cross pattern to help render the fat.

Whisk together the orange juice and zest, soy sauce, honey, ginger, and garlic. Mix half the marinade with the ducks and refrigerate, covered, for at least 2 hours and up to overnight. Mix most of the remaining marinade (reserving about $1/4$ cup) with the figs.

Bring 2 cups of water to a boil, stir in the tea leaves, and leave to brew for about 5 minutes. Pour the tea into the bottom of a large pot with the steamer rack inside. Or, pour the tea into the bottom of a wok and place an Asian bamboo steamer inside. Arrange the duck breasts in the pot or steamer, cover, bring the liquid to the boil, and steam duck breasts 10 to 15 minutes until rare inside. Remove from steamer and cool. This can be done up to one day ahead.

Combine the soaked figs with any liquid with most of the remaining marinade and blend or process to a puree. Transfer to a small pot, bring to the boil, and keep warm.

When ready to serve, preheat broiler to high. Brush the duck breasts with a little of the reserved marinade and broil for about 5 minutes or until well browned. Cool the duck slightly, carve into thin slices, and serve with the served sauce.

Lapsang Souchong Tea

Lapsang souchong is a bold, assertive tea that originated in the Fujian province of China, originally considered a "man's tea." The best Lapsang is produced in the Wuyi mountains where high mountains, thick pine forests, and heavy mist make an ideal environment for growing tea. This special tea is producing by withering tea leaves over resinous pine or cedar fires. After several more steps, it is fully dried in bamboo baskets over burning pine, giving it its characteristic smoky flavor. Lapsang souchong goes well with spicy or salty foods.

Homemade Duck Confit

If you're an ambitious cook, or just happen to have a lot of duck legs, try making this rich, spiced, garlicky preserved duck, a specialty of Gascony in Southwestern France, land of the Three Musketeers. Confit is a traditional method of preserving meats, especially the tough legs and gizzards of fat-rich ducks and geese, which end up fork-tender. It's really not worth making confit unless you have at least ten pounds of duck legs, because they will shrink by half. The confit will keep for up to six months in the refrigerator as long as it's protected by a layer of fat. The only downside is that the confit must ripen and mellow in the refrigerator for at least two weeks before eating. Although the larger Moulard duck legs are ideal, you can make perfectly good confit using smaller and more common Pekin duck legs. I use crushed rather than finely ground spices here to make a kind of crust on the duck.

MAKES 5 POUNDS, ABOUT 15 TO 20 PEKIN LEGS OR 8 TO 10 MOULARD LEGS

$1/2$ cup Crystal brand kosher salt
  or $1^1/2$ cups Morton's brand kosher salt
$1/4$ cup crushed coriander seed
$1/4$ cup grated fresh ginger
2 tablespoons crushed fennel
2 tablespoons crushed allspice berries
2 tablespoons crushed bay leaf
2 tablespoons cracked black peppercorns
10 pounds duck legs, preferably from Moulard ducks
6 cups duck fat
1 cup whole peeled garlic cloves

Combine the salt, coriander, ginger, fennel, allspice, bay leaf, and pepper. Rub the mixture all over the duck legs, coating completely. Arrange the duck legs in a single layer on a wire rack set over a pan. Leave to cure in the refrigerator for 48 hours, turning after 24 hours. Drain and discard any liquid.

Preheat the oven to 275°F. Rinse the legs and pat dry with paper towels. Place in a large roasting pan (or two, if necessary), add the duck fat and garlic cloves to the pan and cover with foil. Bake for 2 to 3 hours (Pekin legs will take less time; Moulard about an hour longer). Test for tenderness by jiggling the leg bone at the joint where it meets the thighbone. It should move easily. Remove pan from the oven and cool the duck in its fat.

Using a cook's fork or tongs, remove the duck legs from the pan and transfer to a container just large enough to hold them. Strain the fat and juices from the pan through a sieve. Bring the fat to the boil in a pot and simmer, skimming off any impurities, until only the clear golden fat is left. Take care not to burn the fat.

Pour the fat over the legs. You should have enough to cover them completely. Push the legs down into the fat if necessary and weigh them down with a plate. (If you don't have quite enough fat, supplement with vegetable oil.) Cool and then refrigerate to cure, leaving at least 2 weeks before using.

As needed, remove the legs from the container, wiping or melting off the excess fat. The confit legs can be pan-fried over low heat or baked at 400°F. until crisp. Restaurants often deep-fry confit to crisp it quickly.

380

Duck Confit with Tomato, Olive, and Preserved Lemon Sauce

For several years, I worked for two Tunisian-born Israeli brothers who taught me how to make my own preserved lemons and fiery red harissa sauce along with many other dishes from this now-trendy cuisine. This dish combines the North African flavors of green olive, ginger, and preserved lemons with the duck confit of Southwest France to make a satisfying dish full of deep, mellow flavor. You can purchase duck confit in specialty markets or by special order, though it won't have the full, aromatic character of the homemade version in the recipe above. Restaurant-style, the sauce is finished with butter to smooth out the flavors and bring them all together. Omit the butter, if desired. Serve with steamed couscous or rice pilaf to soak up the juices.

SERVES 6

6 large legs or 12 small legs Homemade Duck Confit
  (*see* previous page)

2 cups diced tomatoes (one 15-ounce can)

2 tablespoons grated ginger

1 preserved lemon, seeded and diced (*see* Preserved
  Lemons, page 212)

$^1/_2$ cup sliced green olives

$^1/_4$ cup dry white vermouth

2 tablespoons each: chopped Italian parsley and cilantro

2 tablespoons unsalted butter, for finishing sauce
  (optional)

A pinch of kosher salt and freshly ground black
  pepper to taste

Preheat the oven to 400°F. Remove the duck legs from their fat, wiping off the excess, and transfer to a metal baking dish. Bake 10 to 15 minutes or until well browned and crispy.

Meanwhile, in a large skillet, bring the tomatoes, ginger, lemon, olives, and vermouth to the boil. Simmer until thickened, about 10 minutes.

Just before serving, add the chopped parsley and cilantro, swirl in the butter, and season with salt and pepper. Spoon rice or couscous onto serving plates, arrange the duck confit on top, ladle the sauce over all and serve.

DUCK FAT AND CRACKLINGS

You can buy duck fat from specialty stores, though it may need to be specially ordered. I save all the fat packets I pull out of the inside of chickens, geese, and ducks, along with fresh pork trimmings. When I have a nice amount, at least 2 to 3 pounds, I cook it all in a covered Dutch oven in a low (250°F.) oven for about an hour, or until the fat is rendered and it makes a crackling sound. The delicious, though naturally high in fat, small crisp bits that remain are called *cracklings*, for their sound—*gribnis* in Yiddish for poultry cracklings, and *chicharrones* in Spanish for pork cracklings.

381

EGGPLANT

EGGPLANT

Eggplant can be the best of vegetables or the worst of vegetables. When it's good, it's very, very good, but when it's bad, it's horrid! I'm here to help you avoid leathery eggplant, soggy eggplant, bitter eggplant, and grease-laden eggplant. Is it worth the trouble? I happen to adore eggplant, but it's important to know how to handle it. Good eggplant is creamy, with a melting texture and a meaty, satisfying mouth-filling quality shared by few other vegetables.

One of the first three cookbooks I owned, Claudia Roden's *A Book of Middle Eastern Food*, is still a treasured and well-thumbed companion. In it Roden says of eggplant, "The appearance of this vegetable, shiny at times, subtle and gentle in color, but more often fierce and blue-black, has stirred the imagination of the people who have given it, in turn, gentle virtues and malicious magical powers." According to Roden, people in Egypt believe that it's best not to grow eggplants in case an evil fruit might spring up bearing the curse of female infertility. As a result, women in some Middle Eastern countries will be reluctant to eat a particularly black or a strange-looking purple eggplant. On the other hand, a folk cure for female sterility is a walk through a field of eggplants.

A fourteenth-century medical teacher in Bologna (home of a great medical center and university since the Renaissance) gave this warning to his students: "Eat egg-plant for nine days straight and you will go mad." Even eggplant's name in Italian, *melanzane*, is mysterious. Some people think it comes from *melo insano* (the apple of poor health or insanity).

Italians long believed eggplants, along with other vegetables with seeds (like tomatoes and peppers), to be poisonous. Carmelite monks who had enjoyed eggplant in the Orient without any bad effects helped popularize them, especially in Southern Italy. When the Saracen Arabs conquered Sicily in the Middle Ages, they brought eggplants with them, and their taste for eggplant lives on in Sicilian cooking today. Eggplant may be devilish, a carrier of infertility, or a cause of insanity, but it's also a staple in China, India, Japan, the Middle East, North Africa, Italy, Spain, and Southern France. For many people, eggplant is "poor man's meat" or "poor man's caviar," proof of its versatility.

In Italy, Jews originally brought to Rome as slaves from the conquered land of Israel developed their own cuisine during their 2,000-year history in that city. They are credited for popularizing both eggplant and fennel, both essential to modern Italian cooking, and with perfecting the art of deep-frying. Pellegrino Artusi refers to both vegetables in his hugly influential Italian cookbook *La Scienza in Cucina e l'arte di mangiar bene* (The Art and Science of Eating Well), published in fourteen editions

384

beginning in 1891. He tells us, [my own translation] "Eggplant and fennel, forty years ago or so one could scarcely see them in the market in Florence. They were held to be vile foods of the Jews, which only shows how, as in other important matters, they have always had a better nose for good things than Christians."

Along with other late-summer vegetables, like peppers and tomatoes, eggplants belong to the Nightshade (or *Solanum*) family. The vegetable is a native of India, little known in the ancient Mediterranean until Arab traders introduced it to Spain and North Africa in the Middle Ages. Today it is cultivated in almost all warm regions of the world, but India and the Asian countries still use it most.

There are many different kinds of eggplants and ways to cook them. About the only way an eggplant isn't good is raw, though it makes a delicious pickle buried in vinegar and hot peppers. Chinese and Japanese varieties are long and thin, ranging from deep purple to variegated lavender and white. They have delicate, firm flesh, tiny, unnoticeable seeds, and are easy to cook, because they don't tend to absorb oil. The Chinese have purple calyxes; the Japanese is topped with bright green. Our most popular eggplants are deep purple with names like Black Beauty, but variegated purple and white, orange Thai eggplants, and other exotic and heirloom varieties now show up at farmers' markets.

White Eggplants

If you ever see white eggplants, you'll know where the eggplant got its name. Quirky Philadelphia-area farmer Paul Tsakos definitely has a green thumb when it comes to growing Mediterranean produce, maybe because he's half Greek and half Neapolitan. About twenty-five years ago, he arrived at the kitchen door of the restaurant where I cheffed, DiLullo's, to show off his wares. I took one glance at his pint-baskets full of egg-colored, egg-sized, and egg-shaped vegetables and exclaimed, "So that's why they call them egg-plants!" The only way I could really tell the difference was the green calyx topping his "eggs." After seeing them, of course I had to have them, so we established a weekly delivery for special vegetables and lots and lots of the fresh herbs characteristic of the Italian kitchen.

Less familiar, even scary-looking, white eggplants look a little too much like ghosts to be accepted by most Americans. For those in the know, Italian farmers have long been raising white eggplants for local farm markets. White eggplant is smooth and creamy when cooked, without the bitterness sometimes found in dark varieties. Its only drawbacks are a somewhat tough skin and rather large seeds.

Choosing Eggplant

Whatever color you buy, look for firm, almost hard egg-plants without any wrinkles. Just picked, an eggplant's skin is firm and shiny. As it ages, the skin becomes soft and wrinkly. Be wary of large, overgrown eggplants because they can be bitter and spongy. Unfortunately, sometimes baby eggplants can be bitter, too. Look for purple (or white) all the way to the stem, without green. An eggplant is no good if it's either under-ripe or over-ripe. Eggplant will keep for about four to five days in the refrigerator but will begin to shrivel as it ages.

COOKING EGGPLANT

Two characteristics of eggplant tend to discourage the cook. It sometimes contains bitter juice, and it seems to have an amazing power of absorbing large quantities of oil when frying. If your eggplants are on the large side, sprinkle them with salt to drain for about half an hour.

When frying, cook the eggplant at moderately high heat. Eggplant drinks up so much oil because of its spongy texture. But when the cell structure beings to collapse, like a squeezed sponge, the eggplant gives back most of the oil.

To grill eggplant, slice it lengthwise into long "steaks." Cut evenly so it will cook evenly. Brush the cut sides with olive oil mixed with chopped garlic and rosemary with a little hot pepper added. Place the eggplant slices diagonally across the grill bars, then grill on both sides. Turn the eggplant slices criss-cross after several minutes so that they cook through. They will burn if you don't turn them often, so don't be tempted to walk away. Burnt eggplant is almost as bad as raw eggplant. But it's hard to beat the smoky-sweet flavor of fire-cooked eggplant.

To roast whole eggplant, prick a whole eggplant all over and roast on a baking tray in a 425°F. oven until soft when pierced. Scoop out the flesh with a large spoon and use for Rumanian Chopped Eggplant Salad (*see* next page). Mix the same roasted eggplant flesh with tahini (sesame paste), lemon, and garlic to make the Middle Eastern favorite, Eggplant Baba Ghanouj (*see* next page).

To fry eggplant for a pasta sauce or for a ratatouille vegetable stew, cut the eggplant into 1-inch dice. Heat about 1/4 inch of oil in a large, heavy skillet until shimmering hot but not smoking. Add the eggplant and continue to cook at high heat so the oil won't be absorbed. Toss frequently so the eggplant will cook evenly. Don't try to cook too much eggplant at once or you'll just get steamed eggplant.

THE CONTROVERSIAL EGGPLANT

Perhaps because of their dramatic, dark coloring and often humanoid shape, eggplants seem to invite controversy. Acclaimed Italian restaurateur Tony May is author of a professional's reference called *Italian Cuisine, Basic Cooking Techniques*. In it he says, "Bitterness is often found in less mature eggplants." But, according to *Food Lover's Companion* by Sharon Tyler Herbst, eggplants become bitter with age. She also tells us, "Male eggplants have fewer seeds (which are often bitter) than the female of the species. They have a rounder, smoother blossom end or base. The blossom end of a female eggplant is generally indented." In *Big Flavors of the Hot Sun*, by Chris Schlesinger and John Willoughby, under "Sex, Lies and Eggplant," I find the opposite opinion. "The rumor is that male eggplants (detectable mainly by the lack of an 'innie,' as in belly buttons) have fewer seeds and are therefore less bitter. There is actually no such thing as a "male" or "female" eggplant, because they are produced when male pollen fertilizes the female parts of the flower. So all I can say it that according to folk wisdom, eggplants with a round dimple at the bottom have more seeds and are less meaty than those with an oval dimple.

Eggplant Baba Ghanouj

Baba ghanouj originated in Lebanon; in Israel and Palestine, a similar dish is called mutabbal. *Because eggplant is so porous, it absorbs smoky flavors readily. If possible, roast the eggplants using a covered charcoal grill or a smoker. Next best is oven-roasting them at high temperature. According to Clifford Wright, scholar and author of the monumental study of Mediterranean cooking,* The Mediterranean Feast, *baba means* father, *perhaps referring to the important place of eggplant as the "father of vegetables," and* ghanouj *means* coquettish *or* soft, *so that anyone who is enticed into eating it will be spoiled by how meltingly soft and good it is. Sprinkle the baba with ruby-red pomegranate seeds, if they're in season. Serve with fresh pita bread; even better would be the* za'atar *(herb mix) sprinkled pita sold in some Lebanese markets.*

MAKES ABOUT 3 CUPS

2 large eggplants (about 2 pounds total), pricked all over

1/2 cup tahini paste

1/2 cup extra-virgin olive oil

1/2 cup lemon juice

Kosher salt to taste

1 tablespoon finely chopped garlic

1/2 teaspoon Aleppo pepper, or hot red pepper flakes

1/2 cup chopped Italian parsley

1/4 cup chopped mint, or 1 bunch scallions, thinly sliced (optional)

Seeds of one pomegranate, for garnish (optional)

Preheat a charcoal grill or smoker, or preheat the oven to 425°F. and roast the eggplants until soft when pricked, about 20 minutes, depending on size. Remove from the oven and cool. Split the eggplants in half lengthwise and scoop out flesh. Drain in a colander at least 30 minutes to remove any bitter juices and to make a creamier salad.

Meanwhile, prepare the dressing: Whisk together the tahini paste, olive oil, lemon juice, salt, garlic, and hot pepper.

Chop up the drained eggplant flesh. Mix with the dressing, parsley, mint, and scallions. If the mixture is very thick, thin with a little water to spreadable consistency. Garnish with the pomegranate seeds, if desired.

Rumanian Chopped Eggplant Salad

Romania was long the garden of Europe, growing vegetables in abundance that were in all sorts of dishes. Its cooking has been influenced by the Turks, Romans (who brought the national dish, mamalinga, *a variation of polenta), Gypsies (who brought their skills in grilling meat over charcoal), Greeks, Russians, Germans, Hungarians, and even the French. This easy-to-make salad combines roasted eggplant with roasted peppers in a vinaigrette dressing. According to a Rumanian proverb, one should "Eat well, drink moderately, and love to your heart's content," which sounds like good advice for all. Serve as an appetizer salad.*

SERVES 6 TO 8

2 large eggplants, (about 2 pounds total) pricked with a fork

2 green bell peppers

2 red bell peppers

1 red onion, quartered

3/4 cup olive oil

¼ cup cider vinegar

1 tablespoon chopped garlic

2 teaspoons kosher salt

1 tablespoon granulated sugar

Preheat a charcoal grill or smoker, or preheat the oven to 425°F. and grill or bake the eggplants until soft when pricked. Remove from the oven and cool. Split eggplants in half lengthwise and scoop out flesh. Drain the flesh in a colander at least 30 minutes to remove bitter juices, and then chop.

Meanwhile, roast the peppers and onion directly on a grill or broil until evenly charred. When cool enough to handle, remove seeds and spongy white tissue from peppers. Trim onion root and dice.

Whisk together the olive oil, vinegar, garlic, salt and sugar. Combine eggplant, peppers, onions, and dressing. If convenient, marinate overnight to mellow flavors, but bring salad to room temperature before serving.

Haitian Roasted Eggplant Salad

I adapted this boldly seasoned, Asian-Caribbean fusion eggplant salad from a recipe of Chef Guillermo Pernot's in the James Beard award-winning book I co-authored with him called Ceviche: Seafood, Salads, and Cocktails with a Latino Twist. *While he boils his eggplants, I roast them to intensify their flavor and get rid of excess liquid. I'm not quite sure that this is a traditional Haitian dish. As a teenager growing up in Washington, D.C., I was friends with a number of Haitians, one of whom was my next-door neighbor, who was the son of the Military Attaché at the Haitian Embassy. While I ate and enjoyed lots of Haitian food then and frequented Haitian restaurants and clubs, I never tasted anything like this dish. In any case, Asian eggplants work beautifully here, because they are so creamy and mild, and because the salad combines Asian and Caribbean flavors. Serve as part of a an array of salads and appetizers or with crostini or pita chips for a quick hors d'oeuvre.*

SERVES 6

4 tablespoons extra-virgin olive oil, divided

1 tablespoon chopped garlic

3 pounds Asian eggplant, diced

1 red bell pepper, diced

1 (2-inch) section ginger, grated (about 2 tablespoons)

1 minced habanero or Scotch bonnet chile, substitute serrano or jalapeño for less heat

3 tablespoons natural sesame seeds, lightly toasted

¼ cup red wine vinegar

2 tablespoons Japanese toasted sesame oil

Juice of 2 limes

Kosher salt to taste

1 bunch scallions, thinly sliced

2 tablespoons each: chopped Italian parsley and cilantro

Preheat the oven to 425°F. Combine 2 tablespoons of the olive oil with the garlic and toss with the eggplant. Spread the eggplant in a single layer on a metal baking pan. Roast about 15 minutes, or until well-browned and soft throughout. Remove from the oven, cool, and reserve.

In a medium bowl, combine the red pepper, ginger, habanero, sesame seeds, vinegar, remaining 2 tablespoons of olive oil, sesame oil, lime juice, and salt to taste. If serving immediately, add the scallions, parsley, and cilantro.

388

Otherwise, cover and refrigerate until ready to serve, up to two days, and add the scallions, parsley, and cilantro just before serving. If making ahead, taste for seasoning; the salad may need extra vinegar and salt, because flavors tend to fade in the refrigerator.

Grilled Eggplant with Mint Pesto and Sumac

Make this easy appetizer when you're grilling. Like many Mediterranean-style vegetable dishes, this one tastes best at room temperature. The sprinkle of tart, tangy sumac adds a sprightly note and a bit of bright color. I have the feeling that sumac is going to be the next big seasoning. It's quite versatile with a beautiful deep burgundy color and is inexpensive. Look for sumac at Middle Eastern groceries and specialty spice purveyors. See the sidebar below for more about sumac.

SERVES 8 TO 10

Eggplant

2 large, plump eggplants (about 2 pounds total), sliced on the diagonal into even $3/8$-inch thick slices

$1/2$ cup olive oil

$1/2$ cup extra-virgin olive oil

$1/4$ cup lemon juice

Kosher salt and freshly ground black pepper to taste

Lightly brush each eggplant slice with olive oil. Place diagonally on the grill and turn halfway through to make criss-crisscross grill marks. Then turn over and grill again until softened. Remove from grill; arrange in a single layer on a platter. Whisk together the extra-virgin olive oil, lemon juice, salt

and pepper. Brush the mixture onto each slice of eggplant.

Mint Pesto and Garnish

$1/2$ cup extra-virgin olive oil

1 tablespoon coarsely chopped garlic

Kosher salt and freshly ground black pepper to taste

1 cup Italian parsley leaves

$1/2$ cup fresh mint leaves (or 2 tablespoons finely crumbled dry mint)

1 bunch scallions, thinly sliced

$1/2$ cup diced tomatoes

1 tablespoon ground sumac

Blend together the olive oil, garlic, salt, and pepper to a very smooth puree in a food processor. Add the parsley and mint, process again briefly until the mixture is bright green and fairly smooth, and reserve.

Arrange the eggplant slices on a large decorative serving platter and drizzle the mint pesto over the eggplant. Sprinkle with the scallions, tomatoes, and sumac, and serve while still warm.

SUMAC

Sumac, *Rhus coriaria*, is a popular condiment in Turkey, Lebanon, and Iran, and is sprinkled on foods like kebabs and salads for its fruity, tart, and tangy flavor. It has a salty aftertaste from the salt used as a preservative. Available in Middle Eastern groceries and specialty spices stores, it is a coarse-textured, moist, burgundy-red powder. Sumac trees grow wild in the Mediterranean and the Middle East. Mixed with ground sesame seeds and the herb *za'atar* (in the marjoram family) for the seasoning mixture also called *za'atar*, it is sprinkled on yogurt and pita bread.

Eggplant Parmigiano al Forno

This is my nontraditional "eggplant parm" and is well worth trying because it's both flavorful and lighter than the more traditional recipe. If you have individual oven-proof casserole dishes, this dish makes a beautiful presentation. I bake it in small Spanish terra-cotta cazuelas, shallow casserole dishes available inexpensively at Spanish specialty stores and well-stocked kitchenware stores. In my last restaurant, I would roast the eggplant and then bake it in the wonderful wood-oven I had to add an extra layer of smoky flavor. But it's well worth making, even baked in a conventional oven. Best of all is to make it in summer when gold and red beefsteak tomatoes are in season. If you want to prepare the dish ahead of time, refrigerate it up to two days ahead of time, and allow about 45 minutes for baking.

SERVES 8

Roasted Eggplant Slices

1/2 cup olive oil

1 tablespoon chopped garlic

3 tablespoons chopped oregano (or 1 tablespoon dried)

3 tablespoons chopped rosemary (or 1 tablespoon dried)

Kosher salt and freshly ground black pepper

2 large eggplants, sliced

Preheat the oven to 425°F. Combine the olive oil, garlic, oregano, rosemary, salt, and pepper. Brush eggplant slices on both sides with mixture. Arrange eggplant slices in a single layer on a metal baking pan. Roast about 15 minutes, or until well-browned on top and soft throughout.

Ricotta Cheese Mix

1 pound ricotta cheese

3 eggs

1/2 cup grated Parmigiano-Reggiano or Grana Padano

1/2 cup chopped Italian parsley

1/4 cup shredded basil

1/2 pound fresh mozzarella, finely diced

Kosher salt, freshly ground black pepper, and nutmeg to taste

Mix all ingredients together and keep refrigerated until ready to use, up to one day ahead of time.

Assembly

2 tablespoons olive oil

1 cup homemade breadcrumbs, made from country-style Italian bread

2 teaspoons chopped garlic

Roasted Eggplant Slices

Ricotta Cheese Mix

2 red and 2 yellow (or all red) ripe round tomatoes, sliced

1/2 pound fresh mozzarella, sliced

1/2 cup grated Parmigiano-Reggiano or Grana Padano

Preheat the oven to 400°F. In a small pan, heat the olive oil, and then mix in the breadcrumbs and garlic. Cook, stirring, until the breadcrumbs are nicely browned.

Sprinkle the bottom of individual shallow casserole or large baking dish with a layer of breadcrumbs. Arrange a layer of eggplant slices over top. Sprinkle with a layer of breadcrumbs. Spread an even layer of the Ricotta Cheese Mix over the breadcrumbs. Cover the top with alternating slices of eggplant, yellow tomato slices, mozzarella slices, eggplant, and red tomato. Sprinkle with the grated cheese, and bake 30 minutes, or until browned and bubbling.

Japanese Eggplant Chips with Nanami Togarashi

Japanese eggplants are incredibly tender and creamy, with firm texture and tiny seeds. Breaded with extra-crunchy Japanese panko breadcrumbs, available at Asian markets, their melting insides contrast perfectly with their crunchy outsides. Simply sprinkle them with the Japanese seasoning mix called Nanami Togarashi, *also available in Asian markets, and serve with lemon wedges. For more about Japanese Nanami Togarashi, see* below.

SERVES 6

3 eggs

¼ cup soy sauce

1 pound Japanese eggplant, bias cut in ½-inch thick slices

¼ pound (1 cup) all-purpose flour

2 cups Japanese panko breadcrumbs

3 cups peanut or soy oil

Nanami Togarashi

Lemon wedges, for garnish

Lightly beat together the eggs and soy sauce. Dip the eggplant slices in the flour, shake off excess, and dip them into the beaten egg mixture. Let excess liquid drip off, then coat the eggplant in panko. Arrange eggplant slices in a single layer on wax-paper-lined trays. Chill eggplant slices 30 minutes to set crust.

In a large, heavy-bottomed pot, an electric deep-fryer, or a wok, heat the oil until shimmering (365°F. on a frying thermometer). Working in 3 to 4 batches, fry the eggplant slices, laying them into the oil one by one. Fry about 7 minutes, or until browned and crispy on both sides. Using a wire skimmer, remove the eggplant from the oil and drain on a wire rack, keeping warm in a 200°F. oven until all the eggplant has been fried.

Sprinkle with Nanami Togarashi and serve with lemon wedges.

391

JAPANESE NANAMI TOGARASHI

Togarashi is the Japanese word for chiles, so this popular seasoning mix always includes chiles. Along with ground red chile pepper, it generally includes *sansho*, a native Japanese spice related to Szechuan pepper, dried tangerine peel, garlic, *nori* (toasted seaweed), black sesame seeds, and white poppy seeds. Sold in small glass jars ready for sprinkling, Nanami togarashi works well with fatty foods such as the fried eggplant slices above, *shabu shabu* (small bits of food simmered in rich broth), noodle dishes, and *yakitori* (grilled dishes).

Sicilian Eggplant Caponata

Caponata is a traditional Sicilian relish with a long, rich history that originated with the fisherman's caponata alla marinara, *made with seafood. These days, caponata is usually made with eggplant, but it always includes capers, the basis of its name. Sicily's cuisine is a fascinating mélange of Italian, Arab, and Spanish culinary traditions, closely linked to local crops, like the eggplant and capers featured here. Caponata gets its typical sweet-and-sour flavor from a little sugar mixed with red wine vinegar. It will keep up to 10 days if refrigerated, but should be brought back to room temperature for best flavor. Serve with crostini as an hors d'oeuvre, or heat to simmering and serve as a bed for grilled tuna, mahi-mahi, bluefish, or other oil-rich dark-meat fish.*

392

MAKES 1 QUART, SERVES 6 TO 8 AS AN APPETIZER

2 large eggplants (about 2 pounds total), diced

8 tablespoons olive oil, divided

1 red onion, diced

1 red bell pepper, diced

1 yellow bell pepper, diced

3 to 4 ribs celery, diced

1 (28-ounce) can diced tomatoes or 1 (26-ounce) box
   chopped Pomi (in an aseptic box)

3/4 cup sliced green olives

1/4 cup drained capers

3 tablespoons red wine vinegar

1 tablespoon granulated sugar

Kosher salt and freshly ground black pepper, to taste

1/2 cup chopped Italian parsley

2 tablespoons chopped fresh oregano

Preheat the oven to 425°F. Toss eggplant with 6 tablespoons of the olive oil and spread onto a baking pan. Roast about 20 minutes, or until eggplant is browned and soft.

Meanwhile, combine onion, red and yellow peppers, and celery. Sauté in a large skillet or Dutch oven in remaining 2 tablespoons olive oil until crisp-tender.

Separately, combine tomatoes, olives, capers, vinegar, sugar, salt, and pepper. Add to sautéed vegetables. Stir in roasted eggplant. Bring to the boil and simmer together about 15 minutes, or until thickened. Cool and then stir in parsley and oregano. Serve at room temperature.

CAPONATA VARIATIONS

Caponata recipes abound and the dish may be varied almost endlessly by adding toasted pine nuts or almonds, artichokes, hard-cooked eggs, orange juice, anchovies, basil, and even bitter chocolate. Sicilian restaurants sometimes add swordfish, shrimp, or baby octopus and top it with shaved *bottarga* (dried, salted and pressed tuna or gray mullet roe).

EGGS
SAVORY DISHES

EGGS
SAVORY DISHES

For a quick and delicious meal that can suit any mood, minus the hard-to-find or highly perishable ingredients, why not cook eggs tonight? In fact, eggs are one of the few food bargains to be had today. From the colorful layered Torta Milanese, to spicy Mexican Huevos Rancheros with its requisite and filling side of refried beans, to the Spanish egg cake called a *tortilla* (small torta) and nothing at all to do with the Mexican flatbread of the same name, to baked eggs Florentine style (which always means spinach), and a simple but tasty zucchini and dill egg cake from the island of Crete, egg cookery beyond breakfast offers so many possibilities.

One of the best things about egg dishes, as anyone who has put together a restaurant lunch menu knows, is that almost any small bits and pieces of leftovers can be artfully combined with eggs for a frittata, baked eggs, a savory soufflé, or an omelet. Bits of browned sausage, cheese, cooked vegetables, mushrooms, leftover baked potatoes, fried onions, roasted peppers, ham, chopped herbs, and more all work well.

Americans are accustomed to eating eggs for breakfast only and cooked in butter, although in all but the best restaurants, that means a "butter-flavored" commercial oil product. Mediterranean egg dishes are often cooked in flavorful extra-virgin olive oil. Because olive oil has a high burning point, eggs can be cooked at higher tem-

perature, making for the crisp, lacy edges and golden crusts that are so appealing.

Chicken breeds with white feathers and earlobes, such as Leghorns, lay white eggs; breeds with red feathers and earlobes, such as Rhode Island Reds and Plymouth Rocks, lay brown eggs. White eggs are most in demand in America though in New England, brown shells are preferred. Because brown-egg layers are larger birds and require more food, brown eggs are usually more expensive and have thicker shells. Simply for the sensory pleasure of handling these warm brown eggs, I always choose well-protected brown eggs.

We buy eggs by grade, according to the thickness of the shell and the firmness of the white. AA is the best, followed by A (most supermarket eggs), while B-grade eggs have thin shells and watery whites. You can buy perfectly adequate inexpensive tray eggs (30 to the tray) in warehouse clubs, but note that tray eggs will have thin, easily broken shells. Eggs are sized from medium to jumbo (as in condoms, there is no such thing as small), with pee-wees at less than 1 pound per dozen the exception to the rule. At the other end of the size spectrum, jumbos weigh 2 pounds per dozen. See the box on the next page for more about egg sizes.

The albumen, or egg white, accounts for two-thirds of an egg's liquid weight and contains more than half the egg's protein and minerals. Because egg whites tend to thin out as an egg ages, fresh eggs sit up tall and firm in the pan, while older ones tend to thin and spread out. Fresh albumen looks cloudy because it contains carbon dioxide. As the egg ages, the carbon dioxide escapes, so the white of older eggs is more transparent.

The chalazae is the ropy strand of egg white that anchors the yolk in place in the center of the white. The more prominent the chalazae, the fresher the egg. It's perfectly fine to eat, but the more squeamish might prefer to remove this cord, or strain it out of beaten eggs before cooking for a perfectly smooth texture.

The yolk, or yellow, makes up the remaining third of the egg's liquid weight and contains all of the fat, a little less than half the protein, and most of the egg's vitamins. Hens that are fed yellow corn and alfalfa meal lay eggs with medium-yellow yolks, while eggs from hens that eat wheat or barley have lighter-colored yolks. I found it hard to bring myself to eat the unappetizingly pale yolks served to me in London. In Italy, the yolks are such a deep orange color that they are called the "red" instead of the "yellow." These rich-tasting eggs are the secret of the exquisite hand-rolled pasta of Bologna and the custard-based gelato found all over Italy. To achieve the same richness, look for double-yolk eggs sometimes found at farmers' markets.

The calcium-rich eggshell is the egg's first line of defense against bacterial contamination. The shell itself is covered with a protective coating which helps to preserve freshness and prevent contamination. Thousands of tiny pores in the shell allow moisture and carbon dioxide out and air in. The air forms the air cell, the empty space between the white and shell, usually (though not always) at the large end of the egg. The size of the air cell is one basis for determining grade: the smaller the cell, the higher the grade.

395

Egg Sizes and Equivalents

I use extra-large eggs for all my recipes, but never fear, you can easily substitute if your eggs are a different size.

- One whole extra large egg equals 4 tablespoons, about $2^{3}/_{4}$ tablespoons white and $1^{1}/_{4}$ tablespoons yolk. Five extra-large eggs, beaten, equal $1^{1}/_{4}$ cups.

- One whole large egg equals $3^{1}/_{4}$ tablespoons, about $2^{1}/_{4}$ tablespoons white, and 1 tablespoon yolk. Five large eggs, beaten, equal 1 cup.

- One medium egg equals 3 tablespoons, about 2 tablespoons white and 1 tablespoon yolk. Five medium eggs, beaten, equal a bit more than $^{3}/_{4}$ cup.

Checking Eggs

Check each egg in the carton to make sure you don't have any broken shells (not safe). Move each egg in its cup to make sure it hasn't stuck because of a crack or leak on the bottom.

Fertilized Eggs

The little red spot you sometimes see comes from a fertilized egg. The red is a small amount of male hormone. Fertilized eggs are not at all harmful but are not kosher. When I was growing up in a kosher household, we would carefully separate eggs, one at a time into a dish to make sure none of them had the telltale blood spot. Any with the spot had to be discarded.

HOW TO TELL IF AN EGG IS HARD-COOKED OR RAW

Separate hard-cooked from raw eggs by spinning the egg. A cooked egg spins smoothly; a raw egg spins unevenly, because its liquidy inside will keep spinning if you stop the egg.

EGGS THAT REFUSE TO PEEL

What about shells that won't peel? Although incredibly frustrating if you're trying to peel them, it's a sign of a fresh egg, because the shells tend to stick to new eggs with their higher pH. So, let your eggs age if you're going to hard-cook them. Hard-cook eggs in salted water to help them separate from their shells, and peel while still warm.

Freshness of Eggs

How recently an egg was laid has a bearing on its freshness but is only one of many factors. The temperature at which it is held, the humidity, and the handling all play their part. A one-week old egg, held under ideal conditions (temperature under 40°F. and humidity of about seventy-five percent) can be fresher than an egg left at room temperature for one day. Most eggs reach supermarkets within a few days of leaving the laying house.

Egg cartons display the date the eggs were packed in the form of a Julian date representing the consecutive days—January 1 is one, December 31 is three-hundred and sixty-five. You can keep fresh eggs stored in the refrigerator for four to five weeks beyond this date with minimal quality loss.

A fresh egg will sink to the bottom of a bowl of cold water; an old egg will float or turn sideways. Eggshells are porous and in time, an air pocket forms inside that grows bigger as the egg gets older.

There is nothing like a real farm-fresh egg, especially for poached or pan-fried eggs. The yolk stands up in the middle, nestled in a thick white that surrounds the yolk without running.

STORING EGGS

Keep eggs cold at all times and don't use cracked eggs. Store eggs large-end up to keep them fresher by keeping the pointy bottom filled. The yolks will stay centered (which only matters if you're making hard-cooked eggs).

FREEZING EGG YOLKS

Egg yolks must be mixed with either sugar or salt to stabilize before freezing. Add a teaspoon of sugar for every yolk for sweet dishes or $1/4$ teaspoon of salt for every yolk for savory dishes. Pour the stabilized yolks into an ice tray and freeze. Transfer to a zip-top freezer bag and freeze for up to 2 months. Thaw in the refrigerator if possible, or else, drop the well-sealed bag into a bowl of warm water, shaking the contents of the bag occasionally for even thawing.

Broccoli and Aged Gouda Cheese Soufflé

In this quick but impressive soufflé, I combine small bits of broccoli with deep orange-colored, richly flavored, dense aged gouda cheese that has enough potency so that its flavor comes through clearly in the finished soufflé. Aged gouda from Holland can be found in many supermarket cheese sections. I like the extra flavor of three-year-aged cheese. Note that while soufflé waits for no one, any leftovers can be reheated in the microwave, although it won't be as airy as the original. See the sidebar on page 398 for more about soufflés.

SERVES 4 TO 6

2 tablespoons + 4 tablespoons unsalted butter

$1/4$ cup finely grated dry cheese (such as Romano, Asiago, or Dry Jack)

$1/2$ pound (about 2 cups) broccoli florets, cut up

5 tablespoons all-purpose flour

1 cup whole milk, scalded

6 egg yolks

$1/2$ pound (about 2 cups) shredded aged Gouda cheese

Kosher salt, freshly ground black pepper, grated nutmeg, and cayenne to taste

8 egg whites

Using the 2 tablespoons butter, generously butter a large baking dish (either one with straight high sides for a traditional soufflé, or one with shallower sides and bigger surface for a quicker cooking, crustier soufflé) that holds about $2^1/2$ quarts. Sprinkle evenly with the grated cheese and reserve.

Steam, boil, or microwave the broccoli until crisp-tender and emerald green. Rinse under cold water to cool, then drain, and place in the bowl of a food processor. Briefly process to chop up into fine bits and reserve.

In a heavy-bottomed saucepan, melt the remaining 4 tablespoons butter. Stir in the flour and cook 3 to 4 minutes on medium low heat while constantly stirring to cook out the raw flour flavor. While whisking, pour in the hot milk and bring the sauce to the boil, whisking often, until the sauce is smooth and thick.

Pull the pan off the heat, add the egg yolks, and immediately whisk vigorously to combine well so that the yolks don't curdle. Stir in the broccoli and Gouda, season with salt, pepper, nutmeg, and cayenne, and reserve.

Preheat the oven to 400°F. In a dry, clean bowl, beat the egg whites until they're white and fluffy and stick to the sides of the bowl. Fold one quarter of the whites into the broccoli-cheese mixture, repeat, and then fold the remaining half into the mix. Spread the mixture into the prepared baking dish. If using the deep dish, reduce the heat to 350°F.; if using the shallow dish, reduce the heat to 375°F. Bake for 25 to 30 minutes, or until puffed and moist but not liquidy in the center. Serve immediately.

397

ABOUT SOUFFLÉS

There are so many variations that can be made following one basic soufflé recipe. The soufflé can be baked either in a straight-sided classic French soufflé dish or a shallower baking dish, for more crust and quicker cooking.

First, make a thick white sauce (milk thickened with a paste made from equal weights of clarified butter and flour) enriched with egg yolks.

Next, fold in about one pound altogether of additions, like cheese, cooked vegetables (such as asparagus, mushrooms, or spinach) minus excess water, or chopped, poached fruit (such as pears, apricots, or cherries), liqueur, chocolate, citrus juice and zest, or praline paste for a dessert soufflé.

Finally, fold in fluffy beaten egg whites, using more whites than yolks for lightness, and bake in a preheated 375°F. oven until just set. Note that in France, where soufflés originated, the preference is for a liquidy center.

Serve immediately!

Goat Cheese and Hazelnut Soufflé

Following the directions above, substitute $1/2$ pound of toasted ground hazelnuts for the broccoli and $1/2$ pound of mild goat cheese for the gouda. Coat the buttered baking dish with a mixture of $1/4$ cup breadcrumbs and $1/4$ cup of the hazelnuts.

Torta Milanese with Eggs, Spinach, and Peppers

This extravagant torta is related to the Medieval custom of layering all sorts of elaborate fillings inside a tall pastry crust—think of "four-and-twenty-blackbirds baked in a pie." In earlier recipes, the crust was only meant to hold the filling, not to be eaten; eventually the crusts became richer and shorter and good to eat. Here, colorful layers of eggs fragrant with basil, roasted peppers, spinach, ham, and cheese are enclosed in a deliciously flaky short crust pastry made with buttermilk. If you prefer, you can use Brioche Dough (see page 987), or even layers of buttered phyllo dough. While it's a fair bit of work to assemble all the layers, once made, the torta will serve 12 to 16 very happy people, perhaps for brunch, and it makes a dramatic presentation for a party.

MAKES ONE LARGE TORTA, 12 TO 16 SERVINGS

3 cups lightly beaten eggs (12 to 15, depending on the size)

$1/4$ cup heavy cream

$1/2$ cup shredded basil leaves

Kosher salt and freshly ground black pepper to taste

2 tablespoons + 2 tablespoons unsalted butter

$1/2$ cup grated Parmigiano-Reggiano or Grana Padano

2 tablespoons olive oil

1 tablespoon chopped garlic

$1/2$ pound spinach, stems removed

1 pound Buttermilk Pastry Dough (*see* next page)

$1/2$ pound shredded Italian Fontina

$1/2$ pound sliced smoked ham

$1/2$ pound roasted peppers (homemade or purchased)

1 egg, lightly beaten with 1 tablespoon water, for the egg wash

Lightly beat together eggs, cream, basil, salt, and pepper. Melt 2 tablespoons of the butter and cook the egg mixture over moderate heat until only half-cooked. Stir in the Parmigiano and set aside to cool.

Heat the olive oil and the garlic until the garlic is sizzling. Add the spinach and cook 2 to 3 minutes over high heat, or until barely wilted. Remove the spinach from the pan and spread out on a metal baking pan to col.

Rub a 10 x 3-inch springform pan generously with the remaining 2 tablespoons butter. Roll out the Buttermilk Pastry Dough about $1/4$ inch thick. Cut out a circle about 18-inches in diameter. Lay the circle into the pan, pressing well into the pan without stretching. You should have about 1 inch of pastry overlapping the edge. Trim pastry to an even 1-inch edge using scissors. Roll out and cut a 10-inch circle of the Buttermilk Pastry Dough. Chill the pastry-lined pan and the 10-inch circle until ready to fill.

Evenly spread the following in layers in the pastry-lined pan in order:

$1/2$ of the egg mixture

$1/2$ of the spinach mix

$1/2$ of the Fontina

$1/2$ of the ham

All of the peppers

$1/2$ of the ham

$1/2$ of the Fontina

$1/2$ of the spinach mix

$1/2$ of the egg mix

Fold the overlapping pastry over the top, brush the exposed 1-inch overlap with the egg wash, and position the pastry circle over top. Press down to seal. Brush the tops with egg wash and cut a criss-cross pattern lightly through the top. Using scissors, snip about 6 small v-shaped vents in the top. Chill the torta at least 1 hour.

Preheat the oven to 375°F. Place the torta on a metal baking tray to catch any drips and bake 45 minutes to 1 hour, or until the pastry is golden brown and the filling is bubbling through the top. Remove from the oven and cool until warm before cutting into wedges. Serve warm.

Buttermilk Pastry Dough

I've discovered that dry buttermilk powder made by the Saco Company and sold in many well-stocked supermarkets and specialty food stores is a wonderful product to have on hand for baking. Not that different from the idea of powdered milk, this buttermilk powder makes a particularly flaky short crust dough. If you can't find the buttermilk powder, substitute $1/2$ cup liquid buttermilk mixed with 1 egg for the $1/2$ cup beaten eggs. This dough freezes quite well if double-bagged in heavy zip-top freezer bags. Defrost overnight in the refrigerator when ready to use.

MAKES ABOUT ONE POUND

$3/4$ pound (3 cups) unbleached all-purpose flour

2 teaspoons salt

$1/4$ cup dry buttermilk powder

$1/4$ pound (1 stick) unsalted butter, cut into bits

$1/2$ cup eggs (about 3 large eggs), lightly beaten

In the bowl of an electric mixer, combine the flour, salt, and buttermilk powder and mix together lightly. Top with the butter bits but don't mix. Place the bowl in the freezer for 30 minutes, or chill for 1 hour if you're working on a really hot day.

Beat the chilled flour mixture until it resembles cold and crumbly oatmeal. Pour in the eggs and beat until the mixture just comes together into a ball.

Transfer to a large zip-top bag or wrap in plastic and then flatten the dough to fill the bag. Chill for at least 30 minutes, or until firm but still malleable, before rolling out. The dough can be refrigerated for up to 2 days before using.

Huevos Rancheros

This dish of "ranch-style eggs" is my all-time favorite egg dish. Perhaps because I first ate it during my oh-so impressionable youth during two summers living in Mexico. All the flavors and texture work so beautifully together and with the requisite side dish of frijoles refritos (refried beans), it's really quite a filling and balanced meal. So much tastier to serve beans instead of the usual American potatoes or grits served with eggs, although they are optional. Leftover refried beans make a great topping for nachos, and the spicy ranchero sauce is also good served with fajitas or baked enchiladas.

SERVES 4

Ranchero Sauce

1 large onion, peeled

4 cloves garlic, peeled

2 jalapeño peppers, trimmed and seeded

1 (28-ounce) can diced tomatoes

$1/2$ teaspoon allspice

$1/2$ teaspoon cinnamon

2 tablespoons lard, bacon fat, or olive oil

2 tablespoons canola or vegetable oil

$1/2$ cup chopped cilantro

Kosher salt to taste

Process onion, garlic, and jalapeños together until chunky. Add tomatoes, allspice, and cinnamon and process again. Fry the tomato mixture in lard, stirring carefully as it will spatter. Keep cooking until the sauce is thick enough so that the oil separates and rises to the top, about 20 minutes. Reserve.

Refried Beans (Frijoles Refritos)

These mashed and fried beans are called refritos *because they are "recooked" by frying after the first preliminary cooking stage. Although lard, which is called for here, has a bad reputation, it provides wonderful flavor and is actually lower in cholesterol than hydrogenated fats like margarine and shortening. Though completely nontraditional, I've also used duck fat with excellent results. I always make a large batch of refried beans because they freeze so well. Don't hesitate to use canned beans here. Frying them with the onion gives them plenty of flavor.*

SERVES 8

$1/4$ cup lard, melted duck fat or olive oil

1 cup finely chopped onion

6 cups cooked pinto beans

Heat the lard in a large cast-iron or nonstick skillet. Add the onion and cook for 2 to 3 minutes, or until transparent but not browned. Stir in one-fourth of the beans. As the beans begin to bubble, crush them with a potato masher. Cook the beans until thickened, stirring often with a wooden spoon and mashing.

400

Add another one-fourth of the beans and repeat, cooking until thickened. Add the remaining beans in the same fashion. Cook the beans until they resemble mashed potatoes. These beans reheat quite well in the microwave and freeze perfectly.

Assembly

Canola or vegetable oil

8 corn tortillas

2 cups Ranchero Sauce

8 eggs

1/4 pound (about 1 cup) Monterey Jack or
   Cheddar cheese, grated

2 cups Refried Beans (*see* previous page)

Preheat the broiler. Heat a thin film of canola or vegetable oil in a heavy skillet (cast-iron is best). Toast one tortilla at a time for 1/2 minute on each side. Place 2 tortillas per portion on the bottom of individual shallow baking dishes or a single large, shallow baking dish.

Spread sauce over tortillas, and then carefully break two eggs per person onto the sauce. Sprinkle with grated cheese. Place under the broiler and cook 8 to 10 minutes or until the cheese is bubbling and the egg whites are set but the yolks are still liquid. Serve with refried beans.

Spanish Potato and Chorizo Tortilla

Many years ago in Barcelona, when my funds were extremely limited, I tasted a wonderful tortilla studded with golden-brown fried artichokes. I still remember how good it was, especially for an artichoke fiend like me. Like its cousin, the Italian frittata, a Spanish tortilla is a cooked egg cake, similar to a flat omelet. Unlike an omelet, the eggs in a tortilla are fully cooked. A tortilla is often served in wedges at room temperature for a quick appetizer or for tapas. It is a substantial dish, loaded with sliced potatoes here, in one of the most common versions. Chorizo adds smoky, spicy flavor, but it could be omitted. Roasted peppers, fried onions, cooked green beans, or browned sliced squash would all be delicious.

SERVES 6

2 pounds gold or all-purpose potatoes,
   peeled or not, as desired

2 tablespoons olive oil

Kosher salt and freshly ground black pepper to taste

1 tablespoon sweet Spanish paprika

1 teaspoon pimentón

1 pound Spanish chorizo sausage (substitute hot
   Italian sausage)

1/2 cup roughly chopped Italian parsley

8 eggs, lightly beaten

Preheat the oven to 400°F. Cut potatoes into 1/2-inch thick slices. Toss with olive oil, salt, pepper, paprika, and pimentón. Roast 30 minutes. At the same time, prick the chorizo and roast in the oven until browned. Remove the potatoes and sausage from the oven. Drain off any fat, and slice the chorizo. Combine potatoes, chorizo, and parsley with the eggs.

Pour mixture into a lightly oiled cast-iron skillet or a shallow 8- to 9-inch oiled casserole. Place on the top shelf of the oven and bake until the eggs are set, about 15 minutes. Cool slightly, cut into wedges and serve.

401

Dad's Venetian Eggs

My late father, Dr. Melville Green, was the archetypical absent-minded scientist who would forget his car fare and have to borrow money nearly every day, or wear mismatched socks because he'd never notice what he was wearing. His attention was entirely concentrated on the rarified world of theoretical physics, where the only people who understand what you're talking about are other physicists. He had a couple of culinary specialties, including these eggs poached in a garlicky tomato sauce, that would make a very nice supper dish, with Italian bread toasts.

SERVES 4

1 large red onion, diced

1 tablespoon thinly sliced garlic + 1 clove garlic, cut in two

1/4 cup extra-virgin olive oil

1 (28-ounce) can diced tomatoes

6 bay leaves

Kosher salt and freshly ground black pepper to taste

1/2 cup chopped Italian parsley

1 loaf Italian bread, cut on the diagonal into

 1/2 inch-thick slices

8 eggs

Preheat the oven to 350°F. In a wide, shallow pan with a lid, cook the onion and sliced garlic in olive oil until the onion is transparent. Add the tomatoes, bay leaves, salt and pepper, and bring to the boil. Keep cooking until the sauce is thick enough so that the oil separates and rises to the top, about 20 minutes. Stir in the parsley.

Meanwhile, rub the bread slices with the cut sides of the garlic cloves, and then brush with olive oil. Toast for about 10 minutes, or until lightly browned.

Break the eggs into the sauce and allow them to cook 2 to 3 minutes to partially set, and then stir to break up a little. Cover and continue to cook until the whites are set but the yolks are still runny. Spoon into wide, shallow bowls and serve with garlic toasts.

402

Baked Eggs Florentine

The people of Florence have long been known for their love of soft, tender spinach. Catherine de' Medici, the Italian bride of Henry II of France, was a hearty eater and drinker. Upon her marriage to the French king, she brought her skilled Florentine cooks and pastry makers along with her taste for sweet peas, artichokes, and spinach. Ever since then, any dish in French cuisine called "Florentine" is sure to be made with spinach. In this simple dish, a bed of sautéed spinach is topped with eggs, crème fraiche (or sour cream), and grated Parmesan cheese. Also in the Florentine style is the use of nutmeg that is an invariable seasoning for spinach.

SERVES 4

2 pounds prewashed spinach, full-sized
   and trimmed of stems, or baby spinach

1 large onion, diced

2 tablespoons olive oil

Kosher salt, freshly ground black pepper,
   and grated nutmeg to taste

8 eggs

1 cup crème fraiche, or sour cream

¹/₂ cup grated Parmigiano-Reggiano cheese

Preheat the broiler. Lightly cook the spinach by placing it in a large pan with a sprinkling of water. Heat just until the leaves wilt, 2 to 3 minutes. Remove from heat, run under cold water to stop the cooking, then squeeze out the extra water. (If using frozen, just defrost and squeeze out the extra water.)

Cook the onion in the olive oil for 3 to 4 minutes, or until slightly softened, then toss with the spinach. Season with salt, pepper and nutmeg. Spread spinach mixture on the bottom of four individual casserole dishes or a shallow baking dish. Using the back of a spoon, form 8 "nests" (depressions) in the spinach. Carefully break one egg into each nest.

Top with dollops of crème fraiche, then sprinkle with Parmesan cheese. Place under the broiler and cook 7 to 8 minutes, or until cheese is bubbling and the egg whites have set but the yolks are still liquidy. Serve while piping hot.

403

EGGS AND FOOD SAFETY

Protein-rich animal foods can carry microorganisms that cause disease or spoil the food. Salmonella is typically found in the gastrointestinal tract of warm-blooded animals. Although Salmonella may not make the carrier animal ill, it can make people ill. An intact shell egg has many chemical and physical properties that deter bacterial growth. However, in rare instances (about 1 in 20,000 eggs in the U.S.), the Salmonella bacteria can be found inside the egg white.

Although the number of bacteria per egg is likely to be very low (because the egg white discourages bacterial growth), once the shell is cracked and the yolk mixed with the white, bacteria grow with great ease. If the yolk deteriorates because it's old or has been stored as room temperature, bacteria can grow inside the intact shell egg.

For those whose immune resistance is compromised, the very young and the very old, it's best not to eat raw or undercooked eggs. To kill salmonella, cook eggs to 160°F. (the temperature at which yolks start to thicken). Because egg whites set at about 145°F., a cooked white is hot enough to kill salmonella.

404

FENNEL

FENNEL

I'd like to introduce you to one of my favorite vegetables: fennel (also known as sweet anise, Florence fennel, or *finocchio*). If you've never cooked fennel or simply crunched on a mouth-tingling wedge of raw fennel, now is the time to start. This Italian favorite has a clean, light licorice flavor, and a crisp, biting texture. (Fennel seeds are considered so cleansing to the palate that people in India chew them instead of after-dinner mints.) Its flavor is similar to licorice and anise, though lighter and less persistent, becoming even more delicate and elusive when cooked. Perhaps because Americans generally don't eat anise-flavored foods, we find fennel a bit strange. Its spiky look can be a little scary too, but fennel is easy to prepare and delicious, whether raw or cooked.

Fennel, *Foeniculum vulgare*, is a member of the *Apiacea* family, along with parsley, carrots, dill, celery, and other vegetables that have umbrella-like seedpods (they used to be called *Umbelliferae*). There are three main types: bitter or wild fennel and sweet fennel are grown for their seeds, while Florence fennel, sometimes called sweet anise, is used as a vegetable/fruit. Fennel has been used in Europe for at least 2,000 years, although cultivated sweet fennel originated in Italy, where it is still loved best and used most.

Wild fennel is native to Southern Europe and also grows abundantly along the highways in California. It is a tall, relatively thin-stemmed plant with slightly bitter seeds, like celery seed. Sweet fennel, with sweeter, less-intense seeds, is grown in moderately warm regions worldwide. Florence fennel has an enlarged bulb-shaped base to its stems, thickened into a solid, overlapping mass and may be as large as a fist. A special type of fennel called *carosella* that has an extra-thick stalk is a traditional salad vegetable around Naples.

Fennel has an honored place in Greek history and mythology. In Greece, the vegetable is called *marathon*, because it grows in abundance near the village of Marathon about 26 miles from Athens, where the Athenians defeated the Persians in 490 B.C.E. A long-distance runner brought the great news back to Athens and thereby inspiring today's marathon races. According to Greek mythology, Prometheus hid the fire he stole from the gods in a hollow fennel stalk.

Roman cooks often used fennel; it is even mentioned by Apicius, the first-century author of an ancient Roman cookbook. In Medieval times, fennel was a symbol for flattery and was said to be an aphrodisiac. It was also believed to be the favored food of snakes, and was believed to help them shed their skin in the spring, giving them a sleek and youthful appearance.

In the ninth century, the Holy Roman Emperor Charlemagne ordered fennel to be grown in the south of

France; after that, sweet fennel gained popularity rapidly. Arab traders spread it all over the Middle East and to India and China. These days, fennel is cultivated primarily in Italy, France, Greece, and the United States.

Thomas Jefferson grew fennel in his diverse garden at Monticello from Italian seeds sent to him in 1824 by the American consul in Leghorn (Livorno). In a letter to the consul, Jefferson gives a heartfelt description of this oddball vegetable: "The fennel is beyond every other vegetable, delicious. It greatly resembles in appearance the largest size celery, perfectly white, and there is no vegetable equals it in flavor. It is eaten at dessert, crude [raw], and with, or without dry salt, indeed I preferred it to every other vegetable of to any fruit." I feel the same way.

FINOCCHIO AND FINOCCHIO'S

Finocchio, the Italian name for fennel, is also a friendly slang name for a homosexual person. Coincidentally, "Finocchio's" was the name of the fabled female-impersonator club in San Francisco, started by Joe Finocchio, which closed in 1999 after 63 years in the same location.

FENNEL SEASON

It used to be that fennel was difficult to find except in season from Italian growers. Now supermarkets carry it almost year-round, though the quality varies greatly. Look for locally grown fennel, at its best when in season from September to Thanksgiving, or California-grown fennel which is available year-round. In wintertime, you may find very white bulb-only fennel that is greenhouse-grown and imported from Holland. It's generally high priced.

GROWING FENNEL

Two important growers of fennel, one in New Jersey and one in California, are both run by third-generation Italian immigrants. Andy Boy is the brand name for fennel grown by D'Arrigo Brothers of Salinas, California (*see* Andy Boy Broccoli Rabe and Fennel, page 164). Formisano Farms, in Buena, New Jersey, has been growing fennel and other Italian greens for three generations since 1908. Ralph Formisano still runs the same farm originally planted by his grandfather, an Italian immigrant who worked the railroads until he saved enough money to buy a farm. Formisano is so well known for his fennel that the late, legendary food writer, James Beard, once took a train down from New York to have lunch at the farm and sample the fennel, which he had previously never tasted. Formisano's fennel is fresh picked and shipped to market within days. It has smaller bulbs, deeper color, and the more pronounced anise flavor sought after by the large Italian community in the region.

CHOOSING FENNEL

Choose larger, squat bulbs with fluffy green fronds and a pearly sheen that don't have any splitting, drying, browning, or soft spots. Sometimes the fronds are removed and only the bulb portion is sold. Aside from the difference in aesthetic quality, the lack of fronds is a sign that the fennel is getting old, because the fronds deteriorate first.

Preparing Fennel Bulbs

If your fennel has feathery stalks, cut them off diagonally, forming a V-shape at the point where the bulb enlarges. The fronds of sweet fennel have little flavor, but still look nice chopped up for a garnish. To prepare the bulb, trim off a thin slice from the bottom end and discard. Pull away the first layer, which is likely to be stringy and tough. Soak the cut fennel in cold water mixed with a little lemon juice to prevent it from darkening. Like many white vegetables, fennel will oxidize or turn brown if cut and exposed to air.

Using Fennel Stalks

Fennel stalks are quite stringy and need special attention. Separate the dark green outer and upper stalks from the light-colored, more tender portions. Cut the green stalks into short lengths and chop them into small chunks in a food processor. Cook with leeks or onions and potatoes in chicken stock until soft and then blend and strain to make a simple soup. Add lighter-colored portions to chicken or fish soups for a hint of sweetness. Or thinly slice and add with chopped onions and garlic when making tomato-based pasta sauces or seafood dishes. The single upright bushy frond found in the center of each bulb makes the most beautiful garnish.

Using Fennel Raw

Among the most versatile of vegetables, fennel is just as good raw as cooked. Fennel wedges are invariably included in *pinzimonio,* an Italian dish of raw vegetables dipped in extra-virgin olive oil, sea salt, and freshly ground pepper. I always include fennel in my Caesar salad, slicing it paper thin with a French mandolin or a Japanese Benriner cutter, soaking it in ice water until it curls, and then draining it. Fennel has a definite affinity for fish and seafood. Throughout the Mediterranean, fish soups, from bouillabaisse to *zuppa di pesce*, contain fennel.

More Fennel Cooking Ideas

Sauté fennel in olive oil until deliciously caramelized, or braise slowly until meltingly tender. Cut into flat slices, coat in breadcrumbs and then pan fry in olive oil. Or, layer the breaded fennel with marinara sauce and cheese and then bake like Eggplant Parmesan.

408

Tuscan Tuna Salad with Fennel

I developed this light and tasty Italian-style tuna salad for Parma, an Italian fresh-made fast-food company that had quite a successful run in Philadelphia, including Air Parma at the airport. The salad is light because the tuna is dressed with olive oil and fresh lemon juice instead of the usual mayonnaise. The fresh herbs give it brightness, and the red bell peppers and purple olives make for a colorful and appetizing presentation. The important thing here is to use the tasty tuna packed in olive oil enjoyed through-out the Mediterranean region, rather then the drier, rather mealy white tuna packed in water.

SERVES 6

Tuna Salad

$^{3}/_{4}$ cup extra-virgin olive oil

$^{1}/_{2}$ cup fresh lemon juice

Kosher salt and freshly ground black pepper to taste

2 tablespoons chopped tarragon (or 2 teaspoons dried)

$^{1}/_{4}$ cup chopped Italian parsley

2 (6-ounce) cans tuna in olive oil, drained

1 small head fennel, chopped

2 ribs celery, chopped

$^{1}/_{2}$ of a small red onion, chopped (about 1 cup)

Using a whisk or an immersion blender, combine the olive oil, lemon juice, salt, pepper, tarragon, and parsley. Lightly chunk the tuna, then toss it with the fennel, celery, onion, and most of the dressing. Reserve.

Salad Mix

1 pound mixed greens (romaine, butter lettuce, radicchio, and arugula) or spring mix

Tuna Salad

1 red or orange bell pepper, cut into matchsticks

$^{1}/_{2}$ cup pitted Kalamata olives

If you're using mixed greens, trim, wash, dry, and slice them cross-wise into 1-inch-wide strips. Toss the mixed greens or spring mix with the remaining dressing. Arrange on serving plates. Top with the Tuna Salad, and garnish with the bell pepper and olives.

Chicken Salad with Fennel, Lemon Zest, and Currants

This sprightly chicken salad is lively because of the fresh lemon juice and zest. The tiny, fruity, and slightly sweet currants add visual interest, soft and buttery toasted pine nuts give it that all-important contrast of texture, while crunchy fennel makes the salad light and fresh. Roasting the chicken breasts on the bone results in the juiciest white-meat chicken salad. Don't forget to save the deli-cious pan juices—the essence of the chicken—and the bones, for the stockpot. Serve the salad on a bed of greens or in a sandwich of toasted focaccia or brioche bread, or on its own, perhaps accompanied by fresh fruit salad. (See page 775 for more about currants.) Use a good-quality rotisserie chicken here to save time.

SERVES 6

2 pounds bone-in chicken breasts (or 1 rotisserie-
   roasted chicken)

Kosher salt and freshly ground black pepper to taste

1/2 cup mayonnaise

Juice and zest of 1 lemon

1/2 cup pine nuts, lightly toasted in a 300°F. oven

1/2 cup Zante currants

1/2 fennel bulb, finely chopped

1/2 bunch scallions, thinly sliced

1/4 cup chopped Italian Parsley

3 heads fennel, cut into thin wedges

Juice of 1 lemon

1/4 cup + 1/4 cup extra-virgin olive oil

1 pound white onion, thinly sliced

2 tablespoon chopped garlic, divided

Kosher salt and freshly ground black pepper to taste

1 (28-ounce) can whole plum tomatoes, cut into
  halves and seeded

2 cups country-style white breadcrumbs

1 tablespoon chopped fresh thyme leaves

Preheat the oven to 400°F. Season the chicken breasts with salt and pepper, and roast for 20 to 30 minutes, or until firm to the touch. Cool; remove the meat from bones and then shred. Using a rubber spatula, scrape up any pan juices and add to the chicken.

Whisk together the mayonnaise, lemon juice, and zest. Combine with the shredded chicken, pine nuts, currants, fennel, scallions, and parsley, and season to taste with salt and pepper. Store in the refrigerator for up to four days.

Preheat the oven to 375°F. Soak the fennel wedges in a bowl of water with lemon juice added until ready to cook. Combine 1/4 cup of the olive oil, the onions, and half the garlic in a skillet. Cook slowly about 10 minutes, or until softened but not browned. Spread this mixture on the bottom of a large, shallow ceramic baking dish, and season with salt and pepper.

Lightly steam the fennel wedges until slightly softened, about 5 minutes. Drain and arrange over the onions, alternating with tomato halves. Sprinkle with salt and pepper to taste.

In a small bowl, mix the breadcrumbs, remaining olive oil, and thyme. Sprinkle a generous layer on top of the vegetables. Bake 45 minutes, or until the mixture is bubbling and the crumbs are golden brown. Serve hot or at room temperature.

Fennel and Tomato Tian

Like casserole, marmite, and gratin, the Provençal dish called a tian *is named after the special shallow earthenware baking dish used to bake it. Here, rosemary-infused onions are topped by fennel wedges interspersed with plum tomato halves and finished with a garlicky bread crumb crust. Serve the tian hot in winter, and at room temperature in summer.*

SERVES 8

Braised Fennel with White Wine, Bay, and Thyme

Braising is just a fancy way of saying that you're slow-cooking in a small amount of richly flavored liquid. Here, sweet fennel is slowly braised in butter, a little chicken stock (which you could leave out or substitute with vegetable stock), white wine, and lemon juice. It is scented with the oh-so-adaptable thyme (which many chefs consider the most useful herb in the kitchen) and sweetly aromatic bay leaves, and slowly baked. The result is meltingly tender, well-flavored fennel. Braised vegetables like this reheat quite well. Serve with fish, seafood, or chicken. Use the same recipe to braise halved Belgian endive spears or quartered celery hearts.

SERVES 6

3 large fennel bulbs

3 tablespoons unsalted butter

$\frac{1}{2}$ cup dry white wine

$\frac{1}{2}$ cup chicken stock

2 tablespoons granulated sugar

$1\frac{1}{2}$ teaspoons chopped fresh thyme
    (or $\frac{1}{2}$ teaspoon dried)

3 bay leaves

Juice of 1 lemon

Kosher salt and ground white pepper to taste

Preheat the oven to 300°F. Trim off a slice from the bottom portion of each bulb so it can sit flat. Peel off any tough-looking outer layers. (Keep these to add to a fish, seafood, or chicken stock.) Place each bulb on its flat bottom, then, using a sharp knife, cut into thin wedges.

In an ovenproof casserole with a lid, add the butter and sliced fennel and cook 5 minutes, or until crisp-tender. Add the remaining ingredients and bring to the boil. Cover and transfer to the oven. Bake 1 hour, or until the fennel is quite tender and the liquid is syrupy. Remove from the oven and serve immediately.

Whole Grilled Red Snapper Stuffed with Fennel

I spent two weeks on the island of Corsica in 1964 in a small, family-run hotel on the coast, not far from the western capital of Ajaccio, birthplace of Napoleon. Every morning, the proprietor would venture out in his small boat, and whatever he caught was lunch. To this day, I can taste the rouget, *a dense and succulent red-gold-sheened Mediterranean fish (red mullet in English) that he grilled on a fire of wild fennel wood. It was a perfect marriage of fennel, from the rocky terrain of the island, and the rouget found among the rocks of the Mediterranean Sea. If you have access to vividly colored American red snapper, this is an ideal way to prepare it, but sea bass, striped bass, or a small Pacific snapper would also work. The cultivated fennel bulb found in the supermarket is much milder than its wild cousin, but the stalks have the strongest licorice-like flavor. Pernod, actually made from the related anise and the unrelated but similarly flavored Chinese star anise, enhances the taste.*

SERVES 4 TO 6

411

1 (2- to 3-pound) red snapper, cleaned, scaled, and fins
    trimmed
Juice of 2 lemons, divided
Kosher salt and freshly ground black pepper to taste
2 cups finely chopped fennel stalks
$1/4$ cup olive oil
1 tablespoon chopped garlic
$1/2$ cup homemade breadcrumbs, made from
    country-style Italian bread
$1/4$ cup Pernod

Cut three parallel slits on both sides of the snapper, with
the deepest slit through the thickest flesh at the head end
and the shallowest at the tail end. Rub the fish all over and
inside the slits with half the lemon juice and sprinkle with
salt and pepper.

Preheat a grill, preferably natural charcoal, or a broiler.
Combine the remaining lemon juice, fennel, olive oil, garlic, and breadcrumbs, and stuff the fish, including the slits,
with the mixture.

If using the grill, it is preferable to enclose the fish in a
special wire fish grate to keep it whole and to prevent
sticking. Place the fish on the grill and close the cover,
grilling about 15 minutes total or until the skin is lightly
browned and the flesh is opaque on the grill side. Turn
over, cover again, and continue cooking about 10 minutes,
or until the flesh is opaque and flaky at the neck end,
where it's thickest.

Remove the fish from the grill and place on a metal baking pan. Pour the Pernod over top and, averting your eyes,
flame. Serve immediately.

RED SNAPPER

The magnificent red snapper, *Lutjanus campechanus*, is
much sought after in the Caribbean, Florida, and along
the Mid-Atlantic coast where it's fished. Prized for its
fine texture and delicate flavor, its flesh is palest pearly
pink. The true American red snapper's closest cousins
are the vermilion or B-line snapper and the yellowtail
snapper, which are somewhat coarser in texture and
flavor. A true American red snapper (name of a species,
not a provenance) will have warm, rosy-red flesh on its
upper half, shading to golden red underneath and small
bright red eyes. It will be longer, rather than football-
shaped as is the smaller vermilion snapper. Most of our
red snappers come from the Gulf Coast and are often
caught near the reefs where they tend to gather. The
spring commercial red snapper fishing season begins on
the first of February; the fall season begins on the first
of October. Fishing is allowed from the first to the
tenth of the month, until the seasonal quota is reached.

FISH

FISH

In my more than thirty years in the food business, the whole world of fish cookery has completely changed. Where once restaurant chefs, as a matter of course, would serve frozen fish, today chefs demand the freshest of day-boat fish for their customers. Day-boat means that the fish was caught in a small boat that fishes close enough to the shore that it will come in to drop off its catch every day. Huge trawlers that go far out to sea for fishing will stay out for days, so that the fish, although technically fresh, may be as much as a week old before it's even landed.

Sushi and related raw fish dishes like ceviche and the newer Italian *crudo* (raw) seem to have taken over the world, so the quality of the fish is even more critical. For the home cook, however, buying and cooking fish presents a bigger challenge. Without access to prime-quality fish, which go to the highest bidder—usually top-grade restaurants—they have to make do with less-then-stellar fish.

Supermarket fish departments are too often staffed by people who know little about how to handle their product and are even less able to give customers advice on how to cook a particular fish. I once did consulting work for a very reputable supermarket where they bought their fish from the best supplier in the city. However, because the fish weren't handled with care and they kept selling them even when the fish was no longer fresh, what started out as high quality was, in the end, to be avoided.

There are, of course, exceptions, but high-quality fish usually comes with a high price tag, discouraging many people from cooking fish at home very often. I find the best prices and freshest fish at my local Korean supermarket, Han Au Reum, where the fish are cleaned, scaled, and prepared to order: filleted, cut into steaks, or simply trimmed so they're ready to cook whole. Best of all, every time, the fish is wrapped and then topped with a plastic bag filled with crushed ice and the whole thing put into a brown paper bag. I wish all supermarkets would take this kind of care with their fish.

In the days before cross-country trucking, most fish was locally caught. West Coast fish, like salmon and halibut, were rare and expensive back East. Aquaculture was nonexistent. On the East Coast, the most popular fish were porgy, sea trout (or weakies), mackerel, croakers, and sea bass. In season, an abundance of the sport fisherman's favorite, the fighting bluefish, appeared. Today, farm-raised fish is the rule and wild-caught fish the luxury exception.

Personally, I would always choose a wild fish, with the firm texture and developed flavor that comes from a life full of movement and a varied diet. However, practically speaking, our choices at the market are more and more farm-raised fish, such as tilapia, hybrid striped bass, freshwater catfish, and of course, salmon (*see* the chapter on Salmon for more on that fish). Note that fish that is frozen at sea and sealed in air-tight cryovac may actually be fresher than the so-called "fresh fish" that may be far from it.

It's also important to know that some fish, especially fillet of flounder, may be treated with a preservative to keep it white and firm. Other fish, though sold fresh, is brought in frozen and defrosted, such as the popular supermarket fish, orange roughy, originally named "slimehead," which is imported from New Zealand. Once frozen and defrosted, fish deteriorates quickly.

In fish, you definitely get what you pay for, but if you are willing to try less-popular varieties, such as porgies, weakfish, or croakers, which may be bony, or darker-fleshed fish like bluefish, mahi-mahi, or mackerel, or unusual fish like skate and monkfish, there are definitely reasonably priced fish for sale. Be flexible: buy the best-looking fish, not necessarily the one you came in for. Many fish can be easily substituted: sea bass, striped bass, red snapper, and hybrid striped bass will all work well for the same dish. Like fresh produce, fresh fish is at its very best when it's in season and plentiful. So, the time to buy is when the price is low.

CHOOSING A FISH MARKET

The most important thing is to choose a store with a high turnover of fish. Asian markets are a good bet, because their customers buy a lot of fish. Many of them have live tanks for even fresher fish.

The seafood counter should be crowded with lots of people buying fish. Talk to other customers; they can probably tell you what's good and if they've had good experiences in the past.

The fish should be neatly, even artfully, displayed and surrounded by crushed ice. A seller who takes pride in his or her offerings will likely have a good product to sell.

The counter and surrounding areas should be sparkling clean, without any pools of murky liquid.

The fish should be handled with care when it is being selected and packed so the flesh is not bruised or torn.

Ask the counterperson for recommendations on which fish to choose and the best ways to cook it. A person who knows how to best cook a particular fish will likely know how to choose it too.

Note that in the interest of marketing, fish may come under many different and deliberately confusing names. A California white sea bass is really a type of croaker, a Pacific snapper is not at all like the East Coast snapper, a salmon labeled "wild caught" will quite often be ordinary farm-raised fish. This is another reason to buy from a knowledgeable and trustworthy fishmonger.

IDENTIFYING FRESH FISH

Learn to identify a really fresh whole fish. Basically, the fish should look alive, with skin and scales that glisten. Ask for the freshest fish, even though it might be a kind you haven't tried before.

A fresh fish will have a clean, bracing smell like the ocean; there should be no strong or unpleasant odor, either at the fish counter or from the individual fish.

For whole fish, look at the eyes: they should be bright and clear. Cloudy, dull, or sunken eyes usually indicates the fish is old, with a few exceptions for deep-water fish, such as grouper or ocean perch.

The gills, which contain a lot of blood, deteriorate very quickly. They should be luminous pinkish-red, never brownish or dried out.

The texture of a fresh fish will be springy, not at all soft. When pressed gently, the flesh should spring back without leaving a depression.

For fish fillets, it's a little more challenging to gauge freshness. As the fish ages, the flesh will turn from almost translucent to opaque. So, the freshest fillet is the clearest. The skin, if present, should be brightly colored, not dull.

Storing Fresh Fish

The key to good fish is keeping it cold, and crushed ice is the best way to do so—cubed ice will bruise the fish's delicate flesh. Once you get your fish home, keep it on ice, or place the fish in a plastic bag, then put it on top of the "blue ice" used in a cooler chest. Store it in the coldest part of the refrigerator: in a drawer, not on the door. In hot weather, super-chill fish by placing it in the freezer for an hour or so first. While cooking it the same day you buy it is best, if the fish is quite fresh and you keep it quite cold, you may cook it within two days of purchase.

CUTS OF FRESH FISH

Whole Round: This is a whole fish that has been gutted and scaled, and perhaps the fins trimmed, but otherwise left alone. For most fish, allow one full pound per serving.

Pan-Dressed Fish: This is a fish that has been gutted and scaled and with the head, tail, and fins removed. Allow one half to three-quarters of a pound per serving.

Fish Steak: These are pan-ready, crosswise slices cut from larger fish, such as salmon, halibut, or cod. Allow one-third to one-half pound per serving.

Fish Fillet: These are pan-ready portions of fish cut lengthwise with the backbone removed. They may or may not have had the pin bones removed (*see* About Pin Bones page 419). Fish fillets with the skin on will cook up juicier; those without the skin will shrink more and dry out more quickly. Allow one-half pound per serving.

416

Frozen Fish

With recent technological advances, fish may be cleaned and flash-frozen (frozen quickly at very cold temperatures) virtually moments after they are caught. These fish are called Frozen-at-Sea (F.A.S.). Flash-freezing instantly freezes the water inside fish tissues, preserving juices and maximizing flavor and texture when cooked. Frozen-at-Sea fish is likely to be in better shape that "fresh" fish that have sat in a hold at sea for days before sale. Some fish is frozen twice—once at sea, once again after it's been filleted.

To determine if a fish has been properly frozen, check its appearance as you would with fresh fish. It should be somewhat shiny and have no white freezer-burn spots. The fish should be hard as a rock, showing no evidence of previous defrosting (although just defrosted F.A.S. salmon is a reasonable choice, if used immediately). Buy frozen fish where there is high turnover. The freezer should be quite cold, clean, and without excessive frost. The package should be well sealed and it should be a maximum of three months old.

Thaw slowly in the refrigerator overnight. If that is not possible, run the sealed fish under cold, not warm, water. Once it is mostly thawed, cook the fish as quickly as possible, because frozen fish will tend to give off its juices. Fully thawed fish may be dry and mushy when cooked.

SUPER-FRESH FISH

Connoisseurs of fish know that how the fish was caught is paramount. Was it line-caught (preferable) or net-caught? Was the fish stunned immediately after being landed? Was it bled and gutted on board as soon as it landed? Was it iced properly, and was it kept cold all the way to market? Most of us don't have access to fish that is treated with such care, although in areas with a high expectation of freshness, such as Seattle, Washington, and Maine, these questions are being asked more and more by buyers of top-quality fish.

Cooking Fresh Fish

For best results when cooking fish, avoid overcooking it. Most fish is quite lean, so that once cooked, it will easily dry out. Fish is ready when it's barely done in the middle, so it's still juicy. When sautéing, be sure to get the pan really hot, so the fish browns well and cooks quickly. The trend has been to cook fish less and less. In many restaurants, tuna is only seared on the outside and salmon is served medium-rare, like a beef steak. At home, you might want to cook the fish fully, but always cook it to the minimum of doneness. A rule-of-thumb is to cook fish ten minutes for every inch of thickness.

With our oceans slowly being depleted of once-abundant fish, choosing the right fish is an important decision. The Chilean sea bass (renamed from Patagonian Toothfish), for example, became such a popular restaurant and banquet item that the once-large fish are now only being caught much smaller. The fish just aren't getting the chance to grow big, and supplies are getting smaller.

A few of the questions that may be asked in the interest of conservation include:

If the fish is farmed, what type of production system is used?

If the fish is wild caught, where was it caught and by what method (line, net, long-line)?

Are there similar fish to choose that are environmentally friendly alternatives?

Some fish, especially very large ones, carry high levels of mercury and PCB's or may harbor parasites, and are best avoided.

Go to www.environmentaldefense.org/documents/1980_pocket_seafood_selector.pdf to download an easy-to-use Pocket Seafood Selector provided by Ocean's Alive, an environmental defense organization to make eco-friendly choices when buying fish and seafood.

Nantucket Smoked Bluefish Paté with Rosemary Crostini

Some years back I was lucky enough to spend several summers on the fish-eater's paradise island of Nantucket. The superb Straight Wharf fish restaurant there serves a version of this smoked bluefish paté. If you don't have access to Jamaican Pickapeppa Sauce, substitute Worcestershire Sauce.

SERVES 8

1 pound smoked bluefish
$^1/_2$ pound cream cheese, softened
1 small sweet or red onion, peeled and quartered
1 tablespoon Jamaican Pickapeppa sauce
  (*see* Pickapeppa Sauce, page 231)
1 tablespoon hot sauce
$^1/_4$ cup chopped dill
$^1/_4$ cup chopped Italian parsley
Rosemary Crostini (recipe follows)

Trim the bluefish by removing the skin, dark flesh, and any bones. Flake the bluefish by hand and reserve.

Whip the cream cheese in a mixer or food processor until smooth and light. Add onion and process again until smooth. Add Pickapeppa and hot sauce and mix for about half a minute. Remove mixture from processor and place in a bowl.

Stir bluefish, dill, and parsley into the cream cheese mixture. Refrigerate, well covered. Serve with Rosemary Crostini.

Rosemary Crostini

1 loaf Italian country bread, sliced $1/4$- to $1/2$-inch-thick, then cut into 2-inch-wide strips

2 tablespoons finely chopped fresh rosemary

$1/2$ cup fruity green olive oil

Preheat the oven to 375°F.

Arrange the bread in a single layer on a baking sheet. Combine the rosemary and oil and brush the mixture lightly on both sides of each slice of bread. Toast for 5 minutes, then turn and toast 5 minutes longer, or until golden.

NANTUCKET-STYLE BROILED BLUEFISH

In this quick dish, spicy-herbal gin cuts the oiliness of the fish. Brush bluefish fillets with melted butter, sprinkle with dried onion flakes, and broil. When the fish starts to brown, mix more melted butter with gin and flame. Serve immediately.

ABOUT PIN BONES

Pin bones bones run crosswise to the backbones, starting from the head end and running about one-third of the way back along the length of the fish. There is one pin bone per muscle layer. Those at the head end of the fish will be larger and tougher to pull out. Ask the fishmonger to remove them, or use needle-nosed pliers, tweezers, or stainless steel fish pliers to pull them out.

Venetian–Style Sole in Sweet and Sour Sauce: Sogliola in Soar

In earlier times, when refrigeration was nonexistent, fish would be fried and then marinated in vinegar to preserve it. This dish was called escabeche. *The sweet-and-sour version here is popular today in Venice, where it is made with the delicately flavored, small, firm sole that are caught in the Adriatic and not in the Mediterranean. It is also prepared with small, fresh sardines, called* sarde. *This is a dish that should made a day ahead of time, but bring it to room temperature before serving. Serve as a first course. True sole only live across the Atlantic in the English Channel and also in the Adriatic. In America, we call several different types of flounder "sole," such as Rex and Petrale Sole on the West Coast and Lemon Sole on the East Coast. (See the sidebar on page 426 for more information about East Coast flounders.)*

SERVES 6

6 small flounder fillets

Kosher salt and freshly ground black pepper to taste

$1/4$ pound (1 cup) all-purpose flour

$1/2$ cup extra-virgin olive oil, divided

1 red onion, thinly sliced

2 to 3 carrots, cut into matchsticks or shredded

$1/4$ cup tarragon vinegar

2 tablespoons granulated sugar

$1/4$ cup currants, soaked in warm water to cover until soft, about 15 minutes

$1/2$ cup pine nuts, lightly toasted at 300°F.

Sprinkle flounder fillets on both sides with salt and pepper. Dust with flour.

Heat $1/4$ cup of the olive oil in a large skillet, preferably nonstick. Brown the fish lightly on both sides. Remove from pan and reserve. To the same pan, add the red onion and carrots and cook briefly. Add the tarragon vinegar, sugar, and salt and pepper and bring the mixture to the boil. Cook 2 to 3 minutes, or until the liquid is thick enough and bubbling all over.

Using a wooden spoon or rubber spatula, scrape up any brown bits from the pan and pour the liquid over the fish. Drizzle the fish with the remaining $1/4$ cup of olive oil, sprinkle with currants and pine nuts, and marinate overnight in the refrigerator before serving.

Sautéed Striped Bass with Artichokes, Lime, and Olives

I served this crowd-pleasing Mediterranean-style dish to hundreds of happy customers at my last restaurant gig. It's actually easy to make at home, once you've got the fish. Substitute hybrid striped bass (a farm-raised fish), sea bass, or red snapper, or even fresh fluke or flounder. Though I love fresh-prepped and cooked artichokes, my kitchen staff rebelled against the endless paring and cleaning necessary. That was one battle I lost and even in the restaurant I would use the high-quality frozen artichoke heart wedges sold by Trader Joe's. Bottled artichokes just won't do. While it gives a richer seafood flavor and more body to the dish, the clam broth can be left out. If you make the dish in the summer when tomatoes abound, use multicolored diced heirloom tomatoes.

Serve with steamed rice or mashed potatoes to soak up the delicious juices.

SERVES 6

6 (8-ounce) portions striped bass fillet

Kosher salt and freshly ground black pepper to taste

$1/2$ cup mixed canola and olive oil, for sautéing

$1/4$ pound (1 cup) all-purpose flour

1 lime, all green skin and bitter white pith cut away, cut into thin slices

2 cups diced fresh tomatoes (yellow and red preferred)

$1/2$ cup sliced green olives

1 cup artichoke wedges (half of a 12-ounce bag)

$1/2$ cup clam broth

$1/2$ cup white wine

4 tablespoons unsalted butter, softened

2 teaspoons chopped thyme

2 tablespoons chopped parsley

Season the fish on both sides with salt and pepper. Heat the oil in a large skillet, preferably nonstick, until shimmering. Dust the fish with flour, shaking off the excess. Place in the skillet, skin side-down, and brown well. Turn over and brown on the flesh side.

Add the lime slices, tomatoes, olives, artichokes, clam broth, and wine. Bring to the boil, add the fish and cook until the fish flakes, about 5 minutes. (If the fish is large and dense, cover, and reduce the heat so it has a chance to cook through.) Just before serving, swirl in the butter, add the thyme and parsley, and serve immediately.

The striped bass, *Morone saxatilis*, is known in the Chesapeake Bay where seventy to ninety percent of the Atlantic stock is born, variously as striper, rockfish, linesider, roller, squidhound, and greenhead. It has been one of the most sought-after fish since colonial times for its succulent, firm, white flesh, marvelous texture, and flavor. If you have the chance to buy a true wild-caught "striper," snap it up. Its smaller cousin, the hybrid striped bass, a cross of a striped bass and a white bass, is an acceptable and more easily found substitute. Striped bass are found from the St. Lawrence River, Canada to the St. John's River, Florida; and from Lake Pontchartrain, Louisiana, to the Atlantic.

Striped bass range in color from light green to olive, steel blue, brown, or black with iridescent silvery white undersides. They get their name from the seven or eight prominent continuous stripes that mark their silvery sides. Although most fish caught today are much smaller, stripers have been known to reach one hundred pounds and nearly five feet in length, and are legendary among sport fisherman for their fighting ability. Overfishing of this prized and high-priced fish in the Chesapeake Bay has made catches smaller. In the interest of conservation, they are available only at certain times and from certain states in limited quantities.

Baked Sea Bass in Cartoccio

In cartoccio is the Italian equivalent of the French en papillote: both are cooked in a parchment paper bag (often substituted by aluminum foil). This is a wonderful way to cook fish, because all the juices stay inside and the fish comes out moist with an incredible fragrance as the paper bag is cut open at the table. It also has the advantage of being made ahead. Just bake the fish at high temperature when you're ready to serve. The inky-black, oil-cured olives come from Southern Italy, Sicily, and North Africa and are pungent in flavor and dramatic in appearance. The combination of flavors here is typical of Mediterranean fish cookery and dates back to my early days as chef of an Italian restaurant. In Italy, orata, or sea bream, is commonly prepared this way, but any mildly flavored, white-fleshed fish will work well. You'll need four sheets of parchment paper, available at baking supply stores, or substitute four large squares of heavy-duty aluminum foil.

421

SERVES 4

4 (6 to 8-ounce) fillets of sea bass, skin-on preferred
Kosher salt and freshly ground black pepper to taste
2 cups Marinara Sauce, homemade (*see* page 895)
   or purchased
2 lemons, all yellow skin and bitter white pith cut away,
   cut into thin slices
$1/4$ cup pitted, halved oil-cured olives
2 tablespoons drained capers
$1/4$ cup chopped Italian parsley

Season the fish with salt and pepper. Have ready four sheets of parchment paper cut into large squares about 18 inches on a side. Fold each paper in half to form a triangle. Place each fillet on one square of paper, just forward of the fold line, along the edge of the triangle.

Spoon one quarter of the sauce onto the fish. Sprinkle each portion with a quarter of the lemons, olives, capers, and parsley, leaving a 1-inch border around the edges.

Form paper packets by folding the paper over top of the fish so that both edges meet. Form pleated folds at one edge, then tuck the folds under all around the outside edge of the paper packet to seal. Keep folding until the packet is completely closed, twisting the end and tucking it underneath. Alternatively, enclose the fish in heavy-duty aluminum foil packets. Although not as esthetically pleasing, the foil is easier to handle and less likely to leak.

When ready to cook, preheat the oven to 425°F. Arrange the packets on a metal baking pan (to catch any leaks) and bake 12 to 15 minutes, or until the liquid inside boils vigorously and the paper puffs up. Serve the packets immediately on large dinner plates, allowing each person to cut open their own.

422

SEA BASS

Black sea bass, *Centropristis striata,* is a popular fish in Chinese restaurants, where it is often fried whole and called Hunan fish. Look for it in Asian markets, especially from September to March, when the catch is largest. Abundant at one time, sea bass have been declining in size and numbers. They are found along the Atlantic Coast from Cape Cod to Florida, and are most abundant between New Jersey and North Carolina.

This stout-bodied fish has a long dorsal fin, large pectoral and pelvic fins, and a rounded tail. Its skin is deep smoky gray and its belly is only slightly lighter in color. The most common-sized sea bass weigh 1 to 2 pounds, small enough to cook whole. This firm, white, lean fish is a kitchen favorite. Sea bass are relatively easy to fillet because of their firm flesh. Take care not to overcook, because this lean fish will easily dry out.

Whole Roasted Sea Bass in Charmoula

Charmoula is a versatile Moroccan spice and herb mixture that lends its bold character here to this whole roasted fish. If sea bass isn't available, substitute red snapper, hybrid striped bass, or even better, Mediterranean branzino. Ask the fish monger to clean and scale the fish only. Save any extra charmoula in the refrigerator and use it for other recipes.

SERVES 4 TO 6

Charmoula Dressing

MAKES ABOUT 1 1/2 CUPS

1/2 cup extra-virgin olive oil

Juice of 2 lemons (about 1/4 cup)

1 tablespoon chopped garlic

2 tablespoons sweet red paprika

1 tablespoon ground cumin, preferably toasted

2 teaspoons Aleppo pepper or other hot red pepper flakes

Kosher salt and freshly ground black pepper to taste

1/4 cup chopped cilantro

1/4 cup chopped Italian parsley

Put the olive oil, lemon juice, garlic, paprika, cumin, hot pepper, salt, and pepper into the bowl of a blender and puree until smooth and creamy. Remove the charmoula from the blender and stir in the herbs.

Fish

1 (2-to 3-pound) whole sea bass, cleaned and scaled
1 cup Charmoula Dressing

Cut three parallel slits into both sides the fish, with the deepest slit cut through the thickest flesh at the head end and the shallowest at the tail end. Rub the fish all over and inside the slits with about $1/2$ cup of the charmoula. Refrigerate while marinating at least 1 hour and up to overnight.

When ready to bake, preheat the oven to 425°F. Place the fish on a rack, if available, or propped up on crumpled aluminum foil over a metal baking pan with a couple of cups of water in it to prevent the drippings from smoking and burning.

Roast 20 to 30 minutes, depending on the size of the fish. Test by cutting a slit into the thickest part of the flesh at the head end. If the flesh is opaque all the way through, the fish is done.

To serve, cut the flesh away from the bone and serve with the remaining charmoula drizzled over top of each portion.

Turkish Baked Bluefish

Bluefish is landed in great quantities near Istanbul along the Bosphorus in season in January, where it is fished with line and lamp. The city of Istanbul occupies a unique location, half in Europe, half in Asia. Splitting the city in half is the Bosphorus, the strait connecting the Mediterranean to the Black Sea. I took a day trip on one of the local ferries that zigzagged back and forth from Europe to Asia, all the way to the mouth of the Black Sea, stopping for a most memorable lunch at one of the numerous outdoor fish restaurants that line the shores. Bluefish weren't in season then (April), so I ate other local, seasonal fish prepared in similar style. I recently prepared this dish with small croakers given to me by my neighbor, who is an avid sport fisherman. Although bony, the small, tasty fish were absolutely delicious. This dish is best suited to a dark, fleshed, oily-type fish of the kind that is so full of beneficial Omega-3's, such as croaker, mahi-mahi, or mackerel. Serve with either the Golden Potato Mash with Garlic and Green Olive Oil or Horseradish Mashed Potatoes (see pages 761 and 762).

423

SERVES 6

2 pounds fillet of bluefish, as young and fresh as possible
2 teaspoons kosher salt
$1/4$ cup fresh lemon juice, divided
1 red onion, cut into strips
2 teaspoons chopped garlic
$1/4$ cup extra-virgin olive oil, divided
1 (28-ounce) can diced tomatoes
  (or one 26-ounce box Pomi)
2 teaspoons paprika
6 bay leaves
$1/2$ cup chopped Italian parsley

½ teaspoon freshly ground black pepper

1 lemon, cut into wedges, for garnish

Trim and de-bone the fish. Rub all over with the salt and 2 tablespoons of the lemon juice and reserve.

Sauté the onion and garlic in 2 tablespoons of the olive oil. Add the tomatoes and paprika and bring to the boil. Boil 5 minutes to thicken lightly.

Preheat the oven to 425°F. Spread half the sauce onto the bottom of a large baking dish. Drain the fish and arrange over top. Spoon the remaining sauce over top. Garnish each fillet with 1 bay leaf. Whisk together the remaining 2 tablespoons lemon juice, 2 tablespoons olive oil, the parsley, and black pepper and drizzle over the fish.

Bake 15 to 20 minutes, or until the fish flakes. Garnish each portion with a lemon wedge and serve.

Bluefish

Bluefish, *Pomatomus saltator,* is a great game fish, well respected for the tremendous fight it gives to the fisherman and renowned for its voracious appetite. Fishing for bluefish progresses up the eastern seaboard of the U.S. from spring to summer to fall. The flavor of bluefish is delicate in pan-sized "snapper" or "snapping" blues; slightly stronger in medium sized "harbor blues," and most pronounced in large fish.

Though both seasonal and local, I found it hard to sell bluefish at Philadelphia area restaurants. Around the Mediterranean, especially in Turkey and Tunisia, people think of the exact same species of fish as exclusively local and it's a favorite at waterside restaurants. The Turks love bluefish so much, they have five specific names, each for a different size of fish. They range from the small "bay leaf fish" to the full-sized "yellow wing."

Bluefish is soft and deteriorates quickly out of the water, so be sure to keep it cold. I often request a bag of crushed ice at the fish counter and keep my fish in a plastic bag, resting on the ice. Plan to cook this inexpensive, omega-3 oil-rich fish the day you buy it, or marinate it and cook the next day.

MAHI-MAHI

Mahi-mahi, *Coryphaena hippurus*, was long known as dolphin or dorado. Although not related to the mammal dolphin, the mahi-mahi has had a name change, using its Hawaiian name, which means "strong-strong," so that people wouldn't get turned of by the idea of eating Flipper. This strikingly beautiful fish has a brilliant iridescent bluish-green and gold body, golden yellow fins, and a forked tail. Mahi-mahi averages three to six pounds, but may reach seventy pounds and five feet in length. It has a distinctive sloped head, with the male's being more rounded in shape.

It is found in the warm tropical and subtropical waters of the Caribbean, Gulf of Mexico, Hawaii, and the Gulf Coast of Florida.

Mahi-mahi are most plentiful in April through August, with May being the heaviest month. In Central and South America its season runs from November until March. Almost always sold in fillet form, the meat should be firm and pink to light beige in color and a clear red, rather than brownish, central blood line. The older and larger the fish, the darker the meat and the stronger the taste. Mahi-mahi is an exceptionally versatile fish with firm, light-colored, moist meat and a pleasing, not-too-strong flavor.

Mahi-Mahi with Corn–Tomato–Red Onion Ragout

Crunchy kernels of milky sweet corn mixed with sweet-tart juicy tomato, and pungently fragrant field-grown basil combine perfectly in a dish of summer perfection here. This is a quick, tasty, and colorful way to prepare fish in summertime. Substitute baby bluefish fillet or even young mackerel.

SERVES 4

4 (6- to 8-ounce) small mahi-mahi fillets
Kosher salt and freshly ground black pepper to taste
$^1/_4$ cup olive oil, divided
1 small red onion, diced
1 cup diced yellow and red tomatoes
Kernels from 2 ears corn
$^1/_4$ cup thin strips of basil
Lime wedges

Sprinkle salt and pepper all over fillets. In a large skillet, preferably cast-iron or nonstick, heat 3 tablespoons of the oil until shimmering, and brown the fillets on both sides, starting with the flesh-side down. Remove from pan, keeping warm.

Pour off any excess oil, add the remaining 1 tablespoon oil and the red onion and fry 1 to 2 minutes, or until fragrant. Add the tomatoes and corn to the pan. Sauté until brightly colored but still firm, season with salt and pepper and stir in basil. Transfer the mixture to a serving plate and top with bluefish. Serve with lime wedges.

Yuca-Crusted Flounder

This is a dish of Nuevo Latino cuisine, where Latin American ingredients are used with modern, often French-inspired techniques. The original dish was made with a potato crust in France. Latino chefs came up with the idea of using yuca to crust the Caribbean fish, red snapper. I tasted it and thought it could be adapted to the more easily found flounder. It's an easy dish to make, because the grated yuca just has to be pressed on to the fish. It is then quickly pan-fried. Serve the fish with fresh, spicy salsa or simply with a wedge of lime. (See the chapter on Yuca on page 1020 for more information on that vegetable.)

SERVES 4

1 yuca
4 (6- to 8-ounce) flounder fillets, trimmed
Kosher salt and freshly ground black pepper to taste
$^1/_2$ cup extra-virgin olive oil, divided
$^1/_4$ cup chopped cilantro
2 limes, cut in half

Have ready a large bowl of cold water. Cut off and discard $^1/_2$ inch off from the tips and bottoms of the yuca. Using a heavy knife, cut the yuca in half lengthwise. Using a sharp paring knife or a potato peeler, pare the yuca of its outer brown skin and inner purple-colored layer until only the white flesh remains. Place peeled yuca in water while preparing so that it doesn't darken. Grate the yuca into thin shreds using the medium-sized hole on a box grater.

Lay the fish fillets flesh-side up on a sheet of wax paper, and season both sides with salt and pepper. Press the shredded yuca onto the flesh on both sides. Pat the yuca into position to seal in and protect the flesh; the yuca is glutinous and will adhere to itself.

Preheat the oven to 350°F. Heat 2 tablespoons of the oil in a large skillet, preferably cast-iron or nonstick, over medium-high heat. Place the fish in the pan without crowding and brown the fish until the yuca is softened and golden brown, 2 to 3 minutes. Turn with a long spatula and brown on the skin side. Remove from the pan and place in a large baking pan, flesh-side up. Repeat with remaining fillets, adding the remaining oil as needed.

When all the fish has been browned, place the baking pan in the oven and bake about 5 minutes, until the flesh is cooked through. Sprinkle with cilantro and serve with lime wedges.

FLOUNDER

Flounder are a highly desirable fish in the kitchen, renowned for their fine, tender, yet firm texture. They have a delicate, sweet flavor that is easily overpowered. Flounder are most often cooked in fillet form. Note that inexpensive flounder fillets may be treated with a preservative. Although relatively innocuous in flavor, flounder has the advantage of being readily available in fish markets up and down the East Coast. Sand dab or petrale sole would be a good West Coast substitute.

Winter flounder, *Pseuopleuronectes americanus*, a brown-skinned flatfish, is the most common shallow-water flatfish in North America. Flounders may be either right or left-sided. Although they start out as round fish with eyes on either side of their head, as they mature, they flatten out and their eyes shift toward one side or the other of the head. Winter flounder is a right-sided flounder, while summer flounder is a left-sided flounder. On some fish, the tail area on the eyeless side is yellow, so that it is sometimes called "lemon sole." The winter flounder spends its adult life in the ocean during the summer, but moves into estuaries in colder weather. It may weigh up to eight pounds and may grow to as much as twenty-five inches in length. Winter flounder produce both a white and a gray fillet from each fish, but both turn pure white when cooked.

Summer Flounder, *Paralichthys dentatus,* has brownish skin with conspicuous black spots on the top side; its bottom side is almost white. However, the fish can use color adaptation to match the bay or ocean bottom and may partially bury itself for camouflage. These fish come close to shore during the summer and in most areas retreat to deeper, warmer waters for the winter. Also called *fluke*, the summer flounder is one of the larger flounders, weighing as much as twenty-six pounds as much as three feet in length. Its meat is delicately flavored, bright white in color, firm, and quite pleasing in flavor. and quite delicious.

Flounder is quite lean, so care must be taken not to overcook it. As soon as the flesh is opaque, it is done. Because it flakes easily, it is not suitable to stir-frying or grilling. It is often stuffed or rolled and baked or poached. Fillets from larger fish may be baked in a sauce or coated and pan-fried as above.

Halibut with Lemongrass Crust and Mango–Mint Chutney

Breadcrumbs flavored with aromatics have become a favorite and easy way to adorn fish, meats, and poultry in many restaurants; the crust also provides moisture, protecting the flesh from drying out, and texture, with that oh-so-important crunch. This Southeast Asian-accented dish was originally made with Chilean sea bass, now in such short supply that I don't recommend using it (see Environmentally Conscious Fish Buying, page 418 for more on this). Large, firm, white-fleshed halibut fillets make an excellent substitute during their season from spring until late fall. Because of the mild flavor of this fish, it shows off the spicy, aromatic lemongrass, ginger, and cilantro featured here. Serve it with Mango-Mint Chutney and fragrant jasmine rice. The halibut can be prepared with its crust up to one day before cooking.

SERVES 6

¹⁄₄ cup roughly chopped shallots

2 tablespoons roughly chopped peeled ginger

2 tablespoons thinly sliced lemongrass hearts

¹⁄₄ cup cilantro leaves

2 tablespoons canola oil

¹⁄₂ cup Japanese panko breadcrumbs

¹⁄₄ cup natural sesame seeds

Kosher salt and freshly ground black pepper to taste

2¹⁄₂ pounds halibut fillet

2 cups Mango-Mint Chutney (*see* page 575)

Process together the shallots, ginger, and lemongrass. When processed to a chunky paste, add the cilantro and process again. Remove the mixture from the processor and stir in the oil, panko, sesame seeds, and salt and pepper. Reserve.

Cut the halibut into equal portions. Season the fish with salt and pepper and allow it to rest about 10 minutes at room temperature. Pat one sixth of the crust all over the top, bottom, and sides of each fillet.

Preheat the oven to 450°F. Arrange fish on a parchment-paper- or Silpat-lined baking pan and bake 15 minutes, or until lightly browned and the fish is opaque and flakes. Remove from the oven and serve immediately accompanied or topped by the Mango-Mint Chutney.

HALIBUT

The largest of the flatfish and cousin to the sole and flounder, halibut (same for both singular and plural) is fished in the cold northern waters of both the North American Atlantic and Pacific Coasts. Halibut is the largest of the flatfish and one of the largest of the salt-water fish that may weigh over six hundred pounds, although the more common-sized fish weighs from five to one hundred pounds.

The Pacific halibut, *Hippoglossus stenolepsis*, is fished extensively in Alaska (where eighty percent of the catch is found) and British Columbia, in season from March 15 through November 15. Halibut is also fished in Russia and Japan and the Bering Strait. Russian and Japanese halibut are smaller, but have higher oil content. The Atlantic halibut, *Hippoglossus hippoglos-sus*, ranges through the deeper waters of the western Atlantic from Labrador to the Gulf of Maine. Halibut are caught largely close to shore and are now also being farmed.

Halibut have a large mouth and a forked tail, with a long body that is greenish-brown to dark brown on its upper-eyed side, with its blind side ranging from white to gray or mottled gray-white. This lean fish has fine-textured, snow-white flesh with few bones; its gray-brown skin is also edible, although it is often removed. Its mild, adaptable flavor and high nutritional value make it a favorite among fish lovers, so that it also commands a high price. When cooked, it is tender and flaky, though still firm, and quite lean, so it is important not to over-cook it. Small halibut are called chicken halibut, while large adults are called whales. Halibut is sold fresh whole, as steaks, and as fillets.

GAME MEATS & BIRDS

GAME MEATS & BIRDS

Game Meats

Unless you're a hunter, any "game" you've tasted has, in all likelihood, been farm-raised—a term that can mean a whole lot of things. Some animals are free to range and eat a varied diet; others are more like farm animals that are caged and eat a limited diet. This makes a big difference in the character of their flavor. Some pheasants may indeed "taste like chicken," because they're fed a grain diet just like a chicken; others are allowed to peck outside and eat what they will so their flavor will be more complex and "gamey." These birds will be more expensive, but also tastier and closer to hunter's fare. The same goes for venison, which may taste "like veal" or like robust game.

Because I don't have many friends who hunt, I've only tasted true wild game while traveling abroad. The recipes in this chapter were tested using farm-raised game. About twenty years ago, companies such as D'Artagnan (www.dartagnan.com) started selling a wide range of game to American chefs and now to home cooks. Today, with the Internet, anyone can now cook up a game dinner, whether you are a hunter or not.

Game is the flesh of wild animals or birds that are hunted for food and sport. However, even in early times, animals and birds were reared especially to provide a stock of game for hunting for the lord of the manor. Although many game animals are indigenous to the U.S. (bear and bison) others (boar and antelope) have been imported to stock large game preserves. Note that it is illegal in the United States to sell wild-caught game meat or birds in a restaurant, though of course, we're allowed to eat wild-caught fish with no problem.

In America, deer is the most widely hunted large game; rabbit and squirrel are the most common small game. Whether the animal comes from the market or the hunter, the quality of the meat is determined by its age, diet, the time of year, and how it was handled after the kill. Game is generally best in the fall, after the animals have enjoyed plentiful spring and summer feeding. Its robust and primeval flavor makes venison and other game perfectly suited to autumnal flavors like wild mushrooms, cranberries, juniper berries, sage, fennel, and savory. Note that the game found in the supermarket or specialty store must be federally inspected just like beef or pork.

Wild game animals will be leaner and tougher than either farm-raised "wild" game or domesticated animals because they get more exercise. They are often aged to help break down their flesh and make it more tender. Younger game animals will be more tender and even leaner. Any fat in wild animals is generally rank-tasting and should be trimmed and discarded. With the exception of the tender "middle meats" including the rib and loin section, game meats should be cooked slowly, being careful not to overcook them. They take well to moist-heat cooking, such as braising, and stewing. Because they have a different diet and lifestyle, farm-raised game animals will be fatter and more tender than truly wild game and are suited to cooking as you would veal, lamb, or pork.

Game Birds

Wild game birds include large birds like wild turkey and goose, medium-sized birds like pheasant and wild duck, and small birds like partridge and quail. Many game birds are farm-raised, including mallard ducks, guinea hen, quail, pheasant, partridge, pigeon, and "wild turkey." Game birds are most often found frozen, though fresh birds may be available by special order. For fresh birds, choose one with a pleasant aroma and moist-looking skin that is not dull or dry.

Young birds will have a flexible breastbone that is cartilaginous at the neck end, not hard and bony. Wild birds are much leaner than domesticated and are usually basted (brushed with fat), barded (wrapped in thin sheets of pork fatback), or larded (stuck with small chunks of fatback or bacon) before roasting to provide moisture in the form of extra fat. Older birds are best braised or cooked in rich, spiced stews.

COOKING GAME BIRDS

Most chefs cook game birds to 170°F. for dark meat and 165°F. for light meat. Farm-raised game birds are usually not crowded into pens and therefore are not as susceptible to salmonella bacteria; this meat can normally be safely cooked to these temperatures. In fact, duck breast is often cooked rare, like a steak. However, for those whose immune system is compromised, follow the U.S.D.A. recommendations. Cook whole birds or dark meat to 180°F. measured at the thickest point of thigh, and cook the breast or light meat to 170°F..

Grilled Quail with Honey-Poached Pears and Watercress Salad

Small, deliciously mild, tender, and juicy quail are marinated with cinnamon and ginger and then broiled or grilled. They are served over a wintertime salad of firm, poached Bosc pears and peppery watercress. By cooking the pear-poaching liquid down to a syrup and adding it to the dressing, all the flavors come together. You can often find glove-boned quail (with the rib-cage removed), which will make the birds easier to eat (see Glove-Boning a Bird, page 261, for directions to do it yourself). As an appetizer, one bird is enough; as a main dish, two quail are the usual portion. I use Bosc pears here for their elegant shape and firm texture. (See the Pears chapter for more about Boscs.)

SERVES 8

Honey-Poached Pears

1 cup white wine

3 bay leaves

2 teaspoons coriander seeds

2 teaspoons peppercorns

$^1/_2$ cup honey

4 Bosc pears

Juice of 1 lemon

Prepare poaching liquid by combining the wine, bay leaves, coriander, peppercorns, and honey and bringing to the boil in a nonreactive pot.

Meanwhile, peel the pears, rubbing each with lemon juice as it's done. Place pears in liquid and bring back to the boil. Reduce heat and simmer 10 to 15 minutes, or until pears are soft when pricked with a skewer. Cool pears in

431

poaching liquid, then strain, reserving the poaching liquid.

When cool, split the pears in half. Remove the center seed section, using a small melon baller for neatest results. Cut the pears into wedges and reserve.

Grilled Quail

8 semi-boneless quail

$^1/_4$ cup canola oil

2 tablespoons honey

1 tablespoon grated ginger

1 teaspoon ground cinnamon

Kosher salt and freshly ground black pepper to taste

Cut the quail open along one side of the backbone, then cut away the backbone and discard. Flatten the quail. Whisk together remaining ingredients and use to marinate quail at least 24 and up to 48 hours.

Preheat a grill, preferably charcoal, or the broiler. Grill quail on both sides, cooking as slowly as possible, with the lid on, until the quail are just cooked through, about 20 minutes total. Alternatively, broil at high heat, turning as necessary, until browned and just cooked through, about 15 minutes.

Assembly

1 cup Pear-Poaching Syrup

3 tablespoons cider vinegar

6 tablespoons walnut oil

1 shallot, chopped

Kosher salt and freshly ground black pepper to taste

1 bunch watercress, large stems discarded

In a small pot, boil the poaching liquid until syrupy. Whisk in the cider vinegar, walnut oil, shallot, salt, and pepper. Dress the watercress lightly and arrange on plates, top with a grilled quail, and serve immediately.

GAME COOKBOOKS

Game cookery is a subject covered best by specialized books. I recommend *The L.L Bean Game and Fish Cookbook* by Angus Cameron and Judith Jones; *Wild About Game* by Janie Hibbler; and *D'Artagnan's Glorious Game Cookbook* by Ariane Daguin, Georges Faison, and Joanna Pruess.

RED FRUITS

In French, *fruits rouges*, or red fruits, refer to a mixture of small red fruits such as cherries, red currants, raspberries, cranberries, and lingonberries, that are often combined in fruit sauces and preserves.

Alsatian Venison Medallions with Red Fruit Mustard Sauce

If you're looking for a good recipe for venison, go no further. This classic venison dish from the French province of Alsace combines the German and French influences of the region that has been, at one time, part of both countries. While no one can say this is a quick and easy dish, it is very satisfying to make, with the depth of flavor of a true reduction sauce infused with the flavors of the forest: juniper, bay leaf, red wine, and brandy. For best flavor, make Game Stock (see page 993); for a milder flavor, substitute chicken stock. Loin of lamb would make the best substitute if no venison can be found. Spaetzle with Brown Butter, Chives, and Toasted Breadcrumbs (see page 172) makes a perfect accompaniment.

SERVES 6

Red Fruit Mustard Sauce

1/4 cup red-currant jelly

2 tablespoons raspberry vinegar

1/4 cup white wine

1 shallot, chopped

2 tablespoons chopped fresh tarragon
   (or 2 teaspoons dried tarragon)

1 cup Game Stock (*see* page 993), veal stock,
   or chicken stock

1/2 cup fruit mustard (such as black currant or raspberry)
   or coarse-grain mustard

2 tablespoons unsalted butter

Splash of brandy

Kosher salt and freshly ground black pepper to taste

In a medium, heavy-bottomed sauce pot, cook the red-currant jelly until it starts to caramelize. Add the raspberry vinegar, wine, shallot, and tarragon. Bring to the boil and continue cooking 5 to 10 minutes, or until the liquid is thick and syrupy.

Pour in the Game Stock and reduce the sauce again until syrupy. Finally, whisk in the mustard, butter, and a splash of brandy, season with salt and pepper, and keep warm.

Place the reserved venison medallions on serving plates and ladle sauce over top.

Venison

2 1/2 pounds boneless venison loin

Kosher salt and freshly ground black pepper to taste

1/4 pound (1 cup) all-purpose flour, preferably unbleached

4 tablespoons unsalted butter

1/4 cup brandy

Cut the venison into 12 to 16 medallions. Using a meat pounder, lightly flatten the venison medallions. Season with salt and pepper and then dust with flour, shaking off the excess.

Heat the butter and then brown the venison on both sides. Remove from the pan and keep warm. Pour off the fat from the pan, and pour in the brandy. Warm it slightly and, averting your eyes, flame the brandy. When the flames have died out, scrape out the contents of the pan and add it to the reserved game stock.

433

Grilled Loin of Rabbit with Leek and Lime Cream Sauce

In Europe, where rabbit is a favorite meat often served for Sunday lunch, it is a barn-yard animal, and its cousin, the dark-meat hare, is considered game. In America, where rabbit has not yet caught on in any big way, rabbit is sufficiently exotic to be termed game. However, with its delicate flavor, especially in the tender, white loin used here, rabbit is easy to love and easy to prepare. The hardest part will likely be getting hold of the rabbit loin. With internet sales so easy, rabbit can be ordered from meat companies that specialize in game, such as D'Artagnan, and will arrive in a day or two in a chilled box, ready to cook.

SERVES 6

2 pounds boneless rabbit loin

$1/4$ cup Dijon mustard, divided

$1/2$ cup shredded basil leaves, divided

$1/4$ cup chopped shallots, divided

4 teaspoons chopped garlic, divided

Grated zest of 1 lime + juice of 4 limes, divided

$1/2$ cup breadcrumbs (homemade or Japanese panko)

Kosher salt and freshly ground black pepper to taste

1 bunch baby carrots, peeled with $1/2$ inch of top left on

3 to 4 small leeks, cleaned and cut into matchsticks

$1/2$ cup dry white vermouth

2 cups heavy cream

Trim rabbit loin of flanks and any connective tissue. (Optional: use trimmings to make a rabbit stock, reduce to a glaze and add to sauce at the last minute.)

Combine 2 tablespoons of mustard, $1/4$ cup basil, 2 tablespoons shallots, 2 teaspoons garlic, the lime zest and the juice of 2 limes, the breadcrumbs, and salt and pepper to taste. Roll the rabbit loins in this mixture and marinate at least 4 hours, or overnight if possible.

Preheat a grill or broiler. Set up a metal basket or bamboo steamer over a pot of boiling water. Add the carrots and leeks, cover, and steam for 3 to 4 minutes, or until they are crisp-tender and brightly colored. Drain and reserve.

Combine the remaining 2 tablespoons shallots, 2 teaspoons garlic, and the vermouth in a medium, heavy-bottomed nonreactive sauce pot. Bring to the boil, reduce heat, and simmer until reduced by half. Pour in the cream and reduce again by half. Season to taste with salt and pepper, stir in the remaining 2 tablespoons mustard and lime juice, and the remaining $1/4$ cup basil, and keep warm.

Grill or broil the rabbit loin until barely cooked through, 5 to 10 minutes. Remove from the heat, drape loosely with aluminum foil, and allow the meat to rest 5 to 10 minutes. Slice on the diagonal into medallions. Pour the reserved sauce onto individual serving plates. Arrange the rabbit over top and garnish with the carrots and leeks.

434

Moroccan Guinea Hen and Pear Tajine

In this delectable tajine, fragrant spices, exotic orange blossom water, firm juicy Asian pears, and prunes are combined with the wonderful African-native bird, the guinea hen, in a superb combination. Although the list of ingredients looks rather formidable, the results are well worth the effort. A tajine is a type of Moroccan stew cooked in a special pot with a conical lid. If you don't have a tajine, you can, of course, still get great results, though the presentation won't be as dramatic. The best substitute is a heavy enameled cast-iron or earthenware casserole that cooks evenly and retains the heat well. (For more about tajines, see page 436.) The use of rare and expensive saffron here shows that this is a dish for a special occasion or holiday. Serve over steamed couscous, following the directions on the package.

SERVES 8 TO 10

Sauce

2 cups chopped onions

2 tablespoons chopped garlic

1/4 cup chopped ginger

1/2 cup duck, or chicken fat, or olive oil, divided
(*see* Duck Fat, page 381)

1 quart chicken stock

1 tablespoon Ras-el-Hanout (*see* Ras-el-Hanout, page 436)

1 teaspoon crushed saffron threads

Kosher salt and freshly ground black pepper to taste

4 Guinea hens, quartered

2 large Asian pears, cut into wedges

1 pound small turnips, peeled, quartered, and soaked
in cold water

2 tablespoons granulated sugar

1/2 cup pitted prunes, cut in half

1/2 cup orange juice

2 teaspoons orange blossom water

1/2 cup almond slices, preferably skin-on, lightly
toasted at 300°F.

1/4 cup natural sesame seeds, lightly toasted at 300°F.

Couscous, steamed according to package instructions

In a tajine or a large casserole dish, cook the onions, garlic, and ginger in 2 tablespoons of the duck fat. Add the chicken stock, ras-el-hanout, saffron, and salt and pepper. Bring to the boil, reduce heat and simmer 15 to 20 minutes or until slightly reduced and well flavored.

In a large skillet, preferably cast-iron or nonstick, heat the remaining 2 tablespoons of duck fat and brown the Guinea hen quarters over medium heat until well-browned and crispy on all sides. Drain and cool.

When the hens are cool enough to handle, remove the rib cage and thigh bones, reserving bones for another stock, if desired. Add the partially boned hen quarters to the tajine (or casserole dish) and cook slowly for 30 minutes, or until the meat is tender.

Meanwhile, wipe out the skillet and brown the pears and turnips in the remaining 1/4 cup of duck fat, sprinkling with the sugar. Cook until the sugar has caramelized. Add the prunes, the orange juice, and orange blossom water and bring to the boil.

Transfer the contents of the skillet to the tajine (or casserole dish) and simmer until the hens, turnips, and pears are tender, and the juices syrupy, about 25 minutes. Sprinkle all with the almonds and sesame seeds and serve with steamed couscous on the side.

ABOUT TAJINES

A *tajine*, like a French *tian* or *étouffé*, is the name for a huge variety of rich Moroccan stews and the distinctive round shallow earthenware cooking pan with a cone-shaped lid in which the tajine is cooked. Its name derives from the Greek *teganon* (cooking pan) and is believed to date back to the small Greek colonies in North Africa. The Italian word *tegame*, or casserole, has the same origin. The rich, full-bodied flavor of a tajine comes from the tall, conical lid that captures the combined steam and juices from all of the ingredients and forces them to drip back into the shallow pan below. Tajines are made from fish, chicken, pigeon, lamb, and other meats and a wide variety of vegetables with lots of fragrant, spicy, and sweet flavoring ingredients such as dried fruits, olives, and preserved lemons. Many kitchen supply stores are now carrying tajines; some of which are meant only for serving and display, so be sure to get a "cooking tajine" meant for use over heat.

Ras-el-Hanout

In Morocco, *ras-el-hanout*, or *head of the market*, is an incredibly complex mixture representing the best the spice merchant has to offer. It may include such exotics as rose and lavender buds, grains of paradise, cubeb pepper, occasionally hashish, and even the notorious and dangerous supposed aphrodisiac, cantharides, better known as Spanish fly. More common spices used are allspice, black pepper, mace, cardamom, nutmeg, saffron, and cinnamon or cassia. Ras-el-hanout may be purchased from specialty spice merchants; substitute Arabic baharat or Indian garam masala.

GUINEA HENS

The guinea hen, *Numidia melagris*, is a medium-large bird, most similar to quail in flavor, with meat that is pinkish and quite lean. Quite meaty for their size, guinea fowl are native to Africa and Madagascar and were domesticated by the ancient Greeks and Romans. They are still popular in Italy—their Italian name, *faraona*, refers to the Egyptian pharaohs, because the birds were prolific in Egypt.

After dying out in Egypt about 2,000 years ago, the birds reappeared on the Guinea (or Western) coast of Africa. In the fifteenth century, the hens were reintroduced to Europe by Portuguese navigators who brought them from Africa. Their names in French and Spanish, *pintade* and *pintada*, mean "painted" or "spotted," and come from their distinctive black plumage which is sprinkled with white dots. Guinea hens, which are a bit smaller than chickens, have seen a recent surge in popularity, especially among restaurant chefs. They are preferred to the pheasant, which they resemble in size and flavor, because they don't have any hard, bony leg tendons. Guinea hens are mostly farm-raised. Confusingly, the term Guinea hen refers to either a male or a female bird.

Venison Sausage with Juniper Berries and Pancetta

One of the easiest things to do with venison is to make this flavored venison sausage, redolent of woodsy porcini mushrooms and resinous juniper berries. Because the shoulder is tougher but more flavorful than the center section, it works well for grinding. If you don't have a small meat grinder (the kind that attaches to a KitchenAid mixer works well), ask your butcher to grind the meat or chop it very finely by hand. A food processor will turn it to pasty mush. Because venison is naturally quite lean, extra pork fat is added to make the ideal sausage ratio of two parts lean to one part fat meat. These sausages go perfectly with Quince Mostarda (see page 770). Complete the dish Madeira-Braised Chestnuts and Brussels Sprouts (see page 276).

SERVES 6

1^1/$_2$ pounds venison shoulder, cut into 1-inch cubes

1 pound pork butt, cut into 1-inch cubes

^{3}/$_4$-pound pork fat back, skin removed and cut into
   1-inch cubes

^{1}/$_2$ pound pancetta, cut into 1-inch cubes

^{1}/$_2$ cup minced garlic

^{1}/$_2$ cup minced shallots

^{1}/$_2$ cup soaked porcini

1 tablespoon finely minced juniper berries

2 tablespoons kosher salt

2 teaspoons freshly ground black pepper

1 tablespoon finely chopped rosemary

2 tablespoons brandy

^{1}/$_2$ cup dry red wine

2 tablespoons unsalted butter

In a large, nonreactive bowl, combine all the ingredients except for the butter. Cover and marinate overnight. The next day, chill the whole mixture in the freezer about 1 hour, or until firm and stiff but not hard. Grind, ideally first using a coarser plate and then grind again using a smaller plate. Form into 2-ounce patties and arrange on wax-paper-lined trays or stuff into casings and refrigerate until ready to cook, up to 2 days.

To finish, heat the butter in a skillet, preferably cast-iron or nonstick, until sizzling. Prick the sausages and add them to the pan. Reduce the heat to medium-low, and brown well on all sides. To test if the sausages are done, prick with a fork. If they are ready, clear juices will spurt out. If pinkish juices come out, cook a few minutes longer. Remove from the pan and serve.

437

GARLIC

GARLIC

It's hard to imagine cooking without garlic, the legendary "stinking rose." With its unmistakable bold, pungent flavor, garlic is indispensable to nearly all the world's cuisines. Garlic, *Allium sativum*, is thought to have originated in the deserts inhabited by the Kirghiz people of Central Asia. Garlic has been known in China since antiquity, and was important to the cooking of ancient Egypt, Greece, and Rome, esteemed for its medicinal and strength-giving properties. It is possible that garlic reached America with the Asian hunters who made their way across the Bering Strait. Or perhaps, the seeds of its pretty white, star-shaped flowers were carried across by the wind? Garlic grows wild in the forests of Quebec, and the native Americans who live in that province eat it a great deal.

The ancient Egyptians fed garlic to the slaves who built the pyramids, believing it increased their physical strength. So when the Israelites fled Egypt in their Exodus, although they were happy to leave the land of their slavery, they looked back with longing for the garlic of Egypt. As written in the book of Numbers 11:5, "We remember the fish, which we did eat in Egypt freely: the cucumbers and the melons, and the leeks, and the onions and the garlic: But now our soul is dried away: there is nothing at all beside this manna, before our eyes."

In ancient Greece, garlic was considered a strengthening food for workers and soldiers, while upper-class people objected to its smell. The Byzantines used garlic lavishly in their cooking. Their garlic sauce, *skoodaton*, was enjoyed by all classes of their society. For this dish they would roast young, tender garlic in the oven and crush it with olive oil and salt, much like today's Skordalia (*see* page 443).

A head of garlic contains anywhere from six to twenty-four individual cloves that release a notoriously pungent aroma when crushed. As revered as garlic has been throughout the centuries, there have been an equal (or at least equally vociferous) number of virulent enemies. A rich and ancient body of folklore surrounds garlic all over the world, much as its penetrating, long-lasting odor surrounds the garlic-eater.

The priestesses of the Roman temple of Cybele forbade entrance to anyone who had just eaten garlic. The Roman poet Horace cursed the garlic eater, saying, "May your mistress repulse your kisses with her hand and flee far from you!" He also warned that garlic "could drive one's lover to refuse a kiss and to retreat to the far side of the bed." Today, members of the Indian Jains sect and Brahmin Hindus in India will not eat garlic—Jains, because they believe in minimizing violence, even to plants like the garlic bulb, which has the potential to develop into a new plant; Hindus, because garlic is thought to be too stimulating.

In 1330, King Alfonso of Castille issued a decree forbidding any knights who had eaten garlic (or onions) to appear at court, or to speak to other court members for four weeks after having eaten the offensive food. King Henri IV of France was renowned as much for his prowess as a lover as for the powerful aroma of garlic he brought to his many assignations. Garlic contains sulfur of allyl, widely held to be an aphrodisiac. The potency of its aroma is therefore both a deterrent and a force for love.

A garlic sauce called *ailée* was very popular in France from the twelfth to the fourteenth century. This soupy sauce was made of garlic and almonds or walnuts and breadcrumbs pounded together and thinned with meat or chicken broth. It was considered extremely beneficial to the health, preventing colds and coughs. (Chicken soup and garlic together in one dish must be a truly formidable weapon against illness.)

Garlic, said to be the poor man's spice in Provence, was also the poor man's medicine and formed part of many remedies, including the prevention of the dreaded plague. When the plague ravaged Marseilles in 1726, four thieves who were robbing corpses seemed to be miraculously (and unfairly) immune. It turned out their secret was garlic steeped in vinegar. If the wearer breathed this "Vinegar of the Four Thieves" from a pad inside a mask, it would supposedly provide protection. Wearing a string of garlic around the neck was another remedy.

Aioli, the "butter of Provence," is a creamy, emulsified garlic sauce made in its simplest form from crushed garlic, sea salt, and fruity olive oil. The nineteenth-century poet of Provence, Frédéric Mistral, asked, "When they are seated around the divine aioli, fragrant aioli, deep in color as a golden thread, where, tell me where, are those men who do not recognize that they are brothers?"

Introduced to Britain by the Romans, garlic was popular throughout medieval and Elizabethan times. By the seventeenth century, opinion began to change, and garlic was thought to be excessively pungent and unsuitable for polite society. John Evelyn in his 1699 *Acetaria*, the classic book about salads, notes, "We absolutely forbid it entrance into our [salad] by reason of its intolerably Rankness.... To be sure, it's not for Ladies Palates, nor those who court them." By the nineteenth century, the reigning Victorian culinary queen, Mrs. Beeton, opined, "The smell of this plant is considered offensive, and it is the most acrimonious in its taste of the whole of the alliaceous tribe."

Although long denigrated in British and American cuisines, with the recent British and American love affair with food and restaurants, we've begun to change our tune. Whole heads of freshly roasted garlic, the cloves squeezed out and spread on toasted bread anointed with olive oil and salt, have become a deservedly lasting symbol of California's culinary renaissance.

441

HARDNECK AND SOFTNECK GARLIC

There are essentially two types of garlic bulbs: older hardneck (or *rocambole*) varieties that have a single hard stem in the center, and newer softneck varieties with soft-stemmed tops that dry into a grasslike top that can be braided. Many cooks prefer the thicker, easier-to-peel skins and more robust flavor of hardneck garlic. This is the type often found in farmers' markets.

CHOOSING GARLIC

When buying mature garlic, choose fresh and plump heads. Examine the cloves: they should be firm and oily to the touch. Garlic bulbs from this year's crop will have plump, hard cloves that fill their skins. As the garlic ages, it starts to shrivel and begins to grow a green sprout in the center of the clove. The green sprout indicates that the garlic is too old and will be bitter. Markets that serve garlic-loving clientele sometimes have the pink-skinned Italian and Spanish garlic that I prefer because it has large, plump cloves with thicker skin that makes it easier to peel. The more common white-skinned garlic has smaller cloves. I don't bother peeling the small, paper-thin-skinned inner cloves but save them to add to a stock or pureed soup.

The Word Garlic

Garlic comes from *gar*, meaning "spear" because of its spearlike leaves or its even more spearlike scapes, and *lic* from leek, used as a base word for many members of the onion family in Anglo-Saxon times.

PRE-PEELED GARLIC

Peeled garlic cloves are now available in large containers in warehouse clubs and in smaller containers in many supermarkets. This garlic has had its skin removed by blowing air and is a convenient way to use fresh garlic. Check that the cloves look plump, like pearly teeth, with no whitish mold. Avoid shriveled cloves or any showing stickiness or white mold. Look for inexpensive peeled garlic in Asian markets, which may be as little as one-quarter the price in supermarkets.

Other Types of Garlic

Garlic Chives: Chinese chives (or *gau choi*) are the long, flat, green leaves of young garlic with no bulbs yet formed. About a quarter of an inch wide, they are dark green with a mild, slightly sharp flavor. Lemon-yellow blanched Chinese chives (*gau wong*) are a delicacy that sell for a relatively high price. These plants are grown without sunlight, resulting in tender and mild (though highly perishable) plants.

Chinese garlic stems: Chinese garlic stems (*suan tai*) are foot-long solid stems that resemble asparagus. They have a strong bite when raw but are sweet when cooked.

Elephant garlic: Elephant garlic is more closely related to leek although it looks like an extra-large garlic bulb. It is quite mild, with potato-like flesh.

Garlic scapes: Garlic scapes are an allium delicacy that is highly prized and traditionally used in Southern and Eastern European and Korean cuisine because of its subtle garlic flavor, tender-crisp texture, and nutraceutical potency. Known as "stems," "scapes," "spears," or "tops," these tender green "flowers" are the seedpods that form on the ends of the central stalk of hardneck garlic plants in June. This delicious asparagus-like stalk has a taste that is milder than the garlic cloves with a broad spectrum of uses from soups to salads to garnishes.

When the scapes are newly budded and still in full curl, they will be tender and provide a delightfully subtle garlic flavor. They are at their best when they curl between one half and three quarters of a turn and resemble a pig's tail. After the scapes have straightened and the flower top has matured, they will be tough.

Garlic scapes store well in the refrigerator for upwards of three weeks, though freshly cut is always the best. Remove the seed pod (*umbel*) before cooking. Don't overcook, as they get tough and/or lose their flavor.

GREEN GARLIC

We are most familiar with fully mature garlic, picked when the bulb containing many cloves has formed. Green garlic is the same plant pulled from the ground at a much earlier stage, before the bulb forms and when the plant resembles a leek with a stalk about $1/2$ inch in diameter. Its mild, fresh flavor is fleeting and herblike rather than oily and lastingly pungent. Until recently, green garlic rarely appeared in the market. Green garlic is a delicacy, unfortunately not very easy to come by, though better known on the West Coast.

Peeling Fresh Garlic

Rub off the papery outer skin, exposing the individual cloves. Pull the cloves off the core and place on a cutting board. Using a meat pounder or the side of a heavy knife, smash down each garlic clove to break open its skin. Remove the skin from individual cloves. I either use a garlic press or slice the cloves thinly before cooking.

Greek Skordalia with Beets and Asparagus

I devoured the most wonderful plateful of steamed baby beets arranged around a wagon wheel of tender springtime asparagus spears with a big dollop of freshly made, still-warm skordalia for dipping at New York's Molyvos Restaurant. This is my version of this dish that was perfect in every way: flavor, simplicity, seasonality, and appearance. Skordalia, a traditional Greek garlic sauce, is thickened with potatoes and enriched with olive oil and cream. Like many potato-based dishes, it tastes best when freshly made, because potatoes tend to get heavy and mealy once they're cold. To make this into a more substantial meal, serve with hard-cooked egg quarters (see How to hardcook, not boil, eggs, page 168 for the method). As is preferred in Europe, the eggs will taste best if not fully cooked through, so that the yolks are still brightly colored and almost liquid in the center.

443

SERVES 6

Skordalia

1 pound (2 to 3 large) Yukon Gold or other gold-fleshed potatoes

$3/4$ cup heavy cream, scalded

Kosher salt to taste

$1/2$ cup cut up stale substantial Italian or French bread without any crusts

6 large cloves garlic

2 tablespoons red wine vinegar

$1/2$ cup extra-virgin olive oil

Bring a pot of salted water to the boil, add the potatoes and boil until tender, but not mushy. Drain, peel while still warm, and put through a potato ricer. Beat in the scalded cream and salt to taste.

Meanwhile, soak the bread in cold water to cover, until soft, about 15 minutes. Squeeze out the water and reserve.

Put the garlic cloves through a garlic press and transfer to the bowl of a food processor. Add the squeezed-out bread and the vinegar, and process briefly to combine. Slowly pour in the olive oil so that it is absorbed and the mixture is creamy.

Scrape the garlic mixture into the reserved potatoes and beat together to combine. Reserve and serve at room temperature.

Beets and Asparagus and Assembly

2 bunches baby beets, red and gold, or just red

Kosher salt to taste

1 tablespoon red wine vinegar

1 pound (1 bunch) young green asparagus, trimmed

Skordalia

Hard-cooked eggs, peeled and quartered, optional

Trim the tops of the beets, if any, leaving 1 inch of stem attached to prevent bleeding. Bring a pot of salted water to the boil, add the vinegar and the beets, and cook at moderate heat for 20 to 30 minutes, or until soft when pierced. Drain and rinse under cold water until cool enough to handle. Rub off the outer skin and beet tops, then trim any remaining skin and root ends. Cut the beets into 4 to 6 wedges each and reserve.

Meanwhile, steam the asparagus until crisp-tender, about 5 minutes, and drain. Rinse under cold water to set the color, and reserve.

On a large serving plate, set a bowl filled with the skordalia in the center. Arrange the beets, asparagus, and eggs in an attractive pattern surrounding the sauce, and serve.

Fried Rice with Garlic Scapes and Shrimp

Make this dish in summertime when garlic scapes can be found in Asian and farmers' markets. And, of course, that's when you'll find the more fragrant field-grown basil, juicy vine-ripened tomatoes, and sweet corn. Fried rice is often made from leftover day-old rice, so if you happen to have about four cups-worth, use it here. Or, make the rice the day before, cool, and then chill in the refrigerator. This Asian-American fusion recipe was inspired by the delicious fried rice served at Susanna Foo's eponymous restaurant in Philadelphia.

SERVES 6

2 cups medium- or short-grain white rice (rice for risotto or paella work well)

1 teaspoon kosher salt

4 tablespoons canola oil, divided

4 large eggs, lightly beaten

1 cup finely diced red onion

1 cup diagonally sliced garlic scapes

$1/2$ pound diced smoked ham and/or small (raw) shrimp, cleaned

$1/4$ pound snow peas, cut on the diagonal into thirds

2 cups white corn kernels, preferably fresh (substitute frozen)

1 cup diced fresh tomato

$1/2$ cup finely shredded basil

Kosher salt and freshly ground black pepper to taste

Rinse the rice to wash off the surface starch in several bowlfuls of cold water until the water runs clear.

In a medium pot with a lid, bring 3$\frac{1}{2}$ cups water to the boil with 1 teaspoon salt. Add the rice and bring back to the boil. Cover and reduce the heat to a bare simmer and cook for 20 minutes, or until the water has been absorbed and the rice is tender but still firm. Turn off the heat and allow the rice to steam for 10 minutes, then fluff and spread out onto a large baking pan to cool.

Heat 2 tablespoons of the oil in a large, nonstick skillet. Add the eggs and cook over medium heat until set, stirring with a wooden spoon to break them up into small bits. Continue to cook until the eggs have browned lightly, then remove from the pan and reserve.

Wipe out the skillet, add the remaining 2 tablespoons of oil, and heat. Add the onion and garlic scapes and stir-fry over high heat until soft and lightly browned.

Add the ham and/or shrimp, snow peas, and corn kernels and stir-fry until the shrimp are opaque and the snow peas brightly colored, about 3 minutes. Add the tomato, rice, egg, basil, salt, and pepper and stir-fry briefly to combine the flavors. Serve immediately.

GARLIC-IN-OIL AND BOTULISM

It's not a good idea to mix chopped garlic and oil and store it for long periods of time, because there is a small risk of botulism in this anaerobic (no air) mixture. Acid prevents the growth of botulism, so always add vinegar, lemon juice, or citric acid to the mixture of garlic and oil to insure food safety.

Caesar Salad with Roasted Garlic Dressing

Caesar Salad is a member of a select group of dishes invented by restaurateurs and later immortalized. Beef Carpaccio from Harry's Bar in Venice, Lobster Newburg from Delmonico's in New York, and Oysters Rockefeller from Antoine's in New Orleans are all members of this club. I can't think of a restaurant that doesn't serve a version of Caesar Salad, with or without grilled chicken on top (a recent addition). And, as many times as I've eaten the innumerable versions of it, I still love a good Caesar Salad, especially if prepared tableside with the whole baby romaine leaves used in the original. In this version, I fry garlic in olive oil until golden brown and use it to thicken the dressing in place of the traditional eggs. The rosemary croutons add crunch and a woodsy fragrance.

SERVES 6

Roasted Garlic Cloves

1 cup peeled garlic cloves
1 cup canola oil

In a small, heavy-bottomed pot, slow-fry the garlic in oil for about 15 minutes, or until golden brown. The oil should be hot enough for the garlic to bubble, but not so hot that it browns too quickly. When cooked, the garlic should be browned on the outside and soft and creamy on the inside. Remove the pot from the stove and drain, reserving both the garlic and the oil. Allow both garlic and oil to cool.

445

Rosemary Parmesan Croutons

1 tablespoon finely chopped rosemary

$^{1}/_{2}$ cup olive oil

3 cups stale Italian bread cubes, preferably from
 semolina bread

Preheat the oven to 350°F. Combine rosemary and oil. Toss with the bread cubes. Spread in a single layer on a metal baking pan, such as a paella pan, and bake 15 minutes, until lightly browned, stirring once or twice. Cool and then store in a in tightly covered container for up to 3 days.

Golden Garlic Caesar Dressing

MAKES 1 QUART, ENOUGH FOR 12 SALADS

1 (5-ounce) can anchovy fillets, including oil

1 cup Roasted Garlic Oil (from above)

About 1 cup olive oil

$^{1}/_{2}$ cup Roasted Garlic Cloves

2 teaspoons chopped garlic

3 tablespoons Dijon mustard

2 tablespoons Worcestershire sauce

1 teaspoon freshly ground black pepper

1 tablespoon kosher salt

1 cup freshly squeezed lemon juice

Drain the anchovies, reserving both the fish and the oil. Mix the anchovy oil with the garlic oil and add enough olive oil to make 2 cups total.

Place the anchovies, garlic cloves, chopped garlic, mustard, Worcestershire sauce, pepper, and salt in a food processor and process to a smooth puree.

Using a rubber spatula, scrape the mixture from the processor bowl to a deep bowl (if you have an immersion blender) or to a blender jar. Add the lemon juice, then slowly beat in the oil until the mixture is thick and creamy. Store in a tightly covered container for up to 1 week.

Caesar Salad

$1^{1}/_{2}$ pounds (3 to 4 heads) romaine hearts, whole with
 leaves separated or sliced into 1-inch-wide strips

2 cups Golden Garlic Caesar Dressing

$^{1}/_{2}$ cup grated Romano cheese

$^{1}/_{2}$ cup grated Parmigiano-Romano or Grana Padano

2 cups Rosemary Garlic Croutons (recipe above)

Toss the romaine with the dressing until lightly but evenly coated. Toss again with the cheeses and the croutons and serve immediately.

WHERE DID CAESAR SALAD COME FROM?

According to John Mariani's *Dictionary of American Food and Drink*, Caesar Salad was created by Caesar Cardini, an Italian immigrant who opened a series of restaurants in Tijuana, Mexico, just across the border from San Diego. The story goes that on the Fourth of July weekend in 1924, Cardini created the salad with whole romaine leaves on the plate so that people would eat them with their fingers. Movie people who visited Tijuana brought the salad back to Hollywood, where it started appearing on menus. Cardini's original salad did not include anchovies (though the Worcestershire he did use includes anchovy as an ingredient). He also insisted on using Italian olive oil and imported Parmesan cheese.

Rosemary Roast Chicken with Garlic, Potatoes, and Artichokes

This is a take-off on the Provençal French dish of chicken with forty cloves of garlic. The chicken is roasted along with potatoes, artichoke wedges, golden potatoes, and whole garlic cloves for an easy one-dish meal with the French favorite, thyme, adding its slightly peppery aroma. The buttery-tasting gold potatoes don't need peeling, and if you use good-quality frozen artichoke hearts, it's even easier. When roasting, it's important to use a metal pan that will conduct the heat, so that the contents brown well and the potatoes crisp up. A large paella pan, metal baking pan, or lasagna pan would all work. The pan should be just large enough to hold all the ingredients; any bare spots in the pan would tend to burn. Substitute chicken quarters, chicken legs, or chicken thighs (all on the bone for moistness), if desired, adjusting the cooking time as needed.

SERVES 6

6 chicken breast halves on the bone
Kosher salt and freshly ground black pepper to taste
1$\frac{1}{2}$ pounds gold potatoes, unpeeled and cut up
   into large chunks
1 (12-ounce) package frozen artichoke hearts
1 tablespoon finely chopped thyme
2 tablespoons chopped rosemary
$\frac{1}{2}$ cup garlic cloves, peeled or unpeeled
$\frac{1}{2}$ cup extra-virgin olive oil

Preheat the oven to 450°F. Season the chicken breasts with salt and pepper and let them rest at room temperature for 30 minutes.

In a large bowl, combine the chicken, potatoes, artichokes, thyme, rosemary, garlic, olive oil, and a bit more salt and pepper.

Transfer the mixture to a large roasting pan and roast, turning the contents of the pan several times during cooking to allow potatoes and artichokes to brown evenly. Roast until chicken is completely cooked (165°F. on a thermometer when measured at the thickest part of the thigh) and the potatoes and artichokes are brown. Transfer the contents of the pan to a serving platter and serve immediately.

Penne with Grilled Portabellas, Chicken, and Roasted Garlic

A real winner, this is a pasta dish for garlic lovers, with meaty herb-and garlic-roasted portabella mushrooms caps, grilled chicken, and roasted garlic cloves. Like most pasta dishes (except those made with seafood) it's finished with grated cheese. The cheese acts as a binder, tying the whole dish together and making a creamy, slightly thickened sauce from the pan juices and the chicken stock.

SERVES 4 TO 6

1 pound boneless, skinless chicken breasts
Kosher salt and freshly ground black pepper to taste
1 tablespoon + 2 tablespoons olive oil
$\frac{1}{2}$ cup peeled garlic cloves
1 pound penne pasta, preferably ridged (*penne rigate)*
6 Roasted Portabella Mushroom Caps, diced
  (recipe follows)

1 cup chicken stock

1 cup grated Parmigiano-Reggiano or Grana Padano

Rub the chicken breasts with salt and pepper and leave to season about 10 minutes. Preheat a grill (if available) or a broiler. Brush the chicken breasts with 1 tablespoon of olive oil and grill or broil until barely cooked through, about 6 minutes. Remove from the heat, cool slightly, and then slice into strips, and reserve.

If using the broiler, reduce the oven heat to 425°F.; otherwise, preheat the oven to 425°F. Combine the garlic cloves with the remaining 2 tablespoons olive oil. Spread onto a small metal baking pan, such as a paella pan. Bake 10 to 15 minutes, stirring occasionally, until the garlic is well-browned.

Bring a large pot of salted water to the boil. Add the penne and cook until *al dente*, firm and bouncy, and still yellow in color. Drain and reserve.

Meanwhile, combine the mushrooms, chicken, roasted garlic cloves and any pan juices in a large casserole. Pour in the chicken stock and cook all together until everything is hot and the pan juices are syrupy, about 5 minutes. Toss the contents of the pan with the drained pasta, add the cheese, mix well, taste for seasoning, and serve, preferably on heated plates.

Roasted Portabella Mushroom Caps

$1/4$ cup olive oil

1 tablespoon chopped garlic

2 tablespoons chopped resinous herbs (such as rosemary, sage, thyme, savory, and oregano)

Kosher salt and freshly ground black pepper to taste

6 large portabella mushroom caps

Preheat a grill or broiler to high. Whisk together the olive oil, garlic, herbs, salt, and pepper. Rub the mixture all over the mushroom caps. Grill the mushrooms, or arrange in a single layer, gill-side down, on a metal baking pan and broil on high until well browned on top, about 5 minutes, then turn over and broil until well browned on the bottom, about 5 minutes.

Cool mushrooms, cut into cubes, and reserve.

448

GOAT CHEESE

GOAT CHEESE

With its tangy, clean flavor and creamy texture, goat cheese has become one of America's favorite cheeses, appearing on menus from coast to coast. A mixed spring greens salad with baked goat cheese often coated with crunchy breadcrumbs became the iconic dish for the "new American cooking" that was really launched in California, especially the Bay Area. I started serving my version of that salad about twenty years ago, and neither customers nor I ever tired of it.

Today, goat cheese appears in dishes as varied as salads, crostini toppings, vegetable terrines, sandwiches, pasta fillings and sauces, and even desserts. Goat cheese works well with French and Italian dishes, but is quite adaptable, so that it also complements Mediterranean, Californian, and even Latin American-style dishes. Years ago, there were a very few artisanal goat cheese producers, including Laura Chenel's famed products in California, Coach Farms in New York, and Douglas

Newbold's delicately tangy Greystone Chevratel near Philadelphia; today, there are goat cheese producers all over the country too numerous to name. Artisan goat cheeses are not usually aged, so they are fresh, bright white in color, and creamy looking with a fairly mild, tangy, slightly salty flavor, and crumbly texture.

European aged goat cheese can smell like a goaty barnyard with a taste to match. In fact, one of France's most popular goat cheeses is Crottin de Chavignol, named for its resemblance to a piece of horse dung, or "*crottin*"! The French definitely don't share American squeamishness about food or sex—and the two are inevitably closely related. Locals in France often select crottin cheeses when they are well-aged and have developed a dark brown crust, which could be said to resemble their namesake. But, never fear, for the kitchen, the best goat cheese is the freshest one with mildly tangy, adaptable flavor.

CHOOSING AND STORING GOAT CHEESE

Fresh goat cheese should be moist, not bloated (a sign of excess gas fermentation), moldy (unless it is a deliberately moldy cheese such as a blue goat), or leaky in its package. Store goat cheese well-wrapped in the refrigerator for up to 1 month (fresher cheeses keep less well; drier, more aged cheeses will keep longer.) Unlike many cheeses, goat cheese does take well to freezing. In fact, much of the more reasonably priced imported goat cheese has been frozen and defrosted. Thaw overnight in the refrigerator.

COOKING WITH GOAT CHEESE

Mild, fresh goat cheese is best for cooking, as heat intensifies flavors. Because goat cheese can become grainy if overheated, heat just long enough to melt. Unlike cow's milk cheese, goat's milk cheese is curdled (or thickened) with acid, instead of animal rennet (a substance found in a calf's stomach). Because the acid interferes with the formation of stringy protein molecules, goat cheese melts readily when mixed into sauces and gets soft and creamy while maintaining its shape when baked.

NIGELLA SEEDS

No wonder there's so much confusion about nigella, *Nigella sativa*, also known as black caraway (though unrelated to caraway), black cumin (though this is actually another plant called *kala jeera* in India), onion seed (though unrelated to onion), *charnushka* in Russia and Eastern Europe, and *kalonji* in India. The small, matte-black, hard, and sharp-cornered seeds are used for their hauntingly aromatic smoky and sharply resinous scent, and pleasingly acrid and slightly bitter flavor. Nigella is an ancient seed spice, which has been found in Egyptian tombs and pyramids. It is thought that the "black cumin" mentioned in the Old Testament is actually nigella. Not surprisingly, nigella gets its name from the Latin *nigellus*, meaning "black." It can be found in Eastern European and Indian markets and from specialty spice companies.

Wilted Cabbage Salad with White Truffle Oil and Goat Cheese

Here's a hearty, warm, wilted cabbage salad best suited for wintertime and redolent of enticingly earthy truffle oil. Small bits of crisp pancetta (the Italian equivalent of bacon, dry-cured with salt and pepper instead of being smoked) add intense, meaty flavor with a salty aftertaste, while mild goat cheese adds tang and lightness. Although not necessary, I like to sprinkle this salad with tiny jet-black nigella seeds both for their eye appeal and for their pleasingly acrid flavor. (See the sidebar to the left for more about one of my favorite seed spices, nigella.)

SERVES 4

1/4 pound pancetta, frozen until firm, then cut into small cubes

1/4 cup Champagne vinegar

3 tablespoons finely chopped shallots

Kosher salt and freshly ground black pepper

4 (2-ounce) slices mild goat cheese

1/4 cup extra-virgin olive oil

2 tablespoons nigella seeds, lightly toasted in a dry skillet

4 cups finely shredded cabbage (savoy, kale, or napa)

8 teaspoons white truffle oil

Place the pancetta in a small pan on the stovetop or in a 350°F. oven, and render the fat. Drain the fat and reserve both fat and pancetta bits in separate containers. Whisk together the fat, vinegar, shallots, salt, and pepper, and reserve for dressing.

Brush the goat cheese rounds with olive oil, place in an

oiled pan, and bake about 10 minutes, or until cheese is hot. Remove from oven and sprinkle with nigella seeds.

Meanwhile, heat the remaining olive oil and sauté cabbage until wilted and shiny but still somewhat crisp. Sprinkle in pancetta bits and, at the last minute, toss with the reserved dressing. Place cabbage in the center of 4 serving plates. Top with goat cheese and drizzle each portion with truffle oil. Serve immediately.

Goat Cheese and Vegetable Terrine

This vegetable terrine makes a colorful first course on its own, drizzled with olive oil and a touch of balsamic vinegar, accompanied by thick rounds of crusty French bread or a small salad of spring greens. For best flavor, arrange the cold terrine slices on individual serving plates and let them come to room temperature about 20 minutes before serving.

SERVES 8

1 large eggplant, cut lengthwise into even $^3/_8$-inch-thick slices

$^1/_4$ cup + $^1/_4$ cup extra-virgin olive oil

Kosher salt and freshly ground black pepper to taste

2 large zucchini and/or yellow crookneck squash, cut lengthwise into $^3/_8$-inch-thick slices

1 pound mild goat cheese, room temperature

2 tablespoons chopped fresh thyme

1 roasted red bell pepper, purchased or homemade (*see* Roasted Peppers, on page 66), diced

$^1/_2$ cup pitted and chopped Kalamata olives

1 large bunch fresh arugula, roughly chopped

$^1/_4$ to $^1/_2$ teaspoon freshly ground black pepper

Whole arugula leaves for garnish

Preheat the broiler. Brush both sides of the eggplant slices with oil and sprinkle with salt and pepper. Repeat with the zucchini. Arrange the eggplant slices and the zucchini slices in a single layer on two separate baking pans. Broil the eggplant about 3 minutes, turn them carefully, and finish broiling until cooked through and golden on second side. Drain on paper towels. Repeat with the zucchini. Cool before handling.

Place the goat cheese in the bowl of a food processor and process until smooth and creamy. With the processor running, pour in $^1/_4$ cup of olive oil and the thyme. Remove the mixture from the processor, season with pepper and stir in the roasted peppers and olives.

Lightly brush a 9x5-inch metal loaf pan with olive oil, then line it with plastic wrap, leaving a 4-inch overhang all around. Arrange a single layer of eggplant slices crosswise over the bottom and up the sides, overlapping the edge by about 2 inches. Trim with scissors as needed. Spread one-third of the cheese mixture over top. Sprinkle with one third of the arugula, then cover with a layer of zucchini, arranged lengthwise. Spread one-third more of the cheese mixture over top and cover with one third more of the arugula. Cover with a second layer of zucchini and/or yellow squash arranged lengthwise. Spread the remaining cheese over top, cover with the remaining arugula and finish with the remaining zucchini.

Fold the edges of the eggplant over top. Fold the plastic over to cover and press down gently to flatten the terrine. Bang the terrine pan down on the counter several times to eliminate any air holes and refrigerate for at least 6 hours, preferably overnight, until firm.

To serve, carefully peel back plastic wrap and turn the terrine upside down onto a rectangular serving platter garnished with arugula leaves. Using a sharp knife dipped into hot water and wiped clean each time, cut the terrine into $3/4$- to 1-inch) slices.

Herbed Goat Cheese Ravioli with Tomato–Thyme Sauce

This is a dish for a day when you're feeling rather ambitious. Though the ravioli suggests an Italian origin, with its herb- and shallot-flavored tomato sauce enriched with butter, this dish belongs more to French cuisine. (Remember that the area around Nice was part of Italy until 1870, so that ravioli, called raioles, are common.) Although it admittedly takes a fair amount of time to prepare, the results are extraordinary. Once you get the hang of it, it's fun to make the ravioli, and it's something that kids enjoy doing. With their smaller fingers, they can get great results. This is one of the few restaurant-style dishes included in this book. It's just too good not to try, especially in summer, when herbs are abundant and fully fragrant and tomatoes are juicy. Note that purchased pasta-dough sheets won't work well here, because they tend to be too dry. Follow the recipe on page 986 for the pasta dough and detailed instructions on forming the ravioli. Make the dough just a bit softer and moister for the ravioli so that the edges will stick together readily.

MAKES ABOUT 36 RAVIOLI, SERVES 6

Goat Cheese Filling

$1/2$ pound fresh goat cheese

$1/4$ pound whole milk ricotta cheese

1 egg

2 tablespoons each: chopped basil, Italian parsley, thyme, and tarragon

2 tablespoons chopped shallots

$1/2$ teaspoon freshly ground black pepper and a little kosher salt

1 pound Fresh Pasta Dough (*see* page 986)

Combine the goat cheese, ricotta, egg, herbs, shallots, black pepper, and a bit of salt and beat together until well combined and no goat cheese lumps remain. Transfer to a container or bowl and chill well.

Follow the directions on page 986 for forming ravioli, using the filling above.

Sauce and Assembly

$1/2$ cup chopped shallots

4 tablespoons unsalted butter, divided

$1/4$ cup dry white vermouth

1 tablespoon chopped thyme

4 cups peeled and diced plum tomatoes (*see* Peeling fresh plum tomatoes, page 86)

Kosher salt and freshly ground black pepper to taste

Ravioli (from above)

In a medium, heavy-bottomed sauce pot, cook the shallots in 2 tablespoons of the butter until softened, but not browned, about 5 minutes. Add the vermouth and thyme, and cook over high heat until the liquid has mostly evaporated, about 5 minutes. Add the tomatoes and cook again over high heat, stirring occasionally, until the sauce has

453

thickened, about 5 minutes. Whisk in the remaining butter, and season to taste with salt and pepper. Transfer sauce to a large skillet and keep warm.

Meanwhile, bring salted water to the boil in a large pot with a wide opening. Drop in the ravioli, one by one, so that they don't stick to each other. Cook 3 to 5 minutes, or until the ravioli float to the top and the dough in the doubled portion along the borders is barely cooked through. Using a wire or perforated skimmer, remove the ravioli from the water, shaking lightly to drain. Add to the sauce in the pan, shaking to combine. Continue until all the ravioli have been drained and mixed with the sauce. Serve immediately.

HOMEMADE CRÈME FRAICHE

Crème fraiche is easy to make at home. You'll need 1 cup of buttermilk and 4 cups heavy cream. In a clean stainless steel bowl, stir together the buttermilk and heavy cream. Cover tightly with plastic wrap and leave at cool room temperature (68°F. to 72°F.) for 24 to 48 hours. The cream will thicken as its rests. Check after 24 hours; if it is not thick enough, allow it to thicken for another 24 hours and then refrigerate. If the air temperature is too hot, the crème fraiche can develop a bitter-tasting pink mold on top. If this happens, throw it out. Once thickened, the crème fraiche will keep for about 3 weeks refrigerated, continuing to thicken as it sits. You may need to drain off the whey that falls to the bottom of the container.

Goat Cheese Coeur à la Crème

Coeur à la Crème, which translates to "cream heart" from the French, is an easy-to-make sweetened cream cheese mousse that's drained overnight to remove excess liquid. Here, a delightful mélange of cream cheese, crème fraiche (French thickened cream), and goat cheese make a tangier version. The bright white color of the mousse is accented by the deep jewel tones of the fruit, while the soft texture and acidic edge of the berries cuts the richness of the cheese. While it's not absolutely necessary to use whole vanilla beans here, the miniscule black specks and warm, tropical fragrance take this simple dessert to a higher level. You'll need six individual perforated heart-shaped Coeur à la Crème molds, or a single larger mold. Improvise by poking holes into disposable foil custard cups or a double layer of pleated foil muffin molds. Serve with sugared quartered strawberries, blackberries, and/or raspberries as the perfect accompaniment.

SERVES 6

1½ pounds cream cheese
1 cup confectioners' sugar
2 vanilla beans, seeds scraped out
1 cup crème fraiche, purchased or homemade (*see* Homemade Crème Fraiche, at left)
½ pound fresh mild goat cheese
2 cups heavy cream

Beat cream cheese, confectioners' sugar, and vanilla together in a mixer until smooth and creamy, scraping down the sides of the mixer several times to break up any small lumps. Stir in the cream fraiche and goat cheese, and beat

454

again until smooth.

Separately, whip the heavy cream until light and firm. Fold into cream cheese mixture.

Line heart molds with cheesecloth and then fill generously with the mixture. Drain in the refrigerator for 48 hours before serving with berries and berry coulis.

Dream Cookies

These truly dreamy cookies have a delectably sophisticated filling of creamy, mild goat cheese and raspberry preserves, making for a beautiful duo of colors and flavors. Even the easy food-processor cookie dough contains goat cheese. Use a fresh goat cheese here with mildest flavor and best-quality raspberry preserves, such as that made by the Swiss company, Hero, that contains only raspberries and sugar.

MAKES ABOUT 36 COOKIES, INCLUDING RE-ROLLED DOUGH SCRAPS

$^1/_2$ pound (2 sticks) unsalted butter

6 ounces + 6 ounces mild goat cheese

1 pound (4 cups) all-purpose flour, preferably unbleached

Pinch of kosher salt

1 egg, lightly beaten

Confectioners' sugar for rolling

$^1/_4$ cup raspberry preserves

Combine butter, 6 ounces of the goat cheese, the flour, and salt in the food processor, and process until the mixture resembles oatmeal. Add the egg and process only

long enough for a relatively smooth dough to be formed. Transfer the dough to a zip-top bag, form into a rectangular shape, and chill until firm, 1 hour in the refrigerator or 30 minutes in the freezer.

Preheat the oven to 350°F. Roll out the dough in portions, sprinkling top and bottom with confectioners' sugar to keep it from sticking to the board. If the dough gets sticky, refrigerate again until firm. Using a (2-inch) biscuit or cookie cutter, cut out circles of the dough and arrange them on a parchment-paper- or Silpat-lined baking sheet. Place a dab of goat cheese and a dab of raspberry preserves in the center of each dough circle. Fold in half and press edges together to seal. Prick each cookie with a fork to allow steam to escape.

Bake 20 minutes, or until the cookies are lightly browned. Cool completely before serving these fragile cookies. Dust with confectioners' sugar before serving.

455

GREENS FOR COOKING

GREENS FOR COOKING

Cooking greens are any of a whole slew of dark, leafy vegetables with strong, assertive flavors and often tough, fibrous leaves. They are some of the oldest members of the cabbage family, descended from the wild or sea cabbage that grows in coastal areas of Europe and resembles leafy kale. Many of these greens are at their best in winter months, and all are high in vitamin A. The older the green, the tougher and more strongly flavored it will be. Cooking greens are slow-cooked to help break down their fibrous texture and mellow their bitter flavor, resulting in tender, succulent leaves with a flavorful bite and satisfying texture. Because of their own strong flavor, they are often paired with potent garlic, hot peppers, vinegar, and smoked pork or turkey.

While a partner at the White Dog Cafe, I prepared an enormous batch of mixed cooking greens for a Southern Dinner in celebration of Martin Luther King's Birthday. They were absolutely delicious, but I was amazed at how so many cases of greens could cook down to such a small pot. So, be sure to buy plenty of these inexpensive, vitamin-packed vegetables. Look for great selection and fresh-picked quality at farmers' markets in the fall.

Asian cooking greens, such as bok choy and Chinese mustard, belong to the same huge cabbage family, but their leaves are milder and juicier in flavor and less fibrous; many kinds are tender enough to cook in quick stir-fries. They have light, sweet flavor, crisp texture, and are similarly high in nutritional value. Bok choy was introduced to Europe in the 1800s and is now grown in the U.S. and Canada. Readily available in most supermarkets, it is still considered suitable primarily for Asian dishes.

CHOOSING AND STORING GREENS

Look for fresh, plump, crisp leaves with an intense color. It's normal for mustard greens to show a slight bronze tint. Choose greens with fresh-looking, brightly colored leaves with no sign of wilting or fading. Avoid greens with yellowed, flabby, or pitted leaves, or thick, fibrous stems, or an unpleasant sulfurous odor.

Refrigerate in a plastic bag for up to 5 days. Or, trim and wash first, drain well, wrap in paper towels, place in a plastic bag, and store.

Note that because they're mostly water, all greens will shrink considerably when cooked. Two large bunches of greens will serve as a side dish for four people.

Varieties of Cooking Greens

Bok choy and other Asian greens: There are as many types of Asian cooking greens in the cabbage family as there are those of European origin. Bok choy has stems that may be long or short, thick or thin, green or pearly-white, ending in deep green leaves. Shanghai Choy has light apple-green stalks and deeper apple-green leaves. You may also find baby Shanghai, or bok choy, a miniaturized version small enough to cook whole, in season in spring. *Choy sum* (choy means cabbage; sum means heart) or Chinese flowering cabbage has light green leaves and tiny yellow flowers. *Tat soi* has large, flat dark green rosette-shaped leaves; when young, it is used as a salad green.

Collard greens: Collards look like large, deep green, flat cabbage leaves. They are most popular in the South, where majority of the American crop is grown, but are not as well known elsewhere. Collards can usually be found in markets with a significant African-American clientele. They are available all year round with peak season from December through April and are less common in hot summer months. Collards are quite substantial and fibrous and are best braised (slow-cooked in flavorful liquid) until tender. They are often combined with smoked pork neck bones or ham hocks. The tasty liquid produced is called "pot liquor" and is traditionally sopped up with cornbread.

Dandelion: Dandelion gets its name from the French *dent de lion*, meaning "lion's tooth," referring to its characteristic deeply jagged edges. The bright green leaves have a bitter, tangy flavor that adds interest to salads when very young, especially wilted salads with bacon. When it gets to be a little older, dandelion should be cooked. Dandelion greens are available sporadically year-round, with peak season in April and May and limited availability from December through February. It is most tender in the early spring, before the plant begins to flower. Note that much of the "dandelion" sold at farmers' markets and specialty stores is actually similar-looking but milder catalonia, a member of the chicory family. (For more information, *see* Indivia and Radicchio chapter, page 490.)

Flowering Kale: Colorful and almost too pretty to eat, kale resembles a huge, ruffled flower with "petals" that range in color from white and pink to lavender and violet, all enclosed by deep bluish-green leaves. Because of its striking appearance but tough texture, it is often used as a garnish. Salad Savoy is another name for this plant. It is often used as a decorative plant for fall gardens. Look for dense, full heads with crisp leaves, bright color, and no yellowing or wilting.

Kale: Kale has deep green, long, thin leaves with ruffled edges, tough central ribs, mild flavor, and a semi-crisp texture. Its flavor is closest to the leaves of broccoli and is milder and less "cabbagy" than other cooking greens. It is popular in Scandinavia, Germany, Holland, and Scotland and was brought to the U.S. in the seventeenth century. Like many cooking greens, kale has been considered a food of the poor. It is a big favorite in Portugal, where braganza kale, *couve tronchuda* in Portuguese, goes into the national soup, *Caldo Verde*. Portuguese colonists brought their kale to Brazil, where today it accompanies Brazil's national dish, *Feijoada*, an elaborate dish originated by slaves, made up of black beans simmered with pork parts and served with kale and toasted manioc. Kale is most abundant December through February.

Mustard Greens: Mustard greens are a rich, dark green and have a sharp mustard flavor. They are a popular soul food in America and also common in Indian cooking. Red mustard is sharper in flavor but less coarse in texture. Small leaves of red mustard often appear in "spring mix" greens. Peak season for mustard greens is December through April, although they can be found in July and August. Mustard greens are the most pungent of the cooking greens and lend a peppery flavor to food. They originated in the Himalayas more than 5,000 years ago. The greens have light textured, crumpled, or flat leaves with frilled edges.

Turnip Greens: Turnip greens are similar to mustard greens but with a purplish tint and mellower, slightly sweet, turnip-like flavor when young, rather than sharp mustard-like flavor. They can become quite tough and strong-tasting as they age. Turnip greens are in peak season October through March.

Tuscan Kale: Also known as lacinato kale, dinosaur kale, or black cabbage (*cavolo nero* in Italian), Tuscan Kale is an heirloom green from Italy that is a winter staple in that region. Quite attractive and distinctive, it has deep blue-green, almost black leaves that are about a foot long and are heavily savoyed (crinkled). Its flavor is sweet and mild, particularly after frost. Tuscan kale is in season in the winter months and works well as a braised side dish or in hearty soups.

Preparing and Cleaning Greens

Cut off and discard the stems. If the greens have thick ribs, which can be tough and woody, remove them by folding the leaves in half along the rib and ripping them out.

Wash the greens in a large amount of lukewarm water, swishing vigorously to dislodge sand or dirt.

Rinse the greens but don't dry them if you're cooking them right away, because the water that clings to the leaves will help them wilt as they cook.

Simmered Greens with Sweet Onion and Pancetta

When making greens, the more different kinds you use, the better the flavor and more interesting the texture. Here the greens are mellowed by sweet onions. I use Georgia's Vidalia onions (pronounced, as I was directed in Atlanta, Vi-day-li-a), in summer and Oso Sweets from Chile in winter. Small bits of salty cured pancetta enrich the greens while tongue-tingling hot red pepper is paired with a splash of cider vinegar to sharpen the flavor. Mop up the "pot liquor" (the juices of the cooked greens) with a square of Confetti Cornbread (see page 344) or Buttermilk Cornbread (see page 341).

Substitute the meat cut from smoked turkey legs cut into bits for the pancetta, if desired. These greens reheat very well, in fact many believe the flavor is best after a few days.

SERVES 6 TO 8

1 bunch mustard greens

1 bunch kale

1 bunch turnip greens or collards

$1/4$ pound pancetta, frozen until firm, then cut into small squares

1 large sweet onion, diced

2 tablespoons cider vinegar

1 teaspoon red pepper flakes

Kosher salt and freshly ground pepper to taste

Strip all the leaves off their ribs. Wash in a large bowl of lukewarm water, swishing around vigorously. Scoop the leaves from the water, leaving any sand on the bottom.

Place the leaves in a large pot with a lid. Cover and heat just long enough for the greens to wilt, stirring once or twice. Drain and run under cold water to set the color. Drain again and squeeze out the excess liquid with your hands. Cut the cooked leaves into 1-inch strips and reserve. (This step can be done 1 to 2 days ahead of time, if kept refrigerated.)

Render excess fat from the pancetta by slowly cooking it until brown in a small skillet or in a metal pan in a 350°F. oven. Drain off fat, reserving both pancetta bits and fat.

Sauté the onion in the pancetta fat until the onion is transparent. Add the greens and vinegar, toss together and season with red pepper flakes, salt, and pepper. Garnish with crispy pancetta bits just before serving.

Greek Mixed Greens Pie with Poppy Seed Topping

461

Several years ago, I traveled to the Kalamata region of Greece, where the famous pointy purple olives are found along with some of the best olive oil in Greece. On our last night, we ate dinner in a most elegant restaurant in Piraeus, the port of Athens, and tasted a wonderful dish that inspired this recipe. The restaurant, Varoulko, which has since moved to downtown Athens, has recently been awarded a Michelin star. Its chef, Lefteris Lazarou, is renowned for his seafood cookery. At the restaurant, the chef prepared individual round pies for each person; lovely, but a little too much work for the home cook. I especially loved his use of poppy seeds, to give that tiny bit of crunch and sweetly rich flavor for the topping. All kinds of wild greens, called horta (as in horticulture), are gathered in Greece and combined in pies like this one. The rich, fruity olive oil from Kalamata would be perfect here.

1 pound fresh spinach, trimmed of stems

1 pound swiss chard, stalks removed

1 bunch watercress or arugula, stems trimmed off

1 bunch dill, leaves roughly chopped

2 cups roughly cut fennel stalks

2 bunches scallions, sliced

2 tablespoons + $^1/_2$ cup extra-virgin olive oil

2 eggs, lightly beaten

$^1/_2$ pound (2 cups) crumbled feta cheese

Freshly ground black pepper to taste

1 pound phyllo dough, defrosted if frozen, and at room
   temperature

2 tablespoons poppy seeds

462

Combine the spinach, chard, watercress, and dill in a large bowl of lukewarm water. Swish around vigorously to dislodge any sand. Scoop the greens from the bowl. If there is more than a tiny bit of sand left in the bowl, repeat the process.

Transfer the cleaned greens to a large pot. Cover and heat until the greens are just barely wilted, turning them around once or twice so the greens on top cook also. Drain and rinse under cold water. Squeeze out the excess water, slice the greens into 1-inch-wide strips, and reserve.

Preheat the oven to 375°F. Chop the fennel stalks in the food processor (or by hand) into small bits. In a large, heavy skillet, cook the scallions and fennel in 2 tablespoons olive oil until crisp-tender, about 5 minutes and reserve.

Combine the cooked greens with the fennel mixture. Add most of the eggs (reserving about 2 tablespoons for the egg wash), the feta, and plenty of freshly ground pepper to taste. The feta is salty, so salt isn't necessary.

Layer 8 sheets of phyllo, folded to fit, on the bottom of a buttered 9 x 13-inch metal baking pan or a large, rectangular, shallow decorative ceramic baking dish, brushing every other sheet lightly with oil. Spread half the filling evenly over the phyllo. Cover with 8 more sheets of phyllo, brushing with oil in between every other sheet. Spread the remaining half of the filling over top. Finally, layer with 8 sheets of phyllo, folded to fit, brushing those pairs with olive oil, too.

Mix the remaining 2 tablespoons of beaten egg with 1 tablespoon water. Brush the top of the pie with the egg wash and sprinkle evenly with the poppy seeds. Gently score the pie on the diagonal into serving pieces.

Bake 45 minutes, or until the phyllo is crisp and golden. Cool somewhat before cutting into serving pieces, and serve.

OLIVE OIL FROM KALAMATA

I have used, and served to many happy customers, a wonderful olive oil made by Grigoris Lefas, a company that has been selecting and producing olive oil for over one hundred and fifty years. It has very low acidity and is the first cold press of the Koroneiki olives widely grown for oil production in the southern mainland region of Greece called the Peloponnesus, of which Kalamata forms one province.

Braised Tuscan Kale

Tuscan kale is quite the fashionable green these days. First because of its name—anything Tuscan is automatically stylish—and second, because of its dramatic, deep greenish-black color and highly savoyed (crinkled) long, slender leaves. But, best of all, its flavor is full-bodied without bitterness and has a nutty aftertaste. It's wonderful in hearty soups like wintertime minestrone and is excellent added to pasta. Here, it's prepared in a simple braise flavored with the best olive oil, lots of garlic, and chicken stock to give it a foundation of rich, mellow flavor. Tuscan kale is mild and not too fibrous, so it doesn't need blanching (or precooking in boiling water). In the style of Tuscan cooking, fresh olive oil is drizzled over the kale just before serving. If you have some good balsamic vinegar, sprinkle a few drops over top for a bit of extra pizzazz.

SERVES 4

2 bunches Tuscan kale

³/₄ cup extra-virgin olive oil, plus more for garnish

3 tablespoons thinly sliced garlic cloves

¹/₂ cup chicken stock

Kosher salt and freshly ground black pepper to taste

Strip the leaves off their ribs. Wash in a large bowl of lukewarm water, swishing around vigorously. Scoop the leaves from the water, leaving any sand on the bottom, and drain. If the leaves are long, tear into 4- to 5-inch lengths.

In a large skillet or Dutch oven with a lid, heat the olive oil, add the sliced garlic, and cook, stirring, until it sizzles and releases its fragrance. Add the kale and cook, stirring, until it wilts and sizzles in the hot oil. Reduce the heat,

cover, and simmer the leaves until tender, about 10 minutes.

Add the chicken stock and salt to taste and continue to cook until the leaves absorb the liquid and are tender, about 15 minutes longer. Just before serving, drizzle with olive oil and sprinkle with freshly ground black pepper.

Braised Escarole alla Romana

Escarole, Cicorium endivia, is another member of the Chicory family, a large family of leafy vegetables not that well known in the U.S. Escarole has broad, lightly ruffled leaves that form an open, flattened head; it ranges in color from light yellow to deep green. Most popular in Italian cooking, it is also called Batavian Endive after the ancient tribe that occupied Holland. Unlike some of the more bitter chicories, escarole is quite mild in flavor, with a wonderful, melting texture when cooked. Two very different styles of cooking are known as "alla Romana": the first is artichokes with lots of mint and garlic (see Artichokes Roman Style, page 58), the second one as here, refers to greens braised with pine nuts, garlic, and golden raisins. I prefer to use small dried currants because they are less sweet. Note that unlike many vegetables, this escarole reheats quite well.

SERVES 4

2 large heads escarole, outside leaves trimmed off

¹/₄ cup extra-virgin olive oil

1 tablespoon chopped garlic

¹/₄ cup lightly toasted pine nuts

¹/₄ cup Zante currants

Kosher salt and freshly ground black pepper to taste

463

Cut out and discard the core of the escarole. Slice into 1-inch-wide strips and place in a large bowl of lukewarm water. Swish around vigorously to release any dirt. Let the water settle for a few minutes to allow the dirt to sink to the bottom. Scoop the escarole from the bowl, draining off the excess water. With just the water clinging to the leaves, wilt the escarole in a large skillet. Then cool and gently squeeze some of the liquid from the escarole and reserve. (This step may be done a day or two ahead.)

In a large skillet, heat the olive oil with the garlic and cook together until the garlic sizzles and turns light golden brown. Immediately add the escarole, pine nuts, and currants, and season with salt and pepper. Toss well to combine, and cook over low heat about 10 minutes untill the escarole is soft and well-flavored with the garlic and olive oil. Serve immediately.

464

Swiss Chard Ribs au Gratin

Although they are technically not a green, but rather a deliciously nutty stalk, Swiss chard ribs come free when you buy a large bunch of chard. The leaves can be cooked like a firmer, less collapsible, spinach, while the ribs baked in a creamy gratin have a flavor somewhere between artichoke and celery. You'll need two bunches of large-leafed chard to get enough ribs to make this dish. Swiss chard is at its best in early fall and may be found at farmers' markets in hugely extravagant bunches. The BrightLights chard, with multi-colored creamy white, gold, rose, and deep magenta ribs, will work well and will be extra eye-appealing.

Serves 6 to 8

5 tablespoons unsalted butter

6 tablespoons all-purpose flour

3 cups milk

$^1/_2$ cup heavy cream

1 small onion, peeled and roughly chopped

1 teaspoon ground coriander

$^1/_2$ teaspoon ground nutmeg

1 tablespoon chopped fresh thyme,
   or 1 teaspoon dried thyme

$^1/_4$ teaspoon ground cloves

$^1/_4$ teaspoon cayenne pepper

2 bay leaves

$^1/_2$ pound shredded cheese (a mixture of
   Cheddar, Monterey Jack, and Parmesan is good)

2 bunches Swiss chard stalks

In a large saucepan, melt the butter and stir in the flour. Cook over moderate heat for 5 minutes, stirring occasionally.

Meanwhile, combine the milk and cream with the onion, coriander, nutmeg, thyme, cloves, cayenne, and bay leaves and scald. Whisk the hot milk mixture into the roux (the butter and flour paste). Bring slowly to a boil, stirring frequently to be sure not to burn the bottom of pot. Simmer 15 minutes. Remove from heat and strain sauce through a sieve, discarding solids. Stir in most of the cheese and reserve the sauce.

Meanwhile, boil the Swiss chard stalks for 5 minutes or until tender only halfway through. Drain and cool slightly.

Preheat the oven to 350°F. In a large baking dish, spread a layer of about 1 cup of the sauce. Next spread a layer of stalks and then cover with more sauce. Continue layering, ending with a layer of sauce. Sprinkle with the remaining cheese and bake 40 minutes or until browned and bubbling. Remove the dish from the oven and allow to cool about 10 minutes before serving.

HAZELNUTS

HAZELNUT

You say hazelnut, I say filbert, but the two are essentially the same. The filbert gets its name either in honor of the seventh-century Saint Philibert, whose August 22 feast day marks the beginning of the hazelnut season in England, or for the appearance of its husk, noted by farmers for having a "full beard." Native North American hazel trees produce small, thick-shelled nuts. European trees produce larger, thin-shelled nuts. At first, the name filbert was used for smaller American nuts, while hazelnut was reserved for European nuts. That distinction has disappeared and today, filbert is a name used only in Oregon in America.

Out of all the nuts, and believe me it's hard to choose, I'd have to pick the sweet and rich, small, helmet-shaped hazelnut—its English name derived from Greek and Anglo-Saxon words for helmet. In France, an old name for the hazelnut was *avelline*, from the town of Avellino in Campania famed for its hazelnuts, also commemorated in its scientific name *Corylus avellana*. In Italy, hazelnuts are called *nocciole*, a diminutive of *noci*, used for all nuts in general and walnuts in particular.

Hazelnuts or filberts have grown wild since the ice age. Today, they are grown commercially on a large scale in four countries: Turkey, Italy, Spain, and the United States. The majority of the world's crop comes from Turkey, where the nuts are picked by hand. America grows only three percent of the world's crop. Almost all American hazelnuts come from Oregon. As does Oregon, the Turkish growing region along the Black Sea has a temperate climate with mild winters and moderate summers. Turkish hazelnut trees often grow in the wild, where the Oregon trees are cultivated. Italy is the second-largest producer of hazelnuts but consumes virtually all of its own production; the U.S. is third, and Spain ranks fourth.

Early western American explorers, like Lewis and Clark, were given hazelnuts revered by Pacific Northwest Indians among other foods gathered from the wild. Shortly after 1847, an early Oregon nurseryman imported cultivated cob nuts (yet another name for the hazelnut) from England and "Red Aveline" nuts from Austria. In 1885, a French nurseryman started selling specific varieties of hazelnut trees throughout the Northwest, including the cultivar "Barcelona," which is widely planted in Oregon today along with the "Ennis."

Americans haven't taken to hazelnuts the way Europeans have, partly because they are not part of our culinary heritage and partly (probably mostly) because we don't grow nearly as many hazelnuts as we do almonds, walnuts, and pecans (pecans, hickory nuts, and black walnuts are native to America). Germany, France, Italy, Switzerland, Austria, and Belgium use hazelnuts in generous quantities in chocolates, cakes, cookies, and

466

other dishes. They are often paired with chocolate in Italy, France, and Switzerland, and the famed tortes of Vienna wouldn't be the same without the intense flavor of the hazelnuts that helps balance their richness.

Hazelnuts have a distinctive flavor, accentuated by toasting. They pair well with chocolate, but also with raspberries, cherries, pears, and dried fruits. They also work well in savory dishes, combined with artichokes and cardoons, because they share a nutty character, with greens, and with poultry.

FORMS OF HAZELNUTS

Hazelnuts are available in many forms, though many are hard to find. It's even a challenge to find good-quality hazelnuts at the supermarket, at least on the East Coast. I've found the best are sold by Trader Joe's with large size and fresh, never rancid flavor.

I prefer to buy whole hazelnuts with their skin, because the skin adds flavor, even when most of it is rubbed off. Blanched hazelnuts are the most common form of whole shelled nut. Though easier to use because their skins don't need to be rubbed off, I find their flavor a bit insipid. I like the edge of bitter earthiness imparted by the skin. Sometimes preroasted hazelnuts (unsalted) can be found. These are delicious, because roasting accentuates their sweetly nutty flavor, and saves a step at home.

Sliced hazelnuts, if you can find them, are wonderful for sprinkling on cookies, salads, or green vegetables like green beans, and for finishing the sides of a chocolaty cake or torte, or hazelnut buttercream cake.

Hazelnut paste is used by many bakers to flavor cake fillings, ice cream, gelato, chocolate fillings, and more. It is a combination of caramel mixed with toasted hazelnuts and ground to a fine, sticky paste.

Hazelnut oil is outstanding for seasoning salads, though rather expensive. Keep it refrigerated so it won't get rancid.

Hazelnut butter may be found in natural foods stores. It adds richness, smoothness, and lots of flavor to sandwiches, dips, and desserts.

Hazelnut flour, or finely ground hazelnuts, goes into nut meringue cake layers and Viennese tortes.

467

Toasting Hazelnuts

Preheat the oven to 350°F. Spread the hazelnuts out in a single layer on a metal baking pan. Roast about 20 minutes, or until the skins darken and crack open and the nuts are a warm golden brown. You can live dangerously and roast them at higher temperatures for a shorter time or microwave on full power for 3 to 4 minutes, but be sure to use a timer; once you smell the nuts, it's too late to save them from that bitter burnt taste.

Turkish hazelnuts have more papery skins; Oregon hazelnuts have skins that adhere firmly to the nut. To remove the skin, pour the still-hot nuts onto a clean kitchen towel and pull up the four corner points to make a sack. Rub the nuts vigorously against each other for several minutes to loosen the skin. Shake in a wire fry basket or a Chinese brass wire skimmer to let the skin flakes fall out of the openings or carefully pour out into a bowl, leaving the skins behind in the towel. It's okay to leave bits of skin attached, but too much will give a bitter taste.

Storing Hazelnuts

Storing shelled hazelnuts in an airtight bag or container in a freezer will keep them fresh and flavorful for a year or more, or store hazelnuts in the refrigerator in an airtight and odorless container. Allow nuts to warm to room temperature before using them in baking or cooking.

MORE HAZELNUT IDEAS

Mix hazelnut oil with pomegranate molasses and use as a quick tasty dip for chicken kebobs. Brown hazelnuts in butter and add them to green beans or Brussels sprouts. Sprinkle toasted hazelnuts on winter squash soup, add to turkey stuffing, use them to sprinkle on green salad, mix ground hazelnuts with breadcrumbs and use for a crunchy crust on trout or salmon fillets.

Hazelnut Romesco Sauce

Romesco is a characteristic sauce or dip of Catalonia, the area of Spain surrounding Barcelona that has its own distinct culture and language. It is a thick, pounded mixture of fried bread, garlic, roasted peppers, hazelnuts and/or almonds, plus paprika and chile all made into a smooth paste diluted with wine vinegar and traditionally served with fish. This is my version, with roasted hazelnuts, smoky pimentón paprika, and sherry vinegar. Serve with simple roast or grilled fish or seafood, as a dip for vegetables, or as a spread on garlic toasts.

MAKES 2 1/2 CUPS SAUCE, ENOUGH FOR 10 PEOPLE AS AN APPETIZER

2 large whole roasted red peppers, purchased or home-made (*see* page 66), peeled and seeded

6 large cloves garlic

1/2 cup + 1/2 cup extra-virgin olive oil

1 (1-inch thick) slice French baguette bread, crust removed, cut into rough cubes

1/4 pound whole hazelnuts, toasted and skins rubbed off (*see* Toasting Hazelnuts, page 467)

1 1/2 teaspoons Pimentón dulce + 1/2 teaspoons cayenne or 1 1/2 teaspoons hot paprika

1/4 cup Spanish sherry vinegar

Kosher salt to taste

Purée the peppers and their juice in the bowl of a food processor. Without washing the bowl, transfer the purée to a small pot and then cook slowly until it's thick enough to hold its shape, about 10 minutes. Place the garlic cloves and 1/2 cup of the olive oil in a small pot and cook together until the garlic is lightly browned, about 10 minutes. Add the cubed bread and cook 2 minutes longer or until lightly browned.

Place the pepper paste, hazelnuts, and the garlic and bread cubes and their cooking oil back into the food processor. Process to a chunky paste, then add the Pimentón (or other hot paprika), sherry vinegar, and salt. Process again, then drizzle in the remaining olive oil to make a thick sauce with a consistency like mayonnaise. Store in the refrigerator for up to 2 weeks.

About Romesco

Patience Gray tells us about the making of romesco in her classic memoir/cookbook about her life in five rural areas of the Mediterranean, *Honey from a Weed*. "The variations of this sauce are legion, secrecy surrounds the method and there is no common agreement among fishermen or cooks about its creation. The annual 'romescada' near Tarragon is a challenge to fisherman to produce the best romesco." During this festival, which takes place in April, master romesco makers crouch over their mortars at little stands, surrounded by as many as four thousand onlookers, each showing off his or her own "best" version.

Country Paté with Hazelnuts

Patés have gone out of style as of late, but I suppose that means that we'll soon be inundated with newly stylish versions, because "everything old is new again," especially in food, fashion, and music. Actually a fancy, heavily seasoned and enriched meatloaf, this is an easy-to-make country-style paté, where everything is mixed together, rather than done in the more painstaking way of layering the ingredients to make an interesting mosaic. This paté is flavored with brandy-soaked currants, toasted hazelnuts, and a broad palette of sweet and aromatic spices. Keep in mind that the paté is to be served cold and should therefore be generously seasoned, because cold dulls flavor. For moist results, a paté should be about one-third fat. Pork imparts flavor and richness; veal makes the paté more delicate. Accompany with coarse-grain mustard, fruit mustard, sliced cornichon pickles, or fruit chutney, if desired. The paté will fit perfectly in a 1/2-quart French terrine mold, such as the kind sold by Le Creuset.

Makes one 6-cup paté

3/4 cup zante currants or dried blueberries

6 tablespoons brandy

1 1/2 pounds fatty ground pork

1/2 pound ground veal

2 eggs

3/4 cup heavy cream

1 teaspoon chopped garlic

1 1/2 teaspoons ground fennel seed

1/2 teaspoon ground nutmeg

1/4 teaspoon ground cloves

1 teaspoon ground cinnamon

1 teaspoon ground allspice

Kosher salt and freshly ground black pepper to taste

1 cup hazelnuts, toasted and roughly chopped

$1/2$ pound thin-sliced bacon, or fatback for lining terrine

Plump currants by soaking in brandy until soft, about 20 minutes.

Beat together pork, veal, eggs, cream, garlic, fennel, nutmeg, cloves, cinnamon, and allspice. Season generously with salt and pepper. Add the currants and their soaking liquid and the hazelnuts and mix again.

In a small skillet, fry up a small sample to check the seasonings. (You don't want to sample raw pork.) Refrigerate for a few hours to combine flavors.

Preheat the oven to 325°F. Line a 6-cup terrine mold with overlapping strips of the bacon so they hang over the edge by about 2 inches. Fill mold with the paté mixture and bang down once or twice to eliminate any air holes. Top with a layer of bacon strips so the whole paté is enclosed. Cover the mold with aluminum foil, poked with a few holes for air vents.

Make a water bath by pouring hot water into a pan that is larger than the terrine dish so that it comes about 2 inches up the sides. Reduce oven heat to 300°F. and bake for 1 hour, or until the paté has shrunk away from the walls of the mold, is firm all the way through, and reads 150°F. on a meat thermometer inserted into the center.

Allow the paté to cool to room temperature, and then unmold. Wipe off any excess fat and refrigerate until completely cold. The bacon may be removed or left on as desired. Cut into $1/2$-inch-thick slices and serve.

PATÉS AND TERRINES

Patés have long been the staple of French chefs and *charcutiers* (those that work with *char cuit*, or cooked meat. America's closest equivalent is a deli.). To the ever-thrifty though luxury-loving French, pâtés provide an opportunity to use small bits of meat and animal parts, like pig's liver, that are difficult to serve on their own. Herbs, spices, wild mushrooms, wine, brandy, pistachios, and if you're lucky, black truffles, are typical additions. Patés are baked in heavy rectangular or oval ceramic or enameled cast-iron terrine molds, usually lined with thin sheets of lard, bacon, or pastry, for a fancier *paté en croute*. Strictly speaking, the paté is the filling and the terrine is the mold, but both terms are commonly used.

Hazelnut–Lime Cheesecake

This delectable cheesecake combines two opposing qualities at once: it's both creamy and rich yet light, because cream cheese imparts the richness, while ricotta lightens the texture. Richly nutty toasted hazelnuts and the unexpected punch of the lime and aromatic lime zest take it way beyond ordinary. You'll need a 10-inch springform pan to make the cake.

MAKES ONE 10–INCH CHEESECAKE

Hazelnut Crust

1 cup toasted, ground hazelnuts

1 cup breadcrumbs

$1/4$ cup granulated sugar

$1/4$ pound (1 stick) unsalted butter, melted and cooled

Preheat the oven to 375°F. Combine hazelnuts, bread-crumbs, sugar, and butter, and press into the bottom of a 10-inch springform pan. Chill 30 minutes and then bake 25 minutes, or until lightly browned. Cool.

Hazelnut–Lime Filling

1 pound cream cheese

1 pound whole-milk ricotta cheese

$1/2$ cup sour cream

4 eggs

4 egg yolks

$3/4$ cup granulated sugar

1 tablespoon vanilla extract

$1/4$ cup lime juice + grated zest of 1 lime

$1/4$ pound lightly toasted hazelnuts, skins rubbed off and coarsely chopped

Beat cream cheese using the paddle attachment, until smooth, scraping down the sides several times. Beat in ricotta and then gradually beat in sour cream.

Meanwhile, using a whisk, beat together the eggs, yolks, sugar, vanilla, and lime juice until light and fluffy. Pour egg mix into the cream cheese mixture and beat together to combine. Stir in the hazelnuts and then pour mixture into baked hazelnut crust. Cover outsides of the pan with heavy-duty aluminum foil to prevent leakage.

Preheat the oven to 350°F. Bake cheesecake in a water bath about $1^1/2$ hours, or until set in the middle. Cool to room temperature before removing from pan. Using a sharp knife dipped in hot water and wiped dry in between each cut, slice into 12 portions.

Frangelico Semifreddo with Mocha Chocolate Sauce

Definitely a dessert for grown-ups, with the benefit of being made ahead, this semifreddo is a frozen mousse, called "semi-cold" in Italian because it has a softer texture than frozen gelato. Sweet hazelnut-infused Frangelico liqueur is heightened by toasted hazelnuts in a light, creamy confection. To gild the lily, a warm sauce of bittersweet chocolate, more Frangelico, and coffee is poured over top, giving it that palate-stimulating combination of hot and cold in one dessert.

SERVES 12

1 tablespoon hazelnut oil, or bland vegetable oil, for oiling the mold

8 eggs

1 cup granulated sugar

$3/4$ cup +$1/4$ cup Frangelico liqueur

$3/4$ pound (about $2^1/2$ cups) lightly toasted hazelnuts, finely chopped

1 cup heavy cream

$1/2$ pound bittersweet chocolate, chopped

4 tablespoons unsalted butter

$1/2$ cup strong coffee

Prepare a 2-quart decorative metal mold or a metal loaf pan by rubbing it all over with the oil, and reserve.

In a large stainless steel bowl, whisk the eggs with the sugar and $3/4$ cup of the Frangelico. Set the bowl over a large saucepan of simmering water and whisk constantly until the mixture lightens and thickens, about 15 minutes. You should eventually see streaks in the mixture. Do not let the eggs get too hot or they will scramble.

471

Remove the bowl from the heat and continue whisking for a few minutes to cool the mixture slightly. Place the bowl onto a second, larger bowl filled with ice and water and cool, whisking occasionally until the mixture is cool and then fold in the hazelnuts.

In a separate bowl, beat the cream until firm and then fold by thirds into the egg mixture. Spoon the semifreddo into the prepared mold, cover with plastic wrap, and freeze until firm, preferably overnight.

Meanwhile, melt the chocolate over low heat, and add the butter, the remaining $1/4$ cup of Frangelico, and the coffee, stirring occasionally. Keep warm.

To serve, wipe the outside of the mold briefly with hot towels to loosen it, and invert onto a large serving platter. Place back in the freezer for about 30 minutes, or until quite firm.

Serve the semifreddo in slices or wedges, drizzled with the chocolate sauce.

472

FRANGELICO HAZELNUT LIQUEUR FROM ITALY

Frangelico liqueur is flavored with hazelnut and is part of my favorite cocktail, what I call an "Italian Kiss" after the world-famous blue-foil wrapped Perugina chocolate made from hazelnuts called *baci* or *kisses* in Italian. To make it, mix 2 ounces vanilla vodka with no more than a half-ounce of Frangelico. Chill until ice cold and serve in a chilled martini glass. It tastes like the best hazelnut gelato, reserved for grown-ups.

The Ginevra Cake

About thirty years ago, I first gazed upon the small, hauntingly beautiful portrait of Ginevra da Benci, one of the most gifted intellectuals of her time, by Leonardo da Vinci. This painting hangs in its own room at the National Gallery of Art in Washington, D.C. (where I grew up). It was purchased in 1967 for, at that time, the most ever paid for a painting, a mere five million dollars. Painted about 1474, it has as much impact today as it did then. At that moment, I vowed to myself that if I ever had a daughter, her name would be Ginevra. Today, Ginevra Sarah Reiff (my daughter) is a young woman of many talents. This is her favorite cake, requested for birthdays. Dark chocolate and coffee combine in a cake as sophisticated and multidimensional as she is, finished with the glossy shine of a chocolate ganache icing, and edged with rough jewel-like hazelnut praline. Like my Ginevra, the cake conceals a sweet inside that makes it all work. And, I suppose, also like my daughter, the cake is something of a challenge, though completely rewarding.

MAKES ONE 9-INCH LAYER CAKE, SERVING 12

Dark Chocolate Cake

2 ounces ($1/2$ cup) Dutch-processed cocoa

1 cup hot, freshly brewed, extra-strong coffee

6 ounces ($1^1/2$ cups) all-purpose flour, preferably unbleached

1 teaspoon baking soda

$1/2$ teaspoon baking powder

1 teaspoon kosher salt

$1/4$ pound (1 stick) unsalted butter, softened

1 cup dark brown sugar, packed

$1/2$ cup granulated sugar

2 eggs

Preheat the oven to 350°F. Spray a 9-inch springform pan generously with nonstick spray and set aside.

In a small bowl, whisk together the cocoa and the coffee, making sure to break up any lumps, and set the mixture aside to cool to room temperature.

In a separate bowl, whisk together the dry ingredients: flour, baking soda, baking powder, and salt and reserve.

In the bowl of an electric mixer and using the paddle attachment, cream together the butter, brown sugar, and granulated sugar until creamy and light. Beat in the eggs, one at a time, continuing to beat until completely absorbed.

Alternating, add the dry ingredients and the coffee mixture to the butter and sugar mixture, beginning and ending with the dry ingredients. Beat well after each addition.

Pour the batter into the prepared pan. Bake for 40 minutes, or until the cake comes away from the sides of the pan and forms a slightly rounded top, and a toothpick inserted into the center comes out clean.

Cool in the pan on a wire rack. Remove the sides of the springform pan and refrigerate the cake until chilled before filling, preferably overnight.

Hazelnut Praline

MAKES ABOUT 3 CUPS (ENOUGH FOR TWO CAKES)

2 cups granulated sugar

1 cup water

$1/2$ pound (about $1^1/2$ cups) toasted hazelnuts
   (*see* Toasting Hazelnuts, page 467)

Prepare a metal baking tray with shallow sides by spraying generously with nonstick spray and reserve.

In a medium, heavy-bottomed (preferably copper for best heat conduction) pot with a lid, mix the sugar and water together, taking care not to splash up the sides. Cover and heat on low to moderate heat until the sugar melts entirely and the liquid is clear.

Raise the heat to medium-high and continue cooking with the lid on, checking often. The sugar will first start to show thick bubbles all over and then will start to brown lightly at the edges. This is when the extremely hot caramel can burn easily. The caramel is ready when it is a deep brown color with just a hint of redness. PAY CAREFUL ATTENTION HERE AS CARAMEL IS EXTREMELY HOT.

Mix the nuts with the caramel, using a wooden spoon, and while it is still hot, pour the mixture out onto the prepared tray. Allow the praline to cool at room temperature until hard.

Break up into shards by hand, and then break up further using a meat pounder or a hammer. Place the broken-up pieces in the bowl of a food processor and process until the praline is in fine pieces. Remove from the processor and reserve.

Nutella Cream Filling

$1/2$ cup Nutella

$1/4$ pound (1 stick) unsalted butter, softened

1 cup Hazelnut Praline (recipe above)

In the bowl of an electric mixer and using the paddle attachment, cream the Nutella and the butter until light and fluffy. Add the praline and beat again until combined. Remove from the mixer, transfer to a bowl, and chill until ready to use.

Chocolate Ganache Icing

1 1/2 cups heavy cream

12 ounces semisweet couverture chocolate,
  coarsely chopped

Place the cream in a Pyrex measuring bowl (or other
microwaveable container) and heat to scalding or steaming hot in the microwave. Add the chopped chocolate and
allow it to melt in the heat of the cream. Stir until completely melted. (If not completely melted, microwave for
30 seconds longer and then stir again until melted.)

Cool at room temperature, stirring occasionally until
cool and the icing has reached a spreadable consistency,
about 30 minutes, but is still glossy.

Assembly

Dark Chocolate Cake

Nutella Filling

Chocolate Ganache Icing

1 cup Hazelnut Praline

Using a long, serrated knife, cut the cake horizontally
into two layers. Spread the filling on 1 layer. Top with the
second layer. Smooth the sides and chill the cake for 20
minutes in the freezer.

Remove cake from the freezer and spread the top and
sides with the icing. Press the praline into the sides and
refrigerate again until ready to serve.

Cut the cake using a sharp knife dipped in hot water
before each cut, and wipe the blade clean after cutting
each piece. Serve at room temperature for best flavor and
shiny icing.

GIANDUIA, A HAZELNUT CONFECTION FROM TORINO

Gianduia comes from the Northern Italian city of
Torino, close to the mountainous regions of Switzerland where they really love hazelnuts. First made there,
but now popular throughout Italy, gianduia is made
from a combination of toasted hazelnuts, milk chocolate, and caramel all ground until smooth as silk. Yum!
Block gianduia can be purchased from bakery-supply
companies and makes a superb ganache icing melted
with cream and cooled until spreadable, or gianduia
gelato, following a basic gelato recipe.

HONEY

HONEY

"You're my honey bun," "it's a honey," "honey-mouthed," "honey-tongued," and "sweet as honey" are just a few of the honeyed phrases we use without thinking. Though we mostly use sugar for sweetening these days, honey-sweetness forms part of our consciousness that goes way back. For tens of thousands of years, honey—the viscous, sweet liquid made by bees from flower nectar—was almost the only available source of sweetening. Ancient civilizations looked on the making of honey as a miracle, and even today, after much scientific research, honey remains something of a mystery.

Honey has been around since as far back as recorded history. In Biblical times, Israel was referred to as "the land flowing with milk and honey" (Exodus 3:8). In Babylon 4,000 years ago, for the first month after a couple's wedding, the bride's father would supply his son-in-law with all the mead—a honey-based beer— he could drink. Because the Babylonian calendar was lunar based, this period was called the "honey month" or what we know today as the "honeymoon."

The ancient Egyptians were fond of honey and baked special honey cakes as offerings to placate their gods. The Greeks, who made their own honey cakes and offered them to their own gods, viewed honey not only as an important food, but also as a healing medicine. They mixed honey and cheese to make the cheesecakes described by Euripides in the fifth century BC as being "steeped most thoroughly in the rich honey of the golden bee." The Romans used honey for their personal use and as a gift to the gods, and the art of beekeeping flourished throughout the Roman Empire.

Once Christianity was established, both honey and beeswax production increased greatly, with the beeswax needed to meet the demand for church candles. Honey continued to be of major importance in Europe until Renaissance times when sugar began to arrive from Arab lands. By the seventeenth century, the use of honey was in decline. Because honey has so many subtle nuances of flavor and sugar is one-dimensional (except when caramelized), with the decline of honey we became less discerning in our collective sweet tooth.

In the sixteenth century, conquering Spaniards found that the natives of Mexico and Central America had already developed beekeeping. A distinct family of honeybees was native to the Americas. About 1638, European settlers introduced European honeybees to New England. North American natives called these honeybees "white man's flies."

Honeybees make honey from the nectar that they collect from flowers, and "manufacture" it in the beehive. The nectar itself is a thin, sweet liquid produced by flowering plants to attract insects in order to pollinate them.

Bees may travel as far as fifty-five thousand miles and visit more than two million flowers to gather enough nectar to make just one pound of honey.

Bees have been producing honey just as they do today for at least one hundred and fifty million years as food for the hive during the long months of winter when flowers aren't blooming and little or no nectar is available. Cave paintings in Spain from 7000 BC show the earliest records of beekeeping. European honeybees, *Apis mellifera*, produce an abundance of honey, far more than the hive can eat, and humans harvest the excess. European honeybees can be found in beekeepers' hives around the world.

Honeybees are social insects that live in colonies and include a queen, drones, and workers. The largest bee, the queen, is the only sexually developed female in the hive. A two-day-old larva is selected by the workers to be reared as the queen. She will emerge from her cell eleven days later to mate in flight with approximately eighteen drones. These stout, male bees have no stingers and their sole purpose is to mate with the queen. If the colony is short on food, drones are often kicked out of the hive.

Fifty to sixty thousand smaller worker bees feed the queen and larvae, guard the hive entrance, and help keep the hive cool by fanning their wings. These "busy bees" also collect nectar for honey and produce the hexagonal wax comb cells, with walls that are only two-thousandths of an inch thick, but able to support twenty-five times their own weight.

In the kitchen, this miraculous substance presents its own challenges and rewards. When cooking with honey, remember that honey is twice as sweet as sugar because of its higher fructose content. It imparts a pronounced and distinctive flavor rather just adding sweetness, especially in darker varieties. I usually combine honey and sugar, because honey alone tends to dominate. Also, honey burns more easily than sugar, so reduce the heat when cooking or baking.

As sweet as it is, honey goes into savory as well as sweet dishes. Spiced honeyed lamb is a classic dish in Morocco, salad dressings benefit from the thickening power and flavor of honey, hams and turkeys may be glazed with honey, and honey is often the secret ingredient in barbecue sauce. Vegetables, like small onions, carrots, parsnips, and yams, take well to honey and many a pot of baked beans gets its sweetness from honey. Honey has a special affinity with nuts, which are often glazed with honey, or mixed together in cakes and other sweets, such as the Jewish Honey Cake (*see* page 485).

HONEY AND BABIES

Take care and note that honey should never be fed to infants under one year of age. Honey can contain bacterial spores that cause Infant Botulism—a rare but very serious disease that only young babies can get. Honey is a safe and wholesome food for children over the age of one year.

WHAT IS HONEY MADE FROM?

Honey, which contains much less moisture than the original nectar, is primarily composed of fructose, glucose, and water. It also contains other sugars as well as trace enzymes, minerals, vitamins, and amino acids. Although relatively low in nutrients, honey contains more than refined sugars. Darker honeys generally contain higher amounts of minerals than lighter honeys.

FORMS OF HONEY

Honey comes in a variety of forms, including liquid, whipped, and comb. Liquid honey is extracted from the comb in the hive by centrifugal force, gravity, straining, or other means. Whipped honey (also known as creamed honey or Canadian-style honey) is finely crystallized so that it remains creamy and spreadable. Comb honey is honey that comes just as it was produced—in the honeybees' wax comb.

Substituting Honey for Sugar

When substituting honey for sugar in recipes, substitute honey for up to half of the sugar called for in the recipe. When baking with honey, remember the following: Reduce any liquid called for by $1/4$ cup for each cup of honey used. Add $1/2$ teaspoon of baking soda for each cup of honey used to neutralize its acidity. Reduce oven temperature by 25°F. to prevent over-browning. You can use less honey than sugar to achieve the desired sweetness.

Storing Honey

Store honey at room temperature—your kitchen counter or pantry shelf is ideal. If you store it in the refrigerator, the honey will tend to crystallize—a natural process in which liquid in honey becomes solid. If your honey crystallizes, simply place the honey jar in warm water and stir until the crystals dissolve. Or place the honey in the microwave with the lid off and microwave it, stirring every 30 seconds, until the crystals dissolve. Be careful not to boil the honey, which will cause it to bubble up and make a big mess, or scorch the honey by heating to too high a temperature.

MEASURING HONEY

When measuring honey, coat the measuring cup with nonstick cooking spray or vegetable oil before adding the honey. The honey will slide right out. Or, heat the jar in the microwave on medium power for 1 minute to warm and liquefy the honey, making it easy to pour.

COLOR AND FLAVORS OF HONEY

The colors and flavors of honey differ depending on the source of the nectar—the blossoms. Honey color ranges from almost colorless to dark amber brown and its flavor varies from delectably mild to richly bold. In general, lighter colored honeys are milder; darker honeys are usually more robust. There are more than 300 kinds of honey in the United States alone.

478

Honey Varieties

Alfalfa Honey: The most important honey plant of the western states, alfalfa is a legume with blue flowers which produces white or extra-light amber honey with good body and fine flavor.

Avocado Honey: An uncommon honey, it is gathered from California avocado blossoms. Avocado honey is dark in color, with a rich, buttery taste, and is worth seeking out.

Basswood Honey: The Basswood tree grows from Southern Canada to Texas. Basswood honey is characterized by its distinctive biting flavor. The flowers are cream-colored; the honey is water-white with a strong flavor.

Blueberry Honey: Taken from the tiny white flowers of the blueberry bush, blueberry honey is light amber in color and has a full, well-rounded flavor. Blueberry honey is produced in New England, Michigan, and also in South Jersey by growers like Fruitwood Orchards.

Bitter Honey: Originating in Sardinia, *Miele Amaro* (bitter honey) has a unique sweetness, followed by a slightly bitter aftertaste. This honey is collected after three months of pollination on flowers of the "strawberry tree," *Arbutus unedo,* and is a specialty of the island of Sardinia, where it tops ricotta cheese.

Buckwheat Honey: Buckwheat plants grow best in cool, moist climates and yield a dark brown honey of strong, distinct flavor.

Chestnut Honey: Quite popular in Italy and elsewhere in Europe, this slightly crystalline, not very sweet, nutty-tasting honey is quite wonderful, because of its balance of flavors. Not inexpensive, I buy mine at my local Korean market.

Clover Honey: Clovers are the most popular honey plants in the U.S. Depending on location and source, clover honey varies in color from water-white to extra-light amber and has a mild, rather innocuous, flavor.

Eucalyptus Honey: Eucalyptus honey varies greatly in color and flavor, but in general, it tends to be a bold-flavored honey with a slightly medicinal aftertaste. It is Australia's main source of honey.

Fireweed Honey: Fireweed honey is light in color and comes from a perennial herb that grows in the Northern and Pacific states and Canada. Fireweed grows in the open woods, reaching a height of three to five feet and has attractive pinkish flowers.

Greek Thyme Honey: This legendary honey, produced from the blossoms of wild thyme and other herbs, originates on the slopes of Mount Hymettus and is also produced in Crete and elsewhere in Greece. My favorite brand available in the U.S. is Attiki.

Linden Honey: The small fragrant blossom of linden trees, *tilleul* in French, is the source for this wonderful honey. Intense floral notes, sweet creaminess, and a subtle echo of litchi make this honey unforgettable. It has a rich cream color and is very viscous due to the presence of naturally occurring beeswax and pollen.

479

Orange Blossom Honey: Orange blossom honey is often produced from a combination of citrus flowers. Orange blossoms are a leading honey source in southern Florida, Texas, Arizona, and California. Orange trees bloom in March and April and produce a white to extra-light amber honey with a distinctive flavor and the aroma of orange blossoms.

Sage Honey: Sage honey can come from different species of sage, which grow in abundance along the California coast and in the Sierra Nevada mountains. Sage honey has a mild, delicate flavor and is generally white in color.

Tasmanian Leatherwood Honey: The leatherwood tree grows in Tasmania, an island south of Australia. It bears an abundance of extremely delicate white flowers with a fresh, piquant scent, and produces honey that has been appreciated by connoisseurs for over 100 years.

Tulip Poplar Honey: Tulip poplar honey is produced from southern New England to southern Michigan and south to the Gulf states east of the Mississippi. The honey is dark amber in color; however, its flavor is milder than one might expect from a dark-colored honey.

Tupelo Honey: Tupelo honey is produced in the southeastern United States. In southern Georgia and northwestern Florida, tupelo is a leading honey plant, producing tons of white or extra-light amber honey in April and May. The honey has a mild, pleasant flavor and will not granulate.

BEES AS EMBLEMS

Bees were thought to have special powers and were often used as emblems. The bee was the sign of the king of Lower Egypt during the First Dynasty, 3200 BCE. In the third century BCE, the bee was the emblem used on coins in the Greek city of Ephesus. The bee was the symbol of the Greek goddess Artemis and the emblem of Eros or Cupid. Napoleon's flag carried a line of bees in flight, and his robe was embroidered with bees. Today in France, the bee marks the best-known brand of Roquefort and appears on all the famed pocket knives and corkscrews produced in the town of Laguiole, France.

HONEY OUTSIDE OF THE KITCHEN

Honey's unique composition makes it an effective antimicrobial agent, useful for treating minor burns and scrapes, and for aiding the treatment of sore throats and other bacterial infections. Beeswax candles are associated with both Catholic and Jewish rituals. The often intricately braided candle lit to symbolize the division between the holy Sabbath and the weekday must be made of beeswax.

480

Spring Mix Salad with Honey–Spice Almonds and Manchego Cheese

Salads that combine nuts and cheese are always popular in restaurants, most commonly featuring walnuts and blue cheese. In this salad, honey-spice-glazed almonds and salty, mildly pungent Manchego cheese from Spain accent spring greens tossed in a honey and sherry vinegar dressing. This can be served as either a first course or a combination cheese and salad course after the meal. Because sherry vinegar is high in acid, you'll only need a couple of spoonfuls here. If you can get it (and afford it), aged sherry vinegar, which may be as much as twenty-five years old, is wonderfully rich and complex.

Serves 4

6 ounces Spanish Manchego cheese, trimmed of rind

6 tablespoons extra-virgin olive oil

2 tablespoons Sherry vinegar

1 tablespoon coarse-grain mustard

1 tablespoon honey

2 teaspoons chopped fresh rosemary

1 teaspoon kosher salt

Freshly ground black pepper to taste

$^3/_4$ pound spring mix

Honey-Spice Almonds (*see* below)

Cut cheese into thin shavings using a cheese shaver or the side of a box grater and reserve. Whisk together olive oil, vinegar, mustard, honey, rosemary, salt, and pepper. Toss greens with dressing. Divide into serving bowls. Top each serving with several shavings of the cheese and a sprinkling of the almonds.

Honey–Spice Almonds

$^1/_4$ pound whole blanched almonds

1 tablespoon honey

1 tablespoon granulated sugar

$^1/_2$ teaspoon ground cinnamon

$^1/_4$ teaspoon paprika

$^1/_4$ teaspoon kosher salt

1 pinch cayenne pepper

Preheat the oven to 325°F. Spread the almonds onto a baking pan and toast for 15 minutes, or until lightly and evenly browned. Remove from the oven and cool. Mix together honey, sugar, cinnamon, paprika, salt, and cayenne. Toss cooled nuts in honey mixture. Arrange on a nonstick-sprayed baking pan and bake again for 15 minutes, or until nuts are shiny and glazed.

481

Grilled Sweetbreads with Apricots and Honey Mustard

Soft and creamy in texture and mild and delicate in flavor, you may have tasted sweetbreads, which are found in young calves and lamb, while traveling in Europe, where they are highly prized (see Sweetbreads, page 482). In most recipes, the sweetbreads are poached, peeled, and then weighted down to make them firm. Are they worth the effort? If you've ever tasted sweetbreads, you'll know the answer is a resounding yes! If not, here's your chance to try an easy-to-love animal delicacy. Once prepared, they cook very quickly. In this California-style dish, they are glazed with honey and mustard and accompanied by spiced fresh apricots. Serve with steamed spinach, Swiss chard, or broccoli florets. You'll need to precook the sweetbreads several hours ahead of time.

SERVES 4

Juice of 2 lemons

2 bay leaves

3 sprigs fresh thyme

$1\frac{1}{2}$ to 2 pounds fresh sweetbreads

2 tablespoons + 2 tablespoons honey

1 tablespoon + 1 tablespoon coarse-grain mustard

1 tablespoon + 1 tablespoon Dijon mustard

$\frac{1}{2}$ cup canola oil, divided

Kosher salt and freshly ground black pepper to taste

4 tablespoons unsalted butter, softened

1 teaspoon ground cinnamon

$\frac{1}{4}$ teaspoon ground cloves

$\frac{1}{2}$ teaspoon ground allspice

$\frac{1}{2}$ pound (4 to 8) fresh apricots, halved and pitted

In a large pot, make a *court bouillon* (*see* below) by combining 1 quart water, the lemon juice, bay leaves, and thyme. Simmer 20 minutes, then add the sweetbreads. Bring back to the boil, simmer for 5 minutes, or until sweetbreads are firm. Remove the pot from the heat and allow sweetbreads to cool in the broth.

Remove sweetbreads from liquid and peel off the outer membrane, trying to maintain sweetbreads as whole as possible, while also making sure to remove any gristly portions. Wrap in plastic wrap or place inside a plastic zip-top bag and weight with a flat, heavy object such as a pot or a baking dish with a couple of cans inside, for several hours least, or overnight if possible, refrigerated.

Meanwhile, whisk together 2 tablespoons honey, 1 tablespoon each coarse-grain and Dijon mustards, $1/4$ cup oil, and salt and pepper to taste. When ready to cook, coat the sweetbreads with this mixture.

Cream the butter and the remaining 2 tablespoons honey, the remaining 1 tablespoon each coarse-grain and Dijon mustard, and the cinnamon, cloves, and allspice. Use this soft butter to coat the apricots.

Have a hot charcoal fire going and when the flames have completely died down, grill the sweetbreads and apricots. The honey coating should be well caramelized on both the sweetbreads and apricots, although the total grilling time should be no more than 10 minutes. Alternatively, broil the sweetbreads and apricots. Serve immediately.

Sweetbreads

Veal and lamb sweetbreads are the most desirable and highest priced of all variety meats. Sweetbreads are the culinary term for two glands that lie in the young calf or lamb's throat or heart; they shrink as the animal grows older, becoming almost nonexistent in older animals. Throat sweetbreads are elongated and narrow; the more tender heart sweetbreads are plump and rounded.

Their uncharacteristically euphemistic name in French is *ris de veau* (or rice of veal). In Spanish, they're called *mollejas* (also used for poultry gizzards) and in Italian, *animelle* (also used for testicles). Sweetbreads are usually sold in pairs. Veal sweetbreads are larger, multi-lobed, and pinkish-white in color; lamb sweetbreads are smaller and lighter in color and not quite as delicate. Like all organ meats, sweetbreads are highly perishable, so they are often sold frozen. They freeze well; defrost overnight in the refrigerator.

483

COURT BOUILLON

Translating to *short-boiled*, from the French, this is a quick-cooking light stock combining an acid, such as white wine, lemon juice, or vinegar, and aromatic spices and herbs. It is used to flavor and quick-cook fish, seafood, and other light-colored foods such as sweetbreads, cauliflower, and endive.

Moroccan Spiced Lamb Tajine with Honey

Make this lamb tajine and your house will be filled with the enticing aromas of sweet spices (see About Tajines, page 436, for more information). Like many Moroccan dishes, this one calls for a long list of ingredients to give the full, rounded flavors of the both sweet and savory characteristics of this sophisticated cuisine that shows strong Moorish influences (the Moro in Morocco means "moor"). Most ingredients come from the pantry, making it a bit easier to prepare. Lamb shoulder is preferable to lamb leg for stews because it's not as lean and has plenty of connective tissue to melt into the juices for lip-smacking richness. Accompany with steamed couscous or rice, following the directions on the package.

SERVES 6

484

2 tablespoons olive oil

1/2 cup diced onions

2 teaspoons chopped garlic

2 1/2 pounds of lamb shoulder, cut into 1 1/2-inch cubes

Flour for dusting

1 cup lamb or chicken stock

1 cup diced tomatoes, canned or fresh

2 teaspoons ground cumin

2 teaspoons ground coriander

2 teaspoons ground turmeric

1 tablespoon grated fresh ginger

Kosher salt and freshly ground black pepper to taste

2 tablespoons honey

1/4 cup golden raisins

1/4 cup quartered, dried Mission figs

1/4 cup chopped cilantro

Honey for drizzling

In a tajine or Dutch oven, heat the olive oil and brown the onions and garlic. Remove from pan and reserve. Dust the lamb with flour. In the same pan, brown the lamb well on all sides, working in batches, if necessary. Pour off the fat, add the reserved onions and garlic to the browned lamb and cook for 5 minutes.

Add the stock, tomatoes, cumin, coriander, turmeric, ginger, and salt. Stir, cover, and cook over low heat very slowly until the lamb is tender and the pan juices are syrupy, about 45 minutes.

Stir in the honey, raisins, and figs and continue to cook 15 minutes until the flavors have combined. Stir in the cilantro just before serving. Drizzle each portion with a small amount of honey just before serving.

Greek Honey Cake with Semolina: Revani

While traveling in Greece with the International Olive Oil Council, I had the pleasure of tasting this moist, slightly crunchy, and all-around delicious cake at a lovely mountain taverna, called Oinotherapeftirio, in a picturesque small town on the way to Kalamata. It is a popular home-style cake made with semolina used for crunch and soaked in sugar syrup for juiciness in the style of Eastern Mediterranean and North African pastries like baklava and boureko. Look for fine semolina in Italian, Greek, and Middle Eastern markets. Cream of Wheat cereal makes the best substitute. For another semolina-based pastry, see the Galataboureko recipe on page 176 (for more information on semolina, see page 177). This cake is often served with tart Greek sheep and/or goat's milk yogurt to cut its richness.

6 ounces (1^1/$_2$ cups) all-purpose flour

8 ounces (2 cups) fine semolina

1 teaspoon baking soda

2 teaspoons baking powder

Pinch of salt

^{1}/$_2$ pound (2 sticks) unsalted butter

1 teaspoon vanilla extract

5 eggs, separated

^{1}/$_2$ cup + ^{1}/$_2$ cup + 1^1/$_2$ cups granulated sugar

^{1}/$_4$ cup honey

Preheat the oven to 350°F. Prepare a 12-inch diameter cake pan or a 9 x 13-inch rectangular pan by spraying with nonstick spray.

Whisk together the dry ingredients: flour, semolina, baking soda, baking powder, and salt and reserve.

In an electric mixer and using the paddle, beat the butter until light and fluffy. Add the vanilla and beat a little more, until the vanilla has been absorbed. Scrape the mixture out into a large mixing bowl and reserve.

Clean out the electric mixer bowl and, again using the paddle, beat the egg yolks with ^{1}/$_2$ cup of the sugar until light-colored and the mixture forms a ribbon. Fold into the butter mixture and reserve.

Again cleaning out the electric mixer bowl, but using the whisk, beat the egg whites until light and fluffy, sprinkle in ^{1}/$_2$ cup sugar, and continue beating until firm and glossy.

Alternating, fold the dry mixture and the egg whites into the butter mixture, beginning and ending with the dry ingredients.

Pour the batter into the pan and bake about 45 minutes, or until set in the middle, springy to the touch, and the

cake has started to come away from the sides of the pan. Remove cake from the oven.

Meanwhile, bring the remaining 1^1/$_2$ cups sugar, the honey, and 2 cups of water to a boil. Reduce heat and simmer for 5 minutes, skimming off the foam. Remove from the heat and reserve.

When the cake has cooled slightly, poke holes into it with a toothpick. Pour the hot syrup over the cake and into the holes very slowly. Let the cake stand for at least two hours to absorb the syrup before serving. Remove the cake from the pan, cut into portions, and serve.

Jewish Honey Cake

As early as the twelfth century in Germany and Eastern Europe, it was the custom for young boys attending Heder (Jewish religious school) to bring a piece of honey cake on the first day of school to sweeten their learning. Coffee, rum, spices, and orange zest balance the sweetness of the honey in this moist cake. Honey cake should be made 2 to 3 days before eating to mellow the flavors. I usually double the recipe because the cake keeps so well. This cake is ideal to bake in the decorative shaped paper pan-liners from Italy sold at upscale kitchen supply stores. Bring along an extra cake to a friend to serve with tea or coffee. The cake freezes perfectly and will keep, if well-wrapped, for up to one week refrigerated.

MAKES 2 SMALL LOAF CAKES

2 eggs

1 cup granulated sugar

485

1/2 cup vegetable oil

1 cup honey

2 tablespoons brandy or rum

1/2 cup strong black coffee

Grated zest of 1 orange

3/4 pound (3 cups) all-purpose flour, preferably
   unbleached

1 teaspoon baking powder

1/2 teaspoon baking soda

1/4 teaspoon kosher salt

1 teaspoon ground cinnamon

1/4 teaspoon ground cloves

1/2 cup sliced almonds

Preheat the oven to 350°F. Spray two 6-cup loaf pans generously with nonstick spray. Using the whisk attachment of a mixer, beat the eggs and sugar until creamy and light. Beat in the oil, continuing to beat until the oil has been completely absorbed.

In a separate bowl, whisk together honey, brandy, coffee, and orange zest. In another bowl, mix together the dry ingredients: flour, baking powder, baking soda, salt, cinnamon, and cloves. Alternating and beginning and ending with the dry ingredients, fold the honey mixture and the dry ingredients into the eggs.

Using a rubber spatula, scrape the mixture into both pans. Sprinkle the tops with the sliced almonds, and bake for 1 hour, or until the cake puffs up in the middle and has begun to come away from the sides of the pans. Cool before removing from the pans.

Note: Use aluminum or other light-colored pans for this cake. Dark pans will result in an overly dark outer crust. Fill the pans no more than two-thirds of the way up the sides, to leave room for expansion. If the cakes darken too much, reduce the oven to 325°F. for the last 20 minutes of baking.

Citrus Zests and Oils

The finely grated, oil-rich, colorful skin of citrus fruits provide the best "free" seasoning in your kitchen. Use a Microplane® zester to remove just the colored portion of the skin; the white pith that lies below will be bitter. Tangerines are especially rich in fragrant oils while the zest of Meyer lemons, available only during their short season in winter, have a wonderful lemon-orange flavor. If you don't happen to have fresh citrus fruit on hand (and note that it is difficult to zest fruits if they are not firm), try the excellent-quality pure citrus oils sold by the Boyajian company available in many specialty stores or through the Internet. Use in tiny amounts as the oil is quite concentrated.

HONEY AND JEWISH HOLIDAYS

Honey has special significance for Jews at Rosh Hashanah, the Jewish New Year, in September or October. Honey appears in several guises in Rosh Hashanah dinners, symbolizing the wish for a sweet year. The holiday meal typically begins with the dipping of apple slices in a bowl of honey, and honey appears in the ring-shaped challah and the honey cake—or *lekach*—for dessert. Honey cakes have been eaten at all joyful Jewish celebrations since the early Middle Ages in Germany and a bit later in Eastern Europe.

486

Honey–Anise Gelato

In my years at Ristorante DiLullo from the late seventies to mid-eighties, I must have made at least three thousand gallons of gelato in every flavor imaginable. I had a wonderful floor-standing vertical gelato machine made by Carpigiani in Italy. The results were ultra-smooth, rich yet light gelato, with the sophisticated flavors popular in Italy including hazelnut, bittersweet chocolate, espresso, pistachio, almond, crema (vanilla and orange zest), caramel, rum and golden raisin, and gianduia (see page 474). Here, honey makes for an incredibly silky texture, and anise, a seed spice characteristic of southern Italian desserts, gives it extra zip. Start the gelato a day ahead to give the anise time to steep in the milk. Like all gelati, this one should be tempered by transferring it to the refrigerator about 1 hour before serving.

SERVES 8

2 tablespoons anise seed, lightly toasted

2 cups milk, scalded

8 egg yolks

³/₄ cup granulated sugar

¹/₂ cup honey

1 cup heavy cream

1 to 2 teaspoons anise extract, if desired

Crush the anise seeds with a mallet, or grind in a coffee or spice grinder, and add to the milk. Cool, and then steep overnight in the refrigerator.

Beat the egg yolks with the sugar and honey. In a large Pyrex measure or bowl, scald the milk with the anise seed and the cream in the microwave. Whisk a little of the hot milk-cream mixture into the egg yolks to temper. Beat in the remaining hot cream and transfer egg mixture into a medium, nonreactive pot. Cook, whisking, until the custard reaches 165°F., or until it thickens visibly.

Remove from the heat and strain through a fine sieve to remove the anise seeds. Add anise extract to taste, if you like a stronger flavor. Cool over ice and then chill in the refrigerator (*see* Cooling Foods, page 238, for directions). Freeze in an ice cream freezer.

487

INDIVIA & RADICCHIO

INDIVIA & RADICCHIO

Some of the most strikingly beautiful, elegant, and, naturally high-priced vegetables belong to the chicory family. From the long, creamy-white spears called *indivia* in Italian, *witloof* (white leaf) in Flemish (Belgium), *endive* (on-deev) in French, and Belgian endive in English, to the blazing scarlet, rounded heads and long spears of radicchio, they add a note of Continental sophistication wherever they appear.

The endives, *Cichorium endivia*, and their close cousins, the chicories, *Cichorium intybus*, are groups of leafy vegetables in the sunflower family that share a tendency to be bitter and fibrous. Both the endives and the chicories (including radicchio) have their roots in wild chicory, familiar as the ragged-petalled blue wildflower often seen by the side of the road. In classical Greece and Rome, young wild chicory was used as a vegetable and for salad in much the same ways that cultivated chicories and endives are used today.

Belgian endive is probably the best-known member of the chicory tribe. Its smooth, slightly bulging, ivory-colored shoots consist of pale yellow-edged, tightly wrapped, spear-shaped leaves. Their pleasingly bitter flavor and crisp, juicy texture when raw is transformed when cooked into a mild, faintly bitter flavor and softly melting texture.

To produce Belgian endive, chicory plants are harvested in the fall and their leaves cut off. The remaining roots are then planted in a dark cellar, where they then sprout into the shoots that we know as Belgian endive in what is traditionally a two-year cycle. Because of this labor-intensive growing method, it is fairly high-priced, especially the authentic Belgian import packed in deep inky-blue waxed paper to protect it from light. An American version is now being grown hydroponically (in water and nutrients with no soil) in the darkness in greenhouses. Belgian Endive is a winter and early spring vegetable but is available almost year with American endive available in summer and fall.

ORIGIN OF BELGIAN ENDIVE

Belgian endive is an invented vegetable that doesn't exist in nature. The story goes that a farmer returning from the wars to his farm near Brussels in 1830 found chicory roots he had stored in his cellar, intending to dry and then roast them and use them as a coffee substitute. (The same roasted chicory root flavors New Orleans-style coffee.) Instead of drying out, the roots sprouted into the small, white-leafed shoots called *chicons*. By 1846, this Brussels endive was being sold in the city's market stalls. When introduced to Paris in 1872, this new vegetable earned the nickname "white gold" because of its popularity.

Other Types of Endive

Curly endive: Rather tough and decidedly bitter, curly endive grows in bunches of thin, white ribs with leaves that curl at the tips. The heart of the endive bunch will be pale yellow; the outer leaves deep green and sturdy. Curly endive is best braised or cooked in hearty vegetable soups and goes well with creamy white beans. Curly endive is most abundant in winter and spring.

Frisée: This European specialty takes curly endive one step further by blanching it (keeping it out of chlorophyll-producing light). Called *riccia* (curly) in Italian and *frisée* (also curly) in French, it is smaller, lighter and more delicate that its sun-grown forebear. The heads have an opened, flattened shape because they are pressed down while growing and slim, ragged-edged leaves that range from ivory to pale apple-green. Frisée is a common addition to spring mix salad greens, works beautifully in warm salads, such as the classic Salad Lyonnais (with bacon and poached eggs), and is very popular as a restaurant garnish. Because of its demanding growing process, it is expensive and not commonly found in supermarkets.

Escarole: Escarole, *scarole* in Italian, has broad, wavy leaves that form an open, flattened head ranging in color from pale yellow-green in the center to medium green on the outside. Its older name, Batavian endive (after the ancient tribe that occupied Holland), has fallen out of use. Mild in flavor, though fibrous in texture when raw, escarole is especially popular in Italy, where it goes into Italian Wedding Soup and bean soups, and is often served as a cooked green salad

(*insalata cotta*), steamed and dressed with olive oil, lemon, salt, and pepper. It makes a wonderful a melt-in-the-mouth side dish when slow-cooked.

Catalonia: Catalonia, another member of this family of Italian origin, has various cultivars with diverse appearances and characteristics. Its long, relatively thick white stalks and narrow, spiked leaves often resemble dandelion, and in fact, much of the "dandelion" sold in the U.S. is actually cultivated catalonia.

Puntarelle: Puntarelle, meaning shoots, a specialty of Rome, has pale white ribs and long, thin leaves that can be fairly smooth or deeply notched and light to deep green in color. This mild green is now being raised on a limited basis in the U.S. and can sometimes be found in specialty markets.

California Red Belgian Endive: A cross of Belgian Endive and radicchio developed in California and marketed as Red California endive, is a look-alike of Belgian endive but with scarlet-edged leaves. It is now also sometimes found in specialty markets; Endigia is a similar American creation (*see* Endive and Radicchio in California, page 493).

ESCAROLE AND CAST IRON

Avoid cooking any chicory in cast iron because they have a tendency to blacken, especially noticeable in escarole.

RADICCHIO

After traveling to Italy to study with Marcella Hazan in her Bologna cooking class, I knew I had to have radicchio for the menu at the newly opening Ristorante DiLullo. This was in 1979, when I had gotten my first big chef job. I finally convinced a local importer of specialty foods, Joe Assouline (today the owner of the highly successful Caviar Assouline in Philadelphia, www.caviarassouline.com) to risk bringing in a shipment of small European cases of radicchio. I was thrilled when it showed up and immediately started incorporating it into my menu; he was not so happy, because he ended up throwing out the rest of the cases—no one else wanted them! Today, even the salad at McDonald's includes radicchio.

Radicchio has a distinctive, bitter flavor due to intybin, which savvy Italians know stimulates the appetite and digestive system. Raw radicchio is fine, but only in small portions. It is at its best simmered in risotto Venetian style, braised, and grilled—although the gorgeous color turns to reddish-brown in the cooking process.

This strikingly beautiful vegetable began its life as a wild chicory on the plains of the Veneto surrounding Venice, still the most important production area for radicchio. Modern radicchio, with its rich, wine-red, white-ribbed leaves, was developed in the 1860s by applying new techniques, similar to those used to force Belgian endive, to the plants long grown around Treviso.

In Italy, there are at least fifteen well-known varieties of radicchio, from the flat, dark rosettes of Ceriolo to the long, thin leaves of Selvatico da Campo, and the variegated pink and pale green of Castelfranco.

Varieties of Radicchio

Rosso di Chioggia: Radicchio Rosso di Chioggia is by far the most common, being practically synonymous with radicchio in the U.S. It resembles a compact though lightweight head of cabbage with dark magenta-red leaves and white ribs, pronounced bitterness, and fibrous texture.

Rosso di Treviso: Radicchio Rosso di Treviso comes in two varieties: *Precoce* (early) and *Tardivo* (late). Precoce, which is known simply as Treviso when grown in the U.S., has narrow, pointed, fleshy red leaves with white ribs and forms a compact bunch shaped like a tapered head of romaine.

Radicchio di Verona: Radicchio di Verona, which is uncommon in the U.S., has burgundy-red leaves with creamy white ribs. It grows in a small, loose head resembling an elongated butterhead lettuce with tender but firm leaves with a slightly bitter flavor.

Tardivo: Radicchio Tardivo, the later season Treviso, has much more pronounced pearly-looking ribs with thin, splayed leaves that resemble exotic feathers and deep red color on the edges. Tardivo is flavorful, with stronger bitter accents than Treviso.

Variegato di Castelfranco: Radicchio Variegato di Castelfranco resembles a head of butter lettuce with deep wine-red speckles on an eggshell background. Also known as the "edible flower," it's a cross between radicchio and round-headed endive and is mild in flavor and tender in texture.

When I started buying radicchio, it was all imported from Europe. Today, two companies based in California dominate the American market. In the early 1980s a young chef started the company that became California Vegetable Specialties, a producer of red and white endive and their new Endigia. This is their proprietary forced red chicory, developed through years of crossing white endive and red Italian radicchio. You won't see this magenta and pearly-white vegetable in stores, because to date, it is only being sold to chefs.

The J. Marchigini company, started appropriately enough by Italian immigrants, raises round, Chioggia-type radicchio, long-leafed Treviso, and mild speckled Castelfranco radicchio in California's Central Coast and in Chile with year-round production. The company also raises other hard-to-find Italian specialty vegetables including Tuscan kale (*see* page 460), Fennel (*see* page 407), Roman Puntarelle (*see* Other Types of Endive, page 491), and cardoons (long white stalks related to artichokes; *see* page 55).

Indivia, Artichoke, and Prosciutto Salad

Belgian endive leaves are combined here with artichokes (both in the huge sunflower family) and thinly sliced prosciutto for a satisfyingly hearty winter salad. Fragrant tarragon and Dijon-style mustard flavor the bold dressing. Some American-made prosciuttos (the plural is actually prosciutti *in Italian) are of good quality. I recommend Citterio, made in the mountains of Pennsylvania. But, there is nothing like the silky smooth, perfectly balanced flavor of the real thing, prosciutto di Parma, from Italy, made from pigs that are fed the whey left from making Parmigiano-Reggiano cheese.*

SERVES 6

1 tablespoon Dijon mustard

2 tablespoons tarragon vinegar

1 tablespoon chopped tarragon, or 1 teaspoon
  dried tarragon

6 tablespoons + 2 tablespoons extra-virgin olive oil

2 tablespoons chopped shallots

Kosher salt and freshly ground black pepper to taste

1 (12-ounce) package frozen artichoke wedges

$1/2$ cup dry white wine

Juice of 1 lemon

6 heads Belgian endive, cored and cut into 2-inch strips

6 ounces thinly sliced prosciutto

Make the dressing by whisking together mustard, vinegar, tarragon, 6 tablespoons olive oil, shallots, and salt and pepper to taste and reserve.

In a medium, nonreactive pot, place the artichokes, wine, lemon juice, remaining 2 tablespoons olive oil, and a little salt. Bring to the boil and cook over high heat,

493

shaking occasionally until the juices cook away and the artichokes are tender and shiny, 5 to 10 minutes.

Toss endive leaves with the dressing, spoon the artichokes over top, and drape the prosciutto attractively around the plates. Serve immediately.

Treviso, Avocado, and Orange Salad

Make this strikingly beautiful cold weather salad when you can get the long, thin spears of Treviso or substitute red endive spears. Blood oranges are in season in the winter months (see page 657 for more information). Choose blood oranges with a red blush on their skin for deepest and more dramatic color. The avocados should be firm but ripe, just giving when pressed. If the small stem end left on the tip of the avocado when picked pulls out easily, the avocado will be perfectly ripe (see page 83 for more information).

SERVES 4

6 tablespoons + 2 tablespoons extra-virgin olive oil

2 tablespoons sherry vinegar

Grated zest of 1 orange

Kosher salt and freshly ground black pepper to taste

1 fennel bulb, trimmed

Juice of 1 lemon

2 blood oranges, pared of all flesh and white pith and cut into 1/4-inch thick rings

2 firm but giving avocados, cut into 1/2-inch slices

12 oil-cured black olives, halved

4 heads Treviso radicchio, cut into 1-inch-wide strips

Prepare dressing by whisking 6 tablespoons of the olive oil, the vinegar, orange zest, and salt and pepper, and reserve.

Slice the fennel thinly and then cut it into matchsticks. Combine the remaining 2 tablespoons olive oil with the lemon juice, and salt and pepper to taste. Marinate the fennel for 30 minutes.

Arrange blood orange slices in a ring around the outsides of 4 large serving plates. Arrange avocado slices in between the orange rings. Place 1 olive half into the center of each orange slice.

In a medium bowl, toss the fennel and Treviso with most of the dressing. Mound into the center of plate. Drizzle the orange and avocado slices with a little bit of the dressing and serve immediately.

Salad Lyonnais

This is a classic dish characteristic of the hearty cooking of the French city of Lyons, famed as the home of many of France's most important chefs, including Georges Perrier. Chef Perrier serves a delicious version of this salad at the small, chic Le Bar Lyonnais, downstairs from his oh-so-elegant and always delightful Le Bec-Fin Restaurant in the heart of Philadelphia's Restaurant Row. I've freely adapted his recipe here. I've always loved eggs in salad, whether poached as here, or in a variation of this salad served in Bergamo made with pancetta and mixed young greens, or barely hardcooked in a Salad Niçoise. The key to this salad is to make everything à la minute, just-in-time, so the eggs are warm and liquidy in the center, the bacon crisp, and the frisée barely wilted. The egg yolks then enrich and thicken the dressing. Try applewood- or maple-smoked bacon here.

494

3 tablespoons unsalted butter

2 large gold potatoes, peeled and cut into small cubes

1/2 pound thick-sliced smoky bacon, cut into thin strips

6 tablespoons olive oil

1/4 cup aged red wine vinegar

2 teaspoons Dijon mustard

Kosher salt and freshly ground black pepper to taste

1 tablespoon white vinegar

4 extra-large very fresh eggs

2 heads frisée, trimmed, washed, drained, and cut
     into 2-inch strips

In a large skillet, preferably nonstick, heat the butter until sizzling, then add the potatoes. Cook over medium heat until golden brown all over and soft in the center, shaking occasionally so the potatoes brown evenly. Drain, sprinkle with salt to taste, and reserve, keeping warm.

Brown the bacon, either in a small pan, or in the microwave, draining off the excess fat occasionally, until well-browned and crisp. Drain bacon, reserving 2 tablespoons of the fat, and reserve.

Whisk together the reserved bacon fat with the olive oil, vinegar, mustard, and salt and pepper to taste, and reserve.

Bring a small pan of water with the white vinegar to a full rolling boil. Carefully break open each egg and drop, one at a time, into the center of the pan. After all the eggs are in the water, turn the heat down and poach the eggs gently for about three minutes, or until the whites have set, but the yolks are still liquid. Drain the eggs using a slotted spoon, patting dry with a paper towel, and reserve.

Toss the frisée with the dressing and divide among 4 large salad plates. Place one egg in the center of each salad, as in a nest, sprinkle with potatoes and bacon, and serve immediately.

Grilled Radicchio with Balsamic Syrup

Next time you've got the grill going, try this recipe for grilled radicchio with a drizzle of sweet-tart balsamic syrup. Although they require close attention, grilling vegetables is a wonderful way to cook. Because most vegetables are quite porous, they pick up smoky flavors easily. Now, if I only could figure out a way to get soft, fully-cooked radicchio to keep that magenta color, instead of turning brown . . . .

SERVES 4

2 large heads round radicchio or 4 heads Treviso radicchio

2 tablespoons extra-virgin olive oil

Kosher salt and freshly ground black pepper to taste

6 tablespoons Balsamic Syrup (*see* page 596)

Preheat the grill or broiler. Trim the root ends of the radicchio and cut into thick wedges. Brush lightly with olive oil and sprinkle with salt and pepper.

Grill the radicchio on each side for 2 to 3 minutes, or until browned and slightly wilted. Remove from the grill and transfer to a plate. Cover with a bowl and steam until wilted, about 5 minutes. Drizzle each serving with Balsamic Syrup and serve.

495

Pappardelle Pasta with Radicchio

Pappardelle are inch-wide strips of pasta, most commonly found in game-loving southern Tuscany, in the area of Siena and Arezzo, where it is often tossed with a wild boar or wild hare ragù. The word comes from pappare, *which means to gobble-up or feast. It's uncommon to find pre-cut pappardelle, so either make your own (see* Pasta Dough *recipe on page 986), or purchase sheets of fresh pasta and cut your own. Simply roll up like a rug and cut slices about three-quarters of an inch wide. Unroll each slice, fluff the pasta gently, and reserve. Note that the wider the pasta strip, the more brittle it will be, so that once cut and unrolled, the pappardelle should be cooked within the hour. You may substitute fresh fettuccine, or even dried linguine.*

SERVES 4

$1/2$ pound pancetta or bacon, frozen until firm and
   cut into small cubes

1 small red onion, diced

2 small heads radicchio, cored and shredded

$1/2$ cup dry red wine

1 cup diced tomatoes

1 pound pappardelle pasta, substitute fettucine

$1/2$ cup heavy cream

Kosher salt and freshly ground black pepper to taste

$1/2$ cup grated Parmigiano-Reggiano or Grana Padano +
   extra for serving

Bring a large pot of salted water to the boil.

In a large skillet, brown the pancetta until crispy. Scoop out the pancetta bits and reserve. In the fat that remains (about 4 tablespoons), sauté the onion until it is lightly browned, then stir in the radicchio. Sauté until the radicchio has wilted, about 5 minutes. Pour in the red wine and cook over high heat until it evaporates, about 5 minutes. Add the tomatoes to the sauce and cook over high heat for about 5 minutes, until they are soft, but haven't lost their shape and reserve the sauce.

Add the pasta to the boiling water and cook 3 to 4 minutes, stirring often, until just cooked through.

Just before serving, add the cream to the sauce, and season to taste with salt and pepper. Bring the sauce back to the boil, pull off the heat, and stir in the cheese. Drain the pasta, toss with the sauce, and serve immediately, preferably on heated plates. Serve extra cheese on the side for sprinkling at the table.

JICAMA & WATER CHESTNUTS

JICAMA & WATER CHESTNUTS

Jicama and water chestnuts,

two totally unrelated vegetables, one Mexican and the other Asian, are combined in this chapter because they resemble each other in their culinary uses. Both are sweet, crunchy, nutty, and juicy and work well in Mexican, Latin American, and Asian cooking.

Jicama

The jicama, *Pachyrhizus erosus*, is native to Mexico and northern Central America, where it is widely cultivated. It is now also quite common in Southeast Asia. Related to the sweet potato, this underground tuber is also called the Mexican yam bean root, Mexican water chestnut, and the potato bean. Although jicamas commonly weigh less about one half pound, they may grow as large as six pounds. This large, dusty-brown, papery-skinned root is shaped like a beet root with a pointy tap root. Inside is crunchy, juicy, cream-white flesh with an apple-like nutty flavor. Most jicama is imported from Mexico and South America and is available year-round.

Jicamas couldn't be easier to prepare. Just peel away the skin and cut up as desired, using it raw in salads and salsas or cooking it briefly. Jicama makes an excellent substitute for fresh Chinese water chestnuts in stir-fries. Or, mix with mango, watermelon, papaya, pineapple, a squeeze of lime, and other tropical fruits to make a Mexican-style fruit salad.

Water Chestnuts

Many people have never tasted a fresh water chestnut because they are so commonly found in those little cans in the supermarket "Asian" aisle. The first time you taste this sweet, nutty, ultra-crunchy vegetable fresh, it will be almost impossible to go back to the canned version. Fresh Chinese water chestnuts, *Eleocharis dulcis*, resemble small, flattened tulip bulbs called "corms" (the swollen tip of an underground stem) with deep brown, scaly skin and are often sold complete with their imported Asian mud. Inside, the ivory flesh is quite firm, with something of the character of fresh coconut. They have been eaten in China since ancient times.

Water chestnuts are the roots of an aquatic plant that grows in freshwater ponds, marshes, lakes, and slow-moving rivers and streams in Japan, Taiwan, China, Thailand, and now Australia. Because they are difficult to harvest, fresh water chestnuts are something of a rarity, though not very expensive. Even a handful, peeled and halved, sliced or quartered will add wonderful texture to a cooked dish. Stir-fry whole or sliced water chestnuts until just heated through but still crunchy. Boil or steam briefly and add to salad.

Most water chestnuts, called *ma tai* in China, are imported from China or Japan, but they have recently been cultivated in the southeastern United States. Fresh

498

water chestnuts are found in Asian food markets and are most plentiful in summer and fall.

CHOOSING WATER CHESTNUTS

Because of their high sugar content, fresh water chestnuts tend to get moldy. Choose the largest, smoothest water chestnuts that are quite firm and heavy for their weight. Press each one to check for soft spots, an indication of decay. Buy more than you think you'll need to allow for loss from spoilage and for shrinkage in peeling.

STORING WATER CHESTNUTS

Store water chestnuts, washed and dried, but unpeeled, in a loosely closed plastic bag in the refrigerator for up to two weeks. Store peeled water chestnuts in a bowl of cold water, refrigerated (for up to one week), changing the water daily.

Preparing Water Chestnuts

Wash water chestnuts thoroughly in cold water to get rid of any mud. Using a small, sharp paring knife, peel, cutting away any soft or greenish spots until only creamy-white, firm chestnut remains. Place immediately in a bowl of fresh, cold water.

THE UNUSUAL WATER CALTROP

Have you ever been curious about the small, black-shelled vegetable that resembles a water buffalo head or a small bat with outstretched wings? Its woody, sculptured surface immediately brings to mind the face of a bat. That most unusual vegetable is a water caltrop or European water chestnut, *Trapa natans*. This hard-shelled, ebony fruit is related to the chestnut, and has two prominent, downward-pointing horns that are sharp enough to do some real damage.

The water caltrop's large black seed capsules have four spikes, which inspired their English name. The *caltrop* was a vicious medieval weapon with four iron points, made in such a way that at least one point was always up. The weapon would be thrown in front of the feet of horses in battle. The vegetable's Chinese name, *ling ko*, means "ram's horn nut." It is also called Singhara nut, Jesuit's nut, ling nut, and the "peanut in water." Water caltrops grow abundantly in Taiwan where, during the region of Kuantien's Water Caltrop Festival, eager visitors gather the caltrops themselves and eat them in great quantities.

Water caltrops can be found in Asian food markets in September when they are harvested and eaten to celebrate the overthrow of the Mongolians in ancient China. Choose water caltrops that fill out their shells completely; as the meat dries out inside the shell, it rattles if shaken. There is also a slate-brown European caltrop that has been eaten like chestnuts and acorns in Europe since prehistoric times.

Illegal in some parts of the U.S., the water caltrop must be cooked before eating to neutralize the toxins it contains. Although starchier and harder to peel than Chinese water chestnuts, they are often boiled or steamed in the shell as a snack. They may also be roasted and have a taste reminiscent of chestnuts.

499

Yucatan-Style Jicama Sticks

I visited the Yucatan Peninsula first when I was about eleven years old. Regrettably, I still remember refusing to get up and trudge through the hot sun to see the legendary green jaguar at Chichen Itza. I also remember enjoying this delicious low-fat snack sold by street vendors. It couldn't be easier to prepare once you've got the jicama. Crunchy sticks of jicama are marinated in pure ground hot chile, salt, and lime. If you like really hot foods, sprinkle these sticks with hot sauce as well. The fiery-hot Yucatan brand is made with habañeros and comes in green and red versions, with the green being the hottest. The sticks are especially good served with margaritas and beer, perhaps with a bowl of salted, roasted pepitas (pumpkin seeds).

SERVES 6

Juice of 2 limes

1 teaspoon kosher salt

1 tablespoon chili powder

1 teaspoon ground cumin

Hot sauce to taste

1 large jicama root, pared and cut into sticks

Combine lime juice, salt, chili powder, cumin, and hot sauce to make a strong marinade. Mix well with jicama sticks and marinate for 1 hour. Serve as an appetizer.

Shrimp Salad with Jicama, Mango, and Peanuts

This is a festive and colorful first-course salad with the beguiling flavors of Southeast Asia, including the Jicama which, though originally Latin American, has been eagerly embraced there. The smaller and neater the cubes of mango and jicama, the more elegant-looking the salad will be. The same salad can be made with fresh crabmeat instead of shrimp. Chopped roasted peanuts provide crunch and rich, nutty flavor along with the deep toasted flavor of the Asian sesame oil. Kadota from Japan is considered to be a high-quality sesame oil. It is available in Asian markets at a low price.

SERVES 6 TO 8

1 pound small raw shrimp, cleaned

Kosher salt and freshly ground black pepper to taste

1 tablespoon canola oil

Juice of 2 limes

2 tablespoons roasted sesame oil

1 firm but ripe mango, peeled and cut into small cubes

1 small jicama, peeled and cut into small cubes

$1/2$ cup chopped roasted peanuts, preferably salted

$1/4$ cup roughly chopped cilantro

Sprinkle the shrimp with salt and pepper to taste and then sauté in the oil over high heat until pink and opaque, about 2 minutes. Reserve.

Whisk together the lime juice, sesame oil, and salt and pepper to taste. Toss with the shrimp, mango, and jicama. Arrange on individual salad plates, garnish by sprinkling with the peanuts and cilantro, and serve.

500

Asian Duck and Vegetable Salad with Cilantro–Macadamia Pesto

My friend Chef Phillip Chin, now of the restaurant Bambù in Augusta, Georgia, created the original version of this salad. Restaurant style, this salad has several components, but once prepped, it all goes quickly and the delicious results are well worth it. Thinly sliced, pan-seared duck breast tops colorful and crunchy Asian vegetables tossed in a simple dressing. A cilantro pesto, buttery with macadamia nuts, adds another layer of texture and flavor, and a final sprinkle of chopped macadamias and sesame seeds bring the whole dish together. Add a bowl of soup, perhaps Chinese-style egg drop or hot and sour soup, and you've got a fine meal. Serve any leftover pesto over grilled fish or chicken, seared scallops, or steamed vegetables. Note that lean Muscovy duck breasts work well here (see page 375 for more information about Muscovy ducks).

SERVES 6 AS AN APPETIZER

Cilantro–Macadamia Pesto

MAKES 1¼ CUPS

1/2 cup canola or soy oil

1 cup (1/4 pound) macadamia nuts

2 cups (1 small bunch) cilantro leaves

Small handful crushed ice (optional)

Kosher salt and freshly ground black pepper to taste

Combine the oil and macadamia nuts in the bowl of a food processor and process until smooth and creamy. Add the cilantro and the crushed ice (to keep the pesto cold and keep the cilantro from oxidizing), and salt and

pepper to taste and process until the pesto is bright green and chunky-smooth. Reserve.

Duck and Vegetables

1 pound Muscovy duck breast

Kosher salt and freshly ground black pepper to taste

Juice of 2 limes

2 tablespoons soy sauce

1 tablespoon roasted sesame oil

1 tablespoon grated ginger

2 teaspoons hot chili sauce (like Sriracha from Thailand or Crystal from Louisiana)

1 small head Napa cabbage, shredded

1 cup shredded carrot

1 cup shredded jicama

1 cup snow peas, cut into thin strips, if desired

1 cup fresh bean sprouts

Cilantro-Macadamia Pesto

2 tablespoons each: toasted sesame seeds and chopped macadamia nuts, for garnish

Use a sharp knife to score the skin of the duck to the flesh in a diamond pattern. Do not pierce the flesh (if you're using a fatty duck breast, you may pull off all the skin and fat after cooking). Season on both sides with salt and pepper and rest for about 10 minutes at room temperature.

Combine the lime juice, soy sauce, sesame oil, ginger, and chili sauce, and reserve.

Heat a large skillet with about 1 inch of water. Add the cabbage, carrot, jicama, snow peas, and bean sprouts and cook, stirring, for about 2 minutes, or until barely wilted and brightly colored. Drain and rinse under cold running water to set the color, drain again, and reserve.

Place the duck in a heavy-bottomed skillet and cook

501

over medium heat until most of the fat has cooked away, leaving a crispy brown crust, about 8 minutes. Turn the duck over and cook for another 3 minutes, or until medium-rare. Remove from the pan and allow it to rest at room temperature.

Toss the vegetables with the reserved sauce and arrange on 6 large salad plates. Slice the duck breast into thin strips. Arrange the duck slices around the vegetables and drizzle with the pesto. Sprinkle with the sesame seeds and macadamia nuts, and serve.

Pork Loin and Water Chestnut Stir-Fry

Like all wok-cooked food, this dish cooks in minutes once you've got the prep done. Now, if only there was someone to peel, chop, and dice.... Here, thin strips of pork loin are combined with Chinese vegetables in a simple soy and sesame sauce. Serve over steamed rice and eat while piping hot.

SERVES 4

$^1/_2$ pound trimmed pork loin

$^1/_4$ cup soy sauce

$^1/_4$ cup molasses (not blackstrap), or 2 tablespoons
  dark brown sugar, packed

1 tablespoon roasted sesame oil

2 teaspoons cornstarch

1 teaspoon hot red pepper flakes

3 tablespoons soybean oil, divided

1 tablespoon chopped ginger

1 tablespoon chopped garlic

$^1/_4$ pound water chestnuts, trimmed and quartered

$^1/_2$ bunch scallions, cut into 1-inch lengths

$^1/_4$ pound shitake mushrooms, caps sliced

$^1/_4$ pound snow peas, trimmed

$^1/_4$ pound fresh water chestnuts, trimmed and quartered

Place the meat in the freezer and leave it about 45 minutes until firm but not hard. Cut into thin slices and then into finger-shaped strips and reserve.

Combine soy sauce, molasses, sesame oil, cornstarch, and hot red pepper in a small bowl and reserve.

Heat the wok until it just begins to smoke. Add 2 tablespoons of oil, pouring it down the sides and swirling so it coats the whole wok. Add the pork and stir-fry until browned and fully cooked, about 5 minutes. Remove from pan and reserve.

Add remaining 1 tablespoon oil to the wok, swirl around, and add the ginger and garlic. Cook until fragrant, for 1 minute.

Add the water chestnuts, scallions, and mushrooms and stir-fry for 1 minute, then add the reserved pork and snow peas. Bring to the boil, then pour in the sauce mixture. Bring the sauce to the boil while stir-frying, so that the cornstarch thickens. Serve while piping hot.

WOK HISTORY AND "MA"

The wok, traditionally made from carbon steel, originated in China during the Han Dynasty, about 2,000 years ago, to conserve precious fuel. Little has changed in the wok through the centuries because it is a perfectly functional design. The wok is surrounded by the leaping flames of special recessed wok stoves in Chinese restaurants at temperatures up to four times as great as a conventional stove. The deep, bowl-shaped, quick-conducting wok allows high heat to focus on small areas so that the flavors are concentrated during the quick cooking process. Many years of practice are needed to perfect the art of wok cookery and obtain the sought-after wok *ma*, the breath of the wok. See *The Breath of a Wok*, by Grace Young, for more about *ma*.

Wok Cookery Tips

For home use, a standard 14-inch carbon-steel wok is best. Some people prefer the kind with a flat bottom for use on a home stove, especially if you're cooking on an electric range.

Because everything is cooked in minutes at highest temperature, all ingredients should be cut into small, even pieces and arranged in small bowls in order of use in the recipe.

Heat the dry wok until lightly smoking. Pull off of the flame and pour in the cooking oil, allowing it to run down the sides of the wok and swirling so the oil coats the wok evenly.

Put the wok back on the heat and don't add too much food, which would drop the temperature so the food steams instead of sears. Use a curved metal wok spatula to turn the food in the pan, and shake often. If your heat source is not that strong, make two batches.

To clean the wok, hold onto the handle with a hot pad and rinse under hot water, allowing the heat to bubble up the contents of the pot. Drain, wipe dry with a towel, and place back on the heat. In Chinese restaurants, long swinging faucets are close at hand to do just the same thing.

When adding the sauce mixture, pour down the side of the wok so the temperature doesn't drop. Eat the stir-fry immediately, while still piping hot.

CHOOSING AND STORING JICAMAS

Choose medium-size jicamas with smooth, unblemished skins and no stickiness. Store like potatoes in a cool, dry place for several weeks, refrigerating after being cut for up to 3 weeks. Too much moisture will cause the jicama to develop mold (which can be cut away).

Crispy Black Sea Bass with Chinese Black Vinegar and Fresh Water Chestnuts

A delicious sauce flavored with Chinese black vinegar and French-style brown butter is served here with cornstarch-crisped black sea bass—a firm, lean, white-fleshed fish well-loved in Chinese cuisine. The vinegar can be found in Asian markets; it's thick, dark, and syrupy, reminiscent of balsamic vinegar. This Asian-accented dish was inspired by one served at Philadelphia's legendary French restaurant, Le Bec-Fin.

SERVES 4

Fish

1 cup rice wine

1/2 cup soy sauce

1 tablespoon grated ginger

Kosher salt and freshly ground black pepper to taste

4 (1/2-pound) fillets black sea bass, skin on and pin
  bones removed (*see* About Pin Bones, page 419,
  and Removing Pin Bones, page 833, for directions)

Combine the rice wine, soy sauce, ginger, salt, and pepper. Mix with the fish and marinate at least 4 hours and up to overnight, refrigerated.

Sauce

4 tablespoons unsalted butter

1/2 cup soy sauce

1/4 cup Chinese black vinegar

Juice of 1 lime

1 teaspoon hot pepper sauce

Cook the butter in a small, heavy-bottomed pan over low heat until medium-brown in color and nutty-smelling. Note that then when butter starts to brown, it browns quickly. Remove from the heat, pour off and reserve the browned butterfat, leaving behind the small browned bits.

Combine the soy sauce, vinegar, lime juice, and hot pepper sauce in a small pot and warm over low heat. Transfer to the jar of a blender. Slowly pour in the butter and blend until creamy and smooth. Transfer back to the pot and keep warm.

Vegetables and Assembly

3 tablespoons unsalted butter, divided

Several drops roasted sesame oil

1/2 pound fresh water chestnuts, pared, quartered,
  and covered with cold water

1/4 pound snow peas, trimmed

1 bunch scallions, sliced on the diagonal

Marinated Fish (from above)

1/2 cup cornstarch

2 tablespoons soy or canola oil

Sauce (from above)

Place 1 tablespoon of the butter, a few drops sesame oil, and two tablespoons of water in a medium skillet, preferably nonstick. Bring to the boil, add the drained water chestnuts, snow peas, and scallions, and cook over high heat until the liquid evaporates and the vegetables are glossy and crispy, about two minutes. Reserve.

Remove the fish from the marinade and pat dry. Dust with cornstarch, shaking off the excess.

In a large, nonstick skillet, heat the remaining 2 tablespoons of butter and the soy oil until sizzling hot. Place the fish fillets into the pan skin-side down. Brown over high heat for about 2 minutes, then turn over and cook 2 minutes longer. The fish should be crispy and brown, but still juicy.

Divide the vegetables among four serving plates. Cover with a portion of fish, drizzle with the sauce, and serve immediately.

504

KASHA & BUCKWHEAT

KASHA & BUCKWHEAT

Growing up, I enjoyed eating steaming-hot kasha as a cereal with milk and sugar, and in *kasha varnishkes*, mixed with lots of browned onions and bow-tie-shaped egg noodles, dishes evocative of my Eastern European Jewish heritage. Kasha is most often made from roasted buckwheat, *Fogypyrum esculentum*, which is unrelated to wheat, but rather a member of the rhubarb family. Though in America, kasha means only buckwheat groats, in Russia, kasha may also refer to millet or oat porridge.

Buckwheat is quite well known in certain places in the world, many of them cold and unsuited to growing much else, and is practically unknown elsewhere. It is native to Siberia and reached Japan from Korea. For long centuries, buckwheat was the main food of the mountainous regions of Northern Japan, where rice wouldn't grow. Japanese *soba* noodles made from buckwheat flour were first produced there in the seventeenth century.

Buckwheat reached Eastern Europe from Russia during the Middle Ages and was brought to Europe by crusaders who had been introduced to it in their travels to the east. By the fifteenth century, it was known in Germany and not much later was found in Italy and France, where its name reflects its connection with the East—Saracen grain (*sarrasin* in French and *saraceno* in Italian). In the Atlantic province of Brittany, large, thin crepes are made with buckwheat flour in a dish thought to be adapted from the *blini* of Russia, perhaps brought to Brittany by sailors. Today, the largest producers of buckwheat are Russia and Poland. In Italy, *grana saraceno* is buckwheat that has been ground very finely into flour. As in Japan, it is a traditional food of the high mountains, the Valtellina, where it is made into a special pasta called *pizzocheri* and is also cooked into polenta. Dutch colonists originally brought buckwheat to North America and planted it along the Hudson River, where it was one of the first crops to be cultivated. Today, buckwheat is grown primarily in Northern states such as New York and is most commonly used for pancakes.

In America, kasha is roasted buckwheat kernels that are packaged whole, or in coarse, medium, and fine grain. The buckwheat groats can be steamed, boiled, or baked, seasoned and served as a side dish, especially good for anyone who is wheat intolerant. Kasha also makes a very good stuffing for poultry or vegetables such as squash and peppers.

Buckwheat Blini with Caviar and Sour Cream

Buckwheat blini *are small, butter-cooked and butter-anointed yeast-risen pancakes served in Russia as* zakuski *(or hors d'oeuvres). They are the traditional accompaniment for sturgeon caviar, whether beluga, sevruga, or ossetra. However, because beluga sturgeon is now on the U.S. endangered list and other types are quite expensive, I would substitute American paddlefish caviar. Blini make the most elegant party fare, perhaps for New Year's Eve with champagne. The batter rises three times, each time gaining more flavor and lightness. Blini are easiest to make in a special cast-iron blini pan with six 2-inch depressions to hold the batter. If you don't have one, the next best alternative is to cook them on a flat griddle.*

SERVES 6

1 package (2^1/4 teaspoons) dry yeast

^{1}/2 cup lukewarm water

^{1}/2 cup buckwheat flour, divided

^{1}/2 pound (2 cups) all-purpose flour, preferably unbleached

2 cups lukewarm milk, divided

3 eggs, separated

1 teaspoon kosher salt

2 teaspoons granulated sugar

4 tablespoons unsalted butter, melted and cooled

^{1}/4 cup + 1 cup sour cream

1 cup clarified butter, for frying (*see* Making French-style Clarified Butter, page 170)

2 to 3 ounces American paddlefish caviar

Dissolve the yeast in the water, then set in a warm spot until the mixture bubbles up and doubles in volume, about 5 minutes.

In a mixing bowl, combine ^{1}/4 cup of the buckwheat flour with the all-purpose flour. Pour in the yeast mixture and 1 cup of the milk. Beat together until the mixture is smooth. Cover the bowl with plastic wrap and set aside to rise in a warm, draft-free spot until the mixture doubles in volume, about 2 hours.

Stir down the batter and beat in the remaining ^{1}/4 cup buckwheat flour. Cover and let rise again.

Stir down the batter and beat in the remaining 1 cup milk, the egg yolks, salt, sugar, butter, and ^{1}/4 cup sour cream.

Beat the egg whites until firm and fold into the batter. Let the batter rest in the warm spot for 30 minutes longer.

Heat the blini pan and brush with a small amount of clarified butter. Pour in enough batter to fill each round. Cook on moderate heat until bubbles form across the surface of the blini, then turn, using a cook's fork, and continue cooking on the other side for 1 to 2 minutes, or until lightly browned.

507

Remove the blini from the pan and brush each one with melted butter. Spread onto a parchment-paper-lined sheet pan and cover lightly with foil. Keep warm in a 200°F. oven until ready to serve, no more than one hour.

Serve the blini topped with small dollops of sour cream with the caviar spooned onto the white cream.

Buckwheat Pizzocheri with Fontina Cheese

This hearty pasta dish is a specialty of the Alpine Valtellina region in Northern Italy. The pizzocheri are pasta ribbons made from a mixture of one part buckwheat and two parts unbleached flour. (The buckwheat has no gluten of its own to form the structure of the pasta, so it must be mixed with wheat flour.) The pasta is cooked and mixed with sautéed savoy cabbage, which originated in the area (also called Savoy) and a local cheese called bitto, *which is somewhere between Gruyere and Parmigiano in flavor. Because this cheese is not usually exported, I substitute Italian Fontina since it melts so beautifully and has a luscious texture and enticing aroma (see* Fontina Cheese, *page 198 for more information).*

SERVES 4

2 tablespoons + 4 tablespoons unsalted butter

2 to 3 gold potatoes, peeled and cut into small cubes

2 leeks, thinly sliced

1 small head Savoy cabbage, cut into 1-inch thick strips

4 cloves garlic, thinly sliced

2 tablespoons shredded sage

Kosher salt and freshly ground black pepper to taste

1 pound fresh Buckwheat Pizzocheri (recipe follows)

1 cup grated Fontina cheese

Butter a (1½- to 2-quart) shallow casserole with 2 tablespoons of butter and reserve. Preheat the oven to 375°F.

Bring a large pot of salted water to the boil. Add the potatoes and boil until fully cooked, about 8 minutes. Using a skimmer, scoop the potatoes from the water, drain, and reserve.

Meanwhile, in a large Dutch oven, melt the remaining 4 tablespoons of butter and cook until it browns and has a hazelnut-like aroma. Add the leeks and cabbage and cook, stirring occasionally, over medium heat until soft, about 6 minutes. Add the garlic and sage and cook 2 or 3 minutes more, or until the garlic is fragrant. Remove pot from the heat and mix with the potatoes. Season to taste with salt and pepper and reserve.

Bring the pot of water back to the boil, add the Buckwheat Pizzocheri and cook 3 to 4 minutes, or until fully cooked but still firm. Drain. Spoon the cabbage mixture, the pasta, and the cheese into the casserole in layers, ending with the cheese. Cover with foil and bake 10 minutes, just long enough for all the ingredients to meld together. Remove from the oven and serve immediately, preferably in heated pasta bowls.

Buckwheat Pizzocheri Pasta

3 eggs

4 ounces (1½ cups) durum wheat flour

4 ounces (1½ cups) all-purpose flour, preferably unbleached

4 ounces (1½ cups) buckwheat flour

Extra flour (in equal quantities) if needed

Beat the eggs in a mixer using the paddle attachment. Change to the dough hook and start adding the durum flour, all-purpose flour, and buckwheat flour, one cup at a time while beating, until flour is completely absorbed. Keep beating until the dough is well mixed, elastic, and quite firm, and comes away cleanly from the side of the bowl. Add extra flour if necessary, keeping in mind that the dough will soften as it rests. Wrap dough in plastic and allow to rest for at least 30 minutes at room temperature.

Flatten out a small piece of dough by hand into a rough rectangle. Using a hand-cranked pasta sheeter on the lowest number setting (the largest opening between the rollers), flatten out the dough.

Continue to roll out the dough, adding a little flour to keep the dough from sticking, until a long, tongue-shaped piece is obtained that is about three times as wide as the dough slot. Fold the tongue in three, lengthwise, and place crosswise in the slot of the pasta sheeter. (The object is to get an even, wide piece of dough.)

Continue to roll, notching up one number each time, until you reach the next-to-the-highest number, which is almost the smallest opening between the rollers. (Usually the highest setting will yield a too-thin dough, unless the dough you're working with is extremely firm.) The finished dough should be quite thin, but not transparent.

Cut the dough into even lengths of about 1 foot each. Roll each up like a rug and cut slices about three-quarters of an inch wide. Unroll each slice, fluff the pasta gently, and reserve. Note that the wider the pasta strip, the more brittle it will be; once cut and unrolled, the pizzocheri should be cooked within the hour.

Pizzocheri Variation

Cook artichoke hearts and cardoon stems in browned butter until soft and lightly browned. Separately brown venison sausage removed from the casing and chopped into bits. Add sliced red onions and brown lightly. Toss the artichokes, cardoons, venison, and onions with grated Fontina cheese. Layer in a casserole dish, finishing with a layer of cheese. Bake as in the recipe on the left to meld flavors, and serve.

Kasha Varnishkes

This old-time dish of kasha mixed with browned onions and bow-ties is delicious and easy to make. The word kasha *itself comes from a Russian word for cereal, referring to toasted buckwheat groats. Kasha was indispensable to the poor Jewish peasants of Russia and Poland, because it can be grown in poor soil and cold-weather conditions. Immigrants to America brought kasha with them as a taste of the old world of the* shtetl *(the traditional Eastern-European Jewish village) they mourned. Gathering wild mushrooms for drying is a traditional pastime in Poland. You may add dried and reconstituted wild mushrooms, along with some of their soaking liquid to the kasha for a taste of the woods, or sauté fresh wild mushrooms separately and mix them with the kasha just before serving.*

SERVES 6

1 pound box medium kasha

1 egg, lightly beaten (or 2 egg whites)

Kosher salt and freshly ground black pepper to taste

1 quart chicken or vegetable stock, simmering

1 pound egg pasta bow ties

1 large onion, diced

3 tablespoons unsalted butter

1 bunch scallions, thinly sliced

2 teaspoons chopped garlic

$1/4$ cup chopped dill

Preheat the oven to 350°F. Mix kasha, egg, salt, and pepper very well, so that each grain is coated with egg. Spread out into a metal baking pan and bake in the oven, stirring occasionally so that kasha grains are lightly toasted and separate, about 10 minutes.

Bring chicken stock to the boil, add kasha, and transfer to a baking dish. Cover and bake 10 minutes. Remove from the oven, fluff the kasha, cover again, and bake until kasha is soft and fluffed, about 15 minutes more.

Bring a large pot of salted water to the boil. Boil the bow-ties until *al dente*, firm and bouncy, and still yellow in color. Drain, rinse, and reserve.

Meanwhile, brown the onion well in butter, then add the scallions and garlic and cook briefly until the garlic is fragrant. Mix the kasha, onion mixture, bow ties and dill. Serve immediately.

ABOUT VARNISHKES

Varnishkes seems to have originally referred to a dumpling filled with kasha (like a knish filled with kasha; *see* Potato-Onion Knishes on page 759). This transformation into a dish that is easier to prepare is similar to the way gefilte fish originally referred to a stuffed fish (*gefilte*) and eventually to the filling itself minus the fish.

Salmon Coulibiac

Years ago, I would invite my kitchen staff to an annual New Year's Day night (when restaurants usually close) party featuring one magnificent dish like paella, cassoulet, or this coulibiac, an elaborate and impressive Russian fish pie dating from Czarist Russian times. Russian cooking is characterized by savory filled pies. Fittingly, the most elegant of these, known as kulebyaka, was adopted into French cuisine as coulibiac. It is sometimes filled with eel and sturgeon, but most commonly salmon, layered with hard cooked eggs, kasha or buckwheat blini, and mushrooms and traditionally vesiga, the gelatinous marrow inside the spinal cord of a sturgeon, to lend richness and body. The whole pillow-shaped assembly is enclosed in brioche dough, then baked to a magnificent shiny brown, and served with great ceremony. If you'd like, substitute the kasha filling with layers of the buckwheat blini in this chapter.

SERVES 12

1 pound Whole Wheat Brioche dough (*see* page 988), chilled until firm

1 cup medium kasha

1 egg

Kosher salt and freshly ground black pepper to taste

1 bunch scallions, thinly sliced

$1/4$ cup chopped Italian parsley

1 cup sliced shallots

$1/4$ pound (1 stick) unsalted butter

$1 1/2$ pounds assorted sliced mushrooms, such as baby bella, shiitake, pleurottes, and button

$1/2$ cup white wine

6 hard-cooked eggs, peeled, cut into thick slices

1/4 cup chopped dill

Flour and oil for preparing the pan

1 (3- to 3 1/2- pound) side salmon fillet, pin bones removed (see About Pin Bones, page 419, and Removing Pin Bones, page 833, for directions) and trimmed into a compact shape

1 egg, lightly beaten with 2 tablespoon milk, for egg wash

Divide the dough in two sections, one about two-thirds and one about one-third. Roll out the large section into a rectangle about 10 x 16 inches, cover, and refrigerate. Roll out the smaller section into a rectangle about 8 x 14 inches, cover, and refrigerate.

Preheat the oven to 350°F. Mix together the kasha and egg until the grains are well coated. Heat a large skillet and then add the egg-coated kasha. Toast the kasha, separating grains with a fork, about 4 minutes, or until the grains are separate and toasty-smelling. Add 2 cups cold water, cover and bring to the boil, then simmer 10 minutes or until kasha is fluffy. Season to taste with salt and pepper, stir in the scallions and parsley, cool, and reserve.

In a separate skillet, sauté the shallots in butter until softened. Add the mushrooms and wine. Cook over high heat until the mushroom liquid evaporates, about 8 minutes. Season to taste with salt and pepper, remove from the heat, cool, and reserve.

Combine the hard-cooked eggs and dill, season with salt and pepper, and reserve.

Place the larger piece of chilled dough on a floured sheet of parchment or wax paper laid on top of a baking pan. Have ready a second baking pan that has been covered with parchment paper or a Silpat sheet, or is lightly oiled and dusted with flour. Arrange the kasha in a compact rectangular shape in the center of the dough, leaving a 1-inch border at the edges.

Season the salmon on both sides with salt and pepper and arrange it, flesh-side down, on top of the kasha. Cover with the mushrooms and finally make a layer of the eggs, again leaving a border.

Brush the exposed edges of the dough with the egg wash, and cover the coulibiac with the second, smaller oblong of dough. Bring the edges of the bottom layer up over the top layer, enclosing the whole thing, and press to seal at the edges.

Place the second pan on top of the coulibiac. Hold both pans firmly and flip over so that the coulibiac rests right- side up on the second pan. Brush all over with the remaining egg wash, and cut small slits over the top for air holes. If desired, use any dough scraps to cut out decorative shapes, arrange the shapes on the dough and brush with egg wash. (At this point, you may refrigerate the coulibiac up to overnight before baking. Bring out of the refrigerator at least 1 hour before baking to allow the dough to rise and for the fillings to lose their chill.)

Bake the coulibiac for one hour, or until the filling bubbles up in the slits and the pastry is nicely browned. Cover the coulibiac with foil during the last 15 minutes of baking to keep it from overbrowning. Remove from the oven and allow the coulibiac to cool about 20 minutes before cutting into slices for serving.

511

COULIBIAC AT A RUSSIAN BANQUET

One of my personal pleasures is searching the shelves at used book stores where I have found treasures like a first edition of culinary luminary M.F.K. Fisher's 1946 book, *Here Let Us Feast: A Book of Banquets.* The book is described on the cover as "an epicure's zestful visit to the festive boards of ancient & modern literature." Fisher quotes a mouthwatering description of coulibiac in Nikolai Gogol's *Dead Souls* in which Pyotr Petrovitch, described by M.F.K. Fisher as "a fat generous man who loves company," instructs his cook: "And make a four-cornered fish pasty; in one corner put a sturgeon's cheeks and the jelly from its back, in another put buckwheat, mushrooms and onions and sweet roe, and brains and something else—you know. . . . And let it be just a little colored on one side, you know, and let it be a little less done on the other. And bake the underpart, you understand, that it may be all crumbling, all soaked in juice, so that it will melt in the mouth like snow."

512

LAMB

LAMB

Lamb is the meat of choice for those who enjoy its pronounced flavor and the bold seasonings that complement it best. Because I love these flavors, many of them typical of the Middle East, the Mediterranean, and India, lamb is my favorite red meat. The meat gets most of its distinctive flavor from the gamey-tasting fat, which can be trimmed off. Americans eat little lamb: a bit more than three-quarters of a pound a year per person as compared to about sixty pounds of beef. Lamb is the favored meat in India (where Muslims don't eat pork and Hindus don't eat beef), Pakistan, Central Asia, all over the Middle East, the Gulf States, Indonesia, North Africa, Greece, Turkey, the Balkans, and parts of China, especially in Western China, where there is a large Muslim population, and Mongolia.

Lamb works best with seasonings that are, in themselves, potent enough to stand up to the meat's strong flavor. Popular spices and seasonings for lamb include garlic mixed with resinous herbs like rosemary, thyme, and oregano and with lemon, vinegar, or wine, or other tart flavors like pomegranate molasses and tamarind. It is wonderful with warm spices like coriander, cinnamon, cumin, fenugreek, nigella, and fennel, and also works well with tomato-based sauces, oil, and brine-cured olives, capers, and preserved lemons.

Lamb, *Ovis aries*, or young sheep, are in the *Bovidae* family along with goats and cattle. These small animals were among the earliest of domesticated animals, starting about 10,000 years ago. For humans, raising sheep has many benefits. They can be herded easily, tolerate a wide range of weather conditions, and provide their meat, their valuable and renewable wool, and milk for cheese and yogurt. Lamb is traditionally served on both Easter and Passover, both of which fall in the spring, when young lamb is in season. During the Muslim holiday of Aid el Kabir, which commemorates the willingness of Abraham to sacrifice his son Isaac, an animal, usually a lamb, is ritually slaughtered and then eaten.

The introduction of sheep into American cattle herds in the west during the nineteenth century caused much divisiveness and helps explain why lamb has never been embraced in the United States. Even today, the Western sheep industry is dominated by Basque immigrants who brought their knowledge of sheepherding to the west and later went on to own their own herds. The American lamb flock was at its peak of fifty-six million in 1942; by 2002 the flock was at less than seven million. The main sheep-raising states are Texas, California, Wyoming, South Dakota, and Colorado.

The great majority of American lamb are grain-fed, making them milder in flavor; lamb imported from Australia and New Zealand is grass-fed and may have a more pronounced flavor. China is the world's largest producer of lamb, followed by Australia. Imported lamb is lower in price and smaller in size than domestically raised lamb—it is one-half to two-thirds the weight of domestic lamb. Imported Australian and New Zealand lambs are the kind found in many warehouse club stores. American lamb is highly appreciated by top chefs and connoisseurs and is often found on the menus of top restaurants, but is more costly.

When buying lamb, remember: the lighter the color, the younger the meat. Look for light red, finely textured meat, bones that are reddish, moist, and smooth, and white (not yellowed) fat. Avoid lamb that is overly dark in color, has dry, white bones, and yellowed or strong-smelling fat. Lamb has red bones; as lamb grows older, blood recedes from the bones, so mutton has white bones. The bone at the joint of a leg of lamb is serrated, while in mutton it is smooth and rounded.

AMERICAN LAMB BREEDS

English breeds, which are named for their place of origin (such as Southdown, Suffolk, and Cotswold), formed the basis of the earliest American lamb herds in the East, brought by colonists as early as 1640. Sheep in the west developed from the interbreeding of three types of sheep: the original Spanish Churro sheep, brought to North America in 1540 by the Spanish explorer, Francisco Vasquez de Coronado; the Merino, a Spanish breed known for its soft, fine wool; and the Rambouillet, a French variety developed from the Merino with good wool and good meat that adapts to a range of climates. These original churro sheep are now being raised again in the Southwest in an effort to conserve and develop our native heritage breeds.

Lamb Age, Inspection, and Grading

Inspection is mandatory, while grading is voluntary. USDA-graded lamb sold at the retail level is Prime, Choice, or Select. As with beef, most of the lamb in supermarkets is Choice or Select, with Prime going to fancy butcher shops, restaurants, and hotels. Prime lamb has more fat marbling, so it is the most tender and flavorful grade, though it is higher in fat. Choice is not commonly found in supermarkets. Select and lower grades are mainly ground or used in processed meat products. Retail stores may use other terms or brand names for their lamb. The protein, vitamin, and mineral content of lamb are similar in all grades.

515

Baby lamb, hothouse, or suckling lamb is milk-fed lamb that is less than ten weeks old and weighs less than twenty pounds. It is called *abbacchio* in Italian and is a Roman delicacy. Its meat is pale pink, relatively lean, and delicately flavored, and it is usually roasted whole.

Spring or Easter Lamb is several months old and weighs twenty to forty pounds. It is only available fresh between March and the beginning of October. It is a favorite for festive occasions and is often spit-roasted.

French *pré-salé* (salty pasture) lamb grazes on the salty shores of Brittany and Normandy and is considered by connoisseurs to be the finest in the world, although rarely, if ever, available in the U.S.

The most common type of lamb is five months to one year old and is hearty enough not to be overpowered by bold and exotic seasonings and can be cooked by most methods including grilling, broiling, pan-searing, roasting, stewing, and braising.

Yearling (sometimes called hogget) is lamb that is one to two years old. Its meat is darker and more flavorful than lamb. A wether is a castrated sheep.

Mutton is at least two years of age and should be aged, like beef, for at least two weeks, resulting in juicy, well-flavored meat that is firm but not tough. The cuts are larger, the color darker red, and the flavor more pronounced. Although once more common, mutton is not widely available in the U.S. today. It is especially good in English-style meat pies, Irish lamb stew, slow-cooked curries, spicy Middle Eastern dishes, and braised dishes like tajines.

516

Whole Lamb and Cuts

Even full grown, lamb are on the small side, about one tenth the size of beef cattle. A domestic lamb weighs about 120 pounds, yielding about half that much in retail cuts. Smaller lambs are sometimes cooked whole, especially spring lamb and suckling lamb.

In the U.S., lamb is usually divided into five more manageable "primal cuts" at the slaughterhouse for shipping to retail stores and wholesalers. These are the breast and foreleg, the chuck (or shoulder), the rib section, the loin, and the leg.

Horseradish–Crusted Roast Rack of Lamb

Rack of lamb is quite a luxurious cut and therefore expensive. It's best roasted whole and then cut into individual chops to cut down on shrinkage. Ask the butcher to remove the chine bone—the small bones sticking up from the spine—to make it easier to carve. Allow two whole racks to serve four people, or possibly to serve five or six, if you're serving larger American lamb. Some imported lamb is so small that one rack will serve one person, albeit generously. An oven-ready American rack of lamb weighs about 2 pounds; an imported rack of lamb from Australia or New Zealand may weigh less then 1 pound. The general rule is to allow $3/4$ to 1 pound of bone-in lamb per person. Here the lamb is seasoned then pan-seared just until brown on the outside. It is then covered with a mixture of egg and mustard, which acts as the "glue," and then rolled in a horseradish and breadcrumb mixture before being roasted at high heat to make a nice brown crust.

2 racks of lamb (2 portions), trimmed

Kosher salt and freshly ground black pepper to taste

2 tablespoons olive oil

2 eggs, lightly beaten

$^1/_4$ cup Dijon mustard

$^1/_4$ cup prepared horseradish, well-drained

$^3/_4$ cup homemade-style breadcrumbs

Juice and grated zest of 1 lemon

2 tablespoons chopped shallots

1 tablespoon chopped thyme, or 1 teaspoon dried thyme

Rub the lamb all over with salt and pepper and allow it to rest at room temperature for about 20 minutes.

Heat the oil in a large heavy skillet, preferably cast iron, until shimmering. Brown the lamb on all sides. Remove the lamb from the heat, pat dry, and paint with a mixture of the eggs and mustard.

Preheat the oven to 450°F. Combine the horseradish, breadcrumbs, lemon juice and zest, shallots, and thyme. Pat the crumbs all over the lamb.

Place the lamb in a roasting pan just large enough to hold it and roast bone-side up for 10 to 15 minutes, then turn over and roast flesh-side up for another 10 to 15 minutes, or until the lamb reaches 135°F. when measured at the thickest portion.

Remove the lamb from the oven, drape with foil, and allow it to rest 10 minutes.

Cut into chops and serve immediately.

Herb-Roasted Leg of Lamb with Fennel Stuffing

A roast leg of lamb is an excellent choice for a springtime dinner. If boned and stuffed, the lamb is easy to carve and easy to cook, because it will all be about the same thickness. A whole leg of lamb may weigh anywhere from 5 to 15 pounds, depending on where it was raised and on how it has been cut (American lamb is much larger than Australian, and New Zealand is smallest of all). For bone-in leg of lamb, allow about $^3/_4$ pound per person; for boneless leg of lamb allow about half a pound per person. Ask the butcher to bone the leg and remove the shank meat, which is too tough to roast, but is excellent ground or braised, and to butterfly it, cutting the leg open so it can be spread out. Lemon, dill, mint, and olive oil, typical simple flavors of the Greek countryside, are used here, yielding an aromatic, juicy dish that is sure to please. Serve with Rice Pilaf with Toasted Vermicelli (see page 816) and Tomatoes Provençale with Black Olives (see page 639).

517

SERVES 8 TO 10

Lamb Marinade

$^1/_4$ cup extra-virgin olive oil

1 small onion, quartered

1 tablespoon coarsely chopped garlic

$^1/_2$ cup each: coarsely chopped mint and dill

Juice and grated zest of 1 lemon

1 tablespoon ground cumin

Kosher salt and freshly ground black pepper to taste

1 (7- to 8-pound) leg of lamb, boned and butterflied open trimmed of all fat (but not tied)

Combine oil, onion, garlic, mint, dill, lemon juice and zest, cumin, and salt and pepper in the bowl of a food processor. Process to a fine paste. Rub mixture all over lamb, cover, and marinate overnight in the refrigerator, turning once or twice.

Lamb Stuffing and Assembly

1 tablespoon coarsely chopped garlic

1 head fennel, coarsely chopped, including stalks

$1/2$ cup each: coarsely chopped mint and dill

2 bunches scallions, sliced

1 cup homemade-style breadcrumbs

Kosher salt and freshly ground black pepper to taste

2 tablespoons olive oil

Combine garlic, fennel, mint, dill, scallions, and breadcrumbs in the bowl of a food processor. Process to a chunky paste and reserve.

Preheat the oven to 400°F. Drain the lamb, discarding the marinade. Pat the lamb dry and season both sides generously with salt and pepper. Spread the stuffing all over the inner side of the lamb. Roll up the long way, as tightly as possible. Secure either with kitchen string or silicon FoodLoops (*see* Tying Birds for Roasting, page 261).

Heat oil in a large heavy skillet, preferably cast-iron until shimmering. Brown lamb on all sides. Transfer to a roasting pan and roast, turning once, until a thermometer inserted into the thickest part of the lamb reads 135°F. for medium-rare. Remove lamb from the oven, drape with foil, and allow the meat to rest about 15 minutes before slicing thinly. Serve immediately.

Spicy Lamb Burgers

We don't usually think of lamb for burgers, but in the Middle East, where they really know lamb, ground lamb is made into flavorful patties like these and then grilled. Lamb has a forthright flavor that takes very well to bold spices, and the heavenly aroma of these burgers is reason enough to make them. Serve the lamb burgers in Indian naan bread or pita bread topped with tart, yet creamy cucumber relish that cuts the richness of the lamb perfectly, the Greek Tzatzik or Indian Raitai (see page 358).

SERVE 6

1 egg

$1/4$ cup homemade-style breadcrumbs

1 teaspoon finely chopped garlic

1 small red onion, finely chopped

1 tablespoon chopped fresh mint, or 1 teaspoon dried

$1/2$ teaspoon each: red pepper flakes, cinnamon, and allspice

1 teaspoon kosher salt (more for grilling)

2 pounds ground lamb

Olive oil, for brushing

Combine the egg, breadcrumbs, garlic, onion, mint, pepper flakes, cinnamon, allspice, salt, and black pepper. Add lamb and knead mixture until well combined. Form into 6 oblong patties, arranging on a wax-paper-lined tray. Chill patties for at least 1 hour.

When ready to cook, preheat a grill or broiler. Lightly brush the patties with olive oil and sprinkle lightly with kosher salt to help keep them from sticking. Place the patties on an angle on the grill and cook 5 to 7 minutes or

518

until they release freely from the grill when you try to turn them. Rotate the patties a half-turn to make criss-cross marks and continue to grill for 5 minutes, then turn them over and repeat, cooking for another 5 to 7 minutes, or until medium, so that they are fully cooked inside but still juicy and faintly pink.

Jamaican Curried Lamb

Premade curry powders originated with British manufacturers who sought to concoct a spice mixture equivalent to the kari podi *(powder) essential to the hot and spicy cooking that British colonists learned to love in Southern India. Jamaican curry powder, or* poudre de Colombo, *originated with Sri Lankans who immigrated to Jamaica and Trinidad in the West Indies in the years after slavery was abolished in the 1830s . Colombo is the capital of Sri Lanka. In Jamaica, baby goat would be used to make this rich curried stew, but lamb works quite well, too. Look for baby goat in Italian, Latin American, and Middle Eastern markets. Serve this with saffron rice and mango chutney, and sprinkle freshly grated coconut on top.*

SERVES 10 TO 12

4 pounds shoulder of lamb (or baby goat), trimmed
   of fat and connective tissue, cut into 1-inch cubes
$1/4$ pound (1 stick) unsalted butter, clarified
4 cups finely chopped onions
2 tablespoons Jamaican curry powder
2 tablespoons finely chopped fresh hot chiles,
   preferably Scotch bonnet

$1^1/2$ teaspoons ground allspice
Kosher salt and freshly ground black pepper to taste
2 (13.5-ounce) cans coconut milk
2 cups chicken stock
4 bay leaves
$1/4$ cup fresh lime juice

Brown the lamb cubes in the butter, coloring on all sides. Remove the lamb from pan, pour off excess fat and add the onions. Cook until softened. Add the curry, chiles, allspice, and salt and pepper. Simmer for 2 to 3 minutes. Return the lamb to the pan, stir in the coconut milk, stock, and bay leaves. Bring to the boil. Reduce the heat, cover tightly, and simmer for 1 to $1^1/2$ hours, or until the lamb is tender. Stir in the lime juice.

519

Excellent Greek Moussaka

On my first trip to Greece in 1969, I almost landed in jail when I got to Piraeus, the port of Athens, with my peace-sign stickered suitcase. After searching through my bags and confiscating books the customs officials considered subversive, they finally allowed me to enter the country. It was the time of the right-wing military junta known as "the generals", and all over Greece, there were large banners across the road declaring, "Good Greeks aren't Communists," and other such mottos. In spite of my less than cordial welcome, I absolutely loved the food—laden with olive oil and redolent of fresh herbs. I especially loved the rich casserole called moussaka. All these years later, it's still a favorite dish of mine and always gets raves when I serve it to others. Because the recipe makes a rather large quantity, it's best made for a big group or a party. On the bottom is a layer of oven-roasted eggplant, next is a layer of ground lamb simmered with red wine and tomato and seasoned with oregano and cinnamon. The topping is a luscious savory custard with cheese.

SERVES 12

Lamb Mixture

1 large onion, diced

2 tablespoons chopped garlic

$1/4$ cup olive oil

$1^{1}/_{2}$ pounds ground lamb

1 (28-ounce) can chopped plum tomatoes or
   1 box aseptic-packed chopped tomatoes such as Pomi

2 cups dry red wine

2 tablespoons chopped fresh marjoram or oregano,
   or 1 tablespoon dried oregano, preferably Greek

1 teaspoon ground allspice

1 teaspoon ground cinnamon

Kosher salt and freshly ground black pepper to taste

Sauté the onion and garlic in the oil. Add the lamb and brown, then add tomatoes, red wine, oregano, allspice, cinnamon, and salt and pepper. Cook until thickened, about 15 minutes, and ladle off excess fat. Remove from the heat and reserve.

Creamy Topping

$1/4$ pound (1 stick) unsalted butter

$1/4$ pound (1 cup) all-purpose flour

1 quart whole milk

1 cup heavy cream

2 teaspoons ground coriander

1 teaspoon ground nutmeg

$1/2$ onion, peeled and stuck with 4 whole cloves

$1/2$ teaspoon cayenne pepper

2 bay leaves

12 egg yolks, lightly beaten

Melt the butter and stir in the flour to make a roux (cooked butter and flour paste), then cook over moderate heat for 10 minutes, stirring occasionally. Meanwhile, scald the milk and cream, and add the coriander, nutmeg, onion and cloves, cayenne, and bay leaves.

Whisk the roux into the milk mixture and bring to the boil slowly (making sure not to burn the bottom of pot). Simmer for 15 minutes, stirring often, then remove from the fire and strain the sauce through a sieve, discarding the solids. Add a little bit of the hot milk mixture to the egg yolks and whisk together to warm. Add the yolk-sauce mixture into the milk mixture, and stir quickly to combine. Set aside, covering with a lid to prevent a skin from forming.

520

Assembly

2 large eggplants (about 2 pounds), cut into cubes

1 tablespoon chopped garlic

3 tablespoons olive oil

Lamb Mixture (from above)

Creamy Topping

1 cup grated Parmesan cheese

Preheat the oven to 425°F. Combine eggplant, garlic, and olive oil in a large bowl. Pour mixture out in a single layer onto a metal baking pan. Roast for about 25 minutes, or until soft and browned.

Reduce the oven to 350°F. Pour the roasted eggplant mixture into a large lasagna pan, and cover with the lamb mixture. Spoon the Creamy Topping evenly over top and sprinkle with Parmesan cheese. (You can refrigerate the moussaka at this point for up to 2 days before finishing.)

Bake in the middle shelf of the oven until the topping is browned and bubbling, about 45 minutes. Remove from the oven and allow to cool about 20 minutes so the Moussaka sets before cutting into squares.

WHERE DOES MOUSSAKA COME FROM?

Greeks think of moussaka as a dish of Arabic origin, brought to them along with the eggplant, but Arabs, especially in Lebanon, think of it as a Greek dish, perhaps brought by Greek immigrants to Asia Minor. Another possibility is that Turks adapted it from the Greeks and they spread it across the Levant and as far as Egypt, where it is also made with cauliflower. In Arabic, its name is spelled something like *musakka'a*. The creamy French-style béchamel topping was added to the Greek version about one hundred years ago by the famous Greek chef, Nikos Tselementes, who had trained in France.

LEEKS

LEEKS

Consider the leek: it's big, beautiful, and inexpensive. Both milder and sweeter than its cousin, the onion, leeks don't even make you cry. In a single stalk, the colorful leek ranges from creamy white and lemony-green through deep green, almost to blue. In Europe, leeks are considered indispensable to cooking, especially in northern France, Belgium, and the Netherlands, the world's leading producers. This adaptable Allium provides the sweet-savory underlying flavor in many slow-cooked dishes, especially stews and soups.

Native to the broad region stretching from Israel to India, leeks have been cultivated since at least 3000 BCE. Phoenician traders introduced the leek to Wales when they traveled to the British Isles to trade for tin. Legend has it that in 640 CE, the Welsh wore leeks in their hats to distinguish themselves from the invading Saxons and won a great victory over their enemies. Since that time, the Welsh have proudly eaten and worn the leek. Starting during the Industrial Revolution, growers in Welsh mining towns have competed to grow the biggest leeks and win prizes.

Though Americans don't use leeks every day like the cooks in Europe, one of our most famed dishes is made from leeks. Somewhere between 1917 and 1920, a French chef transplanted to the United States—Louis Diat—created an internationally famous soup made from white leeks, and served it at the Ritz-Carlton Hotel in New York.

In his 1941 book, *Cooking a la Ritz*, Diat tells us that his mother would often make a leek and potato soup for her children. Diat says, "But in summer, when the soup seemed to be too hot, we asked for milk with which to cool it. Many years later, it was this memory which gave me the inspiration to make the soup which I have named *Crème Vichyssoise*."

Though not normally sold in the United States, in Northern France and Belgium, a special kind of leek is raised to produce a much higher percentage of white. These leeks are transplanted into drilled holes to keep them away from the sunlight that turns them green. Known in France as *Plante' a Trou*, leeks of this type are usually marked on their box and fetch a high price. The deep, sandy soil of Flanders is ideal for the cultivation of these large leeks with long, white stems most appreciated by European chefs.

Why do Americans give leeks less attention than they deserve? First, leeks are just about the most troublesome vegetable as far as grit because of the way they're grown. To maximize the stalk size, leeks are grown either in trenches or with soil mounded around each plant. Some of this soil inevitably winds up between the layers of the leaves. New Jersey is a major supplier of leeks raised in the sandy soil of the southern part of the state. It takes special care to wash out the grit, but once you've cleaned the leeks using the directions ion the next page, they're easy to use. Second, in America, leeks are too often over-grown until they're too dark, too tough, and too fibrous, and in some places, where there's not enough turnover, they may be on the slimy side.

LEEK SEASON AND CHOOSING LEEKS

The peak season for leeks begins in late April and lasts through early February. Although they are available year-round, leeks are at their best in cold weather.

Choose leeks that are firm and smooth, free of blemishes, with crisp, brightly colored leaves. Avoid leeks with rounded instead of flattened bulb bottoms (an indication of an overgrown leek) or if they have withered, yellowed, or slimy leaves.

Sometimes you'll find leeks that are so overgrown that the inner layers of leaves get bunched up and start to fold in on themselves. The center stalk may have a hard, woody core that must be discarded before using. These leeks belong in the stock pot.

When I see younger leeks with thin stalks, similar in size to a large asparagus, and brightly colored, light green tops, I snap them up. I know these leeks will be tender and sweet and excellent if simply steamed and drizzled with vinaigrette, as in the "Poor Man's Asparagus" Vinaigrette (see page 526).

Cleaning Leeks

Cut off and discard the tough, very dark tops, cutting in an inverted v-shape to follow the shape of the leek. I usually expose the layers by opening up the tops and save the lighter green inner layers because I like their color and flavor. It's also less wasteful. European chefs normally use only the milder white to pale green bottom portions of the leeks.

Your next step depends on the way you're going to use the leek. For leek halves, slice them in half lengthwise and then run your fingers in between the layers to open them up and expose the grit.

Or cut off about a half-inch slice from the root end of the leek. (I save these root ends and any lighter green trimmings to impart their delicate sweetness and onion flavor to my chicken stock.) Then cut the leeks into matchsticks, squares, or rings, depending on your recipe.

Fill a large bowl (or your sink) with cold water. Place cut leeks into the water and swish around vigorously to encourage the sand to wash away and drop to the bottom of the bowl.

Scoop out the leeks and transfer to a colander to drain. If the bowl of water has a lot of grit on the bottom, repeat the process. Leeks will be especially gritty if they have been harvested in wet weather.

You can clean leeks ahead of time, drain them and roll in paper towels before storing in a plastic bag in the refrigerator for several days.

"Poor Man's Asparagus" Vinaigrette

In Europe, asparagus was a food of the rich, while leeks were a food of the poor. But the poor didn't always lose out. In this dish, with its tongue-in-cheek name, young leeks are steamed or boiled and then dressed in a coarse-mustard vinaigrette. Simple, but if the leeks are of the best quality, usually those found in farmers' markets, they're delicious as can be. In France, asperges du pauvre (poor man's asparagus) refers to leeks; in Great Britain, the same term in English refers to rock samphire, also known as sea bean, a plant that grows along rocky cliffs near the seashore.

SERVES 4

1 pound young leeks
6 tablespoons extra-virgin olive oil
3 tablespoons aged red wine vinegar
1 tablespoon coarse-grain mustard
1 tablespoon chopped fresh tarragon, or 1 teaspoon dried
Kosher salt and freshly ground black pepper to taste

Trim the leeks, cutting away just at the point where the rootlets attach to the body of the leek. Split the leeks in half lengthwise and wash vigorously in a large bowl of cold water.

Bring about 2 inches of salted water to the boil in a large, nonreactive skillet. Add leeks and return to a boil over medium-high heat, then reduce and simmer for 10 minutes, or until the leeks are limp and tender when pierced. Drain well and allow them to cool to room temperature. Pat dry with paper towels and arrange in a single layer on an attractive serving platter.

Lightly whisk together the oil, vinegar, mustard, tarragon, and salt and pepper. Drizzle over the leeks and serve. Note that the marinated leeks will keep quite well if refrigerated for 2 to 3 days; bring to room temperature before serving.

Crispy Fried Leeks

These crispy fried leeks are delicious sprinkled as a garnish, on creamy thick soups like Artichoke and Toasted Hazelnut Soup (see page 56), Curried Pumpkin and Apple Soup (see page 184), Creamy Carrot-Dill Soup (see page 211), Creamy Three Celery Soup (see page 220), Shaker Herb and Cheddar Cheese Soup (see page 226), and Clam and Mushroom Soup with Riesling (see page 304). I always topped my Grilled Wild Salmon with Braised Green Lentils (see page 549) with these leeks for restaurant service. The crispy leeks can be made several days ahead of time. Store in layers of paper towels at room temperature. Because the leeks shrink so much, it's best to fry a bigger quantity than you think you need.

SERVES 4 TO 8

2 bunches leeks, trimmed and cut into 3- to 4-inch lengths
1 quart peanut oil, for frying

Cut leek sections in half lengthwise and then cut into thin strips, called julienne. Wash, following the directions on page 525, Cleaning Leeks. Drain well and spin dry in a salad spinner or spread out onto a clean kitchen towel or paper towels and cover with another layer of towers and pat dry.

In a large, heavy-bottomed pot, an electric deep-fryer,

or a wok, heat the oil until shimmering (365°F. on a frying thermometer). Add the leeks a few at a time because the oil will bubble up. Keep adding leeks until the whole surface of the oil is covered. (The bubbling will die down as the water boils out of the leeks.) Fry the leeks, stirring often, until they are light brown and crispy. Drain on a wire rack or a paper-towel-lined pan. Store at room temperature, layered with paper towels in an air-tight container, for up to 4 days.

Alsatian Leek and Bacon Tart: *Flammekueche*

In the French-German border region of Alsace, the cooking shows influences of both cultures. This traditional pizza-like dish is flammekueche (its German name) or tarte flambe (its French name) originated at a time when the pie was baked in a wood-fired oven. Although, alas, most of us do not have access to a wood oven (still my favorite way to cook), even baked in a conventional oven, this has a full-bodied, rustic tart filling that is perfectly balanced by the nutty-tasting dough that absorbs the delicious juices.

MAKES 2 TARTS, SERVING 8 TO 12

1/2 pound double-smoked thick bacon,
   cut into 1-inch slices

1 tablespoon unsalted butter

1 1/2 pounds onions, thinly sliced

3/4 cup fromage blanc (*see* sidebar on page 528)

1/2 cup sour cream

1/2 cup heavy cream

2 egg yolks

1 1/2 pound Whole Wheat Brioche Dough (*see* page 988)

Kosher salt, grated nutmeg, ground white pepper, and
  cayenne pepper, to taste

Cornmeal or semolina, for sprinkling

Preheat the oven to 500°F. about 45 minutes before baking. In you have one, place a pizza stone in the oven when you first begin to preheat.

In a large skillet, cook the bacon until limp and about half the fat has been rendered out. Remove the bacon and reserve. Pour off most of the fat. Add the butter and the onions and sauté until golden brown, about 10 minutes, and reserve. Lightly beat together the fromage blanc, sour cream, heavy cream, egg yolks and seasonings and reserve.

Roll the dough and then pull out by hand into 2 long, tongue-shaped tarts.

If you're using a baker's peel, sprinkle it with cornmeal or semolina. Arrange one tongue-shaped dough piece on the peel. Alternatively, roll out the dough into 2 long tongue shapes and transfer them to a cornmeal-dusted metal baking pan (a paella pan works well here).

Spread the dough with half the cream mixture, then sprinkle with half the browned onions. Finish by sprinkling with half of the bacon. If you're using the peel, transfer the tart to the stone by placing the peel at a low angle to the stone and giving the peel a fast, vigorous thrust forward and then back, so that the tart jumps onto the stone. If you're using pans, simply place them in the oven. Repeat with second tart.

Bake for 8 to 10 minutes, or until the top is bubbling and brown and the crust is golden. Remove from oven and cut down the middle and then into 8 slices each, and serve immediately.

527

528

Swiss Roesti Gold Potato and Leek Cake

The recurring leek and potato theme turns up here as a large grated potato cake from Switzerland made in a cast-iron skillet for best crustiness. Serve wedges of the cake to accompany roast veal or beef, or top with grated Italian Fontina, Swiss Emmenthal, or bits of blue cheese, and melt under the broiler. Topped with fried or scrambled eggs, roesti makes a simple supper dish. Vary the roesti by adding small amounts of grated celeriac, sweet potato, or rutabagas to the potato mixture.

SERVES 6

2 large leeks, cut into thin slices, washed and drained
2 pounds gold potatoes, peeled and coarsely grated

$^{1}/_{2}$ cup clarified butter (or whole butter mixed with vegetable oil)
Kosher salt and freshly ground black pepper to taste

Bring a pan with about 2 inches of salted water to the boil. Add the leeks; bring the water back to the boil, stirring until the leeks are all brightly colored, about 3 minutes. Drain and rinse under cold water and reserve.

Using about one quarter of the potatoes each time, place the potatoes in a towel, roll up and squeeze out as much liquid as possible. Toss with salt, pepper, and reserved leeks.

Heat $^{1}/_{4}$ cup of the butter in a steel or nonstick skillet with a lid, about 9 inches in diameter, and pan-fry over medium heat, covered, until crispy on bottom, about 10 minutes, shaking once or twice to release the potatoes. Using a spatula or spoon, press down on the potato mixture to form a firm cake.

Remove the skillet from the heat and then, holding a large platter directly over the pan, flip over onto the platter. Add the remaining $^{1}/_{4}$ cup of butter to the pan and heat. Flip the potato cake back into the pan and cook on its second side until crispy.

Turn out from pan, cut into wedges, and serve immediately.

Trio Fries with Leeks, Boniatos, and Gold Potatoes

The most successful dish I've ever created has been, without a doubt, the prize-winning Trio Fries (now trademarked) served at the Dock Street Brewpub and Restaurant, which had quite a successful run starting about 1990. These fries are a crunchy combo of Idaho potatoes, the starchy Caribbean sweet potatoes called boniatos *or* batatas, *and most importantly, leeks for their wonderful sweet, oniony flavor. For extra crispness, the potatoes and batatas are soaked in cold water overnight, so you'll need to start a day ahead. Don't miss the Trio Fries Cooking Tips on the next page.*

SERVES 4 TO 6

1 pound large gold potatoes

1 pound boniatos (*see* Boniatos, at right)

1 bunch leeks, trimmed and cut into 3- to 4-inch lengths

1 quart peanut oil, for frying

Popcorn (or flour) salt, or fine sea salt, for sprinkling
  (*see* Popcorn Salt, at left)

Without peeling, cut the potatoes and batatas into long, ¼-inch-thick sticks and soak in a bowl of cold water 4 to 6 hours, or up to overnight, to wash off the surface starch.

Cut leek sections in half lengthwise and then cut into thin strips, called julienne. Wash, following the directions on page 525, Cleaning Leeks. Drain well and spin dry in a salad spinner, or spread out onto a clean kitchen towel or paper towels and cover with another layer of towers and pat dry.

Drain the potatoes and batatas, spread them out onto a clean kitchen towel or paper towels, cover with another layer of towels, and pat dry. Combine the leeks, potatoes, and batatas.

In a large, heavy-bottomed pot, an electric deep-fryer, or a wok, heat the oil (filled no more than one-third of the way up) until it reaches 300°F. on a frying thermometer. Add the vegetables a few at a time because the oil will bubble up. Keep adding the vegetables until the whole surface of the oil is covered. (The bubbling will die down as the water boils out.) Cook 2 minutes, or until slightly limp but not at all brown. Reserve the oil in the pot.

Scoop the cooked vegetables from the pot, preferably using a Chinese brass wire skimmer, and drain in a colander. Spread the cooked and drained vegetables out in a shallow layer on a metal baking pan and reserve at room temperature for at least 30 minutes and up to 2 hours at room temperature, or else refrigerate overnight.

Heat the reserved oil to 375°F. Add the vegetables in batches and fry a second time until golden brown and crispy on the edges, 3 to 4 minutes. Scoop from the pot and drain. Transfer to a large bowl lined with paper towels and while still hot sprinkle with salt to taste. Serve immediately.

BONIATOS

Boniatos, also known as *batatas*, are starchy white to rose pink-skinned sweet potatoes with yellow flesh. They have a dry, fluffy texture flavor reminiscent of chestnuts. Boniatos are a staple in countries from Mexico to Vietnam and can be found in Caribbean, Latin American, and Asian markets. Look for firm boniatos with smooth, unbruised skins and without cracks, or any stickiness. Store in the refrigerator for up to five days.

529

530

Sautéed Salmon with Creamy Leek and Tarragon Sauce

This lovely "pretty in pink" salmon topped with a pale, spring-green leek and tarragon sauce and served over vivid green spinach is as much of a pleasure to the eye as it is to the palate. The mild, sweet, lightly oniony leeks are perked up with the delicate licorice flavor of tarragon in a French-style sauce flavored with vermouth and enriched with a little cream. Accompany with roasted gold potatoes or steamed new potatoes. The granulated flour called for here is sold under the brand name Wondra, and is used because it makes a crisper crust.

SERVES 4

4 tablespoons unsalted butter, divided

2 large leeks (white and light green parts only), sliced and washed

1/2 cup dry white vermouth

1/2 cup heavy cream

2 tablespoons chopped fresh tarragon or 2 teaspoons dried tarragon

Kosher salt and freshly ground black pepper

4 (6- to 8-ounce) salmon fillets, skinned if desired

Granulated flour (Wondra)

1 bunch (or 10-ounce bag) spinach, stems removed, washed and drained

Melt 2 tablespoons of the butter in a large skillet over medium-low heat. Add leeks and sauté until soft and transparent, about 10 minutes. Remove leeks from the pan. To the same pan, add vermouth and boil over high heat until liquid is reduced to 2 tablespoons, about 5 minutes. Add cream and boil again until thickened to sauce consistency, about 5 minutes. Stir in leeks and tarragon. Season to taste with salt and pepper. Remove from heat, and cover to keep warm.

Melt remaining 2 tablespoons butter in a large skillet, preferably non-stick. Sprinkle salmon with salt and pepper and dust lightly with flour, shaking off excess. Place the salmon in the pan, skin side down. Cook over medium-high heat until lightly browned, about 3 minutes, turn over and then brown again until almost cooked through, about 3 minutes.

Meanwhile, place the spinach with any water clinging to its leaves into a pot just large enough to hold it. Heat, stirring often until the spinach has just wilted. Drain spinach well and divide among 4 dinner plates. Place one salmon fillet in the center of each plate. Spoon reserved sauce over top and serve immediately.

LEMONS

LEMONS

Many years ago, I hitchhiked across Europe on my own, staying in youth hostels, where I would cook my own meals. I kept two foods in my backpack at all times: (they really had to be significant because I had to schlep them everywhere) several lemons and a head of garlic. With those two ingredients, I could cook dishes that would make me happy at the end of a long day of walking and sightseeing. Even today, I can't eat fish or seafood or even steamed vegetables unless I have a nice fat wedge of lemon to squeeze over top. I find that almost anything I put in my mouth tastes livelier and fresher finished with a squeeze of lemon.

Say lemon and words like refreshing, juicy, tart, sunny, light, and sunshine-bright come to mind. The lemon is grown primarily for its acidic juice, but the oil produced by its perfumed yellow peel is almost as important as a flavoring, and is prized in the perfume industry. In the countries surrounding the Mediterranean, grated lemon zest is essential for flavoring sweet pastries and other dishes like pasta fillings, fish, and chicken marinades.

It's hard to imagine life without the lemon because we use it so frequently in foods both savory and sweet, hot and cold. I never use bottled lemon juice because I find the flavor one-dimensional with a metallic aftertaste. I look for big, plump, firm lemons to squeeze for juice. My simple orange plastic juicer, made by Sunkist, is still the best design around, though I've tried many others. (Sometimes Sunkist products come with an offer to buy this inexpensive juicer.)

Don't forget the zest; I use my nifty new Microplane zester to remove just the bright yellow oil pockets located on the skin of the lemon for its uplifting, mind-cleansing fragrance. (You can buy the Microplane, a simple metal rod with sharp fine holes, perfect to remove only the zest, at kitchen supply stores.) Because the skins of most lemons are treated with preservative chemicals, it's a good idea to buy organic when you're planning to use the zest (though even I don't stick to that rule—if I need zest, I'll use whatever lemons I have on hand, washing them first).

The lemon, *Citrus x limon*, is a close relative of the lime and both their names derive from the same source: the Arabic word, *limah*, meaning citrus fruit. The word *lemon* reached the English language towards the end of the thirteenth century via the Old French *limon*, which in modern French now means lime. The lemon is known in Italy as *limone*; in most Spanish-speaking areas as *limón*, *limón agria* (sour lemon), *limón real* (true lemon), or *limón francés* (French lemon). In German, the same fruit is a *limonen*; in French, a *citrónnier*; in Dutch, a *citroen*. In Haiti, it is *limon France* (French lemon), and in Puerto Rico, *limon amarillo* (yellow lemon).

As ubiquitous as they are, we don't always love

532

lemons; sometimes their sourness is associated with negative things. In the United States, lemon has a negative secondary meaning, something defective, as in a new car that doesn't work, called a lemon. Think of the folksong, "Lemon tree is very pretty and the lemon flower is sweet but the fruit of the poor lemon is impossible to eat." In Australia and New Zealand, "to go lemony at someone" is to get angry with them. In Britain, a lemon means someone who is lacking in intelligence and vitality.

The true home of the lemon is unknown, though it may have originated in northwest India. The fruit traveled west along with the Arabs, from Persia (today's Iran) and the Middle East to Europe, reaching southern Italy by about 200 CE and was already being cultivated in Iraq and Egypt by 700 CE. It also traveled eastward, reaching China somewhere before 1000 CE.

A fruit that resembles a lemon is depicted in mosaics at Pompeii, although the lemon wasn't well known during the Roman Empire. The Crusaders who first encountered lemons in the Holy Land in the late twelfth century helped to popularize the fruit in Europe. At first, lemons were a rare and expensive luxury. By the end of the fourteenth century, when supplies became more regular and plentiful, lemons started to become an essential item in the kitchen, especially for making drinks.

Towards the end of the sixteenth century, the usefulness of lemons and limes in preventing scurvy (a severe vitamin deficiency) began to be realized. However, the British Admiralty did not act on this knowledge for another two hundred years. It was not until 1795 that lemon juice was officially issued to British sailors. In the following twenty years, well over one million gallons of lemon juice was drunk by sailors.

Christopher Columbus carried lemon seeds to the island of Hispaniola in 1493, and Spaniards included lemons among the fruits they introduced to St. Augustine, Florida, about 1565. The lemon reached California about 1769 when the Franciscan fathers started establishing their mission there. Both Florida and California began raising lemons commercially to offset America's heavy imports of lemons from Sicily. Following the devastating freeze of 1894–95, the lemon was abandoned as a crop in Florida. In 1953, lemon-growing was revived in Central Florida to take advantage of the demand for frozen concentrate and for natural cold-pressed lemon oil. At that time, Florida was importing lemons from Italy for processing.

Lemons grow on a small, widely branched thorny evergreen tree that grows 10 to 20 feet high. The lemon tree is not very cold hardy, which restricts its area of its cultivation. About one fourth of the world's lemons are grown in the United States, mostly in California, though Arizona now also has a significant lemon crop. Southern Mexico and Guatemala have become major growers of lemons, primarily used for lemon oil and for dehydrating into lemon powder. In South America, Argentina is the leading producer, with Chile a distant second. Growing lemons has long been a commercial industry in Spain, Portugal, Italy, Sicily, and Corsica. At present, the leading producing countries are the United States, Italy, Spain, Argentina, Greece, and Turkey.

The lemon tree flowers continuously and has fruit in all stages of development most of the year. A single tree may bear as many as 3,000 lemons in one year. Because most lemons ripen naturally in autumn and winter, when market demand is low, growers pick the lemons green and store them for sale in the spring and summer. These lemons are cured and ripened in storehouses

533

where the fruit shrinks a little; the skin becomes thinner and tougher and develops a silky finish. When the process is completed, the lemons are washed, dried, and sometimes wrapped. They can be kept in this condition for months where they will maintain all their flavor along with their rich supply of vitamin C.

Lemon Varieties

American Lemons: America's most common variety, the Eureka lemon, originated from seed taken from an Italian lemon (probably the Lunario) and planted in Los Angeles in 1858. The tree is vigorous with few thorns, the fruits are good sized with few seeds, and the pulp is very juicy with a high acid content, making it more "lemony" tasting. The Armstrong resembles the Eureka except that it usually bears seedless or near-seedless fruits. The Lisbon lemon (perhaps the same as the Portugal lemon in Morocco and Algeria) originated in Portugal, from where it traveled the world, reaching Australia in 1824, Massachusetts in 1843, and California about 1849. This lemon bears fruit almost identical to the Eureka.

European Lemons: The Fino lemon is a Spanish variety that produces a tree with lots of thorny shoots. The lemons are on the small side, with a smooth, thin rind and a medium number of seeds. The oval-shaped Verna has a pronounced nipple, short neck, a rough, medium-thick peel that is tightly clinging, and few or no seeds. The Verna ripens mostly in winter and is the leading variety of Spain and important in Algeria and Morocco. The Femminello Ovale, one of the oldest Italian varieties, still accounts for three-quarters of Italy's total lemon production. It is short and rounded in shape, with a blunt nipple and rounded base. This lemon is a medium-sized fruit that is tender, juicy, and high in acid. It is considered to be of excellent quality.

Indian Lemons: There are also a number of close lemon relatives that originated in India. The Rough Lemon, which is perhaps a lemon-citron hybrid, is believed to have originated in northern India, where it grows wild. It was carried around 1498 by Portuguese explorers to southeastern Africa, soon taken to Europe, and brought by Spaniards to the New World. The scant pulp and juice limit the rough lemon to home use. The Sweet Lemon is a general name for certain non-acid lemons favored in the Mediterranean region and in southern coastal regions of India.

Preserved Meyer Lemons

You'll need to start these cured lemons about 3 weeks ahead of time. You can use either fragrant, relatively sweet Meyer lemons or common lemons to make this condiment from North Africa. These preserved lemons are cured in salt and lemon juice or olive oil until they are soft and mild. Only the rind is eaten; the inner pulp is too salty to eat. Modern chefs are using preserved lemons in all sorts of dishes, not necessarily North African in origin. Note that you use only the peel, discarding the pulp.

MAKES ABOUT 3 CUPS

6 Meyer lemons, preferably organic (substitute lemons)

1¹/₂ cups kosher salt

1 cinnamon stick, lightly crushed

5 whole cloves

2 tablespoons coriander seeds

2 tablespoons black peppercorns

2 bay leaves

¹/₂ cup freshly squeezed lemon juice, or Meyer lemon juice

Rinse the lemons in hot water. Quarter the lemons from the top to within ¹/₂ inch of the bottom, sprinkle salt on the exposed flesh, then reshape the lemons. Place a layer of salt on the bottom of a glass, ceramic, or plastic container. Pack in the lemons and, pushing them down, add more salt and the spices between layers. Press the lemons down to release their juices and to make room for more lemons. Add freshly squeezed lemon juice to cover the lemons. Let the lemons ripen in a warm place, turning the container upside down each day to redistribute the salt and juice. Let ripen for 3 weeks. Refrigerate in a tightly covered nonreactive glass, ceramic, or plastic container, up to 6 months after the lemons have fully ripened.

To use, rinse the lemons as needed under cold water, remove and discard the pulp. Scrape off the inside white pith and discard. The preserved lemon is delicious chop-ped up and sprinkled on fish, added to a pot of steamed clams, and mixed into salads, such as tuna and chicken.

The pickling juice can be saved, boiled, and reused for the next batch of lemons.

MEYER LEMONS

The Meyer lemon, possibly a hybrid of a lemon and a mandarin orange, was introduced into the United States by the agricultural explorer, Frank N. Meyer, who found it growing as an ornamental pot-plant near Peking, China, in 1908. The Meyer lemon became a garden tree planted in California backyards. Culinary innovator Alice Waters of Chez Panisse fame brought the Meyer lemon to the restaurant table, collecting the lemons from friends who grew them in and around Berkeley. Pastry chef Lindsey Shere, wrote in her fruit-laden book, *Chez Panisse Desserts*, "Meyers have a more delicate, complex perfume and a sweeter flavor than the Eureka, the usual market variety [of lemon], so I cook with them as often as possible."

The complex flavor and aroma of the Meyer hints of sweet lime, lemon, and mandarin, with a pronounced floral fragrance from the rind. A good Meyer will be succulent, juicy, and highly aromatic.

Look for bright, shiny Meyer lemons with richly colored orangey-yellow rind, indicating that the fruit was picked when fully ripe. Meyer lemons deteriorate quickly—after a few days they begin to shrivel, and the rinds become hard and dry. They're usually fine on the inside, however.

Angel Hair with Prosciutto and Lemon Zest

This is a delicious and easy-to-make dish created by Thai chef, Kamul Phutek, previously chef of the Philadelphia favorite French-Asian restaurant, Alouette, and now owner of Nan in West Philadelphia's University City neighborhood. The dish combines the Thai custom of combining hot, salty, and tart flavors in a simple dish that's ready in minutes. If Meyer lemons are in season, they are an excellent substitute. Fresh thyme and high-quality prosciutto are essential here.

SERVES 4

2 tablespoons chopped fresh garlic
1/2 pound imported prosciutto, sliced thin, rolled up and cut into thin strips
1/4 cup extra-virgin olive oil
Juice and grated zest of 2 lemons
1 pound angel hair pasta
1/2 cup chopped Italian parsley
2 tablespoons finely chopped thyme
Hot sauce to taste
Freshly ground black pepper to taste

Bring a large pot of salted water to the boil.

Sauté the garlic and prosciutto in the olive oil, until the garlic sizzles and gives off its aroma. Pour in the lemon juice and zest and bring mixture to the boil.

Meanwhile, cook the pasta *al dente*, until firm and bouncy, and still yellow in color.

Add the parsley, thyme, hot sauce, and salt and pepper to the garlic sauce. Toss with cooked, drained pasta. Form pasta into "nests" on four serving plates, preferably heated, and serve immediately.

Cinnamon and Preserved Lemon Roast Chicken

I served this crowd-pleasing golden aromatic chicken at A'propos on Broad Street in the mid-1980s. Although the restaurant is long gone, I still make this dish especially for a large group of friends in summertime when I've got the charcoal grill going. The chicken is marinated in a heady North African mixture of preserved lemon rind, saffron, cinnamon, ginger, and cilantro. (Go easy on the salt because the preserved lemon is salty.) The chicken just gets better if you leave it in the marinade for several days. Serve with steamed couscous or rice pilaf. North African preserved lemons are cured in salt and lemon juice or olive oil until they are soft and mild. Only the rind is eaten; the inner pulp is too salty to eat. Buy preserved lemons from specialty markets or make your own following the recipe on page 535. They're so good to have on hand to add sparkly, tart flavor to sauces, fish and seafood dishes, and chicken.

SERVES 4 TO 6

2 preserved lemons, drained, pulp and pith
  discarded, roughly chopped (substitute grated
  zest of 2 lemons)

$1/2$ cup freshly squeezed lemon juice

1 teaspoon saffron

2 cinnamon sticks, crushed

1 (2-inch) piece ginger, peeled and grated

$1/2$ bunch cilantro, leaves picked and chopped

1 tablespoon ground coriander seed

Freshly ground black pepper (no added salt because
  the lemons are salty)

5 pounds chicken, thighs and/or breasts, on the bone

Process in a food processor the preserved lemon rinds, lemon juice, saffron, cinnamon, ginger, cilantro, coriander seed, and pepper to a rough paste. Cut several slashes into each chicken piece (so marinade will penetrate better). Rub the chicken pieces with the marinade and leave to marinate in a container in the refrigerator for 24 to 48 hours.

When you're ready to cook the chicken, light a hot charcoal fire in an outdoor grill (or preheat a gas or electric grill). Place the chicken skin-side down on the grill, cover, and grill over moderate heat until the chicken is nicely browned, about 15 minutes. Turn the chicken over, cover the grill, and cook about 15 minutes longer, or until thoroughly cooked. The juices should run clear, rather than pink, when the chicken is pierced.

Sweet and Sour Meatballs with Lemon

My mother was never what you'd call a typical Jewish cook. From her many years of travel and living abroad, she learned to make dishes as varied as Dutch boeterkok (see page 174), Mexican Chiles Rellenos (see page 844), and Moroccan couscous. This homey but delicious dish comes from her Polish-Jewish heritage, although the barbecue sauce is an American adaptation. It would be served at a Jewish wedding at the "smorgasbord," the huge, groaning table of delicacies, hot and cold, eaten before sitting down to the full-course meal. Serve with steamed rice, kasha, or barley. These meatballs freeze quite well. Defrost overnight in the refrigerator and then heat thoroughly before serving.

SERVES 6

537

Meatballs

$1/2$ cup homemade-style breadcrumbs

$1/2$ cup hot chicken stock

2 pounds ground beef (or turkey, mixed dark and light)

1 onion, diced

2 eggs

Kosher salt and freshly ground black pepper to taste

Combine the breadcrumbs with the chicken stock to moisten. Place in an electric mixer, or mix by hand with ground beef, onion, eggs, and salt and pepper, and beat until well combined. Form into walnut-sized meatballs.

In a large skillet, preferably nonstick, brown the meatballs on all sides and reserve.

Sauce and Assembly

2 lemons, sliced thin and pitted

$1^{1}/2$ cups chicken stock

$1^{1}/2$ cups barbecue sauce

$1/4$ cup brown sugar, packed

$1/4$ cup canola oil

1 tablespoon cornstarch

$1/2$ cup golden raisins

Bring a small pot of water to the boil. Add the lemon slices, bring back to the boil and cook 2 to 3 minutes, or until softened but not falling apart. Drain and reserve.

In a large casserole dish, combine the chicken stock with the barbecue sauce, brown sugar, and oil, and bring to the boil. Combine the cornstarch with 2 tablespoons cold water and stir this slurry into the pot. Bring the liquid back to the boil while stirring and then add the reserved meatballs, raisins, and lemon slices. Simmer 30 minutes, or until the sauce has thickened and the meatballs and lemon slices are soft and tender.

Lemon–Caper Relish

This tangy, salty summertime relish is a simple mixture like a salsa that works perfectly spooned over grilled fish like mahi-mahi, tuna, swordfish, or salmon, or over grilled chicken or grilled asparagus. Substitute chopped red onions for the shallots, and fresh oregano or thyme for the marjoram, if desired. Sometimes summer lemons are really the pits, especially during the time when American lemons are out of season and lemons are imported from Spain and elsewhere. You may then substitute limes here, but use only a scant teaspoon of the rather bitter lime zest. Store the relish in the refrigerator up to 2 days, but no longer, or it will lose its fresh lively character.

MAKES 2 CUPS

3 whole lemons, 1 grated for its zest

1 roasted red bell pepper, finely diced

$1/2$ cup chopped mixed green, red, and black olives

$1/4$ cup drained capers

$1/2$ cup minced shallots

$1/2$ bunch Italian parsley, chopped

2 tablespoons chopped marjoram

$1/2$ cup extra-virgin olive oil

$1/4$ cup red wine vinegar

Freshly ground black pepper to taste

Pare away both the yellow rind and the white pith from the lemons, leaving only the yellow flesh. Cut into a small dice, removing and discarding any pits. Combine the lemons, zest, bell pepper, olives, capers, shallots, parsley, marjoram, and season with pepper. Whisk together the vinegar and oil and combine with the chunky vegetable mixture.

538

Preserved Lemon Dressing

Preserved lemons, whether purchased or homemade, make a delicious, creamy salad dressing that works well drizzled over greens, cut-up tomatoes, cucumbers, or cold cooked green vegetables such as broccoli and asparagus. The pleasing bitter aftertaste of the preserved lemon gives a special flavor to the dressing.

MAKES 1½ CUPS

½ preserved lemon, pulp and pith discarded, roughly chopped

½ cup freshly squeezed lemon juice

½ cup sour cream

Freshly ground black pepper

¼ teaspoon cayenne pepper

½ cup olive oil

Kosher salt, as needed

Place the preserved lemon skin and lemon juice in the bowl of a processor and puree to a chunky paste. Add the remaining ingredients and process again to combine. You will most likely not need salt, since preserved lemons tend to be very salty, but add to taste if you think more is needed.

Meyer Lemon Tart with Pasta Frolla Crust

Make this simple and deliciously tangy tart when Meyer lemons are in season, usually in January until about March. The sweet and enticingly aromatic lemon-orange flavor of this tart comes from these special lemons (see Meyer Lemons, page 536, for more information). If Meyers aren't available, mix the juice of 1 orange with the juice of 4 lemons and add the zest of 2 lemons mixed with about 1 tablespoon orange zest to approximate the flavor. The buttery-rich, cookie-like pasta frolla *used here is the Italian equivalent of the French* pate brisée *(crumbly) with the special flavor of dry Marsala from the island of Sicily. (Note that Marsala comes in two versions: dry and sweet. The dry type is preferred here. If it isn't available, substitute with sweet Marsala and cut down on the sugar to 1 tablespoon.) This dough freezes very well, so I usually double the recipe and freeze half. Defrost in the refrigerator until cold and firm and then press into the pan or roll out between two sheets of wax paper.*

SERVES 8

1 pound Pasta Frolla (*see* page 989)

4 eggs

4 egg yolks

1 cup granulated sugar

1½ cups Meyer lemon juice (5 to 6 lemons)

Grated zest of 2 Meyer lemons

6 tablespoons unsalted butter, softened

Press the dough into a 10- to 11-inch fluted French tart shell pan with a removable bottom. Trim the edges even

539

with the top of the pan, then chill for 30 minutes in the freezer, or 1 hour in the refrigerator.

In a mixing bowl, whisk together the eggs, egg yolks, sugar, and lemon juice. Transfer to a two-quart nonreactive pan. Whisk over medium heat until light and the whisk leaves tracks in the foam. Remove from the heat, then whisk in the lemon zest and the butter.

Transfer to a metal bowl and place inside a second, larger bowl filled with ice and water. Stir the filling occasionally to cool evenly and prevent a skin from forming.

Meanwhile, bake the shell: Preheat the oven to 375°F. Line the tart shell with heavy-duty foil, then fill with dried beans. Bake 25 minutes, removing the foil and weights when the dough is partially baked, but no longer raw. Continue baking without the weights until the pastry is light golden brown, pricking the bottom with a fork if it bubbles up, about 15 minutes longer.

Cool the shell to room temperature before filling. When the filling is lukewarm, pour into the prepared shell. Chill about 2 hours or until the filling is set and firm before serving.

540

Homemade Limoncello from Don Alfonso

This recipe was given to me when I visited the farm and incredible wine cellar of the renowned Michelin three-starred restaurant, Don Alfonso. This establishment is in the small town of Sant'Agata sui Due Golfi, which is situated in the center of the Sorrento Peninsula, so that one can see both the Bay of Naples and the Bay of Amalfi. While we didn't get to sample the cuisine because the restaurant was closed for renovations, I was happy to have this recipe for the lemon-zest-scented liqueur that is served after the meal everywhere in this spectacularly beautiful region. You must use pure grain alcohol (190-proof, sold as "Everclear") to extract the volatile oils from the lemons. Increase the amount of sugar syrup, if you prefer a sweeter, less potent liqueur. Organic lemons are best here, because you are only using the rind, which can also contain insecticides and preservatives. If they are not available, scrub your lemons especially well in hot, soapy water and rinse well before using.

MAKES 3 QUARTS

2 pounds (8 to 12) lemons, well scrubbed, preferably organic
1 quart grain alcohol (190 proof)
2 cups granulated sugar

Carefully zest the lemons, using a potato peeler, so there is no white pith on the peel. Mix the lemon zest with the grain alcohol, allowing it to infuse for 48 hours at room temperature. Strain, discarding the peel.

Meanwhile, heat the sugar with 6 cups water until boiling and clear. Cool the syrup to room temperature. Add to the strained lemon-infused alcohol, and transfer to an attractive bottle.

Keep in the freezer until ready to serve in small liqueur glasses.

Frozen Limoncello Soufflé

Limoncello is a liqueur made in Sorrento in Campania where the Sorrento Oval lemon grows in trees overlooking the Mediterranean. It is also produced on the nearby magical island of Capri. It is always served chilled, over ice or neat, or perhaps mixed with a little acqua minerale *(sparkling water). Here it's used to flavor a light, luscious, and easy-to-make frozen soufflé that can be served with fruit* macedonia, *the Italian name (*macedoine *in French) for a mixture of cut-up fruits named after the multi-lingual, multicultural region of Macedonia across the Adriatic from Italy. Limoncello can be found in most larger liquor stores or you can make your own. This dessert is made to look like a baked soufflé, including the paper collar around the top, but it is really more like a frozen mousse.*

SERVES 8

Zest of 3 lemons, cut off in thick strips using
 a potato peeler
1 teaspoon vegetable oil
1 cup granulated sugar
$^1\!/_2$ cup water
8 egg yolks
$^1\!/_2$ cup Limoncello liqueur
$^1\!/_2$ cup lemon juice
2 cups heavy cream

Bring a small pot of water to the boil. Add the lemon zest and boil 5 minutes. Drain and rinse under cold water to cool. Cut the zest strips into very thin slices. Boil again in fresh water for about 3 minutes, then drain and reserve.

Wrap a one-quart soufflé dish in aluminum foil to give it a high collar, then lightly oil the collar. Combine the sugar and water in a small, heavy-bottomed pot with a lid. Bring to the boil, stirring until the sugar is dissolved. Cover and continue to boil until it reaches 250°F. on a candy thermometer (the firm-ball stage).

Meanwhile, place the egg yolks in the bowl of a mixer. Using a wire whisk, beat the yolks lightly by hand just enough to liquefy them. Slowly stream the hot syrup into egg yolks while whisking vigorously by hand. (This method keeps the syrup off of the sides of the mixing bowl.)

When the syrup has been incorporated, switch to the wire whisk attachment of the mixer and beat at medium speed for about 10 to 15 minutes, or until the mixture is cool and very thick. Gently fold in the liqueur, lemon juice and zest.

Beat the cream in a chilled bowl to soft peaks. Fold the whipped cream into the egg mixture in thirds so as not to deflate the mixture. Pour into the prepared dish. For best appearance, the soufflé should come at least 1 inch above the rim. Freeze at least 4 hours until firm or overnight. Then, peel off the foil collar to give the effect of a soufflé. Serve frozen.

541

LENTILS

LENTILS

People are very literal when it comes to lucky foods and lentils are no exception (we choose things that look like the things we want.) In many places, eating lentils is believed to bring good luck because of their coin-like shape. Italians serve lentils for New Year's to ensure good fortune for the year ahead. They are served with *cotechino*, a thick pork sausage with a rich filling, or *zampone*, a pig's trotter stuffed with the same filling. The dish must be served precisely at midnight, with the lentils representing the piles of coins to come; the zampone the container that will hold the wealth. Both pork-based dishes are eaten for the New Year because it is said that the pig, an animal that moves forward while eating, brings good luck.

Even if lentils don't bring you monetary riches, their versatility, easy digestibility, and great flavor are guaranteed to help you eat better and enjoy doing so. Their high protein content (almost twenty-five percent), along with their decidedly meaty character may account for their being a favorite food during Lent in the Roman Catholic countries of Europe. Lentils are quick-cooking, don't need soaking, and are among the easiest of all legumes to digest, especially if they are skinned.

Lentils, *Lens culinaris* or *Lens esculenta*, were, and still are, an important, indeed essential, plant in the ancient world, especially the Middle East, where they have been cultivated for close to 10,000 years. The seeds of a small shrub that are dried after harvesting, lentils are thought to have originated along the Indus River in today's Pakistan. The dish of rice and lentils called *mujaddara*, which is still eaten today in the Middle East, is likely not much different from the "pottage" (thick soup or porridge) for which the biblical Esau traded his birthright.

Lentils get their name from their shape—inside their skin, they are made up of two lens-shaped sides. Lentils range from the earth-brown round that are the largest variety and most common in the U.S., to the slightly smaller green lentils popular in the Latin American community, to the smallest black beluga lentils.

SORTING LENTILS

Because lentils are so small, it's easy for bits of dirt or spoiled lentils to get mixed in with the batch. Sort dried lentils by spreading them in a single layer on a tray or platter. Pick through and discard any discolored or misshapen beans and any bits of dirt. Rinse the lentils under cold water and then cook them. Most lentils cook in 30 to 45 minutes and do not need soaking.

Lentil Varieties

Beluga Lentils: These fancy, petite lentils fetch a high price. Their name is a play on their resemblance to Beluga caviar, the smallest, blackest, and most expensive sturgeon caviar. Beluga lentils, which are shiny, jet-black, and more rounded in shape than other varieties, have a mild flavor. They hold their shape well and are a good choice for lighter soups and salads. They are often served with fish and seafood dishes.

Brown Lentils: These are the most common and inexpensive sort of lentil found in every supermarket and are also known as continental, Indian brown, German, and Egyptian lentils. With their mild flavor and soft, somewhat mealy texture, they are best used for soups, where they will disintegrate and help thicken the broth. Brown lentils can easily turn mushy if overcooked and are not the best choice for salads or any dish where a whole shape is important.

Castelluccio Lentils: These small, brown, firm, nutty-tasting lentils are famed in Italy for their delicate taste and tiny size. They are only produced along the hillsides of Castelluccio in the central Italian province of Umbria and have been awarded the I.G.T., or Protected Geographical Indication. Cultivation has always been organic using centuries-old traditions of crop rotation.

French Green Lentils: Called *lentilles du Puy*, these special lentils were first raised in the Puy region of southwest France. They are small, speckled deep green, and firm when cooked, which only takes a short time. Because of their attractive appearance, nutty flavor, and ease of cooking, they are the darlings of French and American chefs, especially in the iconic *nouvelle cuisine* dish of salmon on a bed of lentils. French green lentils are now being raised in Canada, almost entirely in Manitoba and Saskatchewan, so they are becoming more common.

Petite Crimson Lentils: These tiny red lentils, which are about one-third the size of regular lentils, originated in Turkey, Egypt, and India and are now domestically grown. They are skinned, so they are easily digested and cook in five minutes and can be mixed with rice or made into thick soups. Orange or red lentils are most commonly used in Middle Eastern and Indian food.

Red Chief Lentils: Red chief lentils are medium-sized, deep orange to salmon-red in color, with a mild, earthly flavor and soft texture, best suited to soups and purees. They are also called pink lentils and Egyptian lentils. In India, the light-brown unhulled red lentil is known as the *masoor* and the hulled red lentil known as *masoor dal*.

Spanish Pardina Lentils: Known as Spanish brown lentils or continental lentils, these small lentils are small and richly colored (ranging from earthy brown to moss-green with streaks of black), and hold their shape very well when cooked. This variety is often served with duck, chicken, turkey, or game birds.

Split Yellow Lentils: The split yellow lentils found in Indian markets are skinned green *mung* (or *gram*) beans, called *moong dal*. They are the same bean used to sprout for the Chinese mung bean sprouts. Or, they may be the skinned and split small golden chickpea called *channna dal.* A third possibility is that they are actually yellow split peas. Or they may be the skinned and split small tan beans called pigeon peas or gandules in the Caribbean where they're used whole to make rice and beans. In Indian markets, these are called *toor dal* or *tuvar dal.* They have a mild, nutty flavor, and are often cooked as a side dish or ground into flour.

Split White Lentils: These lentil-like beans popular in India have strong and earthy-tasting black skins covering creamy white interiors. They are closely related to Asian red and green mung beans. When whole they are called black urad or black gram and are often used in curries. When skinned and split, their creamy white, slightly oblong inner beans are called *urud dal* or *kali dal.* They are very quick-cooking and have a rather innocuous flavor and slightly sticky consistency.

LENTILS IN INDIA

India accounts for about half the world's consumption of lentils and therefore has developed its own lexicon and classification for their most popular legumes, based on culinary use rather than botanical category. *Gram* is an Indian term used for legumes that are whole, rather than split, such as black gram or mung bean, green chickpea, and green mung bean. All small split legumes are called *dal,* although they may be in fact be lentils, pigeon peas, chickpeas, gram beans, or lablab beans. In the north of India and Pakistan, the Muslim population mainly eats whole pink lentils; in the south, split lentils are more popular.

Tunisian Mahammass Soup with Israeli Couscous, Lentils, and Chickpeas

Years ago, I worked at the "hot" restaurant, A'propos Bistro, on what is today Philadelphia's Avenue of the Arts. From the owners, two Tunisian brothers, I learned about the special foods of Tunisia's once large Jewish community. I later became friendly with another Tunisian, Taieb Dridi, who imports magnificent hammered-copper couscousiers and has worked with the Culinary Institute at Greystone in Napa Valley demonstrating Tunisian cooking. Through the years, I picked up an affinity for that country's earthy, hot, and spicy cuisine with a strong bias towards vegetables. This soup is based on one I had while attending a conference on Mediterranean flavors, given by the Tunisian chef, Abderrazak Haouari. This hearty soup is prepared with a whole garden of vegetables, three different legumes, and the large balls of toasted couscous known as mahammass in Tunisia.

SERVES 8 TO 10

1/2 cup skinless, dried split favas

1 cup dried chickpeas

1 cup lentils

2 tablespoons tomato paste

1/2 cup fresh tomato puree

1 tablespoon Harissa sauce (prepared or homemade, *see* page 703)

1/4 cup extra-virgin olive oil

1 cup chopped onion

3 tablespoons ground fenugreek

2 teaspoons ground caraway

Kosher salt and freshly ground black pepper to taste

1 pound Israeli couscous

3 tablespoons chopped garlic

1 rib celery, diced

1/2 pound spinach, stems trimmed

3 to 4 carrots, peeled and diced

1 to 2 turnips, peeled and diced

2 medium gold or all-purpose potatoes, peeled and diced

2 lemons, cut in quarters, to serve

Soak the favas and chickpeas overnight in cold water to cover. Drain and rinse. Place favas, chickpeas, and lentils in a large soup pot, and cover with cold water by about 3 inches. Bring to the boil, skimming as necessary, and reduce heat to a simmer.

After about 1 1/2 hours, when the legumes are half cooked, add the tomato paste, tomato puree, Harissa, olive oil, onion, fenugreek, ground caraway, and salt and pepper.

Meanwhile, bring a large pot of salted water to the boil. Boil the couscous until fully cooked but still firm, about 20 minutes. Drain, rinse, and reserve.

When the legumes are three-quarters cooked, about 1/2 hour more, add the fresh vegetables and the cooked couscous. Simmer together about 15 minutes longer, or until the legumes are quite soft. Taste for seasoning and serve the soup very hot accompanied by lemon quarters.

FENUGREEK

The small, pebble-hard seeds of the fenugreek plant, *Trigonella foenum-graecum*, are brownish-gold in color and have a pleasing, acrid flavor and an aroma that immediately brings to mind curry powder. The angular seeds are often roasted to enhance their pungent aroma. The seeds are used in Indian, Ethiopian, Yemeni, and North African cookery. In India, the leaves, called *methi*, are used fresh as a vegetable, or dried as an herb. They are also popular in Iran. Ground fenugreek quickly loses its potency, but the whole seeds are challenging to crush. Use a mortar and pestle or a spice grinder.

Beluga Lentil Salad with Crispy Salami Bits and Tomato

This salad is a variation of a salad included in my book, Beans, that was so popular at cooking classes, I came up with this Italian-accented version featuring the elegant black beluga lentils now sold in many supermarkets and natural foods stores. This appetizing salad of small, inky-black lentils marinated in red wine vinaigrette is colorful because of the red and gold tomatoes and the green chives. Turn this into a main dish by topping each portion with a crisp, oven roasted Homeade Duck Confit (see page 380), or pan-seared oily fish, such as tuna, salmon, mahi-mahi, or black cod. Instead of the more common bacon bits, I crisp-up small cubes of Italian salami to add texture and a burst of salty-savory flavor in the mouth.

547

SERVES 4 TO 6

2 cups (1 pound) beluga lentils

1/2 cup extra-virgin olive oil

1/4 cup red wine vinegar

2 teaspoons crushed garlic

Kosher salt and freshly ground black pepper to taste

2 tablespoons canola oil

1/2 pound thickly sliced Genoa salami, cut into small cubes

2 ripe red and/or yellow tomatoes, diced

1 bunch scallions, thinly sliced

1 cup chopped Italian parsley leaves (about 1 bunch)

2 tablespoons chopped marjoram

Prepare the beluga lentils following the directions in the recipe for Braised Green Lentils, page 550. Reserve in a medium bowl.

Prepare the dressing by whisking together the olive oil, vinegar, garlic, and salt and pepper to taste. Pour the dressing over the lentils while they're still warm, tossing to coat well.

Heat the canola oil over moderate heat in a small, heavy-bottomed pot, and add the salami, cooking until crisp and browned, then drain on paper towels. Add most of the salami, tomatoes, scallions, parsley, and marjoram to the lentils, reserving some of each ingredient for garnish. Taste for seasoning, correcting if necessary.

Serve at room temperature, garnished with the reserved salami, tomato, and scallions, parsley, and marjoram.

Neapolitan Lentil and Chestnut Soup

My first night in the tumultuous urban center of Napoli, I ate this hearty, comforting peasant soup in the style of today's sought-after "cucina povera," dishes that were once only eaten by the poor and often prepared with wild and other local ingredients. This simple thick zuppa *is prepared from two of my favorite ingredients: chestnuts and lentils. In this case, dried chestnuts are used, which are simply soaked to soften. It is difficult to get dried* castagne *(chestnuts); rather, Chinese dried chestnuts are most common—they are sweeter and less richly dense. In Italy, special varieties of lentils have been grown in particular regions for countless generations; I have a special bag of lentils from the lentil-growing town of Onano in Italy that are just right for this soup. Note that this soup is quite*

thick, almost a vegetable stew. Also, use your best hand-crafted olive oil here to drizzle on top at the table. This step enriches the soup and adds a wonderful aroma to the air as you stir it in.

SERVES 8 TO 10

$1/2$ pound dried chestnuts

2 bay leaves

$1/4$ cup fatback, prosciutto fat, or bacon fat, or $1/2$ cup small diced bacon

2 cups finely chopped sweet onion

1 pound European small lentils (French green, Italian Castelluccio, or Spanish Pardina)

$1/2$ cup dry Marsala wine

Kosher salt and freshly ground black pepper to taste

Best-quality extra-virgin olive oil, for garnish

Soak the chestnuts in water to cover overnight. Discard the water.

In a large soup pot, cover the chestnuts with 3 quarts cold water, add the bay leaves, and bring to the boil. Simmer about 2 hours, or until soft, but still whole.

Meanwhile, in a covered pan over low heat, cook the fatback and onion together, stirring occasionally until the onions are softened and lightly browned, about 15 minutes.

Add the onion mixture to the pot along with the lentils. Bring back to the boil, reduce heat to a simmer, and cook about 45 minutes longer, or until the lentils are soft, but still whole and the chestnuts have broken apart into bits. Season with salt and pepper and pour in the Marsala, thinning the soup with a little water if necessary, and serve immediately, accompanied by a bottle of your best olive oil to drizzle into the soup at the table.

Grilled Wild Salmon with Braised Green Lentils

This is reprise of the famed French nouvelle cuisine dish of salmon on a bed of lentils that I served with great success while chef at Stella Notte in Chestnut Hill. I would serve them with a lagniappe of crispy fried leeks (see page 526). The rich, oily flesh of the salmon contrasts beautifully in color, texture, and flavor with the firm, nutty lentils. The lemon-mustard mayonnaise brings the whole dish together. Black beluga lentils would also work well here. Take James Bond's advice and shake but don't stir (the lentils, not the martini), to avoid breaking them up.

SERVES 6

Lemon–Mustard Mayonnaise

2 egg yolks

Juice and grated zest of 1 lemon

2 tablespoons coarse-grain mustard

1 tablespoon Dijon mustard

Kosher salt and freshly ground black pepper to taste

1 cup canola or soybean oil

In a food processor, combine the egg yolks, lemon juice, and zest, both mustards, salt, and pepper until sticky. Then, with the processor still running, slowly pour in the oil until it has all been absorbed. If the mayonnaise gets too thick, thin with a tablespoon or two of warm water. Keep refrigerated until ready to use.

Assembly

6 (6- to 8-ounce) portions salmon fillet

Kosher salt and freshly ground black pepper to taste

2 tablespoons canola oil

1 bunch scallions, sliced

2 tablespoons unsalted butter

6 cups Braised Green Lentils (*see* page 550)

2 cups diced round tomatoes, mixed yellow
   and red if possible

1 tablespoon each: chopped dill, parsley, and tarragon

Lemon-Mustard Mayonnaise, in squeeze bottle if desired

Crispy Fried Leeks (optional, *see* page 526)

Preheat the grill or broiler. Sprinkle the salmon with salt and pepper and allow it to rest at room temperature for about 20 minutes. Rub lightly with oil and grill to desired doneness, starting with the skin-side down.

549

Meanwhile, in a large skillet, sauté the scallions briefly in butter, add the lentils and tomatoes, and simmer together several minutes until hot and somewhat thickened. Just before serving, add the herbs and taste for seasoning.

Spoon a portion of lentils on each plate. Arrange salmon over top. Drizzle Lemon-Mustard Mayonnaise over top, garnish with Crispy Fried Leeks, and serve immediately.

Braised Green Lentils

This is a good basic recipe for cooking those delicious little French lentils. Use either chicken or vegetable stock for the best flavor. Once cooked and cooled, these lentils freeze beautifully in double plastic zip-top bags. Rinse off any frost and allow the lentils to defrost at room temperature for about half an hour before adding to any dish.

SERVES 6 TO 8

1 pound (2 cups) French green lentils

1 quart chicken or vegetable stock

1 whole peeled onion

Zest of 1 lemon

2 bay leaves

3 to 4 sprigs thyme, tied with kitchen string

Kosher salt and freshly ground black pepper to taste

In a medium, heavy-bottomed pot with a lid, bring everything but the salt and pepper to the boil. Skim as needed, reduce heat to a simmer, and cover. Cook until about half-cooked, about 30 minutes, then add the salt and pepper, cover and cook 10 to 15 minutes longer, or until lentils are tender but still firm. Remove from the heat and allow to cool before stirring or draining. Reserve.

550

LIMES

LIMES

Why is it that just about anything with lime in it tastes so good? It seems that the concentrated acidity and slightly bitter flavor of lime gives the needed sharp edge to sweet and highly aromatic tropical foods. Lime is essential to cocktails from the daiquiri to gin and tonic, the mojito, the caipirinha, rum and coke, and more. It flavors ceviche and salsas, grilled fish and seafood. Cut-up fruit like mangoes, melons, pineapples, papayas, and bananas all reach their peak of flavor with a squeeze of lime. And, can anyone pass up a freshly made Florida Key lime pie? (*See* page 556 for a delectable Key Lime Meringue Pie with Coconut-Cashew Crust.)

Limes, *Citrus aurantifolia*, are native to Southeast Asia. Along with the closely related lemon, they made their way to the eastern Mediterranean with the Arabs, and to the western Mediterranean with the returning Crusaders. Columbus introduced citrus fruits to the West Indies on his second voyage, and limes quickly spread. These limes, which predominate in the world outside the U.S., are what Americans call Key limes.

In the eighteenth century, it was learned that citrus juice would prevent scurvy, a disease which had devastated the British navy more than any enemy. Britain imported limes cheaply from its colony of Jamaica, and they became the citrus of choice for sailors who became known as "limeys."

Key limes grow on thorny trees which are quite sensitive to cold weather. They are small, a bit larger than a walnut, rounded in shape, with a thin yellowish rind that is prone to splotchy brown spots. They are aromatic and very juicy, with a stronger and more complex acidic flavor than Persian limes. Their flesh is greenish-yellow and full of seeds; their juice content is high, well over forty percent. Both Persian and Key limes have a higher sugar and citric acid content than lemons, and Key limes are more acidic than Persian. Key limes were grown commercially in southern Florida and the Florida Keys until the 1926 hurricane wiped out the citrus groves. Currently, Mexico is the leading producer, with the West Indies and Egypt next. The majority of Key limes found in supermarkets come from Mexico and Central America.

The most common lime in the United States, the "lime green" Persian lime, *Citrus latifolia*, is probably a hybrid of the Key lime and the citron. Botanists believe this variety was introduced to the Mediterranean via Persia (now Iran) and was then carried to Brazil by Portuguese traders. They eventually made their way to California in the latter half of the 1800s via a round-about route through Australia and Tahiti. The Persian or Tahitian lime, which is almost always seedless, is shaped like a lemon, is larger than the Key lime, and has a thick rind and juicy, pale green pulp. Persian limes are deliberately

552

picked slightly immature, while they are still green, partly to distinguish them from lemons. Today, Florida grows ninety percent of the U.S. crop.

The sweet lime, *Citrus limettoides*, is thought to be another hybrid. It has a somewhat lower sugar content than the other limes but almost no acidity. This juicy fruit is popular in the Middle East and India. In the Middle East and Southern Asia, dried limes called *omani* are indispensable to meat stews, to which they give a pleasantly musty, tangy, sour flavor.

CHOOSING LIMES, SEASON, AND STORAGE

Look for brightly colored, smooth-skinned limes that are heavy for their size. Small brown areas on the skin won't affect the flavor of either Persian or Key limes. Choose Key limes with light yellow, fine-grained skin that are heavy for their size. Avoid limes or Key limes with hard or shriveled skin or those that don't give at all when squeezed, which are likely to be full of dry pulp with little juice.

Persian limes are available year-round. Peak season for Key limes is June through August, but they are available year-round from Mexico and Central America, especially in Latin American markets.

Refrigerate Persian limes in a plastic bag in the refrigerator for up to 10 days. Key limes are more perishable; store refrigerated in a plastic bag for up to 5 days. Store cut limes in a plastic bag for up to 3 days.

Chayote Stuffed with Seafood Ceviche

Ceviche, also spelled seviche *or* cebiche *depending on which part of South America's Pacific Coast it comes from, is best served as a first course with cocktails or beer. Seaside towns in Peru, parts of Chile, Ecuador, and Honduras are ceviche headquarters, although the dish has traveled to Mexico's Pacific Coast and the Caribbean including Yucatan. There is a theory that pre-Hispanic peoples marinated fish with a fruit called* tumbo. *The Incas ate salted fish and a chicha-marinated fish dish (chicha is a beer made from corn that is widely enjoyed in Central and South America). As Latin American flavors have become more and more important to the American palate, we have started to incorporate ingredients like passion fruit, tamarind pulp, nopales (cactus paddles), conch, calabaza squash, yuca root, myriad chiles, and the chayote used here into the food we cook.*

553

SERVES 6

6 chayote squash, split

1 cup freshly squeezed lime juice

$^1/_2$ cup orange juice

2 jalapeño peppers, seeded and finely chopped

$^1/_2$ cup finely chopped white onion

2 teaspoons kosher salt

2 pounds sea scallops, trimmed of connector

1 pound very fresh white-fleshed fish (red snapper, sea bass, or hybrid striped bass)

1 pound shrimp, peeled, deveined, and poached in Seafood Stock (*see* page 994)

1 colorful bell pepper, seeded and finely diced

Grated zest of 1 lime and 1 orange

$^1/_2$ cup chopped cilantro

Bring a large pot of salted water to the boil. Add the chayote and simmer for 15 minutes, or until crisp-tender. Drain and refresh under cold running water. Scoop out and discard some of the inside flesh, leaving a wall about $1/2$ inch thick, and reserve.

Whisk together the dressing ingredients: lime juice, orange juice, jalapeño, and onion, season to taste with salt, and reserve.

Prepare the scallops and fish by removing bones and cutting into 1-inch cubes. Toss scallops and fish with half the dressing. Allow to cure in the refrigerator for 24 hours, stirring once or twice, until meat has become more opaque than translucent. Drain seafood and mix with cooled shrimp, the bell pepper, the cubed chayote, the cilantro, and the remaining dressing.

Spoon the ceviche into the reserved chayote squash and serve immediately.

554

> ## CHAYOTE
>
> The chayote, *Sechium edule,* is an uncommon member of the gourd family, with one large, edible seed inside a plump, pear-shaped vegetable with shallow furrows running its length. Its name is Aztec in origin, and it is native to Mesoamerica and was eaten by both Mayas and Aztecs. Chayotes range from cream to celadon to zucchini-green in color, with a taste and texture between cucumber and apple.
>
> In the U.S., the most common chayote is light green with relatively smooth skin and weighs about half a pound, although the larger, dark green spiny porcupine-like chayote preferred in Mexico is starting to show up in American supermarkets, especially where there is a large Mexican community. Chayote is quite versatile and can be eaten raw, and is substituted for apples and pumpkins in pies in Latin America.

Crab Salad in Mint and Lime Citronette

One of the greatest delicacies of the American East Coast is blue crab, here combined with juicy, crunchy vegetables in a light, lime-y salad. The salad will only be as good as the crab you use. Unfortunately, it's rare to find really good, fresh, unpasteurized (not in a can) crabmeat in the supermarket. High-quality crabmeat is mostly reserved for restaurants, who will pay top dollar for top quality. Pasteurized crabmeat may be your best bet. The salad can also be made with West Coast Dungeness crab or even with poached, diced scallops or small shrimp.

SERVES 4

$1/2$ pound fresh water chestnuts
1 chayote squash, peeled, cut into small dice
  and boiled briefly
1 pound jumbo-lump crabmeat, cleaned
1 red bell pepper, diced
$1/2$ cup olive oil
$1/4$ cup lime juice
2 tablespoons shredded mint
2 tablespoons thinly sliced chives
Kosher salt and freshly ground black pepper to taste
1 bunch baby arugula

Pare and quarter the water chestnuts (*see* Preparing Water Chestnuts, page 499, for directions). Bring a small pot of salted water to the boil. Cook the water chestnuts in the water until tender, about 4 minutes, then scoop from the water and reserve. Add the chayote to the same water and boil about 2 minutes, or until tender. Drain and reserve.

Combine the water chestnuts, chayote, crabmeat, and red pepper and reserve.

Whisk together the olive oil, lime juice, mint, and chives and season with salt and pepper. Use most of the dressing to toss with the crab mixture, reserving a small amount to toss with the arugula.

Place crab salad in a mound in center of salad plate. Toss arugula lightly with the remaining dressing and arrange in two small bunches on either side of the crab salad, and serve.

OTHER NAMES FOR CHAYOTE AND WHERE IT'S GROWN

The chayote goes by many names, variously called mango squash, vegetable pear, *mirliton* in Louisiana and Haiti, *christophine* in France and Trinidad, *chocho* in Brazil and West Africa, custard marrow in Great Britain, and *xuxu* in Vietnam. The chayote is now cultivated in the subtropics worldwide, but is especially popular in Latin America and the Caribbean with California, Florida, Costa Rica, and Mexico as the main American suppliers.

Salmon Tiraditos with Blood Orange and Key Lime

The word tiraditos *means ribbons or strips in Spanish. It has become the latest rage in ceviches, inspired by Japanese sashimi. Here, thin ribbons of salmon are dressed with a Latino-Asian combo of citrus juices and rice wine vinegar. The chipotles (smoked jalapeños) add a welcome hot, smoky note underscored by the fresh red jalapeño. Note that wild-caught salmon must be frozen for 2 days to kill any parasites before defrosting and preparing this dish. It is not necessary to do this with farm-raised salmon.*

SERVES 4

$1/2$ pound sushi-grade salmon fillet, skinned with pin bones removed (*see* About Pin Bones, page 419, and Removing Pin Bones, page 833, for directions)

2 tablespoons kosher salt

$1/4$ cup rice wine vinegar

$1/4$ cup blood orange puree

2 tablespoons freshly squeezed Key lime juice (or lime juice)

2 tablespoons freshly squeezed lemon juice

1 teaspoon sauce from canned chipotles in adobo

Pinch sea salt

2 Key limes, seeded and thinly sliced

1 red jalapeño, thinly sliced

To prepare the fish, rub the salmon all over with salt and leave to rest at room temperature for 40 minutes. Rinse off the salt by rubbing with the rice wine vinegar and then rinse lightly with cold water and refrigerate.

To make the sauce, combine the blood orange puree, Key lime juice, lemon juice, sauce from chipotles in

555

adobo, and sea salt to taste.

When ready to serve, cut the fish on the diagonal into approximately 16 thin slices. Arrange 4 slices for each person onto large individual serving plates. Spoon the sauce over and around the fish. Garnish each fish slice with a ring of Key lime topped with a ring of red jalapeño and serve immediately.

Pan-Fried Flounder with Lime and Cilantro

This simple dish couldn't be easier to make and sacrifices nothing in flavor. Tender, fast-cooking flounder fillet is complemented by sweet onion and red bell pepper with the kick of jalapeño, the tangy citrus flavor of freshly squeezed lime, with an underlying layer of pungent earthiness from the cilantro. Flounder fillet can be found in many supermarkets (for more information, see Flounder, page 426). On the West Coast, substitute another flat fish, such as sand dab or petrale sole. In the Midwest, substitute lake whitefish fillet.

SERVES 4

2 pounds flounder fillet

Kosher salt and freshly ground black pepper to taste

$1/4$ cup all-purpose flour, preferably unbleached

1 tablespoon canola oil

1 tablespoon + 2 tablespoons unsalted butter

1 red bell pepper, seeded and diced

1 jalapeño (fresh or pickled), trimmed, seeded, and minced

1 medium sweet onion, thinly sliced

Juice of 1 lime

$1/4$ cup chopped cilantro

Season the fish on both sides with salt and pepper. Next, dust the fish with flour, shaking off the excess.

Meanwhile, heat the oil in a large, preferably nonstick, skillet over high heat. Add the flounder, starting with the flesh-side down, and sauté 1 minute on each side. Remove the fish from the pan and drape with foil to keep warm. Pour off and discard the oil.

In the same pan, melt 1 tablespoon of the butter and add the bell pepper, jalapeño, and onion. Cook 2 minutes, or until crisp-tender, add the lime juice, and bring to the boil. Cook 2 minutes longer, or until the juices are syrupy. Stir in the cilantro, season with salt and pepper and the remaining 2 tablespoons butter. Arrange the fish on serving plates, preferably heated, pour the sauce over top, and serve immediately.

Key Lime Meringue Pie with Coconut-Cashew Crust

To make the pie, egg yolks and extra-sour Key limes are combined; the yolks are thickened by their reaction with the acidic limes. The easy-to-make graham cracker crumb crust is now the standard, but the crunchy coconut-cashew crust I use here takes the pie down into the tropics. As in most recipes today, the pie is baked to thicken it further and to eliminate any potential salmonella. If fresh Key limes are not available, substitute limes and add 1 teaspoon grated lime peel. The cloud-light Italian meringue topping complements the rich custard filling (and uses up some of those extra egg whites).

MAKES ONE 9-INCH PIE

Coconut–Cashew Crust

$^1/_2$ pound frozen fresh grated or dessicated coconut
  (*see* Frozen Fresh Grated Coconut, page 311, for more
  information)
$^3/_4$ pound cashews, ground
$^1/_2$ cup granulated sugar
12 tablespoons ($1^1/_2$ sticks) unsalted butter,
  melted and cooled

Combine coconut, cashews, and sugar, then mix well with the add cooled butter. Press into a 9-inch-diameter pie pan, preferably metal, and chill 30 minutes in the freezer or 1 hour in the refrigerator.

Preheat the oven to 350°F. Bake the crust for 30 to 40 minutes or until it is dry and lightly but evenly browned. Remove from the oven and, using the back of a spoon, re-press the crust firmly into the pan before cooling.

Filling

1 (14-ounce) can sweetened condensed milk
4 egg yolks
$^1/_2$ cup plus 2 tablespoons fresh Key lime juice

Whisk together the condensed milk and egg yolks in a bowl until combined well. Add the Key lime juice and whisk until combined well (mixture will thicken slightly).

Pour filling into the baked crust and bake at 350°F. for 15 minutes, or until the filling starts to bubble. Cool the pie completely on a wire rack (filling will set as it cools).

Italian Meringue Topping

1 cup granulated sugar
$^1/_2$ cup egg whites
$^1/_4$ teaspoon salt

In a small, heavy-bottomed pot, combine sugar with 1 cup water and bring to the boil, shaking to combine without forming crystals until the mixture forms a clear syrup. Continue to cook until thickened and bubbling all over (238°F. or soft ball stage).

When the sugar is almost ready, beat the egg whites and salt together to form medium peaks. With the mixer going, beat in the hot sugar syrup. Continue to beat until the meringue is firm, glossy, and at room temperature.

Spoon the meringue over the cooled pie or transfer the meringue to a large pastry bag fitted with a large star-shaped tip and pipe over top in an attractive pattern. Either place under a hot broiler for 2 to 3 minutes, watching carefully so it doesn't burn, or use a blow-torch to brown the top. Chill at least 4 hours before cutting into serving portions and serving.

557

Key Lime Pie History

What started out as the official dessert of Key West, the very tip of the long chain of keys (small islands) that stretch south towards Cuba, has now become a ubiquitous dessert in restaurants around the country. Key lime pie developed because the Florida Keys were quite isolated until the railroad was built in 1912, so that the canned sweetened condensed milk (invented by Gail Borden in 1859) was a boon. With the juice of the extra-sour Key limes—widely grown in the Keys until they were wiped out by the hurricane of 1926—egg yolks, and a crust made from boxed graham crackers, the Key lime pie was born.

Italian Meringue

Italian meringue is made with a simple recipe, two parts sugar to one part egg whites, but what makes it special is that it is partially cooked, resulting in a meringue that is firmer with finer air bubbles, and less liable to break-down and "weep." It takes a bit of care to get the timing right, because you have to beat the egg whites to soft peaks and then pour the hot sugar syrup into the whites as they're beating. Although a candy thermometer will make it easier, it's not necessary. Just boil the syrup until the surface is covered by thick, clear bubbles. Also, because Italian meringue must be continuously beaten until it cools to room temperature, it's difficult to make without a standing mixer.

USING A BLOW-TORCH IN THE KITCHEN

An ordinary hardware store blow-torch has many uses in the kitchen. There are also smaller home kitchen versions sold in many kitchen supply stores, although I haven't found that they work as well. The torch allows you to control perfectly the browning of meringue tops and the caramelizing of sugar for crème brulée. Always take care when using a torch, working in an area where there is nothing flammable nearby. Follow the safety instructions that come with the torch.

LOBSTER

LOBSTER

When I first started my kitchen career, I was more than a little frightened of handling live lobsters. The first time I had to kill one, it was with much trepidation but also with the determination to conquer my fear that I did so. Unlike at home, where most lobsters are thrown into a pot of boiling water, in restaurants, lobsters are usually killed and then immediately cut up. Years later, when I foolishly decided to put homemade lobster ravioli on the menu for New Year's Eve, I spent the whole night frantically hacking at the claws to pull out the stubbornly stuck small pieces of meat I needed to fill yet more ravioli. Fifty lobsters later, my hands were as red as my aquatic victims.

There is good reason that lobster is so highly valued. Nothing makes a better-tasting soup, sauce, or stew, because of the intensely lobster-rich flavor imparted by the bodies and shells. I am always amazed by the scary beauty of these creatures, of which only the small stomach sac is inedible. As a chef, it's a totally satisfying experience to transform a lobster into a delectable dish fit for the finest table.

The regal lobster, *Homarus americanus*, also called the American lobster, Atlantic lobster, or true lobster, is a slow-growing, prized creature of the sea found in the Atlantic waters of the American and Canadian Eastern seaboard. It closely resembles its European cousin, *Homarus gammarus*, though the American lobster has more robust tearing and crushing claws. In France, it is called *homard*; in Germany, Denmark, Sweden, and Norway, it is called *hummer*. Lobsters are the basis of the French lobster bisque and lobster Thermidor, and American steamed lobster with drawn butter, lobster Newburg, and New England lobster roll sandwiches.

Hundreds of years before the colonists reached our shores, Native American tribes of the Eastern seaboard fished for lobsters so plentiful that they often were found on the beach at low tide, and washed up on shore in large storms. Known as *wolum keeh* to the Mic Mac Indians, lobsters were eaten for food, their shells used for ornament, and their bodies for fertilizer.

It's hard to believe, but in colonial times, lobsters were so plentiful that in the nineteenth century, a family being housed in the Plymouth, Massachusetts, Poor House complained when they were fed lobster three times in a week. In the eighteenth century, lobsters were considered to be fit only for the poor; it wasn't until the second half of the nineteenth century that the American lobster industry began to flourish. Higher and higher demand has led to higher and higher prices and smaller sizes and smaller harvests.

The Breton lobster, found off of France's Atlantic coast in Brittany, has been highly prized in France since the 1400s. When caught, these lobsters were shipped directly

560

to Paris, where the high price they received helped these fisherman earn a good living. Nicknamed "the cardinal of the sea" because of their bright red color when cooked, French lobsters are generally smaller than their American cousins.

American lobsters can be found in shallower water, especially in rocky areas where they hide in the crevices, in the Atlantic as far north as Labrador and as far south as North Carolina. Lobsters from colder waters are more highly regarded. In earlier times, lobsters were fished from the shallow waters by spearing or gaffing them as they crawled around in search of food on calm evenings.

When the commercial market for lobsters started to develop, the lobsters were worth more if there were no spear marks in them, so fishermen began using wire cages, adapted from the Europeans, who used them to catch crayfish and spiny lobsters.

The largest lobster ever recorded weighed in at forty-four pounds, six ounces and measured three-and-a-half feet from the tip of the largest claw to the tip of its tail. It was caught off southern Nova Scotia in 1977 and sold to a restaurant in New York City. But, a million years ago, lobsters were five to six feet long! These days a three-or four-pound lobster is unusual.

LOBSTER TRAPS

The traditional wooden-lath lobster trap consists of a "kitchen" and a "parlor." The lobster enters the trap through funnel-shaped "doors" in search of the bait, located, naturally enough, in the "kitchen." The doors are shaped so that it is easy for the lobsters to enter but difficult to exit. When the lobster tries to escape, it is led through another door into the parlor. Small vents in the parlor allow undersize lobsters to escape, but larger lobsters are trapped to await their fate.

Lobster Anatomy

Lobsters are actually closely related to insects, with whom they share an exoskeleton (outer skeleton or shell) and jointed appendages (legs, arms, or claws). A lobster's body is divided into two main parts: the head and thorax (midsection) and the abdomen (called the tail) with its small feelers.

The first set of legs with the largest and sharpest pincers are called the claws. One claw is the pincer claw; the other is called the crusher claw. The larger, harder crusher claw, resembles a human molar tooth and is more powerful. It is used to crush the shells of the lobster's prey. The pincer claw is like a fine-toothed razor and is used to tear the flesh of the prey. Surprisingly, lobsters can be right or left-handed, determined by which side the crusher claw appears on. Behind the claws are several pairs of pincers, sharp, small, scissor-like claws used in handling food.

The tail meat is the most highly valued and can usually be pulled out whole after cutting open the shell on the underside. The claws have stringier, but well-flavored meat, harder to extract because of the extra-hard shells, especially on the crusher claw. The small pincers also contain long, narrow, finger-shaped meat that can be extracted with patience.

LOBSTER COLOR

The color of live lobsters varies from olive green to dark greenish-brown with orange, reddish, dark green, or black speckles and bluish joints. The darker the live color, the brighter the cooked color. But, the redness is also determined by the cooking temperature. Lobsters cooked at high heat, either in oil or by steam, will be brightest. About one in two million lobsters is actually bright blue in color, due to a genetic defect. There is also an unrelated blue spiny lobster that is found in the warm waters of the Indian Ocean.

CHOOSING AND STORING LOBSTERS

A live lobster should look lively, wiggling its claws. Its tail should spring right back when straightened, and the shell should be hard and thick. Lobsters must be alive immediately prior to cooking. A lobster can live out of the water for two to three days if kept in a moist and cool place because it can extract the oxygen from the air, but in order to do this its gills must be kept moist. Note that hard-shelled lobsters can live longer than those with soft shells. Lobsters are often sold commercially packed in damp layers of newspaper, or better, in layers of fresh seaweed.

To store a live lobster, put it in a box or shallow pan in the refrigerator and cover with a dampened cloth or layers of damp newspaper for one to two days. Do not store the lobster in fresh water or ice. Cooked lobster meat may be stored in the refrigerator for up to two days.

Hard-and Soft-Shelled Lobsters

A hard-shelled lobster, one with a fully-hardened shell, will yield the highest percentage of meat. A soft-shelled lobster, one that has recently molted (or shed its shell), will have watery meat that doesn't fill its shell and is not as desirable. Soft-shelled lobsters are also more perishable.

MALE AND FEMALE LOBSTERS

I prefer to buy female lobsters if possible because they are plumper and will usually carry the dark green coral or roe (actually the unfertilized eggs) that turn brilliant vermilion red when cooked and add a special flavor to any lobster dish. Look at the first set of feelers below the thorax on the underside of the body. They are soft on a female, hard on a male. Female lobsters also have noticeably shorter, wider tails than males.

Buying Culls

A cull is a lobster with one or both claws missing, or with the tiny replacement claws that the lobster is able to regenerate when a claw is torn off. Sometimes fish markets sell culls, which are less expensive and suited to any dish where the meat is removed from the lobster. Culls must be cooked the same day they're purchased, as they will not live long.

Lobster Sizes and Yields

A chicken or chix lobster is one that is between one and one and a quarter pounds, the minimum size sold, and less desirable, because the proportion of meat is low. A one-and-a-half pound lobster is the most commonly available size and works well for most recipes. Larger lobsters not only weigh more, but also cost more per pound, so they will be quite a bit more expensive. The exception to this is if you can buy a large lobster that is a "cull" (*see* Buying Culls, left)).

A one-pound lobster will typically yield a quarter pound of cooked meat; a one-and-a-half pound lobster will yield between six and eight ounces of meat.

Lobster Tomalley

The tomalley, usually called the liver, is a set of glands. The greenish-brown soft tomalley has the texture of scrambled eggs. It turns light green when cooked and is considered a delicacy by lobster lovers. However, because of its strong taste, it's best used in smaller quantities to enrich and flavor sauces and soups.

How to Tell When a Lobster Is Cooked

A lobster is cooked when it is bright red and when the legs and antennae can be pulled off easily. The tomalley should be green and firm, the roe bright red, and the meat white, elastic, and opaque. The tail shell should be curled, but not too tightly, an indication that it has been overcooked. The large crusher she; will take the longest to cook.

SPINY LOBSTERS AND TRUE LOBSTERS

Another kind of edible lobster is called the spiny lobster or rock lobster. There are many species, all of which lack the large crusher and pincer claws of the true lobster, have spines all over their bodies, and live in subtropical and tropical oceans. These are the lobsters usually served in restaurants and sold frozen as lobster tails. Their texture is not as firm, and their flavor is milder and less distinctive. To me, the only lobster worth eating is a true lobster.

CUTTING UP A LIVE LOBSTER BEFORE COOKING

Grip the lobster on the back of its thorax, or main body shell, just behind the front of the head. Look for the place where the head shell connects to the main thorax, or body shell. Plunge the point of a sharp and heavy chef's knife between the shell sections. This will kill the lobster instantly, although it may continue to move briefly.

Twist off the tail where it meets the body of the lobster. Remove and reserve the dark green roe sacs at the center of the tails. Split the tail lengthwise, then remove and discard the (usually clear) intestine that runs down the center. Loosen but do not remove the tail meat from its shell and reserve. Remove the tomalley, if desired, to add to a sauce; otherwise discard.

563

Poached Lobster

Poaching (slowly simmering) lobsters in a flavorful liquid, gives the lobsters flavors from the cooking broth while at the same time imparting their lobster flavor to the broth. Once the lobsters are cooked, strain the liquid and either use it once more for poaching or especially if you've just poached lobster, shrimp or scallops—or as the base for a seafood chowder or stew. The strained broth may also be frozen for later use, such as in the recipes for Lobster Risotto (see right) and Lobster or the Linguine with Lobster, Corn, Tarragon and Creamy Tomato Sauce (see page 567).

MAKES 4 COOKED LOBSTERS AND 3 QUARTS BROTH

3 quarts Seafood Stock (*see* page 994)
4 (1½ pound) live lobsters

Bring the Seafood Stock to a boil in a large pot.

Kill the lobsters following the first half of directions in Cutting Up A Live Lobster Before Cooking, page 563. Drop the lobsters into the boiling liquid, cover, and cook 4 minutes, stirring once. The lobsters should be bright red with lightly curled tail shells.

Remove the lobsters from the pot and either serve them as is with drawn butter, or cool them in a large bowl of ice mixed with water and then follow the directions in Removing the Meat From A Cooked Lobster, right. Strain and reserve the broth. Cool and chill or freeze for use another time.

REMOVING THE MEAT FROM A COOKED LOBSTER

Twist off the claws where they meet the body of the lobster. Using a mallet or the back of a heavy knife, crack the claw shells without breaking them up too much. Remove the claws from their shells, trying to leave them intact as much as possible. Reserve. Pull off the tail from the body and, using scissors, cut along the underside of the shell. Pull off the tail shell, leaving the tail meat intact. If desired, twist off the small pincers from the body and pull out the long, thin meat on the inside. (This is only worth doing on a larger lobster.)

Lobster Risotto

Lobster makes a wonderful risotto, redolent of the flavor of this regal sea creature. It's a good way to make one larger or two smaller lobsters feed a larger group. Start by poaching the lobsters following the recipe for Poached Lobster (left) to obtain the flavorful cooking liquid needed here. Cool the lobsters and remove their meat. Don't throw away the carcasses, though—freeze them and use them to make another batch of lobster stock for next time.

Seafood risottos (risotti is the Italian plural) are, by tradition, not seasoned with cheese, which is thought to take away from the delicate flavors of the seafood. Here, the lobster is finished with lobster butter, lobster coral, and fragrant herbs.

SERVES 4

564

1/4 cup each: finely chopped shallots, carrots, and fennel

2 tablespoons extra-virgin olive oil

1 cup Italian risotto rice

1/2 cup dry white vermouth

3 to 4 cups simmering Lobster Broth (from Poached
  Lobster, page 564)

Kosher salt and freshly ground black pepper to taste

1 cup lobster meat, cut into bite-sized pieces

2 tablespoons Lobster Butter (recipe follows), substitute
  unsalted butter

1 tablespoon each; chopped tarragon or chervil
  and sliced chives

In a 3- to 4-quart heavy-bottomed sauce pot, cook the shallots, carrots, and fennel in the olive oil until transparent, about 3 minutes. Add rice and cook, stirring, until rice is transparent, about 3 minutes. Pour in vermouth and stir.

Raise the heat, bring to the boil and cook until liquid is absorbed, about 4 minutes. Reduce heat to a healthy simmer and one ladle at a time, add simmering stock to rice. Stir after adding stock, and then allow stock to be fully absorbed before adding a second ladle. Season to taste with salt and pepper.

Continue adding the liquid, one ladleful at a time, until it has all been absorbed. The rice should be firm and fully cooked with no hard white center to the grain. At the last minute, stir in the lobster meat, lobster butter, herbs, and taste for seasoning. Serve on hot plates; risotto tastes best piping hot. (If you want a stronger lobster flavor, add about 2 tablespoons of the green tomalley in the last few minutes of cooking.)

Lobster Butter

MAKES ABOUT 1 1/4 CUPS

Cooked shells and bodies from 2 lobsters (meat
  removed and reserved for another use)

1/4 pound (1 stick) unsalted butter

Any dark green lobster roe

Remove and discard the small sand sack (the stomach) from inside the heads of the lobsters, just behind the eyes. Chop up the lobster bodies into smaller pieces, using a heavy chef's knife or a meat mallet.

Put the lobster pieces through the large holes of a meat grinder or chop coarsely by hand, then place in a food processor and grind very fine, working in several batches if necessary. Mix the ground lobster bits with the butter and transfer to a medium pot. Simmer very slowly for 30 minutes to extract the lobster flavor. Strain through a fine sieve and reserve.

Meanwhile, cook the reserved lobster roe in a small amount of water in the microwave for 1 to 2 minutes, or until the roe turns bright red.

Wash out the processor bowl. Scrape the strained lobster butter back into the bowl of the processor, add the cooked lobster roe and any cooking liquid, and process again so that the roe separates out into tiny, bright red bits. Remove the finished lobster butter from the processor and reserve.

Store, refrigerated, in a covered container for up to 1 month.

565

Grilled Lobster with Herbed Crème Fraiche

In my days as chef of a California-style restaurant, we would grill everything on our heavy steel Wolf grill fired with desert mesquite wood. I still love fire-cooking and admire the skill it takes to control the heat source, though these days, I prefer to cook over fruitwood like cherry or apple or oak. I find that mesquite, which burns extremely hot, gives too strong a taste to the food. Lobsters on the grill (or on the barbie, as they say in Australia) are absolutely delicious and not that hard to make.

SERVES 4

1 cup chilled crème fraiche

2 tablespoons + 2 tablespoons extra-virgin olive oil

2 tablespoons champagne vinegar

2 roasted red peppers, peeled, seeded and finely chopped (purchased or homemade, *see* page 66)

$1/4$ cup finely chopped fine herbs: tarragon, chives, chervil, parsley, and thyme

Kosher salt, freshly ground black pepper, and cayenne pepper to taste

4 (1-to $1/4$-pound) lobsters, preferably female (*see* Male and Female Lobsters, page 562)

Beat the crème fraiche until slightly thickened, then add 2 tablespoons of the olive oil, the vinegar, red peppers, and herbs. Season to taste with salt, pepper, and cayenne. Reserve in the refrigerator up to one day ahead of time.

Grip the lobster on the back of its thorax, or main body shell. Look for the place where two sections of shell meet. Plunge the point of a sharp chef's knife between the shell sections. This will kill the lobsters instantly, although they may continue to move briefly.

Split the lobsters entirely in two, lengthwise. Remove the stomach (located directly behind the eyes) and any visible intestine, and discard. Remove the green tomalley and roe, and remove the dark green coral and reserve separately. Using a meat pounder or a meat mallet (or a hammer) break the claw shells without mashing them up.

Meanwhile, light a hot charcoal fire, preferably using natural charcoal. Brush the lobster halves with olive oil, and season with salt and pepper. Grill, using indirect heat (with the lid closed) at moderate heat, so that the lobster will pick up the smoky wood flavor. Cook about 15 minutes, turning once or twice. The claws, especially the larger crusher claw, will be the last part of the lobster to cook through. The claw meat should be opaque and the tail meat opaque and lightly curled. Remove from the fire and serve with the reserved sauce.

566

Linguine with Lobster, Corn, Tarragon, and Creamy Tomato Sauce

This is not an everyday pasta, but it sure is wonderful. I would make it every summer for my restaurant customers when lobster, local tomatoes, fragrant tarragon, and sweet Jersey or Pennsylvania corn were all in season. The best time to buy lobsters is usually around the Fourth of July, when many supermarkets run loss-leader sales, during which they sell certain items at extra-low prices.. Once the lobsters have been cooked and their meat removed (the hard part), the whole dish comes together very quickly.

SERVES 4

1 cup sliced scallions

2 tablespoons unsalted butter

1 cup Lobster Broth (from Poached Lobster, page 564)

2 cups fresh corn kernels (cut from about 4 ears young corn)

2 cups diced fresh round tomatoes

1/4 cup freshly chopped tarragon

1 cup heavy cream

Kosher salt and freshly ground black pepper to taste

1 pound linguine

2 cups cooked lobster meat (from 2 live lobsters, 1 1/4 to 1 1/2 pounds each, poached according to Poached Lobster recipe, page 564, and meat removed; (*see* Removing the Meat from a Cooked Lobster, page 564)

Bring a large pot of salted water to the boil and reserve. In a large, heavy casserole, lightly cook the scallions in the butter, about 2 minutes, or until wilted and bright green.

Add the lobster broth, corn, tomatoes, tarragon, cream, and salt and pepper to taste. Bring the sauce to the boil and cook over high heat until the juices are syrupy, about 5 minutes.

Meanwhile, cook the linguine in the boiling water until *al dente*, firm and bouncy, and still yellow in color. Drain and reserve briefly.

Add the lobster meat to the sauce, heat thoroughly, and toss the completed sauce with the pasta. Arrange on 4 large plates or pasta bowls, preferably heated, and serve immediately.

Lobster and Shrimp Cioppino

Cioppino is a San Francisco Italian seafood stew based on the many regional fish soups and stews of Italy from Zuppa di Pesce (fish soup, but really a fish and seafood stew), to Brodetto (a fish stew). It was developed by the Italian immigrant fisherman who settled in the city's North Beach section. Serve with a loaf of San Francisco sourdough bread to soak up the delicious juices. This is one of those dishes that just isn't worth making in small quantities. The flavors and textures of all the different types of seafood give an incredible complexity of flavor and interesting textures. Use only the freshest of seafood here; perhaps while on vacation at the beach, close to where the seafood is caught. Substitute Dungeness crabmeat for the calamari, if desired, and add mussels and/or clams.

SERVES 8 TO 10

1 quart Lobster Broth (from Poached Lobster recipe, page 564), substitute fish stock or bottled clam juice

2 (1¼- to 1½-pound) live lobsters

½ cup extra-virgin olive oil

2 medium red onions, chopped

1 cup chopped celery

1 cup chopped fennel, stalks preferred

12 plump, fresh cloves garlic, thinly sliced

2 (28-ounce cans) diced tomatoes

4 sprigs thyme, tied with kitchen string

2 bay leaves

1 teaspoon hot red pepper flakes

2 cups dry white wine

¼ cup Pernod (optional)

Kosher salt and freshly ground black pepper to taste

2 pounds shrimp, peeled to the last tail shell
and deveined (*see* Cooking Shrimp, page 865 for
more information)

1 pound large sea scallops, trimmed of their hard
adductor muscle

2 pounds red snapper fillet (substitute another lean fish
with firm, white flesh), cut into strips

1 pound small calamari cleaned, cut into thick rings
(optional)

1 cup shredded basil

2 tablespoons chopped fresh oregano, or 2 teaspoons dried

½ cup chopped Italian parsley

2 tablespoons unsalted butter

Bring the Lobster Broth to the boil in a large pot. Kill the lobsters as follows: Grip the lobster on the back of its thorax, or main body shell. Look for the place where the two sections of shell meet. Plunge the point of a sharp chef's knife between the shell sections. This will kill the lobster instantly. Add the lobsters to the pot and cook 5 minutes, or until the tails shells start to curl (the lobster

shouldn't be completely cooked).

Remove the lobsters from the pot, using a pair of tongs, and reserve the liquid in the pot. Cool the lobsters by placing in a large bowl of ice mixed with water. Working over a large bowl or tray to catch all the juices, twist the tails and large claws off the lobsters. Using a meat pounder or the side of a heavy cleaver, crack the claws. Slice each tail into rings of meat surrounded by shell. Reserve the lobster pieces in a bowl, and strain any juices over top.

In a large braiser (shallow wide pot with a big capacity) or a soup pot, heat the olive oil. Add the onion, celery, fennel, and garlic and sauté until crisp-tender, about 5 minutes. Add the tomatoes and their juice, the thyme, bay leaves, hot red pepper, the reserved Lobster Broth, white wine, and the Pernod. Bring to the boil and simmer 20 minutes, to combine flavors. Season to taste with salt and pepper.

Add the shrimp, scallops, snapper, calamari, and cut-up lobsters in their shells. Bring the whole stew to the boil, stirring the seafood so it cooks evenly. Just before serving, add the basil, oregano, parsley, and butter, and stir to combine. Serve immediately in large bowls, preferably heated.

ABOUT CIOPPINO

Like its forebears in Italy, cioppino was originally prepared on board boats while still out at sea. It later became a restaurant standard in "the city by the bay," San Francisco. The name cioppino (cha-pee-no) derives from *ciuppin*, a name for the local seafood stew prepared in the port city of Genoa, which sent so many sailors around the world, including the explorers John Cabot (Giovanni Caboto), who traveled to Newfoundland, and Christopher Columbus.

MANGOES

MANGOES

The luscious mango is, without a doubt, a divine fruit. For good reason, mangoes are one of the most popular fruits in the world, eaten with great pleasure by about one fifth of the people on this planet. Enjoying the exquisite, perfumed flesh of the mango is the ultimate tropical indulgence. To millions of people living in Southeast Asia, the mango has been a basic and precious fruit for as long as anyone can remember. Many believe that the "apple" Eve picked from the tree of knowledge was a mango. Its Latin name, *Magnifera indica*, means the great fruit bearer.

For thousands of years mangoes have been the "food of the gods" to the people of India. They are significant in Indian mythology and in the Vedas, a Hindu scripture dating from 4000 BCE. In religious ceremonies all over India, mango blossoms symbolize abundance and divine sweetness. It is said that Buddha himself was presented with a mango grove in which to find repose in a shady area, and while resting in its shadow, Buddha praised the tree because of its longevity.

In the fourteenth century, the Persian poet Amir Khusur wrote, "The mango is the pride of the garden, the choicest fruit of Hindustan; other fruits we are content to eat when ripe, but the mango is good in all stages of growth." And in the sixteenth century, the Persian emperor Akbar planted a famous orchard of 100,000 mango trees.

The mango, which is distantly related to the cashew and the pistachio, originated in Southeast Asia, especially Burma and eastern India, where it has been grown for over 4,000 years. From India, mangoes traveled throughout the whole tropical and subtropical world, including the Mediterranean and the Canary Islands. However, India still produces an estimated two-thirds of the world's mangoes—about fourteen million ton a year.

There are believed to be more than a thousand mango species, which all fall into two main branches of mango varieties, one from India and the other from the Philippines and Southeast Asia. The Indian mango doesn't tolerate humidity and bears regularly shaped, brightly colored fruit. The Philippine mango can tolerate excess moisture and has pale green, elongated kidney-shaped fruit.

Buddhist monks are thought to have to have taken the mango on voyages to Malaysia and Eastern Asia as early as the fourth century BCE. The Persians are thought to have carried it to East Africa about the tenth century CE. The Portuguese brought the mango from their colonies in southern India to West Africa and Brazil early in the sixteenth century. After becoming established in Brazil, the mango was carried to the West Indies, first to Barbados about 1742 and later in the Dominican Republic. Early in the nineteenth century, the mango reached Mexico from both the east, via the Philippines, and the west, via the Caribbean.

Mangoes were imported into Florida as early as 1833 but in spite of trying again and again, most of the trees died. Of six grafted trees that arrived from Bombay in 1889, only one lived to bear fruit nine years later. Seeds from this tree were planted by a Captain Haden in Miami and bore fruit some years after his death. His widow gave the name "Haden" to the tree with the best fruit.

Mango trees often reach 120 feet high, with a top as much as 30 feet wide. A beautiful tree with shining, dark green leaves, it is appreciated in the tropics for casting a great, cool shadow. The fruits ripen in three to six months and hang from the tree on long stems. The smallest mangoes are no larger than a hen's egg, while the largest can weigh up to five pounds. Each mango has a single, flat, tongue -shaped seed, surrounded by flesh, which is either yellow or orange, and rich in vitamins A, C, and D. Because the fruit is easily bruised, mangoes are usually harvested by hand. Buy organically grown mangoes if possible because many imported tropical fruits have been treated with pesticides that have been outlawed in the United States.

Some people call the mango "bath tub fruit," since it is a good idea to eat them while naked since the juicy flesh can cause spots on your clothes that you may not be able to remove. In the tropics, mangoes are therefore often handed to children when they are naked. While most of the time, you'll probably be fully clothed when eating mango, keep in mind that the fruit is juicy, slippery, and a little hard to handle.

MANGOES AND PAISLEY

In India, paisley is known as the *kalka*, or mango design. This pattern originated in ancient Babylon and spread into India and prehistoric Europe. Starting in the late seventeenth century, the paisley design was widely woven into delicate and intricate shawls from Kashmir, in northern India. The shawls became the rage in eighteenth-and-nineteenth century Europe. Surprisingly, the motif is named not for Kashmir, but for a city in Scotland called Paisley. During the height of their fashion, a copycat factory in that city produced imitations of these shawls with Kashmiri techniques and wool from imported Himalayan goats.

Mango Chutney

Mango chutney became a mainstay of British cookery when British colonialists brought back cooked chutneys from India. Chutney, or *chatni* in Hindu, is a relish made from fresh fruits and spices that may be either raw or cooked. (I give a recipe for a fresh Mango-Mint Chutney on page 575.) During the long journey to England from India the concept of chutney changed, until 'Major Grey's,' the commercially made mango chutney made from cooked mangoes, spices, and raisins, became the British standard. Major Grey is a probably mythical colonial British officer who made his own chutney to accompany curries (no one has a copyright on the name, so anyone can use it).

MORE WAYS WITH MANGOES

Try a fresh mango daiquiri: Puree the mango pulp with lime juice, ice, and rum in a blender.

Make a salad with mango, alternating with slices of avocado, and dress it with lime juice and olive oil.

A sorbet made with mango always stays smooth, never crystallizes.

Mix mangoes with papayas and pineapples for a delicious fruit salad, or juice them with other tropical fruits such as kiwi, passion fruit, papaya, and pineapples. Frozen chunks of mangoes may be put through a juicer.

Dried mangoes are also delicious. Soak dried mangoes in water to cover overnight, mix them with grated almonds, and form "bliss balls" by rolling them in sesame seeds or shredded coconut.

TO RIPEN A MANGO

Like all tropical fruits, mangoes must be fully ripened before eating. To expedite ripening, place the mango in a paper bag for a few days and leave at cool room temperature until the flesh is yielding but not mushy. A perfect mango is yielding but still firm, fragrant and sweet without any of the overripe "turpentine-like" smell that develops when mangoes ferment naturally. When the mango is ripe you'll be able to smell its perfume. A scattering of small black spots is also an indication of ripeness. Avoid sunlight or high humidity when ripening mangoes. Its skin should be waxy and slightly loose, rather than shiny and tight.

Mango Varieties

Alphonso Mango: The Alphonso mango is renowned for its sweet taste, buttery texture, and intense fragrance. It is the most-sought after variety in India, where they really know their mangoes. This small, rounded, almost heart-shaped variety is often used for frozen and canned mango.

Ataulfo: This Indonesian-type mango originated from a Hawaiian seedling. The fruit is a small, flat, oblong in shape and weights 6 to 12 ounces. It is greenish-yellow to deep golden when ripe, with delectable, very sweet, rich flavor and an almost buttery texture. It is compact and delicate, with skin that ripens to a golden yellow. When treated properly and sold ripe, the inside is velvety and smooth, with almost no fibrous texture and a wafer-thin pit. Unfortunately, it is often sold hard and green and never fully ripens.

Champagne Mango®: Champagne mangoes are of the golden *Ataulfo* variety, grown in two areas of Mexico that are particularly suited for this sumptuous fruit. It is distinguished by its rich golden color, velvety texture, and sweet taste. Snap them up if you see these small, luscious fruits.

Green Mango: Green mangoes, usually either of the Keitts or Kents variety, are purposely picked prematurely and will not color or ripen. In the west, green mangoes are grown in Florida and Puerto Rico. The unripe flesh of the green mango is popular in Thailand, India, and Malaysia for salads, soups, and relishes. The flesh contains enzymes that aid in tenderizing meats. In sun-dried, powdered form, green mango is used as a yellow-brown seasoning called *amchur* used in Indian and Asian cooking for its tart flavor and to tenderize meats. Green mangoes are often combined with vegetables and lentils.

Haden: Of six grafted trees that arrived in Florida from Bombay in 1889, only one lived to bear fruit nine years later. Seeds from this tree were planted by Captain Haden in Miami and bore fruit some years after his death. For many years, this variety was regarded as the standard of excellence, and it is still popular for shipping because of its tough skin. It is medium-sized, yellow in color with a red-orange blush, mild in flavor and has a moderate amount of fiber. Hadens are in season from February through June.

Kent: This large mango is oval in shape, with plump cheeks, greenish-yellow color and red shoulders. It is fiberless and juicy with a sweet, rich flavor and a soft, butter-like texture when ripe and slices clean to the pit. Because it is soft and bruises easily, Kents should not be put to the squeeze test. Kents are available June through August.

Keitts: This large mango of Indian origin is green with yellow cheeks ripening to orange-yellow. It is juicy and low in fiber, with rich flavor and a small pit. A tapering oval in shape, it has a small, nose-like protuberance above its tip. Its firm flesh has a piney sweetness and minimal fiber surrounding the seed area. A late-fruiting mango, it is available from July through September.

Pango Mango: Frieda's Produce is now distributing an especially sweet and juicy mango called the Pango™ which has been grown in Puerto Rico for over 20 years. It has a smooth, succulent texture, no strings and is very tasty. Its flesh is mostly green with a reddish blush and has twice the shelf life as other mangoes. Pango Mangoes will ripen at room temperature in about one week.

Tommy Atkins: The Tommy Atkins cultivar, which now dominates the world market for mangoes, was especially developed for commercial export, and it stores well. This brightly colored mango has thick skin than is red with purplish bloom, ripening to yellow. Medium to large in size, it has firm flesh, with a small pit and medium fiber. Somewhat oblong in shape with a rounded base, it has a stout stem inserted obliquely into a shallow cavity. It is in season from April through July.

573

PREPARING A MANGO TWO WAYS

Once you know how, preparing mangoes is easy. The mango has one large, tongue-shaped pit in its center. If you hold up a mango you can see that the fruit is flattened on one side and slightly rounded on the other. The pit parallels the shape of the fruit.

Place the mango stem-side down on a cutting board. Slice off one half-inch slice from the top and bottom of the mango, exposing the ends of the pit. Using a potato peeler or paring knife, pare away thin strips of the skin going from top to bottom. Turn the mango upside down, and pare away any remaining bits of skin.

Cut away the flesh from both sides of the pit to make two rounded dome shapes. Cut around the sides of the pit to remove any remaining flesh. Do not cut too closely to the pit because the flesh will be stringy. The mango flesh may then be thinly sliced or diced.

There is a second easy way of preparing mango where the fruit is not peeled, but is cut into cubes:

Slice off the mango flesh as far as the pit on both sides. Turn each dome-shaped piece upside down, exposing the flesh side. Now you will have two halves of mango with skin on one side and flesh on the other. Using a sharp paring knife, make parallel cuts about one inch apart lengthwise on the flesh side without cutting through the skin. Now make parallel cuts crosswise resulting in mango halves with cut squares.

Bend the cut fruit backwards pushing up the underside of the mango to make a bow-shape. The cubes of mango that are still attached to the skin will pop out. Serve the mango as is with a squeeze of lime, using a knife and fork to cut away the cubes, or cut away the cubes and use as desired.

Freezing Mango

You can freeze mango purée, slices, or dice for up to six months. Peel mangoes, remove the pulp from the seed, and use a food processor fitted with a steel blade to puree the fruit. Pour the puree into ice cube trays and freeze. Pack cubes into freezer bags, or pour puree directly into freezer bags and freeze as a block. Frozen mango puree slices easily with a sharp knife and there is no need to thaw it. Return unused, frozen mango puree immediately to the freezer. Use frozen mango puree in sorbet, salad dressing, marinades, and drinks. To freeze mango slices or seal them tightly in freezer bags or containers, mix with a little sugar and/or lime juice, if desired.

Grilled Shrimp with Mango–Mint Chutney

When mangoes are at the height of their season, why not make this light and spicy dish of grilled shrimp with cool mint-flavored mango chutney. It is also delicious served with grilled chicken, scallops, salmon, swordfish, tuna, or with Halibut in Lemongrass Crust (see page 427). I prefer using white or pink shrimp because they are firmer and tastier than the less-expensive tiger shrimp from the warm waters of Southeast Asia. I find the best selection of shrimp at my local Korean market. Unfortunately, many supermarkets only carry tiger shrimp. The prepeeled and deveined shrimp found in the freezer case are an easy choice, though will not be as moist as the kind you peel yourself (see the Shrimp chapter, page 863, for more information). The chutney will keep well refrigerated for two to three days.

574

SERVES 4

Shrimp

1½ pounds large shrimp, preferably white or pink

2 tablespoons olive oil

2 tablespoons lime juice

1 teaspoon of kosher salt and freshly ground black pepper

Mango-Mint Chutney (recipe follows)

Examine the head end of the shrimp. If it is dark (containing dirt), cut through the shell along the back and then pull out and discard the vein. Using scissors, cut off and discard the feelers alongside the inside curved shell of the shrimp.

Whisk together the olive oil, lime juice, salt and pepper, and toss with the shrimp. Marinate the shrimp, refrigerated, for at least 30 minutes or up to overnight.

Preheat a grill, preferably using natural charcoal, to hot. Alternatively, preheat the broiler on high. Remove the shrimp from the marinade, allowing excess to drip off.

Grill shrimp (or broil) on both sides, until curled and lightly charred, about 3 minutes per side. Divide the chutney among 4 serving plates and then top with the shrimp. Serve a bowl alongside for the shrimp shells.

Mango–Mint Chutney

2 large mangoes, firm but ripe

Juice of 2 limes

Kosher salt and freshly ground black pepper to taste

2 tablespoons honey

¼ cup diced red onion

½ cup diced red bell pepper

1 jalapeño pepper, seeded and minced

2 tablespoons each: shredded mint and cilantro

Cut the mangoes into small, even cubes and combine with the lime juice, salt, pepper, and honey. Toss together with the red onion, red bell pepper, jalapeño, mint, and cilantro and reserve.

Thai Green Mango and Jicama Slaw

When green, mangoes are treated like a vegetable, as in this light but flavorful Thai slaw. Green papayas may be used the same way. Although native to Mexico and Central America, jicama has become very popular in Southeast Asian cooking. If you have a French mandoline or Japanese Benriner cutter, use it to make neat restaurant-style matchstick cuts of the mango and jicama. Otherwise, use the large-holed side of a box grater or the vegetable shredder attachment to a food processor or mixer. Typical of Southeast Asian cooking, this slaw depends on lots of fresh, aromatic herbs for zest and roasted peanuts for crunch.

SERVES 6

½ cup fresh lime juice (about 4 limes)

2 tablespoons fish sauce

2 tablespoons dark brown sugar, packed

1 green mango, peeled

1 jicama, pared

1 fresh green chile, such as serrano or jalapeño, trimmed and thinly sliced

½ bunch scallions, thinly sliced

1 tablespoon shredded basil

1 tablespoon shredded mint

575

2 tablespoons shredded cilantro

¹/₄ cup chopped roasted peanuts

Combine lime juice, fish sauce, and brown sugar and reserve. Toss the mango, jicama, chile, scallions, basil, mint, and cilantro with dressing.

Divide the slaw among six serving plates, top each portion with some of the peanuts and serve immediately.

Asian Fish Sauce

Fish sauce is a salty, pungent-smelling, thin, clear brown liquid made from fermented fish. It is the single most important flavoring ingredient in Thai cooking and is also well-loved in Laos, Cambodia, Vietnam, Burma, and the Philippines. Used like salt in western cooking and soy sauce in Chinese cooking, its closest equivalent in western cooking is salted anchovies. It is directly related to the *garum* made in classical times by the Romans.

The best fish sauce is made with the freshest fish. As soon as fishing boats return with their catch, the fish are rinsed and mixed with sea salt and then packed into large, earthenware jars for fermenting. The jars are covered and left in a sunny location for nine months to a year, occasionally opened to expose the fish to sunlight to help break it down into liquid form.

Use fish sauce in small quantities to start; its bark is worse than its bite. It's mildly salty, fishy taste is belied by its potent and unmistakable aroma. Squid brand is good quality and widely available.

Mango–Rose Dessert Salad

This exotic salad combines two flavors of India—mango and rose water—in a simple but lovely-looking salad. Serve it with crisp biscotti or shortbread cookies and/or scoops of rich vanilla ice cream for a killer dessert that can be assembled and served in under 15 minutes. If you or a neighbor grow roses, sprinkle the salad with a few fresh petals. Avoid commercially grown rose, unless they're meant for eating, because they may contain undesirable pesticides. Look for edible dried rose petals in Middle Eastern and Indian groceries.

Serves 6

4 large firm but ripe mangoes

Juice of 2 limes

2 tablespoons honey

1 teaspoon rose water

1 tablespoon edible rose petals, either fresh or dried

Cut the mangoes in the following way to produce slices: slice a thin piece off the top and bottom of the mango. Using a sharp paring knife cut away long thin strips off the skin of the mango, continuing until all the skin has been removed. Cut away on both sides from the long, thin tongue-shaped pit concealed in the mango. (You can see the placement of the pit at the cut-away top.)

Lay down the two halves of the mango on their flat sides with their rounded tops up. Following the length of the mango, cut even, thin tongue-shaped slices. Arrange the mango slices attractively on a slightly dished (concave) platter.

Combine the lime juice, honey, and rose water. Spoon

this sauce over the mango slices and sprinkle with rose petals if serving immediately. If you'd like to serve this dish a few hours later, cover the platter tightly with plastic wrap and refrigerate up to 3 hours, sprinkling with the petals just before serving.

Mango Flan

I learned to make this delectably, velvety smooth flan (baked egg custard) while working as a cook at Philadelphia's wonderful French country restaurant called The Garden back in the 1970s. At the restaurant, we served it as an accompaniment to braised and then glazed duck. The savory duck meat was well complemented by the sweet, fruity flan, but it also works as a dessert. Serve with a simple passion fruit sauce (mix passion fruit puree—found frozen in Latin American markets—with sugar syrup and a splash of rum or tequila). Use the refrigerated mango slices found in the supermarket produce refrigerated section to make it even easier. Raw mango contains an enzyme that prevents the custard from setting, so it must be brought to a boil first.

SERVES 8

2 large ripe mangoes, cut into slices, or 1 (16-ounce) jar refrigerated mango slices, well drained

$1/4$ cup honey

$1/4$ cup granulated sugar

1 tablespoon grated ginger

8 eggs

2 cups heavy cream

Pinch kosher salt

Preheat the oven to 325°F. Spray 8 (6-to 8-ounce) custard cups, coffee cups, or other small molds thoroughly with nonstick spray and reserve.

Place mango slices, honey, sugar, and ginger in the bowl of a food processor and process to a fine puree. Scrape the mango puree into a medium mixing bowl. You should have about $1/2$ cups liquid. If using fresh mango, bring the mixture to the boil in a small pot (or in the microwave) before proceeding.

Remove from the heat and whisk in the eggs, cream, and salt until well blended. Pour the liquid into molds as full as possible because the flans will shrink as they cook. Place the molds into a baking pan. Pour hot water two-thirds of the way up the sides of the molds.

Bake for about 45 minutes, or until the custard is just set. Remove the pan from oven. Using tongs (or hot pads), remove the custard cups from the water bath and cool slightly.

Shake molds back and forth to loosen the contents. Remove flans from molds by turning them upside-down. Serve warm for a savory side dish, or warm or cold for dessert.

577

Mango Cheesecake

I make this sinful cheesecake with a crunchy Brazil-nut crumb crust and a filling studded with diced dried mango. Buy the dried mango in the produce department at many supermarkets or in Indian and Asian markets. The Philippine brand of dried mango sold in many warehouse club stores is excellent. For even more mango punch, serve the cake accompanied by sliced fresh mango or a simple mango sauce made by combining mango puree, sugar syrup, and a squeeze of lime.

Crumb Crust

$3/4$ cup Grape Nuts cereal

1 cup Brazil nuts

$3/4$ cup dark brown sugar, packed

1 teaspoon ground cinnamon

$1/4$ pound (1 stick) unsalted butter, melted and cooled

Process cereal, nuts, sugar, and cinnamon until finely chopped but not pasty. Pour in butter and process until well combined.

Preheat the oven to 350°F. Press the crumb mixture into the bottom of a 9-inch springform pan. Bake 15 to 20 minutes, or until lightly browned. Cool and reserve.

Filling

$1^3/4$ pounds cream cheese

$1/2$ cup granulated sugar

$1/2$ cup sour cream

3 eggs

2 teaspoons vanilla extract

$1/2$ teaspoon ground cardamom

$1/4$ pound dried mango, diced

Preheat the oven to 300°F. Beat the cream cheese and sugar until smooth, scraping down the sides of the mixer bowl once or twice. Gradually add the sour cream, eggs, vanilla, and cardamom, beating until smooth.

Stir in the diced mango and pour into the crumb-crust lined pan. Bake at 300°F. in water bath, for 1 hour. Remove and cool 30 minutes before removing from pan.

578

MOZZARELLA

MOZZARELLA

Is there anything better-tasting or more appealing to the eye than a plateful of fresh mozzarella, sliced, juicy, never-been-refrigerated vine-ripened tomatoes, anointed with top-quality fruity extra-virgin olive oil, and interleaved with fragrant, field-grown basil? Called *Insalata Caprese* in Italy, this delicacy originated on the dreamy Mediterranean isle of Capri, off the coast of Campania, the province that is home to Italy's exquisite *mozzarella di bufala*, made from the milk of water buffaloes. Melted on a thin-crust pizza, inside a *panino* (panini is plural) sandwich, baked in lasagna, cannelloni, stuffed shells, or eggplant Parmigiano, it's delicate, mild, and creamy, formed into its characteristic long, elastic strings.

Pearl-white mozzarella made and eaten the same day can't be beat for delicacy of flavor and texture; to preserve it any longer, more salt must be added, causing the curd to firm up and the whey to drain out, making for a drier and less delicate cheese. The mozzarella familiar from American sandwich shops and pizzerias is called "low-moisture" mozzarella"—I call it "rubber mozz"—and has less then fifty percent moisture, so that it keeps well and doesn't "weep" when baked on pizza. American mozzarella is usually made from cow's milk.

Mozzarella has been made in Italy in the region of Campania, near Naples, from the rich, tangy milk of water buffalos imported from India at least as far back as the beginning of the fifteenth century, and was originally called simply "mozza," from the verb *mozzare,* meaning "to cut by hand." In fact, the best mozzarellas are still cut by hand today. The water buffaloes have lived in that area since the second century; during World War II, the Nazis destroyed many herds, but the Italians replaced and expanded the herd, bringing them again from India more then seventeen hundred years later.

Because it was made from raw milk and refrigeration was limited or nonexistent, mozzarella was seldom found outside its region of origin. As technology, refrigeration, and transportation systems developed, the taste for and availability of mozzarella cheese spread to other regions of Italy in tandem with the large numbers of southern Italians moving to the industrial north in search of jobs.

Even today, the finest artisanal *mozzarella di bufala* is produced near the towns of Battipaglia and Caserta where it was first produced and customers come to purchase it daily. It is soft and moist, light and milky tasting, with an almost spongy texture that oozes with milk. In Italy, fresh cow's milk mozzarella is called *fior di latte* (flower of the milk), sometimes spelled as one word. Note that even in Italy, *mozzarella di bufala* is made from a combination of cow and water buffalo milk, because there is simply not enough supply for the demand.

Today *Mozzarella di Bufala Campana* has been awarded

D.O.P status (protected designation of origin). Another special type, called *mozzarella nella mortella,* is wrapped in myrtle branches so that the porous cheese absorbs its fragrance and flavor. The wonderful Italian *burrata* or *burrino* from the province of Puglia is made by forming a thin "bag" of mozzarella stuffed with curds and cream and then knotted at the top. It is occasionally exported and is also being produced on a small scale in America, particularly in California.

In the U.S. today, there are three types of mozzarella called variously fresh, soft, wet, or high-moisture, produced in both salted and unsalted versions. The industrially produced fresh mozzarella found in many supermarkets and warehouse club stores is vacuum-packed in its original container, though it may be repacked at store level. This type became possible only in the last ten years or so, when new developments in industrial machinery allowed the curd to be stretched mechanically; without the bacteria from human hands, the cheese lasts much longer.

Fresh mozzarella curds are sold to Italian delis and specialty shops to mix with hot water and make their own mozzarella. Handmade artisanal mozzarella, closer to the Italian original, is produced by specialty cheese companies. A very small amount of buffalo-milk mozzarella is produced in the U.S.; most of it is imported from Italy and South America and sometimes cow's and goat's milk is combined to make the cheese.

Mozzarella is an incredibly adaptable cheese that can be stretched out like bread dough and layered with sun-dried tomatoes, basil pesto, or prosciutto and then rolled up like a rug. It can be smoked, either naturally (the type found in ball form) or by coating it with liquid smoke (the type found in block form). The curds can be flavored with fresh herbs or even chili peppers before forming them into their final shape.

MAKING FRESH MOZZARELLA

Cheese consists of a just a handful of ingredients. Read the label and you'll see just milk, cream, enzymes, culture, and salt. The enzymes and culture curdle the milk. The salt slows down the starter and dries the curd, allowing more whey to drain out. The compressed curds contain nearly all the casein (the cheese protein) and most of the fat.

To make mozzarella, the curds are cooked. Step one is to cut the curds (*mozzare*) into small chunks for even heating. The curd is then mixed with vegetable rennet and lightly heated, while constantly stirring. Once the curds go into the hot water, the shiny, smooth, fresh mozzarella is ready in just ten minutes. Heating and agitation causes it to fuse into tiny filaments of protein. Italians classify mozzarella as *pasta filata* or string cheese. Scamorza and provolone are aged "pasta filata" cheeses.

The next step is to cool the curds until they clump together. The critical time is determining the perfect moment for forming the string: too long, and the cheese will be mushy, too early, and the cheese will be tough and dry. The "dough" is then kneaded and stretched to accentuate the fibers of the cheese. When the right smooth, elastic consistency is reached, the curds are formed by hand or machine into various-sized balls ,which are then tossed into cold water to set their shape.

Like kneaded dough, mozzarella can be molded into various shapes, including a braid, the traditional top-knot, *ciliegine* (cherries), *bocconcini* (bite-size), or the slightly larger *ovoline* (eggs). The finished mozzarella is then salted and packaged. The whole process takes less than eight hours from milk to cheese.

The Best Mozzarella I've Ever Tasted

On a Slow Food Philadelphia chapter trip to Campania, Italy, we visited an outstanding water buffalo farm called Vannulo. There, four hundred happy buffaloes, of which about two hundred and forty are adult (all but a few are female; the lucky males "service" all those females, who line up for their turn), live in luxury, including rubber mattresses in each stall for comfort during love-making, a pool to cool themselves off, showers, and a system of brushes so they can rub their bodies clean.

Each buffalo is known to the workers by name. They produce their incredibly rich milk (9.5 percent butterfat), as compared to common cow milk (3.5 percent), and every day it is made on the premises into superb *mozzarella di bufala*. Their product is so sought-after that people line up to get their share, taking numbers as they wait in line (and no one is allowed to buy more than 5 kilos), hoping to get to the front before it's all sold out. The milk is completely organic, and the cows are treated homeopathically if they are ill.

The cheese is made entirely by hand, and it takes just twelve hours to go from "milk to money," as I was told at the farm. There are no machines in the dairy, only highly qualified workers, in whose careful hands and in very hot water the cheese is prepared each day. When there is enough production, the farm also produces buffalo-milk yogurt, ricotta, and the best gelato you've ever (or never) tasted in your life.

The incredibly light, tangy cheese oozed droplets of milk, a sign of freshly made cheese, and the skeins of cheese thread (the *pasta filata*) were clearly visible. As the cheese ages, these threads start to come together into one mass. The farm is not far from the famed Greek ruins at Paestum and is a must if you are in the area. For more information go to www.tenutavannulo.it.

FRESH MOZZARELLA FROM TEXAS

Mozzarella maven Paula Lambert first tasted fresh mozzarella while traveling in Italy in 1962, where it appeared in tomato salads. She wanted to be able to reproduce the cheese she had enjoyed and believed that others in her home town of Dallas would want to buy fresh mozzarella if they had it available to them. So, in 1982, she founded The Mozzarella Company, located in a small factory in the historic Deep Ellum area of Dallas. More than twenty years later, Lambert has expanded her line to include American-made *mozzarella di bufala*, cow and goat's milk mozzarella, goat's milk cheeses, and more, all hand-crafted. For more information, go to www.mozzco.com

582

CHOOSING GOOD MOZZARELLA

Good mozzarella should taste fresh and reminiscent of milk, with mild and delicate flavor and just a hint of acidity.

The color should be white, although it may vary to a more buttery color, according to the diet of the animal. *Mozzarella di bufala* may have a faint greenish-yellow tint.

The fresher the mozzarella, the more elastic and springy the curd. As the cheese ages it becomes softer until, finally, it disintegrates.

When sliced, the cheese should ooze droplets of whey and the stringy grain should be visible, as if cutting through a rubber band ball.

Note that imported *mozzarella di bufala* may not be in prime condition if the store doesn't have quick enough turnover. It gets mushy as it ages. Also, buffalo-milk mozzarella will have a distinctively tangy flavor and rich consistency. Buy it and eat it the same day or the next.

Pizza Margherita

This classic pizza was created for the Italian King Umberto and his wife, Queen Margherita di Savoia, while they were visiting Naples in 1889. The king invited the most renowned pizzaiolo (pizza-maker), Raffaele Esposito, to prepare his specialties. He served three pizzas: one with melted pork fat (strutto in Italian), cheese, and basil; one with tomatoes, olive oil, and garlic; and the third with red tomatoes, white mozzarella, and green basil—the colors of the Italian flag, which, of course, was the queen's favorite. He then dedicated this pizza to her, beginning the worldwide craze for fresh mozzarella on pizza.

MAKES ONE 14-INCH PIZZA, TO SERVE 4

2 tablespoons extra-virgin olive oil

2 teaspoons crushed garlic

Cornmeal

1 pizza round (about 1 pound) purchased or homemade
  (*see* Cornmeal Pizza Dough, page 985)

1 cup Pizza Sauce (recipe follows)

1 yellow (or red) tomato, sliced

1/4 cup mixed grated Romano and Parmigiano-Reggiano cheese

1/4 pound drained, sliced fresh mozzarella

8 to 12 whole basil leaves, divided if large

Preheat the oven to 500°F., if possible with a pizza stone in the oven. Mix together the olive oil and garlic.

Sprinkle a wooden peel lightly with cornmeal. Stretch out the pizza round to the size of the peel. Alternatively, roll out the pizza and transfer it to a cornmeal-dusted metal pizza pan. Brush lightly with the olive oil mixture, especially on the edges.

Spread a thin layer of the pizza sauce over the dough using the back of a ladle to smooth it out, leaving a 1-inch border at the edges. Arrange the tomato slices in a circle around the pizza. Sprinkle the pizza with the grated cheese, and arrange the mozzarella slices attractively over top.

If using the peel, transfer to the pizza stone by placing the peel at a low angle to the stone and giving the peel a fast, vigorous thrust forward and then back, so that the pizza jumps onto the stone. Bake until bubbling and well browned, about 6 minutes. If you're baking this in a pan, place the pan in the oven and bake until bubbling and well-browned, about 8 minutes. Arrange basil leaves over top just before serving, then cut into 8 to 12 wedges and serve immediately.

583

Pizza Sauce

MAKES 1 QUART

1 tablespoon chopped garlic
1/4 cup extra-virgin olive oil
1 (28-ounce) can chopped plum tomatoes
1/4 cup shredded basil
2 tablespoons chopped Italian parsley
1 tablespoon chopped fresh oregano, or 1 teaspoon dried
Kosher salt and freshly ground black pepper to taste

Cook garlic in the olive oil until it sizzles. Add the tomatoes and bring to the boil. Simmer 20 minutes and remove from fire. Add herbs and seasonings and cool.

REHEATING PIZZA

To reheat leftover pizza, preheat the oven to 450°F. Wrap the pizza in aluminum foil and bake about 6 minutes, or until quite hot. Uncover the top and bake about 2 minutes longer, or until bubbling hot.

Pizza in Naples and America

In the late nineteenth century, pizza was sold in the streets of Naples at breakfast, lunch, and dinner. It was cut from a large tray that had been cooked in the baker's oven. Pizza was sold by peddlers out of cylindrical copper drums with a bottom section packed with charcoal from the oven to keep the pizzas hot. The name of the pizzeria would be embossed on the drum. I sampled the real thing at Da Michele, one of Naples's most venerable and justly famous pizzerias. I had the simplest pizza (tomato puree and fresh mozzarella) on the lightest yet chewy dough—made twice a day and baked in a wood-fired oven. There are only two kinds offered: the other, Pizza alla Romana has tomato, chunks of garlic, and oregano. Pizza migrated to America with the Italians in the second half of the nineteenth century, and until returning American soldiers brought back their taste for pizza, was only found in cities with a large Italian immigrant community until World War II.

584

Spinach and Portabella Pizza

This pizza was a real winner at both A'propos in the mid 1980s and at Stella Notte twenty years later. At both restaurants, I was lucky enough to have a wood-burning pizza oven, something I miss every time I make pizza at home. Even without the underlying flavor and fragrance of hardwood smoke, this makes a delicious "white" pizza (no tomato sauce). The smaller crimini mushrooms, sometimes called "baby bellas," would also work well here, as would a combination of shiitakes and portabellas. And, if you happen to have some genuine wild mushrooms (as apposed to these cultivated exotics), this pizza would be a wonderful way to enjoy them. Here, I use the pizza-shop standard "low-moisture" mozzarella found in block form to compensate for the liquid contained in the spinach and the mushrooms.

MAKES ONE 14–INCH PIZZA, TO SERVE 4

1/2 pound spinach, fresh or frozen

1 tablespoon crushed garlic

2 tablespoons + 2 tablespoons + 1 tablespoon
  extra-virgin olive oil

2 ounces pancetta, cut into small cubes (substitute bacon)

1 small red onion, cut into 1/2-inch thick slices

Kosher salt and freshly ground black pepper to taste

1 pizza round (about 1 pound) purchased or homemade
  (*see* page 985)

1 cup diced Roasted Portobella Mushroom Caps
  (*see* page 448)

1 cup shredded low-moisture mozzarella

Place the spinach in a bowl and microwave briefly just long enough to wilt it, or wilt in a pan with a small amount of water. Run under cold water to cool, and then squeeze out the water.

Heat the garlic in 2 tablespoons of olive oil until sizzling, then add the spinach and sauté 2 to 3 minutes, or until shiny. Remove from the heat, spread out to cool, and reserve.

In a small pot, brown the pancetta until crispy. Drain, discard the fat (or reserve for another use), and reserve.

Preheat a grill or broiler. Brush the red onion slices with 2 tablespoons olive oil and sprinkle with salt and pepper. Grill or broil the onions until well-browned and reserve.

Preheat the oven to 500°F., if possible with a pizza stone in the oven. Sprinkle a wooden peel lightly with cornmeal. Stretch out the pizza round to the size of the peel. Alternatively, roll out the pizza and transfer it to a cornmeal-dusted metal pizza pan. Brush lightly with the remaining 1 tablespoon olive oil, especially on the edges.

Arrange the spinach on the pizza, spreading evenly. Top with the pancetta, red onions, and portabella mushrooms, and sprinkle with the mozzarella.

If using the peel, transfer to the pizza stone by giving placing the peel at a low angle to the stone and giving the peel a fast, vigorous thrust forward and then back, so that the pizza jumps onto the stone. If you're baking this in a pan, place the pan in the oven and bake until bubbling and well-browned, about 8 minutes. Bake until bubbling and well browned, about 6 minutes. Cut into 8 wedges and serve immediately.

Eggplant Tortino Layered with Salsa Verde, Tomato, and Fresh Mozzarella

I started making this rich and delectable dish—which can be served as an appetizer, a main dish for lunch on its own, or perhaps with a soup or salad for dinner—in my years as chef of a wonderful Northern Italian restaurant, and it's as good today as it was then. A torta *is a cake, related to the French* tarte *and the Austrian* torte, *although there is no cake or pastry involved in this colorful vegetable assembly. A* tortino *is a friendly diminutive, so that this makes small individual layered tortas. The salsa verde, or green sauce, is versatile on its own. Try it as a topping for grilled salmon, tuna, or swordfish. If you have access to fresh* mozzarella di bufala, *its exquisite taste and creamy texture will make a truly extraordinary dish.*

586

SERVES 6

Salsa Verde

1 cup Italian parsley leaves

2 tablespoons extra-virgin olive oil

2 tablespoons anchovy fillet

2 teaspoons chopped garlic

1/4 cup drained capers

Puree all ingredients in a food processor until pasty but still somewhat chunky, and reserve.

Tortino

1/4 cup extra-virgin olive oil, divided

2 teaspoons crushed garlic

Kosher salt and freshly ground black pepper to taste

1 large eggplant, cut in 1/2-inch rounds

Salsa Verde

1/2 pound fresh mozzarella cheese, or imported
    Mozzarella di Bufala, cut in 1/2-inch rounds

2 to 3 large ripe beefsteak tomatoes, cut in 1/2-inch slices

1/4 cup homemade-style breadcrumbs

1/4 cup grated Parmigiano-Reggiano or Grana Padano

Preheat a grill or broiler to high. Whisk together 2 tablespoons of the olive oil, the garlic, and salt and pepper. Brush the mixture on both sides of the eggplant slices. Grill the eggplant slices, or arrange in a single layer on a metal baking pan and broil on high until well-browned on top, about 5 minutes, then turn over and broil until well-browned on the bottom, about 5 minutes.

Preheat the oven to 425°F. Place 6 eggplant rounds on a baking sheet. Spread each round with a layer of Salsa Verde, cover with a slice of mozzarella and a slice of tomato. Repeat eggplant, salsa, cheese, and tomato, making two layers of each.

Combine breadcrumbs and Parmesan cheese with remaining olive oil and cover tops of tortinos with an even layer of crumbs. Bake until bubbling hot, about 12 minutes, and serve immediately.

Pan–Fried Mozzarella di Bufala with Anchovy Sauce

In another dish that dates back to my days as an Italian chef, this dish is a real case of gilding the lily. It's a bit tricky to make, because here the mozzarella slices are dusted with flour and then dipped in a rich egg-and-cheese batter, and pan-fried until the cheese starts to ooze out of its cheesy coating. The cheese is "gilded" with the batter, and then the golden-brown, lusciously melting cheese is anointed with an anchovy butter sauce. Exquisite! Although the dish can be made with fresh cow's milk mozzarella, it you have access to mozzarella di bufala, *by all means, use it here for its slightly tangy, ineffably creamy and delicate flavor. Serve small portions because of its richness, but don't miss this winner of a dish.*

SERVES 4 TO 6

4 eggs

$^1/_2$ cup + $^1/_2$ cup all-purpose flour

2 ounces Parmigiano Reggiano or
 Grana Padano cheese, grated

$^1/_4$ pound (1 stick) unsalted butter, softened

Juice of 2 lemons

1 bunch Italian parsley, roughly chopped

$^1/_4$ cup nonpareil capers, drained

4 whole salt-pack anchovies, rinsed, filleted and chopped

4 tablespoons olive oil

$^1/_2$ pound round of Buffalo mozzarella, cut
 in $^1/_2$-inch slices

Preheat the oven to 400°F. Make a thick batter of the eggs, $^1/_2$ cup of flour, and Parmesan cheese, and reserve.

To make the anchovy sauce, cream the butter, then beat in lemon juice, parsley, capers, and anchovies.

Heat olive oil in a heavy sauté pan. Dip slices of mozzarella in remaining $^1/_2$ cup of flour, shake off excess, and then dip into egg batter, making sure to coat the mozzarella completely. Sauté the mozzarella at moderate heat until browned. Carefully flip mozzarella over to other side and brown about 2 minutes longer. Remove from the pan, and drain on paper towels. Place each portion on an oven-proof plate. Top with approximately 1 tablespoon of anchovy sauce and place in oven for several minutes, to melt the butter. Serve immediately.

SALT–PACK ANCHOVIES

The salt-pack anchovies called for in this recipe come from Sicily and are packed whole (minus their heads but including innards) in large tins layered with sea salt. To prepare them, rinse under tepid water, discarding the bones and innards. Surprisingly, these anchovies are quite mild and firm in texture, much more so than the standard oil-packed anchovies. The best alternative is the oil-and-vinegar-packed white anchovies, commonly found as *boquerones*, imported from Spain. Ordinary anchovies are the third-best choice; it you do use them, drain their oil and rinse under tepid water.

Anchovies are a small, warm-water fish related to the herring of Northern Europe. Like herring, anchovies are salt-packed to preserve them. In Italy, salt-packed anchovies are preferred for their meatier flavor and firm texture. Excellent-quality salted anchovies from Agostino Recca of Sicily are imported to America and can be found in Italian delis and from online specialty food suppliers in $1\frac{1}{2}$-pound cans. Store the closed can in the refrigerator, because anchovies, even though canned, can still deteriorate in a warm environment. Once the can is opened, transfer the entire contents of the can to an airtight container and refrigerate, where they will keep for several months.

588

MUSHROOMS

MUSHROOMS

For anyone who loves earthy and woodsy flavors, mushrooms are a wonderful treat, whether cultivated, common or exotic, or truly wild. Cultivated mushrooms are available year-round, while wild mushrooms must be foraged in season in the special areas where specific varieties grow. Wild mushrooms often grow in the same place year after year, but these locations are often kept secret so that other eager mushroom pickers don't get there first. In the U.S., the temperate, rainy woods of the Northwest are prime mushroom-hunting areas, although plenty of wonderful mushrooms can be found elsewhere. In fact, we have more wild mushrooms than can be sold in America, because many people don't know how to use them, and much of our harvest is exported, especially to Europe, where they can't get enough of them.

In the kitchen, mushrooms can be used in their fresh form; dried whole, in slices, and powdered; or frozen. Porcini and other highly prized wild mushrooms are the ones found frozen; most others are used fresh or dried. Mushroom powder can flavor pasta dough, bread dough, sauces, or soups. Dried mushrooms can be reconstituted in water and then further cooked; their soaking liquid, called *mushroom liquor*, carries most of their flavor.

Mushrooms are a huge group of edible fungi that are grown, picked, and eaten around the world. Mushrooms have been eaten since earliest times but not by everyone and not everywhere. The rarest and finest mushrooms, including the rare truffle, were highly esteemed in classical Greece and Rome. The word *mushroom* was first recorded as an English word as far back as the ninth century and probably came from the French *mousseron*, a word that referred to various small mushrooms.

Scientists use the term *mushroom* to denote only the fruiting body of either *Agarics* (the familiar white mushrooms and brown field mushrooms) or *Boletes* (the fabulous cèpe or porcini). But, in everyday usage, a mushroom is any edible fungus having a round cap and usually a stalk. There are now about three hundred types of cultivated mushrooms along with myriad wild mushrooms.

Mushrooms—especially wild ones—are indeed mysterious things, with their ephemeral nature, apparent lack of roots, hallucinogenic properties of some kinds, and poisonous properties of others. Wild mushrooms grow and are eagerly gathered in most parts of the world. The most desirable mushrooms grow in wooded areas: coniferous for chanterelles and Japanese matsutakes; deciduous for cèpes and black trumpets. Species of mushrooms tend to have a wide distribution in the world because their spores are so small they are easily carried from one continent to another.

Every year, more varieties of cultivated mushrooms come to market. These mushrooms are raised on pasteurized compost in conditions that replicate damp, autumn mornings and take about six weeks to grow before they're picked by hand. The Chinese and Japanese have been raising shiitakes on rotting logs for thousands of years. Modern European mushroom cultivation started in the mid-seventeenth century near Paris with *Agaricus bisporus*, our common white mushroom, known then and now as *champignons de Paris*.

As a rule, if a mushroom is larger, darker, and has more open gills, it will have a deeper and more profound flavor. The smaller, paler, and less open the mushroom is, the more delicate and subtle it will be. Freshly picked mushrooms with closed caps are preferred for salads. White mushrooms, crimini, portabellas, and enoki are frequently used raw, although some people may not digest raw mushrooms well. The flavors of specialty mushrooms are generally enhanced by cooking, and almost all wild mushrooms should be cooked.

Mushroom Varieties

Black Trumpets: Black Trumpets, *Craterellus fallax*, are sometimes called "trumpets of death" because of their color: grayish brown to very dark brown or almost black. They are distinctively aromatic and have an elegant, buttery flavor. Their flesh is thin and brittle, their caps wavy-edged, and their outer surface smooth or wrinkled. Black Trumpets grow under deciduous trees throughout North America in the summer and fall, sometimes in great quantity. Black Trumpet mushrooms are in season in late summer to late autumn in Europe and late autumn to late winter in America. They can be found midsummer through mid-autumn in specialty produce markets.

Beech Mushrooms: Beech, or *Hon-Shimeji*, mushrooms, *Hypsizygus tessulatus*, are petite, with either all-white or light brown button-caps all joined in a clump at the base. All *Hon-Shimeji* are cultivated. They have small, thin caps with sharply defined ivory gills and thick, tender stems. These mushrooms are

crunchy in texture, with mild flavor that can be slightly bitter and fleshy juicy texture.

Chanterelles: *Chanterelle* refers both to the golden chanterelle, *Cantharellus cibarius*, and to close relatives such as red, trumpet (or funnel), and white chanterelles. Depending on the variety, the cap can be yellow, orange, white, brownish gray, or black. The caps are wavy, cup-shaped, and firm, and wrinkled on their underside, rather than gilled. Chanterelles are noted for their soft flesh and apricot-like fragrance. Chanterelles grow in forests in temperate regions. Most chanterelles are 3 to 5 inches high from root to cap. Choose chanterelles with spongy, firm, and fleshy caps. Wet or slippery chanterelles indicate deterioration. Chanterelles that are overly dirty will be difficult to clean. Although available dried, they don't have much flavor in this form.

Crimini: Crimini, *Agaricus silvaticus*, are similar in appearance to White mushrooms because they are closely related. They have naturally light-tan to rich

591

brown caps, and deeper, denser, earthier flavor than White mushrooms. Crimini are very firm, and they have good keeping qualities and a reasonable price. Substitute crimini for White mushrooms if a deeper mushroom flavor is desired.

Enoki: Enoki Mushrooms, *Flammulina velutipes,* are a Japanese variety that grow in small clusters of fragile and flower-white stems topped by tiny caps. They have a mild, light flavor with a slight crunch. They are usually eaten raw in salads or as a garnish.

Hedgehogs: Hedgehog mushrooms, *Dentinum repandum,* have buff-to tawny-colored caps with pale stems. Tiny, spine-like teeth (instead of gills) fill the undersides of the caps. They have a mild, sweet flavor and firm, chewy texture. Hedgehogs are picked wild, not cultivated, and should be cooked before eating. Hedgehog mushrooms are available December through March from California and Oregon.

Lobsters: Lobster Mushrooms, *Hypomyces lactifluorum,* get their name from their knobby appearance and bright orange to reddish color. They have a minutely pimpled surface and fishy—some say lobstery—aroma. Lobster mushrooms, with their crisp, white flesh and bright fluorescent color, are among the most spectacular wild mushrooms. Lobster mushrooms are found primarily in the Northwest region from August through October.

Maitakes: Maitakes, *Grifola frondosa,* grow in clusters of dark fronds with firm, supple texture at the base and slightly brittle, crumbly texture at the edges. They have

a distinctive aroma with a rich, woodsy taste that is enhanced by cooking. The prized Maitake is indigenous to the northeastern part of Japan and are both cultivated and wild. The botanical name of Maitake refers to the gryphon: a mythical beast which is half-lion and half-eagle. Sometimes maitakes grow to over 50 pounds, why they are called the "King of Mushrooms."

Matsutakes: The Matsutake mushroom, *Tricholoma magnivelare,* is a dark brown Japanese wild mushroom with a dense, meaty texture and nutty, fragrant flavor much prized by Japanese and Koreans. The American matsutake grows wild under the old needles of pine and fir trees. It has firm flesh and an intoxicatingly potent, spicy aroma that is somewhat fruity, but also stinky. It is often sold still sprinkled with pine needles. Matsutake mushrooms are in season from late fall to midwinter, especially in Japanese markets or specialty produce stores.

Morels: Morel mushrooms, *Morchella esculenta* and other species of Morchella, may be tan, yellow, or black in color with short, thick, hollow stems topped with sponge-like pointed caps. Morels have rich, nut-like flavor and woodsy fragrance that may be nutty and slightly smoky, but it is their texture with its honeycomb whorling, that combines softness with crunchiness that is most distinctive. Morels flourish in most temperate parts of the world and those on the market in the U.S. may be imported. Wild morels are in season in earliest spring and are abundant in the American Midwest. Although morels have been cultivated, their flavor is rather insipid and efforts have mostly been abandoned.

Pleurottes: Pleurottes, *Pleurotus ostreatus,* are fluted and graceful, ranging in color from soft brown to gray and from one to three inches in diameter. Also known as oyster mushrooms, they have a delicate, mild flavor and velvety texture and are best if cooked. These mushrooms are cultivated. The stems are tough and form a large portion of the mushroom when purchased; only the furled cap portion should be used. The stems may be chopped or ground for stuffing or used for stock. The large, thick-stemmed, light-colored variety known as Korean Mushrooms are a type of pleurotte.

Porcini: Porcini mushrooms, *Boletus edulis,* are rich, meaty, and amazingly versatile, delicate enough for an elegant ragout or sauce, and yet vigorous enough to stand up to grilled steak. The legendary porcini (or cèpe) have fat, firm, curved, white stalks and broad dark brown caps with a spongy layer of long, miniscule tubes beneath the cap. Although wild porcini and other members of the *Bolete* family can be found in North America, many of ours are imported from Europe and elsewhere. They are one of the few wild mushrooms that can be eaten raw. Porcini mushrooms are available in May and June and again in October and are sometimes found frozen from specialty suppliers. Porcini should be firm, with opulent white stalks and brown caps that are whole, not nicked or broken. Avoid porcini if the undersides of the caps have a yellowish-brown tinge or black spots, indicating spoilage. Inspect the stems for worms (actually maggots) which are harmless but unpleasant.

Portabellas: Portabella mushrooms, *Agaricus bisporus,* are larger, hardier relatives of Whites and Crimini with caps that can reach six inches in diameter. Portabellas have a long growing cycle resulting in a solid, meat-like texture and flavor. These incredibly popular mushrooms are available as whole Portabellas (caps including their large, heavy stems), caps only, and sliced. Choose portabellas with pink to brown coloring, dry, and shapely gills and firm, plump caps. Black, wet, or dented gills and wrinkly or shriveled caps indicate age or spoilage.

Shiitakes: Shiitakes, *Lentinus edodes*, originated in Japan and are still most popular in Japanese and Chinese cooking. They range in color from tan to dark brown with broad, umbrella-shaped caps that are dark above and white inside, with wide open veils and tan gills. The caps are soft and spongy in texture, with a meaty, slightly chewy texture when cooked. They have a distinctive nutty-smoky aroma. Their stems are too woody to eat as is, though flavorful if ground finely or used for stock. Those grown on oak are best.

White: White mushrooms, *Agaricus bisporus,* are the most well-known mushroom in Europe and America. They range from creamy white to beige in color. They are good both raw and cooked; their flavor intensifies when cooked. Freshly picked white mushrooms have closed veils (caps that fit closely to the stem) and delicate flavor; mature whites, with open veils and darkened caps, develop a richer, deeper taste. Whole white mushrooms range in size from small (button), suitable for slicing raw in salads, to jumbos, suitable for stuffing and baking.

STORING MUSHROOMS

Most mushrooms are very perishable. The exception is some of the drier, firmer types such as shiitakes and crimini. Handle mushrooms with care, as they bruise easily. Once purchased, put them in a paper bag in the salad drawer of the refrigerator and eat them within three days. If you buy them in a prepack, take off the cling film and put the mushrooms into a paper bag, or wrap them in absorbent kitchen paper.

Enoki mushrooms are generally packaged in 3- to 5-ounce vacuum-sealed packages and can last up to two weeks if refrigerated. Fresh shiitakes and dry firm morels can last up to two weeks if refrigerated.

Pleurottes and chanterelles can last up to 7 days if refrigerated.

Maitakes and beech mushrooms can last up to 10 days if firm and dry.

Fresh whole portabellas and portabella caps remain fresh for up to 1 week. Sliced Portabellas should be used within 3 days.

Fresh whole white mushrooms, crimini, and baby bellas will remain fresh 5 to 7 days when stored properly. Sliced White mushrooms are best used in 3 to 5 days.

Cleaning Mushrooms

Some people peel mushrooms before using them, although this is not necessary, especially for cultivated mushrooms. Trim off the end of the stems (saving for soup stock, if desired). For mushrooms with tough stalks, like shiitakes, remove the stalks, which are too tough to eat as is, though they can be ground and cooked for stuffings.

You may rub the mushrooms with either a paper towel or a brush if they are relatively clean.

If the mushrooms are dirty, quickly rinse them under cold running water just before you use them and drain them. Dry washed mushrooms on absorbent paper towels. Shiitakes and crimini generally don't need washing or wiping.

To prepare fresh porcini, scrape any dirt you may find off the stalks and wipe the mushrooms clean with a damp cloth—only wash them if you absolutely must, and never in hot water. They should be used as soon as possible. If you must wait, stand the mushrooms on their caps to prevent any of the tiny worms which sometimes inhabit their stalks from traveling upward.

Before using fresh chanterelles, rinse them quickly though carefully, especially inside the wrinkles. Drain them immediately, and dry them with a cloth or paper towel.

Hungarian Mushroom Soup: Gombaleves

The recipe for this deep, dark soup was given to me by a Czech friend who got it from a Hungarian cookbook. I have further adapted it to use portabella mushroom caps for their earthy flavor and meaty texture. I'm a big fan of the sour cream so prevalent in Central European cooking. Here, bright white dollops add a light tang, enrich the soup, and contrast with its dark color. The soup is easy to make and freezes very well, so I suggest doubling the recipe and freezing half.

Serve 6 to 8

$1/2$ cup dried porcini mushrooms (about $1/2$ ounce by weight), soaked in warm water to cover until softened, about 20 minutes

1 small onion, chopped

1 tablespoon chopped garlic

3 tablespoons unsalted butter

1 pound portabella mushroom caps, diced

1 tablespoon sweet Hungarian paprika

Kosher salt and freshly ground black pepper to taste

3 tablespoons all-purpose flour

4 cups chicken stock, simmering

$1/4$ cup chopped Italian parsley

1 cup sour cream, for garnish

Lay a dampened paper towel in a sieve set over a bowl. Scoop out the soaked porcini, chop up into small bits and reserve. Strain the mushroom "liquor" through the paper towel to remove any sand particles and reserve.

In a large, heavy soup pot, sauté the onions and garlic in the butter. When the onions are translucent but not browned, add the portabellas and reserved chopped porcini, and cook until the mushrooms give off their liquid. Stir in the paprika, salt and pepper to taste, and the flour.

Pour in about half the stock, and bring to a boil while stirring until thick and smooth. Pour in the remaining stock, bring back to a boil, and stir in the parsely. Serve each portion topped with a dollop of sour cream.

POISONOUS MUSHROOMS

Many common types of wild mushrooms can be readily identified by a mycologist (someone who studies mushrooms) or by those familiar with that particular mushroom. It is imperative to hunt mushrooms with someone knowledgeable to begin with or join a mushroom-hunting club in your area.

In Italy, wild mushrooms are so sought-after that every small village has a mushroom specialist—who can identify edible mushrooms (usually either a pharmacist or priest). Even so, Italians are such avid wild mushroom hunters that an average of fifty people a year die from eating poison mushrooms.

This is partly because one of the favored varieties is called ovoli, *Amanita caesarea*, which is edible and extraordinarily delicious (I've had the pleasure of eating them in season in Northern Italy), but they are closely related to other *Amanita* mushrooms that are the deadliest of mushrooms. I believe that part of the pleasure here is the danger; just like eating Japanese blowfish.

Spiced Button Mushrooms

Now that we have such a varied choice of mushrooms, we sometimes neglect the firm, mild white button mushroom, called champignon de Paris, *that was the first type of mushroom cultivated near Paris. Here, their delicate flavor and firm texture are highlighted by simmering them in an aromatic mixture of vermouth, spices, and herbs. The flavorful cooking liquid is then reduced to a syrup, in a restaurant-style method, and then mixed with olive oil and prepared horseradish. These mushrooms are perfect to serve as an hors d'oeuvre on toothpicks with wine or cocktails before dinner and keep quite well. Like all good starters, whether Italian* bocconcini *(mouthfuls), French hors d'oeuvres (apart from the main dish), Spanish tapas (toppers for small glasses of sherry), or Middle Eastern mezze (taste, relish, or a nibble), the spiced mushrooms are strong in flavor, but not overly filling.*

MAKES 6 CUPS

3/4 cup dry white vermouth

6 tablespoons cider vinegar

1 onion, peeled and cut into quarters

1/4 bunch thyme, tied with kitchen twine

2 teaspoons coriander seed

1 teaspoon black peppercorns

2 teaspoons yellow mustard seed

2 teaspoons kosher salt

2 1/2 pounds button mushrooms, trimmed and washed briefly

6 tablespoons extra-virgin olive oil

1 tablespoon prepared horseradish

Bring vermouth, vinegar, onion, thyme, coriander, peppercorns, and mustard seed to the boil. Simmer 30 minutes, then remove and discard the onion quarters and thyme.

Add the salt and mushrooms and bring back to the boil. Remove the pot from the heat and, using a slotted spoon, remove the mushrooms to a separate bowl and reserve. Strain the remaining liquid through a sieve, then pour back into the pot and heat, reducing the liquid until thick and syrupy. Whisk together the mushroom liquid, olive oil, and horseradish. Combine with mushrooms and marinate in the refrigerator for at least 1 day (or up to 2 weeks) before serving.

Warm Roasted Wild Mushroom Salad with Balsamic Syrup

As is apparent by the number of components, this is a dish with restaurant origins. Don't be deterred, however, because it is absolutely delicious, full of earthy flavor and fragrant with pungent truffle oil. The balsamic syrup can also be used to dress caramelized Brussels sprout halves (see page 198) or caramelized cauliflorets. The caramelized shallots are wonderful sprinkled on top of steak or hamburger, as are the roasted mushrooms. If you happen to have the grill on, roast the mushrooms on a metal pan placed over the grill with the lid on. Because mushrooms are so porous, they readily pick up wood smoke flavors.

SERVES 6

Balsamic Syrup

1/2 cup brown sugar, packed

1 cup balsamic vinegar

2 tablespoons honey

Combine all ingredients in a medium, heavy-bottomed pot, bring to the boil, then reduce heat and simmer until bubbling and thickened to a light syrup, about 10 minutes. Store at room temperature.

Caramelized Shallots

1 quart canola oil
2 cups sliced shallots

In a large, deep pot, heat the oil (filled no more than halfway up the sides) to 365°F., or until shimmering hot. Add the shallots a few at a time, stirring as the oil bubbles up, then adding more until all the shallots have been added. Fry over high heat until the shallots are brown and crispy, stirring occasionally, about 15 minutes. Remove from oil using a wire skimmer, and drain on paper towels. Store at room temperature for up to 5 days.

Roasted Mushrooms

$1/2$ pound shiitake mushrooms, caps only
1 pounds crimini mushrooms, trimmed and quartered
$1/2$ pound oyster mushrooms, stems removed and sliced
$1/2$ pound portabella mushrooms, quartered
3 tablespoons olive oil
2 teaspoons kosher salt
$1/4$ teaspoon finely ground black pepper
$1/2$ cup Balsamic Syrup (from above)

Preheat the oven to 450°F. Combine mushrooms with oil, salt, pepper, and syrup. Spread out in a thin layer on a metal baking pan, and roast until well browned, turning once or twice, about 10 minutes.

Mixed Greens with Lemon Dressing

2 tablespoons freshly squeezed lemon juice
$1/4$ cup olive oil
Salt and pepper to taste
3 cups spring mix salad greens

Whisk together lemon juice, olive oil, salt, and pepper. Toss greens lightly with dressing.

To Serve

Roasted Mushrooms
Mixed Greens with Lemon Dressing
Caramelized Shallots
Black Truffle Oil

Arrange roasted mushrooms over mixed greens, top with a spoonful of caramelized shallots and sprinkle with black truffle oil. Serve immediately.

597

Morel Turnovers in Cream Cheese Pastry: Piroshki

Only a crazy chef would insist on cooking for their own wedding. This is what I did when I married Don Reiff, architect of the restaurant where I was then chef. I couldn't bring myself to hire a caterer, so I devised a mostly make-ahead menu and hired several people to help finish the dishes and serve. The food was delicious, not that I tasted much of it, and I paid the price of working so hard by getting sick on my honeymoon in Paris. These morel turnovers, called piroshki *in Russian, were on the menu, along with a full kilo (!) of Russian sevruga caviar that disappeared quickly, and the biggest lobster I've ever cooked.*

MAKES ABOUT 75 TO 100 MINI PASTRIES

Cream Cheese Pastry

$1/2$ pound (2 sticks) unsalted butter

$1/2$ pound cream cheese

$1/4$ cup heavy cream

$3/4$ pound (3 cups) unbleached all-purpose flour

1 teaspoon kosher salt

Cream the butter and cream cheese together, beat in the cream, and add the flour and salt, beating only long enough to combine the ingredients. Form into a flattened rectangle, wrap well, and refrigerate for at least 1 hour to relax the gluten in the dough, or freeze for at least 30 minutes.

Morel Mushroom Filling

3 pounds mushrooms

$1/4$ pound dried morels or 1 pound fresh if in season

$1/4$ pound (1 stick) unsalted butter

$1/2$ cup shallots, chopped (about 2 ounces)

$1/2$ cup brandy

1 cup heavy cream

Kosher salt and freshly ground black pepper to taste

1 tablespoon chopped fresh thyme, or 1 teaspoon dried

To make the filling, chop the mushrooms. If you're using dried morels, soak them in warm water for about 15 minutes, then remove and discard the tough stems. Strain the soaking liquid through a damp paper towel and reserve. Melt the butter, and sauté the mushrooms, morels, and shallots over medium heat until liquid is released from the mushrooms. Then increase the heat and cook to evaporate excess liquid, stirring frequently. Add the brandy and, averting your eyes, ignite carefully. Allow the alcohol burn off,

then add the cream and reserved soaking liquid. Cook the mixture until quite thick but not dry. Season with salt, pepper, and thyme, and chill in the refrigerator for about 1 hour. (This step, too, can be done a few days in advance.)

Assembly and Baking

2 egg yolks

2 tablespoons water

Flour, for rolling

Chilled Cream Cheese Pastry

Chilled Morel Filling

Mix together the egg yolks and water and reserve.

Roll out the pastry dough to a thin, even sheet, dusting it with flour to prevent sticking. Cut into 2- to 3-inch rounds with a biscuit or cookie cutter. Place one spoonful of filling on each circle of dough, fold the circle in half, and crimp or roll the edges, making sure that the pastries are well-sealed. As they are completed, place them on a metal baking pan, and brush with the egg wash. Prick the pastries with a fork. (If you're not baking immediately, freeze the pastries on the pan and then transfer to an airtight plastic container with waxed paper separating the layers of pastry, and freeze for up to 3 months.)

When ready to bake, preheat the oven to 375°F. Arrange the *piroshki* on a baking sheet and bake until browned and the filling starts to bubble out of the pricked holes, about 20 minutes. If the pastries are frozen, do not defrost, simply bake at 350°F. for about 35 minutes. Serve immediately.

Wild Mushroom Flan
with Cilantro Pesto

This recipe was given to me by Chef Adan Saavedra, a native of Michuoacán, Mexico, who serves it at his charming and intimate restaurant, Paloma, in Philadelphia. The chef combines his years of experience in French kitchens with the flavors of his native Mexico. Here a classic French savory flan is flavored with exotic mushrooms and the wildly pungent herb, epazote, that is often combined with mushrooms in Mexico (see Epazote, page 603, for more information). The topping of cilantro pesto adds an extra level of flavor and nutty texture. You'll only need half the pesto for this recipe. Serve the rest as a topping for grilled chicken, fish, or skirt steak. Saavedra often makes the flan and the pesto a day ahead of time, making things a bit easier.

SERVES 4

1 tablespoon each olive and vegetable oil

$1/2$ cup each trimmed, thinly sliced shiitake (caps only), crimini, and oyster mushrooms

2 cups heavy cream

1 tablespoon finely chopped epazote

Kosher salt and freshly ground black pepper to taste

2 whole eggs

2 egg yolks

1 cup Cilantro Pesto (recipe follows)

Spray four large ramekins, coffee cups, or glass custard cups with nonstick spray. (Your containers should hold about 1 cup.) Preheat the oven to 350°F.

Heat the oil in a medium pot and add the mushrooms. Cook 5 minutes over medium high heat, or until the mush-

rooms are soft and most of their liquid has evaporated. Add the cream and epazote. Bring to the boil and simmer for 5 minutes, or until thick bubbles appear on the surface. Remove from the heat and season generously with salt and pepper.

In a bowl, lightly beat together the whole eggs and the yolks. While still beating, pour in the hot cream-mushroom mixture, beating to combine well. Taste for seasoning, adding more salt and pepper if necessary.

Ladle the mixture into the prepared ramekins. Place the ramekins into a large cake or baking pan and then fill the pan with hot water about two-thirds of the way up the sides. Cover with foil slashed several times to release the steam and bake 30 to 35 minutes, or until the custards are set and firm in the middle. Remove the pan from the oven. Carefully remove the ramekins from the pan, and reserve at room temperature if serving within 2 hours.

To serve the flans, run a thin, sharp knife or an icing spatula around the sides of the custard cups. Give each flan several vigorous shakes from side to side to encourage it to separate from the mold. Turn each flan upside down onto a plate, knocking the bottom of the flan so that it drops onto the plate. (You may have to repeat the shaking and knocking until the flan comes away from its mold.)

Warm the reserved Cilantro Pesto in a small pan and then drizzle about 2 tablespoons onto each flan. Serve immediately.

To reheat, preheat the oven to 350°F. Unmold the flans onto heatproof plates and then warm in the microwave on medium power for 1 to 2 minutes and then transfer to the oven. Heat for 5 to 10 minutes, or until the center of the flan is hot when stuck with a thin metal skewer. Meanwhile, warm the pesto in a small pan, and drizzle all around the flans.

Cilantro Pesto

Leaves from a large bunch fresh cilantro,
 washed and dried

$1/4$ cup pine nuts

$1/4$ cup each: olive oil and vegetable oil, divided

6 to 8 cloves garlic

Juice of $1/2$ lime

Kosher salt and freshly ground black pepper to taste

Heat a small saucepan of water to boiling. Add the cilantro leaves and then immediately turn off the heat. Stir until the cilantro wilts and turns brilliant green. Drain immediately in a colander and run under cold water to set the color. Squeeze excess moisture out of the leaves.

Place the pine nuts in a small skillet with 1 tablespoon of olive oil and lightly toast, shaking often until the pine nuts start to brown, watching carefully so that the nuts don't burn. Remove from heat and cool.

Place the cilantro, pine nuts and their cooking oil, garlic, and lime juice into the bowl of a food processor. Process 1 minute or until everything starts getting chopped up. With the machine still running, slowly drizzle in the remaining oil. Remove the pesto from the processor, season with salt and pepper, and reserve.

600

Chicken Fricassee with Meatballs and Mushrooms

Chicken fricassee is an old French dish originally consisting of a white meat stewed in stock and served in a white sauce that was adapted by the English by 1600. Somehow this dish became the utmost in elegance in the American Jewish immigrant community, often combining the chicken with meatballs and mushrooms. It was made for special occasions by my aunt in Boro Park, a center of orthodox Jewish life. For authentic flavor, make the fricassee with a kosher chicken and use chicken fat. I like to flavor the sauce with the rich, earthy liquor given off by dried porcini mushrooms when soaked in tepid water to cover. Being that chicken fricassee is enjoyed by Jews of Eastern Europe where wild mushrooms abound, this is a very appropriate adaptation. Serve over cooked egg noodles, or with mashed potatoes, or spaetzle (see page 172).

SERVES 8

$1/2$ cup dried porcini mushrooms

1 ($2^{1}/2$- to 3-pound) whole chicken

Kosher salt and freshly ground black pepper to taste

1 cup all-purpose flour, for dusting

1 cup chicken fat, or canola oil, divided

2 pounds uncooked Meatballs (*see* page 848)

1 onion, diced

1 green pepper, diced

1 pound quartered crimini mushrooms

1 cup chicken stock

Soak the porcini in warm water to cover until soft, about 20 minutes. Scoop out the mushrooms, chop finely, and reserve.

Strain the mushroom "liquor" through a dampened paper towel laid into a sieve to remove any sand, and reserve.

Cut the chicken up as follows: remove the backbone and wing tips (reserving for stock). Cut into portions including two legs, two thighs, two wings, and four pieces of breast (each half cut into half) for a total of 10 pieces per chicken (*see* Cutting Up a Bird in Eight Pieces, page 259, for more detailed instructions). Season the chicken pieces with salt and pepper and roll in flour. Shake off excess flour and brown in 6 tablespoons of the fat or oil in a large skillet. Continue to cook until well browned. Remove chicken from the pan and reserve.

Add 6 tablespoons more fat or oil to the pan. Dust the meatballs with flour, shaking off the excess, and brown well on all sides. Remove from pan and reserve.

Pour off the fat, add the remaining fat or oil to the skillet, and sauté the onion, green peppers, and crimini mushrooms. Brown lightly and then add the chicken stock and the porcini mushroom liquor. Bring to the boil, then add the chicken pieces and the meatballs. Bring back to the boil, then simmer 30 minutes, or until the chicken is cooked through and the liquid has thickened. Serve over cooked egg noodles, if desired.

Chicken Fricassee from Fannie Farmer's 1918 Cookbook

"Dress, clean, and cut up a fowl. Put in a kettle, cover with boiling water, and cook slowly until tender, adding salt to water when chicken is about half done. Remove from water, sprinkle with salt and pepper, dredge with flour, and sauté in butter or pork fat. Arrange chicken on pieces of dry toast placed on a hot platter, having wings and second joints opposite each other, breast in centre of platter, and drumsticks crossed just below second joints. Pour around White or Brown Sauce.

Reduce stock to two cups, strain, and remove the fat. Melt three tablespoons butter, add four tablespoons flour, and pour on gradually one and one-half cups stock. Just before serving, add one-half cup cream, and salt and pepper to taste; or make a sauce by browning butter and flour and adding two cups stock, then seasoning with salt and pepper.

Fowls, which are always made tender by long cooking, are frequently utilized in this way. If chickens are employed, they are sautéed without previous boiling, and allowed to simmer fifteen to twenty minutes in the sauce."

AMERICAN JEWISH CHICKEN FRICASSEE

Samuel Chotzinoff, who first tasted this dish at a fancy wedding, tells us in his 1955 memoir *A Lost Paradise*, "I had known chicken exclusively in its austere boiled state, garnished with whole, waterlogged onions or accompanied by masses of noodles. But chicken fricassee was so special a form as to make it seem improbable that it could ever be served in any home. . . . It was known by reputation to most of the children of the neighborhood, but only a few had ever come face to face with it. I could now testify that it deserved its fame."

Wild Mushroom Quesadilla

This hearty and well-flavored vegetarian dish will satisfy even the most inveterate meat eater. It dates back to my days as chef and partner at Philadelphia's now nationally known White Dog Café. Because of the social activist atmosphere and its location surrounded by the University of Pennsylvania, the restaurant attracted a large vegetarian clientele. While I am omnivorous, my preferred foods are vegetables, mushrooms, starches, and cheese. If you don't want to go to the trouble of making both the deep red-brown chile ancho sauce and the pumpkin seed-green tomatillo sauce, make one or the other. If you do make both sauces, note that they freeze well and can be served with fajitas, enchiladas, or nachos. Epazote has a real affinity for wild and exotic mushrooms, but cilantro or oregano can be substituted. (See Epazote, page 603, for more information.)

SERVES 6 TO 8

Chile Ancho Sauce

1 pound plum tomatoes

4 whole shallots, unpeeled

1/2 head garlic, unpeeled

2 whole chile anchos, stemmed, seeded and soaked in warm water

1 cup vegetable stock, liquor from dried mushrooms, or chicken stock

1/4 cup olive oil

1/2 teaspoon allspice

Preheat the oven to 400°F. Place the tomatoes, shallots, and garlic in a metal roasting pan and roast 20 minutes, or until well-browned. Remove from the oven and transfer to the jar of a blender. Blend the roasted vegetables, the soaked chile anchos, and the stock until smooth.

Heat the olive oil in a medium, heavy-bottomed pot. Add the contents of the blender, and fry over moderate heat until the oil rises to the top, stirring occasionally. Strain, season with salt, and reserve.

Pepita Sauce

1 white onion, diced

1 tablespoon chopped garlic

1/4 cup olive oil

1 pound tomatillos, skinned and chopped

1 cup lightly toasted pumpkin seeds (pepitas)

1 tablespoon chopped epazote (or oregano)

2 tablespoons chopped cilantro

1 jalapeño, stemmed and seeded

1 cup vegetable stock, liquor from dried mushrooms, or chicken stock

Cook the onion and garlic in olive oil until transparent, about 5 minutes. Add the remaining ingredients, simmer for 15 minutes until the tomatillos are soft. Transfer to a blender and blend until smooth.

Filling

1/2 cup peeled and sliced shallots

1/4 cup olive oil, divided

2 tablespoons thinly sliced garlic

1 pound shiitake mushrooms, stems removed and caps sliced

1 pound crimini mushrooms, sliced

2 poblano chiles, roasted, peeled, seeded, and sliced

1 pound aged Gouda, grated

1 pound package white corn tortillas

2 tablespoons chopped epazote (substitute cilantro or oregano)

Kosher salt and freshly ground black pepper to taste

Preheat the oven to 400°F. Brown shallots in 2 tablespoons of the olive oil, then add garlic, cook until fragrant, about 3 minutes, and reserve.

Toss mushrooms in the remaining 2 tablespoons olive oil and salt and pepper to taste. Spread out in a single layer in a metal roasting pan and roast about 15 minutes, or until browned, then cool.

Combine the shallot mixture, the mushrooms, poblanos, cheese, epazote, salt and pepper, and reserve.

Divide the filling among the tortillas, then fold each tortilla in half and press together to seal. (You may reserve the quesadillas up to 2 days at this point.)

Garnishes and Assembly

1 to 2 tablespoons canola oil, for griddle

Pepita Sauce

Chile Ancho Sauce

1/4 cup sour cream

1/2 cup lightly toasted pumpkin seeds (pepitas)

1/4 cup chopped cilantro

2 diced tomatillos

Preheat the oven to 350°F. When ready to cook, preheat a cast-iron griddle or skillet and cover with a thin layer of oil. Cook quesadillas on griddle, then transfer to a metal baking pan and bake just long enough to melt the cheese, about 5 minutes. Serve drizzled with the chile ancho and pepita sauces, dot with the sour cream, and sprinkle with the pumpkin seeds, cilantro, and tomatillo. Serve immediately.

Mushroom Lasagna

A good lasagna is never a simple thing to make, but the aromas that fill your house are only a prelude to bringing out the big pan of bubbling hot deliciousness. This Northern Italian-style lasagna is a wonderful version for winter made with layers of porcini mushroom ragù (a chunky sauce), layered with sliced plum tomatoes, a lusciously rich and creamy Fontina cheese sauce, and fresh egg pasta sheets. Although it is a vegetarian dish, this lasagna is quite hearty, with the flavors of the woodsy mushrooms and the rosemary and sage often paired with game in Italy. A good alternative to the fresh pasta is the precooked lasagna sheets produced by several Italian companies, such as Del Verde. The sheets just need to be briefly cooked to soften them. Assemble the lasagna a day or two ahead, if desired, allowing about 30 minutes extra time, and bake at 350°F.

SERVES 12

Mushroom Ragù

$1/2$ cup dried porcini

$1/2$ cup dry Marsala

6 tablespoons olive oil

$1^1/2$ cups thinly sliced red onions

2 tablespoons thinly sliced garlic

2 pounds assorted wild and domestic mushrooms,
    trimmed and sliced

2 tablespoons each: chopped rosemary and sage

$1/4$ cup chopped Italian parsley

Soak the porcini in the Marsala for at least 1 hour or until plump and softened. Scoop out the porcini from the liquor, squeezing out the excess liquid. Strain the liquid through a paper-towel-lined sieve. Combine the strained liquid with the porcini and reserve.

Heat the olive oil in a large casserole dish and sauté the onions and garlic until lightly browned. Add the mushrooms and continue to cook over high heat until browned. Add the porcini and their liquor, plus the rosemary and thyme, and cook until the liquid has completely evaporated. Cool and reserve. Stir in the parsley just before assembling lasagna.

Fontina Cheese Sauce

3 tablespoons unsalted butter

$1/2$ cup all-purpose flour, preferably unbleached

1 cup heavy cream, scalded

2 cups milk, scalded

Kosher salt, freshly ground black pepper, grated nutmeg,
    and cayenne to taste

$3/4$ pound imported Italian Fontina cheese, frozen and
    then shredded

In a medium-sized, nonreactive pot, heat the butter, stir in the flour and cook together until the flour is very lightly browned. Pour in the cream and milk and whisk together vigorously. (Avoid using aluminum here, which will discolor the sauce.) Bring sauce to the boil, simmer for about 15 minutes, and then remove from heat.

Stir in the seasonings and the cheese, whisking together until completely combined. Cool the sauce, and dot with bits of butter, which will melt and prevent formation of a skin. It's best to work with the sauce at room temperature or slightly warm. If cold, it will be too thick to spread.

Assembly

Mushroom Ragù

Fontina Cheese Sauce

1 (28-ounce) can whole peeled plum tomatoes,
    drained, sliced, and drained again

1 pound fresh egg pasta sheets, cut into lengths to just fit
    the lasagna pans

1 cup grated Parmigiano-Reggiano

Bring a large pot of salted water to the boil. Gently lay in individual sheets of pasta, boiling only until half-cooked. Drain and lay out on waxed paper. Assemble lasagna as soon as possible after cooking.

Ladle a thin layer of Fontina sauce on the bottom of a large lasagna pan. Cover with a layer of slightly overlapping pasta sheets. Spread one third of the mushroom mixture over top. Cover with another layer of pasta, then top with a thin layer of sauce, and cover with a thin layer of tomato slices. Continue until all the pasta and filling has been used. End by spreading a thin layer of sauce and tomato slices over top of the last pasta layer. Sprinkle with the grated cheese.

Bake at 375°F. for about 45 minutes, or until browned and bubbling on top and when a skewer stuck into the center is hot to the touch. Remove from the oven and allow the lasagna to cool for about 10 minutes so it sets up before cutting and serving.

MUSSELS

MUSSELS

In cities where there is a large Italian community, many people make a regular ritual of going out to restaurants for steamed mussels "in red" or "in white" sauce. We might not think of making steamed mussels at home, but they make a fast, flavorful meal in a bowl that's low in cost and high in protein. Mussels are a way of life on the west coast of France in Brittany, and in Belgium, where they are often steamed with white wine. In France, mussels are served without utensils. Instead, a handy set of empty hinged mussel shells are used to remove the tender mussel meat from the remaining shells, and a single empty shell makes a perfect scoop to get at the last spoonful of delicious broth.

When I first started cooking in the early seventies, mussels were delivered to restaurants in large burlap net bags. These wild-harvested mussels were often muddy and encrusted in barnacles that had to be laboriously pried off one at a time. At that time, chefs and home cooks really had to be determined to serve mussels. Now, it's so much easier; almost every supermarket fish department sells clean, shiny blue-black farm-raised mussels that are inexpensive and quite adaptable.

Mussels range all the way from the southern Arctic to the Carolinas and also throughout the Mediterranean. In Italy, where the small mussels are prized, they are known as *mitili* or *cozze*, in France and Belgium, they are *moules*, and in Spain, *mejillón*. While there are many places where mussels can be gathered wild, these can be dangerous to eat because mussels are susceptible to pollution and disease. It is a good idea for both taste and health to eat only cultivated and/or precleaned mussels. Not only will they be consistently plump and sweet, they also arrive at the market prescrubbed, debearded, and pan-ready.

The oldest method of cultivation first developed in the 1200s by an Irishman named Walton, the sole survivor of a shipwreck off the coast of France. He first tried to use nets supported by poles fixed in the water to catch the birds who flew across the mud flats. He then realized that he could better harvest the mussels that spawned and grew onto the poles. This method is still used in France today to raise mussels. In Holland and Denmark, protected areas of the seabed called mussel "parks" are used for cultivation. In Spain, a leading world producer of mussels, mussel-growing ropes are suspended from large floating rafts.

Prince Edward Island in Canada is a large producer of rope-grown mussels, which tend to be smaller in size. The Great Eastern Company in Maine gathers larger wild mussels, then washes, debeards, and purges them in water until they are clean and sand-free. Another producer of mussels that uses a similar method of washing and purging wild mussels is the White Water company, which gathers them from the calmer waters off the coast of Rhode Island.

I consider the flavor of mussel "liquor," the juice inside of fresh mussels, to be the sweetest and tastiest of all sea offerings. Mussels have long been sold in mega-quantities in Europe, especially in Italy, and on the Atlantic coast of France. They are the national obsession of Belgians, who eat them steamed in every way you can imagine accompanied by crispy fresh-made *frites* (French fried potatoes). American diners didn't much go for mussels years ago. Because most mussels are now cleaned, plump, and barnacle and dirt-free, they have gained quite a following.

THE BEST MUSSELS

One of the most knowledgeable and respected people in the seafood business in the Philadelphia region is Sammy D'Angelo, the third generation in the family-owned business started on a pushcart by his grandfather, an Italian immigrant. Today, D'Angelo is owner of Samuels and Son Seafood, a regional wholesale supplier to fine restaurants. According to him, the best-tasting mussels in America come from the waters between the islands of Nantucket and Martha's Vineyard and the shores of Rhode Island. These Nantucket shoals are loaded with nutrients, enriching the flavor of the mussels and also making them larger and meatier than mussels from the northern waters of Prince Edward Island and Maine. It's all a matter of taste, and you might prefer the smaller mussels sought after by French and Belgian mussel-lovers.

Cleaning and Storing Mussels

Look for cleaned mussels in a two-pound net bag in the fish department of your local supermarket. The best thing is to cook them the day you buy them. Otherwise, store for one day or at most two days in the refrigerator.

Mussels attach themselves to their perch with a "beard," the tuft of fibers sticking out of the shell. Because the beard is the mussel's lifeline, they will stay alive longest if their beard is attached. Most likely, the mussels you buy will already have the beard removed. If not, pull off and discard the hairy beard that sticks out of the mussel.

Sort the mussels, discarding any that are broken or not tightly closed. If the mussels are just slightly open, try pressing their edges together. If the mussel closes up, it is alive and healthy. Discard any mussels that either gape open or contain sand. Scrub, using a brush, under cold running water. Keep cold until ready to steam.

Billi Bi

This delectable soup is based on a traditional dish of Normandy, on France's western coast, where it is called mouclade. *It is said to have been created by chef Louis Barthe in 1925 at the famed Maxim's of Paris for one of his restaurant's regular customers, William B. Leeks, Jr., an American industrialist who was inordinately fond of it, although its true origins aren't clear. In any case, it's easy to make, and most elegant to serve, because the mussels are pureed and then strained out, in French restaurant style, leaving only their fabulous flavor for the diner to enjoy. Save a few whole cooked mussels in or out of their shells for garnish, if desired.*

SERVES 8

2 cups dry white wine

2 pound mussels, well-scrubbed

3 to 4 sprigs thyme

$1/2$ teaspoon crushed red pepper flakes

2 tablespoons olive oil

1 cup thinly sliced celery

1 cup finely diced onion

1 tablespoon chopped garlic

2 tablespoons all-purpose flour

1 cup chopped plum tomatoes

$3/4$ cup brandy

2 cups fish stock or clam broth

1 quart heavy cream

Kosher salt and freshly ground black pepper to taste

Place the white wine, mussels, thyme, and red pepper flakes in a large soup pot. Cover and steam over high heat until all the mussels open, about 10 minutes, shaking the pot occasionally. Scoop the mussels from the broth, reserving the liquid.

Remove the meats from the mussel shells, reserving the meat and discarding the shells. To ensure that no sand remains in the mussel liquor, pour it through a dampened coffee filter or a paper towel placed inside a sieve.

Meanwhile, in a second large stock pot (or wash out and reuse the first pot), heat the olive oil over medium heat. Add the celery, onion, and garlic, and sauté until fragrant, about 3 minutes. Stir in the flour and cook for 2 to 3 minutes, then add the tomatoes and continue cooking for a total of 5 minutes, or until the vegetables are crisp-tender. Pour in the brandy and cook for 3 to 4 minutes, until the flavors are combined. Then add the reserved mussels, strained mussel juice, and the fish stock or clam broth to the pot. Bring to the boil and simmer together 5 minutes. Add the cream, bring back to the boil and simmer 2 to 3 minutes longer, stirring constantly. Season to taste with salt and pepper. (If using the clam broth, salt will probably not be needed.) Blend the soup, strain, taste again for seasoning, and serve immediately.

610

Steamed Mussels with Saffron, Leeks, and Tomato

This Italian-style dish of steamed mussels includes saffron threads, a natural partner to seafood from Italy, to Southern France and Spain. The saffron imparts its own, slightly acrid flavor along with a rich golden color to the broth. The leeks are sweet and tender and also soak up the delicious mussel liquor. I prefer to use dry white vermouth, a fortified wine infused with herbs (such as the Italian brands Cinzano, Martini and Rossi, and Stock, or the French Nouilly Prat), instead of white wine, because it is inexpensive and keeps well without refrigeration.

SERVES 4

$1/2$ teaspoon saffron threads

1 cup dry white vermouth (or dry white wine)

1 bag (2 pounds) cultivated mussels, well scrubbed
  with an abrasive scouring pad

2 tablespoons extra-virgin olive oil

3 leeks, cut into small squares and soaked in a large bowl
  of water to clean

$1/2$ teaspoon hot red pepper flakes

1 tablespoon chopped garlic

2 cups tomato sauce

1 tablespoon chopped fresh marjoram, or 1 teaspoon
  dried marjoram

$1/4$ cup chopped Italian parsley

Soak the saffron threads in the wine for 10 minutes, or until the wine turns yellow. Make sure the mussels are all tightly closed.

In a large, heavy soup pot with a lid, heat the olive oil and add the leeks and stir-fry for 2 minutes, or until bright green. Stir in the pepper flakes and garlic and cook for 1 minute, or until the aromas are released. Add the wine with the saffron, the mussels, and the tomato sauce to the pot. Cover tightly and steam about 5 minutes. Shake frequently until the mussels open (discard any mussels that stay closed). Sprinkle in the chopped herbs and shake to mix with sauce. Serve in heated bowls topped with a crostino.

Crostini

2 tablespoons extra-virgin olive oil

1 tablespoon crushed garlic

1 loaf stale Italian bread, cut into $1/2$-inch-thick slices

Preheat the oven to 350°F. Combine the olive oil and garlic and brush onto both sides of each slice of bread. Arrange in a single layer on a baking sheet. Place in the oven and toast 10 minutes, or until the crostini are browned and crispy.

611

Saffron

Saffron, *Crocus sativus*, is the three brilliant orange-red stigmas of the autumn flowering crocus flower in the iris family, which gets its name from Arabic words meaning "yellow thread." Saffron has a distinctively pungent, earthy flavor and an acrid, hay-like aroma. Native to the Mediterranean and domesticated by Bronze Age Greeks, saffron was known to the Sumerians almost 5,000 years ago, and Alexander the Great found it growing in Kashmir on his travels through India more than 2,800 years ago. The Arabs brought saffron to Spain, which remains one of the world's top producers, along with Iran.

Saffron is legendary as the most expensive spice in the world. However, because it is so concentrated, a pinch of threads can flavor and color an entire dish. Saffron is essential for Mediterranean fish and seafood dishes like French *bouillabaisse*, Spanish *paella alla Valenciana*, and Italian *risotto alla Milanese*. Buy whole saffron threads and expect to pay a high price. As with any rare and expensive spice, there are inexpensive substitutes, such as safflower, marigold petals, or ground turmeric. The world's best saffron comes from Kashmir, in India, and Iran. It includes only the pure deep red-orange stigmas; less-expensive saffron bulks up with the flavorless yellow stamens. Look for saffron in Indian, Iranian, and Spanish markets.

I buy a full-ounce metal tin of Spanish saffron (about $45) and store it in the freezer. Well-sealed, it will keep well for at least one year. Perhaps a group of friends can share a tin; saffron in the tin will likely be fresher (the tins are marked with their harvest date) and will be much less expensive than buying it in by the gram, often in small glass vials (about $5 a gram, and there are 28 grams in an ounce).

Mussels Steamed in Beer

In Belgium, where they say "everyone eats well," wonderful beers, steamed mussels, and frites *(French fries) are a national obsession. For this Belgian-inspired dish, I prepare a sharp and tangy mustard butter to enrich the mussels, which are first steamed in beer. For an all-around Belgian meal, serve the mussels accompanied by crispy shoestring French fries. Don't forget a loaf of crusty bread to mop up the delicious juices. The mustard butter is also excellent on beef steak or pork chops.*

SERVES 4

Mustard Butter

$1/4$ pound (1 stick) unsalted butter

3 cloves garlic

Juice of 1 lemon

1 tablespoon soy sauce

1 tablespoon Dijon mustard

1 teaspoon dry mustard

$1/4$ cup Italian parsley leaves

1 tablespoon fresh thyme leaves, or 1 teaspoon
  dried thyme

Place all the ingredients into the bowl of a food processor and process all together until creamy. (To prepare by hand, soften the butter and beat in remaining ingredients.)

Remove the Mustard Butter from the processor and form into a log shape. Wrap well in plastic wrap, chill, and reserve. Note that the recipe will make more than you need for the mussels. Rewrap and freeze any extra butter for later use.

Mussels Steamed in Beer

1 bag (2 pounds) cultivated mussels

2 teaspoons crushed garlic

2 crushed bay leaves

1/2 teaspoon red pepper flakes

1/2 teaspoon ground allspice

2 tablespoons olive oil

1 bottle (12-ounces) dark beer

Make sure all of the mussels are closed, discarding any that are open.

In a large, heavy soup pot, sauté the garlic, bay leaves, red pepper flakes, and allspice in the olive oil over high heat for 2 minutes to release flavors. Add the beer and mussels. Cover and steam over high heat, shaking occasionally until the mussels open, discarding any shells that remain closed.

Serve the mussels with their juices, topping each portion with a spoonful of the mustard butter over top, accompanied by crusty bread to soak up the juices.

Steamed Mussels with Potatoes and Harissa

I developed this dish for the opening menu of a Moroccan-inspired restaurant in Philadelphia called Tangerine. The spicy aromatic flavors of North Africa—including preserved lemons, Harissa sauce, coriander seed, and cilantro leaf— work together to make a wonderful dish. Potatoes are cooked in a flavorful broth, then mussels are added and steamed open, lending their sweet-salty broth to the dish. You can either buy or make the Harissa and the preserved lemons (see pages 703 and 212), or simply substitute grated lemon zest for the preserved lemon. Bottled clam broth helps accent the flavors of the sea, although fish stock would also work.

SERVES 4

1 cup dry white vermouth

2 cups clam broth

1 tablespoon chopped garlic

1 preserved lemon, rind only, diced

1 tablespoon Harissa Sauce
 (purchased or homemade, *see* page 703)

1 tablespoon ground coriander

1 tablespoon ground fennel

4 star anise pods

1/4 cup extra-virgin olive oil

1 pound gold potatoes, diced

1 bag (2 pounds) cultivated mussels

2 tablespoons chopped cilantro

Juice of 1 lemon

613

In a large pot, simmer the vermouth, clam broth, garlic, lemon rind, Harissa, coriander, fennel, anise pods, olive oil, and potatoes for 20 minutes, or until the potatoes are tender.

Add the mussels, cover, and steam open over high heat. Add the cilantro and lemon juice, and toss to combine. Remove any closed mussels, and serve immediately.

Baked Mussels with Spinach and Saffron Cream

Mussels and saffron have a special affinity, because the more delicate flavor of the mussels doesn't overwhelm the saffron, and the sweet licorice-like flavor of the fennel is another perfect complement. Here, I steam the mussels (larger ones work best), remove the meats, and then cook down their wonderful "liquor" with other aromatics and cream until thickened. Next, I mix this tasty cream with mild, herbal spinach, fill the mussels, and top them with breadcrumbs for crunch. This makes a very good appetizer or hors d'oeuvre with drinks and can be made up to one day ahead of time up to the point of baking them, which only takes about ten minutes.

SERVES 6

1 bag (2 pounds) cultivated mussels

$1/2$ cup dry white vermouth

2 tablespoons chopped shallots

$1/4$ cup finely chopped fennel

$1/2$ teaspoon crumbled saffron threads

1 cup heavy cream

$1/2$ pound spinach leaves, wilted and with water squeezed out

2 tablespoons Pernod

Kosher salt and freshly ground black pepper to taste

$1/4$ cup Japanese panko breadcrumbs

1 tablespoon unsalted butter, melted

Place the mussels and vermouth in a large, heavy soup pot, cover and steam open over high heat, shaking occasionally until the mussels open, about 5 minutes, discarding any unopened shells.

Strain the mussel juices through a dampened paper towel set into a sieve to remove any sand. Place the strained mussel juice in a medium, nonreactive pot along with the shallots, fennel, saffron, and cream. Bring to the boil, taking care that the liquid doesn't boil over. Reduce the heat to medium and continue cooking until the liquid has thickened to a thick cream. Remove from heat, stir in the spinach and the Pernod. Season to taste with salt and pepper.

In a separate bowl, mix the breadcrumbs with the butter. Preheat the oven to 425°F. Remove one shell from each mussel, discarding the extra shell. Spoon a portion of the spinach mixture over the mussels in their shells. Sprinkle with the breadcrumb mixture. Bake on a baking sheet for 10 minutes, or until the mussels are bubbling and the crumbs are lightly browned, and serve immediately.

NECTARINES & PEACHES

NECTARINES & PEACHES

I can hardly wait each year for the arrival of luscious summer fruits, fully ripened to bring out the most natural fruit sugars. Perfectly ripened peaches and nectarines are the most luscious and sensuous of the summer fruits. Treat these precious but perishable fruits with plenty of TLC. Slow down and take pleasure in the giving feel in the hand of a tree-ripened, locally grown peach. Using sensitive fingertips, caress the light fuzz, reminiscent of the delicate velvety down on a young child's face. Inhale their evanescent fragrance, better than any perfume. And all this before you've even taken a bite! Be sure to handle even hard, unripe peaches with gentle hands, because any bruises will show later.

Of all fruits, the peach, *Prunus persica*, most closely resembles human flesh. Imagine the texture of a "pinch ripe" peach. Warm, golden-skinned peaches blushed with deeper rose seem painted just for the pleasure of the eye. The delicate cleft that divides the peach in two plump halves suggests inevitable comparisons. No fruit is more laden with erotic metaphor. The French variety, *Téton de Venus* (breast of Venus) says it all.

It's no wonder peaches have long inspired artists. Renoir told young artists, who longed to paint rosy-blushed female breasts as he did, to first learn to paint peaches in a bowl. To a Japanese poet, they recalled the "the left cheek of my girl." Chinese myth and poetry are filled with tales of the mythical peaches of immortality, which bear fruit every six thousand years, so that the gods can eat them and continue to live forever.

The nectarine, *Prunus persica Nucipersica group*, is a fruit all its own whose origin is still a mystery. It is thought to have originated as a mutant of the peach and gets its name from the Greek *nekter*, meaning sweet liquid, like the "nectar of the gods." Nectarines were first described in print in England in 1587; peaches are much older. Nectarines and peaches are genetically very similar but nectarines have smooth skin and peaches have fuzz. (Although today much of the fuzz has been bred out; it seems like fuzz means flavor, and older, fuzzier varieties just taste better.) Fuzziness is genetically dominant, but sometimes fuzzy peach trees bear a few smooth nectarines or the other way around. Many nectarine varieties have a spicy "zing" to their taste, and they may be either white or gold-fleshed.

All the stone fruits (including apricot, cherry, peach, and plum) belong to the rose family, which also includes apples and pears. Wild peaches originated in China and were small, sour, and hairy. Though wild peaches still grow in China, people in many parts of the world have been cultivating and improving peaches for at least 2,000 years.

The cultivated peach traveled westward to Persia, where it flourished so well that people assumed it was a native

616

Persian fruit (its Latin name, *Prunus persica,* means Persian Plum). The Spaniards brought the peach back from the East and from there sent them to the New World. In modern times, American growers in California, which has a perfect climate for peaches, have shaped the world market. The U.S. provides about one quarter of the world's supply of fresh peaches, about half of that from California, followed by South Carolina, Georgia, New Jersey, and Pennsylvania. Most Southern peaches go to the fresh market, accounting for about half the fruit available.

To be at its best, a peach must ripen on the tree. To me, the two most important categories of peaches are "woolly and inedible" or "juicy and ripe." More than likely you've bitten into a peach and gotten a mouthful of "wool" instead. By picking the fruit too early and keeping it in cold storage for weeks, commercial shippers transform peaches into disappointingly dry, mealy rocks. Frequent local farmers' markets for the best in peaches and nectarines, and avoid refrigerating them, at least until they're fully ripe.

CLINGSTONE AND FREESTONE PEACHES

Peaches are either Clingstones or Freestones. Both can have either pinky-white or yellow-orange flesh. Clingstones ripen earlier in the season, and even when ripe, their flesh sticks to the stone. The first modern peach variety was the Elberta, a clingstone. Peaches in cans tend to be clingstones, because they're quite firm. Much of the world's production of peaches ends up in cans, because they survive canning better than most fruits.

Freestones, which ripen later in season, have flesh that easily pulls away from the stone when ripe. These firm beauties are commercially less common because Clings are firmer, easier to transport, and deeper colored (more like apricots). My favorite is the late season, intensely flavored Red Havens. These red Freestones have prominent red streaks radiating out from the pit, are tart, firm and juicy at the same time, and peel easily.

Peaches in Pennsylvania

Glenn Brendle is a Chester County specialty farmer, owner of Green Meadow Farm in Gap, Pennsylvania, an area filled with old peach trees. Says Glenn, "A shipped peach isn't even worth talking about. You can't pick and haul a peach that's really ripe for more than one day. If it wasn't ripe to begin with, to hell with it!" Glenn concurs with many when he declares, "Peaches are the most erotic fruits there are, with juices than run down your chin. They're never cloyingly sweet; they have character. A ripe peach is a good as it gets."

The Amish in his area of Pennsylvania and else-where can hundreds of quarts of peaches every summer. These home-canned peach halves serve as the wintertime "workhorse dessert." After canning, Brendle's mother would throw out hundreds of peach pits. Out of those pits that sprouted, she would choose the tallest one to plant. Every summer, throughout his childhood, Glenn ate these cross-bred peaches. His earliest recollection is sitting under a peach tree, waiting for peaches to drop off as they attained the utmost in ripeness. Favorite old-time peaches include "Belle of Georgia," an heirloom variety that probably dates from the time of the Civil War, and the tender white peaches named "White Lady" and "White Hale."

617

WHITE PEACHES AND NECTARINES

White-fleshed peaches and nectarines are savored by connoisseurs for their sweet, luscious flavor, tantalizing fragrance, and novel color. White-fleshed fruits have been cultivated for hundreds of years and have occurred in nature for thousands. Records of white-fleshed peach varieties can be traced to the mid-1600s, and white-fleshed nectarines to the late 1700s. Until recently, supermarkets wanted only firm, yellow-fleshed fruit; the whites were too easily bruised. But in the 1980s, when the Asian markets opened up, they demanded white-fleshed fruits with low-acidity and paid top dollar for them, so they became more common.

Donut Peaches

These small, odd-looking, but intriguing flat peaches are descendants of the flat peaches of China, first grown in America in the 1800s. These so-called "donut" peaches are freestones that are flattened, round and drawn in at the center, with an almost round pit. Their skin is pale yellow with a red blush, with exquisitely sweet and juicy flesh, intense peach flavor, and hauntingly perfumed fragrance.

Locally Grown Fuzzy Peaches

Look for locally grown fruits, best found at farm stands. They may be a bit spotty, or even have a bruise to be cut away, but they'll be satisfying, fragrant, and juicy. Consumers unfamiliar with tree-ripened fruit are reluctant to buy a fuzzy peach, so smoother varieties have been developed. Don't be put off by the fuzz; you might miss an exquisite peach.

PEACHES AND JANE GRIGSON

The late Jane Grigson, British literary food writer, tells us that today's all-too-often disappointing peaches are "the children of arranged marriages" in her wonderful *Jane Grigsons' Fruit Book*. In search of the perfect peach, she explored Montreuil, near Paris, an area known from the time of King Louis the XIV for its legendary peaches grown on *espaliers* (wall trellises). Years ago, in fine restaurants, each peach would be presented gem-like at the table in its own blue-lined wooden box. Grigson favors the French *Pêches de Vigne*, covered with soft gray down, that ripen with the grape harvest. French vineyard varieties ripen late and are sometimes called blood peaches (like blood oranges) because of their deeply streaked red color, most similar to the Red Haven and other late-harvest American varieties.

Choosing and Ripening Peaches and Nectarines

Choose peaches without green shoulders. Look at the stem end of the peach. It should be yellow or creamy-colored. Don't choose it if the area surrounding the stem end is greenish. This is a sign of a prematurely plucked peach that will rot before it ripens. Ripen peaches in a cool room, stem-end-down. When you can smell the peaches and they give just slightly, the fruits are ready to eat.

To Pit Peaches

Use a sharp paring knife. Start at the stem end and cut through the natural cleft all the way around, ending at the stem end. Make sure to cut all the way to the stone. Firmly grasp the two halves and twist the two halves in two different directions, clockwise and counterclockwise. One half will pop off, leaving the second half with the stone. Use a spoon to scoop out the stone.

Or, cut the second half-peach in half again, cutting through to the stone. Twist off the first wedge. The remaining wedge will have the stone attached. Twist the stone off the remaining wedge.

Bellini Cocktail

Sitting at the bar at Harry's Bar and Grill overlooking Venice's Grand Canal, I sipped my Bellini cocktail, and was in heaven. It was my first trip on my own to Italy and I was thrilled to have a chance to eat at this rightly famed restaurant. Although an unknown young woman, I was treated like royalty with the best and most attentive of service by those smooth-talking, good-looking Italians. At that time, I had been studying Italian for less than a year, but drinking a glass of wine or a cocktail like this relaxed me, loosened my tongue, and eliminated my fear of making a fool of myself. Who cared if my grammar wasn't perfect? All I had to do was say a few words and people around me would compliment me on my fluency. Prosecco, used to make a Bellini, is quite popular today in America and can be found at reasonable prices in many wine shops. Most American bars use frozen peach puree today, but fresh white peaches in season will make a drink to remember.

Serves 2

$1/2$ cup fresh white peach nectar, chilled
2 teaspoons freshly squeezed lemon juice
2 tablespoons peach schnapps, or brandy
1 cup Prosecco, chilled

Mix the peach nectar with the lemon juice and schnapps and pour into two chilled champagne flutes. Top with the Prosecco and serve immediately.

619

Now a world-wide classic, the Bellini was invented in 1934 by the incredibly creative Harry Cipriani, owner of Harry's. The classic Bellini, named after the fifteenth-century founder of the Venetian school of painting, is made with pureed white peaches or white peach nectar and Prosecco, the lightly sparkling wine produced in the Veneto, the region surrounding Venice. When white peaches are in season, put them through a juicer or blend and strain through a fine sieve to make this exquisite drink.

To Peel Peaches

Bring a large pot of water to the boil. Gently drop in firm, but ripe peaches. Leave in the water for about half a minute. Remove one peach. You should be able to slide the skin away from the flesh. If not, leave in water a minute longer.

Skim the peaches out of the water and gently place in a colander. Run cold water over them to stop them from cooking. Rub off the skin. Under the skin, the peaches should be shiny from juice, with a lovely blush.

620

Peach–Mustard Glazed Corned Beef

In my years as local chairperson of the American Institute of Wine and Food, our chapter sponsored a wonderful annual pot luck dinner, where each of us tried to outdo other food-fiends in bringing our best dishes. One member brought this southern-style corned beef glazed with peaches, ketchup, brown sugar, vinegar, and mustard, and it was a big hit. I believe that this dish originated as a Jewish alternative to the popular southern glazed ham made using the same recipe in an effort to fit in with the locals. Sometimes corned beef comes in a vacuum-packed bag with the pickling spices already included. In that case, simply cover the meat and the contents of the bag with cold water and simmer until tender, omitting the pickling spice and bay leaves from the recipe.

SERVES 12

2 tablespoons pickling spice

2 bay leaves

1 corned beef brisket, about 6 pounds

1 cup peach preserves

$1/4$ cup brown sugar, packed

2 tablespoons dried mustard

2 tablespoons cider vinegar

1 teaspoon freshly ground black pepper

$1/2$ teaspoon ground allspice

Bring a large pot of water to the boil with the pickling spice and the bay leaves and simmer 15 minutes. Add the corned beef, bring to the boil, skimming as necessary. Reduce the heat to a bare simmer, cover, and cook $2^1/2$ to 3 hours, or until the meat is tender when pierced but not falling apart. Remove from the heat and allow the meat to cool in the liquid.

Preheat the oven to 350°F. Mix together the peach preserves, brown sugar, mustard, vinegar, pepper, and allspice. Remove the brisket from the liquid, pat dry with paper towels, and coat with the glaze.

Transfer to a roasting pan, and bake for 30 minutes. Reduce the heat to 325°F., and continue cooking for 1¹/₂ hours, or until nicely glazed. Remove from the oven, and allow the corned beef to cool about 15 minutes.

If the drippings in the pan haven't gotten overly dark and bitter, add about 1 cup of water to the empty pan, and place the pan back in the oven for about 10 minutes to soften, then scrape the glaze out of the pan into a small pot. Bring to the boil and whisk to combine.

Meanwhile, slice the beef thinly across the grain, pour the juices over top, and serve.

CORNED BEEF

Corned beef gets its name from Anglo-Saxon times when meat was *corned* or salted using the small grains of salt that were known as *corns*—the same derivation as the English word for the grain corn. Today, the beef, usually brisket from the beef forequarter, is brined in a mixture of salt, water, and pickling spices. Corned beef is associated with the cooking of the British Isles. Corned beef and cabbage was the traditional rural Irish Easter dinner. Because brisket is a forequarter cut and can therefore be kosher-slaughtered, corned beef is hugely popular as Jewish deli fare. Uncooked corned beef is often sold in a pouch complete with pickling spices.

Upside-Down
Spiced Nectarine Cake

Upside-down cakes became popular in the 1930s because they were easy to make in a cast-iron skillet. The pineapple version is the best known, but this nectarine cake hints of the East with its mysterious faint perfume of roses from the rose water. Like other cakes from the eastern end of the Mediterranean, this one includes yogurt; buttermilk makes a good substitute. Nectarines work well here, because I don't peel the fruit and their skins are thin and tender. Make it when the best late-season summer freestone nectarines are in season. Serve warm with vanilla or cinnamon ice cream, and garnish with sliced nectarines, if desired. To ensure that the nectarines don't stick to the pan, it's best to line it with a circle of parchment paper. If you happen to have some extra egg whites in the freezer, now's the time to use them, allowing 2 tablespoons per white.

621

MAKES ONE 9-INCH CAKE, TO SERVE 12

6 to 8 freestone nectarines, ripe but still firm

¹/₄ cup + ¹/₂ cup + ¹/₄ cup granulated sugar

Juice of 1 lemon

¹/₂ pound (2 cups) all-purpose flour

1 teaspoon baking soda

1 teaspoon baking powder

1 teaspoon ground cinnamon

1 teaspoon kosher salt

3 egg yolks

¹/₂ cup whole-milk plain yogurt

2 teaspoons rose water

¹/₄ pound (1 stick) unsalted butter

¹/₄ cup honey

6 egg whites

$^{1}/_{2}$ cup peach or apricot jam, strained and melted

Preheat the oven to 350°F. Prepare a 9-inch springform pan by lining the bottom with a circle of parchment paper. Cut the nectarines into $^{1}/_{2}$-inch-thick wedges and mix with $^{1}/_{4}$ cup sugar and the lemon juice. Arrange in concentric circles, as tightly as possible (the fruit will shrink in the oven) over the parchment paper.

Combine the dry ingredients: flour, baking soda, baking powder, cinnamon, and salt, and reserve. Separately, whisk together the yolks, yogurt, and rose water, and reserve.

Cream the butter, $^{1}/_{2}$ cup sugar, and the honey until light colored and the mixture forms a ribbon. Beat in the yolk mixture.

Beat the egg whites until white and fluffy, and then gradually sprinkle in the remaining $^{1}/_{4}$ cup of sugar. Continue beating until firm and glossy. Fold into the batter in thirds.

Pour the batter over the nectarines in the pan and bake for 45 to 50 minutes, or until set in the middle. Remove the cake from the oven, cool to room temperature on a wire rack, and then turn upside down onto a serving platter.

Heat the strained jam until it's runny, then brush lightly over the nectarines. Cool until set, then serve.

Peach and Pearl Tapioca Pudding

In this grown-up version of the childhood favorite, creamy tapioca pudding is studded with diced peaches and spiked with a dash of Amaretto liqueur. The pearly-white grains used to make tapioca are produced in a complex process from the roots of the cassava, also known as yuca. Yuca, Manihot esculenta, a root native to Brazil, is called man-ioc there, a name given it by Amazonian Indians. Tapioca mostly comes from manioc planted in Southeast Asia and Indonesia. Here I call for the large pearl tapioca because I prefer its prominent "fish-eye" appearance and slightly chewy consistency. It's the same tapioca used to make the wildly popular Asian bubble teas. Look for inexpensive tapioca in Asian markets. You'll need to soak the tapioca overnight before making the pudding.

SERVES 6

$^{1}/_{2}$ cup large pearl tapioca

2 cups cold water

2 cups milk

$^{1}/_{4}$ teaspoon kosher salt

$^{1}/_{2}$ cup granulated sugar

2 eggs

1 teaspoon vanilla extract

1 cup heavy cream, chilled

4 ripe peaches, peeled and diced

2 tablespoons Amaretto liqueur

Soak tapioca in water overnight in refrigerator. Drain and rinse.

Preheat the oven to 325°F. Combine the soaked tapioca

622

with milk, salt, sugar, and eggs. Mix well, transfer to a heavy-bottomed, nonreactive Dutch oven (with a lid), and bring to the boil over low heat, stirring occasionally. Cover and place in the oven. Bake 45 minutes, or until the pearls are translucent, stirring once or twice. Remove from oven and stir in vanilla. Cool to room temperature, then chill in the refrigerator.

When ready to serve, whip the cream until firm and fold into the pudding. Fold in the peaches and Amaretto, and serve immediately.

Peaches and Raspberries in Amaretto

One of my earliest kitchen jobs was to work the all-important salad and dessert station at the wildly busy Garden Restaurant in Philadelphia, which had a lovely enclosed garden that was filled to the max every day of the week. At that time, about 1977, there were few, if any, other restaurants where you could eat outside. One of my jobs was to make this delectable, simple dessert to order scooped into large stemmed wine glasses. Make it with late-season freestone peaches, which are easier to remove from their pit and have gorgeous red streaking that works perfectly with the equally striking red raspberries.

SERVES 6

$^1/_4$ cup Amaretto

2 tablespoons granulated sugar

Juice of 1 lemon

6 large firm but ripe peaches

$^1/_2$ pint raspberries

1 cup heavy cream, chilled

$^1/_4$ cup confectioners' sugar

6 sprigs mint (optional), for garnish

Mix together the Amaretto, sugar, and lemon juice. Using a sharp knife, slice the peaches into thin slices, pulling them away from the pit. Toss lightly with the Amaretto mixture.

Layer the peaches with their juices alternating with the raspberries in tall parfait glasses or large wine glasses.

Meanwhile, beat the cream until soft and fluffy. Sprinkle in the confectioners' sugar and continue beating until firm, but not stiff. Spoon over the fruit, garnish with mint sprigs, and serve immediately.

623

OATMEAL & BARLEY

OATMEAL & BARLEY

The children's song that begins "watch our oats and barley grow" is a reminder of the importance of these two rather neglected grains of northern latitudes that deserve a closer look. Both have a nutty quality when baked and a creamy quality when cooked. Both have the additional benefit of thickening a soup without turning to mush. For this reason, I add cooked barley to my vegetable soups, especially minestrone. Both oatmeal and barley can also be cooked risotto style for a change of pace.

Because both oats and barley contain little gluten (the stretchiness that forms into bubbles filled with fermented gasses that produces lighter wheat bread), breads made from them are coarse and dense. In Europe, barley is added to soups and stews, made into porridges, and of course, alcoholic drinks, such as beer and Scotland's famed *usquebaugh* (whisky). The *praximades* of Greece are an ancient barley cake that are still made today.

Oats, *Avena sativa*, are grains that grow well in moist, cool climates, and thrive in conditions in which even barley won't grow, such as Scotland, Wales, and Ireland. Wild oats (just like those proverbially sown by the young) drop off their heads and scatter as soon as they ripen, so they spread easily but are difficult to harvest. Cultivated oats keep their heads much longer. Oats have been eaten by humans as far back as 400 BCE, while barley has been a part of our diet for much longer.

Oats and barley were cultivated in classical time by Greeks and Romans, who regarded them as coarse fare, fit only for their animals. However, the Romans did cultivate oats in Great Britain, where they became hugely important in Scotland. There seems to be an affinity between oats and people of Celtic origin; Irish steel-cut oats are famed. Elsewhere in Europe they are less important. Oats did well in the New World thanks to Scottish immigrants who planted them in Massachusetts in 1602.

In Scotland, where oatmeal is a staple, it is ground into a coarse powder. Various grades are available, depending on the thoroughness of the grinding, including coarse, pin(head), and fine. It is commonly held that the large success in business achieved by the Scots can be accredited to their diet of oats. There, oatmeal is used in baking; to make bannocks or oatcakes; to stuff poultry; as a coating for Caboc cheese; as the main ingredient of the Scottish *skirlie*, or mealie pudding (related to the Pennsylvania Dutch scrapple).

The steel-cut oats from Ireland found in American specialty stores first have their hulls removed, leaving the oat groat. The groats then pass through a cutting machine where rotating steel discs cut each groat into about four small angular pieces called pinhead or steel-cut oats. While they take much longer to cook than the familiar American quick-cooking oats, steel-cut oats have a distinct nutty flavor and firm texture.

Quaker Oats, officially formed over one hundred years ago, but with much older roots, is the United States' leading maker of oatmeal. Oats are among the most nutritious of cereals, containing about sixteen percent protein. After reports found that oats can help lower cholesterol, an "oat bran craze" swept the U.S. in the late 1980s. The fad was short-lived and faded by the early 1990s. The popularity of oats again increased after the FDA (Food and Drug Administration) ruled in 1997 that foods high in oats can carry a label that it may reduce the risk of heart disease when combined with a low-fat diet. Oats have long been a staple of many athletes' diets, especially those of weight trainers, because of their high level of complex carbohydrates and fiber, which encourage slow digestion.

In America, oats are mainly eaten as a hot breakfast cereal, and are frequently found in granola bars and streusel toppings for bar cookies. Oats are also used in breads, muffins, and cookie mixes because they have moisture-retention properties that help keep baked goods fresh longer. Oat flour goes into baby cereals and facial cleansers.

Barley, *Hordeum vulgare*, is the oldest cultivated cereal in the Middle East and Europe and may predate the cultivation of rice, dating back as far as 6000 BCE. It was once the staple grain of the ancient world and was one of the seven biblical fruits mentioned in the Old Testament. In biblical times, barley was the poor-man's staple, eaten as porridge and barley cakes, and fed to cattle and other livestock.

Barley reached Spain about 5000 BCE and from there, spread north into France and Germany. It did not reach Great Britain until about 500 BCE. Eastward, barley reached India about 3000 BCE and China around 2000 BCE. Today, its primary use is for animal fodder. It is also used for malting (sprouting) to make beer, barley syrup, barley sugar, and such, and as a grain. One of its most important uses in Scotland is as malted barley, which is distilled into Scotland's renowned whisky.

PAXIMADI

The cuisine of the Byzantine Empire formed a bridge between the foods of the ancient world and those of modern Greece and Turkey. In 470, when the future emperor Justin II walked from his Dalmatian homeland to the capital of Byzantium, Constantinople, as a penniless young man, he had nothing but army barley biscuits called *paximadion* to keep him alive. A classical Roman invention, these biscuits have many modern descendants including the Arabic *bashmat*, the Turkish *beksemad*, the Serbo-Croat *peksimet*, the Romanian *pesmet*, and the modern Greek *paximadi*. Today, these crunchy barley rusks accompany the wonderful Greek yogurt, so rich that the top layer consists of creamy yellow cream, and its equally superb herb-scented honey in a traditional Greek breakfast that I enjoyed every morning while traveling in Greece.

FLAVORING HOT OATMEAL CEREAL

Add any of the following to hot oatmeal cereal: salt, sugar, brown sugar, honey, maple syrup, butter, milk or cream, toasted almond slices, diced apples, raisins, dried cherries, dates, dried currants, chopped candied ginger, and cinnamon.

Oats in Samuel Johnson's Dictionary

In the famed English dictionary written in 1755, Samuel Johnson defined oats as, "A grain, which in England is generally given to horses, but in Scotland supports the people." His biographer, James Boswell, is said to have retorted: "Which is why England is known for its horses and Scotland for its men."

BELILA

Claudia Roden tells us in her *Book of Jewish Food*, that at one time in Syria, cooked young green wheat (called *freek*) and barley soaked in sweet syrup were sold on the street. People would buy it and decorate it with nuts, dried fruits, tiny edible silver balls, and flavor it with orange blossom water. Called *belila*, this was the traditional offering to friends and neighbors who stopped in to help celebrate a happy event, such as a baby cutting her first teeth. To further mark the occasion, the sweet pudding would be served in a silver bowl.

MAKING SCOTCH WHISKY

Scotch malt whisky (its proper spelling in Scotland) derives from *usquebaugh*, a term of Celtic origin meaning *water of life*, like Scandinavian *aquavit*, and is made from just barley and water. Grain whiskies are usually blends and are partly distilled from wheat.

To make whisky, barley is first malted to convert its starches into sugar by soaking until it sprouts. It is then dried in a kiln traditionally heated by peat (partially decayed vegetable matter that forms in wetlands called bogs, moors, or fens), giving it its smoky character. The milled malted barley is then mixed with hot water and fed into the mash tun, where revolving paddles stir the mixture for several hours, dissolving the sugars. The liquid, called the *wort*, is drawn off, and the process repeated twice more, increasing the temperature each time. After cooling, the wort is passed into large vessels called *wash backs*, traditionally made from wood. There, yeast is added and fermentation begins, converting the sugars into alcohol. After two days, the liquid has a low strength of alcohol similar to beer and is now called *wash*.

Malt whisky is usually distilled twice in copper-pot stills. The first one is called the *wash still* and the second, the *spirit still*. The stills are heated, and as the steam rises up and passes over the neck of the still, it condenses. The collected liquid is then transferred to the second still, where the same process is repeated. The new-made whisky is then filled into oak casks and, by law, left to mature for three years, during which time, the compounds present in the wood help flavor the whisky. Each year, the whisky loses two percent of its volume due to evaporation. This is called the *Angels' Share*.

Winter Minestrone Soup with Barley

There are probably as many ways of making minestrone as there are cooks in Italy. A minestra in Italian is a simple soup with only a few ingredients; a minestrone is a large-size complex minestra with lots of ingredients. This wintertime version includes white beans, pancetta (salt and pepper-cured bacon), curly Savoy cabbage, and barley for thickening. Barley freezes quite well, unlike the potatoes or pasta often included in minestrone, so make extra and freeze for another time. Like the Simon and Garfunkel song, this soup is flavored with parsley, sage, rosemary, and thyme, mixed with the pancetta and aromatic vegetables to make what is called a battuto, the seasoning mixture that is the base of the soup. Canned beans work quite well here; include their liquid, which is full of soluble fiber.

SERVES 8 TO 10

1 cup pearl barley

¼ pound pancetta, frozen until firm and cut into small cubes

2 carrots, roughly chopped

2 ribs celery, roughly chopped

1 fennel bulb, roughly chopped

1 tablespoon roughly chopped garlic

1 tablespoon each: chopped sage, rosemary, and thyme

½ cup extra-virgin olive oil

1 red onion, diced

1 (28-ounce) can diced tomatoes

1 small Savoy cabbage, cored and shredded

3 cups (two 16-ounce cans) cooked cannellini beans

Kosher salt and freshly ground black pepper to taste

½ cup chopped Italian parsley

¼ pound shredded aged Pecorino Toscano (aged sheep's milk cheese)

Bring 1 quart of salted water to the boil, add the barley, cover, and cook over low heat for 30 minutes until half-cooked. Drain and reserve.

Chop together (either by hand or using the food processor) the cubed pancetta, carrots, celery, fennel, garlic, sage, rosemary, and thyme to form a chunky paste. Place the mixture in a large, heavy Dutch oven and add the olive oil and onion. Cook over medium heat for several minutes, or until the aromas are released. Stir in the tomatoes, cabbage, the half-cooked barley, and the beans with their liquid. Bring to a boil, stirring occasionally, then season with salt and pepper. Simmer for 20 minutes or until the barley is tender. The soup can be cooled, covered, and refrigerated for up to 2 days at this point before serving.

When ready to serve the soup, bring it back to a boil, sprinkle with parsley, and serve immediately accompanied by a bowl of the cheese.

629

SCOTCH BROTH

Scotch broth, a term that dates back to at least the early eighteenth century, is also known as "the porridge of the evening." This hearty soup is made by boiling mutton and barley and then adding root vegetables like carrots, rutabagas, turnips, parsnips, onions, and leeks, with parsley and leek greens stirred in just before serving.

Mushroom–Barley Soup

A Jewish deli staple, mushroom barley soup can also be found in Polish restaurants. This hearty soup gets its flavor from beef stock (homemade is best, see page 990 for a recipe). Although beef stock is more expensive to make than chicken stock, it is needed here for the robust flavor it lends to this soup. Barley comes in different sizes: small, medium, and large pearl. Medium pearl is the most useful size, small takes less time, and large must be cooked longer. Any of them will work here. Garnish the soup with a dollop of sour cream, if desired.

SERVES 10

2 quarts beef stock, purchased or homemade (*see* page 990)

1/2 pound medium pearl barley

1 onion, diced

1 bunch leeks, quartered lengthwise, then diced crosswise to make small squares, and washed well

1 tablespoon chopped garlic

2 tablespoons chopped savory (and/or thyme, marjoram, or sage)

1/4 cup canola oil

1/2 pound each: button mushrooms and crimini (or baby bella) mushrooms, trimmed and sliced

1/2 pound shiitake mushrooms, caps only, sliced

Kosher salt and freshly ground black pepper to taste

Bring the beef stock and barley to the boil and simmer 45 minutes, or until barley is tender.

   Meanwhile, sauté the onion, leeks, garlic, and savory until transparent in the oil, about 5 minutes, then add the mushrooms and cook until softened. Add the vegetables to the barley-stock mix and bring to the boil, season with salt and pepper and remove from the heat. Serve immediately.

Oatmeal Meatloaf

I have served this meatloaf in many a restaurant, where its full-bodied flavor and moist texture made it a real winner. Oatmeal is the secret ingredient, making it light and nutty. Add your favorite kind of barbecue sauce here, purchased or homemade. Worcestershire and soy sauce make it dark and savory, while ground pork gives it a more rounded flavor. You may substitute ground dark meat turkey with good results. Because I have herbs growing in the herb garden that fronts my kitchen window, I tend to use a big variety of them. While four herbs are used here, you may substitute parsley plus one of those listed to make it easier. Dried herbs are a reasonable but just adequate substitute. A final coating of barbecue sauce makes a shiny, spicy glaze.

SERVES 8 TO 10

2 teaspoons chopped garlic

2 ribs celery, roughly chopped

2 carrots, roughly chopped

1 onion, peeled and quartered

1/2 pound white mushrooms

2 tablespoons bacon fat, or canola oil

2 pounds ground beef

1/2 pound ground pork

1 cup oatmeal

1/2 cup + 1/2 cup barbecue sauce

2 eggs

2 tablespoons Worcestershire sauce

2 tablespoons soy sauce

2 tablespoons each: chopped Italian parsley, marjoram, sage, and thyme

Kosher salt and freshly ground black pepper to taste

Chop all the vegetables to small bits in a food processor or by hand. Sauté the vegetables in the bacon fat until softened, about 5 minutes. Remove from the pan and cool to room temperature.

Beat together by hand, or in a mixer using the paddle attachment, the ground beef and pork, the vegetables, oatmeal, 1/2 cup of barbecue sauce, eggs, Worcestershire, soy sauce, herbs, and salt and pepper. Sauté a small spoonful of the mixture and taste for seasoning (it's not a good idea to eat anything with raw pork).

Preheat the oven to 375°F. Using your hands, form the mixture into a large meatloaf, shaping as evenly as possible on a nonstick-sprayed baking pan. Bake 45 minutes, then brush with the remaining 1/2 cup of barbecue sauce and bake again for about 15 minutes, or until well-browned and cooked through, measuring 150°F. on a meat thermometer. Remove from the oven and cool about 10 minutes so the loaf will set. Slice and then serve.

Toasted Grain, Fruit, and Nut Granola

I am a member of the "crunchy generation" who, for many years, wore Earth shoes and Clark's desert boots in my quest to be "unisex" and to be taken seriously for the male jobs I sought. I was a mail carrier for one summer, the only female on the job, and later went to work in restaurants where I was often the only woman, including my most recent chef position only a few years ago. For long years, I wore no make-up lest I be thought frivolous. While I'm perfectly happy these days to dress up in heels and mascara, I still admire the ideals of those years and love to make foods like this homemade granola, an archetypical dish of

the era. Visit a natural foods store, now mainstream rather than fringe, as they were in the sixties and seventies, to buy the ingredients. If you've never tasted homemade granola, this delicious recipe, crunchy of course, and full of cinnamon and orange zest, will be a revelation. Although I'm in favor of all-natural ingredients, I still buy my yellow-colored dried fruit like golden raisins and apricots treated with sulfites to keep their attractive color.

MAKES 2 QUARTS

1 cup light brown sugar, packed

1 cup canola oil

2 tablespoons cinnamon

2 tablespoons vanilla extract

Grated zest of 1 orange or tangerine

1 teaspoon kosher salt

1 1/2 cups unsweetened coconut flakes, called dessicated coconut

1 1/2 cups natural sliced almonds

6 cups old-fashioned rolled oats

1 1/2 cups wheat germ

1/2 cup of each of 4 kinds of dried fruit, 2 cups total: diced dried papaya, golden raisins, diced dried pineapple, dried cherries, cut-up California apricots, dried blueberries, or dried strawberries

Preheat the oven to 350°F. In a medium, heavy-bottomed nonreactive saucepan, combine the brown sugar, oil, cinnamon, vanilla, orange zest, and salt and cook until the sugar is dissolved, stirring constantly.

Mix together the coconut, almonds, oats, and wheat germ in a large bowl. Scrape the brown sugar mixture into the bowl and toss well and vigorously, so the syrup coats everything well. Spread the mixture out in a single layer on 1 or 2 large

631

metal baking pans and bake 15 to 20 minutes, or until the mixture is well-browned, stirring once or twice. Remove from the oven and cool to room temperature. Break up large chunks by hand, stir in the dried fruits, and store in an airtight container at room temperature up to 2 weeks.

Oatmeal Crispies

Oatmeal makes these cookies crisp and nutty; molasses makes them moist with a deep, dark, rounded flavor. Chopped dates, walnuts, and golden raisins make them sweet and chewy. Altogether a wonderful cookie recipe that freezes well either as batter or as finished cookies. These cookies would be perfect to take along on one of those long airplane flights where they serve only a tiny packet with about ten small pretzels. If you don't have molasses, substitute dark corn syrup, maple syrup, or honey. (See sidebar at right for more about molasses.) These chunky, filling cookies are best made in cold weather when the humidity is low, so they will stay crisp.

MAKES 6 TO 8 DOZEN

10 ounces (2^1/$_2$ cups) all-purpose flour

2 teaspoons baking soda

1 teaspoon each: cinnamon and allspice

2 teaspoons kosher salt

3 cups rolled oats

1 pound (4 sticks) unsalted butter

3 cups granulated sugar

^{1}/$_2$ cup molasses, not blackstrap

1 tablespoon vanilla extract

4 eggs

1^1/$_2$ cups golden raisins

2 cups chopped walnuts

1 cup chopped dates

Preheat the oven to 350°F. Whisk together the flour, baking soda, cinnamon, allspice, and salt. Stir in the oats and reserve.

Cream the butter and sugar together until the mixture is light and fluffy. Beat in the molasses and vanilla, and then beat in the eggs, one at a time. Spoon in the flour mixture, beating until barely mixed. Stir in the raisins, walnuts, and dates by hand so as not to toughen the dough.

Drop by scant tablespoons onto parchment-paper- or Silpat-lined baking sheets, at least 2 inches apart because they will spread. Bake 12 minutes, or until the edges brown, turning the trays around halfway through to ensure even baking.

Cool thoroughly before storing in a tin for up to 1 week, or freeze.

MOLASSES

To make sugar, the raw juice pressed from sugar cane is separated into brown liquid molasses and sugar crystals by boiling up to three times. The highest grade of molasses is made from clarified, reduced, and blended sugarcane juice without any sugar extracted. This is the kind called for here and found in supermarkets (but not natural foods stores) under the brand name Grandma's Molasses. Bitter-tasting blackstrap molasses is obtained from the last boiling and contains the least sugar and the most vitamins, minerals, and trace elements, but is too strong for most kitchen use. (Brown sugar is simply white sugar mixed with molasses, with smaller amounts mixed in for light brown sugar, larger amounts for dark brown sugar.)

OLIVES & OLIVE OIL

OLIVES & OLIVE OIL

Whether green, light violet, gold, purple, red, brown, or black, whether brine-cured, oil-cured, salt-cured, lye-cured, or water-cured, olives are intense, powerful, and addictive. Long a symbol of peace, the olive branch brings us a marvelous, healthy fruit that must be carefully treated to make it not only edible, but also appetizing and delicious.

The use of the ancient and revered olive tree, *Olea europaea*, for eating and extracting its rich oil dates far back into history. The olive and its oil are mentioned numerous times in the Bible. The land of Israel is described in the Old Testament book of Deuteronomy as, "A land of wheat, and barley, and vines; of fig trees and pomegranates; a land of olive oil and honey." The olive appeared in Egyptian records almost 4,000 years ago, and was well known throughout the ancient Mediterranean world. The word *olive* derives from the Latin *olivea*, and first appeared in English around 1200 CE. The Hebrew word is *zayit*, cognate to the Arabic word, *zeytun*.

King Solomon paid with olive oil for the cedar wood used for the building of the first temple. The Maccabees used olive oil to light their way for eight days, later commemorated in the Jewish holiday of Chanukah. Olives, together with bread, dry cheese, and vinegar, were mainstays in the diets of the poor shepherds and field hands,

then and even now. Olive oil was and still is used to cook, to light lamps, and as soap and skin conditioner. For the poor peasant, cured and sun-dried olives were a gift from heaven. They are nutritious, relatively high in fat, and rich in minerals, and their pungent, salty flavor helps to season an otherwise monotonous diet of bread and grains.

The average life expectancy of an olive tree is 300 to 600 years, but when I traveled in Israel about thirty years ago, I was taken to see an olive tree said to be 1,000 years old. Gnarled, many-branched, and long-living olive trees cover the hillsides of the Mediterranean region. The tree's narrow leaves, gray-green on the surface and silver underneath, flutter and turn with the breeze, so both colors show at once. An olive branch is a longtime symbol of peace, and its distinctive, densely whorled grain wood is perfect for making tools of peacetime: spoons, cutting boards, and other kitchen tools.

I can remember, years ago, when the small, ridged, and cone-shaped glass jars of Progresso olive oil were the only choice of oil available at our local supermarket. We'd have to go to the local barrel-filled Greek grocery for more choices. Today, however, olive oil has become more popular because of the health benefits. Warehouse club shelves carry large, reasonably priced, three-liter containers of extra-virgin, virgin, and light olive oil,

634

while supermarkets have an even bigger selection.

The olive is native to the Mediterranean region and, still today, the largest producers are Italy and Spain, where olives are a mainstay, often served as a bite-sized snack with wine or other drinks. Olive trees were introduced to California about 1769 by the Spaniards, where they flourished. California now provides almost 200,000 tons of commercial olive crops per year, mostly as dyed black unripe olives, for clean pitting and canning.

In the ancient method used to make extra-virgin olive oil, ripe olives are crushed between heavy stone disks to extract their oil. As in winemaking, virgin olive oils are affected by the soil and climate where they are grown, as well as the variety of olive. Virgin oils are cold-pressed, crushed without heat to preserve all the fruity flavor of the olives. To squeeze out more oil after the first (or virgin) cold-pressing, the olives are heated. This type of oil must then be refined to eliminate any undesirable flavors.

Extra-virgin olive oil has to have less then one percent acidity, while virgin may have up to three percent. Many popular supermarket brands are blends of refined oil mixed with a little virgin oil for flavor. "Light" olive oils, unfortunately, have no fewer calories than other oils (about 120 per tablespoon); they are simply more highly filtered, so their flavor is lighter. This kind of oil is appropriate when you want a more neutral oil. The filtration process also gives it a higher smoke point than regular olive oil so it can be used for high-heat frying, whereas regular olive oil is better suited for low- to medium-heat cooking, and for use in uncooked foods, such as salad dressings and marinades.

For frying, the International Olive Oil Institute recommends what is now labeled simply *olive oil*. Once called *pure olive oil*, this is a combination of refined olive oil and virgin or extra-virgin oil. The flavor of extra-virgin olive oil tends to break down at frying temperatures, making the added expense for this oil a waste. I prefer to mix my highly flavored extra-virgin olive oil with a more neutral oil when frying.

Like vintage wines, virgin oils vary greatly by year or region, while blended oils always taste the same. You may prefer milder blended oil to stronger-tasting cold-pressed oil. It's simply a matter of taste. Color is a clue to flavor: yellow oils are mild, green oils are stronger. Because I love bold flavors, I use stronger, deeper green extra-virgin oils.

What makes those beautiful bottles of olive oil sold in gourmet stores so expensive? These artisanally produced oils are carefully extracted in small batches and are often unfiltered. Filtering is done to prevent spoilage and removes any small particles from the oil. Unfiltered olive oil can be made only from perfect, blemish-free fruits. Buy fine olive oils in small bottles and experiment to find the ones you like best. Save these to be sprinkled on foods at the last minute.

STORING OLIVE OIL

Olive oil should be stored in a cool, dark place for up to six months and always kept out of the light. It can be refrigerated, in which case it will last up to a year. Chilled olive oil solidifies and is too thick to pour. However, when brought to room temperature, the oil will clear and become liquid again.

635

Cooking with Olive Oil

Don't use fine extra-virgin oils for cooking, since subtleties of flavor are destroyed by heat. Refined olive oil, simply labeled as "olive oil", is best for frying, because it can reach high temperatures without burning.

Drizzle "a hair" of best-quality extra-virgin olive oil over pasta, cooked vegetables, and hearty vegetable and bean soups just before serving, so that the subtle aromatic qualities are released by the heat without being destroyed by cooking.

When grilling or sautéing, use a pastry brush to spread oil evenly and sparingly.

Perk up grilled fish or chicken with a simple sauce from Sicily called *Salmoriglio*: Chop plenty of parsley and oregano, mix with fresh lemon juice and virgin olive oil, and serve.

Instead of using butter, sprinkle olive oil on bread, adding fresh herbs for extra flavor.

CHANUKAH AND OLIVE OIL

After 500 years of servitude to the Greeks, the Jews finally regained their freedom and the use of their holy Temple. Jewish law required that they purify the temple with oil, but they only had a meager amount left. Miraculously, this small amount burned for the eight consecutive nights required by Jewish law to perform the purification ceremony. The eight day holiday of Chanukah, "the festival of lights," commemorates this joyful event. Olive oil is symbolic of the Jewish people. Do you know how you get the finest oil from an olive? You've got to press it really hard, with perseverance.

A VISIT TO PIETRO CORICELLI, AN UMBRIAN OLIVE OIL PRODUCER

A morning spent at the family-owned olive oil production company in Spoleto, Italy, taught me how exacting is the process by which fine-quality oils are produced, whether on a large scale, as here, or by smaller artisanal producers. Every step of the process is carefully monitored by a combination of scientific instruments and the all-important human palate. I participated in a formal olive-oil tasting but was told that official tasters can be no more than forty years of age, so their palates are fresh (I'm no longer eligible). The company was founded by Signore Pietro Coricelli sixty years ago. Today, his son, also Pietro Coricelli, and his three grandchildren, including Pietro the third, and the youngest, Chiara Coricelli, work together to maintain the family's high standards in a modern environment.

The company produces six main types of oil including a DOP (*denominazione di origine protetta*, protected place of origin) using only local Umbrian olives, an organic oil (called *biologico* in Italy), a nonfiltered olive oil with all the complex flavors of the fruit, and a refined pure olive oil best for cooking and making the lightest fried foods you've ever tasted. They also produce small quantities of the unfiltered Novello oil, made from just-picked olives and sold only from November until December 20, just after the late fall harvest. Fine oils like this one are best used as a condiment, drizzled on soups, fish, meats, and vegetables just before serving.

Note that the "burning" sensation at the back of the throat produced by some olive oils is a sign that they are full of beneficial antioxidants. For more about their oils, go to www.corcicelli.com.

636

Table Olive Varieties

Alphonso: This large Chilean olive is cured in a wine or wine vinegar solution, which gives it a beautiful dark purple color and tart flavor. Its flesh is very tender and slightly bitter.

Amfissa: A mottled light to deep brownish-black, medium-sized ripened olive from the Amfissa valley in Greece. It is large and plump with mild flavor, rather soft flesh, and tough skin.

Arbequina: A small, marble-sized, greenish brown, smoky-tasting Spanish olive from the province of Catalonia. It is the classic oil olive of the region. Prepared as a table olive, it has an intense, herby, floral flavor and is often found with its stem still attached.

Bella di Cerignola: These red, black, and green large, firm olives hail from the southern Adriatic coast in the region of Puglia, Italy. They are the largest olives commonly found and are packed in salted brine. The red olives are colored using natural ingredients in a special process. Their mild flavor and meaty flesh make them excellent table olives and they are well suited to marinating.

Gaeta: A black olive from the region of Lazio, south of Rome. It may be found dry-salt cured and then rubbed with oil, in which case it will be shiny black in color and wrinkled in appearance, with mild flavor and often packed with rosemary and other herbs. Gaetas are also found brine-cured, in which case they are smooth and plump with a deep purplish-black color. They are also grown in Morocco.

Kalamata: A very popular Greek olive from the valley of Messina in the Peloponnesus peninsula near the town of Kalamata. They are harvested fully ripe and are deep purple in color, with a pointed tip. The olives are then slit and cured in a red-wine vinegar brine that gives them a rich and fruity flavor and soft texture. Kalamatas are easy to pit and may also be found pitted. Over-ripe Kalamatas can be mushy. Hand-picked Kalamatas will be of higher quality.

637

Liguria: An Italian black olive from the province of Liguria, whose capital is Genoa. It is salt-brine cured, with a lively flavor, and is sometimes packed with its stem.

Manzanilla: This Spanish green olive is commonly found in jars in the supermarket and is available unpitted and/or stuffed with anything from pimentos to garlic and anchovies. It is lightly lye-cured then packed in a salt and lactic acid brine.

Nafphlion: A medium-sized dark green to brown olive from the valley of Argos in the Peloponnesus peninsula of Greece that is cracked to allow brine to penetrate. It has a strong smell, meaty, crisp texture and spicy, tart flavor.

Niçoise: A petite French black olive from the region of Provence near the city of Nice. It is harvested fully ripe and has a nutty, mellow flavor and a high pit-to-meat ratio. It is often packed with herbs and its stems intact.

Nyons: These Provençal olives are dry-cured, then aged in brine. They are small, plump, and wrinkled, with large, smooth pits. Authentic Nyons olives are matte rather than shiny and have a rich, fruity, full-bodied flavor.

Oil-Cured Olives: These shiny, wrinkly olives may come from Sicily or Morocco. They are full-ripened, salt-cured, and inky-black in color. Their flavor is strong and pungent, with an oily finish. Because they are ripe and soft, they are easily pitted.

Picholine: These torpedo-shaped Provençal French green olives are brine-cured and have a subtle, lightly salty flavor. Those from Provence are usually marinated with coriander and herbes de Provence; for the American market, they are preserved with citric acid.

Ponentine: An Italian black olive that is salt-brined, cured, then packed in vinegar. It is mild in flavor.

Sevillano: These green California salt-brine cured olives are preserved with lactic acid. They have a very crisp texture.

Souri: The souri, which means *Syrian*, is a small, light purplish-brown colored Middle Eastern variety from Israel. It is brine-cured and has a firm, textured meat with delicate flavor.

638

Tomatoes Provençale
with Black Olives

This dish is well-known for a good reason. It's delicious, easy to make with easy to find ingredients, and it complements many other foods, including broiled steaks and fish. But, the breadcrumbs must have some body and texture. They should preferably be homemade from a French baguette, Italian bread, or sourdough bread. The garlic must be fresh, without sprouts, which would make it bitter. Most of all, the tomatoes must be round, ripe, firm, beefsteak-type tomatoes. An insipid tomato will make an insipid dish. While not traditional, I like to add shiny, wrinkled black Sicilian or Moroccan oil-cured olives for their intense flavor, slightly chewy texture, and dramatic look. Like other Mediterranean baked, stuffed vegetables, these tomatoes taste good hot or at room temperature.

SERVES 4 TO 6

1 cup homemade-style breadcrumbs

¼ cup pitted and chopped oil-cured black olives

¼ cup extra-virgin olive oil

2 tablespoons chopped garlic

1 tablespoon chopped fresh thyme, or 1 teaspoon dried thyme

¼ cup chopped Italian parsley

2 pounds ripe beefsteak tomatoes, cut in half through the middle, seeds removed

Preheat the oven to 400°F. Combine the breadcrumbs, olives, olive oil, garlic, thyme, and parsley. Fill the tomatoes with the crumb mixture, pressing into seed pockets and sprinkling evenly over top. Arrange on a lightly oiled metal baking pan just large enough to hold the tomatoes and bake 20 minutes, or until crumbs have browned and tomatoes are bubbling hot inside, Serve immediately, or serve at room temperature.

Trenette con Salsa Cruda

If I had to choose only one tomato dish, this would be it (although it would be a hard choice indeed). There is nothing like the flavor of warmed, rather than cooked tomatoes, marinated with olive oil, garlic, and basil. For a really eye-catching dish, make it in summer when farmers' markets have opal (purple) basil and golden tomatoes, or other colors of heirloom tomatoes. And, please don't refrigerate your tomatoes. The best pasta to use here is fresh thinly cut trenette (like fine linguine), because the fresh egg pasta will absorb the excess juices; next best is dried cappellini pasta. Just make sure not to overcook it, which can happen very quickly. It should be firm and still yellow when you drain it. For a real treat, splurge here on Mozzarella di Bufala (see page 583 for more information).

SERVES 4

1 cup basil leaves

1 cup opal (purple) basil leaves, if available (substitute green if unavailable)

1 pound fresh mozzarella cheese

2 pounds very ripe red beefsteak tomatoes, seeded and cut into small dice

2 pounds ripe yellow or orange tomatoes, seeded and cut into small dice (substitute red if unavailable)

639

1 red onion, cut into small dice

1 tablespoon chopped fresh garlic

$1/2$ cup extra-virgin olive oil

Kosher salt and freshly ground black pepper to taste

$1^1/_2$ pounds fresh egg Trenette pasta or 1 pound dried cappellini

Gently wash the basil leaves and roll them up in paper towels to dry. Roll the leaves up like a cigar, one inside the other. Then slice crosswise, using a sharp knife, into thin shreds. Cut the mozzarella cheese into small cubes and reserve.

To make the Salsa Cruda, combine diced tomatoes, onion, garlic, olive oil, basil, and salt and pepper in a large bowl. Marinate at room temperature for 1 hour, then drain off the excess liquid (discard or save to add to tomato sauce or soup).

Bring a large pot of salted water to the boil. When ready to serve, heat the Salsa Cruda until hot to the touch. Cook the pasta and drain.

Combine the cooked pasta, half the sauce, and half the mozzarella cubes. Place on hot plates. Make a "nest" in the middle, garnish with the remaining sauce and cheese cubes, and serve immediately.

STORING OLIVES

Unopened jarred olives can be stored at room temperature up to two years. Opened olives should be refrigerated in their own liquid in a non-metal container and will last up one to two months before starting to get mushy.

Spiced Seville Olives

I adapted the recipe for these pungent, herb-flavored olives from a recipe of Penelope Casas, the renowned writer about Spanish food. I've been making it for years, especially to serve as tapas with drinks. I first started to serve tapas at the Mediterranean bistro, A'propos, in the late 1980s. It's only in the last couple of years that tapas like this one have finally started to take off. Either the large green whole Spanish queen olives (not pitted) or the large, mild Cerignola olives work well here. The only hard part is breaking the olives so that their inner flesh is exposed and will absorb the marinade. Allow at least three to four days for the olives to marinate before serving. They will keep perfectly for at least two months, refrigerated. Serve with a glass of dry Sherry and some toasted Spanish Marcona almonds.

SERVES 8 TO 12 AS TAPAS

2 pounds large green olives with pits

1 teaspoon ground cumin

1 teaspoon dried oregano

1 tablespoon chopped fresh rosemary

1 tablespoon chopped fresh thyme

4 crushed bay leaves

1 tablespoon whole fennel seed

4 garlic cloves, thinly sliced

$1/2$ cup red wine vinegar

1 (2-ounce) can anchovy fillets in olive oil, well-drained

Drain the olives, discarding the liquid. Then, using a heavy cleaver or meat pounder, lightly crush the olives so that the skin breaks open. Combine remaining ingredients and toss in a bowl with the cracked olives.

Place olives and marinade back into the olive jar and add enough cold water to cover. Cover tightly, and refrigerate to marinate at least 3 to 4 days.

New Orleans Olive Salad

The city of New Orleans has an incredible culinary heritage, which I only hope will survive the devastations of Hurricane Katrina. While attending a culinary conference there about ten years ago, I realized after a couple of days that I had only seen the inside of the hotel ballroom, so I gave myself permission to play hooky for the day and wandered throughout the marvelous French quarter. On the day of my flight back, I knew I couldn't leave without sampling the famous muffaletta sandwich. So, on the way to the airport, I stopped at the Central Grocery and had them wrap up a large rounded bread stuffed with this olive salad, sliced Italian meats, and cheeses. By the time I arrived in Philadelphia, the entire airplane was filled with the pungent aromas of cured meats, sharp cheese, garlic, herbs, and vinegar, but my family sure enjoyed our New Orleans take-out treat.

MAKES ABOUT 1 QUART

2 pounds mixed olives (Kalamata, green, black oil-cured, Gaeta, Alphonso)

$1/4$ cup extra-virgin olive oil

$1/4$ cup red wine vinegar

1 tablespoon chopped garlic

$1/2$ head celery, diced

1 fennel bulb, diced

$1/2$ cup chopped Italian parsley

2 tablespoons chopped marjoram

$1/2$ teaspoon freshly ground black pepper

Pit the olives as necessary and then chop into large bits. Make the dressing in the jar of a blender by combining the olive oil, vinegar, and garlic and pureeing until well-combined. Remove the dressing from the blender jar and mix together with the olives, celery, fennel, parsley, marjoram, and pepper. Store in the refrigerator for up to 1 month.

Olivada

Called either pesto, which just means "paste," or olivada in Italy, or in a somewhat different version, tapenade in the south of France, this pungent, fragrant spread is so versatile. Spread it on toasted crostini, use it as a sandwich spread, dot it onto a salad or grilled fish, serve as a dip for vegetable crudités, or drizzle it over sliced tomatoes and fresh mozzarella. I use a combination of salty, oil-cured olives and tangy, wine-vinegar-packed Kalamata olives here. They can both be found already pitted at Trader Joe's stores and elsewhere. The spread is easy to make; everything is just processed together. However, I've invariably found at least one stubborn pit in every batch, so check the olives to make sure one hasn't inadvertently been left. (Of course, I make batches about twelve times the size of this one, so it was more likely that one olive would be left unpitted.) The olivada keeps quite well in the refrigerator. Just allow it to come to room temperature before serving.

641

1 cup pitted Kalamata olives

1 cup pitted oil-cured black olives

2 teaspoons ground fennel seed

Juice and grated zest of 1 orange

$^1/_4$ cup lemon juice

$^1/_4$ cup extra-virgin olive oil

Freshly ground black pepper (no salt)

Combine all the ingredients in the bowl of a food processor and process to a chunky paste. Serve as desired, or refrigerate until needed.

642

Chicken Rivierasca

Rivierasca *means "Riviera style" in Italian. Though the French Riviera is better known, there is a stretch of Italian Riviera in the province of Liguria stretching from Monaco to Genoa called the* Riviera del Ponente. *Below Genoa, it is called the* Riviera del Levante. *While not strictly traditional, this chicken sauté combines many typical flavors of the region, including basil, orange zest, olives, tomatoes, and garlic. Chicken breasts cooked on the bone will be juicier, though boneless, skinless breasts may be substituted. There are so many delicious little tomatoes found now in farmers' markets and some supermarkets. Use anything from currant, to grape, to cherry, to mini-pear tomatoes here, but be sure to halve them. Whole cherry tomatoes are difficult to spear at the table, and they may explode with steamy juice. Serve with steamed rice.*

1 cup fresh basil

4 tablespoons olive oil, divided

3 pounds chicken breasts on the bone, skinned, with all visible fat cut away

Kosher salt and freshly ground black pepper

2 ounces ($^1/_2$ cup) all-purpose flour

1 red onion, cut in thin slices

6 to 8 cloves garlic, peeled and thinly sliced

Pinch of ground cloves

$^1/_2$ cup chicken stock

Juice and grated zest of 1 orange

$^1/_4$ cup cured black olives, pitted and halved

1 pint ripe cherry tomatoes, cut in half

Gently wash the basil leaves and roll them up in paper towels to dry. Roll the leaves up like a cigar, one inside the other. Then slice crosswise, using a sharp knife, into thin shreds, and reserve.

Heat 2 tablespoons of the olive oil in a large, heavy skillet (preferably cast-iron for the best browning). Meanwhile, season the chicken with salt and pepper and dust in flour, shaking off any excess. Carefully place each chicken breast in the hot pan and brown well on both sides.

Remove the chicken from the pan and reserve. Drain off the oil. To the same pan, add the remaining 2 tablespoons olive oil along with the red onion, garlic, and cloves. Sauté several minutes until the onions are crisp-tender.

Add chicken stock, orange juice and zest, black olive halves, and reserved chicken to the pan. Bring to the boil and simmer 15 to 20 minutes, or until the juices are syrupy and the chicken nearly cooked. Add the tomatoes, black pepper, and the basil and simmer 10 minutes longer, or until the chicken is fully cooked and the tomatoes have collapsed but haven't disintegrated.

ONIONS

SWEET & STORAGE

ONIONS
SWEET & STORAGE

I totally agree with the late, great Julia Child who said, "It's hard to imagine a civilization without onions." And, Brillat Savarin, the French gastronome and author of the 1825 book, *The Physiology of Taste*, declared, "The onion is the truffle of the poor." No matter where in the world, be it rich or poor, onions are essential to every savory kitchen.

In my days as a television food stylist, I had the pleasure of preparing onion-centric dishes from *Onions, Onions, Onions*, a wonderful cookbook all about onions by Linda and Fred Griffith. Onions are prominent in nearly every cuisine worldwide, where they provide the underlying rounded, sweet-savory flavor to cooked foods and welcome edge of sweet-sharp flavor when raw. While acting as a national spokesperson for the super high-quality Oso Sweet onions from Chile, a winter sweet onion equivalent to summer's Vidalia and Walla-Walla sweets, I learned to love onions even more, especially because Oso Sweets don't even make you cry.

The onion, *Allium cepa*, a member of the lily, or *allium*, family, is one of the oldest-known cultivated vegetables and among the world's most popular, with nearly fifty million tons grown annually. It is a bulb that may be white, golden, or red in color, round, flattened, or elongated in shape, marble- to grapefruit-sized, and sharply pungent to mild when raw and savory to sweet when cooked. By the first century CE, long, round, red, yellow, white, strong, and mild onions were already known.

Onions probably originated in Central Asia although they now grow throughout the world. Indeed, onions have so long been part of humankind's diet that ancient names for the onion in Sanskrit, Hebrew, Greek, and Latin are unrelated, showing that onions have been cultivated independently in far-flung places as far back as prehistoric times. The origin of the name "onion" comes from the Latin, *unio*, meaning union, because the onion grows as a single bulb. In ancient Egypt, the onion symbolized eternity because of its circle-within-a-circle structure.

Onions were planted in Chinese gardens as much as 5,000 years ago, and they are referred to in some of the oldest Indian writings. An ancient Sumerian text, dated to about 2500 BCE, tells of someone plowing over the city governor's onion patch, while the Mesopotamians from the ancient city of Ur left accounts from about 2100 BCE of onions being grown in gardens.

Egyptian leaders took an oath of office with their right hand on an onion. Egyptian onions, said to be large, white, and mild, were adopted by frugal peasants to relieve the monotony of their diet, and were often eaten raw. The Pharaoh Cheops paid for labor on the Great Pyramid in onions, garlic, and parsley. As early as the building of the Pyramids, the onion was a part of the basic rations for sailors because it helped to prevent scurvy during long voyages without fresh foods. Army quartermasters valued it for the same reasons. Egyptian mummies set out for the afterlife with a stock of onions carefully wrapped in bandages, looking like another little mummy.

Upon leaving Egypt, the ancient Hebrews wept for the lack of onions they had become accustomed to eating in that land. In the book of Numbers, the children of Israel lament the meager desert diet enforced by the Exodus: "We remember the fish, which we did eat in Egypt freely, the cucumbers and the melons and the leeks and the onions and the garlic."

The onion was an essential part of the diet of the Phoenicians and Greeks. Before competition at the Greek Olympic Games, athletes would consume pounds of onions, drink onion juice, and rub onions on their bodies. The Romans were passionately fond of onions, which they pickled in honey and vinegar. Roman soldiers carried onions with them on journeys to their colonies in England and Germany. Pliny the Elder, Rome's keen-eyed observer, wrote of Pompeii's onions and cabbages before he was killed during the volcanic eruption in 79 CE. Excavators at Pompeii found gardens where onions had grown: the bulbs had left behind telltale cavities in the ground. The Franks are said to have eaten onions as avidly as they drained tankards of beer.

The onion was introduced by the Spanish into the West Indies and from there, it soon spread to all parts of the Americas. The first Pilgrims brought onions with them on the Mayflower, and onions were eaten at the first Thanksgiving dinner. The colonists planted bulb onions in 1648, as soon as they were able to clear the land. Native Americans used wild onions in a variety of ways, eating them raw or cooked, as a seasoning or as a vegetable, in syrups, as poultices, for dyeing, and even as toys. George Washington enjoyed onions cored, stuffed with mincemeat, and baked like apples. During the Civil War, General Ulysses S. Grant sent an urgent message to the War Department: "I will not move my army without onions." The very next day, three trainloads of onions were on their way to the front. Maybe onions are what kept the American union intact.

SWEET AND STORAGE ONIONS

Onions are of two general categories: summer/fall storage onions and spring/early summer fresh or sweet onions. Fresh onions are yellow, white, and red with varied shapes—flat, top-shaped, and round. These mild, early-maturing onions have thin, light-colored skin and are often used raw. They bruise easily.

Extra-mild sweet onions are by necessity fresh, because they're just too sweet and juicy to keep well, and they get extra tender loving care in handling.

Sweet onions have a crisp, firm texture and mildness that make them perfectly suited to use raw in relishes, marinades, cold soups and salads, or to top sandwiches and burgers. Their ready ability to caramelize adds wonderful deep flavor to recipes from French onion soup to mashed potatoes. And, their firm texture, large size, and high sugar content make them excellent candidates for grilling.

Most sweet onions are hybrids of the Yellow Granex type. Their sugar content may actually be lower than other onions. However, they have a lower content of the pyruvic acid that causes onions to taste "hot" and are exceptionally juicy, with large thick rings and thin inner skins separating the layers. The sweet onion's delicate nature requires that they be harvested by hand, thoroughly dried, and treated gently during grading and packaging.

Storage onions are yellow, white, and red but always round, and are protected by several layers of thick, dark skin. These moderate to strong, full-flavored onions have thicker skins and denser flesh; they're meant to be stored over the long, cold winter. Storage onions are typically much harsher when eaten raw, though they may be the sweetest when cooked.

Onion Types

Picklers, pearls, creamers, standards, and jumbos are simply size names for the same variety of onion, planted differently and picked at different times for size.

Boiling Onions: These are egg-sized onions, perfectly proportioned to cook whole in stews, such as the French *boeuf à la Bourguignon*. They are more common in cold-weather months.

Green Onions: Green onions (also called scallions) are pulled while the tops are still green and before a large bulb has formed.

Pearl Onions: Pearl onions are tiny versions of the same *Allium cepa*. They stay small because they are planted tightly together and picked early. They are as pungent and storable as larger onions. Pearl onions are in season beginning with whites in July and followed by the red and gold pearls. Availability typically continues through March, with greatest availability from September through the holidays.

Spring Onions: Spring onions have formed bulbs but their tops are still green. They are sweet and sharp and must be used quickly.

Onion Varieties

Apaz Onions: Apaz onions are wild onions that resemble pearl onions topped with a green stalk. They are in season in Oregon in June.

Bermuda Onions: Imported from England in 1616, the Bermuda onion was grown from seeds brought from the Spanish and Portuguese islands of Tenerife and Madeira. The Bermuda onion became so famous along the U.S. East Coast that people from Bermuda became known as "Onions." Starting in the 1930s, Bermuda's onion exports declined due to high tariffs, competition from similar onions grown in Texas and elsewhere, and the limited arable land on the island. The Texas sweet onion industry began when the Bermuda onion was introduced into South Texas in 1898.

Cévennes Onion: A highly prized hand-harvested sweet onion grown on steep-terraced hillsides in the mountains of south-central France. The sweet onion of the Cévennes, long admired for its delicious, mild taste, has been awarded an *Appellation d'Origine Controlee* (AOC) from the French government. The delicate and sweet *oignon doux des Cévennes* is medium in size and rounded, with pearly color, shiny skin, and easily peeled thin layers.

Cipolline: Cipolline (meaning *small onions* in Italian— *cipolla* is onion) are distinct, flattened, flying-saucer-shaped onions from Italy, now being grown in the U.S. by specialty farmers. They are complex, mellow, and unusually rich and sweet in flavor, but more perishable than round pearls. The Borettano is a variety of cipolline. Cipolline are often glazed in a sweet and sour sauce.

Italian Red Onion: Italian red onions are flattened in shape with definite ridges and thick layers. The inner skin layers are deep purple. They don't store well but have sweeter flavor and crunchier texture than other red onions. Italian red onions are in season in California from April through August. Other red onions are more rounded, not as deep on color, and smoother.

Maui Onions: Maui, Hawaii, is the home of the famous sweet Maui onion with a crisply moist texture. Mauis can range in color from white to pale yellow and are usually shaped like a slightly flattened sphere. Mauis are available on a very limited basis outside of the West Coast from April to July.

Oso Sweets: Oso Sweets from Chile are large, high-quality, extra-sweet onions shipped to the U.S. for sale January through March. They are hand-packed in sturdy wood crates, which allows good air circulation and maintains their high quality. They contain up to fifty percent more sugar than other sweet onions. (Go to www.sweetonionsource.com for more about Oso Sweets and other types of sweet onions.)

Spanish Onions: Spanish or yellow onions are a large category of generally mild, globe-shaped onions. They are the most common onion at the market and may be found in a large range of sizes, from very small to the gigantic ones used for restaurant-style deep-fried blooming onions.

Texas 1015s: Texas 1015s are large, sweet, round yellow onions harvested in the Rio Grande Valley of Texas and are in season March through June. They get their name from the date they are planted: October 15. Onions are the number one agricultural product in Texas and the Texas-bred Granex hybrid has been popularized worldwide under many different names.

Tropea Onion: Tropea in Calabria, Italy, is famous for its pungent, football-shaped red onion, now grown by a few specialty farmers in the U.S. The history of the Tropea onion in Italy can be traced back to its introduction by the Phoenicians around 2,000 years ago.

Walla-Wallas: Walla-Walla Sweets were brought to Walla-Walla, Washington, from Corsica at the beginning of the twentieth century. This French onion developed over several generations so they areexceptionally sweet, jumbo-sized, and round in shape. They are in season in June and July

Vidalia Onions: Vidalia onions are Georgia-grown and known for their sweet, mild flavor, partly due to the unique combination of soils and climate in the production area. In 1952, the Granex hybrid was shipped from Texas to Georgia where they were first grown in Toombs County, near the town of Vidalia, and became known as Vidalias. Vidalia onions are harvested from late April through mid-June but retailers usually have fresh Vidalias available through mid-July. With modified-atmosphere long-term storage, they are now available much of the year, although at lesser quality.

White Onions: White onions are quite mild in flavor with papery white skins. They can be quite large, round in shape, and good both raw and cooked. They are the preferred onion of Mexico.

CHOOSING AND STORING ONIONS

Look for onions that are dry, firm, and shiny, with a thin skin. The necks should be tightly closed with no sprouts emerging. The outer skins should be papery and can be loose.

Avoid onions with dark patches, soft spots, and black mold (usually found on white or red onions). The sprout end of Italian red onions is often sunken, and this is where the first signs of spoilage begin. Onions with green sprouts will taste bitter.

Store onions loose or in the net bag they're sold in, in a cool, dark, dry, and well-ventilated area. For long-term storage, wrap each onion separately in foil and refrigerate. Do not store onions under the sink or with potatoes because potatoes give off moisture that can cause onions to spoil.

How to Ask for an Onion in . . .

Arabic, *basal*; Chinese, *chung*; Danish, *løg*; French, *oignon*; German, *zwiebel*; Greek, *kremmidi*; Hebrew, *bazal*; Hindi, *piaz*; Italian, *cipolla*; Japanese, *tamenegi*; Spanish, *cebolla*; Swahili, *kitunguu*; Thai, *ton hom*; Yiddish, *tsibele*.

Senegalese Chicken Yassa

This well-known Senegalese dish from the west coast of Africa consists of marinated chicken that is either broiled or browned and then simmered with lots of onions and fresh lemon juice. It is often served over broken rice, which has a special couscous-like texture all its own. While this custom began because broken rice was cheaper, it is now preferred. Look for broken rice, sometimes called "Mali rice," in African and Asian markets. The broken rice in Africa is fragrant Jasmine rice imported from Thailand.

SERVES 4

3 cups (about 2 large onions) sliced white onions

1 tablespoon finely chopped garlic

2 teaspoons finely chopped fresh hot green chiles

1 teaspoon ground ginger

3 bay leaves

1 tablespoon chopped fresh thyme, or
  1 teaspoon dried thyme

1 teaspoon coarsely ground black pepper

Kosher salt to taste

1 cup fresh lemon juice

1 cup water

$\frac{1}{2}$ cup canola or vegetable oil, divided

1 (2$\frac{1}{2}$- to 3-pound) fryer chicken, cut into 8 pieces

In a shallow, nonreactive (not aluminum) baking dish, combine the onions, garlic, chiles, ginger, bay leaves, thyme, pepper, and salt. Add the lemon juice, water, and $\frac{1}{4}$ cup oil. Marinate in the refrigerator at least 4 hours, or up to overnight.

Remove the chicken from the marinade and pat dry

648

with paper towels. Strain the marinade liquid, reserving both liquid and solids.

Heat $\frac{1}{4}$ cup oil in a large, heavy skillet (cast-iron preferred) and brown the chicken on all sides. Transfer the cooked chicken to a plate.

Pour off most of the oil from the skillet. Add the reserved solids to the pan and cook for about 5 minutes over moderate heat, or until the onions are soft and lightly colored. Return the chicken (and any juices) to the skillet. Add the marinade, bring to the boil, then reduce the heat to low and simmer about 25 minutes, or until the chicken is tender. Serve with hot boiled rice.

ONIONS AND SHARPNESS

The bite of raw onions is due to sulphur compounds. When an onion is cut, the crushing of the cells and contact with air allows an enzyme to work, releasing allicin—the substance that causes tearing.

Chill an onion before chopping to lessen tearing and use a sharp knife, dicing rather than chopping. Note that if you wear contact lenses, you can chop onions with impunity: the lenses prevent tearing.

To cut an onion, trim off the top, slice it in half vertically, and peel the outer layers while leaving the root end whole. Lay the halves down on their flat sides, and cut thin, parallel slits from the root outward toward the top. Then cut perpendicular slices, releasing the onion bits. The root end contains the most sulfuric compounds, which causes tearing.

To cut down on the sharpness of raw onions, slice or dice and soak in ice water for 30 minutes and then drain.

Onions in Brittany

The French province of Brittany has been famous for growing onions for many years. In the nineteenth century, one town, Roscoff, would send thirty or forty ships laden with onions to England. An enterprising Frenchman from Roscoff asked a visiting Englishman to translate for him the French phrase "the English onion is not good." Three days later, the Frenchman left for London with a sloop laden with onions. Upon arrival, he headed straight to the busiest market and displayed a placard on which was written in big letters: THE ENGLISH ONION IS NOT GOOD. Underneath, he placed a little barrow full of French onions. After a fight with an Englishman to gain the right to sell his French onions, Londoners bought all of his onions that day. From that time even until the 1970s, French onion-sellers from Roscoff and other towns in Brittany would bicycle around English towns peddling their wares.

649

ONION GARNISHES IN FRENCH CUISINE

In French cuisine, glazed (or caramelized) onions form part of several classic garnishes:

Bourguignon: glazed onions, fried mushrooms, and bacon dice

Nivernaise: glazed onions, carrots and turnips, braised lettuce, and boiled potatoes

Bourgeoise: glazed onions, carrots, and bacon dice.

"Mine eyes smell onions: I shall weep anon."

—*All's Well that Ends Well* by William Shakespeare

"An honest laborious country-man with good bread, salt, and a little parsley, will make a contented meal with a roasted onion."

—John Evelyn, seventeenth century writer and gardener

"It was for bringing the cook tulip-roots instead of onions."

—Why the Queen of Hearts wants to behead the Seven-of-Spades, *Alice's Adventures in Wonderland* by Lewis Carroll

"For this is every cook's opinion,
No savoury dish without an onion;
But lest your kissing should be spoiled,
Your onions should be thoroughly boiled."

—Jonathon Swift, Irish satirist

"Onion skins very thin,
Mild winter coming in.
Onion skins very tough,
Coming winter very rough."

—English proverb

"Life is like an onion.
You peel it off one layer at a time;
And sometimes you weep."

—Carl Sandburg, American poet

650

Pissaladière Niçoise

Pissaladière is a caramelized-onion-topped savory pie that is a close cousin of the pizza. It gets its name from pissala, a traditional Niçoise fish paste made from anchovies, and is usually served as an appetizer in small portions. Like pizza, it is traditionally made with a bread dough crust that soaks up the onion juices, though sometimes short-crust pastry or even puff pastry is used for more refined versions. I make it with a generous layer of slow-cooked sweet onions, mingled with the rich flavors of garlic, thyme, black olives, and black pepper. Strips of flat anchovy fillets decorate the top.

SERVES 12 TO 16

1 pound Spanish onions, thinly sliced
1 pound red onions, thinly sliced
1 pound white onions, thinly sliced
$1/4$ cup extra-virgin olive oil
2 tablespoons chopped fresh thyme
  (or 2 teaspoons dried thyme)
$1/2$ teaspoon ground allspice
Kosher salt and freshly ground black pepper to taste
1 pound Pizza Dough (purchased or homemade,
  see page 985)
$1/2$ pound anchovy fillets packed in olive oil, rinsed and
  patted dry
$1/2$ pound dry-cured black olives, pitted and halved
$1/2$ cup chopped Italian parsley

In a large, heavy-bottomed pot, cook all of the onions in the olive oil, until the juices are released, about 10 minutes. Then add the thyme, allspice, and salt and pepper (keeping in mind that the olives and anchovies are salty), and cook together for 25 to 30 minutes, or until the onions are lightly browned and soft and the liquid is mostly evaporated. Cool the filling to room temperature.

Preheat the oven to 400°F. Roll out the Pizza Dough into a large blue steel Sicilian square pizza pan (*see* sidebar below), an aluminum half-sheet pan, or a 14-inch round pizza pan. Spread the onion filling on the dough, up to 1 inch from the edge, smoothing out the surface. Arrange the anchovies in a diagonal crisscross pattern across the dough. At every X, place an olive half. Allow the pissaladière to rise (about 30 minutes) in a warm place.

Bake about 20 minutes, or until the dough is lightly browned and the top is bubbling and browned. Sprinkle with the parsley, cut into serving pieces, and serve.

PIZZA PANS

Square Sicilian pizza pans made from dark blue steel are ideal for making pizza. They brown the dough best for excellent and authentic results. These pans can be found in specialty kitchen stores, such as Philadelphia's own 100-year-old Fante's (www.fantes.com), in the historic Italian market. A round pizza pan or even an aluminum half sheet pan will also work well.

ONION DOMES

The onion was an ancient symbol of eternity because of the concentric circles that it contains. For this reason, Russian and other orthodox churches are designed with onion domes, a bulb-shaped dome with a pointy top.

Alpine Mushroom Pizza

This richly indulgent pizza has a base of slow-cooked onions similar to the Pissaladière above. I use a very special pizza dough here from the Austrian-influenced Alto-Adige region made with rye flour and riced potatoes. It makes a flavorful, light, and moist dough, but you may certainly substitute either purchased dough, or another recipe for pizza dough. What makes it really special are the toppings: roasted mushrooms, lusciously melting Italian Fontina from the Alps, and a final sprinkle of pungently earthy white truffle oil (white truffles come from the same region). The more kinds of mushrooms you use here, the better this pizza will be. I suggest a combination of baby bellas, shiitakes, and oyster mushrooms.

MAKES ONE 12-INCH PIZZA

651

Caramelized Onions

2 tablespoons canola or vegetable oil

2 pounds yellow onions, thinly sliced

1 tablespoon chopped thyme

Kosher salt and freshly ground black pepper to taste

Heat oil in large skillet, add onions and brown well over high heat, stirring often until onions are evenly and deeply browned. Stir in the thyme, season with salt and pepper, and cool. Store in covered container up to 5 days.

Roasted Mushrooms

$1/4$ cup olive oil

1 tablespoon chopped garlic

2 tablespoons chopped resinous herbs
   (such as rosemary, sage, thyme, and oregano)

Kosher salt and freshly ground black pepper to taste

2 pounds assorted exotic and wild mushrooms, trimmed
and sliced

Preheat the broiler to high. Whisk together the olive oil, garlic, herbs, and salt and pepper. Combine with the mushrooms. Arrange in a single layer on a metal baking pan and broil on high until well browned on top, about 5 minutes, then turn over and broil until well browned on the bottom, about 5 minutes. Cool and reserve.

Pizza Dough with Potato and Rye

1 ($2^1/_4$ teaspoon) package dry yeast

3 ounces milk, warmed

$^1/_4$ cup beer

1 tablespoon extra-virgin olive oil

$^3/_4$ cup Idaho potato puree (boiled in skin, peeled, and
passed through a food mill while still hot)

$^1/_4$ cup dark rye flour

10 ounces ($2^1/_2$ cups) unbleached all-purpose flour

1 tablespoon kosher salt

Dissolve the yeast in the milk. Beat in the beer and allow the yeast to bubble up. Beat in the olive oil and potato puree.

Combine the rye flour, all-purpose flour, and salt in a bowl. Combine the dry ingredients with the wet ingredients in the bowl of a standing mixer fitted with the dough hook attachment, and beat until smooth and elastic. Transfer the dough to an oiled bowl and cover with plastic wrap. Allow to rise at room temperature for about 1 hour, or until doubled in size. Punch the dough down and roll it into a ball. Oil the dough lightly and replace in the bowl, covering again with plastic wrap. Allow the dough to rise again,

for about 1 hour, until doubled. Punch down and then either roll out or refrigerate overnight, covered, for later use. Bring to room temperature before rolling out and filling.

Assembly

1 (12- to 14-inch) round of pizza dough

Olive oil for brushing

1 cup shredded Fontina

1 cup Caramelized Onions

2 cups Roasted Mushrooms

White Truffle Oil, for sprinkling

Chopped parsley, for garnish

Preheat the oven to 450°F., if possible with a pizza stone in the oven. Lightly sprinkle a wooden peel with cornmeal, then stretch out the pizza round to the size of the peel. Alternatively, roll out the pizza and transfer to a cornmeal-dusted metal baking pan (a paella pan works well here). Brush lightly with olive oil, especially on the edges. Sprinkle with the Fontina, then top with dollops of onions, and arrange mushrooms over top.

If you're using the peel, transfer to the pizza stone by placing the peel at a low angle to the stone and giving the peel a fast, vigorous thrust forward and then back, so that the pizza jumps onto the stone. Otherwise, place the pan in the oven. Bake until bubbling and well browned, about 6 minutes. Cut into 8 to 12 wedges. Sprinkle with truffle oil and parsley and serve.

Crunchy Panko Sweet Onion Rings

It's so rare to find really good homemade onion rings. The old Corned Beef Academy in Philadelphia made them just the way I like them: in thick rings, coated in crispy, rough breadcrumbs. Because the restaurant, actually a small chain, doesn't exist anymore, I've had to recreate them for myself. But this recipe makes something that is even better than regular onion rings, if there could be such a thing: sweet onion rings. The crunch comes from Japanese panko, easy to find in Asian markets. Peanut oil is excellent for deep-frying for crisp texture and nutty flavor, without any of those nasty trans-fats we've been hearing about. However, if you or someone close to you is allergic, substitute soy or canola oil.

SERVES 6 TO 8

2 eggs, lightly beaten

2 tablespoons soy sauce

$^1/_4$ cup water

$^1/_4$ pound (1 cup) all-purpose flour

2 cups Japanese panko breadcrumbs, divided

3 sweet onions, cut in $^1/_2$-inch-thick slices and separated into rings (save small inner rings for another use)

3 cups peanut oil

2 tablespoons roasted Japanese sesame oil

Combine the eggs, soy sauce, and water. Set up 3 bowls: one with flour, the second with the egg mix, and the third with half the panko. First, dip each onion ring into the flour and shake off any excess. Second, dip the onion into the egg mixture and let the excess liquid drip off. Finally, dip the onion in panko crumbs, coating well on all sides. (Add the second half of the panko to the bowl as needed, so the crumbs stay dry.) Arrange breaded onion slices on a wax paper-lined baking sheet and chill for at least 30 minutes and up to overnight.

Combine the oils and heat in a wok (or heavy skillet), then wok-fry the onion rings a few at a time. Drain, preferably on a wire rack. Keep warm in a 250°F. oven until ready to serve.

Oven-Roasted Sweet Onion Wedges

When sweet onions are in season—whether they are winter imports from South America, such as my favorite Oso Sweets, or one of the newer summer regional onions like Pennsylvania's new Simply Sweets and New York's Empire Sweets—this is an easy and delicious way to prepare them. Serve the roasted onions with steaks or use as a topping for salads and sandwiches.

SERVES 8

$^1/_2$ cup olive oil

2 tablespoons chopped garlic

Kosher salt and freshly ground black pepper to taste

2 tablespoons chopped mixed fresh herbs (or 2 teaspoons dried mixed herbs), such as thyme, oregano, rosemary, and marjoram

4 sweet onions, peeled and cut into wedges, trimming the rootlets, but leaving the root section attached

Preheat the oven to 425°F. Whisk together the olive oil,

653

garlic, salt and pepper, and herbs. Toss with the onions and arrange in a single layer on baking pans. Roast 20 minutes, stir and then roast 10 minutes longer, or until browned and crusty. Serve hot or at room temperature.

Belgian Beef, Beer, and Onion Stew: Carbonade a la Flamande

This typical Belgian beef stew gets its rich sauce from the famed dark Belgian beer, and its sweetness from lots of simmered onions. A little cider vinegar and brown sugar give the stew a sweet and sour tang. Serve with egg noodles in brown butter and parsley, or with spaetzle (see page 172), or with mashed potatoes (see page 762). Like all stews, this one tastes even better made a day or two ahead and reheated. It also freezes beautifully, so you may want to double the recipe. I always do.

SERVES 6 TO 8

$1/4$ pound bacon, cut into thin strips

3 pounds onions, sliced thinly

3 pounds beef chuck, cut across the grain in

$1/3$-inch thick slices, or into cubes

$1/4$ pound (1 cup) flour (for dusting) + 2 tablespoons flour

2 (12-ounce) bottles dark beer

2 tablespoons cider vinegar

2 tablespoons dark brown sugar, packed

1 tablespoon chopped fresh thyme, or 1 teaspoon dried

Kosher salt and freshly ground black pepper to taste

4 bay leaves

In a large, heavy skillet, preferably cast-iron, brown the bacon until the fat is rendered. Remove the bacon bits and half of the fat and reserve both. Sauté the onions in the remaining half the bacon fat until well browned. Remove the onions from the pan and reserve. Add the remaining bacon fat to the pan.

Dust the beef with flour, shaking off the excess. Brown the beef well on all sides, working in batches, if necessary. Remove beef slices from pan. Add the 2 tablespoons flour to the fat remaining in the pan. Add the vinegar, brown sugar, thyme, salt and pepper to taste, and bay leaves. Bring the liquid to the boil.

Layer the beef, onions, and liquid in a large casserole dish and bring to the boil on top of the stove. Cover and place in a 300°F. oven for 2 to $2^1/2$ hours, or until the beef is tender when pierced. Remove from the oven and serve.

AVERAGE ONION CONSUMPTION

Average per person annual onion consumption world-wide is about 13.7 pounds of onions; in the U.S. it is about 18.6 pounds, while Libya has the highest consumption with an astounding 66.8 pounds. Men eat 40 percent more onions than women, according to the USDA.

654

ORANGES & TANGERINES

ORANGES & TANGERINES

Oranges

Just gazing upon a brightly colored orange or tangerine is enough to cheer anyone up in the dead of winter, when the fruits are at their best. In Victorian England, when oranges were rare and expensive, a single orange would be a much-longed-for gift. Today, because they're so abundant and our access to them is greater due to ease of transportation, we tend to take oranges for granted. Their sunshine-colored rinds are covered with tiny pockets filled with fragrant oil that makes them a pleasure to handle, but are also the source of one of the best seasonings around—their grated zest.

Oranges, tangerines, and other citrus fruits are equally well-suited for dinner and dessert. Many of the myriad fish and seafood stews of the Mediterranean get their characteristic aroma from orange juice and zest; in Chinese cooking, dried tangerine peel imparts its bittersweet aroma and taste to many dishes, especially those with beef. When it comes time for dessert, beautifully cut *suprêmes* of orange—the French way of completely trimming all pith and skin, leaving only the sections of shiny, juicy brightly colored fruit—make a beautiful garnish for everything from wintertime salads to duck and duck confit, to chocolate cake and tangerine cheesecake.

The orange, *Citrus sinensis*, is a small, round, orange-colored citrus fruit full of sweet, juicy, bright-orange flesh.

It can be both cooked and eaten raw. Its name comes from the Sanskrit word *naranga* used in ancient India.

The bitter orange, *Citrus aurantium*, has sour juice and an aromatic rind, and is usually a cooking orange, used for salsas, marinades, and dressings. The orange's wild ancestors are thought to have come from China and India, but the earliest oranges eaten in China were actually mandarins or tangerines. Today, Brazil and the U.S. together produce more than two-thirds of the world's orange crop.

The sour orange was the first to travel westward and was being grown in Sicily by the eleventh century. The sweet orange followed about five hundred years later, when the Portuguese discovered the sea route around Africa in 1498 and brought back sweet oranges from the east. Columbus brought orange seeds to Haiti in 1493 and oranges were being raised in Florida by 1565. In California, oranges were being grown in the southern part, now Mexico, by 1739. Oranges began to be cultivated in southern Africa in 1654 and Australia after 1788.

Most American oranges come from Florida and California. Due to differences in soil and climate, Florida and California oranges—even those of the same variety—vary in color, texture, and juiciness. Florida oranges are thin-skinned, very juicy, and easy to squeeze. They are less than picture perfect, with thin orange, yellow, and green skins marked with blemishes, and juicy flesh, so they excel for juicing. California oranges usually have full orange color (due to a drier climate with cooler nights), thicker skin, and less juiciness, and are best for eating.

Oranges are available year round, though most of the American crop starts appearing in October and runs through March or into early April. The peak season for oranges in Florida and Texas is November through May. In California and Arizona, peak season is December through May.

Tangerines

Tangerines are a group of small, flattened citrus fruits with highly fragrant skin and sweet-tart, juicy flesh. They are distinguished by their zipper skin which allows you to easily separate the skin from the fruit. They're also easily separated into segments. Often darker in color than oranges, tangerines are also smaller and less acidic. They normally contain more water and less sugar than oranges, so their juice is more concentrated. The first of these fruits were grown in the U.S. in the 1840s, and were all known then as *mandarins*. The name *tangerine* originated toward the end of the nineteenth century, when mandarins, which were thought to come from Tangiers in Morocco, became common.

All tangerines are mandarins, but not all mandarins are tangerines. Some types are still known as mandarins (especially the peeled segments found in small cans). Mandarins have light orange-colored smooth skin, a mild sweet flavor, and few seeds. Their Latin name, *Citrus reticulata*, comes from the word *reticulated*, or netted, because of the fibrous strands of pith under the loose rind. The original wild citrus, from which mandarins are descended, probably grew in northeast India, where wild mandarins are still found. They were first cultivated in China thousands of years ago, but it was not until 1804 that mandarins were first brought to the west from China to England, where they became known as *mandarins*.

Satsumas, which were developed in Japan in the sixteenth century, are sometimes placed in a separate species, *Citrus unshiu*. Tangors, *Citrus x nobilis*, are a cross between tangerines and oranges and tend to be large and similar to oranges in flavor. Tangelos, *Citrus x paradisi x Citrus reticulata*, are hybrids between grapefruits and tangerines and noted for their juiciness and mildly sweet flavor.

Orange Varieties

Blood Orange: The mutation which produced the blood orange's ruby-red color probably arose in the seventeenth century in Sicily. The best-known varieties include the round, early-season Moro, and the midseason Tarocco (named for its resemblance to a child's toy), and the highly prized Sanguinaccio. These small to medium-sized fruits with moderate amounts of seeds have tangy juice that is concentrated in flavor and body. Blood oranges are imported from Mediterranean countries and are now also grown in California. They are in season from California mid-December through mid-April.

Cara Cara Orange: The Cara Cara Orange originated at the Hacienda de Cara Cara in Venezuela. Cara Caras are medium in size, have bright orange peels with pink- to raspberry-colored flesh, and are usually seedless. These juicy oranges have a sweet flavor with undertones of grapefruit and are best eaten fresh. Cara Caras are available late December through March from specialty growers.

Hamlin Orange: The Hamlin is an early-maturing orange grown primarily in Florida. Although Hamlins are practically seedless, their flesh is rather pulpy, so they are best for juicing. Small in size, Hamlins have a very thin, pale-orange rind and no seeds. Their juice is light, sweet, and refreshingly clear. Hamlins are in season from October through December.

Jaffa Orange: The Jaffa, or Shamouti, has been famed since the late nineteenth century. Fragrant, sweet, and juicy, Jaffas are easy to peel, have no navel, and are almost seedless. They keep quite well and are very popular as eating oranges in Europe. They are now also grown in the western U.S. but come from Israel mid-December through mid-February.

Navel Orange: The Navel orange originated in Bahia, Brazil, and is now the most important eating orange in the world. Navels thrive in the Mediterranean, Australia, California, and Argentina. Navel oranges have an unmistakable "baby fruit" imbedded in its blossom end, mature early, are typically large and seedless, easy to peel, and easy to segment. They have a rich, tart flavor. California navels are somewhat more flavorful than those grown in Florida. If used for juice, they should be squeezed as needed because their juice turns bitter quickly, even when refrigerated. American navels are in season November through April. The Chinese Navel orange has sweet flavor with low acid content. It is grown in California, but most are exported to Hong Kong.

Pineapple Orange: The Pineapple orange is similar to the Hamlin in appearance. These oranges, named for their aromatic quality, are seedy with juicy, sweet, and rich flavor. Though best for juicing, they are good for eating if you don't mind the seeds. They are bright yellow-orange with a smooth, thin rind and have bright orange flesh with some seeds. Pineapple oranges are in season December through February.

Seville, Bigarade, or Bitter Orange: Seville oranges have a thick, rough skin and an extremely tart, bitter flesh full of seeds. Because of their high acid content, Sevilles are used for making marmalades, salsas, and marinades, as well as liqueurs. They are an essential seasoning in Spanish and Latin American cuisine, especially in Cuba. The bulk of the Spanish crop is shipped to Britain to be made into marmalade. Seville oranges are also grown in Florida and are in season in Florida from December through April. Look for them in Latin American markets.

Sweet Orange: Sweet oranges are small fruits with a pebbly rind and juicy, soft-textured flesh, insipidly sweet because they're very low in acid, and faintly bitter. Vainiglia, or Maltese, and Vainiglia Sanguigno (or Mango Orange), which has pink flesh and tastes like a melon, are two varieties from Italy. Look for sweet oranges in specialty stores and Middle Eastern and Indian groceries.

Valencia Orange: The Valencia, which came from the Azores and is probably Portuguese in origin, leads production in both California and Florida, and accounts for about half the crop produced each year. Medium to large in size, Valencias have a thin rind that is not difficult to peel when mature, plenty of well-colored juice, and two to four seeds. They are good for both eating and juicing. Florida Valencias are considered the best juice oranges. Valencias are in season March through June.

Volcano Orange®: Volcano Oranges® are raised only along the slopes of the Sicilian volcano, Mount Etna.

These deep red oranges are sweet and juicy with a distinct flavor. This rare variety is excellent for making the Italian *spremuta* or fresh-squeezed red orange juice, and can be found in glass bottles in the U.S. at specialty stores. Volcano oranges come into season in mid-March. Look for them at specialty stores.

CHOOSING ORANGES

Oranges are always picked when they are ripe, and each variety will be at its best at the midpoint of its growing season. Choose oranges that are firm, heavy for their size (they will be juiciest), and evenly shaped. Their skin should be smooth rather than deeply pitted, although juice oranges are generally smoother than navels.

Thin-skinned oranges will be juicier than thick-skinned varieties, and small to medium-sized fruits are sweeter than the largest oranges. Superficial brown streaks don't affect flavor or texture, but oranges that have serious bruises or soft spots, or feel spongy, should be avoided.

Skin color is not a good guide to quality. Some oranges are artificially colored with a harmless vegetable dye (this is permitted in Florida, but not in California or Arizona), while others may show traces of green although they are ripe. Florida oranges are likely to be slightly greenish, while California oranges are usually a solid orange color. Through a natural process called *regreening*, the skins of ripe oranges sometimes revert to green if there are blossoms on the tree at the same time as the fruit. Oranges that have regreened may actually be sweeter because they are extra-ripe.

Cutting an Orange

Halve unpeeled oranges crosswise for juicing, or halve them either crosswise or lengthwise and then cut each half into thirds, for eating.

For garnishing, halve an orange "through the poles," then cut each half crosswise into slices.

CUTTING AN ORANGE "TO THE QUICK"

To cut an orange "to the quick," cut a round of peel from the top and bottom so the flesh is exposed. Cut slices of peel longitudinally from top to bottom through to the flesh. For orange rings, slice the peeled fruit crosswise. To section, run a sharp knife along the sides of dividing membranes to the core; twist the knife at the core to release the sections, working over a bowl to catch the juices.

STORING ORANGES AND TANGERINES

Oranges keep well for up to two weeks in the refrigerator but they keep almost as well at room temperature with no wrapping. They will also yield more juice at room temperature. If oranges are placed in unperforated plastic bags, the moisture trapped inside may encourage mold growth. Remove and discard any oranges with mold so the mold doesn't spread to the rest of the fruit. If you like to eat oranges chilled, by all means refrigerate them. Store tangerines for up to one week in a plastic bag in the refrigerator. Clementines deteriorate quickly and should be eaten within four or five days. They are usually stored at room temperature.

ZESTING AN ORANGE OR TANGERINE

Orange zest is the aromatic orange-colored part of the peel. To remove this for use in baking or cooking, be sure to scrub oranges with hot soapy water first. You'll also want to check that the oranges have not been artificially colored or waxed. You can use a variety of tools to scrape different sizes of zest from the orange: the fine side of a hand grater, a special zesting tool, a Microplane zester, a sharp paring knife, or a vegetable peeler will work. Scrape just the colored part of the peel, avoiding the bitter white pith underneath. The oil contained in the zest is highly fragrant. Grate tangerines with light pressure because they are soft and giving.

TANGERINE SEASON

Florida tangerines are in season November through March, California tangerines, January through May.

Tangerine and Mandarin Varieties

Clementine: Tiny, seedless Clementines are the most important early ripening mandarin of the Mediterranean. They are usually only found in the early months of the year and are sold by the case in small wooden crates. These small, light orange-colored, largely seedless fruits have thin, loose zipper-skins. Their flesh is deep-orange and they have tangy-sweet, juicy flesh. Clementines are highly perishable because of their tender skin. Examine the stem ends and make sure they're not softened before purchase. Clementines come from Chile, Morocco, and Spain, and peak season is November to February.

Dancy: The Dancy is one of the oldest tangerine varieties in Florida. It was very popular at one time, but has mostly been replaced by new tangerine hybrids. This medium-sized oblong to pear-shaped fruit has a deep orange to red peel and smooth, thin, leathery skin. Its rich-flavored pulp is dark orange, with 10 to 14 segments and 6 to 20 small seeds.

Fairchild: The Fairchild tangerine is a Clementine and Orlando hybrid grown in California. This tangerine is the first of the season and known for its loose zipper skin that is often pebbly and firm yet tender flesh. The fruit is medium in size, with bright deep orange-colored skin, juicy flesh, few seeds, and excellent flavor. Fairchilds are in season from mid-October through February.

Sunburst: The Sunburst is a medium-sized, oblong fruit with orange to scarlet skin, pulp that divides into 11 to 15 segments, abundant colorful juice, and 10 to 20 seeds. It is in season from mid-November to mid-December.

Tangor and Tangelo Varieties

Honeybell: The sought-after delectable Honeybell, named for its unique bell-like shape, is easy to peel, extremely juicy, and honey-sweet. It has a short season in January and is available in limited quantity from specialty growers.

Honey Mandarin: The Honey Mandarin is a tangor—a hybrid between a Mediterranean orange and a King Mandarin. It has thin, glossy skin and a slightly flattened shape with no neck. Its rind is light yellowish-orange, faintly pebbled, and peels easily. Its pulp is very aromatic with a distinctive rich flavor. The Honey is often confused with the Murcott from Florida and is grown in California, with its season lasting from late January through April.

Honey Murcott: The Honey Murcott is a tangor, which is a tangerine and orange hybrid, grown in Florida. (It is often confused with the California Honey Mandarin.) The fruit is yellow-orange, smooth, and glossy, with 18 to 24 seeds per fruit. It has very sweet flesh and a thin, easily removable peel. The fruit has higher soluble solids than oranges and, because of this, has a unique tender, but almost meaty texture. In season January to March, it is one of the latest-maturing fruits of the mandarin hybrids.

Minneola: Minneolas are a cross between a grapefruit and a mandarin and are the most important and plentiful tangelo grown in the West, though they are also grown in Florida. The fruit tends to be large, with a deep red-orange exterior and a distinctive knob-like formation at the stem end. Minneolas are smooth to slightly pebbled in texture, peel easily, and have few if any seeds. They have a delicious tart-sweet flavor and a strong aroma. Minneolas are in season from February through April in Florida and December through April in California.

Ortanique: The Ortanique is believed to be a chance cross of sweet orange and tangerine, discovered in Jamaica in the early 1900s. The fruit closely resembles the Temple, oblong in shape with deep-orange, thin, adherent (rather than "zipper"-type) skin. Its pulp is divided into 16 segments and is very juicy, with distinctive, acid-sweet flavor. It is either seedless or has few seeds and needs special handling because it is vulnerable to cold. It is mostly grown in Jamaica and now also in Florida and is in season in March and April.

Orlando: The Orlando tangelo is a cross between a tangerine and a grapefruit. It is flat-round in shape and rather large in size, with color and texture closer to that of an orange. Orlandos have a bright orange exterior color, a smooth to slightly pebbled texture, juicy, mild, sweet flavor, few to many seeds, and a tight-fitting rind. They are in season November through January.

Satsuma Mandarin: Satsumas are a distinctive type of Japanese mandarin that are highly sought after in

Japan. The Satsuma is the first mandarin of the season available from the western U.S. The fruit has a pebbly textured skin, light orange color with some green, mild sweet flavor, and virtually no seeds. It is known for easy peeling and segmentation and is in season October through December.

Temple: The temple is a tangor, a cross between a mandarin and a sweet orange, that reportedly originated in Southeast Asia. It resembles an orange that is large in size but with a rounder shape. It has a red-orange color, slightly rough skin, and few seeds. It is easy to peel, with a spicy, tart-sweet flavor. Temples are in season January through March.

662

Choosing and Storing Tangerines

When selecting tangerines, look for fruit that fills its skin. Avoid hollow-feeling fruits or fruits with soft or dented spots or any visible mold. Tangerines sold with stems and leaves are found mostly in the winter holiday season and are typically of very high quality.

PREPARING TANGERINES

Most tangerines are full of seeds. To remove them, cut a small slit in the inside center of each segment and squeeze out the seeds that surround the opening. Alternatively, cut the tangerine in half through its equator, exposing the seeds. Use the tip of a sharp knife to pick out the seeds.

Orange–Dressed Duck Confit Salad

Duck à l'orange is such a famed dish that at Paris' renowned restaurant, La Tour d'Argent, they have been serving the same dish for almost one hundred years. Classically, bitter orange (bigarade in French) is used to make the sauce. In America, where fresh bitter oranges are only now starting to appear regularly in markets, the sauce is generally made with sweet-tart navel oranges. In this warm salad, which also combines duck and oranges—crispy duck confit over the light-colored bitter European curly endive called frisée *(curly) in France—I like to combine orange and tangerine juice, for the extra-concentrated flavor and aroma of the tangerine. Use purchased duck confit (salt-cured, slow-cooked duck from the southwest of France) or see the recipe on page 380. Use the extra orange dressing for freshly shaved fennel and watercress salad, or to dress pan-fried or grilled fish.*

SERVES 6

Orange Dressing
MAKES 1¼ CUPS

1 cup squeezed orange juice (or use part tangerine juice)

2 tablespoons + 2 tablespoons chopped shallots

1 teaspoon each: crushed black peppercorns
   and coriander seed

2 bay leaves

2 sprigs thyme

2 tablespoons Sherry vinegar

½ cup olive oil

Zest of 1 orange (and/or tangerine zest)

Kosher salt and freshly ground pepper to taste

Combine orange juice, 2 tablespoons of shallots, peppercorns, coriander, bay leaves, and thyme in a medium, nonreactive pot. Reduce slowly until thick and syrupy, and about $1/2$ cup of liquid remains. Whisk together with the sherry vinegar and olive oil. Stir in remaining chopped shallots and the orange zest, and season with salt and pepper. Reserve. Refrigerate for up to 2 weeks in the refrigerator.

Duck Confit Salad

6 duck confit legs (purchased or homemade,
  see page 380)
3 heads frisée greens, cored and cut into smaller pieces
$3/4$ cup Orange Dressing

Preheat the oven to 400°F. Wipe off any excess fat from the duck legs. Arrange them on a metal baking pan and bake about 15 minutes, or until crisp and browned. (Restaurants often deep-fry confit to crisp it quickly.)

When ready to serve, toss the frisée with most of the dressing and arrange on serving plates. Arrange the duck legs on top, or if desired, remove the meat from the bones, discarding any fat pockets or connective tissue, and divide among the plates. Drizzle the salads with the remaining dressing, and serve immediately.

DUCK À L'ORANGE

In the early nineteenth century, during the French Third Republic, the famed maitre d', Frédéric Delair, of the equally famed restaurant, La Tour d'Argent (in business since 1600), created the ritual of the *Canard au Sang a l'orange au poivre*, in which the juices from the duck bones are extracted using an elaborate silver duck press to thicken and flavor the orange- and peppercorn-infused sauce.

In a brilliant public relations move, M. Delair decreed that each duck would be numbered and a card be given to the guest bearing its number. Since then, every *Caneton Tour d'Argent* has been registered. By 1929, the numbers were well over one hundred thousand. Number 328 was served to King Edward VII of England in 1890, number 40,312 was served to King Alphonse XIII of Spain in 1914, and number 53,211 was served to Emperor Hiro Hito of Japan in 1921.

Oranges à l'Orientale: Caramelized Oranges Scented with Orange Blossom

In this classic French dessert, inspired by the orange salads of Morocco and Algeria, oranges are first cut a vif (to the quick) to remove all their rind, bitter white pith, and inner skin. An orange caramel is made from sugar syrup cooked until it caramelizes, orange juice, zest, and the fragrant orange-blossom water, a favorite in the Arabic world. The oranges, cut into thick slices, are briefly browned in butter and then mixed with the caramel sauce. This is an easy-to-make dessert, but it does require attention at the stove so as not to burn the caramel. (If it gets too dark, discard it and start again—all you will have lost is a half cup of sugar.) If you have a copper pot, this is the time to use it; because copper is such a good heat conductor, the caramel will brown evenly and will have less tendency to burn. Accompany with fine-quality chocolate bon-bons and bittersweet chocolate truffles. Garnish the oranges Arabic style if desired by sprinkling with pomegranate seeds.

SERVES 6

6 brightly colored juicy navel oranges, well scrubbed

$1/2$ cup granulated sugar

1 cup orange juice, preferably freshly squeezed

2 tablespoons unsalted butter

Grated zest of 1 orange

1 teaspoon orange-blossom water

$1/2$ cup pomegranate seeds, optional, for garnish

Cut the peel and all the bitter white pith from the oranges, following the directions above in Cutting an Orange "To the Quick," page 659. With all its flesh exposed, cut each orange crosswise into three thick slices and reserve.

Meanwhile, bring the sugar and $1/2$ cup of water to the boil over moderate heat in a medium, heavy-bottomed nonreactive saucepan with a lid, stirring occasionally until the sugar has dissolved and the syrup is clear. Bring the syrup to the boil, cover, and cook over moderate heat, shaking the pot occasionally, until the syrup just begins to color. Continue to cook, swirling the syrup so that it cooks evenly, until it is a slight reddish-brown. Immediately, but carefully, pour in the orange juice—it will bubble up vigorously, harden, and create hot steam, so take care. Simmer, stirring with a wooden spoon or silicone spatula, until the hardened caramel has completely dissolved, about 4 minutes. Boil the orange caramel about 5 minutes longer, or until thick and syrupy, and reserve.

In a large skillet, preferably nonstick, heat the butter until it starts to brown and smells nutty. Add the orange slices and cook over moderate heat until just starting to brown, about 2 minutes on each side, working in batches if necessary and removing the oranges as they brown.

Pour the reserved orange-caramel into the pan and heat until bubbling. Slip the orange slices back into the pan, shaking to coat with the caramel. Add the orange zest and orange-blossom water and shake again to combine the flavors. Serve immediately, pouring a portion of the pan juices over each serving. Lightly sprinkle with the pomegranate seeds just before serving.

Candied Tangerine Cheesecake

The oil-filled pockets in the skin of a brightly colored tangerine are full of the most wonderfully slightly bitter perfumed flavor. I take advantage of both the zest and juice of tangerines when they're in season to make this outstanding wintertime cheesecake. Because most tangerines are full of seeds, I find it easiest to use them in dishes like this one, where I grate off their zest and squeeze their juice. I use a potato peeler to remove the zest in long strips that can be candied, rather than using a special zester. I like to use a crunchy biscotti crumb crust, using either purchased or homemade biscotti. It's a good way to use the funny-shaped end pieces from homemade biscotti. Graham cracker or zwieback crumbs can be substituted.

Makes one 9–inch cake, to serve 12 to 16

Biscotti Crumb Crust

2 cups crushed biscotti cookies

$1/4$ cup granulated sugar

4 tablespoons unsalted butter, melted and cooled

Combine the cookie crumbs, sugar, and butter, then press into the bottom of a 9-inch springform pan. Chill for 30 minutes to set the crust. Preheat the oven to 375°F. and bake the crust for 25 minutes, or until lightly browned. Cool and reserve.

Filling

Juice and zest strips of 3 tangerines, peeled with a potato peeler

$3/4 + 1/4$ cups granulated sugar

$1^1/_2$ pounds cream cheese

$1/2$ cup sour cream

$1/2$ cup heavy cream

3 eggs

1 tablespoon vanilla extract

Bring a small pot of water to the boil. Meanwhile, trim the zest strips into even rectangles and then cut into small squares. Add the zest squares to the water, bring back to the boil, and cook about 2 minutes, or until slightly softened. Drain and reserve.

In a small, heavy-bottomed nonreactive saucepot, combine the reserved zest, the juice, and the $3/4$ cup sugar. Cook over moderate heat until the mixture comes to the boil and the syrup is clear. Reduce heat and simmer, uncovered, until the zest is tender, and liquid is reduced to a thick syrup, about 20 minutes, shaking the pot occasionally to prevent sticking. You'll need about $3/4$ of a cup of the candied zest to make the cake. Drain the candied zest and reserve (the syrup will be rather bitter and should be discarded).

Preheat the oven to 300°F. In the bowl of a mixer, beat the cream cheese alone until smooth, scraping down the sides of the mixer once or twice. Gradually beat in the $1/4$ cup sugar, the sour cream and the heavy cream, beating until smooth and scraping down the sides of the mixer once or twice to ensure that no small lumps remain. Beat in the eggs one at a time, and then beat in the vanilla and the reserved candied zest and any syrup sticking to it. Pour the mixture into the baked biscotti crumb crust.

Bake 1 hour, or until the cake is just barely set in the middle. Cool before removing from the pan. Chill and then cut using a knife dipped in hot water and wiped dry in between each cut.

Chocolate–Orange Pound Cake

While working as a freelance television food stylist for the QVC network, I had the honor of cooking for Anne Willan, author of the fantastic Look and Cook *series, which work so well for the beginning or unconfident cook. One of the recipes I prepared for her appearance was this moist, chewy, chocolate-orange pound cake. I've since adapted the recipe to make it easier, at least for me, with the same classic flavor combination of chocolate and oranges. This rich cake freezes quite well, so consider making a double recipe. You can substitute good-quality purchased candied orange peel to make it easier. To accent this combination of chocolate and oranges, serve each slice accompanied by a portion of the Oranges à l'Orientale from page 664.*

MAKES ONE 8–CUP LOAF CAKE

Candied Oranges

2 navel oranges, well scrubbed
1 cup granulated sugar

Bring about 6 cups water to the boil in a medium heavy-bottomed nonreactive saucepan. Meanwhile, prick the oranges several times with a fork or skewer. Add the oranges and enough additional water to barely cover them, and simmer about 1 hour, or until tender when pierced. Drain the oranges, cut into rough chunks, transfer to the bowl of a food processor, and chop until chunky (like mar-malade).

Combine the chopped oranges with the sugar and 1 cup of water in a medium-sized, nonreactive pan. Bring to the boil and simmer together 1 hour, or until the liquid has mostly been absorbed. Shake occasionally so that the oranges don't burn. Remove from heat, cool to room temperature, drain, and reserve.

Chocolate–Orange Cake Batter

$1/4$ pound (1 cup) all-purpose flour, preferably unbleached
$1/2$ cup Dutch-process cocoa
2 teaspoons baking powder
$1/2$ teaspoon kosher salt
13 tablespoons unsalted butter
1 cup granulated sugar
3 eggs
1 cup chopped candied oranges (substitute $3/4$ cup chopped candied orange peel)

Preheat the oven to 325°F. Sift together flour, cocoa, baking powder, and salt. Prepare an 8-cup loaf pan by greasing it with 1 tablespoon of butter and sprinkling with some of the flour mixture, shaking out the excess.

Cream the remaining butter and the sugar until light and fluffy. Beat in the eggs, one at a time, until absorbed. Stir in the candied oranges and then fold in the remaining flour mix. Pour the batter into the prepared pan and bake 45 to 50 minutes, or until the cake begins to come away from the sides of the pan and a toothpick stuck in the center comes out clean. Cool before removing the cake from the pan. Slice with a serrated knife and serve.

Orange–Almond Layer Cake with Cinnamon–Orange Buttercream

Buttercream cakes have gotten a bad reputation because they are so often made not with butter, but some trans-fat-laden butter substitute. Real butter is, of course, more expensive and more challenging to work with, but it's the only way to go. Why bother wasting precious calories on fake flavors? The icing here is classic French cooked-sugar buttercream—it's silky smooth, and disappears in your mouth, filling it with orange and cinnamon flavors. The vanilla layer cake is adaptable; serve dusted with confectioners' sugar, with summer fruit salad (see page 941), with Vanilla Custard Sauce (see page 990), or ice it with chocolate ganache (see page 474) and serve it for a special children's birthday cake. I normally use unbleached all-purpose flour for all my baking, but here it is important to use bleached cake flour for extra lightness. An alternative is to use all-purpose flour, substituting cornstarch for 1/4 cup of the flour. You can also bake this cake batter as cupcakes in muffin-paper lined tins.

Cinnamon–Orange Buttercream Icing

TO ICE ONE 10-INCH LAYER CAKE

1 cup granulated sugar

1/2 cup water

2 eggs

1 pound (4 sticks) unsalted butter, slightly softened, but not greasy, cut up

2 teaspoons vanilla extract

1 teaspoon ground cinnamon

Zest of 1 orange

In a medium, heavy-bottomed nonreactive saucepan, heat the sugar with 1/2 cup of water to boiling. Continue cooking until the syrup reaches 238°F. on a candy thermometer, or when a soft ball forms when dropped in ice water. (Another way to tell when the sugar is ready is the entire pan will be covered with thick-walled bubbles.)

Meanwhile beat the eggs until light. With the mixer on low speed, carefully pour in the hot sugar syrup and continue beating until the mixture is at room temperature and thick, like mayonnaise. Beat in the butter, bit by bit, until it has been fully absorbed. Add the vanilla, cinnamon, and orange zest and beat briefly. Chill the buttercream for at least 1 hour, tightly covered, before using. The buttercream freezes well; cover tightly and freeze up to 2 months. Defrost in the refrigerator before using.

Vanilla Layer Cake

3/4 pound (3 cups) cake flour

1 tablespoon baking powder

1/2 teaspoon kosher salt

1/2 pound (2 sticks) unsalted butter

2 cups granulated sugar, divided

4 eggs, separated

2 teaspoons vanilla extract

2 tablespoons brandy

1 cup milk

Prepare a 9-inch cake pan by spraying generously with nonstick spray. Preheat the oven to 350°F. Whisk together the dry ingredients: flour, baking powder, and salt.

Cream butter and 1 cup of the sugar until light and fluffy. Beat in the egg yolks, one at a time, and beat until creamy. Add the vanilla and brandy. Alternating, beat the flour mixture and the milk into the creamed mix.

In a separate, clean bowl, beat the egg whites with the remaining 1 cup of sugar until firm and glossy. Fold by thirds into the batter. Pour batter into the prepared pan and bake for 45 minutes, or until the cake is set in the middle and begins to come away from the sides of the pan. Cool, then cut the cake down the middle into two rounds, then ice.

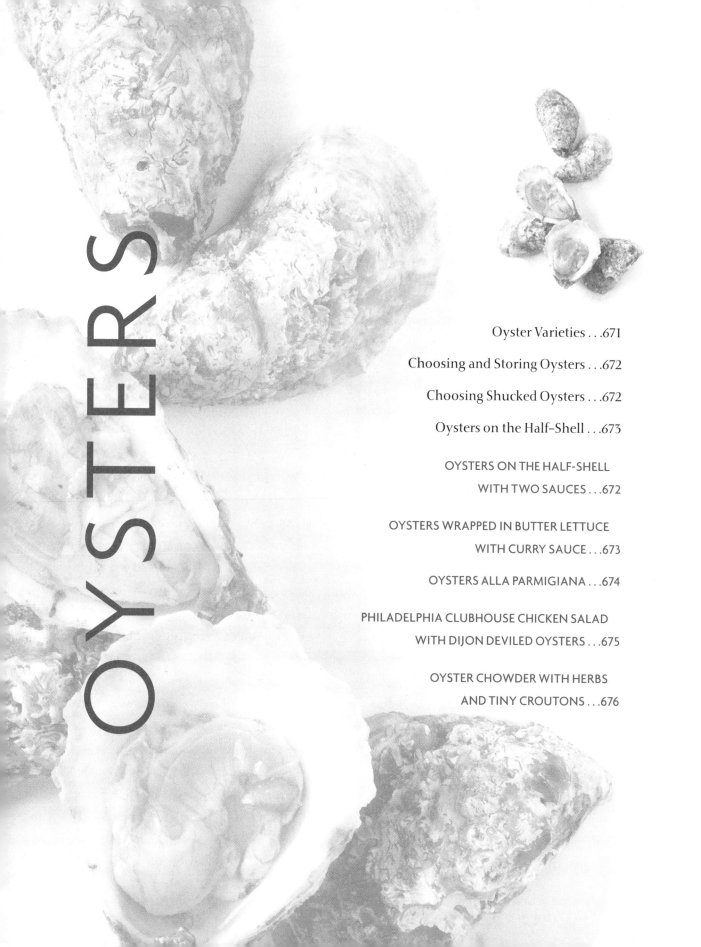

OYSTERS

OYSTERS

My upbringing in a kosher home did nothing to prepare me for eating oysters. I had always found them rather intimidating, both in the shell and out. At age twenty-five, during a trip to Quebec at Oyster Festival time, I finally succumbed to their allure. Bravely, I sampled briny, sparkling oysters nestled on a bed of seaweed; succulent oysters suspended in creamy stew; and delectably crunchy pan-fried oysters, and finally understood why people are so crazy for them. Then, about twenty years ago, I experienced a transcendent oyster stew made from poached thimble-sized Olympias out of Puget Sound, the first course of a superb meal at Chez Panisse, which I've never forgotten. While I'm hardly a maniac, like Henry IV, who ate three hundred oysters a day, or Casanova, who ate fifty nightly with his evening punch, I'm now an oyster fan.

Like clams, mussels, and scallops, oysters are saltwater bivalve mollusks. In her book, *Consider the Oyster*, the great American food writer, M.F.K. Fisher, describes our subject at its best and worst. She tells us, "A perfect oyster, healthy, of fine flavor, plucked from its chill bed and brought to the plate unwatered and unseasoned, is more delicious than any of its modifications. On the other hand, a flaccid, moping, debauched mollusk, tired from too much love and loose-nerved from general world conditions, can be a shameful thing served raw upon its shell."

Up until early historic times, a great barrier reef made of European flat oysters ran from Scandinavia through the Mediterranean as far as Greece. When the supply started to disappear, the Greeks began raising oysters on lime-filled shards of broken pottery. The Romans adored oysters and delighted in trying native oysters in new regions they conquered. Their express service transported them across Europe in winter, loaded in ice-filled carts that were replenished from icehouses along the way.

In modern times, the complexities of oyster cultivation in Brittany were poetically described in Eleanor Clark's fascinating book about life among the oyster farmers, *The Oysters of Locmariaquer*. Oysters produce millions of larval oysters, which start out free-swimming but soon anchor themselves to a support. The Bretons place special hollow tiles in the water in June. After eight to ten months, they strip off the oyster "spats" and move them elsewhere to finish their maturation. For three to four years they live in various fattening beds, often located at the mouth of a river. And then, once again, the Bretons move these oysters to refine their quality before finally packing them for sale.

Though the oyster's reputation as an aphrodisiac is, no doubt, quite undeserved, many people believe that oysters are a stimulant. You've probably seen the bumper sticker that says "Eat Oysters, Live Longer, Love Longer." Perhaps this explains why raw oyster bars continue to boom. And after all, with aphrodisiacs, believing is seeing (if you believe it will work, it will work).

Aside from that, wild oysters are back in vogue. A few years ago it seemed that farm-raised oysters were the crest of the wave. Now people want wild because they have better flavor and texture. In recent years, because of strict guidelines and monitoring of oyster beds, the risk in eating wild oysters is rapidly diminishing. Because of better management, supplies of once-disappearing wild oysters are growing.

While the cold slows down their growth, the oysters develop flavor. An oyster that takes five years to grow to maturity in Cape Cod is full-sized in only three in the Gulf of Mexico. Oysters tend to grow to fit their habitat so slow-growing Northerns are more regular, which makes them popular for the restaurant "half-shell trade."

In the old days, the rule—never eat oysters in the months without an "R"—made sense. Oysters spawn during summer months and, though edible, tend to be flabby and insipid. Farm-raised oysters allow us to eat them all year round. Oysters are at their best in season in the winter months. Because oysters filter so much seawater through their system, they are high in minerals like iron, potassium, and zinc. They're a good source of protein and are low in fat, so why not indulge?

Oyster Varieties

European Oyster: The European oyster can be found from the Norwegian Sea to Morocco. Up and down the European Atlantic coast, in Britain, France, Belgium, the Netherlands, and Denmark, people cultivate these oysters. The Portuguese Oyster, native to the Iberian Peninsula, now thrives in France as the result of a happy mishap. When a Portuguese ship, anchored in the French harbor to weather a storm, threw its cargo of rotting oysters overboard, a few robust oysters survived and multiplied. The French prize a flat Breton oyster, called the Belon, which grows in deep, cold water and develops a strong iodine taste. American entrepreneurs now farm these exquisite, though expensive, beauties in cold-water Maine.

American Oyster: The American Oyster, or Eastern Oyster, thrives from New Brunswick to the Gulf of Mexico. Oysters over a foot long astounded the first Europeans in America. The abundant oysters in New York Bay were part of the reason the Dutch bought both Manhattan and Oyster (now Ellis) Islands. Oysters were a great favorite with the native peoples, who only ate them cooked. They taught the settlers how to make Oyster Stew. Even now, Americans eat more cooked oysters than Europeans. Beginning in 1842, express wagons carried oysters across the Alleghenies to be served at oyster feasts like Abe Lincoln's famous oyster parties.

Japanese Oyster: The Japanese Oyster, found along the Pacific seaboard, even now grows as big as a foot long. At the other extreme, in their shell, Olympias from Washington's Puget Sound measure only about $1^1/_2$ inches across. More than 1,400 of these thimble-sized beauties are required to make a gallon.

672

Oysters on the Half-Shell with Two Sauces

Oysters on the half-shell are for the purist and the lover who believes them to increase his potency. Whatever your motivation for eating these, following are detailed instructions on how to open an oyster and two classic sauces to spoon on top just before slipping the freshly exposed oyster into your mouth.

SERVES 12

French Mignonette Sauce

1 cup aged red wine vinegar

1/2 cup chopped shallots

1 teaspoon each: crushed white and black peppercorns

Stir ingredients together and leave at room temperature for 30 minutes to develop flavor. Top ice-cold fresh-shucked oysters with a spoonful of sauce.

Tomato-Horseradish Sauce

2 pounds plum tomatoes

2 pounds red peppers, stemmed and seeded

1/2 cup olive oil

1/4 cup cider vinegar

Splash of Tabasco

2 tablespoons prepared horseradish, preferably with beets

1/4 cup finely chopped onion

1 teaspoon dry mustard

Kosher salt and freshly ground black pepper to taste

Preheat the oven to 400°F. Arrange the tomatoes and red peppers in a metal roasting pan just large enough to hold them. Roast about 20 minutes, or until softened and their skins are well browned.

Blend or process the tomatoes and peppers and then strain through a food mill or a sieve to remove the skins and seeds. Transfer to a small pot and cook off excess liquid, stirring frequently, for about 10 minutes, or until thickened.

Whisk in remaining ingredients, cool to room temperature, and serve with oysters on the half-shell. Refrigerate any remaining sauce for up to two weeks.

OYSTERS ON THE HALF-SHELL

You will need to buy an inexpensive oyster knife, available at kitchen-supply stores and some fish and seafood markets. Using an abrasive pad, scrub the oysters under cold running water before opening them.

Turn the oyster over so that its flat side is facing up and the pointy end is facing you. The pointy end curves slightly just beyond the tip at the point the oyster shells are joined together.

Stick the end of the oyster knife into the edge of the oyster just beyond the tip, angling down. Pry and jiggle the knife until the knife slips inside.

Now, twist the knife vigorously to separate the two shells, popping them apart. Scrape the knife across the inside top of the shell to release the oyster meat from the shell and then remove and discard the top shell.

Scrape the knife against the bottom shell, cutting underneath the oyster to release it from its shell without piercing the oyster meat. If you are using shucked oysters, remove the oyster from its shell, place in a clean container, and then strain the oyster juices through a sieve onto the oyster.

If serving on the half-shell, give the opened oyster a quick rinse under cold water to rinse off any shell bits that might have broken off. Don't rinse more than necessary because you don't want to wash away the precious juices.

Oysters Wrapped in Butter Lettuce with Curry Sauce

This delicate dish gets its flavor from the cooked-down oyster juices mixed with curry powder and enriched with cream. It is a modern French dish that I adapted from one in Georges Perrier: Le Bec-Fin Recipes, the first book I worked on. The oysters are lightly poached, then wrapped in tender Boston lettuce leaves, also rightfully called butter lettuce for its melting texture. Use freshly shucked oysters, which you can buy from a good fishmonger, and preferably those from cold water, because they are firmer with better flavor.

SERVES 4

12 freshly shucked oysters + their juices (about $^1/_4$ cup)

$^1/_4$ cup dry white wine

2 tablespoons chopped shallots

1 small celery root, pared and julienned or shredded

1 carrot, julienned

1 tablespoon + 4 tablespoons unsalted butter

2 heads Boston lettuce

Kosher salt and freshly ground black pepper to taste

2 teaspoons curry powder

$^1/_4$ cup heavy cream

In a small, heavy-bottomed nonreactive saucepan, combine the oyster juice with the white wine and shallots. Bring the liquid to a boil, add the oysters, and reduce the heat to a simmer. Poach the oysters, cooking them just until their edges curl. Scoop out the oysters and reserve both the oysters and the pot with the poaching liquid.

Heat 1 tablespoon of butter in a small skillet, add the celery root and carrot, cook 2 minutes, or until crisp-tender, and reserve.

Unfurl the leaves of the Boston lettuce. Choose 12 large, perfect outer leaves and reserve the hearts of lettuce for another use. Bring a medium pot of salted water to the boil. Add the leaves and cook 10 seconds, or just until they wilt. Drain and run under cold water to chill.

Arrange each leaf with the heavy rib-side down and the leaf completely spread open. Place a small amount of the vegetable julienne in the center of each leaf, seasoning to taste with salt and pepper. Place an oyster on the vegetables and wrap the lettuce leaf around it. Repeat to make 12 packets. Keep warm in a 200°F. oven.

Meanwhile, add the curry powder to the reserved poaching liquid and reduce the liquid by half. Stir in the cream and again reduce by half. Whip in the remaining 4 tablespoons butter, season with salt and pepper, and strain the sauce, if desired.

Divide the oyster packets among 4 serving plates, preferably heated, drizzle the sauce over top, and serve immediately.

Oysters alla Parmigiana

Although oysters were well loved by the ancient Romans, they are not that common in contemporary Italian cuisine.

This is one easy way to prepare oysters, by stuffing them with spinach and glazing them under the broiler with a mixture of butter and Parmigiano-Reggiano or Grana Padano cheese. Spinach and oysters make a natural pair and also appear together in the famed New Orleans dish of Oysters Rockefeller, there flavored with licorice-like Pernod. Have your fishmonger pop open 16 to 20 oysters, leaving them in their shells. At home, remove and discard the upper shells.

SERVES 4

1/2 pound fresh spinach
1 tablespoon chopped garlic
2 tablespoons olive oil
Kosher salt and freshly ground black pepper to taste
16 to 20 oysters on the half-shell
1/4 pound Parmigiano-Reggiano or Grana Padano, grated
2 tablespoons unsalted butter

Wilt the spinach briefly, either by cooking in the microwave for 1 to 2 minutes or placing in a skillet with about half an inch of boiling water and stirring until evenly wilted. Drain, rinse under cold water to chill, and squeeze out the excess water.

Preheat the broiler. In a large skillet, cook the garlic in the olive oil until aromatic, about 1 minute, then stir in spinach. Cook until the spinach starts to sizzle, about 5 minutes, and then season to taste with salt and pepper.

Arrange all the oysters with their juices on a metal baking pan. Place a mound of spinach on each oyster. Sprinkle generously with the cheese and dot with butter. Place under the broiler for about 8 minutes, or until oyster juices bubble. Serve immediately.

Philadelphia Clubhouse Chicken Salad with Dijon Deviled Oysters

For many years, Philadelphia was not at all known for its restaurants. The best food to be had in "the Quaker City" was at private clubs, such as the Philadelphia Club, the Vesper Club, and the Union League. One of the favored club lunch dishes was chicken salad accompanied by fried deviled oysters. Although the city is now one of the top culinary destinations in the country, this salad is still a local favorite on club menus along with other stalwarts like snapper soup and pepper-pot stew. Either the oysters or the chicken salad are delicious on their own. Buy fresh-shucked oysters from your fishmonger. The best crust for the oysters is from processed or blended crustless, firm, white sandwich bread. Commercial white bread will be too mushy. Pepperidge Farm or Whole Foods white sandwich bread is perfect.

SERVES 4 TO 6

Chicken Salad

1 cup mayonnaise, purchased or homemade
Juice of 2 lemons
2 tablespoons chopped dill
2 tablespoons chopped Italian parsley
1 bunch scallions, thinly sliced
2 pounds cooked chicken meat, either white
  or dark or a mixture
3 ribs celery, diced
Kosher salt, freshly ground black pepper,
  and cayenne pepper to taste

Whisk together the mayonnaise, lemon juice, dill, parsley, and scallions. Mix with the chicken and celery, season with salt, pepper, and cayenne, and reserve.

Dijon Deviled Oysters and Assembly

$^1/_2$ cup Dijon mustard
$^1/_2$ cup sour cream
2 eggs
$^1/_2$ teaspoon cayenne pepper
3 cups fresh breadcrumbs, divided (*see* headnote)
24 shucked oysters
1 cup canola or vegetable oil, for frying
1 head Boston or other soft lettuce, separated into
  individual leaves

Whisk together the mustard, sour cream, eggs, and cayenne and transfer to a small bowl. Place half the breadcrumbs in a second bowl.

Dip each oyster into the mustard mix, coating on all sides. Roll the coated oyster in breadcrumbs, then shake off excess and arrange in a single layer on a wax-paper-lined tray. Refrigerate until ready to cook, up to 1 day.

Heat the oil in a large, heavy skillet, preferably cast-iron, until shimmering. Place the oysters, one at a time, into the oil and pan fry until crunchy and brown on both sides. Drain on a wire rack or paper towels, keeping warm in a 200°F. oven, if desired.

Line 4 to 6 plates with lettuce leaves. Place a portion of the chicken salad over top, arrange the oysters around the salad, and serve immediately.

675

Oyster Chowder with Herbs and Tiny Croutons

In this recipe, I tried to recreate the rich and creamy oyster chowder served to me years ago during a marvelous oyster festival held in Quebec City that featured the wonderful cold-water oysters of the Saint Lawrence Seaway. Another inspiration was the delectable Olympia oyster chowder I enjoyed long ago at Berkeley's rightly legendary Chez Panisse. There, the tiny, bite-sized oysters were barely poached and each was an exquisite mouthful. Celery root adds a marvelously nutty yet cleansing note to this chowder.

SERVES 8

Tiny Croutons

$^1/_2$ loaf firm homemade-style white sandwich bread, preferably day-old

4 tablespoons unsalted butter, melted

2 teaspoons finely chopped thyme

Preheat the oven to 350°F. Cut off and discard the crusts from the bread and cut them into small cubes. Toss with the melted butter and thyme and arrange on a metal baking pan. Toast 10 to 15 minutes, shaking once or twice, until the croutons are nicely browned. Remove from the oven and reserve.

Aromatic Milk Broth

6 cups milk

1 cup heavy cream

1 onion, stuck with 4 cloves

3 bay leaves

1 teaspoon mace

$^1/_2$ teaspoon freshly ground black pepper

2 teaspoons dry mustard

1 teaspoon ground coriander

1 teaspoon fennel seed

1 teaspoon celery seed

Scald the milk and cream with the remaining ingredients. Allow the mixture to steep for 1 hour, discard the onion, and then strain through a food mill or sieve, discarding the solids. Wipe out the pot, return the liquid to it and keep it warm.

Chowder

1 celery root, pared and diced

4 carrots, peeled and diced

2 leeks, cut into $^1/_2$-inch squares and washed

1 white onion, peeled and diced

4 tablespoons unsalted butter

$^1/_4$ cup all-purpose flour

3 dozen shucked small oysters + oyster liquor

2 tablespoons chopped fresh marjoram

$^1/_4$ cup chopped Italian parsley

Aromatic Milk Broth, heated

1 cup heavy cream

Kosher salt and freshly ground black pepper to taste

In a large soup pot, cook the celery root, carrots, leeks, and onion in butter until softened, about 10 minutes. Stir in the flour and cook together 2 to 3 minutes to get rid of raw flour taste. Add the shucked oysters, any oyster liquor, the marjoram, parsley, hot Milk Broth, and cream, and season with salt and pepper. Bring the liquid just to the boil, cooking only until the edges of the oysters curl. Serve immediately.

PEANUTS

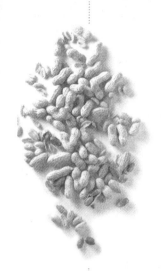

PEANUTS

Peanuts are so ingrained in American culture, it's hard to believe they were once scorned as a food fit only for slaves or animals. They're eaten at baseball games and at the circus, fed to elephants at the zoo, served at taverns with beer, and on airplanes as snacks. They go into countless childrens' lunch boxes as peanut butter and jelly sandwiches (a combination I particularly disliked and refused to eat as a child). The combination of peanuts and chocolate goes as far back as their origins in South America, and is seen in the chocolate-covered peanuts called "Goobers" and such iconic candies as Reese's peanut butter cups, both well-loved in America. We also top the list as the world's largest consumer of peanut butter.

Peanuts, *Arachis hypogaea*, probably originated in Brazil or Peru and for about 3,500 years—as long as people have been making pottery in South America—they have been making jars shaped like peanuts and decorated with peanuts. Graves of ancient Incas found along the dry, western coast of South America often contained jars filled with peanuts to provide food in the afterlife. Peanuts were grown as far north as Mexico by the time of the Spanish conquest. Spanish and Portuguese explorers took peanuts back to Europe. From there, traders and explorers took peanuts to Asia, and Africa, where they became common in the tropical regions of West Africa. Many Africans regarded the peanut as one of several plants possessing a soul.

African slaves from the west coast brought peanuts along with them to America, and planted them throughout the southern states. The word *goober* comes from the Congo name for peanuts, *nguba*; *pindar* is another name for the peanut with an African origin. In the 1700s, peanuts, then called "groundnuts" or "ground peas," were regarded as excellent food for pigs. By 1800, they were already being grown commercially in South Carolina. Because of their connection to the slave trade, peanuts were regarded as food only for the poor. During the Civil War, soldiers on both sides ate peanuts. By the second half of the nineteenth century, peanuts were eaten as a snack, sold freshly roasted by street vendors and at baseball games and circuses, a habit we still follow today.

Unlike any other legume, after its flower is fertilized, the peanut buries itself in the soil, where the fruit or pod develops underground, hence its other common name, groundnut. Once difficult and time-consuming to harvest, with new mechanical equipment built around 1900, peanuts came into demand for their oil, as roasted and salted nuts, and for peanut butter and candies. George Washington Carver, who was born during the tumultuous years of the Civil War, began his research into peanuts in 1903 at the Tuskegee Institute, where he served as the school's Director of Agriculture for forty years. Carver came up with more than three hundred uses for peanuts and developed the crop rotation method, which revolutionized southern agriculture by educating farmers to alternate soil-depleting cotton with soil-enriching crops like peanuts, peas, soybeans, and sweet potatoes.

Many types of peanuts are raised in the United States, where about one-tenth of the world's crop is grown. Nearly half the United States crop is grown in Georgia. The number of kernels in a pod ranges from two to three in some varieties to as much as from five to seven in others. Peanuts are nutritious and high in energy, containing forty to fifty percent oil and twenty to thirty percent protein. About half the peanuts grown in the United States are made into peanut butter and one-quarter more are sold roasted.

Elsewhere in the world, peanuts are grown in the warm climates of Asia, Africa, Australia, and North and South America. India and China together account for more than half of the world's production. Other major peanut-growing countries include Senegal, the Sudan, Malawi, Nigeria, Brazil, and Argentina, and South Africa.

Peanut Varieties

Runner: The attractive uniform kernel size and large yield of Runners has led them to become the dominant type of peanut, with the introduction in the early 1970s of a new runner variety, the Florunner. More than half the runners grown are used for peanut butter. They are grown mainly in Georgia, Alabama, Florida, Texas, and Oklahoma.

Spanish: Spanish-type peanuts have smaller kernels covered with a reddish-brown skin. In America, they mostly go into peanut candies, but are also used for snacks and peanut butter. They have higher oil content than other types of peanuts, so they are also crushed for their oil. They are primarily grown in Oklahoma and Texas.

Valencia: Valencias contain three or more small kernels to a pod and are covered in a bright-red skin. They are quite sweet and are usually roasted and sold in the shell or used for the fresh, boiled peanuts eaten as a snack in the south. New Mexico is the primary producer of Valencia peanuts.

Virginia: The Virginia peanut, also called the Virginia bunch peanut, has the largest kernels and provides most of the peanuts eaten whole in the United States, both shelled and in the shell as "ballpark" peanuts. Virginias are grown mainly in Virginia and parts of North and South Carolina.

679

PEANUTS AND PEANUT PRODUCTS

Buy raw, shelled peanuts in bags at a natural foods store. Use these peanuts when you're going to further toast or fry the nuts. If you live in a part of the country that grows peanuts, you might be able to buy green peanuts in their shell. These are boiled for a long time in salted water and eaten as a snack in the low country regions of South Carolina and Georgia, as the Japanese do with salted green soybeans called edamame. Dry-roasted peanuts are roasted without any additional oil, but they are not especially low in calories, because the peanut itself is high in fat.

Peanut Butter

Peanut butter was first concocted in the early 1900s and quickly became an American staple. Other cultures, particularly Indonesian and Thai, have long used ground peanuts as a key ingredient to enrich and thicken their sauces.

Natural peanut butter can be kept on the pantry shelf for one year; once opened, store in the refrigerator. Stir vigorously to recombine the peanut paste with the oil from which it eventually separates.

PLANTERS PEANUTS

An Italian immigrant by the name of Amadeo Obici started the Planters Peanut Company in 1906. In 1916, their beloved mascot, Mr. Peanut—with his top hat, monocle, and cane—was created as the winning entry in a contest Mr. Obici offered to school children.

Storing Peanuts

Peanuts can keep for up to 12 months if stored properly. Raw peanuts should be stored in the refrigerator in a tightly covered container to prevent spoilage. Store roasted peanuts in a porous bag, such as a brown paper bag. Keep them in an upper cupboard away from moisture so that mold doesn't form. To maintain good air circulation, don't store them in a plastic bag or plastic container.

DEEP FRYING IN PEANUT OIL

Many chefs, including myself, insist on peanut oil for deep frying because of its high smoke point and pleasing nutty flavor. It is considered the top-of-the-line frying oil and is more expensive than hydrogenated (transfat) soy or other vegetable oils commonly used in less highly reputed establishments. Unrefined peanut oil (the kind sold at natural foods stores) has a relatively low smoke point of 320°F., making it best suited for sautéing. Light-colored refined peanut oil has a much higher smoke point, at 450°F., so it is suitable for deep-frying, which is done at 365 to 375°F.

West African Peanut Soup

Peanut soup appears on the menu in many African countries. This smooth, creamy version, thickened with both peanuts and peanut butter, gets its sweetness from yam. Colored a warm, reddish brown, the soup is fragrant with sweet spices, intensely flavored, earthy, and piquant. Europeans brought peanuts from South America to Africa in the early 1500s where they caught on quickly because of their similarity to the native African bambarra groundnut. In the U.S., it has become traditional to serve this soup when celebrating the seven days of Kwanzaa. Substitute vegetable stock for a deliciously rich vegetarian soup.

SERVES 8

2 tablespoons vegetable oil

1 large onion, chopped

1 tablespoon each: chopped garlic and ginger root

2 teaspoons each: ground cumin and ground coriander

1/2 teaspoon ground cinnamon

1 pinch each: ground cloves and cayenne pepper

1 (15-ounce) can chopped plum tomatoes,
  or 2 cups fresh diced tomatoes

2 large yams, peeled and cut up

6 cups chicken stock (or vegetable stock), simmering

3/4 cup roasted peanuts

1/2 cup peanut butter, crunchy or creamy

1/2 bunch cilantro, leaves chopped

Kosher salt and freshly ground black pepper, to taste

Optional garnishes: diced fresh tomato, cilantro sprigs,
  and chopped roasted peanuts

Heat the oil in a large Dutch oven over medium heat. Sauté the onion until lightly browned, about 8 minutes. Stir in the garlic, ginger, cumin, coriander, cinnamon, cloves, and cayenne. Sauté together 2 to 3 minutes to release their fragrance. Stir in the tomatoes and yams and continue to cook about 5 minutes, stirring occasionally to meld the flavors.

Add the hot stock and peanuts, bring to a boil, reduce heat, and simmer for 30 minutes. Remove the soup from the heat. Using a food processor, blender, or immersion blender, puree the soup until smooth. For extra-smooth soup, strain it through a sieve. Return the soup to the saucepan. Whisk in the peanut butter and cilantro, season with salt and pepper, and heat through. Top each serving with the garnishes. Serve piping hot.

ROASTING PEANUTS

To roast raw peanuts in the shell, spread them out on a shallow baking pan, one or two layers deep, and roast, turning occasionally, in a 350°F. oven for 25 to 30 minutes, or until nutty-smelling and evenly browned.

To roast raw, shelled peanuts, first remove the skins by blanching. Bring a pot of salted water to the boil. Add the peanuts, turn off the heat, and leave to steep for about 3 minutes. Drain, and slip off the skins. Pat dry with paper towels and then spread them out in on a baking pan and roast at 350°F., turning them occasionally until nutty-smelling and evenly browned, about 15 to 20 minutes.

Rad Na Thai Chicken

The Continental, at Philadelphia's 2nd and Market Streets and now with a second location at 17th and Chestnut Streets, was the pioneer restaurant in the now-booming area of Old City. In 1995, nationally known restaurateur and former rock-concert promoter Steven Starr took over the old Continental Diner, hired a designer from New York's Soho, and reinvented The Continental as a highly popular restaurant and Martini Bar with a giant green olive as its symbol. This Rad Na Chicken was brought to the restaurant by its longtime Chef de Cuisine, Raul Bacordo, of Philippine and Laotian background. While Bacardo has since moved on, he was responsible for tilting the menu in the direction of Asia with dishes like this one, which he grew up eating as an everyday dish made by his mom.

SERVES 4

Rad Na Sauce

6 tablespoons Chinese oyster sauce (purchased)

3 tablespoons Asian fish sauce (purchased)

3 tablespoons granulated sugar

3 tablespoons rice wine vinegar

Combine all the ingredients in a small pot and bring to the boil. Reduce heat and simmer 5 minutes. Cool before storing in the refrigerator for up to 1 week.

Chicken

$1/4$ cup canola oil

$1/2$ pound boneless, skinless chicken breasts, cut into thin strips

2 eggs, lightly beaten

1 pound Rad Na noodles (*see* Rad Na or Chow Fun, below)

$1/2$ teaspoon crushed red pepper flakes

Rad Na Sauce

1 bunch scallions, thinly sliced

$1/2$ pound fresh mung bean sprouts

1 cup roasted salted peanuts

1 head romaine lettuce, outer leaves removed and cut into squares

Heat a skillet or wok until smoking hot. Add the oil and heat again until smoking. Add the chicken strips and stir. When the chicken is half-cooked, after about 3 minutes, add the eggs. Stir vigorously to break up the eggs as they cook.

Add the noodles, crushed pepper, and Rad Na Sauce. Stir to combine and coat the noodles. When the noodles are hot and coated with the sauce, add most of the scallions, most of the sprouts, and most of the peanuts. Stir well and remove from heat.

Divide the lettuce between 4 bowls. Top with the hot noodle mixture and garnish with the remaining scallions, bean sprouts, and peanuts. Serve immediately.

RAD NA OR CHOW FUN

These are wide strips of fresh rice noodles, sold at room temperature at Asian markets. The noodles may need to be cut into half-inch-wide strips before proceeding with the recipe. While Rad Na are preferable, you may substitute wide rice noodles, soaked in cold water for two hours then drained before using. Thai or Vietnamese Fish Sauce (*Nam Plah*), rice wine vinegar, and oyster sauce may also be found at Asian markets.

Thai Peanut Slaw

This crunchy, colorful slaw is easy to make and works well as an accompaniment to Asian dishes. Although it can be served with Szechuan Duck Spring Rolls (see page 376), it is good enough to serve on its own, perhaps topped with chicken or beef strips marinated briefly in a little soy sauce and a few drops of sesame oil and then stir-fried, or topped with pan-fried crabcakes (a variation on American crabcakes with cole slaw). Common green cabbage can be substituted for the more delicate napa cabbage, just be sure to remove and discard the tough central veins, which have a strong cabbagey flavor.

SERVES 6 TO 8

$1/2$ cup rice wine vinegar

$1/2$ cup Thai or Vietnamese fish sauce

2 teaspoons chili paste

$1^1/2$ teaspoons granulated sugar

Freshly ground black and/or white pepper to taste

1 head napa cabbage, shredded (about 3 cups)

1 cup shredded carrot

$1/2$ cup thinly sliced scallions

1 cup chopped roasted peanuts

$1/2$ cup shredded Thai basil (substitute basil and/or combine with mint)

Whisk together the vinegar, fish sauce, chili paste, sugar, and pepper. Combine the cabbage, carrot, scallions, peanuts, and Thai basil and toss with the dressing. Cover and refrigerate for at least 1 hour and up to 24 hours to combine flavors before using.

Chocolate–Peanut Brownies with Fudge Icing

While we may think of chocolate and peanuts together as a quintessentially American combination, it is actually said to date back to the Incas, who flavored their pounded peanuts (a rough type of peanut butter) with ground cocoa beans. Chocolate and peanuts may be a long-lived combo, but brownies with peanuts are American all the way. Brownies have been an American favorite since the nineteenth century, first appearing in print in the 1897 Sears Roebuck and Company catalogue. Salted or unsalted nuts both work here, according to your taste.

MAKES 24 BROWNIES

1 pound semisweet chocolate, in small discs or chopped

$3/4$ pound (3 sticks) unsalted butter

1 pound (4 cups) all-purpose flour, preferably unbleached

2 ounces ($1/2$ cup) Dutch-process cocoa

2 teaspoons baking powder

Pinch of salt

10 eggs

1 pound ($2^1/4$ cups) dark brown sugar, packed

1 cup granulated sugar

$1^1/2$ pounds chopped toasted peanuts, salted or unsalted

Fudge Icing (recipe follows)

Place the chocolate and the butter in a large, microwaveable bowl. Melt on medium power for 3 to 4 minutes, then stir and heat again until the chocolate has mostly, but not entirely melted. Stir the mixture until the chocolate melts and allow it to cool to room temperature.

683

Preheat the oven to 325°F. Whisk together the dry ingredients: flour, cocoa, baking powder, and salt, and reserve.

Beat the eggs and sugars together until light colored and the mixture forms a ribbon. Stir in the chocolate mix, and then fold in the dry ingredients and 1 pound of the peanuts.

Scrape onto a parchment-paper or Silpat-covered 18 x 12-inch half sheet pan or two 13 x 9-inch rectangular baking pans. Bake 20 minutes or until the brownies are mostly set, but still moist in the center.

Remove from the oven and cool to room temperature. Spread with Fudge Icing and sprinkle with chopped toasted peanuts. Chill at least 1 hour and then cut into 24 squares.

Fudge Icing

1 pound semisweet chocolate, in small discs or chopped

$^3/_4$ pound (3 sticks) unsalted butter

6 ounces ($^3/_4$ cup) Dutch process cocoa

1 cup dark corn syrup

8 egg yolks

$^3/_4$ cup confectioners' sugar

Place the chocolate and butter in a microwaveable bowl. Melt on medium power for 3 to 4 minutes, then stir and heat again until the chocolate has mostly, but not entirely, melted.

In a medium, heavy-bottomed nonreactive saucepan, whisk together cocoa, corn syrup, and $^1/_2$ cup of water and heat until bubbling and thickened, about 5 minutes. Remove from heat and stir in the chocolate, whisking until the mixture is completely smooth.

Beat the egg yolks and confectioners' sugar together until light colored and the mixture forms a ribbon, then beat in the chocolate mixture. The icing should be thick enough to show streaks when stirred.

Allow the icing to cool to room temperature before spreading on the cooled brownies. Note that the icing can be reheated over hot water, whisking until smooth and shiny.

684

Peek–A–Boo Peanut Butter and Jelly Sandwich Cookies

When I was a child, if my mother dared to send me to school with a peanut butter and jelly sandwich for lunch, I would immediately find someone else to trade with. Somehow however, in cookie form, I find the combination irresistible. I first made these cookies for a television presentation during my years as a food stylist for QVC. To shape the cookie dough, you will need a fairly large (4-inch) round cutter, fluted if possible, and a small (1-inch) round cutter, or the bottom of a metal pastry tip. You can also use a smaller cutter and sandwich two cookies together with the jam filling without cutting out the peek-a-boo hole. This recipe is also great for simple fork-flattened peanut butter cookies.

MAKES 2 DOZEN LARGE SANDWICH COOKIES

1 1/4 pounds (5 cups) all-purpose flour, preferably unbleached

1 tablespoon baking powder

1 teaspoon baking soda

1 teaspoon kosher salt

1 teaspoon ground cinnamon

2 cups chunky peanut butter

3/4 pound (3 sticks) unsalted butter

1 pound (2 1/4 cups) dark brown sugar, packed

2 cups confectioners' sugar

3 eggs

2 tablespoons vanilla extract

1 (15-ounce) jar best-quality raspberry or strawberry jam

Whisk together the dry ingredients: the flour, baking powder, baking soda, salt, and cinnamon, and reserve.

In the bowl of an electric mixer, beat together the peanut butter, butter, brown sugar, and confectioners' sugar until light and fluffy. Beat in the eggs, one at a time, until completely absorbed and creamy, and then add the vanilla. Stir in the dry ingredients, then transfer the dough to a zip-top bag and flatten to a rectangular block. Refrigerate for about 1 hour, or until firm.

Preheat the oven to 325°F. Divide the dough into 4 portions. On a lightly floured board, roll out a portion of the dough to about a 3/8-inch thickness. Using a 3- to 4-inch round cutter, cut out circles and place them 2 inches apart on baking sheets lined with parchment paper. Repeat with remaining portions of dough. You should have about 48 cookie rounds.

Refrigerate the rounds for about 30 minutes, or until firm. Cut out the centers of half the rounds using with a 1-inch round cutter. (Reroll these small dough rounds or bake as is, for mini cookies.)

Bake the cookies for 20 to 25 minutes or until lightly browned on the edges, turning the baking sheets after about 7 minutes for even browning. Remove from the oven and cool the cookies to room temperature on a rack.

Warm the jam for 2 minutes in the microwave oven or over low heat in a small saucepan for 2 minutes, until runny but not hot to the touch. Spoon 1 tablespoon of the warm jam into the center of each solid cookie round. Cool slightly to set, then lay a cutout top over the jam, pressing and twisting to adhere. Chill before serving for about 30 minutes to set the filling, and serve at room temperature.

PEARS

PEARS

Pears are automatically elegant.

Make a dish with apples and it'll be homey; switch the apples to pears and instantly, your dish is refined. We inevitably associate anything with panache with the French, including high fashion, fine restaurants, and even pears. France is the great country for pear lovers. We've imported some of their best, including the Williams (or Bartlett), the Comice, and the Anjou.

King Louis the XIV knew a perfect pear has no peer. Pears were the supreme fruit of the age in the seventeenth century. At that time, the French knew three hundred varieties of pears, though they considered only twenty-five worth eating. The King loved pears. He would meticulously peel the fruit so that he could rewrap its skin back into place. He would bestow these artfully peeled pears upon those currently in his good graces.

The King's pears were not only tricky to ripen, they were challenging to raise. In the open orchards of the time, the fruits ripened unevenly, instead of all at once. The *espalier* technique transformed pear growing close to Paris. This technique involves manipulating trees to grow against a wall, almost like a vine. This allowed the *cultivateur* to control his harvest. In the 1850s, horticulturists in the French province of Anjou began cultivating the *Doyenne du Comice* (just Comice in this country), to this day the queen of pears. We still eat D'Anjou pears, first

known as *D'Anjou Beurré* (buttered pear of Anjou) as our most common winter butter pear.

People have been eating both fresh and dried pears for thousands of years. The word *pear* appears to originate from some Mediterranean language even older than our Indo-European ancestral language. Versions of the same word appear in the French *poire*, the Italian and Spanish *pera*, and the Dutch *peer*. Proud backyard pear cultivators used to savor and compare pear varieties as seriously as wine at tastings. To me, pears make the best dried fruit. I eat them as is or diced and added to cakes and cookies and homemade granola.

The Romans introduced the cultivated pear to Britain, and it quickly became the second most widely grown and consumed fruit after apples. Though their history is older, pears have never been as popular as apples, probably because they don't store well. Pears have a short shelf life and will get mealy if ripened on the tree. The saying goes that one must sit up all night to catch a pear at its precise moment of ripe perfection.

The two main types of pears are the granular Hard or Winter pears, suitable for poaching, and the soft, melt-in-your-mouth Butter or Beurre pears. Shakespeare often referred to the Warden, a hard cooking pear that was the most commonly grown pear for centuries in England. The hundreds of varieties of Asian pears are

688

in-between apples and pears. Also sold as Apple-Pears, their shape is like an apple; their skin is like a pear. The most common variety of Asian pear, the Japanese variety called Twentieth Century (*Nijisseiki* in Japanese), has papery russet skin like a Bosc. Asian pears are great for eating straight, though their slightly gritty texture might take a little getting used to. They taste especially good in savory dishes. Eat them raw, and they'll be crunchy and juicy. Cook them, and they'll never lose their shape.

Winter Pear Varieties

Bosc: These large, firm, winter pears are known as the aristocrat of the pear family, The unmistakably shaped Bosc sits on a fat bottom that tapers up to a curved point at the tip, and has russeted yellow-brown skin, which does not change colors as its ripens. Its firm, crisp, creamy-white flesh tastes sweet and spicy. Its highly aromatic, dense flesh is ideal for baking and cooking. Boscs may be poached, roasted, grilled, baked, or sautéed and caramelized before eating, and go well with blue cheese and nuts.

Kieffer Pear: The Kieffer is squat and rounded in shape, small to medium in size, and has golden yellow-skin with a crimson blush. Its flesh is crisp and juicy with a musky flavor, white color, and coarse texture. This hybrid pear, named in 1876 by Peter Kieffer, is probably a cross between the Chinese sand pear and the Bartlett.

It was grown extensively in the United States in the first part of the 1900s and can still be found in small orchards and at farmers' markets. It is a late pear, in season from mid-September to mid-October.

Seckel Pear: The smallest of all commercially grown pears, Seckels have olive-green skin with a prominent red blush. Their firm, sweet, spicy flesh makes them excellent for cooking, pickling, or canning, and their small size and attractive appearance makes them ideal for autumn holiday garnish. The texture of Seckels is grainier than other European pears, giving them the nickname "sand pear." Seckels don't change color when they ripen. Seckel pears came originally from Delaware and were named by an American named Seckel, who discovered and propagated the pear that carries his name. Because they're rather grainy, people usually cook these almost miniature fruits. Seckels make perfect pickled spiced pears.

A TORTUROUS PEAR

A famous early pear variety called the *Poire d'angoisse* (pear of anguish) dates from medieval times. It was named after an instrument of torture in which a pear-shaped metal contraption was inserted into the victim's mouth and expanded. Street hawkers sold *poires d'angoisse*, the fruits, on the streets of Paris as early as the thirteenth century.

Summer (or Butter) Pear Varieties

Anjou and Red Anjou: The Anjou pear is the second most popular pear in America after the Bartlett. Egg-shaped and relatively hardy, Anjous are sweet and juicy, with mellow flavor and pale green or red skin. They do not change color as they ripen. Anjous are firm pears and good choices for both cooking and for eating.

Barlett and Red Bartlett: The Bartlett Pear, called Williams Pear in England and France, is to me, just about the finest eating pear (excluding the all-too-rare Comice). Given the choice between a Bartlett and an Anjou, often for sale at the same time, I'll always choose the Bartlett. I find Anjous to be a bit dull. Seventy-five percent of all pears grown in the United States are Bartletts, with their classic plump-bottomed, slender-necked "pear shape." They have smooth buttery texture, juicy flesh, and light green skin that turns to a warm yellow when ripe. Ripe Bartletts give off a distinctive pear aroma that can fill the room. Much of the Bartlett harvest goes to canning. The fruit is lightly chewy and sweet when dried, and is the same pear you find in a bottle of Swiss *Poire Eau de Vie*. This clear "water of life" liquor is a personal obsession of mine. However, I don't buy the one with the pear, even though it's as surprising as seeing a ship in a bottle. Unfortunately, the pear in the bottle tastes terrible. When I savor a small glass, chilled until icy, I'm not sure which is better, the taste or the aroma. Bartlett Pears now come in the beautiful red-skinned variety that taste similar to yellow Bartletts, but which cost more. I've found them to be uneven in quality.

Comice: Rightly known as the "Queen of Pears," the Comice, short for the French *Doyenne de Comice*, is generally considered to be the best eating pear. It is a fat, lumpy-looking, blunt, yellowish-green French pear variety with a russet or red blush. Large and exquisite, this pear has buttery smooth, sweet flesh and a fruity fragrance. Comices have almost no color change when ripe. Its smooth, creamy mouth-feel is unequaled, as is its sweet and juicy taste. Its enticing perfume helps make the Comice the eating pear par excellence.

Forelle Pear: The green and red speckled Forelle pear is also known as the "trout pear" (*forelle* is the German word for trout) because its markings are similar to those on the fish. The Forelle originated in Saxony in the early eighteenth century. It is the size and shape of a small Bartlett, with beautiful bright yellow skin freckled with crimson when ripe. Forelles are sometimes tricky to ripen, but can be very sweet and juicy with firm, slightly grainy flesh.

Packham Pear: The Packham pear, originally bred in Australia in 1897, is the Australian pear of choice. A late-season pear, Packhams have the overall shape and size of an Anjou, with bumpy green skin. When fully ripe, they are juicy and sweet. Packham pears are excellent eaten out-of-hand, but are also suitable for cooking. When cooking Packhams, select slightly underripe, firm pears.

RESCUING ANTIQUE PEAR VARIETIES IN UMBRIA

Isabella dalla Ragione and her father, Livio, have made it their mission to rescue disappearing antique pear and other fruit trees in their native region of Umbria, in central Italy. They have named their farm and their work the *Associazione Archeologia Arborea* (Archeological Arbor Association; www.archeologiaarborea.org). On a charming old farm up a steep, rocky road, the Association's central farmhouse is centered around a huge fireplace embellished with old farm and kitchen tools. They research the pears, plant and propagate old varieties, and write about them so that they will be better known.

On one miraculously sunshiny day in November 2005, I visited their farm and learned why they are so obsessed with this important work. Pears, which may be as much as two hundred and fifty years old, are among the most long-lived fruit trees; only olives live longer. The cultivation of pears is especially embedded into the culture and cuisine of this part of Umbria, close to neighboring Tuscany. Pears were used in savory dishes, roasted with pork, cooked with beef and poultry, and in general were an important ingredient in earlier times. The dalla Ragione's also grow old varieties of peaches, cherries, apples, medlars, quince, plums, figs, and grapes. It is possible to adopt a tree by paying for its upkeep. The tree would bear the adoptive parent's name.

Poaching Pears

Select hard winter pears, like Bosc or Seckel, or use firm but not hard buttery pears. Make a light sugar syrup, enough to cover the pears, using equal quantities of sugar and water (two cups of each is a good amount to start with). Add flavorings as you wish: a whole vanilla bean split lengthwise, soft cinnamon sticks, whole allspice berries, lemon or orange zest, cardamom seeds, and/or several whole cloves, along with the juice of one lemon. Bring the liquid to a boil. You may also substitute honey for part of the sugar. Use half as much honey as the sugar it is replacing (honey is twice as sweet as sugar) when making the syrup. Peel the pears and split them in half from the stem to the bottom, leaving the stems attached, and, using a melon baller, scoop out around the round ball of flesh containing the seeds. Everything else is edible. Place the pears in the liquid. Slowly bring to a boil. Simmer until the pear is almost tender through when pricked. Turn the fire off and let the pears cool in the liquid.

691

Substitute Asian pears or hard pears for any apple recipe. Ripe butter pears will tend to disintegrate, so use either butter pears that are quite firm but juicy, winter hard pears, or Asian pears.

Try an old-fashioned apple cake or tart made with pears instead. Combine a few varieties for fullest flavor and interesting variations in texture.

Sauté pear slices in whole butter, then sprinkle with sugar, swirling until the sugar melts and caramelizes. Carefully (from a measure, not from the bottle) pour in several spoons of brandy, rum, or liqueur and flame. This is exquisite with ice cream or pound cake.

Pears have a special affinity with chocolate. *Poires Belle-Helene* sounds intimidating, but it's just poached butter pears, such as Comice or Bartlett, topped with warm chocolate sauce and served over vanilla ice cream.

For a cold-weather snack, preferably in front of a roaring fire, serve buttery Bartlett or Comice pear wedges with fresh walnuts in the shell, and a wedge of room-temperature Roquefort or Gorgonzola cheese.

Author Jane Grigson makes a divinely simple British-style savoury (a tasty morsel served at the end of a formal meal) by toasting white bread and covering it with watercress and thin slices of Comice pears. After topping it with Stilton cheese slivers, she broils the toast until the cheese melts.

Asian Pear and Cabrales Salad with Fig–Port Wine Vinaigrette

Instead of ending a meal with a plate of fruit and cheese, serve this elegant winter salad made with crunchy, juicy Asian pears and figs. The burgundy-streaked long spears of radicchio di Treviso are very similar to red Belgian endive, which makes a good substitute (see the Indivia and Radicchio chapter, page 490, for more information). Dried figs, preferably the dark purple-black mission figs, are simmered in port wine, puréed, and then added to the dressing. Cabrales cheese, a hearty blue cheese from the north of Spain, has a sharp, biting flavor and buttery texture that works perfectly here (see the Blue Cheese chapter for more about Choosing and Storing Cabrales, page 242).

SERVES 6

3 dried figs, preferably Black Mission

1/2 cup ruby port wine

Kosher salt and freshly ground black pepper, to taste

6 tablespoons grapeseed oil, or another neutral salad oil

2 tablespoons cider vinegar

2 tablespoons finely chopped shallots

2 heads Belgian endive

1 head radicchio di Treviso

1 large Asian pear

Juice of 1/2 a lemon

1/2 pound Cabrales cheese, cut into 6 slices

Trim off and discard the stems from the figs. Cut the figs into 6 to 8 pieces each. Heat the port wine until hot to the touch, turn off the heat, then add the figs. Allow the figs

692

to soak in the port for 2 hours, or until softened.

Place the figs and their soaking liquid in a food processor or blender and puree until smooth. Strain the mixture through a sieve, pushing on the solids with a spatula to extract all the juices. Discard the solids. Stir enough water (about $1/4$ to $1/3$ cup) into the puree to thin it to dressing consistency. Season with salt and pepper and reserve.

Whisk together the oil, vinegar, and shallots. Season with salt and pepper and reserve.

Cut the endive and radicchio into 1-inch-wide strips, discarding the hard cores. (It's not normally necessary to wash these salad greens.)

Remove the core from the Asian pear, cut into thin wedges, and toss with lemon juice. Toss the endive, radicchio, and pears with the vinaigrette. Divide among 6 salad plates.

Drizzle the reserved fig and port wine dressing over the salads. Top each salad with a slice of Cabrales cheese and serve immediately.

Roasted Pear Salad with Rosemary, Honey, and Fennel

Pears are at their best here, marinated in olive oil, honey, and rosemary and then broiled until the edges caramelize. When I can, I roast the pears in a wood-burning oven for an incomparable flavor. Broiling works just fine, but be sure to keep a careful eye on the pears so they don't burn. Baking at a high temperature will also work, but the pears will tend to cook softer without as much caramelization. The juicy, deep-flavored pears are accented here by thinly shaved, sweet, crunchy fennel bulb and sweet toasted hazelnuts. Bosc pears, hazelnuts, and fennel are in season in the late fall and winter, so they all work well together. Although raspberries are in season in the summer and early fall, I find that this vinaigrette, made with raspberries and rosemary, works very well using frozen raspberries. Frozen raspberries have better flavor than the fresh, because only the ripest, hard-to-sell berries are frozen.

SERVES 4

Roasted Pears

2 Bosc pears

1 tablespoon chopped rosemary

2 tablespoons olive oil

1 tablespoon honey

1 teaspoon kosher salt

$1/4$ teaspoon freshly ground black pepper

Preheat the broiler to high. Cut the pears in half and remove the seed section using a melon baller (or tomato shark). Cut the pears into thin, $1/4$-inch-wide wedges. Toss with the remaining ingredients and spread in a single layer on a sheet pan. Broil 5 to 8 minutes, turning once or twice until well browned at the edges, about 10 minutes. Cool to room temperature and reserve.

Assembly

$3/4$ pound spring mix greens

1 head fennel, shaved and soaked in ice water

2 tablespoons chopped toasted hazelnuts
  (hand-chopped)

1 cup Raspberry Vinaigrette (*see* page 791)

Roasted Pears

$1/2$ pint fresh raspberries

693

Lightly toss the greens with the fennel, hazelnuts, and most of the dressing, making sure that fennel shows around bottom edge of salad. Arrange on salad plates. Place Roasted Pears up against the side of the salad. Drizzle each plate with the remaining dressing and garnish with raspberries. Serve immediately.

Walnut Mascarpone– Filled Pears with Pear Caramel Sauce

I served this dessert in my days at the Bolognese-style Ristorante DiLullo, where I served as chef for six years. While Italy is filled with fancy pasticcerie (pastry shops, where people traditionally buy stylishly wrapped delicacies to bring home to the family on Sundays), homestyle desserts like this one are usually based on fruits. Here, pears are first poached in a lemon, vanilla, and cinnamon-flavored vermouth syrup and then hollowed out from the bottom. For the filling, ultra-rich, super-smooth mascarpone—a type of ripened, thickened cream cheese—is mixed with toasted walnuts and flavored with pear eau de vie, made by distilling the pears to create a highly fragrant, unsweetened essence of pear. Topping the stuffed poached pears is a luscious caramel sauce made by simply cooking down the pear-poaching liquid until it thickens and then caramelizes.

SERVES 8

Vermouth Poached Pears

$1/4$ cup dry white vermouth

Juice of 1 lemon

1 cup granulated sugar

1 vanilla bean, split

1 cinnamon stick, crushed

8 Bosc pears with stems (no bruises)

In a large, nonreactive pot, place the vermouth, lemon juice, sugar, vanilla bean, and cinnamon stick, plus 1 cup of water, and bring to the boil.

Meanwhile, peel the pears evenly. Add the pears to the syrup and bring to the boil again. Reduce heat to a bare simmer. Cover pears with a plate to weigh them down into the syrup. Simmer about 20 minutes, or until tender when pierced with a skewer. Cool in syrup and then drain, reserving syrup. Hollow out the inside from the bottom up. Cut off a thin slice from the bottom so that the pears will stand upright.

Pear Caramel

Pear poaching liquid (from above)

2 cups heavy cream

Juice of 1 lemon

Water as needed

Transfer poaching liquid to a large pot and reduce over medium heat until the syrup just begins to caramelize. Continue to cook until the syrup is a deep golden color and just beginning to turn red. Slowly pour in the cream, taking care, as the cream will bubble up vigorously. Whisk if necessary to keep the syrup from overflowing. Cook until the caramel is dissolved and the sauce is thick and smooth.

Remove from heat, stir in the lemon juice and reserve. Store refrigerated, heating gently to rewarm and adding water as needed to thin to pouring consistency.

Mascarpone Filling

1 cup Mascarpone

¼ cup confectioners' sugar

2 tablespoons Poire William Eau de Vie

1 cup walnuts, toasted and finely chopped

Whip the Mascarpone until light and fluffy, being careful not to overbeat. Add confectioners' sugar, eau de vie, and walnuts. Transfer mixture to a pastry bag.

Assembly

Mascarpone Filling

Poached pears

Pear Caramel

Toasted whole walnut halves, for garnish

Pipe the Mascarpone Filling into the bottoms of the drained poached pears. Arrange on individual serving plates. Spoon warm Pear Caramel over top. Garnish with walnut halves.

Red Wine and Cinnamon–Poached Pears

Pears are also wonderful poached in spiced red wine mixed with honey. The pears will continue to absorb the color and flavor of the syrup after poaching as they marinate for up to five days, so this is an excellent choice for a make-ahead dessert. Serve as is, warm or cold, or to accompany with a rich, flourless chocolate cake, such as Chocolate Strega Cake (see page 291), with Bittersweet Chocolate Soufflé (see page 296), or with Frangelico Semifreddo with Mocha Chocolate Sauce (see page 471).

SERVES 8

2 cups dry red wine

½ cup granulated sugar

½ cup honey

2 bay leaves

1 cinnamon stick, lightly crushed

4 whole cloves

Juice of 1 lemon

8 Bosc pears

695

Combine the wine, sugar, honey, bay leaves, cinnamon, cloves, lemon juice, and 2 cups of water. Bring to the boil in a large, nonreactive pot.

Meanwhile, pare off the skin of the pears, then cut into halves, removing the seed core with a melon baller (or a tomato shark). Place the pear halves in the syrup and bring back to the boil. Reduce heat and gently poach for about 15 minutes, or until pear halves are close to tender when pricked with a skewer.

Remove the pears from the pot and arrange in a glass or ceramic bowl. Pour the poaching liquid into a bowl, wipe out the cooking pot, and strain the poaching liquid back into the pot. Heat to boiling and then reduce to medium heat. Cook the liquid for about 15 minutes, or until it has reduced by about half and is thick and syrupy. Pour the thick syrup over the pears, cool and then serve, or refrigerate for up to 5 days before serving.

Sautéed Bartlett Pears in Chocolate Sauce

The classic combination of pears and chocolate makes a most elegant, yet easy-to-make dish. For good results, all you need are firm, but ripe, pears and best-quality chocolate. Bartlett pears work best here because of their intoxicating fragrance and firm, juicy texture. Fannie Farmer gives a variation on this dish in her Boston Cooking School Cookbook. *I adapted this recipe from her book.*

SERVES 6

2 cups milk

$1/4$ pound semisweet chocolate, disks or chopped

2 teaspoons cornstarch

1 cup light cream

$1/4$ pound (1 stick) unsalted butter, divided

$1/2$ cup confectioners' sugar

1 teaspoon vanilla extract

4 to 6 firm, but ripe Bartlett pears, peeled, seeded, and quartered

Scald the milk, either in the microwave, or on top of the stove. Stir in the chocolate and allow it to melt from the heat of the milk. Stir again until completely smooth. (Heat gently and briefly if the chocolate has not fully melted.)

Make a slurry by combining the cornstarch and cream. Whisk into the melted chocolate and transfer to a medium, heavy-bottomed, nonreactive pot. Cook, while stirring often, over moderate heat until smooth and just beginning to bubble.

Meanwhile in a small, heavy pot, cook 4 tablespoons of the butter together with the confectioners' sugar, stirring until caramelized. Scrape this caramel into the chocolate mixture and stir in the vanilla. Keep the sauce warm.

Heat the remaining 4 tablespoons butter in a large, nonreactive skillet until sizzling and just beginning to brown. Add the pear quarters and sauté over high heat until browned, about 5 minutes. Serve hot with warm chocolate sauce drizzled over top.

Baked Bosc Pears
with Almond Streusel

*I've been making fruit crisp variations since I was a preco-
cious baker at age eleven. Bosc Pears with Almond Crisp
Topping is hard to beat. In this simple pear crisp, the pears
are baked until juicy and bubbling, and the topping is
browned and crisp. I prefer to use skin-on sliced almonds
because they have more flavor and their appearance is
more dramatic than the finer blanched, skinned, and sliced
almonds. I buy them at Trader Joe's and at warehouse club
stores like BJ's and CostCo. Feel free to substitute blanched
almonds or even better, sliced skin-on hazelnuts, sometimes found in specialty stores.*

SERVES 6 TO 8

1 cup light brown sugar, packed

$1/2$ pound (2 cups) all-purpose flour, preferably
   unbleached

1 teaspoon cinnamon

$1/2$ pound (2 sticks) unsalted butter, cut into bits
   and chilled

1 cup sliced almonds, preferably skin-on

6 Bosc pears, peeled, seeded, and cut in wedges

Preheat the oven to 400°F. In a bowl, combine the sugar,
flour, and cinnamon. Cut in the butter until the mixture is
crumbly. Stir in the sliced almonds.

   Lightly butter a shallow baking dish. Arrange the pears
on the bottom. Cover generously with the almond topping and bake for 30 minutes, or until brown and bubbling.
Serve hot.

PEPPERS

PEPPERS

In my early years as a chef, I traveled to Italy to learn more about its cuisine, and was knocked out by the then-unusual yellow bell peppers I saw everywhere. I just had to have them. At that time, no one grew them in the U.S., at least not in Pennsylvania. I secreted packets of seeds in my luggage, and upon my return, found several farmers to raise them for me. I was so excited when I got my first crop. Now, colorful bell peppers are so common as to be almost ubiquitous and overused for the sake of their color, without consideration for whether their strong flavor is appropriate to the dish. Whether grilled, roasted, marinated, sliced into julienne for a salad, diced and sautéed with other vegetables, made into a sweet vegetable-based sauce, or stuffed, peppers are extremely versatile, easy to find, and work well with dishes from just about anywhere around the Mediterranean, the Balkans, Mexico, and South America.

All peppers, whether hot or sweet, are perennials in the genus *Capsicum* and—along with tomatoes, potatoes, and eggplant—belong to the larger *Solanaceae* family. Peppers originated in South America and were eventually spread, probably by birds, throughout South and Central America. Over time, peppers have traveled around the world, where unique peppers have been bred and incorporated into local cuisines. Sweet bell peppers are large and blocky in shape, with thick flesh

walls and sweet flavor, and are available in many colors—green (or unripe), red, yellow, orange, purple, white, and even brown (unfortunately the purple and white colors tend to disappear with cooking). The color depends on the variety and the stage of ripeness. Almost all peppers start out as green—a few start as yellow—and ripen to another color.

The most common sweet bell peppers are green, which are fully developed but not yet ripe. Red, orange, and yellow peppers are riper, sweeter, and pricier than green peppers. Suntan peppers are harvested when red or another color just starts to develop, leaving most of the pepper green. Many peppers on the market come from hothouses in Holland, Israel, Mexico, and Canada. These peppers are evenly sized, have thick, juicy flesh, and sweet flavor. Their calyxes are noticeably fleshy and firm. Longer, thinner-walled yellow and red domestic peppers mostly come from California and may not be as brightly colored throughout. Sweet mini peppers are bred from bell peppers and hot peppers to develop a small, sweet pepper with relatively few seeds. These finger-sized peppers are sweet and crunchy. They sell for a relatively high price and are usually packed in clear plastic "clamshell" containers.

Peppers seem to have been designed specifically for stuffing—what other vegetable is both hollow inside

700

and perfectly sized for an individual portion? It was in Istanbul during the nearly 700-year-long regime of the Ottoman Empire (which lasted from the 1299 to 1923) that stuffed vegetables were first treated as a regular culinary genre. Stuffing peppers came later to the Ottomans, after the discovery of the New World, when peppers were brought to Turkey from their place of origin, South America. It's likely that peppers were already being stuffed in the New World long ago, but it was in the Old World that sweet peppers began showing up with all manner of stuffings.

Stuffing peppers, whether sweet or hot, is a natural way to make a more expensive filling go further, and there are countless creative variations on this culinary theme. Sometimes the peppers are hot; sometimes they are sweet and they can be served either hot or cold, depending on the filling. Like many homestyle dishes, stuffed peppers take well to advance preparation and slow oven cooking that doesn't take a watchful eye. When I was growing up, my mom's stuffed peppers were filled with a mixture of browned onions, beef, rice, and maybe a few raisins, all simmered in tomato sauce. If you come from an Italian background, you may have been served the same dish made with sweet and hot sausage, oregano, and garlic.

In the Umbrian hill town of Orvieto, Italy, at the charming restaurant La Volpe e la Uva (The Fox and the Grape), I ate an old-time dish of stuffed narrow, long peppers with a very finely ground veal and pork filling. Now, all I have to do is find a recipe for this unpretentious dish (the kind that doesn't usually find its way into books) so I can try making it for myself. In Italy, another version of the stuffed pepper, filled with anchovies, capers, and garlic, is served as a simple but popular antipasto.

If you go out drinking in bars, you're sure to have seen and/or experienced one of the latest rages, often called "shooters" or "poppers"—hot cherry peppers or jalapeño peppers stuffed with cheese or other things, then battered and fried. Unfortunately, most of these come straight out of the freezer into the fryer. To me, these snacks are a commercial iteration of the classic Mexican *chile relleno* (stuffed hot pepper), not as good as the real thing, but obviously enticing for their name, shape, and fieriness (a test of *machismo*).

CHOOSING PEPPERS FOR STUFFING

When buying peppers for stuffing, choose evenly sized and shaped peppers. The best shape is either short and blocky, which can stand up in the baking dish, or long and tubular, which can lay sideways in the pan. The more expensive hothouse bell peppers, available in bright colors from Holland, Israel, Canada, and Mexico, are excellent candidates for stuffing. They look very appealing if you cut off the tops, stuff the peppers, and bake the tops alongside the peppers. When serving the dish, place the pepper tops back on top (if you bake the peppers with their tops on, the tops are apt to burn because they'll stick up too much). Thinner-skinned light greenish-yellow Cubanelles, light green Italian frying peppers, or Hungarian banana (yellow) or wax peppers are also good choices for stuffing. These long peppers have much thinner walls of flesh, so they are more delicate and a little harder to handle.

Sweet bell peppers are in season year round with peak season from May through August. At different times of year there may be domestic or imported hothouse peppers on the market. Hothouse peppers sell for a higher price but also have greater yield.

Sweet peppers will keep in the refrigerator for three to four days, depending on their freshness when they were purchased. Because red peppers are riper than green ones, they will spoil faster. Mini peppers will keep up to two weeks.

Choosing Peppers

Choose fresh, firm, brightly colored peppers with taut, shiny skin, thick flesh and a firm green calyx. Peppers should feel heavy for their size. Avoid peppers with wrinkled skins or any brown or soft spots. Many colorful peppers are now greenhouse-grown in Holland, Israel, Mexico, and Canada. They are often of very high quality, with dense, meaty flesh. However, they may be sold when they are well beyond their prime; pass up peppers with flabby, wrinkly skin.

702

Piquillo Peppers with Boquerones Anchovies

The marvelous heart-shaped piquillo peppers come only from the northern Spanish region of Navarre, once the Kingdom of Navarre, which borders France and the Basque country. These vermilion-colored peppers are sweet and slightly piquant, with thin flesh walls and intensely fruity flavor. A popular tapas, they are stuffed with all manner of things from Serrano ham to Manchego cheese, creamed salt cod, crab or lobster, tuna in olive oil, or fresh white cheese, or simply marinated as here, with the lightly cured anchovies called boquerones. *Only sold roasted and canned, piquillos can be purchased from specialty food suppliers like La Tienda (www.latienda.com) and The Spanish Table (www.spanishtable.com) and now at many well-stocked supermarkets.*

Serves 6 as tapas

3 tablespoons extra-virgin olive oil

2 teaspoons sherry vinegar

2 teaspoons finely chopped or pressed fresh garlic

Kosher salt to taste

12 ounces (about 1 jar or can) roasted piquillo
    peppers, drained

2 ounces boquerones anchovies

2 tablespoons finely chopped Italian parsley

Lightly whisk together the olive oil, vinegar, garlic, and salt. Place the peppers on a flat serving platter. Arrange the anchovies in an attractive pattern over top. Drizzle with the dressing, sprinkle with the parsley, and serve immediately.

Harissa Sauce

Harissa is Tunisia's basic seasoning paste, consisting of sweet and hot peppers boldly flavored with garlic and ground caraway. It is served with kebabs and appears on the table in a small dish to be added to the cooking juices of couscous and to spread sparingly on casse-croute sandwiches. It is also delicious on crusty bread with hummus. Prepared Harissa may be found in tubes or cans; the best comes from Tunisia. Ground caraway is essential to the flavor of this condiment, though it may be hard to find. Use about 1½ tablespoons of whole caraway seeds, ground in a clean coffee grinder or finely crushed using a mortar and pestle.

MAKES ABOUT 3 CUPS

¾ pound (2 to 3 large) sweet bell peppers, roasted
   and peeled
2 ounces (2 to 3 small) chile peppers, such as red Serrano,
   jalapeño, or Holland red peppers, roasted and peeled
½ cup sweet Spanish paprika
¼ cup extra-virgin olive oil
4 large cloves garlic, crushed
2 tablespoons ground caraway seed
Kosher salt to taste

Combine all above ingredients in the bowl of a food processor and puree to a fine paste. Store tightly covered in the refrigerator for up to 3 weeks.

Fettuccine all'Catunzein with Roasted Peppers and Sausage

This simple but satisfying dish came from a well-known restaurant in Italy's gastronomic capital of Bologna. The restaurant was a symbol of deluxe living and was "liberated" in the late 1970s by leftist student rebels to feed their comrades. I served this dish for years at Ristorante DiLullo, where it fit right in with its Bolognese menu. Combining fresh and hot sausage gives the best of both worlds—if you use all hot sausage, the dish is too spicy; all sweet, and the dish doesn't have enough bite. As with all fresh egg pasta dishes, it's important to serve this very hot; fresh pasta turns gluey and heavy as it cools.

SERVES 4

½ pound hot Italian sausage, removed from its casing
½ pound sweet Italian sausage, removed from its casing
1 red onion, diced
4 roasted red bell peppers, peeled, seeded and diced
2 cups Marinara sauce (*see* page 895)
1 pound fresh egg fettuccine
½ cup chopped Italian parsley
¼ pound freshly grated Parmigiano-Reggiano or
   Grana Padano cheese

In a heavy-bottomed skillet, preferably cast-iron, render out the fat and brown the sausage evenly, breaking it up with a spoon as it cooks. Remove the browned sausage from the pan and reserve. Pour off any excess fat and discard, leaving a thin film of fat in the pan.

   In the same pan, stir-fry the onion until lightly browned, then add the peppers and tomato sauce. Bring to the boil and simmer together 15 minutes, stirring occasionally, until thickened.

Meanwhile, bring a large pot of salted water to the boil. Add the fettuccine and cook until tender yet still firm. Drain gently, so as not to break up the pasta.

Add the parsley to the sauce. Toss the fettuccine with half the sauce and half the cheese. Make a nest of fettuccine in each of 4 plates, preferably heated. Spoon more sauce into the middle of each plate and sprinkle with the remaining cheese to taste. Serve immediately, while piping hot.

DOLMA: STUFFED PEPPERS AND OTHER VEGETABLES

Long ago, I made a trip to Istanbul, the home of the stuffed vegetable, known as *dolma*. I can still picture appetizing round trays in restaurant windows covered with warm, stuffed vegetables—including eggplant, tomato, grape leaves, onions, zucchini, and of course, peppers. There are two main categories of dolma. Those with meat stuffing—usually including some type of grain such as rice or bulgur wheat—are served hot with a sauce. Those with rice-based stuffings—often including nuts, raisins, or legumes such as lentils or chickpeas—are served cold (actually cool room temperature) and dressed with olive oil. Dolmas are found in Turkey, the Balkans, Lebanon, the southern Caucasus, Iran, Central Asia, Egypt, the countries of the Fertile Crescent, and Arabia, all places touched by the far-reaching Ottoman Empire.

BRUSCHETTA WITH ROASTED PEPPERS, MOZZARELLA, AND ANCHOVIES

To make this popular Italian antipasto, divide roasted red and/or yellow bell peppers into wide sections along their natural break lines. Stuff them with a mixture of chopped anchovy, breadcrumbs, garlic, parsley, and of course, olive oil. Baked them in a hot oven until browned and slightly shriveled. Serve at room temperature.

GENIE IN A PEPPER

Claudia Roden, in her *New Book of Middle Eastern Food,* describes the charming folk belief in the existence of *djinns* (spirits) who inhabit vegetables like peppers. "These spirits are seasoned and spiced, and given piquant, naughty, or gentle personalities." Better treat your vegetables right!

Shrimp Chiles Rellenos

When I lived in Mexico in the early 1960s, one of the first dishes I learned to prepare (and still adore) was the classic, Chiles Rellenos. It is made with hot but not fiery dark green poblano chiles that are grilled, peeled, seeded, stuffed, and then dipped in the lightest egg-foam batter, deep-fried, and then finally simmered in a richly spiced tomato sauce. Yes, it's a lot of work. But every once in a while I get ambitious and make this slightly updated version of a genuine Mexican classic. I deep fry the peppers here restaurant-style so the peppers are nice and firm with skin that easily slips off. You can also grill or broil the peppers before peeling.

Serves 6

1 quart peanut oil, for frying

6 poblano chile peppers, preferably large and long in shape (substitute Anaheim or Pasilla peppers)

$1/2$ cup each: diced red bell pepper, red onion (and/or scallions), jicama, carrot, and whole corn kernels

2 teaspoons chopped garlic

2 tablespoons olive oil

$1/2$ pound small shrimp, chopped into bite-size pieces

$1/2$ pound shredded Chihuahua or Monterey Jack cheese

3 cups Mexican Tomato Sauce with Allspice (*see* page 897)

6 eggs, separated

Kosher salt to taste

Flour, for dusting

Heat the peanut oil to 365°F. or until shimmering and hot to your hand held about 2 inches from the oil. Add the poblano peppers and deep-fry long enough to blister the skin. Remove peppers from the oil, reserving the oil. Rinse the peppers under cold water until cool enough to hold. Peel and seed the peppers by making a small slit in the side of the pepper, leaving the stem intact, and reserve. Alternatively, you can grill or broil the peppers until they are charred all over, then peel them.

In a skillet, sauté the chopped vegetables, corn, and garlic in the olive oil until crisp-tender. Remove from the oil and reserve. Add the shrimp to the same skillet and sauté 2 to 3 minutes, or until just opaque.

Mix the vegetables, shrimp, and cheese together. Cool the mixture to room temperature and then use to stuff the reserved peppers. Press the slit edges of the peppers closed as much as possible and secure with a toothpick. Chill until set, about 30 minutes.

Bring the tomato sauce to a bare simmer in a wide casserole and reserve.

Heat the peanut oil again to 365°F. Meanwhile, beat the egg whites and a pinch of salt until firm and glossy. In a separate bowl, lightly beat the egg yolks just to liquefy them. Fold into the egg whites.

Pat the stuffed peppers dry with paper towels and remove the toothpicks. Dust lightly with the flour, shaking off the excess. Then roll in the egg batter and place, one by one, into the oil to deep-fry. Fry about 5 minutes, turning so the peppers cook evenly, or until they are nicely browned. Drain on paper towels and then add to the simmering tomato sauce. Simmer about 15 minutes, or until the cheese starts to melt out. Serve the peppers with the sauce.

705

Grilled Roasted Pepper and Eggplant Sandwiches

These delicious sandwiches were a winner at A'propos, the Mediterranean bistro where I cheffed on what is now Philadelphia's booming Avenue of the Arts. In these sandwiches, grilled eggplant slices take the role of the meat. The Pepper Jack cheese is mild, melting Monterey Jack, spiked with bits of hot pepper. Substitute plain Monterey Jack if you'd like. These sandwiches would also work well cooked in an electric panini maker, something that didn't exist when I was a chef, at least in America. Semolina, the inner kernel of the same durum wheat flour used to make dried pasta, goes into the deliciously nutty, golden-hued bread I like to use for these sandwiches.

SERVES 6

2 tablespoons olive oil

1 tablespoon chopped garlic

2 tablespoons chopped fresh marjoram (or oregano)

Kosher salt and freshly ground black pepper to taste

2 pounds eggplant, cut lengthwise into $1/2$-inch-thick slabs

2 to 3 large red bell peppers

1 loaf Italian bread, sliced diagonally, preferably semolina bread

$1/2$ pound Pepper Jack cheese, shredded

Heat a charcoal or other type of grill until quite hot. Combine the olive oil, garlic, marjoram, and salt and pepper. Brush the eggplant slices on both sides with most of the olive oil mixture, reserving the remainder. Grill the eggplant, turning often, so that char-marks appear, but the eggplant doesn't burn. Grill the red peppers until charred on all sides. Cool and peel the peppers. Cut into strips.

Preheat the oven (or toaster oven) to 400°F. Cover a slice of bread with one grilled eggplant "steak," then top with roasted peppers. Cover with shredded cheese. Top with a second slice of bread. Repeat until you have 6 sandwiches. Brush the sandwiches with the remaining olive oil mixture, place on a baking sheet, and bake for about 10 minutes, or until the cheese melts. Cut each sandwich in half diagonally and serve.

Macedonian Frying Peppers Stuffed with Cheese and Chiles

Peppers are used in many ways in the food of Macedonia, a small Balkan country surrounded by Greece, Albania, Serbia, and Bulgaria. In this make-ahead mezze (small appetizer), long, thin, frying peppers are stuffed with a mixture of hot green chiles, salty strong feta cheese, and mild, rich manouri cheese and seasoned with oregano. Greek or Italian branch-dried oregano has the best flavor. Look for it in Italian and Greek groceries.

SERVES 6 TO 8

3 pounds long, thin, Italian green frying peppers or Cubanelle peppers

$1/4$ cup olive oil, divided

2 cups finely diced onion

$1/4$ cup finely minced green chile such as jalapeño or serrano

706

½ pound feta, soaked in cold water for 15 minutes, drained, and crumbled

½ pound Manouri cheese, crumbled (substitute diced Mozzarella)

3 eggs, beaten

2 tablespoons crumbled dried oregano, preferably Greek

Use a small knife to cut a slit halfway around the stem of each pepper, leaving the stem attached. Cook the peppers in boiling water about 5 minutes, or until limp (or cook in a little water in the microwave). Remove the seeds by rinsing the peppers one at a time in a bowl of water. Drain well.

In a small skillet, cook 2 tablespoons of the olive oil with the onion and chile for 5 minutes, or until the onion and chile are soft. Set aside.

In a shallow bowl, crush the two cheeses with a fork; add the contents of the skillet, the eggs, and the oregano. Place the mixture into a pastry bag with a large open tip and carefully fill each pepper. Alternatively, use a spoon to stuff the peppers. Brush the peppers with the remaining olive oil, then place in a single layer on a foil-lined tray and refrigerate for up to 2 days.

Preheat a grill or broiler to hot. To finish, grill or broil the peppers until tender and spotted black, about 6 minutes, then gently turn over, brush with the remaining oil and broil on the second side for about 4 minutes, or until the cheese starts to ooze out. Remove from the oven and cool slightly. Cut the peppers into diagonal slices, place a toothpick in each slice, and serve.

Hungarian Stuffed Peppers with Veal, Pork, and Bacon

The Turkish Ottomans brought both peppers and stuffed vegetables to Hungary during their occupation of that country in the sixteenth and seventeenth centuries. Since that time, the Hungarians have made stuffed peppers an art form of their own. In this dish, the peppers are stuffed with a tasty mixture of ground veal and pork along with rice, topped with strips of bacon, and then simmered in tomato sauce. Use a package of six hothouse-grown peppers, two each of red, yellow, and green, for an eye-catching, colorful dish. To make a vegetarian variation, mix sautéed fresh mushrooms and dried, reconstituted wild mushrooms with rice, sautéed onions, and eggs, then stuff into the peppers and simmer in tomato sauce. Ice water makes the pepper stuffing more firm, so the peppers are easier to stuff and the filling is lighter in texture.

SERVES 6

¼ pound smoky bacon

1 cup diced onions, divided

1 (28-ounce) can chopped plum tomatoes or 1 box Pomi chopped tomatoes

¾ pound ground veal

¼ pound sweet Italian pork sausage, removed from casing

1 egg + 1 yolk

½ cup cooked rice

2 tablespoons chopped Italian parsley

1 teaspoon kosher salt

¼ teaspoon freshly ground black pepper

6 large red bell peppers

707

1 cup sour cream

$^1/_4$ cup half-and-half

Cut the bacon into 2-inch-long strips. Place in a large skillet in a single layer and heat gently until the fat melts out of the bacon—you'll need to use about 2 tablespoons of that fat. Remove the bacon and fat from the pan and reserve both separately. Heat 1 tablespoon of the bacon fat and add $^1/_2$ cup of the onions. Cook until transparent, about 5 minutes, and then add the tomatoes. Simmer over low heat for 30 minutes and reserve.

Meanwhile, heat the remaining bacon fat and cook the remaining onion until transparent, about 5 minutes. Remove from heat and cool.

In a bowl, mix together the ground veal, pork sausage, egg and yolk, rice, parsley, salt, and black pepper. When the onion mixture has cooled, add to the meat mixture along with $^1/_4$ cup of ice water.

Preheat the oven to 400°F. Cut the peppers in half lengthwise and remove the seeds and white connective tissue. Fill each half with a portion of the stuffing.

Pour the reserved tomato sauce into a large baking dish. Place the pepper halves over top. Lay a bacon strip onto each pepper. Whisk together the sour cream and half-and-half and spread over top of the peppers.

Bake for about 1 hour, or until the bacon is browned and the filling is bubbling hot.

PINE NUTS

PINE NUTS

Native Americans, Mediterraneans, and Asians all have a venerable tradition of gathering and eating the nuts enclosed in the cones of special varieties of pine. Lately, pine nuts seem to be everywhere in the United States, especially in restaurants of the Mediterranean persuasion. Pine nuts, pine seeds, pine kernels, piñon, pinyon, pignoli, and pignoles are all names for the small, edible seeds extracted from between the scales of pinecones of many species of pine tree. Difficult to cultivate commercially, pine nuts are sweet, mild, and have good keeping and nutritional qualities. Mediterranean pine nuts contain about thirty percent protein, while the American ones have less protein and more oil. There are about 1,500 American pine nuts in a pound. Most pine nuts for sale in America are smaller, rounded ones imported from China.

Not only are they delicious, pine nuts have a reputation as a powerful aphrodisiac throughout the Mediterranean and in Asia. In *Ars Amatoria* (The Art of Love), the Roman poet Ovid recommends "the nuts that the sharp-leafed pine brings forth" as an aphrodisiac. Apicius, in his Roman cookbook, *De Re Coquinaria*, suggests pine nuts with onions, white mustard, and pepper to enhance physical love.

Galen, a Greek of the second century, advises that eating a mixture of pine seeds, honey, and almonds before bedtime for three consecutive evenings might produce desirable effects. The early sixteenth century Sheik Nefzaoui wrote in *The Perfumed Garden*—the Arabic love guide—"He who feels that he is weak for coition should drink before going to bed a glassful of very thick honey and eat twenty almonds and one hundred grains of the pine tree."

Many believe that the most effective pine nuts for love come from the Chilgoza Pine or Noosa Pine, *Pinus gerardiana*, which grows only at extremely high elevations in the northwestern Himalayas from Afghanistan to Tibet. Chilgoza pine nuts are a staple food for the inhabitants of Kunawar, a Himalayan region known for its high birthrate. Attempts have been made to cultivate the Chilgoza pine outside the Himalayas, but without success. I don't know if pine nuts work as a stimulant, but they're legal, fun to eat, and couldn't do any harm.

The long, thin, oval-shaped seeds of the Stone Pine, *Pinus pinea*, which grows at quite low altitudes, are prized throughout the Mediterranean. Evidence of their use in the Middle East goes back to biblical times. Mediterranean *pignoli* resemble almonds in their flavor and dense texture, but they are more resinous and spicy. The highly resinous wild pine nut, called *zgougou* in North Africa, or Aleppo pine nut, has dark brown to black seeds.

During the summer holidays in the Lebanese mountains, Anissa Helou, author of the outstanding cookbook, *Lebanese Cuisine*, used to gather pinecones. "After we gathered enough cones, we sat by a flat stone and with another small stone, we started cracking the hard kernels open. The secret was how to scale the strength of the hit so that we broke the shell without crushing the nut, a feat we occasionally achieved." They would also eat soft immature or "green" pine nuts dipped in salt.

The Swiss Stone Pine has a range that extends eastwards from the Alps, while another bears nuts in Korea. In the Southern Hemisphere, in Australia, Chile, and Brazil, other types of edible pinenuts grow which tend to be larger. We have two main varieties of pinenut trees in North America, the *Pinus edulis* and the Mexican pinyon, *Pinus cembroides*. In the course of 180 million years, the original tall pines of northern Asia ended up as little desert trees in Mexico and the American Southwest. For the Pueblo and Navajo people, *piñons* were a staple eaten raw, roasted, boiled, ground into flour, or mashed and spread on corn cakes like peanut butter.

Pine nuts used to be hard to find, and were sold in small glass jars for an outrageously high price. Lately, warehouse markets have been selling inexpensive large bags of Chinese pine nuts. It is very difficult to find authentic Mediterranean pine nuts and if you do find them, they will be expensive. I was happy to notice genuine Mediterranean *pignoli*, called *s'noobar* in Arabic, at Bitar's, a Lebanese market in Philadelphia and at the Spanish Table in Seattle. They are rather expensive but are the only nuts to make an authentic Genoese pesto. They are so flavor-packed, with a firm, almost chewy texture, that it's hard to go back to the ordinary, blander nuts. Store pine nuts in the freezer to prevent the oil-rich nuts from getting rancid.

711

TOASTING PINE NUTS

Toasting pine nuts brings out their flavor. There are many ways of toasting nuts, all of which require close attention because nuts burn very easily. For the most evenly browned nuts, roast pine nuts in oil. Place 1 cup of pine nuts in a very small saucepan and cover with a neutral oil (such as canola). Heat the pot and cook over low heat until the nuts are golden brown, shaking occasionally, about ten minutes. Be careful once the nuts start to take on some color because they quickly pass from golden and nutty to black and bitter.

After straining the nuts from the oil, pour the oil into a glass jar and allow the solids to settle to the bottom. Use this pine nut-flavored oil for salad dressings.

Oven-toast pine nuts by placing them in a baking dish large enough to hold them in a single layer. Bake at 300°F. oven for 10 minutes, then shake and place back in the oven for 5 minutes longer, until light golden brown. Use a timer, because if the pine nut aroma is powerful enough for you to notice, it's probably already too late.

Pan-Fried Soft-Shell Crabs with Pine Nuts, Cilantro, and Tomato

This is a wonderfully flavorful way to prepare those delectably rich soft-shell blue crabs. Here, a simple combination of soft, rich pine nuts, refreshing lime, pungent cilantro, and fresh tomato make a perfectly balanced dish. Because soft-shells are so rich, you might serve a single one for an appetizer or as part of a multi-course meal. Finishing the sauce with butter is a French technique for smoothing, thickening, and enriching; it's one reason restaurant sauces just taste so good. It is optional.

SERVES 4

8 large soft-shell crabs (called whales or jumbos), cleaned (*see* Cleaning Soft-Shell Crabs, page 153)

Kosher salt and freshly ground black pepper to taste

1/2 cup canola oil, divided

1/4 pound (1 cup) flour

4 tablespoons unsalted butter, divided

1/4 cup pine nuts

1/4 cup freshly squeezed lime juice

1 cup diced fresh tomato

2 tablespoons chopped cilantro

Sprinkle the crabs with salt and pepper. Heat half the oil in a large skillet, preferably nonstick. Dust each crab with flour and then sauté in hot oil starting with the topside down (stand clear because soft-shells tend to pop and splatter). When the crabs are well browned, after 3 to 4 minutes, turn them over and cook on the second side about 2 to 3 minutes. Remove from the pan, drain on paper towels, and keep in a warm place. Repeat with the second batch of crabs.

Pour off any excess oil from the pan and melt 2 tablespoons of the butter over low heat. Add the pine nuts and, shaking constantly, brown evenly. As soon as the pine nuts reach a golden brown, add the lime juice and tomato, shaking the pan to dislodge any browned bits.

Raise the temperature to high and allow the liquid to come to the boil. Cook until the liquid is slightly thickened, about 5 minutes, then add the crabs to the pan. Heat the crabs thoroughly in the pan sauce, shaking occasionally. Sprinkle with cilantro, stir in the remaining 2 tablespoons of butter and swirl around to incorporate into sauce. Serve the crabs with sauce poured over top.

Lebanese Chicken Cutlets with Pine Nuts and Orange

Sautéed chicken breasts get a brand-new treatment in this dish from Lebanon. The cutlets are dipped in a mixture of eggs and the thick, cheese-like yogurt called labne *and then coated with a mixture of ground walnuts, breadcrumbs, and garlic. The cutlets are then pan-fried in olive oil until they're brown and crunchy. A simple pan-sauce is made from orange juice and chicken stock flavored with lemon and orange zest (the best free flavors around). "Naked" sections of orange and lemon (all white pith and membrane removed) and toasted pine nuts add texture, a sharp edge of fruity acidity, and juicy crunch. Serve with Rice Pilaf with Toasted Vermicelli (see page 816).*

SERVES 4 TO 6

8 boneless, skinless chicken breasts,
  trimmed and butterflied

Kosher salt and freshly ground black pepper to taste

2 cups fresh soft breadcrumbs

1 cup ground walnuts

2 tablespoons minced garlic

2 eggs

1/4 cup labne

1/4 cup olive oil

1/2 cup orange juice

1 cup chicken stock

Zest of 1 orange

Zest of 1 lemon

2 oranges, cut into suprêmes (*see* page 659)

2 lemons, cut into suprêmes

1/4 cup toasted pine nuts

Fresh mint sprigs, for garnish

Season the chicken with salt and pepper. Combine the breadcrumbs, walnuts, and garlic. Combine eggs and labne. Dip the chicken breasts into the egg mix, drain, and press crumb mixture evenly over breasts. Chill for 30 minutes to set the crust.

Heat the olive oil in a large, nonstick sauté pan. Brown the chicken cutlets evenly on both sides, then remove from pan and drain on paper towels. Pour off the fat from the pan. Add the orange juice and chicken stock and bring to the boil. Cook 5 minutes, or until thickened, then add the zests, suprêmes, and pine nuts and heat.

Place cutlets on serving plates and pour sauce over top. Garnish with mint sprigs.

PINE NUTS IN THE MEDITERRANEAN

The *Flavors of the Mediterranean* conference in Napa Valley I attended in 2000 was a haven for pine nut fiends like myself. In four days, I began to understand the adaptability of the tiny but never insignificant pine nut. Spanish Chef Norberto Jorge prepared tuna escabèche in sherry layered with pine nuts, garlic, and parsley as well as squid in onion and red wine sauce with pine nuts. The late Jean-Louis Palladin made a lovely Provençal pine nut, lemon, and lavender-honey tart. Chris Veneris served Cretan sea bass glazed with a pine nut-thickened garlic sauce called *skordalia*. Chef Haouari Abdezzarak made *Titma*, an unusual Tunisian sweet of crushed fried brik pastry in rose-water syrup with almonds, hazelnuts, and pine nuts, and *Assida Zgougou*, a crushed wild Aleppo pine nut custard scented with rose geranium, served with Tunisian mint tea, and garnished with toasted pine nuts. Sicilian cookbook author Anna Tasca Lanza shared her recipe for Sicilian ricotta cheesecake, studded with candied pumpkin, chocolate, and pine nuts.

Pan-Fried Trout
with Lemon and Pine Nuts

Almost all trout eaten in America is farm-raised, and unless you're a fisherman (or fisherwoman) yourself, it's likely that this dish will be made with one of the two main products of Idaho: Idaho potatoes and farm-raised rainbow trout. Because farm-raised fish is not quite as firm and doesn't have the subtleties of flavor of its wild cousin, it works well in this dish from Spain that enhances its flavor. Small, sweet-but-earthy currants are soaked in brandy, and a lemon juice and zest butter is made to enrich the sauce, which is added to the pan, along with toasted pine nuts and diced tomato. This dish was inspired by a recipe in Paula Wolfert's newly re-released book, Cooking of Southwest France. *The flavors are simple, but all work beautifully together. Serve the fish with roasted or baked potatoes. Use grape tomatoes in wintertime, because they seem to have good flavor even in cold-weather months.*

SERVES 4

$^1/_2$ cup Zante currants

$^1/_2$ cup brandy

2 tablespoons butter, at room temperature

1 tablespoon fresh lemon juice

2 teaspoons finely grated lemon zest

4 boneless trout, heads removed if the fish are large

Kosher salt and freshly ground black pepper to taste

Flour, for dusting

2 to 4 tablespoons extra-virgin olive oil

$^1/_2$ cup pine nuts

$^1/_2$ cup diced fresh tomato

Preheat the oven to 200°F. Soak the currants in the brandy. Using a fork, mash together the butter, lemon juice, and zest until the liquid is absorbed and the butter is creamy. Reserve.

Open up the fish so they lie flat. Season the fish with salt and pepper and dust lightly with flour, shaking off the excess. In a large skillet, preferably nonstick or cast-iron, heat the olive oil over medium-high heat. Brown 2 of the fish on both sides until cooked through, about 4 minutes on each side. Remove from the skillet and keep warm in the oven on a plate. Repeat with the remaining 2 fish, adding a little fresh olive oil if necessary.

Reduce the heat to low and pour off any excess fat. Add the pine nuts and brown lightly, shaking often. Add the currants and brandy. Averting your face, flame the liquid. Shake the pan and cook until the flames die down. Add the diced tomato, heat gently, then remove the skillet from the heat. Stir in the reserved lemon butter, pour the pan sauce over the fish, and serve immediately.

714

Pinolate
(Sicilian Pine Nut Macaroons)

Mixed almond and hazelnut macaroons studded with pine nuts, pinolate, *are a classic of the island of Sicily. Marzipan and other delicacies like these macaroons trace their origins back to the Arabic* martabān *almond paste brought to Sicily during the Saracen reign. The Arabs who gave us the word* sugar, *from the Arabic* sukkar, *had planted sugar cane in Sicily by the end of the ninth century. The special skill in making intricate pastries and highly realistic marzipan fruits, vegetables, and small creatures is an art that developed in Sicily's convents. Today, Sicilian pastries like cassata and cannoli are famous throughout Italy and much of the rest of the world.*

Makes 2 dozen

$1/4$ pound (about 1 cup) blanched almonds

$1/4$ pound (about 1 cup) skin-on almonds

$1/4$ pound (about 1 cup) lightly toasted hazelnuts
   with skins rubbed off

3 cups granulated sugar

3 tablespoons unsalted butter, at room temperature

1 tablespoon honey

1 cup egg whites, divided, at room temperature

$1/2$ pound (about 2 cups) pine nuts

Grind the almonds, hazelnuts, and sugar in the food processor as finely as possible. Add the butter, honey and $3/4$ cup of the egg white. Continue processing until the mixture comes together to form a stiff paste. If the mixture is crumbly, add the remaining egg white, a bit at a time, until the mixture resembles stiff cookie dough.

Preheat the oven to 350°F. Have ready either lightly buttered or parchment paper-lined baking sheets. Place the pine nuts in a bowl. Roll the dough into walnut-sized balls and press into the pine nuts, flattening and coating well on the top. Arrange the pinolate on the baking sheets and bake until the pine nuts are golden, about 15 to 20 minutes. Cool on racks. These cookies will keep quite well in an airtight cookie tin for up to 2 weeks.

PINEAPPLE

PINEAPPLE

The magnificent pineapple, *Ananas comosus,* is native to Brazil and was spread by the Indians up through South and Central America to the West Indies. Pineapples were once a favorite of the fierce Carib Indians who inhabited the islands of the Caribbean Sea. Portuguese sailors who traded to and from Brazil spread the name used by the Brazilian Tuli Indians for the fruit–*anana,* meaning "excellent fruit." Today this name is still used in most languages to refer to the pineapple.

On his second voyage to the Caribbean, in 1493, Christopher Columbus and his crew explored the lush, volcanic island of Guadaloupe, where they found a deserted Carib village. They saw cookpots filled with human remains and, more pleasingly, fresh vegetables and fruits, including pineapples. The fruits were eaten and enjoyed by his sailors, who described the unusual new fruit as having a rough, segmented exterior like a pinecone and a firm interior like an apple.

In Europe, the rare new pineapple, so full of natural syrupy-sweetness, was prized by royalty and envied by the hoi polloi. In the 1600s, King Charles II of England posed for an official portrait receiving a gift of "the fruit of kings," the pineapple, as a symbol of royal privilege. In the new American colonies, where the home was the center of community social life, the pineapple was held in high esteem and became symbolic of hospitality and gracious-ness. A pineapple would crown the most important feasts, placed on a special pedestal on the table. So important was this fruit's symbolic value that they were rented out by the day to decorate hostess tables. Later, the same fruit would be sold to other, wealthier customers who would actually eat the fruit. Pineapples also became a favorite motif of American craftspeople, decorating gateposts, weather vanes, china, and tablecloths, and were painted onto the backs of chairs and onto chests.

While ships brought preserved, candied, and glazed pineapples from Caribbean islands as expensive sweet-meats, the fresh fruit was even rarer. Only the fastest ships in the best weather conditions could deliver fresh, unspoiled pineapples to the finest shops of colonial America. The search for a way to grow pineapples in England stimulated the development of the greenhouse, although it would be two hundred years before pineapples were successfully reproduced. Pineapples spread around the world on sailing ships that carried the fruit as protection against scurvy. The Spanish introduced it into the Philippines and may have taken it to Hawaii, now the world's leading producer, early in the sixteenth century.

Toward the end of the nineteenth century, James Dole, a horticulture graduate of Harvard University, arrived in Hawaii and within fifteen years had developed the pineapple into Hawaii's second-largest industry (after sugarcane).

By the 1950s, pineapple was practically synonymous with Hawaii, which then accounted for about eighty percent of world production. Hawaii still leads production in fresh pineapples in the U.S.; the best are jetted to the mainland.

In the kitchen, pineapples add color, sweetness, acidity, and firm texture to fruit salads. Pineapples are versatile enough to grill in slices as an accompaniment to pork or poultry; they may be caramelized and flamed with rum for a simple dessert, arranged on the bottom of a cake for an old-fashioned pineapple upside-down cake, added to cake batters such as carrot cake or the Jamaican pineapple roulade which follows, and cooked into a spicy chutney.

Pineapple Varieties

Baby Sugar Loaf Pineapple: This variety originated in Mexico, where it is still grown. It was taken to Hawaii, where it is sweeter, meatier, and more yellow in color. It can be picked ripe and shipped without reducing its shelf life.

Del Monte Gold™: This pineapple, introduced by Del Monte in 1996, is twice as sweet as common white-fleshed pineapples, has up to four times the amount of vitamin C, and is low in acid. It is plumper and heavier than traditional pineapples with a square, barrel-like appearance, chunky shoulders, and a juicy, deep-gold flesh.

Kona Sugarloaf: This pineapple from Hawaii is too tender for shipping. Round to conical in shape, it weighs 5 to 6 pounds and has white to yellow flesh that is very sweet and juicy. Its leaves pull out easily.

Natal Queen: This conically shaped South African pineapple is small in size, weighing 2 to 3 pounds, with spiny leaves, dark yellow skin, and deep eyes. Its golden yellow flesh is crisp in texture, with delicate, aromatic flavor. Its core is small and tender, and it keeps well after ripening.

Red Spanish: This pineapple is the most popular cultivar in the West Indies, Venezuela, and Mexico, and is well adapted for shipping to distant markets. It weighs 2 to 4 pounds, has pale yellow flesh with a pleasant aroma, and is squarish in shape with a large core. Its leaves are spiny; its orange-red skin has deep eyes.

Smooth Cayenne or Sweet Spineless: This is the most widely planted pineapple from Hawaii, and the most easily obtainable in the U.S. Introduced from Cayenne, French Guyana, in 1820, it is cylindrical in shape and has smooth leaves, an orange rind, and shallow eyes. Weighing 5 to 6 pounds, it has pale yellow flesh that is low in fiber. Its flesh is juicy and rich and has mildly acidic and quite sweet flavor.

South African Baby Pineapple: Sweeter than Hawaiian Baby Sugar Loaf Pineapples, this South African variety has been grown year-round since the mid-1980s. The entire pineapple measures just 5 inches in length and 3 inches in width, with golden-colored skin and a bright yellow interior. It is sweet, very juicy, and tender and has a crunchy, edible core.

719

Grilled Tuna with Pineapple–Poblano Salsa

When I first went to work for A'propos Bistro, Shimon and Koby Bokovza, the Tunisian-born Israeli owners wanted to have "the most unusual food in Philadelphia." This indeed became our reputation and this dish, unusual as it is, was one that just kept selling. This chunky, sweet-hot salsa was originally developed by the restaurant's consultant, Chef Jonathan Waxman, who gained his reputation in California and first brought his cooking to the East Coast in the 1980s at New York City's Jam's.

SERVES 6

Pineapple–Poblano Salsa

1 golden pineapple, cut into $1/2$-inch dice

2 tablespoons olive oil, divided

Kosher salt and freshly ground black pepper to taste

3 poblano chile peppers

$1/4$ cup canola oil

$1/4$ cup whole peeled garlic cloves

$1/2$ cup chopped cilantro

Juice of 2 limes

$1^1/2$ teaspoons ground cumin, preferably toasted

Preheat the oven to 450°F. Toss the pineapple with 1 tablespoon of the olive oil and the salt and pepper. Spread in a single layer onto a metal baking pan. Roast about 20 minutes, or until browned on the edges. Remove from the oven and reserve.

Preheat a grill or broiler to high. Brush the poblano peppers with the remaining 1 tablespoon of olive oil. Grill or broil on all sides until the skin blisters and blackens.

Remove from the heat, cool and then peel, seed, and remove the stem. Dice and reserve.

Meanwhile, combine the canola oil and garlic cloves in a small, heavy-bottomed pot. Heat over moderate heat and fry until the garlic cloves are light golden in color. Remove from the heat and drain, reserving the garlic-flavored oil for another use (use to cook the vegetables for Marinara Sauce, page 895, if desired). Chop the garlic cloves and reserve.

Combine the pineapple, poblano, garlic, cilantro, lime juice, and cumin and reserve at room temperature for up to 3 hours, otherwise refrigerate until needed.

Tuna and Assembly

3 pounds center-cut tuna loin, cut into 8-ounce portions
Kosher salt and freshly ground black pepper to taste
Canola oil
Pineapple-Poblano Salsa, room temperature

Preheat a grill or broiler to high. Sprinkle the tuna with salt and pepper and leave to season for 15 to 20 minutes. When the grill (or broiler) is hot, brush the tuna with oil and grill on both sides to desired doneness (no more than medium-rare for juiciness).

Spoon the salsa over the grilled tuna and serve immediately.

Hawaiian Chicken Salad with Pineapple

Because Hawaii is so often associated with pineapple—after all, it once grew eighty percent of the world's pineapple—this Hawaiian chicken salad includes pineapple. It's an easy salad to make, especially if you use the precut fresh pineapple cubes available in many supermarket produce sections. Usually, the precut pineapple is made from the gold type. I prefer gold pineapple because it is more colorful, lower in acidity, and quite a bit sweeter than the usually less-expensive white pineapple. Serve the salad on butter lettuce leaves sprinkled with toasted, chopped macadamia nuts.

Serves 6

1 pound boneless, skinless chicken breast
$1/4$ pound (about 1 cup) snow peas, trimmed
$1/2$ cup canola oil
$1/4$ cup rice wine vinegar
$1/2$ white onion, grated
2 tablespoons honey
2 tablespoons Dijon mustard
2 tablespoons grated ginger
Kosher salt and freshly ground black pepper to taste
1 red bell pepper, diced
1 bunch scallions, thinly sliced
1 pound unsweetened pineapple cubes
1 head butter-type lettuce (Boston or Bibb), washed, dried, and separated into leaves
$1/4$ cup chopped, toasted macadamia nuts (optional garnish)

Set up a steamer basket with steaming water on the bottom and add the chicken to the steamer. Steam 5 to 10 minutes, or until the chicken is opaque and firm, but still juicy. Remove the chicken from the basket, cool, and then dice. Add the snow peas to the same basket and steam briefly over high heat for 1 to 2 minutes, or until brightly colored. Remove snow peas from the steamer and run under cold water to set the color. (Reserve the steaming liquid to use as chicken stock, freezing if desired.)

Whisk together the oil, vinegar, onion, honey, mustard, ginger, and salt and pepper. Toss with the chicken, snow peas (reserving a few for garnish), red pepper (reserving a bit for garnish), scallions (reserving a few for garnish), and pineapple. Arrange the lettuce leaves in nest shapes on 6 individual salad plates. Top with the salad, sprinkle with the macadamia nuts, and serve.

722

Jamaican Spiced Pineapple Roulade with Guava Sauce

This tropical cake, flavored with native Jamaican allspice, gets its richness from its moist, chunky filling. A roulade is an easy-to-make, fancy-looking cake that is rolled up like a rug, enclosing its filling. When cut on the diagonal, the slices will look like spirals, showing off the chunky pineapple-coconut-walnut filling. For best results, use the precut fresh golden pineapple found in supermarket produce sections, either the type in a plastic bag or container, along with the frozen fresh grated coconut sold in most Asian markets. The guava paste was originally made in Spain with quince; the same type of thick fruit paste was adapted in Latin America to use native guava fruit.

SERVES 12

Pineapple Filling

$3/4$ pound (3 sticks) unsalted butter

1 cup dark brown sugar, packed

$1/4$ cup grated fresh ginger

3 cups chopped pineapple, preferably golden
   (about 1 pineapple)

3 cups chopped toasted walnuts

1 pound frozen grated coconut, defrosted and fluffed

In the bowl of an electric mixer and using the paddle, cream butter and sugar until light and fluffy. Stir in the remaining ingredients, scrape out, stir to combine well, and reserve in the refrigerator.

Guava Sauce

1/2 package (about 1/2 pound) guava paste

2 cups orange juice

Combine the guava paste and orange juice in a medium saucepan over low heat. Whisk together while heating slowly until the mixture boils. Add enough water to make a sauce that pours easily (the sauce will thicken as it cools), remove from the heat and reserve.

Cake Batter and Assembly

18 ounces (4 1/4 cups) all-purpose flour, preferably
  unbleached

1 tablespoon ground allspice

1 tablespoon baking soda

Pinch of kosher salt

3 cups pineapple juice

3 cups sweetened condensed milk

1 tablespoon vanilla extract

9 eggs

Pineapple Filling

Guava Sauce

Preheat the oven to 350°F. Prepare one 18 x 12-inch half sheet pan or two 13 x 9-inch rectangular cake pans by spraying with nonstick spray.

Whisk together the dry ingredients: flour, allspice, baking soda, and salt. Combine the pineapple juice, condensed milk, and vanilla, and reserve.

In a clean mixer bowl, beat the eggs until light and fluffy and the mixture forms a ribbon. Fold in the dry mixture alternating with the wet mixture, beginning and ending with the dry mixture. Spread the batter into the reserved pan(s). Bake for 20 minutes, or until set in the middle and the batter has begun to shrink away from the sides of the pan. Cool to room temperature. Flip the cake over onto parchment or wax paper. Spread with the reserved Pineapple Filling. Roll up tightly and chill at least 1 hour to set. Cut into slices on the diagonal and serve with the Guava Sauce.

PLUMS & PRUNES

PLUMS & PRUNES

The newest fashion color in Italy is *prugne* (prune), a lusciously deep, dark rosy-brown violet, exactly the color of the plump dried prunes enjoyed in Europe, though often denigrated in America. Whether green, yellow, red, blue, purple, or even almost black, the plum is such a luscious and sought-after fruit that for at least 200 years, the word *plum* has often been used to describe something very desirable, as in "a plum job." In the Middle Ages, *plum* referred to virtually any dried fruit, including raisins. Stalwart British sweets—like plum pudding, plum cake, and Little Jack Horner's plum pie—all contain dried fruit such as raisins, but no plums.

The plum, *Prunus domestica*, forms another branch of the *Prunus* family that also includes cherries, apricots, peaches, and nectarines. Plums and cherries are close cousins; the main difference is in size, so that plums may be substituted for cherries in many recipes (*see* the Cherries chapter for ideas). Hybrid plumcots (plum and apricot), like the speckled Dinosaur Eggs, have started to appear in our markets.

Wild plums are common throughout the temperate parts of the Northern Hemisphere. It seems likely that *Prunus domestica* is indigenous to Central Europe, although the time and manner of its origin are uncertain. Plums were known in Egypt; prunes (dried plums) have been found among the provisions for the afterlife stored in the tomb of Kha, the architect of Thebes. The earliest cultivation of plums took place in China. Plum trees must be grafted onto rootstock because plum trees grown from seeds revert back to the wild blackthorn that has grown wild in the forests of western Asia for thousands of years.

The Etruscans knew of the wild plum and the Roman natural historian Pliny speaks of the "great crowd of plums" that was the glory of Roman orchards. According to Roman physician and philosopher Galen, prunes from Spain were the best. The Iberians of Catalonia probably improved on wild plums brought to them by the Phoenicians and Greeks.

Plums were cultivated in the gardens of medieval monasteries in England and Chaucer refers to a garden with "ploumes" and "bulaces" (bullace is another kind of plum). By the early seventeenth century, the British were importing the best plums in Europe, reputed to grow in the Balkans and Southern Europe, particularly Moravia, in Southern Germany. Plum cultivation became increasingly important in the seventeenth and eighteenth centuries in England and Western Europe. The famed French Reine-Claude plum commemorates Queen Claude, wife of Francois I. She was described as "far from pretty, but so good, kind and sweet" that the naturalist Francois Belon thought of her at once when he needed a name for the plum he had brought back from the East to the French province of Touraine. During the eighteenth century, Sir William Gage took the Reine-Claude to England, where it acquired a new British name, the Green Gage.

The Damson, a small oval plum and the somewhat rounder bullace are classified as *Prunus institutia*. This species native to Eastern Europe and Western Asia is considered to be older then *Prunus domestica*, the plum proper. Growing wild in hedgerows, it is small and sour, suited to making jam. The damson had been known in Western Europe since prehistoric times—remains have been found in excavations of prehistoric Swiss lake dwellings—but it was also grown in the Near East. It received its name because it was from Damascus, in Syria, that the damson reached Italy well over 2,000 years ago. About the year 1200, the Duke of Anjou brought the Damascene plum back to France from a Crusade. Older fruits of the same species already known in Europe were called "Damson." The British took a prominent role in improving damsons, developing varieties from it that include the Farleigh and Bradley's King along with the Black and White bullaces. Damsons are also made into damson "cheese," a stiff fruit paste reminiscent of the Spanish quince membrillo paste and the Latin American guava membrillo paste.

Ever since medieval times, the English word *prune* has meant an extra-sweet variety of plum that has been dried. In France, the fresh fruit is called *prune* and the dried fruit is *pruneau*. Prunes all come from a group of oval, black-skinned plums with a very high level of sugar that allows them to be sun dried without fermenting and a "free" or easily detached pit, uncommon among plums. Prunes turn black in drying as the result of enzyme action. It takes about three pounds of fresh plums to produce one pound of prunes.

There was a time when people would snigger at the mention of prunes, which they associated with old age and the prune's laxative qualities. In France and other places known for prunes, they know better. The superb *Prune d'Agen* comes from a town in Aquitaine in the southwest of France. The Agen plum came from Damascus during the Crusades and ended up in Agen, where it was known in the early eighteenth century as *robe de sergent* (sergeant's coat) because it had the same color as police officer uniforms of the time. If you ever get to try prunes macerated in Armagnac, the special brandy also from this region, you'll know why they are so prized.

The Agen plum, now grown all over western France, is not picked; the trees have to be shaken. The fallen fruits are then sorted on cloths spread under the trees. Before they ripen, the plums have already been thinned on the tree in order to encourage larger fruits. Once the plums are gathered, they are set out to dry for several days and turned frequently. This same French variety was taken to California by a Frenchman in the nineteenth century and is now prominent in the California prune industry.

In America, several varieties of indigenous wild plums well known to Native Americans before the arrival of Europeans to the continent are still common and often made into jam or jelly. The best-known wild plum is the beach plum, *Prunus maritima*, found growing in beach dunes from New England to Virginia. The cherry-sized crimson or purple fruits were among the first foods that the early colonists adapted to their own recipes. Because of their tartness and high pectin (fruit jelly) content, they make an excellent jelly, and are sometimes served with soft-shell crabs because they both share the same season.

Inland, the American wild plum, *Prunus americana*, sometimes called "sloe," is widespread. In the north, the hardy Canadian plum, *Prunus nigra*, is common. In the southeast, the Chickasaw plum, *Prunus angustifolia*, often produces large, red plums. Several of these native plums, edible even in the wild, have been the source of cultivated varieties, especially in the southern states where *Prunus domestica* will not thrive.

The early colonists brought European plums along with them to the east coast. The first kinds they raised were a mixture of European and native plums and some of these persist. In 1790, William Prince planted the pits of 25 quarts of Green Gage plums; these produced trees yielding fruit of every color. By 1828, Prince's nursery offered one hundred and forty different kinds of plums for sale. The opening up of California coincided with the introduction of the Asian plum, *Prunus salicina*, from Japan. Plums of oriental origin such as the Burbank, Santa Rosa, El Dorado, and President dominate the California crop, by far the largest in North America.

The Quetsche, the pride of Alsace, is a delicious plum, elongated like the Agen plum, juicy and fragrant. The true Alsatian Quetsche, when bought in France, should have its place of origin specified on its packaging. If it is anonymous, it may well have come from Italy, where the French claim the variety has less flavor, scent, and sugar. Not far from Alsace is Lorraine, home to the Mirabelle plum of Nancy. Deep golden, with a fine perfume, mirabelles should be savored before they are actually eaten.

Plums end up distilled into potent liquor in Alsace and Lorraine and in bordering Germany. Both Quetsch and Mirabelle are distilled into *eau de vie*, or clear white liqueur. Mirabelle eau de vie has been known since the sixteenth century and makes a softer and more full-bodied liqueur than Quetsch.

The Bokhara plum, *Prunus bokhariensis*, is dried extensively for use in the cuisines of Central Asia, Georgia, and the northern fringe of India. Some plums, such as the Portuguese Elvas, are candied to make the fabled "sugarplums." Georgian cooking has a classic sauce based on sour plums called *tkemali* that is the universal condiment in Georgia. Used as much as American ketchup, tkemali is made from plums flavored with coriander seed and leaf, fennel, garlic, hot pepper, salt, and mint. Sour plums also marry well with fatty meats and end up in goose stuffing and pork stews in Central Europe.

CHOOSING, RIPENING, AND STORING PLUMS

When selecting plums, look for plump, shapely fruit that is well-colored, firm to the touch, and without cracks or blemishes. If they are particularly soft or hard, look elsewhere. If they are still somewhat hard, keep them out but once they are ripe, refrigerate them and they will hold for four or five days. Once the skins lose their shine and begin to look duller, the plums are ripe.

More Plum Types

Angeleno: The Angeleno is a huge purple plum with yellow flesh, very sweet and meaty. When fully tree-ripened, it develops a full, robust flavor and is quite versatile. It is in season from mid-August through the beginning of September.

Black Amber: This super-large, super-beautiful plum with shiny black skin has a slightly floral bouquet. Best used for pies and sauces, Black Ambers should be cooked with the skin left on because it will color the flesh a deep, stained-glass red and add tartness. This plum is in season mid-June through mid-July.

Burbank: The famed Burbank plum was imported by Luther Burbank from Japan. It has red and golden yellow skin and apricot-colored flesh, which is firm, sweet, aromatic, juicy, and uniquely flavored. A semi-freestone, the Burbank is in season in mid-August.

Casselman: This bright red plum is considered to be the best-tasting late season variety. Its deep amber flesh is very sweet and meaty. It has an old-fashioned tangy taste, similar to some French plums. It is in season in late August to late September.

Dinosaur Egg Pluot: The fancifully named Dinosaur Egg is a hybrid of a plum and an apricot, commonly known as a pluot, that mainly retains the characteristics and flavor of a plum. Its skin is a light reddish-yellow in color with small but noticeable speckles. It is very sweet and tends to bruise easily when ripened, so handle with care. It is in season from August through September.

El Dorado: This plum is dark with nearly black skin and firm, amber-colored flesh. Medium to large in size, with a flattened shape, it has pleasing flavor and sweetness and will still be firm when fully ripe. The El Dorado has bright red to reddish skin with purple highlights and amber flesh with mellow, sweet flavor. It stays firm during cooking, making it a great plum for canning. It is in season in mid-July.

Elephant Heart: Often found at farmers' markets, the delicate skin of this variety requires very gentle handling. A large, heart-shaped plum, it has dark reddish-purple mottled skin and sweet, juicy, richly flavored, firm red flesh. Look for it beginning the third week in July.

Friar: This large, deep blue to purplish black-skinned plum has amber-fruited, sweet, juicy flesh. An excellent eating plum, it is also recommended for preserves, sauces, and tarts. Friars are sweetest and most delicious late in its season, which begins in August and ends in the fall.

Italian Prune Plum: As it ripens, this small, slender plum's color changes from a reddish blue to a purple-blue, showing a powder-white bloom when fully ripe. Its flesh is rich in flavor and very sweet when fully ripe and is excellent for cooking and preserving. A freestone plum, it is in season in late summer and is very popular in areas with large Italian communities.

Kelsey: A distinctively heart-shaped plum with thin, greenish-yellow skin blushed with red, it is large, firm, and aromatic with rich flavor. It tends to have a hard supplementary core near the pit that must be cut

729

away before eating. It is low in acid, has a small pit, and is a freestone. The Kelsey is in season the third week in June and keeps well.

Laroda: This is a dark reddish-purple plum similar to Santa Rosa, but larger, and is harvested approximately five to six weeks later. Not quite round in shape, the highly flavored Laroda is quite tart but develops wonderful sweetness when fully tree-ripened. It is in season the second week in July.

Nubiana: This farmers' market favorite is an old-fashioned plum with delightful flavor. Flattened in shape, its skin is shiny black, and its flesh is deep amber. Its flavor is slightly wild with a hint of musk. It is fragrant and holds very well after being picked in late July.

Red Beauty: A fully tree-ripened Red Beauty plum will be dark red-purple in color and slightly soft to the touch. Its amber flesh is sweet, aromatic, and juicy; its skin is slightly tart. This plum is almost exclusively used for fresh eating and it keeps quite well. It is in season from mid-May through the beginning of June.

Santa Rosa: Often considered to be the queen of all plums, the Santa Rosa, developed by Luther Burbank, is the most popular plum in California and Arizona. Juicy, tangy, and flavorful, its skin is reddish-purple and its amber flesh is tinged red. Santa Rosas account for more than one-third of the California plum harvest. Among the most flavorful plums in the world, the Santa Rosa has only a twenty-four-hour window between being too green and too ripe. Its season begins in early July.

Satsuma Plum: A longtime favorite plum in California, this Japanese plum is mottled maroon over green skin and dark red meaty flesh. Its flavor is sweet, mild, and not tart, and it is excellent for jam. It is in season in late July.

Wickson Plum: This large, heart-shaped, greenish-yellow plum has very sweet, amber-yellow, and translucent flesh and little or no tartness at the skin or the pit. Its flesh is a bit coarse, somewhat fibrous, and firm, and it keeps and ships well. Its season begins the third week in June.

Chicken Marbella with Olives, Prunes, and Capers

This rich-tasting, fancy-looking chicken dish is a make-ahead classic named after a resort town on Spain's Costa del Sol. It has appeared on buffet tables ever since a recipe appeared in the incredibly popular Silver Palate Cookbook. *I got the recipe when it was reprinted in the* New York Times Magazine *some years ago. Olives, prunes, and capers might not sound like the most likely combination, but salty, sweet, and tangy combine beautifully here. I recommend using high-quality, grain-fed, boneless, skinless chicken thighs for best flavor. Because the fat absorbs any off flavors, commercial chicken thighs may be overly strong in flavor. Use scissors to trim off any visible fat from the chicken, and remove the skin, if bought with skin on. Serve with steamed rice to soak up the deliciously rich and hearty juices. Be sure to use plump, soft prunes; avoid dried out or hard prunes here.*

730

1 cup dry white wine

$^{1}/_{2}$ cup dark brown sugar, packed, divided

$^{1}/_{2}$ cup olive oil

$^{1}/_{2}$ cup red wine vinegar

2 tablespoons chopped garlic

2 tablespoons fresh oregano, or 2 teaspoons dried

Kosher salt, hot red pepper flakes, and freshly
  ground black pepper to taste

12 boneless, skinless chicken thighs, excess
  fat trimmed off

4 bay leaves

1 cup pitted prunes

$^{1}/_{2}$ cup pitted green olives

$^{1}/_{2}$ cup drained capers

$^{1}/_{4}$ cup chopped cilantro

Whisk together the wine, $^{1}/_{4}$ cup brown sugar, the olive oil, vinegar, garlic, oregano, salt (the olives and capers are salty, so salt judiciously), hot pepper flakes, and black pepper. Place the chicken into a large nonreactive bowl, toss with the marinade, cover and marinate overnight in the refrigerator.

Preheat the oven to 375°F. Arrange the chicken, along with any pan juices, in a single layer in 1 or more nonreactive metal baking pans. Add the bay leaves, prunes, olives, and capers, sprinkle the remaining $^{1}/_{4}$ cup brown sugar over top. Bake 1 hour, basting often, until the chicken is fully cooked and tender and the pan juices are syrupy. Remove the chicken from the oven and sprinkle with the cilantro before serving.

Alsatian Pork Loin Stuffed with Prunes and Apricots in Riesling Wine

This richly flavored stuffed pork loin comes from the region of Alsace, which has a cuisine that owes as much to Germany as to France. The Riesling wine used here originated in Germany's Rhine and Mosel river valleys, but is also raised extensively in Alsace, where it is the region's finest wine. In Alsace, Rieslings are exclusively dry, but elsewhere they may be anywhere from dry to quite sweet. Riesling is highly aromatic with fruity apple, peach, melon, and pear flavors and delicate floral and herbal undertones. It marries perfectly with the prunes and apricots used here and, of course, is the wine that should be served with the dish. Accompany the pork with a substantial cooked whole grain such as barley, kasha, or hulled wheat berries. A make-it-and-forget-it dish, this stuffed pork loin is fancy enough to be served for company. Try making it with best-quality natural pork and you'll see just how good and juicy it can be.

731

SERVES 8

$^{3}/_{4}$ pound (about 1$^{1}/_{2}$ cups) pitted prunes

$^{3}/_{4}$ pound (about 1$^{1}/_{2}$ cups) apricots, preferably
  California (*see page 43 for more information*)

12 ounces Riesling wine

3 pound boned pork rib roast (with its bones)

Kosher salt and freshly ground black pepper to taste

$^{1}/_{4}$ pound bacon, cut into small bits

1 onion, finely chopped

3 to 4 ribs celery, finely chopped

4 to 5 carrots, finely chopped

¼ cup whole peeled garlic cloves

¼ cup canola oil

3 bay leaves

1 tablespoon chopped fresh thyme leaves

1 cup veal stock (substitute chicken stock)

¼ pound (1 stick) unsalted butter

Place the prunes in one bowl and the apricots in a second bowl and cover both with Riesling. Soak several hours or up to overnight at room temperature until softened and plump. The next day, drain both the prunes and apricots, reserving the wine.

Season the pork on all sides with salt and pepper. Using a sharpening steel or a wooden dowel, make a hole in the center end of the loin all the way through and stuff it with prunes and apricots, alternating fruits (reserve fruit that won't fit into the pork). Roll and tie the roast into a compact shape (or use silicone FoodLoops, *see* Tying Birds for Roasting, page 261).

Preheat the oven to 325°F. In a large casserole dish, heat bacon and render out most of the fat. When the foaming subsides add the onion, celery, carrots, and garlic. Cover and cook for 5 to 8 minutes, or until the vegetables are crisp-tender. Remove them with a slotted spoon and reserve.

Add the canola oil to the same casserole dish and heat until shimmering. Add the pork loin and brown on all sides, including the ends. When the pork has browned, remove it to a plate, cover, and reserve.

Pour off any excess fat from the casserole. Spoon the reserved cooked vegetables, the bay leaves, and thyme into the bottom of the casserole dish. Place the meat on top and add any extra prunes and apricots. Pour in the reserved wine from the marinade and the veal stock over top. Cover and bake for 1 hour or until the juices run a clear yellow and the internal temperature measures 150°F. at the thickest part.

Remove the casserole from the oven, transfer the pork, apricots, and prunes to a serving platter, and drape with foil to keep warm. To make the sauce, strain the juices into a heat-resistant cup and discard the solids. The fat will rise above the juices; discard it. Return the defatted juices to the casserole and boil down until thickened. Just before serving, beat the butter into the sauce.

To serve, remove and discard the string around the pork. Cut into slices about ½ inch thick and arrange on plates. Spoon any extra fruit around the meat and ladle the sauce over top.

Deep-Dish Plum Pie

Deep-dish pies are so satisfying to make, and with their higher proportion of fruit to pastry, they are best made when fruits are abundant. Make this pie later in plum season, when freestone varieties like Santa Rosas, Friars, Damsons, and Italian prune plums come into season. Mixed varieties make an even better pie, because some will hold their shape and some will collapse into sauciness. Use a 9-inch diameter deep fluted French quiche pan, deep-dish pie pan, or a round casserole dish about 2 inches deep.

SERVES 8

Sugar Crust Pastry Shell

¾ pound (3 cups) all-purpose flour, preferably unbleached

½ cup granulated sugar

¼ pound (1 stick) unsalted butter, chilled and cut into ½-inch cubes

½ cup heavy cream, chilled

732

In the bowl of a food processor, combine the flour, sugar, and butter. Process briefly, pulsing, until the mixture resembles oatmeal. With the motor running, pour in the cream and continue processing only long enough for the dough to come together into a ball.

Transfer the dough to a large plastic zip-top freezer bag or wrap in plastic wrap, flatten to a rectangular shape and chill 2 hours, or until firm. Divide the dough into 2 pieces, one with about one-third of the dough, and the other with the remaining two-thirds. Roll out the smaller portion into a circle about 12 inches in diameter, large enough to cover the inside of a deep 9-inch pie plate or casserole dish. Without stretching the dough, press the dough into the pan. Chill for 30 minutes in the freezer or 1 hour in the refrigerator. Roll out the second portion of the dough into a round about 10 inches in diameter for the top. Cover with wax paper and chill until needed.

Plum Filling and Assembly

1 cup granulated sugar

$1/2$ cup brown sugar, packed

1 tablespoon vanilla extract

2 teaspoons + 1 teaspoon ground cinnamon

3 pounds slightly underripe plums, red flesh preferred (Santa Rosa), cut into $1/2$-inch-thick wedges

2 ounces ($1/2$ cup) all-purpose flour, preferably unbleached

1 egg yolk, lightly beaten with 1 tablespoon water

4 tablespoons raw or crystallized sugar

Combine the sugars, the vanilla and 2 teaspoons of cinnamon in a large bowl. Add the plum wedges and toss together to combine well. Sprinkle in the flour and toss again to combine. Reserve at room temperature.

Preheat the oven to 375°F. Line the dough in the pie plate with heavy-duty aluminum foil and fill with dried beans. Bake for about 25 minutes, or until the pastry is lightly browned. Once the dough is set and no longer wet, remove the foil and beans and continue to bake until the pastry is evenly browned, 5 to 10 minutes longer. Remove the shell from the oven and cool to room temperature, then fill with the plum filling, being careful not to wet the edge of shell.

Brush the egg yolk mixture along the inside top edge of the shell. Place the reserved dough round over top, pressing to join the edges. Using scissors, cut away any excess dough. Brush the remaining egg yolk mixture over the top of the shell.

In a small bowl, combine the raw or crystallized sugar with the remaining 1 teaspoon of cinnamon. Sprinkle the mixture over the top of the pie, and then cut 6 to 8 small slits into the top of the pie. Place the pie on a baking pan to catch any drips. Bake for 20 minutes, and then lower the heat to 350°F. and bake 40 minutes longer, or until the pastry is brown and the filling is just bubbling. Cool until warm and serve.

733

Rustic Plum Tart with Slivovitz

This country-style tart is easier and less intimidating to make than a fancier tart made in a fluted flan ring. A Slivovitz-flavored almond cream is layered inside a pizza-like pastry shell, plums cover the top, and skin-on raw, sliced almonds for a crunchy texture are sprinkled over top and an interesting look.

SERVES 12

Almond Filling

1 ounce (¼ cup) all-purpose flour

½ cup almonds, whole or sliced

¼ pound almond paste

4 tablespoons unsalted butter

¼ cup granulated sugar

2 eggs

¼ cup Slivovitz (substitute kirsch or brandy)

Grind the flour and almonds in a food processor until finely ground. (The flour keeps the almonds from turning oily.)

Cream together the almond paste, butter, and sugar. Beat in the eggs, one at a time. Add the flour and almond mixture to the creamed mix. Stir in Slivovitz and reserve. (Refrigerate if making ahead, up to 4 days.)

Sweet Pastry and Assembly

12 tablespoons (1½ sticks) unsalted butter

2 tablespoons granulated sugar

½ pound (2 cups) all-purpose flour

½ teaspoon ground cinnamon

½ teaspoon kosher salt

3 tablespoons ice water, as needed

Almond Filling

6 to 8 large plums, thinly sliced

2 tablespoons milk

1 egg

1 cup sliced almonds (skin-on preferred)

1 cup strained plum or apricot jam (optional)

Cream the butter and sugar. Stir in the flour, cinnamon, and salt. Add enough ice water for the dough to form a ball. Chill.

Preheat the oven to 350°F. Roll the dough into a large circle (about 16 inches in diameter) and place onto a round pizza pan at least 12 inches in diameter or shape one out of several layers of heavy-duty aluminum foil). Spread a ¼-inch-thick layer of filling over the pastry, leaving a 1½-inch border all around. Arrange the plums in tight concentric rings over the filling. Fold the edges of the dough up, pleating as you go to form a rough border. Trim excess dough with scissors.

Lightly beat together the milk and egg to make an egg wash. Use it to brush the dough border, then sprinkle with the sliced almonds. Bake for about 45 minutes, or until the pastry edges are brown and the filling is bubbling.

In a small pot or in the microwave, melt the jam until just hot to the touch. Remove the tart from the oven, cool and then brush with the jam.

SLIVOVITZ: BRANDY DISTILLED FROM PLUMS

Slivovitz, is or was originally, the local fruit brandy of Serbia and Bosnia-Herzegovina. It is made from a black plum called Madjarka, which imparts a richly heady scent to the spirit. These black plums are crushed along with their stones and fermented very slowly for about three months. It is double-distilled and then aged in casks of Slovenian oak. Sometimes, whole plums are thrown in to macerate in the spirit while it ages about five years.

POMEGRANATES

POMEGRANATES

Of ancient origin and rightly celebrated in myth and art, the pomegranate is regally beautiful. A native of Persia (now Iran), the pomegranate is one of the seven fruits mentioned in the Old Testament (including dates, figs, olives, grapes, barley, and wheat). Multitudes of shiny, ruby-red seeds have made the pomegranate the symbol of fertility in legends around the world. The plump, round, dappled scarlet fruit is also a symbol of Aphrodite, the Greek goddess of love.

The Romans called the pomegranate a Punic apple because it arrived in Italy via Carthage (Punic), hence its Latin name, *Punica granatum* (Carthage seeds). Many Italian Renaissance fabrics boasted a decorative pattern of pomegranates. The Moors brought pomegranates to Spain around 800 CE; in fact, the city of Granada was named for the pomegranate. Chaucer, Shakespeare, and Homer all extolled its virtues, while the French called their hand-tossed explosive a grenade after the seed-scattering properties of the fruit.

Pomegranates are nearly round and may be as large as five inches in diameter. Their leathery skin ranges from pink to rich crimson over yellow. Inside, pods of ruby-red kernels, each containing a hard seed, are enclosed in a thin membrane surrounded by white, acrid spongy pith. A prominent turreted calyx that resembles a small crown tops this truly regal fruit.

Spanish settlers first brought pomegranates to California in 1769; they are now grown in the drier parts of California and Arizona. Pomegranates are also grown in the Middle East, Africa, India, Malaysia, and southern Europe. The many varieties of pomegranates include Balegal, Early Wonderful, Fleshman, Green Globe, Phoenicia, and Wonderful.

Almost all of America's pomegranates come from the San Joaquin Valley, where hot, dry summers yield sweet, attractive fruit. The west side of the valley, where cool night air coming off the hills helps the fruit to deepen in color, is the preferred location. By far, the most widely planted and leading variety in California is the large, glossy, deep red or purplish red Wonderful, first propagated from a Florida cutting in 1896 by a Porterville, California, farmer. The Wonderful yields a large crop of large, shiny, magenta fruits, full of juice, deep ruby-colored arils that are high in sweetness, acidity, and flavor. This variety is also resistant to cracking, which happens when ripe pomegranates split open after rain. While split fruit may taste fine, it spoils quickly.

Pomegranates have an indescribable taste that is sweet and tart with a wine-like, intense but refreshing flavor. They are not the easiest fruit to eat and can be quite messy, which may explain why many Americans have never tasted one. Good pomegranate juice will be rich-flavored, with a pleasing tannic tinge and a lingering aftertaste, but without being overly sweet. Bottled pomegranate juice was once only available at Middle Eastern and health food stores, but today, you can find Pom Wonderful juice available in many supermarkets.

Once the arils (the membrane-covered seeds enclosing the ruby-red juice) have been extracted, they are easy to sprinkle on salads, dips, chicken, turkey, and pork dishes. The seeds are a traditional and eye-pleasing garnish throughout the Middle East, where they are sprinkled onto hummus (chickpea spread), tahini (sesame seed spread), and other small salads. Pomegranate seeds are often sprinkled with sugar, lime juice, or rose water in North Africa, the Arab world, and India.

CHOOSING, RIPENING, AND STORING POMEGRANATES

Fresh pomegranates are in season from August through December and into January, but peak availability is in October and November. Generally they're sold ripe and ready to eat, because once picked, the fruit won't ripen any further. The best pomegranates are large, heavy, and deeply colored, with taut and unbroken rinds. Pomegranates keep several months in the refrigerator, but eventually dry out and lose their sprightly flavor.

Avoid bruised, shriveled, or hard pomegranates or those with dull skin. Overripe fruits will tend to crack open. Freeze pomegranate seeds for up to three months.

Preparing a Pomegranate

To peel a pomegranate, first cut off the crown and gently scoop out some of the spongy white center core. Using a small, sharp paring knife, score just through the outer rind to mark the fruit in quarters. Place your thumb in the center of the core and gently pull apart the sections. Peel away the white pith and discard. Invert the skin inside out and pop out the seeds.

To separate the seeds from the attached white membrane, place the sections of pomegranate in a bowl of cold water and gently separate the juicy seeds. Discard the membrane pieces that float to the top.

To juice a pomegranate, put the seeds through a juicer, or ream the halved fruits on an orange juice squeezer, without squeezing too hard, which will release bitter juices from the pith. Or, warm the fruit slightly and roll it between your hands to soften the interior. Cut a hole in the stem end and place over a glass. Let the juice run out, squeezing the fruit to extract it all.

Avoid using aluminum and carbon steel knives or pots as they can turn the juice bitter.

To Eat or Not to Eat the Seeds

Most aficionados swallow the nutty-flavored seeds, which are small and edible, but those who find them objectionable spit them out. I will eat small amounts of the seeds, but if I'm eating a whole pomegranate, I will generally spit them out after extracting all the delicious flavor of the surrounding juice.

Pomegranates in Biblical Times

In Biblical times, the pomegranate was used for making wine and for seasoning and was also used as a dye. Then, as now, it was appreciated for its aesthetic qualities, particularly the crown near the stem. Tradition has it that a pomegranate has 613 seeds to represent the 613 commandments in the Torah (five books of Moses sacred to Jews). The decorative silver crowns that top the two scrolls of the handwritten parchment Torah scroll are often made in the shape of pomegranates.

Pomegranates in Israel

Fittingly enough, pomegranate trees are prevalent today in Israeli gardens. The tree has rich green leaves and red flowers that bear fruit just in time for Rosh Hashanah, the Jewish New Year, celebrated in the fall (September or October, depending on the lunar calendar). The plump red fruits are often plucked to decorate the *sukkah* (small harvest hut) built during the feast of *Sukkot* (Tabernacles).

Healthy Pomegranates

Long reputed to have beneficial health properties, today, pomegranate juice is the latest miracle food. Lynda and Stewart Resnick, owners of the Franklin Mint outside of Philadelphia and other successful businesses, predicted that pomegranate fruit and juice could be the next big thing. Starting in 2002, they planted 6,000 acres of pomegranates in California's San Joaquin Valley, which will almost quadruple America's production of pomegranates in the next five years. These pomegranates are being juiced and sold as their Pom Wonderful brand juice, a refrigerated premium juice high in beneficial antioxidants. Maybe Americans will finally start to love this superb but challenging fruit. (Go to www.pomwonderful.com for more information.)

738

Crunchy Cauliflower with Pomegranate Sauce

Cauliflower, which originated in Egypt, is still quite popular in the Arab world. Simply steamed, cauliflower may be rather bland. Once breaded and fried, its interior becomes creamy yet light, with a delicately vegetal flavor. Even better, the simple sauce—made from bottled pomegranate molasses, a little garlic, and olive—adds a tart edge of flavor and bold color to the dish. If you're staying away from frying, steam the cauliflower until crisp-tender, drain, and serve with the Pomegranate Sauce.

SERVES 6

1 teaspoon finely chopped garlic

2 tablespoons pomegranate molasses

6 tablespoons extra-virgin olive oil

2 eggs, lightly beaten

$1/2$ cup milk

Kosher salt, freshly ground black pepper, grated nutmeg, and cayenne pepper to taste

$1/4$ pound (1 cup) all-purpose flour

3 cups Japanese panko or soft breadcrumbs (made from firm white sandwich bread with the crusts cut off)

1 head cauliflower, cut up into florets about 1 inch all around

1 cup canola oil

Whisk (or blend) together the garlic, pomegranate molasses, and olive oil until thick and creamy, and reserve at room temperature.

In a medium bowl, lightly beat together the eggs, milk, salt, pepper, nutmeg, and cayenne. Place the flour in a second bowl and the breadcrumbs in a third bowl.

Dip the florets, one at a time, into the flour, shaking off the excess. Next dip the florets into the egg mixture, letting the excess liquid drip off, then coat evenly with the breadcrumbs. Arrange the florets on a wax-paper-lined baking sheet in a single layer without touching each other, and chill in the refrigerator to set coating about 30 minutes (or up to 2 days ahead).

When ready to cook, heat the oil in a heavy skillet or a wok until lively bubbles form when a piece of cauliflower is placed in the oil. Fry the florets in small batches for about 5 minutes, or until golden brown on all sides. Drain on paper towels, sprinkle with salt and pepper, and serve with the pomegranate sauce.

Muhammara (Red Pepper and Pomegranate Dip)

This Turkish dip gets its name from brick, which it resembles in color. A tangy, easy-to-make combination of roasted red bell peppers, walnuts, pomegranate molasses, and cumin, it will be a welcome change on your table from the more common hummus and tahini dips. Serve the muhammara with vegetable crudités, toasted pita bread, or as part of a selection of mezze (small Middle Eastern appetizers). Pomegranate molasses is available at Middle Eastern markets and from many specialty stores. It is reasonably priced and lasts indefinitely in the cupboard, so it's worth having on hand. (Try using it instead of vinegar for your next salad dressing.)

MAKES 3 CUPS

2¹/₂ pounds, (3 to 4) red bell peppers

1 tablespoon Turkish red pepper paste (bottled)

6 ounces walnuts, coarsely ground

¹/₂ cup wheat crackers, crumbled

1 tablespoon lemon juice

2 tablespoons pomegranate molasses

1 teaspoon ground cumin

1 teaspoon kosher salt

2 tablespoons olive oil

2 tablespoons chopped pistachios (for garnish)

Roast the peppers on a grill or under the broiler. Process the peppers, pepper paste, walnuts, crackers, lemon juice, pomegranate molasses, cumin, and salt until ground and creamy. Spread onto a serving dish. Drizzle with olive oil and chopped pistachios. Serve with pita crisps.

740

Dawood Basha (Lebanese Meatball Stew with Pine Nuts)

Dawood Basha is the name of the much-admired, tolerant Ottoman Turkish governor who restored peace and unity to Lebanon in the late 1800s, so that the country experienced a long period of civil harmony. This tasty meatball stew, scented with cinnamon and allspice, consists of seasoned beef and/or lamb balls browned and then simmered in a rich and tangy tomato and pomegranate molasses sauce, studded with rich pine nuts. In Lebanon, the flavorful, almost chewy, long, thin Mediterranean pine nuts would be used. Unfortunately, they are hard to find and quite expensive in America. The meatballs in sauce also freeze quite well. Serve with Rice Pilaf with Toasted Vermicelli (see page 816), or with steamed bulgur wheat or kasha. The seltzer makes the meatballs lighter, but either sparkling or plain water can be substituted.

SERVES 6 TO 8

Meatballs

1 cup grated onion

2 pounds coarsely ground beef

2 teaspoons ground cinnamon, divided

2 teaspoons ground allspice, divided

1 teaspoon freshly ground black pepper, divided

4 teaspoons kosher salt, divided

¹/₄ cup seltzer water (substitute sparkling or plain water)

6 tablespoons olive oil, divided

1 pound peeled shallots, quartered, including trimmed root end

2 tablespoons all-purpose flour

2 cups chopped plum tomatoes

1 tablespoon pomegranate molasses

1/2 cup pine nuts

Place the onion, ground beef, 1 teaspoon each of cinnamon and allspice, 1/2 teaspoon of pepper, 2 teaspoons of salt, and the seltzer in the bowl of a mixer. Beat to combine well (or mix by hand). Cook a small amount to check the seasonings. Using a small ice-cream scoop, shape into walnut-sized balls, and chill until ready to cook (up to 1 day, if covered and refrigerated). Heat 2 tablespoons of olive oil in a large skillet and brown the meatballs well on all sides, working in batches. Remove the meatballs from the pan and reserve. Reserve the skillet and any fat also.

In the reserved skillet, heat 2 tablespoons more olive oil and then brown the shallots well. Remove from pan and reserve.

Add the flour to the pan; stir to mix with the fat, and brown lightly. Add the remaining 1 teaspoon of cinnamon and allspice, the remaining 1/2 teaspoon of black pepper, and the remaining 2 teaspoons of salt, 1/4 cup of seltzer, the tomatoes, and pomegranate molasses. Bring the sauce to the boil; add the browned meatballs and shallots. Simmer together 15 minutes.

Meanwhile, in a small skillet, heat the remaining 2 tablespoons of olive oil and cook the pine nuts, stirring often, until golden brown. Stir half the pine nuts into the sauce; reserving the remainder to sprinkle on top for garnish.

Pomegranate Sorbet

As a young, driven, and uncompromising chef, I would buy cases of Wonderful pomegranates, split them open so their ruby juice would run all over the place, and patiently extract the seeds, separating them from the attached bits of bitter white pith. I would then crush them and make them into the most wonderful sorbetto you've ever tasted. You have to be at least a little bit crazy to be a good chef. Today, fresh refrigerated and bottled pomegranate juice, frozen pomegranate puree, and the cooked-down sour pomegranate juice called dibs rimonim or pomegranate molasses, are all available at the market, so it's relatively easy to make wonderful pomegranate dishes without all the fuss—but without some of the fun, too!

SERVES 6

741

4 large juicy pomegranates, or 3 cups juice, preferably fresh refrigerated type

2 cups freshly squeezed orange juice

2 cups granulated sugar

1 teaspoon orange-blossom water (optional)

Fill a large bowl with cold water. Cut the pomegranates in quarters. Holding the fruit under the water, break it apart, separating the seeds from the tough red outer skin and the bitter white pith. The seeds will fall to the bottom of the bowl; the pith will float to the top. Skim off and discard the pith and drain the seeds. Place the seeds in a blender along with the orange juice and purée until smooth.

Strain the juice mixture through a sieve, pressing with the back of a wooden spoon to extract as much liquid as possible (or strain through the finest screen of a food mill). Stir in the sugar and orange-blossom water. Transfer the mixture to an ice-cream maker and run until firm but not stiff. Store, tightly covered, in the freezer until firm. Temper by leaving in the refrigerator for 30 minutes before serving.

PORK

PORK

How can a Jewish woman raised in a kosher home bring herself to cook, eat, and write about pork? Although I still get a pang of guilt every time I sample a pork product, I believe that all the riches of our mother earth were meant to be treated with respect, learned about, and enjoyed. In my quest to become the best chef I could be, I've been determined to learn as much as I could about every kind of food. From China to France, Spain to Latin America, so much of the world's cuisine depends on this smart, emotional animal that it behooves any chef to learn how best to use it.

Pork is the meat of pigs usually slaughtered before they are one year old. A pig is a young animal, six to eight months old; a hog is a mature pig. Pork is a perennially popular menu item because of its relative low cost and because its mild yet distinctive flavor blends well with a myriad of seasonings. With the exception of beef, Americans consume more pork than any other meat. Pork is generally very tender with a delicate flavor and can be eaten any way but raw, whether fresh, cured, salted, or smoked.

The pork we eat today is leaner and healthier than it once was because of advances in animal husbandry, although fully fattened specialty breeds are making inroads because less fat unfortunately means less flavor and succulence. Because pigs are slaughtered at a young age, their meat is generally very tender and delicate in flavor. The meat is well suited to a variety of cooking methods. More than 60 percent of pork marketed in the United States is cured to produce products such as smoked hams and bacon.

The domestic pig, *Sus scrofa*, belongs to the *Suidae* or swine family along with the wild boar and warthog. It is descended from the European wild boar and the Asian wild boar. Wild boars were an important—and dangerous—prey for prehistoric hunters. A wild boar hunt is depicted in the prehistoric cave paintings at Lascaux, France. Pigs were domesticated as early as ten thousand years ago, around the same time as the sheep. The early Greeks valued pork for its nutritious qualities, succulent flavor, and versatility—the same reasons we eat it today. In Roman times, Apicius the epicure provided many recipes for pork and suckling pigs, and hams were already being exported from Gaul (now France) to Rome.

From early times, in Europe pigs were traditionally slaughtered at midwinter when the weather was cold so the meat wouldn't spoil. This occasion became an annual festival, where every part of the pig was consumed or prepared for preserving, from the snout to the tail. For the poor, this annually slaughtered pig was often the only source of meat. Pigs came to the Americas with Columbus, Cortes introduced them to Mexico, and

DeSoto brought them to Florida in 1539. Escaped pigs from DeSoto's herd formed the basis of the semi-wild razorback hogs that became an important food for hunters in the American South. Pork—fresh and cured—is still a main source of protein in the region.

English colonists brought pigs to Jamestown, Virginia, in 1607, and kept them on what is still known as "Hog Island." On Manhattan Island, a long, solid wall was constructed to control roaming herds of pigs; this area is now known as Wall Street. Settlers in the Midwest brought pigs with them and Cincinnati (called "Porkopolis") and later Chicago ("hog butcher of the world") became the center of pork processing. The refrigerated railroad car transformed the meat industry after the Civil War: as a result, the upper Midwest (the "Corn Belt"), where feed grains were produced, became known as the "Hog Belt." Iowa is still the largest pork-producing state.

Worldwide, pork is eaten throughout Europe, North and South America, China, Southeast Asia, and Indonesia. Pork is forbidden to Jews and Muslims, perhaps because pork spoils quickly in hot weather or because pigs are scavengers. Today, Americans eat about 65 pounds of pork a year per person. Europeans eat a lot more pork than Americans, with Denmark eating the highest amount, followed by Spain and Germany. In Asia, people in Hong Kong eat the most pork, followed by Taiwan and China. However, pork accounts for over sixty percent of all meat consumed in China, down from eighty percent as recently as the 1980s.

PORK BREEDS

In Denmark, Landrace pigs became the basis of the Danish bacon industry. They are fed the skim milk created during cheese production (similar to the relationship of Parma pigs, which eat the whey from making Parmigiano cheese). The famed Iberian or Pata Negra pig, which may be a direct descendent of the original Mediterranean wild boar, is prized for the fine, rich, incredibly flavorful ham it produces. There are many different breeds of Chinese pigs, because of varied geography and climate.

In Britain and the U.S., pigs are classified as lard or bacon breeds. Lard breeds, which are compact and thick, with short legs and deep bodies, are fattened quickly on corn. Long, lean, and muscular bacon pigs are fed a high-protein diet, so they grow more slowly and put on more muscle. When the market for lard collapsed after World War II, American breeders needed to produce leaner meat. Today, the pork industry relies on a three-way cross between the Duroc, Hampshire, and Yorkshire breeds.

745

KUROBUTA OR BERKSHIRE BLACK PORK

Black Berkshire hogs are the oldest recognized breed in today's world and prized for the quality of their meat for three hundred and fifty years. Berkshire pork is distinctive with rich, darker-colored meat that is well marbled and quite juicy, with a unique flavor. The pigs are raised on specialty farms where they are fed corn and soybeans without the use of hormones or rendered by-products, so the pigs are healthier and the meat is antibiotic-free.

The same breed is known in Japan as *Kurobuta*, which means "black pork," because the pigs themselves are black and their meat is darker in color than that of other breeds. Look for this specialty pork on restaurant menus and at specialty retail markets, but expect to pay a high price for it. It is considered to be the "Kobe of pork."

Raising Pork

A pig weighing about two hundred and forty pounds will yield a carcass of about one hundred and eighty pounds, with about one hundred pounds of meat, much of which is cured and made into ham, bacon, and sausage. Pigs can forage for their food, eating anything from household waste to grass, and thrive, but these days, most American pigs are corn-fed. Today's pig has fifty percent less fat compared to the pig of the 1950s. China is the world's top pork producer, followed by the European Union and the U.S., which produces about ten percent of the world's supply.

Pork Safety

Trichinosis is a parasite that lives in pork. Although people may contract trichinosis, this disease is now quite rare. To be absolutely certain to remove all traces of the parasite, according to the U.S. Food Safety and Inspection Service, pork should be cooked to 160°F. Because trichinosis is destroyed at 140°F, many chefs recommend cooking quick-cooking cuts (such as chops and roasts) to 150°F. so they're slightly pink and still juicy, and cooking slower-cooking cuts from the shoulder and leg to 165°F. (Because many thermometers are not accurate, it's best to allow a 10-degree Fahrenheit margin for error.) Because pork these days is younger and leaner, it should not be cooked to 180°F. as recommended in older recipes or it will get hard and tough.

SUGGESTED BARBECUE SAUCE ADDITIONS

- A-1 sauce
- Asian chile paste
- Bourbon or dark rum
- Canned chipotles in adobo
- Canned tomatoes
- Chili sauce
- Chinese Hoisin sauce
- Chopped garlic
- Chopped pickled ginger
- Dark brown sugar
- Grated ginger root
- Guava paste
- Honey
- Lime or lemon juice
- Liquid smoke
- Maple syrup
- Mango chutney
- Marmalade or preserves
- Molasses
- Orange juice
- Pickapeppa sauce
- Pickled jalapeño peppers
- Prepared horseradish
- Prepared mustard
- Sweet pickle relish
- Vinegar
- Worcestershire sauce

Kitchen Sink Barbeque Ribs

Ribs always taste better if you rub them first with spices and then slow-bake them before finishing them on the grill. Spice the ribs up to two days before cooking them for even better flavor. This recipe comes from the fact that everyone seems to have a refrigerator door full of half-used bottles of sauces, relishes, and condiments. To make "kitchen sink" sauce, start with this basic barbeque sauce and start adding ingredients, tasting as you go, keeping a balance of sweet, hot, pungent, and savory ingredients. Of course, it will be impossible to duplicate this wonderful concoction next time. If you end up with a bigger batch than you need, store in the refrigerator up to 1 month, or up to 6 months in the freezer.

SERVES 6 TO 8

Rib Spice Rub

$1/4$ cup chili powder

$1/4$ cup brown sugar, packed

$1/4$ cup kosher salt

2 tablespoons paprika

2 tablespoons garlic powder

1 tablespoon ground cumin

1 tablespoon dry mustard

1 tablespoon oregano

1 tablespoon freshly ground black pepper

6 to 8 pounds ribs (baby back, spareribs, or country style)

Combine all of the dry ingredients in a bowl. Rub each rack of ribs all over with about $1/4$ cup of the spices. Marinate in the refrigerator at least 1 hour, but preferably overnight. Wrap in heavy-duty foil and bake at 300°F. for 2 hours, or until the ribs are tender when pierced. (This step may be done up to 2 days ahead. Cool, then refrigerate, preferably overnight. Remove and discard any congealed white fat.)

Basic Barbeque Sauce

1 quart barbeque sauce (purchased)

1 quart ketchup

1 cup soy sauce

1 small onion, finely chopped

1 tablespoon ground cumin

1 tablespoon ground allspice

2 tablespoons dry mustard

In a medium heavy pot, bring all the sauce ingredients to the boil. Reduce the heat and simmer for 1 hour, stirring occasionally.

Finishing Ribs

Preheat a grill or broiler to hot. Dip each rib rack into the sauce and then grill over medium-low heat, turning often, until glazed and shiny. Cut into sections, 2 ribs per section, and serve with extra sauce for dipping.

DOUSING A GRILL FLAME

Keep a plastic spray bottle of water near a charcoal grill. If you have any flare-ups of fire, just spray with water to douse the flame. (Don't do this with an electric or gas grill.)

747

Spareribs, Back Ribs, and Country–Style Ribs

Baby Back Ribs: Baby back ribs are not actually from baby pigs. They are pork chop bones from the upper (or back) portion of the ribs left after the loin meat has been cut away. They are smaller and leaner than spareribs but relatively expensive. Look for lean ribs with plenty of meat on them.

Country-Style Ribs: Country-style ribs are pork chops from the blade (or shoulder) end of the loin that have been split in half and butterflied. They are meaty as well as inexpensive.

Spareribs: Spareribs are the 14 ribs from the belly of the pig—the part that's left after the bacon is cut away. The best slabs weigh more than three pounds. Look for ribs that are not too fatty. St. Louis-style ribs have been trimmed into a compact shape.

Philippine Pork Inihaw

Philippine cooking may be the original fusion food. It is basically the cooking of Malaysians who reached the Philippines during prehistoric times, mixed with the foods of the Spanish colonists who ruled for around 400 years. But the food also has other influences, including Chinese, Japanese, Southeast Asian, American, and even Mexican. It is characterized by strong contrasts in flavors, and vinegar is an important seasoning. Sweet and savory Pork Inihaw is a Philippine favorite, perfect for pulutan, the savory dishes served with drinks. To make Pork Inihaw, the meat is marinated for up to 24 hours. After grilling, the pork ends up with a shiny, slightly charred crust. It is then sliced and served on a bed of steamed vegetables and drizzled in soy vinaigrette.

SERVES 6

Soy Vinaigrette

6 tablespoons cane vinegar

3 tablespoons soy sauce

1 large clove garlic, thinly sliced

2 scallions, sliced

2 tablespoons finely diced onion

$1/2$ teaspoon Sambal Oelek (or other hot red chile paste)

1 teaspoon hot red pepper flakes

1 tablespoon granulated sugar

1 teaspoon kosher salt

$1/2$ teaspoon black pepper

Combine all of the ingredients in a container and marinate at room temperature for at least 4 hours and up to 2 days before using. Store covered, in the refrigerator for up to 1 month.

Pork and Vegetables

$1^1/2$ pounds boneless pork butt

6 tablespoons vegetable oil

2 tablespoons roasted sesame oil

1 tablespoon Chinese oyster sauce

6 tablespoons soy sauce (Kikkoman preferred)

¹/₄ cup cane vinegar

6 tablespoons Philippine banana sauce (substitute ketchup)

2 tablespoons granulated sugar

1 tablespoon kosher salt

¹/₂ teaspoon garlic powder

2 tablespoons chopped garlic

¹/₂ teaspoon freshly ground black pepper

3 cups assorted vegetables, cut into bite-size pieces (such as Napa cabbage, green and red bell peppers, sugar snap peas, onion, and/or celery)

Soy Vinaigrette

Optional garnishes: sliced white onion, thin carrot sticks, sliced scallions

Wrap the pork in plastic wrap and freeze for 1 hour, or until firm. Using a very sharp knife, cut the pork against the grain into thin slices ¹/₄- to ¹/₈-inch thick (or ask your butcher to do this step for you). Filipinos often prefer the fatty parts; you may choose to trim the fat.

Place the pork slices into a large container and add the vegetable oil, sesame oil, oyster sauce, vinegar, banana sauce, sugar, salt, garlic powder, garlic, and black pepper. Mix until well combined. The meat should be "swimming" in the marinade. Cover and refrigerate at least 4 hours, but preferably overnight.

To cook, preheat a grill until red-hot. Drain the pork and grill each slice over moderate heat until shiny and slightly charred on both sides. Reserve the grilled pork in a 200°F. oven while you briefly steam the vegetables.

Arrange the steamed vegetables in a mound in the center of each of 6 plates. Slice the pork into thin, crosswise strips and arrange over top of the vegetables. Drizzle about 2 tablespoons of the Soy Vinaigrette over each portion and serve immediately topped with garnishes.

PHILIPPINE INGREDIENTS

To make this dish authentically, you'll need two unique Philippine ingredients: cane vinegar distilled from sugarcane (you can substitute white vinegar) and banana sauce, a ketchup-like thick, red sauce made from bananas, tomatos, and spices. Look for the banana sauce (Jufran brand is recommended) and cane vinegar in well-stocked Asian markets.

Spanish Roast Pork Tenderloin in Pimentón–Oregano Crust

This simple Spanish-style roast is flavored with smoked paprika, oregano, plenty of garlic, and olive oil and then roasted at high heat so that it comes out browned and crusty and juicy on the inside. Pork tenderloin is one of the butcher's last great bargains and it's so easy to prepare, with little to no trimming needed. Because most pork tenderloins come packed in twos, this recipe is designed to use one of those packages. Rub the pork the day before and refrigerate overnight, if desired. Be sure to let the pork come to room temperature before roasting.

SERVES 6

1/4 cup extra-virgin olive oil

1 tablespoon chopped garlic

2 tablespoons sweet Spanish paprika

1 tablespoon pimentón

2 tablespoons chopped fresh oregano, or
   2 teaspoons dried

1 teaspoon kosher salt

1/2 teaspoon freshly ground black pepper

2 whole pork tenderloins

Whisk the olive oil, garlic, paprika, pimentón, oregano, salt and pepper, and reserve.

Trim the pork of all connective tissue and fat, including the silverskin (the shiny material that encloses the muscle meat). Rub the meat with the above mixture, coating evenly. Refrigerate and leave the meat to marinate overnight (or up to 2 days).

Preheat the oven to 450°F. Fold the thin end of the pork tenderloins underneath. Place both in a roasting pan and roast for 20 to 30 minutes, turning once, until meat is cooked through and reads 160°F. on a meat thermometer at the thickest point. Remove from the oven and allow the meat to rest for 10 minutes to re-absorb its juices. Slice thinly, drizzle with the pan juices, and serve.

Hungarian Pork Goulash with Potato Dumplings

Fiery-looking paprika powder is the national spice of Hungary, brought there in the seventeenth century by Bulgarians who got it from Turks, who perhaps encountered the spice in Portuguese settlements in Central Asia. In Hungarian cuisine, six grades of paprika are produced in two main growing areas: Szeged and Kalocsa. The Hungarian "national dish" is gulyás (cattleman), a thick and spicy soup made from beef and vegetables and seasoned with plenty of paprika. Here, steaming fluffy potato dumplings dropped on top complete a perfect symphony of ingredients.

SERVES 4 TO 6

2 pounds pork shoulder cubes

Kosher salt and freshly ground black pepper to taste

2 ounces (1/2 cup) all-purpose flour

About 1/4 cup canola oil

1 red onion, cut into thin strips

2 large carrots, cut into diagonal half-moons

1 red bell pepper, cut into strips

1 green bell pepper, cut into strips

2 teaspoons chopped garlic

1 teaspoon ground cumin

2 tablespoons paprika

1 (15-ounce) can diced tomatoes

1/4 cup chopped dill

Potato Dumplings (recipe follows)

Season the pork with salt and pepper, then dust with flour, shaking off the excess. Using a large braising pan, brown the pork cubes on all sides in 3 to 4 batches over high heat in the oil.

In the same pan, sauté the vegetables until transparent, about 6 minutes. Add the garlic, cumin, and paprika and sauté 2 to 3 minutes longer. Add the tomatoes and salt and pepper. Bring to the boil. Place in a casserole dish, cover, and bake at 300°F. for 1 1/2 hours, or until pork is tender when pierced.

Prepare the Potato Dumplings while the casserole is bak-

750

ing. Remove the casserole from the oven, allow the goulash to cool slightly and then spoon into serving plates. Top with the Potato Dumplings and serve immediately.

Potato Dumplings

1 pound Idaho potatoes, steamed or baked in skins
    until soft (2 medium potatoes)

1 egg, lightly beaten

1 ounce ($1/4$ cup) all-purpose flour

Kosher salt to taste

$1/4$ cup breadcrumbs

2 tablespoons chopped parsley

Extra flour for dusting

Bring a large wide pot of salted water to the boil. Cool potatoes until they can be handled. Remove and discard potato skins and put the potatoes through a ricer or food mill into a medium bowl. Add the egg and mix by hand to combine. Add flour, salt, breadcrumbs, and parsley, and mix by hand to combine.

Dust your hands with flour and form the mixture into approximately 16 (1-inch diameter) dumplings. Drop one by one into the boiling water. Boil gently over moderate heat until the dumplings rise to the top. Turn over so they cook evenly and continue boiling about 4 minutes, or until light and fluffy all the way through (undercooked dumplings will be dense in the middle). Scoop out with a slotted spoon or a skimmer—they are too fragile to dump into a colander—and serve on top of the goulash.

PIG NAMES

A *barrow* is a castrated male hog, or boar. A *gilt* is a young female, while a *sow* is a female that has born a litter.

Jamaican Jerked Pork

Jerk is a style of cooking native to Jamaica in which meats are dry-rubbed with a fiery spice mixture of aromatic seasonings and then cooked in a pit, on a grill, or on an open fire. Fiery jerk pastes featuring native Jamaican allspice (called "pimento" there), thyme, and Scotch bonnet chiles are used to marinate pork, goat, or chicken before barbecuing, preferably over an allspice-wood fire. The meat may also be stuffed or wrapped with allspice leaves to give it an even more aromatic flavor. The soft-stick or "true" cinnamon called for here is milder and more subtle than the stronger cassia bark often sold as cinnamon. Look for it in Latin American or Asian groceries.

SERVES 6 TO 8

3 tablespoons whole allspice

3 bay leaves, crumbled

1 stick soft-stick cinnamon (canela)

2 teaspoons black peppercorns

$1/2$ cup malt or cider vinegar

1 Scotch bonnet, or 2 to 3 serrano or other hot chiles,
    seeded and minced

1 bunch scallions, thinly sliced

Kosher salt to taste

3 pounds pork shoulder, trimmed of excess fat and
    cut into thin strips

2 tablespoons canola oil

Heat the spices in a small dry skillet, shaking over the heat for several minutes, or until the fragrances are released. Cool to room temperature and then grind in a spice grinder or crush using a mortar and pestle, and reserve.

Whisk together the vinegar, $1/2$ cup of water, the chile peppers, scallions, crushed spices, and salt.

In a large, nonreactive bowl, combine the marinade with the pork. Cover and marinate overnight, covered, in the refrigerator.

When ready to cook, preheat a grill or broiler to high. Drain the pork strips, then thread them an S-shape onto skewers, making sure to skewer each piece 3 times so it doesn't turn around on the skewer. Brush the skewered meat with oil. Grill indirectly in a covered grill about 20 minutes, or until browned on all sides and cooked through but still juicy, or broil, watching carefully so the pork doesn't burn. If desired, toss 1 teaspoon of whole allspice berries into the fire halfway through the cooking time.

SCOTCH BONNET PEPPERS

Essential to the flavor of jerk are Scotch bonnet peppers, the fiery light green, yellow, or red bonnet-shaped peppers named for their resemblance to a Scotch tam o'shanter hat. The Carib Indians used them for torturing captives and for seasoning their pepper-pot stew. Aside from providing heat and a unique fruity-fiery flavor, these chiles helped preserve foods and aided in digestion. For less heat, omit the seeds. The heat of chiles is measured in Scoville units. Jalapeños measure about 5,000 while Scotch Bonnets range from 100,000 to as much as 350,000, so treat them with the respect they deserve.

HANDLING HOT CHILES

Use care when handling fresh chiles. Protect your hands from the capsaicin, the oil contained in hot chilies that produces their heat, by wearing rubber gloves, or coat your hands with oil, which native cooks have done for centuries, and avoid inhaling the fumes. Once your hands or gloves have been in contact with the chile, don't touch your lips, eyes, face, or delicate body parts. To prevent burning those sensitive areas later, scrub your hands and arms vigorously with plenty of hot, soapy water.

ABOUT JERK SEASONING

The term *jerk* is said to come from the work *charqui*, a Spanish term for salted, dried meat, which eventually became *jerky* in English. Another theory is that the name refers to jerking or poking of the meat to produce holes that were filled with the spices. The origins of jerk pork can be traced back to the Cormantee of West Africa through to the Maroons, who were Jamaican slaves that escaped from the British during the invasion of 1655.

POTATOES

POTATOES

French fries, mashed potatoes, baked potatoes with sour cream, stuffed potato skins, home-fried potatoes, roasted potatoes, potato salad . . . it's hard to imagine a world without potatoes. However, until the exploration of the New World starting in the late fifteenth century, the potato was unknown outside of Latin America. The humble potato, *Solanum tuberosum*, is a starchy tuber that may be as small as a marble or large as a brick. It may be smooth or lumpy, fresh-dug for creamy smoothness or aged to increase its starch content.

Native tribes in the Andes began cultivating the wild potatoes they found high in the mountains as early as 7,000 years ago. Even today, Peru is the world's potato capital with a huge diversity of native potatoes in odd shapes and strange colors, although two-thirds of the world's potato crops originate in Europe. These early potatoes were small, knobby, and bitter. Amerindians used special techniques to remove their bitterness. Wild potatoes continue to be eaten in the Andes and are known as *papas criollas* (native potatoes). Potatoes in today's market may be lumpy or smooth, leather-skinned or paper-skinned, small as 1 ounce or large as 1½ pounds, in colors ranging from cream to rose to yellow, red, brown, purple, and blue, and gold to brown, and they are used in every part of the meal—including dessert.

The Spanish brought the potato back to the Old World about 1570, and from there potatoes spread throughout much of the world, eventually becoming a staple food, especially for the poor. Like tomatoes, potatoes were thought to be poisonous because both are members of the family that includes deadly nightshade. Indeed, the leaves of the potato plant are poisonous, as are potatoes left in the light long enough to turn green, which indicates the presence of solanine, a substance that causes illness and, in large quantities, can be toxic.

In the Spanish Colonies, potatoes were considered food for the poor. In the Old World, they were first used to feed hospital inmates. It took two centuries before the potato was commonly accepted. The British King Charles II recommended that large quantities be grown in case of war or famine. About 1780, the people of Ireland adopted the rugged food crop and by the mid-nineteenth century, the vast majority of the Irish population had become totally dependent on the potato for food. When the potato blight destroyed crops in the years 1845, 1846, and 1848, thousands starved to death while others emigrated, mainly to North America and Britain.

In France, the potato was introduced by Antoine Augustin Parmentier, who became a great champion of the new vegetable and encouraged the French to use it in their cuisine. Any French dish that bears the name *à la Parmentier* is sure to include potatoes. Potatoes became fashionable in France after the French court of Louis XVI started promoting them.

754

Types of Potatoes

There are innumerable varieties of potatoes in supermarkets and at farmers' markets, but they fall into several general categories:

All-Purpose Potatoes: As their name implies, these are potatoes that are medium in starch level and have smooth, light tan skin and white flesh. Several varieties of all-purpose potatoes, which may be called round whites, Irish, Chef's, Maine, or Katahdin potatoes, are grown and used most often in the Eastern United States as an "all-purpose potato" suitable for anything the chef can dream up, except perhaps for French fries. They are creamy in texture, hold their shape well after cooking, and are available year-round at a reasonable price. If you simply buy "potatoes," this is the kind you'll get.

New Potatoes: New potatoes are freshly dug potatoes that have not reached their maturity and have never been kept in storage. They have a thin skin and fine-textured, quick-cooking, creamy flesh. They are in season from late winter or early spring through mid-summer and are often found fresh-dug at farmers' markets.

Starchy Potatoes: Starchy or mealy potatoes, such as Russets, are known more commonly as Idaho potatoes. The potato cells in starchy potatoes separate more easily upon cooking because of their high starch levels. When cooked, they have a glistening appearance and a dry, fluffy texture, making them suitable for baking or mashing. Because they're starchy, they're well suited for making gnocchi and potato dumplings, and chefs love them because they absorb that much more butter and cream in dishes like the classic French *Gratin Dauphinoise*, made with four Idaho potatoes and one quart of cream.

These potatoes, especially when well aged, have a lower sugar content, so they will not brown excessively if deep-fried. Steakhouses like Ruth's Chris and others are known for the large size of their steaks and their equally large potatoes. While most restaurants serve an eight- to one hundred-count potato (the number per fifty-pound case), steakhouses will serve potatoes as large as forty-count (more than one pound per potato). I'm not sure if bigger is better here, though. Size isn't everything, at least in potatoes.

Waxy Potatoes: Waxy Potatoes, such as red-skinned potatoes, are lower in starch. They have a smooth, creamy, and moist texture when cooked. The cells in these potatoes have greater tendency to adhere, helping them to hold their shape well. This quality makes them ideal for boiling and steaming and for potato salads. They are sold in three size grades: A, which is large; B, which are smaller at $1^1/_2$ to 2 inches in diameter; and C, also called "creamers" or "baby potatoes," which are marble-sized.

Potato Varieties

All Red: These potatoes have brilliant red skin and pinkish-red to red flesh. They are very popular for California-style potato pizzas and to make pink-tinted mashed potatoes and potato salads. The All Red is harvested by late August to early September and October.

Papas Criollas: In the Andes of Bolivia, Ecuador, and Peru, farmers grow varieties of potatoes that are never seen outside the region. These native Andean potatoes display extraordinary diversity of taste and texture and come in a fascinating array of shapes and colors. For perhaps as long as 8,000 years, these native potatoes have been important in the nutrition and economy of Amerindians. Huño is a freeze-dried potato traditionally made by Quechua and Aymara Indians in Peru and Bolivia, made in a five-day process in the dry air of the mountains, by freezing the potatoes at night and then drying them in the sunlight. They may be found in Latin American markets.

Purple Peruvian: This exotic potato has a subtle nutty, earthy flavor with thin, cream-colored skin, blue-violet to purple flesh, and an unusual number of deep eyes running in a spiral pattern. It ranges from two to six inches in length and is mostly available in the fall.

Fingerlings: These small, thin-skinned potatoes are long, lumpy, and slender, resembling a fat finger. There are many varieties of Fingerlings, include French Fingerlings, Ruby Crescents, and Russian Bananas. Most have yellow flesh with a rich, buttery texture. Fingerling potatoes are excellent for baking, roasting, grilling, and steaming and are available October through April.

German Butterball: This medium round to oblong heirloom potato from Germany has smooth golden skin with deep-golden flesh that is more yellow than butter-colored. The German Butterball is harvested by late August/early September.

Long White: The Long White, mostly grown in California, is a versatile all-purpose potato with medium

756

starch content. These warm-weather summer potatoes can't be stored for long because they have a tendency to turn green (the green portion, called "solanine," is inedible). Long whites are available spring through summer, especially in California. They have thin, light tan skin, brilliant-white to cream-colored flesh, and a firm, creamy texture. Long whites are a favorite on the West Coast from May through July.

Ozette: This historic heirloom is said to have been brought from Peru in the late 1700s by Spanish explorers and traded to the Ozette Indian tribe of the Olympic Peninsula in Washington State. The Ozette is harvested by late September/early October. It is a fingerling potato that ranges in length from three to seven inches with an undulated surface, a thin skin similar to that of new white potatoes, and a light yellow to tan color. Its flavor is earthy and nutty, reminiscent of cooked dried beans, with a firm texture that becomes creamy in the mouth. It is one of the foods in Slow Foods' Ark of Taste, which works on "saving cherished Slow foods, one product at a time." (For more information, *see* Slow Food and the Ark of Taste, page 758.)

Round Red or Red Bliss: Because of the ease of preparing them (they don't need peeling) and their attractive appearance, these popular potatoes may be seen on the plates at many restaurants. Round reds have rosy-red skin and dense, waxy white flesh. Their firm, smooth, and moist texture that keeps its shape makes them well-suited for salads, roasting, boiling, and steaming. They are in season mostly in the late summer and early fall.

Russian Banana: Developed in the Baltic region, these fingerlings are medium-sized tubers with banana-yellow skin and flesh, firm waxy texture, and great flavor. They are the most popular fingerling potato in the U.S. today. Russian Bananas are excellent for salads and are a favorite among chefs and at farmers and specialty markets. Because of their relatively high price, they are often split and roasted and served as part of a garnish in restaurants to show off their interesting shape. The Russian Banana is harvested by late August/early September.

Russet, Russet Burbank, Baking, or Idaho Potatoes: Russet potatoes are the most widely used potato variety in the United States, with the great majority grown in the Northwest. Note that "Idaho potato" is a registered trademark; the same potato grown outside of Idaho must be called a Russet. These large, elongated potatoes have thick, netted, dull-brown skin and white flesh. Their low moisture and high starch content makes them cook up light and fluffy. They are excellent for baking, for making French fries, and for mashing. European chefs often return home with a bag of russets, because they are unlike any European potatoes. Russet potatoes are available year-round and are the best for fries.

Yukon Gold and other yellow potatoes: Gold potatoes are very popular in Europe and increasingly so in the United States, although still not grown in large quantities. Their dense, creamy texture and buttery flavor makes them excellent for mashing, roasting in chunks, and for salads. The Yukon Gold was developed at the University of Guelph in Canada after years of experiments. Success was finally achieved by crossing a North American white potato with a wild South American yellow potato. The result was the Yukon Gold, the first Canadian-bred potato to be marketed and promoted by name, which started to be exported to the U.S. in 1980.

Yukon Golds are slightly flat and oval in shape, with thin, light gold skin and light yellow flesh. They can be identified by the rosy pink color of their shallow eyes. They are in season in the late summer and early fall. There are other gold-fleshed varieties on the market, including Yellow Finn, Michigold, Donna, Delta Gold, Banana, and Saginaw Gold, but none are as famous as the Yukon Gold.

SLOW FOOD AND THE ARK OF TASTE

Founded by Carlo Petrini in Italy in 1986, Slow Food is an international association that opposes the standardization of taste, protects food and gastronomic traditions, and food and agricultural biodiversity worldwide. Eighty-three thousand international members are organized into local groups called *convivia*, which organize courses, tastings, dinners, and other food and wine events. The Ark of Taste was founded as part of Slow Food to discover, catalogue, and safeguard small quality food products and defend biodiversity. I have led several programs for the Philadelphia convivium, and traveled with the group to Campania, Italy, in the fall of 2005 to visit local producers, including producers of Sorrento lemons and organic mozzarella di bufala. For more information, go to www.slowfood.com.

Rosemary and Garlic Roasted Gold Potatoes

This recipe is so easy as to not really need to be written out, but it's so good that it's worth reading just to get the small details right. With buttery-tasting, firm-fleshed gold potatoes now available almost everywhere, this is an easy side dish to make that's sure to please. Don't peel the potatoes, both because it tastes so good with the peel and also because that's where all the nutrients lie. As with any simple dish, the few ingredients here have to be the best: the garlic should be freshly peeled, without any bitter green sprouts, the olive oil of high quality and fruity flavor, the rosemary fresh, and the pepper freshly ground. If you use a steel paella pan or a cast-iron skillet for roasting, you'll get the crustiest brown edges.

SERVES 6

2 pounds Yukon gold (or other yellow) potatoes,
  unpeeled and cut into 1-inch cubes
1/4 cup extra-virgin olive oil
1/4 cup garlic cloves, cut into slivers
2 tablespoons chopped rosemary, or 2 teaspoons dried
Kosher salt and freshly ground black pepper to taste

Preheat the oven to 425°F. Toss the potatoes with the olive oil, garlic, rosemary, and salt and pepper. Transfer to a metal roasting pan, just large enough to hold the potatoes in a single layer.

Roast for 30 to 40 minutes, or until well browned and crusty on the outside and tender when pierced on the inside. Turn the potatoes several times during cooking with a metal spatula to allow them to brown evenly.

Potato-Onion Knishes

The delectable hockey-puck-shaped knish is a pastry of Eastern European Jewish origin consisting of a flaky dough enclosing a filling of mashed potatoes with lots of browned onions; kasha (buckwheat groats) and onions; liver and onions; farmer cheese, dill, scallions; and more. Anything but light, these portable meals are well suited to eating on the go. During the early part of the twentieth century, when hundreds of thousands of Eastern European Jews immigrated to America and settled in New York City, they brought with them their family recipes for knishes. It's important to use Idaho or other starchy Russet potatoes here, as others would make a watery filling.

MAKES 8 KNISHES

1¹⁄₂ pounds Idaho potatoes

¹⁄₂ pound (1 large) diced onion

4 tablespoons unsalted butter

Kosher salt and freshly ground black pepper to taste

¹⁄₄ cup lightly beaten egg (about 2 eggs)

1 pound Cream Cheese Pastry (*see* page 597)

1 egg, lightly beaten (for egg wash)

Preheat the oven to 300°F. Steam the potatoes until quite soft. Drain well and then dry out in the oven for 15 minutes, or until no longer wet. When the potatoes are cool enough to handle, peel off the skin by hand, and cut into large chunks.

Meanwhile, brown the onion in the butter until well caramelized, about 15 minutes, turning often until evenly browned. Combine the potato chunks, onions and their cooking liquid, salt and pepper, and the ¹⁄₄ cup of egg in the bowl of a mixer. Beat using the paddle until creamy but some chunks of potato remain. Taste for seasoning and cool to room temperature.

Roll the Cream Cheese Pastry out thinly and cut into 6-inch rounds. Fill the center of each round with about ¹⁄₄ pound of the potato-onion filling, leaving a 1-inch border all around.

Fold over the dough to enclose the filling completely, then turn over with the seam-side down. Brush with egg wash and cut a small, v-shaped slit into the top of each knish. Bake 30 to 40 minutes at 350°F., or until lightly browned and the filling is bubbling up through the slits. Serve immediately. Any leftover knishes can be refrigerated up to 3 days. To reheat, wrap in foil and then heat in a 350°F. oven for about 20 minutes.

759

Yonah Schimmel's Knishes

In 1890, Yonah Schimmel, a rabbi from Romania, began to sell his knishes at New York's Coney Island and from a pushcart on the Lower East Side. By 1910, he had opened his original knish bakery still located on East Houston Street. Today, Yonah Schimmel's sells potato, kasha, red cabbage, mushroom, sweet potato, vegetable, and broccoli knishes.

French Gold Potato Salad with Fines Herbes (and Truffles)

If you're feeling especially generous, add chopped black truffles in whatever form you can afford to this salad. It will make a delicious salad that is out of this world, or maybe under this world, because the truffles are dug from the earth by highly skilled dogs. With or without truffles, the salad will be light but flavorful with all the aromatic herbs to brighten it up. If you do use truffles, substitute the juice from a can of truffles for some of the chicken stock, substitute truffle oil for some of the olive oil, and add small bits of truffle (called "breakings") or truffle paste (usually mixed with mushrooms) to the salad. Note that this salad, like all potato salads, tastes best at room temperature.

SERVES 6

1½ pounds Yellow gold potatoes, cut into ½-inch thick half moons

1½ cups rich chicken stock, homemade if possible (*see* page 991)

6 tablespoons red wine vinegar

Kosher salt and freshly ground black pepper to taste

¾ cup extra-virgin olive oil

½ cup chopped mixed tarragon, chervil, and thyme, parsley, and/or chives

1 bunch scallions, thinly sliced

Set up a steamer basket and steam the potatoes until soft when pierced. Drain well, allowing the potatoes to dry out a bit. While still hot, mix the potatoes with the chicken stock, and vinegar, and season to taste with salt and pepper. Allow the mixture to marinate 10 to 15 minutes.

Meanwhile, whisk together the olive oil, herbs, and scallions. Toss this mixture with the marinated potatoes, taste again for seasoning, and serve immediately.

Matzo Meal

Matzo meal is ground flakes of the unleavened bread made from only flour and water that is eaten by Jews at Passover in commemoration of their escape from slavery in Egypt. It is sold already ground in boxes in many supermarkets, especially at Passover time, in the spring. If you do see it then, buy a box and keep it in the freezer, because it is harder to find at other times of year, except in a kosher market. It is the secret to light latkes, because it absorbs excess liquid to yield a perfect texture. Whole matzos may be ground in a food processor to make your own.

Potato Latkes

The instantly intoxicating and nostalgic smell of onion-laden potato latkes frying in oil is something I have to immerse myself in—it's a warm bath in the best memories of the holiday of Chanukah, celebrated for eight wonderful nights. In my childhood, when my zeida, otherwise known as my great-grandfather and unquestioned patriarch of the family, was still alive, we would go to my great-aunt's house and join with the families of all six of his children for the holiday. Needless to say, we ate a lot of latkes. Much later, I gave a big Chanukah party one year and had people lining up for the latkes as soon as they came out of the pan. Two cooks couldn't keep up the demand! Even if you aren't Jewish, making latkes may become a tradition in your family too. Serve the latkes with applesauce (homemade is best) and sour cream. The sour salt is crystallized citric acid, used in areas where lemon is not easily found.

SERVES 8

2¹/₂ pounds Idaho potatoes, peeled

1 pound onions

¹/₄ teaspoon sour salt (substitute 1 teaspoon lemon juice)

1 cup matzo meal

2 eggs

Kosher salt and freshly ground black pepper to taste

Peanut oil, for frying

Applesauce, for serving

Sour cream, for serving

Grind together the potatoes, onions, and sour salt in a meat grinder, food processor, or blender until fine but not pasty. Drain well, pressing out the excess liquid.

Beat together the matzo meal and eggs, and season to taste with salt and pepper (the potatoes suck up salt). Combine with the potato-onion mixture and allow it to rest 10 minutes to thicken.

When ready to fry, spoon the mixture into 2-inch cakes and pan-fry in a cast-iron skillet in peanut oil until crispy and reddish-brown on all sides, about 3 to 4 minutes per side. Drain on a wire rack and keep warm in a 200°F. oven (if they last that long), until all the latkes have been fried. Serve immediately accompanied by cold applesauce and sour cream.

Golden Potato Mash with Garlic and Green Olive Oil

Ever since I first started using Yukon gold potatoes when they first became available in the early 1980s, I have become completely enamored of them. Their buttery-earthy flavor, fluffy consistency, and beautiful color make me want to use them all the time. They do make outstanding mashed potatoes, beautiful to look at and even better to eat. Here, I use extra-virgin olive oil to flavor the potatoes. This is a place to use your best oil—because it is simply warmed enough to release its volatile aromas, you'll really take advantage of its subtle and fleeting character.

SERVES 4

1 pound Yukon Gold or other gold potatoes, peeled

1/4 cup extra-virgin olive oil

1 cup half-and-half

Kosher salt and freshly ground black pepper to taste

Bring a pot of salted water to the boil. Add the potatoes and cook until quite soft, 20 to 25 minutes. Meanwhile, heat the olive oil and half-and-half, and season with salt and pepper.

Scoop the potatoes from the water (saving the hot water in the pot) and drain well, shaking to remove any water. Immediately put through a potato ricer or a food mill. Transfer to a large bowl and slowly pour in the hot olive oil-cream mixture, gradually beating until incorporated and smooth. Taste and correct the seasoning if necessary and serve immediately.

To keep the mashed potatoes warm, place the bowl in the pot of hot water and cover with a lid or foil. If the potatoes get too thick, thin them with a little of the starchy potato water.

762

FLUFFY MASHED POTATOES

For the fluffiest mashed potatoes, it's important to pass the potatoes, while they're still piping hot, through a potato ricer or a food mill. If these tools are not available, mash them with a potato masher or a heavy whisk. If you wait until the potatoes start to cool, they may get unpleasantly gluey when mashed.

Horseradish Mashed Potatoes

Horseradish really livens up a bowl of mashed potatoes and complements steaks and beef roasts particularly well. Buy a small jar of prepared horseradish (mixed with vinegar) in the dairy aisle at the supermarket. It will keep in the refrigerator almost indefinitely. Idaho or Russet potatoes work best here, because they have the highest levels of starch and potato solids and therefore absorb the most liquid. Also, their white color works best with the white horseradish. For lighter potatoes, use milk instead of half-and-half. You may, of course, use salted butter here; simply omit the salt. I base all my recipes on unsalted butter, because it is by necessity fresher without the salt to help preserve it, and it's versatile enough to use in both sweet and savory dishes.

SERVES 4

1 pound Idaho potatoes, peeled and cut into large chunks

1 cup half-and-half

4 tablespoons unsalted butter

2 tablespoons prepared horseradish

Kosher salt and freshly ground black pepper to taste

Bring a large pot of salted water to the boil. Add the potatoes and boil until quite soft, 20 to 25 minutes. Meanwhile, heat the half-and-half, butter, and horseradish and reserve.

Drain the potatoes well and transfer to the bowl of a mixer. Using the paddle attachment, beat the potatoes to break them up into small chunks. Next, while beating on slow speed, pour in the hot cream mixture gradually, beating until the liquid is incorporated and the potatoes are relatively smooth. Season with salt and pepper and serve immediately.

Yukon Gold Potato and Sweet Onion Pizza

During my days as a television food stylist, I did most of my work for the fabulously successful QVC network. In those days (starting in 1993), the network was growing at an incredible rate and it felt like the Wild West because of its free and easy, yet challenging atmosphere. I would work endless shifts (up to 30 hours) anywhere in the 24 hour day, 7 days a week. For the first few years, I was about the only food stylist on hand, and I got to work with most of the great culinary luminaries of the day. I particularly enjoyed working with chef/owners Johanne Killeen and George Germon's cookbook, Cucina Simpatica, *based on the robust trattoria cooking of their Providence restaurant, Al Forno. This carb-laden pizza adapted from their book is absolutely scrumptious. Serve it in small portions with drinks or wine before dinner.*

SERVES 6

1¹/₂ pounds Yukon gold potatoes

¹/₂ cup sour cream

4 tablespoons extra-virgin olive oil, divided

Kosher salt and freshly ground black pepper to taste

¹/₂ cup chopped parsley

1 bunch chives, thinly sliced

1¹/₂ pounds sweet onions, sliced into strips

¹/₂ cup dry white vermouth

2 tablespoons chopped rosemary

2 tablespoons chopped thyme

1¹/₂ pounds Cornmeal Pizza Dough (*see* page 985)

¹/₂ pound Italian Fontina cheese, shredded
(freeze first to firm)

Preheat the oven to 450°F. Set up a steamer basket and steam the potatoes until soft when pierced. Allow the potatoes to cool enough to be handled (use gloves to make this easier), then pull off the peel and mash the potatoes. Meanwhile, heat the sour cream, 2 tablespoons of the olive oil, and salt and pepper. While the potatoes are still hot, add the hot sour cream mixture and beat to combine. Add most of the parsley and most of the chives, reserving some for garnish. Cool the mixture and reserve at room temperature.

Meanwhile, cook the onions in the remaining 2 tablespoons olive oil. When crisp-tender, add the vermouth and bring the mixture to the boil over high heat. Cook together, stirring occasionally, until the liquid is thick and syrupy. Stir in the rosemary and thyme, season with salt and pepper, and reserve at room temperature.

Roll out the pizza dough into a large square (to fit into a Sicilian pizza pan) or a large circle (to fit into a circular pan), or make 2 smaller pizzas. Sprinkle the pans with a little cornmeal and spread the dough to reach the edges. Cover the pizza with a layer of the potato mixture, leaving a 1-inch border at the edge, and top with a layer of the onion mix. Sprinkle with the shredded Fontina. Bake until bubbling and well browned, about 8 minutes. Remove from the oven and garnish by sprinkling with the remaining parsley and chives. Allow the pizza to cool somewhat, cut into portion sizes, and serve.

763

Ricotta-Stuffed Potatoes

Is there anyone who doesn't love double-baked stuffed potatoes? Anyone who has only eaten dense but smooth piped-in restaurant-style stuffed potatoes will absolutely adore this slightly lumpy but lighter version made with ricotta cheese. It's important to use whole-milk ricotta and to allow it to drain for about one hour in a sieve, otherwise the filling will be watery. Serve the potatoes as soon as they come out of the oven, as they will deflate as they cool. Make variations by adding chopped basil, marjoram, and/or parsley, or sauté finely chopped shallots and firm vegetables such as celery root, carrots, peppers, and/or zucchini until crisp-tender and fold into the potato filling before baking.

SERVES 6

6 Idaho potatoes, washed, dried, and rubbed with olive oil

1 pound whole milk ricotta, drained

2 teaspoons finely chopped garlic

2 tablespoons unsalted butter, softened

Kosher salt, grated nutmeg, cayenne pepper, and freshly ground black pepper to taste

$1/4$ cup Japanese panko breadcrumbs

2 tablespoons olive oil

1 bunch chives, thinly sliced

Preheat the oven to 400°F. Roast the potatoes about 45 minutes, or until soft all the way through when pierced. Remove the potatoes and cool somewhat. Split open, being careful to stay away from any hot steam that the potatoes will release. Using a spoon, scoop out the flesh, leaving a wall about $1/4$-inch thick. Place the potato flesh in a bowl and mash in the ricotta, garlic, chives, and butter using a potato masher or a heavy whisk. Season generously to taste with salt, nutmeg, cayenne, and black pepper (the potatoes will continue to absorb the seasonings as they bake).

Spoon the filling back into the reserved skins. Mix together the breadcrumbs and olive oil and sprinkle over top of the potatoes. Bake again at 400°F. for 30 minutes, or until browned and bubbling. (The potatoes may be stuffed and set aside for finishing later; if the weather is warm, refrigerate them, allowing them to come to room temperature before baking. If the weather is cool, allow them to rest at room temperature for several hours before baking.) Serve while still hot.

CHOOSING AND STORING POTATOES

Choose potatoes that are firm, smooth, and fairly clean, with few eyes and good color. All potatoes should be firm and blemish-free. Select regularly shaped potatoes for less waste in peeling. Avoid potatoes with wrinkled skin, cut surfaces, soft dark areas, a green tint, or visible sprouts.

Like a bad apple, one bad potato can spoil the barrel, so separate out any potatoes with signs of spoilage for immediate use (after trimming) or discard. Store potatoes in a cool, dark, well-ventilated place for up to two weeks. It is possible to refrigerate potatoes, but low temperature (below 40°F.) can cause the potatoes to convert their starch to sugar, giving them a sweet taste and a soft texture when cooked. Always trim off any sprouts and green portions before using potatoes.

Ethiopian Potatoes and Vegetables with Ginger: Yataklete Kilkil

Ethiopia—the oldest independent country in Africa and one of the oldest in the world (at least 2,000 years)—has sent many immigrants to the United States and Canada in recent years. Vegetarian dishes are plentiful there because their ancient Coptic religion calls for many meat-free days. This lively vegetable stew is flavored with ginger, garlic, and hot chile peppers. The potatoes are sometimes cut in a special decorative pattern; I've given directions below. Carrots, green beans, onions, peppers, and scallions all make for a colorful, multitextured dish that works well on its own or as an accompaniment to a simple roast chicken.

Serves 6

6 large, evenly shaped all-purpose potatoes (if cutting into the decorative shape) or 6 red bliss potatoes, whole if small, quartered if larger

3 carrots, peeled, quartered, and cut into 2-inch-long sticks

1/2 pound green beans, trimmed and cut into 2-inch sections, and/or 1/2 pound okra, trimmed and split lengthwise

1/4 cup vegetable oil

1 onion, cut into thin wedges

1 large green pepper, cut into 2-inch-long strips and/or 1 poblano pepper, cut into 2-inch-long strips

2 whole fresh hot chile peppers

1 tablespoon each: finely chopped garlic and ginger

Kosher salt and white pepper to taste

6 scallions, trimmed, halved lengthwise, and cut into 2-inch lengths

Bring a medium pot of salted water to the boil. Add the potatoes and boil for 5 minutes, or until partially cooked. Add the carrots and green beans to the pot and boil for 5 minutes longer, or until the potatoes and vegetables are almost tender. Drain (saving the cooking liquid if desired for vegetable stock) and run under cold water to stop cooking.

In a Dutch oven, heat the oil and add the onion, green pepper, and chiles and cook for 5 minutes, stirring often, until the vegetables are soft but not brown. Add the garlic, ginger, salt and pepper, and stir together for 1 minute. Add the reserved vegetables and cook for about 10 minutes over low heat, stirring occasionally. Add the scallions and stir to wilt slightly. Serve immediately.

Decorative Potatoes

Start with 6 large, evenly shaped boiling potatoes. Trim off the tops and bottoms to make flattened surfaces, and then peel the potatoes. Lightly score the flat surface of the potatoes into 8 sections. Continue scoring lightly down the sides of the potatoes to provide guidelines for cutting. Cut out lengthwise wedges in between the scoring lines, leaving ridges of potatoes in a wheel-shaped pattern. Place into a bowl of cold water to keep the potatoes from darkening.

QUINCE

QUINCE

The mysterious fruit, sometimes seen at farmers' markets or in Asian groceries, that looks something like a large, lumpy apple or a squat pear with yellow skin and white flesh, is actually a quince. This old-time cousin of the pear and apple has been neglected in modern times, partly because it must be cooked to be softened, and partly because it's often covered with thick, tan-colored fuzz that can be a little daunting. But for those adventurous enough to try them poached or baked, the quince turns a lovely carnelian color, somewhere between pink and orange, and has a firm texture and wonderfully concentrated jammy flavor.

The quince, *Cydonia oblonga*, is one of the earliest-known fruits, and is native to the Caucasus. Many believe that the forbidden fruit in the Garden of Eden was a quince. In Greek legend, the Trojan war began when Paris gave a quince to the Goddess Aphrodite, naming her more beautiful than the goddess Athena. In England, in Tudor and Stuart times, quince marmalade wrapped in gold foil was regarded as an aphrodisiac.

The fruits, which weigh up to one pound, are pear- or apple-shaped depending on the variety, bright yellow, and covered by a characteristic felty coating. This coating wipes off easily, revealing the wax-coated skin which emanates a sweet, fresh fragrance when rubbed. Although mankind has cultivated it for thousands of years, the quince has undergone little change in breeding, largely retaining the character of a wild fruit. The fruit's unique fragrance, hinting of pineapple, guava, and pear, can perfume a room.

Quince's sharp, distinctive flavor complements a wide variety of dishes, including savory meat, poultry, and even fish dishes. In the past, quince was an important fruit, but its popularity has declined greatly in most regions because sweeter, softer fruits like pears and apples took its place. Today, only a small portion are consumed as fresh fruit; the majority go into mustards, preserves, jellies, and liqueurs. The quince is popular in parts of Mexico and in Latin America, especially in Uruguay, where there are large plantations. In Spain, it is made into a quince paste eaten with cream cheese, simply called *membrillo*, also the Spanish name for quince. When cooked, the hard, dry flesh of the quince turns light pink to purple and becomes softer and sweeter. It is a favorite for baking and preserving because of its sweet-sour flavor and high levels of pectin.

The main variety available in American supermarkets is the Pineapple Quince, grown in California. It looks like a knobby pear, though large, smooth, and golden yellow in color, with a distinct pineapple aroma (as long as it's not picked too green). The flesh has a white color, with faint flavor of pineapple.

The Perfumed Quince has an oval shape with tapered ends. The skin is smooth and yellow in color, and the flesh is white. A few small growers offer Orange Quince, several similar varieties of nearly round, bright-colored fruit. A late-season variety is the Champion, a very fuzzy, pear-shaped, delicately flavored variety. The very rare Portugal is giant, bulbous, and football-shaped with a particularly deep, rich flavor.

Choosing and Ripening Quince

Quince are usually lumpy in shape, so if you buy a small one, there won't be much edible fruit left after trimming. Instead, choose quince that are hard and firm, yellow rather than green, and as large as possible. Quince ripen slowly at room temperature, turning from green to yellow, with the flesh remaining firm. Note that although quince bruise easily, any small marks on the skin won't affect their quality. Avoid softened, shriveled, or overly bruised quince, and look for the best quality at Asian, especially Korean markets, where these fruits are in high demand.

Storing and Preparing Quince

Stored in a cool place without touching each other, quince can keep for up to ten weeks without spoiling. The fruit should be peeled before eating, either before or after cooking. Peel with a potato peeler or a small, sharp paring knife, and cut the fruit away from its large, fibrous seed pocket. Or, simmer first whole until half-cooked, then remove from the liquid, cool somewhat and then peel and cut up. Peeling will be much easier with softer, partially cooked fruit.

Tunisian Fish Couscous with Quince and Raisins

This unexpectedly delicious couscous was prepared at a conference I attended at the Culinary Institute of America's Napa Valley campus. The chef, Haouari Abdezzarak, is the owner of a well-regarded restaurant (Chez Haouari) on the island of Djerba, off the coast of Tunisia. This region has an incredibly old Jewish community, and this dish incorporates many of that community's flavors and ingredients, such as preserved lemons, spicy harissa sauce, and several types of couscous. The flavors and textures all worked together so beautifully, I had to recreate the dish on my own.

Serves 6 to 8

2¹/₂ pounds cod fillets

Kosher salt and freshly ground black pepper to taste

2 teaspoons ground cumin

1¹/₂ cups chopped onion

4 tablespoons extra-virgin olive oil, divided

1 cup fresh or canned tomato puree

2 tablespoons tomato paste

1 to 2 tablespoons Harissa Sauce (to taste), purchased or homemade (*see* page 703)

2 large ripe quince, peeled, cored, and cut into wedges

6 tablespoons crushed garlic

³/₄ cup raisins, soaked in warm water to cover

2¹/₄ pounds couscous

Sprinkle the fish on all sides with salt, pepper, and cumin, and reserve.

In a large casserole, cook the onion in 2 tablespoons of olive oil, and then add the tomato puree, tomato paste,

769

and Harissa. Season to taste with salt and pepper. Moisten the mixture with about $^1/_2$ cup of water, reduce the heat, and cook for 10 minutes, or until thickened again.

Moisten again with about $^1/_2$ cup of water and add the quince and the garlic. Cook over moderate heat until the quince are almost tender, about 20 minutes, and then add the fish and the soaked raisins, and finish cooking about 10 minutes longer, or until the fish is opaque and the sauce has thickened somewhat.

Meanwhile steam the couscous, tightly covered, until fluffy, about 15 minutes, then remove from the heat. Transfer the couscous to a large bowl, add the remaining 2 tablespoons olive oil and salt to taste, and mix well.

Place the seasoned couscous back in the steamer and steam a second time. When the couscous is soft and fluffy, about 15 minutes more, transfer it to a large serving platter, form into a large mound, and dress it with a bit of the sauce. Arrange the fish and the quince around the couscous and ladle the sauce over top. Serve more Harissa on the side for those who like it hot.

Quince Mostarda

Mostarda is a spicy-sweet fruit relish used in Italy as a condiment for the dish of boiled meats called Bollito Misto. *Serve mostarda as one element in a cheese, fruit, and nut plate. You can also serve this mostarda with Venison Sausage with Juniper Berries and Pancetta (see page 437). Mostardas are also made with grapes, figs, tart apples, and pears, but quince works particularly well because it stays firm and its naturally spicy character is enhanced by the sweet seasonings.*

MAKES ABOUT 2 QUARTS

2 cups dry white vermouth

2 cups granulated sugar

$^1/_2$ cup lemon juice

Grated zest of 1 lemon

Grated zest of 1 orange

2 tablespoons grated ginger

2 tablespoons yellow mustard seeds

1 cinnamon stick

1 teaspoon whole cloves

1 teaspoon whole peppercorns

$^1/_2$ teaspoon crushed red pepper flakes

5 pounds whole quince, washed well

$^1/_2$ cup finely diced candied ginger

In a large, nonreactive ovenproof casserole with a lid (such as a Le Creuset pot) combine 1 quart of water with the vermouth, sugar, lemon juice, lemon and orange zests, ginger, mustard, cinnamon stick, cloves, peppercorns, and red pepper flakes. Bring to the boil, stirring occasionally, and simmer for 10 minutes, or until clear and slightly thickened.

Add the quince to the pot, bring back to the boil and

simmer, covered, for 20 minutes, or until the quince are half-cooked. Remove the quince from the pot and drain, reserving both the syrup and the quince. Allow the quince to cool. Meanwhile, strain the syrup, pressing well to extract all the juices, and discard the solids.

Preheat the oven to 300°F. Cut the quince into a small dice, discarding the center hard seed pocket. In the same pot, combine the diced quince with the syrup. Bring the syrup back to the boil, and then cover and place in the oven to cook 30 minutes, or until quince are tender and the syrup has reduced until it is thick and has mostly been absorbed.

Remove the pot from the oven, stir in the candied ginger, and cool to room temperature. Transfer to glass jars and store in the refrigerator for up to 3 months. Bring to room temperature before serving.

MORE ABOUT MOSTARDA

Although the name mostarda sounds like mustard and does actually contain whole yellow mustard seeds, its name ultimately derives from the French *mout ardent*, or "fiery must," made by cooking down grape must with powdered mustard seed to make a spicy condiment. (Prepared mustard is called *senape* in Italian.) The most famous mostarda comes in large tins from the town Cremona in the Northern Italian region of Lombardy. It consists of chunks of brightly colored apricots, cherries, figs, tangerines, pears, peaches, and pineapples simmered in a thick honey-and-spice syrup seasoned with sharp mustard oil.

In some regions, the fruit is cooked in grape must, the sweet and syrupy reduction of the juice of wine grapes. Although mostarda has been made for hundreds of years in Cremona, it was only in 1780 that the first recipe was published in a book.

Quince Crema Catalana

Crema Catalana is a typical dessert of Catalonia, the region of Spain that includes the wonderful city of Barcelona. It is the Spanish equivalent to France's crème brulée. Here, I combine quince wedges poached in white wine and honey with a rich custard topping and bake it in a water bath. The final touch is to sprinkle the top with superfine sugar, also known as bar sugar, and caramelize it. An ordinary blow-torch works just fine; I find the smaller crème brulée torches sold in specialty kitchen stores to be less effective. Just be sure to work in an area that is free of anything that might catch fire, and have a fire extinguisher or box of baking soda nearby, just in case.

SERVES 8

Poached Quince

1 cup white wine

$^1/_2$ cup granulated sugar

$^1/_2$ cup honey

1 cinnamon stick

1 vanilla bean, split open

Juice of 1 lemon

4 to 6 quince

Combine the wine, sugar, honey, cinnamon stick, vanilla bean, lemon juice, and 2 cups of water in a non-reactive pot, and bring to the boil. Add the whole quince to the pot, and bring back to the boil. Lower the heat and simmer, covered, for 20 minutes, or until the quince are half-cooked. Remove the quince from the syrup, and remove and reserve the vanilla bean and cinnamon stick for use in the custard (below).

Strain the syrup and save for another use (you may poach other fruits, such as hard pears or Asian pears in the same syrup and then cook it down to make a caramel sauce).

Custard

2 cups heavy cream

2 cups half-and-half

Reserved vanilla bean and cinnamon stick (from above)

8 egg yolks

1 cup granulated sugar

Poached Quince

Extra-fine sugar (bar sugar), for sugar crust (substitute granulated sugar, process until fine)

Preheat the oven to 325°F. In a medium, heavy-bottomed nonreactive pot, scald the cream, half-and-half, and the reserved vanilla bean and cinnamon stick.

Meanwhile, lightly beat the egg yolks with the granulated sugar until light and lemon-colored. Temper the hot cream mixture into the egg yolks by adding a little cream mixture at a time to warm the eggs slowly. Then fully combine the eggs and cream mixture. Pour this custard back into the pot and heat until it visibly thickens and reaches 165°F. on a thermometer, then immediately remove from the heat.

Cut the quince in half, scoop out the seed portion using a melon baller, and cut the quince into fans or thin wedges. Arrange the quince in an attractive pattern on the bottom of 5-inch-diameter porcelain crème brulée dishes, or in a larger, shallow, ovenproof casserole dish. Strain the custard slowly over the fruit, being careful to avoid dislodging the quince.

Place a water bath (a larger rimmed baking pan or lasagna pan works well) in the oven, then place the cus-

tard dish(es) in it. Pour enough hot water in the pan to come halfway up the sides of the baking dish(es). Cover the large pan with foil that has been slashed in several places to allow steam to escape. Bake about 45 minutes, or until the center of each custard is just barely set. Carefully remove from the oven and cool. (This can be done early in the day or even the day before serving.)

When ready to serve, use a sieve to cover the top of each baked custard with a thin, even layer of extra-fine sugar. Place the custard under a hot broiler until the sugar is browned and bubbling, or glaze quickly with a blowtorch.

Quince and Cherry Chutney

This sweet-spicy cooked chutney, accented with tamarind, comes from India. Chatni (its Hindu name) is a relish usually made from fresh fruits and spices. During the colonial era in India, returning Britons brought home their taste for this intriguing condiment, which evolved into the cooked and bottled mango chutney called Major Grey's. Similarly, this chutney is cooked in a spiced syrup based on unsulphured molasses (the first boiling of sugar cane syrup), most commonly found in supermarkets under the Grandma's label. The thick, dark blackstrap molasses sold in natural foods stores is too strong to use here. Small pieces of firm quince are accented here with tart sun-dried cherries in a nontraditional but nevertheless delicious condiment. Store the chutney in the refrigerator for up to four months and serve with pâtés, on burgers, on turkey sandwiches, with cooked sausages, or to liven up melted cheese toasts.

772

Spice Mix

2 tablespoons strained tamarind pulp

  (*see* About Tamarind, right)

$^1/_2$ cup granulated sugar

$^1/_4$ cup cider vinegar

$^1/_2$ cup unsulphured molasses (Grandma's brand)

2 tablespoons peeled and chopped ginger

1 tablespoon hot red pepper flakes

1 tablespoon ground allspice

Kosher salt and freshly ground black pepper to taste

2 tablespoons black mustard seeds

1 cinnamon stick

Fruit

3 pounds quince, peeled and diced

$^1/_4$ pound sun-dried cherries

Place the Spice Mix ingredients in a heavy-bottomed saucepan, add 1 cup water, and bring to a boil, stirring occasionally. Add the diced fruits and bring back to the boil. Simmer together until thick, about 1 hour.

ABOUT TAMARIND

Tamarind comes from the fruit pod of a tree native to tropical Africa. The tree had already spread to India by prehistoric times and today grows throughout the tropical and subtropical regions of the world. The deep-brown-colored pulp of the fruit has hints of prune and orange and is used in hot regions much as we use lemon and vinegar. Tamarind gets its name from the Arabic *tamar hindi* which means *Indian date*. Its thick, deep-brown pulp reminded Arabs, who began importing tamarind from India long ago, of the more familiar date. Spanish and Portuguese explorers brought the tamarind to the New World, where it is incredibly popular, especially thinned out and served as a refreshing juice or in frozen fruit pops.

773

TO PREPARE TAMARIND

Tamarind is commonly sold in rectangular blocks that weigh about a pound and keep indefinitely. To prepare dried tamarind, soak a piece of the block in hot water to cover for about 30 minutes, or until the tamarind has softened. Break up the pulp with your hands to speed the process. Rub the tamarind with its liquid through a sieve or food mill, discarding the fibers and large seeds. The resulting pulp is ready to use, and will keep for at least one month in the refrigerator, or it can be frozen indefinitely.

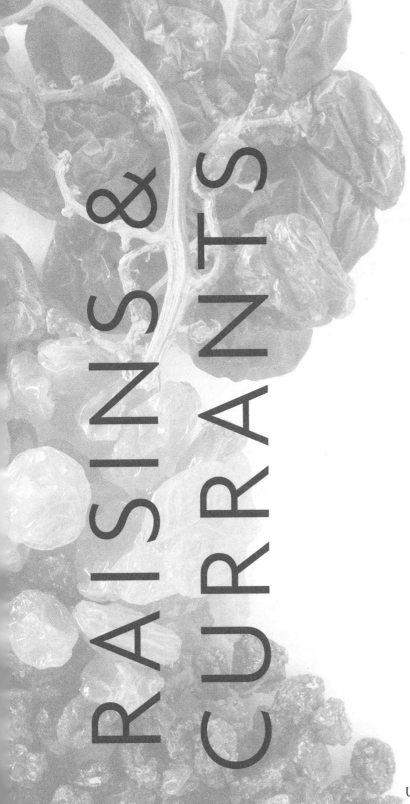

RAISINS & CURRANTS

RAISINS & CURRANTS

My memories of my great-grandmother are few and rather fuzzy (she died when I was about thirteen), but those that remain are inevitably connected to food. Every Friday, in preparation for Shabbat (the Sabbath), she would prepare a pair of large, braided challah breads studded with plenty of golden raisins. To this day, the only challah that tastes right to me contains those raisins, and the only raisins that taste right to me are those golden beauties, although with new types of raisins on the market—like the large Monukka and the Red Flames sold by Earthbound Farms—I'm learning to expand my repertoire.

In the winter months of times past, when supermarket aisles full of fresh (though often flavorless) produce didn't exist, people relied on dried and preserved food from their pantries and cold cellars to carry them through until summer's bounty ripened. The small, chewy, dense, and sweet dried grapes called raisins were used in both sweet and savory dishes to take advantage of their ability to plump up by absorbing liquids. Raisins are quite concentrated: it takes four and a half pounds of fresh grapes to produce one pound of raisins.

The word *raisin* comes from the Latin *racemus* and means *a cluster of grapes or berries*. Note that in Great Britain and its former colonies, raisins are commonly known as *sultanas* (which in America refers to a particular type of

raisin); and in France, *raisins* are fresh grapes, while raisins are *raisins secs*. In the United States, the term *raisin* refers to any form of dried grape. In Australia and other countries, specific varieties are given separate names, so in Australia, *raisins* are largest, *sultanas* are medium-sized, and *currants* are the smallest.

Humans probably discovered raisins when they happened upon grapes drying on a vine. The peripatetic trading Phoenicians established the earliest vineyards in Greece and southern Spain, while Armenians created vineyards in Persia (parts of today's Turkey, Iran, and Iraq). These areas not only had perfect climates for growing raisins, but they were also close to the important markets in Greece and Rome. Phoenicians and Armenians traded raisins with the Greeks and Romans, and the fruit soon became a favorite in these regions. The Roman Emperor Augustus feasted on small roasted birds stuffed with raisins, and Hannibal brought raisins as rations to feed his troops while as they crossed the Alps (perhaps creating the first "trail mix"). Greeks and Romans decorated places of worship with raisins and handed them out to winners in sporting contests. Roman physicians prescribed raisins to cure anything from mushroom poisoning to old age.

Crusader knights first introduced raisins to Europe in the eleventh century, when they returned home from the

776

Eastern Mediterranean. Because raisins were easy to pack and ship, they were soon found throughout northern Europe. By the fourteenth century, raisins had become an important part of European cuisine, and raisin prices skyrocketed. The English, French, and Germans all attempted to grow grapes for raisins, but their climates were too cold for drying the fruit.

In Greece today, raisins, mainly sultanas, are produced in the areas of Peloponnesus, Crete, and the smaller islands. The larger and darker Corinthian, or black raisin, is cultivated near the city of Corinth. Farmers on the Ionian island of Zakynthos (Zante in English) first raised the tiny, seedless, tangy dried black grapes called currants when dried. Their name in many languages reflects their origin. Often known as *Zante currants*, these treats are made from the tiny, so-called Champagne grapes often used to garnish cheese trays. Currants are wonderful in savory dishes because they are less sweet than raisins and their tiny size imparts just a small, intense flavor accent. Currants are better known in Europe, where they go into English currant cakes and scones. They are not the same as the black currant or cassis, a type of berry.

Muscat grapes from the vineyards of Spain eventually ended up in California, brought by missionaries sent to Mexico by Spain's Queen Isabelle. Missionaries who raised grapes for sacramental wine passed on their knowledge of viticulture and planted these same Muscat grapes for raisins. But it wasn't until 1851 that farmers near San Diego, California, began growing a commercially marketed raisin grape, the Egyptian Muscat. Eventually, because San Diego did not have enough water, the farmers moved to the San Joaquin Valley, perfect for growing, with its long, hot growing season and plenty of sunshine. In 1873, a massive heat wave hit the San Joaquin Valley just before harvest. Most of the grapes that had been planted to make wine dried on the vine, spelling financial disaster throughout the region. In desperation, enterprising growers took their dried grapes to San Francisco, where they were marketed as "Peruvian Delicacies." They were the hit of the season and sold out immediately.

By the late 1800s, many Armenians—descendents of the same people who cultivated the earliest vineyards in Persia—began settling the San Joaquin Valley. The development of this area of California as the world's largest producer of raisins can be credited, in great part, to these Armenian growers who still dominate the industry.

DRYING RAISINS

Most raisins are dried in the vineyards naturally, by sun, although some are mechanically dehydrated. Once they are sun dried, a process that takes two to four weeks, they are then graded, cleaned, and packed. Light-colored raisins are kept golden in color with the addition of sulfur dioxide (sulfites).

Seedless and Seeded Raisins

Seedless raisins are made from grapes that contain no seeds. Seeded raisins are made from grapes that contain seeds, which have been removed. Seeded raisins are more difficult to find and may be found during the autumn and winter holiday season.

Raisin Varieties

Monukka: These large, dark, seedless raisins come from the grapes of the same name. They're produced in limited quantities and can be found at natural foods and specialty stores.

Muscat: Large and brown, with an intensely fruity flavor, these premium raisins are made from large, greenish-gold Muscat grapes. They are mostly used in baking and can be found at natural foods and specialty stores.

Sultana: More popular in Europe, these raisins come from a seedless yellow grape and are usually softer and sweeter than other varieties. The American variety of sultana grape is the Thompson seedless golden raisin that is kept from darkening by the use of sulfur dioxide.

Thompson Seedless: Also known as the Oval Kishmish or Sultanina, these are entirely seedless yellow grapes with low acidity that were introduced in California in 1876 by a Scottish farmer named William Thompson. When sun dried, these grapes become the dark raisin so familiar to Americans today. Later, it was discovered that they would keep their original light gold color if processed with the use of sulfur. Today, ninety-five percent of both light and dark California raisins are made from Thompson seedless grapes grown in the San Joaquin Valley.

Spanish Malaga: Also called Muscatels, white Muscats, or Muscats, these are oversized, thin-skinned raisins with lots of seeds and superb flavor. Light in color with firm, rich flesh, these raisins are specially oven-dried (rather than by the sun), and are treated to retain their light color.

Smyrna Sultana: Smyrna Sultanas, from the Western Coast of Turkey, are seedless and pale yellow, with a fine flavor.

Zante Currant: Not to be confused with the red, black, or white currant in the *Ribes* genus, Zante currants are small black grapes originally grown in the Eastern Mediterranean area for drying and now marketed as Champagne grapes when fresh.

RAISINS DRIED ON THE BRANCH

In Europe, bunches of raisins are dried whole on their branches, a practice that was once more common in the United States, especially at holiday season. Australia is starting to export small bunches of these branch-dried raisins to the U.S., and they are wonderful to garnish a cheese plate or a holiday roast turkey. While in Italy in late November, I stayed in the Umbrian town of Spoleto in a converted Renaissance palazzo. On the carved dark-wood sideboard was a curved silver candelabra draped with bunches of dried grapes that could well have been displayed the exact same way for hundreds of years.

Carrot–Currant Salad with Rosemary

This easy-to-make and colorful salad just gets better as it marinates. A combination of shredded carrots, mild rice vinegar, piney but sweet fresh rosemary, and tiny, tangy-sweet currants give it a rounded sweet-and-sour flavor. Many supermarkets carry the bright orange box of Zante currants packed by Sun-Maid in California. I used to buy inexpensive, high-quality currants from Trader Joe's, but they have (as of this printing) unfortunately discontinued them due to lack of demand. Maybe Zante currants will all of a sudden become a new (rather, old) hot ingredient. Serve this salad on the side with a sandwich like the Smoked Turkey Reuben (see page 917).

SERVES 6 TO 8

$1/2$ cup rice wine vinegar

$1/2$ cup grapeseed or vegetable oil

2 teaspoons kosher salt

$1/2$ teaspoon freshly ground black pepper

1 pound carrots, peeled and shredded

$1/4$ cup Zante currants

2 tablespoons finely chopped shallots

2 tablespoon finely chopped rosemary

Whisk together the vinegar, oil, salt, and pepper. Toss with the carrots, currants, shallots, and rosemary. Mix very well so the currants are evenly distributed. Marinate at least 1 hour before serving. This salad keeps well for up to 1 week, refrigerated.

Sicilian Pasta alle Sarde (with Sardines and Currants)

This pasta dish is a classic of Sicilian cooking that combines canned sardines and anchovies, lots of licoricey fennel, a bit of saffron, and currants. In a typical Sicilian garnish, toasted breadcrumbs are sprinkled onto the dish just before serving, lending their crunchy, browned flavor to the sauce while soaking up some of the delicious juices. This dish provides you with the perfect opportunity to use potently flavored wild fennel, which grows in Sicily. And if you can get hold of it, sprinkle some superbly fragrant wild fennel pollen, sold in Italy and now being produced from domestic fennel in California, over top just before serving, so its fragrance is released at the table.

SERVE 4

Stalks from 2 heads fennel, plus any fennel leaves

2 tablespoons + 6 tablespoons extra-virgin olive oil

$1/2$ cup breadcrumbs from country-style bread

$1/2$ small onion, finely diced

4 anchovy fillets, chopped

$1/2$ cup tomato puree, fresh or canned

1 pinch saffron threads, crumbled

$1/4$ cup lightly toasted pinenuts

$1/4$ cup Zante currants

2 ($3^3/4$-ounce) cans imported sardines packed in olive oil, drained and broken up

1 pound bucatini or perciatelli pasta (hollow spaghetti)

$1/4$ cup finely chopped dill

Bring a large pot of salted water to a boil. Add the fennel stalks and cook for 10 minutes, then scoop out with a strainer or wire skimmer, keeping the cooking liquid in the pot. Finely chop the fennel and reserve.

In a small skillet, heat 2 tablespoons of olive oil with the breadcrumbs and cook, stirring often, until the breadcrumbs are nicely browned. Remove from the heat and reserve.

In a large skillet, cook the onion in the remaining 6 tablespoons of olive oil until softened but not browned, then add the fennel and the anchovies and continue cooking 5 minutes, or until the mixture is fairly dry. Add the tomato puree, saffron, and 1/2 cup of the reserved fennel water and cook 5 minutes, or until the mixture has thickened. Add the pinenuts, currants, and sardines and then remove the sauce from the heat.

Bring the fennel water back to the boil. Add the perciatelli and cook until *al dente,* firm and bouncy, and still yellow in color. Just before the pasta is ready, add the dill and fennel leaves and reheat the sauce. Drain the pasta and toss with the sauce. Divide among 4 plates, sprinkle each portion with toasted breadcrumbs, and serve immediately.

Sweet Noodle and Cheese Kugel with Golden Raisins

This lusciously tender Ashkenazi-Jewish-style noodle pudding is tangy and rich with small-curd cottage cheese and sour cream, and fragrant with cinnamon, vanilla, and lemon zest. Plump golden raisins give each mouthful a burst of fruity-sweet flavor. Is it a dessert or a main dish? That's up to you. Sweet as it is, this kugel is often served for a main dish, especially on the holiday of Shavuot, the feast of sheaves, during which dairy dishes are traditionally served. It also makes a wonderful make-ahead brunch dish.

SERVES 8

1 pound egg noodles

3 eggs

1/4 cup granulated sugar

2 teaspoons vanilla extract

Grated zest of 1 lemon

4 tablespoons + 2 tablespoons unsalted butter, melted and divided

1/2 pound small-curd cottage cheese

1/2 cup sour cream

1 cup golden raisins

1/2 cup Japanese panko or homemade-style breadcrumbs

1/2 teaspoon cinnamon

Preheat the oven to 350°F. Bring a large pot of salted water to the boil. Add the egg noodles and cook until firm. Drain and reserve.

Meanwhile, lightly beat together the eggs, sugar, vanilla, lemon zest, and 4 tablespoons of butter. Combine with the cottage cheese and sour cream. Stir in the noodles and the raisins.

Butter a 6- to 8-cup baking dish and fill with the noodle mixture. Combine the breadcrumbs, the remaining 2 tablespoons of butter, and the cinnamon and sprinkle over top of kugel. Bake for 40 minutes, or until the kugel is set and the topping is golden brown. Remove from the oven, cool slightly, cut into serving portions, and serve.

Sour Cream Raisin Bars

Bar cookies are about the easiest way to satisfy a sweet tooth. I tasted these delicious bars at an event sponsored by the California Raisin Marketing Board and found them to be perfectly balanced, moistly chewy, fruity, and nutty. Soaking the raisins in bourbon first is a small extra step that elevates these bars to a higher level of sophistication. Brandy or gold rum make good substitutes, but there is no doubt that the American-made bourbon complements the raisins perfectly.

MAKES 48 BARS

$3/4$ pound golden raisins

$1/2$ cup bourbon

$1/2$ pound rolled oats

$1/2$ pound (2 cups) all-purpose flour

1 teaspoon baking soda

1 cup dark brown sugar, packed

$1/2$ pound (2 sticks) unsalted butter, softened

2 egg yolks

2 cups sour cream

$1/2$ cup granulated sugar

2 tablespoons cornstarch

2 teaspoons vanilla extract

Soak the raisins in the bourbon until plump and most of the liquid has been absorbed, at least 30 minutes. Preheat the oven to 350°F.

Whisk together the oats, flour, baking soda, and brown sugar. Beat in the butter, continuing to beat until the mixture forms into dough. Press half the mixture into the bottom of a 18 x 12-inch half sheet pan or two 9 x 13-inch rectangular baking pans lined with parchment paper or Silpat sheets. Bake for 15 minutes, or until lightly colored, then remove from oven and cool.

Meanwhile, whisk together the egg yolks, sour cream, granulated sugar, and cornstarch in a medium, nonreactive saucepan. Heat over moderate heat while constantly whisking until the mixture thickens and begins to bubble. Remove from the heat and stir in the raisins with any soaking liquid, and the vanilla.

Pour the filling into the partially baked crust. Top with the remaining crumb mixture, crumbling it over top. Bake for 30 minutes longer, or until the top begins to brown. Cool and then refrigerate until cold before cutting into 48 bars. Bring to room temperature before serving.

Rugelach with Dark Raisins, Walnuts, and Cinnamon

Starting at about age ten, I learned to bake from my mother. These were one of her holiday specialties. Like any rolled cookie, they are more involved to make, but rolling out a series of circles and then cutting long, thin, triangular wedges makes the task much easier. The filling couldn't be simpler—chopped walnuts, raisins, and cinnamon—but combined with the rich, flaky cream-cheese pastry, they are truly out of this world. The cream-cheese dough is a pleasure to work with because it stretches and rolls out easily without breaking.

MAKES 6 DOZEN

2 cups finely chopped walnuts

1 cup dark raisins, chopped up

1 tablespoon cinnamon

1 1/2 pounds Cream Cheese Pastry Dough (*see* page 597)

1 cup confectioners' sugar

Mix together the walnuts, raisins, and cinnamon and reserve.

Divide the dough into eight even sections. Press each section into a flattened round and then roll it out into a circle about 9 inches in diameter and about 1/8 inch thick. Sprinkle one-eighth of the nut mixture all over the dough, leaving a 1-inch border at the edge. Using a rolling pin, roll over the filling so it adheres to the dough. With a heavy chef's knife, cut the dough circle into 12 long, thin, triangular wedges. Roll up the dough tightly from the wide end towards the point, as if making a croissant, making sure that the filling is enclosed. Repeat with the remaining filling and dough.

Preheat the oven to 350°F. Arrange the cookies with their points tucked under on baking pans, about 1 inch apart. Refrigerate to set shape while preparing the remaining cookies. (Note that formed but unbaked cookies can be frozen. Bake from frozen at 325°F. for about 35 minutes.) Bake the cookies for about 25 minutes, or until lightly golden. Cool on racks, sprinkling with confectioners' sugar while still warm.

ORIGINS OF RUGELACH

There is fierce disagreement as to the origin of these delectable pastries and the real way to make them. Most say that the word *rugelach* comes from the Yiddish and means *little twists*, but other sources say that the word *rugel* means *royal*. These same croissant-shaped, filled cookies are known as *kipfel* in Germany and *kifli* in Yugoslavia. Hungarian-Jewish immigrants, renowned for their skill at baking, probably introduced the first recipes for these delectable cookies to America. In Europe, the dough was yeast-risen and included sour cream. The cream-cheese dough used in America may have been developed by the Philadelphia Cream Cheese Company. An early version of this dough appears in my copy of *The Perfect Hostess*, written in 1950 by Mildred Knopf, sister-in-law of publisher Alfred Knopf. She recalls that the recipe came from Nela Rubenstein, wife of the famous pianist Arthur Rubenstein. But, it was Mrs. Knopf's friend and baker extraordinaire, Maida Heatter, who put rugelach on the culinary map, using her grandmother's recipe. It was the most sought after of all Mrs. Heatter's recipes and appeared in her book, *Cookies*.

Philadelphia Cream Cheese

In 1872, American dairymen, who were trying to recreate the French cheese, Neufchâtel, invented American-style cream cheese. Philadelphia Brand Cream Cheese was introduced in 1880 and was named after Philadelphia, a city well known for dairy products. James L. Kraft invented pasteurized cheese in 1912, leading to the development of pasteurized Philadelphia Cream Cheese, originally made by the Phenix Cheese Company, which was bought by the Kraft Cheese Company in 1928. Today, Philadelphia Cream Cheese is one of the world's most popular cheeses, with a special importance in Spain, and is made worldwide.

Cream Cheese and Golden Raisin Strudel

This strudel has a simple, tangy-rich cream-cheese and golden raisin filling that is enclosed in layers of flaky dough. Austrians, Germans, Hungarians, and people from the Balkans take considerable pride in making their own superb strudels made from thin, flaky, hand-stretched dough surrounding any number of fillings, both sweet and savory (see page 193 for a savory Cabbage and Caraway Strudel). The word strudel *comes from German and means "whirlpool," because the pastry is spiraled around its filling. Strudel is closely related to the paper-thin sheets of phyllo dough used to form pastries from Greece to Turkey, Lebanon, and Syria, and all the way across North Africa. Several different countries claim to have invented strudel, but most likely it is an ever-present reminder of Turkish influences on Hungarian food from the time of Turkey's occupation of Hungary in the sixteenth century.*

SERVES 8 TO 10

Golden Raisin Filling

3/4 cup golden raisins

1/4 cup dark rum

1 1/2 pounds cream cheese

1/2 cup honey

2 eggs

1/4 cup fine semolina, substitute Cream of Wheat cereal

1/2 teaspoon cinnamon

Soak the raisins in the rum, at least 1 hour and up to overnight, or until soft and plump. Beat the cream cheese until light, add the honey, eggs, semolina, and cinnamon, and beat again until creamy. Stir in the raisins and any soaking liquid, and reserve.

Strudel with Phyllo Dough

1 pound phyllo pastry, defrosted in the refrigerator overnight, if frozen

1/2 cup fine dry breadcrumbs

2 tablespoons unsalted butter, at room temperature , + 4 tablespoons unsalted butter, melted and cooled

Confectioners' sugar, for dusting

Allow the package of phyllo dough to come to room temperature, about 30 minutes, to make the dough more pliable. Open the package of phyllo dough and carefully unroll the pastry leaves. Place the flat leaves on the kitchen counter and keep covered with a damp kitchen towel while working.

In a small skillet, cook the breadcrumbs in 2 tablespoons of butter over moderate heat, stirring constantly until they are golden, then transfer them to a large bowl and reserve.

On a work surface, arrange an 18-inch-long piece of wax paper with a long side facing you. Cover the paper with 2 sheets of the phyllo, and brush lightly with some of the melted butter and some breadcrumbs. Layer 8 more sheets of phyllo over the first sheet in the same manner, brushing every other each sheet lightly with melted butter and more breadcrumbs. Spread the filling mixture evenly in a line along the long side facing you, leaving a 1-inch border at each end.

Preheat the oven to 375°F. Using the wax paper as a guide, roll the strudel tightly away from you. With the seam-side down, fold the ends under to enclose the filling. Transfer the strudel carefully to a lightly buttered jellyroll pan,

783

forming it into a horseshoe shape to fit into the pan. Brush the strudel with melted butter. Cut diagonal slashes about 1 inch apart halfway through the strudel.

Bake the strudel for 45 minutes, or until it is golden brown and crispy. Remove from the oven, cool on the pan, and then dust with confectioners' sugar. Transfer to a serving platter, using long spatulas, and cut into slices with a serrated knife.

Note that you can prepare and bake the strudel up 2 days ahead of time. Reheat in a preheated 375°F. oven for 15 to 20 minutes, or until the pastry is crispy and the filling piping hot. (Stick a metal skewer into the center of the strudel, remove it, and tap it against the back of your wrist to check if the filling is hot enough.)

Using Phyllo Dough for Strudel

While I admire anyone who has the ambition to make their own strudel dough, in my recipes, I call for packaged phyllo dough. When buying phyllo dough, it's important to buy it from a store that maintains high quality. Dough that has been frozen for too long, or frozen, partially defrosted, and frozen again will be frustrating to use. If you open the package and the sheets stick together or crumble right away, the dough is old or has been improperly handled. The best phyllo dough that I've used is sold fresh in the refrigerator, never frozen, and comes from a Lebanese grocery.

OTHER KINDS OF STRUDEL

In George Lang's *Cuisine of Hungary*, he lists eleven kinds of strudels: walnut, almond, potato, wine (with browned breadcrumbs), chocolate, Varga (from the restaurant that created it early in the century) with sweetened cottage cheese, sour cream and golden raisins, pot cheese, cabbage, and mushroom. A Balkan favorite is cherry strudel with cinnamon. Other fillings use ground walnuts, boiled poppy seeds, sweetened cottage and other fresh cheeses, or cream cheese and golden raisins as here.

STRUDEL FROM GUNDEL OF BUDAPEST

I had the pleasure of tasting a classic Hungarian apple strudel, served warm, made by the chefs of Budapest's famed Gundel Restaurant. The Gundel chefs consider a strudel that is anything past just out of the oven to be not worth eating. Karoly Gundel, the great Hungarian restaurateur and son of the founder of the world-renowned restaurant, attributed the success of strudel in his country to the excellent quality of Hungary's wheat flour, which, he said, should be neither wet nor freshly ground. He recommended using smooth wheat flour. In 1991, Ronald Lauder (son of Estée) and George Lang purchased and completely restored the Gundel Restaurant, open since 1894.

HANDMADE STRUDEL DOUGH

Hungarians mix two types of flour—always aged first—for the dough: bread flour, for stretching ability, and softer pastry-type flour, for the starch that gives body and allows the dough to be stretched out as thin as onionskin. The basic dough is made from flour, egg, butter, and a little vinegar (to encourage elasticity) mixed to a dough with water, then kneaded until silky smooth and then rested. The dough is then placed on a floured cloth on a large table, rolled out a little and then hand-stretched by placing the knuckles of the hand underneath and pulling the dough gently toward to edge of the table until it forms a huge, thin sheet, ideally without any holes. When the strudel dough is properly pulled out, you should be able to read a newspaper through it. To make the pastry into a long roll, it is brushed with melted butter, scattered with breadcrumbs, and the chosen filling is placed at one end of the sheet of dough. The cloth is lifted so the pastry rolls up to the other end of the table. It is then curved around into a horseshoe shape, brushed with more melted butter, and baked.

785

RASPBERRIES

RASPBERRIES

With their velvety, tender texture, unique concentrated fruity-acidic flavor, and jewel-like color, raspberries induce rapture, though it may be fleeting. Delicate, highly perishable, and much sought-after, raspberries automatically transform any dish they're served with into a special event. Raspberries actually consist of soft, multiple fruits clumped together in a slightly conical helmet shape around their stem. The fruits are usually deep blue-tinted red, though golden and black (or purple) varieties exist. Their tart, intensely flavored pulp, a magnificent color fit for royalty, surrounds a small but noticeable hard seed.

In the restaurant and hotel business, serving raspberries is a must for any place with high-level ambitions. These fruits are highly perishable, especially so if picked during the wet weather that is characteristic of their best growing regions, and are equally difficult to transport. This means that raspberries are always high-priced, except perhaps at a farmers' market in their season of abundance (early summer with a smaller crop in the fall) and that the market is highly volatile. A case of twelve half-pints of raspberries may sell for over one hundred dollars when they're scarce; the same case one or two days later could be worth less then ten dollars, because the fruits break down and develop mold so quickly that it would only be suitable for sauces and purees, and that only after a lot of picking through them.

In Belgium, raspberries are used to flavor the typical fruit beer called *lambic framboise*. In Germany, raspberry juice is added to make a red-tinted version of the Berlin-style white wheat beer enjoyed for its refreshing tartness in the summer. In American colonial times, raspberry shrub—a syrup of raspberries, vinegar, and sugar—was thinned with about eight parts liquid to one part shrub to make a refreshing summer beverage.

The red raspberry is indigenous to Asia Minor and North America. Two thousand years ago, the people of Troy, in Asia Minor, gathered the fruit from the wild. Records of raspberry domestication were found in the fourth-century writings of Palladius, a Roman agriculturist, and seeds have been discovered at Roman forts in Britain, so the Romans are given credit for spreading their cultivation throughout Europe. In Medieval Europe, only the rich ate raspberries. While today, their enjoyment is certainly more widespread, raspberries are still a food for the privileged.

By the seventeenth century, British gardens were lush with raspberry bushes, which flourished in the country's cool, moist climate; by the eighteenth century, raspberry cultivation practices had spread throughout Europe. When the colonists came to America, they brought the European cultivated raspberry, *Rubus idaeus*, with them, but found Amerindians drying the native American wild raspberry, *Rubus strigosus*, to preserve for ease of transport for their nomadic lifestyle. In 1761, George Washington moved to his estate in Mount Vernon, where he began to cultivate berries in his extensive gardens. By 1867, over forty varieties of raspberries were known in America.

There are three main types of raspberries: black, golden, and the most common, the red raspberry. Red raspberries thrive in the relatively cool, moist, coastal climate of the Pacific Northwest, west of the Cascades. The Meeker, a late season productive summer fruiting variety with full raspberry flavor is the most widely planted raspberry in that region. About ninety percent of the fresh-market red raspberries are grown in California, Washington, and Oregon, with Michigan and New York producing more limited quantities. Washington accounts for nearly sixty percent of the U.S. production of red raspberries and has a strong reputation for the high quality of its berries.

Raspberry Types

Black Raspberries: Black raspberries, *Rubus occidentalis*, known as *blackcaps* by growers, are native to North America and common in the eastern U.S. and Canada. They are usually purplish black, with small seeds and a hollow core, though yellow and red forms exist, with whitish blooms on the outside of the berry. Black raspberries have a distinct and moderately tart jammy flavor, small seeds, and, like the red raspberry, grow around a core that is hollow once the berry has been picked off. Black raspberries are in season in July.

Golden Raspberries: Golden raspberries are a relatively new variety that is much rarer and always more expensive than their red cousins. They are a naturally occurring variant of red raspberries, ranging in color from clear, light yellow to golden to a gorgeous rosy-tinged apricot. Their luscious flavor and texture brings to mind soft, yielding, and delicately perfumed apricots. Golden raspberries are available in limited quantity from June to October. Look for them in farmers' markets and specialty stores.

Red Raspberries: Raspberries are medium to light to deep red depending on the variety and where they're grown. Red raspberries are available year-round throughout the United States, especially to the restaurant trade, but peak season is June and early September. Limited quantities are available December through March from Chile and Southern California. Raspberries imported in winter from Chile sometimes show individual fruits that are pale or even colorless, with equally pallid flavor.

789

CHOOSING RASPBERRIES

If the berry fruit pulls away cleanly and easily from its protruding stem, the fruit has reached its perfect point of ripeness. Raspberries are delicate. The best-tasting ones will have been handled very carefully. Look for berries that are full and round, not flattened. The walls of a fine berry should be full and meaty, not skimpy. The best berries have a hazy, soft gloss. Avoid raspberries with pale coloring, dents, or bruises, or berries that are broken apart. Check the bottom of the container. If it is stained red, this is a sign of overripe or softened and decayed berries.

STORING RASPBERRIES

Raspberries are quite perishable and must be refrigerated. Keep them cold but not too cold, because they are very sensitive to freeze damage. Moisture will hasten the decay of your raspberries, so keep them dry, and do not wash them until just before serving. Spreading them out on paper towels will help keep them from spoiling. Unless they are in exceptionally fine condition, store raspberries no more than one to two days in the refrigerator.

Names for the Raspberry

Lampone: Italian

Framboise: French

Frambozen: Flemish (Belgium)

Himbeere: German

Frambueso: Spanish

Razuberi: Japanese

TOP FIVE RASPBERRY-PRODUCING COUNTRIES

As of 2002, Russia produced twenty-four percent of the world's raspberry crop, followed by Serbia and Montenegro at twenty-three percent, the U.S. at thirteen percent, Poland at eleven percent, and Germany at seven percent.

THE JUSTLY FAMOUS RICHTER RASPBERRIES

As a restaurant chef, I was privileged to be able to buy George Richter's fabulous raspberries in their beautiful little green, metal-edged balsa-wood crates whenever they came into their short (six-week) season. Justly rated as some of the best in the country, these berries are sold exclusively to high-end restaurants and hotels and specialty food markets.

According to Mr. Richter, a third-generation raspberry grower, the sandy, slightly acidic soil of Washington's Pullyup Valley yields plump berries ripe with true raspberry flavor. Richter grows mostly the Tulameen raspberry, a variety bred in British Columbia in the 1980s that is so venerated in England, they are sold under that name instead of as raspberries. (Britain's former Prime Minister Margaret Thatcher once brought a flat of Richter raspberries home after eating them during an international summit in Houston.) Although sixty percent of his sales is in raspberries, Richter also raises blackberries, nectarberries (a kind of hybrid boysenberry), tayberries (a raspberry-blackberry cross), gooseberries, red, black, and white currants, and hothouse rhubarb in the winter. If you see his raspberries, don't miss the chance to taste what may be the berry-best berry you've ever tried!

Raspberry Shrub from Tait Farms

Pennsylvania's Tait Farms produces a contemporary raspberry shrub based on a Colonial recipe (available at www.taitfarmfoods.com). Try it in sparkling wine or added to vinaigrette dressing, or mix with sparkling water to make a refreshing raspberry cooler.

Raspberry Vinaigrette

Either fresh or frozen raspberries will work well for this lovely, rose-red vinaigrette. Because of the pectin in the fruit and the thickness imparted by the walnuts, it is a thick, creamy style dressing, best drizzled over the salad and then mixed at the table just before serving so it doesn't weigh down the greens. Serve this dressing with green salads, especially those containing fruits such as apples, pears, or berries, or drizzle it over steamed, cooled greens beans. Grapeseed oil has a light fruity-nutty flavor, making it well suited to mixing with acidic fruits.

MAKES 1½ CUPS

1 (½ pint) container raspberries
6 tablespoons raspberry-flavored red wine vinegar, white balsamic, or cider vinegar
2 tablespoons chopped, toasted walnuts
2 tablespoons honey
2 teaspoons finely chopped rosemary
1 cup grapeseed or canola oil
Kosher salt and freshly ground black pepper to taste

Place the raspberries, vinegar, walnuts, honey, and rosemary in a blender jar and puree until smooth. Gradually pour in the oil and season to taste with salt and pepper, pureeing again until smooth. If desired, strain through a sieve or food mill to extract the seeds. Reserve refrigerated for up to 1 week.

Raspberry–Lemon Bread Pudding with Lemon Sauce

Raspberries and lemons work together to enhance this soft and tender bread pudding. Either fresh or frozen raspberries will work here, although frozen berries do tend to bleed, streaking the pudding with red. The braided, egg-enriched Jewish bread called challah makes wonderful bread pudding, but it, like all bread for puddings, works best when stale (drier bread cuts more easily into even cubes and absorbs the delicious custard mix better). French brioche, which is similarly egg-enriched, also works well. If you can't find either, substitute firm white sandwich bread. You can also use the Brioche Dough on page 987 if desired for this pudding. Serve the pudding sprinkled with a handful of fresh raspberries, if available. Raspberry leaves also make a lovely garnish and are edible.

SERVES 8 TO 10

1 cup milk
1 cup heavy cream
Grated zest of 1 lemon
6 eggs
2 cups granulated sugar
1 tablespoon vanilla extract
1 teaspoon grated nutmeg
Pinch kosher salt
1 large loaf challah bread (about 1½ pounds), diced
2 pints raspberries, picked over, washed, and drained
Lemon Sauce (recipe follows)

In a large Pyrex measure or bowl, scald the milk and cream with the lemon zest in the microwave.

Meanwhile, beat together the eggs, sugar, vanilla, nut-meg, and salt. Temper the hot cream into the egg mix by beating a small amount into the eggs first and then beating in the remainder. Toss this mixture with the diced bread and allow the whole pudding mix to soak at room temperature until liquid has been absorbed, about 30 minutes. Toss with the raspberries.

Preheat the oven to 300°F. Spoon the pudding mix into a nonstick-sprayed 13 x 9-inch baking pan. Make a water bath by pouring hot water into a pan that is larger than the baking dish so that it comes about 2 inches up the sides. Cover with aluminum foil and bake about 30 minutes. Remove the foil and raise the oven heat to 350°F. for 15 minutes to crisp the top. The pudding is done when it is just barely set in the middle. Remove from the oven, cool slightly, and cut into serving portions. Serve accompanied by the Lemon Sauce.

Lemon Sauce

3 eggs

$1/2$ cup granulated sugar

$1/2$ cup freshly squeezed lemon juice (about 4 lemons)

Grated zest of 1 lemon

2 tablespoons unsalted butter, melted

Beat together the eggs and sugar until light. Beat in the lemon juice, zest, and butter. Make a double boiler by bringing about 2 inches of water to the boil in the bottom of a medium pot. Transfer the lemon mixture to a stainless steel bowl or a nonreactive pot that can fit on top of the second pot without touching the water. Cook over medium heat, stirring constantly, until the sauce thickens. Remove from the pot, transfer to a bowl, and place plastic wrap directly on the custard to keep a skin from forming. Keep warm until needed.

Raspberry and Lemon Verbena Granita

A granita is just what it sounds like: a grainy ice, made by freezing the mixture and breaking it up with a fork as it crystallizes. What makes this granita special is the lemon verbena, a wonderful herb for lemon lovers that deserves a larger place in the kitchen. In fact, many chefs are starting to incorporate this highly fragrant herb into both sweet and savory dishes. Lemon verbena has a strong affinity to fresh fruits; its bright lemon taste emphasizes fruit flavors such as the raspberries used here. Frozen raspberries will work well in this recipe, although only fresh will do for garnish. Serve as is or top with unsweetened whipped cream garnished with fresh raspberries and sprigs of lemon verbena or small strips of lemon zest.

SERVES 6

1 cup granulated sugar

2 cups water

1 tablespoon finely shredded lemon verbena

4 ($1/2$ pint) containers raspberries (about 2 cups)

Fresh raspberries and lemon verbena sprigs, for garnish

Combine the sugar, water, and shredded lemon verbena in a medium saucepan. Stir over medium heat until the sugar dissolves and the liquid is clear. Bring to the boil, simmer briefly, and remove from the heat. Cool and then chill the syrup until quite cold.

Meanwhile, puree the raspberries in a blender or food processor, and then mix in the chilled sugar syrup. Pour the mixture through a strainer, pressing on solids to extract as much liquid as possible. (You may have to do this twice to remove stubborn raspberry seeds.) Pour the mixture into a shallow metal baking dish. Freeze about 2 hours, or until almost firm, stirring occasionally with a fork to break up ice crystals that form on the edges. Continue freezing granita until firm (do not stir), at least 3 hours or overnight. This granita can be prepared 3 days ahead. Just cover it and keep it frozen.

To serve, temper the granita by transferring it to the refrigerator for about 1 hour. Then, using a heavy fork, scrape the surface of the granita to form crystals. Scoop the crystals into glasses, keeping them in the freezer until just before serving. Garnish each portion with raspberries and lemon verbena.

LEMON VERBENA

Native to South America, lemon verbena, *Lippia citriodora*, has long, narrow, rough-textured apple-green leaves that give off an intense lemony-floral fragrance. The herb is relatively easy to grow and grows quickly, though it isn't winter-hardy. (I do well with it, and I can't grow anything that requires TLC.) The leaves are best used fresh, though they may occasionally be found dried.

Raspberry Mascarpone Cheesecake

Do I really need another cheesecake recipe in this book? Aren't Amaretto Cheesecake with Chocolate-Amaretti Crust (page 23), Hazelnut-Lime Cheesecake (page 470), Mango Cheesecake (page 578), and Candied Tangerine Cheesecake (page 665) enough? Apparently not. I just had to include this lusciously light, over-the-top cheesecake dotted with raspberries. It makes a striking impression when guests cut into the cake and find the surprise of whole raspberries baked into the batter. Tart raspberries balance the richness of the mascarpone cheese used here, while a drizzle of the simple raspberry sauce accents the raspberries and makes an even more eye-catching presentation. Splurge on a whole vanilla bean here, scraping out the insides to flavor the cake with the miniscule black specks of vanilla seeds. Note that although frozen raspberries will make an excellent sauce, they are not suitable to fold into the cake, because they will collapse and bleed into the creamy white batter.

MAKES ONE 10-INCH CHEESECAKE, TO SERVE 12 TO 16

Biscotti Crumb Crust

2 cups crushed biscotti cookies, preferably almond
$1/4$ cup dark brown sugar, packed
1 teaspoon ground cinnamon
4 tablespoons unsalted butter, melted and cooled

Prepare a 10-inch springform pan by placing a parchment paper round on the bottom. Preheat the oven to 350°F.

Place the biscotti, sugar, and cinnamon in a food processor. Process together until fine crumbs are formed, then pour in the butter and process for 1 more minute or until combined but not pasty. Press the crumb mixture into the bottom of the prepared pan and chill for 30 minutes. Bake 15 minutes, or until lightly browned. Cool and reserve.

Filling

1^1/$_2$ pounds cream cheese, at room temperature

1 cup Mascarpone

Grated zest of 1 orange

^{3}/$_4$ cup granulated sugar

4 eggs

Scrapings of 1 vanilla bean, or 2 teaspoons vanilla extract

2 (^{1}/$_2$ pint) containers fresh raspberries

Lower the oven temperature to 300°F. Beat the cream cheese until smooth, scraping down the sides of the bowl once or twice with a rubber spatula. Add the Mascarpone and beat again until smooth. Add the orange zest, sugar, eggs, and vanilla bean scrapings to the bowl and beat until smooth.

Spoon one half of the batter into the baked crumb crust and bake 20 minutes, or until set. Sprinkle in half of the raspberries, cover with the remaining batter, and top with the remaining raspberries.

Bake the cheesecake for about 45 minutes, or until just set in the middle. Check carefully near the end of the baking time to be sure the filling doesn't overbake and begin to over-rise and crack. Remove from the oven and cool to room temperature. Meanwhile, prepare the topping.

Topping and Raspberry Sauce

^{1}/$_2$ cup Mascarpone

2 tablespoons + 1 cup granulated sugar

2 tablespoons Framboise or Kirschwasser

2 (^{1}/$_2$ pint) containers fresh raspberries, or 1^1/$_2$ cups frozen
   raspberries

Preheat the oven to 400°F. Whisk together the Marscapone, 2 tablespoons of sugar, and the liqueur briefly, just until smooth. Spread the topping evenly over top of the cheesecake and bake for 6 minutes, or until the topping has set. Remove from the oven, cool to room temperature, and then refrigerate until cold.

In a small, heavy-bottomed nonreactive saucepan, combine the raspberries, the remaining 1 cup sugar, and 1 cup water. Heat gently until the sugar dissolves and the liquid just comes to the boil. Remove the sauce from the heat, strain through a sieve or food mill and cool. If desired, transfer to a plastic squeeze bottle.

Serving

Chill the cake before serving and cut into 12 or 16 portions with a knife rinsed under hot water in between each cut. Serve each slice garnished with a crisscross drizzle of Raspberry Sauce, or simply spoon some of the sauce next to each slice.

RASPBERRY LAMBIC FROM BELGIUM

In a practice that dates back to long before the use of hops, various fruits like peach, cherry, and black currants were used to flavor beer. In order to be labeled *Lambic*, the beer must be spontaneously fermented by wild yeasts. Belgium's raspberry lambic has a full-bodied, fruity aroma with a delicate raspberry flavor and undertones of fruity acidity. It matches well with rich, dense, dark chocolate desserts, crème caramel, baked Alaska, and even oysters and caviar. It should be served chilled in special stemmed Lambic glasses with a full, rounded bowl.

794

RHUBARB

RHUBARB

One definition of *rhubarb* is a heated dispute or controversy. Perhaps this is why the plant that bears the same name inspires such strong reactions, as well. The first question it elicits is: Do you love it or hate it? In my family, my mom loved rhubarb and my dad wouldn't eat it, so when she made her favorite stewed rhubarb, the two of us would enjoy its tart flavor and unique smooth, melting consistency. The second question is: Is it a fruit or a vegetable? While looking up information about this plant in my own *Field Guide to Produce*, I couldn't remember whether it was listed under fruits or vegetables. I found it under vegetables, but it could just have easily been included with the fruits. In fact, in 1947, the U.S. Customs Court in Buffalo, New York, ruled that rhubarb is a fruit, since that is how it was mainly used.

The scientific name for rhubarb, *Rheum rhabarbarum*, originated from the Latin meaning *root of the barbarian*, so even from earliest times, this unusual plant had negative connotations. It comes originally from Asia and is related to sorrel and buckwheat. Rhubarb was used as a medicinal tonic rather than a food until the nineteenth century. Popularly known as the "pie plant," rhubarb is one of spring's earliest earthly gifts, its rosy-red color a harbinger of spring. The edible portion of the plant is its thick red fleshy stalks, which are topped by inedible wide leaves. Rhubarb is always cooked with sugar or other sweeteners to balance its intense acidity and most often shows up in pies, often mixed with spring's other fruit specialty, fresh local strawberries.

There are two basic types of rhubarb: hothouse (or strawberry rhubarb) and field grown (or cherry rhubarb). Hothouse rhubarb tends to have smoother flesh, more delicate texture, and less acidity than field grown. Field-grown rhubarb has deeper color, more juice, and bolder acidity. Green rhubarb is also available. Rhubarb is so versatile, it can be used both for savory dishes and for desserts, especially when paired with other fruits, such as apples, raspberries, or strawberries.

RHUBARB SEASON

Rhubarb is in season from the spring into the early parts of summer. Hothouse rhubarb is available from Washington, Michigan, and Ontario from mid-January through mid-April, field-grown rhubarb starts to come into season in April and is available, depending on the part of the country, until September.

Preparing Rhubarb

If your rhubarb has noticeable strings, you may wish to pare the stalks or pull off the strings as you would for celery. I prefer not to do so, because I don't want to lose any of its superb deep color. Hothouse rhubarb generally does not need peeling.

Cut rhubarb into thin slices, on the diagonal if desired, against the grain of the stalk. Be sure to cook in nonreactive pots, such as enamel or stainless steel, because the highly acidic rhubarb will react with the metal, and shake, rather than stir, to keep it from disintegrating.

RHUBARB IN CHINA

During the Song dynasty (960-1127), rhubarb was taken in times of plague. Later, the emperor of Guangzong (1620) was miraculously cured with rhubarb of an illness he contracted after enjoying himself with four(!) beautiful women sent to him by a high official.

In 1828, the Emperor of China declared that no more tea and health-giving rhubarb would be sold to British "barbarians." About ten years later, the Chinese imperial commissioner was sent to Canton to put an end to Great Britain's fantastically profitable opium trade. He wrote to Queen Victoria pointing out that the foreigners (the British) would surely die without Chinese tea and rhubarb and that, therefore, the Queen should stop the wicked British merchants from trading in opium in return for a continued supply of rhubarb and tea. Victoria seems never to have had the letter translated and when, later the same year, the commissioner told British merchants in Canton that an end to the rhubarb trade would surely end in their death, they responded with cannons. Perhaps the Opium Wars should be called the Rhubarb Wars.

CHOOSING AND STORING RHUBARB

Choose rhubarb with firm, crisp, brightly colored stalks, avoiding those with bruises or blemishes, or stringiness at the ends of the stalks. Store rhubarb in a plastic bag in the refrigerator for up to one week.

RHUBARB ON STAGE

Stage and movie directors would have actors repeat the word "rhubarb" over and over to simulate background conversations or mutterings of a surly crowd.

Rhubarb Reaches Europe and America

Marco Polo talked about rhubarb at length in the accounts of his travels in China at the end of the thirteenth century. In the early thirteenth and fourteenth centuries, Venice was an extremely important trading center and, as a result of trade with Arabs, Chinese rhubarb was already widely used in European pharmacies. A planting of rhubarb in Italy was first recorded in 1608. Even at that time, in the kitchen, rhubarb was mainly used as a tart and pie filling. About 1777, a Banbury apothecary named Hayward began cultivating rhubarb in England from Russian seeds, from which he produced a drug that was sold by men dressed up as Turks.

Rhubarb reached the American colonies in Massachusetts in the early years of the nineteenth century. By 1822, it was found in produce markets.

Baked Rhubarb
with Cardamom

I like to bake rhubarb, so that it maintains something of its firm texture and chunky quality. Here I mix in a small amount of sweetly spicy cardamom, a spice that is well-suited to rhubarb, with sugar to balance the plant's aggressive acidity. Serve the baked rhubarb as a side dish to accompany game birds like Guinea hen, duck, or quail, or to cut the fattiness of roast pork.

SERVES 6

1 tablespoon canola or vegetable oil

2 bunches rhubarb, cut into 1-inch pieces

1 cup granulated sugar

1 teaspoon ground cardamom

Preheat the oven to 375°F. Lightly oil a large shallow metal baking pan. Combine the rhubarb, sugar, and cardamom and spoon the mixture into the pan, spreading it out in a single layer. Cover with aluminum foil and bake for 30 minutes, or until the rhubarb is tender but still holds its shape. While the rhubarb is baking, don't mix it, but give the pan an occasional shake so the rhubarb doesn't stick. Remove the pan from the oven, cool slightly, and then transfer the rhubarb to a serving bowl, taking care not to break it up. Serve warm or at room temperature. Store in the refrigerator for up to 4 days before serving.

ABOUT CARDAMOM

Cardamom, *Elettaria cardamomum*, is a fragrant seed that is usually sold enclosed in its fibrous, lantern-shaped pod. The almond-sized pods range from lime-green to pale green to creamy-white in color, depending on their freshness and whether the pods have been bleached (a practice that is now out of favor). The small, dark brown, pebbly inner seeds impart their potent fragrance and slightly astringent, warming spiciness to foods and Turkish coffee. Native to India, it is called the "queen of the spices" there. Cardamom was grown only in India and Sri Lanka until about one hundred years ago, when German immigrants brought cardamom to Guatemala, now the world's largest producer. Because it must be hand-picked, cardamom is among the most expensive spices and is most common in the Arab world, India, and much further north, in Scandinavia, where it is commonly used to flavor sweet baked goods.

798

Salmon with Rhubarb and Pea Tendrils

Here are three springtime treats in one dish—salmon, pea shoots, and rhubarb. Because the salmon is rich and oily, the sprightly pea tendrils and the sweet-tart rhubarb scented with cleansing Chinese star anise cut the richness of the fish and balance the flavors. Pea tendrils are the unfurling, tender leaves and shoots of young pea plants usually culled from immature snow peas. They are a spring delicacy in China and may be found at Asian grocery stores in the spring. They are sweetly tender with a pronounced pea flavor. If they're not available, substitute snow peas. This eye-catching dish is cooked quickly and would go well with steamed jasmine rice.

SERVES 4

1 tablespoon canola or vegetable oil

1 bunch rhubarb (about 1 pound), trimmed and
  cut into 1-inch lengths

2 bay leaves

$1/4$ cup honey

2 star anise pods, lightly crushed

Kosher salt and freshly ground black pepper to taste

$1/2$ cup heavy cream

4 (8-ounce) portions salmon fillets

1 cup trimmed pea shoots or snow peas

Preheat the oven to 375°F. Lightly oil a large shallow metal baking pan. Combine the rhubarb, bay leaves, honey, star anise, and salt and pepper, and spoon into the pan in a single layer. Cover with aluminum foil and bake, without stirring, but giving the pan an occasional shake so the rhubarb doesn't stick, 30 minutes, or until the rhubarb is tender but still holds its shape. Remove and discard bay leaves and star anise. Transfer the reserved rhubarb to a small, nonreactive pot, add the cream and gently heat together, shaking rather than stirring to combine, and keep warm.

Meanwhile, lightly oil the salmon fillets and season both sides with salt and pepper. Preheat a large, nonstick pan over medium heat. Arrange the salmon in the pan, skin-side down, and cook until the skins are well browned and crisp, about 4 minutes. Turn and cook on the other side until the salmon is medium to medium-rare. Remove from the pan and drain on paper towels. Pour off the fat from the pan, add the pea tendrils and heat about 1 minute, or until barely wilted.

Ladle the reserved rhubarb sauce onto four large, heated dinner plates. Place one portion of salmon, skin-side up, on each plate. Surround the salmon with the pea tendrils, and serve immediately.

799

NEVER EAT RHUBARB LEAVES

Rhubarb leaves contain so much oxalic acid that they are toxic. Normally the leaves are removed before being sold except for a small portion resembling a webbed duck's foot at the top. If you grow your own, be sure to remove the leaves before cooking.

Alsatian Strawberry–Rhubarb Strudel with Warm Custard Sauce

This springtime dessert combining rhubarb with strawberries comes from Alsace, the portion of Eastern France that was long part of Germany and still retains its taste for German-style foods like strudel. It's hard to remember, but strawberries were once available only during their short season, making them a very special treat, perfectly timed to match with the availability of rhubarb. Start the rhubarb the day before, to give it time to soak with the sugar and release its juices. The tart fruit is mellowed here by the smooth, mild vanilla custard sauce. You'll need cake crumbs made from stale sponge cake or from packaged ladyfingers to help soak up the juices and keep the strudel from getting soggy.

SERVES 6 TO 8

Rhubarb and Strawberries

2 pounds rhubarb, sliced
$1/2$ cup + $1^1/_2$ cups granulated sugar
1 pint strawberries, sliced

Combine the rhubarb with $1/2$ cup of sugar and allow it soak overnight at room temperature.

The next day, drain the rhubarb and transfer it to a heavy-bottomed, nonreactive saucepan and add $1^1/_2$ cups of sugar. Cook for 2 minutes, then add the strawberries and stir together, cooking 2 more minutes, or until the strawberries have started to soften. Strain the mixture, reserving both the fruit and the liquid. Transfer the liquid to a small, heavy-bottomed, nonreactive saucepan and cook down over high heat to a thick syrup, about 5 min-

utes. Mix this thick syrup back into the fruit and cool to room temperature.

Strudel with Phyllo Dough

1 pound phyllo pastry, defrosted in the refrigerator overnight if frozen
$1^1/_2$ cups fine cake crumbs, made from sponge cake or ladyfingers
2 tablespoons unsalted butter, at room temperature + 6 tablespoons, melted and cooled
2 cups Vanilla Custard Sauce, for garnish (*see* page 990)
1 pint strawberries, halved, or quartered if large
$1/4$ cup granulated sugar
Confectioners' sugar, for dusting

Allow the package of phyllo dough to come to room temperature, about 30 minutes, to make the dough more pliable. Open the package of phyllo dough and carefully unroll the pastry leaves. Place the flat leaves on the kitchen counter and keep covered with a damp kitchen towel while working.

In a small skillet, cook the cake crumbs in 2 tablespoons of butter over moderate heat, stirring, until they are golden, then transfer them to a large bowl and reserve.

On a work surface arrange an 18-inch-long piece of wax paper with a long side facing you. Cover the paper with 2 sheets of the phyllo, and brush lightly with some of the melted butter and sprinkle with cake crumbs. Layer 8 more sheets of phyllo over the first sheet in the same manner, brushing every other each sheet lightly with melted butter and more cake crumbs. Spread the rhubarb and strawberry mixture evenly in a line along the long side facing you, leaving a 1-inch border at each end.

Preheat the oven to 375°F. Using the wax paper as a guide,

roll the strudel tightly away from you. With the seam-side down, fold the ends under to enclose the filling. Transfer the strudel carefully to a lightly buttered jellyroll pan, forming into a horseshoe shape to fit into the pan. Brush the strudel with melted butter. Cut diagonal slashes about 1 inch apart halfway through the strudel.

Bake the strudel for 45 minutes, or until it is golden brown and crispy. While the strudel is baking, prepare the Vanilla Custard Sauce (*see* page 990).

Combine the strawberries with the granulated sugar and allow them to macerate about 15 minutes.

When the strudel is done, remove it from the oven, cool in the pan, and then dust with confectioners' sugar. Transfer to a serving platter, using long spatulas, and cut into slices, using a serrated knife. Serve with the warm Vanilla Custard Sauce and the sugared strawberries.

RABARBARO, AN ITALIAN RHUBARB BEVERAGE

In Italy, *Rabarbaro* is an alcoholic beverage produced using the native Chinese variety of rhubarb, *Rheum Palmatum*. Rhubarb is considered to be beneficial to the liver and has long been used in traditional Chinese medicine. In Italy, *Rabarbaro* was often prescribed by doctors in the past for digestive ailments. Today, it is drunk either as an *aperitivo*, to stimulate the appetite before eating, or as a *digestivo*, to help digest the meal. The *Rabarbaro* produced by Ettore Zucca is one well-known brand.

Rhubarb and Blackberry Fruit Terrine

I got the idea for this lovely magenta terrine when I was working with satiny red rhubarb and happened upon some gorgeous plump, soft-textured blackberries. The rhubarb and blackberry combine to make a delicious and enticing dessert, good enough to make the most die-hard rhubarb-o-phobe a rhubarb-o-philiac. Because both fruits are soft, the terrine is easy to slice into even slices that make an eye-catching mosaic. This terrine really calls for the fully developed flavor and deep red color of field-grown rhubarb.

SERVES 12

3 pounds rhubarb, cut into 1-inch lengths
1 cup orange juice, divided
1$^1/_2$ cups granulated sugar
1 teaspoon vanilla extract
3 ($^1/_2$ pint) containers blackberries
2 envelopes unflavored powdered gelatin
  (2 scant tablespoons)
Vanilla Custard Sauce (optional) (*see* page 990)

Preheat the oven to 300°F. In a large bowl, toss the rhubarb with $^1/_2$ cup of the orange juice, the sugar, and vanilla. Transfer to a Dutch oven, cover and bake for 30 minutes, or until the rhubarb is soft but still holds its shape. Remove from the oven and, using a slotted spoon, scoop out about one third of the rhubarb and reserve. Add 1 container of blackberries to the Dutch oven, cover, and place back in the oven. Bake for 30 minutes longer, or until the fruit is very soft.

In a glass or ceramic bowl, sprinkle the gelatin into the remaining $1/2$ cup of orange juice and allow the gelatin to "bloom" for about 5 minutes, or until it swells and absorbs the liquid. Heat at medium power in the microwave for 1 minute, or until the liquid is clear, and reserve.

Remove the Dutch oven from the oven. Place a wire sieve over a large bowl. Pour the contents of the Dutch oven into the sieve and press down lightly to extract the juice. Discard the fruit pulp. You should have about $3^{1}/2$ cups of liquid. Add the melted gelatin and stir vigorously to make sure the gelatin dissolves completely in the hot liquid.

Line an 8-cup loaf pan with plastic wrap. Pour about $1/2$ cup of the liquid mixture into the bottom of the loaf pan. Chill until barely set. Spoon half of the reserved rhubarb pieces into the pan, and cover with about $1/2$ cup more liquid. Chill until barely set, top with 1 container blackberries, cover with $1/2$ cup more liquid, and chill again. Repeat with the remaining rhubarb, and another $1/2$-cup layer of liquid. Chill until barely set, then top with the remaining blackberries, and the remaining layer of liquid. Chill for 4 hours or overnight.

To serve, allow the terrine to come to room temperature, about 15 minutes, then unmold by turning upside down onto a flat serving platter. Unmold the terrine, discarding the plastic wrapping. Using an electric knife, if possible (for cleaner cuts), cut the terrine into $1/2$-inch-thick slices and place on individual serving plates. Serve, if desired, with the Vanilla Custard Sauce on page 990.

Rhubarb and Raspberry–Filled Hazelnut Shortcakes

I often combine rhubarb with berries, not only because they go so well together, but because the presence of the "sexy" berries help encourage wary guests to give rhubarb a try. I first tasted shortcakes made using James Beard's recipe (in which he enriches the dough with crumbled cooked egg yolks) at Larry Forgione's restaurant, An American Place, on New York's Upper East Side. As I dined with a group of fellow chefs at the restaurant the very first week it was open, I was lucky enough to encounter Mr. Beard enjoying a meal at his protégé's restaurant. I added hazelnuts to his recipe on my own. For best flavor and texture, serve this dessert while the biscuits and rhubarb filling are still warm, topped with the chilled whipped cream.

SERVES 8

Hazelnut Shortcakes

$1/2$ pound (2 cups) unbleached all-purpose flour

3 tablespoons granulated sugar

$1^{1}/2$ teaspoons cream of tartar

1 teaspoon baking soda

1 teaspoon kosher salt

$1/2$ cup finely ground toasted hazelnuts

2 hard-cooked egg yolks, pushed through a sieve

$1/4$ pound (1 stick) unsalted butter, chilled and cut into bits + 2 tablespoons unsalted butter, melted

$3/4$ cup heavy cream

Place the flour, sugar, cream of tartar, baking soda, salt, hazelnuts, and egg yolks in the bowl of a food processor. Process to combine, then add the chilled butter and process until the mixture forms oatmeal-like flakes. Pour in the heavy cream and continue to process just long enough for the mixture to come together.

Preheat the oven to 375°F. On a floured surface, roll the dough out about ³⁄₄ inch thick. Using scalloped cutters, cut into 8 rounds about 3 inches in diameter and another 8 rounds about 2 inches in diameter. Arrange the rounds on a baking sheet and brush them with melted butter. Bake 15 minutes, or until lightly browned on the edges. (Note that the dough may be cut into the rounds and then refrigerated until later in the day to bake.)

Filling, Whipped Cream, and Assembly

1 pound rhubarb, cut into 1-inch pieces

1 cup light brown sugar, packed

1 teaspoon ground cardamom

¹⁄₂ pint raspberries (or 1 cup defrosted frozen raspberries)

1 cup heavy cream, chilled

¹⁄₄ cup confectioners' sugar + extra for dusting

¹⁄₂ cup sour cream, chilled

1 teaspoon vanilla extract

Preheat the oven to 375°F. Combine the rhubarb, brown sugar, and cardamom. Place in an ovenproof casserole dish and cover. Bake for 30 minutes, or until the rhubarb is softened. Remove from the oven, cool to room temperature. Drain the liquid from the rhubarb mixture into a medium pot, reserving the rhubarb. Cook the rhubarb liquid over high heat until thickened but still brightly colored, about 8 minutes. Pour the liquid back over the rhubarb to intensify its flavor and gently fold in the raspberries.

Beat the heavy cream until soft peaks form. Add the confectioners' sugar and beat again until quite firm but still bright white and not at all buttery-looking. Fold in the sour cream and vanilla and reserve.

To serve, arrange the larger biscuits on serving plates. Spoon the rhubarb-raspberry mixture over top, cover with whipped sour cream, and top with the smaller biscuits. Dust with confectioners' sugar and spoon extra juice around the outside of each cake. Serve immediately.

803

RICE

BROWN, WHITE, RED, BLACK

RICE
BROWN, WHITE, RED & BLACK

What's not to like about rice? This soft, absorbent, mildly flavored grain is a staple food for more than half of the people on our planet, which helps explain why all those electric rice cookers are for sale. "Don't mess with my rice and beans," they say in the Caribbean, because these are the basic foods of life. Louis Armstrong would sign his letters, "Red beans and ricely yours," celebrating New Orleans's traditional Monday's wash-day dish. And Maurice Sendak's children's classic is called *Chicken Soup with Rice* because of how comforting this simple food can be to children of all ages.

Warm, soft, sweet, and comforting, rice pudding is one of those "nursery foods" that grown-ups in Great Britain and elsewhere still love to eat. But, rice pudding served Empress Style is studded with a royal treasure house of candied and glazed fruits, while the same idea is expressed in the Chinese Eight Treasures Rice, this time enhanced candied lotus seeds, dried red dates, candied kumquats, and more. Endlessly versatile, with an amazing variety of colors, shapes, and textures, rice can be cooked whole—whether hulled, as in white rice, or unhulled, as in brown rice—made into flour, flakes, wine, cakes, vinegar, milk, noodles, and even paper. Fermented rice flavors Japanese *miso*, so rice even ends up as a condiment.

In India and Asia, rice is the most important food crop, essential to the meal, sopping up the juices of curries, dals, and stir-fries. But beyond its place as a simple accompaniment to other dishes, rice is essential to some of the most famous dishes of the world. The elaborate rice pilafs of Persia (now Iran) are legendary, fragrant with some of the world's best saffron, native green pistachios, and raisins. In Spain, *paella alla Valenciana*, made from special short, pearl-shaped rice, gets its flavor from the marvelous mixture of juices from its additions, along with the same saffron that goes into Persian pilafs, showing the legacy of the long years of Moorish occupation in the south of Spain. A paella may include chorizo sausage, chicken, snails, rabbits, clams, baby octopus, mussels, mushrooms, roasted peppers, artichokes, peas, and more. In Northern Italy, especially the Veneto and Lombardy, creamy risotto, cooked in flavorful broth that soaks up into the pearly grains, can be made in endless variations. Risotto is a dish that I never tire of making and eating.

Rice is a grass plant with long, slender leaves and small seeds native to tropical and subtropical southeastern Asia, where it grows in wetlands. Its cultivation is best-suited to regions with high rainfall and low labor costs, as it is very labor-intensive to cultivate and requires plenty of water for irrigation. However, rice can be grown practically anywhere, even on steep hillsides, though usually with the help of insecticides. Rice is the world's third-largest crop, behind maize (corn), and wheat. Although it is native to South Asia and parts of Africa, long centuries of trade and exportation have made rice common practically everywhere in the world.

Rice is often grown in paddies—shallow flooded fields—taking advantage of the rice plant's tolerance to water as well as the benefits the water adds in preventing weeds. Once the rice has established dominance of the field, the water can be drained in preparation for harvest. Rice paddies are an important habitat for birds, such as herons and warblers, and a wide range of amphibians and snakes. Whether it is grown in a paddy or a field, rice requires a great amount of water, making it a controversial crop in some areas, particularly in the United States and Australia, where rice farmers use large amounts of water to generate relatively small crop yields. However, in places that have a periodical rainy season and typhoons, rice paddies help keep the water supply steady and prevent floods from reaching dangerous levels.

Rice cultivation probably began simultaneously in many countries over 6,500 years ago. Two species of rice were domesticated: Asian rice, *Oryza sativa*, and African rice, *Oryza glaberrima*. Common wild rice (not related to the dark brown grains of American native wild rice, see the chapter on Wild Rice, page 975, for more information) was likely the ancestor of Asian rice, which appears to have originated around the foothills of the Himalayas.

In Japan, dry-land rice was introduced about 1000 BCE, and wet-paddy rice agriculture was brought to Japan about seven hundred years later. African rice, which originated in the Niger River delta as far west as Senegal, has been cultivated for 3,500 years. However, this variety never developed far from its original region. Instead, its cultivation declined in favor of Asian rice,

possibly brought to Africa by Arabs between the seventh and eleventh centuries. Rice was adapted to farming in the Middle East and Mediterranean around 800 BCE. The Moors brought it to Spain about 700 CE, and after the middle of the fifteenth century, its cultivation spread throughout Italy and then France.

Rice first reached the United States in 1694 in South Carolina, probably from Madagascar. Colonial South Carolina and Georgia grew and amassed great wealth from huge rice plantations cultivated by slaves from the Senegambia area of West Africa. At the port of Charleston, through which passed forty percent of all American slaves, Senegambian slaves brought the highest prices because they were experienced in the complex techniques of rice culture.

From the slaves, plantation owners learned how to dike the marshes and periodically flood the fields. At first, the rice was milled by hand with wooden paddles, then winnowed in sweetgrass baskets, handmade using another skill brought by the slaves. The invention of the rice mill increased the profitability of the crop, and water power for the mills was another step forward. With the loss of slave labor after the Civil War, rice production became less profitable and it died out in its original region about one hundred years ago. There is a movement today to bring back this tradition of rice to the region from Carolina Plantation Rice (go to www. carolinaplantationrice.com for more information).

To prepare rice for eating, the seeds of the rice plant are first milled to remove the outer husks of the grain, creating brown rice. If the process is continued so that the germ and the remaining husk (now called bran) are removed, white rice is created. Most varieties of rice are processed into white rice at the mill, where the grains are

807

polished to remove the husk, bran, and part of the germ. This processing strips some of the nutrients, but makes the rice tender and fast-cooking. Many producers sell enriched white rice, which restores some of the nutrients lost in processing.

Rice is often classified by its shape and texture. Thai Jasmine rice is long-grain and cooks up fluffy. Chinese restaurants usually serve long-grain as plain unseasoned steamed rice. Japanese *mochi* rice and Chinese sticky rice are short-grain. Japanese table rice is a sticky, short-grain variety, while sake is distilled from another type. Indian rice cultivars include *Basmati* (grown in the North), long and medium-grained *Patna* rice, and short-grained *Masoori*.

THE WORLD'S TOP PRODUCERS, IMPORTERS, AND EXPORTERS OF RICE

The top three rice producers (in 2004) in the world were China, with thirty-one percent of world production; India with twenty percent; and Indonesia with nine percent. The top three exporting countries were Thailand, twenty-six percent; Vietnam, fifteen percent; and the United States, with eleven percent; while the top three importers were Indonesia, fourteen percent; Bangladesh, four percent; and Brazil, at three percent.

RICE AND THOMAS JEFFERSON

Thomas Jefferson, our third president, was truly a renaissance man and a pioneer of plant improvement. He traveled all the way to Piedmont in Northern Italy to find out why Italian rice fetched a higher price in the market at Paris than American-grown Carolina rice, and then resourcefully smuggled seeds out in his pockets, which he planted in America.

Other Forms of Rice

Rice bran, called *nuka* in Japan, is a valuable commodity in Asia. It is the moist and oily inner layer of rice that is heated to extract rice bran oil, sold in Asian markets.

Raw rice may be ground into flour for many uses as well, including making beverages like *horchata*, rice milk, and sake.

Remember the grain of rice shooting out of a cannon on the television ads for puffed rice cereal? Rice, like other cereal grains, can be puffed (or popped), taking advantage of its inner moisture content. It typically involves heating grain pellets in a special chamber.

Pinipig, also called rice flakes, is pounded dried glutinous rice used by Filipino cooks to make desserts and drinks.

In East and South India, rice is usually boiled in large pans immediately after harvesting and before removing the husk. It is then dried and the husk removed later. This rice often shows small red speckles and has a pronounced smoky flavor from the fire.

INSTANT AND CONVERTED RICE

Instant or precooked rice is white rice that's been pre-cooked and dehydrated so it later cooks quickly. It's relatively expensive, though, and you sacrifice both flavor and texture. White instant rice cooks in about five minutes, brown in about ten. Minute Rice is a well-known American brand.

Converted rice or parboiled rice is steamed before it's husked, a process that causes the grains to absorb many of the nutrients from the husk. When cooked, the grains are more nutritious, firmer, and less clingy than white rice grains. Uncle Ben's is a well-known American brand.

LONG, MEDIUM, AND SHORT-GRAIN RICE

American long-grain rice (which includes Carolina rice) has long, slender kernels that stay separate and fluffy after cooking, and have a somewhat bland flavor. It is the best choice if you want to serve rice as a side dish or as a bed for sauces.

Medium-grain rice is shorter, plumper, and stickier than long-grain rice and works well in paella and risotto.

Short-grain rice, also known as round grain rice or pearl rice, is almost round in shape, with moist grains that stick together when cooked. It is best suited for paella, rice puddings, and molded salads. It is also good for making sushi and also works pretty well in a risotto.

BROWN RICE

Brown rice isn't milled as much as white, so it retains much of the outer bran and germ, making it fiber-rich, nutritious, and chewy. Brown rice takes about three times as long to cook as white rice. Many rice varieties come as either brown rice or white rice. Unfortunately, it doesn't perform as well as white rice in many recipes. Long-grained brown rices aren't as fluffy and tender, and short-grained types aren't as sticky. Brown rice also has a much shorter shelf life (because of the oil in the germ). Keep it in a cool, dark place for not more than three months, or freeze.

Broken Rice

In Senegal and other parts of Western African, broken rice, the small bits of rice produced during processing, is preferred. While the custom began because broken rice was cheaper, it is now sought-after, especially broken Jasmine rice from Thailand, also known as *Mali* rice. Its texture and flavor when cooked are reminiscent of couscous, because this rice absorbs cooking juices so well.

Rice Varieties

American Basmati: Also called "popcorn rice" or "della rice," this is a hybrid of basmati and American long-grain rice. Common brands include Texmati, Delta Rose, and Cajun Country Popcorn Rice. When cooked, this rice expands similar to long grain rice, both lengthwise and widthwise, and becomes dry and fluffy, with distinct separate grains and a nutty fragrance.

Basmati Rice: Sometimes called the "Prince of Rice," basmati is a very long, slender-grained, highly aromatic rice grown mainly in the foothills of the Himalayas in India and Pakistan. The cooked grains are lightly dry and fluffy. Aged basmati rice is better but more expensive. In Indian recipes, basmati is often cooked with whole spices, like cinnamon and cloves, to enhance its aromatic properties. The spices are left in the rice to enhance its appearance but aren't meant to be eaten. Brown basmati is also available.

Bhutanese Red Rice: This red short-grain rice is a staple in rural areas of Bhutan, high in the Himalayas. It has a strong, nutty flavor and works well with other bold seasonings. It is quite firm in texture.

Risotto Rice: Risotto rice, also called "Piedmontese" (like the kind that Thomas Jefferson found), are plump kernels of white medium-long rice that can absorb lots of liquid while keeping its texture, so it's best for making risotto. Grown in Piedmont and Lombardy, risotto varieties are graded, with the highest grade being *superfino*, followed by *fino*, *semi-fino*, and *commune*. *Arborio* is the best known variety, but *Carnaroli*, *Roma*, *Baldo*, *Padano*, and *Vialone Nano* are highly regarded.

Arborio is the risotto rice most widely available outside Italy. It is wider and longer than other risotto rices and has a high starch content so it thickens and holds together beautifully while still retaining bite in the middle. When cooked in risotto, it has creamy, evenly cooked grains. Baldo is a relatively new variety derived from Arborio and most comparable to it in shape and starchiness. It's the quickest cooking of the risotto rices. Carnaroli, sometimes called the "king" or the "caviar" of Italian rice, is the preferred risotto rice in most regions of Italy. It has longer, elegant grains and produces a very creamy risotto, yet is resistant to overcooking. Vialone Nano is the preferred rice of the Veneto region, where risotto is king. A smaller, sturdier grain with a rounded edge, it can absorb twice its weight in liquid, and with its high starch content, it produces a very creamy risotto.

Jasmine Rice: Also known as Thai basmati rice, this is a long-grain rice produced in Thailand with a subtle floral aroma, sold in both brown and white forms. Unlike other long-grain rices, it has a soft and slightly sticky texture when cooked. It works best with Chinese and Southeast Asian food.

Japonica Rice: This short- and medium-grain rice is grown mainly in California and comes in a variety of colors, including red, brown, and black, with Cal Rose the predominant Japonica variety. It is popular in Caribbean and especially Japanese cuisines because of its characteristic clingy, moist, and firm nature when cooked. Sushi in Japan, Taiwan, and Korea, and the U.S. is likely made with Japonica rice grown in the Sacramento Valley, because it is grown and processed to satisfy the most discriminating rice connoisseurs. American producers use Japanese polishing methods, including sanding or bathing it in hot uncooked tapioca after milling to remove remaining dust or bran and produce a sparklingly white finish. Black japonica rice, or "black forbidden rice," has short grains that turn a beautiful indigo-blue when cooked.

Kalijira Rice: This tiny aromatic rice from Bangladesh cooks up quickly and is especially good in rice puddings.

Spanish Rice: The Moors first introduced rice to Spain over 1,000 years ago. Since then, rice has become integral to Spanish cuisine, especially in the southern Arab-influenced regions of Andalusia and Valencia. The best Spanish rice comes from an area in Murcia near the town of Calasparra. Although Valencia produces virtually all of the rice grown in Spain, a small amount of the very best rice, including two historic varieties— *Sollana* (called *Callasparra* rice) and the coveted *Bomba*—are grown in nearby Nurcia. There, the rice grows in cool mountain water made possible by Moorish irrigation. Calasparra is an old strain of small-grained rice that grows very slowly, producing kernels that are exceptionally well dehydrated and perfect for absorbing the cooking juices of paella.

Bomba is another ancient strain of rice that matures very slowly, so it produces an extremely hard and absorbent grain, because it has taken such a long time to mature. It expands in width, like an accordion, rather than in length, as do other rice strains. It absorbs three times its volume in broth while the grains remain distinct, so it is also perfectly suited to absorbing all the juices in paella. Bomba had all but disappeared from the market because it requires such intensive care, but with renewed interest in heritage Spanish foods, Bomba is once again available. This high-quality rice is, not surprisingly, also high in price, with each bag individually numbered and harvest-dated by the producer.

Sticky Rice: This very sticky, short-grain rice is widely used in Asia for sushi and to make various desserts. It may be found as either white or black (actually rust in color). It is also known as glutinous rice, sushi rice, sweet rice, Chinese sweet rice, waxy rice, botan rice, mochi rice, Japanese rice, and pearl rice.

Thai Purple Sticky Rice: Also known as Thai black sticky rice or Thai black glutinous rice, this firm-textured rice turns a rich dark purple when cooked. The color bleeds, so it's best to pair it with other dark ingredients. In Thailand, it is often used in desserts.

Wehani Rice: This russet-colored rice is another aromatic rice that is related to basmati rice. When cooked, it splits lengthwise and resembles American wild rice, and has a popcorn-like fragrance.

Wild Pecan Rice: Also known as pecan rice, this chewy, nutty-tasting hybrid is only partially milled, so it retains some of the bran and has a nutty, pecan-like flavor. This aromatic rice comes from Louisiana and is a basmati hybrid.

Cretan Rice, Cabbage, and Raisin Pilaf

Diane Kochilas, a well-known Greek cookbook author, says about Crete, "In many respects its [Cretan] cuisine can be seen as an unbroken continuum from prehistoric times to the present. . . . The land is still blessed here, and the traditional foods of Crete remain to this day simple and seasonal, based on faith in the time-tested triad of grains, vegetables, and olive oil." Here, this triad appears as a simple, hearty vegetarian pilaf prepared at a food conference in Napa Valley by Cretan chef and cooking teacher, Chris Veneris.

SERVES 6

2 tablespoons olive oil

1 cup coarsely chopped onion

2 cups finely shredded green cabbage

1 cup long-grain white rice

1 cup peeled and diced fresh plum tomatoes (*see* Peeling Fresh plum tomatoes, page 86, for directions)

Kosher salt and freshly ground black pepper to taste

$1/2$ teaspoon ground cinnamon

$1/2$ cup dark raisins

$1/2$ cup pine nuts, lightly toasted

In a medium saucepot, heat the olive oil and cook the onion until slightly softened, but not browned. Add the cabbage and cook, stirring, over medium heat, until a bit limp. Add the rice and cook, stirring constantly, several minutes, or until the rice is shiny and somewhat transparent. Add the tomatoes and $2^{1}/2$ cups water. Bring to a gentle boil, season with salt, pepper, and cinnamon, and cover. Reduce heat to low and cook until all the liquid has been absorbed, about 15 minutes total. After 5 minutes cooking, stir in the raisins and add the pine nuts. Continue cooking until the rice is tender, turn off the heat, and allow the rice to steam for 5 to 10 minutes before fluffing and serving.

RICE AND GMOS

Texmati, a hybrid cultivar from America, is a genetically modified patented cultivar that is creating great controversy because of concerns about the long-term effects on the planet and our seed stock from these permanently changed seeds. Personally, I find it to be one of the best-tasting varieties of rice, easiest to cook up fluffy without being sticky. In another controversial procedure, scientists are working on golden rice that is genetically modified to produce beta carotene, the precursor to vitamin A.

812

Risotto with Two Variations

Pasta is wonderful but risotto is even better. Why? Because the rice swells as it absorbs the flavors of its cooking liquid, producing a marvelously creamy, fragrant dish that, at its best, forms l'onda, *the wave—so firm and yet simultaneously fluid that it moves from side to side like a wave, while holding its shape without mushiness. Having made this bold statement, I have to add the caveat that risotto, when good, is very, very good, but when bad, it is awful. Most important is to use the proper kind of Italian risotto rice, whether the more common Arborio, or the rarer and more sought-after Carnaroli and Vialone Nano, used extensively in the Veneto. Next, pay attention to the details: The broth must be simmering as it's added to the rice, allowing it to be absorbed into the inner portion of the kernel, rather than remaining on the outside. And remember, risotto waits for no one; once it's ready, serve immediately on heated plates, so that it's hot and steaming and marvelously fragrant.*

SERVES 4

¼ cup chopped shallots

4 tablespoons unsalted butter, divided

1 cup risotto rice

¼ cup dry white vermouth (or white wine)

3 cups simmering chicken stock

Kosher salt and freshly ground black pepper to taste

Garnish (*see* Risotto Variations at right)

¼ cup freshly grated Parmigiano-Reggiano or
   Grana Padano cheese

In a medium, heavy-bottomed nonreactive saucepan with a lid, cook the shallots in 2 tablespoons of the butter until transparent. Add the rice and cook, stirring, about 3 minutes, or until the rice is transparent. Add the vermouth and stir. Bring to the boil and cook over moderately high heat until liquid is absorbed. One ladle at a time, add the simmering stock to the rice. Stir after adding the stock, allowing the stock to be fully absorbed before adding a second ladle. After three ladlefuls have been absorbed, start checking the rice for consistency—this is the key! The rice should be firm but starting to soften. Stir in the remaining broth, season to taste with salt and pepper, and stir in the garnishes. Simmer uncovered for about 10 minutes, stirring occasionally, until the rice is tender but still firm, and the broth has been almost complete absorbed. Just before serving, vigorously stir in the cheese and the remaining 2 tablespoons of butter (to form "the wave"). Serve immediately, preferably on heated plates.

Risotto Variations

Risotto Primavera: About 5 minutes before the risotto is ready, add tiny cubes of lightly cooked carrot, zucchini, and thinly sliced green beans, cut crosswise, along with shredded spinach, snow peas cut into thin strips, and sliced scallions. Finish with Parmigiano-Reggiano or Grana Padano and butter.

Risotto with Spring Greens: Just before serving, stir in a mixture of shredded arugula, spinach, watercress, leek, scallions, endive, and romaine leaves. Add Parmigiano and tiny dice of fresh mozzarella, stir and serve.

813

Louisiana Dirty Rice

Clams, chicken livers, Andouille sausage, onions, peppers, and seasonings give this dish of white rice a dark brown "dirty" look. To make a good dirty rice, the flavoring ingredients should be cooked as dark brown as possible over high heat to concentrate the flavors. By the time the clams have all opened, all the liquid should be absorbed. The rice grains should be firm and separate but loaded with the delicious juices given off by the clams and the andouille sausage. You'll need to purchase Cajun seasoning or make your own following the recipe in my Field Guide to Herbs & Spices. *Like Chinese-style fried rice, this dish works best with precooked white rice, so cook it a day ahead of time, cool, and refrigerate.*

SERVES 4 TO 6

1 tablespoon unsalted butter

1^1/$_2$ cups long-grain white rice

3 tablespoons canola oil

^{1}/$_2$ cup diced green pepper

^{1}/$_2$ cup diced onion

1 cup sliced andouille sausage

1 tablespoon chopped garlic

3 tablespoons Cajun seasoning

^{1}/$_2$ cup chicken livers, cut into small pieces

24 littleneck clams, scrubbed

2 cups chicken stock

In a medium, heavy-bottomed nonreactive pot, bring 4 cups of water to the boil along with the butter. Add the rice, then reduce the heat, cover, and simmer about 12 minutes, or until firm but cooked through. Drain and rinse under cold water and reserve.

In a large skillet (or chicken fryer) with a lid, heat the oil over high heat. Add the green pepper and onion and sauté until softened and just beginning to brown, about 5 minutes. Add the sausage, garlic, and Cajun seasoning and sauté 2 to 3 minutes, or until the sausage begins to brown. Add the chicken livers and sauté 2 to 3 minutes longer, or until the spices and the chicken livers brown well and start to stick to the bottom of the pan. Add the clams, cooked rice, and chicken stock to the pan. Shake the pan to combine the ingredients. Bring to the boil over high heat and then cover and reduce the heat to medium. Continue cooking, shaking the pan occasionally, until the clams have opened and all the moisture has been absorbed. Transfer the dirty rice to large, shallow bowls (preferably heated) with the clams arranged on top of the rice. Serve immediately.

CUTTING UP CHICKEN LIVERS

Place the chicken livers in a small bowl and use a pair of scissors to cut them into bits. It's easier and cleaner than chopping them on a cutting board.

Arancini: Truffled Risotto Oranges

In the fanciful minds of Sicilians, these deep-fried stuffed rice balls resemble the oranges that grow all over the island, so they're called arancini, *which means "little oranges." Traditionally filled with a rich meat ragù, these fritters are consumed by Sicilians as snacks. This one dish demonstrates much of Sicily's diverse culinary heritage—the canestrato fresco, a fresh, mild, firm cheese closest to mozzarella, comes from the Greeks; the rice and saffron from the Arabs; the meat ragù or ragout from the French; and the tomato sauce from the Spanish. In Rome, similar rice balls are called* suppli al telefono *or "telephone wires", because when the balls are pulled open, the melted mozzarella within forms long, thin strings. Although not traditional, my version with truffle oil, truffle paste, and Italian Fontina is pretty wonderful. Use refined olive oil, labeled simply olive oil, for frying here. Unlike extra-virgin, this oil has been treated and filtered so it can reach high temperatures without burning.*

MAKES ABOUT 16

1/4 pound shallots, chopped

2 tablespoons unsalted butter

1 cup Arborio or Canaroli rice

1/2 cup dry white vermouth

3 cups chicken stock, simmering

2 tablespoons truffle paste

1 tablespoon truffle oil

1 bunch chives, thinly sliced

Kosher salt and freshly ground black pepper to taste

1 cup grated Parmigiano Reggiano

1/4 pound Italian Fontina, cut into 16 cubes

2 eggs lightly beaten and mixed with 2 tablespoons water

2 cups homemade-style breadcrumbs or Japanese panko

Refined olive oil for frying

Combine the shallots and butter in a large casserole dish. Cook over moderate heat until transparent, stirring often, about 3 minutes, then add rice. Cook again until the rice grains are shiny and a bit transparent, about 3 minutes, then add the vermouth and bring to the boil. Cook together until the vermouth evaporates. Add the stock, one ladle at a time, cooking until the stock is absorbed by the rice; then continuing until all the stock has been absorbed. Stir in the truffle paste and oil, chives, salt and pepper, and Parmigiano Reggiano. Spread out into a thin layer on a parchment-lined sheet pan to cool, about 2 hours. Chill in the refrigerator, then scrape into a container. When cold, form the rice into 1-inch balls, then flatten into a pancake shape. Place a Fontina cube in the center of the flattened rice, then enclose the cheese with the surrounding rice, forming a ball.

Roll the rice balls in the egg wash, draining the excess, then in the breadcrumbs. Arrange on a wax-paper-lined tray, and refrigerate until ready to fry, up to 2 days ahead of time.

In a large, heavy-bottomed pot, a wok, or an electric fryer, preheat the olive oil to 365°F. on a frying thermometer, or until the oil is thin and almost watery looking and shimmering. Lay the arancini one by one into the oil, without splashing and without crowding, and fry until golden brown, about 6 minutes, or until the balls stop releasing steam and the cheese just begins to ooze out. Drain on a wire rack and keep warm in a 200°F. oven. Serve immediately.

815

Rice Pilaf with Toasted Vermicelli

Whether spelled pilaf *or* pilau, *this dish of rice simmered in flavorful broth and containing bits of other prized ingredients comes from Persia, today's Iran. The word* pilaf *was imported into English by travelers in this part of the world. Today, it is one of the most popular dishes in Turkey and other parts of the former Ottoman Empire, like Lebanon. In the sixteenth century, ordinary rice came from Egypt and was paid as tribute to the emperor. But, the highly prized extra-long-grain rice, best used for pilaf, came all the way from Anatolia and Persia, so the dish was served as a symbol of plenty. I like to use Texmati rice to make this simple Lebanese rice pilaf with its toasted pasta.*

SERVES 4 TO 6

1 cup white long-grain rice

2 tablespoons unsalted butter

$^3/_4$ cup crushed cappellini pasta, about $^3/_4$ inch in length

1$^3/_4$ cups chicken stock

2 bay leaves

Kosher salt to taste

Wash the rice and drain well. In a medium, heavy-bottomed pot with a lid, melt the butter and add the capellini. Brown over moderate heat, stirring constantly until deep golden brown. Stir in the rice and stir until well coated with the butter, but not at all browned. Add the stock, bay leaves, and salt, and cover, then bring to the boil. Reduce the heat to a bare simmer and cook for 15 minutes, or until the liquid has been absorbed. Remove from the heat and allow the rice to steam for 5 minutes longer before serving.

Honey-Caramel Rice Pudding

This is no ordinary rice pudding. Here firm, absorbent arborio rice from Italy is simmered and then flavored with aromatics like vanilla, cinnamon, nutmeg, and lemon zest. Then a hot honey caramel is used to line the pan and the pudding is slowly baked until it sets up. Just like a Spanish flan (baked egg custard), the pudding soaks up some of the honey syrup, giving it a deep golden-brown outside contrasting beautifully with its soft, creamy, yet fluffy, inside. Unmold the pudding onto a large, shallow serving plate and dig right in.

SERVES 8

4 cups cold water

4 tablespoons unsalted butter

2 teaspoons kosher salt

1 pound (2 cups) Arborio rice

2 cups + 1 cup granulated sugar

$^1/_2$ cup honey

Juice and grated zest of 1 lemon

3 cup milk

2 cups heavy cream

6 whole eggs + 2 egg yolks

1 tablespoon vanilla extract

$^1/_2$ teaspoon ground cinnamon

$^1/_2$ teaspoon ground nutmeg

In a medium saucepan, bring the water, butter, and salt to the boil. Add the rice, cover, and bring back to the boil. Reduce the heat to so the liquid barely simmers, then cover and cook for 20 to 25 minutes, or until all the liquid has been absorbed. To keep the grains nice and whole, allow the rice to cool to room temperature before stirring. Reserve the rice.

Have ready a 9- or 10-inch round metal cake pan. In a small, heavy pot, whisk together 2 cups of the sugar, the honey, and lemon juice and zest. Heat slowly until the mixture melts and the liquid is clear. Raise the heat to medium and continue to cook until the mixture caramelizes or turns medium golden brown in color. Carefully pour the caramel into the cake pan, rotating the pan to cover the bottom evenly. Reserve the pan.

Preheat the oven to 325°F. Place the milk and heavy cream in a glass measure and scald (or heat until steaming) in the microwave, or heat in a small pot. Meanwhile, whisk together the remaining 1 cup of sugar, the eggs, yolks, vanilla, cinnamon, and nutmeg. Pour the milk mixture into the egg mixture, constantly stirring, until well combined. Add the cooked rice and stir until well combined. Pour the pudding mixture into the caramel-lined cake pan.

Make a water bath by placing the cake pan inside a larger pan. Fill the larger pan with hot water so it reaches about halfway up the sides of the cake pan. Place in the oven and bake for 45 minutes, or until the pudding has set in the middle. Cool to room temperature before unmolding and then serve immediately, spooning some caramel syrup over each portion.

CREAMY RICE PUDDING

What makes rice pudding creamy? It turns out that there are three main types of rice—short, medium, and long grain—and it's important which you choose for your pudding. The key here is the type of starch, which acts as a thickener in the pudding. Plants store glucose sugars as starch—sugar molecules hooked together to make bigger molecules—in either long, straight chains (*amylose*), or in small, branched shapes (*amylopectin*). When amylose has been heated, it thickens. When it cools and dries, it forms hard crystals. So, if you use long-grain rice for pudding, it can become very hard when chilled because of this crystallized amylose. The solution is to switch to medium- or short-grain rice, both of which have less amylose than long-grain rice does.

817

RICOTTA & OTHER FRESH WHITE CHEESES

RICOTTA
& OTHER FRESH WHITE CHEESES

Little Miss Muffett *sat on a tuffet, eating her curds and whey*. Until the spider came along, Miss Muffett couldn't stop eating her fresh white cheese. What's the connection between Miss Muffet's cheese and Mexican *Queso Blanco*, German *Quark*, Lebanese *Labne*, Indian *Panir*, French *Fromage Blanc*, Russian Farmer Cheese, and English Cottage Cheese? They're all the simplest kind of cheese: fresh, unaged "farmhouse" or "cottage" cheeses; curds and whey.

Cheese is either fresh, aged, or (heaven forbid!) processed by chemical means. To make cheese, first you need milk, a total food, meant to nourish the young of all mammals. Americans mostly eat cow's-milk cheese, but around the world, people enjoy cheese made from the milk of sheep, goats, mares, water buffalos, and yaks. Milk contains two main proteins: casein, which thickens and solidifies; and whey, which remains suspended in liquid.

The first step to making cheese is to culture the milk with a "friendly" bacteria strain that thickens it and forms curds. The milk or cream sours as it thickens. Depending on the culture, it can turn the milk into cheese or other dairy products. For instance, different strains of bacteria transform milk into French Crème Fraiche, Italian Mascarpone, American buttermilk, German quark, Greek and Middle Eastern yogurt, and Devonshire clotted cream. Fresh cheeses made from milk, not cream, are naturally low in fat.

Traditionally, after churning butter, a farmer or, more likely, his wife would make cottage cheese from the buttermilk. First she would skim the cream off the top. Then she would set the skimmed milk in a warm place (such as the back of a wood stove) until the milk had clabbered (or curdled). She would pour the warm curds and whey into a cheesecloth sack and hang it up to drain. After mixing the soft curds with a little salt and fresh cream, the cheese was ready to chill. Cottage cheese, pot cheese, farmer cheese, fromage blanc, and other traditional white cheeses are all made essentially the same way.

For centuries, fresh white cheeses were a staple food of the poor, sometimes called "white meat." Fermented and aged cheeses were a luxury food reserved for the rich. People living close to the edge couldn't wait two to three years (as for Parmigiano or extra-sharp Cheddar) to eat their cheese. They also couldn't invest the huge quantities of milk needed to produce this kind of cheese. Typically, the amount of an aged cheese weighs only ten percent of the original amount of milk, and hard long-aged cheeses, like Parmigiano and Romano, can yield as little as one percent of the milk.

Cheesemaking is so old, we can't tell when it started. Like wine, beer, and sourdough bread, aged cheese is a fermented food that probably first occurred naturally. Only later did people learn how to control fermentation. The words for cheese in many languages share one of two roots: the English word *cheese*, the Spanish *queso*, and the German *käse* all come from the Latin *caseus* for curd; the French *fromage* and Italian *formaggio* come from the Latin *forma*, for the mold where the cheese drains.

We're each loyal to our own version of white cheese, depending on our ethnic heritage. Southern Italian immigrants brought over the techniques for making fresh ricotta and hand-kneaded mozzarella, while Armenians brought their own string cheese, often flavored with small black nigella seeds. With my Eastern European (Polish and Lithuanian) background, I grew up eating lots of cream cheese, farmer cheese, and sour cream, all of which contain no animal rennet, forbidden to strictly Orthodox Jews, because of the mix of an animal product with its milk. In a religious culture that separates milk and meat, a whole cuisine of dairy dishes evolved. Blintzes, cheesecake, potato latkes (pancakes) with sour cream, bagels with cream cheese, and cheese kugel all share this history.

I still can't seem to get enough of sour cream. I serve it to garnish nachos and enchiladas, stirred into borscht and schav soups, or to dip strawberries: first in sour cream and then dark brown sugar. I'd probably be better off if I liked my Grandmother's homemade sour milk because it's lower in fat than the sour cream, in which I indulge all too often. She used to set the (most likely raw) milk mixed with a little vinegar out for several days at room temperature until it naturally soured and thickened. Somehow I could never bring myself to drink it.

Originally brought to market wrapped in banana leaves, Latin American fresh cheeses were made by local artisans. Like other fresh cheeses before modern sterile cheesemaking techniques, they had a shelf-life of less than a week. What makes these Hispanic cheeses different is that they keep their shape when heated. Especially popular among Dominicans, cubes of *Queso Para Freir* are browned by cooking them directly on a griddle, similar to the way Greek *kasseri* is pan-fried and then flamed in Ouzo for the dish called *saganaki*.

Middle Eastern cheeses tend to be unaged, acidic, and fresh because of the region's low production of milk, poor pasturage, and hot climate. Lebanese *Labne* (meaning *white*) is a tangy drained yogurt cheese; Broccio, a sheep's milk ricotta, comes from Corsica; Mascarpone is a Northern Italian cream cheese thickened with tartaric acid. Feta from Greece and Bulgaria is unaged, though heavily salted to preserve it. The French enjoy fresh cheese for dessert such as *Petit-Suisse*, which is often topped with strawberries. *Fromage blanc* is sweetened and then drained in special heart-shaped ceramic molds for the exquisite Goat Cheese Coeur a la Crème or cream heart (*see* page 459).

Ricotta, which means *recooked* in Italian, originated as a thrifty way to use the whey left over from making cheese. After the first cooking to separate the curds and whey, the cheesemaker adds an acid, like vinegar, to the whey. After the whey is heated to a higher temperature, the fine whey curds separate out. True whey cheeses (sometimes called *ricotone*) are now rare, because American, and much Italian, ricotta is manufactured from whole or part-skim milk. Ricotta cheeses differ immensely among regional brands. Some are unpleasantly pasty, others mealy, others exquisitely and delicately flavored, with a pleasing, finely grained texture.

Try mixing farmer cheese or creamy cottage cheese with fresh fine herbs (tarragon, chervil, parsley, and chives). Season the cheese with a little salt, freshly ground pepper, and a pinch of cayenne. Serve the herb cheese to top baked potatoes or spread on chewy, country-style bread.

FARMER CHEESE

Since childhood, I've loved dense, tangy, firm, old-fashioned farmer cheese. The oldest company that makes it is the Friendship Dairy of Friendship, New York. Founded more than 80 years ago, this family business specializes in the dairy products beloved by Eastern European Jews. After all these years, they still do most of their sales around New York, in certain Philadelphia neighborhoods, and in Miami (go to www.friendship-dairies.com for more information). There are now some smaller Russian companies making farmer cheese, sold in Russian specialty stores.

You can't make authentic blintzes or pierogies without farmer cheese, with its tangy flavor and firm texture. Because of its short shelf life, you may have to go to an ethnic market to find farmer cheese cut from the old-fashioned three-pound loaf. Made from just milk, cream, salt, and culture, the curd is drained overnight in special canvas "socks." The next day, the firm, oddly shaped three-pound loaves are taken out of their socks and wrapped for sale.

Lioni Latticini Fresh Ricotta

My favorite ricotta these days is the fresh type made by the Lioni Latticini Company in Brooklyn and sold packed into perforated metal containers. This hand-packed product is highly perishable, but better than any other ricotta I've ever tasted in the U.S. It is sold at Whole Foods in the fancy Cheese Department (go to http://lionimozzarella.com for more information).

Hispanic White Cheeses

Panela: The most popular fresh cheese in Mexico, this cheese is mild, white, and crumbly. Like *Queso Blanco*, it will get soft and creamy but will not lose its shape when heated. Panela is used in Mexico for many cooked dishes and is crumbled over salads, tacos, chili, and burritos.

Queso Añejo: This cheese, also known as Cotija cheese, is an aged, salted white cheese similar to feta, with a much stronger flavor. It is often crumbled or grated over Mexican dishes.

Queso Blanco: This mild-tasting cheese is the most popular Latin American cheese, both for snacking and cooking. It is wonderful for cooking, because it becomes soft and creamy when heated, but will not melt.

Queso Fresco: Very popular among many people of Mexican descent, this fine-grained cheese is often crumbled over salads or refried beans.

Queso Para Freir: This cheese is quite popular among people from the Caribbean and is frequently used for frying—its name means *cheese for frying*— because it resists melting even more than *Queso Blanco*, due to its high levels of rennet. It is actually a variation of *Queso Blanco* that is similarly white and crumbly, but saltier.

For more information on Hispanic and Middle Eastern cheeses, go to www.specialcheese.com.

Middle-Eastern and Indian White Cheeses

Ackawi: Ackawi is a soft, white cow's-milk cheese native to Lebanon and Syria, though popular throughout the Middle East. It is brined to give it its traditional salty taste.

Basket Cheese: This white, soft cheese is formed in a circular basket shape and has a salty taste. Because of the cheese's distinctive form, it is difficult to mass produce, and the genuine product is easily recognizable.

Kashta: This thickened heavy cream, also known as *Kishta*, is very popular in the Middle East and most resembles Devonshire clotted cream or Italian mascarpone. Traditionally, it is made by skimming the thickest part of the cream from whey cream. It has no more than a five-day life. Kashta is used in cooking and is mixed with honey to be eaten as an incredibly rich dessert.

Kenafa: Kenafa is an unsalted, very fresh, soft cheese that melts easily and freely. It is used to make the popular Middle Eastern cheese-filled dessert, also called *Kenafa*. It can be used as a base for other sweet cheese desserts and is sold frozen because it contains no salt for preserving.

Halloumi: This dense, creamy, and mild cheese from Greece is quite versatile in the kitchen and deserves to be better known. The cheese, which originated in the Eastern Mediterranean, has a pleasant, refreshing taste and a firm texture because it is boiled. It is also made in a mint-flavored version by folding in spearmint leaves after it has been boiled.

Jibneh Arabieh: This simple cheese is found all over the Middle East but is particularly popular in Egypt and the Arabian Gulf. The cheese, which began as Bedouin goat- or sheep's-milk cheese, is now widely made with cow's milk. It has an open texture, a mild taste, and is widely used in cooking and snacking.

Naboulsi: Naboulsi is made by boiling fresh Ackawi cheese in a fragrant mixture of gums, spices, and seeds. Popular in Syria, Lebanon, and Jordan, it is packed in brine.

Paneer: This light-textured and mild-flavored, rather jiggly fresh cheese from India is also known as *Panir*, and is often cooked in curry with peas or in samosa fritters.

823

GERMAN QUARK

Quark (not the quark that is one of the two basic constituents of matter in particle physics) is an essential ingredient in German cuisine, accounting for half the country's total cheese consumption. Quite tangy and thick, quark has a tart flavor and smooth, soft, creamy texture. It is now being produced in America. (Trader Joe's sells it under their house brand.)

Baked Potato Gnocchi with Ricotta

Like most extremely simple dishes, gnocchi can be a challenge to make, especially for those without experience. Luckily, if you don't want to or don't have time to make your own, there are some very good packaged gnocchi available in the clear-plastic-covered modified atmosphere packaging used to extend the shelf-life of perishable foods. Buy this, and all you have to do is boil the gnocchi, drain it, mix it with the cheese, and bake until bubbling. When making gnocchi yourself, use well-aged dry and firm Idaho potatoes, so your gnocchi will come out light and still hold together. Large, well-aged, gold-fleshed potatoes with a thick skin are another good choice. New potatoes or waxy-type potatoes like red bliss are not suitable for gnocchi.

SERVES 4 TO 6

1 pound large, well-aged Idaho potatoes with thick skin

2 egg yolks

2 tablespoons thinly sliced chives (optional)

1 teaspoon kosher salt

$1/4$ teaspoon ground white pepper

4 to 6 tablespoons unbleached all-purpose flour
  + extra for rolling

$1/2$ pound whole milk ricotta

$1/2$ cup heavy cream

2 eggs

Kosher salt, grated nutmeg, and freshly ground
  black pepper to taste

$1/4$ pound mozzarella, diced

$1/2$ cup grated Parmigiano-Reggiano or Grana Padano

Steam the potatoes in their skins, or boil them in salted water until quite tender but still firm enough to hold their shape, about 40 minutes. Drain and cool them just long enough to be able to handle them, then peel the potatoes and put them through a potato ricer or food mill while still hot.

Mix together the egg yolks, chives, salt, and white pepper, and mix into the potatoes. Form the potato mixture into a ring and place the flour in the middle. Gently, only using your fingertips, mix the flour into the potato mix to make a fairly firm mass that doesn't stick to the surface, working until just combined. Throw a little flour onto your work surface and gently roll the dough into six $3/4$-inch-thick logs. Cut off pieces about 1-inch long. Dust each piece lightly with flour and roll up along the inside tines of a dinner fork to form ridged, pillow-like gnocchi. Set aside on a floured board.

It is best to cook the gnocchi as soon as they are formed, or they might get sticky and soft. Bring salted water to the boil in a wide, shallow pot. Boil the gnocchi until they float to the top, and then cook 2 to 3 minutes longer, until cooked through but still firm. Drain and reserve.

Preheat the oven to 400°F. Meanwhile, combine the ricotta, cream, eggs, salt, nutmeg, and black pepper. Mix in the mozzarella and combine with the gnocchi. (At this stage, you can refrigerate the gnocchi and bake it later or the next day. Allow the dish to come to room temperature before baking.) Spread the gnocchi into a shallow ceramic casserole dish and top with the grated cheese. Bake 20 to 25 minutes, or until browned and bubbling. Remove from the oven and serve immediately.

824

GNOCCHI

Gnocchi (pronounced N-yukky) is the Italian word for *dumplings*; in Italian, *gnocchi* is the plural of *gnocco*, which literally means *lump*. The word *gnocco* derives from a Germanic word for a *knot* (as in wood). In colloquial Italian, a *gnocco* is a stupid person; while in Emilia-Romagna's dialect the word means *a blow with a fist* (shaped like a gnocco). These small, hand-formed dough lumps are one of the oldest forms of pasta, with the first recipes recorded as far back as the thirteenth century. They are popular in German-speaking countries as *kneidl*, the very same term used for the matzo balls traditionally served in chicken soup by Jews of Eastern European background.

Gnocchi can be made of potato, semolina wheat (Roman style), chestnut flour, ricotta cheese (with or without spinach), or more fanciful ingredients. In Tuscany, spinach-and-ricotta gnocchi are called *strozzapreti*, or *priest-stranglers* (because legend tells of a priest who choked upon eating too many gnocchi). The same mixture is also called *ravioli nudi* or *naked ravioli*, because the filling is not clothed in pasta dough.

Hungarian Liptauer Cheese Spread

Called Liptauer *in Austria, the special sheep's-milk cheese that is the traditional base of this spicy spread came from Liptó, in Hungary. According to the champion of Hungarian cuisine, George Lang, the basic musts are fresh sheep's-milk cheese, paprika, onion, and caraway seeds. Because fresh sheep's-milk cheese is hard to find in the United States, I substitute farmer cheese and add a bit of butter for richness and body. Hungarian aristocrats served Liptauer cheese topped with Beluga caviar. Lacking a generous supply of Beluga, I serve it with black or pumpernickel bread, garnished with radish flowers, scallion tassels, and whole black and green olives.*

MAKES 8 TO 12 SERVINGS

825

1 pound Farmer Cheese (substitute tangy, small-cured cottage cheese, well-drained)
1/4 pound (1 stick) unsalted butter, softened
2 tablespoons sweet Hungarian paprika
Kosher salt and freshly ground black pepper to taste
1 1/2 tablespoons caraway seeds
1 tablespoon dry mustard
2 tablespoons chopped capers
2 tablespoons finely chopped onion
1 bunch thinly sliced chives
1/2 cup sour cream

In the bowl of a food processor, process the farmer cheese until smooth, remove, and set aside. Place the butter, paprika, salt and pepper, caraway seeds, mustard, capers, and onion in the processor bowl and process until smooth. Beat the 2 mixtures togetherand add the chives. Stir in the sour cream, thinning to a spreadable consistency, then transfer to an attractive crock, and refrigerate until ready to serve. The spread will keep well for up to 1 week, refrigerated.

Spinach–Ricotta Cannelloni Glazed with Lemon Cream Sauce

Save this luscious dish for a special group of hedonistic friends. It is admittedly rich, though, so serve it in small portions, but it's well worth the indulgence. This recipe is a mélange of two extraordinary dishes: a ricotta and mascarpone-filled cock's-comb-shaped pasta called cresce I ate *in Parma, Italy; and an extraordinary lemon-creamglazed spinach and ricotta cannelloni I had at a dinner party. Together, they make a dish that is out of this world.*

SERVES 8 TO 12

$1/2$ pound baby spinach

2 eggs

$1/2$ cup fine breadcrumbs

1 pound fresh whole-milk ricotta

$1/2$ pound finely chopped + $1/2$ cup grated
   Parmigiano-Reggiano or Grana Padano

1 cup Mascarpone

2 tablespoons finely chopped Italian parsley

1 tablespoon finely grated lemon zest + juice and
   grated zest of 1 lemon

1 teaspoon freshly grated nutmeg

Kosher salt and freshly ground black pepper

$1/4$ cup chopped shallots

2 tablespoons unsalted butter

1 cup heavy cream

16 (5-inch) squares fresh egg pasta (about 1 pound
   fresh pasta sheets)

Wilt the spinach either in a small amount of boiling water or in the microwave. Immediately run under cold water to set the color. Squeeze out the excess water and chop.

Beat together the eggs and breadcrumbs to a paste. Combine the ricotta, chopped Parmigiano, Mascarpone, parsley, 1 tablespoon of lemon zest, nutmeg, and salt and pepper to taste, then beat in egg mixture and spinach, and reserve.

In a medium, heavy-bottomed nonreactive saucepot, cook the shallots in the butter until softened but not browned. Add the cream and bring to the boil. Simmer for 5 minutes, or until the cream has thick bubbles throughout its surface. Remove from the heat, stir in the lemon juice and remaining zest, season to taste with salt and pepper, and keep warm.

Preheat the oven to 375°F. Bring a large pot of salted water to the boil. Adding one square at a time to the pot so they don't stick together, cook 4 to 6 cannelloni squares for about 3 minutes, or until softened but not mushy. Repeat with remaining squares. Scoop the squares out of the water using a wire skimmer or slotted spoon, rinse under cold water, and lay them out on a work surface. Place about $1/2$ cup of filling across one edge of each pasta square. Roll up tightly in a flute shape and place seam-side down onto a wax-paper-covered work surface.

Spread a thin layer of the Lemon Cream Sauce on the bottom of a large, shallow baking dish. Place the cannel-

826

loni rolls in a single layer on top, keeping the seam-sides down. Cover with the remaining sauce and sprinkle with the grated cheese. (The dish may be prepared ahead of time up until this point, keeping refrigerated until ready to bake. Allow it to come to room temperature before baking.)

Bake until bubbling, about 40 minutes, making sure the filling is hot. Remove from the oven and cool for 10 to 15 minutes before serving so the cannelloni will get a little firmer, then serve.

BLINTZES IN HISTORY

Although many countries lay claim to originating the Jewish crepe-like filled pancake, it probably originated in the late nineteenth century in the Austro-Hungarian Empire. In Hungary, pancakes of every kind with various fillings called *palacsinta* are common. A blintz can be filled with cheese, meat, apricot compote, even chocolate and chestnut paste, but to me, the only real blintz is a farmer-cheese blintz. Blintzes became a specialty for the Jewish holiday of Shavuot, the feast of sheaves, when it is customary to eat dairy dishes.

Cheese Blintzes

My recipe for cheese blintzes is adapted from the large-batch (144 at a time) quantities and method used by Miriam Perloff for the 45-year-old Jewish-American eatery, The Country Club Diner and Bakery. Though it still has the same name, this Philadelphia institution, a unique combination diner and kosher-style restaurant, has since been sold. Mrs. Perloff and her husband founded the Country Club, first as a lunch counter in his pharmacy, later as a beautiful stainless steel diner, and then, in the early 1960s, as a huge (second-largest diner ever built) "moderne" diner with lots of flash. Glitz or no glitz, the blintzes stayed the same, and people kept eating them. You can take a shortcut here by buying frozen crepes instead of making your own.

SERVES 8

6 eggs
$1/2$ pound (2 cups) all-purpose flour
1 teaspoon kosher salt
2 pounds Farmer Cheese
$1/2$ teaspoon cinnamon
$1/2$ cup granulated sugar
$1/2$ cup sour cream, for serving
1 tablespoon each: butter and vegetable oil, for cooking

Beat together 4 of the eggs and 3 cups of water in a blender. Add the flour and salt and blend until smooth. Chill for 30 minutes before using the batter. Meanwhile, combine the farmer cheese, cinnamon, sugar, and sour cream in a bowl and beat until smooth.

To make blintzes, heat a small, nonstick frying pan with a tablespoon of vegetable oil. Ladle in a small amount of batter (about 2 tablespoons). Swirl around until the batter coats the bottom of the pan. Cook for 1 to 2 minutes, or until the top looks set. Turn out of the pan and repeat with more batter, layering the cooked blintzes on top of each other on a plate. (Freeze any extra blintzes to use for cannelloni or crepe dishes.)

Fill the pan-cooked side of the blintzes with the filling, using about 1/4 cup for each one and placing the filling in the center in an oblong shape. Fold the short sides over the ends of the filling, then roll up, envelope-style. Store the blintzes seam-side down. At this point, you can refrigerate the blinzes for up to 2 days, until you're ready to serve them.

To finish, in a large, preferably nonstick skillet, heat the butter mixed with vegetable oil until it foams. Lightly brown the blintzes, cooking seam-side down, then turning them over to brown on the second side. Serve hot with cold sour cream as a topping.

Ricotta Cheese Soufflé Pancakes

Almost as good as blintzes are these light and airy ricotta cheese soufflé pancakes, which I developed for the opening menu at Azalea Restaurant at the Omni Hotel at Independence Park. The pancakes get their ethereal texture from ricotta and from egg whites beaten to a meringue and folded in at the last minute. Grated nutmeg and lemon zest give them a characteristic Italian flavor in honor of Philadelphia's large Italian community, while vanilla is added just because it tastes so good. Serve the pancakes with sugared berries and/or pure maple syrup.

SERVES 8

1/2 pound whole-milk ricotta cheese
1/4 pound (1 stick) unsalted butter, melted and cooled
5 eggs, separated
Scrapings of 1 vanilla bean, or 1 teaspoon vanilla extract
1 teaspoon freshly grated nutmeg
Grated zest of 2 lemons
2 ounces (1/2 cup) all-purpose flour
2 tablespoons granulated sugar
Canola oil + unsalted butter, for cooking
Pure maple syrup, for serving
Berries mixed with granulated sugar, for garnish

Drain the ricotta in a sieve for several hours, or up to overnight, to remove any excess liquid.

Purée the drained ricotta in a food processor until smooth and shiny. Add the butter, egg yolks, vanilla, nutmeg, and lemon zest and process briefly to combine. Remove the mixture from the processor and fold in the flour.

In a separate, clean bowl, beat the egg whites until soft and fluffy, then beat in the sugar. Continue beating until firm and glossy. Fold the egg white mixture into the ricotta batter by thirds

Heat a griddle or large, preferably nonstick skillet, with a little oil and butter. Ladle in the batter to make medium-sized pancakes, and cook over moderately high heat until lightly browned on the bottom and bubbles show all around the outsides of the top. Turn over and brown lightly for 1 to 2 minutes longer, or until set in the middle. Keep warm in a 200°F. while preparing the remaining pancakes.

Serve immediately on heated plates, accompanied with warmed pure maple syrup and sugared berries.

Sicilian Cassata

The classic Sicilian cassata *is an elaborate layered cake that originates in the Arabic* qas'ah, *a word that refers to the terra-cotta bowl originally used to shape the cake. Try to find high-quality naturally colored, undyed candied fruit, which is usually available during the winter holiday baking season. If you don't care for or can't find candied fruits like glacé cherries, candied citron, and orange rind, other possibilities are dried pineapple, mango, papaya, cherries, and raisins, all found in many natural foods stores. You should start this cake two days before you wish to serve it, since there are a few steps that require some time. The dried fruits need to be soaked in liqueur a day ahead so they get plump and soft. Also, the cake needs to set up in the refrigerator overnight.*

MAKES 1 LARGE TERRINE, TO SERVE 16

Savoy Cake

8 eggs, separated

5 eggs, left whole

1 tablespoon vanilla extract

Grated zest of 1 orange

1 cup + 1/4 cup granulated sugar

1/2 pound (2 cups) pastry flour

Pinch of kosher salt

Preheat the oven to 375°F. Prepare an 18 x 12-inch half sheet pan or two 17 x 12-inch jelly roll pans by lining them with parchment paper.

In the bowl of an electric mixer, using the paddle attachment, beat together the 8 egg yolks, whole eggs, vanilla, and orange zest for 10 minutes. Add 1 cup of sugar and beat again until light and fluffy. Sift the flour and salt together and fold into the egg mixture.

In a separate, clean bowl, beat the egg whites until light and fluffy, and then sprinkle in the remaining 1/4 cup sugar and beat again until firm and glossy. Fold the meringue into the yolk mixture by thirds. Spread the batter into the prepared pan(s) and bake for 20 minutes, or until the cake is springy and lightly browned. Cool before removing it from pan. If the cake is thick, split it horizontally into 2 thin layers when it is cool.

Ricotta Filling

1/2 cup diced candied fruits

2 tablespoons Strega liqueur, substitute rum or brandy

1 1/4 pounds fresh whole-milk ricotta, drained lightly

2 tablespoons heavy cream

6 tablespoons granulated sugar

1/2 cup chopped semisweet or bittersweet chocolate

1/2 cup coarsely chopped pistachios

Soak the fruits in the liqueur until soft and plump, overnight if possible. Place the ricotta in the bowl of a food processor and process until smooth. Pour out into a bowl and add the heavy cream, sugar, and any soaking juices from the fruits. Do not overbeat. Fold in the soaked candied fruit, the chocolate, and the pistachios and reserve in the refrigerator.

Assembly

1 cup granulated sugar

1/2 cup liqueur of choice: Strega, Cointreau, or gold rum

Savoy cake, split if thick

Ricotta Filling

829

In a small pot, bring the sugar and 1 cup of water to the boil. When the liquid is clear, remove it from the heat and stir in the liqueur, and set aside.

Line a large terrine mold or loaf pan with plastic wrap. Remove and discard any hardened crusts from the cake.

Cut 1 layer of cake into a piece large enough to cover the bottom and sides of the terrine. Cut the remaining cake into pieces the same size as the terrine mold. Fit the large layer of cake into the bottom of the terrine and up the sides of the mold. Moisten by brushing with the sugar and liqueur syrup. Spread one-third of the Ricotta Filling over top and cover with another strip of cake. Continue the layers, finishing with a layer of moistened cake. Chill the cassata overnight so that it sets up.

Mocha Icing and Finishing the Cassata

12 ounces semisweet chocolate, chopped into bits

$3/4$ cup espresso (or strong black coffee)

$1/2$ pound (2 sticks) unsalted butter, chilled
and cut into bits

Melt the chocolate and coffee together in the microwave. Beat in the chilled butter bits until the mixture is completely smooth. Chill until it is firm enough to spread, but still glossy, and reserve at room temperature.

Unmold the cassata, and then spread with the icing, piping rosettes along the center, if desired. Chill at least 1 hour to set the icing, and then slice using a knife that has been dipped in hot water and wiped dry in between each cut. Serve the cassata at room temperature.

830

SALMON
WILD & FARMED

SALMON
WILD & FARMED

I had my first unforgettable taste of wild salmon in 1962, the year of the World's Fair, when I spent a summer living in Seattle. We took a trip out to Tillicum Village on Blake Island in Puget Sound, one of the first facilities to recreate a Native American-style potlatch for the public. There, I enjoyed a meal under the stars, starring the wonderful wild salmon cooked on alderwood planks. This meal has remained my benchmark for salmon.

The potlatch was a big feast and celebration, usually held in the winter months by coastal Native American groups on the West Coast of North America from Alaska to Washington State. You can still visit Blake Island, thought to be the old hunting grounds of the tribe of Chief Seeahth (Seattle) and experience the traditional method of cooking salmon on alderwood planks alongside an open fire.

Since the advent of farm-raised salmon in the mid-1980s, which has come to dominate the market, I rarely get excited about the once anticipated spring-summer salmon season. However, true wild salmon is now increasingly being served in restaurants and sold in specialty markets. Food aficionados who have found out how good wild salmon tastes are now searching them out in the market, choosing fish by variety name, like King salmon or Sockeye, or by provenance, like Copper River or Colombia River.

Each variety of salmon has a different look, flavor, and texture, and the fun is in trying them all and deciding which one is your own particular favorite. Several years ago, I tasted a huge gorgeous Alaska King salmon baked in a salt crust prepared by the late legendary chef, Jean-Louis Palladin. No one I know would have an oven large enough to bake this fish whole, but it was a taste well worth remembering.

True salmon, *Salmo salar* in Latin, all swim in the temperate or cold waters of the Northern Hemisphere. Members of two different families of the same fish, salmon have a long history in both the Atlantic and Pacific Oceans. Salmon is an anadromous fish, spawning in fresh water but spending much of its life at sea. These fish get their color from eating a crustacean—krill—from, which they draw a pigment that makes them pink to red. (Of course, no one has told me where the crustaceans get their color.)

The extraordinary life cycle of the salmon has brought it up against man-made obstacles in the last two centuries, and in many places, it has tragically disappeared. The salmon's sensitivity to environmental changes and dependence upon both fresh and saltwater habitats has made it particularly vulnerable. Numbers have dropped greatly in the past fifty years, and the number of adult fish returning to North American rivers is estimated to have dropped from approximately 200,000 to only 80,000.

In both the Atlantic and the Pacific, the salmon has generated a rich cultural heritage, based on recreational fishing and on the mystique of the fish itself. Flashing silver as it jumps a waterfall, the salmon is a symbol of wildness and healthy river systems, and of the importance of looking at a species in a truly international way. The wild Atlantic salmon is a world traveler with a historic range on both shores of the North Atlantic Ocean from Canada to Connecticut in North America, and from Russia's White Sea to Portugal on the European coast. Many runs are now reduced or extinct, but limited quantities of Atlantic salmon can still be found in the rivers of the British Isles, Scandinavia, Russia, France, Spain, Canada, and the United States. The wild Pacific salmon ranges from Alaska as far south as California.

Some Atlantic salmon groups never go to sea, inhabiting lake and river systems in areas bordering the North Atlantic. These smaller fish migrate between deep-lake feeding areas and spawning grounds along shorelines or in tributaries. A close relation of the salmon is the sea or salmon trout, *Salmo trutta*. The same species includes not only the sea trout, which behave like salmon, but also the brown trout of rivers, which are different in both behavior and flavor.

The Pacific wild salmon season starts in June with large Kings, followed by brilliant orange-red Sockeyes through August and smaller Coho's into September. The quality of a wild salmon is directly related to the length of its native river. The longer it takes a salmon to reach its spawning grounds, the higher its oil content and the better its flavor.

While you can count on finding farm-raised salmon year-round in your local fish market, be sure to seek out a true seasonal specialty: wild salmon, which in the United States is almost invariably from the Pacific. When preparing a prime wild salmon, it's best to go as simple as possible; pan-searing, broiling, or grilling the fish and serving it with a little herb butter or good olive oil and a wedge of lemon or lime.

833

CHOOSING AND STORING SALMON

Whether you're serving wild or farmed salmon, the key is to get the freshest, firmest fish possible with lively looking bright eyes. While salmon is an oily fish, it should smell briny, not "fishy." Keep the fish cold as can be, and serve it within two days of purchase. If the weather is hot, I ask my fishmonger to give me a package of crushed ice to keep the fish cold on the trip home. When I refrigerate the fish, I top it with a package of "jelly ice" placed inside a zip-top plastic bag to keep it at that extra-cold temperature (close to 32°F.) that maintains the fish at its best.

Removing Pin Bones

Be sure to remove the pin bones from the salmon. These slender bones stick up into the flesh, one bone to each muscle layer, and run from the head to about one-third of the way toward the tail. The bones nearer the head are larger and stiffer. If you're lucky, your fishmonger or market may remove the pin-bones. If not, invest in a special pair of stainless steel fish pliers to make an easy job of picking out the bones. Or, use a pair of ordinary needle-nose pliers. Your fingers will also do the job, although more bones will tend to break rather than come out clean and whole (*see* About Pin Bones, page 419, for more information).

The Five Types of Pacific Salmon

Sockeye Salmon: The sockeye salmon, whose name is a mistranslation of the Native American word *suk-kegh*, which means red fish, is about 34 inches long. At spawning time, the male is bright red and has developed a hooked lower jaw and a somewhat humped back. Its deep red, firm flesh is incredibly beautiful, though its lean meat and pronounced flavor make it less versatile.

Chinook or King Salmon: The Chinook, also called King salmon, may be up to 51 inches long and has dark spots on its fins and its back. This richly flavored salmon is fatty enough not to get dried out in cooking, and its milder flavor is appealing to a great many people.

Chum Salmon: Chum salmon can be up to 38 inches long. It is also known as dog salmon because the males have greatly enlarged, canine-like teeth at spawning time. With its light color and low fat content, this salmon is not as sought after, though it does well for smoking.

Coho or Silver Salmon: Coho or silver salmon, up to 35 inches long, is a deep-bodied fish with some black spots on its fins. It has light to deep pink flesh and is quite succulent. This same salmon has been introduced to some lakes and is being farm-raised in small sizes for individual portions.

Humpback or Pink Salmon: Humpback or pink salmon, up to 30 inches long, are the smallest of the fall-spawning Pacific salmon species. Valued on the Asian side of the North Pacific, it is commonly used for canning. Its mild meat is relatively lean, so it can be on the dry side if overcooked.

Moroccan Cured Salmon

This version of Scandinavian gravlax, or cured salmon, has become all the rage in restaurants and at catered events along with pastrami-cured salmon. How this traditional dish of Northern Europe—where native wild salmon are cured with a mixture of salt, sugar, and dill—became transformed into this version involving a whole slew of spices is something of a mystery, though I do know that New York celeb-chef David Burke is given credit for coming up with the pastrami cure for salmon. Perhaps he had a Jewish clientele who he felt would respond to the flavors of pastrami? From there, it was only a matter of time until we had Moroccan cured salmon and now, Tequila-Cilantro Salmon, and others. Maybe I'll try Ethiopian Berberé cured salmon using the recipe for the spice mixture in my Field Guide to Herbs & Spices *next. Serve the salmon on crostini spread with a thin layer of Olivada, or on buttered toasts.*

SERVES ABOUT 12

1 teaspoon whole allspice berries

1 (3-inch) stick cinnamon, crushed

2 teaspoons black peppercorns

20 threads saffron

2 teaspoons ground cardamom

2 teaspoons ground ginger

2 tablespoons sweet red paprika

2 teaspoons turmeric

2 teaspoons ground nutmeg

1 (2½- to 3-pound) side of wild salmon, cut in 2 (or 2 small sides of salmon or Coho salmon fillets) with skin on

½ cup kosher salt

½ cup light brown sugar, packed

Heat a small skillet, preferably uncoated steel or cast-iron, without any oil, until quite hot. Add the allspice berries, cinnamon, and black peppercorns and toast, shaking occasionally until the spices are lightly browned and fragrant. (Watch the spices carefully at this point; you don't want blackened, bitter spices.) Add the saffron threads and toast 1 minute longer. Remove from the pan and stir in the cardamom, ginger, paprika, turmeric, and nutmeg. Cool to room temperature and then grind in a small coffee grinder, preferably reserved for spices. Alternatively, crush the seeds using a mortar and pestle.

To prepare the salmon: remove the line of pin bones running from the head end to halfway toward the tail using needle-nosed pliers (*see* About Pin Bones, page 419, and Removing Pin Bones, page 833, for directions). Combine the spice mixture, salt and brown sugar. Spread the mixture on the flesh side of the salmon pieces. Cover one piece of salmon with the other, end to end, flesh sides together.

Enclose the salmon with cheesecloth and place cans on top to weight. Place on a wire rack with a pan underneath to collect the juices. Leave the salmon for 24 hours, then turn over and reweigh, leaving for another 24 hours. Drain off any excess liquid that accumulates and discard. Leave the salmon to cure fully, at least 3 days or until firm to the touch. The salmon will keep about 5 days in the refrigerator. Slice thinly to serve.

835

Salmon in Cartoccio with Summer Vegetables

While this dish does take a bit of time and organization to prepare, once all the fish and vegetables are enclosed in their parchment paper envelopes, all you need to do is slip them in a hot oven to bake, then serve. Everything is already inside the packets—the fish, the vegetables, potatoes, and seasonings—making it easy for you, the host. You'll need 6 sheets of parchment paper, preferably heavy-duty (the more expensive kind, also called vegetable parchment) or 6 large squares of heavy-duty aluminum foil.

SERVES 6

Tarragon–Chive Pesto

1 bunch tarragon, leaves picked

1 bunch chives, thinly sliced

$1/2$ bunch Italian parsley, leaves picked

Grated zest of 1 lemon

1 cup extra-virgin olive oil

1 tablespoon kosher salt

$1/2$ teaspoon freshly ground black pepper

$1/4$ cup crushed ice

Place all the pesto ingredients in the jar of a blender, including the crushed ice, and blend all until a smooth, green, loose paste results. (The ice keeps the mixture cool so it maintains its emerald-green color.) If desired, transfer to a plastic squeeze bottle with large tip opening, or else transfer to a measuring cup with a pouring spout, and reserve.

Assembly

3 to 4 gold and/or pink beets, trimmed

4 yellow potatoes, cut into $1/2$-inch-thick slices (unpeeled)

1 bunch broccolini, trimmed and cut into 2-inch lengths

2 small yellow squash, sliced into $3/8$-inch-thick slices

Kernels cut from 2 ears corn

1 pint mixed cherry tomatoes, halved

6 sheets parchment paper, cut into squares, folded into triangles, with 2 inches off tips of triangle shapes cut away, opened into square shape

6 (8-ounce) salmon fillets, cut on the bias, into slices about 1 inch thick

Kosher salt and freshly ground black pepper to taste

2 lemons, pared and thinly sliced, all pits removed

Tarragon-Chive Pesto, in a squeeze bottle

Dry white vermouth, in a squeeze bottle

Bring a medium pot of salted water to the boil. Add the beets and simmer until tender when pierced, about 20 minutes depending on their size and age. Drain, cool, and rub off the peels. Cut into wedges and reserve.

Meanwhile, bring a second pot of salted water to the boil. Boil the potatoes until they are barely cooked through and still firm in the middle. Scoop from the water and cool. To the same water, add the broccolini and blanch for about 2 minutes, or until it is brilliant green. Scoop from water and run under cold water. To the same boiling water, add the yellow squash and blanch for 1 minute, scoop from the water and cool.

To assemble, have ready the beet wedges, potatoes, broccolini, yellow squash, corn, and cherry tomatoes. Arrange the parchment paper sheets on a work counter. Place 1 salmon fillet on each sheet, just forward of the fold line. Sprinkle with salt and pepper. Arrange 2 to 3 lemon slices over top. Squeeze about 3 tablespoons of the Tarragon-Chive Pesto over top. Arrange about 4 potato slices on each portion. Top with about $1/2$ cup yellow squash slices, $1/4$ cup of cut broccolini spears, about 12 cherry tomato halves, 3 beet wedges and finally, top with about $1/4$ cup of corn kernels. Sprinkle all with salt and pepper again and squeeze about 2 tablespoons more Tarragon-Chive Pesto over top.

Form paper packets by folding the paper over top of the fish so that both edges meet. Form pleated folds at the edge, tucking the folds under all around the outside edge of the paper packet to seal. Just before closing it up, pour $1/4$ cup vermouth into the opening. Fold until the packet is completely closed, tucking the finished edge underneath. Keep folding until the packet is completely closed, twisting the end and tucking it underneath. Alternatively, enclose the fish in heavy-duty aluminum foil packets. Although not as asthetically pleasing, the foil is easier to handle and less likely to leak.

When ready to cook, preheat the oven to 425°F. Arrange the packets on a metal baking pan (to catch any leaks) and bake for 12 to 15 minutes, or until the liquid inside boils vigorously and the paper puffs up. Serve the packets immediately on large dinner plates, allowing each person to cut open his or her own.

Pickled Salmon Salad

Growing up, I would attend synagogue every Saturday morning. Afterwards we would have a small kiddush, *with the blessing of the wine accompanied by pickled herring and egg* kichels, *light egg biscuits. I wanted to re-create the flavor of that herring here using salmon. The salmon cubes make a terrific* nosh *(a small snack) and are low in fat, unless, of course, you accompany them with cream-cheese-slathered bagels, or top them with sour cream. Once pickled, the salmon will keep quite well for at least 1 week, refrigerated.*

SERVES 8 TO 10

1 quart cider vinegar

3 cups water

$3/4$ cup granulated sugar

$1/4$ cup kosher salt

1 ($2^1/2$-to 3-pound) salmon fillet, skinned

$1/4$ cup pickling spice

12 bay leaves

4 white onions, sliced $1/4$ inch thick

Bring the vinegar, water, sugar, and salt to the boil. Let the mixture cool completely.

Remove the pin bones (and skin, if necessary) from the salmon and cut into 1-inch cubes (*see* About Pin Bones, page 419, and Removing Pin Bones, page 833, for directions). In a large, nonreactive bowl (such as glass, ceramic, or stainless steel), place a layer of salmon pieces, a sprinkling of pickling spice, some bay leaves, and a layer of onions, continuing until all ingredients are used. Pour the cooled marinade over fish. Cover and refrigerate for 3 to 4 days to develop the flavor. Serve as a *nosh* with cocktail picks.

Grilled Salmon in Grape Leaves with Tomato Jam

Wrapping salmon in grape leaves not only keeps it moist and juicy, but also imparts a delicate vineyard flavor. Grape leaves are sold in brine in jars and are available at most well-stocked supermarkets or at Greek or Middle Eastern groceries. The salmon packets can be assembled up to 1 day ahead of time and then either grilled or broiled. The sweetly aromatic tomato jam, with its edge of balsamic vinegar, accents the salmon. The tomato jam will keep quite well refrigerated for up to 3 weeks, or in the freezer. Serve it with grilled steak, chicken, or pork chops, or use it to top burgers. Serve the salmon on a bed of steamed pearl barley or whole wheat couscous, if desired.

838

SERVES 4

Salmon in Grape Leaves

Juice of 2 lemons

$1/4$ cup finely chopped shallots

1 tablespoon finely chopped thyme

$1/4$ cup extra-virgin olive oil

Kosher salt and freshly ground black pepper to taste

4 (8-ounce) fillets of salmon, skinless

12 preserved grape leaves, soaked in water, rinsed and dried

Tomato Jam (recipe follows)

Combine the lemon juice, shallots, thyme, olive oil, and salt and pepper. Rub all over the salmon and allow to marinate for 2 hours, refrigerated. Arrange the grape leaves, overlapping and rib-side up to form a rectangle about 10 x 8 inches.

Lay 1 salmon fillet in the middle, flesh-side down, fold the leaves up to enclose it in a neat package, and press to seal. Repeat with the remaining grape leaves and salmon fillets.

When ready to serve, preheat a grill or broiler to hot. Grill or broil the salmon packets, starting with the seam-side down, for about 10 minutes, or until the salmon feels firm inside the packets. Serve immediately, topped with spoonfuls of the tomato jam.

Tomato Jam

$1/4$ cup extra-virgin olive oil

1 tablespoon chopped garlic

2 tablespoons chopped ginger

$1/4$ cup Balsamic vinegar

1 (28-ounce) can diced tomatoes

$1/4$ cup dark brown sugar, packed

2 tablespoons honey

1 teaspoon ground cinnamon

1 teaspoon ground cumin, preferably toasted

$1/2$ teaspoon ground allspice

Kosher salt, cayenne pepper, and freshly ground black pepper to taste

Combine the olive oil, garlic, and ginger in a medium, heavy-bottomed, nonreactive saucepan. Cook together until softened, about 5 minutes, stirring often. Add the vinegar and cook until the liquid is syrupy, about 5 minutes. Add the tomatoes, brown sugar, honey, cinnamon, cumin, and allspice. Season to taste with salt, cayenne, and black pepper and cook together very slowly for 1 hour, or until the tomato juices have evaporated and the sauces is thickened, stirring occasionally. Cool the jam before storing in the refrigerator for up to two weeks.

Salmon Loaf with Cucumber–Dill Sauce

Often made with canned salmon back when fresh salmon was still a rare and expensive indulgence, this salmon loaf is even better made with the fresh salmon sold in every supermarket today. If your market sells the tail sections for less money, buy them, because you'll be baking and then flaking the salmon before using it anyway. Note that the loaf will also work well made with the high-quality canned red salmon that comes from Alaska. For a perfect complement, serve this with the Cucumber-Dill Sauce on page 361. For a fancier presentation, prepare 8 small (8-ounce) molds by brushing with melted butter and then fill with the salmon mixture and bake for about 30 minutes, or until barely set in the middle. Any leftovers reheat very well in the microwave.

SERVES 8

1¹/₂ pounds salmon fillet

Kosher salt and freshly ground black pepper to taste

4 eggs

4 tablespoons + 2 tablespoons unsalted butter, melted

1 tablespoon Worcestershire sauce

Juice and grated zest of 2 lemons

¹/₄ cup chopped dill

2 teaspoons paprika

³/₄ cup soft breadcrumbs

¹/₂ cup sour cream

1 bunch scallions, thinly sliced

1 red bell pepper, finely diced

1 small fennel bulb, finely diced

Preheat the oven to 350°F. Season the salmon with salt and pepper to taste, place in a baking dish, cover with foil and bake for about 15 minutes, or until it is barely cooked. Remove from the oven and cool. When cool enough to handle, flake the salmon into large chunks, discarding skin, any bones, and dark flesh.

Meanwhile, whisk together the eggs, 4 tablespoons of the butter, the Worcestershire sauce, lemon juice and zest, dill, and paprika. Add the breadcrumbs, sour cream, scallions, red pepper, and fennel and reserve. The mixture should be soupy. Stir in the salmon flakes and reserve.

Brush an 8-cup loaf pan with the remaining 2 tablespoons of melted butter. Fill with the salmon mixture. Bake for 40 minutes at 350°F., or until set in the middle and the loaf has started to come away from the sides of the pan. Remove the loaf from the oven, cool, and then unmold and slice. Serve with Cucumber-Dill Sauce (*see page 361*), or else accompany by wedges of lemon.

839

SAUSAGE

SAUSAGE

Full of flavor, tender, quick-cooking, and inexpensive, sausage is as popular today as it was in old times, if not more so. Sausage-making originated as a way of preserving small bits and pieces of meat, especially from the pig slaughtered annually in many parts of Europe. The word *sausage* derives from the Latin word *salsus*, which means *salted* or *preserved*, and probably first referred to all kinds of preserved meats.

Sausages are made from ground meat mixed with fat, salt, and other seasonings depending upon where in the world they are made. The ratio is generally seventy percent lean to thirty percent fat. Different regions produce their own distinctive types of sausage, both fresh and dry, influenced by the availability of ingredients as well as the climate. In parts of the world with periods of cold climate, such as northern Europe, people were able to keep their sausage fresh without refrigeration during the cold months. They developed the smoking process to help preserve the meat during the warmer months. In the hotter climates of southern Europe, dry-cured fermented sausage was developed that did not need to be kept cold. This dry sausage developed along with the discovery of new spices, which helped to enhance, flavor, and preserve the meat. In fact, herbs, spices, and seasoning mixes are essential to the art of sausage-making.

Although sausages are made from poultry, game, beef, fish, and seafood, the vast majority are made from pork.

Pork is naturally suited to sausage-making because it is easy to raise in the farmyard, has an abundance of fat and soft-textured meat, and has a rounded, highly adaptable flavor. Beef makes a very hard, dense sausage, so it is often mixed with pork or made into cooked sausage like kosher salami. Lamb makes a very gamey-tasting sausage, because the fat carries all its strong flavor, which is intensified in the sausage-making process. Veal makes a good, but expensive sausage and is used in such delicate specialties as French *boudin blanc* and German *weisswurst*.

Almost three thousand years ago in Greece, the sausage peddler made use of all that was left after the prime meat was removed by the butchers. Perhaps the original fast food, sausages were peddled in the aisles to be eaten as snacks during Greek theater presentations. In the second century CE, the cooked-meat shops of Alexandria, Egypt, specialized in sausages and offal. Similarly, in France, the *charcutiers* who organized into a guild in the fifteenth century were first allowed to sell only cooked pork and raw pork fat.

During the years of the Roman Empire, two types of sausages came into being that still survive, including *salsicia*, from which many modern names, including the English *sausage*, are derived. A recipe for *lucanica* was recorded by the Roman epicure Apicius and was said to be invented by the Lucanians, who lived in southern Italy at the time of the Greek settlement and the Roman Republic. Modern descendents include Portuguese *linguica*, Spanish *longaniza*, Italian *luganega*, and Greek *loukanika*, which are made in long, thin rings and stuffed into lamb castings and sold fresh by the length.

With the advent of Christianity, sausages became a problem because of their association with pagan phallic rites in an inevitable association of like form. The Roman Emperor Constantine banned sausages in 320 CE because of this link to pagan festivals, although the ban was eventually lifted. Some of the earliest types of sausages were blood sausages made from the fast-spoiling blood of animals, forbidden in the Old Testament and in the early Church. Today, these sausages are popular as *boudin noir* in Frances, *morcilla* in Spain, and *boudin rouge* in Lousiana. Sausages were common in medieval Europe but were and still are little used in the Arab world, partly because the pig, forbidden to Jews and Muslims, is so well-suited to sausage, with every part of the animal except the "oink" usable.

In recent years, sausages have suddenly become suitable for the most discerning person's table, with chefs experimenting with all sorts of never-before-tasted combinations such as Burmese chicken, Cajun alligator, roasted red pepper with corn, spinach and feta, and Thai sausage with coconut and lemongrass—this last is actually a traditional sausage. Turkey and chicken sausages abound, and sausages go upscale with additions of truffle and porcini mushrooms. Celeb-chefs, especially in California, have taken to making their own soppressata, salami, and every other kind of *salumi* (cured meat), especially those in the vast Italian repertoire.

Sausage Casings

At its simplest, sausage is a chopped-meat mixture stuffed into a tubular casing, originally made from the cleaned and then salted intestines (beef for large sausages like mortadella, pork for medium sausages like salami, and sheep for small sausages like chipolata), although bladder is used for Scottish haggis and pig's trotter for zampone. Some of today's artificial sausage casings are of good quality and are made from natural collagen; others are made from manufactured substances and are overly thick and tough. The artisanal sausages made by specialty companies and chefs are generally in natural casings, which give flavor and body to the sausage and keep them from sticking in the pan when browning.

Preparing Fresh and Cured Sausage

Preparing fresh sausage is relatively simple: the meat is cut up, seasoned, and ground—usually with ice to provide moisture and keep the meat cold. Preparing cured sausage is more complex because it must first be salted, then dried (and sometimes smoked). It depends on controlled lactic-acid fermentation to achieve particular results. Potassium nitrate (saltpeter) is added to keep the meat an attractive pink color (rather than brown or gray) and also inhibit the growth of dangerous bacteria. Once the cured sausage has been properly fermented and dried, it may develop a harmless white "bloom" made of yeast cells on the outside.

BASICS TYPES OF SAUSAGE

There are thousands of different types of sausages worldwide (1,000 in Germany alone!), but they fit into three main categories: *fresh sausages* (like Italian *salsiccia* and American breakfast link sausages) that must be cooked; *cured sausages* that are meant for long storage and are eaten without cooking (such as Italian and Hungarian salami, and German *landjaeger*); and *cooked sausages* that are either meant to be eaten cold (Italian mortadella and American bologna) or further cooked and eaten hot (German frankfurters and bratwurst). Broadly speaking, sausages for cooking and eating hot are mostly found in Northern countries (bockwurst, boudin blanc, haggis). Sausages that are cured and air-dried without cooking (*saucisson sec*, pepperoni, and soppressata) are traditional to areas with cool, dry wind. Many types of sausages are also smoked, especially those of German origin (*bierwurst* and *braunschweiger*).

Chiles Rellenos with Cheese, Corn, and Chorizo

I couldn't resist a second variation of chiles rellenos in this book (see Shrimp Chiles Rellenos on page 705). Although classically, the chiles are roasted, peeled, cleaned, stuffed, dipped in an egg batter, fried, and then finally simmered in a spicy tomato sauce, here I simply bake the roasted stuffed chiles for a deliciously spicy dish that's easy to make. Here the chiles are stuffed with a mixture of browned Mexican chorizo sausage, crunchy sweet corn kernels, and cheese, eggs, and breadcrumbs to bring it all together. If you don't eat pork, substitute turkey chorizo. When I prepared this dish for an audience of 150 people, it was gone before I could get a bite myself. If you don't like hot chiles, substitute milder Anaheims or even Italian frying peppers or cubanelles, which are similar in shape and texture.

SERVES 4 TO 6

8 Poblano chiles (or substitute Anaheims)

$1/2$ pound fresh chorizo sausage

4 eggs

1 cup fresh soft breadcrumbs

$1/2$ pound provolone cheese, shredded

$1/2$ pound Monterey Jack cheese, shredded

2 ears corn, kernels cut off (or substitute 2 cups frozen corn kernels)

$1/4$ cup chopped cilantro

3 cups Mexican Tomato Sauce with Allspice (*see* page 897)

Grill the chiles over an open flame until the skins are blackened. Cool, and rub off the skins. Cut a slit lengthwise in each pepper and pull out and discard the seeds and connective tissue. Using scissors or a sharp paring knife, slit the sausage casing lengthwise. Remove the casing and discard. Slice the chorizo and then brown well in a small pan. Drain off the excess fat and reserve the chorizo.

Preheat the oven to 400°F. Combine the eggs and breadcrumbs, then stir in both cheeses, the corn kernels, cilantro, and chorizo. Open up the peppers and stuff them with the cheese mixture. Press the edges of the peppers back together to reform into a pepper shape.

Spoon the tomato sauce onto the bottom of a large ceramic or Pyrex baking dish. Arrange the stuffed poblanos over top. Bake for 25 minutes, or until the filling begins to ooze out of the peppers. Remove from the oven and cool slightly, so that the peppers firm up before serving.

Polish *Bigos*: Sauerkraut, Smoked Pork, and Sausage Hunter's Stew

Bigos is a multi-ingredient stew of meats and cabbage typical of Polish and Lithuanian cuisine that may be considered Poland's national dish. It is said to have been brought to Poland by Wladislaus II, a Lithuanian prince who became king of Poland in 1385. He is said to have served it to his hunting party guests. Metaphorically, bigos can also mean confusion or trouble in Polish, because it is a dish in which so many foods are mixed together. The original preserved cabbage dish that the German and Alsatian choucroute garni, bigos, and like dishes are based

on, is thought to have originated in Asia, may be related to Korean kimchi, and it was introduced in Europe by invading Asiatic tribes.

SERVES 10 TO 12

1 ounce dried porcini or other wild mushroom

¼ pound thick-sliced bacon

1 pound bottom round of beef, cut into 2-inch cubes

1 pound loin pork chops

1 pound pork spare ribs

1 pound smoked pork butt

2 pounds sauerkraut

1 head green cabbage, shredded

1 cup chopped onions

4 tablespoons all-purpose flour

1 pound smoked kielbasa, skinned and sliced

1 (28-ounce) can crushed tomatoes

Kosher salt and freshly ground black pepper to taste

Soak the porcini in warm water to cover until soft, about 20 minutes. Scoop out the mushrooms, chop finely, and reserve. Strain the mushroom liquor through a dampened paper towel laid into a sieve to remove any sand, and reserve.

In a large Dutch oven, cook the bacon over moderate heat until the fat has rendered out and the bacon is crisp. Remove and reserve the bacon. Pour off and reserve about half the fat, leaving half in the pot. Brown the beef, pork, and spareribs in the remaining fat. Transfer the browned meats and the smoked butt to a separate large pot with a lid, add 1 cup of water, cover, and simmer until tender.

Meanwhile, pour off all the fat from the first pot and

845

add the sauerkraut, cabbage, and 1 cup of water. Cover and cook until cabbage is tender, about 30 minutes. Crumble the reserved bacon and add to the sauerkraut.

As each type of meat is done, remove it from the pot and reserve: the pork chops should be ready after about 30 minutes, the pork butt and beef after 1 hour, and the spareribs after 1 1/2 hours. When the meat is cool, trim off any excess fat and bones and cut into small pieces. Add the meats to the sauerkraut.

In a third pan, heat the remaining bacon fat and fry the onions until they just brown, then stir in the flour. Cook together 3 to 4 minutes, then scrape the mixture into the pot with the sauerkraut mixture. Add the kielbasa and the mushrooms and their liquor to the sauerkraut mixture along with the tomatoes. Season with a small amount of salt and pepper (the sauerkraut and meats are quite salty). Bring the entire mixture to a boil, simmer 15 minutes, until the flavors come together, and serve immediately.

846

MORE ABOUT BIGOS

This stew combines fresh and fermented white cabbage (sauerkraut), tomato, different kinds of pork, including smoked and cured, or venison, and wild mushrooms. It may be seasoned with pepper, caraway, marjoram, allspice, dried or smoked plums, and red wine. It is usually served with bread to mop up the juices, and with dry white wine or vodka as an accompanying beverage. Like most stews, *bigos* get better when reheated and take well to freezing. Because sauerkraut is rich in vitamin C, *bigos* are a traditional part of the Polish winter diet, when other sources of the vitamin, like fresh fruits, are not available.

Choucroute Garni

Choucroute, a statement of Alsatian identity on a plate, is a hearty dish of sauerkraut laden with cured and boiled meats: for those with large appetites. Choucroute is the French translation of the German sauerkraut or sour cabbage. Though classically garnished with smoked sausage, ham knuckles, pork belly, and other such meats, it is also made in a seafood version with salmon sausage, cod, haddock, scallops, smoked herring, and even salmon caviar. The more ingredients you use, the more flavor the sauerkraut will soak up, so make it when you're expecting a large group. Juniper berries are a classic seasoning, while apples add sweetness and moisture.

SERVES 10 TO 12

2 pounds fresh sauerkraut

1 pound lean salt pork

2 cups finely chopped onions

1 cup carrot chunks

1 tablespoon finely chopped garlic

1/4 pound lard (or bacon fat)

2 apples, peeled, cored, and diced

2 cups chicken stock

1 bottle light beer

2 tablespoons finely chopped juniper berries

Kosher salt and freshly ground black pepper to taste

3 bay leaves

2 pounds uncooked smoked garlic type sausage (Kielbasa or saucisson)

10 to 12 slices smoked ham, cut 1/2 inch thick

Rinse the sauerkraut in fresh water, then squeeze it dry. Blanch the salt pork in the water for 15 minutes, then drain and reserve.

Preheat the oven to 325°F. Sauté the onions, carrots, and garlic in the lard until soft but not browned. Stir in the apple, then the sauerkraut. Cover and reduce the heat to low and braise the vegetables for 15 minutes. Then add the chicken stock, beer, and juniper berries. The stock should almost cover the sauerkraut. Season with salt and pepper and add the bay leaves. Bring to the boil on top of the stove, cover, and place in oven. Bake for 3 hours.

Prick the sausage all over with a fork, then add to the pot. Cook for 30 minutes more, then spread the ham slices over the sauerkraut. Cover and cook about 20 minutes longer. Serve in an individual casserole dish with a slice of ham and several slices of smoked sausage for each person.

JUNIPER BERRIES

Small, meaty, blue-black Juniper berries come from the evergreen juniper, *Juniperus communis*. Because these slow-growing berries must be hand-picked among needle-like leaves, they are relatively expensive. They are the only spice in the evergreen family, although we also eat pinenuts from the piñon pine. Soft and easily crushed, juniper berries have a nutty, slightly astringent flavor and a resinous aroma. Juniper complements game, smoked and cured meats, and even oily fish like salmon and bluefish. In Holland, where gin originated as *genever*, the liquor is boldly flavored with juniper.

Country Breakfast Sausage Patties

Sausages are just the thing for a leisurely weekend breakfast, and if you make your own, you can be sure that all the ingredients are fresh and no preservatives or chemicals have been used. This recipe is easy to make, because the sausages don't have to be stuffed into casings. You roll up the mixture, freeze it until firm, and then cut slices ready for the pan. Serve with pancakes (see the Ricotta Cheese Soufflé Pancakes on page 828 or the Blueberry Buttermilk Pancakes on page 137), fried or scrambled eggs, and/or French toast. Ask the butcher to double-grind the pork so it is extra-smooth and fine and the fat and lean are mixed well together.

SERVES 8   847

1/2 cup chopped onions

1 tablespoon chopped garlic

2 tablespoons each: chopped fresh sage, thyme, marjoram, and Italian parsley

1 1/2 teaspoons chili powder

1/2 teaspoon hot red pepper flakes

2 teaspoons kosher salt

2 pounds double-ground pork

Oil for the pan

Combine the onions, garlic, herbs (sage, thyme, marjoram, and parsley), chili powder, red pepper flakes, and salt in the bowl of a food processor. Process until a fine, but slightly chunky paste results. Transfer the seasoning mixture to a mixer bowl and add the pork. Beat about 5 minutes, using the paddle attachment, until the mixture is well-combined and fluffy. Fry up a small sample to check the seasonings. (You don't want to sample raw pork.)

Shape into a 2-inch diameter roll, rolled up in parchment paper, wax paper, or plastic wrap. Freeze until firm, for several hours, then unwrap and slice into $1/2$-inch-thick rounds. Or, freeze until ready to use, up to 1 month. Once sliced, reserve the sausage patties in the refrigerator until ready to use.

When ready to cook, heat a griddle or large skillet, preferably cast-iron or nonstick, and oil lightly. Add the sausage patties and brown well on both sides over moderate heat, cooking 3 to 4 minutes per side, until the patties are firm but still juicy.

Spaghetti with Meatballs in Gravy

This truly Italian-American dish doesn't exist in this form in Italy but rather developed here when immigrant Southern Italians found that meat was much more affordable than in the Old Country where it was reserved for the rich or holidays. The first Italian restaurants in America appeared about 100 years ago, and did not serve their spaghetti with meatballs; meatballs were added to satisfy the American hunger for red meat. It seems that people from Naples brought the first recipes for spaghetti and sauce to America. Late nineteenth- and early twentieth-century American cookbooks often refer to recipes for spaghetti and meat sauce as Neapolitan spaghetti, while recipes for spaghetti and meatballs begin to show up in American cookbooks during World War II to satisfy the tastes of returning American soldiers who had learned to love Italian food during the war.

SERVES 8 TO 10

1 cup chopped onion

1 rib celery, chopped

1 carrot, chopped

$1/2$ cup chopped mushrooms or mushroom stems

1 tablespoon chopped garlic

2 tablespoons olive oil

1 pound ground beef

$1/2$ pound each: hot and sweet Italian sausage, removed from casing

2 eggs

$1/4$ cup breadcrumbs

$1/2$ cup grated Romano cheese

1 tablespoon chopped marjoram

2 teaspoons finely chopped rosemary

2 tablespoons chopped Italian parsley

Kosher salt and freshly ground black pepper to taste

4 cups Marinara Sauce (*see* page 895)

Preheat the oven to 400°F. Grind the onion, celery, carrot, mushrooms, and garlic in a processor to fine chunks. Sauté in the olive oil until softened but not browned. Cool and then chill and reserve.

Place the beef and sausage meat in the bowl of a mixer. Add the chilled vegetable mix, the eggs, breadcrumbs, cheese, marjoram, rosemary, and parsley, and season with salt and pepper. Fry up a small sample to check seasonings. (You don't want to sample raw pork sausage.)

Form into walnut-sized meatballs using a disher (ice cream scoop) if desired. Arrange the meatballs in a single layer on a metal baking pan. Bake for 20 minutes, turning once, or until the meatballs are well browned on all sides. Remove the meatballs from the pan and simmer in marinara sauce for 30 minutes.

SPAGHETTI AND TOMATO SAUCE IN NAPLES

Because tomatoes originated in the New World, it was not until Spanish explorers brought them back to Europe that tomato sauce was introduced to Italy in the eighteenth century. Naples, at the time, was ruled by the Spanish. The first tomato sauce recipe for pasta appears in the enormously influential Neapolitan cookbook, *Cucina teorico pratica*, written by Ippolito Cavalcanti in 1839. Spaghetti was first produced on a large scale in Naples about 1800, made by extruding the dough using a wooden screw press, and the long strings were hung out like laundry to dry in the sun. The dough was kneaded by hand until 1830, when a mechanical kneading trough was invented. Bringing the two elements together, spaghetti with meat in tomato sauce most likely originated in Naples.

Thirteen–Layer Neapolitan Meat Lasagna

This over-the-top Neapolitan-style lasagna may overflow in your pan unless you use a deep, specially made lasagna pan. Thirteen lucky layers bulge with sausages, meatballs, ricotta, mozzarella, hard-cooked eggs, sauce, pancetta, and of course, lasagna noodles. Because lasagne requires a baking oven, which during most of Italian history were found only in the kitchens of the wealthy, the dish was considered to be a lavish one. While this is not a dish to make on the spur of the moment, it can be made ahead and will feed a large crowd of very happy people, pleasing the kids as much as the grown-ups.

SERVES 12

Meat Layer

$1/2$ cup + $1/2$ cup extra-virgin olive oil

2 red onions, finely diced

2 tablespoons minced garlic

$1/2$ pound pancetta, diced

Kosher salt and freshly ground black pepper to taste

$1^1/2$ cups red wine

2 (28-ounce) cans chopped plum tomatoes

$3/4$ pound ground beef

$1/2$ cup grated Romano-Parmigiano

2 eggs

1 tablespoon garlic

1 cup chopped parsley

$1/2$ cup all-purpose flour

$1/2$ pound each: Italian hot and sweet sausage, removed from the casing

In a large Dutch oven, heat $1/2$ cup of the olive oil with the onions, garlic, and pancetta, cooking until the onions are wilted but not browned. Season with salt and pepper. Add the wine and cook until it has mostly evaporated, about 20 minutes, stirring occasionally. Add the tomatoes and simmer, covered, stirring occasionally, for 1 hour, or until the sauce has thickened enough for the oil to rise to the top.

Meanwhile, combine the ground beef, cheese, eggs, garlic, and parsley and form into 1-inch balls. Dust the meatballs with flour and brown well in a large skillet in the remaining $1/2$ cup olive oil. Remove the meatballs and reserve. In the same pan, brown the sausages well, breaking them up with a spoon as they brown. Coarsely chop the meatballs and sausage and add to the sauce.

Simmer for 1 hour until the sauce has thickened enough

849

for the oil to rise to the top. Strain the sauce, reserving both sauce and meats separately. Divide the sauce portion into two portions, one about one-third and one about two-thirds. Add the meats to the larger portion of the sauce, divide into two equal portions and reserve. Divide the smaller portion of the sauce and reserve. You should end up with a smaller portion of sauce divided in two and a larger portion of meat sauce divided in two.

Cheese Layer

1$\frac{1}{2}$ pounds ricotta

3 eggs

1 cup each: grated Parmigiano-Reggiano or Grana Padano
   and grated Pecorino Romano cheese

$\frac{3}{4}$ cup chopped parsley

$\frac{3}{4}$ cup shredded basil

$\frac{1}{2}$ pound fresh mozzarella, finely diced

Combine the cheese layer ingredients and divide into 2 equal parts (for 2 layers). Reserve.

Finishing Lasagna

1 pound egg pasta sheets, cut to fit or ready-to-bake
   lasagna sheets

6 hard-cooked eggs, roughly chopped
   (eggs cooked partially, about 6 minutes)

$\frac{1}{2}$ cup each grated Parmigiano-Reggiano or Grana Padano
   and grated Pecorino Romano cheese

$\frac{1}{2}$ pound fresh mozzarella, finely diced

Preheat the oven to 350°F. In a large lasagna pan or a rectangular roasting pan, layer as follows: a layer of plain sauce, a layer of pasta sheets, half the meat sauce, half the chopped eggs, a layer of pasta sheets, the cheese layer, a layer of pasta sheets, the second half of the meat sauce, half the chopped eggs, a layer of pasta sheets, a layer of the plain sauce, and finally the mozzarella and grated cheese.

Bake the lasagna for 1 hour, or until the top is browned and crispy on the edges and the filling is bubbling hot inside. Remove from the oven and allow the lasagna to rest at room temperature for 20 minutes to set up before cutting into 12 or more serving portions. Serve with any remaining plain tomato sauce.

THE ORIGINS OF LASAGNA

Surprisingly *lasagne* (plural for *lasagna*) were probably the earliest forms of pasta. Its remote ancestor may have been the Greek *laganon*, which was a flat baked cake, rather than a boiled noodle. In classical Rome, the *laganon* was cut into strips and became known as *lagani* (plural). Cicero (first century CE) was known to have been particularly fond of lagani. So was the Roman poet Horace, of the same century. He cited them as an example of peasant's food while boasting of his simple way of life. In earlier times, the dough sheets were laid out to harden in the hot sun and cut with simple rollers designed to create a curly, interlocking edge. The dough was interleaved with a savory mixture and baked in the oven. Medieval lasagnas were typically creamy, sweet, and layered with cheese, and to be eaten during Lent. Something more like modern lasagne had appeared in Italy by the thirteenth century.

850

SCALLOPS

SCALLOPS

Like other chefs, I always loved serving scallops, because they are easy to prepare and make a beautiful presentation, especially if pan-seared until deep-brown and crusty on the outside and barely cooked on the inside. Because of their medium-bodied sea-flavor, more distinctive than crab and milder than mussels, clams, or shrimp, scallops are always a big seller. They match well with a whole array of foods and cuisines, from Chinese and Southeast Asian to French, Italian, Spanish, and Nuevo Latino, and lend themselves to the most creative presentations a chef can dream up.

The scallop is best known for its beautiful and distinctive scallop-edged and ridged pearly-white shell, featured in works by Titian, and especially the famed *Venus on the Half-Shell* by Botticelli that hangs in the Uffizi Gallery in Florence, Italy. The subtle beauty of this sea creature's shells has long been appreciated. Buildings in ancient Pompeii and Herculaneum were decorated with scallop-shell ornaments.

Marco Polo mentioned scallops as one of the seafoods sold in the marketplace in Hangchow, China, in the thirteenth century. Probably the most famous scallop dish is *Coquille St.-Jacques*, a name that sometimes just refers to the scallops themselves. The word *coquille* means *shell* in French and the lovely scallop shell was used as a symbol by pilgrims visiting the Spanish shrine of St. James (*St. Jacques* in

French) at Lourdes, France. The famous dish is a rich mixture of scallops in a lusciously creamy sauce baked in the scallop's own shell to a fine browned and bubbling glaze.

Scallops are bivalve mollusks living in their large, hard white shells marked by radiating ribs and concentric growth rings. Near the hinge, where the two valves (shells) meet, the sides flare out, forming small "wings." The entire scallop within the shell is edible, but it is the marshmallow-shaped adductor muscle, called the *nut*, that is eaten in the U.S. In Europe, the neon orange *coral* is also eaten. The adductor muscle is more developed in the scallop than in oysters and clams because scallops are active swimmers, gliding through the water by snapping their shells together.

Scallops range in size from the tiny, tender bay scallop to the larger, meatier deep-sea scallop. With the advent in 1965 of new equipment able to process deepwater mollusks, calico scallops became a major harvest off the shores of North Carolina and Florida. Scallops are primarily harvested by dredging and are shucked soon after capture. Because scallops cannot hold their shells closed, once they are out of the water, they lose moisture quickly and die, so they are shucked right on board the ships, placed in containers, and refrigerated.

The sea scallop, *Plactopecten magellanicus*, is the largest of the scallops, most commonly sized at between 20 and 40

852

to the pound, though much larger scallops are sold, at a much larger price. Scallops freeze well. Raw scallops will be creamy-white to beige in color and sometimes the females are tinted orange due to the algae they eat, though this does not affect their texture or flavor. Scallops have a distinct, sweet odor when they are fresh and the fresher the scallop, the more translucent it will be. Beware of bright white scallops; these have been treated with a chemical to bleach their color and make them soak up more liquid so they'll weigh more for sale.

There are many ways to prepare scallops, all of which call for cooking them quickly, as they shrink up and toughen easily. As soon as they lose their translucence and turn opaque, they are done. Sea scallops may be broiled, kabobed, stir-fried, baked, or steamed. If you plan to put them in a sauce, it's best to cook the scallops and the sauce separately and then combine them; otherwise, water will cook out of the scallops and make your sauce runny.

The only difficult thing about cooking sea scallops is getting high-quality fresh ones. They are one of the easiest seafoods to prepare from fresh, because all you need to do is remove the small hard muscle on the side of the scallop. If you have access to Nantucket bay scallops, in season in late fall, try them. They are exquisitely tender and sweet. If you can't find them fresh, ask your fishmonger for "dry-pack" scallops, which contain only natural, untreated scallops.

The texture of fresh raw scallop meat should be firm and smell pleasing and mild. A healthy scallop whose shell is open should close tightly when tapped. The season for fresh sea scallops and bay scallops runs from October through March, while fresh calico scallops are available from December through May.

Types of Scallops

Bay Scallops: The small bay scallop, Argopecten irradians, lives in bays and estuaries from New England to the Gulf of Mexico. Only about one-half inch in diameter, there are between fifty and ninety per pound. These soft, fleshy, and delicately mild, sweet scallops are enjoyed by even those who don't much care for seafood. These small scallops, harvested from Maine to the Carolinas, are often called "Nantucket" or "Cape Bay" scallops. Bay scallops are not as abundant as larger sea scallops and are usually more expensive. Bay scallops are known for their sweet flavor and delicate texture and because of their small size, are best suited for stir-frying, salads, stews, and casseroles.

Calico Scallops: Calico scallops are one of the smallest species available. Calicos are harvested primarily in the South Atlantic and Gulf of Mexico. Due to their small size, seventy-plus meats per pound, calicos are landed in the shell for dockside shucking. The heat treatment used for opening the shells causes the tips of calico scallops to appear white. Though more commonly available, they are not as highly regarded as bay scallops.

Pink and Spiny Scallops: The small and lovely Pink scallop, Chlamys rubida, and Spiny scallops, Chlamys hastata, are harvested off the coast of Washington and British Columbia. Similar in appearance, the pink scallop is about the same size and shape as the spiny, but has prominent ruffles or spines on the ribs. Their shells are about two inches in diameter and are easily recognized by their pink shells. They yield about twenty to twenty-five scallop meats per pound. They are typically eaten whole, either steamed or raw. Their meat color ranges from ivory to pinkish-white, and they have a tender and moist, but sometimes chewy, texture with a sweet flavor.

NANTUCKET BAY SCALLOPS

The best scallops I have ever tasted were not even cooked, but were rather marinated and served in the freshest tomato-based ceviche. They were the Nantucket Bay Scallop, Pecten irradians, that resides in Nantucket Bay, harvested from the pristine shores and bays of Nantucket Island and Cape Cod. The flavor of the just-shucked small, plump muscle is stellar. These petite beauties have an exquisitely delicate, sweet flavor and firm, resistant texture. There are generally thirty to forty to the pound. During their season, which lasts from the first of November until the end of March, bay scallops are in high demand by New Englanders who know a good thing, and by chefs in New England and New York.

The scallops are primarily dredged using small day boats, with a daily five-bushel limit (there are about eight pounds of scallops per bushel). They are hand-opened and rushed daily to markets where they fetch a high price. It is risky to venture onto frigid North Atlantic waters in small boats during the harsh winter months, but the fisherman can be rewarded with a highly profitable catch. As recently as the 1980s, the bay scallop fishery on Nantucket thrived. Unfortunately, catches have been in decline in the past twenty years, and although there are many theories, no one knows for sure why.

Diver Scallops

These premium sea scallops are harvested from the ocean by divers who hand-pick each scallop. The majority of scallops on the market are harvested by boats that drag heavy chain sweeps across the ocean floor, so they are often gritty. These scallops may be gray in color and are often soaked in a chemical solution to preserve them. Diver scallops won't have this grittiness and they're a much more ecologically friendly way of harvesting scallops.

The diver descends to the ocean floor, usually fifty to one hundred feet down, and picks the larger scallops off the rocks one by one. The scallops are then placed into bags. When the bag is full, the diver signals the boat above to hoist up the sack and send an empty one down. At best, a diver can harvest about one hundred pounds of scallops in one day, though most times yields are much lower.

Scallops that grow in a fast-water current are best, because the water brings them an abundance of food. They will also have firm flesh with very little, if any grit. Those from areas where there is little water movement can be soft and grainy. The season for diver scallops is from November 1 to April 15, although scallops may be dragged year round as long as it is past the three-mile point from shore.

Be aware that a good portion of the scallops sold as "diver scallops" are not that at all. There are just not that many of them to go around, so in many cases, they will actually be dry-pack scallops.

Scallops in Corn Cream with Summer Vegetables

As delicious as fresh corn munched off the cob is, this dish of scallops and summer vegetables poached in a jalapeño-spiked creamy corn puree is well worth the task of preparing the corn. I served this dish in summer at West Philadelphia's multicultural, ecocentric, fair-labor, social-activist White Dog Café, with vegetables and the all-important corn brought to me every few days from local organic farms. As in the best French kitchens, every bit of good-tasting trimmings is used, including the corn cobs, tomato seeds and juice, and herb stems.

Serves 4 to 6

6 ears young sweet corn, shucked

1 pound fresh sea scallops, small connecting muscle removed and reserved, halved or quartered if large

1 jalapeño, seeded and cut up

2 large beefsteak-type tomatoes, yellow and red, if possible, seeded and diced, with trimmings reserved

1/2 cup mixed chopped tender herbs: tarragon, thyme, chives, parsley, basil, mint, and/or marjoram, stems reserved

2 bay leaves

1 quart half-and-half

1 cup heavy cream

Kosher salt and freshly ground black pepper to taste

4 cups summer vegetables in small pieces: summer squash, zucchini, yellow and red bell peppers, young green beans or wax beans, shelled limas or edamame (can be frozen)

Prepare the corn cream: Cut the kernels off the corn cobs, then scrape down the cob with the edge of a knife to extract the corn milk. Cut the cobs into large chunks and reserve one quarter of the corn kernels. Place the cobs and three quarters of the corn kernels into a medium, heavy-bottomed, nonreactive saucepan along with the scallop trimmings, jalapeño, tomato trimmings, herb stems, bay leaves, and half-and-half. Bring to the boil, reduce the heat, and simmer for 20 minutes, stirring occasionally.

Remove from the heat, and fish out and discard the corn cobs, herb stems, and the bay leaves. Puree the remainder in a blender, then strain through a food mill or sieve, pressing down hard to extract all the liquid.

Transfer the liquid to a large skillet, preferably nonreactive, and bring to the boil. Add the heavy cream and season with salt and pepper and bring to the boil again. Add the tomatoes and summer vegetables, and simmer until almost crisp-tender, than add the scallops, and remaining corn kernels, and simmer just long enough to cook the scallops until barely opaque. Sprinkle with the chopped herbs, stir to combine, and serve immediately in large bowls.

Warm Bay Scallop, Red Banana, and Clementine Salad

This warm salad, which dates from my days at A'propos, makes a striking presentation and takes advantage of three wintertime fruits and mild-tasting bay scallops, which are at their best in cold weather. Because it is sometimes hard to find good quality-bay scallops, you may substitute larger sea scallops, cut into bite-size pieces.

SERVES 4

¼ cup extra-virgin olive oil

Juice and grated zest of 2 tangerines

2 shallots, chopped

2 tablespoons Champagne vinegar

Kosher salt and freshly ground black pepper, to taste

4 firm but ripe red bananas

4 tablespoons unsalted butter, divided

¾ pound bay scallops, small hard adductor muscles removed

4 Clementine oranges, or 4 navel oranges, peeled and divided into segments

1 head radicchio, cored and shredded

Whisk together the olive oil, tangerine juice and zest, shallots, and vinegar. Season with salt and pepper and reserve.

Peel the bananas and cut them in two lengthwise and crosswise, so that you have four sections for each banana. Just before serving, quickly sauté the banana sections in half the butter until browned. Remove the bananas from the pan and keep warm. To the same pan, add the remaining butter. When the butter is sizzling and lightly browned, add the scallops. Cook over high heat until barely opaque in the center.

Add the clementine sections to the scallops at the end of cooking, just long enough to heat through. Transfer the scallops and clementines to a bowl and reserve. Heat the tangerine dressing in the same pan, swirling it to allow the mixture to emulsify. Toss most of the dressing with the scallops and clementines.

Place a bed of radicchio on each individual serving plate. Top with a mound of scallops and clementines, and arrange the banana halves around the edges. Drizzle with the remaining dressing and serve immediately.

ECO-FRIENDLY SCALLOP HARVESTING

In Japan, they constantly replenish their stock of scallops to maintain supply. For many years in the U.S., divers would take only the larger scallops so there would always be plenty. Proof of the effectiveness of this is that divers could harvest from the same location year after year. In recent years, divers have been taking smaller, immature scallops, hurting their potential for healthy survival. The most common method of scallop harvesting, dragging the bottom, not only hurts the scallop population, but all the shellfish that lie in their path.

856

Scallop and Wild Mushroom Ring

I adapted this wonderful recipe for scallops and wild mushrooms from the book I co-authored, Georges Perrier: Le Bec-Fin Recipes. *Although it is suitable for serving to the most demanding guests, it is pretty easy to make and perfect if you have a source of wild-foraged mushrooms. Although one comes from the earth and the other from the sea, both wild mushrooms and scallops are in season in the fall and winter and go quite well together. While chanterelles are wonderful here (see page 591 for more information), other, more easily found, mushrooms such as baby bellas and pleurottes (also known as oyster mushrooms) will also work well. Although I'm not usually a fan of white pepper, which is the hotter, less aromatic inner kernel of common black pepper, I use it here because of its more concentrated potency and because white pepper doesn't detract from the pristine white scallops. To be fancy here, you'll need four large, stainless steel ring molds, about 3 inches in diameter. Glass custard cups will do in a pinch for molding, but 4 well-cleaned empty tuna cans with both ends cut off are even better.*

SERVES 6

2 large gold potatoes, peeled and cut into very small cubes

4 tablespoons unsalted butter, divided

3 tablespoons red wine vinegar, divided

Kosher salt and freshly ground white pepper to taste

2 tablespoons thinly snipped chives

$1/2$ pound Chanterelle mushrooms or other firm, meaty mushroom

$1/2$ pound Shiitake mushrooms, stems removed for another use

1 pound large fresh sea scallops, trimmed

2 tablespoons olive oil, divided

In a large, nonstick skillet, sauté the potatoes in 2 tablespoons of the butter until browned, then add 1 tablespoon of the vinegar and shake to combine. Season with salt and white pepper, stir in the chives, remove from the pan, and keep warm.

Carefully clean the chanterelles, wiping clean and trimming off any sandy parts. Cut both types of mushrooms into small cubes. Wipe out the skillet, add the remaining 2 tablespoons butter and the mushrooms and sauté 3 minutes, or until firm and lightly browned. Sprinkle with 1 tablespoon of vinegar. Remove from the pan and keep warm.

Cut the scallops into small cubes and pat dry, if wet on the outside. Sprinkle the scallops with salt and white pepper. Wipe out the skillet, and then heat 1 tablespoon of olive oil until shimmering. Sauté half the scallops in the oil over high heat until browned on the outside, but still moist, remove from pan and reserve, then sauté the remaining half in the remaining 1 tablespoon olive oil. Deglaze the pan with the remaining 1 tablespoon vinegar; shake to combine with the juices, pour over the scallops, and reserve.

Have ready 4 large ring molds, set on 4 serving plates. Layer $1/4$ of the scallops on the bottom of each ring, top with $1/4$ of the mushrooms and finally, top with $1/4$ of the potatoes. Press down gently and evenly to shape, then pull off the rings. Serve immediately.

857

Scallop and White Corn Chowder with Poblano Chiles

This is another big pot of chunky soup, loaded with sweet scallops and white corn kernels, with a spicy edge of mildly heated, peppery-tasting poblano chiles. The small, hard muscle kernels that must be removed from the edge of the scallop are loaded with flavor. Never throw them out, but save them to enhance a fish or seafood broth, or just add them to the chicken stock as here for more scallop flavor.

SERVES 8 TO 12

1 quart chicken stock

2 pounds naturally packed bay scallops, with trimmings reserved

2 large sprigs thyme

2 bay leaves

1 sweet onion, diced, with trimmings reserved

1 pound yellow potatoes, peeled and diced

4 tablespoons unsalted butter

$1/4$ cup all-purpose flour

1 pound white corn kernels (frozen or fresh)

2 poblano chiles, roasted, peeled and diced

Kosher salt and freshly ground black pepper to taste

In a large soup pot, combine the chicken stock, scallop trimmings, thyme, bay leaves, and any trimmings from the onion. Bring to the boil, reduce the heat, cover and simmer for 30 minutes. Strain the broth and place back in the cleaned pot. Add the potatoes to the broth and simmer until soft but not mushy, about 15 minutes.

Separately, cook the onions in the butter until transparent. Stir in the flour and cook for 3 to 4 minutes to cook out the raw taste, then scrape the mixture into the broth. Add the corn kernels, and roasted chiles, and bring to a boil, stirring until the broth is smooth, about 5 minutes.

At the last minute, add the scallops, cooking only long enough for them to firm, about 2 minutes and stirring so they cook evenly. Season the chowder with salt and pepper and serve immediately.

858

Broiled Scallops with Linguine in Cherry Tomato Sauce

This is one of those easy-to-make dishes that gives back much more than it takes. Prepare it in summer when all kinds of farmers' market cherry tomatoes are available. It is a light, colorful dish with plenty of garlicky flavor that is sure to please everyone. I served a version of this dish at several restaurants and always had good success. Save the small, hard side muscle pieces from the scallops in the freezer to add to the broth for a fish or seafood stew; they are loaded with scallop flavor. The basic method of marinating the seafood in a mixture of olive oil, garlic, and breadcrumbs, which magically makes all the flavor adhere, comes from the Adriatic coast of Italy near the towns of Rimini and Cesanatico, home of Marcella Hazan, who shared this method of preparing them, along with some of her immense knowledge of la cucina Italiana *with me many years ago.*

SERVES 4

Marinated Scallops

$^3/_4$ cup Japanese breadcrumbs

1 tablespoon chopped garlic

6 tablespoons olive oil

Kosher salt and freshly ground black pepper to taste

1 tablespoon finely chopped thyme

$1^1/_2$ pounds "dry" sea scallops, hard outer muscle removed

Process together the breadcrumbs, garlic, olive oil, salt, pepper, and thyme. Toss with the scallops and marinate for several hours, refrigerated, or up to overnight.

Assembly

1 red onion, thinly sliced

1 tablespoon chopped garlic

$^1/_4$ cup extra-virgin olive oil

$^1/_2$ cup dry white wine

2 pints ripe cherry tomatoes quartered

Kosher salt and freshly ground black pepper to taste

2 handfuls basil leaves, rolled up like a cigar and sliced into thin strips

1 pound linguine

Marinated Scallops

Preheat the broiler to high. Bring a large pot of salted water to the boil.

In a large nonreactive skillet, sauté the red onion and garlic in the olive oil until transparent, about 3 minutes. Add the white wine and tomatoes and bring to the boil. Season with salt and pepper and cook for 2 to 3 minutes or until slightly thickened.

Add the linguine to the water and cook until al dente, firm and bouncy, and still yellow in color. Drain and toss with the sauce. Add the basil.

Meanwhile, arrange the scallops in a single layer on a metal baking pan and broil for 10 minutes, or until scallops are barely opaque inside and crumbs are brown.

Twirl the pasta into nests in the center of 4 large dinner plates, preferably heated. Top with the scallops and serve immediately.

859

SHRIMP

SHRIMP

Although I've never been a shrimp lover and can't really understand the American obsession with this all-too-often frozen seafood, when I get the chance to sample fresh, sweet shrimp, simply prepared, they are absolutely delicious. Traveling down the Sorrento Peninsula and then the spectacular Amalfi coast in the fall with the Philadelphia chapter of Slow Food, I ate superb, sweet, fresh, firm, and succulent shrimp—everything you want a shrimp to be.

As a restaurant chef, I would buy fifty-pound cases of fresh shrimp out of the Carolinas and serve them as fast as I could. Like other seafood, shrimp are extremely perishable, so fresh shrimp are normally found only near where they're caught, or at very high-level restaurants who pay for quick shipment. While this is more work than most people want to do, I would freeze the remainder myself. Even out of the freezer, these shrimp still tasted sweet and pleasing, much better than any commercially frozen product. Years ago, my importer would occasionally bring in French *crevettes grises*. The first time I tasted these tiny grey shrimp from the Mediterranean, I realized that they were the epitome of shrimp, with an intense, concentrated flavor of the sea. I wanted more.

Unfortunately, the choices of shrimp for the home cook are not the best. Most, if not all, supermarket shrimp have been frozen and defrosted, and the longer they sit, the more juices they lose. Also, unless you shop in a high-end store, the only shrimp likely to be found are the black-striped tiger shrimp from Asia. To my taste, these farmed, warm-water shrimp don't have the pleasingly firm texture and well-developed flavor of the higher-priced white and pink wild shrimp harvested from the Gulf of Mexico on both the American and South American shores.

There is a vast number of different kinds of shrimp throughout the world, all divided into three basic categories: cold-water or northern; warm-water and southern or tropical; and freshwater. I prefer firm textured cold-water shrimp to the softer warm-water shrimp. Cold-water shrimp from the northern Atlantic are called *Pandalus borealis* while those that inhabit the northern Pacific are called *Pandalus jordoni*. Atlantic cold-water shrimp are found in northern waters anywhere from Alaska and Canada on the Western coast to Cape Cod all the way to Greenland and across to Norway. Cold-water shrimp that inhabit the northern Atlantic and northern Pacific are generally very small and do not have to be deveined before eating.

Just to make things more confusing, the terms *prawn* and *scampi* are often used interchangeably with shrimp: *prawn* commonly refers to freshwater shrimp or large saltwater shrimp; *scampi* is often used by restaurateurs to describe shrimp cooked in butter and garlic. You may find all three

862

categories in your local market. Warm-water shrimp from the Gulf states of Florida, Alabama, Mississippi, Louisiana, and Texas represent the overwhelming majority of domestic shrimp caught in the U.S. The three major species are brown, white, and pink shrimp.

Shrimp Varieties

Black Tiger Shrimp: The best things about these shrimp are their name and their relatively low price. The black tiger shrimp, *Penaeus monodon*, is Asia's most important species of farmed shrimp. The largest of more than three hundred commercially sold shrimp species worldwide, tiger shrimp can be as much as one foot long. They are found in east and southeast Africa, the Red Sea, and the Arabian Gulf, around India, through the Malays to northern Australian and the Philippines. Farmed black tigers have a mild, rather bland flavor, and their texture is softer. Although chemical-free black tigers are available, some treat these shrimp with sulfites to prevent deterioration; indications are pitted shells and a soapy flavor. Cook these shrimp only long enough for them to turn opaque; they quickly overcook and toughen.

Chinese White Shrimp: Chinese white shrimp, *Penaeus chinensis*, are similar to Pacific and Gulf whites. They are farmed and wild-caught by trawlers in China and along the Korean coast. They have fragile, mild meat that is softer in texture than that of Gulf or Pacific whites. They sell for much less than other whites, so they are sometimes passed off as the more expensive Gulf or Pacific whites.

Giant Freshwater Shrimp: Known as Malaysian prawns, Hawaiian blue prawn, or giant river prawn, this shrimp, *Macrobrachium rosenbergi*, is found in the wild from Pakistan and India, to Malaysia and as far as Australia. In the U.S., they are commercially farmed in Hawaii, California, and other states. These fast-growing shrimp can be over a quarter-pound each. Freshwater shrimp are more perishable than other types and have a delicate sweet flavor and firm, white flesh. Their tail, long legs, and antennae are bright blue. They maintain their flavor best if cooked whole, with their heads on. This is the way they're usually presented at high-end restaurants.

Gulf Brown Shrimp: Brown shrimp, *Penaeus aztecus*, are found off the Texas-Louisiana coast. They have reddish-brown shells, and their meat has a stronger flavor than that of white or pink shrimp because of their higher iodine content. As a result, brown shrimp are generally less expensive than Gulf white or pinks. Brown shrimp have a special groove in the last tail segment that differentiates them from the more expensive whites.

Gulf Pink Shrimp: Gulf pink shrimp actually come in a variety of colors, including, pink, brown, white, brownish-pink, and lemon yellow. All Gulf shrimp are harvested from the wild using trawl nets. Pink shrimp, *Penaeus duorarum*, are the largest Gulf specifies, reaching eleven inches, and are usually sold with their

863

heads on because two-thirds of their body length is in the head. They are tender and sweet, with firm texture. They are found on Mexico's Gulf Coast.

Gulf White Shrimp: Gulf white shrimp, *Penaeus setiferus*, were the first important commercial shrimp to be harvested in the U.S., as far back as 1709. They are found south of the Carolinas and are common in Florida waters, with the main harvest from the Gulf of Mexico. Whites are the most sought-after of the Gulf shrimp and have sweet, firm meat. Although classified as white, the shells of some shrimp are actually greenish-gray.

Northern Pink Shrimp: Found in most northern waters in both the Atlantic and Pacific, pink shrimp are just about the most important commercial shrimp in the world. Known as salad shrimp, they used in inexpensive shrimp salad and such things as Chinese egg rolls. They are quite small, usually about fifty per pound. They are hermaphrodites, spending their early part of their lives as males, then turning into females. A special variety, *Penaeus Jordani*, is found only along the Pacific Coast from Alaska to San Diego.

Panamanian White Shrimp: The highly appreciated large, mild, and sweet Panamanian white shrimp, *Penaeus vannamei*, is, not surprisingly, a specialty of Panama. These white-fleshed tropical shrimp are flown to America during their short season in the summer and are served in top-tier restaurants. Native to the Pacific Coast of Central and South America (from Mexico to Peru), this is the leading farm-raised species in the Western Hemisphere.

Rock Shrimp: Rock shrimp, *Sicyonia brevirostris*, are a fairly recent introduction into the American market. Rock shrimp get their name from their hard shell. The meat of rock shrimp is very firm, more lobster-like, and lower priced than other shrimp. This deep-water cousin of pink, brown, and white shrimp has a hard shell is similar to that of other deep-water crustaceans like lobster. Look for rock shrimp with transparent or clear white flesh and a mild, oceanic smell. They are sold already peeled and cleaned, making them a cinch to cook. Because of their small size, they cook very quickly.

Santa Barbara Spot Shrimp: The Santa Barbara spot shrimp, *Pandalus platyceros*, also called "California spot prawn," are named for the four bright white spots on their bodies located on both sides of the first and fifth shell segments. They are called *tarabaebi* in Japanese and they are a highly prized sushi bar item. Spot shrimp have pink to red shells with spots and sweet, firm flesh. Commonly found from Alaska to San Diego, spot prawns inhabit rocky areas. In Monterey, California, fishermen trap spot prawns year round. In southern California, trawlers fish for spot prawns during the summer. If you find spot shrimp, look for the delicious roe under their belly shells—it's great as a garnish for ceviche.

864

DRIED SHRIMP

Tiny, pungent dried shrimp are a popular seasoning in Asia, West Africa, and in the Afro-Brazilian cuisine of Bahia, in Brazil. They are available in Asian and Latin American markets. They are usually toasted in a dry pan to crisp them up and release their potent flavor.

Shrimp Sizes and Brands

Like eggs and condoms, there is no such thing as a small shrimp, at least in retail markets, where they are sold as large, extra-large, jumbo, and colossal. In the food trade, shrimp are sold by count, a range of shrimp per pound. The most common size in restaurants is 16-20, meaning there are 16 to 20 headless shrimp per pound. The smaller the count per pound the larger and more expensive the shrimp. In the market, you may also see descriptive size names such as small, medium, large, or jumbo. Shrimp in their standard frozen form, in five-pound boxes, are sold in the following sizes: under 10, under 12, under 15, 16-20, 21-25, 26-30, 31-35, 36-40, 41-50, 51-60 count. Ocean Garden from Mexico and BG from South America are two top names in frozen shrimp. When buying shrimp, compare the prices based on actual count per pound, because these size descriptions vary greatly. It all depends on your point of view.

Cooking Shrimp

Shrimp cooked with the shell on will not shrink as much and will be more flavorful, though it is more pesky to remove the inner vein once they're cooked. It's important not to overcook shrimp, as they quickly become rubbery and mealy. Cook only until the flesh just becomes opaque and the tails begin to curl.

Don't discard the shells, which are loaded with flavor. Cover them with cold water, add pickling spices, garlic, lemon and/or white wine, and a bit of onion, celery, carrot, and fennel if desired. Bring to the boil, skim as necessary, and simmer about 30 minutes, or until the vegetables are soft. Strain and use for a cooking liquid for poaching shrimp, for fish or seafood chowders, and for seafood stews. Cool and then freeze for up to 3 months.

Shrimp will shrink by half their weight in cleaning and cooking, so that 2 pounds of raw shrimp will yield 1 pound of cooked and peeled shrimp.

THE WORD SHRIMP

The word *shrimp* is Middle English and may derive from the German word *schrimpen*, which means to *shrink up*, used to describe small, weak things, the way we might describe someone small as a "shrimp."

Shrimp Giardiniero

This dish of shrimp poached in a flavorful liquid and then tossed with a chunky, country-Italian-style vinaigrette can also be made with scallops or served with half of each. The shrimp don't even boil; once they're added to the boiling liquid, they are removed from the fire, covered, and allowed to set in the heat of the liquid. This will work fine unless you have unusually large shrimp, which may need to be brought to the boil and then removed from the heat. Shrimp cooked like this will be quite tender and juicy. The most important thing about any marinated seafood salad is that it is best served warm, just after marinating. After a while, the acid in the dressing "cooks" the seafood so that it becomes hard in texture, and chilling dulls the delicate flavors. You'll need to buy a jar of the pickled Italian vegetables called "Giardiniero," usually found in the Italian section of the supermarket or in an Italian grocery.

SERVES 6

Poached Shrimp

1 tablespoon pickling spice

1 teaspoon hot red pepper flakes

2 tablespoons kosher salt

2 sprigs thyme

2 lemons, cut in half

1½ pounds large shrimp, peeled and deveined, last tail shell segment left on

1 tablespoon hot sauce

In a large pot, combine 6 cups of water with the pickling spice, red pepper flakes, salt, thyme, the juice from the lemons, and the lemon halves. Bring to the boil, then reduce the heat to a simmer. Simmer 30 minutes to flavor the liquid, then strain, discarding the solids.

Add the shrimp to the hot liquid, stir vigorously, cover, and then take off the heat. Allow the shrimp to set in the hot liquid until opaque, about 3 minutes longer. Drain well and immediately toss with the vinaigrette and hot sauce. Serve while still warm.

Chunky Vinaigrette

½ cup extra-virgin olive oil

Juice of 2 lemons + grated zest of 1 lemon

2 tablespoons red wine vinegar

2 teaspoons crumbled dry oregano leaves

Kosher salt and freshly ground black pepper to taste

¼ cup finely diced Giardiniero vegetables

½ cup diced roasted red peppers

2 tablespoons drained capers

2 firm but ripe avocados, sliced into wedges, for garnish (optional)

Whisk together the olive oil, lemon juice and zest, vinegar, oregano, and salt and pepper. Stir in the Giardiniero, roasted peppers, and capers. Toss with the shrimp. Garnish each plate with the avocado slices.

Shrimp with Green Goddess Dressing

This famous dish with the intriguing name was created at San Francisco's Palace Hotel in the 1920s. George Arliss, star of the popular play that takes place in India, The Green Goddess, *was staying at The Palace Hotel during the run of the play there in 1923. In preparation for a banquet in Arliss's honor, the Executive Chef of the hotel, Philippe Roemer, created a totally green salad dressing with lots of fresh herbs to suggest the name of the play. The dressing, which works especially well with the seafood for which San Francisco is famous, is regarded as the hotel's signature salad dressing and for decades has been served in its Garden Court Restaurant. It is on the lunch menu of the Garden Court Restaurant today with Dungeness crab. The dressing always includes anchovies, mayonnaise, vinegar, scallion, garlic, parsley, tarragon, and chives.*

SERVES 6

³/₄ cup mayonnaise

¹/₄ cup sour cream

Juice of 2 limes

2 tablespoons cider vinegar

1 teaspoon crushed garlic

Kosher salt, cayenne pepper, and
 freshly ground black pepper to taste

1¹/₂ pounds shrimp, poached

¹/₂ pound cold boiled green beans

1 pint cherry tomatoes, halved

¹/₄ cup chopped Italian parsley

1 bunch chives, thinly sliced

2 tablespoons chopped tarragon

¹/₂ cup thinly sliced scallions

Lemon wedges, for garnish

Combine the mayonnaise and sour cream with the lime juice, vinegar, and garlic, and season to taste with the salt, cayenne, and black pepper. Chill the dressing. Arrange the shrimp, green beans, and cherry tomatoes attractively on serving plates. Add the parsley, chives, tarragon, and scallions to the dressing, and serve in a small bowl in the middle of each plate for dipping. Accompany by lemon wedges.

Gambas a La Planxa

867

Gambas, *the Spanish word for shrimp, are prepared* a la planxa, *that is, seared on a seasoned cast-iron griddle, so that all their flavor is concentrated and the outside is browned and crusty. The shrimp are marinated up to overnight in a simple mixture of cumin, saffron, and garlic in olive oil before cooking. They are best served simply with a wedge of lemon. If you and your guests are willing to shell them at the table, use shell-on or, even better, whole head-on shrimp for this dish. Or else, leave the brightly colored last tail-shell segment on the shrimp to keep the shrimp juicy and serve as a built-in handle. Serve as a tapas with drinks.*

SERVES 6 TO 8

1 1/2 pounds shrimp (21-25 count)

1 1/2 teaspoons ground cumin

1/2 teaspoon cayenne pepper

1/2 teaspoons saffron threads, crushed

2 tablespoons chopped garlic

Kosher salt and freshly ground black pepper to taste

1/4 cup olive oil

2 lemons, cut into wedges

Peel and devein the shrimp, leaving the last tail-shell segment and its pointy tail attached to use as a handle. To devein, use a small, sharp knife and cut a shallow line down the back of the shrimp, exposing the intestinal vein inside. Pull out and discard the vein. Some shrimp may not have a dark vein; these do not need cleaning.

Place the cumin, cayenne, saffron, garlic, salt and pepper, and olive oil in a food processor and process until smooth and pasty. Combine the shrimp and marinade, coating the shrimp evenly. Leave to marinate overnight.

Heat olive oil in a cast-iron skillet or a griddle. Place the shrimp in the skillet and cook over high heat until the shrimp are half-cooked, then turn them and cook until just barely cooked through. Serve immediately with lemon wedges.

Thai Tamarind Grilled Shrimp

Hot, sour, sweet, and salty dancing in your mouth all at once: that's Thai food. Hotness comes from tiny fiery chilies; sourness from lime, tamarind, and vinegar; sweetness from sugar, especially palm sugar; and saltiness from sea salt and fish sauce, the clear, concentrated liquid made from fermented fish called nam plah. *Fresh cilantro, Thai basil, and lemongrass are used in abundance, while garlic, shallots, ginger, and* galangal *round out the flavors. Here, canned Thai red chile paste, which includes most if not all the above ingredients, along with coconut milk, lime juice and its fragrant zest, and the strong spicy-minty leaves of Thai basil make an intriguing marinade for shrimp. The shrimp are skewered on water-soaked bamboo skewers and then grilled. Serve with the Thai Cucumber Salad on page 360.*

SERVES 8

1 package bamboo skewers

1 tablespoon Thai red chili paste

2 tablespoons soy or vegetable oil

2 tablespoons tamarind puree

   (*see* Preparing Tamarind on page 772)

1/2 cup unsweetened coconut milk

Juice of 2 limes and the grated zest of lime

2 tablespoons molasses, not blackstrap

   (*see* Molasses on page 632)

2 teaspoons kosher salt

2 pounds peeled and deveined shrimp (21-25 count)

   with the final tail shell segment left on

1/4 cup shredded Thai basil leaves,

   or substitute a combination of basil and mint

1/4 cup shredded cilantro leaves

Soak the skewers in water for several hours. Combine the red chile paste, oil, tamarind, coconut milk, lime juice and zest, molasses, and salt. Marinate the shrimp in this mixture for at least 4 hours and up to 24, then add the herbs: Thai basil, and cilantro.

Preheat a grill to hot. Drain the shrimp, then thread onto water-soaked bamboo skewers. Grill on both sides until the shrimp are crusty on the outside and barely opaque on the inside, about 6 minutes total. Serve with Cucumber Salad (page 360).

Crispy Coconut–Beer Shrimp

Fried, breaded shrimp keep all their juices inside and don't shrink much, hence their popularity in restaurants, although they usually are of the out-of-the-freezer-into-the-fryer type. Here the shrimp are dipped in a beer batter, coated in dried coconut, then fried and served with a simple tangy sweet-and-sour dip made from ginger, horseradish, mustard, and marmalade. Serve with beer, naturally.

SERVES 8

Beer Batter

3 eggs

4 cups light beer

½ pound (2 cups) all-purpose flour

Lightly beat together the eggs and beer. Place the flour in a mixing bowl, making a well in the middle. Pour the egg-beer mixture into the well, whisking to combine with the flour. Refrigerate batter for 20 minutes.

Shrimp

2 pounds extra large shrimp (16-20 count)

½ pound (2 cups) seasoned flour (season all-purpose flour to taste with salt, pepper, and cayenne pepper)

4 cups flaked unsweetened coconut

Peel and devein the shrimp, leaving the last tail-shell attached. Split the shrimp down the middle, cutting as far as the tail shell, to butterfly. Open up and spread the shrimp as flat as possible. Set up 3 bowls: one of flour, the second of batter, the third of coconut. Dip each butterflied shrimp first into flour, shaking off the excess. Then dip into the batter, allowing the excess to drip off. Then, place the shrimp into the bowl of coconut, patting all over so that the coconut adheres well. Repeat until all the shrimp are coated. (You can refrigerate the shrimp at this point for cooking later in the day or the next day.)

869

Dip and Assembly

2 tablespoons powdered ginger

3 tablespoons prepared horseradish

2 cups good-quality orange marmalade

1 cup Dijon-style mustard

1 quart peanut or canola oil, for frying

Whisk together the ginger, horseradish, marmalade, and mustard and set aside.

Heat the peanut oil until it registers 365°F. on a frying thermometer. Fry the shrimp in several batches, adding only enough shrimp at a time so they don't crowd the pot. This will keep your shrimp light without absorbing excess oil. Cook until they are golden brown and crispy. Serve with a bowl of the dip.

Shrimp Provençal

A quick shrimp sauté with lots of fresh vegetables, this sprightly and brightly colored dish should be served with steamed rice. Brine-cured Kalamata olives, garlic, fennel seed, and thyme give it that Mediterranean flavor. Shrimp work well for sautéed dishes because they do best with quick-cooking methods. Once everything is cut up, the dish can be ready to serve in less than 15 minutes.

MAKES 6 SERVINGS

3 tablespoons olive oil

1 1/2 pounds uncooked large shrimp, peeled, deveined

2 cups thinly sliced red bell peppers

1 cup thinly sliced red onion

1 tablespoon finely chopped fresh thyme or
  1 teaspoon dried

1 tablespoon chopped garlic

2 teaspoons ground fennel seeds

1 (15-ounce) can diced tomatoes

1/2 cup pitted Kalamata olives, in halves

1/2 cup dry white wine

Kosher salt and freshly ground black pepper to taste

1/2 cup chopped fresh basil

Heat the olive oil in a large, preferably nonstick, skillet, over medium-high heat until fragrant and shimmering. Add the shrimp and sauté just until pink, about 1 minute, turning often. Using a slotted spoon, transfer the shrimp to a bowl and reserve.

To the same pan, add the bell peppers, onion, thyme, garlic, and fennel seeds. Sauté until the onion and peppers are crisp-tender, about 5 minutes. Add the tomatoes with their juices, the olives, and wine. Season with salt and pepper and bring the liquid to the boil. Reduce the heat to medium-low, cover, and simmer until flavors blend, about 5 minutes.

Add the shrimp; simmer uncovered until they are heated through and just opaque in the center, about 2 minutes. Just before serving, stir in the basil and serve immediately.

Shrimp Adriatic Style

This is a perfect dish for a summer night when you're planning to grill. Serve the skewered shrimp as an appetizer or with drinks. They pick up the smoky flavor from the grill and end up crusty and brown, with a golden color imparted to the pink shrimp from the saffron. I've been making this dish of marinated and grilled shrimp so long, but it still tastes and looks as good as can be. The shrimp are marinated in a mixture of saffron, lemon juice, garlic, thyme, hot peppers, and olive oil, with some breadcrumbs to bind the flavors to the shrimp. If you happen to have some fragrant fennel pollen, sprinkle it over the shrimp just before serving.

SERVES 8

$1/2$ teaspoon crumbled saffron

Juice of 2 lemons

$1/4$ cup homemade-style breadcrumbs

2 tablespoons extra-virgin olive oil

1 tablespoon chopped garlic

1 tablespoon chopped fresh thyme

$1/2$ teaspoon crumbled hot pepper flakes

Kosher salt and freshly ground black pepper to taste

2 tablespoons chopped Italian parsley

$2^1/2$ pounds shrimp, (16-20 count) peeled and
  deveined, tail shells left on

Soak the saffron threads in the lemon juice for about 10 minutes, or until the juice is bright gold in color.

Place the breadcrumbs, olive oil, lemon juice with saffron, garlic, thyme, pepper flakes, and salt and pepper into the bowl of the food processor, and process to a fine paste. Remove the mixture from the processor and add the parsley, then toss the mixture with the shrimp. Marinate the shrimp for at least 2 hours and up to 24 hours, and then thread on skewers without pushing the shrimp too close together (so they would tend not to cook).

When ready to cook, preheat a grill to hot. Grill the skewers until the shrimp are opaque and have started to curl. Serve immediately, allowing about 5 shrimp per person.

871

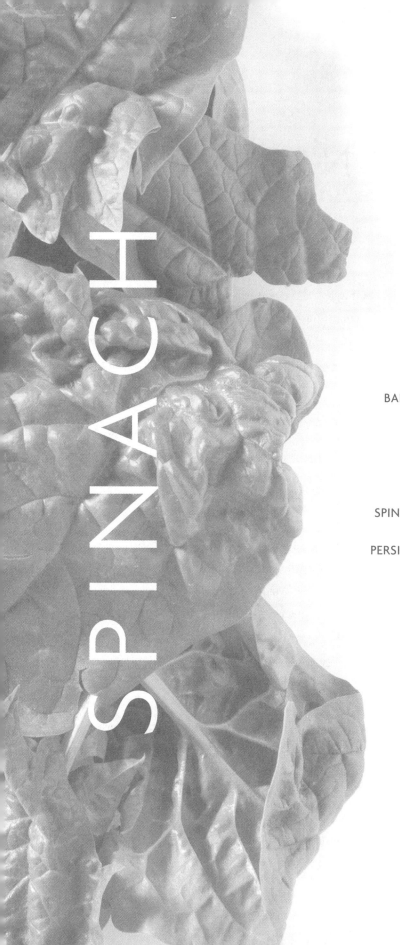

SPINACH

SPINACH

Do you say "yuck" or "yum" when you hear that spinach is on the menu? Although I'm of the "yum" persuasion, many people find spinach mundane, at best, and hardly a vegetable of romance. In spite of, or perhaps because of, the fact that Popeye ate spinach to make him strong, spinach is still a vegetable famously despised by children.

However, in many countries and cuisines, spinach is cherished for its subtle, faintly bittersweet taste and arresting deep green color. Spinach is incredibly versatile, adaptable to everything from egg dishes like omelets and soufflés to soups, both cold and hot; salads, raw and cooked; tarts, savory and sweet; spreads, sauces, and dips; or as a brightly colored addition to pilafs, stir-fry's, curries, and noodle dishes.

The Persians, who were great gardeners, cultivated spinach in Persia (now Iran) as early as the fourth century CE. From Persia, spinach was exported eastward to China via Nepal. In the seventh century, the Chinese emperor T'ai Tsung asked rulers of other lands to send him the best plants their countries grew. The King of Nepal sent him spinach, which had only recently arrived from Persia. Spinach is still known in Chinese as Persian vegetable.

The Arabs, who were also avid gardeners, adapted spinach along with its name—*esfenaj*. They showed their high regard for this mild-mannered green by designating it "the prince of vegetables." Spinach traveled across the Mediterranean in the eleventh century with the Arabs, who brought it along with them when they conquered Spain. Spain became the first center of European spinach production. From there, it was adapted by the French, who called it at first *erbe d'Espaigne*.

In Europe in Medieval times, spinach was often used in sweet dishes, combined with ingredients like honey, eggs, and almonds to make a pie filling. The Provençal *Tarte aux Épinards*, a survivor of these times, is still served in that region as part of the long, elaborate meal preceding Midnight Mass on Christmas Eve. The tarte is made from cooked spinach mixed with sweet pastry cream, flavored with lemon zest, vanilla, and candied melon.

Our own habit of seasoning spinach with nutmeg—a very suitable and long-lasting marriage—is probably another remnant of Medieval tastes in modern times. Perhaps the Greek *spanakopita* (small envelopes of phyllo dough wrapping a spinach filling) also derives from this tradition. In French haute cuisine, any dish *à la Florentine* invariably includes spinach, because cooks from Florence brought their sophisticated methods of cooking spinach to France.

The well-deserved reputation of spinach as "good for you" was promoted in eighteenth century England, where it was recommended to "eat largely of spinach."

874

And in modern times, according to esteemed culinarian and author Jane Grigson, in Britain, spinach was "shoveled into children as if their survival depended on it." And of course, Popeye merely had to consume a can—to my taste, the worst way to eat spinach—and his biceps would grow enormously large, enabling him to rapidly vanquish his foes. Later, in America in the 1930s and '40s, spinach became a colloquial term for nonsense, because of the caption in a *New Yorker* magazine cartoon which declared, "I say it's spinach."

There are two main types of spinach on the market today: flat-leafed and curly (or Savoy). The flat-leafed type is more tender and milder in flavor, especially the prewashed baby variety sometimes marketed as Popeye spinach. I prefer the bouncing, firm, dark leaves of Savoy spinach, especially the locally grown type from South Jersey sold in wired bunches. Curly spinach has a stronger "iron" flavor with a very slight bitter aftertaste and a crunchy texture.

The disadvantage of bunch spinach, much of it grown in the sandy soil of South Jersey, is that it harbors sand in its curls and whorls—especially if picked soon after a heavy rain—and needs several good soakings to get it clean. Because I get such satisfaction out of prepping beautiful vegetables, I find it's well worth the extra effort. The bags of washed spinach sold in many supermarkets can be a good product, but because the brittle leaves often crumble, it's best to use this type for cooked dishes rather than salads.

The other thing about spinach is that, unfortunately, a lot goes but a little way. Buy several pounds of spinach; cook it in a large pot, and you'll only end up with a couple of cups of spinach. If your recipe calls for squeezing out the excess water, as many do, you might have as little as one cup of spinach in the end. While I prefer the bright, iron-laden flavor of fresh spinach, I do occasionally use frozen spinach, especially the whole-leaf type. Frozen chopped spinach generally contains too many stems and tends to be unpleasantly stringy. I've found the whole-leaf organic frozen spinach sold by Trader Joe's to be the best on the market.

Cleaning Spinach

To clean fresh bunch spinach, pull off the leaves and discard the stems (though in Italy, the stems are often cooked separately, like Swiss chard stalks). Fill a large bowl or a sink with cold water and swish the spinach leaves around vigorously. Scoop the spinach from the water, allowing any sand to sink to the bottom. If you see a lot of sand on the bottom, wash the spinach again. Flat-leafed spinach is easier to clean because there's no place to catch and hold the sand. (The main thing I remember about an otherwise perfect meal at a multi-starred restaurant in Montreal is the sandy spinach that came with the quail.)

CHOOSING AND STORING SPINACH

Because spinach is a tender green, it will spoil quickly. Avoid buying spinach with any yellowed leaves. If it's at all questionable, sniff it; if the spinach has deteriorated, you will quickly detect an unpleasant odor. Because it has been prewashed to make it easier for the cook, bagged spinach can be less than fresh if it sits on the shelves at the supermarket for more than a day or two. If you want to keep the spinach a few days longer, steam it, chill it, and bag it. When you're ready to serve it, recook the spinach with a little garlic and olive oil, or shallots and butter.

Baby Spinach Salad with Sweet and Sour Mustard Vinaigrette

Baby spinach is tender and mild and usually prewashed, so all you have to do is open up the bag, toss the leaves with the dressing, and top with the warm sautéed mushrooms, and onions. The spinach will wilt slightly and get shiny, but once assembled, the salad should be served immediately so that the spinach doesn't collapse. The dressing gets its sweetness from honey, its bite from two kinds of mustard, and a nutty edge from Asian roasted sesame oil.

SERVES 6

2 tablespoons olive oil

$1/2$ pound baby bella mushrooms, quartered

1 red onion, sliced into rings

6 tablespoons canola oil

3 tablespoons cider vinegar

1 tablespoon honey

1 tablespoon coarse-grain mustard

1 teaspoon dry mustard

1 tablespoon dark roasted sesame oil

1 teaspoon hot sauce

Kosher salt and freshly ground pepper to taste

1 pound baby spinach leaves, cleaned

In a large skillet, preferably cast-iron or nonstick, heat the olive oil until fragrant and shimmering, then sauté mushrooms over high heat until browned. Remove from the pan and reserve. Add the onion to the same pan and sauté over high heat until browned on the outside but still crispy.

Whisk together the dressing ingredients: canola oil, vinegar, honey, both mustards, sesame oil, hot sauce, and salt and pepper to taste. Toss with the spinach, top with onions and mushrooms, and serve immediately.

Spinach Salad with Grilled Spiced Chicken

Spinach and mushrooms do have an affinity. Spinach salad with bacon, mushrooms, and eggs is a restaurant menu perennial and can be very good, as long as the eggs don't have that all-too-common green edge from old or over-cooked eggs. This spinach salad topped with meaty grilled portabella mushroom strips and spice-marinated grilled chicken makes a light but satisfying salad meal. Use the recipe for the fragrant spiced grilled chicken to serve on its own, perhaps with a fruit chutney or salsa, or to add it to sandwiches.

SERVES 8

Marinated Chicken

1 tablespoon whole coriander seed

1 tablespoon juniper berries

2 teaspoons black peppercorns

1 tablespoon fennel seed

2 pounds boneless, skinless chicken breast

In a spice grinder or mortar and pestle, crush the coriander, juniper, peppercorns and fennel seeds together until fine, but still a little chunky. Rub the chicken breasts with the spices and marinate, refrigerated, for at least 1 hour, but preferably overnight.

876

Spinach Salad

$1/2$ pound shallots, cut into $1/4$-inch-thick rings

$1/2$ cup peanut oil

$1/2$ cup balsamic vinegar

1 tablespoon Dijon Mustard

$1/2$ teaspoon crushed red pepper flakes

Salt to taste

Marinated Chicken

1 pound Portabella mushroom caps

2 pounds spinach leaves, cleaned

1 large roasted red pepper, cut into thin strips

In a small pot, fry the shallot rings in peanut oil, over moderate heat, until browned and crispy, about 10 minutes. Remove from the heat and drain, reserving both the shallots and oil. Drain shallots on paper towels and allow the oil to cool to room temperature.

Whisk together the balsamic vinegar, reserved shallot cooking oil, Dijon mustard, red pepper flakes, and salt.

When ready to serve, preheat a grill or broiler to hot. Grill the chicken breasts, then cool and cut into finger-size strips. Brush the mushroom caps with a little of the dressing and grill or broil. Cool slightly, then cut into 1-inch-thick strips.

Toss the spinach with the remaining dressing. Arrange the mushrooms, roasted red pepper, and chicken strips over the spinach. Sprinkle with crispy shallots just before serving.

Spinach and Bowties
Pasta Salad

I'm not normally much of a pasta salad fan, finding this American invention too often bland and mushy. But, there's always an exception. The key is not to overcook the pasta, to dress it right away, and serve the same day. Pasta will always keep absorbing liquid, so it will inevitably get soft if kept for the next day. Bow-tie pasta seems to have the perfect shape to hold the dressing and garnishes and it won't slip out of the fork or mouth, like the more commonly used rotini or penne will. This is perfect picnic fare and makes a good addition to a potluck dinner table. Use colorful heirloom-type tomatoes in the summer for an even prettier salad.

SERVES 6 TO 8

1 pound bow-tie pasta

$1/4$ cup red wine vinegar

$1/2$ cup olive oil

2 tablespoons chopped fresh oregano,
    or 2 teaspoons dried oregano

Kosher salt and freshly ground black pepper to taste

1 pound cleaned baby spinach leaves

1 large ripe red tomato, diced

1 large ripe yellow tomato, diced

1 small red onion, cut into thin strips

$1/2$ cup each: grated Parmigiano-Reggiano
    or Grana Padano and Pecorino Romano cheese

Bring a large pot of salted water to the boil. Cook the bow-ties until cooked quite *al dente*, firm and bouncy, and still yellow in color. Drain the pasta, rinse under cold water, and drain again.

Meanwhile, whisk together the vinegar, oil, oregano, and salt and pepper. Toss with the drained pasta. Add the spinach, tomatoes, and onion. Sprinkle the salad with grated cheese just before serving.

Persian Spinach Dip with Caramelized Onions & Yogurt

This classic Iranian dish is easy for Americans to like, because it is simply a mixture of sweet caramelized onion, spinach, and yogurt sprinkled with chopped, toasted walnuts. It is served as a dip with veggies and/or pita bread. Our English name for spinach originated from the Persian esfenaj. In Persian (now Iranian) cooking, known for its large repertoire of spinach dishes, any dish of vegetables mixed with yogurt is named borani. *It is named after Queen Poorandokht, who ruled Persia 1,300 years ago and was said to be especially fond of yogurt dishes.*

SERVES 6

2 pounds fresh spinach, washed (or two 12-ounce boxes frozen spinach)

2 sweet onions, diced

2 tablespoons unsalted butter

1 pint plain yogurt

Kosher salt and freshly ground pepper to taste

$^1/_2$ cup chopped walnuts, lightly toasted in a 300°F. oven

Assorted vegetables and pita bread wedges for dipping

In a large pan, cook the spinach in the water that clings to the leaves until it wilts. Drain, rinse under cold water, and gently squeeze out the excess liquid. Chop finely and reserve. (Run frozen spinach under warm water until room temperature, then squeeze out liquid.)

In a medium pan, cook the onions in the butter over medium heat until well caramelized and golden brown. Cool and then mix with the spinach, yogurt, and salt and pepper. Sprinkle with toasted walnuts and serve as an appetizer or as a dip for pita bread and crudités.

Suggested vegetables include colored pepper wedges, Belgian endive and/or Treviso spears, celery lengths, cucumber boats, snow peas, sweet onions cut into single-layer wedges, scooped-out tomato wedges, and any colorful vegetable that is more or less boat-shaped to hold a chunky dip.

Ukrainian Spinach &
Egg Noodle Casserole

This is one of my all-time favorite noodle dishes, which I've been making for at least 20 years. I adapted this delicious vegetarian recipe from the Time-Life Foods of the World series book on Russia. I rank this series as the best ever for international foods, even 30 years after they were first published. At the time they came out, I would longingly eye my neighbor's copies as they arrived each month in the mail. At the time, I just couldn't afford them. Since those years, I've managed to obtain a full series through searches at used book stores. Although the dish may come from far away, the ingredients are easy to find: egg noodles, onions, cheese, and spinach. It follows the same theme as the Persian Spinach Dip above, combining sweet, butter-cooked onions with lots of spinach, this time combined with soft egg noodles.

SERVES 6 TO 8

3 cups cooked and drained egg noodles
  (12 ounce package)

8 tablespoons unsalted butter, melted, divided

1 cup grated Swiss cheese, divided

2 teaspoons kosher salt, divided

1/2 teaspoon freshly ground black pepper, divided

1 cup finely chopped onions

2 pounds fresh spinach, cooked, squeezed,
  and finely chopped

1 cup soft breadcrumbs

2 hard-cooked eggs, chopped

Preheat the oven to 350°F. In a large bowl, toss the cooked noodles, 2 tablespoons of the melted butter, half of the cheese, and half of the salt and pepper.

Melt 3 tablespoons of butter in a medium skillet. Add the chopped onions and cook over medium heat, or until the onions are soft but not brown. Stir in the chopped spinach; raise the heat to high and cooked uncovered until the moisture has completely evaporated, stirring often, about 5 minutes. Stir in the remaining salt and pepper.

Brush the bottom and sides of a 2-quart baking dish with 1 tablespoon butter. Arrange one-third of the noodle mixture on the bottom, top with half the spinach mixture, a second layer of noodles, the remaining spinach, and top with the remaining noodles.

Melt the remaining 2 tablespoons of butter in a heavy skillet and remove from heat. Stir in the breadcrumbs and the remaining grated cheese. Sprinkle the crumb mixture over the casserole and bake 30 minutes, or until browned and bubbling. Serve garnished with the chopped egg.

879

STRAWBERRIES

STRAWBERRIES

What's so special about strawberries? Supermarket produce aisles are loaded with green plastic strawberry crates 52 weeks a year. Almost invariably, you'll find commercial berries bred to ship well and keep well. Produce managers find it much easier to sell these berries because the supply is reliable year-round. But, those often overgrown, hollow-centered, spongy-textured berries are just an imitation of the real thing. You owe it to yourself to seek out the red-ripe, juicy berries that are a magnificent gift of June in many regions across the country.

One day in June my mother said to me, "When I eat strawberries, they don't taste at all like the ones I remember. What happened?" I handed her a basket of locally grown small, cone-shaped berries, ruby red, tinted with orange and still fragrant from the early summer heat. She tasted them and exclaimed, "Now *these* are strawberries!"

It's easy to recognize locally grown berries if you know the clues. Look first at color and size: These luscious strawberries are a deep, intense red from tip to stem. You'll never see the "white shoulders" that adorn the long-distance berries. Though small, these petite beauties are solid-fleshed from skin to heart and jam-packed with sweet flavor. Since berry season is short and intense, these berries are often packed in large green cardboard quart-sized punnets. Because of their juicy contents, red streaks often stain the cardboard containers.

Supermarket strawberries are picked green and super-cooled to extract field heat, then packed in plastic. Trucks from California, Mexico, and Florida carry these berries cross-country. In wintertime, they are air-freighted in from New Zealand and Chile, halfway around the world. Something irreplaceable is lost in this process.

My friends, who raise strawberries organically in Bucks County at Branch Creek Farm, explained to me why it's such a labor of love. Strawberries have only a three-week growing season; not much yield for so much work. In the first year, they must constantly baby the plants and keep them covered since they are so vulnerable to frost. Strawberries don't bear any fruit at all until their second year. By the third year, the plants are no longer very productive. To get a good crop, farmers have to plant strawberries each year. Harvesting strawberries is demanding and labor intensive. After picking one season's strawberry crop, one of their workers declared, "I'll never complain about the price of strawberries again." Luckily, there are a few perks to sweeten the work: picking berries warm and fragrant from the sun and overeating all the ones that aren't perfect.

Ask for locally grown berries at your produce market. Look for them at roadside farmers' market stands, or take the family for a pick-your-own outing in June. To savor fresh-picked strawberries at their best, don't chill them and eat them, right away. Field-grown, sun-ripened strawberries are a not-to-be-missed all-American delicacy.

883

Strawberry and Cointreau Jelly

I just knew that, one day, jellies would come back into fashion. (In some places, they never went away. Lime green and other rather garishly colored Jell-O molds are still quite popular at church suppers in the South.) But, once upon a time, jellies were made from scratch and that included simmering gelatin-rich calves feet with sweet aromatics, straining, and then clarifying (removing the cloudy bits) until the jelly was sparkling clear. We can now buy powdered gelatin, and even better and more refined European-style sheet gelatin, to make natural fruit jellies like the one below. Make this lovely, jiggly jelly when fresh local strawberries are abundant, sweet, and intensely colored. Strawberries and bitter orange-flavored Cointreau

make a lovely match, but less-expensive Triple Sec may be substituted. Dessert jellies have the advantage of being fat-free, unless of course, you top them with whipped cream.

SERVES 8

4 pint containers red ripe strawberries
  (2 pounds), hulled and sliced

1 cup granulated sugar

Juice of 1 lemon

2 envelopes unflavored powdered gelatin
  (2 scant tablespoons)

1/4 cup Cointreau liqueur

Preheat the oven to 300°F. Toss the strawberries with the sugar and transfer to a Dutch oven. Add 2 cups of water, cover and bake for 1 hour, or until the fruit is quite soft and has given off its liquid. Remove the casserole from the oven. Place a wire sieve over a large bowl. Pour the contents of the casserole into the sieve and press down lightly to extract all the juices. (Note that the more pressure you exert, the cloudier the result). Discard the fruit pulp.

In a glass or ceramic bowl, combine the lemon juice with 2 tablespoons of water. Sprinkle the gelatin into the liquid and allow the gelatin to "bloom" for about 5 minutes, or until it swells and absorbs the liquid. Heat at medium power in the microwave for 1 minute or until the liquid is clear.

Add the melted gelatin or gelatin sheets to the strawberry juice and stir in the Cointreau. Strain the liquid through a double layer of cheesecloth. Pour into decorative stem glasses and chill until set, several hours or overnight, and then serve.

884

Strawberry Tiramisu

Anyone who has dined out in the last 15 years has no doubt encountered the classic Tiramisu, flavored with espresso and lemon zest. For more about this restaurant-invented dessert, see the recipe for Tiramisu with Espresso Syrup on page 331. This pink-and-white-layered strawberry version is best made in June, when small, succulent strawberries are in season at farmers' markets. Frozen strawberries can be substituted; their flavor is usually quite good, because only ripe fruit is frozen, however, they tend to be a bit mushy.

SERVES 8

1 pound Mascarpone

4 tablespoons white rum, divided

3 egg yolks

2 tablespoons + 1/4 cup + 1 cup granulated sugar

2 teaspoons vanilla extract

Grated zest of 1 lemon

2 egg whites

1 (12-ounce) package ladyfingers

1 quart strawberries, preferably small, locally grown and red ripe, sliced

In a large bowl, lightly beat together the mascarpone and 2 tablespoons of the rum and set aside.

In a medium, stainless steel bowl, beat the egg yolks with 2 tablespoons of sugar, the vanilla and lemon zest until thick and light. Set the bowl over a large saucepan of simmering water and whisk constantly until the mixture lightens and thickens, about 10 minutes. You should be able to see definite streaking when the whisk is dragged through the mixture. Do not let the eggs get too hot or they will scramble. Remove the bowl from the heat and continue whisking for a few minutes to cool the mixture slightly. Place the bowl onto a second, larger bowl filled with ice and water and cool, whisking occasionally until the mixture is cool. Fold into the reserved mascarpone mixture in thirds.

In a separate, clean bowl and using the whisk attachment to a mixer, beat the egg whites until fluffy, and then gradually beat in 1/4 cup of sugar. Continue beating until the whites are firm and glossy and stick to the sides of the bowl.

Meanwhile, in a small pot, bring the remaining 1 cup of sugar and 1 cup of water to the boil. When the liquid is clear, remove it from the heat and stir in the remaining 2 tablespoons of rum and reserve.

Line the bottom of an 8-inch casserole dish with ladyfingers. Brush the ladyfingers with syrup, top with one third of the strawberries, and layer with half the mousse. Repeat with remaining ladyfingers, one third more strawberries, and the remaining mousse. Arrange the remaining berries over top in a decorative pattern. Chill well and keep tightly covered until ready to serve, at least 2 hours or overnight.

Tres Leches Cake with Strawberries

Here is a cake for those days when you have a sweet tooth to satisfy. While there are innumerable variations on this Latin American favorite, consisting of a simple white cake soaked in rich, milky-creamy-sweet syrup, this one is an easy-to-make, delicious treat with a strawberry topping that lightens and brightens the plate (and could also be made from frozen strawberries). Try the cake when local strawberries are in season—they may be small and short-lived but they are also juicy, red, and sweet. While the amount of almond extract is small, don't leave it out, because its flavor really makes the cake special. Best of all, this cake can be made several days before serving if well-wrapped in plastic and kept refrigerated.

SERVES 6

Tres Leches Cake

$1/2$ pound (2 cups) all-purpose flour

2 teaspoons baking powder

$1/2$ teaspoon baking soda

$1/2$ teaspoon kosher salt

6 eggs, separated

$1^1/2$ cups granulated sugar

$1^1/2$ cups water

1 teaspoon almond extract

Milk Mixture (recipe follows)

Preheat the oven to 350°F. Spray a 13 x 9x 2-inch (3-quart) baking dish generously with nonstick spray. In one bowl, combine the dry ingredients: flour, baking powder, baking soda, and salt. In a separate bowl, beat the egg whites, adding sugar gradually, and continuing to beat until firm and glossy. Add the yolks to the egg whites one at a time, beating well after each addition. Mixing on low speed, sprinkle in the flour mixture and then add $1^1/2$ cups of water and almond extract. Pour into the prepared pan and bake for 30 to 40 minutes, or until a cake tester comes out clean.

Milk Mixture

1 can (13-ounce) evaporated milk

1 can (14-ounce) sweetened condensed milk

1 cup heavy cream

Pour both milks and the cream into a blender and puree. With a toothpick, punch holes in the cake while it is still warm; then pour the sauce over the cake and allow the cake to cool in the refrigerator.

Strawberries

1 pint strawberries, locally grown if at all possible

2 tablespoons granulated sugar

Trim and slice strawberries and mix with sugar. Cut cake into portions, making sure to include some of the milk syrup with each portion. Top with sliced strawberries just before serving.

Quick Strawberry Shortcake

There is a perennial argument between those who prefer their shortcake made with biscuits, the more old-fashioned way, and those who prefer it made with layer cake in the more modern style. As a kid, my mom made me the most wonderful birthday party in Rock Creek Park in my hometown of Washington, D.C., where we all got to ride ponies and gorge ourselves on cakey strawberry shortcake. These days, I go for the less sweet, biscuit type with the added contrast of texture from the dry-ish biscuit and the tender, juicy strawberries, and of course, the soft, fluffy whipped cream. I'm usually one to make things from scratch, because I avoid processed foods. However, these ultra-light biscuits made from Bisquick baking mix are quick, easy, and delicious. Of course, I add sour cream or buttermilk to the mix for tangy flavor and extra tenderness from the acid, and use pure vanilla. The filling will only be as good as the quality of the strawberries.

SERVES 8

Vanilla Cream

1 cup heavy cream, chilled

$1/4$ cup confectioners' sugar

$1/4$ cup sour cream

2 teaspoons vanilla extract

1 teaspoon almond extract

Biscuits

$1/2$ cup sour cream (or buttermilk)

$1/4$ cup granulated sugar, divided

1 teaspoon vanilla extract

2 cups Bisquick baking mix

2 tablespoons unsalted butter, melted

Crushed Strawberries

2 pints red ripe strawberries

$1/2$ cup granulated sugar

$1/4$ cup Amaretto liqueur

Preheat the oven to 375°F.

Beat the heavy cream until firm; add the confectioners' sugar and beat again for 1 minute, then fold in the sour cream and vanilla and almond extracts. Chill the cream, tightly covered with plastic wrap, until ready to serve, up to 2 hours ahead.

Stir together the sour cream, half of the sugar, and the vanilla and beat briefly into the Bisquick. Roll out the dough about 1 inch thick and cut into 8 large biscuit rounds. Brush the tops with melted butter and sprinkle with the remaining sugar. Bake for 15 minutes, or until puffed and lightly browned.

Meanwhile, clean and hull the strawberries. Place them in a mixing bowl along with the sugar and Amaretto. Using a potato masher or a heavy whisk, crush the berries until they are in small chunks surrounded by plenty of juice.

When the biscuits are ready (they're best warm) split them in half, fill with the crushed strawberries, top with Vanilla Cream, and serve immediately.

886

Strawberry–Amaretto Sauce

Make this quick-as-can-be sauce when you've got some overripe strawberries. Nothing beats a fresh-made strawberry sauce that's never been heated. It has all the fresh, fruity flavor of the berries without the cooked "jammy" flavor of the longer-keeping simmered sauce. This sauce will keep for 2 to 3 days in the refrigerator. Serve over ice cream, angel food cake, or pound cake, or drizzle over fruit salad. The almond-flavored Amaretto makes a dreamy-tasting sauce. Serve the sauce to someone you love.

MAKES 1 PINT

1 pint red, ripe strawberries, cleaned

$1/4$ cup water

$1/4$ cup Amaretto liqueur

$1/4$ cup confectioners' sugar

887

Combine all the ingredients in the jar of a blender. Blend until completely smooth, stirring once or twice.

That's it! If the strawberries are truly ripe, this is strawberry sauce at its best. The sauce will keep for about 1 week in the refrigerator or for 2 to 3 months in the freezer.

TOMATOES

TOMATOES

Every year in late July, I succumb to "tomato fever." I eat them every day and every which way, never tiring of these enticing, juicy fruits. No other vegetable (technically the fruit of a tomato plant) generates so much strong feeling. In late summer, I end up with piles of diverse tomatoes: beefsteaks for slicing on sandwiches, plums for sauce, heirlooms for incredible salads, and sweet cherries for snacking, and I can't wait!

I look outside my kitchen window and see a row of tomato plants full of lush, bitingly fragrant leaves—in my neighbor's front-yard garden. The stalks dangle green tomatoes just beginning to blush. Like so many Philadelphia-area tomato fanatics, my neighbors plant tomatoes every spring. Since I don't have a sunny yard, I grow the herbs. We exchange basil, rosemary, and thyme for tomatoes; a fair trade by my estimation.

Scattered in neighborhoods in Philadelphia and other cities are community gardens, small home plots, and windowsill planters full of tomatoes. The urge to raise tomatoes strikes over and over, again and again. Jersey tomatoes are renowned across the country, but Pennsylvania-grown tomatoes, in season a month or so later, have their own diehard fans. Tomatoes have long been part of the scene in Philadelphia. Hucksters have been touting the superiority of their tomatoes in Philadelphia markets for at least one hundred and fifty years.

Called *pommes d'amour*, or *love apples* in Southern France, and *pomodori* or *golden apples* in Italy, tomatoes once enjoyed a reputation as a powerful aphrodisiac. The Spanish brought tomatoes back to the Old World after their early explorations. Shortly thereafter, they carried them to Naples, then a Spanish colony. Italian tomatoes today closely resemble early European varieties.

The English name for this golden apple—the tomato—comes from the Aztec *tomatl*. In England, tomatoes ended up as the primary ingredient in ketchup, along with sugar, vinegar, and spices, and in America, we still consume innumerable bottles of tomato ketchup yearly. Perhaps because they are so seductive-looking, people in the New World at first feared tomatoes. Early botanists recognized them as members of a plant family that includes poisonous Belladonna and Deadly Nightshade. In the 1500s, when tomatoes first appeared in Europe, people regarded eating tomatoes as a risky and dangerous activity. By the 1800s, tomatoes were considered safe to eat, but only after they had been cooked for hours, to destroy any "poisons."

Tomatoes come in all sizes, shapes, and colors. We compare tomatoes to a panoply of fruits: plums, currants, pears, grapes, and cherries. There are fig tomatoes and even yellow-striped pineapple tomatoes. I search out Sweet 100s, a cherry tomato that grows in cascading clusters of cherry-red sweet fruit. Because old-time varieties produce far fewer tomatoes per vine than hybrid varieties, you get more flavor in each tomato. Each plant might produce five flavor-packed tomatoes, instead of fifty watery-tasting tomatoes. Tomato plants generate flavor and fragrance in volatile oils like those used to blend perfumes.

Long before there was such as thing as commercially propagated tomatoes, home gardeners were cultivating them. Tomatoes are still, by far, the most common home-grown vegetable. We think of golden tomatoes as an exotic new variety, but they are actually the ancestor of our modern tomato, which originated in Peru. Collecting heirloom varieties of tomatoes is a popular avocation in our area, with some gardeners growing twenty to thirty varieties. Lately, the hottest "new thing" on restaurant menus has been heirloom tomato salads! While chefs used to look for perfectly matched firm, if mealy, tomatoes, now they're out searching for the oddest and lumpiest of tomatoes—the weirder, the better. You might be served brilliant Yellow Taxi Tomatoes, Green Grape and fuzzy, pink-blushed Peach Tomatoes, tiny yellow and red Currant Tomatoes, and even red- and orange-streaked Pineapple or Tigerella Tomatoes. Heirloom gardeners plant green- and red-striped Mr. Stripy's and the unexpected yellow-skinned, green-fleshed Evergreen Tomato. So you've seen red, yellow, orange, and green tomatoes, but how about white and black tomatoes? The White Queen reigns as the best white tomato, while the Black Krim, actually an intensely deep purple, is an old variety from St. Petersburg, Russia.

Home gardeners and small specialty farmers keep these old-fashioned varieties alive for future generations to enjoy and save. That's why William Woys Weaver, culinary historian and heirloom gardener, raises about 75 kinds of tomatoes in his Devon garden. As a child, Weaver loved his grandmother's special Yellow Ruffles tomato preserves, spiced with cardamom and ginger. She sold her preserves at the family's stand at Reading Terminal Market for "pin-money." When he later inherited her cookbooks, he became more and more interested in food history. Culinary history led him to heirloom gardening, to learn firsthand about the foods that formed our history. I'm crazy about his Garden Peach tomatoes, complete with peachy coloring and faint fuzz.

Today, tomatoes are once again provoking controversy, but for a twentieth-century reason. Tomatoes were the first genetically engineered food approved by the U.S. Food and Drug Administration. Scientists have altered the ripening gene in tomato seeds named "Flavr Savrs." These tomatoes can ripen on the vine longer and still remain firm enough to ship cross-country. Genetically altered tomatoes may give us a better-tasting tomato for the winter months, although many people are concerned about the long-term effects of genetic engineering. It's hard to believe that they will ever compete with old-fashioned tomatoes in season.

Not long ago, the only tomatoes in supermarkets came three to a plastic box, covered in cellophane. These cello-packed tomatoes were specially bred to be long lasting, with thick skins for ease of transport and regular size for easy machine packing. It is true that local varieties require tender loving care. Because of their thin skins and plentiful juices, they are prone to splitting and bruising. Sometimes you'll notice "cat-facing" or dark streaks radiating from the stem end of the tomato, a result of cold mornings.

I asked Mark Dornstreich of Branch Creek Farm, Philadelphia's premier organic specialty farmer, what made often-lumpy heirloom tomatoes so different? His simple answer is that old-fashioned tomatoes are open-pollinated varieties. Heirloom or old-plant tomatoes can self-fertilize without the intervention of modern plant science. If you save the seeds of an open-pollinated variety, like Mark's sought-after *Cuore di Bue* (beef heart) tomatoes, the plants you get will vary, but they'll all be basically similar.

Old varieties are the product of natural selection from locally grown plants. Plant breeding was an extension of what existed, rather than entirely new laboratory creations. Instead of simpler human selection, plant geneticists breed hybridized tomatoes based on desired characteristics from a worldwide gene pool. Modern tomato varieties, such as the Burpee Big Boy, came about through controlled laboratory experimentation and manipulation of plant genetics. These plant hybrids won't self-fertilize. If you save and plant their seeds, you'll get a mixed bag of results.

I asked Mark whether he prefers heirloom or hybridized tomatoes. He told me he grows heirloom varieties, such as Brandywine Pinks, Red and Yellow Currants, and Sicilian Plums along with hybrid tomatoes. His thin-skinned, plump, juicy garden tomatoes are truly vine-ripened and organically grown in specially prepared soil. So just because a tomato is a hybrid, doesn't mean it's a bad guy. He says it's hard to beat varieties like Burpee's Big Boy, developed for our own particular

conditions and tastes. These tomatoes ripen evenly and have the consistency needed for commercial production, even on his smaller scale.

Because Mark is an organic farmer, he looks for disease-resistant varieties. Heirloom varieties can be more prone to disease, a significant factor for a farmer who uses no chemical insecticides. As a chef, I was overjoyed to be able to get any of his luscious tomatoes. My personal favorites are his Red and Yellow Currant Tomatoes. These tiny, ruby- or golden-colored beauties make cherry tomatoes look big. Each one pops open in your mouth with a burst of intense, sweet-tart flavor. I recently had the pleasure of polishing off a basket of superb cherry-sized golden and red tomatoes from Kauffman's stand at Reading Terminal Market.

Real tomatoes are vulnerable and behave best if treated gently. Always ripen tomatoes with their stem-side down. Since this is the last part of the tomato to ripen, it can best support the weight of a ripe tomato without collapsing. Please don't refrigerate tomatoes unless it's absolutely necessary and then wait until they're finally ripened before subjecting them to the cold. Buy locally grown tomatoes whenever possible and help support your regional food economy.

I could eat tomatoes every day for the whole summer. I try not to waste any part of the tomato, since they all contribute flavor. I save tomato skins, seeds, and cores in small, heavy-duty bags and put them in my freezer. Whenever I'm making soup or sauces, I add a bag or two of concentrated natural flavor.

The UglyRipe Tomato Controversy

The UglyRipe Tomato, a firm, lush, vine-ripened, lumpy-looking tomato with firm yet yielding texture is quite different from the common smooth, round, evenly shaped, often mealy and tasteless tomatoes grown in Florida for sale up north in the cold weather months. UglyRipe tomatoes actually taste good. However, the Florida Tomato Committee, a trade group that controls interstate sales and shipments of round tomatoes, has determined that the brand does not meet its standards. (In past years, the Committee had granted an exception.) As a result of this decision, an editorial appeared in the *New York Times* on December 23, 2004, titled "The Unshapely Tomato," in which the editors said, "Perhaps it's time for the Florida Tomato Committee—the trade group that controls the sales and shipping of Florida tomatoes— to take a new name. It could call itself the Florida Round Red Tomato Committee. Or perhaps the Tasteless Winter Supermarket Tomato Committee. Then it would be perfectly justified in preventing, as it has, the shipment of the UglyRipe tomato variety— so called because its flesh is deeply ridged."

Mr. Joe Procacci of Procacci Brothers of Philadelphia, which grows UglyRipes in Florida, contends that the committee is afraid of the competition from a tomato whose sales have tripled in the past few years, especially in winter. In Florida, where seventy percent of the fresh tomatoes sold in the United States in winter are produced, the round tomato is the standard. Because the UglyRipe does not meet it, they cannot be sold in the interstate market. Because of this, Mr. Procacci has reduced his plantings of this tomato from 700 acres to only 100 acres for the 2004 winter season, mostly to sell in Florida. No more ugly-but-good tomatoes for anyone outside of Florida, at least in winter, unless the situation changes.

Tomatoes on Mount Vesuvius

In the region of Naples in the foothills of the magnificent volcano, Mount Vesuvius, the special small, pointy-tipped heirloom called *Pomodorino del Vesuvio* hang in large, full, drooping red clusters over the rafters to preserve them for the winter. Napolitani (the proud people of Naples) are adamant that these native tomatoes are the only ones suitable for their recipes. The small, red fruits are squarish around the stem, with thin skin, a distinctive small pointy tip, firm compact flesh, and most importantly, a delicious, sweetly acidic flavor.

The best terrain is also the most difficult to reach, often way up high, where during the long centuries since the last major eruption, the hillsides of lava have been transformed into dark earth, grainy but fertile soil rich in potassium and calcium and ideal for growing these tomatoes. Even in areas that risk eruptions, the country people stubbornly continue to return with seeds selected from the year before to plant their precious tomatoes. The deep color of these tomatoes is also a gift of the volcano. According to the elders, the roots of the tomato are nourished by the very same lava of Vesuvio. Vesuvius has erupted about three dozen times since 79 CE, most recently from 1913 to 1944, thought to be the end of a cycle of eruptions that began in 1631.

Costoluto Tomatoes

I remember huge mounds of deeply ridged, convoluted tomatoes resembling a peeled orange at the San Lorenzo Market in Florence. These were probably the famous *Costoluto Genovese*, which have been enjoyed for many generations in Italy, where tomatoes are part of almost every meal. They are large, deep-red in color, with a deeply ridged and heavily lobed surface. They are delicious eaten fresh, have a firm, meaty texture, and make beautiful scallop-edged slices.

Heirloom Tomato Seeds

Lancaster County boasts the Landis Valley Farm Museum with gardens. Its Heirloom Seed Project maintains a seed bank for home gardeners. They specialize in "German" tomatoes with potato-plant-shaped leaves and the deep lobes characteristic of older strains. These old varieties (called *bammerans*, *bommerans*, or *gummerans* in Pennsylvania German dialect) appear much the same as they did a hundred years ago. Look for Pink Brandywine, which originated in Chester County, Pennsylvania, renowned for its mild, sweet flavor and firm flesh; Red Brandywine; and the Amish Paste Tomato seeds in their catalog. A list of heirloom varieties and an order form are available at no charge by calling 717-569-0401 ext. 204. You may order by phone, fax (717-560-2147), or e-mail: c-bleensva@state.pa.us.

To Skin or Not To Skin (Tomatoes)

I don't skin thin-skinned round tomatoes. Plum tomatoes have thicker skins that can be unpleasant unless peeled. The best way to peel tomatoes is to drop them whole into a large pot of boiling water. Check them after two minutes. The tomatoes are ready when you can slide their skin easily over their flesh. Remember, the riper the tomato, the easier they will be to peel. When they're ready, drop the tomatoes into a large bowl of ice water to stop the cooking. Then slip off their skins. When you have great tomatoes, heirloom or not, the simplest dishes are the best.

Cutting Tomatoes for Salad

I learned the best way to cut tomatoes for salad from Toto Schiavone, owner of Moonstruck Restaurant in Philadelphia and a native of Calabria in Southern Italy. First, remove the core, using a sharp paring knife (or make it easy on yourself to remove the core by investing about $1.00 in a little tool called a Tomato Shark. Then, cut rough, scallop-shaped 1-inch pieces, cutting around the tomato in a spiral-fashion around the outside of the tomato. You end up with firm, roughly round tomato chunks that you can toss with dressing without them falling to pieces.

Marinara Sauce

About 10 years ago, I developed recipes for a company called Northern Italian Foods. One of my missions was to come up with the recipe for a killer marinara sauce. I tasted every brand of canned tomato available, then created the recipe below. There are some excellent brands of Italian canned San Marzano plum tomatoes, but they can be pricy. Lots of rich, fruity olive oil is another secret to a good sauce. Make sure your garlic is fresh, not dried out or sprouted and bitter, and don't stint on the basil. Fresh oregano gives it an even better flavor, and don't even think about using dried basil, which to my taste, bears no resemblance at all to the fresh. Note that tomato sauce sticks and burns easily, so prepare it in a heavy-bottomed pot and stir often, using a wooden spoon, so you don't scrape up any metal. The sauce is ready when it has thickened enough so that the oil floats to the top.

MAKES ABOUT 2 QUARTS

$^1/_2$ cup extra-virgin olive oil

1 large red onion, diced

1 tablespoon chopped garlic

$^1/_2$ cup diced celery

$^1/_2$ cup diced carrots

1 cup shredded basil

2 tablespoons chopped fresh oregano,
   substitute 2 teaspoons dried

1 (28-ounce) can chopped plum tomatoes

1 box Pomi tomatoes or 1 (28-ounce) can chopped plum
   tomatoes (see The Best Processed Tomatoes, at right)

Kosher salt and freshly ground black pepper to taste

In large, heavy-bottomed saucepot, heat the olive oil and then sauté the onion, garlic, celery, and carrots until lightly browned. Add the remaining ingredients, and bring to the boil, then reduce the heat and simmer for 1 hour, stirring frequently.

The sauce is ready when the oil starts to separate out and is visible at the top, indicating that the sauce is sufficiently thickened. Cool, then refrigerate in a covered container for up to 1 week. The sauce can also be frozen, if desired, once cooled.

THE BEST PROCESSED TOMATOES

After tasting can after can of commercially packed plum tomatoes and rejecting many, I agree with many others in the business that the best American canned tomatoes are those packed by the Stanislaus Company of Modesto, California. The company, which does nothing but plant and pack tomatoes, was started in 1942 by immigrant Italians from Tuscany and Liguria and is still owned by the same Cortopassi family. Unfortunately, their products are only sold in large cans (108 ounces, about four times the size of a large, 28-ounce can found in the supermarket) and are available only from wholesale distributors. The next-best choice is Pomi tomatoes from Parma, Italy, packed in 26-ounce aseptic boxes and found at many supermarkets, including Whole Foods. Because of this special packaging, they do not need the addition of large amounts of citric acid for preservation, so they are sweeter and firmer, with the closest taste to fresh of any packaged tomato I've had to date.

895

Tomato Kasundi

*I was given the recipe for this hot and spicy tomato chut-
ney by organic/biodynamic farmer and longtime friend,
Judy Dornstreich, who learned to make it while living on
an ashram in Northern India. There, it is known as* tamtar
kasaundi. *It has an incredible depth of mysterious flavors
that maintain their distinct character, yet at the same
time seamlessly blend with one another. In India, it would
accompany a main dish with* naan *or paratha bread. For
the American table, it is sensational on burgers and works
well as a topping for grilled fish or chicken. Try it as a
spread on cold-cut sandwiches.*

MAKES ABOUT 1 QUART, SERVES 16

1/2 cup tamarind puree

   (*see* To Prepare Tamarind, page 773)

1 large onion, diced

2 tablespoons coarsely chopped garlic

1/4 cup canola or vegetable oil

2 tablespoons black mustard seeds

1 1/2 teaspoons ground cardamom

1/2 teaspoon ground cloves

1 tablespoon ground cumin

1 tablespoon kosher salt

1/2 teaspoon cayenne pepper

1 1/2 teaspoons Garam Masala

1/2 teaspoon ground cinnamon

1/2 teaspoon freshly ground black pepper

2 (28-ounce) cans chopped plum tomatoes

2 teaspoons granulated sugar

1 bunch cilantro, chopped

In a food processor, process the onion and garlic to
a paste.

Heat the oil, add the mustard seeds and cover, cooking
until the seeds pop. Add the cardamom, cloves, cumin,
salt, cayenne, garam masala, cinnamon, and black pepper
to the pan, stir to combine, and then add the onion-garlic
paste. Fry the paste in the spices for 5 minutes. Add the
reserved tamarind pulp, tomatoes, and sugar and cook all
together at low heat for 30 minutes, stirring frequently or
until thickened. Remove from the heat and stir in the
cilantro. Chill and then refrigerate to store.

GARAM MASALA

Garam masala is the best known of India's spices
mixes and comes from Northern India's Persian-
derived Mogul cuisine. It can be purchased from
specialty spice purveyors such as Vann's Spices
(www.vannsspices.com), or you can make your own
following the recipe in my *Field Guide to Herbs &
Spices*. In a pinch, you can substitute French *quatres
epices*, or even Chinese five spice powder.

896

Mexican Tomato Sauce with Allspice

This spicy, aromatic sauce gets its flavor from jalapeño chiles, pork fat, cinnamon, and allspice. Use it for any Mexican dish that calls for tomato sauce, like enchiladas or Huevos Rancheros, or use it to top nachos or to dip tortilla chips. It also goes with the Shrimp Chiles Rellenos on page 705, and with the Chiles Rellenos with Cheese, Corn, and Chorizo on page 804. Substitute olive oil for the bacon or lard if desired and substitute one canned chipotle in adobo for the fresh jalapeño for a smoky flavor. The sauce is easy to make if you have a food processor, because all the vegetables are processed together to a chunky, soupy paste and then fried and simmered together until thickened.

MAKES 3 CUPS

1 small onion, cut up

2 cloves garlic

1 jalapeño pepper, trimmed and seeded

1 (28-ounce) can chopped plum tomatoes

1/2 teaspoon each: allspice and cinnamon

1/4 cup lard, bacon fat, or olive oil

Kosher salt and freshly ground black pepper to taste

Process the onion, garlic, and jalapeño together until chunky. Add the tomatoes, allspice, and cinnamon and process again. In a large saucepan, fry the liquid in bacon fat, lard, or olive oil, stirring carefully as it will spatter. Simmer until the sauce has thickened enough for the oil to rise to the top, about 20 minutes. Puree the sauce in a blender until smooth, and season with salt and pepper. Cool and then refrigerate for up to 1 week, or freeze if desired.

Sun-Dried Tomato Pesto

Make this flavorful, pungent tomato pesto as a spread for crostini (Italian bread toasts brushed with olive oil and garlic), but only if your sun-dried tomatoes are soft, pliable, and bright red. If you are using the kind that are marinated in a jar, drain well before proceeding with the recipe. All too often, the sun-dried tomatoes I see at the market are dried out and an unpleasant brown color. You can also use this to spread on eggplant strips for rollatini and to mix with tomato sauce for pizza. The pesto also makes a good house gift packed in a pretty jar. The recipe for the roasted garlic and oil called for here can be found on page 445, as part of the recipe for Caesar Salad with Roasted Garlic Dressing. Roasted garlic can now be purchased in small, clear plastic jars at many supermarkets in the produce aisle. If you use this kind, substitute extra olive oil for the recipe.

MAKES ABOUT 6 CUPS

1 pound sun-dried tomatoes, soaked in warm water to dehydrate and then drained, or drained marinated sun-dried tomatoes

3/4 cup roasted garlic oil

1/4 cup roasted garlic puree

1 1/2 cups extra-virgin olive oil + extra

1 teaspoon hot red pepper flakes

1 (2-ounce) can anchovies, drained

2 tablespoons capers

3 tablespoon red wine vinegar

1/4 cup chopped Italian parsley

Juice of 1 lemon

Kosher salt and white pepper to taste

Combine all of the ingredients above in the bowl of the food processor. Process, scraping down the sides once or twice, until well-combined and pasty. Transfer into glass jars or plastic containers. Cover each container of pesto with a layer of olive oil (to protect from mold). Store in the refrigerator, tightly covered, for about 2 months. Allow the pesto to come to room temperature before using, because the oil will congeal in the refrigerator.

Golden Tomato Gazpacho

Gazpacho comes from Spain, and is Andalusia's best-known dish. It probably originated in the Middle Ages when Spain was part of the Islamic world. In a well-made gazpacho, no one ingredient stands out. Before Columbus brought tomatoes to the Old World, gazpacho was a simple mash of olive oil, bread, and garlic with vinegar. Modern recipes for Gazpacho in the Andalusian style, served as refreshing cold soup with finely chopped garnishes, include the New World tomato. Here, I use golden tomatoes and bell pepper along with crumbled saffron for a beautiful and delicious variation. Golden tomatoes are available from farmers' markets in season and sometimes in supermarkets. You may, of course, substitute red, juicy tomatoes or purchase golden tomato juice or puree, sometimes found in specialty stores.

Makes 2 quarts, serves 6 to 8

1/4 cup toasted garlic croutons (*see* page 267)
1/4 teaspoon crumbled saffron threads
2 teaspoons red wine vinegar
2 1/2 pounds golden tomatoes, cored and chopped
1 yellow bell pepper, seeded and chopped
1 teaspoon chopped garlic
1 English cucumber, peeled and chopped
1/2 cup chopped red onion
1 teaspoon Pimentón (smoked paprika)
6 tablespoons extra-virgin olive oil
Kosher salt and freshly ground black pepper to taste
Garnishes: finely diced red and/or yellow pepper, tomato red onion, and cucumber, and more garlic croutons

Soak the croutons and saffron in the vinegar until the bread is soft and the mixture is bright yellow. Combine the soaked croutons and any remaining liquid, golden tomatoes and their juice, bell pepper, garlic, cucumber, onion, pimentón, and olive oil in the jar of a blender. Blend and then strain. Season with salt and pepper and chill for about 2 hours before serving. Serve chilled and garnish with a spoonful of combined diced pepper, tomato, onion and cucumber along with a tablespoonful of croutons.

Cream of Jersey Tomato Soup with Tarragon

The Campbell's Soup Company, still headquartered in Camden, New Jersey, made its name with its soup made with Jersey tomatoes. The familiar red and white can immortalized by Andy Warhol has been around since 1897. Inspired by the iconic Campbell's Cream of Tomato, I make my own using the incomparable Jersey tomato. I have to admit that red, ripe, homegrown or farmers' market tomatoes from other parts of the country will also produce a

898

delicious soup, but there's something magical about these jolie-laide *tomatoes (the French phrase means* ugly-beautiful*).* Delicate tarragon gives a slightly sweet licorice flavor to the soup. Substitute vegetable stock for a vegetarian soup.

MAKES 3 QUARTS, ENOUGH TO SERVE 10 TO 12

4 tablespoons extra-virgin olive oil, divided

1 large white onion, cut into chunks

3 cloves garlic

3 pounds ripe Jersey or other round, rich, beefsteak-type tomatoes, cut up into large chunks + 1 pound tomatoes, diced

$1/4$ cup white rice

$1/4$ cup tarragon leaves + 2 tablespoons chopped tarragon

1 quart chicken stock

1 bunch leeks, washed and drained, cut into $1^1/2$-inch dice

1 cup heavy cream

Kosher salt, cayenne pepper, and freshly ground black pepper to taste

In a large soup pot, heat 2 tablespoons of the olive oil; add the onion and garlic and cook until softened but not browned, about 6 minutes. Add the beefsteak tomatoes, the rice, $1/4$ cup of tarragon leaves, and the chicken stock. Bring to the boil and simmer until the rice is creamy and quite soft, about 20 minutes.

Transfer to a blender jar and puree until smooth. Strain, discarding any solid bits and reserving the liquid. Wash out the pot, then add the strained liquid and reserve.

Meanwhile, in a large skillet, sauté the leeks in the remaining 2 tablespoons of olive oil until transparent, then add the diced tomatoes and cook together for 5 minutes,

or until the tomatoes are softened but still hold their shape. Scrape the mixture into the reserved tomato liquid and bring to the boil. Add the heavy cream, season with the salt, cayenne, and black pepper, and serve immediately.

Pan-Fried Beefsteak Tomato Slices with Fresh Mozzarella and Basil

It's hard to imagine anything better than this simple dish of pan-fried vine-ripe tomato slabs topped with sliced milky-fresh mozzarella, then heated in the oven. Use an old-fashioned cast-iron skillet for the crispiest coating, and top with fresh basil leaves just before serving. I've been a committee member of the annual New Jersey Tomato Festival in charge of chef demonstrations and farmers for the past 2 years on Camden, New Jersey's, waterfront. For my own demonstration, I prepared these crispy, juicy tomatoes. I didn't get to even taste my own dish, because they were snapped up so fast. Although green tomatoes are more traditionally fried, especially after having been immortalized in a book and movie, to my taste, ripe tomatoes are even better.

SERVES 6

4 ounces (1 cup) all-purpose flour

2 eggs, lightly beaten

2 teaspoons kosher salt

$1/2$ teaspoon freshly ground black pepper

$1/4$ teaspoon cayenne pepper

4 cups Japanese panko breadcrumbs

TOMATOES

1 pound large ripe beefsteak tomatoes,
    sliced ½-inch thick
2 cups canola oil, for frying
½ pound fresh mozzarella, drained and cut into slices
1 bunch basil, large leaves picked off

Set up three bowls: one with the flour, one with the eggs seasoned with the salt, black pepper and cayenne and one with the panko. Dip the tomato slices first into the flour, then the eggs, and then coat with the crumbs. Place in a single layer on a wax-paper-lined tray, and chill until you're ready to cook them.

Heat ½ inch of oil in a heavy skillet until shimmering but not smoking, then gently place the tomato slices in the pan without crowding. Pan-fry until the edges are golden, then turn, using a spatula or tongs, and brown on the other side. Drain the tomatoes on paper towels and continue with another round of tomatoes, adding more oil as needed.

When you're ready to serve them, preheat the oven to 400°F. Arrange the fried tomatoes in a baking pan and top each slice with a slice of mozzarella. Bake for 10 minutes, or until the cheese starts to melt. Serve immediately, each slice topped with a basil leaf.

Linguine with Chicken Cacciatore Sauce

Cacciatore *means* hunter's style *in Italian, so chicken cacciatore has the woodsy flavors of mushrooms and rosemary. Cacciatore is usually served as a stew made from a cut-up chicken; here, I call for diced chicken breast tossed with pasta. It's a dish to please kids and grown-ups equally. I served it at Parma, the "old-world fast-food" chain for which I developed recipes, where it was one of the most popular dishes. Make it with gemelli or rotini if your kids are too young to handle string pasta like linguine. The Marsala is optional, though it does give a subtle nutty sweetness to the sauce.*

SERVES 4

1 red onion, sliced
2 cups quartered white mushrooms
1 tablespoon chopped garlic
1 tablespoon chopped rosemary
¼ cup olive oil
¼ cup dry Marsala wine
2 cups Marinara sauce (purchased or homemade,
    see page 895)
2 pounds chicken breast, roasted on the bone and diced
Kosher salt and freshly ground black pepper to taste
1 pound linguine, cooked and drained
¼ cup chopped Italian parsley
1 cup grated Parmigiano-Reggiano or Grana Padano

Bring a large pot of salted water to the boil. In a large, heavy skillet, sauté the red onion, mushrooms, garlic, and rosemary in the olive oil until softened, about 6 minutes. Add the Marsala to the pan and bring to the boil. Add the marinara sauce and the chicken, season with salt and pepper, and reserve.

Meanwhile, cook the linguine until *al dente*, firm and bouncy, and still yellow in color. Drain well, toss with the sauce and the parsley, sprinkle with cheese, and serve immediately, preferably in heated pasta bowls.

TUNA
CANNED & FRESH

TUNA
CANNED & FRESH

Only a few years ago, if you said tuna, any American would automatically assume it came from a can. More recently, the opposite has been true. Say tuna and we think of rare, sushi-grade tuna. Unfortunately, most home cooks don't have access to the freshest or highest-grade tuna, or if we find it, it's prohibitively expensive. There is an excellent alternative. In the Mediterranean, along with its 2,000-year-old tuna fishing industry, there is also a longtime tradition of preserving tuna by canning it in olive oil. For many classic Mediterranean dishes, such as *Salade Niçoise* and *Vitello Tonnato*, tuna from a can has the right taste and rich texture. The best tuna canned in olive oil can be likened to a confit of tuna, oil-poached tuna that melts in your mouth with a meaty, satisfying texture. I've never tasted better canned tuna than the one hand-carried to me from Tunisia called *Sidi Jabeur*. Use canned tuna to make mixed salads, stuffed vegetables, hors d'oeuvres, or on sandwiches such as *pan bagnat* (the Provençal version of a hoagie filled with tuna, eggs, and peppers) and in spreads like tapenade.

To preserve this great fish, the Phoenicians would salt and smoke tuna. The Greek writer Archestratus recommended the great tuna from the islands of Samos and Sicily and said that tuna from North Africa are the best. Maybe this is why there are still so many dishes using tuna in the cuisine of Tunisia. Pliny believed that the Golden Horn, the entrance into the Bosphorus, was given its name to mark the abundance of tuna in this area of Byzantium.

Tuna are migratory fish that travel in dense shoals. As early as the second century BCE, the Greeks knew of their migratory habits, which are still not fully understood. Not until the nineteenth century was evidence shown that the majority of tuna in the Mediterranean stay there throughout the year. In Provence, until the end of the nineteenth century, the approach of shoals of tuna was heralded by lookouts blowing their horns.

In the Mediterranean, tuna fishing is of great antiquity and considerable commercial importance. Bluefin tuna are still caught in special tuna traps during their breeding migrations, although the numbers of these traps is dwindling. Comparable traps were probably used in Neolithic times and were well-established by classical times. A long net stretches out to sea, intercepting the migrating fish and diverting them into a series of ponds. They end up in the net where the fish are finally captured and taken from the nets with gaffs.

Early in this century, fishing for bluefin tuna was still done on a small scale and restricted to the Mediterranean, whereas fishing for albacore tuna was modernized around 1850 and thrived in the Bay of Biscay. The first boat designed for fishing tuna for the canning industry was built in 1906. Today, tuna fishing is industrialized and scientific, and uses helicopters or even satellites to locate the migrating shoals.

Different methods are used to catch different tuna. Purse seining is used to catch the skipjack and yellowfin tuna that make up the majority of the light canned tuna pack. Vessels with mile-long nets encircle the tuna and are then closed off by drawstrings, much like a drawstring purse. Longlining is used to fish for larger albacore , with 60-mile and longer mainlines with branch lines and baited hooks catch two to three fish per 100 hooks. Trolling is used for fishing smaller albacore using eight to twelve lines with baited hooks tow the fish that are then pulled on board.

Butchering a tuna is similar to butchering a cow in that each part and muscle is treated differently in cut and how it is prepared. One Spanish company, Salazones Ramon Asensio S.A., shows just how seriously canned and other forms of preserved tuna are taken in this part of the world. "Our piece of the Mediterranean Sea is protected as a world natural preserve for its beauty and originality. The warm and constant winds that come from the North of Africa that mingle with the aroma and coolness of our protected, clean, and crystalline waters create a sea breeze that engulfs our products, giving them an exclusive, incomparable, and unique savor. Our company was created to continue our land's tradition of curing, ventilation, drying, maceration, and smoking of fish which goes back to the Roman epoch." They sell a large assortment of tuna cuts, including Cured Fillets, Roe, Bellies (Ventresca), Neck, and Tenderloin, just as if they were selling beef, to upscale gourmet stores in Europe.

903

The Five Kinds of Tuna

Five main species of tuna that are fished are albacore, blackfin, bluefin, skipjack, and yellowfin.

Albacore: The albacore, *Thunnus alalunga*, averages from ten to thirty pounds and is a fish of the seven seas. Its creamy white, slightly rose-tinted meat resembles veal and was once nicknamed "veal of the Carthusians," as it could be eaten by Carthusian monks on meatless days. It has a mild, rich taste and firm, steak-like texture with large, moist flakes. It is less dense than bluefin, though it is high in fat and has the highest amount of beneficial Omega-3 oils than any of the other tunas. Because it is less firm than yellowfin or bluefin, it is not suited to sushi. Albacore is widely canned and is the only tuna that can be labeled "white meat tuna." Found off the western coast of Italy, around Sicily, and in Greek waters, it can be easily recognized by its extra-long pectoral fins.

Bigeye (or Blackfin Tuna): Bigeye (or Blackfin) *Tunnus Obesus*—about 200 pounds—is caught in the same areas as the yellowfin and is often eaten fresh. Bigeye tuna congregate in schools and swim along the edges of warm underwater streams in search of food.

Bluefin Tuna: The bluefin, *Thunnus thynnus*, the biggest member of the tuna family, is called "giant" by fisherman, and for good reason. It is a rapid, powerful swimmer that lives in temperate and tropical waters worldwide. Over half the global catch comes from the biologically separate groups of fish from the eastern and western Atlantic Ocean. The Mediterranean is also a historic area for bluefin, in parts where the water is deep enough for this huge fish. When young, its belly has green stripes; later it has a dark blue back. Bluefin average about 250 pounds, but can weigh as much as 1,400 pounds. Bluefin is fished in deep water areas of the Mediterranean and in the Bay of Biscay and is usually sold fresh. Its flesh is dark red, very firm and compact, and rather heavy. Because of its high fat content, bluefin is especially prized for use raw in sushi, ceviche, and tartars. It is best served raw or seared on the outside and raw to rare on the inside, because it can quickly dry out. Bluefin is graded by taking sample "plugs" out of its flesh to test for color and fat content, critical to its price. Those with the best color and richest fat return very high prices. Bluefin is sold in three grades: Number 1, *sashimi-grade*, is destined for the Japanese market, which pays the highest price for the fish, often bought right from the boats off Montauk Point in Long Island, New York. Number 2, or *grill-grade*, is the second best, while Number 3 is lower in quality.

Skipjack Tuna: Skipjacks, *Tunnus Katsuwonus pelamis*, are small, usually between five and eight pounds, but can be as large as forty pounds. Nearly half of the catch of the five main tuna varieties is skipjack, making it a staple of global tuna fisheries.

Yellowfin Tuna: The yellowfin, *Thunnus albacares*, has a long, bright-yellow dorsal fin and a yellow stripe down its side with a steel-blue back, grayish sides, and a silvery belly. It's thinner than the bluefin and is not as large, running up to two hundred pounds, though most fish in the market are quite a bit smaller. This tuna is called *ahi* in Hawaii, meaning *fire*, because its golden color glows at night when the fish feeds. Yellowfin is fished in tropical waters and is widely canned as "light tuna." Its meat is mild, similar to swordfish, with more flavor than albacore but leaner than bluefin. More than any other kind of tuna, fresh yellowfin is susceptible to developing histamines if improperly handled, which will cause scombroid poisoning. Buy tuna from a reputable fishmonger to avoid a potential problem. Avoid bargain tuna and choose yellowfin with glistening flesh and bright, clear, reddish-pink color, and fresh smell.

CHOOSING CANNED TUNA

When buying canned tuna, there are so many possibilities it can get confusing. Although water-packed solid white meat tuna has been the gold standard in America, to me it is mealy and dry. I choose yellowfin, also called light tuna, packed in olive oil, as is done throughout the Mediterranean, where they eat a lot of canned tuna. Canned tuna is sold solid-pack (larger pieces tightly packed together) and chunk, which is in small fragments.

My top choice is the very reasonably priced Genova Tonno, yellowfin tuna packed in olive oil, sold by Trader Joe's. Star-Kist Gourmet's Choice Solid Light Tuna in Olive Oil is another good brand. Look for large hunks of tuna packed in olive oil in glass jars from Spain and Italy. I also use the local Cento brand light tuna in olive oil for my recipes because it is fairly easy to find on supermarket shelves and has a good flavor. Try a few brands, including imported Italian and Spanish, to find your favorite.

904

Tuna and Caper Spread

I learned to make this delicious, flavor-packed tuna spread from Lauren Groveman, author of Lauren Groveman's Kitchen, *although I've naturally adapted it to my own taste. Light tuna packed in olive oil is a must here for moistness. Just like Caesar Salad dressing, the key ingredient here is anchovies, and if your friends don't like anchovies, or think they don't, I say what they don't know won't hurt them. It's funny that America's most popular salad dressing is made from anchovies and yet if asked, most people would say that they hate anchovies. This spread is outstanding on crackers, pita chips, or crostini, or used as a dip for crudités. It will keep 2 weeks in the refrigerator.*

MAKES 2 CUPS, ENOUGH TO SERVE 12

2 (6-ounce) cans light tuna in olive oil, drained

3 tablespoons coarse-grain mustard

1/4 cup sliced shallots

4 anchovy fillets, chopped

1 1/2 teaspoons crushed garlic

Juice and zest of 1 lemon

2 tablespoon drained capers

6 tablespoons mayonnaise

Freshly ground black pepper to taste

2 tablespoons chopped parsley

Place the tuna, mustard, shallots, anchovies, garlic, and lemon juice, and zest in the bowl of a food processor. Process briefly, just until chunky. Add the capers and process briefly, just to break them up. Remove the mixture from the processor and beat in the mayonnaise , black pepper, and parsley. Keep refrigerated for up to 5 days.

Mechoui: Roasted Vegetable Salad with Tuna

Mechoui *is the Arabic word for* charcoal grill, *also spelled* meshwi. *In this Tunisian salad, grilled peppers, tomato, and onion are spiced with caraway, coriander, and garlic and then chopped to combine the flavors. Garnished with canned tuna, black olives, and hard-cooked eggs, it makes a colorful and satisfying main dish salad. When I served this dish at a recent party, it disappeared quickly.*

SERVES 6

2 cloves garlic

1 1/2 teaspoons ground caraway

1 1/2 teaspoons ground coriander

Kosher salt to taste

1/2 pound red bell peppers

1/2 pound green Italian frying peppers, or poblano peppers, or Anaheim chiles

1/2 pound plum tomatoes

1 red onion, quartered

1/4 cup extra-virgin olive oil

Juice of 1 lemon (about 1/4 cup)

1 (6-ounce) can tuna in oil, preferably olive oil

1/2 cup mixed cured olives, pitted

2 hard cooked eggs, quartered

Chop the garlic cloves together with the caraway, coriander, and salt.

Preheat a grill or a broiler. Rub the red and green peppers, tomatoes, and onion quarters with a little of the oil. Grill or broil the vegetables on all sides until blistered. Cool the vegetables, then rub off the skins. Remove the seeds from the tomatoes. Trim and discard the seeds and white membrane from the peppers. Chop all the vegetables or slice into thin strips.

Combine the vegetables with the garlic and spice mixture. Arrange on a serving platter then drizzle with the lemon juice and the remaining olive oil. Garnish with chunks of the tuna, the olives, and the egg quarters. Accompany with grilled or toasted pita bread or Italian bread.

Brik de Maman with Tuna and Egg Filling

In Tunisia (long ruled by the Ottoman Turks) the Turkish borek became brik—*a national snack food. Large round brik leaves, somewhere between crepe and phyllo, filled with all kinds of stuffings, are quickly fried until crispy on the outside and hot inside. This recipe comes from Tunisian chef Haouari Abdezzarak's mother. Buy brik leaves from North African markets or specialty retailers such as Kalustyans in New York (www.kalustyans.com) or use defrosted unsweetened crepes or even phyllo dough.*

MAKES 8

1/2 pound potatoes

2 tablespoons drained capers

1/2 cup chopped Italian parsley

1/2 cup finely chopped onion

1 (6-ounce) can tuna in oil, preferably olive oil

1 teaspoon harissa

2 eggs, lightly beaten

Kosher salt and freshly ground black pepper to taste

8 brik leaves, or phyllo dough, or crepes

1 quart olive oil, for frying

Lemon quarters

Steam the potatoes, then rub off the skins, and press through a ricer into a bowl. Add the capers, parsley, onion, tuna, harissa, eggs, and salt and pepper. Divide the filling among the brik leaves. Fold in quarters, press the edges to seal, and pan fry in oil until crispy. Drain on paper towels and serve with lemon quarters.

Italian Tuna Loaf

Polpettone (or meat loaf) is made in all sorts of forms in Italy, using ground pork, turkey, veal, chicken, and, as here, tuna. I adapted this recipe from one in Edda Servi Machlin's wonderful memoir and cookbook, The Classic Cuisine of the Italian Jews. *In the original recipe, the mixture is formed into a loaf that is wrapped in cloth, tied, poached like a large sausage and then served with a pungent lemon, anchovy, and caper sauce. Polepettone de Tonno makes a good picnic or buffet dish, and can be made several days ahead and sliced as needed. Use any extra sauce as a sandwich spread.*

SERVES 6

Tuna Loaf

2 teaspoons chopped garlic

2 tablespoons extra-virgin olive oil

2 (6-ounce) cans light tuna in olive oil, drained

1/2 cup country-style breadcrumbs

¼ cup grated Parmigiano-Reggiano or Grana Padano

3 eggs, slightly beaten

½ cup chopped Italian parsley

Kosher salt and freshly ground black pepper to taste

Preheat the oven to 325°F. In a small pan, cook the garlic in olive oil until light gold in color. Crumble the tuna and combine with the breadcrumbs, cheese, eggs, parsley, and the garlic along with its cooking oil. Season with salt and pepper, then pack the mixture into a nonstick-sprayed 6-cup loaf pan, then cover with foil. Bake for 45 minutes, or until the loaf is set in the middle and a skewer stuck in the middle comes out clean. Remove from the oven, cool, and slice, reserving any pan juices for the sauce.

Sauce and Assembly

Pan juices, from above

1 egg

1 tablespoon capers, drained

4 fillets anchovy

Juice of 1 lemon

¾ cup extra-virgin olive oil

¼ oil-cured black olives, pitted and halved

1 lemon, sliced

Prepare the sauce as for a mayonnaise: place any pan juices, the egg, capers, anchovies, and lemon juice in the jar of a blender. Blend until smooth, then slowly pour in the olive oil until the sauce has thickened.

Serve the tuna loaf slices with sauce drizzled over top. Garnish with black olives and lemon slices.

Tuna Ceviche with Apple and Soy

This recipe came from the Japanese sushi chef, Taka (Eji Takase) of Sushi Samba in New York. Chef Taka has been artfully incorporating Latin American flavors into his sushi partly as a result of a trip to Brazil with the owners and chefs of the restaurant, superstar bistro-chef Tony Bourdain, and myself. In this ever-popular Peruvian-Japanese fusion ceviche, tuna is dressed with a slightly sweet mixture of soy sauce, sake, and mirin, flavored with fresh apple, ginger, and a bit of garlic. Chef Taka prefers Japanese Yamasu soy sauce for this ceviche because it is less salty. Be sure to buy the finest sushi-grade tuna and keep it icy cold until ready to serve.

SERVES 4

¼ cup saké

2 tablespoons mirin

1 Granny Smith apple; peeled and cored, half cut into rough chunks, half cut into tiny cubes

2 teaspoons grated ginger

1 teaspoon chopped garlic

½ teaspoon sea salt

¼ cup rice wine vinegar

½ pound sushi-grade Ahi tuna

¼ cup soy sauce, preferably Japanese Yamasu

Combine the saké and mirin in a small pan and warm over medium heat. Light the heated liquid and allow it to burn until the alcohol has burned off.

Place the rough apple chunks, ginger, garlic, salt, and vinegar in the jar of a blender and puree until smooth.

Remove the mixture from the blender, combine with the saké mixture and soy sauce, and reserve until ready to serve.

Using a sharp, thin-bladed knife, cut the tuna into $1/4$-inch-thick slices, then cut the slices into 1-inch squares. Lightly toss the tuna squares with the reserved sauce, divide among 4 serving plates and serve immediately garnished with the apple cubes.

SUSHI SAMBA

At Sushi Samba, sushi and ceviche (or *seviche*) are served from a central bar where the chefs work in front of customers to the tune of Brazilian samba. There are now five Sushi Samba locations: two in New York, one in Chicago, one in Miami, and the newest in Tel-Aviv. The stylish food inspired by the cuisines of Japan, Peru, and Brazil is presented in an up-to-date, energetic, and artfully designed ambiance. (Go to www.sushi samba.com for menus, culture, music, and more.)

Seared Tuna Niçoise on Potato Slices

Serve these tidbits of Niçoise-style seared tuna on potatoes as an hors d'oeuvre for your next gathering. Your guests will love them. Use the freshest sushi-grade tuna here and sear it the same day you're planning to serve the canapés. The special rectangular blocks of Saku tuna sold in cryovac packaging will also work here. Idaho potatoes are the best choice, because they are relatively even in size and can be cut into nice, round, matching slices. Tiny string-like haricots verts will make the most elegant topping, but slender, young green beans will also work well. The Niçoise olives called for here are small, deep brown, and mild in flavor. Press down on each olive to break it open and remove the pit.

MAKES 50

8 tablespoons extra-virgin olive oil, divided

1 tablespoon sherry vinegar

1 tablespoon finely chopped shallots

Kosher salt and freshly ground black pepper to taste

$1/4$ pound haricots verts, cut into thin strips

4 large Idaho potatoes

$1^1/2$ pounds center-cut tuna loin

1 red bell pepper, finely diced

$1/2$ cup Niçoise olives, pitted and halved

2 teaspoons finely chopped thyme

1 tablespoon shredded basil

Whisk together 3 tablespoons of olive oil with the sherry vinegar, shallots, and salt and pepper, and reserve.

Bring a large pot of salted water to the boil. Add the

haricots verts (or green beans) and cook for 2 minutes, or until bright green. Scoop the beans from the water and run under cold water to cool and set the color.

Meanwhile, peel the potatoes and cut them into slices a bit thicker than $1/4$ inch. Drop in the same boiling water, cook for 1 minute, and then drain immediately. Run under cold water to rinse off any surface starch, and reserve.

Trim the tuna of any dark spots. Cut into long sections about $1^1/4$-inches on a side. Season the tuna with salt and pepper and rub with 1 tablespoon of the olive oil.

Meanwhile, heat a large heavy skillet, preferably cast-iron until just beginning to smoke. Sear the tuna on all sides and immediately remove from the pan (the tuna should be rare inside). Cool and then reserve.

Wipe out the skillet, add 2 tablespoons olive oil and brown the potato slices on both sides. Remove the slices, add the remaining 2 tablespoons of olive oil and brown the remaining potatoes. Arrange in a single layer on a large wax- or parchment-paper-lined tray.

Mix together the haricot verts, red pepper, olives, thyme, and basil. Slice the tuna as thinly as possible. Place one slice of tuna on each potato slice and top with the haricots verts mixture. Drizzle with the vinaigrette and serve immediately.

Grilled Tuna with Red Wine and Green Peppercorn Sauce

Tuna, especially if prepared on a charcoal grill, is quite steak-like. This dish, fit for the most determined meat-and-potatoes eater, especially of the male variety, is hearty as can be. Cut the tuna at least $3/4$-inch thick (preferably 1-inch thick), so that it can be crusty on the outside and rare to medium-rare and juicy on the inside. Keep the tuna quite cold until you're ready to cook it, so that it stays rare. The sauce is a multistage recipe that is admittedly time-consuming. However, none of the steps need much attention and once made, the sauce can be served another night with a big, juicy, grilled New York strip steak. The surprising heat of the small, unripe green peppercorns here contrasts with the unctuous richness of the sauce. It is difficult, if not impossible, to make the sauce in a tiny quantity, but it will keep quite well refrigerated for up to 2 weeks, or in the freezer for up to 3 months.

909

SERVES 4

Red Wine and Green Peppercorn Sauce

1 cup + $1/4$ cup sliced shallots

2 tablespoons unsalted butter

1 rib celery, sliced

1 bay leaf

2 cups sliced mushroom stems and trimmings, preferably from shiitakes and/or portabellas, substitute chopped mushrooms

3 sprigs fresh thyme

$1/2$ teaspoon crushed black peppercorns

2 cups dry red wine

1 quart Demi-Glace (purchased or homemade,
  see page 115)
¼ cup balsamic vinegar
2 tablespoons Green Peppercorns in brine, drained
Kosher salt to taste

In a large, heavy nonreactive saucepan, brown 1 cup of the
shallots in the butter until deep brown. Add the celery, bay
leaf, mushrooms, thyme, and crushed peppercorns. Sauté
together until browned. Add the red wine and Demi-Glace
and simmer for 1 hour, or until the sauce has good body
and is beginning to get syrupy. Strain, add the vinegar and
remaining ¼ cup shallots to the sauce, and reduce again
until the sauce is the consistency of syrup. Stir in the green
peppercorns, salt to taste, and keep warm.

Tuna and Assembly

4 (8-ounce) portions of tuna, at least ¾-inch thick
1 tablespoon canola or vegetable oil
Kosher salt and freshly ground black pepper to taste
1 cup thinly sliced strips of colorful sweet bell peppers
1 cup Red Wine and Green Peppercorn Sauce

Preheat a grill or broiler until hot. Rub the tuna with oil,
then season on both sides with salt and pepper. Place on
the grill crosswise, then turn as needed to make crisscross
marks on both sides. Cook the tuna to desired temperature, preferably no more than medium-rare.

Meanwhile, heat the pepper strips in the sauce. Serve
the tuna topped with a portion of the peppers and sauce.

GREEN PEPPERCORNS

Green peppercorns are the same dried fruits of the
pepper plant, Piper nigrum, more familiar as black peppercorns. They are hand-picked when full-sized but not
yet ripe, so they are always more expensive. To keep
them green, the enzyme present in the fruits that turns
them black is kept from activating, either by brining, or
by boiling and then oven-drying, or by freeze-drying.
Highly aromatic and less pungent, with a fresh, herbal
character, green peppercorns are used mostly in European and American cooking to season mustard, steak
sauces, and pâtés. Here I call for brined peppercorns
sold in small cans for the sauce, because they have a
softer quality, though crunchier freeze-dried green
peppercorns can be substituted. I recently bought fresh
green peppercorns on the branch at a specialty spice
store in Canada, so they may start showing up in the
States soon.

910

TURKEY

TURKEY

Look at the cover of any food magazine in November and, lo and behold, they'll show yet another beauty shot of a big, beautiful, roast turkey. Their challenge is to come up with a new-ish take on the bird every year, one that will set their magazine off from its competitors, yet will be mainstream enough for most readers. Roast turkey makes a magnificent centerpiece for most of our Thanksgiving dinners, though depending on our ethnic backgrounds we might accompany it with lasagna, spaetzle, tamales, or fried rice. However, there is a lot more to turkey than a once- or twice-a-year bird. Chefs and consumers are starting to discover the versatility of these birds. Turkey consumption has more than doubled over the past twenty-five years because people are now using turkey parts for their recipes, rather than limiting themselves to buying the whole bird.

Native to North America, turkeys are now farmed and used around the globe. The word *turkey* was originally a prefix to the terms *cock*, *hen* and *poult* (a young bird, as in the word *poultry*) but now stands on its own. *Turkey* came from the English, who may have had their first birds brought by Turkish or Levantine merchants, so they called them *turkey-cocks*.

The original wild turkeys of North America are much leaner and more streamlined birds than their modern descendants. In their natural state, turkeys live in flocks, roosting in swampy areas and feeding on woodland berries and seeds. They are awkward in flight but run fast. Two distinct races of wild turkey are known—one which originally ranged throughout eastern North America and is our American wild turkey. Until recently, these birds were disappearing in the United States. When the National Wild Turkey Federation was founded in 1973, there were only 1.3 million turkeys throughout the United States. That number now stands at five million.

The second kind of wild turkey came from further south, around the Gulf of Mexico. This Mexican variety appears to have been quite adaptable and was easily domesticated by the Aztecs and other native peoples. Turkey is thought to have been first domesticated late in the second millennium BCE somewhere in Central America. The Aztecs, who enjoyed a variety of wild animals, ate a great deal of turkey. By the time of the Spanish Conquest, turkeys were being reared as a table bird and eaten by royalty. The Spaniard Bernardino de Sahagún had good things to say about turkey, writing in 1529, "the meat of the hens [are] as fat and savory." According to him, turkeys were already being included in tamales, a dish still in Mexico's culinary repertoire today.

Despite the availability of wild fowl and then of domesticated ducks and chickens introduced by the Spaniards, the turkey survived as an important food in

912

Mexico. Besides being served in tamales, one of the most famed dishes in Mexican cuisine is turkey in molé, a complex sauce with as many as one hundred ingredients.

We all probably learned the story of the first Thanksgiving dinner in America in 1621 from elementary school. Ten years earlier, the inhabitants of Jamestown, reduced almost to starvation, were kept alive by gifts of wild game, including "turkies" given to them by Native Americans. In 1621, the Plymouth colonists and the Wampanoag Indians enjoyed an autumnal feast which became famous as The First Thanksgiving. According to an account of the period, "They dined on wild fowl and on venison; ducks, geese, and turkey shot by the colonists, and five deer provided by Massasoit's men, and other foods besides."

Because Europeans believed turkeys to have originated in the East, they called the bird names like the French *coq d'Inde* (Indian cock), later shortened to the modern *dinde* or *dindon* in French. When turkeys first arrived in Europe, they were confused with Guinea fowl and peacocks, two exotic birds that were highly prized at the time. Turkey's Latin name is *Meleagris gallopavo*: *meleagris* is the Roman name for guinea fowl; *gallo* means chicken, and *pavo* means *peacock* in Latin and Italian.

Turkeys were quickly adapted in the Old World. By the 1550s, their price was fixed in the London markets and they were already the bird of choice for Christmas dinner. Not much later, during the reign of Elizabeth I, turkeys were already being made into English-style meat pies. In a cookbook of the time, Gervase Markham recommended that turkeys be roasted and served with a sauce of onions, flavored with claret [Bordeaux wine], orange juice, and lemon peel. In France, Queen Marguerite of Navarre raised turkeys at Alençon in 1534

and sixty-six turkeys were served at a feast given for Catherine de Medici in 1549.

By 1570, there were several recipes for turkey in Italy, including spit roasted, and a more elaborate dish where the bird was stuffed, stuck with cloves, enclosed in a crust with its head exposed, and then baked. Turkey recipes appeared later in France, during the culinary renaissance of the seventeenth century. The famed La Varenne gave several recipes including one with a truffled bouillon. From the eighteenth century onwards, turkeys were firmly established in Europe. Originally a dish with high status, turkeys were soon being served at the tables of the bourgeoisie and in more recent times at everyone's table, at least for special occasions. Because France, Italy, and Great Britain adopted turkey early, they developed a large repertoire of turkey dishes for the bird and thus more occasions for eating them.

Surprisingly, Americans are not the world's top consumers of turkey. That title goes to Israel at nearly thirty pounds per year, much of it eaten as *shwarma*. This large, layered vertical spit-roasted meat, sliced hot for sandwiches, was originally made with lamb only, but now generally combines turkey and lamb. In Israel, a small country with little grazing land for cattle, turkey has become the meat of choice. Pastrami made from turkey meat is an Israeli innovation.

Roast turkey is still the American holiday meat of choice, with more than five hundred million pounds consumed on Thanksgiving, twenty-two million pounds at Christmas, and almost that much at Easter. Americans generally prefer the white meat, while other countries choose dark meat. A fifteen-pound turkey typically is about seventy percent white meat and thirty percent dark meat, although the "heritage breeds" now

913

being raised are higher in dark meat. Why not help support this American movement to bring back our heritage of diverse and tasty turkeys this Thanksgiving?

WHITE AND DARK MEAT TURKEY

White meat has fewer calories and less fat than dark meat, but those who prefer dark meat say it has more flavor. White meat is milder in flavor and is a good counterfoil to flavors like tomato, Marsala, lemon, mushroom, and apples, though it can be dry if overcooked. Dark meat holds up well in rich marinades and is a perfect choice for grilling and barbecuing and makes very rich, tasty ground meat.

Beyond Roast Turkey

Boneless, skinless breasts are perfect for poaching to make turkey salad or marinating and then barbecuing or slicing for sandwiches. Ground turkey meat—whether light or dark or mixed—is suited to dishes like spaghetti and meatballs, meatloaf, picadillo, and stuffed peppers. Sweet and spicy turkey sausage is a delicious alternative to pork-based sausages. Smoked turkey drumsticks are inexpensive and flavorful, excellent when cooked with bean or other hearty soups giving that smoky, meaty flavor without using pork products.

Ben Franklin and Turkey

Benjamin Franklin, who proposed the turkey as the official United States' bird, was dismayed when the bald eagle was chosen instead. Franklin wrote to his daughter, referring to the eagle's "bad moral character," saying, "I wish the bald eagle had not been chosen as the representative of our country! The turkey is a much more respectable bird, and withal a true original native of America."

DEEP-FRYING TURKEY CAJUN STYLE

Deep-frying turkeys is a Southern tradition that has gained national attention in the last few years. By deep-frying, the inside of the bird remains very juicy and the skin develops a crisp texture. Commercial catering operations in the South commonly offer deep-fried turkey, and restaurants feature the golden crisp bird during the holidays. At tailgate parties, outdoor church suppers, and neighborhood parties, people set up large, deep stock pots on low gas burners. They fill the kettles with fresh peanut oil, pat the turkeys dry, put on long, heavy-duty gloves and cook these juicy, deep-brown turkeys.

If you'd like to try your own deep-fried turkey, you'll need to buy a special turkey deep-fryer pot along with several large containers of peanut or vegetable oil. A 26-quart Turkey Fryer with a deep pot, lid, rack, grabbing hook, and thermometer costs about $120 from www.Cajunmarket.com, and I've seen them for sale at warehouse club stores like BJ's in Thanksgiving season.

Turkey Waldorf Salad

Here is a variation on the ultra-simple classic Waldorf salad created in the 1890s at New York's Waldorf-Astoria hotel by the legendary maître d', Oscar Tschirky. This one uses turkey instead of chicken and creamy walnut oil vinaigrette rather than the original mayonnaise. The original recipe in his 900+ page 1896 The Cook Book by Oscar of the Waldorf reads as follows: "Peel 2 raw apples, cut into small pieces about $1/2$-in. square, cut some celery the same way, and mix with the apple. Add 'a good mayonnaise'."

SERVES 6 TO 8

$1/2$ cup each: walnut oil and canola or vegetable oil

$1/2$ cup cider vinegar

2 tablespoons honey

2 tablespoons finely chopped shallots

2 teaspoons kosher salt, divided

Freshly ground black pepper to taste

2 cups chicken broth

1 pound turkey breast

1 crispy red apple (Stayman Winesap or Fuji) and 1 tart green apple (Granny Smith)

Juice of 1 lemon

1 cup halved red and/or green grapes, seeded if necessary

1 cup chopped walnuts, lightly toasted in a 300°F. oven until medium brown

4 ribs celery, diced

$1/4$ cup chopped Italian parsley

Place the oils, vinegar, honey, shallots, 1 teaspoon of the salt, and the pepper into the container of a blender (or use an immersion blender) and puree until creamy and smooth, and reserve.

Bring the broth and the remaining 1 teaspoon of salt to the boil. Add the turkey and enough water to barely cover. Poach about 15 minutes, or until turkey is firm and no longer pink in the middle. Allow the turkey to cool in the broth, and then cut into 1-inch cubes. (If desired, strain the cooking liquid and reserve for another use, such as soup.)

Cut the apples into small cubes and toss with the lemon juice. Combine the turkey cubes, grapes, walnuts, celery, apples, parsley, the dressing, and more black pepper to taste. Serve immediately, or refrigerate and serve within 2 days.

TURDUCKEN

In America, we have our own regional specialties using turkey. In Louisiana's Cajun country, a special way of treating turkey has developed. This is a turducken, which is a deboned chicken, stuffed into a deboned duck, which is then stuffed into a deboned turkey. A properly prepared turducken provides rich slices that present all three birds' meat in layers.

Turduckens are becoming one of Louisiana's biggest poultry exports, their popularity exploding in the last three years. One processor has built a turducken plant, which produces more than 30,000 of these turkeys every year for customers across the United States.

Heritage Turkey Breeds

Heritage turkeys are bred to be true to one of the older registered "standard breeds" of turkeys and must be able to breed naturally, grow slowly, and live seven to nine years. The modern commercial turkey, the Broad-Breasted Bronze and Large White, became the dominant commercial turkey in American during the second half of the twentieth century, selected because it could produce a lot of meat quickly. Through breeding, their body shape was altered so that they have heavy breasts and short legs. They cannot breed naturally or fly, they have short lives, and tend to be innocuous in flavor.

Because heritage turkeys grow more slowly than modern commercial varieties, they tend to have more intrinsic flavor, but how they are raised and what they eat is also important. The recent revival of heritage turkeys came about through a program of Slow Food USA, in which a market was developed for varieties of turkeys that were threatened with extinction. This preserves genetic variety and also keeps alive an American culinary tradition. To learn more and to purchase heritage breed turkeys, go to www.slowfoodusa.org/ark/turkeys.html.

Maple–Apple Smoked Turkey Breast

Try this recipe and see if it isn't the best smoked turkey you've ever tasted. My super critical son thought so and I agree. It's moist, juicy, and tender, with a delicious, deep brown crusty glaze of apple cider and maple, two of America's best native flavors. Serve the turkey in salad, or on sandwiches, and don't throw away the bones. Save them to make Roasted Chicken or Turkey Stock following the recipe on page 991. Use the stock for delicious bean soups such as Cuban black bean or split pea soup. If you don't have a smoker, use the same recipe to brine your turkey breast, then simply roast it the next day. Double the recipe and it will be enough to brine your Thanksgiving turkey; guests won't believe how juicy this turkey will be.

Serves 6 to 12

1 quart apple cider

1/4 cup kosher salt

1/4 cup chopped ginger root

1 teaspoon ground allspice

1 cup maple syrup

1/2 cup soy sauce

1 turkey breast on the bone (about 6 pounds)

Bring 1 cup of apple cider to the boil and dissolve the salt in it. Mix with the remaining cider, the ginger, allspice, maple syrup, and soy sauce, and cool to room temperature.

Place the turkey breast in a large, deep bowl or nonreactive pot, cover with the marinade and refrigerate overnight. Weigh the turkey down with a plate to keep it submerged. The next morning, turn the turkey over and marinate all day.

Set up your smoker using cherry or apple wood if possible. Drain the turkey, discarding the marinade. Hot-smoke for about 2 hours, or until the turkey registers 165°F. on a meat thermometer stuck into the thickest part of the breast.

Cool before slicing, reserving the carcass for soup stock, if desired. The smoked turkey will keep up to 2 weeks in the refrigerator.

Smoked Turkey Reuben Sandwich

An ooey, gooey sandwich, the Reuben is a classic that doesn't have to be reserved for your next visit to the local deli. Use either the homemade smoked turkey breast on the previous page, or purchased smoked turkey breast, but try to get the natural kind. Many packaged types of smoked turkey have lots of preservatives, and the gelatin added to keep it moist gives it a rubbery quality. The fresh sauerkraut found refrigerated in the dairy aisle is crisper and less sharp than the canned type. I'm not much of a fan of the "Russian Dressing" served in most restaurants, which consists of ketchup and mayonnaise mixed together with maybe a little pickle relish thrown in. This one, made with cognac (or brandy) and flavored with tarragon, is a winner. Serve any extra dressing on cold-cut sandwiches.

SERVES 6

Cognac–Tarragon Russian Dressing
MAKES 2 CUPS

1 cup mayonnaise

1/2 teaspoon crushed garlic

Juice of 1 lemon

1 teaspoon paprika

1/4 teaspoon cayenne pepper

2 tablespoons Cognac

2 tablespoon finely diced white onion

2 tablespoons each: chopped tarragon and Italian parsley,
  and sliced chives

1 small roasted red pepper, diced

Kosher salt and freshly ground black pepper to taste

Combine all of the ingredients and season to taste with salt and pepper. Store tightly covered in the refrigerator for up to 2 weeks.

Assembly

1 loaf marble rye bread, sliced

3/4 cup Cognac-Tarragon Russian Dressing

1 1/2 pounds sliced Maple-Apple Smoked
  Turkey Breast (*see* previous page)

1 pound fresh sauerkraut, rinsed, drained,
  and the excess liquid squeezed out

1 pound sliced Gruyere cheese

1 tablespoon vegetable oil, for the griddle

Lay out 6 slices of bread. Spread each slice with Russian Dressing, and top with 3 ounces of turkey for each sandwich. Cover with sauerkraut and then the cheese. Spread 6 more slices of bread with Russian Dressing and cover the sandwiches, pressing lightly.

Preheat a griddle and brush lightly with oil, and cook the sandwiches on both sides until the bread is toasty and the cheese is starting to melt. Remove the sandwiches from the grill, slice in half on the diagonal, and serve cut-side outwards.

917

918

Turkey Scaloppine with Porcini and Marsala Wine Sauce

Dried porcini mushrooms, called cèpes *in French, maintain all the inimitable woodsy aroma of the fresh porcini that are so hard to find unless you're good friends with a mushroom forager or are one yourself. Lots of these mushrooms grow in America, especially in the moist, temperate forests of the Northwest, but not many people know how to find them, so they're typically quite expensive and rarely found in the market. Here, reconstituted dried porcini flavor the pan-sauce for inexpensive, tasty turkey cutlets along with nutty, slightly sweet, dry Marsala wine. (It comes in two types: sweet and dry; the dry is best for savory dishes.) One year I made this dish at the Philadelphia Flower Show for a demonstration and then served samples to more than 100 people. I didn't see anything but empty plates. Butter added at the end enriches the sauce, smoothes it out, and generally brings the whole dish together, but you can leave it out for a lighter dish.*

SERVES 4

$1/2$ cup dried porcini mushrooms

1 pound turkey scaloppine (thinly sliced turkey breast cutlets)

Kosher salt and freshly ground black pepper to taste

2 tablespoons olive oil

$1/4$ pound (1 cup) all-purpose flour

2 tablespoons thinly sliced shallots

$1/2$ cup dry Marsala

2 tablespoons chopped Italian parsley

Squeeze of fresh lemon juice

2 tablespoons unsalted butter (optional)

Soak the dried porcini in hot water to cover until soft and pliable, about 20 minutes. Remove the mushroom pieces from their liquor and reserve. Strain the liquor through a sieve lined with a dampened paper towel to remove any sand, and reserve the liquid.

If necessary, pound the scaloppine lightly to flatten. Sprinkle on both sides with salt and pepper and reserve.

Heat the olive oil in a large skillet until shimmering. Lightly dust the scaloppine with flour, shaking off the excess. Sauté about 1 minute on each side, or until opaque, then remove from the pan and reserve on a plate.

Add the shallots to the pan and cook for 2 to 3 minutes, or until softened but not brown. Pour in the Marsala and flame (to cook off the alcohol). Add the reserved porcini liquor and pieces. Boil until the liquid has reduced enough to form bubbles that cover the whole surface of the pan. Add the scaloppine back to the pan, shaking to heat evenly, and coat with the pan sauce. Add the chopped parsley, a squeeze of lemon juice, and swirl in the butter. Serve immediately.

CHOOSING DRIED PORCINI

Look for whole pieces, mostly caps, edged with their brown, tube-like gills rather than the tougher, stalky-looking stems. Lots of broken pieces are an indication of lesser quality. The aroma should be potent enough to escape from the bag when handled. Occasionally, I see good buys on dried porcini at warehouse club stores, so I'll make sure to buy a package to keep in my pantry. Store the dried porcini at room temperature in a cool, dark place for up to six months.

Turkey Burger with Grilled Vegetable Salsa

Turkey can make a most delicious, moist, and juicy burger, but only if you include at least a portion of dark meat. I like to mix the ground turkey with seasonings to give it a little extra oomph. Also, because it is important to cook turkey to medium, it tends to dry out more than beef burgers, which are often cooked to a juicier rare or medium-rare. These days, most supermarkets sell white or dark meat ground turkey, in clear-plastic-covered modified-atmosphere packaging to give it a longer shelf life. The all-white is more delicate and lower in fat; dark is richer and more flavorful. I like to buy one pound of each and mix the two, but it's your choice. Top the burgers with the delicious grilled vegetable salsa and your family will ask for more.

919

SERVES 6

2 teaspoons each: garlic powder, onion powder, paprika, and dried oregano
1 teaspoon kosher salt
$1/2$ teaspoon freshly ground black pepper
1 egg
$1/4$ cup breadcrumbs
1 tablespoon Worcestershire Sauce
2 pounds freshly ground turkey
1 tablespoon olive oil, for brushing
Kosher salt, for grilling

Mix together the garlic powder, onion powder, paprika, dried oregano, salt and pepper, egg, breadcrumbs, and Worcestershire sauce, whisking to combine well. Mix in the ground turkey, combining thoroughly. Form into

6 turkey patties, arranging on a wax-paper-lined tray. Chill the patties for at least 1 hour. (Note that you don't want to sample the raw turkey; to check for seasoning, cook a small spoonful and then taste.)

When ready to cook, preheat a grill or broiler. Lightly brush the patties with olive oil and sprinkle lightly with kosher salt to help keep them from sticking. Place the patties on an angle on the grill and cook for 5 to 7 minutes or until they release freely from the grill when you try to turn them. Rotate the patties a half-turn to make criss-cross marks and continue to grill for 5 minutes, then turn them over and repeat, cooking for another 5 to 7 minutes, or until medium, so they are fully cooked inside but still juicy and faintly pink.

Spicy Grilled Vegetable Salsa

6 ripe plum tomatoes

1 red bell pepper

1 red onion, quartered

2 poblano chiles

1 tablespoon vegetable oil

$1/4$ cup lime juice

Kosher salt to taste

$1/4$ cup chopped cilantro

Preheat a grill or broiler. Rub the vegetables with oil. Grill well on all sides. Cool and then peel off most, but not all, of the blackened skin. For a chunky texture, grind the vegetables in a meat grinder, process, or chop by hand.

Combine the lime juice and salt and toss with the vegetables and cilantro. Store any extra salsa in the refrigerator for up to 5 days.

Arepas with Turkey Picadillo

Picadillo, made in many versions throughout Latin America, is a tasty mixture of ground meat, often beef, simmered with aromatics like onion and garlic, and the bold flavors of cumin and sherry vinegar. It may include raisins, currants, olives, toasted almonds, or pine nuts. The word picadillo *comes from the Spanish* picar, *which means* to cut into small pieces. *This delicious mixture may be used to stuff peppers, simply served over rice, or as here, served on top of the corncakes called* arepas. *Popular in Colombia and Venezuela, arepas are made in innumerable variations and are the specialty of small restaurants called* areperas. *Here, the arepas are made from three types of corn: fresh (or frozen) corn kernels, cornmeal, and masa harina, cornmeal made from lime-treated corn (not the fruit, but the mineral) to make it more nutritious. Grated cheese and sugar flavor the batter, which is then cooked on a griddle, like American-style pancakes.*

SERVES 6 TO 8

Turkey Picadillo

1 quart chicken stock

1 tablespoon kosher salt

1 bay leaf

6 turkey thighs

2 tablespoons olive oil

$1/2$ cups finely diced red onion

$1/2$ cup finely diced red and yellow bell peppers

1 tablespoon chopped garlic

1 cup chopped plum tomatoes, fresh or canned

2 teaspoon ground cumin, preferably toasted

$1/4$ cup Zante currants

$1/4$ cup chopped pitted green olives

2 tablespoons sherry vinegar

Kosher salt and freshly ground black pepper to taste

2 tablespoons chopped cilantro

Bring the chicken stock, salt and bay leaf to the boil in a large pot. Add the turkey thighs, bring back to the boil, and then reduce the heat to a bare simmer. Simmer for 1 hour, or until the meat is quite tender, and then remove from the heat. Allow the thighs to cool for about 30 minutes and then remove from the pot, reserving the liquid for another use. Remove and discard the turkey skin. Pick the turkey meat off the bones, and pull into shreds. Reserve.

Heat the olive oil in a large skillet. Add the onions, peppers, and garlic, and cook together until lightly browned. Add the tomatoes and cumin and bring to the boil. Simmer together for 30 minutes, or until the sauce is thickened.

Stir in the turkey, currants, olives, and vinegar and bring back to the boil. Remove from the heat and season with salt and pepper. Stir in the cilantro and keep warm.

Arepas

1 pound frozen white corn

$^1/_2$ cup ground yellow cornmeal

$^3/_4$ cup Masa Harina

$^1/_4$ pound (about 1 cup) grated aged cheese such as
   Mexican Queso Añejo, Dry Jack, Asiago, or aged Gouda

$^1/_4$ cup milk

2 tablespoons granulated sugar

2 teaspoons kosher salt

$^1/_2$ cup clarified butter (*see* page 170,
   Making French-style clarified butter

Place the corn in a food processor and grind until a rough puree results. Transfer to a mixing bowl, and stir in the corn-

meal, masa harina, grated cheese, milk, sugar, and salt and mix very well. Cover the mixture and refrigerate for at least 1 hour.

Heat a griddle and lightly brush with clarified butter. Spoon the batter into small cakes, flattening slightly with the back of a spatula so they are $^1/_2$-inch thick. Brown lightly on both sides and keep warm in a 200°F. (Be attentive so the Arepas do not burn.) Serve immediately topped with the reserved Turkey Picadillo.

Stuffed Turkey with Achiote and Cornbread–Jicama Stuffing

My deep-red, crusty, slow-roasted turkey is rubbed inside and out with Achiote Condimentado, a blend of spices from Yucatan that uses mild red annatto (or achiote) seed as its main ingredient. You can buy this inexpensive flavoring at Mexican groceries or from www.delmayab.com (six 3.5-ounce bricks that keep indefinitely cost $10 including shipping). The flavorful stuffing is made from cornbread studded with crunchy, nutty jicama root, a root vegetable also known as Mexican yam bean that resembles water chestnuts in both flavor and texture. Simply marinate the turkey without stuffing, if desired.

SERVES 12 TO 15

Achiote Marinade

$^1/_2$ cup Achiote paste

$^1/_4$ cup vegetable oil

$^1/_2$ cup cider vinegar

1 tablespoon ground toasted cumin

921

2 tablespoons finely chopped garlic

1 tablespoon dried oregano

1 teaspoon ground allspice

2 teaspoons salt

Blend together all the marinade ingredients: achiote paste, oil, vinegar, cumin, garlic, oregano, allspice, and salt and reserve. Freeze any extra achiote paste and use to marinate chicken.

Cornbread–Jicama Stuffing

$1/4$ cup olive oil

1 cup chopped onions

1 cup diced red bell peppers

2 tablespoons chopped garlic

2 cups diced jicama root (about 1 jicama)

Turkey liver (optional)

1 bunch cilantro leaves, chopped

6 cups crumbled Buttermilk Cornbread, purchased or
   homemade (*see* page 341)

Kosher salt, freshly ground black pepper,
   and cayenne pepper to taste

Heat 3 tablespoons of the olive oil and cook the onions, red pepper, garlic, and jicama until softened but still brightly colored. Separately brown the turkey liver in the remaining tablespoon of olive oil until firm but still pink inside. Cool and dice the liver, and add it to the vegetable mixture. Remove the mixture from the heat and stir in the cilantro. Crumble the cornbread and add it to the mixture. Season with salt, pepper, and cayenne. Cool and reserve.

Assembly and Roasting the Turkey

1 (12- to 15-pound) turkey, rinsed thoroughly and patted
   dry with paper towels, giblets, neck, and tailpiece
   removed and reserved

$1^1/2$ cups Achiote Marinade

1 recipe Cornbread Stuffing

3 tablespoons cornstarch

Place the turkey giblets, neck, and tailpiece in a pot with water to cover (don't add the liver, because it will make the sauce cloudy). Bring to the boil, skim off any white scum, reduce the heat, and simmer while the turkey is roasting.

Heat the oven to 425° F. Rub the turkey inside and out with the Achiote Marinade. Stuff the turkey (not too tightly because it will expand) in both the neck and stomach cavities with 8 to 12 cups of the Cornbread Stuffing depending on the size of the turkey. (Bake any extra separately, moistening with extra turkey stock, and serve alongside.) Using string or trussing needles, tie the turkey into a compact shape.

Place the turkey in a roasting pan just large enough to hold it (a double disposable foil roasting pan works well). Roast the turkey for 30 minutes, then reduce the oven temperature to 350°F. and roast for $1^1/2$ to 2 hours, depending on the size of your bird, or until a thermometer inserted into the inner part of the thigh (the last place to finish cooking) reads 165°F. Remove the turkey from the oven and allow it to rest about 20 minutes before serving.

To make the pan gravy, strain the turkey broth, discarding the solids. Scrape the pan drippings into a medium saucepan, skimming off and discarding the fat. Add about 4 cups of turkey broth to the pot and bring to the boil, skimming off any scum and remaining fat. Simmer about 15 minutes, or until the liquid is rich and flavorful. Mix the cornstarch with 3 tablespoons cold water and gradually stir into the pot. Bring the gravy back to the boil and simmer until the sauce thickens slightly. Strain through a sieve and serve with the turkey.

TURNIPS, RUTABAGAS, & KOHLRABI

TURNIPS,
RUTABAGA & KOHLRABI

Have you ever wondered about that strange-looking vegetable with stalks sticking out all over the place, topped by broccoli-like leaves? Whether it's a lovely shade of deep violet or pale green, it's kohlrabi, *Brassica oleracea*, whose German-derived name translates to *cabbage turnip*. In Italy, where they really know their vegetables, the same vegetable is known as *cavolo rapa* (also cabbage-turnip), describing its flavor perfectly. Covered with a tough outer skin, the knob of both the violet and green varieties is the same whitish-green color inside. To me, kohlrabi tastes like crunchy, juicy broccoli stems (always my favorite part of the broccoli) with a bit of the hotness of radish and the sweetness of turnip.

Yet another member of the large and vitamin-rich *Brassica* family—which includes broccoli, cauliflower, and cabbage—that we should all serve more often, kohlrabi may not be the most universally praised vegetable, but it is among the most versatile. People of Middle European, French, Italian, and Chinese descent are familiar with the virtues of this uncommon vegetable. It is two vegetables in one: both the root and the leaves are delicious but completely different in flavor and texture. Give kohlrabi a try if you like celery root, the stems of broccoli, and cabbage.

Turnips, *Brassica rapa*, and Rutabagas, *Brassica napus*, are fellow members of the sometimes denigrated *Brassica* family. They are round, firm, root vegetables with a biting flavor between cabbage and mustard. Turnips, known in Latin as *rapa* or *napus*, have been cultivated since ancient times; many distinct kinds were known to the Romans and Greeks. In Middle English, *napus* evolved into *nepe*, which combined with the word *turn* (as in *make round*) became the word *turnip*. Rutabaga gets its name from the Swedish *rotabagge*, suggesting a Scandinavian origin as does its common name—Swedes. Both white and yellow-fleshed rutabaga varieties have been known in Europe for more than three hundred years.

Although closely related, turnips and rutabagas are distinctly different. Most turnips are white-fleshed and most rutabagas are yellow-fleshed, but confusingly, there are also white-fleshed rutabagas and yellow-fleshed turnips. Turnips and rutabagas have a different number of chromosomes. Botanical studies indicate that a rare hybridization between a cabbage and turnip resulted in the new species, rutabaga, which was probably first found in Europe in the late Middle Ages. Rutabagas are also known as Swedes because of their popularity among Swedish people in the American Upper Midwest.

Turnips are smooth and have several circles of ridges at the base of their leaves with white flesh and white, purple-tinged skin. Small young turnips are delicate and slightly sweet; as they age, their taste becomes stronger

924

and their texture almost woody. Red-skinned, purple-tipped, pearl-white, pink, and golden turnips can be found in some markets. Small White Tokyo turnips, a Japanese variety, are sold in bunches with their greens. These bite-sized turnips are tender and mild enough to eat raw, and are absolutely delicious glazed with a bit of butter, sugar, salt, and pepper.

Rutabagas are larger, rounder, denser, and sweeter than turnips and are often sold with an unappealing wax coating to help preserve them. Underneath that disguise is a delicious yellow-orange vegetable that holds its beautiful color when cooked and is surprisingly mild in flavor.

BABY TURNIPS: A SIMPLE HORS D'OEUVRE

One of the best and simplest hors d'oeuvres I've ever eaten was served to me at the renowned Four Seasons Restaurant in New York. A small plate arrived at the table including wedges of peeled white baby turnip, ripe cherry tomatoes, and juicy Kalamata olives, all to be nibbled on before the meal. Try serving it at home in summer when baby turnips and all kinds of cherry tomatoes can be found at local farmers' markets.

CHOOSING TURNIPS, RUTABAGAS, AND KOHLRABI

Young turnips are sold in spring. Look for small turnips that feel heavy for their size, are smooth and firm with unblemished skin and fresh, green leaves. Avoid shriveled turnips or those with greens that have spoiled. Turnips larger than three inches in diameter are apt to be woody. Turnips are available year-round, with peak season October through March.

Look for firm, smooth-skinned rutabagas that feel heavy for their size. They are in season from September through June. Avoid bruised or cut rutabagas as these will have been in storage too long.

Look for small to medium-size kohlrabi with small, smooth bulb-stems and firm, green leaves. Avoid large kohlrabi, which will be tougher and stronger-tasting.

Preparing Turnips, Rutabagas, and Kohlrabi

To prepare any of these three firm, substantial roots, you can either steam them whole (in their "jackets") or pare away the tough outer skin before cooking. Because they are so firm, all three are ideal to cut into fancy shapes, especially easy if you own a French mandoline, Japanese Benriner, or a Japanese spiral vegetable cutter. It's not necessary to soak cut kohlrabi and rutabagas in water, however it is best to soak white turnips to keep them from discoloring. For kohlrabi, remove the leaves, discarding the stems and any tough center ribs, and then shred them. Pare the root and cut into slices, dice, half-moons, or thin wedges.

926

Passato di Verdure: Italian Winter Vegetable Puree

This is one of those dishes where the whole is greater than the sum of its parts. An easy-to-make, creamy-textured soup with no cream, it is a combination of humble vegetables including kohlrabi, turnips or rutabagas, along with potatoes, carrots, and onions, finished with strips of escarole. All the vegetables are simmered together in chicken stock until nice and soft. The soup is then pureed and strained to make it smooth, and then soft, mild escarole is stirred in and simmered until meltingly tender. Once the soup is seasoned, it's ready to serve. It will leave people guessing as to its delicious flavor. Note that soups like this one, made with potato, don't freeze well.

SERVES 12

1 large onion, peeled and chopped

1 pound (2 to 3) Idaho potatoes, peeled and chopped

2 each: kohlrabi, turnip, or rutabaga, peeled and chopped (or a mixture of any two)

1/2 pound carrots, peeled and cut into rounds

1/2 bunch thyme, tied in kitchen twine

2 quarts homemade-style chicken stock (*see* page 991)

Kosher salt, grated nutmeg, cayenne pepper, and freshly ground black pepper to taste

1 head escarole, cut into 1/2-inch shreds and washed

Combine the onion, potatoes, kohlrabi, parsnips, carrots, thyme, and chicken stock in a large, heavy-bottomed pot. Bring to the boil. Simmer for 30 minutes or until the vegetables are quite soft, stirring occasionally to prevent sticking and burning.

Remove the thyme, purée or blend the soup in a food processor or blender and strain through a sieve or food mill. Transfer back into the pot and bring to the boil. Season with salt, nutmeg, cayenne, and black pepper. Stir in the escarole and cook about 5 minutes, or until the escarole has wilted. Serve immediately or cool to serve later. Store in the refrigerator for up to 5 days before reheating and serving.

Scalloped Kohlrabi and Potatoes

To many of us, a dish of bubbling brown scalloped potatoes is cause for delight. Here, kohlrabi is layered with potatoes for a dish that has an extra-elusive dimension in flavor. Your guests will probably not be able to identify the special taste of this dish, but they'll be sure to enjoy it. Substitute turnip, rutabagas, or celery root for the kohlrabi, or mix them together for a variation.

SERVES 6 TO 8

5 tablespoons unsalted butter

6 tablespoons all-purpose flour

3 cups milk

$1/2$ cup heavy cream

1 small onion, peeled and quartered

1 teaspoon ground coriander

$1/2$ teaspoon ground nutmeg

1 tablespoon chopped fresh thyme (or 1 teaspoon dried thyme)

$1/4$ teaspoon ground cloves

$1/4$ teaspoon cayenne pepper

2 bay leaves

$1/2$ pound shredded sharp cheese (a mixture of cheddar, Jack, and aged Gouda is good)

$1^1/2$ pounds kohlrabi knobs (about 2 bunches), pared

2 pounds Idaho or golden potatoes, peeled

In a large saucepan, melt the butter and stir in the flour. Cook over moderate heat for 5 minutes, stirring occasionally to make a *roux*.

Meanwhile, combine the milk and cream with the onion and seasonings and scald (heat until steaming). Whisk the hot milk mixture into the roux . Bring slowly to a boil, and simmer for 15 minutes, stirring frequently to be sure not to burn the bottom of pot. Remove from the heat and strain the sauce through a sieve, discarding the solids. Stir in most of the cheese and reserve.

Preheat the oven to 375°F. Meanwhile, steam or boil the kohlrabi and potatoes for 15 minutes, or until tender only halfway through. Drain, cool slightly, and then slice thinly.

Spread about 1 cup of the sauce in the bottom of a large baking dish. Next spread a layer of kohlrabi and potatoes and then cover with more sauce. Continue layering, ending with a layer of sauce. Sprinkle with the remaining cheese and place in the oven. Bake for 35 minutes, or until browned and bubbling. Remove the dish from the oven and allow to cool about 10 minutes before cutting into serving portions.

927

Stir-Fried Kohlrabi Knob and Greens with Ginger

This simple, fresh-tasting stir fry combines crunchy kohlrabi knob with its mild-tasting green leaves. Substitute turnips with their greens, especially the mild, tender Japanese Tokyo turnips. Rice wine, soy sauce, ginger, garlic, five-spice powder, and sesame oil are the bold seasonings.

SERVES 4

1 pound kohlrabi with its greens

¼ cup rice wine (or saké or dry sherry)

2 tablespoons soy sauce

2 teaspoons cornstarch

1 teaspoon Chinese five-spice powder (or a pinch each of cinnamon and cloves)

2 tablespoons soy or vegetable oil

2 tablespoons finely chopped ginger

1 tablespoon chopped garlic

1 teaspoon dark roasted sesame oil

1 bunch scallions, sliced on the bias into 1-inch pieces

Using scissors, snip off the stems from the kohlrabi knob. Now, strip off the green leaves from the stems and discard the stems. Cut the leaves into 1-inch-wide strips. Wash the greens in a large bowl of water, then scoop out and drain in a colander. Using a sharp paring knife, cut away the outer layer of skin from the kohlrabi knob. Cut the knob in half and then cut each half into thin slices to form half-moon shapes.

To make the sauce, in a small bowl, stir together the rice wine, soy sauce, cornstarch, and five-spice powder and reserve. In a wok or a large sauté pan, heat the oil, and then add the ginger and garlic and stir-fry for 1 minute to release the flavors. Add the kohlrabi knob slices and stir-fry for about 5 minutes, or until the kohlrabi begins to soften.

Add the greens and the reserved sauce mixture, stirring up just before adding in case the cornstarch has settled to the bottom. Cook all together until the liquid boils and the greens wilt. Add the sesame oil and the scallions and cook together 1 minute longer. Serve immediately.

PEELING GINGER

As delicious and versatile as fresh ginger is, it's also pesky to peel and grate. To get the most out of your ginger, use the edge of a tablespoon to scrape away the brown skin only. For larger quantities, pare off the outer skin and small knobs, saving them if desired to make ginger-infused sugar syrup for bar drinks, to add to hot tea, or to mix with fresh fruit salad. If the ginger is tender, and creamy-white in color rather than greenish, grate it using the fine side of a box grater. For ginger that is older and more fibrous, grate and then place the grated ginger in a small piece of cheesecloth, squeeze out the juice, and discard the stringy remains. Try grating ginger on the special ceramic graters sold in Asian markets and some cookware stores.

928

Vegetarian Chili with Butternut and Rutabagas

This hearty and satisfying chili will satisfy even the most carnivorous person. Like most chilis and stews, it really can't be made in small quantities, but luckily, it freezes beautifully. How nice to have a ready-made dinner in the freezer for that day when cooking is just too much to handle. Serve the chili with lots of garnishes to make it fun for kids and grown-ups. Canned beans and frozen corn work very well together in this cold-weather dish. Accompany with tortilla chips or steamed rice, if desired.

SERVES 8 TO 10

2 tablespoons canola oil

1 sweet onion, chopped

3 carrots, diced

1 tablespoon chopped garlic

1 (28-ounce) can chopped tomatoes

1 small butternut squash, peeled and diced
  (or 1-pound package diced butternut)

1 rutabaga, peeled and diced

1 (1-pound) bag frozen corn

1 (15-ounce can or 20-ounce jar) each: dark red kidney
  beans and black beans

$1/4$ cup chili powder

2 chipotle chiles in adobo, chopped

Kosher salt to taste

Garnishes: diced fresh tomatoes, shredded extra-sharp
  cheddar, diced avocados, chopped cilantro, diced red
  onion, tortilla chips

Heat the oil in a large Dutch oven. Add the onion, carrots, and garlic and cook over medium heat for 5 minutes, until crisp-tender. Add the tomatoes, butternut squash, and rutabaga, and bring to a boil. Cover and simmer for 20 minutes, or until thickened, stirring occasionally.

Stir in the corn, beans, chili powder, chipotles, and salt. Bring to a boil, reduce the heat and simmer for 20 minutes longer, stirring occasionally, until the chili has thickened. Serve with small bowls of the garnishes.

929

UGLI®

& OTHER UNUSUAL FRUITS

UGLI®
& OTHER UNUSUAL FRUITS

Tropical markets are full of fragrant, brightly colored, exotic fruits in odd shapes that most people in the United States never get to see, but luckily in recent years, with the growing influence of Latin American and Asian immigrants, the selection is getting bigger and the quality is getting better. While we may never have the opportunity to taste the delicious cashew fruit that grows at the end of the nut and goes into the wonderful and potent Brazilian cocktail called a *caipirinha*, ugli fruit, passion fruit, guavas, and papayas are becoming more common. Go to a Latin American, Asian, or Indian market to find even more unusual fruits to try, like the creamy vanilla monstera fruit and the extraordinary spiky red rambutan.

UGLI® FRUIT

Usually marketed under the trademarked name Ugli fruit, Uniq fruits were developed by the English in Jamaica and are a type of tangelo: a cross between a grapefruit and a tangerine that is in season in winter starting in December. Ugli fruits are indeed rather ugly in that they are lumpy, misshapen, and are covered with an odd-looking thick, baggy rind with a pulled-up appearance at the top. The fruits can be quite large, and their meat is juicy and abundant, though much of their bulk consists of thick peel. Uglis are easily peeled and have a fine fragrance of citron. The segments separate freely and taste like honey and apricot with a refreshing tartness and a slightly bitter aftertaste, like a grapefruit. They come in all sizes and range in color from green to yellow and yellow-orange. The fruits are tree-ripened and whatever their skin color, their flesh is pink-tinted orange to deep orange in color.

Passion Fruit

The purple passion fruit, Passiflora edulis, is native to southern Brazil and was given its name by Portuguese colonists to whom its flower's elaborate and prominent five spiky stamens symbolized the five wounds received by Jesus during his passion on the cross. It is a subtropical fruit and is widely grown in California, Hawaii, and Australia. The yellow passion fruit is tropical and grows in Hawaii and Fiji.

Whether purple or yellow, passion fruits resemble a dented egg with a tough, waxy skin that becomes brittle and wrinkled when ripe. Inside, it is filled with yellowish, jelly-like pulp surrounding an abundance of black, edible seeds. The musky, tart flesh has a luscious, intoxicating scent that is decidedly tropical.

Fresh passion fruits are sporadically available, more commonly on the West Coast. Yellow passion fruit is generally larger than the purple variety, but the pulp of the purple is less acidic, richer in aroma and flavor, and has a higher proportion of juice.

CHOOSING AND RIPENING PASSION FRUIT

Choose passion fruit that is heavy for its size, large, and plump. When ripe, it is fragrant with a shriveled, wrinkled shell that is rich in color. Any mold on the shell does not affect quality and can be wiped off.

If the skin is smooth, ripen at room temperature, turning occasionally. Passion fruit is ripe when it is dented. Store in the refrigerator up to 1 week. Passion fruit is available year-round from Florida, February to July from New Zealand, and July to March from California.

Guava

The guava, *Psidium guajova*, is a plum-sized tropical fruit with yellow, red, or purple-black skin and white, yellow, or red flesh studded with small seeds and a sweet, highly aromatic flavor. It gets its name from the Arawak Indian language and is the fruit of a small, shrubby tree native to Central America and the West Indies and now grown in tropical and subtropical regions around the world. Guavas are especially popular in Mexico, where they are made into blocks of fruit paste called *membrillo* and sold in *palletas* (frozen fruit pops). Europeans first encountered guavas on the earliest voyages to Haiti, and Spanish and Portuguese mariners soon spread the fruit to other regions. By the seventeenth century, the guava was well established in India and Southeast Asia and has remained popular there ever since.

Guavas may be as small as a plum or as large as an apple, and may be round or pear-shaped, rough- or smooth-skinned with skin that is greenish-white, yellow, or red and flesh that is yellow, bright pink, or red and filled with small, hard seeds. At its best, a guava will be soft and creamy with a rind that softens enough to be fully edible. Large, pear-shaped white fruits are considered the best. The aroma of a ripe guava is sweet, flowery yet musky, pungent, and penetrating. The seeds are numerous but small and, in well-ripened fruits, fully edible. The taste is sweet to sour with an unusual spiciness due to eugenol, the same essential oil found in cloves. Guavas are in season from June to August and from November to March from Florida, with some fruits coming from California and Arizona.

933

CHOOSING AND RIPENING GUAVAS

Choose guavas that give to gentle palm pressure but that have not yet begun to show spots. Avoid spotted or mushy guavas or underripe guavas that are too green. Choose tender fruits with some yellow color. Store at room temperature until soft. Refrigerate ripe fruit in a plastic or paper bag for up to two days.

PAPAYA

The papaya, *Carica papaya*, is a large, tropical, pear-shaped fruit with soft, juicy, and silky-smooth flesh, a delicate, rather innocuous flavor, and a center full of edible black seeds. Native to Central or South America, the papaya gets its name from the Carib Indians.

Papayas now grow in Hawaii, Mexico, Puerto Rico, Florida, and southern California. Brazil is the largest papaya producer, and Mexico is second. Most papayas grown in the United States come from Hawaii, while Florida produces a small quantity. The fruit (and leaves) of papaya contain papain which helps digestion and is used to tenderize meat. The edible seeds have a spicy flavor somewhat reminiscent of black pepper.

There are two types of papayas, Hawaiian and Mexican. The smaller Hawaiian papaya is pear-shaped, weighs about one pound, and has green skin that ripens to yellow. Its flesh is bright orange to pinkish-orange with small black seeds clustered in the center. The much larger Mexican papaya may weigh up to twenty pounds. It commonly has a dark green skin with flesh that ranges from salmon-red to bright orange and a musky, less sweet taste.

Papayas of various varieties are available year-round with the best selection at Latin American markets.

Papaya Varieties

Maradol: This large, football-shaped Mexican-type papaya can weigh ten pounds or more. It has salmon-red flesh and smooth, thin skin that goes from green to burnt orange when ripe. It will often be displayed cut in pieces and wrapped in plastic. It has the same smooth texture as smaller papayas, but its flavor is earthier and less sweet.

Solo: The Solo papaya grows in Hawaii, introduced there from Barbados. It resembles a pear and has smooth, greenish-yellow skin that turns yellow as the fruit ripens. The flesh is a golden orange color with a juicy, very sweet melon-peach flavor and small black seeds in the center. Firmer than most papayas, the Solo can withstand the stress of shipping.

Sunrise: The reddish-orange-fleshed Sunrise papaya, a Hawaiian-type fruit, is the most exported papaya in the world. It weighs three to five pounds and is shaped like an elongated melon. Its skin is green when unripe, but turns yellow to orange with a few freckles once it matures. Sunrise papayas have soft, juicy flesh that is salmon-pink or red in color with a sweet, melon-peach flavor.

Waimanolo: The Waimanalo is a round Hawaiian papaya with a short neck, averaging one to two pounds. Its skin is smooth and glossy; its inner cavity is star-shaped. It has thick, firm flesh that is orange-yellow in color; it has good flavor and keeps well.

CHOOSING AND RIPENING PAPAYAS

When selecting Hawaiian papayas, look for plump fruit that is mostly warm yellow in color with smooth, unblemished skin. The neck will still be somewhat green when the rest is ripe. Papayas have little aroma, even when ripe. Avoid hard or shriveled papayas or fruit that is mushy, bruised, or has a fermented aroma. Papayas with dark spots should be avoided because those spots often extend beneath the skin's surface and spoil the flavor.

Mexican papayas may remain mostly green even when fully ripe. When selecting a Mexican papaya that is already cut and wrapped, choose the one that has the deepest salmon-red color. When choosing a whole, uncut fruit, select the one that has the deepest skin color and the most giving flesh.

Papayas are ripe when they emit a soft, fruity aroma and will give slightly. An underripe papaya will be unpleasantly astringent, especially at the neck. Often the fat part of the papaya will be ripe while the neck never fully ripens. Cut off and discard that part of the neck that is still firm. Ripen papayas in a paper bag with a banana to speed ripening. Refrigerate ripe fruit in a plastic or paper bag for up to three days.

Cherimoya

The cherimoya, *Annona cherimola*, which gets its name from the Andean Quechua language, tastes like a delicate combination of pineapple, papaya, and banana. This large tropical fruit is shaped like a plump heart with scaly, leathery green skin marked with overlapping thumbprint indentations. The flesh, peppered with large, shiny, black seeds, is cream-colored and has the texture of firm custard.

The cherimoya and its close relatives—atemoya, sweetsop, and soursop—are Annonas, a genus of tropical fruit tree which originated in the Andean valleys of Ecuador, Peru, and Chile. Cherimoyas have been introduced to subtropical regions around the world and were first planted in California in 1871. Today, Spain is the largest cherimoya producer in the world. Because this luscious fruit is in high demand, most fruit never leaves California, the only producing state. Cherimoyas command high prices because of their scarcity and because they must be individually harvested as they ripen.

CHOOSING AND RIPENING CHERIMOYAS

Choose cherimoyas that are firm, heavy for their size, and without skin blemishes. To ripen, leave at room temperature to soften (they will give slightly with soft pressure). The skin may turn brownish as the fruit ripens; this doesn't affect the inside. Once ripe, refrigerate for up to four days, wrapped in a paper towel.

UGLI & OTHER UNUSUAL FRUITS

Sea Scallop Ceviche with Ugli® Fruit

Scallops are perhaps the easiest of seafoods to make into ceviche, which is made of fish and seafood, usually raw, marinated in citrus juice, and spiked with chile, here smoky chipotle flakes. The Spanish contributed the Mediterranean custom of using lemons and onions to make the simple marinated fish eaten along the Pacific Coast of Latin America. Here, three kinds of citrus fruits—limes, oranges, and ugli fruit—provide the acid balance for the scallops, while fresh herbs lend their fragrance and cleansing flavor to the dish. Serve on natural scallop shells for a beautiful, perfectly suited presentation.

SERVES 4

$1/4$ cup + 2 tablespoons fresh lime juice

$1/4$ cup fresh orange juice

$1/2$ teaspoon chipotle chile flakes, substitute 2 teaspoons chopped seeded canned chipotle in adobo

1 teaspoon kosher salt

$1/2$ pound fresh untreated sea scallops, trimmed of hard muscle

2 ugli fruit

6 red radishes, trimmed and thinly sliced

1 tablespoon shredded basil

1 tablespoon shredded fresh mint

Whisk together $1/4$ cup of the lime juice, the orange juice, chipotle flakes, and salt. Divide the mixture in half. If the scallops are large, slice them crosswise into 2 thin rounds. In a nonreactive bowl, toss the scallops with half of the marinade, cover, and refrigerate for 1 hour to marinate.

Meanwhile, using a sharp paring knife, cut away all of the skin and the thin outside layer of membrane enclosing the ugli fruit sections. Cut out each section of fruit from between the membrane on both sides.

Drain the scallops and toss with the remaining marinade, the radishes, and the basil and mint. Arrange the ugli fruit segments in an attractive pattern around the scallops, drizzle the ceviche with ugli fruit juice, and serve immediately.

Lobster Salad with Grilled Papaya and Passion Fruit Dressing

Bahia is the province of Brazil most influenced by Africa. It is renowned for its imaginative, highly seasoned cooking, which evolved from slave plantation cooks improvising on African, Amazonian, and traditional Portuguese dishes with locally available ingredients, usually the parts discarded by the owners. Seafood, like the Bahian spiny lobster, and tropical fruits, like passion fruit and papaya, are menu staples. In Brazil, they would use the native clawless spiny lobster, which populates the warmer waters of the Caribbean and the South Atlantic. I prefer the firmer flesh and more distinctive flavor of native American lobster. Frozen passion fruit puree is available in Latin American markets.

SERVES 4

2 firm but ripe papayas, or 1 large ripe green papaya

Kosher salt and freshly ground black pepper to taste

4 tablespoons olive oil, divided

2 (1½ pound) cooked lobsters

½ cup passion fruit puree

2 tablespoons chopped shallots

Preheat a grill until white-hot. Halve the papayas, then dig out and discard the seeds. Cut each half into three wedges. Trim off the ends, and pare off a thin strip along the length of both sides of each papaya wedge. There should be no skin along the edges, only on the bottom of each wedge. Sprinkle the papaya wedges with salt and pepper and rub lightly with 2 tablespoons of the oil. Grill by placing the cut edges against the grill, gradually turning 90 degrees to form cross-hatched grill marks, and reserve. Cut away the remaining skin of the papaya, and cut each wedge into 3 to 4 sections.

Pull the claws off the body of each lobster, then twist and pull off the tail portion. Cut the tail section, with the shell on, into 1-inch rings. Divide the claw from the knuckle. Reserve the knuckle arm section for another use. Crack the claws by tapping them gently with the side of a heavy chef's knife. Remove the bottom half of claw shells. (The pointy pincer claw has a thinner, easier-to-crack shell. The larger rounded masher claw has a very thick shell.) Arrange the lobsters on a large oval platter. Place the papaya wedges along either side of the lobster.

In a small bowl, whisk together the passion fruit puree, the remaining olive oil, shallots, and salt and pepper. Drizzle the mixture over the lobster and papaya and serve immediately.

Guava–Glazed Barbecue Ribs

I first prepared Steve Raichlan's version of these tropical-style barbecued pork ribs for his appearance on QVC during my years as a television food stylist. The sweet-tart guava flavor, heated up with ginger and smoky chipotle chiles and laced with molasses-flavored dark rum, is a perfect foil to the rich, fatty ribs. Of course, I had to make my own changes to the recipe. I prefer to use the thin, less-fatty back ribs, sometimes called baby back ribs, although they are less meaty than either spare ribs or country-style ribs. (For more about ribs, see page 748.) Bake the ribs a day ahead of time, so that they can set up in the refrigerator, discarding any hard white fat that forms. Five pounds may sound like a lot of ribs, but one person can easily put away close to a pound. Also, ribs do reheat very well. Wrap in aluminum foil and heat in a 400°F. oven for about 15 minutes until quite hot, unwrapping the foil for the last 5 minutes, so the ribs will crisp up.

Ribs

2 tablespoons chopped garlic

2 teaspoons chipotle chile flakes, or 1 seeded, chopped chipotle in adobo

4 bay leaves, crushed

2 tablespoons ground cumin

1 tablespoon kosher salt

5 pounds back ribs

Combine the garlic, chipotle flakes, bay leaves, cumin, and salt. Rub the ribs all over with the mixture. Leave to marinate at least 1 hour at room temperature, but preferably overnight, refrigerated. Wrap in heavy-duty foil and bake at 300°F. for 2 hours, or until the ribs are tender when pierced. (This step is best done at least 1 day and up to 2 days ahead. Cool and then chill. Remove and discard any congealed white fat.) Cut into 2-rib sections.

Guava Barbecue Sauce

9 to 10 ounces (about half of an 18- to 21-ounce
   package) guava paste

$3/4$ cup cider vinegar

$1/2$ cup dark rum

1 (15-ounce) can crushed tomatoes

$1/2$ cup lime juice

$1/4$ cup soy sauce

$1/4$ cup ketchup

2 tablespoon Worcestershire sauce

1 small red onion, diced

$1/4$ cup finely chopped ginger

2 tablespoon chopped garlic

2 whole chipotle chiles in adobo
   (including sauce from the can)

2 tablespoons kosher salt

$1^1/2$ teaspoons freshly ground black pepper

In a large, heavy Dutch oven, combine all the ingredients and bring to the boil. Reduce the heat and simmer for 1 hour, stirring often. Remove the sauce from the heat and cool.

When ready to serve, preheat the oven to 350°F. Brush the rib sections generously with the sauce and bake 2 hours, turning after 1 hour and brushing with more sauce. Serve with extra sauce for dipping.

938

GUAVA MEMBRILLO

The thick, shimmering, jellied fruit paste made from sweetened, cooked-down guava puree is a Latin American take on the original quince version from Spain. Also called "guava paste" (*pasta de guayaba* in Spanish) the kind sold in a flat, round can imported from Brazil and sold under the Goya name is an excellent choice. La Fe and La Costena are other good brands. Look for it in Latin American supermarkets. Mango paste, made by many of the same companies, is a good substitute.

Passion Fruit Mousse

Passion fruit has such a concentrated, passion-inspiring flavor that it works well in a frozen mousse because, even though lightened with meringue and whipped cream, its distinctive tangy flavor comes through loud and clear. While fresh passion fruit makes the best mousse, with the added bonus of the decorative shiny black seeds to sprinkle over top, there are some excellent frozen purees available. For those in the restaurant business or if you have a large freezer, the Perfect Puree company of California sells passion fruit puree in a 30-ounce container (www.perfectpuree. com). I find inexpensive packages of frozen passion fruit puree under both the Goya and the La Fe names at my local Latin American market. (For more information about sheet gelatin, see page 135.)

SERVES 6

1 tablespoon vegetable oil

5 leaves gelatin (or 2 teaspoons powdered gelatin)

14 ounces pure passion fruit puree
  (1 package Goya or La Fe frozen)

$1/4$ cup + $1/2$ cup granulated sugar

2 tablespoons light corn syrup

2 egg whites

1 cup heavy cream

Rub the oil in a 4- to 6-cup metal mold. Soak the gelatin leaves in cold water to cover until softened, about 10 minutes (or soak the powdered gelatin in warm water to cover until softened), and then gently heat until clear, and reserve.

Bring the passion fruit puree to the boil with $1/4$ cup of the sugar, and then remove from the heat. Drain the soaked gelatin leaves and stir into hot passion fruit puree (or stir in the bloomed gelatin). Stir vigorously until the gelatin has completely dissolved. Cool the liquid in an ice bath until it just begins to get jiggly.

Meanwhile, bring the remaining $1/2$ cup of sugar, the corn syrup, and $1/4$ cup of water to the boil in a medium, heavy-bottomed pot. Continue to boil until the syrup reaches 240°F. on a candy thermometer (soft-ball stage). When the sugar is almost ready, start beating the egg whites with the whisk attachment. Beat until a meringue is formed, then reduce the speed to low. While continuing to beat, pour in the hot sugar syrup. When all the syrup has been added, raise the speed to high and continue to beat until the meringue is at room temperature, stiff and glossy. Fold the meringue by thirds into the thickened passion fruit puree.

Beat the heavy cream until firm but not stiff. Fold into the passion fruit mixture. Pour the mousse into the pre-pared mold. Chill in the refrigerator at least 2 hours, or preferably overnight, until set. To unmold, heat the outsides of the mold with a small blowtorch or wrap the mold in a kitchen towel soaked in hot water. Shake the mold from side to side to break the seal and turn over onto a serving platter. Chill again before serving, topped with a little fresh passion fruit puree if desired.

PREPARING FRESH PASSION FRUIT

You'll need 2 fruits. Cut open horizontally in 2 half shells, and spoon out the soft, seedy pulp, which should yield about $1/4$ cup per fruit. Strain if desired, though it's not necessary for this recipe. Frozen passion fruit puree, called *parcha* in Spanish, can be found in 14-ounce bags in Latin American markets and from specialty suppliers.

Cherimoya Flan

With its custardy flavor and texture, cherimoya makes an excellent flan (or baked egg custard). Like the classic Spanish and Latin American flan, this one is baked in a caramel coating that forms its own sauce. Because cherimoyas have a very delicate flavor, make sure that they are fully ripened to make this home-style dessert.

SERVES 6

1/4 cup granulated sugar

2 very ripe cherimoyas

3 cups heavy cream

8 eggs

1/4 cup dark rum

Juice of 1 lime

In a 3- to 4-quart heavy-bottomed, nonreactive pot with a lid, mix 1 cup of sugar with 1/2 cup of water. Bring to the boil, then cover and cook over moderate heat, shaking occasionally until the water cooks away and the sugar browns and just begins to redden in color. Working with care (caramelized sugar is as hot as frying oil), pour the hot caramel into the bottom of an ovenproof dish, such as a gratin, quiche, or soufflé dish (10 x 2 inches in diameter) and reserve.

Peel the cherimoyas, remove the seeds, puree the pulp in a food processor, and reserve.

Preheat the oven to 325°F. Heat the cream to scalding. Meanwhile, beat eggs, the remaining 1/4 cup sugar, and rum together until light. Temper the hot cream, adding a little at a time to the egg mixture. Stir in the cherimoya puree and the lime juice, then strain through a sieve to remove any fibers.

Pour the mixture into the caramel-lined dish. Cover with foil cut with several slits to allow steam to escape. Place the dish in a water bath (a large pan half-filled with hot water) and bake for 45 minutes, or until the center of the custard is set. Allow the custard to cool somewhat, then turn upside-down onto a large, flat serving dish with a lip, unmold, and serve. The flan will keep in the refrigerator for up to 3 days.

Tropical Fruit Salad with Poppy Seed–Honey Dressing

Take advantage of the best tropical fruits, usually for sale in wintertime, to make this light, colorful salad. Even if you can't get to a tropical paradise, you can still dream about one with the help of these juicy, fragrant tropical fruits. When choosing the fruits, consider texture, color, and flavor, and try to contrast all three elements. Firm but ripe fruits work best here. Toss with the Amaretto-flavored citrus dressing, and if you'd like, serve with a scoop of ricotta cheese for a fresh and easy lunch, perfect for a wedding or baby shower.

SERVES 8

Juice of 2 limes

Juice 1 orange

2 teaspoons grated orange zest

2 tablespoons honey

2 tablespoons amaretto

$1/2$ teaspoon grated nutmeg

1 tablespoon poppy seeds

2 mangoes, peeled and diced

1 red papaya, peeled and diced

1 starfruit, sliced and seeded

1 golden pineapple, peeled and diced

4 kiwis, diced

2 red bananas, diced

$1/4$ cup sliced almonds, skin on, lightly toasted at 300°F.

Whisk together the lime juice, orange juice and zest, honey, amaretto, nutmeg, and poppy seeds. Toss lightly with the fruits, sprinkle with the toasted almonds, and serve immediately

941

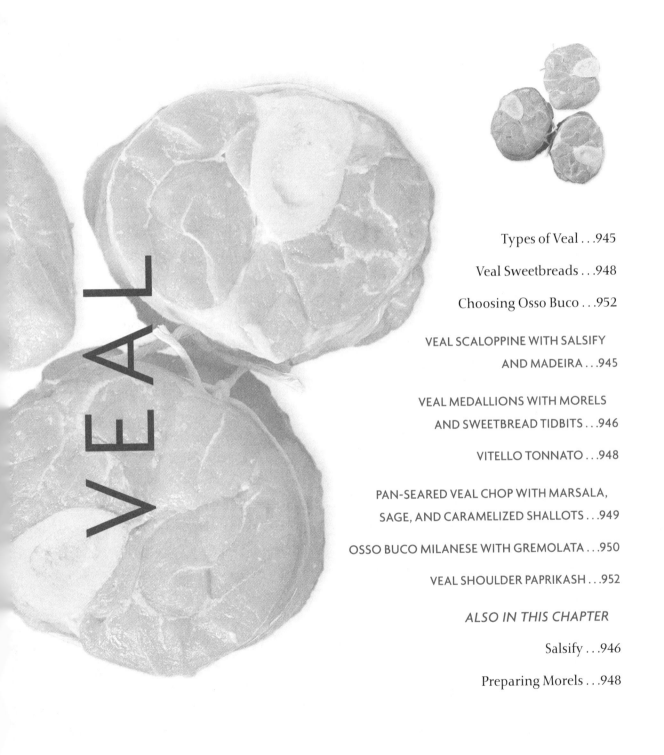

VEAL

VEAL

Perhaps the most controversial meat on the menu, veal is a dining-out favorite, especially in Italian restaurants, which often have a whole menu section just devoted to veal specialties. Many of these dishes don't exist in Italy, but have been developed to suit American palates. Veal is simply the meat of young beef cattle and gets its name from the Latin *vitellus*, meaning *calf*. Veal has always been a luxury item, because it is the meat of such a young animal sacrificed to the table before it reaches anywhere near its full potential in size. In Roman times, the huge appetite for veal and other suckling animals had to be controlled by a decree forbidding their slaughter; not enough were being left to replenish stocks.

Veal is important in the cuisine of the Netherlands (where the formula-fed veal industry began), France, Italy, Germany, and Switzerland. Italian and German immigrants to the U.S. in the late nineteenth and early twentieth century brought with them a taste for veal. But even so, Americans eat less than one pound per person per year of veal, whereas Italians eat more than fifteen pounds per person per year.

Veal production in America is tied to the dairy industry, and veal calves are primarily raised in major dairy states. To be efficient milk producers, dairy cows must give birth once a year. Female calves, or heifers, are raised to give milk, but until the advent of "special-fed" veal, male Holstein calves were simply killed because they were not suitable for beef production. Now, the great majority of male Holstein calves are raised by veal farmers, mostly small family farms that use one or another of the special feed programs to keep their veal light in color, the way Americans prefer it.

Light-colored veal developed in the 1950s, when American dairy farmers sold inexpensively large surpluses of skim milk to veal producers in the Netherlands. Dutch veal producers found that feeding their veal calves this milk led to increased weight and an improved quality of veal. With an increase in production, there was a concurrent increase in demand for this "milk-fed" veal first in Europe and then in America. This mildly flavored, pale pink-colored veal has subtle flavor that makes it adaptable to many styles of cuisine.

Veal consumption has been affected by objections, especially in Britain and the U.S., to the practice of raising calves in restricted spaces with no exercise or sunlight and an iron-deficient diet. However, improved animal care and feeding practices have evolved. Today, most veal calves are raised in well-lit, climate-controlled, and ventilated barns. The well-fed calves are housed in specially constructed, individual stalls large enough to allow the calves to stand, stretch, lie down, and groom themselves. There has been a new interest in restaurants in serving pasture-fed veal, which is darker in color and stronger in flavor, but is likely to have led a less confined and more enjoyable life.

944

Types of Veal

Bob Veal: These calves are milk-fed and are about three weeks old at slaughter. They usually weigh less than one hundred and fifty pounds and have light pink meat without much flavor and a soft, rather mushy texture. Though this type of veal represents about fifteen percent of American totals, much of it is processed.

Grain-Fed Veal: These calves are first fed milk, and then a diet of grain and hay. Their meat is dark pink to red with firm texture and is somewhat marbled. This type of veal, sometimes called "pasture-fed," has a stronger and more beef-like flavor and meat that can be slightly chewy. These calves are marketed at about six months of age and weigh about five hundred pounds. About one-third of American veal is of this type. For grain-fed (range-fed or grass-fed) veal, look for slightly moist, light reddish-pink meat with pale yellow fat. This is the type of veal that is found on the menus of eco-conscious restaurants and is often purchased direct from the farmer.

Special-Fed Veal: This is the type of veal found on the tables at fine restaurants. Special-fed calves are fed a nutritionally complete milk supplement until they reach four to five months of age and weigh about four hundred pounds. The meat is ivory to creamy pink, with a firm, fine, and velvety texture; because of its larger size, it can be found in larger cuts suitable to scaloppine. About half of U.S. veal calves are of this type, which is the main type that is exported.

Look for special-fed veal in fancy markets, and expect to pay a premium price. The meat should be pale pink and moist but not wet or drippy. Any fat should be smooth and white. This type of veal is highly perishable, so be sure it is not old, discolored, and gray on the edges, and that you serve it within two days of purchase. The best selection of veal is usually to be found in Italian butcher shops.

Veal Scaloppine with Salsify and Madeira

Salsify is a wonderful, nutty-tasting, long, white root that is not nearly as popular in America as in Europe. Here, it is cut into thin coins, then simmered until tender. Quickly sautéed veal scaloppine are glazed with Marsala wine, lemon, and butter and mixed with the salsify for a simple yet elegant dish. Note that turkey or pork scaloppine can be prepared the same way and, while they won't be quite as delicate in flavor, their lower cost is a major bonus.

SERVES 4

Juice of 1 lemon

1 bay leaf

1 pound salsify roots, ends cut off and roots peeled

1 pound thin veal scaloppine

Kosher salt and freshly ground black pepper to taste

4 tablespoons unsalted butter, divided

$1/4$ pound (1 cup) all-purpose flour

$1/2$ cup Madeira wine

1 wedge lemon

1 tablespoon chopped Italian parsley

In a medium, nonreactive pot, bring 1 quart of salted water to the boil with the lemon juice and bay leaf. Boil the salsify for 15 to 20 minutes, or until tender when pierced. Drain, reserving the liquid and the salsify. Cool the salsify, then cut into thin coins and reserve.

Sprinkle the veal on both sides with salt and pepper. Heat 2 tablespoons of the butter in a large, heavy-bottomed skillet, preferably nonstick, until sizzling and just starting to brown. Meanwhile, dust the veal with the flour, shaking off the excess. Add the veal to the pan without crowding and sauté for about 1 minute on each side, or until opaque, then remove from the pan and reserve on a plate. Pour off and discard any fat from the pan.

Add the Madeira to the pan and flame (to cook off the alcohol). Now add the salsify and about 2 tablespoons of its cooking liquid and boil for 2 to 3 minutes with the Madeira, until syrupy. Add the reserved veal back into the pan, season to taste with salt and pepper, shaking to heat evenly and coat with the pan sauce. Finish the sauce by swirling in the remaining 2 tablespoons butter with a squeeze of lemon juice. Sprinkle with the chopped parsley and serve immediately.

946

SALSIFY

Salsify, *Tragopogon porrifolius*, is a hardy, long, edible white root vegetable with light-tan skin that resembles a thin parsnip or a thin white carrot. Its roots are often forked and covered with scraggly rootlets. Native to the Mediterranean region, salsify is in the huge Compositae (or sunflower) family. Often called "oyster plant" because of its oyster-like color, salsify is firm in texture and has a nutty, artichoke-like flavor with a sweet aftertaste. Although now rare in America, salsify was common in Thomas Jefferson's era. This delicious root, in season in the winter, deserves to be rediscovered.

Veal Medallions with Morels and Sweetbread Tidbits

This is a refined restaurant-style dish, suited for the most discerning of palates and the best wines. It makes a wonderful special-occasion dish, perhaps for New Year's Eve or a special Valentine's Day dinner. Wild morels, truly one of the world's great mushrooms, are sautéed with bits of sweetbread and used to top medallions of veal from the loin, the most expensive part of the animal and the equivalent to a New York strip steak in beef. Sweetbreads call for some special preparation techniques. They are soaked in water, then simmered, cooled, trimmed, and weighted so they're nice and firm. The sweetbreads are delicious on their own and so are the morels, but together with the veal, the whole dish is extraordinary. Start the dish a day ahead to prepare the sweetbreads.

SERVES 6

Sweetbreads

1 pound calf's sweetbreads

2 tablespoons each: olive oil and unsalted butter

1/4 cup each: chopped carrot, celery, and onion

1/4 cup Madeira

2 tablespoons brandy

1/4 cup veal Demi-Glace, purchased or homemade
(*see* page 115)

Soak the sweetbreads in cold water for 2 to 3 hours, then drain and discard the water. Place the sweetbreads in a sauté pan, cover with cold water, and bring to the boil. Simmer for 5 minutes, then drain and cool. Pull off and discard the outer skin and any hard connective tissue. Wrap the sweetbreads in plastic and place them in a flat dish. Cover with a heavy weight, such as a can of tomatoes, to compress and firm the sweetbreads. Refrigerate overnight.

The next day, in a medium sauté pan, brown the sweetbreads on all sides in olive oil and butter. Add the carrot, celery, and onion and brown together lightly. Add the Madeira and brandy and bring to the boil over high heat. Add the demi-glace, bring back to the boil, and then reduce heat to braise slowly, either on top of the stove or in a 300°F. oven, for about 20 minutes, or until the sweetbreads are firm and the liquid is syrupy.

Allow the sweetbreads to cool in the cooking liquid, then remove from the liquid and pull apart into small nuggets. Strain the cooking liquid and reserve to add to the sauce below.

Veal with Morels and Sauce

4 tablespoons unsalted butter, divided

1/2 pound fresh morels (substitute 2 ounces dried morels)

1 1/2 pounds boneless loin of veal, cut into 2-ounce
medallions

1/4 pound (1 cup) all-purpose flour

1 tablespoon olive oil

2 tablespoons finely chopped shallots

1/2 cup dry white wine

1/4 cup Madeira wine

1/2 cup cooking juices from the sweetbreads above

Kosher salt and freshly ground white pepper to taste

Melt 2 tablespoons of butter in a medium sauté pan. Add the morels and cook, covered, over medium heat, for 6 to 7 minutes, or until firm and the pan juices have mostly evaporated. Remove from the heat and keep warm.

Dust the veal medallions in flour, shaking off the excess. In a large, heavy-bottomed skillet, preferably nonstick, heat 1 tablespoon of butter and the olive oil until sizzling. Sauté the veal on both sides until well browned. (Do not crowd the pan with veal so that it will brown well.) Remove the medallions from the pan and keep warm.

Pour off the fat from the pan and add the shallots, stirring and cooking for 1 minute, or until fragrant. Add the white wine, Madeira, morels, and the sweetbread cooking liquid to the pan and bring to the boil. Cook to reduce the liquid slightly. Season with salt and pepper.

Return the veal medallions and the cooked sweetbread tidbits to the pan to heat. Swirl the remaining tablespoon of butter into the sauce to finish. Arrange the veal medallions on a serving platter, ladle the sauce and a portion of morels and sweetbreads over each serving, and serve immediately.

Veal Sweetbreads

Sweetbreads are the most sough-after of "variety meats"—the euphemistic American name for organ meats. (Our more earthy, Anglo-Saxon forebears called them offal, for off fall, because they were allowed to fall to the ground during slaughter.) Sweetbreads are, of course, neither sweet nor bread, but one of two glands that shrink as the calf gets older. In a further euphemism, they are known as ris de veau in French, meaning veal rice, a term often used in English, especially at fancier establishments. Throat sweetbreads are plump and rounded; heart sweetbreads are elongated and narrow. Because of their appealing mild flavor and soft, creamy texture, sweetbreads are often expensive, like other rare ingredients such as wild mushrooms and truffles. Look for them at fancy butcher shops or order them from your own market. They usually come frozen, because, like all organ meats, they are quite perishable.

948

Preparing Morels

Trim off the bottom $1/2$-inch of the morel stems and discard. Place morels in a bowl filled with cold water. Let them soak for 10 minutes. Remove the morels from the water. Rub the morel caps with your fingers. If you feel any sand, wash the caps again in cold water. Cut the morel caps lengthwise into halves and reserve. (If you're using dried morels, follow the direction in Reconstituting Dried Porcini, page 304.)

Vitello Tonnato

This classic Italian dish comes from up in the mountainous north of Piedmont, where it is a summertime favorite. It tastes best served at room temperature, preferably outdoors with a fresh breeze blowing and lots of white wine, if that can be arranged. Although tuna and capers don't sound like they'd go very well with veal, the mild flavor and tender consistency of the veal are contrasted to the creamy aioli-like sauce flavored with pungent anchovies and capers, with the light but meaty tuna giving body and rounded flavor to the sauce. The top round is the largest single muscle in the veal calf (or in beef, lamb, and pork); it is the large inner muscle at the top inside of the leg, placed where it gets little exercise, so it stays nice and tender. Look for the best veal at Italian butcher shops or order it from your local market, but expect to pay a premium price for this sought-after cut, used for high-quality scaloppine.

Serves 8

1 quart chicken stock

1 cup white wine

1 small onion, peeled and stuck with 2 whole cloves

1 celery stalk

1 carrot

2 bay leaves

2 garlic cloves

2 pounds top round of veal

1 (6-ounce) can tuna in olive oil

6 anchovy fillets

4 tablespoons capers, divided

2 egg yolks

Juice of 2 lemons

½ cup extra-virgin olive oil

2 tablespoons chopped Italian parsley

1 thinly sliced lemon

In a large casserole dish, bring the chicken stock, white wine, onion, celery, carrot, bay leaves, and garlic to the boil. Simmer for 20 minutes, then add the veal. Bring the liquid back to the boil, reduce the heat, and simmer very slowly until tender, about 45 minutes. Remove from the heat and cool the veal in its cooking liquid. Strain the liquid and skim off the fat. Reserve 1 cup of the cooking liquid, chilling or freezing the remainder to use as a sauce base, if desired.

Blend the reserved cup of liquid in a food processor with the tuna and its oil, the anchovies, 2 tablespoons of the capers, and the egg yolks. Add the lemon juice and then pour in the olive oil in a slow, steady stream, blending until a thick, creamy sauce is obtained.

Slice the cooled veal into thin slices. Spread a thin layer of sauce onto a large serving platter. Cover with a layer of veal. Continue in the same fashion, ending with a layer of sauce. Sprinkle the sauce with the remaining capers and the parsley, and decorate the edge of the platter with the sliced lemon. Serve immediately at room temperature or refrigerate for serving within the next day or two, but bring the dish to room temperature before serving.

Pan–Seared Veal Chop with Marsala, Sage, and Caramelized Shallots

If you really want to splurge, go all out and buy large, thick veal porterhouse steaks, including parts of both the buttery tenderloin and the full-bodied sirloin strip. Each steak will cost about 15 dollars, but that's a whole lot less than you'd pay in a restaurant, and they're easy to prepare. The crispy brown fried shallots are optional or you could brown them in a skillet, but they add wonderful crispness and all-over caramelized flavor to the veal. Serve with best-quality full-bodied white wine or a light red. Whole sage leaves give a light, resinous edge to the sauce; once fried, they become quite mild and delicious eaten whole.

SERVES 4

949

Caramelized Shallots

4 cups canola oil for deep frying

4 cups thinly sliced shallots

Heat the oil in a large, deep saucepot or a wok filled no more than one-third full with the oil. The oil should be shimmering and the air above the oil should feel hot. Add the shallots in batches, stirring and allowing them to bubble up. As the bubbles die down, add more shallots until they are all in the pot. Keep frying over moderately high heat, stirring often until the shallots are evenly browned and crispy, about 10 minutes. Take care, because once they start to brown, they can burn easily. Drain on paper towels and store, tightly covered, at room temperature for 3 to 4 days.

Veal Chops

4 (14-ounce or larger) veal porterhouse steaks

Kosher salt and freshly ground black pepper to taste

2 tablespoons olive oil

2 tablespoons unsalted butter

1 tablespoon shredded sage leaves

$^1/_2$ cup dry Marsala

$^1/_4$ cup Demi-Glace, purchased or homemade
  (*see* page 115)

Caramelized Shallots, for garnish (optional)

Preheat the oven to 350°F. Sprinkle the veal on all sides with salt and pepper and allow the meat to rest at room temperature for about 20 minutes. Preheat a large, heavy-bottomed skillet, preferably cast-iron, until it just begins to smoke. Rub the veal chops with the olive oil and brown on both sides, two at a time, until well-browned all over. Remove from the pan, and repeat with the remaining veal chops. Arrange the veal chops on a metal baking pan and place in the oven to finish cooking, for about 10 minutes, or until the juices in the inside run light pink when pierced.

   Meanwhile, pour off the fat from the pan, wipe out, and heat the butter until sizzling. Add the sage leaves and heat briefly until sizzling, then add the Marsala and the Demi-Glace. Boil for about 5 minutes, or until the sauce is thickened and syrupy. Remove the veal from the oven, arrange on serving plates, and ladle the sauce over top. Sprinkle with the caramelized shallots and serve immediately.

Osso Buco Milanese with Gremolata

When I first started to serve osso buco, "the hollow bone," at restaurants in the late 1970s, it was a relatively inexpensive cut, as tougher cuts usually are. Today, the price has gone up because this dish has become so popular, especially in restaurants. It can be made ahead, and makes a striking presentation, with the bone sticking up in the air, and is a whole meal on a plate. In Italy, special long spoons with a small bowl meant to dig out the best part, the meltingly creamy and impossibly rich marrow, are sold. Substitute iced-tea spoons or demi-tasse spoons. Classic Milanese-style osso buco is served on a bed of rich, golden risotto, cooked in times past with marrow fat for even more richness. The final touch is the sprinkling of fragrant gremolata, *a mixture of grated citrus zests, finely chopped raw garlic, and plenty of Italian parsley, without which osso buco is a much more ordinary dish.*

SERVES 6

6 osso buco, tied with butcher's string
  to ensure they stay whole

Kosher salt and freshly ground black pepper to taste

$^1/_4$ pound pancetta, cut into small cubes

$^1/_2$ cup canola or vegetable oil

$^1/_4$ pound (1 cup) all-purpose flour

2 ribs celery, diced

2 carrots, diced

1 red onion, diced

1 tablespoon chopped garlic

1 tablespoon chopped rosemary

1 (28-ounce) can diced tomatoes

950

1 cup white wine

3 cups chicken or veal stock

2 tablespoons chopped Italian parsley

Preheat the oven to 300°F. Sprinkle the osso buco on all sides with salt and pepper and leave at room temperature for about 20 minutes. Meanwhile, cook the pancetta in the vegetable oil until the bits are crispy and brown. Drain, reserving both the pancetta and the oil.

In a large, heavy Dutch oven, heat about half the reserved oil. Dust the osso buco with flour, shaking off the excess. Brown the osso buco very well on all sides (this step is key to the richness of its flavor). Remove the osso buco and reserve. Pour off and discard fat from pan.

Heat the remaining fat in the pot and add the celery, carrots, onion, garlic, and rosemary. Sauté until the vegetables are crisp-tender, about 5 minutes. Pour in the tomatoes with their juices, the white wine, the chicken stock, and parsley, and bring the liquid to the boil.

Add the browned osso buco to the pan, bring back to the boil, and then cover. Place the pot in the oven and simmer, turning once, for about 2½ hours, or until the meat is tender when pierced with a fork but still holds it shape. Remove the shanks from the oven and allow to cool slightly before serving.

Meanwhile, prepare the Gremolata and Saffron Risotto.

Gremolata

Grated zest of 1 orange

Grated zest of 2 lemons

1 cup chopped Italian parsley

2 tablespoons chopped garlic

Combine all the ingredients and chop them together to bring the flavors together. Cover and keep refrigerated until ready to serve.

Risotto alla Milanese and Assembly

½ cup dry white wine

½ teaspoon crumbled saffron threads

4 tablespoons unsalted butter, divided

½ cup finely diced onion

1 cup risotto rice

Kosher salt and freshly ground black pepper to taste

1 quart chicken stock, simmering

½ cup freshly grated Parmigiano-Reggiano cheese

In a small bowl, combine the wine and saffron, soaking until the liquid is golden yellow, about 15 minutes.

In a medium, heavy-bottomed saucepot, heat 2 tablespoon of butter until sizzling. Add the onion and cook for 3 to 4 minutes or until softened, but not browned. Add the risotto, stirring for 1 to 2 minutes, until the rice is shiny and slightly clear. Pour in the wine-saffron mixture and season with salt and pepper. Raise the heat to high and cook until the wine evaporates. Reduce the heat so the rice is bubbling nicely.

Start adding the hot broth, one ladleful at a time. Keep cooking, stirring occasionally until the broth is absorbed, then add another ladleful. Continue until all the broth has been absorbed by the rice. Turn off the heat, and stir in the grated cheese. Season with salt and pepper and let the rice sit a few minutes until the cheese melts.

The risotto should consist of firm but cooked grains of rice suspended in a creamy liquid. Just before serving, stir in the cheese and the remaining 2 tablespoons of butter. Top each portion with a piece of osso buco, remove the string, ladle over the cooking juices and a portion of the vegetables. Serve immediately, preferably on heated plates, (and pass around a bowl of gremolata for sprinkling.)

Veal Shoulder Paprikash

Like goulash, veal paprikash is a rich, hearty stew from the complex cuisine of Magyar Hungary. Here, the sauce is flavored with paprika and garlic, but is enriched and lightened with sour cream. Veal cubes from the shoulder will be less expensive than those cut from the leg, and will also be more succulent, though more fatty. If you'd like, prepare the paprikash a day ahead of time up to the point of adding the flour and sour cream. Cool and then chill overnight. Remove and discard any solidified fat on the top of the stew, reheat gently, and then proceed with the recipe. Serve with buttered egg noodles tossed with poppy seeds or with the Spaetzle with Brown Butter, Chives, and Toasted Breadcrumbs (see page 172).

SERVES 6

2^1/$_2$ pounds veal shoulder cubes

Kosher salt and freshly ground black pepper to taste

^{1}/$_4$ pound (1 cup) + 2 tablespoons all-purpose flour

^{1}/$_4$ cup rendered bacon fat, divided

^{1}/$_4$ cup unsalted butter, divided

2 white onions, thinly sliced

1 tablespoon chopped garlic

3 tablespoons sweet Hungarian paprika

2 cups chicken stock

2 cups sour cream

2 tablespoons chopped parsley

Sprinkle the veal cubes with salt and pepper and allow them to rest at room temperature for about 15 minutes. Lightly dust the veal cubes with flour, shaking off the excess.

Heat about half the bacon fat and half the butter in a large, heavy Dutch oven. Brown the veal in batches, without crowding, repeating until all the veal is done, remove, and reserve.

Add the remaining bacon fat and butter to the same pan, stir in the onions and fry until lightly colored. Add the garlic and cook, stirring, for 1 minute, or until fragrant, then stir in the paprika, coating the onions well. Add the chicken stock and bring the liquid to a boil. Add the veal cubes, bring back to the boil, then reduce the heat to a simmer, and cover. Simmer for about 1 hour, or until the juices are syrupy and flavorful, and the veal is tender when pierced.

To finish the sauce, whisk 2 tablespoons of the flour with the sour cream, then stir the mixture into the sauce and simmer for 6 to 8 minutes longer, or until thickened and creamy. Taste for seasoning, and serve immediately, topped with parsley.

952

WALNUTS, BLACK WALNUTS, & PECANS

WALNUTS
BLACK WALNUTS, & PECANS

I'm a nut-a-holic, I admit. It all goes back to one of my early tasks in a very influential kitchen: toasting walnuts with a great deal of trepidation to make sure I didn't burn a whole expensive batch. It had long been my goal to work at Kathleen Mulhern's The Garden restaurant in Philadelphia, and I finally landed a job in the pantry, just in time for their madly busy summer. At the time, The Garden was just about the only restaurant around that boasted an outdoor garden, and it was always mobbed for lunch, especially by expense-account business people. One of my jobs was toasting a huge tray of walnuts every day for the chicken salad. Perhaps because I didn't get much time to eat anything else, except the toasty ends of French baguette, I managed to gorge myself daily on those soft, buttery-tasting toasted nuts. They are still among the foods that I can't resist.

The walnut tree, which grows widely in temperate zones throughout the world, goes so far back in human history that no one knows where it originated. The name *walnut* derives from the corruption of *Gaul nut*, coined by the French. It's easy to imagine why ancient Romans considered the walnut to be a tree version of the human brain. The shell represented the skull, while the two nut halves resembled a miniature brain.

The most common walnut in America is called the Persian or English walnut. Walnuts were brought to Europe through Persia in early history and got their name, English walnut, because they were brought from Asia Minor to England aboard English boats. The Carpathian walnut is a cold, hardy strain found in the northern states of the American Midwest. Walnuts are so basic that they are simply known as nuts (*noci*) in Italian, French (*noix*), and Spanish (*nuez*).

Eastern Black Walnuts are native to the central and eastern United States and have a robust and distinct flavor that sets them apart. However, black walnuts are notoriously difficult to crack, with thick, ridged shells, and hulls that adhere to the shell. Black walnuts are especially favored for baking and are used to flavor ice cream.

Americans love golden-brown pecans for good reason—butter pecan ice cream is still my favorite, and it seems that every restaurant in America serves pecan pie. The pecan is native to the Mississippi River Valley and is a member of the hickory family, known more for its wood, used for smoking, than its difficult-to-shell nuts. For years, pecans were known as Mississippi nuts or Illinois nuts until the native American name, *pecan*, gained widespread use. Pecans, which were important to the Native American diet and were a staple food in winter months, were introduced by locals to the early settlers of Georgia and were exchanged for tools and trinkets.

Thomas Jefferson—president, horticulturist, and food connoisseur—was fond of pecans and planted trees from Louisiana at Monticello. The first successfully grafted pecan tree was made by a Louisiana slave named Antoine in 1846 and by 1871, several good-sized groves had been planted in most of the southeastern states, including Georgia. Today, Georgia, Oklahoma, and Texas all produce large amounts of pecans.

WALNUTS AND PECANS IN THEIR MANY FORMS

Faced with such a slew of nuts in so many forms, it's confusing to choose the right kind. Whole shelled nut halves are the top-of-the-line nut; the most expensive but also the sweetest and freshest. Packages of walnut and pecan pieces are perfect for cookie making. For the best taste and quality, nuts should be purchased fresh from the current harvest beginning in late fall. At holiday time, nuts in their shells appear on produce-aisle shelves.

There is no doubt that nuts taste their best right out of the shell. Don't choose nuts that rattle in their shells, since they will be dry instead of plump and meaty. Cracking nuts is not only fun, but you have to work really hard to eat too many. Set out a basket of nuts and nut-crackers. Add a hunk of blue cheese and wedges of apple or pear to make a perfect fireside treat.

If you use a lot of nuts, buy them from a specialty supplier that has quick turnover. If possible, taste nuts before buying them because their high fat content makes them prone to rancidity, especially in hot-weather months. Place nuts in heavy-duty zip-top freezer bags and squeeze out all the air before sealing. Stored this way in the freezer, the nuts will stay fresh for six months. You don't have to defrost them before using.

Light-colored whole walnuts will be most expensive, but also sweeter. Small bits and pieces can be just right for baking because they cost less and don't have to be chopped.

Choosing Shelled Walnuts and Pecans

Select walnuts that are full and plump-looking, with light-colored skins and no powdery bits of broken nuts and skin in the bag. Warehouse club stores are good places to buy nuts, especially in the fall and winter. Trader Joe's sells high-quality nuts, and their high turnover ensures that the nuts are fresh. Natural foods markets also sell good-quality nuts, though prices will generally be higher.

Select plump pecans that are uniform in golden brown color and in size. The color of a pecan in its shell should be light brown, and the shell should be smooth, with no evidence of holes or other damage. Some black markings occur on the shell and vary with the variety of nut. The newer varieties, called "paper-shell pecans," have thin shells that you can break with your fingers and contain larger nut meats.

956

Walnut–Grapefruit Salad

I'm especially fond of nuts in salads, perhaps a result of my days in the salad station, where I could munch away on toasted nuts. Here, tangy, bittersweet ruby grapefruit sections are combined with mixed greens, toasted walnuts, and scallions in a walnut-oil-based dressing for an easy, tasty winter salad that's as pretty as it is good to eat. Walnut oil makes a wonderful rich, smooth dressing, but because of its penetrating flavor, you can mix it with a bland oil such as soy or canola to cut the price of the salad.

SERVES 6

1 cup walnut oil, substitute half walnut oil and
 half vegetable oil
$1/4$ cup Sherry vinegar or rice wine vinegar
Sprinkle of Tabasco sauce
Kosher salt and freshly ground black pepper to taste
2 Ruby grapefruits
$3/4$ pound mixed salad greens: Romaine, Boston lettuce,
 endive, watercress, spinach, Treviso
$1/4$ pound (1 cup) walnuts, lightly toasted
$1/2$ bunch scallions, thinly sliced

Whisk together the oil, vinegar, Tabasco, and salt and pepper and reserve.

Using a sharp paring knife, slice off about $1/2$ inch from the top and bottom of the grapefruits, exposing the flesh. Cutting down, remove strips of the rind, the pith (thick, spongy white membrane), and the skin covering the grapefruit sections. You should end up with a small pink ball. Then, cutting in between the skin, remove the sections of grapefruit and reserve.

Toss the greens with about $^{1}/_{2}$ cup of the dressing. Arrange the grapefruit sections, walnuts, and scallions over top, sprinkle with any grapefruit juice, and serve immediately.

WALNUT OIL

Walnut oil is pressed from lightly toasted walnuts and has a full-bodied nut flavor that is full and warm with a smooth finish. France's Dordogne, also known as the Périgord, has been the heart of French walnut country for centuries, and is equally famed for its black truffles. There is evidence that walnut trees have existed in this part of the world for more than 17,000 years, and they have long been essential to the region's economy. In earlier times, walnut oil was considered to be as precious as gold, and the nuts were used to pay off debts and were tithed to the church. There is an old saying in the region that nothing is lost of the walnut but the sound of its shell being cracked. Whole walnuts go to fine restaurants to be added to green salads and used in desserts. Broken nuts are pressed at walnut mills into the oil essential to Périgord cooking and salad dressing.

Pecan Red Rice

Use nutty-tasting Bhutanese short-grain red rice for this dish. This special rice is grown at 8,000 feet in the Himalayan Kingdom of Bhutan and irrigated with glacier water rich in trace minerals. When cooked, this earthy-tasting rice has a soft texture and a beautiful red russet color. The nutty-tasting rice and the rich, buttery pecans work together to make a wonderful side dish, suitable for the holiday table with a roast turkey, goose, or duck. Brown short- or medium-grained rice makes the best substitute, but barley, kasha, or hulled wheat berries would also work well.

SERVES 4 TO 6

2 tablespoons unsalted butter
$^{1}/_{4}$ cup finely chopped shallots
$^{1}/_{4}$ pound (1 cup) roughly chopped lightly
    toasted pecans, divided
1 cup red rice
3 cups chicken stock, simmering
Kosher salt and freshly ground black pepper to taste

Melt the butter and lightly brown the shallots in a medium sauté pot. Add half the pecans and cook together until the pecans are lightly browned. Add the rice and sauté until translucent, about 4 minutes. Add the simmering stock and season with salt and pepper.

Cover and bring to the boil. Reduce the heat to low (or place in a moderate 325°F. oven), simmer and cook for 45 minutes, or until the rice is tender and fluffy. Serve immediately, sprinkled with the remaining pecans.

957

Walnut–Rosemary Bread

This fragrant, walnutty bread was a big hit in my days at A'propos Bistro in Philadelphia. We made all of our own bread and served it with every meal. I do believe this one was the most requested, with good reason. The richness of the nuts tempered with the piney rosemary make for a perfectly balanced bread. Serve it with a cheese course, especially with stinky washed-rind cheeses such as Italian Taleggio or French Pont L'Evêque or with any of the great blues of the world, which have a particular affinity for walnuts. Any leftover bread makes wonderful toast to be spread with butter, goat cheese, or cream cheese. The larger amount of yeast is to encourage this rather dense dough, heavy with walnuts, to rise properly.

MAKES 1 LARGE LOAF

1$\frac{1}{2}$ cups warm milk (105°F. to 115°F.)

1 tablespoon kosher salt

3 tablespoons granulated sugar

2 packets (2 scant tablespoons) active dry yeast

1$\frac{1}{2}$ pounds bread flour

$\frac{1}{2}$ cup extra-virgin olive oil

$\frac{1}{4}$ cup walnut oil

$\frac{1}{4}$ pound (1 cup) roughly chopped toasted walnuts

2 tablespoons finely chopped rosemary

In a small bowl, whisk together the milk, salt, and sugar. Dissolve the yeast in the milk and allow it to bubble up. Place the flour in the bowl of a mixer with a paddle attachment, and beat in the milk mixture along with the olive oil and walnut oil. Switch to the dough hook attachment and knead until the dough is smooth and elastic and comes away smoothly from the sides of the bowl.

Cover with a damp towel and leave in a warm place, allowing the dough to rise until doubled in volume. Punch the dough down and then knead in the walnuts and rosemary. Shape into 1 large or 2 smaller loaves on a lightly floured baking pan and allow to rise until doubled again.

Preheat the oven to 400°F. Bake the loaf for 20 minutes, then reduce the heat to 350°F. and continue baking for 30 minutes longer, or until the bread sounds hollow when tapped, and reads 200°F. when pierced in the center with a thermometer. Remove the bread from the oven and allow it to cool before slicing and serving.

958

Black Walnut, Goat Cheese, and Honey Tart

This is a deliciously sophisticated variation on the popular favorite, pecan pie, made here with a rich, crumbly, walnut-cookie pastry filled with a transparent and gooey layer of honey, black walnuts, and English walnuts. To put the icing on the cake or to gild the lily, the tart is topped with a cheesecake-like layer of cream cheese mixed with goat cheese. If you cross pecan pie with cheesecake and add distinctively bittersweet native American black walnuts, this tart is the result. Store in the refrigerator for 3 to 4 days.

SERVES 8 TO 12

Walnut Pastry

1 pound (4 cups) all-purpose flour, preferably unbleached

$1/4$ pound (about 1 cup) ground walnuts

$1/2$ cup granulated sugar

Pinch of kosher salt

1 egg + 2 egg yolks

Grated zest of 1 lemon

2 tablespoons dark rum

$3/4$ pound (3 sticks) unsalted butter, frozen until firm and cut into small bits

Combine the dry ingredients: flour, walnuts, sugar, and salt in the bowl of a mixer or food processor. In a separate bowl, whisk together the egg, egg yolks, lemon zest and rum, and reserve.

Add the butter to the dry ingredients and beat or process until the pieces are the consistency of oatmeal. Pour in the reserved egg mixture and beat or process until just combined and the dough forms a ball. Press the dough into a 10- to 11-inch fluted-edge French tart pan and refrigerate until firm, at least 45 minutes and up to overnight.

Preheat the oven to 375°F. Press heavy-duty foil into the shell and fill with beans. (For more information, *see* Blind-Baking with Beans, page 230.) Bake for 25 minutes, or until very lightly browned, but no longer at all raw and pasty. Remove the shell from the oven, and remove the foil and beans as soon as the shell is cool enough to handle. Cool the shell to room temperature and reserve.

Filling

2 eggs

Dash kosher salt

4 tablespoons unsalted butter, melted and cooled

$1/4$ cup corn syrup

$1/2$ cup honey

2 teaspoons vanilla extract

$1^1/2$ cups chopped walnuts

1 cup chopped black walnuts

Reduce the oven temperature to 350°F. Whisk together all the filling ingredients: eggs, salt, butter, corn syrup, honey, vanilla, walnuts, and black walnuts. Place the cooled shell on a metal baking pan (to catch any drips), pour in the filling and bake for 30 minutes, or until the filling is set in the middle. Remove from the oven and reserve.

Topping

$3/4$ pound ($1^1/2$ cups) cream cheese

$1/2$ pound mild goat cheese

2 eggs

2 tablespoons granulated sugar

Grated zest of 1 lemon

1 teaspoon vanilla extract

959

Beat together the cream cheese and goat cheese until smooth and creamy. Add the eggs, sugar, lemon zest, and vanilla and beat together until well-combined, scraping down the sides of the mixer once or twice to ensure smoothness. Pour the topping onto the nut filling and bake for 20 minutes more at 350°F., or until just set in the middle. Cool the tart completely before cutting into portions. Store the tart in the refrigerator for up to 4 days.

Black Walnut Shortbread

This shortbread is meant for black walnut lovers. Maybe you have friends from Missouri, where the majority of America's black walnuts are gathered from backyard trees for sale across the country. The bold, bittersweet flavor of black walnuts is tempered by an equal amount of milder English walnuts to make a well-balanced shortbread, rich with butter. The dough freezes very well, so divide in two, placing one half in a heavy plastic zip-top freezer bag and freeze for up to 3 months.

MAKES 36 COOKIES

2 pounds (8 cups) all-purpose flour

1⅓ cups cornstarch

2 cups granulated sugar

2 cups chopped walnuts

2 cup chopped black walnuts

2 pounds (8 sticks) unsalted butter,
    cut into small pieces and chilled

1 tablespoon vanilla extract

¼ cup heavy cream

1 cup crystallized, or raw, sugar

Preheat the oven to 350°F. Combine the flour, cornstarch, sugar, walnuts, and black walnuts. Cut in the butter as if making pastry dough, mixing until the mixture looks like oatmeal. Sprinkle in the vanilla and the cream and beat again briefly, only until the mixture comes together in a ball.

Chill the dough until firm but still malleable, about 30 minutes, and then roll out slightly less than ½ inch thick. Cut into diamond shapes and sprinkle with crystallized sugar, pressing lightly with your hands so that the sugar adheres. Arrange on parchment-paper-lined baking pans and bake for 20 minutes, or until just beginning to color. Remove from the oven and cool before serving. Store in an airtight container at room temperature for 4 to 5 days.

Walnut–Whiskey Pound Cake

This deliciously moist and liquor-laden cake just gets better as it sits for a few days; the whisky mellows out and the flavors come together in a winner of a cake. This recipe was adapted from one of Edna Lewis' in her book, In Pursuit of Flavor. *A grande dame of Southern cooking, the late Lewis was the founder of the Society for the Revival and Preservation of Southern Food. Here, I've substituted soft, oil-rich walnuts for the harder, more mealy Brazil nuts in her original. I have also made this with pecans and Brazil nuts and it always tastes good. The best pan to use here is a Bundt pan. Unfortunately, only the dark, nonstick-type are available today. Lewis' method of starting the cake in a cold oven and then raising the heat works perfectly.*

MAKES ONE 10–INCH BUNDT CAKE

Unsalted butter and flour for the pan

$^1/_2$ pound (2 sticks) unsalted butter

$1^3/_4$ cups granulated sugar

4 eggs + 1 egg yolk

$^3/_4$ pound (3 cups) all-purpose flour,
  preferably unbleached

$^1/_2$ teaspoon kosher salt

$^1/_2$ teaspoon nutmeg

$^1/_2$ teaspoon cinnamon

1 tablespoon baking powder

$^1/_2$ pound ground walnuts

1 cup whisky

Butter and flour a 10-inch Bundt pan and reserve.

Cream the butter and sugar until light and fluffy, and then beat in the eggs and egg yolk, one at a time. Sift together the dry ingredients: flour, salt, nutmeg, cinnamon, and baking powder. Stir in the walnuts and reserve.

Beginning and ending with the dry ingredients, fold the dry ingredients into creamed mixture alternating with the whisky. Scrape the batter into the prepared pan.

Place in a cold oven and turn on the oven at 275°F. Bake for 30 minutes, then raise the heat to 300°F. and bake for 30 minutes longer. Raise the heat again, this time to 325°F. and bake for 15 minutes longer, or until the cake is set and has begun to come away from the sides of the pan. Cool to room temperature before unmolding. Store the cake at room temperature for 4 or 5 days.

Bourbon Honey Pecan Pie

My husband, Don Reiff, has an insatiable sweet tooth, so I'm always baking for him. There is nothing he likes better than a big piece of this bourbon-spiked, honey-flavored pecan pie. Pecan pie is commonly made with corn syrup, which is sweet, but doesn't have much flavor of its own. By combining dark corn syrup with honey, the honey flavor comes through without overpowering the bourbon and the all-important pecans. For the crust, use either the sweeter Sugar Pastry (page 989) or the unsweetened Buttermilk Pastry (page 988). If you don't want to go to the trouble of making your own dough, use an unbaked store-bought pie crust, and blind-bake the empty pie shell before continuing with the recipe.

MAKES ONE 9–INCH PIE

$^3/_4$ pound pastry, either Sugar Pastry crust (page 989)
  or Buttermilk Pastry (page 988)

6 eggs

$^1/_2$ pound dark brown sugar, packed

$^1/_4$ pound (1 stick) unsalted butter, melted and cooled

$^1/_4$ cup heavy cream

1 cup dark corn syrup

1 cup honey

6 tablespoons bourbon

1 pound whole pecans

Preheat the oven to 375°F. Roll the dough out and use it to line a 9-inch pie pan. Line the pie shell with heavy-duty aluminum foil and fill with beans. Bake for about 25 minutes, or until the pastry is lightly browned. Once the dough is set and no longer wet, you may remove the foil and beans and continue to bake until the pastry is evenly browned, 5 to 10 minutes longer. Remove from the oven, cool, and reserve.

Reduce the oven temperature to 325°F. Beat the eggs and sugar together until light colored and the mixture forms a ribbon. Stir in the butter, cream, corn syrup, honey, and bourbon. Arrange the pecans in the baked pie shell and ladle the filling over the top. Bake about 45 minutes, or until the pie is just set in the center. Cool completely before slicing.

Maple–Pecan Cookies

I adore the all-American flavor of real maple syrup, here mixed with another native American ingredient— pecans—to make buttery, thin, "refrigerator" or "slice- and- bake" cookies. Grade B maple syrup is darker, stronger-tasting, less expensive and best for baking. In fact, it's the only kind I buy, because both grade B maple syrup and large whole pecan meats are to be found at rea- sonable prices in warehouse club stores. The dough for these delicate buttery thins freezes beautifully, so I would wrap one roll and keep it in the freezer for unexpected company. Simply defrost only long enough for the dough to be cold and firm but not brittle, then just slice and bake. Serve a couple of thins on a plate with coffee or tea.

MAKES 6 DOZEN

1 pound (4 sticks) unsalted butter

$\frac{1}{2}$ cup granulated sugar

$\frac{1}{2}$ cup dark brown sugar, packed

2 egg yolks

$\frac{1}{4}$ cup pure maple syrup

2 teaspoons vanilla extract

1 pound (4 cups) all-purpose flour

$\frac{1}{2}$ pound pecans, coarsely chopped

Cream the butter and sugars until light and fluffy. In a separate bowl, stir the egg yolks, syrup, and vanilla together, then beat into the butter mixture. Stir in the flour and then the pecans, beating only long enough for a dough ball to form. Press the dough into a block, wrap well with plastic, and chill for 1 hour, or until somewhat firm. Form into logs, roll into wax paper or plastic wrap, and chill again.

Preheat the oven to 350°F. Slice the cookie dough about $\frac{1}{4}$ inch thick and place on parchment-paper-lined or nonstick-sprayed baking sheets. Bake, turning the cookies halfway through baking, for about 12 minutes, or until lightly browned at the edges. Check the cookies carefully, as they can burn easily. Note that the cookie logs can be frozen very successfully, as long as they are well wrapped. Defrost in the refrigerator.

962

WHEAT

WHEAT

The USDA (United States Department of Agriculture) tells us that we all need to eat more whole grains and legumes to add all-important fiber to our diets. They are right. However, the only way most of us will add these foods to our diet, and keep them there, is if they taste good. This chapter includes some absolutely delicious ways of preparing whole-grain wheat products, including wheat berries, bulgur, and the old cousin of wheat called farro. (Many delicious recipes for oats, barley, and buckwheat—not related to wheat at all—can be found elsewhere in this book. Wheat has long been prized as a grain for the wealthy, while barley, rye, and millet were darker grains for the poor. In fact, the word *wheat* is derived from *white* implying a light-colored, finely milled grain.

Wheat, *Triticum aestivum,* was one of the first of the grains domesticated by humans—only barley is older. Bread wheat is known to have been grown in the Nile valley by 5000 BCE and apparently spread from there to the Indus and Euphrates valleys by 4000 BCE, China by 2500 BCE, and England by 2000 BCE. Since the earliest agriculture, wheat has been the chief source of bread for Europe and the Middle East. It was introduced into Mexico by the Spaniards about 1520 and into Virginia by English colonists early in the seventeenth century.

Wheat was originally a wild grass. Evidence exists that it first grew in Mesopotamia and in the Tigris and Euphrates River valleys in the Middle East nearly 10,000 years ago. As early as 6700 BCE, Swiss lake dwellers used wheat in flat cakes. It was the Egyptians who discovered how to make yeast-leavened breads between 2000 and 3000 BCE. Since wheat is the only grain with sufficient gluten content to make a raised or leavened loaf of bread, it quickly became favored over other grains grown at the time, such as oats, millet, rice, and barley. The workers who built the pyramids in Egypt were paid in bread.

In 150 BCE, the first bakers' guilds were formed in Rome. Roman bakeries produced a variety of breads and distributed free bread to the poor in times of need. In the ashes of Pompeii, buried by the volcano Vesuvius in 79 CE, were found round breads several inches thick, divided into eight sections like a large Kaiser roll. The actual preserved breads can be seen at the National Archeological Museum in Naples, Italy, along with bread-baking tools and petrified grains of wheat.

The Romans were highly dependent on wheat and imported vast amounts from growing regions in their empire. In 1202, England adopted laws to regulate the price of bread and limit bakers' profits. At the time, many bakers were prosecuted for selling loaves that did not conform to the weights required by local laws. As a result of the bread trials in England in 1266, bakers were ordered to mark each loaf of bread. These bakers' marks were among the first trademarks.

Between 1874 and 1884, five thousand Russian Mennonites settled in Kansas, bringing with them Turkey Red Winter Wheat. Scientists at the U.S. Department of Agriculture also introduced wheats from eastern Europe in 1900. These grains provided the basic genetic material for the successful production of hard red winter wheat in the Great Plain, although most of these early wheats are no longer grown for commercial production.

Using scythes or sickles, a farmer could cut only two acres of wheat a day. With Cyrus McCormick's 1831 mechanical reaper, farmers could cut eight acres a day. In 1928, the commercial bread slicer was perfected. By 1930, sliced bread and the introduction of the automatic toaster had increased consumption of toast at breakfast. (Remember the phrase, "the greatest thing since sliced bread"?) But, in 1942, during wartime rationing, the sale of sliced bread was banned in an effort to hold down prices. Now, we pay higher prices for the privilege of cutting artisan-style breads by hand. Wheat is grown on more acres in the United States than any other grain, with somewhere over sixty million acres harvested each year, and modern combines cut an acre of wheat in six minutes or less.

SOFT AND HARD WHEAT; WINTER AND SPRING WHEAT

Soft red winter wheat and soft white wheats are grown east of the Mississippi River. Hard spring wheats are used for bread doughs and noodles; durum goes into dried pasta. Soft wheats are used for cake, pastry, and all-purpose flours. West of the Mississippi, the wheats grown include hard red winter, hard red spring, durum, hard white, and soft white. Soft white wheat is grown in the Pacific Northwest, while hard spring and durum wheats are grown in the Northern Plains.

Farro

Tasty farro, *Triticum spelta*, is an ancient grain that is a cousin to wheat. Known in English as spelt, farro is one of the first grains to be grown by farmers as long ago as 5000 BCE it can be traced back to early Mesopotamia. Called *farrum* by the Romans, spelt's nutty flavor and firm texture have made it long popular in Europe. In Italy, farro is most common in Tuscany. The same grain is called *dinkle* in Germany. This traditional grain is finding renewed popularity today, both in Italy and America.

Unlike the highly cultivated wheat, spelt has retained many of its original traits and remains highly nutritious and full of flavor. It is naturally high in fiber and contains significantly more protein than wheat. Emmer and eikorn are two other early cultivated grains related to wheat. Some people that are gluten-sensitive are able to eat spelt. Spelt has a tough hull, making it more difficult to process, but this hull protects the nutrients, keeps the grain fresh, and discourages insects, allowing growers to avoid pesticides.

BULGUR WHEAT

Bulgur or bulgur wheat is known as *burghul* in the Middle East and North Africa. Burghul is made from wheat berries that are cooked, the bran removed, then boiled, dried, and crushed. Making wheat into bulgur is an ancient process that originated in the Mediterranean and has been an integral part of Middle Eastern cuisine for thousands of years. It may in fact be man's first processed food. Arab, Hebrew, Egyptian, and Roman civilizations record eating dried cooked wheat as early as 1000 BCE.

Because its name is transliterated from the Arabic, the same product may be called *burghul, burghoul, balgour,* and *boulgur.* The Romans called it *cerealis,* among the Israelites it was *dagan,* and other Middle Easterners called it *arisah,* also used in the Bible. According to Biblical archeologists, arisah was a porridge or gruel prepared from parboiled and sun-dried wheat. For primitive people, bulgur was an excellent food that could be stored for long periods of time and quickly prepared by soaking it in water and mixing it with wild herbs for flavor.

Burghul is most commonly found in Middle Eastern and Mediterranean markets, but many supermarkets also carry it. It has a light and nutty flavor and its higher nutritional value makes it a good substitute for rice or couscous. Quite versatile and easy to prepare, bulgur can be used in pilafs, soups, bakery goods, or mixed into stuffing, but is best known as a main ingredient in tabbouli salad (*see* Turkish Red Tabbouli Salad, page 967). Bulgur remained exclusively a traditional food of the Mediterranean region for many years. It was first introduced to America by Middle Eastern immigrants, and is now also manufactured in the U.S.

DURUM WHEAT

Durum wheat, *Triticum durum,* is especially suited to making pasta and has probably been used for this purpose for more than two thousand years. This wheat is physically hard and, when ground, splinters into fine, almost glassy, chips called *semolina* (used in the recipes for Galataboureko, page 176, and Cream Cheese and Golden Raisin Strudel, page 783).

TRADITIONAL WAYS OF PREPARING BULGUR WHEAT

To prepare bulgur the old way, as is still done in small villages of the Eastern Mediterranean, wheat berries are boiled in huge pots until thoroughly cooked. They are then spread out on flat rooftops to dry in the sun. The bulgur is then cracked into pieces of different sizes for different uses, from fine to coarse.

Turkish Red Tabbouli Salad

Tabbouli is a salad based on bulgur wheat, which is precooked and then dried, so that it only needs soaking to be ready to eat. Tabbouli is a dish of the Levant, close to where wheat originated. In this Turkish version, the red color comes from a jam-like red pepper paste flavored with famed hot red Aleppo pepper from the Syrian culinary capital of Aleppo, grated red-ripe tomatoes, and tart, fruity pomegranate molasses. The salad is garnished with romaine lettuce leaves to be used as scoops for the salad. Look for bulgur, Aleppo pepper, and pomegranate molasses at Middle Eastern groceries.

3 roasted red bell peppers, trimmed and seeded

1 teaspoon (or more) Aleppo pepper,
   substitute other hot red pepper flakes

2 cups bulgur wheat (medium)

3 ripe tomatoes

1 bunch scallions, thinly sliced

1 seedless cucumber, peeled, seeded, diced

1 cup chopped Italian parsley

6 tablespoons lemon juice

2 tablespoons pomegranate molasses

1/2 cup olive oil

Kosher salt to taste

2 heads hearts of romaine, separated into whole leaves

Place the red peppers and Aleppo pepper in the bowl of a food processor and process to a paste. Transfer to a small saucepan and cook over medium heat, stirring often, until reduced to a jam-like consistency, about 10 minutes or place in a dish and microwave until thick.

Wash the bulgur in a sieve to remove the dust. Dampen with cold water and let stand 30 minutes, or until plump. Squeeze out any excess moisture and reserve.

Cut the tomatoes in half, seed, and then grate the halves against the coarse side of a grater. (You should be left with just the tomato skin, which should be discarded.)

In a mixing bowl, combine the bulgur, red pepper paste, grated tomatoes, scallions, cucumber, and parsley.

Whisk together the lemon juice, pomegranate molasses, olive oil, and salt. Mix gently into the bulgur, fluff, and serve on a large platter surrounded by the romaine leaves.

Whole Wheat Bigoli with Onion and Anchovy Sauce

This traditional dish of the Veneto, the flatland region surrounding Venice, is so basic that it is simply called bigoli in salsa, *bigoli pasta with sauce. All you need are onions, anchovies, and the whole-wheat pasta. The nutty-tasting, chewy pasta marries perfectly with the sweet, soft onions and the salty anchovies in this age-old dish. Bigoli are closely connected to local specialties of duck—including the eggs, which are used to make the dough— from the wetlands and anchovies from the nearby sea (see* page 968 *for Bigoli Pasta with Duck Ragù). While I have seen the special bigoli machines for sale in Italy, I would suggest using the whole wheat spaghetti made by DeCecco and other Italian pasta companies.*

1 pound whole-wheat spaghetti or linguine

2 cups finely diced yellow onion

4 tablespoons extra-virgin olive oil, divided

2 ounces anchovies in olive oil, finely chopped

Freshly ground black pepper to taste

2 tablespoons finely chopped Italian parsley

Bring a large pot of salted water to the boil. Add the pasta and cook until *al dente*, firm and bouncy, and still yellow in color.

In a large, heavy-bottomed saucepot with a lid, brown the onions well in 2 tablespoons of the olive oil. Add a spoonful of the hot pasta water, cover, and cook about 10 minutes, or until the onions are quite soft. Add the anchovies and cook together, mashing the anchovies into a sauce with the back of a fork. Reduce the heat and stir in the remaining 2 tablespoons olive oil, the black pepper, and the parsley, swirling to amalgamate the sauce.

Drain the pasta well and toss with the sauce. Serve immediately, preferably on heated plates.

968

Bigoli Pasta with Duck Ragù

This rich, hearty duck sauce, a specialty of the Veneto, the flat marshy region surrounding Venice, is served over the special whole wheat pasta called bigoli. *You can substitute purchased whole wheat pasta. In a restaurant, the breasts would be cut off the ducks to use for one dish, while the remainder, including the tough but tasty legs would be used to make this hearty duck ragù, not forgetting the carcasses, which would go into the pot for duck stock. This is a good, hearty, wintertime dish that reheats well. Duck legs can be ordered and will usually be reasonably priced, though they'll probably come frozen. Although not at all traditional, turkey thighs make an excellent substitute. The sauce freezes well, so it's worth making in a bigger batch, as here. Cut the recipe in half if desired.*

SERVES 8

$1/2$ cup dried porcini mushrooms

$1/4$ cup duck fat, or olive oil

8 duck legs and thighs (about 4 pounds), skinned and excess fat trimmed off

1 onion, finely chopped

2 carrots, finely chopped

2 ribs celery, finely chopped

1 tablespoon chopped garlic

2 to 4 finely chopped duck livers, substitute chicken livers (optional)

1 (28-ounce can) diced tomatoes

1 cup dry red wine

1 cup chicken stock

Kosher salt and freshly ground black pepper to taste

1 tablespoon each: chopped sage and rosemary, or

1 teaspoon each: dried sage and rosemary

1 pound Bigoli or whole wheat spaghetti

1 cup grated Parmigiano-Reggiano or Grana Padano

Soak the porcini in warm water to cover until soft, about 20 minutes. Scoop out the mushrooms, chop finely, and reserve. Strain the mushroom liquor through a dampened paper towel laid into a sieve to remove any sand, and reserve.

In a Dutch oven, heat the fat and brown the duck legs and thighs well on all sides. Remove and reserve. Add the chopped porcini, onion, carrots, celery, garlic, and duck livers, and cook until crisp-tender, about 6 minutes. Pour in the tomatoes, wine, chicken stock, and porcini liquor and bring to a boil. Return the duck legs and thighs to the pot, bring to the boil, cover, reduce heat, and simmer for about 1 hour, or until the duck meat is tender and starting to come away from the bones.

Remove the duck from the pot and turn off the heat. When the duck is cool enough to handle, pull off all the meat. Pick through the meat, discarding any fat pads or connective tissue, and return to the pot. Season to taste with salt and pepper and add the sage and rosemary. Simmer uncovered until thick and rich, about 30 minutes, stirring occasionally. Keep warm.

Meanwhile, bring a large pot of boiling salted water to the boil. Add the bigoli and boil until *al dente*, firm and bouncy, and still yellow in color. Drain well and toss with the reserved sauce and the cheese. Serve immediately, preferably in heated pasta bowls.

Tunisian Whole-Wheat Couscous with Winter Vegetables

The first time I tasted couscous, the marvelously complex dish of light and fluffy steamed wheat beads soaked in rich, spicy juices was at a kosher restaurant in the old Jewish quarter of Paris, where houses leaning into the street were propped up by large beams. No more than 12 years old at the time, I've loved it ever since. Couscous is, by its nature, a complex dish with many components, but it is quite forgiving, so vegetables can easily be substituted. Whole- wheat couscous, called asmar, *adds a slightly chewy texture, and a pleasing nutty flavor to the dish. Several natural foods companies make whole wheat couscous including Near East, Casbah, and Trader Joe's. Serve the couscous accompanied by a bowl of Harissa Sauce, either purchased or homemade (see the recipe on page 703) thinned out with some of the cooking juices to a pouring consistency.*

SERVES 8

$1/2$ cup + 3 tablespoons extra-virgin olive oil

6 tablespoons tomato paste

2 tablespoons sweet paprika

Kosher salt and freshly ground black pepper to taste

$1/2$ pound carrots, peeled and cut into sticks

2 turnips, peeled and cut into half-moons

1 fennel bulb, diced

$1/2$ pound small gold potatoes, quartered

1 (15-ounce) can (or one 20-ounce jar) chickpeas

$1/2$ small green cabbage, cored and shredded

1 pound whole-wheat couscous

2 leeks, sliced and washed

1 bunch Swiss chard, shredded

2 long Italian frying peppers, green or red, cut into thin strips

1/2 pound frozen artichoke hearts

1/2 teaspoon ground cinnamon

1/2 teaspoon ground anise seed

2 teaspoons ground coriander

In the bottom of a couscousier, called the *makfoul*, place 1/2 cup of olive oil, the tomato paste, paprika, and salt and pepper. Add the carrots, turnips, fennel, potatoes, chickpeas, and cabbage, and then stir to combine. Gently simmer the vegetables for about 5 minutes, then add 2 quarts of water and heat to boiling. (Note that the liquid should not fill the couscousier more than halfway.)

Meanwhile prepare the couscous: Pour the couscous grain into a large bowl. Add 2 tablespoons of olive oil and mix with your fingers to coat the couscous with the oil. Add a pinch of salt and quickly moisten with 1/2 cup (no more) of cold water. Gently transfer the couscous to the top part of the couscousier, called the *keskes*. Place the lid on top, leaving a small opening so excess steam can escape. This prevents drops of water from falling into the couscous from the lid, making the couscous soggy. (It also allows the fragrance to fill the house and stimulate the appetite!) Cook for 15 minutes after the steam starts to build up.

Remove the top portion of the couscousier and dump upside down into the large bowl. Add the leeks, Swiss chard, and peppers to the bottom of the couscousier. (If the mixture seems dry, add a little water.) Continue cooking. After 10 minutes add the rinsed and drained artichokes to the vegetable mixture in the bottom of the couscousier.

Meanwhile, add another 1/2 cup of cold water to the couscous and fluff it gently with your fingertips. Transfer the fluffed couscous back into the *keskes*, cover with the lid askew, and cook for 20 minutes over medium heat. The couscous grains should bounce back when you tap it lightly and should be firm with separated grains.

Turn off the heat, and dump the couscous upside down again into the bowl. Add 1 tablespoon more olive oil, and the cinnamon, anise, and coriander, and fluff again with your fingertips. Note: You do not add any water at this point. While the grain is still hot, ladle off enough liquid from the vegetable mixture to just cover the couscous. The couscous will actually look soupy, but it will absorb this flavorful liquid as it sits for about 5 minutes. Lastly, use a wooden spoon to stir and aerate the soaked couscous.

To serve, transfer the couscous to a large serving dish, 2 to 3 inches deep. Scoop out the vegetables using a slotted spoon and arrange over top of the couscous. Moisten with some of the vegetable juices, saving any excess for another use. Serve immediately.

IMPROVISING A COUSCOUSIER

If you don't have a couscousier, set up a large soup pot with a tightly fitting lid. Place a bamboo steamer, a perforated pasta cooker, or a metal steamer basket inside the pot, propped up above the liquid with crunched-up aluminum foil. After filling the bottom of the pot with the liquid and filling the steamer with the couscous grain, place a ring of dampened paper towels around the edge of the pot and cover with the lid, so that the steam is trapped inside.

Couscous is a staple food of North Africa that requires little in the way of utensils, so it is ideal for nomads as well as for more settled people. In fact, the grain itself, actually closer to a type of pasta, can be made by hand by rolling moistened grains of semolina in a large, shallow bowl full of flour so that the grains grow like a pearls by adding on thin coats of flour until the desired size is reached. The best and most famous couscous is made from hard wheat but whole wheat, barley, and millet couscous are also made.

The famed fifteenth century Arab traveler Leo Africanus wrote, "Of all things to be eaten once a day it's alcuzcuçu because it costs little and nourishes a lot." It was the traditional food of the nomadic Berbers, who are said to have invented couscous in the eleventh or twelfth century. For centuries, black African women were employed as couscous cooks and even today in Morocco the dada—young black Saharan and sub-Saharan women who serve in the households—are often employed to prepare couscous. For more history and background, go to www.cliffordawright.com or read Wright's superb book, *The Mediterranean Feast*.

OTHER NAMES FOR COUSCOUS

The Arabs call it *alcuzcuçu*, the Berbers call it *sekrou* or *seksu*, while it is known as *maftul* or *maghribiyya* in the countries of the eastern Mediterranean, and *suk-sukaniyya* in the Sudan. Very large couscous grains are called *muhammas* or *burkukis*, while very fine grains, usually used for sweet couscous dishes, are called *masfuf*.

Farro with Broccoli Romanesco and Asiago Cheese

The firm, nutty grains of farro are sautéed pilaf style, then simmered in chicken stock and mixed with broccoli romanesco (the vegetable that looks like broccoli from outer space, with its yellow-green pyramids) and Asiago cheese. Asiago is a grating cheese from the mountains of Italy, often flavored with a tiny amount of blue fenugreek, so that it is flecked with green. Asiago is also made in America, minus the herb. Broccoli romanesco has a flavor halfway between broccoli and cauliflower; in the area of Rome where it is common, it is called simply cavolfiore, *or cauliflower. You'll need to soak the farro at least 24 hours ahead of time to soften it.*

971

SERVES 6

1 small onion, diced

1 tablespoon extra-virgin olive oil

1 pound farro berries, soaked overnight in cold water, substitute whole wheat berries or barley

2 quarts chicken stock, simmering

Kosher salt and freshly ground black pepper to taste

1 head broccoli romanesco, cut into small florets

¼ pound (about 1 cup) grated Asiago cheese

Sweat the onion in the olive oil until softened, then add the drained farro. Cook together for 5 minutes, then add the simmering chicken stock. Cover, bring to the boil, then reduce the heat and simmer for 45 minutes, or until the farro is soft and has absorbed all the liquid. (Add extra water if necessary.)

Season with salt and pepper, stir in the broccoli romanesco florets, and cook for 5 to 8 minutes longer, or until the florets are tender. Remove the farro from the heat, stir in the grated cheese, and serve immediately, preferably on heated plates.

Neapolitan Pastiera

The superb, if disconcertingly named, restaurant, The Pink Garden—in the small town of Terzigno on the slopes of Mount Vesuvius—is run by a quarter of brothers, with the oldest, Salvatore Ascione, acting as lead chef, and numerous other family members running the dining room. After a parade of the house specialties, one better than the next, although I swore I couldn't eat any more, I just had to have a slice of this Neapolitan Pastiera, a specialty of the region often served for Easter. The filling is made from slow-cooked wheat berries mixed with ricotta cheese and candied fruits fragrant with wafts of acqua di fiori d'arancio, *orange blossom water. The candied citron is a must, because some of the best citrons in the world are grown in this region. You'll need to soak the wheat berries at least 2 days to soften them.*

SERVES 8 TO 12

$^1/_4$ pound (1 cup) wheat berries, soaked for 2 days in cold water, then well-drained

2 cups milk

Grated zest of a half an orange

$^1/_4$ cup lard, substitute unsalted butter

1 tablespoons + $^1/_2$ + $^1/_4$ cup granulated sugar

1 teaspoon vanilla extract

1 pound Pasta Frolla pastry (*see* page 989)

$^3/_4$ pound whole-milk ricotta

3 eggs, separated

1 vial Italian acqua di fiori d'arancio, substitute 1 teaspoon orange blossom water

$^1/_2$ teaspoon cinnamon

$^1/_4$ cup minced candied citron

$^1/_4$ cup minced candied orange peel, substitute candied pineapple

$^1/_4$ cup minced candied squash (*cocozzata*, in Neapolitan), substitute candied papaya

1 egg, lightly beaten with 2 tablespoons milk

Drain the soaked wheat berries, rinse, and transfer to a medium pot. Cover with 2 quarts cold water and bring to the boil. Reduce the heat, cover, and simmer for about 2 hours, or until plump. Drain and rinse the wheat.

Preheat the oven to 275°F. Combine the cooked wheat with the milk, orange zest, lard, 1 tablespoon sugar, and the vanilla in a heavy Dutch oven. Bring to the boil, stirring constantly, so the milk doesn't stick. Cover and bake for 4 hours, or until the grains come apart and the milk has been absorbed, so that the mixture is dense and creamy. Remove from the oven and cool to room temperature.

Roll out two-thirds of the pastry dough between 2 sheets of wax paper and use it to line a 10-inch-diameter shallow tart part with a removable bottom. Roll out the remaining dough, again between two sheets of waxed paper, into a roughly rectangular shape, and refrigerate until firm.

Using the paddle, beat together the ricotta and $^1/_2$ cup of sugar, and mix well. Beat in the egg yolks, one at a time, continuing to beat until they are fully absorbed and the mixture is creamy. Beat in the acqua di fiori d'arancio, the cinnamon, and the wheat mixture. Fold in the candied fruits and reserve.

972

Increase the oven temperature to 350°F. In a clean bowl, beat the egg whites until white and fluffy and then gradually sprinkle in the remaining ¼ cup of sugar. Continue beating until firm and glossy. Fold into the ricotta mixture by thirds and reserve. Spoon the prepared filling into the dough-lined pan.

Cut the remaining dough into long strips, preferably using a ridged pasta cutter, about ½ inch wide. Using a long spatula to help support them, lift the strips and, one by one, lay them across the dough spaced about 1½ inches apart. Then, turn the pan around and lay more strips crosswise on the diagonal so that the strips form diamond shapes in the middle. Make a border of the strips on top of the edge of the dough. Brush the strips with the egg wash. Bake for 50 minutes, or until the dough is nicely browned and the filling is puffy, firm, and set. Remove from the oven and cool. Cut into serving pieces and serve at room temperature.

SOAKING AND COOKING WHEAT BERRIES

The amount of soaking and boiling needed depends on the type of wheat berry you've purchased. The hard wheat berries I use require 2 days of soaking in cold water. Then they must be simmered for another 2 hours, and finally they are baked for 4 hours until soft and plump. Soft wheat will be less recalcitrant. Pearl barley and *risotto* both make good substitutes if you don't want to spend the time. The precooked hulled wheat berries from France, called *Ebly*, make a delicious substitute and don't need to be soaked. In Campania and other parts of Italy, precooked wheat berries are sold just to make Neapolitan Pastiera.

CITRON

The citron, *Citrus medica*, which looks like a large, often lightly ridged, rough-skinned lemon, has a very thick rind and is used mostly for preserves and candying. This citrus fruit is native to India, where it was used from early times as a perfume and in medicine. The main producing areas today are Sicily, Corsica, and Crete and other islands off the coasts of Italy, Greece, and France, and the neighboring mainland, especially the region of Amalfi, Italy, which is famed for its citrons.

Most of the citron consists of thick, dense rind; inside, the dryish flesh has a weak lemon flavor. The rind, with its powerful and distinctive fragrance, is used to make thick, light yellowish-green, transparent candied peel, especially popular in the south of Italy and Sicily. In Jewish practice, a particular variety of citron, the *Etrog*, is used during the Feast of Tabernacles (taken from the Biblical phrase "the fruit of a beautiful tree"). These highly prized and highly priced fruits must be carefully tended, because a citron for ritual use must have no blemishes.

973

ORANGE BLOSSOM WATER

This native Mediterranean, Middle Eastern, and Indian flavoring of Arab origin is distilled from the blossoms of the wild or bitter orange tree distilled to make the essential oil, *neroli*, used in perfumery. When the oil is drawn off; the watery portion that remains is orange blossom water. In Italy, packets of glass vials of *acqua fior d'arancio*, each the perfect size for a pastiera, are sold in groceries; the best substitute in America is the more expensive orange blossom water imported from France in small blue bottles, or the more reasonably priced kind imported from Lebanon (Cortas is a good brand) and sold at Middle Eastern groceries.

974

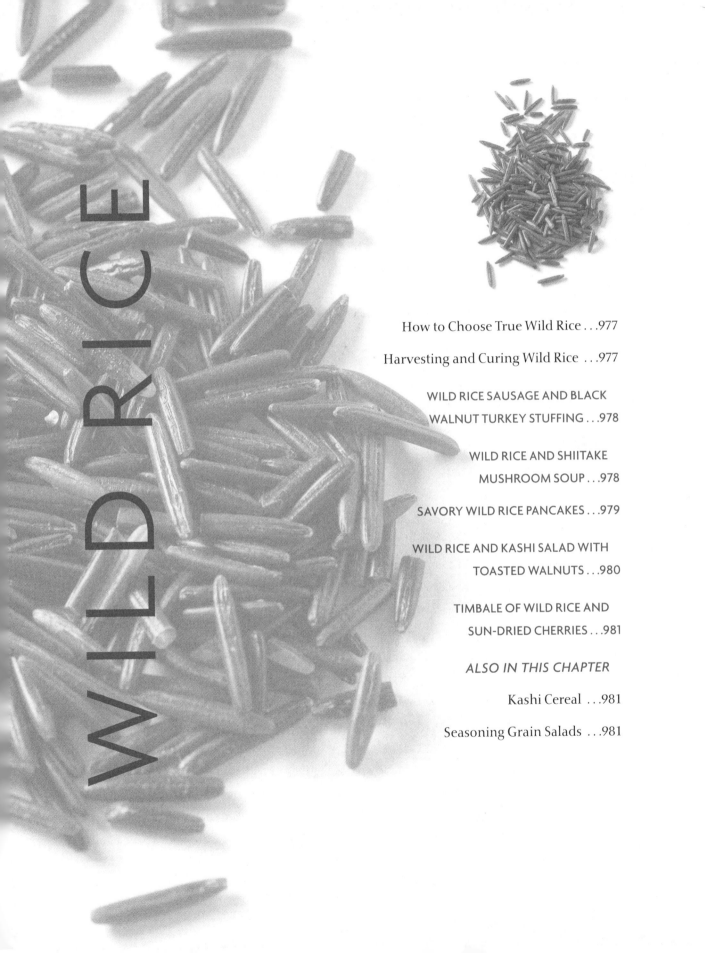

WILD RICE

WILD RICE

Up until the 1960s, wild rice was rare and precious, a truly wild-harvested grain that was reserved for special occasions. Sometime in the years since then, it became a more common, almost boring addition to white rice mixtures or "medleys" sold by large companies such as Uncle Ben's and served at inexpensive banquet meals to show they were special. What happened?

The answer is that up until about forty years ago, most wild rice in the United States was produced in natural stands in lakes, rivers, and streams. Each year, American lake and river foragers harvest about half a million pounds of true "wild" varieties and Canadians harvest another three and a half million pounds. But, in the early 1960s, varieties of wild rice were developed that didn't shatter easily when ripe, scattering their seeds and making them difficult to harvest. By 1999, American farmers were growing about eighteen million pounds annually of this less-expensive "cultivated" or "farm-grown" wild rice, much of it in California. At this time, wild rice started appearing in gourmet markets and started being promoted internationally as an American specialty food.

About twenty percent of the world's wild rice crop is still hand-picked by Native Americans in canoes, who retain exclusive harvesting rights on the reservations along the shores of the Great Lakes. Early North American inhabitants, especially the Ojibway, Menomini, and Cree tribes in the North Central region, used the grain as a staple food, They first introduced the grain to French fur traders, who called it *riz sauvage* (wild rice) or *folles avoines* (crazy oats). Native Americans in the Great Lakes region still use it extensively. Other popular names include Canadian rice, squaw rice, water oats, blackbird oats, and marsh oats.

Many of the Indigenous peoples of North America consider this plant, called *manoomin* or *good berry*, to be a gift from the Great Spirit, so that it is spiritually sacred and quite distinct from the cultivated or farm-grown type. Harvesting wild rice has been a cultural and spiritual tradition of the Ojibwa people for centuries. Now some tribal members worry that natural wild rice could be threatened by genetically modified wild rice. Today in Canada, most wild rice is still produced in lakes and streams that are leased from the government. Although growing wild rice as a field crop was first suggested in 1852, efforts to grow it did not begin until 1950. Commercial production of cultivated or farm-grown varieties has also been established and developed in Hungary and Australia.

This evolutionarily ancient grain has been found in layers of the earth dating back some 12,000 years. In addition to its role as an important food staple for ancestral peoples, it has provided a unique habitat for fish and waterfowl for thousands of years. It is found primarily in areas west and north of the Great Lakes, but there are several other species that grow in limited quantities in parts of North America including New Jersey, Florida, and Texas.

Chinese or Manchurian wild rice, *Zizania latifolia*, or water grass, is a different species of wild rice, native to ecologically similar regions in Asia. Its broad leaves are used for wrapping dumplings, and its young shoots, rather than the full-grown seeds, are eaten in China like asparagus. Wild rice can be used in a multitude of dishes—from everyday cooking to gourmet creations—and triples or more in size, so a little goes a long way! Just be patient when cooking it: cook slowly at a low temperature until the grains are soft enough to split lengthwise.

HOW TO CHOOSE TRUE WILD RICE

True heirloom wild rice grows solely in the northern Great Lakes region. Look for a "hand harvested" or "lake harvested" insignia on the package, which verifies the organic, foraged variety. By purchasing this authentic wild rice, you will be supporting both the economic system of the Native American harvesters and the crop itself, which is ecologically fragile. While shopping for wild rice, you might notice a light-brown "wild rice mix" as well as the more familiar dark variety. This lighter-colored, milder-tasting, paddy-grown grain is not the same thing as authentic Native American wild rice. When purchasing wild rice, look for whole, not broken, grains, and a dark, shiny color with a full-bodied, nutty aroma.

Harvesting and Curing Wild Rice

Wild rice grown on Minnesota state waters is regulated and must be harvested in the traditional Indian way during its season from a canoe, using only a pole for power and two rice-beater sticks to knock the mature seeds into the bottom of the boat. In Canada, there have been recent efforts to seed lakes that were without wild rice. The lakes are then mechanically harvested by airboats equipped with collecting troughs. Once harvested, the rice is placed in long, narrow rows to cure, dissipating the green chlorophyll. From there, the kernels are parched, so they are dried and develop their characteristic roasted nutty flavor. After this, the fibrous hull is removed, exposing the shiny black wild rice seed, now ready for the pot.

Wild Rice, Sausage, and Black Walnut Turkey Stuffing

Make this uncommonly tasty stuffing for your next Thanksgiving turkey, or don't wait that long: use it to stuff a large capon or roaster chicken. This combination of wild rice, sausage, black walnuts, and more features two native American foods: the wild rice and the black walnuts (see the Walnut chapter for more about black walnuts, page 953). Because this recipe makes a large enough quantity to stuff a 20-pound turkey, cut it in half if you're using it to stuff a capon or chicken. The stuffing mixture can also be baked and served with a roast of beef or pork. Use the Country Breakfast Sausage Patties (see page 847) to make your own, if desired.

MAKES 3 QUARTS STUFFING, ENOUGH FOR A LARGE (UP TO 20–POUND) TURKEY, ABOUT 20 SERVINGS

1 (1$^{1}/_{2}$ pound) loaf country-style bread, crusts removed and cut into cubes

$^{1}/_{4}$ pound (1 stick) unsalted butter, divided

1 pound mild pork sausage, removed from its casing

3 ribs celery, chopped

1 onion, chopped

1 cup wild rice, cooked according to package directions

1 cup black walnuts, chopped

3 eggs

$^{1}/_{2}$ cup chopped Italian parsley

$^{1}/_{2}$ cup golden raisins

1 tablespoon each: chopped sage, marjoram, and savory, or 1 tablespoon poultry seasoning

2 cups chicken or turkey broth, simmering

Kosher salt and freshly ground black pepper to taste

Preheat the oven to 350°F. Melt 4 tablespoons of the butter, and toss with the bread cubes, then spread in a single layer in a metal baking pan, stirring once or twice, and toast in the oven for about 15 minutes, or until lightly browned.

Meanwhile, in a large skillet, lightly brown the pork sausage, breaking it up as it cooks. Remove and reserve the sausage. In the same pan, melt the remaining 4 tablespoons of butter, add the celery and onion, and cook until crisp-tender, about 5 minutes.

In a large bowl, combine the bread cubes, sausage, onions and celery with the cooked wild rice and black walnuts. Stir in the eggs, parsley, raisins, and herbs. Slowly stir in chicken broth until the stuffing is moist and holds together. Season with salt and pepper. Cool to room temperature before stuffing in the turkey just before roasting (stuffing ahead of time can lead to food safety dangers). If you're baking this on its own, transfer it to a baking pan and bake for 30 to 40 minutes.

Wild Rice and Shiitake Mushroom Soup

This hearty soup is a grown-up version of chicken soup with rice, with lots of tender, nutty-tasting wild rice kernels surrounded by sliced mushrooms, floating in a robust shiitake mushroom broth. The soup is well suited to a vegetarian version. Make it with Mushroom Stock (page 993) for an extra layer of mushroom flavor, or make it with Vegetable Stock (page 995) for a lighter, more rounded flavor. This soup freezes quite well; just make sure it is cool before placing in the freezer.

MAKES 3 QUARTS, SERVES 10 TO 12

¼ pound dried shiitake mushrooms (or other dried mushrooms)

½ pound fresh shiitake mushrooms, stems and caps separated and reserved

1 cup dry white vermouth

2 quarts chicken stock, vegetable stock, or mushroom stock (see pages 991, 995, and 993)

1 tablespoon fennel seed

1 tablespoon black peppercorns

1 tablespoon coriander seed

4 bay leaves

½ pound wild rice

Kosher salt and freshly ground black pepper to taste

2 bunch scallions, thinly sliced

Combine the dried shiitakes, the fresh shiitake stems, the vermouth, chicken stock, fennel, peppercorns, coriander, and bay leaves in a large soup pot. Bring to a boil, reduce the heat, then simmer slowly for 1½ hours. Remove from the heat and pour the contents of the pot through a sieve, pressing down firmly with the back of a ladle or a large spoon to extract all the liquids. Discard the solids and reserve the liquid. (If the mushrooms were at all sandy, pour the broth through several layers of dampened paper towels lining a sieve and placed over a pot or bowl to catch the liquid.)

Meanwhile, in a medium pot, combine the wild rice, 4 cups of water, and the salt. Bring to a boil, then reduce the heat and simmer for 45 minutes, or until tender but not mushy. Remove from the heat and reserve.

Thinly slice the shiitake mushroom caps. In a large soup pot, combine the mushroom broth, the wild rice with its cooking liquid, and the sliced shiitake caps. Bring to a boil, stir in the scallions, season with salt and pepper, and serve immediately.

Savory Wild Rice Pancakes

Pancakes don't have to be breakfast food. In fact, they make a good and substantial side dish or as a vegetarian main or side dish. These pancakes are particularly good in wintertime, because the wild rice has a robust flavor suited to cold weather. The only time-consuming thing here is cooking the wild rice. Note, however, that once cooked, wild rice freezes quite well, as long as it is well-wrapped. Use either a cast-iron skillet for best browning and crustiness or a nonstick skillet so the pancakes don't stick.

SERVES 6

½ cup wild rice

½ cup diced onion

½ cup diced celery

½ cup sliced scallion

1 tablespoon chopped fresh herbs (sage, thyme, and/or marjoram) or 1 teaspoon dried

¼ pound (1 stick) unsalted butter, divided

1 egg

½ cup milk

½ cup all-purpose flour, preferably unbleached

1 teaspoon baking powder

Bring 1½ cups of salted water to the boil and add the wild rice. Simmer, covered, for about 45 minutes, or until the rice is plumped and most of the kernels have split open. Drain well and cool.

In a medium skillet, cook the onion and celery in 2 tablespoons of butter until crisp-tender. Stir in the scallions and herbs and cool. Combine the rice with the vegetables, the egg, and the milk.

In a separate bowl, whisk together the flour and baking powder and gently stir into the rice mixture, mixing only until smooth.

Heat a portion of the remaining butter in a large skillet, preferably cast-iron or nonstick. Ladle $^1/_4$-cup portions of the batter into the pan and cook over medium-heat until lightly browned on both sides. Repeat with remaining butter and batter. Serve immediately.

Wild Rice and Kashi Salad with Toasted Walnuts

This chunky, substantial salad is suitable for vegetarians if made with vegetable or mushroom stock. Nutty-tasting from both the grains and the toasted walnuts, it's colorful with sweet bell peppers and scallions, and gets a light anise-flavored crunch from diced fennel bulb. Wild rice adds an extra dimension of flavor and texture. You'll need to cook the Kashi and the wild rice in separate pots, because the Kashi takes about 45 minutes to cool while the wild rice may take 1 hour or more, depending on how dry it is. A tangy Dijon mustard and cider vinegar dressing with walnut oil finishes the dish. Substitute toasted hazelnuts and hazelnut oil for a wonderful variation. This salad is a good choice for a potluck dinner or holiday buffet table.

SERVES 6 TO 8

Grains

1 cup wild rice, soaked in cold water to cover for at least 2 hours

1 cup Kashi mixed grain cereal

3 cups + 2 cups chicken stock, substitute vegetable or mushroom stock

Rinse and drain the wild rice. Transfer to a medium pot, add 3 cups of chicken stock and bring to the boil. Reduce heat, cover, and simmer slowly together for about 45 minutes, or until softened but still whole and firm. (Add extra water if needed.) Remove from the heat, keep covered, and allow the rice to steam for 15 minutes to absorb remaining liquid.

In a separate pot, bring the Kashi and the remaining 2 cups of stock to the boil, cover, reduce heat, and simmer for about 30 minutes, or until softened but still whole and firm. (Add extra water if needed.) Remove from the heat, keep covered, and allow the Kashi to steam for 15 minutes to absorb remaining liquid.

Dressing

$^1/_2$ cup canola oil

$^1/_4$ cup walnut oil

$^1/_4$ cup cider vinegar

2 tablespoon Dijon mustard

2 teaspoons ground coriander

Kosher salt and freshly ground black pepper to taste

Whisk together all the dressing ingredients or place them all in a glass measure and blend with an immersion blender. Toss with the grains while they are still warm and reserve.

Vegetables and Herbs

1 small fennel bulb, cut into small dice

Juice of 1 lemon

2 colorful sweet bell peppers, diced

1 bunch scallions, sliced

1 cup chopped walnuts, lightly toasted

1 tablespoon each: chopped thyme and marjoram,
  or oregano

¹/₄ cup chopped Italian Parsley

Combine the fennel and the lemon juice and reserve. When ready to serve the salad, add the vegetables and herbs to the dressed grains, mix well together, taste for seasoning, and serve.

KASHI CEREAL

Kashi cereal is a mixture of seven whole grains including buckwheat, triticale (a cross of durum wheat and rye), rye, wheat, barley, oats, brown rice, and sesame seeds. It can be found in most natural foods markets. The best substitute would be a mixture of pearl barley, brown rice, and buckwheat groats (kasha). Go to www.kashi.com for more information.

SEASONING GRAIN SALADS

Grain-based salads like this one taste best the day they're made and served at room temperature to bring out their flavor and have the best soft texture. If made ahead of time, bring to room temperature and taste for seasoning. You may need to add extra seasonings such as mustard, vinegar, salt, and pepper to bring out the flavor.

Timbale of Wild Rice and Sun–Dried Cherries

A timbale is the French word for thimble, *referring here to the larger individual portion molds made in a thimble shape that hold about ¹/₂ cup. Once packed into the molds, the natural starches help it all to stick together. When ready to serve, cover the mold with a serving plate and, holding both together, flip over, so that the contents unmold into an attractive truncated cone shape. Repeat for each serving. Wild rice and the sun-dried cherries made from tart French Montmorency cherries both come from the Great Lakes region—the wild rice from Minnesota and the cherries from the "Cherry Capital of the United States," Traverse City, Michigan. Restaurants and caterers use 4-ounce foil custard cups to form this and other individual molded dishes. They can sometimes be found at party supply stores.*

981

SERVES 10

³/₄ cup chopped shallots

1 tablespoon chopped fresh thyme, or 1 teaspoon dried

4 tablespoons unsalted butter

1 cup sun-dried cherries

¹/₂ cup dried currants

¹/₄ cup Marsala

1 pound (about 2 cups) wild rice, soaked in
  cold water 2 hours

6 cups chicken stock, simmering

2 bay leaves

Kosher salt and freshly ground black pepper to taste

2 eggs

Sauté the shallots and thyme in the butter until the shallots are transparent, but not browned. Remove them from the heat and stir in the cherries, currants, and Marsala. Reserve.

Separately, cook the wild rice in the chicken stock with the bay leaves, salt, and pepper, until soft and split open but not mushy, about 45 minutes. While still warm, beat in the eggs, and taste for seasoning.

Pack the rice mixture tightly into ten 4- to 6-ounce metal timbale molds, foil cups, or demi-tasse cups that have been sprayed generously with nonstick spray. (The molds may be reserved at this point up to 2 days before finishing.)

Preheat the oven to 350°F. Arrange the molds in a baking pan and fill the pan halfway with hot water to make a water bath. Cover the molds with aluminum foil and bake for 20 minutes, or until set. Remove the molds from the oven and allow the timbales to cool for 5 minutes, then turn them onto serving plates and give a sharp rap to unmold. Serve immediately.

X-TRAS

BASICS & USEFUL INFORMATION FOR THE COOK

X-TRAS
BASICS & USEFUL
INFORMATION FOR THE COOK

This chapter includes the recipes for eight basic stocks along with pizza dough, pasta dough, two kinds of brioche dough, and assorted other useful basic recipes. Although few kitchens these days make the full panoply of individual stocks for each type of meat, there is nothing like the deep, full-bodied flavor of a soup, sauce, or braise made with a real homemade stock. To me, making stocks is one of the most enjoyable tasks in the kitchen. I save plastic freezer bags full of vegetable trimmings, mushroom trimmings, and separate bags of ends of beef, veal, and lamb roasts, and the carcasses of roast chicken, turkey, and duck. Other bags hold fish trimmings from the stringier tail end, the small, hard muscles that attach scallops to their shells, shrimp shells and lobster shells and bodies, when I have them. When I've accumulated enough of any one thing, I make a pot of stock, then cool and freeze it, this time in quart-size zip-top freezer bags, marked with the type and date, ready to pull out and defrost as needed. Extra stock can be boiled, cooled, and refrozen with no loss of flavor. When I make stock, I feel like I'm being extra thrifty, making something out of nothing, like in the fairy tale called *Stone Soup*. This is a very good thing to balance my "Champagne tastes."

Also in this chapter are handy charts, all in one place, for converting American and Metric measures for liquids, weights, and oven temperatures. Another set of charts shows roasting temperatures for meats and poultry, essential if you don't want to waste a lot of money on an overcooked roast or risk a health problem with an undercooked bird or pork dish. The final chart is for sugar syrup temperatures, used for making candies, caramel toppings, buttercream icings, and other desserts that call for cooked sugar syrup.

Two of the most useful investments you can possibly make in the kitchen are a kitchen scale that measures at least five pounds and converts to metric, and a good-quality meat thermometer. Staples sells a ten-pound electronic convertible metric and American weight scale for less than fifty dollars that will work well in the kitchen. Don't be afraid; these are simply tools to make your job easier and they really do help! If the thermometer helps prevent one overcooked roast or undercooked bird, it has already paid for itself. And once you start using the scale for baking, all of a sudden your results will improve and the whole process will be much easier.

984

Cornmeal Pizza Dough

I used this light, but slightly crunchy pizza dough to make hundreds, if not thousands, of pizzas in the wood-burning oven in my last restaurant. Although traditional Neapolitan pizza dough is made only with flour, yeast, salt, and oil, this one, which combines bread flour for strength, all-purpose flour for tenderness, and cornmeal for flavor and texture, makes a delicious dough for any pizza recipe. Pizza dough doesn't freeze very well.

MAKES 2 POUNDS DOUGH, ENOUGH FOR 2 LARGE OR 3 SMALLER PIZZAS

1 cup warm water

1 tablespoon honey

1 package (2$\frac{1}{4}$ teaspoons) dry yeast

2 teaspoons kosher salt

$\frac{1}{4}$ cup warm milk

$\frac{1}{4}$ cup extra-virgin olive oil

10 ounces (2$\frac{1}{2}$ cups) bread flour

10 ounces (2$\frac{1}{2}$ cups) all-purpose flour, preferably unbleached

$\frac{1}{2}$ cup cornmeal

Whisk together the water, honey, and yeast and allow it to proof until bubbling. Beat in the salt, milk, and olive oil. Transfer the liquid to a mixing bowl.

Combine the bread flour, all-purpose flour, and cornmeal using the dough hook. Beat the flour mixture (dry ingredients) into the liquid mixture on low speed for about 10 minutes, or until smooth and elastic. The dough should form a ball and come away from the sides of the bowl. As the dough develops, the dough ball will clean the sides of the bowl. If the dough continues to stick to the bowl after about 5 minutes of beating, add about $\frac{1}{4}$ cup more all-purpose flour and continue beating. The finished pizza dough should be soft and slightly sticky: a finger pressed into the dough should be able to be pulled away cleanly after sticking briefly.

Transfer to a large, oiled bowl. Allow the dough to rise at warm room temperature until doubled in volume, about 1 hour. Divide into portions and form into rounds. Roll out or stretch out by hand intothe desired size: 12 to 14 inches is common.

TEMPERATURE AND HUMIDITY WHEN RISING BREAD

Bread doughs rise best in a warm and humid environment. A hot, sticky day is actually the best day to make bread (although the worst day to make anything crispy like meringue shells or brandy snap cookies). Professional bakers calculate the temperature of the room and the temperature of the dough and adjust the water temperature as needed. If the day is colder, you'll have to compensate by making the liquid a bit warmer than usual; on a hot day, the water can be cooler. Setting up a humidifier in the room will also help get a good rise out of your dough, while spritzing the inside of the oven with water or even throwing a few ice cubes into the oven will keep the crust moist and flexible so that it can continue rising. (Once the crust is hard, it won't rise further.)

985

Fresh Pasta Dough and Forming Ravioli

MAKES ABOUT 1 POUND, ENOUGH FOR 36 RAVIOLI

3 eggs
6 ounces (1½ cups) durum wheat flour
6 ounces (1½ cups) all-purpose flour,
  preferably unbleached
Extra of both kinds of flour, if needed

Beat the eggs in a mixer using the paddle attachment. Combine the flours in a separate bowl. Change to the dough hook and start adding the flour, while beating, one cup at a time, until the flour is completely absorbed. Keep adding flour until dough is well mixed, elastic, and quite firm. Add extra flour if necessary, keeping in mind that the dough will soften as it rests. Wrap the dough in plastic, and allow it to rest for at least 30 minutes at room temperature.

Flatten out a small piece of dough by hand into a rough rectangle. Using a hand-cranked pasta sheeter set on the lowest-number setting (the largest opening between the rollers), flatten out the dough. Continue to roll out the dough, using as little flour as possible to keep the dough from sticking, until a long, tongue-shaped piece is obtained that is about three times as long as the dough slot is wide. Fold the tongue in three lengthwise, and place crosswise in slot. (The object is to get an even, wide piece of dough.) Continue to roll, notching down one number each time, until you reach the next-to-the-highest number, which is almost the smallest opening between the rollers. (Usually the highest setting will yield a too-thin dough, unless you're working with an extremely firm dough.) The finished dough should be quite thin, but not transparent.

Place a length of dough on a lightly floured ravioli plaque, pressing down so that the dough adheres to the plaque. Place spoonfuls of your desired filling into each depression, making sure to keep the filling away from the borders. Using a small brush, brush a thin layer of water along the edges of each ravioli square.

Lay a second sheet of dough on top and press down firmly along all the ravioli square borders to seal. Turn the ravioli plaque upside-down over a lightly-floured board so the ravioli release. Using a sharp knife or ravioli wheel (preferably ridged), cut between the individual ravioli pillows. Continue until all the filling and dough has been used up. As the ravioli are finished, arrange them on a portable wire window screen or a wire cooling rack so that air can circulate all around them. Alternatively, arrange them on a lightly floured parchment- or wax-paper sheet, turning them over every so often so they don't get sticky on the bottom. Leave the ravioli at room temperature for up to 2 hours before cooking, or freeze up to 2 weeks, adding the frozen ravioli directly to the pot of boiling water to cool.

MAKING PASTA DOUGH IN THE FOOD PROCESSOR

To make dough in the food processors use the same ingredients as above. Place both kinds of flour in the bowl. Add two eggs, one at a time, until the dough is crumbly. Add the final egg and process briefly until the dough just forms a ball but is still rough-looking, with some small bits of dough not incorporated. Remove from the processor and knead by hand until smooth. If the dough is still too dry, add a sprinkle of water. Place in a plastic bag and let rest for at least 1 hour before rolling out.

Brioche Dough

This classic dough is best made using a standing mixer, because it takes a lot of beating to fully incorporate the butter. I use it to make my Rich Philadelphia Sticky Buns (page 173) and, if I'm feeling ambitious, or happen to have some on hand, for the Rich Chocolate Bread Pudding (page 288) and the Raspberry-Lemon Bread Pudding with Lemon Sauce (page 791). It is perfect for the elaborate layered Torta Milanese with Eggs, Spinach, and Peppers (page 398) and to make the best sandwiches filled with my Chicken Salad with Fennel, Lemon Zest, and Currants (page 409).

MAKES 2 POUNDS DOUGH

2 packages (4$\frac{1}{2}$ teaspoons) active dry yeast

2 tablespoons granulated sugar

1 teaspoon kosher salt

1$\frac{1}{4}$ pound (5 cups) all-purpose flour, preferably
   unbleached

6 eggs, lightly beaten

$\frac{1}{2}$ pound (2 sticks) unsalted butter, cut up and softened

Make a sponge by dissolving the yeast in $\frac{1}{2}$ cup warm water and then beating in the sugar, salt, and $\frac{1}{4}$ pound (1 cup) of the flour. Allow the sponge to double in volume, then transfer to the mixer bowl.

Beat in the eggs, and then beat in $\frac{3}{4}$ pound (3 cups) of the flour, beating well until the dough is smooth and silky looking and comes away cleanly from the sides of the bowl. Beat in the butter until it has been completely absorbed. Now beat in the remaining $\frac{1}{4}$ pound (1 cup) of flour to form a medium-firm dough.

Cover the bowl with plastic wrap and allow it to rise until doubled in volume. Punch down, divide into two, and wrap each portion in plastic wrap and form into a rectangular shape. Chill dough until firm enough to roll out (or chill overnight).

TYPE OF BREAD YEAST

Yeast is a microscopic single-celled fungus (related to mushrooms) that, when activated by a warm liquid (like water or milk) and fed by sugar or starch, gives off tiny bubbles of carbon dioxide gas. This gas, trapped in the network of gluten molecules formed by kneading the dough, is what makes bread doughs rise and achieve their light texture. Sourdough breads take advantage of wild yeasts floating in the air or on the surface of organic fruits like grapes.

Commercial bread yeasts are specific strains with action that is more easily controlled. Fresh, compressed, or cake yeast has a short life of one to two weeks and must be kept refrigerated. It is crumbled into water and then mixed with the flour. Less commonly found in supermarkets, look for it in the dairy aisle. Active dry yeast is the more familiar type that must be dissolved in warm water and proofed (just a way of checking that the yeast is active) before mixing. Rapid-rise or instant yeast is combined directly with the flour without dissolving first. It is quite vigorous and best for single-rise doughs.

Whole-Wheat Brioche Dough

While white flour brioche is more classic, I prefer to use this earthier whole-wheat brioche dough to wrap the Russian classic Salmon Coulibiac (see page 510) because it goes so well with the flavors of the kasha filling. I also use it for the Alsatian Flammekuche, a pizza-like torte topped with a thin layer of cream, bacon, and leeks (see page 528). I like using white whole-wheat flour, sold by King Arthur flour and other companies, for its light color and more delicate flavor and texture.

MAKES 2¾ POUNDS DOUGH

1 package (2¼ teaspoons) active dry yeast

2 tablespoons honey

2 teaspoons kosher salt

1 pound (4 cups) bread flour, divided

1 cup (5 to 6) lightly beaten eggs

¾ pound (3 sticks) unsalted butter, cut up and softened

¼ pound (1 cup) whole-wheat flour

In the bowl of a mixer, make a sponge by dissolving the yeast in ½ cup warm water and then, using the paddle, beating in the honey, salt, and ¼ pound (1 cup) of the bread flour. Allow the sponge to double in volume before continuing.

Using the dough hook, beat the eggs into the sponge, and then beat in the remaining ¾ pound (3 cups) of the bread flour, beating well until the dough is smooth and silky-looking, but still sticky. Beat in the butter until it has been completely absorbed. Now beat in the whole-wheat flour to form a medium-soft dough that comes away cleanly from the sides of the bowl

Cover the bowl with plastic wrap and allow it to rise until

doubled in volume. Punch down, cover, and chill dough until firm enough to roll out (or chill overnight).

Buttermilk Pastry

This unsweetened pastry dough is made with buttermilk. I've discovered that dry buttermilk powder, made by the Saco company and sold in many well-stocked supermarkets and specialty food stores, is a wonderful product to have on hand for baking. Not that different from the idea of powdered milk, buttermilk powder makes a particularly flaky short crust dough because the acidity in it tenderizes the dough. If you can't find the buttermilk powder, substitute ½ cup liquid buttermilk mixed with 1 egg for the buttermilk and ½ cup beaten eggs in the recipe.

MAKES ABOUT 1 POUND DOUGH

¾ pound (3 cups) unbleached all-purpose flour

2 teaspoons kosher salt

¼ cup dry buttermilk powder

¼ pound (1 stick) unsalted butter, cut into bits

½ cup eggs (about 3 eggs), lightly beaten

In the bowl of an electric mixer, combine the flour, salt, and buttermilk powder and mix together lightly. Top with the butter bits but don't mix. Place the bowl in the freezer for 30 minutes (or chill for 1 hour if you're working on a really hot day).

Using the paddle, beat the chilled flour mixture until it resembles cold and crumbly oatmeal. Pour in the eggs and beat until the mixture just comes together into a ball. Place in a large, resealable plastic food storage bag and then flatten the dough to fill the bag. Chill for at least 30 minutes before rolling out. (The dough can be refrigerated for up to 2 days before using.)

Pasta Frolla

This rich and fragile dough, fragrant with lemon zest and well-flavored with Marsala, is perfect for Italian-style tortas including the Meyer Lemon Tart (see page 539) and the Neapolitan Pastiera (see page 972). It's easiest to press this dough into the tart pan. Roll out and refrigerate the dough until firm again before cutting into strips to top a torta. Dry sherry or Madeira can be substituted for the Marsala. If you're using sweet Marsala, cut the sugar down to 1 tablespoon.

MAKES 1¾ POUNDS

½ pound (2 sticks) unsalted butter, at room temperature

8 egg yolks

3 tablespoons granulated sugar

2 tablespoons dry Marsala

Grated zest of 1 lemon

Pinch kosher salt

¾ pound (3 cups) all-purpose flour, preferably unbleached

Place the butter, egg yolks, sugar, Marsala, lemon zest, and salt into the bowl of a mixer. Using the paddle attachment, beat until light and creamy. Add flour and beat again briefly, until combined. Collect the dough into a ball, wrap in plastic, and refrigerate until needed. Note that this dough is fragile, so it is best used for shallow tarts.

Sugar Pastry

Not quite as fragile as the Pasta Frolla above, this sweet pastry is equivalent to the French pâte brisée. Use it for any fruit tart, pressing it into the shell rather than rolling it out. Note that the more sugar is included with a pastry dough, the more difficult it will be to roll out, due to the soft stickiness of the dough. The almond and vanilla extracts here give the dough a subtle fragrance.

MAKES 1½ POUNDS

½ pound (2 sticks) unsalted butter, cut into bits

½ cup granulated sugar

¾ pound (3 cups) all-purpose flour, preferably unbleached

1 teaspoon kosher salt

1 egg, lightly beaten

1½ teaspoons almond extract

1½ teaspoons vanilla extract

2 to 3 tablespoons ice water

989

In a mixer bowl, combine the butter, sugar, flour, and salt. Chill in the freezer until the butter is firm but not hard, about 30 minutes.

Whisk together the egg, almond extract, vanilla, and 2 tablespoons ice water, and reserve, refrigerated.

Beat the butter and flour mixture until the pieces are the consistency of oatmeal. Pour in the reserved egg mixture and beat or process until just combined and the dough forms a ball. If the mixture is dry, beat in the remaining 1 tablespoon ice water. Form the dough into a flattened round, wrap in plastic, and refrigerate until firm, about 2 hours, before rolling out as needed.

Vanilla Custard Sauce

This versatile sauce is commonly referred to by its French name, crème Anglaise (English cream) and is also called "pouring custard," as opposed to a fully set baked custard. It is typical of the nursery foods served to well-to-do English children, who traditionally ate their meals in the nursery (or children's quarters), fed by their nannies. Use a split-open fresh vanilla bean if at all possible, for its full-bodied fragrance and also for the aesthetic pleasure of the miniscule black seeds speckled into the creamy pale yellow sauce. Note this same sauce can be chilled and run in an ice cream machine to make delectably rich, French-style vanilla ice cream.

MAKES 2 CUPS

3/4 cup half-and-half
3/4 cup heavy cream
8 egg yolks
1/2 cup granulated sugar
1 vanilla bean, split open

Scald together the half-and-half and cream and reserve.

Beat the egg yolks and sugar until light-colored and the mixture forms a ribbon. Pour in about 1/2 cup of the hot cream mixture while continuing to beat, to warm the mixture. Pour in the remaining milk-cream mixture and the split vanilla bean with its contents. Transfer the mixture to a heavy-bottomed, nonreactive pot and heat until the custard visibly thickens and reads 165°F. on a thermometer, stirring often with a wooden spoon or silicone spatula. Immediately remove from the heat. Strain the mixture through a sieve and keep warm. Note that you may rinse off the vanilla bean, refrigerate it and use it again or dry it and then store it in a jar of sugar to give the sugar a vanilla flavor.

Beef Stock

Beef stock is the most challenging stock to make because the bones are usually expensive and it requires a good amount of them to extract enough flavor and body to make a good stock. Look for meaty rounds of beef shank, like giant osso buco, sometimes on special at the meat counter. Freeze until you accumulate enough to make this rich-tasting stock. French onion soup made with real homemade beef stock is like none you've ever had, unless you've eaten it at Les Halles market in Paris.

MAKES ABOUT 6 QUARTS

5 pounds beef back ribs or beef shin (on the bone)
1 onion, unpeeled
3 to 4 whole cloves
2 carrots
3 bay leaves
2 to 3 leeks, white and light green parts
1 teaspoon coriander seed
1 teaspoon black peppercorns

Place the beef in a large soup pot and cover with water. Bring to the boil, skimming as necessary. Stick the onion with the cloves and add to the pot. Add the remaining ingredients, cover, and reduce heat to a bare simmer. Leave to simmer very slowly overnight. Strain, discarding the solids (beef bones are too hard for the disposal), cool, and then chill overnight. The next day, remove and discard the solidified white fat from the top. Freeze, if desired.

Chicken and/or Turkey Stock

Save roasted chicken or turkey carcasses, chicken wing tips, backbones, and other trimmings and supplement as needed with inexpensive chicken legs and thighs or backs and necks. I like to use inexpensive turkey wings to fortify this stock. With their high content of gelatin-producing collagen, they add body and a rich flavor. After cooling the stock, ladle it into plastic 1-quart containers (or even freezer bags, sealed carefully) and freeze. Frozen stock just needs a minute or two in the microwave to melt enough so that it slides right out of the bag into a pot, ready to boil.

MAKES 3 QUARTS

4 pounds mixed chicken parts (necks, backs, wings, and legs), preferably from grain-fed chickens, defrosted if frozen, rinsed and drained

1 pound turkey wings

1 onion, unpeeled

2 carrots, peeled

2 ribs celery, trimmed

3 bay leaves

1 teaspoon each: coriander seed, fennel seed, and peppercorns

A small handful of tender herb trimmings (parsley, chervil, tarragon)

In a large stockpot, combine the chicken parts with 4 quarts water. Bring to a boil, skimming off and discarding the white foam impurities that rise to the surface. Add the remaining ingredients and bring to the boil again. Reduce the heat to a bare simmer and cook, partially covered, for 6 hours, or until the chicken meat falls easily off the bones. Strain through a sieve into a large, stainless steel bowl or another pot, discarding the solids.

In hot weather, place the strained stock into a sinkful of ice mixed with water and cool for about 1 hour. In cool weather, cool at room temperature. Refrigerate overnight. The next day, remove and discard any fat from the surface. If desired, freeze the stock at this point.

ROASTED CHICKEN OR TURKEY STOCK

Never discard the carcass of a roasted chicken or turkey. If you're not ready to cook it at the time, simply wrap in plastic and freeze it. A roasted stock (or *brown stock*, as opposed to *white stock* in French cuisine) works best for gravies and sauces; a white stock, made from uncooked bones and trimmings, works best for soups. But there is no law (at least in America) that says you can't mix them.

Fish Stock

Fish stock is quick and easy to make; it's ready in less than 45 minutes. The only challenge is getting good, fresh-smelling fish "frames": skeletons left after the fillets have been remove; heads, rich in flavor and gelatin but with the pesky sharp gills that must be removed either with a pair of pliers or with your hands wrapped in a towel; or simply trimmings. Make friends with your fishmonger; he or she will usually give you the bones for free and may even clean them if you ask nicely (and buy fish regularly). Use the stock for the New England Style Clam Chowder (see page 305), the Oyster Chowder with Herbs and Tiny Croutons (see page 676), or the Lobster and Shrimp Cioppino (see page 567).

MAKES 3 QUARTS

5 pounds fish bones (clean and sweet-smelling)

2 ribs celery

1 onion

1 sprig fresh thyme

1 bay leaf

10 crushed peppercorns

2 cups white wine

Rinse the fish bones in cold water, cutting off the heads if not already done. Place them in a large stock pot with the remaining ingredients. Add one gallon of cold water and bring to the boil. Skim as necessary and reduce the heat to a bare simmer. Cook slowly for 35 to 40 minutes. Strain the liquid and chill, removing any solidified fat. The stock called *fumet* in French, will not keep beyond three to days. Place in a tightly sealed container and freeze for up to 1 month, defrosting when needed.

Different Fish Make Different Stocks

One of the subtleties of fish cookery is that different fish make different stocks. Flat fish like flounder and halibut make the gelatinous stocks, rich in body. Red Snapper makes a superb light, clear, flavorful stock. Oily fish like salmon or bluefish make a stock that is generally too strong in flavor, though salmon stock may be used as the base for a salmon chowder (follow the recipe for the Pennsylvania Dutch Corn and Potato Chowder on page 341, substituting salmon stock for the milk and adding about 1 pound boneless, skinless salmon cubes to the chowder along with the corn at the end).

Game Stock

While it's probably not often that you will have the ingredients for a game stock, it makes a wonderfully woodsy-tasting stock that will go a long way toward making a superb sauce, fit for the connoisseur. Save the bones of roasted game or trimmings in the freezer until you accumulate enough to make this stock. Extra stock can be brought back to the boil and frozen again.

MAKES 3 QUARTS

5 pounds venison, pheasant, pigeon, rabbit, or other
   game meat bones, mixed with veal bones

4 tablespoons canola oil

1 cup each: chopped onion, celery, and carrot

1 cup red wine

3 sprigs fresh thyme, or 1 teaspoon dried thyme

2 bay leaves

2 tablespoons juniper berries

1 teaspoon crushed peppercorns

1 quart chicken stock

In a large Dutch oven, brown the bones in hot oil, turning often so they brown deeply and evenly without burning. Add the onions, celery, and carrots and brown well. Pour off any excess fat and pour in the red wine, thyme, bay leaves, juniper berries, and peppercorns. Add the chicken stock plus enough water to cover the bones completely. Bring the liquid to the boil, skimming as necessary. Reduce the heat and simmer for 3 to 4 hours. Strain the stock, cool, and then chill.

Mushroom Stock

Use this stock when you want an earthy mushroom flavor, or as an alternative vegetarian stock when a heartier, more robust flavor is called for. It is perfect for a vegetarian version of mushroom soups like the Wild Rice and Shiitake Mushroom Soup (see page 978). The Mushroom-Barley Soup (see page 630), the Clam and Mushroom Soup with Reisling (see page 304), and the Hungarian Mushroom Soup (see page 595) would all benefit by this deep, dark stock. Save any mushroom trimmings and stems in the freezer to use here. Shiitake stems are especially full of flavor and too tough and woody to use easily for other purposes.

MAKES 3 QUARTS

$^{1}/_{2}$ cup dried porcini mushroom (or dried shiitakes)

3 pounds sliced mushrooms or mushroom trimmings

$^{3}/_{4}$ cup dry white vermouth

1 tablespoon fennel seed

1 teaspoon black peppercorns

3 to 4 sprigs thyme, or 1 teaspoon dried thyme

4 bay leaves

Soak the porcini in warm water to cover until soft, about 20 minutes. Scoop out the mushrooms and reserve. Strain the mushroom liquor through a dampened paper towel laid into a sieve to remove any sand, and reserve.

   In a large soup pot, combine the soaked porcini, strained mushroom liquor, mushrooms, vermouth, fennel seed, peppercorns, thyme, and bay leaves. Cover with 3 quarts of water and bring to the boil, skimming as necessary. Simmer about 2 hours, then strain out solids, pressing well to extract all the liquid.

993

Seafood Stock

By poaching (slowly simmering) shrimp, lobsters, or scallops in this flavorful liquid, they pick up flavors from the cooking broth while at the same time the broth picks up the seafood flavor. The stock may be strained, cooled, and then frozen to use once more for poaching. If you happen to have seafood trimmings, such as shrimp shells or scallop trimmings, by all means, add them to the stock. Also, the delicious juices of cooked mussels or clams can be added to the stock.

MAKES 3 QUARTS

1 cup dry white vermouth

1 tablespoon pickling spice

1 tablespoon coriander seeds

1 tablespoon fennel seeds

4 bay leaves

4 sprigs fresh thyme, or 1 teaspoon dried thyme

$1/4$ cup kosher salt

1 teaspoon crushed black pepper

2 lemons, cut in half

In a large pot, combine 3 quarts of cold water with the vermouth, pickling spice, coriander, and fennel seeds, bay leaves, thyme, salt, pepper, the juice squeezed from the lemons, and the lemon halves. Bring to the boil, skimming as necessary, then reduce the heat and simmer for 30 minutes. Strain and cool. You may freeze any extra stock once it reaches room temperature.

994

USING SEAFOOD STOCK

Use seafood stock as the base for a seafood chowder or stew such as the Lobster and Shrimp Cioppino (*see* page 567), the Lobster Risotto (*see* page 564), or Linguine with Lobster, Corn, Tarragon, and Creamy Tomato Sauce (*see* page 567), or substitute the stock for the milk in the Oyster Chowder with Herbs and Tiny Croutons (*see* page 676). Or, use it to poach octopus or calamari for seafood salad. Once used for this purpose, the stock will probably taste too strong and will be cloudy, so it can't be reused. Substitute shrimp for the lobster in the Lobster Risotto and use this stock for a delicious (and less expensive) Shrimp Risotto.

CHOOSING VEGETABLES
FOR VEGETABLE STOCK

To make a good vegetable stock, it's important to have a wide variety of aromatic vegetables and herbs, but it's equally important not to use those that are too strong in flavor. Do not use red onions (which dye the stock an unpleasant color) or members of the *Brassica* family, such as broccoli, cabbage, or cauliflower, which give too strong a taste and smell. Rosemary and sage can be overpowering in this stock, but other, more tender herb stems will give an extra dimension of flavor and aroma. No one vegetable should dominate.

Vegetable Stock

There is no one recipe for making vegetable stock, but this one is a good basic. Note that a vegetable stock will never have the rich body of one made with meat, because the vegetables contain no collagen, which produces gelatin. Substitute part of the water here with the liquid saved from cooking with chickpeas, or drained from a can of chickpeas. It is particularly rich in soluble fiber, or pectin, which mimics the body of meat-based stocks. Vegetable stock is rather perishable, so freeze within 1 to 2 days.

MAKES 3 QUARTS

3 quarts assorted vegetable trimmings including
any or all of the following:
Carrots, including tips and root ends, no peels
Onions, including peels and trimmings of yellow
   or white onions only, no red
Celery, including tips, trimmings, leaves
Scallions, white root ends, not green tips
Mushrooms, especially stems from shiitakes
   and portabellas
Asparagus, any trimmings, including peelings
Pea pods
Red bell pepper trimmings
Fennel stalks
Potatoes, including peelings
Tomatoes, including trimmings
Squash
Corn cobs
1 cup tender herb trimmings such as parsley, thyme,
   basil, marjoram, chives, lovage, or dill
1 tablespoon each: black peppercorns and coriander seeds
4 bay leaves

Combine everything in a large stockpot and cover with about 1 gallon of water. Bring to the boil, reduce heat, skim as necessary, and then simmer for 1 hour. Strain and cool. You may freeze any extra stock once it reaches room temperature.

Smoked Pork or Turkey Stock

Use either smoked pork bones, including inexpensive but meaty and flavorful neck bones. or smoked turkey wings or legs to make this rich-tasting, smoky stock perfectly suited to hearty bean soups.

MAKES ABOUT 3 QUARTS

4 pounds smoked pork bones
   (or smoked turkey wings and/or legs)
1 large unpeeled onion, cup into rough chunks
3 to 4 carrots, cut into rough chunks
3 to 4 ribs celery, cut into rough slices
1 bay leaf
2 sprigs fresh thyme

Place all the ingredients into a large soup or stock pot. Add cold water to cover by about 2 inches. Bring to the boil, then reduce the heat to a bare simmer, skimming to remove any white foam that rises to the top. Simmer about 3 hours, or until the bones are soft enough to fall apart. Cool slightly and then strain, discarding the solids. Refrigerate overnight. The next day, remove and discard any solid fat congealed on the top, and then use or freeze.

AMERICAN AND METRIC MEASURES

AMERICAN	EUROPEAN
$^1/_4$ teaspoon	1 ml
$^1/_2$ teaspoon	3 ml
1 teaspoon	5 ml
1 tablespoon	15 ml
$^1/_8$ cup	35 ml
$^1/_4$ cup	65 ml
$^1/_2$ cup	125 ml
$^3/_4$ cup	190 ml
1 cup	250 ml

AMERICAN AND METRIC WEIGHTS

AMERICAN	EUROPEAN
3 ounces	85 g
4 ounces, $^1/_4$ pound	100 g
8 ounces, $^1/_2$ pound	225 g
9 ounces	250 g
10 ounces	275 g
12 ounces, $^3/_4$ pound	350 g
14 ounces	400 g
16 ounces, 1 pound	450 g
18 ounces	500 g
20 ounces	550 g
32 ounces, 2 pounds	900 g
2.1 pounds	1000 g
64 ounces, 4 pounds	1800 gm
80 ounces, 5 pounds	2.25 k

FAHRENHEIT AND CELSIUS OVEN TEMPERATURES

DESCRIPTION	FAHRENHEIT	CELSIUS
Lowest, use for dehydrating	150°F.	70°C.
Low, use for slow-roasted tomatoes	200°F.	100°C.
Low, use for braising of large cuts of meat	250°F.	120°C.
Low-medium, use for cooking beans	300°F.	150°C.
Moderate, use for most baking	350°F.	180°C.
High, use for roasting potatoes and meats	400°F.	200°C.
Very high, use for roasting vegetables, fish, and small cuts	450°F.	230°C.
Hottest, use for baking pizza	500°F.	260°C.

BAKING BY WEIGHT, NOT VOLUME

People in many other parts of the world are accustomed to measuring by weight, rather than by volume as we do in America. All equivalents are rounded off to make conversion easier.

The unbleached all-purpose flour that I use is milled to yield 19 cups of flour per 5-pound bag. This is just slightly less than $^1/_4$ pound per cup and close enough for normal kitchen use. Because flour volume changes so much according to the weather temperature and humidity, not to mention differences in measuring, once you start baking by weight, your results will be more consistent and you'll understand proportional relations, making it easy to increase or decrease batch sizes.

Meat & Poultry Cooking Tips & Roasting Charts

TIPS FOR COOKING MEATS

Season the meat and poultry on all sides with salt and pepper to taste. Kosher salt is easiest to use, because it can be spread lightly and evenly on the surface.

Depending on the size, allow the meat or poultry to rest at room temperature for 20 minutes for chops, and up to 2 hours for large roasts, so that the meat will cook more evenly. In hot weather, cut the resting time in half. The exception to this is if you want to cook a thin cut (such as flank steak or skirt steak) to rare to medium-rare. In this case, season the meat, but allow it to rest in the refrigerator until ready to cook.

After cooking—whether on a grill, stovetop, oven, or broiler—remove from the heat and allow the meat to rest again for 10 minutes (for chops) and up to 30 minutes (for large roasts) to allow the juices to get reabsorbed into the meat and for the temperature to even out. Drape the meat with foil while it is resting. By including this step, your meats will be juicier and more succulent.

Most chefs prefer meats to be cooked at most to medium-rare, because it will be juicier and more succulent (and shrinks less, so portions don't have to be as large). However, according to the USDA, to be completely safe from dangers of salmonella, meats must be cooked to medium-well. In the following charts, I have listed both chef's ideal temperature and the USDA recommended temperature. People who have compro-mised immune systems or are vulnerable to illness because of pregnancy or reasons of health, would do well to cook their meat to the USDA recommendations.

In general, meats will have a better, more crusty and browned flavor if cooked at higher heat, and will be juicier and shrink less if cooked at lower heat.

When roasting, use a pan that is just large enough to hold the meat or the bird, so that bare areas don't smoke and burn.

Roast meats starting with the fat-side up, so that the melting fat will naturally baste the meat.

When reading the following charts, keep in mind that a centigrade degree is almost twice as large as a Fahren-heit degree. There are 180 Fahrenheit degrees between the freezing temperature of water (32°F.) and the boiling temperature of water (212°F.) and only 100 Centigrade degrees between the freezing point of water (0°C.) and the boiling temperature of water (100°C.).

Note also that for larger roasts, there are two temperatures given. The Cooking Temperature is what the roast should read at the thickest point when it is removed from the oven. The larger the roast, the more "carryover heat" must be allowed for. This is the heat retained in the roast that will continue to cook, raising the temperature to the temperature shown in the chef's ideal temperature column.

997

BEEF AND LAMB STEAKS

Doneness	Description	Chef's Ideal Temp.	USDA Recommended Temp.
Extra-rare (blue, Pittsburgh)	Center soft and raw; outside bright red and juicy	115°F. to 120°F. 52°C.	Not recommended
Rare	Red with cold, soft center	125°F. to 130°F. 55°C. to 58°C.	140°F. 61°C.
Medium-Rare	Red with warm, firmer center	130°F. to 140°F. 58°C. to 61°C.	145°F. 63°C.
Medium	Pink and firm throughout	140°F. to 150°F. 61°C. to 65°C.	160°F. 71°C.
Medium-well	Pink line in center, quite firm	150°F. to 155°F. 65°C.	160°F. 71°C.
Well-done	Gray-brown throughout and completely firm	160°F. to 165° 71°C. to 74°C.	170°F. 77°C.
Ground beef or lamb	Medium (pink and firm throughout)	140°F. to 150°F. 61°C. to 65°C.	160°F. 71°C.

998

BEEF AND LAMB ROASTS

Doneness	Description	Cook Temp.	Resting Time	Chef's Ideal Temp	USDA Reccomended
Rare	Red with cold, soft center	125°F. 52°C.	15 to 30 min.	125°F. to 130°F. 55° to 58°C.	140°F. 61°C.
Medium-Rare	Red with warm firmer center	130°F 55°C.	15 to 30 min.	135°F. to 140°F. 58° to 61°C.	145°F. 63°C.
Medium	Pink and firm throughout	135°F. 58°C.	15 to 30 min.	140°F. to 150°F. 61° to 65°C.	160°F. 71°C.
Medium-well	Pink line in center, quite firm	145°F. 63°C.	15 to 30 min.	150°F. to 155°F. 65° to 68°C.	160°F. 71°C.
Well-done	Gray-brown throughout and completely firm	155°F. 68°C.	15 to 30 min.	165°F. 71° to 74°C.	170°F. 77°C.

VEAL CHOPS

Doneness	Description	Chef's Ideal Temp.	USDA Recommended Temp.
Medium-Rare	Pink with warm center	130°F. to 140°F. 58°C. to 61°C.	145°F. 63°C.
Medium	Pink throughout	140° to 150°F. 61°C. to 65°C.	160°F. 71°C.
Medium-well	Slight pink in center	150° to 155°F. 65°C.	160°F. 71°C.
Well-done	Beige-pink throughout	160° to 165°F. 71°C. to 74°C.	170°F. 77°C.

X-TRAS

VEAL ROASTS

Doneness	Description	Cook Temp.	Resting Time	Chef's Ideal Temp	USDA Reccomended
Medium-Rare	Pink with warm center	130°F. 55°C.	15 to 30 min.	135° to 140°F. 58° to 61°C.	145°F. 63°C
Medium	Pink throughout	40°F. 61°C.	15 to 30 min.	150°F. 66°C.	160°F. 71°C.
Medium-well	Slight pink in center	150°F. 66°C	15 to 30 min.	160°F. 71°C.	165°F. 74°C.
Well-done	Beige-pink throughout	160°F. 71°C.	15 to 30 min.	165°F. 74°C.	170°F. 77°C.

PORK CHOPS

Doneness	Description	Chef's Ideal Temp.	USDA Recommended Temp.
Medium	Pink throughout	155°F. 68°C.	160°F., 71°C.
Medium-well	Slight pink in center	160°F. 71°C.	165°F., 74°C.
Well-done	Beige-pink throughout	165°F. 74°C.	170°F., 77°C.

PORK ROASTS

Doneness	Description	Cook Temp.	Resting Time	Chef's Ideal Temp	USDA Reccomended
Medium	Pink throughout	150°F.	15 to 30 min.	155°F. 68°C.	160°F. 71°C.
Medium-well	Slight pink in center	155°F.	15 to 30 min.	160°F. 71°C.	165°F. 74°C.
Well-done	Beige-pink throughout	160°F.	15 to 30 min.	165°F. 74°C.	170°F. 77°C.

POULTRY AND RABBIT

Meat	Description	Cook Temp.	Resting Time	Chef's Ideal Temp	USDA Reccomended
Rabbit	Opaque throughout	155° to 160°F. 68 to 71°C.	15 min.	160°F. 71°C.	160°F. 71°C.
White meat poultry	Opaque throughout	160°F. 71°C.	15 min.	165°F. 74°C.	170°F. 77°C.
Dark meat poultry	Clear juices in leg, leg jiggles easily in joint	165°F. 74°C.	15 min.	170°F. 77°C.	180°F. 82°C.
Whole bird	Clear juices in leg, leg jiggles easily in joint	165°F. 74°C.	15 min.	170°F. 77°C.	180°F. 82°C.

AMERICAN AND METRIC SUGAR SYRUP TEMPERATURES

Use this chart when cooking sugar syrup to make buttercream icings and candies. A candy thermometer (same as a deep-frying thermometer) makes this task easier, but the tests listed below work very well.

NAME	FAHRENHEIT	CENTIGRADE	DESCRIPTION
Thread	230°F.	110°C.	Makes a 2-inch thread when dropped from a spoon
Soft Ball	234°F.	112°C.	A small amount dropped into chilled water forms a ball, but flattens when picked up.
Firm Ball	244°F.	118°C.	The ball will hold its shape and flatten only when pressed
Hard Ball	250°F.	121°C.	The ball is more rigid, but still pliable.
Soft Crack	270°F.	132°C.	A small amount dropped into chilled water separates into threads that bend when picked up.
Hard Crack	300°F.	149°C.	Separates into threads that harden and are brittle.
Caramel	310°F. to 338°F.	154°C. to 170°C.	Turns light golden to deep reddish-gold
Burnt sugar	350 °F.	177°C.	Black and burnt, sometimes used to color sauces and gravy.

YAM, SWEET POTATO, & BONIATO

YAMS,
SWEET POTATO & BONIATO

Native to the New World (South America) but inextricably bound to American holiday traditions, sweet potatoes are delicious by any name and almost any way they are prepared. Sweet potatoes, *Ipomoae batatas*, are sweet-fleshed, oblong, pointy-ended tubers in the Morning Glory family. They are rich in beneficial beta-carotene and are native to the American tropics. Their skin color ranges from light tan through deep garnet, and their flesh color ranges from creamy tan through deep orange. Note that botanists prefer to call all the members of this family, whether popularly known as sweet potatoes or yams, *sweetpotatoes* (one word) to distinguish them from any regular potato that might taste sweet.

True yams, members of the genus *Dioscorea*, are native to the tropics around the world, and are a staple in Africa. These tubers can grow to enormous size and have rough, bark-like skin. Their flesh is rather bland, so they are usually cooked in a spicy preparation. They are most likely to be found in African, Caribbean, Latino, or Asian markets, usually cut into smaller pieces for sale. The edible, inside portion ranges from light tan or pale yellow to red or purple.

Native Americans were already growing sweet potatoes when Columbus arrived on the northern continent in 1492. Native to the New World, sweet potatoes traveled to the Old World before the unrelated common potato, *Solunum tuberosum*. Sweet potatoes were introduced first to Europe with the name *batata*, which later became *potato*. When the common potato arrived a bit later in Europe, it was given the same name, and sweet varieties began to be distinguished from common, rather than vice-versa. The sweet potato is botanically unrelated to the potato or the African yam. Both Louis XIV and Empress Josephine's fondness for the sweet potato encouraged two short periods of popularity for this tuber in France in the late eighteenth and early nineteenth century, but it has never enjoyed the favor there that it has in the New World and in Asia.

African slaves in the South called the sweet potato *nyami* because it reminded them of the starchy, edible tuber of that name that grew in their homeland. The Senegalese word *nyami* was eventually shortened to the word *yam*. In the 1930s, when Louisiana growers introduced a very sweet, deep-orange-fleshed sweet potato, they decided to call it a Louisiana yam, to take advantage of this association and to distinguish it from the similar, but starchier, more chestnut-like varieties grown up north in New Jersey, Maryland, and Virginia.

In American markets today, *yams*, as we perceive them, are sweet potatoes with vivid orange color, and a soft, moist consistency, and sweet flavor when cooked. The most popular yam is the Beauregard, which is uniform in size and shape, with smooth skin and deep orange flesh. Other varieties include Garnets, which have garnet-colored skin, orange-yellow flesh, and excellent flavor. They are popular with organic growers. Jewels have more orangey skin and deep orange flesh. Dry-fleshed yellow or white sweet potatoes are grown in the northern part of the U.S. These have pale white-to-yellow flesh and beige skin. They appear occasionally at local markets with names such as Nancy Hall and Jersey Yellow sweet potato. All these tubers, whether they're called *yams*, *sweetpotatoes*, *sweet potatoes*, *boniatos*, or *batatas* are varieties within the same species and are cultivars within the species. Only the African yam comes from a different family altogether.

Sweet Potato and "Yam" Cultivars

Asian Sweet Potatoes: Asian sweet potatoes are terms for various rose-skinned, ivory-fleshed cultivars from Asia. They fall between the drier boniato types and the moist-flesh whites. Well above ninety percent of the world's sweet potatoes are grown in Asia.

Boniato: Boniatos, sometimes called *Cuban sweet potato* or *batata*, are short, plump, irregularly shaped tubers with rose-pink thin skin and white flesh. They are somewhat less sweet and are firmer and drier in texture than orange-fleshed types. They are sold at Latin American markets. These starchy, reddish-skinned sweet potatoes have flaky skin and white flesh that is dry and fluffy with delicate, mildly sweet flavor similar to chestnuts. Boniatos are popular in Latin American and Asian markets and are a staple in countries from Mexico to Vietnam.

Hayman: The Hayman sweet potato is an heirloom variety that has been grown for more than a century on the Eastern Shore of the Chesapeake Bay. Smaller than a traditional sweet potato, it has creamy, light-colored flesh that turns pale yellow when cooked, and a lush, sweet flavor. This variety is becoming more common, with about 360,000 pounds sold annually at roadside stands, farmers' markets, and specialty stores along the mid-Atlantic coast. Local lore has it that the potato got its name from a ship captain who brought it to Virginia's shore, but no one is certain.

Louisiana Yams: The most popular Louisiana "yam" is the Beauregard, which is uniform in size and shape with smooth skin and deep orange flesh. Other orange-fleshed varieties include Garnet yams, which have garnet-colored skin, orange-yellow flesh, and excellent flavor, and are a cultivar popular with organic growers. Jewel yams have more orangey skin, deep orange-colored flesh, and account for about seventy-five percent of American commercially grown sweet potatoes.

Okinawa: The heirloom Hawaiian sweet potato called the Okinawa—*poni* in Hawaiian—cooks to an extraordinary deep purple-lilac color and has rich, sweet, slightly sticky flesh.

1005

Sweet Potato Ravioli with Sage and Brown Butter

Some dishes are just so good that their taste remains in memory. I first tasted Parma's specialty: zucca-filled ravioli while on a class trip with Marcella Hazan's cooking school back in 1979. Zucca is a dense winter squash closest to Latin American calabaza. To recreate the dish, I used American sweet potato, because it shared the same color and texture, but wasn't as watery as the American squashes I could get at the time. A simple sauce of butter cooked until the bits of milk solids get brown and "hazelnutty" in flavor (the French call this beurre noisette, hazelnut butter) with whole sage leaves sizzled in the butter and the whole mixed with Parma's world-class cheese, Parmigiano-Reggiano enhances the delightful filling. You'll need to purchase amaretti, found at Italian specialty stores. These macaroons are made from bittersweet apricot pits rather than almonds so they balance the sweetness of the filling.

Sweet Potato Filling

2 pounds sweet potatoes
1 cup Amaretti crumbs
1 cup grated Parmigiano-Reggiano
2 eggs
Kosher salt, grated nutmeg, and freshly ground
  black pepper to taste

Preheat the oven to 400°F. Bake the sweet potatoes about 1 hour, or until tender when pierced. Remove from the oven, cool, and then peel. Mash the sweet potato with the remaining ingredients and chill in the refrigerator. Follow the directions in the X-tras chapter for forming ravioli (page 986), using the filling above.

Brown Butter and Sage Sauce, Ravioli and Assembly

Sweet Potato Ravioli (*see* page 986)

4 tablespoons unsalted butter

2 tablespoons whole sage leaves

1 cup grated Parmigiano-Reggiano

Bring a large pot of salted water to the boil. Add the ravioli one by one, then bring back to the boil, stirring occasionally with a wooden spoon so as not to break open the ravioli. Boil for 3 to 5 minutes or until the dough at the edges of the ravioli feel just tender. Scoop from the water using a wire skimmer or slotted spoon and reserve.

In a large, heavy-bottomed skillet, heat the butter over moderate heat until it turns nutty brown with an aroma of hazelnuts. Add the sage leaves and allow them to sizzle in the butter for 1 to 2 minutes, or until fragrant. Remove the skillet from the heat. Toss gently with the ravioli until well coated with the butter, then toss again with the grated cheese. Serve immediately, preferably on heated plates.

YAM TIPS

Always use a stainless steel knife when cutting a sweet potato; a carbon blade will cause the yam to darken.

Roasted sweet potatoes will keep quite well for two to three days in the refrigerator.

When making mashed sweet potatoes, add one common potato to every three to four sweet potatoes for a firmer, smoother consistency.

Sweet Potatoes in Escabeche

According to scholars, the famed Latin American ceviche is a descendant of the Iberian Spanish escabeche, a word that refers to the technique for flavoring and preserving fried fish, meat, or vegetables in a vinegar-based liquid for several days, or as long as several weeks, allowing the flavors to blend and mellow. Escabeche, in turn, can be traced back to the Arabs, who ruled Spain in medieval times during its "Golden Age," and the Arabic iskibaj, meaning a kind of meat with vinegar. (See Clifford Wright's The Mediterranean Feast for more.) Here, I use sweet potatoes to make a rich-tasting, spicy escabeche that is easy to make, versatile, and even inexpensive. The mild and aromatic true cinnamon, called canela in Spanish, is essential here. The more common hard cinnamon sticks sold in America are actually the stronger and more pungent cassia. (For more on canela, see page 297.)

SERVES 6 TO 8

3 pounds sweet potatoes

1/2 stick canela (soft stick cinnamon), crushed

1 teaspoon whole cumin seeds

1/2 teaspoon whole allspice berries

2 teaspoons dried oregano

2 bay leaves, crumbled

2 tablespoons + 4 tablespoon olive oil

1 red onion, thinly sliced

1 tablespoon chopped garlic

1/4 cup cider vinegar

1 teaspoon chipotle chile flakes (substitute hot red pepper flakes)

Kosher salt and freshly ground black pepper to taste

Preheat the oven to 400°F. Bake the sweet potatoes for about 1 hour, or until tender when pierced. Remove from the oven, cool, and then peel and cut into thick slices.

Meanwhile, in a dry pan, toast the canela, cumin, allspice, oregano, and bay leaves over medium heat until the spices give off their aroma and begin to brown. Cool and then grind in a spice grinder, mortar and pestle, or crush using the side of a heavy chef's knife.

In a large skillet, heat 2 tablespoons of the olive oil. Add the onion and cook over high heat until the onion browns lightly. Add the garlic, toss to combine, and cook 1 minute more, or until fragrant. Pour in the vinegar and shake to combine the ingredients. Add the ground spice mixture, the chipotle flakes, and season with salt and pepper. Add the sweet potato slices and the remaining olive oil, toss to combine, and then remove the pan from the heat. Cool and then chill in the refrigerator for at least 1 day before using so that the flavors mellow and penetrate the sweet potatoes. Bring the escabeche to room temperature before serving. Store in the refrigerator for up to one week.

Mashed Yams with Ginger and Cardamom

This dish of mashed yams, fragrant with ginger and cardamom and sweetened with honey, is easy to make because the mixture can be mashed in the food processor. Because yams don't have the starch content of potatoes, they won't get gluey in the processor, even though I add one potato to the yams to make a creamier mash with more body. I prefer steaming the yams and potatoes here, because they will be firmer and less waterlogged and will therefore absorb the butter and other ingredients better. Any leftovers can be spread into a baking dish, dotted with butter, and then baked at 400°F. until browned and heated thoroughly.

SERVES 8

2 pounds (3 to 5) yams, peeled and cut into large chunks
1 large Idaho potato, peeled and cut into large chunks
2 tablespoons honey
2 tablespoons grated ginger
4 tablespoons unsalted butter
$1/2$ teaspoon ground cardamom
Kosher salt and freshly ground black pepper to taste

Steam yams and the potato until quite soft (about 20 minutes). Meanwhile, combine the honey, ginger, butter, cardamom, and salt and pepper, and heat to steaming. (You can easily do this by placing the ingredients in a glass measure and microwaving about 2 minutes.)

Remove the yams and potato from the steamer, reserving the liquid, and transfer to the bowl of a food processor. While still hot, process until relatively smooth. Gradually add the honey mixture and process until absorbed, scraping down the sides of the processor bowl with a rubber spatula so that the whole mixture is smooth. Thin with some of the reserved liquid to make a nice consistency, season with salt and pepper, and serve immediately.

Blue Ribbon Sweet Potato Pie

I first sampled this sweet potato pie at a Philadelphia Horticultural Association harvest show, where it did indeed win a blue ribbon. Sweet potato pie is a traditional soul food dish that originated in the cooking of American slaves who made brilliant use of foods rejected by white owners. The great African-American agronomist, George Washington Carver, wrote about sweet potatoes in a 1937 bulletin published by the Tuskegee Institute, of which he was the director, called, "How the Farmer Can Save His Sweet Potatoes and Ways of Preparing Them for the Table." He tells us that the sweet potato was known as Indian potato, Tuckahoe, *and* Hog potato, *and writes, "Here in the South, there are but few if any farm crops that can be depended upon one year with another for satisfactory yields, as is true of the sweet potato. It is also true that most of our southern soils produce potatoes superior in quality, attractive in appearance and satisfactory in yields, as any other section of the country."*

MAKES ONE 9–INCH PIE

Shortcrust Pastry Dough

MAKES ABOUT 1 POUND PASTRY DOUGH

$1/2$ pound (2 sticks) unsalted butter,
   cut into bits and chilled
$1/4$ pound (1 cup) unbleached all-purpose flour
$1/4$ pound (1 cup) cake flour
$1/4$ teaspoon salt
$1/2$ cup ice-cold water

Place the butter, flours, and salt in a mixing bowl and chill in the freezer for 30 minutes.

Using the flat beater from an electric mixer, or by hand, cut the butter into the flour until the pieces are the size of peas. Sprinkle the ice water over the flour mixture while tossing with your hands to distribute the water evenly. Pat the mixture together until a ball is formed. If necessary, add a few more teaspoons of water, using only enough to gather in any dry ingredients remaining in the bowl. Wrap in plastic, forming the dough into a flat block, and refrigerate for one hour.

Roll the dough into a circle (about 12 inches in diameter). Pat into a pie plate, forming an attractive border and trimming off any excess dough. Chill while preparing filling.

Sweet Potato Filling

1 pound sweet potatoes, steamed in their skins and
   then peeled
1 cup dark brown sugar, packed
2 teaspoons ground cinnamon
2 tablespoons grated ginger root
Grated zest of 1 lemon
1 teaspoon kosher salt (use only $1/2$ teaspoon of table salt)
2 egg yolks
1 cup heavy cream

1009

¹/₄ cup dark rum

4 egg whites

2 cups granulated sugar

1 rolled-out pie shell (from above)

Vanilla-flavored whipped cream, for topping

Preheat the oven to 325°F. Using an electric mixer with the paddle attachment, whip together the sweet potatoes, dark brown sugar, cinnamon, ginger, lemon zest, and salt until smooth. Beat in the yolks and the heavy cream. Beat in the rum.

Separately, whip the egg whites until soft and fluffy. Gradually beat in the sugar and continue beating until firm and glossy. Fold into the sweet potato mixture. Scrape the mixture into the prepared pie shell and bake until set in the middle, about 1¹/₂ hours. Cool, then serve with whipped cream.

1010

GEORGE WASHINGTON CARVER'S SWEET POTATO PIE RECIPE

PIE (EXTRA FINE)

Boil in skins. When tender, remove skins; mash and beat until light. To each pint of potatoes, add ¹/₂ pint of milk, ¹/₂ pint of cream and four well-beaten eggs; add 1¹/₂ teacups of sugar (less if the potatoes are very sweet). Add spice, cinnamon and ginger to taste; one ground clove will improve it. Bake with bottom crust only.

YOGURT

YOGURT

More than a small container suitable for a quick lunch, yogurt is a way of life in the region stretching from Bulgaria, where it first developed, to Greece, Turkey, Syria, Lebanon, Iran, and into India and Russia. Every morning on a visit to Greece, I enjoyed scoops of incredibly rich yogurt, complete with a thick layer of light gold cream at the top. The sour yogurt drizzled with honey made the perfect breakfast. Yogurt (also spelled *yogourt* or *yoghurt*) is a semi-solid fermented milk product that originated centuries ago in Bulgaria. Although milk of various animals can be used to make yogurt, including the incredibly rich and smooth water-buffalo-milk yogurt I tasted at Vannulo near Paestum in Campania, Italy, industrialized yogurt is generally made from cow's milk.

Yogurt is one of the oldest foods known to man and has been a basic food in East-Central Europe, the Middle East, India, and Central and Western Asia for thousands of years. Ancient Greek doctors, like the famous Galen, were familiar with the health properties of yogurt, and there are references to it by the Greek historian Herodotus, who lived in the fifth century. Yogurt was well known to the Romans, including the scholar and natural scientist Pliny, who lived in the first century CE. Yogurt was widely respected in the Arab world in the Middle Ages, and a book that appeared in Damascus in 633 praised its therapeutic properties.

Yogurt is traditionally believed to be an invention of the Bulgars from Central Asia, about 4,500 years ago. The Bulgars, who were the earliest Turkic-speaking people to migrate to Europe, starting from the second century CE, had settled in the Balkans by the end of the seventh century CE. Yogurt, like other fermented foods, such as bread, beer, and wine, was first probably spontaneously fermented, perhaps by wild bacteria residing inside goatskin bags the Bulgars used for transportation. The word *yogurt* derives from a Turkish word meaning *to blend*, a reference to how yogurt is made.

Yogurt remained primarily a food of the East until the 1900s, when a Russian biologist and Director of the Pasteur Institute in Paris named Ilya Ilyich Mechnikov theorized that a diet rich in yogurt was responsible for the unusually long lifespans of Bulgarian peasants. Mechnikov, who was known for his pioneering research into the human immune system, worked to popularize yogurt throughout Europe and received the Nobel Prize in 1908. However yogurt arrived in Western Europe, it was little-known there until the 1920s. There is a story of an Armenian doctor who advised the French king, Francis I, to eat yogurt, thereby curing him of melancholy and other problems. Another story tells of a Jewish healer from Constantinople who arrived in Europe on foot with

1012

a flock of sheep and goats with which to make yogurt. Yogurt was propagated widely after the First World War by Greek immigrants who made yogurt themselves and served it to customers in their restaurants.

In 1919, a Spanish entrepreneur named Isaac Carasso started the first commercial yogurt plant in Barcelona, naming the business *Danone* after his son. Today, the company is known as *Dannon* in the U.S. Yogurt with fruit preserved was invented and patented in 1933 by a dairy in Prague, Radlická Mlékárna, in an effort to get yogurt to keep longer. The first commercially produced yogurt sold in the U.S. was in 1929 by two Armenian immigrants, Rose and Sarkis Colombosian, whose family business later became Colombo Yogurt.

AMERICAN WATER BUFFALO AND GOAT'S AND SHEEP'S MILK YOGURT

Water-buffalo yogurt is now being made in the U.S. by the Woodstock Water Buffalo Company in Vermont and sold at Trader Joe's. My favorite yogurt of the moment is imported from Greece under the Fage name and is made from sheep's and goat's milk and sold at Whole Foods (Trader Joe's carries other yogurts by this company, but not the top-of-the-line sheep- and goat's-milk type). There are other small producers in the U.S. of goat's- and sheep's-milk yogurt, including the biodynamic one from Seven Stars Farm in Chester County, Pennsylvania, that I used in the kitchen in my restaurant days.

MAKING YOGURT

Yogurt-making involves the introduction of specific "friendly" bacteria into preferably unpasteurized, unhomogenized milk in order to maintain the healthy balance of bacteria and enzymes of milk in its unprocessed state under very carefully controlled temperature and environmental conditions. The bacteria ingest the natural milk sugars and release lactic acid as a waste product; the increased acidity, in turn, causes the milk proteins to tangle into a solid mass, forming a denatured protein called *curd*. The increased acidity also prevents other potentially harmful bacteria from growing.

Yogurt cultures generally include two or more different bacteria for more complete fermentation, most commonly a form of *Streptococcus* and *lactobacillus* such as *acidophilus* and *bulgaricus*. Depending on the particular culture, it can turn into yogurt, buttermilk, or sour cream. Other strains of bacteria transform milk into French *crème fraiche*, Italian mascarpone, and Devonshire clotted cream.

If yogurt is not heated to kill the bacteria after fermentation, it is sold as containing "live active cultures," which some believe to be nutritionally superior. Because live yogurt culture contains enzymes that break down lactose, some individuals who are lactose intolerant find that they can enjoy yogurt without ill effects.

If the fruit is already stirred into the yogurt, it is often called Swiss-style. Most yogurt in the United States has pectin or gelatin added to make it firmer. Greek yogurt and some specialty American yogurts have a layer of thick cream at the top. Wheat berries and cooked rice are added to yogurt in Italy, and in America, it may be flavored with chocolate, coffee, lemon, and various fruit jams.

Kinds of Yogurt

Ayran: This cooling drink, popular in Turkey, is made of yogurt and water wth salt usually added and sometimes black pepper. It usually accompanies kebabs and meat pastries. In Turkey, even McDonalds serves *ayran*. In rural areas of Turkey, ayran is always offered to guests, and in Syria and Lebanon, it is available in all restaurants as well as fast food shops. A similar drink, *doogh*, is found in Iran and is called *tan* in Armenia. It differs from *ayran* because mint and other herbs are usually added, and it is carbonated, usually with seltzer water.

Bulgarian Yogurt: Bulgarian yogurt is often considered the finest, and it is certainly has one of the oldest traditions. It is prized for its specific taste, aroma, and quality and is usually eaten plain. Bulgarian yogurt producers are currently taking steps to legally protect the trademark of Bulgarian yogurt on the European market and distinguish it from other product types that do not contain live bacteria. Bulgarian yogurt is often strained by hanging in a cloth for a few hours to reduce its water content. The resulting yogurt is creamier, richer, and milder in taste because of increased fat content. Hanging overnight is sometimes employed to make a concentrated yogurt similar to cream cheese.

Cacik: This classic Turkish cold soup is known as *tarator* in Bulgaria and *cacık* in Turkey and is similar to but thinner than the Greek Tzatziki (see the recipe on page 358. Also see the Almond Tarator Dip on page 20 for a different version). *Cacik* is served cold in very small bowls as a first course in the summertime. It is made from Ayran, cucumbers, garlic, and ground walnuts. (See the recipe for Chilled Cucumber-Buttermilk Soup with Toasted Walnuts page 359.)

Greek Yogurt: Greek "full" yogurt is made from milk that has been blended with cream to a fat content of exactly ten percent. Standard yogurt at five percent fat, low-fat at two percent, and non-fat versions are also made. Greek yogurt is often served with honey, walnuts, or the soupy Greek fruit preserves known as "spoon fruit" as a dessert.

Kefir: Kefir is a sour, carbonated, slightly alcoholic drink with a consistency like thin yogurt. Kefir originated in the Caucasus. A related Central Asian-Mongolian drink made from mare's milk is called *kumis* or, in Mongolia, *airag*. It is made by mixing cow's or goat's milk with the grains—or "beads"—a combination of beneficial bacteria and yeasts, from previous kefir batches. Most commercially available American "kefir" is neither carbonated nor contains any alcohol, but is rather thinned yogurt. In Chile, this beverage is called *Yogurt de Pajaritos*. Due to the slight amount of alcohol in kefir, Russians often use it as a hangover cure. *Kephir, kewra, talai, mudu kekiya, matsoun, matsoni, waterkefir,* and *milkkefir* are other names for this drink.

Lassi Yogurt: *Lassi* is a yogurt-based beverage, originally from India, where it is made in two versions: salty and sweet. Salty *lassi* is usually flavored with roasted cumin and chile peppers; the sweet kind contains rosewater and/or lemon, mango, or other fruit juices.

1014

Matsoni or Caspian Sea Yogurt: In Japan, Caspian Sea Yogurt is a very popular homemade yogurt believed to have been introduced into the country by a sample brought from Georgia, in the Caucasus region, in 1986. This Georgian yogurt has a viscous, honey-like texture and is milder in taste than many other yogurts. It is easy to make at home and, in Japan, freeze-dried starter is sold, but many people obtain some yogurt from a friend to use as a starter.

Greek Meatballs with Yogurt–Mint Sauce

These small meatballs from Greece are usually made from pork. In nearby countries where similar dishes are made, the meat used is lamb, because of Muslim prohibitions against eating pork and because of regional taste. Pork, beef, or lamb will all work well here. The most important thing is the savory yogurt sauce for dipping the meatballs, flavored with mint and lemon juice for tang. To form the meatballs, use a melon baller to scoop the mixture. Then, dip your hands in water and roll the meatballs into a rounded shape.

MAKES 6 DOZEN SMALL MEATBALLS

1 pint plain whole-milk yogurt

Juice of 1 lemon

1 tablespoon chopped mint (or 1 teaspoon crumbled dried mint)

Kosher salt and freshly ground black pepper to taste

2 slices of bread without crusts, soaked in water until mushy

2 pounds ground beef, lamb, or pork

$\frac{1}{2}$ sweet onion, grated

1 egg

1 tablespoon chopped fresh oregano (or 1 teaspoon dried oregano)

2-4 tablespoons vegetable oil, for browning

Whisk together the yogurt, lemon juice, mint, salt, and pepper. Store in the refrigerator, up to 3 days.

Squeeze any excess moisture from the bread. Mix together the bread, ground meat, onion, egg, oregano, and salt and pepper. Form into 6 dozen small meatballs.

Heat a thin layer of oil in a large skillet over moderate heat and brown the meatballs on all sides. Remove the meatballs and pour off any fat from the pan. Add 1 cup of water to the pan and scrape up any browned bits from the bottom. Add the meatballs to the pan and simmer for about 10 minutes, or until the liquid is syrupy. Serve with toothpicks and dunk in the yogurt sauce.

1015

Yogurt and Herb-Stuffed Grape Leaves

This is an unusual and unexpectedly delicious dish of grape leaves stuffed with a mixture of yogurt cheese (called labne *or* white *in Lebanon), scallions, and dill, and thickened with semolina. The packets are then pan-fried in olive oil, of course, and baked until soft. They are best served at room temperature as* mezze, *an assortment of small salads and dishes served with pita bread as an appetizer or a light meal.*

MAKES 16

1 pound labne

1 cup chopped scallions

1/2 cup snipped dill

2 tablespoons crumbled dry mint

1 teaspoon kosher salt

1/2 teaspoon freshly ground black pepper

1/2 cup semolina or stone-ground cornmeal

16 large grape leaves (1/2 pound)

1/4 cup extra-virgin olive oil

Lemon wedges, to serve

In a food processor bowl, combine the labne, scallions, dill, mint, salt and pepper, and semolina. Process until chunky.

Preheat the oven to 275°F. Spread out 2 grape leaves, shiny-side down, on a work surface. Trim away the stems and the tough ribs near the stem. Form a rough rectangle about 6 x 4 inches. Pat the leaves dry and spread 2 tablespoons of the filling in the center of each leaf. Fold in along sides, then roll up to make a neat oblong envelope. Repeat with the remaining leaves and filling. Refrigerate to firm up the packets, about 30 minutes, up to 2 days.

Heat the oil in a (preferably nonstick) frying pan and gently fry a few grape leaf packets at a time until crisp and crinkly on both sides, 5 minutes. Transfer to a baking dish and bake at 400°F. for 25 minutes longer. Remove and cool to room temperature. Serve with lemon wedges.

Yogurt and Garlic Marinated Chicken Wings

While chicken wings have "taken off" as the ever-present bar food, Buffalo Wings, they are just as good, if not better, marinated for several days in this garlic and hot pepper sea-soned yogurt accented with sweet cinnamon and allspice. The acidic yogurt tenderizes and moistens the wings, so that when grilled or broiled, they come out succulent and juicy. The wings reheat quite well, but if you don't want to make such a big batch, simply cut the recipe in half. Purchase either V-shaped chicken wings, with their third joint already removed, or "Buffalo wings," where the second two joints of the wing have been split. If still attached, the small third joint that tends to burn quickly should be cut off (save it for the stock pot). The wings are superb cooked using indirect heat (with the lid on) in an outdoor grill. Accompany with the Almond Tarator Dip on page 20 if desired.

MAKES 5 POUNDS

1 pound thick plain yogurt, preferably full fat

2 tablespoons crushed garlic

2 tablespoons sweet paprika

2 teaspoons Aleppo pepper, substitute
   hot red pepper flakes

1/2 teaspoon ground allspice

1 teaspoon ground cinnamon

1 tablespoon kosher salt

1/2 teaspoon freshly ground black pepper

5 pounds chicken wings

Mix together the yogurt, garlic, paprika, Aleppo pepper, allspice, cinnamon, salt, and pepper. Mix well with the chicken wings, cover, and marinate for 48 hours, refrigerated.

Preheat the broiler to high. Drain the wings well, discarding the liquid. Allow them to come to room temperature, about 30 minutes. Spread out in a single layer in a metal baking pan. Watching carefully and turning once or twice, broil for about 20 minutes, or until well browned but still moist. The wings should jiggle loosely at the joint. Serve immediately.

Apple-Yogurt Coffee Cake

Like buttermilk or sour cream, yogurt makes for a tender and moist cake. This one has lots of chunky apples, pecans, cinnamon, and vanilla. Make it for brunch or just to have a slice with coffee. I prefer Fuji apples for baking because they combine a crisp texture with a sweet and tart flavor and they keep their shape well. However, a mixture of apples is also good so that some stay firm and chunky and some break down and get rich and saucy. The cake will keep well in the refrigerator for up to 5 days. Allow it to come to room temperature when serving it.

**MAKES ONE 10-INCH ROUND CAKE OR ONE
13 x 9-INCH RECTANGULAR CAKE**

6 ounces (1 1/2 cups) all-purpose flour, preferably unbleached

1 1/2 teaspoons baking powder

1/2 teaspoon kosher salt

1/2 pound (2 sticks) unsalted butter, divided

1 cup + 4 tablespoons granulated sugar, divided

2 eggs

1 cup plain whole-milk yogurt

1 teaspoon baking soda

5 Fuji apples, peeled, cored and sliced

1 tablespoon freshly ground cinnamon, divided

1 cup coarsely chopped pecans

1 tablespoon vanilla extract

Preheat the oven to 350°F. Prepare the cake pan by spraying generously with nonstick coating, or rub with butter and dust with flour.

1017

Whisk together the dry ingredients: flour, baking powder, and salt, and reserve.

Cream 12 tablespoons (1 1/2 sticks) of the butter with 1 cup of the sugar. Beat in the eggs, one at a time, then add the vanilla. Separately, combine the yogurt and baking soda, and then add to the egg mixture. Add the dry ingredients, beating only long enough to combine.

Mix the apple slices with 2 tablespoons of sugar and 1 1/2 teaspoons of cinnamon, and reserve. Toss the pecans with the remaining 2 tablespoons sugar and 1 1/2 teaspoons of cinnamon, and reserve.

Pour half the batter into the prepared pan. Cover with half the apples. Spread the remaining batter over top, cover with the remaining apples, and sprinkle with the pecan mixture. Dot the top with the remaining 4 tablespoons of butter. Bake for 45 minutes, or until just set. Turn off the over, open the oven door, and allow the cake to cool in the oven before removing. Cut into serving pieces, and serve.

~~~~~~

Turkish Apricot, Honey, & Yogurt Swirl

This light and delicious dessert comes from Turkey, where both apricots and yogurt are important ingredients. Make it in apricot season, when fresh, plump apricots, the first of the stone fruits to appear, are in the market. Start by draining the yogurt for at least 4 hours in the refrigerator, or else purchase Lebanese style labne or yogurt cheese. The apricots should be ripe enough to have a sweet aroma but still firm enough to hold their shape.

SERVES 6

2 cups yogurt

1 packet (2$\frac{1}{4}$ teaspoons) unflavored gelatin

$\frac{1}{2}$ cup apple juice

1 pound fresh apricots

$\frac{1}{2}$ cup honey

1 vanilla bean, split open

1 cinnamon stick

3 star anise pods

$\frac{1}{4}$ cup dark brown sugar, packed

Place the yogurt in a piece of dampened cheesecloth, put the cheesecloth package into a sieve, and drain over a bowl in the refrigerator for 4 hours.

Soften the gelatin in the apple juice. In a medium, heavy-bottomed, nonreactive saucepan, simmer together the apricots, honey, vanilla, cinnamon, star anise and 2 cups of water until the apricots are very soft, about 30 minutes. Remove the apricots from the heat and stir in the softened gelatin, stirring well to make sure the gelatin has fully dissolved. Cool at room temperature, then chill in the refrigerator, covered, until the mixture starts to gel.

When the yogurt has drained off about $\frac{3}{4}$-cup of liquid, combine yogurt with the brown sugar. Layer the apricot puree with yogurt in parfait glasses. Alternatively, layer in a footed glass trifle bowl. Cover and chill again about 2 hours, or until set, and then serve.

1018

YUCA & MALANGA

YUCA & MALANGA

Beloved throughout the Caribbean, Central America, South America, and now Indonesia and Polynesia, yuca is a bland, starchy tuber typically about 10 inches long and 2 inches thick. The outside skin of the yuca is brown and bark-like; the inside flesh is very white. Originally from Brazil, where it is known as *apian* when used as a fresh vegetable and *manioc* when used as a processed flour, yuca was first domesticated by the Amazonian peoples thousands of years ago. The Amazon Indian name for manioc, *Seats*, means literally *food*, which shows just how important this plant was in their diet.

Because of its popularity in Cuban cooking, the fruit is commemorated in the acronym, YUCA, Young Upwardly-Mobile Cuban Americans. This group of highly successful people includes Miami restaurateur Efrain Vega, who left Cuba as a child in 1962. He is the owner of Yuca, the elegant restaurant in Miami Beach where super star Latino chef Douglas Rodriguez got his start.

Native Americans from the Amazon originally bred the two main races of yuca: the sweet and the bitter. Both types of yuca plant contain two substances that react together to produce poisonous prussic acid as soon as the tubers are uprooted. The reaction speeds up when they are cut or peeled and exposed to air. Sweet yuca, *Manioc dulce*, the kind sold in American supermarkets, has a lower yield than the bitter but its tubers contain a small amount of poison, which is mostly contained in the skin. After peeling, sweet yuca may be safely eaten as a cooked vegetable.

Bitter yuca, *Manioc utilissima*, has a high yield of large starchy tubers but contains a significant amount of poison. Because prussic acid is easily soluble in water and driven off by heat, the Amazonians developed various soaking and heating methods to remove the poison. You may not realize that you've eaten yuca, but it is the source of tapioca. Tapioca is a product of the bitter yuca treated to form flakes, seeds, and pearls. The name *tapioca* comes from the Tupi-Guarani languages of Brazil. Their word, *tapioca*, refers to the starch produced by processing yuca or cassava roots. The main producers of tapioca are in Africa and Asia, rather than its country of origin, Brazil.

The first European explorers in the West Indies found yuca in use everywhere in the form of meal and dried, flat cakes. Similarly, in the countries of the Caribbean, like Jamaica, moist cassava pulp is used to prepare a thick cake called *balmy* and *casaba*, an unleavened bread. In Puerto Rico, the strong place of yuca in the cuisine is part of the heritage of the now-extinct native Taíno Indians.

In Brazil, the roasted flour made from yuca, *farinha de mandioca*, is transformed into one type or another of *farafo*. These dishes are prepared by either by cooking the farinha in water, by frying the farinha in red palm oil (dendé oil) or in butter, or by stirring the farinha into sauces. It is so important to the cuisine of Brazil that there are specialists in the art of making farofa, called *farofeiros*. On a recent culinary expedition to Brazil, the food was invariably accompanied by bowls of farofa. Sometimes it was crunchy and yellow from *dendé* (red palm oil); sometimes it was fluffy, like couscous, and sometimes it was simply dried and toasty. Each person sprinkles his or her dish with farofa before eating.

In much of Brazil, *pão de queijo* (cheese bread)—made of sweet and sour cassava starches, cheese, and eggs—is a popular fast food, often served for breakfast. *Sour*, a fermented starch extracted from yuca, is used in Colombia to prepare snacks and cheese breads, called *pan de yuca* and *pan de bono* (*see* the recipe below).

Today, Brazil and Indonesia are the main countries producing yuca. When you buy the long, brown-skinned yuca tubers in the market, they are usually waxed to help preserve them. (Yuca is not the same as yucca, though the two are often confused because of the similarity of their names. Yucca is related to the agave plant, from which tequila is distilled.) Yuca is high in carbohydrates but low in protein, so it must be supplemented by protein to make a balanced meal. One reason that yuca spread so far is the fact that, after the tubers have grown, which typically takes only six months, they can be left in the ground for as long as three years without deteriorating. This made yuca an ideal plant to keep in reserve against famine years.

European slavers brought yuca from Brazil to Africa during the sixteenth century, where it quickly became the food of Africans on their way to slave markets. Due to its ease of cultivation—yuca grows well in poor soil, resists drought and insect damage, is easily propagated, and has no specific planting or harvesting season—it quickly spread throughout sub-Saharan Africa.

In Africa, yuca is cooked and pounded to make the fermented porridge called *foo-foo*. Yuca arrived in Malaysia and Indonesia in the eighteenth century. In Indonesia, the Javanese have developed a fermented yuca delicacy called *tapé*, which has a soft texture, juicy consistency, and tangy flavor. During the nineteenth century, yuca became an important food in Hawaii, where it is often used as an alternative to *taro* in making their national dish, *poi*, a fermented porridge.

CHOOSING AND STORING YUCA

Look for firm, evenly shaped spears of yuca at Asian and Latino markets. They keep quite well at room temperature for up to one week.

Cassareep

This thick syrup—made by boiling down yuca juice with sugar, cloves, and cinnamon—is essential to the West Indian Pepper Pot Stew, a dish that traveled to Philadelphia, where it evolved into the classic Philadelphia Pepper Pot Soup. A similar sweet syrup called *tucupi* is used in Brazil. There, the Indian tribes also make cassava beer and boil and eat the young leaves as a vegetable.

MALANGA

If you've ever eaten the crunchy white basket filled with various mixtures at a Chinese restaurant, you've tasted malanga, also known as taro. Thin malanga chips are also prepared, sometimes dyed magenta with beet juice, and served at restaurants and included in packages of Terra Chips. Malanga, *Colocasia esculenta,* is a dense and starchy tuber that ranges in shape from fat oval and almost round to oblong. Its flesh, which can vary from white to yellow to pale pink, turns mauve-gray or violet when cooked and is often speckled with purplish-red or brown, stringy-looking markings. Its flavor and texture fall somewhere between potato and coconut.

Malanga, or taro, is most important in Hawaii, where its cultivation is tied to cultural and religious beliefs. The word *lu'au* refers to the leafy tops of young taro plants cooked in coconut milk; one dish at a traditional feast, the famed *poi,* is made from steamed, mashed taro.

The main tuber of the malanga plant is about the size of a turnip and is covered with shaggy brown skin circled with distinct rings. Along the roots that spread deeper into the soil may be found smaller malanga, called *eddo.* Asian markets carry both the small and large tubers. The large, edible malanga leaves (called *callalou* in the Caribbean) are cooked in soup. This wild, tropical plant native to Asia was first cultivated in India nine thousand years ago. From there, it spread through Asia and South America to the South Pacific islands that today are the largest consumers of malanga. Taro is its name in Hawaii and Asian communities. It is also popular in the Caribbean and Latin America, where it is known as *malanga.*

AFRICAN BATONS DE MANIOC

In Central Africa, yuca is made into *Batons de Manioc,* using a painstaking process. To make them, first the yuca is soaked in a pond or stream for at least 3 days. Next, it is peeled and washed in large tub, changing the water several times. Then, using a mortar and pestle, the yuca is pounded into a thick, smooth paste. The paste is then spread onto banana leaves, which are folded into foot-long packets and tied closed. Finally, the packets are steamed for 8 hours. At least the *Baton de Manioc* is ready to be served with soups and stews. The method here parallels the Mexican and Central American *tamales.*

Choosing and Storing Malanga

Malanga is available year-round, especially in Asian markets. The tubers should be firm to the touch at both ends, with hairy roots. Freshly dug malanga will be pinkish-or whitish-green at the stem end. For a richer and creamier consistency, choose medium to large malanga with a dark, muddy look and clear, reddish veining on white flesh.

Basic Cooked Yuca

What makes yuca so good to eat is its sweet, nutty flavor and creamy, rich texture—as long as it is prepared properly. Be sure to completely peel the pinkish inner skin from the yuca; only creamy-white flesh should remain. There is a set of unpleasantly tough strings running down the center of the root that must be removed. Once cooked according to the recipe below, the yuca will be ready to fry or mash for an unusual but tasty side dish that goes well with Latin American and Caribbean foods such as the Haitian Roasted Eggplant Salad (see page 388), the Caribbean Callalou Soup (see page 311), or the Chayote Stuffed with Scallop Ceviche (see page 553).

SERVES 6

4 large, firm yuca roots
2 tablespoons white vinegar
Kosher salt, to taste

Have ready a large bowl of cold water. Cut off and discard $1/2$ inch from the tips and bottoms of the yuca. Using a sharp paring knife or a potato peeler, pare the yuca of its brown outer skin and purple inner layer until only the white flesh remains. Using a heavy knife, cut the yuca in half lengthwise. Cut each yuca half into 4 lengthwise spears, then cut away and discard the fibrous inner core. Place the peeled yuca in water while preparing so that it doesn't darken.

Bring a large pot of salted water to the boil with the vinegar. Add the yuca spears and boil for 20 minutes, or until tender when pierced with a fork.

Have ready a large bowl of ice mixed with water. Scoop the yuca from the water using a slotted spoon or skimmer and transfer it directly into the bowl of ice water. This will encourage the yuca spears to spread open on their inner sides, creating a creamier texture. Cover and refrigerate cooked yuca spears for up to 1 day before frying or mashing, as in the next recipe.

Crunchy Yuca Spears with Pimentón

I learned the method for making these crunchy yuca spears while working on Ceviche: Seafood, Salads, and Cocktails with a Latino Twist with hot Latino chef, Guillermo Pernot. He first boils yuca in water with vinegar and salt and then immediately plunges the cooked spears into ice water, which encourages the spears to spread open, making them extra tender and appealing to the eye as in the recipe for basic cooked yucca, at left. I especially like the flavor of the oak-smoked pimentón here, a special paprika from Spain that comes in sweet, bittersweet, and hot versions. American or Mexican chipotle powder, made from smoke-dried, red-ripe jalapeños is also delicious. Other ground chile powders, such as chile ancho, New Mexico hot, or even cayenne would also work.

SERVES 6 TO 8

3 tablespoons kosher salt
1 teaspoon granulated garlic or garlic powder
1 teaspoon pimentón (or chipotle powder,
 or other ground hot chile powder)
1 quart peanut oil, for frying, substitute canola or soy
4 Basic Cooked Yucas (at left)

1023

Combine the salt, garlic, and pimentón and set aside.

In a large, heavy-bottomed pot, an electric deep-fryer, or a wok, heat the oil until shimmering (365°F. on a frying thermometer). Working in 3 to 4 batches, add about 6 spears of yuca so that there is plenty of bubbling oil surrounding them. Fry until firm and well-browned, turning with tongs as they brown, about 8 minutes. in all

Using a wire skimmer, remove the yuca from the oil and drain on a wire rack, keeping warm in a 200°F. oven until all the yuca has been fried. Transfer the yuca to a bowl. Sprinkle with the reserved salt mixture, toss together to combine, and serve immediately. Note: Once fried, drained, and seasoned, the yuca can be refrigerated, covered, for up to 1 day and then reheated in a single layer on a baking sheet in a 400°F. oven for about 10 minutes.

1024

Malanga con Mojo

Cubans and other Caribbean people depend on root vegetables, such as boniato, Malanga, and yuca as a diet staple. Yuca con mojo is a popular Cuban dish served during holidays made with mojito *(a diminutive of* mojo *popularly used for the stylish Cuban cocktail made from fresh muddled mint, sugar syrup, and rum). In the kitchen,* mojo *is a strong marinade of olive oil, lemon juice, sliced raw onions, and garlic that gives the rather bland, dense roots a magically spicy flavor. The best mojo is made with fresh sour (or Seville) orange juice, which is difficult to find. These are same type of oranges used to make orange marmalade. For a similar flavor, substitute orange juice mixed with lime juice. Inexpensive bottled mojo already mixed with garlic can be found at Latin American markets as can firm, unblemished Malanga. , also known as Taro in Asian markets.*

SERVES 6

2 tablespoons white vinegar

1 pound Malanga, pared and trimmed

1/4 cup extra-virgin olive oil

2 tablespoons chopped garlic

1 cup bottled sour orange juice (or 3/4 cup orange juice mixed with 1/4 cup lime juice)

1/2 teaspoon freshly ground black pepper

Kosher salt to taste

1 small red onion, thinly sliced and briefly rinsed in cold water

Bring a large pot of salted water to the boil. Add the vinegar and the Malanga and boil like a potato until tender when pierced. Remove from the water, cool, and then slice.

Meanwhile, heat the olive oil in a small frying pan, add the garlic, and cook for 1 to 2 minutes, stirring constantly, or until just beginning to brown. Pour in the orange juice, black pepper and heat until bubbling. Pour over the Malanga, season with salt to taste, and stir in to mix. Serve immediately garnished with the onion.

MOJO AND MOJO

Aside from being the name of a spicy, garlicky sauce, *mojo,* meaning powerful magic has entered the English language from the American south, by West African slaves, referring to a small bag containing protective magical objects with the special powers of voodoo, condomblé, and other religions of African origin. References to *mojo* are common in southern rural blues songs. When these same songs were covered by white rock & roll bands in the 1960s, the word came to refer to male virility: "I've got my mojo working...." I guess it takes magic.

Brazilian Yuca and Cheese Bread Puffs

Called Pão de Queijo *in Brazilian Portuguese, this famous bread from the rich mining state of Minas Gerais is served at most steak houses in southern Brazil. It is unusual in that the recipe calls for native Brazilian manioc starch rather than European wheat flour. They are made on a similar principle to the French choux puffs, with the leavening coming from steam created during baking. These small, round rolls are best consumed hot out of the oven. In Brazil, these rolls would be made with Queijo de Minas, a mild, white cheese similar to Muenster in texture, with its own particular taste. Manioc starch is available at Latin American, especially Brazilian, markets or Web sites.*

MAKES 2½ DOZEN

¾ cup milk

½ cup olive oil

1 pound manioc starch (polvilho)

3 eggs

½ cup grated strong cheese, such as queso añejo,
   Pecorino, aged Gouda

1½ cups grated mild cheese, such as Monterey Jack,
   Mexican Chihuahua, or muenster

Bring the milk and oil to a boil in a small saucepan. Put the manioc in the bowl of an electric mixer. Add the milk mixture, the eggs, and the cheeses and blend well, until smooth and elastic.

Divide into pieces the size of a walnut or small plum. Place a little oil on your hands and round the dough into balls. Arrange on a baking sheet. Bake at 375°F. until puffed and brown, about 15 to 20 minutes. Serve warm.

Mashed Malanga with Browned Garlic Bits

Malanga *is more commonly known as* taro *and it is a regular at Chinese restaurants, grated into a light fried nest.* Malanga *is its name in Latin America. Here, boiled Malanga, with its faint violet color, is mashed with generous amounts of browned garlic and olive oil. Think of this as Latin-style garlic mashed potatoes.*

SERVES 6

8 Malanga, or taro root, peeled and sliced

3 garlic cloves, mashed to paste

4 tablespoons olive oil

Kosher salt and freshly ground black pepper to taste

1025

Boil Malanga in a large pot of salted boiling water until tender. Drain and reserve the cooking water.

Mash and mix the malanga with garlic and olive oil, then season with salt and pepper. If the mixture is too thick, add cooking water or more olive oil to loosen it.

ZUCCHINI
& OTHER SUMMER SQUASH

ZUCCHINI
& OTHER SUMMER SQUASH

The ever–proliferating zucchini is so common that it has become a vegetable to make fun of. Of course, its unquestionably phallic shape also lends itself to humorous references. In Great Britain, huge zucchini are grown and with a different connotation are known as vegetable marrows because of their similarity to large beef marrow bones. There are many types of summer squash, ranging in size from miniscule bite-sized babies to huge baseball bats. It was the Italians who first marketed summer squash in a small size and, as immigrants, they introduced this vegetable to America, where it has taken over summer vegetable gardens. In fact, zucchini grow so fast, that from one day to the next, a nice, firm, adolescent zucchini can all of a sudden grow to be immense, seedy, and watery.

Zucchini is Italian diminutive of *zucca* or *large squash*, although properly speaking, *zucchino* is singular and *zucchini* is plural. The same difference exists in France, where *courgette* is small and *courge* is large. In Spanish, *calabacita* is the diminutive small version of the large *calabaza*.

Zucchini exists in many forms and colors, mostly commonly speckled deep green. (I've had this long-standing vision of a beautiful green tweed suit resembling the skin of a zucchini, although so far I haven't found such a thing.) Large zucchini are only suitable for stuffing. All types of summer (and some winter) squash may also be sold as baby squash, especially in farmers' markets and specialty stores.

BABY ZUCCHINI AT THE VILLA D'ESTE ON LAKE COMO, ITALY

More than twenty years ago, BC (before children), I was lucky enough to stay with my now husband, Donald Reiff, at the world-class Villa d'Este on the shores of spectacular Lake Como in Northern Italy. The former country estate of the princely Este family, built in the sixteenth century, is surrounded by a twenty-five-acre park full of formal gardens, fountains, and statues overlooking the lake. Our large corner room, with balconies facing in two directions onto the lake was the best I've ever stayed in. At one of the hotel's restaurants, I tasted what was to me at the time a new vegetable: baby zucchini, about the size of a small cigar. These sweet, firm beauties were a revelation to me and I was determined to have them on the menu at my restaurant. Back home, I convinced a local farmer to bring me these infant zucchini, only days old, and started serving them to happy customers.

Zucchini Varieties

Costata Romanesca: Costata Romanesca has pale, raised ribs with mottled green color, and is zucchini-shaped, with a slightly bulging bottom. This Roman variety may also be termed *cocozelle*, an older name for zucchini used when they were first introduced into the U.S. in the late nineteenth century. When solid and young, this squash is juicy and sweet, but it quickly turns flabby and can be bland and bitter.

Golden zucchini: Golden zucchini has brilliant, sunny yellow skin which retains its color and fresh light flavor when cooked. This squash starts out yellow rather than ripening from green.

Middle-Eastern Zucchini: Middle-Eastern Zucchini—also known as *Lebanese* or *Egyptian Zucchini*, *Cousa*, *Kula*, and *Magma*—are stocky, pale green tapering cylinders with a thick, darker green stem. They have smooth, shiny skin that bruises easily, solid, crisp flesh, and moist, flavorful flesh. They retain their firm texture when cooked.

Pattypan: Pattypan—or Cymling (Native American), Custard Marrow (British), Pâtisson (French)—Squash have a characteristic scalloped edge and may be flattened or bell-shaped. They may be cream, sunny yellow, celadon, pistachio, or ivy-green in color, and they taste best when small. Solid and smooth-fleshed, they are rather bland in flavor. Scallopini is a cross of zucchini and pattypan.

Round Zucchini: Round Zucchini are dense and heavy for their size, nearly seedless, with smooth-textured flesh. When cooked, the juicy, flavorful flesh has a green tint.

Tatume: Tatume, which are common in Mexico, are shaped like a huge egg and weigh about one pound each. They have dense, smooth flesh and are virtually seedless.

Yellow Crookneck: Older varieties of Yellow Crooknecks have thick, warty skin, heavily curved necks, sweet flavor, and crunchy texture. Newer varieties are straighter with thinner, softer skin and blander flavor.

Zephyr: Zephyr is a hybrid of Yellow Crookneck and a cross between Delicata and yellow Acorn squash (both Winter Squash). It has a sharply defined green lower portion topped with yellow and resembles zucchini with a slightly bulbous bottom.

Zucchini Season and Choosing Zucchini

Summer squash are available all year, but spring to summer is the best season for domestically grown squash. Look for baby squash and squash blossoms at farmers' markets. Choose small to medium-sized squash with shiny, taut skin and solid flesh. Lightly scratched or slightly bruised squash are fine. Avoid overly large squash or squash with pitted skin or flabby, spongy texture. Store squash in plastic for two to three days in the refrigerator.

CHOOSING AND PREPARING SQUASH BLOSSOMS

Open up the squash blossoms and carefully inspect them for insects before using them. Pull off and discard the dark green calyxes. The best blossoms to use are the fruit-bearing female blossoms. The sweet fleshy bottom is the most delicious part. Blossoms keep best if they are kept cool and moist by packing them in layers of dampened paper towels and sealing the container in plastic. However, they are extremely perishable and are best used within one or, at most two days of picking.

Squash Blossoms

Squash Blossoms are an extremely perishable delicacy that may come from many types of squash, including winter squash varieties. There are two types: male blossoms, which grow from the branches, and female blossoms, which bear fruit. Baby squash may be sold with blossoms attached. Female blossoms have a soft, fleshy, delectably succulent center portion that will spoil within one day. They should be picked in the morning, when they open toward the sun, and then sold that day. Male blossoms are hairier and not as fruity but are more plentiful and will last a little longer. Squash blossoms can be found in specialty and farmers' markets, often still attached to small fruits. When I wanted to serve zucchini blossoms, I found a local grower to pick only the plump, succulent female blossoms—not the less-desirable males—in the early hours of the morning and deliver them the same day, so I'd receive these delicate, short-lived beauties fully opened and ready to stuff and serve that same night.

Summer Squash and Corn Soup with Garden Tomatoes

This super-simple soup shows off summer's ripe produce at its best. Go to the farmers' market and buy the smallest yellow squash you can find (because they are the most colorful and the firmest), the biggest, ripest, juiciest red tomatoes, and the youngest, sweetest corn. If your market sells fresh white onions, they are best here. There is no stock used here; it would muddy the clear flavors of the few, but good, ingredients. Although most heavy cream is ultra-pasteurized (cooked at high temperature to kill bacteria), fresh cream, sometimes sold by local dairies, is best. I include the corn "milk" here, obtained by scraping against the cobs, for extra creamy flavor.

MAKES 1 GALLON, SERVES 12

3 pounds small summer squash, grated

1½ pounds white onions, grated

1030

2 tablespoons kosher salt

1 quart water

3 pounds ripe beefsteak tomatoes, diced, juice strained and reserved

10 cups corn kernels & corn milk

1 quart heavy cream

2 bunches fresh basil leaves, chiffonade

Freshly ground black pepper to taste

Combine the squash, onions, salt, and water in a large pot. Bring to the boil and simmer for 30 minutes. Add the tomatoes, corn, and corn milk, and bring to the boil. At the last minute, stir in the cream and basil, then add pepper to taste. Serve immediately or chill over ice, then heat as needed.

Creole–Style Stuffed, Baked Zucchini with Ham, Onions, & Peppers

In the wake of the terrible aftereffects of Hurricane Katrina, New Orleans, America's culinary queen, has been inalterably changed, to the loss of not just natives but all Americans. I'm lucky that, on a visit to New Orleans before the hurricane, I got to walk about in the French quarter where I ate spicy steamed crawfish served on newspapers at a used book store. Just as the Creole language combines the elements of many other languages, Creole cuisine is a combination of French, Spanish, and American with a little Italian thrown in. This dish of stuffed zucchini may also be made with chayote, called mirliton *only in New Orleans.*

SERVES 6

6 medium zucchini

4 tablespoons unsalted butter

1 small red onion, diced

2 ribs celery, diced

1 red and 1 green bell pepper, diced

$1/4$ pound smoked ham

1 bunch scallions, thinly sliced

2 teaspoons chopped fresh thyme, or $1/2$ teaspoon dried

1 tablespoon chopped garlic

4 tablespoons all-purpose flour, preferably unbleached

1 cup half-and-half

Kosher salt, cayenne pepper, and freshly ground black pepper to taste

$1/4$ cup breadcrumbs, if needed

Bring a large pot of salted water to the boil. Add the whole zucchini and bring the water back to the boil. Cook for 2 minutes, or until the zucchini are brightly colored and crisp-tender. Drain and run under cold water to cool. When the zucchini are cool enough to handle, cut them in half lengthwise and scoop out the insides, leaving a wall about $1/4$ inch thick all around. Chop the zucchini flesh and reserve both the shells and flesh.

Preheat the oven to 350°F. In a large skillet, preferably cast-iron, melt the butter and add the onion, celery, peppers, and ham. Sauté until the vegetables are crisp-tender and then add the chopped zucchini flesh, the scallions, thyme, and garlic. Stir and sauté for about 3 minutes, or until fragrant and any juices from the zucchini have evaporated, then stir in the flour. Stir again until the flour has been absorbed and the raw taste is gone, about 2 minutes. Pour in the half-and-half and bring the contents of the

1031

pan to the boil, stirring to combine well. Remove the pan from the heat and season with salt, cayenne, and pepper. Cool the mixture and, if the filling is too watery, add the breadcrumbs.

Stuff the filling into the reserved shells. Arrange the stuffed zucchini boats in a baking pan and bake for 40 minutes, or until browned and bubbling. Remove from the oven and allow the zucchini to cool slightly before serving.

CREOLE AND CAJUN COOKING

Many Creoles were rich planters, and their kitchens aspired to the grande cuisine of their French and Spanish forebears. Their recipes came from France or Spain as did their chefs. By using classic French techniques with local foodstuffs, they created a whole new cuisine—Creole cooking. On the other hand, the Acadians, later contracted to *Cajun*, who were of French-Canadian origin, who lived in strenuous conditions in the low-lying bayous of the region. Cajun food was pungent and peppery, usually made in a single pot (like jambalaya and gumbo), and prepared from locally available ingredients, including alligator, rabbit, turtle, and above all, crawfish.

Farm–Market Pasta with Summer Squash

As a chef, my greatest joy was the deliveries from local farmers like Glenn Brendle of Green Meadow Farm, Mark Dornstreich of Branch Creek Farm, Paul Tsakos of Overbrook Farm, and many others. I couldn't wait to open their boxes, sniffing the fragrance of dirt and fresh-picked vegetables with their incomparable flavor. The subtle and complex flavors of vegetables start fading as soon as they are picked. Until you've tasted a fresh-picked zucchini, sun-warmed tomato, or iron-rich curly spinach, you really don't know vegetables at all. Brilliant colors, odd shapes, and a surprise every week made these visits the high points of the week for me. I couldn't wait to start cooking with them. Because I never knew what would show up, I would make this highly adaptable pasta dish with whatever was abundant, topping it with the light, tangy Greystone Chevratal goat cheese from nearby Chester County. Green spinach pasta underscores the garden-fresh aspect of the dish, but egg pasta can certainly be substituted.

Serves 4

1½ cups Vegetable Stock (*see* page 995)

6 tablespoons extra-virgin olive oil, divided

8 cups colorful assorted vegetables, cut into bite-sized
    pieces including any or all of the following:
    Vidalia onion, cut in half and then sliced into strips
    Yellow and/or red bell peppers, trimmed and cut into
      strips or squares
    Haricot verts or green beans, trimmed and
      cut into short lengths
    Fennel bulb, cut into squares or tender fennel stalks,

thinly sliced and precooked in boiling water until tender

Asparagus, trimmed and cut on the diagonal
into short lengths

Zucchini, trimmed and cut into thin half-moons

Yellow squash, trimmed and cut into thin half-moons

Red ripe beefsteak or plum tomatoes, beefsteaks cut
into thin wedges, plum tomatoes cut into thin rings

Corn kernels cut off the stalks

$1/2$ cup thinly sliced fragrant basil leaves

$1/4$ cup Chinese chives, chives, or scallions, thinly sliced

1 tablespoon chopped fresh thyme leaves

1 pound fresh spinach fettuccine or tagliatelle

Kosher salt and freshly ground black pepper to taste

6 ounces mild goat cheese crumbled

Bring a large pot of generously salted water to the boil for the pasta. Reduce the heat to a simmer while you prepare the vegetables.

In a separate pot, heat the vegetable stock and reserve. In a large skillet, preferably nonstick, heat half the olive oil. Add the onions and sauté over high heat for about 2 minutes or until transparent but still crispy. Add the firmer vegetables, such as peppers, haricots verts or green beans, fennel and asparagus, zucchini, and yellow squash. Sauté quickly for about 2 minutes, tossing and shaking often so the vegetables cook evenly. Add the remaining tender vegetables, including the tomatoes and corn, and the herbs and then heat for 1 minute.

Bring the pasta water back up to boiling and then add the pasta, cooking for about 2 minutes, once the water has come back to the boil. Meanwhile, add the vegetable stock to the pan and boil together for 2 minutes or until the stock has reduced to about half its volume. Season the mixture generously with salt and pepper. Transfer the

vegetable mixture to a large bowl that has been rinsed under hot water to preheat. Drain the pasta and toss with the vegetables and the remaining oil.

Divide among 4 large, preheated pasta bowls, making sure to include a portion of the pan juices and top each serving with the crumbled goat cheese. Serve immediately.

Cretan Zucchini and Dill Egg Cake

This delicious egg cake from the island of Crete is made from just zucchini, dill, eggs, and olive oil. Chris Veneris, Cretan cooking teacher and chef, prepared it for a tasting of typical Cretan dishes at a conference on "Flavors of the Mediterranean: The Garden, The Grove, and The Sea," held at the Culinary Institute of America's campus at Greystone in Napa. If you like the taste of mint, mix a little fresh chopped mint in with the dill. Although Chris' recipe only calls for dill, I swear I tasted mint.

SERVES 4

8 extra-large eggs

$1/4$ cup finely chopped dill

Kosher salt and freshly ground black pepper to taste

$3/4$ pound small zucchini (and/or yellow zucchini),
sliced $1/4$-inch thick

$1/2$ cup extra-virgin olive oil

Beat the eggs lightly with the dill, salt, and pepper. In a 9- or 10-inch skillet, preferably nonstick, cook the zucchini in the olive oil until bright green and somewhat softened.

Transfer the zucchini to a bowl and combine with the egg mixture. Wipe out the pan, oil lightly, and heat. Pour the egg-zucchini mixture back into the pan, and cook over low heat, shaking occasionally until the eggs are set on the bottom and have formed a golden crust, about 5 minutes.

Remove the skillet from the heat, place a large plate over top and flip the eggs onto the plate. Slide the uncooked side of the omelet back into the pan and continue cooking for 5 minutes, or until a light-brown crust forms on the bottom. Turn the egg cake out of the pan, cool slightly, cut into wedges, and serve hot or at room temperature.

Stuffed Squash Blossoms with Orange–Pepper Vinaigrette

Large, succulent female zucchini blossoms are one of the world's delicacies, available only at local farmers' markets or from local growers. The blossoms must be picked early in the day when they are fully opened, so that any insects inside can be removed, and they should be cooked the same day. These flowers are the epitome of evanescence, to be enjoyed for the moment. However, once stuffed, they can be kept refrigerated overnight and fried the next day. With a simple stuffing of tangy, moist mozzarella di bufala, and an orange-colored pepper vinaigrette, they are extraordinary. Substitute a combination of half fresh mozzarella and half mild goat cheese, crumbled, for the mozzarella di bufala.

SERVES 4

12 large zucchini blossoms

6 ounces imported mozzarella di bufala, diced

1 tablespoon fresh marjoram leaves

1 tablespoon lemon thyme leaves

1 red bell pepper

2 yellow bell peppers

2 tablespoons aged Sherry vinegar

$1/4$ cup peanut oil

Kosher salt and freshly ground black pepper to taste

2 tablespoons unsalted butter

Open up each blossom and inspect the inside for any insects. Finely chop the marjoram and lemon thyme (reserving the sprigs for garnish) and mix with the cheese. Stuff each blossom with the cheese and marjoram, without overstuffing. Set aside in the refrigerator.

Meanwhile, grill the peppers on an open gas flame or directly on an electric element. Turn the peppers so that the skin gets evenly blackened. Cool, and then peel the peppers and remove the seeds and ribs. Chop the peppers roughly, and add them to the jar of a blender along with the vinegar, oil, and salt and pepper. Blend and reserve the pepper vinaigrette.

Just before serving, heat the butter until it foams and sauté the stuffed blossoms for about 2 minutes on each side. Spread the orange pepper vinaigrette on large dinner plates. Drain the sautéed blossoms on paper towels and place over sauce. Decorate with a few thyme and marjoram sprigs.

1034

Deep-Fried Zucchini Blossoms for Dessert

I can't say enough about one of my culinary obsessions, zucchini blossoms, here dipped in a light batter and deep-fried for dessert. If you are lucky enough to get some zucchini blossoms, perhaps gathered from your own garden, serve them for dessert to some very good and lucky friends. This dish shows that the simplest of ingredients, often discarded in America, can be used to make the most delectable of dishes.

SERVES 4

$^1/_2$ cup milk

$^1/_4$ cup mild oil, preferably a nut oil such as walnut or hazelnut

1 egg

Freshly grated nutmeg to taste

Grated zest of 1 lemon

$^1/_4$ pound (1 cup) all-purpose flour, preferably unbleached

2 tablespoons baking powder

$^1/_2$ teaspoon kosher salt

1 tablespoon granulated sugar

2 quarts pure peanut oil, substitute soy oil

12 large zucchini blossoms, cleaned

Confectioners' sugar, for dusting

Whisk together the milk, oil, egg, nutmeg, and lemon zest. Whisk together the dry ingredients: the flour, baking powder, salt, and sugar. Slowly sprinkle the dry ingredients over the wet ingredients, whisking together all the while. The batter should have the consistency of slightly thickened heavy cream. Set the batter aside to rest in the refrigerator for at least 30 minutes.

When ready to serve, heat the peanut oil to 365°F. in a wok or a deep, heavy pot, making sure that the oil comes no more than one-third of the way up in the pot. Dip each blossom into the batter, making sure that the batter lightly coats all surfaces of the blossom. Deep-fry the blossoms for about 3 to 4 minutes. Drain well on paper towels. Dust with confectioners' sugar and serve immediately.

LIGHT AND TENDER FRYING BATTER

By allowing batter to rest, the gluten (or elastic protein) developed by beating the flour in liquid can relax, making for a more tender batter. Also, a batter that has thickened in the cold of the refrigerator requires less flour to fully coat the blossoms, making for a lighter batter. In fact, tempura batter often contains small chips of ice for this very reason.

INDEX

1036

1037

1038

1040

1041

1042

1043

1044

1048

1049

1050

1051

1052

1053

1055